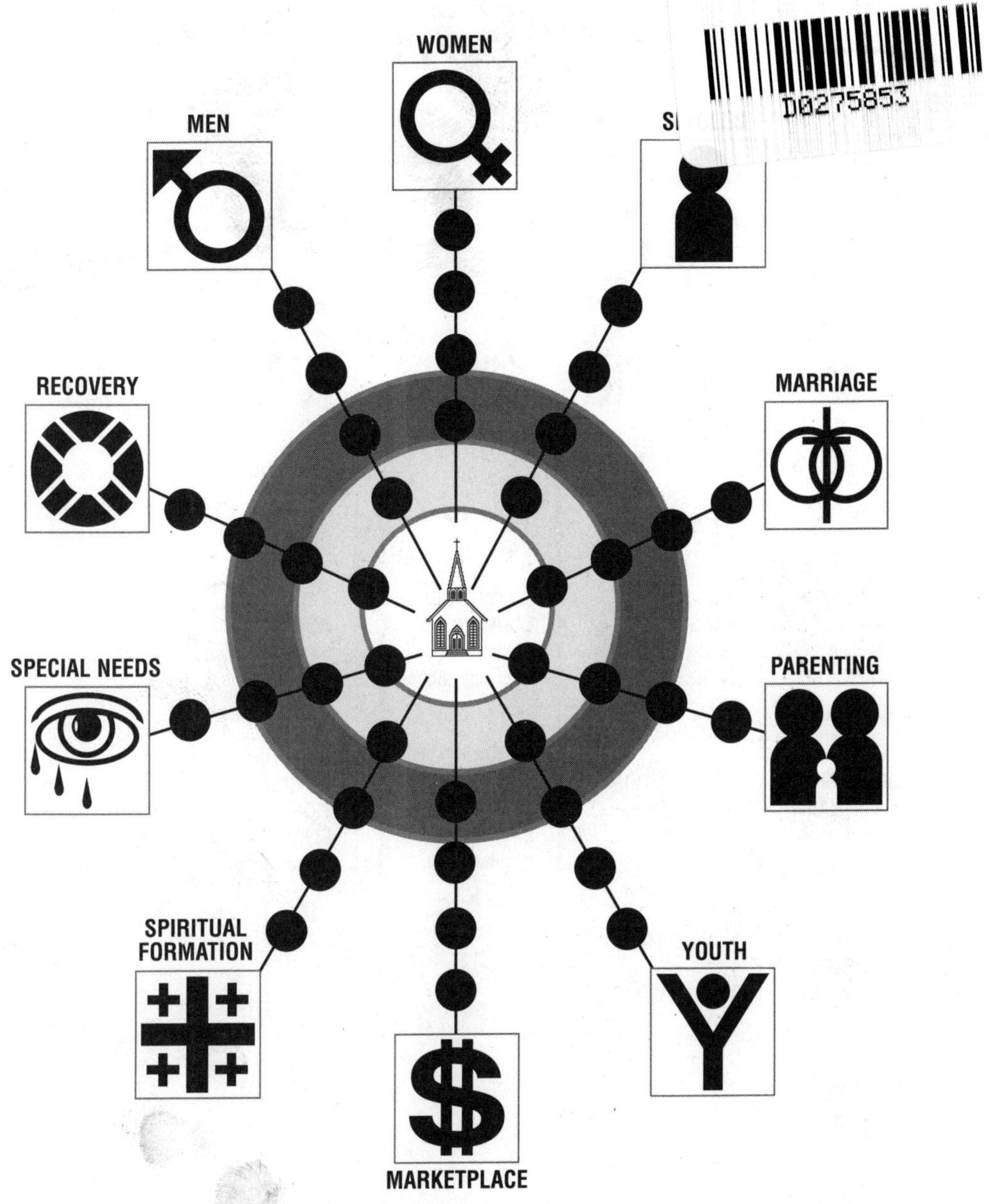

Targeting 10 small group audiences

Find Your Kind of Group

Leading a small group

... and Pick a Course

YOUTH	MARKET-PLACE	SPIRITUAL FORMATION	SPECIAL NEEDS	RECOVERY
(page 24)	(page 26)	(page 27)	(page 28)	(page 29)
13. UP CLOSE Discovering My Real Identity	17. BUSINESS ETHICS A Christian in a Down and Dirty World	19. SPIRITUAL BASICS Becoming a Christian	22. FINANCIAL STRESS Making Ends Meet	24. STRESS MANAGEMENT Living Under Pressure
14. CONFIRMA-TION What Do I Believe?	18. BORED AND BURNED OUT Assessing Your Career	20. MATURING IN CHRIST Called to Discipleship	23. LIVING WITH PAIN Coping With Life's Hurts	25. 12 STEPS The Road to Recovery
15. STRESS Surviving Day to Day		21. COMING HOME Pilgrims on Their Way Back		
16. HASSLES Getting Along With My Parents				

See additional course outlines on pages 33-37.

just got easier!

Serendipity New Testament

10th Anniversary Edition

The NIV® Serendipity Bible, New Testament Edition
10th Anniversary Edition

Published by Serendipity, a publishing house specializing in equipping pastors and church leaders for small group ministry in the local church. A list of training events and catalog of resources can be obtained by writing to: SERENDIPITY HOUSE, P.O. Box 1012, Littleton, CO 80160 *or* call Toll Free: 1-800-525-9563.

96 97 98 99 8 7 6 5 4 3 2 1

You will be pleased to know that a portion of the purchase price of your new NIV Bible has been provided to International Bible Society to help spread the gospel of Jesus Christ around the world!

Serendipity New Testament

10th Anniversary Edition

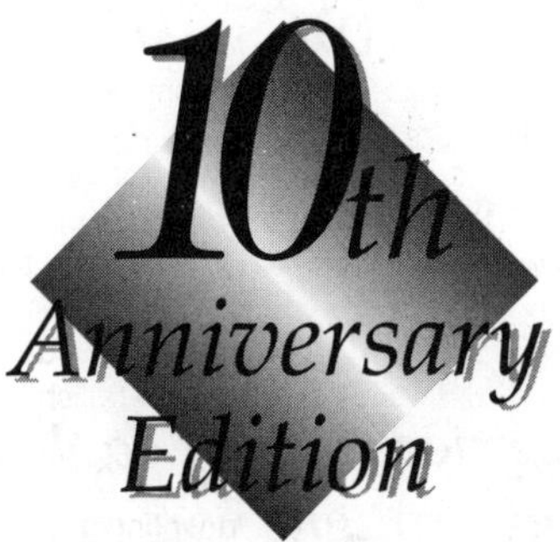

NEW INTERNATIONAL VERSION

Serendipity House / P. O. Box 1012 / Littleton, CO 80160 / TOLL FREE: 1-800-525-9563

Dedicated To:

Kevin Lyman Coleman

1968-1995

"I carried you on eagles' wings
and brought you to myself."
Exodus 19:4

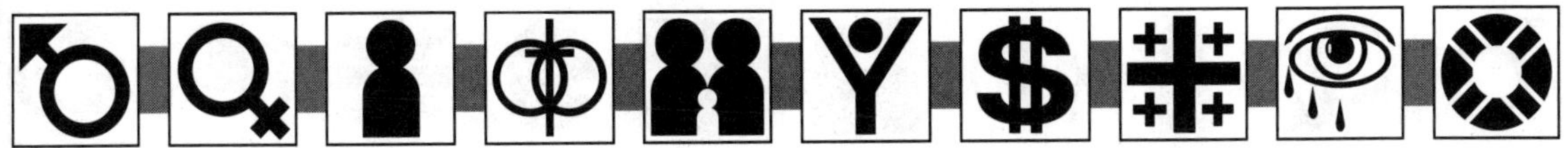

CONTRIBUTORS

EDITOR-IN-CHIEF	Lyman Coleman.
FIRST EDITION EDITORS	Gary Christopherson, Tucson, AZ; William F. Cutler, Auburn, ME; Dietrich R. Gruen, Madison, WI; Mary H. Naegeli, Moraga, CA; Richard V. Peace, Hamilton, MA; Lance Pierson, London, England; Denny Rydberg, Colorado Springs, CO.
10TH ANNIVERSARY EDITION EDITORS	Brenda Quinn, Andrew Sloan, Stephen Sheely, Cathy Tardif, Alfred Shepard.
MARGIN QUESTIONS	**Matthew:** Mari R. Anderson, Lancaster, NY; Mary H. Naegeli, Moraga, CA; James M. Singleton, Jr., South Hamilton, MA; **Mark:** Verne Becker, Wheaton, IL; Mary H. Naegeli, Moraga, CA; James M. Singleton, Jr., South Hamilton, MA; **Luke:** Verne Becker, Wheaton, IL: Carol Detoni, Arcadia, CA; **John:** Mari R. Anderson, Lancaster, NY; William F. Cutler, Auburn, ME; **Acts:** William F. Cutler, Auburn, ME; Doug LaBudde, Beverly, MA; **Romans:** Verne Becker, Wheaton, IL; William F. Cutler, Auburn, ME; **1,2 Corinthians:** John T. Anderson, Lancaster, NY; William F. Cutler, Auburn, ME; Mark Horton, Bethel, CT; **Galatians:** John T. Anderson, Lancaster, NY; John Crosby, Glen Ellyn, IL; **Ephesians:** Mari R. Anderson, Lancaster, NY; John and Fay Winson, Beverly, MA; Steve and Betsy Crowe, Wenham, MA; **Philippians:** Mari R. Anderson, Lancaster, NY; John and Fay Winson, Beverly, MA; **Colossians:** Mari R. Anderson, Lancaster, NY; John and Fay Winson, Beverly, MA; **1,2 Thessalonians:** John and Fay Winson, Beverly, MA; **1,2 Timothy:** Mari R. Anderson, Lancaster, NY; Judy Johnson, Madison, WI; **Titus:** Mari R. Anderson, Lancaster, NY; **Philemon:** John and Fay Winson, Beverly, MA; **Hebrews:** James M. Singleton, Madison, WI; **James:** Mari R. Anderson, Lancaster, NY; **1,2 Peter:** Mark Shepard, Easton, MA; **1,2,3 John:** Bill Tucker, Dubuque, IA; **Jude:** Mari R. Anderson, Lancaster, NY; **Revelation:** Dietrich R. Gruen, Madison, WI.
FIRST EDITION ART DESIGN PRODUCTION TEAM	Billie Herwig, Doug LaBudde, Fay and John Winson at Frontline Marketing, Beverly, MA; Hal Hunt at Autographics, Pomona, CA; Erika Tiepel at Graphics Plus, Littleton, CO.
10TH ANNIVERSARY EDITION ART DESIGN AND PRODUCTION TEAM	Christopher Werner, Erika Tiepel, Sharon Penington, Maurice Lydick.

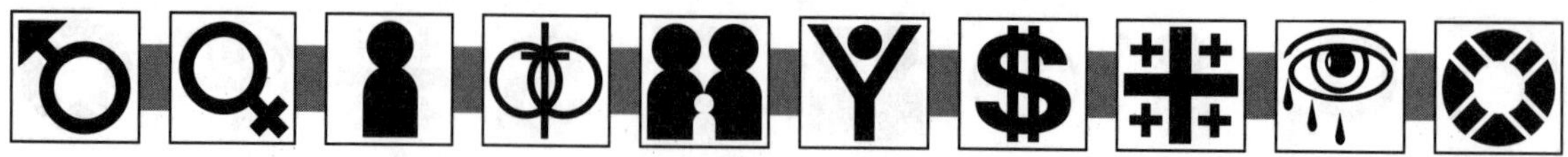

CONTENTS

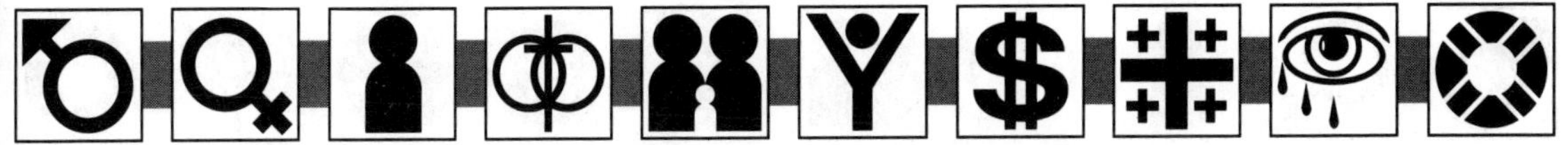

BOOKS OF THE NEW TESTAMENT

Abbreviations Key:

v. – verse
vv. – verses
f – verse following
ff – verses following
ch – chapter(s)
c. – about, approximately
e.g. – for example
i.e. – that is
NT – New Testament
OT – Old Testament
p. – page number

Sample of Ready-made Course Outlines

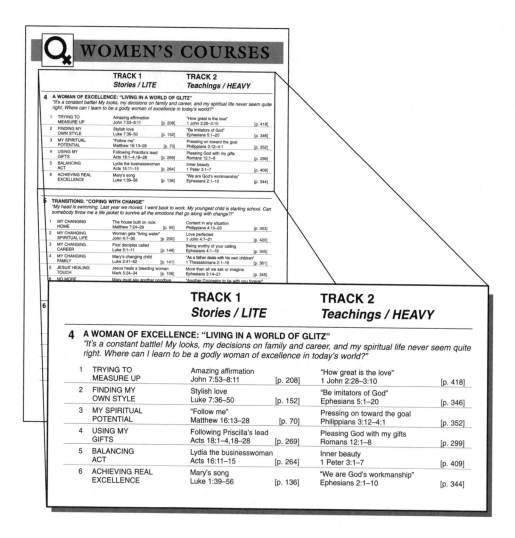

WOMEN'S COURSES

		TRACK 1 *Stories / LITE*	TRACK 2 *Teachings / HEAVY*

4 A WOMAN OF EXCELLENCE: "LIVING IN A WORLD OF GLITZ"

"It's a constant battle! My looks, my decisions on family and career, and my spiritual life never seem quite right. Where can I learn to be a godly woman of excellence in today's world?"

	Session	TRACK 1 Stories / LITE	TRACK 2 Teachings / HEAVY
1	TRYING TO MEASURE UP	Amazing affirmation John 7:53–8:11 [p. 208]	"How great is the love" 1 John 2:28–3:10 [p. 418]
2	FINDING MY OWN STYLE	Stylish love Luke 7:36–50 [p. 152]	"Be imitators of God" Ephesians 5:1–20 [p. 346]
3	MY SPIRITUAL POTENTIAL	"Follow me" Matthew 16:13–28 [p. 70]	Pressing on toward the goal Philippians 3:12–4:1 [p. 352]
4	USING MY GIFTS	Following Priscilla's lead Acts 18:1–4,18–28 [p. 269]	Pleasing God with my gifts Romans 12:1–8 [p. 299]
5	BALANCING ACT	Lydia the businesswoman Acts 16:11–15 [p. 264]	Inner beauty 1 Peter 3:1–7 [p. 409]
6	ACHIEVING REAL EXCELLENCE	Mary's song Luke 1:39–56 [p. 136]	"We are God's workmanship" Ephesians 2:1–10 [p. 344]

5 TRANSITIONS: "COPING WITH CHANGE"

"My head is swimming. Last year we moved. I went back to work. My youngest child is starting school. Can somebody throw me a life jacket to survive all the emotions that go along with change?!"

	Session	TRACK 1 Stories / LITE	TRACK 2 Teachings / HEAVY
1	MY CHANGING HOME	The house built on rock Matthew 7:24–29 [p. 55]	Content in any situation Philippians 4:10–23 [p. 353]
2	MY CHANGING SPIRITUAL LIFE	Woman gets "living water" John 4:7–30 [p. 200]	Love perfected 1 John 4:7–21 [p. 420]
3	MY CHANGING CAREER	First disciples called Luke 5:1–11 [p. 146]	Being worthy of your calling Ephesians 4:1–16 [p. 345]
4	MY CHANGING FAMILY	Mary's changing child Luke 2:41–52 [p. 141]	"As a father deals with his own children" 1 Thessalonians 2:1–16 [p. 361]
5	JESUS' HEALING TOUCH	Jesus heals a bleeding woman Mark 5:24–34 [p. 106]	More than all we ask or imagine Ephesians 3:14–21 [p. 345]
6	NO MORE	Mary must say another goodbye	"Another Counselor to be with you forever"

SINCE YOU ASKED

ABOUT THE READY-MADE COURSES FOR GROUPS

DECIDING

1. **How do you choose what to study?** Review the courses on pages 19–37 and choose one that your group wants to study.

DIFFERENCES

2. **What is the difference between the courses on pages 19–29 and those on pages 33–37?** The first courses, with the 10 different pictograms, are designed for specific needs or kinds of groups. The other more general courses can be used by any group.

DURATION

3. **How long does a study course last?** Six or 12 sessions, depending upon whether you want to study only Track 1—Stories, or Track 2—Teachings, or both. The general courses on pages 33–37 last from seven to 13 weeks.

TWO TRACKS

4. **What is the difference between Track 1 and Track 2?** Track 1 is somewhat easier. All of the studies are taken from stories and have a ready-made questionnaire at the bottom of the text for easy sharing.

TRACK 2

5. **What about Track 2?** Track 2 is somewhat harder than Track 1. The studies are taken from teachings (mostly from the Epistles) and you will use the questions in the margin.

TARGET GROUPS

6. **How did you arrive at the study courses?** We targeted the 10 affinity groups and tried to deal with the most important issues in each group (see the chart in the front of the New Testament).

CONTINUING

7. **What do you suggest after completing a course?** Choose another course or move to a book study—such as one of the shorter epistles like Philippians or James.

BOOK STUDY

8. **How do you organize a book study?** The introduction page to each book in the New Testament contains a study outline. The outlines include two options for study. Choose the option that fits best with your time schedule. The column for Personal Reading indicates what you can read prior to the meeting. The Group Study Passage indicates the passage your group should focus on, using either the corresponding questionnaire (if applicable) or the margin questions.

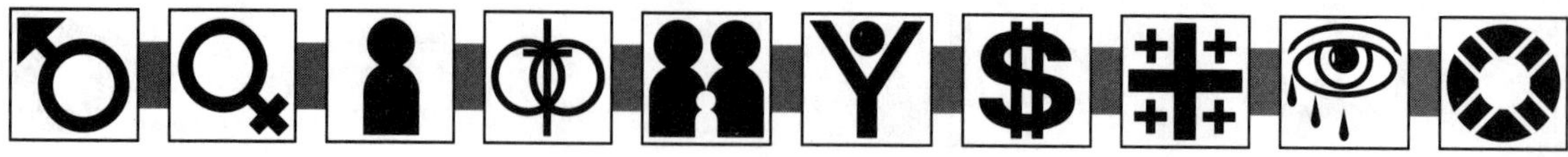

Sample of Questionnaire With Pictograms to Target Special Groups

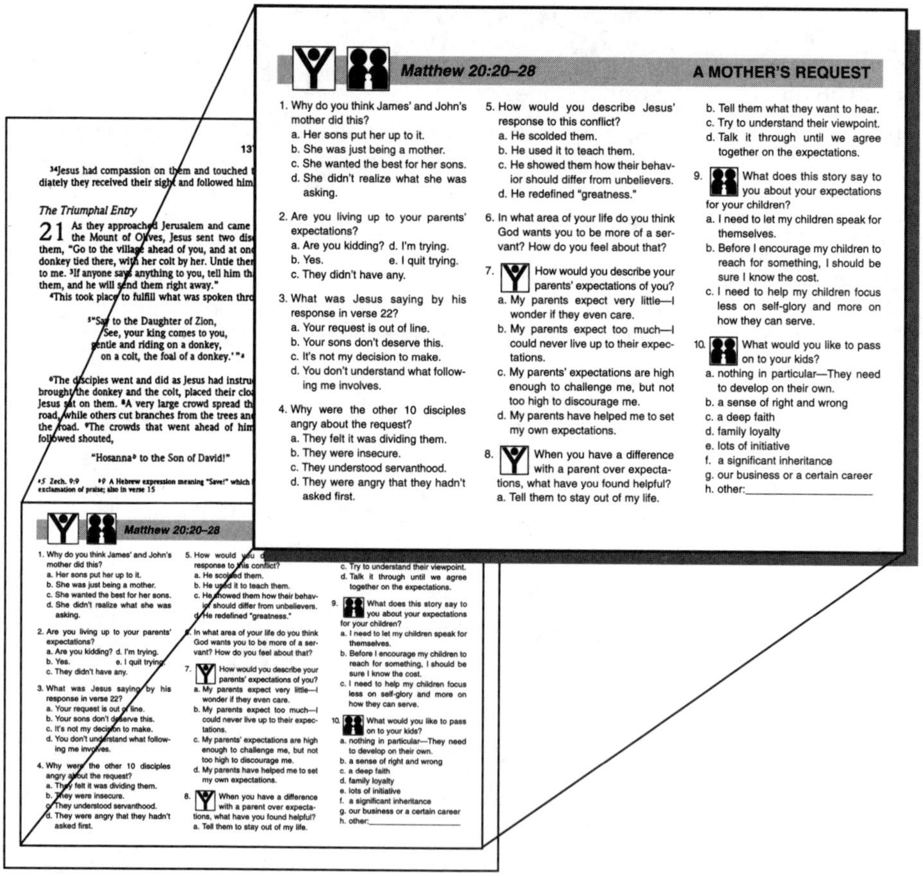

Matthew 20:20–28 **A MOTHER'S REQUEST**

1. Why do you think James' and John's mother did this?
   a. Her sons put her up to it.
   b. She was just being a mother.
   c. She wanted the best for her sons.
   d. She didn't realize what she was asking.

2. Are you living up to your parents' expectations?
   a. Are you kidding?
   b. Yes.
   c. They didn't have any.
   d. I'm trying.
   e. I quit trying.

3. What was Jesus saying by his response in verse 22?
   a. Your request is out of line.
   b. Your sons don't deserve this.
   c. It's not my decision to make.
   d. You don't understand what following me involves.

4. Why were the other 10 disciples angry about the request?
   a. They felt it was dividing them.
   b. They were insecure.
   c. They understood servanthood.
   d. They were angry that they hadn't asked first.

5. How would you describe Jesus' response to this conflict?
   a. He scolded them.
   b. He used it to teach them.
   c. He showed them how their behavior should differ from unbelievers.
   d. He redefined "greatness."

6. In what area of your life do you think God wants you to be more of a servant? How do you feel about that?

7. How would you describe your parents' expectations of you?
   a. My parents expect very little—I wonder if they even care.
   b. My parents expect too much—I could never live up to their expectations.
   c. My parents' expectations are high enough to challenge me, but not too high to discourage me.
   d. My parents have helped me to set my own expectations.

8. When you have a difference with a parent over expectations, what have you found helpful?
   a. Tell them to stay out of my life.
   b. Tell them what they want to hear.
   c. Try to understand their viewpoint.
   d. Talk it through until we agree together on the expectations.

9. What does this story say to you about your expectations for your children?
   a. I need to let my children speak for themselves.
   b. Before I encourage my children to reach for something, I should be sure I know the cost.
   c. I need to help my children focus less on self-glory and more on how they can serve.

10. What would you like to pass on to your kids?
   a. nothing in particular—They need to develop on their own.
   b. a sense of right and wrong
   c. a deep faith
   d. family loyalty
   e. lots of initiative
   f. a significant inheritance
   g. our business or a certain career
   h. other:________________

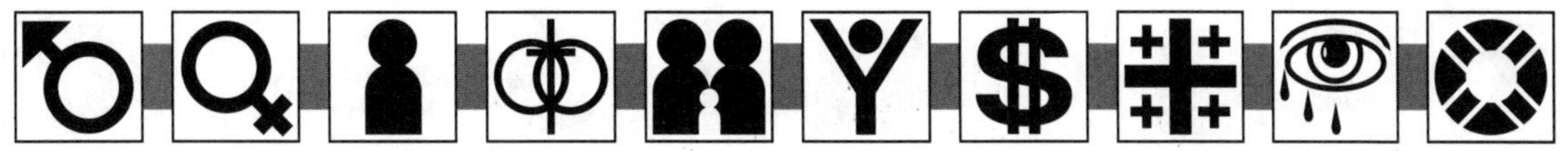

ABOUT THE READY-MADE QUESTIONNAIRES

DISCUSSION QUESTIONNAIRES

9. **What are the questionnaires at the bottom of some of the pages for?** They are especially good for beginning groups and groups that don't know a lot about the Bible.

RIGHT-BRAIN QUESTIONS

10. **How are the questionnaires designed?** The questionnaire is a series of right-brain questions with multiple-choice options that walk you through a Bible story into your own life—how you relate your story with the story in the Bible.

FAVORITE STORIES

11. **How did you go about choosing the stories?** We chose 86 of the favorite stories in the New Testament (see the list on pages 30–32).

EASY SHARING

12. **Why did you choose stories instead of other Bible passages?** It is easier for a small group to relate to a story or parable quickly.

ALL AGES

13. **Who are the questionnaires designed for?** All ages—from youth to senior citizens.

NO CORRECT ANSWERS

14. **In the multiple-choice options, are there any "correct" answers?** Not really. Most of the options could be correct, depending on your perspective. This makes for good sharing.

DISCLOSURE SCALE

15. **Is there any particular flow in the questions?** Yes. The questions are arranged to move across the "Disclosure Scale" from NO RISK at the beginning of the questionnaire to HIGH RISK at the end of the questionnaire.

ESCAPE OPTION

16. **Do you mean that these questionnaires could get a group into hot water?** It's always possible, but not probable. The multiple-choice options always give an escape option. Otherwise, you can choose to pass.

PICTOGRAMS

17. **Why are there pictograms next to some questions?** The pictograms indicate questions that are designed for a particular audience, such as Women, Youth, etc. (see course outlines beginning on page 19). You may want to read the question to see if it still relates to your group.

STUDY COURSES

18. **How long would you want a group to use the questionnaires?** At least six sessions—to get acquainted, share your spiritual story and become a "caring" community.

DEEPER

19. **What if you want to go deeper?** You can always move over to the questions in the margin—especially the BOOK questions. You can also use CUP questions as ice-breakers to open your meeting.

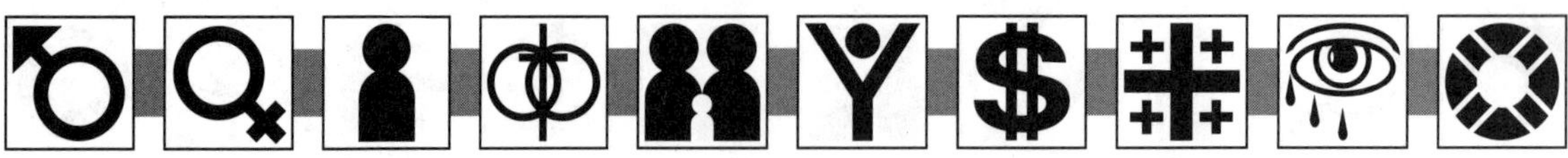

Sample of Margin Questions

To Start:

How would you arrange for a visiting President to have maximum exposure in your town: What parades? What TV talk shows or radio call-in programs? Where would he eat? Stay the night?

To Study:

1. To what town has Jesus come? Why? **2.** Jesus comes on a donkey and not on a stallion. What does that portray? **3.** What kind of kingdom and king were the people expecting? How do their wishes compare with the reality of Jesus? **4.** How might that discrepancy account for the same crowd jeering and shouting later, "Crucify him!"?

To Close:

1. What difference does it make to you that Jesus is a gentle King, and not like the one described in 20:25? **2.** How would you have reacted if you had been there to greet Jesus riding into town? Do you jump on political or religious bandwagons today? Why or why not? **3.** Does Jesus' humility work for you? Why or why not?

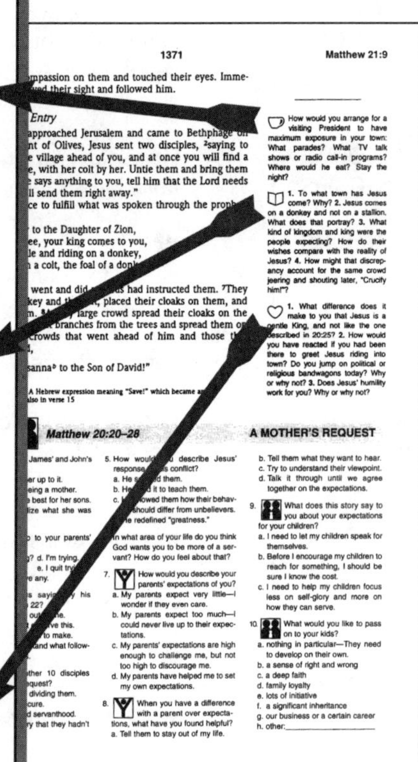

1371 Matthew 21:9

mpassion on them and touched their eyes. Imme-
ved their sight and followed him.

Entry

approached Jerusalem and came to Bethphage on
nt of Olives, Jesus sent two disciples, ²saying to
e village ahead of you, and at once you will find a
e, with her colt by her. Untie them and bring them
e says anything to you, tell him that the Lord needs
ll send them right away."
ce to fulfill what was spoken through the proph

to the Daughter of Zion,
ee, your king comes to you,
le and riding on a donkey,
a colt, the foal of a don

went and did ... had instructed them. ⁷They
key and ..., placed their cloaks on them, and
m. ⁸... large crowd spread their cloaks on the
... branches from the trees and spread them o
crowds that went ahead of him and those t

sanna[b] to the Son of David!"

A Hebrew expression meaning "Save!" which became a
also in verse 15

How would you arrange for a visiting President to have maximum exposure in your town: What parades? What TV talk shows or radio call-in programs? Where would he eat? Stay the night?

1. To what town has Jesus come? Why? **2.** Jesus comes on a donkey and not on a stallion. What does that portray? **3.** What kind of kingdom and king were the people expecting? How do their wishes compare with the reality of Jesus? **4.** How might that discrepancy account for the same crowd jeering and shouting later, "Crucify him!"?

1. What difference does it make to you that Jesus is a gentle King, and not like the one described in 20:25? **2.** How would you have reacted if you had been there to greet Jesus riding into town? Do you jump on political or religious bandwagons today? Why or why not? **3.** Does Jesus' humility work for you? Why or why not?

Matthew 20:20–28 **A MOTHER'S REQUEST**

God wants you to be more of a servant? How do you feel about that?

7. How would you describe your parents' expectations of you?
   a. My parents expect very little—I wonder if they even care.
   b. My parents expect too much—I could never live up to their expectations.
   c. My parents' expectations are high enough to challenge me, but not too high to discourage me.
   d. My parents have helped me to set my own expectations.

8. When you have a difference with a parent over expectations, what have you found helpful?
   a. Tell them to stay out of my life.
   b. Tell them what they want to hear.
   c. Try to understand their viewpoint.
   d. Talk it through until we agree together on the expectations.

9. What does this story say to you about your expectations for your children?
   a. I need to let my children speak for themselves.
   b. Before I encourage my children to reach for something, I should be sure I know the cost.
   c. I need to help my children focus less on self-glory and more on how they can serve.

10. What would you like to pass on to your kids?
   a. nothing in particular—They need to develop on their own.
   b. a sense of right and wrong
   c. a deep faith
   d. family loyalty
   e. lots of initiative
   f. a significant inheritance
   g. our business or a certain career
   h. other:__________

ABOUT THE MARGIN QUESTIONS

SHARING

20. What are the margin questions for? To facilitate sharing in groups with questions on three different levels—(1) to start a meeting, (2) to study together, and (3) to close.

COFFEE CUP

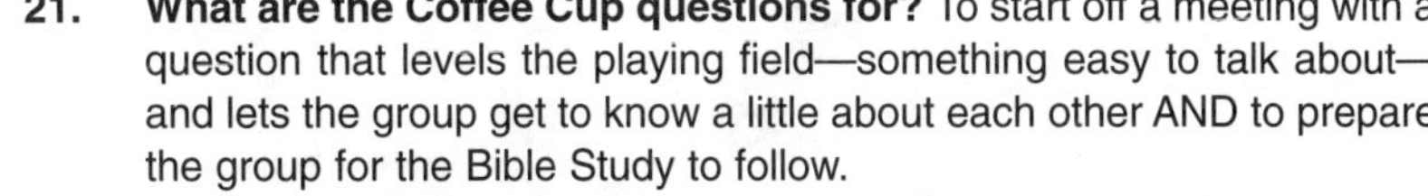

21. What are the Coffee Cup questions for? To start off a meeting with a question that levels the playing field—something easy to talk about—and lets the group get to know a little about each other AND to prepare the group for the Bible Study to follow.

BOOK

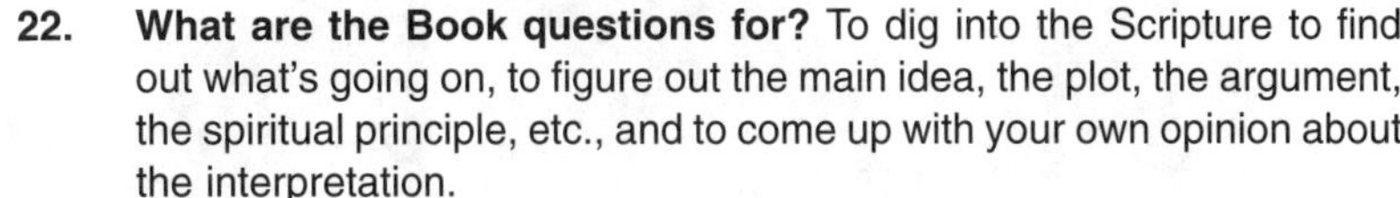

22. What are the Book questions for? To dig into the Scripture to find out what's going on, to figure out the main idea, the plot, the argument, the spiritual principle, etc., and to come up with your own opinion about the interpretation.

HEART

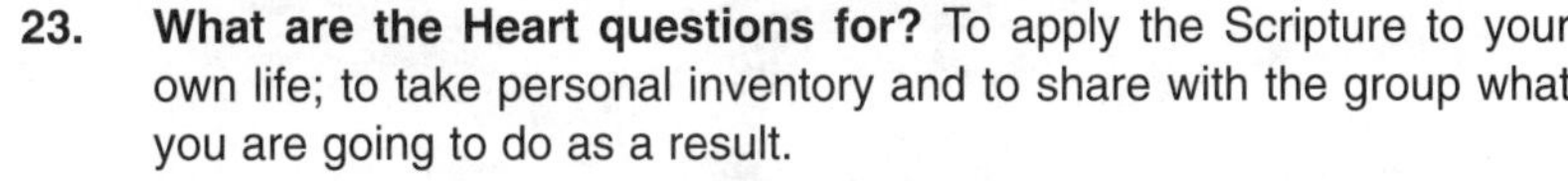

23. What are the Heart questions for? To apply the Scripture to your own life; to take personal inventory and to share with the group what you are going to do as a result.

MODIFYING

24. What if the questions don't fit our situation? Feel free to modify or customize them.

SMALL GROUPS

25. Why a New Testament designed specifically for small groups? Because small groups need special kinds of discussion questions that help the group to relax and share their own life as well as discuss the Scripture.

INTERACTION

26. What do you call this small group interaction? Serendipity.

SERENDIPITY

27. What is "serendipity"? Originally, it meant "the facility of making happy chance discoveries" (Horace Walpole, 1743). Applied to Bible study, serendipity is what happens when a group of people get together to share their lives around the Scripture, and the Holy Spirit does something special.

GROUP BUILDING

28. How does this New Testament fit into this? *The Serendipity New Testament* gives you the tools for building a solid, sturdy, balanced support group.

DREAM

29. What is your hope and dream for this New Testament? To help groups in the church to be part of a Christian community that both studies together and cares for one another.

TARGET COURSES

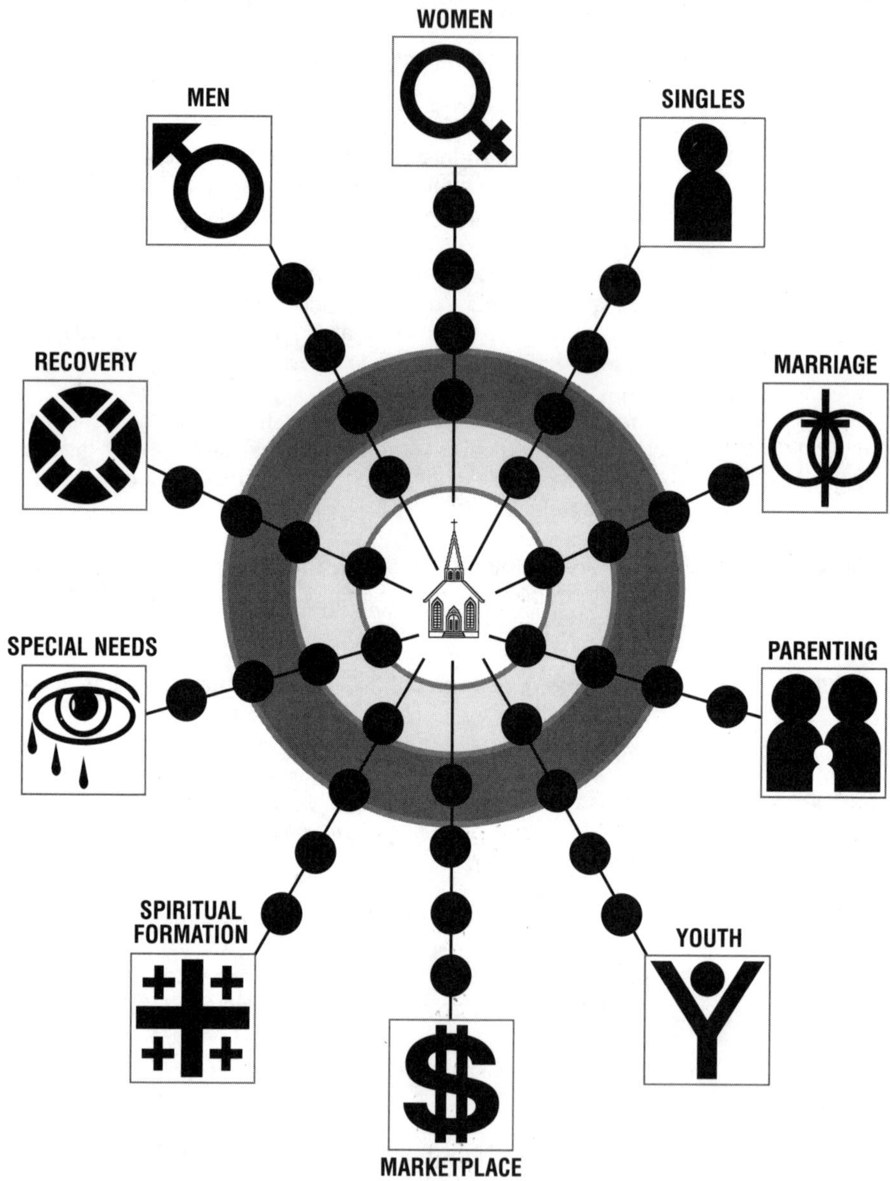

Targeting 10
small group audiences

MEN'S COURSES

		TRACK 1 Stories / LITE		TRACK 2 Teachings / HEAVY	

1 MASCULINITY: "WILL THE REAL JESUS PLEASE STAND UP?"

"I get mixed messages about what a man should be—somewhere between macho and milquetoast. I know Jesus is God, but is he also someone I can look to as the ultimate man?"

		Track 1		Track 2	
1	THE DIVINE JESUS	"God with us" Matthew 1:18–25	[p. 45]	Children of God 1 John 2:28–3:10	[p. 418]
2	THE HUMAN JESUS	"Isn't this Joseph's son?" Luke 4:14–30	[p. 144]	Jesus made like his brothers Hebrews 2:1–18	[p. 387]
3	THE INITIATED JESUS	Baptized and tempted Matthew 3:13–4:11	[p. 48]	Tempted as we are Hebrews 4:14–5:10	[p. 389]
4	THE TOUGH JESUS	Temple cleansing time Mark 11:12–19	[p. 120]	Paul tells it like it is Galatians 1:1–10	[p. 336]
5	THE TENDER JESUS	"Jesus wept" John 11:1–44	[p. 215]	"In his steps" 1 Peter 2:13–25	[p. 408]
6	THE TRIUMPHANT JESUS	Jesus' death Luke 23:44–49	[p. 190]	"More than conquerors" Romans 8:28–39	[p. 294]

2 DISCIPLESHIP: "BEING A MAN AFTER GOD'S OWN HEART"

"Could anyone tell me what it means to be a man of God? I'm tired of pious Jesus talk and Sunday Christians. If I'm going to go for Christianity, I'm going all the way."

		Track 1		Track 2	
1	OPENING UP	A Pharisee and a tax collector Luke 18:9–14	[p. 177]	You are not alone 1 Corinthians 10:1–13	[p. 314]
2	TOTAL COMMITMENT	The rich young man Mark 10:17–31	[p. 117]	Take up your cross Luke 9:18–27	[p. 156]
3	TEACHABLE SPIRIT	Peter's stretching vision Acts 10:1–23	[p. 254]	Obey God and your leaders Hebrews 13:1–25	[p. 398]
4	MY DARK SIDE	Dirty dancing Mark 6:14–29	[p. 108]	A war within Romans 7:7–25	[p. 292]
5	MY DOUBTS	I believe; help my unbelief! Mark 9:14–29	[p. 115]	Real confidence 1 John 5:1–21	[p. 420]
6	SPREADING THE WORD	Don't just stand there Acts 1:1–11	[p. 235]	Christ's ambassadors 2 Corinthians 5:11–6:2	[p. 327]

3 ATTITUDE ADJUSTMENT: "DOWN BUT NOT OUT"

"Pressure is closing in on me. Too many demands. Not enough time. Money. My job. My kids. My marriage. Things are out of control and getting worse. I can't take this rat race anymore."

		Track 1		Track 2	
1	PRESSURES	Stress at work Matthew 20:1–16	[p. 75]	Pressure beyond our ability to endure 2 Corinthians 1:1–11	[p. 324]
2	DEMANDS	Jesus deals with demands Mark 1:29–39	[p. 98]	Paul's boasting 2 Corinthians 11:16–33	[p. 332]
3	CHAOS	Paul and Silas in the slammer Acts 16:16–40	[p. 265]	Fixing our eyes on the eternal 2 Corinthians 4:1–18	[p. 326]
4	BLOWING IT	Peter denies Jesus Luke 22:54–62	[p. 187]	The good news of forgiveness 1 John 1:1–2:14	[p. 417]
5	FAMILY STRESS	Fracas in the family Luke 15:11–32	[p. 171]	Good discipline Hebrews 12:1–13	[p. 397]
6	FOURTH AND GOAL	Peter steps out of the boat Matthew 14:22–33	[p. 67]	Trials and temptations James 1:1–18	[p. 401]

WOMEN'S COURSES

		TRACK 1 *Stories / LITE*	**TRACK 2** *Teachings / HEAVY*

4 A WOMAN OF EXCELLENCE: "LIVING IN A WORLD OF GLITZ"

"It's a constant battle! My looks, my decisions on family and career, and my spiritual life never seem quite right. Where can I learn to be a godly woman of excellence in today's world?"

#	Session	Track 1	Track 2
1	TRYING TO MEASURE UP	Amazing affirmation John 7:53–8:11 [p. 208]	"How great is the love" 1 John 2:28–3:10 [p. 418]
2	FINDING MY OWN STYLE	Stylish love Luke 7:36–50 [p. 152]	"Be imitators of God" Ephesians 5:1–20 [p. 346]
3	MY SPIRITUAL POTENTIAL	"Follow me" Matthew 16:13–28 [p. 70]	Pressing on toward the goal Philippians 3:12–4:1 [p. 352]
4	USING MY GIFTS	Following Priscilla's lead Acts 18:1–4,18–28 [p. 269]	Pleasing God with my gifts Romans 12:1–8 [p. 299]
5	BALANCING ACT	Lydia the businesswoman Acts 16:11–15 [p. 264]	Inner beauty 1 Peter 3:1–7 [p. 409]
6	ACHIEVING REAL EXCELLENCE	Mary's song Luke 1:39–56 [p. 136]	"We are God's workmanship" Ephesians 2:1–10 [p. 344]

5 TRANSITIONS: "COPING WITH CHANGE"

"My head is swimming. Last year we moved. I went back to work. My youngest child is starting school. Can somebody throw me a life jacket to survive all the emotions that go along with change?!"

#	Session	Track 1	Track 2
1	MY CHANGING HOME	The house built on rock Matthew 7:24–29 [p. 55]	Content in any situation Philippians 4:10–23 [p. 353]
2	MY CHANGING SPIRITUAL LIFE	Woman gets "living water" John 4:7–30 [p. 200]	Love perfected 1 John 4:7–21 [p. 420]
3	MY CHANGING CAREER	First disciples called Luke 5:1–11 [p. 146]	Being worthy of your calling Ephesians 4:1–16 [p. 345]
4	MY CHANGING FAMILY	Mary's changing child Luke 2:41–52 [p. 141]	"As a father deals with his own children" 1 Thessalonians 2:1–16 [p. 361]
5	JESUS' HEALING TOUCH	Jesus heals a bleeding woman Mark 5:24–34 [p. 106]	More than all we ask or imagine Ephesians 3:14–21 [p. 345]
6	NO MORE GOODBYES!	Mary must say another goodbye John 20:1–18 [p. 230]	"Another Counselor to be with you forever" John 14:15–31 [p. 221]

6 ASSERTIVENESS: "HOLDING YOUR OWN"

"I feel like I'm always giving and always giving in. I want to be a giving person, but I have needs too. How and when do I speak up for myself?"

#	Session	Track 1	Track 2
1	EMPATHY vs. OBSESSION	Jesus mourns with Mary and Martha John 11:1–44 [p. 215]	The attitude of Christ Philippians 2:1–11 [p. 351]
2	SERVANTHOOD vs. SETTING LIMITS	Mary chooses not to serve Luke 10:38–42 [p. 161]	"Neither do we go beyond our limits" 2 Corinthians 10:1–18 [p. 330]
3	ACCEPTED BY GOD	Affirmed by Jesus Luke 19:1–10 [p. 179]	Chosen and blessed Ephesians 1:1–14 [p. 343]
4	LOVE AND ANGER	Jesus clears the temple Mark 11:12–19 [p. 120]	"Speaking the truth in love" Ephesians 4:1–16 [p. 345]
5	AT PEACE WITH MYSELF	Jesus at peace in the temple Luke 2:41–52 [p. 141]	"Peace I leave with you" John 14:15–31 [p. 221]
6	GIVING AND RECEIVING	The sheep and the goats Matthew 25:31–46 [p. 87]	Equality in giving 2 Corinthians 8:1–15 [p. 329]

SINGLES COURSES

7 LOVE AND LONELINESS: "SOLITAIRE ON A SATURDAY NIGHT"

"I often go for days without a hug or meaningful conversation. Sometimes singleness is like being a social leper. How can I deal with my 'disease'?"

		TRACK 1 Stories / LITE		TRACK 2 Teachings / HEAVY	
1	MY NEED FOR COMMUNICATION	Early connections Acts 2:42–47	[p. 239]	Everybody needs some body 1 Corinthians 12:12–31	[p. 316]
2	MY NEED TO RISK AGAIN	Seventy-seven times Matthew 18:21–35	[p. 73]	"To this you were called" 1 Peter 3:8–22	[p. 409]
3	MY NEED TO INVEST IN OTHERS	The Good Samaritan Luke 10:25–37	[p. 160]	"Love each other deeply" 1 Peter 4:1–11	[p. 410]
4	MY NEED FOR A LOVING TOUCH	A touching act Luke 7:36–50	[p. 152]	Love with actions and in truth 1 John 3:11–24	[p. 419]
5	MY NEED FOR A GOOD MATCH	Priscilla and Aquila: True partners Acts 18:1–4,18–28	[p. 269]	"In knowledge and depth of insight" Philippians 1:1–11	[p. 350]
6	MY NEED TO REACH OUT	Lydia: A servant open to God Acts 16:11–15	[p. 264]	The attitude of Christ Philippians 2:1–11	[p. 351]

8 THE SINGLE JESUS: "BECOMING A WHOLE IN ONE"

"Jesus was single. Is it possible God wants me to remain single for life? How can he call singleness a 'gift'? Couldn't I serve him better with a partner? How can I be 'whole' for him now as a single?"

		TRACK 1 Stories / LITE		TRACK 2 Teachings / HEAVY	
1	DID JESUS EVER FEEL LONELY?	Alone in the wilderness Matthew 3:13–4:11	[p. 48]	A gentle and merciful high priest Hebrews 4:14–5:10	[p. 389]
2	THE *GIFT* OF SINGLENESS?	A high calling Acts 9:1–19	[p. 251]	Happier as a single 1 Corinthians 7:25–35	[p. 311]
3	HOW DO I DEAL WITH BEING ALONE?	Jesus' life of balance Mark 1:29–39	[p. 98]	Each one has his own gift 1 Corinthians 7:36–40	[p. 312]
4	HOW CAN I BEST SERVE?	The greatest servant Mark 10:35–45	[p. 118]	The best kind of service 2 Timothy 2:14–26	[p. 377]
5	HOW SHOULD I PRAY?	Jesus prays for God's will Mark 14:32–42	[p. 127]	"Present your requests to God" Philippians 4:2–9	[p. 353]
6	A WHOLE IN ONE	Transfiguration of Jesus Mark 9:2–13	[p. 114]	"I can do everything ..." Philippians 4:10–23	[p. 353]

MARRIAGE COURSES

		TRACK 1 *Stories / LITE*		TRACK 2 *Teachings / HEAVY*	

9 BALANCING ACT: "WINNING AT WORK WITHOUT LOSING AT HOME"

"We both have so many demands for our time and energy. How can we give our best to our work without it coming at the expense of our family? I don't want to lose what we're supposed to be working for!"

		Track 1		Track 2	
1	WORK AND STRESS	Workers in the vineyard Matthew 20:1–16	[p. 75]	God's rest Hebrews 4:1–13	[p. 388]
2	TEAMMATES	Martha in the kitchen Luke 10:38–42	[p. 161]	"Love is ..." 1 Corinthians 13:1–13	[p. 317]
3	STRESS MANAGEMENT	Jesus deals with demands Mark 1:29–39	[p. 98]	One day at a time Matthew 6:19–34	[p. 53]
4	WHAT ARE WE WORKING FOR?	Parable of the rich fool Luke 12:13–21	[p. 164]	The secret of contentment Philippians 4:10–23	[p. 353]
5	SERVING EACH OTHER	Footwashing John 13:1–17	[p. 219]	Putting your "better half" first Philippians 2:1–11	[p. 351]
6	FAITHFUL AND FULFILLED	Priscilla and Aquilla work together Acts 18:1–14,18–28	[p. 269]	Serving the Lord Colossians 3:1–4:1	[p. 358]

10 COMMUNICATION AND CONFLICT: "LASTING LOVE"

"Whether it's how to spend an evening or how to spend our income tax refund—we have a different point of view. How can we relate to each other in a way that pulls us together instead of apart?"

		Track 1		Track 2	
1	THE POWER OF COMMITMENT	Joseph marries Mary Matthew 1:18–25	[p. 45]	"What God has joined together" Matthew 19:1–12	[p. 74]
2	FAMILY HASSLES	Jesus and his mom at a wedding John 2:1–11	[p. 196]	Taming the tongue James 3:1–12	[p. 403]
3	MONEY HASSLES	Parable of the talents Matthew 25:14–30	[p. 86]	When you don't get your own way James 4:1–12	[p. 403]
4	THE POWER OF SUPPORT	A family turns to the Lord Acts 16:16–40	[p. 265]	Body support 1 Corinthians 12:12–31	[p. 316]
5	THE POWER OF FORGIVENESS	Parable of the unmerciful servant Matthew 18:21–35	[p. 73]	"In your anger do not sin" Ephesians 4:17–32	[p. 346]
6	PULLING TOGETHER	Overcoming differences John 4:7–30	[p. 200]	Mutual respect Ephesians 5:22–6:9	[p. 347]

PARENTING COURSES

		TRACK 1 *Stories / LITE*	TRACK 2 *Teachings / HEAVY*

11 PARENTING: "NOT JUST A STROLL IN THE PARK"

"I got into parenting before I was ready. Dr. Spock makes it sound so easy. My mother just laughs. My grandmother says everything will be okay. But I'm trying to raise my kids without a map. Please help."

		Track 1	Track 2
1	PREPARATION	Mary and Joseph become parents Luke 2:1–20 [p. 138]	The pain and the hope Romans 8:18–27 [p. 294]
2	DEDICATION	Jesus presented in the temple Luke 2:21–40 [p. 140]	Committed to love Romans 12:9–21 [p. 299]
3	EXPECTATIONS	A mother's high hopes Matthew 20:20–28 [p. 77]	High standards Colossians 3:1–4:1 [p. 358]
4	CONFUSING TIMES	Jesus perplexes his parents Luke 2:41–52 [p. 141]	"In your anger do not sin" Ephesians 4:17–32 [p. 346]
5	PAINFUL TIMES	Peter disowns Jesus Luke 22:54–62 [p. 187]	Godly discipline Hebrews 12:1–13 [p. 397]
6	JOYFUL TIMES	Homecoming party Luke 15:11–32 [p. 171]	Hard times/beautiful times James 1:1–18 [p. 401]

12 FAMILY TIME: "MAKING MEANINGFUL MEMORIES"

"We want to live like a ***real*** *Christian family. Will our kids remember their childhood in a way that feels good to them and honors God?"*

		Track 1	Track 2
1	PROPER PRIORITIES	Lord of the Sabbath Mark 2:23–36 [p. 101]	Training for godliness 1 Timothy 4:1–16 [p. 372]
2	TIME TOGETHER	Supper time John 13:1–17 [p. 219]	"Love is ..." 1 Corinthians 13:1–13 [p. 317]
3	FAMILY TRADITIONS	The Last Supper Luke 22:7–34 [p. 185]	Passing on the faith 2 Timothy 1:1–2:13 [p. 376]
4	FAMILY VACATIONS	A "vacation" with 5,000 surprises Mark 6:30–44 [p. 109]	Getting along Ephesians 5:22–6:9 [p. 347]
5	WORSHIPING TOGETHER	The fellowship of believers Acts 2:42–47 [p. 239]	Godly role models Titus 2:1–15 [p. 381]
6	LASTING VALUES	The light of the world John 9:1–34 [p. 211]	Leaving a legacy 2 Timothy 3:10–4:8 [p. 378]

YOUTH COURSES

		TRACK 1 *Stories / LITE*	TRACK 2 *Teachings / HEAVY*

13 UP CLOSE: "DISCOVERING MY REAL IDENTITY"

"I know I'm good at some things and not so good at others. I don't want to be weird, but I do want to be myself. What makes me unique? How can I be all that I was meant to be?"

		TRACK 1	TRACK 2
1	BEING REAL	A Pharisee and a tax collector Luke 18:9–14 [p. 177]	Children of God 1 John 2:28–3:10 [p. 418]
2	MY UNIQUENESS	Zacchaeus Luke 19:1–10 [p. 179]	Finding your place 1 Corinthians 12:1–11 [p. 316]
3	MY PERSONALITY	Mary and Martha Luke 10:38–42 [p. 161]	Don't be ashamed of your youth 1 Timothy 4:1–16 [p. 372]
4	MY ABILITIES	Using your "talents" Matthew 25:14–30 [p. 86]	You and your gifts Romans 12:1–8 [p. 299]
5	FITTING IN	Paul's struggle for acceptance Acts 9:20–31 [p. 252]	Body support 1 Corinthians 12:12–31 [p. 316]
6	GOD'S CALL	Following Jesus Luke 5:1–11 [p. 146]	New creation 2 Corinthians 5:11–6:2 [p. 327]

14 CONFIRMATION: "WHAT DO I BELIEVE?"

"It's easy to let stuff at church, like the Apostles' Creed, go in one ear and out the other. I think it's time to know what I really believe, and really believe what I already know."

		TRACK 1	TRACK 2
1	GOD THE FATHER ALMIGHTY	The Father speaks Matthew 3:13–4:11 [p. 48]	The Father's power Ephesians 3:14–21 [p. 345]
2	JESUS CHRIST	An angel visits Mary Luke 1:26–38 [p. 135]	The supremacy of Christ Colossians 1:15–23 [p. 356]
3	HOLY SPIRIT	The Spirit shakes things up Acts 4:1–31 [p. 241]	Living by the Spirit Galatians 5:16–26 [p. 340]
4	CHRISTIAN CHURCH	The cost in "being there" Acts 4:32–37 [p. 243]	Unity in the body of Christ Ephesians 4:1–16 [p. 345]
5	FORGIVENESS OF SINS	Jesus: My substitute Mark 15:1–15 [p. 129]	God's gift of grace Ephesians 2:1–10 [p. 344]
6	RESURRECTION AND LIFE	A new day dawns Matthew 28:1–20 [p. 94]	Resurrection life 1 Corinthians 15:12–34 [p. 319]

15 STRESS: "SURVIVING DAY TO DAY"

"I have to buy my own clothes. Bum a ride. Make a C average just to stay on the team. Everybody's on my back. And my best friend didn't call tonight. Life stinks."

		TRACK 1 Stories / LITE		TRACK 2 Teachings / HEAVY	
1	STRESSED OUT	Facing storms Mark 4:35–41	[p. 105]	Not to worry Matthew 6:19–34	[p. 53]
2	MAKING THE GRADE	Parable of the talents Matthew 25:14–30	[p. 86]	Attitudes and gifts Romans 12:1–8	[p. 299]
3	FIGHTING THE CROWD	Four friends who cared Mark 2:1–12	[p. 99]	Who is "the wrong crowd"? 2 Corinthians 6:14–7:1	[p. 328]
4	FEELING ALONE	Jesus in Gethsemane Mark 14:32–42	[p. 127]	Devoted to one another Romans 12:9–21	[p. 299]
5	DEALING WITH DISAPPOINTMENT	Jesus betrayed and arrested Matthew 26:47–56	[p. 90]	Hope doesn't disappoint Romans 5:1–11	[p. 290]
6	FACING FAILURE	Peter disowns Jesus Luke 22:54–62	[p. 187]	"More than conquerors" Romans 8:28–39	[p. 294]

16 HASSLES: "GETTING ALONG WITH MY PARENTS"

"In my parents' eyes, I can't do anything right. I don't look right, act right, study right, spend money right or pick friends right. As long as I'm still at home, will I always be wrong?"

		TRACK 1 Stories / LITE		TRACK 2 Teachings / HEAVY	
1	PARENTAL REQUESTS	Jesus and his mom at a wedding John 2:1–11	[p. 196]	"Love is ..." 1 Corinthians 13:1–13	[p. 317]
2	PARENTAL EXPECTATIONS	A mother's dream Matthew 20:20–28	[p. 77]	Harmony at home Colossians 3:1–4:1	[p. 358]
3	FAMILY TENSION	When Jesus didn't come home Luke 2:41–52	[p. 141]	Fights and quarrels James 4:1–12	[p. 403]
4	DEALING WITH FRUSTRATIONS	Jesus and his family Mark 3:20–35	[p. 102]	"In your anger do not sin" Ephesians 4:17–32	[p. 346]
5	ARGUING OVER RELATIONSHIPS	Dirty dancing Mark 6:14–29	[p. 108]	Living to please God 1 Thessalonians 4:1–12	[p. 362]
6	MAKING THINGS RIGHT	A son returns home Luke 15:11–32	[p. 171]	Mending your fences Matthew 5:21–48	[p. 51]

MARKETPLACE COURSES

		TRACK 1 *Stories / LITE*		TRACK 2 *Teachings / HEAVY*	

17 BUSINESS ETHICS: "A CHRISTIAN IN A DOWN AND DIRTY WORLD"

"It sounds easy on Sunday, but Monday morning the rubber hits the road. Slice the meat a little thinner and say your prayers later. Can you live like a Christian in the business world and try to get ahead?"

		Track 1		Track 2	
1	VALUES OF INTEGRITY	Rich fool faces regret Luke 12:13–21	[p. 164]	The love of money 1 Timothy 6:3–10	[p. 373]
2	LACK OF INTEGRITY	Ananias and Sapphira Acts 5:1–11	[p. 244]	Living in the light Ephesians 4:17–32	[p. 346]
3	INTEGRITY AND CONSCIENCE	Parable of the shrewd manager Luke 16:1–15	[p. 172]	The war within Romans 7:7–25	[p. 292]
4	INTEGRITY AND AUTHORITY	Paying taxes to Caesar Mark 12:13–17	[p. 122]	Submission to authorities Romans 13:1–7	[p. 300]
5	RELATIONSHIPS OF INTEGRITY	Who is greatest? Mark 10:35–45	[p. 118]	Harmony at work Colossians 3:1–4:1	[p. 358]
6	INTEGRITY AND COMPETITION	Paul under pressure Acts 18:5–17	[p. 268]	"Live at peace with everyone" Romans 12:9–21	[p. 299]

18 BORED AND BURNED OUT: "ASSESSING YOUR CAREER"

"My job is like a broken record. The same thing over and over. By 10 a.m. I'm already tired. By noon, I'm ready to go home. Is it me ... or my work? Maybe I need an attitude adjustment."

		Track 1		Track 2	
1	WHY WORK?	A beachcomber paralytic John 5:1–15	[p. 202]	A workman not ashamed 2 Timothy 2:14–26	[p. 377]
2	WHY AM I HERE?	Philip does productive networking Acts 8:26–40	[p. 250]	"Perplexed, but not in despair" 2 Corinthians 4:1–18	[p. 326]
3	HOW CAN GOD USE ME?	Peter's windfall Luke 5:1–11	[p. 146]	A living sacrifice Romans 12:1–8	[p. 299]
4	HOW'S MY "SERVE"?	Jesus takes a job beneath him John 13:1–17	[p. 219]	Jesus' attitude Philippians 2:1–11	[p. 351]
5	SHOULD I STEP OUT?	Peter steps out of the boat Matthew 14:22–33	[p. 67]	"Why do you worry?" Matthew 6:19–34	[p. 53]
6	WHAT IS MY PASSION?	Paul's passion revealed Acts 26:1–32	[p. 280]	The secret of contentment Philippians 4:10–23	[p. 353]

SPIRITUAL FORMATION

		TRACK 1 *Stories / LITE*		TRACK 2 *Teachings / HEAVY*	

19 SPIRITUAL BASICS: "BECOMING A CHRISTIAN"

"I feel a little stupid and afraid to ask, but I didn't grow up in a church and I never really heard what it means to become a Christian. How do I get to know someone I can't see, touch or hear?"

		Track 1		Track 2	
1	WHO IS CHRIST?	An angel visits Mary Luke 1:26–38	[p. 135]	Supreme over all Colossians 1:15–23	[p. 356]
2	HOW DO I RESPOND?	Jesus and Nicodemus John 3:1–21	[p. 198]	Confess and believe Romans 9:30–10:21	[p. 296]
3	WHAT ABOUT MY SINS?	Jesus: My Substitute Mark 15:1–15	[p. 129]	God's gift of grace Ephesians 2:1–10	[p. 344]
4	HOW CAN I BE SURE?	An honest doubter John 20:24–31	[p. 231]	Confident faith 1 John 5:1–21	[p. 420]
5	WHAT SHOULD I DO NOW?	Zacchaeus' new life Luke 19:1–10	[p. 179]	Faith and action Acts 2:42–47	[p. 239]
6	WHAT DOES IT COST?	Take up your cross Matthew 16:13–28	[p. 70]	Pressing on toward the goal Philippians 3:12–4:1	[p. 352]

20 MATURING IN CHRIST: "CALLED TO DISCIPLESHIP"

"Now that I have given my life to Christ, what do I do next? I need to think through my priorities. My relationships. My goals in life. And I need a group of people to help stay the course."

		Track 1		Track 2	
1	UNDER NEW MANAGEMENT	Paul's change of direction Acts 9:1–19	[p. 251]	Controlled by the Spirit Romans 8:1–17	[p. 293]
2	ETERNAL VALUES	The rich man and Lazarus Luke 16:19–31	[p. 173]	Counting the cost Luke 14:25–35	[p. 168]
3	KINGDOM PRIORITIES	Parable of the great banquet Luke 14:15–24	[p. 169]	Using your gifts Romans 12:1–8	[p. 299]
4	QUIET TIME	Jesus: A person of prayer Mark 1:29–39	[p. 98]	The Lord's Prayer Matthew 6:1–18	[p. 52]
5	SERVANTHOOD	The Last Supper Luke 22:7–34	[p. 185]	The attitude of Christ Philippians 2:1–11	[p. 351]
6	CALLED TO BE WITNESSES	Don't just stand there Acts 1:1–11	[p. 235]	Called to be change agents 2 Corinthians 5:11–6:2	[p. 327]

21 COMING HOME: "PILGRIMS ON THEIR WAY BACK"

"God, I'm on my way back, but I keep hitting roadblocks. I hear voices from my past reminding me of all the bad things I've done ... and telling me that I will never make it. Please be patient."

		Track 1		Track 2	
1	THE CALL OF LOVE	Parable of the Prodigal Son Luke 15:11–32	[p. 171]	"We love because he first loved us" 1 John 4:7–21	[p. 420]
2	THE CALL TO FOLLOW	Following Jesus Luke 5:1–11	[p. 146]	The Good Shepherd John 10:1–21	[p. 213]
3	RESPONDING TO GOD	Parable of the sower Matthew 13:1–23	[p. 63]	Struggling with sin Romans 7:7–25	[p. 292]
4	RESTORED VISION	On the road to Emmaus Luke 24:13–35	[p. 191]	Seeing the real battle Ephesians 6:10–24	[p. 347]
5	RETURNING TO GOD	Jesus reinstates Peter John 21:1–25	[p. 232]	Living by the Spirit Romans 8:1–17	[p. 293]
6	A CLEAN SLATE	Great love, great grace Luke 7:36–50	[p. 152]	True confessions James 5:7–20	[p. 404]

SPECIAL NEEDS

		TRACK 1 *Stories / LITE*	TRACK 2 *Teachings / HEAVY*

22 FINANCIAL STRESS: "MAKING ENDS MEET"

"I've got the mortgage. The loan to pay off. And now these credit card bills. How did I get myself into this? I could ask a relative for a loan, but I would rather die than admit I've blown it. What do I do?"

		Track 1	Track 2
1	HARD TIMES	Hitting bottom Luke 15:11–32 [p. 171]	Trials and temptations James 1:1–18 [p. 401]
2	FACING THE STRESS	Jesus faces pressure Luke 4:14–30 [p. 144]	Relying on God 2 Corinthians 1:1–11 [p. 324]
3	TAKING RESPONSIBILITY	Parable of the talents Matthew 25:14–30 [p. 86]	God is faithful; we should be too 2 Thessalonians 3:1–18 [p. 367]
4	TOUGH DECISIONS	Parable of the shrewd manager Luke 16:1–15 [p. 172]	Don't worry Matthew 6:19–34 [p. 53]
5	MUTUAL AID	Believers share their possessions Acts 4:32–37 [p. 243]	Giving and receiving 2 Corinthians 9:6–15 [p. 330]
6	IN GOD WE TRUST	The widow's offering Mark 12:41–44 [p. 124]	In plenty or in want Philippians 4:10–23 [p. 353]

23 LIVING WITH PAIN: "COPING WITH LIFE'S HURTS"

"I feel like I'm dragging a ball and chain around. How can I deal each day with the pain I'm in, plus the guilt I feel for being such a burden to others?"

		Track 1	Track 2
1	WHERE IS GOD WHEN I HURT?	The pool paralytic John 5:1–15 [p. 202]	Groaning for redemption Romans 8:18–27 [p. 294]
2	PAIN AND BLAME	Why was he born blind? John 9:1–34 [p. 211]	Patience and forgiveness James 5:7–20 [p. 404]
3	PAIN AND SHAME	Jesus heals an "unclean" woman Mark 5:24-34 [p. 106]	"If God is for us, who can be against us?" Romans 8:28–39 [p. 294]
4	PAIN AND COMFORT	Four friends who cared Mark 2:1–12 [p. 99]	"The God of all comfort" 2 Corinthians 1:1–11 [p. 324]
5	PAIN AND PERSPECTIVE	"Jesus wept" John 11:1–44 [p. 215]	The fruit of suffering Romans 5:1–11 [p. 290]
6	PAIN AND PERSISTENCE	Parable of the persistent widow Luke 18:1–8 [p. 176]	Paul's thorn in the flesh 2 Corinthians 12:1–10 [p. 332]

RECOVERY COURSES

		TRACK 1 *Stories / LITE*	TRACK 2 *Teachings / HEAVY*

24 STRESS MANAGEMENT: "LIVING UNDER PRESSURE"

"The stress I'm under every day is incredible. Deadlines, projects, work relationships—plus home and family. If I don't find a way to release some of this pressure, I'm gonna crack!"

		Track 1	Track 2
1	LIVING WITH STRESS	The storm Mark 4:35–41 [p. 105]	"Perplexed, but not in despair" 2 Corinthians 4:1–18 [p. 326]
2	SETTING LIMITS	Mary chooses not to serve Luke 10:38–42 [p. 161]	"Neither do we go beyond our limits" 2 Corinthians 10:1–18 [p. 330]
3	BALANCING WORK AND REST	Jesus feeds 5,000 Mark 6:30–44 [p. 109]	Rest for the weary Matthew 11:25–30 [p. 60]
4	HEALTHY INVESTMENTS	Parable of the talents Matthew 25:14–30 [p. 86]	A living sacrifice Romans 12:1–8 [p. 299]
5	MY NEED FOR OTHERS	Jesus in Gethsemane Mark 14:32–42 [p. 127]	Passing on God's comfort 2 Corinthians 1:1–11 [p. 324]
6	MY NEED FOR GOD	Paul's vision brings comfort Acts 18:5–7 [p. 268]	Peace of mind Philippians 4:2–9 [p. 353]

25 12 STEPS: "THE ROAD TO RECOVERY"

"I'm hooked, and this thing is stronger than I am. I know I need a 'Higher Power' and I know that 'Higher Power' is God. How can God help me break the stranglehold of this addiction?"

		Track 1	Track 2
1	GOING BEYOND DENIAL	A Pharisee and a tax collector Luke 18:9–14 [p. 177]	Admitting we are powerless Romans 7:7–25 [p. 292]
2	NAMING THE HIGHER POWER	Jesus heals an "unclean" woman Mark 5:24–34 [p. 106]	Confess and believe Romans 9:30–10:21 [p. 296]
3	COMING TO GOD	A possessed man set free Luke 8:26–39 [p. 155]	Submit to God James 4:1–12 [p. 403]
4	CONFESSION	The Prodigal Son comes home Luke 15:11–32 [p. 171]	"Confess your sins to each other" James 5:7–20 [p. 404]
5	MAKING AMENDS	Zacchaeus makes things right Luke 19:1–10 [p. 179]	"Produce fruit in keeping with repentance" Matthew 3:1–17 [p. 47]
6	AN ADDICTION-FREE LIFESTYLE	Peter's deliverance from prison Acts 12:1–19 [p. 257]	"Be careful that you don't fall!" 1 Corinthians 10:1–13 [p. 314]

86 NEW TESTAMENT STORIES WITH READY-MADE QUESTIONNAIRES

In addition to the 25 courses found on pages 19–29, you can design your own small group course using these 86 questionnaires—such as choosing stories from *Jesus' Last Week and Resurrection Appearances* for a Lenten series. Or you can use one of the suggested course outlines at the end of the list of the 86 stories.

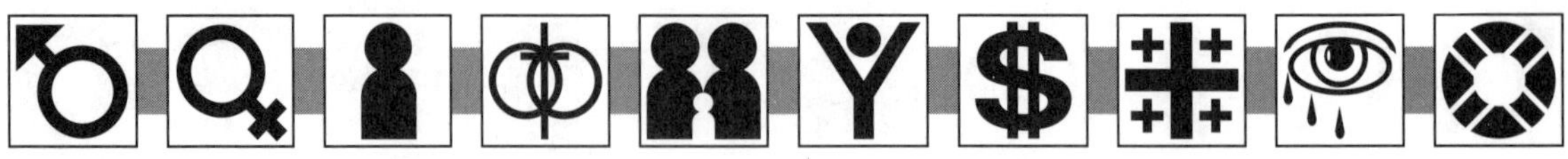

GENERAL COURSES

THE LIFE OF CHRIST

7-wk plan	13-wk plan			Page
1	1	The Birth of Jesus	Lk 2:1–20	138
	2	The Baptism and Temptation of Jesus	Mt 3:13–4:11	48
2	3	Jesus Begins Ministry in His Hometown	Lk 4:14–30	144
	4	Jesus Heals and Prays	Mk 1:29–39	98
3	5	Clashes With the Pharisees	Mk 2:23–3:6	101
	6	The Transfiguration	Mk 9:2–13	114
4	7	The Triumphal Entry	Lk 19:28–44	181
	8	Jesus Clears the Temple	Mk 11:12–19	120
5	9	The Last Supper	Lk 22:7–34	185
	10	Jesus in Gethsemane	Mk 14:32–42	127
	11	Jesus Before Pilate	Mk 15:1–15	129
6	12	The Crucifixion	Jn 19:16–27	228
7	13	Resurrection and Great Commission	Mt 28:1–20	94

JESUS' MIRACLES

7-wk plan	13-wk plan			Page
1	1	The Birth of Jesus Foretold	Lk 1:26–38	135
	2	Jesus Changes Water to Wine	Jn 2:1–11	196
2	3	Jesus Heals a Paralytic	Mk 2:1–12	99
	4	Jesus Walks on Water	Mt 14:22–33	67
3	5	Jesus Calms the Storm	Mk 4:35–41	105
	6	Jesus Heals a Bleeding Woman	Mk 5:24–34	106
4	7	Jesus Feeds the 5,000	Mk 6:30–44	109
	8	The Healing of a Boy With an Evil Spirit	Mk 9:14–29	115
5	9	Ten Healed of Leprosy	Lk 17:11–19	175
	10	The Healing at the Pool	Jn 5:1–15	202
6	11	Jesus Heals a Man Born Blind	Jn 9:1–34	211
	12	Jesus Raises Lazarus	Jn 11:1–44	215
7	13	Jesus Appears to Thomas	Jn 20:24–31	231

	7-wk plan	13-wk plan			Page
JESUS REACHES OUT TO OTHERS		1	Nicodemus	Jn 3:1–21	198
	1	2	Samaritan Woman	Jn 4:7–30	200
		3	First Disciples	Lk 5:1–11	146
	2	4	Levi	Lk 5:27–39	148
	3	5	Anointed by a Sinful Woman	Lk 7:36–50	152
		6	The Rich Young Man	Mk 10:17–31	117
		7	Demon-possessed Man	Lk 8:26–39	155
	4	8	Woman Caught in Adultery	Jn 7:53–8:11	208
	5	9	Zacchaeus	Lk 19:1–10	179
	6	10	Washing the Disciples' Feet	Jn 13:1–17	219
		11	Mary Magdalene	Jn 20:1–18	230
		12	Disciples on the Road to Emmaus	Lk 24:13–35	191
	7	13	Reinstating Peter	Jn 21:1–25	232

	7-wk plan	13-wk plan			
JESUS' TEACHINGS	1	1	Parable of the Pharisee and Tax Collector	Lk 18:9–14	177
		2	Parable of the Prodigal Son	Lk 15:11–32	171
	2	3	The Beatitudes	Mt 5:1–12	50
		4	The Wise and Foolish Builders	Mt 7:24–29	55
	3	5	Parable of the Sower	Mt 13:1–23	63
		6	Parable of the Unmerciful Servant	Mt 18:21–35	73
	4	7	Parable of the 10 Virgins	Mt 25:1–13	85
		8	Parable of the Talents	Mt 25:14–30	86
	5	9	The Sheep and the Goats	Mt 25:31–46	87
		10	Parable of the Good Samaritan	Lk 10:25–37	160
	6	11	Parable of the Rich Fool	Lk 12:13–21	164
		12	Parable of the Great Banquet	Lk 14:15–24	169
	7	13	Take Up Your Cross	Mt 16:13–28	70

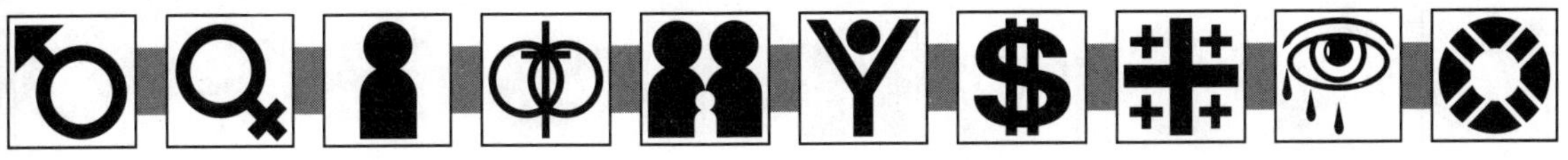

PREFACE

THE NEW INTERNATIONAL VERSION is a completely new translation of the Holy Bible made by over a hundred scholars working directly from the best available Hebrew, Aramaic and Greek texts. It had its beginning in 1965 when, after several years of exploratory study by committees from the Christian Reformed Church and the National Association of Evangelicals, a group of scholars met at Palos Heights, Illinois, and concurred in the need for a new translation of the Bible in contemporary English. This group, though not made up of official church representatives, was transdenominational. Its conclusion was endorsed by a large number of leaders from many denominations who met in Chicago in 1966.

Responsibility for the new version was delegated by the Palos Heights group to a self-governing body of fifteen, the Committee on Bible Translation, composed for the most part of biblical scholars from colleges, universities and seminaries. In 1967 the New York Bible Society (now the International Bible Society) generously undertook the financial sponsorship of the project—a sponsorship that made it possible to enlist the help of many distinguished scholars. The fact that participants from the United States, Great Britain, Canada, Australia and New Zealand worked together gave the project its international scope. That they were from many denominations—including Anglican, Assemblies of God, Baptist, Brethren, Christian Reformed, Church of Christ, Evangelical Free, Lutheran, Mennonite, Methodist, Nazarene, Presbyterian, Wesleyan and other churches—helped to safeguard the translation from sectarian bias.

How it was made helps to give the New International Version its distinctiveness. The translation of each book was assigned to a team of scholars. Next, one of the Intermediate Editorial Committees revised the initial translation, with constant reference to the Hebrew, Aramaic or Greek. Their work then went to one of the General Editorial Committees, which checked it in detail and made another thorough revision. This revision in turn was carefully reviewed by the Committee on Bible Translation, which made further changes and then released the final version for publication. In this way the entire Bible underwent three revisions, during each of which the translation was examined for its faithfulness to the original languages and for its English style.

All this involved many thousands of hours of research and discussion regarding the meaning of the texts and the precise way of putting them into English. It may well be that no other translation has been made by a more thorough process of review and revision from committee to committee than this one.

From the beginning of the project, the Committee on Bible Translation held to certain goals for the New International Version: that it would be an accurate translation and one that would have clarity and literary quality and so prove suitable for public and private reading, teaching, preaching, memorizing and liturgical use. The Committee also sought to preserve some measure of continuity with the long tradition of translating the Scriptures into English.

In working toward these goals, the translators were united in their commitment to the authority and infallibility of the Bible as God's Word in written form. They believe that it contains the divine answer to the deepest needs of humanity, that it sheds unique light on our path in a dark world, and that it sets forth the way to our eternal well-being.

The first concern of the translators has been the accuracy of the translation and its fidelity to the thought of the biblical writers. They have weighed the significance of the lexical and grammatical details of the Hebrew, Aramaic and Greek texts. At the same time, they have striven for more than a word-for-word translation. Because thought patterns and syntax differ from language to language, faithful communication of the meaning of the writers of the Bible demands frequent modifications in sentence structure and constant regard for the contextual meanings of words.

A sensitive feeling for style does not always accompany scholarship. Accordingly, the Committee on Bible Translation submitted the developing version to a number of stylistic consultants. Two of them read every book of both Old and New Testaments twice—once before and once after the last major revision—and made invaluable suggestions. Samples of the translation were tested for clarity and ease of reading by various kinds of people—young and old, highly educated and less well educated, ministers and laymen.

Concern for clear and natural English—that the New International Version should be idiomatic but not idiosyncratic, contemporary but not dated—motivated the translators and consultants. At the same time, they tried to reflect the differing styles of the biblical writers. In view of the international use of English, the translators sought to avoid obvious Americanisms on the one hand and obvious Anglicisms on the other. A British edition reflects the comparatively few differences of significant idiom and of spelling.

As for the traditional pronouns "thou," "thee" and "thine" in reference to the Deity, the translators judged that to use these archaisms (along with the old verb forms such as "doest," "wouldest" and "hadst") would violate accuracy in translation. Neither Hebrew, Aramaic nor Greek uses special pronouns for the persons of the Godhead. A present-day translation is not enhanced by forms that in the time of the King James Version were used in everyday speech, whether referring to God or man.

For the Old Testament the standard Hebrew text, the Masoretic Text as published in the latest edition of *Biblia Hebraica,* was used throughout. The Dead Sea Scrolls contain material bearing on an earlier stage of the Hebrew text. They were consulted, as were the Samaritan Pentateuch and the ancient scribal traditions relating to textual changes. Sometimes a variant Hebrew reading in the margin of the Masoretic Text was followed instead of the text itself. Such instances, being variants within the Masoretic tradition, are not specified by footnotes. In rare cases, words in the consonantal text were divided differently from the way they appear in the Masoretic Text. Footnotes indicate this. The translators also consulted the more important early versions—the Septuagint; Aquila, Symmachus and Theodotion; the Vulgate; the Syriac Peshitta; the Targums; and for the Psalms the *Juxta Hebraica* of Jerome. Readings from these versions were occasionally followed where the Masoretic Text seemed doubtful and where accepted principles of textual criticism showed that one or more of these textual witnesses appeared to provide the correct reading. Such instances are footnoted. Sometimes vowel letters and vowel signs did not, in the judgment of the translators, represent the correct vowels for the original consonantal text. Accordingly some words were read with a different set of vowels. These instances are usually not indicated by footnotes.

The Greek text used in translating the New Testament was an eclectic one. No other piece of ancient literature has such an abundance of manuscript witnesses as does the New Testament. Where existing manuscripts differ, the translators made their choice of readings according to accepted principles of New Testament textual criticism. Footnotes call attention to places where there was uncertainty about what the original text was. The best current printed texts of the Greek New Testament were used.

There is a sense in which the work of translation is never wholly finished. This applies to all great literature and uniquely so to the Bible. In 1973 the New Testament in the New International Version was published. Since then, suggestions for corrections and revisions have been received from various sources. The Committee on Bible Translation carefully considered the suggestions and adopted a number of them. These were incorporated in the first printing of the entire Bible in 1978. Additional revisions were made by the Committee on Bible Translation in 1983 and appear in printings after that date.

As in other ancient documents, the precise meaning of the biblical texts is sometimes uncertain. This is more often the case with the Hebrew and Aramaic texts than with the Greek text. Although archaeological and linguistic discoveries in this century aid in understanding difficult passages, some uncertainties remain. The more significant of these have been called to the reader's attention in the footnotes.

In regard to the divine name *YHWH,* commonly referred to as the *Tetragrammaton,* the translators adopted the device used in most English versions of rendering that name as "LORD" in capital letters to distinguish it from *Adonai,* another Hebrew word rendered "Lord," for which small letters are used. Wherever the two names stand together in the Old Testament as a compound name of God, they are rendered "Sovereign LORD."

Because for most readers today the phrases "the LORD of hosts" and "God of hosts" have little meaning, this version renders them "the LORD Almighty" and "God Almighty." These renderings convey the sense of the Hebrew, namely, "he who is sovereign over all the 'hosts' (powers) in heaven and on earth, especially over the 'hosts' (armies) of Israel." For readers unacquainted with Hebrew this does not make clear the distinction between *Sabaoth* ("hosts" or "Almighty") and *Shaddai* (which can also be translated "Almighty"), but the latter occurs infrequently and is always footnoted. When *Adonai* and *YHWH Sabaoth* occur together, they are rendered "the Lord, the LORD Almighty."

As for other proper nouns, the familiar spellings of the King James Version are generally retained. Names traditionally spelled with "ch," except where it is final, are usually spelled in this translation with "k" or "c," since the biblical languages do not have the sound that "ch" frequently indicates in English—for example, in *chant.* For well-known names such as Zechariah, however, the traditional spelling has been retained. Variation in the spelling of names in the original languages has usually not been indicated. Where a person or place has two or more different names in the Hebrew, Aramaic or Greek texts, the more familiar one has generally been used, with footnotes where needed.

To achieve clarity the translators sometimes supplied words not in the original texts but required by the context. If there was uncertainty about such material, it is enclosed in brackets. Also for the sake of clarity or style, nouns, including some proper nouns, are sometimes substituted for pronouns, and vice versa. And though the Hebrew writers often shifted back and forth between first, second and third personal pronouns without change of antecedent, this translation often makes them uniform, in accordance with English style and without the use of footnotes.

Poetical passages are printed as poetry, that is, with indentation of lines and with separate stanzas. These are generally designed to reflect the structure of Hebrew poetry. This poetry is normally characterized by parallelism in balanced lines. Most of the poetry in the Bible is in the Old Testament, and scholars differ regarding the scansion of Hebrew lines. The translators determined the stanza divisions for the most part by analysis of the subject matter. The stanzas therefore serve as poetic paragraphs.

As an aid to the reader, italicized sectional headings are inserted in most of the books. They are not to be regarded as part of the NIV text, are not for oral reading, and are not intended to dictate the interpretation of the sections they head.

The footnotes in this version are of several kinds, most of which need no explanation. Those giving alternative translations begin with "Or" and generally introduce the alternative with the last word preceding it in the text, except when it is a single-word alternative; in poetry quoted in a footnote a slant mark indicates a line division. Footnotes introduced by "Or" do not have uniform significance. In some cases two possible translations were considered to have about equal validity. In other cases, though the translators were convinced that the translation in the text was correct, they judged that another interpretation was possible and of sufficient importance to be represented in a footnote.

In the New Testament, footnotes that refer to uncertainty regarding the original text are introduced by "Some manuscripts" or similar expressions. In the Old Testament, evidence for the reading chosen is given first and evidence for the alternative is added after a semicolon (for example: Septuagint; Hebrew *father*). In such notes the term "Hebrew" refers to the Masoretic Text.

It should be noted that minerals, flora and fauna, architectural details, articles of clothing and jewelry, musical instruments and other articles cannot always be identified with precision. Also measures of capacity in the biblical period are particularly uncertain (see the table of weights and measures following the text).

Like all translations of the Bible, made as they are by imperfect man, this one undoubtedly falls short of its goals. Yet we are grateful to God for the extent to which he has enabled us to realize these goals and for the strength he has given us and our colleagues to complete our task. We offer this version of the Bible to him in whose name and for whose glory it has been made. We pray that it will lead many into a better understanding of the Holy Scriptures and a fuller knowledge of Jesus Christ the incarnate Word, of whom the Scriptures so faithfully testify.

The Committee on Bible Translation

June 1978
(Revised August 1983)

Names of the translators and editors may be secured
from the International Bible Society,
translation sponsors of the New International Version,
1820 Jet Stream Drive, Colorado Springs, Colorado 80921-3696 U.S.A.

NEW TESTAMENT

INTRODUCTION to

MATTHEW

Book Study Outline: If you are using Matthew for a study course, here is a 7- or 13-week outline. Use the margin questions for your group agenda:

☕ start meeting / 15 min.

📖 read & discuss Bible / 30 min.

♡ close meeting / 15–45 min.

Refer to the Questions and Answers in front of Bible for more information.

7-week plan	13-week plan	Personal Reading	Group Study Passage
1	1	1:1–25	1:18–25/Angel Appears to Joseph
	2	3:1–4:25	3:13–4:11/Baptism &Temptation
2	3	5:1–6:34	5:1–12/The Beatitudes
	4	7:1–9:34	7:24–29/Wise & Foolish Builders
3	5	9:35–11:30	10:1–42/Jesus Sends Out 12
	6	12:1–13:52	13:1–23/Parable of Sower
4	7	13:53–16:12	14:22–33/Walking on Water
	8	16:13–17:27	16:13–28/Christ Must Die
5	9	18:1–35	18:21–35/Unmerciful Servant
	10	19:1–20:34	20:1–16/Workers in Vineyard
6	11	21:1–25:46	25:14–30/Parable of Talents
	12	26:1–75	26:47–56/Jesus Arrested
7	13	27:1–28:20	28:1–20/Jesus' Resurrection

Author: Although not named, a long tradition has assigned it to Matthew, the tax collector who became an apostle.

Date: Uncertain, but probably between A.D. 50–70.

Theme: Jesus, the long-promised Messiah and authoritative teacher.

Historical Background: The first three Gospels cover many of the same events in Jesus' life in the same way. For that reason they are often called the "synoptic Gospels" meaning that they are "able to be seen together." It is generally assumed that Matthew and Luke used Mark as their prime source in compiling their writings. In Matthew nearly 90 percent of the material in Mark is reproduced. These similarities, however, do not mean that the Gospels are merely a restatement of each other. Matthew adds many teaching sections and other details not found in Mark. Matthew slants his material to a Jewish readership as he cites numerous Old Testament prophecies that were fulfilled in Jesus' life and ministry. His purpose was to show that Jesus is the promised Son of David, the Messiah, come to establish the kingdom of God.

Characteristics: Matthew is built around five teaching sections (ch. 5–7; 10; 13; 18; 24–25) which illustrate what life in the kingdom of heaven is all about. Matthew's frequent citation of Old Testament prophecies makes it the perfect book to bridge the Old Testament and the New Testament. While strongly oriented to be a witness to the Jews, Matthew also makes it clear that the Messiah has come for all peoples.

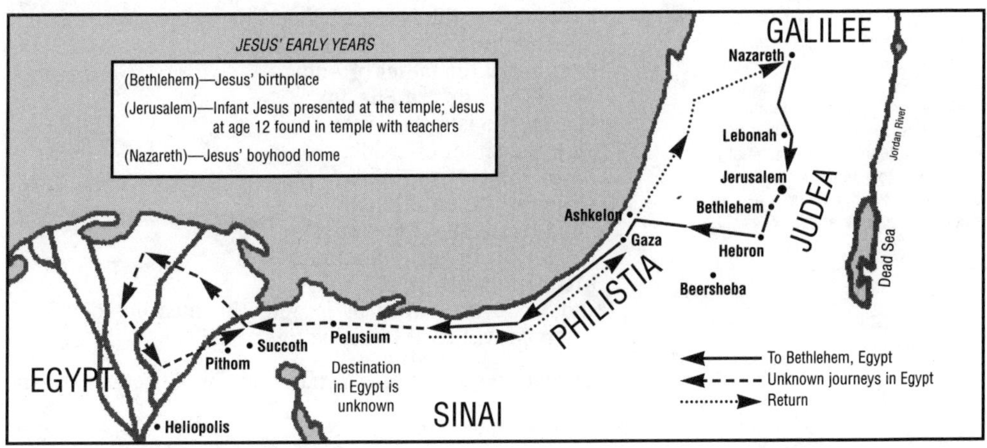

Matthew

1. When you were a child, what did you like best about your grandparents? What is your most vivid memory of any great-grandparents? **2.** What do you know about your genealogy? What would you like to discover about it? **3.** If you could design a coat of arms for your family, what symbols would you choose? Why?

1. What titles does Matthew assign Jesus in verses 1 and 16? What is the meaning of each title? **2.** Which people do you recognize in this genealogy? What do you remember about each of these people? Which people on the list are the most significant in establishing who Jesus is? **3.** Why do you think some women were named when it was not the Jewish custom to include women's names in genealogies? What do you know about these women? **4.** Into what three sections does Matthew divide his genealogical table? What great event climaxes each section? From the promises to Abraham (Ge 12:2–3; 17:6–8), why is it significant that Jesus is Abraham's son (Gal 3:16–18)? From 2 Samuel 7:11–16, why is it significant that he is David's son as well? Of what does that assure us? **5.** If Luke's genealogy (Lk 3:23–38) goes back to Adam to emphasize the universality of the Gospel, what is Matthew's point in beginning with Abraham? What does Matthew's lineage say to Jewish readers?

1. What does it mean to you that God's promises are trustworthy over the generations? **2.** At what point in your life have you most felt Jesus' presence? **3.** Who are the significant people in your spiritual upbringing? What has been passed on to you spiritually from your forebears? What do you know about the ways your ancestors exercised their faith?

The Genealogy of Jesus

1 A record of the genealogy of Jesus Christ the son of David, the son of Abraham:

2Abraham was the father of Isaac,
Isaac the father of Jacob,
Jacob the father of Judah and his brothers,
3Judah the father of Perez and Zerah, whose mother was Tamar,
Perez the father of Hezron,
Hezron the father of Ram,
4Ram the father of Amminadab,
Amminadab the father of Nahshon,
Nahshon the father of Salmon,
5Salmon the father of Boaz, whose mother was Rahab,
Boaz the father of Obed, whose mother was Ruth,
Obed the father of Jesse,
6and Jesse the father of King David.

David was the father of Solomon, whose mother had been Uriah's wife,
7Solomon the father of Rehoboam,
Rehoboam the father of Abijah,
Abijah the father of Asa,
8Asa the father of Jehoshaphat,
Jehoshaphat the father of Jehoram,
Jehoram the father of Uzziah,
9Uzziah the father of Jotham,
Jotham the father of Ahaz,
Ahaz the father of Hezekiah,
10Hezekiah the father of Manasseh,
Manasseh the father of Amon,
Amon the father of Josiah,
11and Josiah the father of Jeconiah[a] and his brothers at the time of the exile to Babylon.

12After the exile to Babylon:
Jeconiah was the father of Shealtiel,
Shealtiel the father of Zerubbabel,
13Zerubbabel the father of Abiud,
Abiud the father of Eliakim,
Eliakim the father of Azor,
14Azor the father of Zadok,
Zadok the father of Akim,
Akim the father of Eliud,
15Eliud the father of Eleazar,
Eleazar the father of Matthan,
Matthan the father of Jacob,
16and Jacob the father of Joseph, the husband of Mary, of whom was born Jesus, who is called Christ.

17Thus there were fourteen generations in all from Abraham to

[a] *11* That is, Jehoiachin; also in verse 12

David, fourteen from David to the exile to Babylon, and fourteen
from the exile to the Christ.[a]

The Birth of Jesus Christ

18 This is how the birth of Jesus Christ came about: His mother
Mary was pledged to be married to Joseph, but before they came
together, she was found to be with child through the Holy Spirit.
19 Because Joseph her husband was a righteous man and did not
want to expose her to public disgrace, he had in mind to divorce
her quietly.
20 But after he had considered this, an angel of the Lord appeared
to him in a dream and said, "Joseph son of David, do not be afraid
to take Mary home as your wife, because what is conceived in her
is from the Holy Spirit. 21 She will give birth to a son, and you are
to give him the name Jesus,[b] because he will save his people from
their sins."
22 All this took place to fulfill what the Lord had said through the
prophet: 23 "The virgin will be with child and will give birth to a
son, and they will call him Immanuel"[c]—which means, "God
with us."
24 When Joseph woke up, he did what the angel of the Lord had
commanded him and took Mary home as his wife. 25 But he had no

What two positive qualities about your mom or dad come to mind as you recall your childhood?

1. How would you feel in Joseph's place in verse 19? In verses 20–21? What would you say to family and friends? To God? **2.** What reason does Matthew give as to why Jesus was born (v. 21)?

1. What is most striking to you in this story of Jesus' conception? How have you experienced Jesus as Immanuel in your life lately? **2.** What do you learn about faith from Joseph?

[a] 17 Or *Messiah.* "The Christ" (Greek) and "the Messiah" (Hebrew) both mean "the Anointed One." [b] 21 *Jesus* is the Greek form of *Joshua,* which means *the LORD saves.* [c] 23 Isaiah 7:14

Matthew 1:18–25 AN ANGEL APPEARS TO JOSEPH

Though a Jewish couple were forbidden to have sexual relations during engagement, they were referred to as "husband and wife," and their relationship could be broken only by divorce.

1. If you had been in Joseph or Mary's sandals, what would have been the most difficult aspect of this situation?
   a. telling Joseph I was pregnant
   b. trusting Mary, and the angel, that no other man was involved
   c. trying to explain the pregnancy to our families
   d. facing the gossip of neighbors because of this early pregnancy

2. What effect do you think these incidents had on Joseph and Mary's future marriage relationship?
   a. It strengthened their mutual trust.
   b. It strained their relationship.
   c. Knowing God had a special task for them brought them closer.
   d. Dealing with a child so soon put a lot of pressure on their marriage.

3. How do you think Joseph and Mary felt about being parents to a child who would "save his people from their sins"?

4. What is the most miraculous aspect of this story to you?
   a. that a virgin could have a baby
   b. that an angel appeared to Joseph
   c. that God came to earth in the person of a baby
   d. that this baby would save people from their sins

5. When did Jesus really become your "Immanuel"—God with *you*? How are you experiencing Jesus "with you" in your life now?

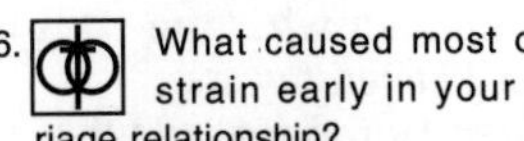

6. What caused most of the strain early in your marriage relationship?
   a. financial struggles
   b. vocational struggles
   c. relational struggles—between us
   d. relational struggles—with others
   e. a pregnancy early in our marriage

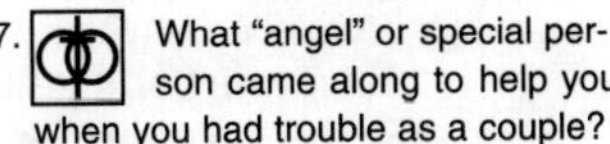

7. What "angel" or special person came along to help you when you had trouble as a couple?

8. The hard times in our marriage have brought us greater commitment as a couple because they helped us:
   a. realize what is important in life.
   b. appreciate each other's strengths.
   c. see that our love is strong enough to last.
   d. be less self-focused.
   e. depend more on God.

9. When you were growing up, who were your most significant masculine role models?
   a. my father
   b. another relative or family friend
   c. a sports or entertainment celebrity
   d. a teacher or coach
   e. a church leader
   f. Jesus Christ
   g. other:__________

10. How do you feel about viewing Jesus as a model of masculinity?
   a. His divine nature makes him too different from me.
   b. His divine nature keeps me from identifying with his human nature.
   c. His divine nature makes him the ultimate masculine role model.
   d. He's the Savior, not a male role model.
   e. He's as much a role model for women as men.

union with her until she gave birth to a son. And he gave him the name Jesus.

The Visit of the Magi

2 After Jesus was born in Bethlehem in Judea, during the time of King Herod, Magi[a] from the east came to Jerusalem 2 and asked, "Where is the one who has been born king of the Jews? We saw his star in the east[b] and have come to worship him."

3 When King Herod heard this he was disturbed, and all Jerusalem with him. 4 When he had called together all the people's chief priests and teachers of the law, he asked them where the Christ[c] was to be born. 5 "In Bethlehem in Judea," they replied, "for this is what the prophet has written:

6 " 'But you, Bethlehem, in the land of Judah,
are by no means least among the rulers of
Judah;
for out of you will come a ruler
who will be the shepherd of my people
Israel.'[d]"

7 Then Herod called the Magi secretly and found out from them the exact time the star had appeared. 8 He sent them to Bethlehem and said, "Go and make a careful search for the child. As soon as you find him, report to me, so that I too may go and worship him."

9 After they had heard the king, they went on their way, and the star they had seen in the east[e] went ahead of them until it stopped over the place where the child was. 10 When they saw the star, they were overjoyed. 11 On coming to the house, they saw the child with his mother Mary, and they bowed down and worshiped him. Then they opened their treasures and presented him with gifts of gold and of incense and of myrrh. 12 And having been warned in a dream not to go back to Herod, they returned to their country by another route.

1. What is your favorite tradition related to Christmas? **2.** Who are three "Magi" or wise men you look to for advice?

1. Why was it important that Jesus be born in Bethlehem? **2.** Since the Magi were pagan astrologers, why would they leave everything in order to follow that star? **3.** Note the responses of the Magi upon seeing Jesus. How is that similar to the response that Christians make to Jesus? How is it different? **4.** What do the star, the Magi, the gifts, the homage, the hostility and the prophecy teach about the significance of Jesus?

1. In your journey toward God, how are you like the Magi? Unlike them? Have you had to leave anything to follow Jesus? **2.** What is the "gold, incense, and myrrh" in your life? How have you offered this to Jesus?

The Escape to Egypt

13 When they had gone, an angel of the Lord appeared to Joseph in a dream. "Get up," he said, "take the child and his mother and escape to Egypt. Stay there until I tell you, for Herod is going to search for the child to kill him."

14 So he got up, took the child and his mother during the night and left for Egypt, 15 where he stayed until the death of Herod. And so was fulfilled what the Lord had said through the prophet: "Out of Egypt I called my son."[f]

16 When Herod realized that he had been outwitted by the Magi, he was furious, and he gave orders to kill all the boys in Bethlehem and its vicinity who were two years old and under, in accordance with the time he had learned from the Magi. 17 Then what was said through the prophet Jeremiah was fulfilled:

18 "A voice is heard in Ramah,
weeping and great mourning,
Rachel weeping for her children
and refusing to be comforted,
because they are no more."[g]

1. If you or your parent(s) decided to move to another country to work or retire, how would you feel? **2.** How far away from where you were born do you now live? Would you go back to your birthplace to live (or retire later)? Why?

1. Based on Herod's response to the news of the coming Messiah, what kind of person do you think he was? What does his response say about his view of the Messiah? **2.** What is Matthew's point in emphasizing God's watchfulness over Jesus? In fulfillment of Hosea's and Jeremiah's prophecies (vv. 17–18,23)? **3.** What relocation options face Joseph? How did God use prophecy, dreams, faith and circumstances to guide him?

1. When, like Herod, have you felt threatened by Jesus' Kingship? How do you react? **2.**

[a] *1* Traditionally *Wise Men* [b] *2* Or *star when it rose* [c] *4* Or *Messiah*
[d] *6* Micah 5:2 [e] *9* Or *seen when it rose* [f] *15* Hosea 11:1 [g] *18* Jer. 31:15

The Return to Nazareth

19After Herod died, an angel of the Lord appeared in a dream to
Joseph in Egypt 20and said, "Get up, take the child and his mother
and go to the land of Israel, for those who were trying to take the
child's life are dead."
21So he got up, took the child and his mother and went to the
land of Israel. 22But when he heard that Archelaus was reigning in
Judea in place of his father Herod, he was afraid to go there. Having
been warned in a dream, he withdrew to the district of Galilee,
23and he went and lived in a town called Nazareth. So was fulfilled
what was said through the prophets: "He will be called a Nazarene."

From Joseph's responsiveness, what do you learn about faith and obedience? How long would it take you to say "yes" if God asked you to relocate?

John the Baptist Prepares the Way

3 In those days John the Baptist came, preaching in the Desert
of Judea 2and saying, "Repent, for the kingdom of heaven
is near." 3This is he who was spoken of through the prophet
Isaiah:

> "A voice of one calling in the desert,
> 'Prepare the way for the Lord,
> make straight paths for him.' "[a]

4John's clothes were made of camel's hair, and he had a leather
belt around his waist. His food was locusts and wild honey. 5People
went out to him from Jerusalem and all Judea and the whole region
of the Jordan. 6Confessing their sins, they were baptized by him in
the Jordan River.
7But when he saw many of the Pharisees and Sadducees coming
to where he was baptizing, he said to them: "You brood of vipers!
Who warned you to flee from the coming wrath? 8Produce fruit in
keeping with repentance. 9And do not think you can say to yourselves, 'We have Abraham as our father.' I tell you that out of these
stones God can raise up children for Abraham. 10The ax is already
at the root of the trees, and every tree that does not produce good
fruit will be cut down and thrown into the fire.
11"I baptize you with[b] water for repentance. But after me will
come one who is more powerful than I, whose sandals I am not fit
to carry. He will baptize you with the Holy Spirit and with fire.
12His winnowing fork is in his hand, and he will clear his threshing
floor, gathering his wheat into the barn and burning up the chaff
with unquenchable fire."

The Baptism of Jesus

13Then Jesus came from Galilee to the Jordan to be baptized by
John. 14But John tried to deter him, saying, "I need to be baptized
by you, and do you come to me?"
15Jesus replied, "Let it be so now; it is proper for us to do this to
fulfill all righteousness." Then John consented.
16As soon as Jesus was baptized, he went up out of the water. At
that moment heaven was opened, and he saw the Spirit of God
descending like a dove and lighting on him. 17And a voice from
heaven said, "This is my Son, whom I love; with him I am well
pleased."

1. What was the longest period of time you spent in the wilderness or away from civilization? What was it like? **2.** When you were baptized, how much water did it take?

1. What was John the Baptist like? Why would anyone go out of their way to hear this radical preacher (v. 7)? Who did they think he was (see 2Ki 1:8)? **2.** How would you paraphrase John's message (v. 2) for people today? What is the "kingdom of heaven"? **3.** What angered John so much about the Pharisees and Sadducees? **4.** What do the images of judgment mean: The coming wrath? The ax? The fire? His winnowing fork? **5.** How do John's and Jesus' ministries compare? **6.** Why did Jesus, who was without sin, come to John to be baptized? What "righteousness" did he fulfill (see Isa 53:12)? **7.** What do you think verse 17 meant to Jesus? How does this set the stage for his ministry to begin?

1. Who has been a John the Baptist in your life? How did he or she prepare you to meet Jesus? **2.** Who are today's Pharisees and Sadducees? **3.** How is repentance linked to your experience of salvation: In the past? Now? Where does repentance, to God and/or others, still need to happen in your life? **4.** How has God affirmed you as his child in Christ?

[a] *3* Isaiah 40:3 [b] *11* Or *in*

What is the longest you ever went without eating? How did it feel?

1. For each of the three temptations: (a) What is its nature? (b) What potentially might appeal to Jesus? (c) What price would there be were he to yield? (d) How does Jesus respond? **2.** What links these temptations with the baptism of Jesus (vv. 1,3,6)? **3.** Of these three, which temptation appears most legitimate? Which one is most shrewd?

1. What human need is at the heart of each temptation? How are these needs evident in your life? How does Satan use these to tempt you? **2.** What is your greatest temptation right now? How can others help?

The Temptation of Jesus

4 Then Jesus was led by the Spirit into the desert to be tempted
by the devil. 2After fasting forty days and forty nights, he was
hungry. 3The tempter came to him and said, "If you are the Son of
God, tell these stones to become bread."
4Jesus answered, "It is written: 'Man does not live on bread
alone, but on every word that comes from the mouth of God.'[a]"
5Then the devil took him to the holy city and had him stand on
the highest point of the temple. 6"If you are the Son of God," he
said, "throw yourself down. For it is written:

" 'He will command his angels concerning you,
and they will lift you up in their hands,
so that you will not strike your foot against a
stone.'[b]"

7Jesus answered him, "It is also written: 'Do not put the Lord
your God to the test.'[c]"
8Again, the devil took him to a very high mountain and showed
him all the kingdoms of the world and their splendor. 9"All this I
will give you," he said, "if you will bow down and worship me."
10Jesus said to him, "Away from me, Satan! For it is written:
'Worship the Lord your God, and serve him only.'[d]"
11Then the devil left him, and angels came and attended him.

---

1. When did you leave home to be on your own for the first time? **2.** Have you ever been fishing? Tell a story about your adventures.

Jesus Begins to Preach

12When Jesus heard that John had been put in prison, he returned to Galilee. 13Leaving Nazareth, he went and lived in Caper-

[a]4 Deut. 8:3 [b]6 Psalm 91:11,12 [c]7 Deut. 6:16 [d]10 Deut. 6:13

Mt 3:13–4:11 BAPTISM AND TEMPTATION OF JESUS

1. What was the purpose of Jesus coming to John to be baptized?
   a. to commit himself to God
   b. to get God's approval
   c. to kick off his public ministry
   d. to be free of sin
   e. to identify with our sin
   f. to set an example for his followers
   g. to be equipped by the Holy Spirit
2. Do you think Jesus needed this affirmation from God (3:16–17) when he began his ministry?
   a. No—it was for the crowd.
   b. Maybe—because of the skeptics.
   c. Yes—just like anyone else.
3. How important was it for Jesus to be tempted by Satan?
   a. Not very important—the Son of God couldn't *really* be tempted.
   b. Somewhat—to toughen him up.
   c. Very important—just like any other "rookie."
4. How would you describe the power struggle going on in this story?
   a. This is the ultimate struggle between good and evil.
   b. Satan is trying to conquer Jesus when he seems weak.
   c. Jesus is being tempted to use his power as God's Son for himself.
   d. This power struggle is no different than those we face daily.
   e. This power struggle is greater than anything we could face.
5. What do you think was appealing to Jesus about the three temptations?
6. What does Jesus' encounter with temptation teach us?
   a. Fasting and prayer make us vulnerable to temptation.
   b. Fasting and prayer enable us to overcome temptation.
   c. It's best to be armed with Scripture when temptation comes.
   d. Satan knows Scripture too.
   e. We need to tell Satan to get lost.
   f. When you resist, God sends help.
7. When do you find yourself most vulnerable to the tempter?
   a. when I'm tired or under stress
   b. when I'm alone or away from home
   c. after a spiritual high
   d. when I'm not expecting it
   e. when I let my mind dwell on certain things
8. What has helped you overcome temptation when it comes?
   a. Scripture (such as:____________)
   b. prayer
   c. telling someone about it
   d. talking myself out of it
   e. running away
9. When have you been alone in the "desert"? How can it help to know Jesus has been there? What is the difference between being *lonely* and being *alone*?
10. In this story God the Father said, "This is my Son, whom I love." Is it possible for us, like Jesus, to have an intimate relationship with God? How do you feel about *your* relationship with God?
11. What is the closest you have come to a time of initiation into manhood? Who was there for you—affirming and cheering you on?

naum, which was by the lake in the area of Zebulun and Naphtali— 14to fulfill what was said through the prophet Isaiah:

15"Land of Zebulun and land of Naphtali,
the way to the sea, along the Jordan,
Galilee of the Gentiles—
16the people living in darkness
have seen a great light;
on those living in the land of the shadow of death
a light has dawned."[a]

17From that time on Jesus began to preach, "Repent, for the
kingdom of heaven is near."

The Calling of the First Disciples

18As Jesus was walking beside the Sea of Galilee, he saw two
brothers, Simon called Peter and his brother Andrew. They were
casting a net into the lake, for they were fishermen. 19"Come,
follow me," Jesus said, "and I will make you fishers of men." 20At
once they left their nets and followed him.
21Going on from there, he saw two other brothers, James son of
Zebedee and his brother John. They were in a boat with their
father Zebedee, preparing their nets. Jesus called them, 22and immediately they left the boat and their father and followed him.

Jesus Heals the Sick

23Jesus went throughout Galilee, teaching in their synagogues,
preaching the good news of the kingdom, and healing every disease
and sickness among the people. 24News about him spread all over
Syria, and people brought to him all who were ill with various
diseases, those suffering severe pain, the demon-possessed, those
having seizures, and the paralyzed, and he healed them. 25Large
crowds from Galilee, the Decapolis,[b] Jerusalem, Judea and the
region across the Jordan followed him.

The Beatitudes

5 Now when he saw the crowds, he went up on a mountainside
and sat down. His disciples came to him, 2and he began to
teach them, saying:

3"Blessed are the poor in spirit,
for theirs is the kingdom of heaven.
4Blessed are those who mourn,
for they will be comforted.
5Blessed are the meek,
for they will inherit the earth.
6Blessed are those who hunger and thirst for
righteousness,
for they will be filled.
7Blessed are the merciful,
for they will be shown mercy.
8Blessed are the pure in heart,
for they will see God.
9Blessed are the peacemakers,
for they will be called sons of God.
10Blessed are those who are persecuted because of
righteousness,
for theirs is the kingdom of heaven.

[a]*16* Isaiah 9:1,2 [b]*25* That is, the Ten Cities

1. How does Jesus react to John's imprisonment? **2.** How had they been living in darkness (v. 16)? What was Jesus' message? What is the relation between repentance, the kingdom of heaven, and the light? **3.** What invitations does Jesus give to these fishermen? What seems unusual about their response? What prior knowledge of Jesus do you think they had (vv. 13,17)? How might Zebedee have felt (v. 22)? **4.** From how far away are the crowds coming (vv. 23–25; see map on page 1337)? What needs do they have? What are they learning about God's kingdom?

1. How has coming to know Jesus been like moving from darkness to light for you? **2.** In what ways does God's kingdom seem present now for you? In what ways does it seem "not yet"? **3.** Spiritually, are you still preparing the nets? Leaving the boat? Following hard after Jesus? Feeling left behind? **4.** If you were in the crowds (vv. 23–25), what would you ask Jesus to heal for you? Why not pray about that as a group?

---

1. When you want to get away from people, where do you go and what do you do? **2.** What saying or bumper sticker do you keep on your desk or car?

1. How do the eight qualities that describe "kingdom people" relate to the promises that follow them? How do they relate to each other? How would you describe the opposite of each quality? **2.** Is Jesus *describing* who his followers *are*? Or *prescribing* what they must *do*? Why do you think so? **3.** How does this "sermonette" explain the nature of the kingdom? How are these Beatitudes related to being salt and light (vv. 13–16)? How are Christians to penetrate society?

1. How do these promised blessings compare with what most people in the world prize? Would "kingdom people" be admired in your society? Why or why not? **2.** Of these eight qualities, which two do you desire most in your life? Why? Who in your group or family do you associate with each? **3.** Which of these qualities are you most tempted to avoid? **4.** Based on the beatitudes, is the light of your life shining like a 300-watt bulb? A 100-watt? A night light? Why? How can Jesus enable you to "shine brighter"?

As a child, what family rule did you love to break? Why?

1. How does Jesus "fulfill" the Prophets and "accomplish everything" in the Law? **2.** What is Jesus' point about the "least" and the "great"? **3.** How do we obtain a righteousness that surpasses the Pharisees?

Consider the Ten Commandments (Ex 20:1–17). Which commandments are most difficult for you? Why?

11"Blessed are you when people insult you, persecute you and falsely say all kinds of evil against you because of me. 12Rejoice and be glad, because great is your reward in heaven, for in the same way they persecuted the prophets who were before you.

Salt and Light

13"You are the salt of the earth. But if the salt loses its saltiness, how can it be made salty again? It is no longer good for anything, except to be thrown out and trampled by men.

14"You are the light of the world. A city on a hill cannot be hidden. 15Neither do people light a lamp and put it under a bowl. Instead they put it on its stand, and it gives light to everyone in the house. 16In the same way, let your light shine before men, that they may see your good deeds and praise your Father in heaven.

The Fulfillment of the Law

17"Do not think that I have come to abolish the Law or the Prophets; I have not come to abolish them but to fulfill them. 18I tell you the truth, until heaven and earth disappear, not the smallest letter, not the least stroke of a pen, will by any means disappear from the Law until everything is accomplished. 19Anyone who breaks one of the least of these commandments and teaches others to do the same will be called least in the kingdom of heaven, but whoever practices and teaches these commands will be called great in the kingdom of heaven. 20For I tell you that unless your righteousness surpasses that of the Pharisees and the teachers of the law, you will certainly not enter the kingdom of heaven.

Matthew 5:1–12 THE BEATITUDES

1. Imagine that you were sitting on the hillside that day with the disciples. What would be your first impression after hearing Jesus' words?
   a. What on earth is he talking about?
   b. This guy doesn't live in the real world.
   c. Jesus had better change his message, or he won't get very far.
   d. I've been searching for this.
2. The Beatitudes are important because they:
   a. are true words spoken by Jesus.
   b. will make me happy.
   c. will help me "get ahead."
   d. are marks of spiritual maturity.
   e. are in the Bible (though they seem unrealistic to me in daily life).
3. Silently rate yourself from 1 (very low) to 4 (very high) on each of the following qualities of the Beatitudes:

POOR IN SPIRIT: I recognize my spiritual bankruptcy and my need for God. Because my relationship with God depends on his grace, I know I'm incapable of earning God's love on my own.

MOURN: I feel the pain that sin, including my own, causes. I can let others know when I am hurting without embarrassment. I can weep like Jesus did.

MEEK: I don't have to be the strong one who is always in control. I can be tender and gentle. I've given control of my life to God and I don't always have to win.

SPIRITUAL HUNGER: I want to know God and his will for my life more than anything—including my own pleasure, status or success. My heart truly longs for God.

MERCIFUL: I can share the feelings of people who are hurting, lonely or distressed, and walk alongside them in their pain. God has given me a sensitivity for the suffering of others.

PURE IN HEART: I am completely honest with God and others. I don't have to put on a false front or pretend to be something I'm not. My life is marked with openness and integrity.

PEACEMAKER: I work hard to keep channels of communication open with others. Rather than allowing anger and conflict to fester, I deal with them constructively. I help those around me work out their differences without hurting one another.

PERSECUTION: I know for whom and for what I am living. And for this I am willing to suffer and (if need be) stand alone for what is right. I can take criticism without reacting defensively or feeling self-pity.

4. Share with the group where you scored yourself the *highest* and where you scored yourself the *lowest.* How can you work on this area?
5. Have one person in your group sit in silence while others share which of the Beatitudes they see most clearly in that person. Go around the group and do this for each member. End with a prayer of thanks for the character qualities God gives and for God's gift of each other.

Murder

21“You have heard that it was said to the people long ago, ‘Do
not murder,[a] and anyone who murders will be subject to judgment.’ 22But I tell you that anyone who is angry with his brother[b]
will be subject to judgment. Again, anyone who says to his brother,
‘Raca,[c]’ is answerable to the Sanhedrin. But anyone who says,
‘You fool!’ will be in danger of the fire of hell.
23“Therefore, if you are offering your gift at the altar and there
remember that your brother has something against you, 24leave
your gift there in front of the altar. First go and be reconciled to
your brother; then come and offer your gift.
25“Settle matters quickly with your adversary who is taking you
to court. Do it while you are still with him on the way, or he may
hand you over to the judge, and the judge may hand you over to
the officer, and you may be thrown into prison. 26I tell you the
truth, you will not get out until you have paid the last penny.[d]

Adultery

27“You have heard that it was said, ‘Do not commit adultery.’[e]
28But I tell you that anyone who looks at a woman lustfully has
already committed adultery with her in his heart. 29If your right
eye causes you to sin, gouge it out and throw it away. It is better
for you to lose one part of your body than for your whole body to
be thrown into hell. 30And if your right hand causes you to sin, cut
it off and throw it away. It is better for you to lose one part of your
body than for your whole body to go into hell.

Divorce

31“It has been said, ‘Anyone who divorces his wife must give her
a certificate of divorce.’[f] 32But I tell you that anyone who divorces
his wife, except for marital unfaithfulness, causes her to become an
adulteress, and anyone who marries the divorced woman commits
adultery.

Oaths

33“Again, you have heard that it was said to the people long ago,
‘Do not break your oath, but keep the oaths you have made to the
Lord.’ 34But I tell you, Do not swear at all: either by heaven, for it
is God’s throne; 35or by the earth, for it is his footstool; or by
Jerusalem, for it is the city of the Great King. 36And do not swear
by your head, for you cannot make even one hair white or black.
37Simply let your ‘Yes’ be ‘Yes,’ and your ‘No,’ ‘No’; anything
beyond this comes from the evil one.

An Eye for an Eye

38“You have heard that it was said, ‘Eye for eye, and tooth for
tooth.’[g] 39But I tell you, Do not resist an evil person. If someone
strikes you on the right cheek, turn to him the other also. 40And if
someone wants to sue you and take your tunic, let him have your
cloak as well. 41If someone forces you to go one mile, go with him
two miles. 42Give to the one who asks you, and do not turn away
from the one who wants to borrow from you.

[a] *21* Exodus 20:13 [b] *22* Some manuscripts *brother without cause* [c] *22* An Aramaic term of contempt [d] *26* Greek *kodrantes* [e] *27* Exodus 20:14 [f] *31* Deut. 24:1 [g] *38* Exodus 21:24; Lev. 24:20; Deut. 19:21

1. How did your parents settle disputes between you and your brother/sister? **2.** What’s the best advice you have been given for dealing with anger?

1. What new standard of right and wrong is Jesus creating (vv. 21–26)? How does he link anger and murder? Why? What inner attitudes is he stressing? **2.** How does Jesus apply the principle in verses 21–26 to the commandment about adultery? What is Jesus’ point in using such exaggerated language (vv. 29–30)? **3.** Some rabbis allowed divorce for nearly any reason if a husband wanted it. What was their casual attitude toward divorce promoting? How are they misusing Moses’ allowance for divorce (see Dt 24:1–4)? What inner quality is Jesus seeking instead? **4.** How do you imagine the OT teaching about oaths is being misapplied (vv. 33–37)? What ought always be true about our speech? **5.** What was the original intent of “eye for eye” and “tooth for tooth” (see Ex 21:24; Lev 24:17–20)? How is this law being perverted? What qualities ought to replace those desires for revenge? **6.** Only the first part of the quote in verse 43 is from the OT. What does this show about the common use of Scripture at this time? In this context, what does the type of love Jesus calls for involve?

1. When it comes to making things right with others, or reconciling, who in your life do you think of? How do verses 21–26 and 43–48 speak to you? **2.** How do you think God wants you to apply verses 29–30 in your life? **3.** Since all of us experience something of anger, lust, divorce, duplicity, revenge, selfishness and hate, what is Jesus saying to us here? Which illustration gets to you the most? **4.** If these standards are like a doctor’s thermometer to show us how sick we are, what is the medicine needed to heal us? How does that relate to the Beatitudes (vv. 3–10)? What is the hope for us here? **5.** Although these standards are not a new law that we must attain *before* God will have mercy on us, what do they suggest about the direction in which God wants us to grow *after* we have received his mercy? Which of these qualities do you want to cultivate most right now? How would your life be different as God helps you to put this quality into action?

Love for Enemies

43“You have heard that it was said, ‘Love your neighbor[a] and
hate your enemy.’ 44But I tell you: Love your enemies[b] and pray
for those who persecute you, 45that you may be sons of your Father
in heaven. He causes his sun to rise on the evil and the good, and
sends rain on the righteous and the unrighteous. 46If you love those
who love you, what reward will you get? Are not even the tax
collectors doing that? 47And if you greet only your brothers, what
are you doing more than others? Do not even pagans do that? 48Be
perfect, therefore, as your heavenly Father is perfect.

Giving to the Needy

6 “Be careful not to do your ‘acts of righteousness’ before men,
to be seen by them. If you do, you will have no reward from
your Father in heaven.

2“So when you give to the needy, do not announce it with
trumpets, as the hypocrites do in the synagogues and on the
streets, to be honored by men. I tell you the truth, they have
received their reward in full. 3But when you give to the needy, do
not let your left hand know what your right hand is doing, 4so that
your giving may be in secret. Then your Father, who sees what is
done in secret, will reward you.

Prayer

5“And when you pray, do not be like the hypocrites, for they
love to pray standing in the synagogues and on the street corners to
be seen by men. I tell you the truth, they have received their
reward in full. 6But when you pray, go into your room, close the
door and pray to your Father, who is unseen. Then your Father,
who sees what is done in secret, will reward you. 7And when you
pray, do not keep on babbling like pagans, for they think they will
be heard because of their many words. 8Do not be like them, for
your Father knows what you need before you ask him.

9“This, then, is how you should pray:

“ ‘Our Father in heaven,
hallowed be your name,
10your kingdom come,
your will be done
on earth as it is in heaven.
11Give us today our daily bread.
12Forgive us our debts,
as we also have forgiven our debtors.
13And lead us not into temptation,
but deliver us from the evil one.[c]’

14For if you forgive men when they sin against you, your heavenly
Father will also forgive you. 15But if you do not forgive men their
sins, your Father will not forgive your sins.

Fasting

16“When you fast, do not look somber as the hypocrites do, for
they disfigure their faces to show men they are fasting. I tell you
the truth, they have received their reward in full. 17But when you
fast, put oil on your head and wash your face, 18so that it will not
be obvious to men that you are fasting, but only to your Father,

---

1. Did you grow up in an openly “religious” home? Or was religion a private matter, unseen by you until later years? **2.** Were you taught any prayers as a child? What was one of the earliest ones you can recall?

1. Jesus continues to describe a righteousness surpassing that of the Scribes and Pharisees (5:20). How have they corrupted giving to the poor? What is their motivation? Their reward? How does their hypocrisy contrast with genuine compassion for the poor? **2.** How does their hypocrisy affect their prayer? How does their reward contrast with that of those who pray sincerely? Why did Jesus warn his followers to avoid wordiness? **3.** In Jesus’ model prayer (vv. 9–13), what three concerns related to God did he pray about first? What personal concerns follow? What is the relationship between forgiveness and prayer? **4.** If our Father knows what we need before we ask, why pray? **5.** How does the fasting of Jesus’ disciples contrast with that of the religious leaders? Why? Why fast?

1. What “religious disciplines” are valued in your circles? In what way can they be used to impress others? When have you given in to that temptation? Why? **2.** Do you tend to join in with public religious displays, or do you avoid such disciplines as fasting, praying or giving altogether? What attitudes does it take to practice these disciplines? How does that relate to the attitudes expressed in 5:3–11? When used properly, what is the value of religious discipline?

---

a43 Lev. 19:18 b44 Some late manuscripts *enemies, bless those who curse you, do good to those who hate you* c13 Or *from evil*; some late manuscripts *one, / for yours is the kingdom and the power and the glory forever. Amen.*

who is unseen; and your Father, who sees what is done in secret, will reward you.

Treasures in Heaven

19"Do not store up for yourselves treasures on earth, where moth and rust destroy, and where thieves break in and steal. 20But store up for yourselves treasures in heaven, where moth and rust do not destroy, and where thieves do not break in and steal. 21For where your treasure is, there your heart will be also.

22"The eye is the lamp of the body. If your eyes are good, your whole body will be full of light. 23But if your eyes are bad, your whole body will be full of darkness. If then the light within you is darkness, how great is that darkness!

24"No one can serve two masters. Either he will hate the one and love the other, or he will be devoted to the one and despise the other. You cannot serve both God and Money.

Do Not Worry

25"Therefore I tell you, do not worry about your life, what you will eat or drink; or about your body, what you will wear. Is not life more important than food, and the body more important than clothes? 26Look at the birds of the air; they do not sow or reap or store away in barns, and yet your heavenly Father feeds them. Are you not much more valuable than they? 27Who of you by worrying can add a single hour to his life[a]?

28"And why do you worry about clothes? See how the lilies of the field grow. They do not labor or spin. 29Yet I tell you that not even Solomon in all his splendor was dressed like one of these. 30If that is how God clothes the grass of the field, which is here today and tomorrow is thrown into the fire, will he not much more clothe you, O you of little faith? 31So do not worry, saying, 'What shall we eat?' or 'What shall we drink?' or 'What shall we wear?' 32For the pagans run after all these things, and your heavenly Father knows that you need them. 33But seek first his kingdom and his righteousness, and all these things will be given to you as well. 34Therefore do not worry about tomorrow, for tomorrow will worry about itself. Each day has enough trouble of its own.

1. If you were walking on a beach and found an ancient chest, what would you hope to find inside? 2. When you were a teenager, what did your parents think of your clothes: Weird? Indecent? Tattered?

1. What alternatives does Jesus propose with respect to treasures (vv. 19–21), desires (vv. 22–23) and masters (v. 24)? 2. What is the link between treasure and heart? Heart and eye? Eye and body? Master and money? How does your choice of treasure, master and perception (vv. 19–24) affect your attitude toward life (vv. 25–27)? 3. What does God's care for the birds and lilies teach you?

1. Considering this past week, is your "bank" on earth or in heaven? What do you need to do to change accounts? Who has been your master lately? Why? 2. Why pray when you can worry? What causes you the most worry? What are the signs that indicate you are worrying too much? What is God saying to you through this passage about handling your particular worry or disappointment?

Judging Others

7 "Do not judge, or you too will be judged. 2For in the same way you judge others, you will be judged, and with the measure you use, it will be measured to you.

3"Why do you look at the speck of sawdust in your brother's eye and pay no attention to the plank in your own eye? 4How can you say to your brother, 'Let me take the speck out of your eye,' when all the time there is a plank in your own eye? 5You hypocrite, first take the plank out of your own eye, and then you will see clearly to remove the speck from your brother's eye.

6"Do not give dogs what is sacred; do not throw your pearls to pigs. If you do, they may trample them under their feet, and then turn and tear you to pieces.

Ask, Seek, Knock

7"Ask and it will be given to you; seek and you will find; knock and the door will be opened to you. 8For everyone who asks receives; he who seeks finds; and to him who knocks, the door will be opened.

1. What was the best gift you ever received from your dad? 2. Have you ever been in a house threatened by a natural disaster or calamity? What happened?

1. This chapter continues to reveal the attitudes and actions "kingdom people" are to have. What connection is Jesus making between the faults we notice in others and our own problems? For those who do "see clearly," what is the meaning of Jesus' warning in verse 6? 2. What is Jesus stressing about God in verses 7–11? What is the guiding principle of prayer here? 3. How does the righteousness described in verse 12 differ from that of the Pharisees? 4. How might verse 12 define what Jesus means by the "narrow gate"? Why is that road less traveled? 5. What are some of the "good fruits" Jesus

[a]27 Or *single cubit to his height*

9“Which of you, if his son asks for bread, will give him a stone?
10Or if he asks for a fish, will give him a snake? 11If you, then,
though you are evil, know how to give good gifts to your children,
how much more will your Father in heaven give good gifts to those
who ask him! 12So in everything, do to others what you would have
them do to you, for this sums up the Law and the Prophets.

The Narrow and Wide Gates

13“Enter through the narrow gate. For wide is the gate and broad
is the road that leads to destruction, and many enter through it.
14But small is the gate and narrow the road that leads to life, and
only a few find it.

A Tree and Its Fruit

15“Watch out for false prophets. They come to you in sheep's
clothing, but inwardly they are ferocious wolves. 16By their fruit
you will recognize them. Do people pick grapes from thornbushes,
or figs from thistles? 17Likewise every good tree bears good fruit,
but a bad tree bears bad fruit. 18A good tree cannot bear bad fruit,
and a bad tree cannot bear good fruit. 19Every tree that does not
bear good fruit is cut down and thrown into the fire. 20Thus, by
their fruit you will recognize them.

21“Not everyone who says to me, ‘Lord, Lord,’ will enter the
kingdom of heaven, but only he who does the will of my Father
who is in heaven. 22Many will say to me on that day, ‘Lord, Lord,
did we not prophesy in your name, and in your name drive out
demons and perform many miracles?’ 23Then I will tell them plainly, ‘I never knew you. Away from me, you evildoers!’

The Wise and Foolish Builders

24“Therefore everyone who hears these words of mine and puts
them into practice is like a wise man who built his house on the
rock. 25The rain came down, the streams rose, and the winds blew
and beat against that house; yet it did not fall, because it had its
foundation on the rock. 26But everyone who hears these words of
mine and does not put them into practice is like a foolish man who
built his house on sand. 27The rain came down, the streams rose,
and the winds blew and beat against that house, and it fell with a
great crash.”

28When Jesus had finished saying these things, the crowds were
amazed at his teaching, 29because he taught as one who had authority, and not as their teachers of the law.

The Man With Leprosy

8 When he came down from the mountainside, large crowds
followed him. 2A man with leprosy[a] came and knelt before
him and said, “Lord, if you are willing, you can make me clean.”

3Jesus reached out his hand and touched the man. “I am willing,” he said. “Be clean!” Immediately he was cured[b] of his leprosy. 4Then Jesus said to him, “See that you don't tell anyone. But go,
show yourself to the priest and offer the gift Moses commanded, as
a testimony to them.”

[a]2 The Greek word was used for various diseases affecting the skin—not necessarily leprosy. [b]3 Greek *made clean*

is looking for? Is evaluating a person's fruit contradicting the mandate not to judge (v. 1)? Why? **6.** What was the fault of the “evildoers” (v. 23)? If the ability to prophesy, drive out demons, and perform miracles is not what Jesus means by doing the will of the Father, what is? **7.** How do the two house builders reflect the people who heard Jesus? What kind of commitment is Jesus calling for here? What is the alternative? **8.** How would you sum up the attitudes Jesus is encouraging in this chapter? Why are these required for “kingdom people”?

1. In living your life, do you tend to walk more on the broad road or the narrow road (vv. 13–14)? What makes the broad road most tempting for you? What makes the narrow road difficult? Rewarding? **2.** Considering the sermon as a whole, is your foundation on solid rock? Or on sand, but with a nice view? What would you have to tear down in order to solidify that foundation? How do you need others to help you in the process? **3.** At this point in your life, is your pressing need to learn more or to practice what you have already learned? Why? How would you like the group to pray for you to that end? **4.** In light of this section's seriousness, what hope do verses 7–9 give you? How about 5:3? What attribute of “kingdom people” will you ask for?

---

1. Would you be more likely to stand in line all night to get tickets to see the Super Bowl, a rock band or Mother Teresa? **2.** Describe a time when you saw a despised or neglected person receive a surprising amount of love and respect.

1. What did it mean to be a leper: Physically? Socially? Spiritually? What is significant about Jesus' touch? Why would Jesus want the cleansing to be cer-

The Faith of the Centurion

5When Jesus had entered Capernaum, a centurion came to him,
asking for help. 6"Lord," he said, "my servant lies at home paralyzed and in terrible suffering."
7Jesus said to him, "I will go and heal him."
8The centurion replied, "Lord, I do not deserve to have you
come under my roof. But just say the word, and my servant will be
healed. 9For I myself am a man under authority, with soldiers
under me. I tell this one, 'Go,' and he goes; and that one, 'Come,'
and he comes. I say to my servant, 'Do this,' and he does it."
10When Jesus heard this, he was astonished and said to those
following him, "I tell you the truth, I have not found anyone in
Israel with such great faith. 11I say to you that many will come from
the east and the west, and will take their places at the feast with
Abraham, Isaac and Jacob in the kingdom of heaven. 12But the
subjects of the kingdom will be thrown outside, into the darkness,
where there will be weeping and gnashing of teeth."
13Then Jesus said to the centurion, "Go! It will be done just as
you believed it would." And his servant was healed at that very
hour.

Jesus Heals Many

14When Jesus came into Peter's house, he saw Peter's mother-
in-law lying in bed with a fever. 15He touched her hand and the
fever left her, and she got up and began to wait on him.
16When evening came, many who were demon-possessed were
brought to him, and he drove out the spirits with a word and
healed all the sick. 17This was to fulfill what was spoken through
the prophet Isaiah:

tified by the priests? **2.** Why is Jesus' offer to go to a centurion's house so remarkable? What does it show about Jesus? **3.** What does the centurion's comment (vv. 8–9) show about his view of Jesus? Why is this so important to Jesus? **4.** Who are the "many" (vv. 11–12)? Who are the subjects of the kingdom? Why is Jesus sharing this with a Jewish audience? **5.** As Peter, what would you think as you watched the scene in verses 14–17? **6.** What do these healings indicate about the kingdom of heaven?

1. Which character are you most like: The leper—"I hope God will help me, but I'm not sure"? The centurion—"I *know* God can meet my need"? Peter's mother-in-law—"I didn't expect to get well *this* fast"? Why? **2.** What hope do these stories give you as you think of the disease of sin in your life? **3.** Both the leper and the centurion were outcasts from the Jews' perspective. Who are the outcasts in your community? How do these stories model the way you might relate to them?

Matthew 7:24–29 THE WISE AND FOOLISH BUILDERS

This parable ends Jesus' Sermon on the Mount, which began in Matthew 5.

1. Who is Jesus addressing here?
   a. people with hearing problems
   b. housing developers
   c. a crowd faced with a big decision
   d. nobody I know
   e. everybody I know

2. What does the rock refer to?
   a. the truth of the Gospel
   b. faith in Jesus
   c. Jesus himself
   d. obedience to Jesus' words

3. What does the sand refer to?
   a. atheism and agnosticism
   b. weak doctrine
   c. wishy-washy commitment
   d. the world's values
   e. disobedience to Jesus' words

4. Why did the foolish man build his house on sand?
   a. He wanted a beach in his yard.
   b. It was an easier place to dig.
   c. He got the land at a bargain price.
   d. Other people were doing it.
   e. He didn't know he was doing it.

5. What is Jesus promising those who are willing to live by his words?
   a. You will never experience storms.
   b. You will experience the same storms as everyone else.
   c. The storms won't destroy your faith.
   d. You will get a new house if the old one collapses.

6. What kind of storm do you think claims the most spiritual casualties?
   a. intellectual doubts
   b. moral failures
   c. relational conflict
   d. personal crises
   e. creeping apathy

7. What's the immediate forecast for the "weather" in your life?
   a. sunny c. thunderstorms
   b. dreary d. hurricane

8. To be a "wise builder" at this point in your life, do you need to learn more or practice what you have already learned?

9. Being totally honest, what is the foundation you depend on?
   a. my abilities e. good health
   b. my status f. my family
   c. wishful thinking g. my resources
   d. self-confidence h. faith in Christ

10. How would you describe your spiritual foundation?
    a. shaky
    b. steady
    c. brand new
    d. temporary
    e. eroding
    f. destroyed, but I'm trying to rebuild

11. What is the message of this parable to you about the realities of life?
    a. If my focus is on the externals of life, the results will be disastrous.
    b. If spiritual foundations are right, circumstances don't really matter.
    c. If I base my life on Christ, he'll make my dreams come true.
    d. If I base my life on Christ, my dreams may not come true, but God will make me content.

> "He took up our infirmities
> and carried our diseases."[a]

What is the best excuse you've heard for not getting work done?

Why did Jesus respond like this? What do his responses teach about discipleship?

How have you learned the cost of following Jesus?

The Cost of Following Jesus

18When Jesus saw the crowd around him, he gave orders to cross to the other side of the lake. 19Then a teacher of the law came to him and said, "Teacher, I will follow you wherever you go."

20Jesus replied, "Foxes have holes and birds of the air have nests, but the Son of Man has no place to lay his head."

21Another disciple said to him, "Lord, first let me go and bury my father."

22But Jesus told him, "Follow me, and let the dead bury their own dead."

When you were a kid, where did you go to hide in the house when there was a bad storm?

1. What are the disciples feeling as this storm begins? As it whips up? When Jesus silences it? **2.** What was Jesus teaching them by sleeping through the storm? By rebuking it? **3.** Is it significant that the possessed man called Jesus the "Son of God"? Why? **4.** What is a modern application of Jesus' power over these demons?

1. When circumstantial clouds darken your life, do you sense the Son still shining? Or does he seem asleep? Why might it feel that way? **2.** What do you learn about Jesus from these stories? How does that relate to the times you face evil? **3.** What "storms" or "demons" seem too much for you to handle now?

Jesus Calms the Storm

23Then he got into the boat and his disciples followed him. 24Without warning, a furious storm came up on the lake, so that the waves swept over the boat. But Jesus was sleeping. 25The disciples went and woke him, saying, "Lord, save us! We're going to drown!"

26He replied, "You of little faith, why are you so afraid?" Then he got up and rebuked the winds and the waves, and it was completely calm.

27The men were amazed and asked, "What kind of man is this? Even the winds and the waves obey him!"

The Healing of Two Demon-possessed Men

28When he arrived at the other side in the region of the Gadarenes,[b] two demon-possessed men coming from the tombs met him. They were so violent that no one could pass that way. 29"What do you want with us, Son of God?" they shouted. "Have you come here to torture us before the appointed time?"

30Some distance from them a large herd of pigs was feeding. 31The demons begged Jesus, "If you drive us out, send us into the herd of pigs."

32He said to them, "Go!" So they came out and went into the pigs, and the whole herd rushed down the steep bank into the lake and died in the water. 33Those tending the pigs ran off, went into the town and reported all this, including what had happened to the demon-possessed men. 34Then the whole town went out to meet Jesus. And when they saw him, they pleaded with him to leave their region.

Which is more home to you: (a) The place you grew up? (b) Where you live now? (c) Other? What makes one place more like "home sweet home"?

1. What did the people expect Jesus to do? Why did Jesus forgive the man's sins instead? **2.** Why would that be considered blasphemy? **3.** How did Jesus demonstrate that he had indeed forgiven the man's sin? How did the people respond? **4.** What is surprising about Jesus' choice of Matthew? Why? What is the irony

Jesus Heals a Paralytic

9 Jesus stepped into a boat, crossed over and came to his own town. 2Some men brought to him a paralytic, lying on a mat. When Jesus saw their faith, he said to the paralytic, "Take heart, son; your sins are forgiven."

3At this, some of the teachers of the law said to themselves, "This fellow is blaspheming!"

4Knowing their thoughts, Jesus said, "Why do you entertain evil thoughts in your hearts? 5Which is easier: to say, 'Your sins are forgiven,' or to say, 'Get up and walk'? 6But so that you may know that the Son of Man has authority on earth to forgive sins. . . ." Then he said to the paralytic, "Get up, take your mat and go home." 7And the man got up and went home. 8When the crowd

[a] *17* Isaiah 53:4 [b] *28* Some manuscripts *Gergesenes;* others *Gerasenes*

saw this, they were filled with awe; and they praised God, who had
given such authority to men.

The Calling of Matthew

9As Jesus went on from there, he saw a man named Matthew
sitting at the tax collector's booth. "Follow me," he told him, and
Matthew got up and followed him.
10While Jesus was having dinner at Matthew's house, many tax
collectors and "sinners" came and ate with him and his disciples.
11When the Pharisees saw this, they asked his disciples, "Why does
your teacher eat with tax collectors and 'sinners'?"
12On hearing this, Jesus said, "It is not the healthy who need a
doctor, but the sick. 13But go and learn what this means: 'I desire
mercy, not sacrifice.'[a] For I have not come to call the righteous,
but sinners."

Jesus Questioned About Fasting

14Then John's disciples came and asked him, "How is it that we
and the Pharisees fast, but your disciples do not fast?"
15Jesus answered, "How can the guests of the bridegroom mourn
while he is with them? The time will come when the bridegroom
will be taken from them; then they will fast.
16"No one sews a patch of unshrunk cloth on an old garment, for
the patch will pull away from the garment, making the tear worse.
17Neither do men pour new wine into old wineskins. If they do,
the skins will burst, the wine will run out and the wineskins will
be ruined. No, they pour new wine into new wineskins, and both
are preserved."

A Dead Girl and a Sick Woman

18While he was saying this, a ruler came and knelt before him
and said, "My daughter has just died. But come and put your hand
on her, and she will live." 19Jesus got up and went with him, and
so did his disciples.
20Just then a woman who had been subject to bleeding for
twelve years came up behind him and touched the edge of his
cloak. 21She said to herself, "If I only touch his cloak, I will be
healed."
22Jesus turned and saw her. "Take heart, daughter," he said,
"your faith has healed you." And the woman was healed from that
moment.
23When Jesus entered the ruler's house and saw the flute players
and the noisy crowd, 24he said, "Go away. The girl is not dead but
asleep." But they laughed at him. 25After the crowd had been put
outside, he went in and took the girl by the hand, and she got up.
26News of this spread through all that region.

Jesus Heals the Blind and Mute

27As Jesus went on from there, two blind men followed him,
calling out, "Have mercy on us, Son of David!"
28When he had gone indoors, the blind men came to him, and
he asked them, "Do you believe that I am able to do this?"
"Yes, Lord," they replied.
29Then he touched their eyes and said, "According to your faith
will it be done to you"; 30and their sight was restored. Jesus
warned them sternly, "See that no one knows about this." 31But
they went out and spread the news about him all over that region.

[a] *13* Hosea 6:6

in Jesus' response to the Pharisees' criticism?

1. If Jesus really does forgive sin, why do many Christians struggle so with their forgiveness? **2.** What is more valuable to you: physical healing or forgiveness? Why? **3.** Who are the "Matthews" around you?

As a kid, did you outgrow your clothes or wear them out?

1. Why don't Jesus' disciples fast now? When will they? **2.** How do unshrunk cloth and new wine relate to fasting, the bridegroom and the kingdom?

What is your "new wine"? Your "old wineskins"?

What are you like when you wake up: (a) Rarin' to go when my feet hit the floor? (b) Give me coffee, and leave me alone?

1. What feelings prompted the ruler to approach Jesus? How about the woman? How would you feel as you reached out to touch Jesus? Just afterward? **2.** Compare the ruler and the woman. What does Jesus' response to both show about the kingdom? **3.** What part does faith play in these healings?

The ruler and the woman were desperate. What is the relationship between desperation and faith? What does this story encourage you to do as you face desperate situations?

Would you describe yourself as gullible or cynical? Why?

1. What is the meaning of the title the blind men use for Jesus (v. 27)? How do they show faith? Why does Jesus want them to keep quiet? **2.** How did the crowds react to Jesus' power? How did the Pharisees react? Why the difference? **3.** How do Jesus' actions prove the Pharisees wrong (vv. 35–36)? **4.** What does Jesus see in the crowds? In the harvest field?

1. How might you still be spiritually "blind" or "dumb"? How can Jesus heal your sight and speech? **2.** From chapter 9, what have you learned about the kingdom? How do these stories demonstrate what it means to labor in the field where God has placed you?

---

1. What is the longest you have hiked or hitchhiked your way across country? **2.** What kind of person would you want in your expedition party (to complement your weakness) the next time you embark on a great adventure? **3.** Who was one of the more unusual house guests you or your family ever entertained?

1. What did Jesus do before sending out his men (v. 1)? How do the disciples' activities here compare with what Jesus had been doing in chapters 8–9? With what he has just seen (9:36)? With what he has prayed (9:38)? **2.** The "zealots" were guerrilla fighters committed to the freedom of the Jews from Rome. Why would Jesus choose one of them to be on the same team with Matthew, a tax collector who had worked with Rome? **3.** What limits did Jesus put on their ministry (v. 5)? Do you think the disciples were disappointed that these groups were excluded? Why? **4.** What was to be their message? What were they to do? **5.** Why do you think that Jesus told them to take nothing more than the clothes on their backs? **6.** What was the basic point of Jesus' preparation speech to the disciples? What problems would they (and future disciples) face? How were they to respond to each problem? **7.** What does it mean to be "like sheep among wolves," "shrewd as snakes," "innocent as doves" (v. 16)? **8.** Who would persecute them? Why? In times of persecution, what could they expect from God? **9.** How might Christ's truth divide a family? What kind of radical commitment does Jesus call for in verses 37–39? **10.** How were the disciples to understand their reception (vv. 40–42)? What confirm-

32While they were going out, a man who was demon-possessed
and could not talk was brought to Jesus. 33And when the demon
was driven out, the man who had been mute spoke. The crowd
was amazed and said, "Nothing like this has ever been seen in
Israel."
34But the Pharisees said, "It is by the prince of demons that he
drives out demons."

The Workers Are Few

35Jesus went through all the towns and villages, teaching in their
synagogues, preaching the good news of the kingdom and healing
every disease and sickness. 36When he saw the crowds, he had
compassion on them, because they were harassed and helpless,
like sheep without a shepherd. 37Then he said to his disciples,
"The harvest is plentiful but the workers are few. 38Ask the Lord of
the harvest, therefore, to send out workers into his harvest field."

Jesus Sends Out the Twelve

10 He called his twelve disciples to him and gave them authority to drive out evil[a] spirits and to heal every disease and
sickness.
2These are the names of the twelve apostles: first, Simon (who is
called Peter) and his brother Andrew; James son of Zebedee, and
his brother John; 3Philip and Bartholomew; Thomas and Matthew
the tax collector; James son of Alphaeus, and Thaddaeus; 4Simon
the Zealot and Judas Iscariot, who betrayed him.
5These twelve Jesus sent out with the following instructions:
"Do not go among the Gentiles or enter any town of the Samaritans. 6Go rather to the lost sheep of Israel. 7As you go, preach this
message: 'The kingdom of heaven is near.' 8Heal the sick, raise the
dead, cleanse those who have leprosy,[b] drive out demons. Freely
you have received, freely give. 9Do not take along any gold or silver
or copper in your belts; 10take no bag for the journey, or extra
tunic, or sandals or a staff; for the worker is worth his keep.
11"Whatever town or village you enter, search for some worthy
person there and stay at his house until you leave. 12As you enter
the home, give it your greeting. 13If the home is deserving, let your
peace rest on it; if it is not, let your peace return to you. 14If anyone
will not welcome you or listen to your words, shake the dust off
your feet when you leave that home or town. 15I tell you the truth,
it will be more bearable for Sodom and Gomorrah on the day of
judgment than for that town. 16I am sending you out like sheep
among wolves. Therefore be as shrewd as snakes and as innocent
as doves.
17"Be on your guard against men; they will hand you over to the
local councils and flog you in their synagogues. 18On my account
you will be brought before governors and kings as witnesses to
them and to the Gentiles. 19But when they arrest you, do not worry
about what to say or how to say it. At that time you will be given
what to say, 20for it will not be you speaking, but the Spirit of your
Father speaking through you.
21"Brother will betray brother to death, and a father his child;
children will rebel against their parents and have them put to
death. 22All men will hate you because of me, but he who stands
firm to the end will be saved. 23When you are persecuted in one
place, flee to another. I tell you the truth, you will not finish going
through the cities of Israel before the Son of Man comes.

[a] *1* Greek *unclean* [b] *8* The Greek word was used for various diseases affecting the skin—not necessarily leprosy.

24“A student is not above his teacher, nor a servant above his
master. 25It is enough for the student to be like his teacher, and the
servant like his master. If the head of the house has been called
Beelzebub,[a] how much more the members of his household!
26“So do not be afraid of them. There is nothing concealed that
will not be disclosed, or hidden that will not be made known.
27What I tell you in the dark, speak in the daylight; what is whispered in your ear, proclaim from the roofs. 28Do not be afraid of
those who kill the body but cannot kill the soul. Rather, be afraid of
the One who can destroy both soul and body in hell. 29Are not two
sparrows sold for a penny[b]? Yet not one of them will fall to the
ground apart from the will of your Father. 30And even the very
hairs of your head are all numbered. 31So don't be afraid; you are
worth more than many sparrows.
32“Whoever acknowledges me before men, I will also acknowledge him before my Father in heaven. 33But whoever disowns me
before men, I will disown him before my Father in heaven.
34“Do not suppose that I have come to bring peace to the earth.
I did not come to bring peace, but a sword. 35For I have come to
turn

“ ‘a man against his father,
a daughter against her mother,
a daughter-in-law against her mother-in-law—
36 a man's enemies will be the members of his
own household.’[c]

37“Anyone who loves his father or mother more than me is not
worthy of me; anyone who loves his son or daughter more than me
is not worthy of me; 38and anyone who does not take his cross and
follow me is not worthy of me. 39Whoever finds his life will lose it,
and whoever loses his life for my sake will find it.
40“He who receives you receives me, and he who receives me
receives the one who sent me. 41Anyone who receives a prophet
because he is a prophet will receive a prophet's reward, and anyone who receives a righteous man because he is a righteous man
will receive a righteous man's reward. 42And if anyone gives even
a cup of cold water to one of these little ones because he is my
disciple, I tell you the truth, he will certainly not lose his reward.”

Jesus and John the Baptist

11 After Jesus had finished instructing his twelve disciples, he
went on from there to teach and preach in the towns of
Galilee.[d]
2When John heard in prison what Christ was doing, he sent his
disciples 3to ask him, “Are you the one who was to come, or
should we expect someone else?”
4Jesus replied, “Go back and report to John what you hear and
see: 5The blind receive sight, the lame walk, those who have leprosy[e] are cured, the deaf hear, the dead are raised, and the good
news is preached to the poor. 6Blessed is the man who does not fall
away on account of me.”
7As John's disciples were leaving, Jesus began to speak to the
crowd about John: “What did you go out into the desert to see? A
reed swayed by the wind? 8If not, what did you go out to see? A
man dressed in fine clothes? No, those who wear fine clothes are
in kings' palaces. 9Then what did you go out to see? A prophet?

[a]*25* Greek *Beezeboul* or *Beelzeboul* [b]*29* Greek *an assarion* [c]*36* Micah 7:6
[d]*1* Greek *in their towns* [e]*5* The Greek word was used for various diseases affecting the skin—not necessarily leprosy.

ing authority does Jesus bestow upon his disciples at the end of his discourse (v. 40), as well as at the beginning (v. 1)?

1. What warnings or encouragements would you need to hear from Jesus in order to go out and represent him? **2.** How has Christ's teaching united the members of your family? How has it divided them? **3.** Under what circumstances do you find it most difficult to talk about your faith? **4.** What does the paradox in verse 39 mean to you? How can you lose yourself for Christ this week? **5.** How can you best represent to your neighbors that the kingdom of heaven is near? **6.** What, besides dust on your feet, will stick with you from this passage?

---

1. (For the married:) When did you know that the person you married was “the one”? What tipped you off? (For the unmarried:) What is the sign you look for in a potential mate to tell you “this is the one”? **2.** When you “church shop,” what three items are on the top of your list?

1. Who questions Jesus (v. 2)? Where is John? How did he land in prison (see 14:1–5)? **2.** How might prison have raised doubts for John (v. 3)? **3.** Does Jesus answer John more with promises or with evidence? Why? How might John, who knew the OT well, have interpreted Jesus' reply (see Isa 35:5–6; 61:1)? **4.** How was John unlike a weak reed or a well-groomed politician? What does Jesus say about John? **5.** How is a NT believer greater than

John (v. 11; see 18:3–4)? **6.** How do the people respond to John? To Jesus? How are they like the children pictured here?

1. What kinds of "prisons" tend to bring out doubts for you regarding Jesus? **2.** In those periods of discouragement and doubt, what most renews your courage and faith? **3.** In what specific way can you be an encourager to someone in church leadership? In your family? Among your friends?

Yes, I tell you, and more than a prophet. [10]This is the one about whom it is written:

> " 'I will send my messenger ahead of you,
> who will prepare your way before you.'[a]

[11]I tell you the truth: Among those born of women there has not risen anyone greater than John the Baptist; yet he who is least in the kingdom of heaven is greater than he. [12]From the days of John the Baptist until now, the kingdom of heaven has been forcefully advancing, and forceful men lay hold of it. [13]For all the Prophets and the Law prophesied until John. [14]And if you are willing to accept it, he is the Elijah who was to come. [15]He who has ears, let him hear.

[16]"To what can I compare this generation? They are like children sitting in the marketplaces and calling out to others:

> [17]" 'We played the flute for you,
> and you did not dance;
> we sang a dirge,
> and you did not mourn.'

[18]For John came neither eating nor drinking, and they say, 'He has a demon.' [19]The Son of Man came eating and drinking, and they say, 'Here is a glutton and a drunkard, a friend of tax collectors and "sinners." ' But wisdom is proved right by her actions."

What is your favorite city? Least favorite? Why?

1. What judgment does Jesus pass on each city mentioned? Why will their judgment be worse than that of the pagan cities of the OT? **2.** If Jesus is rejected, what is the judgment?

What is Jesus' point for you in this warning?

Woe on Unrepentant Cities

[20]Then Jesus began to denounce the cities in which most of his miracles had been performed, because they did not repent. [21]"Woe to you, Korazin! Woe to you, Bethsaida! If the miracles that were performed in you had been performed in Tyre and Sidon, they would have repented long ago in sackcloth and ashes. [22]But I tell you, it will be more bearable for Tyre and Sidon on the day of judgment than for you. [23]And you, Capernaum, will you be lifted up to the skies? No, you will go down to the depths.[b] If the miracles that were performed in you had been performed in Sodom, it would have remained to this day. [24]But I tell you that it will be more bearable for Sodom on the day of judgment than for you."

---

1. Why is the Gospel hidden from the "wise and learned"? Who truly knows God? **2.** What does Jesus mean by taking up his "yoke"? By the "rest" he promises to those who do? Since a yoke unites two animals in common work, what does this imply about discipleship?

1. How are you like the "wise and learned"? Like the "little children"? **2.** Is Jesus' yoke resting lightly on you, or are you struggling to get out from under it? How does taking up his way lead to rest?

Rest for the Weary

[25]At that time Jesus said, "I praise you, Father, Lord of heaven and earth, because you have hidden these things from the wise and learned, and revealed them to little children. [26]Yes, Father, for this was your good pleasure.

[27]"All things have been committed to me by my Father. No one knows the Son except the Father, and no one knows the Father except the Son and those to whom the Son chooses to reveal him.

[28]"Come to me, all you who are weary and burdened, and I will give you rest. [29]Take my yoke upon you and learn from me, for I am gentle and humble in heart, and you will find rest for your souls. [30]For my yoke is easy and my burden is light."

As a child, what was Sunday dinner like? What do you like best about Sundays now? Least?

Lord of the Sabbath

12 At that time Jesus went through the grainfields on the Sabbath. His disciples were hungry and began to pick some heads of grain and eat them. [2]When the Pharisees saw this, they said to him, "Look! Your disciples are doing what is unlawful on the Sabbath."

[a]*10* Mal. 3:1 [b]*23* Greek *Hades*

3He answered, "Haven't you read what David did when he and
his companions were hungry? 4He entered the house of God, and
he and his companions ate the consecrated bread—which was not
lawful for them to do, but only for the priests. 5Or haven't you read
in the Law that on the Sabbath the priests in the temple desecrate
the day and yet are innocent? 6I tell you that one[a] greater than
the temple is here. 7If you had known what these words mean, 'I
desire mercy, not sacrifice,'[b] you would not have condemned the
innocent. 8For the Son of Man is Lord of the Sabbath."

9Going on from that place, he went into their synagogue, 10and
a man with a shriveled hand was there. Looking for a reason to
accuse Jesus, they asked him, "Is it lawful to heal on the Sabbath?"

11He said to them, "If any of you has a sheep and it falls into a pit
on the Sabbath, will you not take hold of it and lift it out? 12How
much more valuable is a man than a sheep! Therefore it is lawful to
do good on the Sabbath."

13Then he said to the man, "Stretch out your hand." So he
stretched it out and it was completely restored, just as sound as the
other. 14But the Pharisees went out and plotted how they might kill
Jesus.

God's Chosen Servant

15Aware of this, Jesus withdrew from that place. Many followed
him, and he healed all their sick, 16warning them not to tell who
he was. 17This was to fulfill what was spoken through the prophet
Isaiah:

> 18"Here is my servant whom I have chosen,
> the one I love, in whom I delight;
> I will put my Spirit on him,
> and he will proclaim justice to the nations.
> 19He will not quarrel or cry out;
> no one will hear his voice in the streets.
> 20A bruised reed he will not break,
> and a smoldering wick he will not snuff out,
> till he leads justice to victory.
> 21 In his name the nations will put their hope."[c]

Jesus and Beelzebub

22Then they brought him a demon-possessed man who was blind
and mute, and Jesus healed him, so that he could both talk and see.
23All the people were astonished and said, "Could this be the Son
of David?"

24But when the Pharisees heard this, they said, "It is only by
Beelzebub,[d] the prince of demons, that this fellow drives out
demons."

25Jesus knew their thoughts and said to them, "Every kingdom
divided against itself will be ruined, and every city or household
divided against itself will not stand. 26If Satan drives out Satan, he
is divided against himself. How then can his kingdom stand? 27And
if I drive out demons by Beelzebub, by whom do your people drive
them out? So then, they will be your judges. 28But if I drive out
demons by the Spirit of God, then the kingdom of God has come
upon you.

29"Or again, how can anyone enter a strong man's house and
carry off his possessions unless he first ties up the strong man?
Then he can rob his house.

[a]6 Or *something*; also in verses 41 and 42 [b]7 Hosea 6:6 [c]21 Isaiah 42:1-4
[d]24 Greek *Beezeboul* or *Beelzeboul*; also in verse 27

1. Regarding the Sabbath, what is the point about David (see 1Sa 21:1–6)? **2.** How had the Pharisees neglected the meaning of "I desire mercy, not sacrifice" (Hos 6:6)? **3.** What does Jesus imply by his claim in verse 6? Verse 8? How do the Pharisees react? How is their question in verse 10 a trap for Jesus? **4.** How does Jesus show that he is the authoritative interpreter of the law? What does the Pharisees' response show?

1. From this section, how important are your needs to God? **2.** When have you fallen into the trap of "offering sacrifice" but "neglecting mercy"? How can you work to reverse that this week?

Where do you go when life gets too heavy for you? Why?

1. In reacting to the Pharisees' hostility (12:14), how does Jesus fulfill prophecy? **2.** How does Jesus treat the wounded and weak?

1. How does Jesus' example encourage you when people are hostile to you? **2.** In telling others about Jesus, what use of the OT do you make? **3.** What is one way Jesus has mended your life?

In describing your conversational style, are you: (a) A gossip? (b) A closed book? (c) Speak your mind? or (d) Nice and easy?

1. How did the people react to Jesus' healing the blind and mute man? How did the Pharisees react? Why are Jesus' miracles open to varied interpretations? **2.** What three defenses does Jesus give in answer to the Pharisees' accusations (vv. 26–27,29)? By implication, what is Jesus saying about his inauguration of God's kingdom? Is neutrality to Jesus possible? Why or why not? **3.** What is meant by "blasphemy against the Spirit" (vv. 31–32)? How have the Pharisees committed this sin? Why is it impossible for this one sin to be forgiven? **4.** What reason does Jesus give for the Pharisees' hostility (vv. 34–37)?

What real difference does Jesus' power make in your daily struggles against evil? In your freedom to be honest to God? In your daily speech with others?

---

1. What bumper sticker or T-shirt design brings a smile to your face when you think about it? **2.** What is one habit or behavior you do which totally annoys others around you?

1. Why do you think the Pharisees wanted to see a miracle? **2.** How does Jesus feel about "this generation" (v. 41)? Why? **3.** What is the "sign of Jonah"? How is Jesus greater than Jonah? **4.** How do the Ninevites and the Queen of the South condemn Jesus' generation? **5.** A person who is reformed but neglectful of God's presence is prey to even greater evil. How do Israel's leaders exemplify this principle? **6.** Why might Jesus' mother and brothers be eager to speak with him (see Mk 3:20–21)?

1. What does Jesus want from you, other than a heart "swept clean and put in order" (v. 44)? **2.** From your life this week, would others see you as a "brother or sister" of Jesus, or a distant relative? Why?

Regarding house plants, do you: (a) Talk and sing to them like friends? (b) Forget about them till their leaves fall off? (c) Just hope no one gives you one?

1. What is a parable? **2.** What four types of soil does Jesus mention? What characterizes each? What happens to the seed in each kind of soil? **3.** What does Jesus' explanation of the parable (vv. 18–23) reveal about the

30"He who is not with me is against me, and he who does not gather with me scatters. 31And so I tell you, every sin and blasphemy will be forgiven men, but the blasphemy against the Spirit will not be forgiven. 32Anyone who speaks a word against the Son of Man will be forgiven, but anyone who speaks against the Holy Spirit will not be forgiven, either in this age or in the age to come.

33"Make a tree good and its fruit will be good, or make a tree bad and its fruit will be bad, for a tree is recognized by its fruit. 34You brood of vipers, how can you who are evil say anything good? For out of the overflow of the heart the mouth speaks. 35The good man brings good things out of the good stored up in him, and the evil man brings evil things out of the evil stored up in him. 36But I tell you that men will have to give account on the day of judgment for every careless word they have spoken. 37For by your words you will be acquitted, and by your words you will be condemned."

The Sign of Jonah

38Then some of the Pharisees and teachers of the law said to him, "Teacher, we want to see a miraculous sign from you."

39He answered, "A wicked and adulterous generation asks for a miraculous sign! But none will be given it except the sign of the prophet Jonah. 40For as Jonah was three days and three nights in the belly of a huge fish, so the Son of Man will be three days and three nights in the heart of the earth. 41The men of Nineveh will stand up at the judgment with this generation and condemn it; for they repented at the preaching of Jonah, and now one[a] greater than Jonah is here. 42The Queen of the South will rise at the judgment with this generation and condemn it; for she came from the ends of the earth to listen to Solomon's wisdom, and now one greater than Solomon is here.

43"When an evil[b] spirit comes out of a man, it goes through arid places seeking rest and does not find it. 44Then it says, 'I will return to the house I left.' When it arrives, it finds the house unoccupied, swept clean and put in order. 45Then it goes and takes with it seven other spirits more wicked than itself, and they go in and live there. And the final condition of that man is worse than the first. That is how it will be with this wicked generation."

Jesus' Mother and Brothers

46While Jesus was still talking to the crowd, his mother and brothers stood outside, wanting to speak to him. 47Someone told him, "Your mother and brothers are standing outside, wanting to speak to you."[c]

48He replied to him, "Who is my mother, and who are my brothers?" 49Pointing to his disciples, he said, "Here are my mother and my brothers. 50For whoever does the will of my Father in heaven is my brother and sister and mother."

The Parable of the Sower

13 That same day Jesus went out of the house and sat by the lake. 2Such large crowds gathered around him that he got into a boat and sat in it, while all the people stood on the shore. 3Then he told them many things in parables, saying: "A farmer went out to sow his seed. 4As he was scattering the seed, some fell along the path, and the birds came and ate it up. 5Some fell on rocky places, where it did not have much soil. It sprang up quickly, because the soil was shallow. 6But when the sun came up, the

[a]*41* Or *something*; also in verse 42 [b]*43* Greek *unclean* [c]*47* Some manuscripts do not have verse 47.

plants were scorched, and they withered because they had no root.
7Other seed fell among thorns, which grew up and choked the
plants. 8Still other seed fell on good soil, where it produced a
crop—a hundred, sixty or thirty times what was sown. 9He who
has ears, let him hear."
10The disciples came to him and asked, "Why do you speak to
the people in parables?"
11He replied, "The knowledge of the secrets of the kingdom of
heaven has been given to you, but not to them. 12Whoever has will
be given more, and he will have an abundance. Whoever does not
have, even what he has will be taken from him. 13This is why I
speak to them in parables:

"Though seeing, they do not see;
though hearing, they do not hear or
understand.

14In them is fulfilled the prophecy of Isaiah:

" 'You will be ever hearing but never
understanding;
you will be ever seeing but never perceiving.
15For this people's heart has become calloused;
they hardly hear with their ears,
and they have closed their eyes.
Otherwise they might see with their eyes,
hear with their ears,
understand with their hearts
and turn, and I would heal them.'[a]

[a]*15* Isaiah 6:9,10

seed? About the various soils? The fruit? The farmer? **4.** What do parables accomplish that simple and direct speech lacks? **5.** How does Jesus' challenge in verse 9 help explain verses 11–12? How does faith open you up to more and more spiritual insight? **6.** How does the quotation from Isaiah (vv. 14–15) explain the difficulty of understanding parables (v. 13)? **7.** In verses 16–17, Jesus gives a new Beatitude. What have these disciples seen and heard that the prophets longed to see and hear? Are we included in this blessing? Why do you think so?

♡ **1.** Can you see and hear Jesus at work in today's world? If so, how? **2.** How would you explain this parable to a bunch of city kids who don't know anything about sowing a field? What modern analogy would you use? **3.** Why do so many people misunderstand the Gospel? **4.** What deep "roots" help to prevent a believer from falling away? What gives you roots? **5.** What worries can choke your growth in Christ? How can you free your life from these "thorns"? **6.** What "crop" does Jesus want believers to yield?

Matthew 13:1–23 PARABLE OF THE SOWER

1. What is your initial reaction to this parable?
   a. This would make a great article for *Better Homes and Gardens.*
   b. I'm glad Jesus interprets it.
   c. Why doesn't Jesus say what he means up front?
   d. Why does Jesus want to keep some people in the dark?
   e. This is really a parable of the soils, more than the sower.
   f. I wonder which soil I am.

2. Why do you think Jesus told this parable?
   a. so those who reject him can be condemned as infertile soil
   b. so those who reject him can understand *why* they reject him
   c. so people will examine their lives
   d. so disciples who sow the word won't get discouraged by results

3. What is the crop that the seed is supposed to produce?
   a. faith
   b. zeal
   c. Christ-like character
   d. good deeds
   e. new converts

4. Which of the four types of soil best describes your response to the Gospel when you first heard it?

5. How would you describe the root system of your spiritual life now?
   a. shallow like an over-watered plant
   b. fairly extensive, but I worry about times of drought
   c. extensive and deep, strengthened by faith and difficulties

6. In the period of your life when your spiritual life was the most unfruitful, what was the main reason?
   a. I had a whole lot of problems.
   b. I didn't know about Christ.
   c. I knew about Christ, but I was taken up with other things.
   d. I lacked a supportive community.
   e. I was living life *my* way.

7. What was the main factor at the time you produced the best crop?
   a. I continually sought God's will.
   b. I had my priorities in order.
   c. I had few distractions in my life.
   d. I had a supportive community.
   e. I had a strong devotional life.

8. Which "thorn of worry" is most likely to choke your faith?
   a. finances
   b. failure
   c. family problems
   d. what others think
   e. health
   f. fear of death
   g. the future

9. What steps could you take to improve the soil of your spiritual life?
   a. plow it up and start over
   b. allow troubles to be fertilizer rather than just "rocky times"
   c. uproot the thorns of the worries and desires of the world
   d. have a refreshing devotional life
   e. surround myself with the rich topsoil of a spiritual community

10. How can you relate to verses 11–17 in your efforts and struggles to respond to God?
   a. I've had trouble seeing, hearing and understanding spiritual things.
   b. My heart has been calloused.
   c. I feel blessed that my spiritual eyes and ears have been opened.
   d. I am longing for God's truth.

What can you do to increase your productivity?

16 But blessed are your eyes because they see, and your ears because they hear. 17 For I tell you the truth, many prophets and
righteous men longed to see what you see but did not see it, and to
hear what you hear but did not hear it.
18 "Listen then to what the parable of the sower means: 19 When
anyone hears the message about the kingdom and does not understand it, the evil one comes and snatches away what was sown in
his heart. This is the seed sown along the path. 20 The one who
received the seed that fell on rocky places is the man who hears
the word and at once receives it with joy. 21 But since he has no
root, he lasts only a short time. When trouble or persecution comes
because of the word, he quickly falls away. 22 The one who received
the seed that fell among the thorns is the man who hears the word,
but the worries of this life and the deceitfulness of wealth choke it,
making it unfruitful. 23 But the one who received the seed that fell
on good soil is the man who hears the word and understands it. He
produces a crop, yielding a hundred, sixty or thirty times what was
sown."

---

1. In your family, who liked to play practical jokes? Any one joke stand out? **2.** What childhood dream has become a reality for you (example—learned to play the piano, became a brain surgeon)?

1. In the parable of the weeds (vv. 24–30 and vv. 36–43), who is the sower? What does the wheat represent? The weeds? The enemy? The harvest? **2.** How does this parable relate to 7:15–20? **3.** Why does this parable so puzzle the disciples? Why is patience and tolerance toward unbelievers difficult for them (and for us)? **4.** What does this passage teach about church purity? Divine patience? Human accountability? **5.** In the parable of the mustard seed and yeast (vv. 31–33), what aspects of Jesus' ministry seem small? What is the promise if the small seed is sown? **6.** How does the kingdom of heaven become evident to others? **7.** What does the summary statement and prophecy here (vv. 34–35) reveal about the way (and the reason) Jesus used parables?

1. In what way can over-zealous judgment of the world and its evils harm our mission as believers? Where is the harvest field God has placed you? **2.** Where (in your life or in your church) have you seen faith like "yeast" or a "mustard seed" have a great impact? **3.** What accountability are you now feeling for yourself? For others? To God? What are you "hearing" God call you to do as a result?

The Parable of the Weeds

24 Jesus told them another parable: "The kingdom of heaven is
like a man who sowed good seed in his field. 25 But while everyone
was sleeping, his enemy came and sowed weeds among the wheat,
and went away. 26 When the wheat sprouted and formed heads,
then the weeds also appeared.
27 "The owner's servants came to him and said, 'Sir, didn't you
sow good seed in your field? Where then did the weeds come
from?'
28 " 'An enemy did this,' he replied.
"The servants asked him, 'Do you want us to go and pull
them up?'
29 " 'No,' he answered, 'because while you are pulling the weeds,
you may root up the wheat with them. 30 Let both grow together
until the harvest. At that time I will tell the harvesters: First collect
the weeds and tie them in bundles to be burned; then gather the
wheat and bring it into my barn.' "

The Parables of the Mustard Seed and the Yeast

31 He told them another parable: "The kingdom of heaven is
like a mustard seed, which a man took and planted in his field.
32 Though it is the smallest of all your seeds, yet when it grows, it
is the largest of garden plants and becomes a tree, so that the birds
of the air come and perch in its branches."
33 He told them still another parable: "The kingdom of heaven is
like yeast that a woman took and mixed into a large amount[a] of
flour until it worked all through the dough."
34 Jesus spoke all these things to the crowd in parables; he did
not say anything to them without using a parable. 35 So was fulfilled
what was spoken through the prophet:

> "I will open my mouth in parables,
> I will utter things hidden since the creation of
> the world."[b]

The Parable of the Weeds Explained

36 Then he left the crowd and went into the house. His disciples
came to him and said, "Explain to us the parable of the weeds in
the field."

[a] *33* Greek *three satas* (probably about 1/2 bushel or 22 liters) [b] *35* Psalm 78:2

37He answered, "The one who sowed the good seed is the Son of Man. 38The field is the world, and the good seed stands for the sons of the kingdom. The weeds are the sons of the evil one, 39and the enemy who sows them is the devil. The harvest is the end of the age, and the harvesters are angels.

40"As the weeds are pulled up and burned in the fire, so it will be at the end of the age. 41The Son of Man will send out his angels, and they will weed out of his kingdom everything that causes sin and all who do evil. 42They will throw them into the fiery furnace, where there will be weeping and gnashing of teeth. 43Then the righteous will shine like the sun in the kingdom of their Father. He who has ears, let him hear.

The Parables of the Hidden Treasure and the Pearl

44"The kingdom of heaven is like treasure hidden in a field. When a man found it, he hid it again, and then in his joy went and sold all he had and bought that field.

45"Again, the kingdom of heaven is like a merchant looking for fine pearls. 46When he found one of great value, he went away and sold everything he had and bought it.

The Parable of the Net

47"Once again, the kingdom of heaven is like a net that was let down into the lake and caught all kinds of fish. 48When it was full, the fishermen pulled it up on the shore. Then they sat down and collected the good fish in baskets, but threw the bad away. 49This is how it will be at the end of the age. The angels will come and separate the wicked from the righteous 50and throw them into the fiery furnace, where there will be weeping and gnashing of teeth.

51"Have you understood all these things?" Jesus asked.

"Yes," they replied.

52He said to them, "Therefore every teacher of the law who has been instructed about the kingdom of heaven is like the owner of a house who brings out of his storeroom new treasures as well as old."

A Prophet Without Honor

53When Jesus had finished these parables, he moved on from there. 54Coming to his hometown, he began teaching the people in their synagogue, and they were amazed. "Where did this man get this wisdom and these miraculous powers?" they asked. 55"Isn't this the carpenter's son? Isn't his mother's name Mary, and aren't his brothers James, Joseph, Simon and Judas? 56Aren't all his sisters with us? Where then did this man get all these things?" 57And they took offense at him.

But Jesus said to them, "Only in his hometown and in his own house is a prophet without honor."

58And he did not do many miracles there because of their lack of faith.

John the Baptist Beheaded

14 At that time Herod the tetrarch heard the reports about Jesus, 2and he said to his attendants, "This is John the Baptist; he has risen from the dead! That is why miraculous powers are at work in him."

3Now Herod had arrested John and bound him and put him in prison because of Herodias, his brother Philip's wife, 4for John had been saying to him: "It is not lawful for you to have her." 5Herod

---

1. What needs sorting out in your garage or basement right now? What is most likely to be found in storage: trivia, trash, or treasure? **2.** With the proceeds from a garage sale or a moving sale, what worthy item would you purchase?

1. What do the parables in verses 44–46 teach about the value of the kingdom? With what emotion and energy should it be pursued? **2.** What does the parable of the net teach about the kingdom of heaven? **3.** How does it compare with the parable of the weeds (vv. 24–30)? **4.** Who are the teachers of the old Law who have been instructed in the new Gospel (v. 52)? **5.** How does the hometown crowd's response to Jesus (vv. 54–58) differ from that of other Israelites? What do they "know"? How does this affect his ministry?

1. Compared to the man and the merchant, how valuable is the kingdom to you and why: (a) It's worth more than anything else. (b) I think I'd miss too many of the other things. (c) I'm not ready to put all my eggs in one basket. **2.** Of the parables in chapter 13, which one is still unclear? All too clear? **3.** Verses 53–58 also applies to any of us who grew up "always knowing Jesus." What does this story teach us about taking Jesus for granted? **4.** What relation does our faith have to Jesus' ability to be at work in our lives? Why does he look for faith?

What would be your "dream" birthday present?

1. Why did Herod fear Jesus? John the Baptist? **2.** Why did Herod behead John? What does this say about his character? **3.** What does Herod seem to fear most: The fame of Jesus?

The ghost of John? The reaction of his dinner guests? His wife?

In what area of your life are your actions governed by fear of what others think? How could Jesus help you?

wanted to kill John, but he was afraid of the people, because they
considered him a prophet.
6On Herod's birthday the daughter of Herodias danced for them
and pleased Herod so much 7that he promised with an oath to give
her whatever she asked. 8Prompted by her mother, she said, "Give
me here on a platter the head of John the Baptist." 9The king was
distressed, but because of his oaths and his dinner guests, he ordered that her request be granted 10and had John beheaded in the
prison. 11His head was brought in on a platter and given to the girl,
who carried it to her mother. 12John's disciples came and took his
body and buried it. Then they went and told Jesus.

1. After a busy day, how do you unwind? 2. If you fed five thousand people at a picnic, what would you serve?

1. Why does Jesus withdraw? How does he react to the interruption? 2. Describe how the disciples might have felt in verse 15. In verses 16–17? In verses 18–21? 3. What new power do the disciples discover in Jesus? 4. What is the lesson here?

1. What insight about Jesus will you remember from this story? 2. How have you seen Jesus stretch your resources beyond what you could imagine?

Jesus Feeds the Five Thousand

13When Jesus heard what had happened, he withdrew by boat
privately to a solitary place. Hearing of this, the crowds followed
him on foot from the towns. 14When Jesus landed and saw a large
crowd, he had compassion on them and healed their sick.
15As evening approached, the disciples came to him and said,
"This is a remote place, and it's already getting late. Send the
crowds away, so they can go to the villages and buy themselves
some food."
16Jesus replied, "They do not need to go away. You give them
something to eat."
17"We have here only five loaves of bread and two fish," they
answered.
18"Bring them here to me," he said. 19And he directed the people to sit down on the grass. Taking the five loaves and the two fish
and looking up to heaven, he gave thanks and broke the loaves.
Then he gave them to the disciples, and the disciples gave them to
the people. 20They all ate and were satisfied, and the disciples
picked up twelve basketfuls of broken pieces that were left over.
21The number of those who ate was about five thousand men,
besides women and children.

1. Of all your adventures in life, which was the most daring? 2. Describe your first experience waterskiing, surfing or ice-skating.

1. Why do you think Jesus wanted to pray alone? What was one of Jesus' concerns about his popularity among the people (see Jn 6:15)? 2. How does public opinion and Jesus' response to it resemble that of the temptations in 4:3–10? 3. Meanwhile, what happens out on the lake to rock the disciples' boat? To stir up their fear? To encourage their faith? 4. What do Peter's actions reveal about his personality? 5. Why do you think Peter asks Jesus to call to him? When did Peter begin to sink? Why then and not earlier? 6. What do the disciples conclude about Jesus as a result of this experience?

Jesus Walks on the Water

22Immediately Jesus made the disciples get into the boat and go
on ahead of him to the other side, while he dismissed the crowd.
23After he had dismissed them, he went up on a mountainside by
himself to pray. When evening came, he was there alone, 24but the
boat was already a considerable distance[a] from land, buffeted by
the waves because the wind was against it.
25During the fourth watch of the night Jesus went out to them,
walking on the lake. 26When the disciples saw him walking on the
lake, they were terrified. "It's a ghost," they said, and cried out in
fear.
27But Jesus immediately said to them: "Take courage! It is I.
Don't be afraid."
28"Lord, if it's you," Peter replied, "tell me to come to you on
the water."
29"Come," he said.
Then Peter got down out of the boat, walked on the water and
came toward Jesus. 30But when he saw the wind, he was afraid
and, beginning to sink, cried out, "Lord, save me!"
31Immediately Jesus reached out his hand and caught him. "You
of little faith," he said, "why did you doubt?"
32And when they climbed into the boat, the wind died down.

[a]*24* Greek *many stadia*

33Then those who were in the boat worshiped him, saying, "Truly
you are the Son of God."
34When they had crossed over, they landed at Gennesaret. 35And
when the men of that place recognized Jesus, they sent word to all
the surrounding country. People brought all their sick to him 36and
begged him to let the sick just touch the edge of his cloak, and all
who touched him were healed.

Clean and Unclean

15 Then some Pharisees and teachers of the law came to Jesus
from Jerusalem and asked, 2"Why do your disciples break
the tradition of the elders? They don't wash their hands before
they eat!"
3Jesus replied, "And why do you break the command of God for
the sake of your tradition? 4For God said, 'Honor your father and
mother'[a] and 'Anyone who curses his father or mother must be
put to death.'[b] 5But you say that if a man says to his father or
mother, 'Whatever help you might otherwise have received from
me is a gift devoted to God,' 6he is not to 'honor his father[c]' with
it. Thus you nullify the word of God for the sake of your tradition.
7You hypocrites! Isaiah was right when he prophesied about you:

> 8" 'These people honor me with their lips,
> but their hearts are far from me.

[a]4 Exodus 20:12; Deut. 5:16 [b]4 Exodus 21:17; Lev. 20:9 [c]6 Some manuscripts *father or his mother*

1. Would you be more likely to stay in the boat or step out of it? Why? **2.** What do you see in your own life that parallels Peter's attempt to walk on water?

---

1. What one family tradition did you observe as a child, still do, and hope to see carried on in the next generation? **2.** On what recent project have you felt like you were "the blind leading the blind"?

1. Jesus addresses three groups here (vv. 1,10,12). Who is Jesus harshest with? Why? **2.** How does Jesus support his charge of hypocrisy? What does the example he uses (vv. 5–6) reveal about their hypocrisy? What does Isaiah say to the Pharisees (vv. 7–9)? To all religious people? **3.** Why does Jesus call them "blind guides"? What's their apparent relationship with God? **4.** What is Jesus' stance on adults caring for their parents? **5.** How is "unclean-

Matthew 14:22–33 JESUS WALKS ON WATER

1. Why did Jesus send the disciples out onto the water without him?
   a. He wanted to get away from them.
   b. He needed to pray alone.
   c. He was setting up this miracle.
   d. He knew they needed to be afraid to realize how much they really needed him.

2. How would you have reacted if you were in the boat during the storm and saw someone walking on the water?
   a. I would have closed my eyes, taken a deep breath and waited for things to return to normal.
   b. I would have had heart failure.
   c. I would have cried out, "Where's Jesus?!"
   d. I would have known it was Jesus.

3. When Peter said, "Lord, if it's you, tell me to come to you on the water," what was he asking for?
   a. the same power Jesus had
   b. an invitation to take a risk
   c. a chance to show off
   d. an opportunity to test his faith

4. What made Peter sink?
   a. His sandals got waterlogged.
   b. He lost confidence in himself.
   c. His focus shifted from Jesus to his circumstances.
   d. His fear was greater than his faith.
   e. He realized how foolish he had been to step out of the boat.

5. When it comes to taking risks, how would you describe yourself?
   a. impulsive—quick to step out
   b. cautious—testing the water first
   c. apprehensive—scared to death
   d. procrastinating—putting it off

6. What is the relationship between risk-taking and faith?
   a. There is no relationship.
   b. It's okay to be a risk-taker if you have faith in Christ.
   c. Risk-taking is good if you have faith in yourself.
   d. A life of faith is a life of risk-taking.

7. Where do you feel God is inviting you to "get out of the boat"?
   a. in my relationships—dealing with a problem
   b. in my future planning—doing something I've been afraid to try
   c. in my inner life—facing a hang-up
   d. in my spiritual walk—putting God first
   e. other:____________________

8. What would be the best way for God to help you in that situation?
   a. be very gentle with me
   b. assure me it's okay to fail
   c. give me a push
   d. give me a lot of support people
   e. get out of the boat with me

9. What is the nature of the storm you fear most right now? In order to be rescued from that storm, what is your next step?
   a. admit that real men have fears
   b. admit that I am sinking
   c. step out and take some risks
   d. reach out to Jesus for strength
   e. stop doubting myself
   f. stop doubting God

10. What dreams do you have for the future—particularly your career? What are the risks? How do those who are close to you feel about those dreams and their risks and potential consequences?

11. What has been the highlight of this course for you? As a way of expressing appreciation for each other, have one person at a time listen as others share an affirmation of that person.

ness" understood by the Pharisees? By Jesus?

1. What traditions in your church might make it difficult for new people to feel at home there? How could you change these things? 2. What is one area in your life that needs changing in order to get your heart and mouth more in line with each other? What has God already done in you along that line?

> 9 They worship me in vain;
> their teachings are but rules taught by men.'[a]"

10 Jesus called the crowd to him and said, "Listen and understand. 11 What goes into a man's mouth does not make him 'unclean,' but what comes out of his mouth, that is what makes him 'unclean.' "

12 Then the disciples came to him and asked, "Do you know that the Pharisees were offended when they heard this?"

13 He replied, "Every plant that my heavenly Father has not planted will be pulled up by the roots. 14 Leave them; they are blind guides.[b] If a blind man leads a blind man, both will fall into a pit."

15 Peter said, "Explain the parable to us."

16 "Are you still so dull?" Jesus asked them. 17 "Don't you see that whatever enters the mouth goes into the stomach and then out of the body? 18 But the things that come out of the mouth come from the heart, and these make a man 'unclean.' 19 For out of the heart come evil thoughts, murder, adultery, sexual immorality, theft, false testimony, slander. 20 These are what make a man 'unclean'; but eating with unwashed hands does not make him 'unclean.' "

For what would you walk 100 miles? Why?

1. How would Jesus' accusers in 15:1 have viewed his 100-mile trip to this area? 2. What do we learn about the woman? About Jesus? About Jesus' attitude toward non-Jews?

1. When you deal with needy people or "outsiders," are you more like the disciples or Jesus? Why? 2. How has God gone a long distance to heal you?

The Faith of the Canaanite Woman

21 Leaving that place, Jesus withdrew to the region of Tyre and Sidon. 22 A Canaanite woman from that vicinity came to him, crying out, "Lord, Son of David, have mercy on me! My daughter is suffering terribly from demon-possession."

23 Jesus did not answer a word. So his disciples came to him and urged him, "Send her away, for she keeps crying out after us."

24 He answered, "I was sent only to the lost sheep of Israel."

25 The woman came and knelt before him. "Lord, help me!" she said.

26 He replied, "It is not right to take the children's bread and toss it to their dogs."

27 "Yes, Lord," she said, "but even the dogs eat the crumbs that fall from their masters' table."

28 Then Jesus answered, "Woman, you have great faith! Your request is granted." And her daughter was healed from that very hour.

What do you often tend to forget: names, birthdays, keys, umbrellas, etc.? Why?

1. How does what Jesus is doing compare with Jewish expectations of the Messiah (see Isa 35:3–6)? 2. How does the feeding of this multitude compare with Matthew 14:13–21? 3. Having already seen a miraculous feeding, how do you account for the disciples' lack of faith? 4. Why does Jesus heal and feed the crowds?

1. When you face overwhelming situations now, how well do you remember God's provision for you in the past? 2. What would stimulate your memory of God's mercy? 3. How helpful is it for you to hear the stories of the way God has worked in the lives of other Christians? Why?

Jesus Feeds the Four Thousand

29 Jesus left there and went along the Sea of Galilee. Then he went up on a mountainside and sat down. 30 Great crowds came to him, bringing the lame, the blind, the crippled, the mute and many others, and laid them at his feet; and he healed them. 31 The people were amazed when they saw the mute speaking, the crippled made well, the lame walking and the blind seeing. And they praised the God of Israel.

32 Jesus called his disciples to him and said, "I have compassion for these people; they have already been with me three days and have nothing to eat. I do not want to send them away hungry, or they may collapse on the way."

33 His disciples answered, "Where could we get enough bread in this remote place to feed such a crowd?"

34 "How many loaves do you have?" Jesus asked.

"Seven," they replied, "and a few small fish."

35 He told the crowd to sit down on the ground. 36 Then he took the seven loaves and the fish, and when he had given thanks, he broke them and gave them to the disciples, and they in turn to the

[a] 9 Isaiah 29:13 [b] 14 Some manuscripts *guides of the blind*

people. 37They all ate and were satisfied. Afterward the disciples
picked up seven basketfuls of broken pieces that were left over.
38The number of those who ate was four thousand, besides women
and children. 39After Jesus had sent the crowd away, he got into
the boat and went to the vicinity of Magadan.

The Demand for a Sign

16 The Pharisees and Sadducees came to Jesus and tested him
by asking him to show them a sign from heaven.
2He replied,[a] "When evening comes, you say, 'It will be fair
weather, for the sky is red,' 3and in the morning, 'Today it will be
stormy, for the sky is red and overcast.' You know how to interpret
the appearance of the sky, but you cannot interpret the signs of the
times. 4A wicked and adulterous generation looks for a miraculous
sign, but none will be given it except the sign of Jonah." Jesus then
left them and went away.

The Yeast of the Pharisees and Sadducees

5When they went across the lake, the disciples forgot to take
bread. 6"Be careful," Jesus said to them. "Be on your guard against
the yeast of the Pharisees and Sadducees."
7They discussed this among themselves and said, "It is because
we didn't bring any bread."
8Aware of their discussion, Jesus asked, "You of little faith, why
are you talking among yourselves about having no bread? 9Do you
still not understand? Don't you remember the five loaves for the
five thousand, and how many basketfuls you gathered? 10Or the
seven loaves for the four thousand, and how many basketfuls you
gathered? 11How is it you don't understand that I was not talking to
you about bread? But be on your guard against the yeast of the
Pharisees and Sadducees." 12Then they understood that he was not
telling them to guard against the yeast used in bread, but against
the teaching of the Pharisees and Sadducees.

What memories do you have of baked goods hot out of the oven? Grandma's homemade rolls? Mom's cookies? Uncle Bob's cornbread?

1. What do you think the Pharisees and Sadducees were actually hoping to see in the sky? How convincing would a sign have been for these religious leaders? **2.** Why do you think Jesus used the word "adulterous" instead of "disloyal" or "unbelieving"? In light of verses 1–4, what is the "yeast" about which Jesus warns the disciples? **3.** What was Jesus' point in the series of questions in verses 8–11? **4.** Why are the disciples so slow in understanding Jesus?

1. How is the "yeast of the Pharisees and Sadducees" working today? **2.** When you aren't understanding Jesus, what helps you to keep on trying?

Peter's Confession of Christ

13When Jesus came to the region of Caesarea Philippi, he asked
his disciples, "Who do people say the Son of Man is?"
14They replied, "Some say John the Baptist; others say Elijah;
and still others, Jeremiah or one of the prophets."
15"But what about you?" he asked. "Who do you say I am?"
16Simon Peter answered, "You are the Christ,[b] the Son of the
living God."
17Jesus replied, "Blessed are you, Simon son of Jonah, for this
was not revealed to you by man, but by my Father in heaven.
18And I tell you that you are Peter,[c] and on this rock I will build
my church, and the gates of Hades[d] will not overcome it.[e] 19I
will give you the keys of the kingdom of heaven; whatever you
bind on earth will be[f] bound in heaven, and whatever you loose
on earth will be[f] loosed in heaven." 20Then he warned his disciples not to tell anyone that he was the Christ.

Jesus Predicts His Death

21From that time on Jesus began to explain to his disciples that
he must go to Jerusalem and suffer many things at the hands of the
elders, chief priests and teachers of the law, and that he must be
killed and on the third day be raised to life.

1. If we polled two good friends from your early teen years, what adjective would they use to describe you? **2.** If you could "gain the world," where would you place your summer and winter castles?

1. Why did people think that Jesus was John the Baptist, Elijah or Jeremiah? **2.** What was significant about Peter's confession? **3.** How do you interpret the insight (v. 17), power (v. 18) and authority (v. 19) given to Peter? What are the "keys" of the kingdom? What do they "bind" and "loose"? **4.** Why does Jesus change the direction of his teaching now? **5.** What kind of Messiah was Peter expecting? Why was Jesus' response to Peter so strong (see 4:1–11)? **6.** What activities and attitudes are at the heart of Christian discipleship? How does a Christian forfeit his life? What might tempt people to lose their life or exchange their soul?

[a] *2* Some early manuscripts do not have the rest of verse 2 and all of verse 3. [b] *16* Or *Messiah*; also in verse 20 [c] *18* *Peter* means *rock*. [d] *18* Or *hell* [e] *18* Or *not prove stronger than it* [f] *19* Or *have been*

1. When and how did you come to recognize Jesus as your Messiah? **2.** In what area does verse 24 strike home to you now? **3.** How does verse 26 influence the way you make priorities?

22Peter took him aside and began to rebuke him. "Never, Lord!"
he said. "This shall never happen to you!"
23Jesus turned and said to Peter, "Get behind me, Satan! You are
a stumbling block to me; you do not have in mind the things of
God, but the things of men."
24Then Jesus said to his disciples, "If anyone would come after
me, he must deny himself and take up his cross and follow me.
25For whoever wants to save his life[a] will lose it, but whoever
loses his life for me will find it. 26What good will it be for a man if
he gains the whole world, yet forfeits his soul? Or what can a man
give in exchange for his soul? 27For the Son of Man is going to
come in his Father's glory with his angels, and then he will reward
each person according to what he has done. 28I tell you the truth,
some who are standing here will not taste death before they see
the Son of Man coming in his kingdom."

1. What was one mountain-top experience in your life? **2.** Of all the places you call "God's country," which is your favorite?

1. It's been six days since Peter confessed Jesus as the Christ and Jesus predicted his own death. Why is that information important for what happens next? Who does Jesus invite as a witness? Why only three? Why these three? **2.** What does it mean to be "transfigured"? **3.** Why Moses? Elijah (see 11:13)? **4.** Why was Pe-

The Transfiguration

17 After six days Jesus took with him Peter, James and John
the brother of James, and led them up a high mountain
by themselves. 2There he was transfigured before them. His face
shone like the sun, and his clothes became as white as the light.
3Just then there appeared before them Moses and Elijah, talking
with Jesus.
4Peter said to Jesus, "Lord, it is good for us to be here. If you
wish, I will put up three shelters—one for you, one for Moses and
one for Elijah."
5While he was still speaking, a bright cloud enveloped them, and

[a]*25* The Greek word means either *life* or *soul*; also in verse 26.

Matthew 16:13–28 CHRIST MUST DIE

1. Why do you think Jesus asked his disciples who people said he was?
   a. He was concerned about what people thought of him.
   b. He was searching for who he was.
   c. He wanted to find out how well he was revealing himself.
   d. He wanted the disciples to think about who *they* thought he was.

2. If you asked the typical person today, "Who is Jesus Christ?" what would he or she say?
   a. founder of a religion
   b. greatest man who ever lived
   c. Son of God
   d. social revolutionary
   e. spiritual philosopher and teacher
   f. Lord and Savior
   g. a swear word

3. What would your answer to this question have been in the past? What is your answer today?

4. Why did Peter get so upset when Jesus told about his future death?
   a. He didn't want to lose his leader.
   b. He didn't want his friend to suffer.
   c. He was afraid that this meant he would suffer too.
   d. He thought that Jesus would be Israel's new ruler.

5. Why did Jesus get so upset with Peter's response?

6. "If anyone would come after me, he must deny himself and take up his cross and follow me" means:
   a. Following Jesus is no picnic.
   b. If you've got any reservations, now is the time to get out.
   c. It's going to cost you everything.
   d. Shape up or ship out.

7. When I compare my spiritual life to Jesus' call to deny myself, take up my cross and follow him, I feel like:
   a. starting over.
   b. running away.
   c. yawning.
   d. going for it.

8. What would it mean for you to "deny" yourself?
   a. stop focusing on my problems
   b. think more about others
   c. never do anything for myself
   d. put Christ's desires above mine

9. What might it mean for you to gain the whole world yet forfeit your soul?
   a. gain the approval of significant people, but give up what I stand for
   b. gain the world's approval, but lose Christ's approval
   c. gain in career or possessions, but lose what's most important in life

10. When Peter declared who Jesus was, Jesus in turn revealed Peter's great potential. What potential has Jesus revealed in you as you have come to follow him?

11. What would taking the next step in your spiritual life mean?
    a. to correct some of my misconceptions of who Jesus is
    b. to do remedial work on the basics—prayer, Bible reading, etc.
    c. to confess my faith publicly
    d. to find my spiritual potential

12. How has this course helped you? How can this group continue to help you—such as continuing to meet or pray for you?

a voice from the cloud said, “This is my Son, whom I love; with
him I am well pleased. Listen to him!”
6When the disciples heard this, they fell facedown to the ground,
terrified. 7But Jesus came and touched them. “Get up,” he said.
“Don’t be afraid.” 8When they looked up, they saw no one except
Jesus.
9As they were coming down the mountain, Jesus instructed
them, “Don’t tell anyone what you have seen, until the Son of Man
has been raised from the dead.”
10The disciples asked him, “Why then do the teachers of the law
say that Elijah must come first?”
11Jesus replied, “To be sure, Elijah comes and will restore all
things. 12But I tell you, Elijah has already come, and they did not
recognize him, but have done to him everything they wished. In
the same way the Son of Man is going to suffer at their hands.”
13Then the disciples understood that he was talking to them about
John the Baptist.

The Healing of a Boy With a Demon

14When they came to the crowd, a man approached Jesus and
knelt before him. 15“Lord, have mercy on my son,” he said. “He
has seizures and is suffering greatly. He often falls into the fire or
into the water. 16I brought him to your disciples, but they could
not heal him.”
17“O unbelieving and perverse generation,” Jesus replied, “how
long shall I stay with you? How long shall I put up with you? Bring
the boy here to me.” 18Jesus rebuked the demon, and it came out
of the boy, and he was healed from that moment.
19Then the disciples came to Jesus in private and asked, “Why
couldn’t we drive it out?”
20He replied, “Because you have so little faith. I tell you the
truth, if you have faith as small as a mustard seed, you can say to
this mountain, ‘Move from here to there’ and it will move. Nothing
will be impossible for you.[a]”
22When they came together in Galilee, he said to them, “The
Son of Man is going to be betrayed into the hands of men. 23They
will kill him, and on the third day he will be raised to life.” And the
disciples were filled with grief.

The Temple Tax

24After Jesus and his disciples arrived in Capernaum, the collectors of the two-drachma tax came to Peter and asked, “Doesn’t
your teacher pay the temple tax[b]?”
25“Yes, he does,” he replied.
When Peter came into the house, Jesus was the first to speak.
“What do you think, Simon?” he asked. “From whom do the kings
of the earth collect duty and taxes—from their own sons or from
others?”
26“From others,” Peter answered.
“Then the sons are exempt,” Jesus said to him. 27“But so that
we may not offend them, go to the lake and throw out your line.
Take the first fish you catch; open its mouth and you will find
a four-drachma coin. Take it and give it to them for my tax and
yours.”

[a]20 Some manuscripts *you.* 21*But this kind does not go out except by prayer and fasting.*
[b]24 Greek *the two drachmas*

ter's response inappropriate? **5.** What is significant in what the voice from the cloud says about Jesus? (See Ex 24:15.) **6.** Why does Jesus silence the disciples?

1. How did you come to realize that Jesus was the one, above all others, that you should listen to? **2.** How has God said to you, "This is my son (or daughter), whom I love, with whom I am well pleased"?

If you could move mountains, which one would you move first: Mt. Everest? Your favorite ski slope? Mountains of paper?

1. Why did demons seem to be more common in Jesus' day? **2.** Who is Jesus describing in verse 17? Why would he say such a thing? **3.** How would you paraphrase verse 20? **4.** What does the disciples' grief reveal about them?

1. When has a mountaintop experience in your life been followed by a valley experience? How did you cope? **2.** In which areas of your life do you long to see more faith?

What wild "fish story" is retold in your family?

1. What was the temple tax (see Ex 30:11–16)? Who was required to pay it? **2.** Why is Jesus exempt from the tax? **3.** What lesson was Jesus teaching Peter by paying the tax anyway?

1. Which freedoms do you enjoy most as a Christian? **2.** What is at stake when we offend someone?

1. Which would best describe you as a child: "Little angel" or "Holy terror"? Why? **2.** Which "woe" would be the worst way to go: (a) Canoe ride over a 250-foot waterfall? (b) Parachute failing to open? (c) Running out of fuel in outer space? (d) Being a late-night snack for a pride of lions?

1. Why would the disciples want to be "the greatest"? **2.** What childlike qualities is Jesus emphasizing? Why do you think this is important for Jesus' kingdom? **3.** Why is causing a child to sin such a serious offense? **4.** Although evil is inevitable (vv. 7–9), how are we still responsible for others' spiritual welfare? **5.** Who are the "little ones" in verses 12–14?

1. What childlike quality do you need to recapture? Why? **2.** When were you a sheep that wandered off? How did God get you back? **3.** What needs to change in your attitude toward those who "wander"? Toward the weak? The powerless? What could be an area in your life that causes problems for others? What will you do about it?

The Greatest in the Kingdom of Heaven

18 At that time the disciples came to Jesus and asked, "Who is the greatest in the kingdom of heaven?"

2He called a little child and had him stand among them. 3And he said: "I tell you the truth, unless you change and become like little children, you will never enter the kingdom of heaven. 4Therefore, whoever humbles himself like this child is the greatest in the kingdom of heaven.

5"And whoever welcomes a little child like this in my name welcomes me. 6But if anyone causes one of these little ones who believe in me to sin, it would be better for him to have a large millstone hung around his neck and to be drowned in the depths of the sea.

7"Woe to the world because of the things that cause people to sin! Such things must come, but woe to the man through whom they come! 8If your hand or your foot causes you to sin, cut it off and throw it away. It is better for you to enter life maimed or crippled than to have two hands or two feet and be thrown into eternal fire. 9And if your eye causes you to sin, gouge it out and throw it away. It is better for you to enter life with one eye than to have two eyes and be thrown into the fire of hell.

The Parable of the Lost Sheep

10"See that you do not look down on one of these little ones. For I tell you that their angels in heaven always see the face of my Father in heaven.[a]

12"What do you think? If a man owns a hundred sheep, and one of them wanders away, will he not leave the ninety-nine on the hills and go to look for the one that wandered off? 13And if he finds it, I tell you the truth, he is happier about that one sheep than about the ninety-nine that did not wander off. 14In the same way your Father in heaven is not willing that any of these little ones should be lost.

What funny things did you and a sibling argue about?

1. How does this passage reconcile with 7:3–5? **2.** This reconciliation process involves what four stages? Why not go public right away? What authority is given to Jesus' followers?

What does this passage say about the importance of counsel through others? Of accountability to a trusted few?

A Brother Who Sins Against You

15"If your brother sins against you,[b] go and show him his fault, just between the two of you. If he listens to you, you have won your brother over. 16But if he will not listen, take one or two others along, so that 'every matter may be established by the testimony of two or three witnesses.'[c] 17If he refuses to listen to them, tell it to the church; and if he refuses to listen even to the church, treat him as you would a pagan or a tax collector.

18"I tell you the truth, whatever you bind on earth will be[d] bound in heaven, and whatever you loose on earth will be[d] loosed in heaven.

19"Again, I tell you that if two of you on earth agree about anything you ask for, it will be done for you by my Father in heaven. 20For where two or three come together in my name, there am I with them."

How many credit cards do you have? When does your credit card tempt you the most?

1. Offenders in Jesus' day were forgiven up to three times; a fourth offense need not be forgiven. What does Jesus' answer say about forgiveness in the kingdom? **2.** How does the parable of the unmerciful servant extend

The Parable of the Unmerciful Servant

21Then Peter came to Jesus and asked, "Lord, how many times shall I forgive my brother when he sins against me? Up to seven times?"

22Jesus answered, "I tell you, not seven times, but seventy-seven times.[e]

[a] *10* Some manuscripts *heaven.* *11The Son of Man came to save what was lost.*
[b] *15* Some manuscripts do not have *against you.* [c] *16* Deut. 19:15 [d] *18* Or *have been* [e] *22* Or *seventy times seven*

[23]"Therefore, the kingdom of heaven is like a king who wanted
to settle accounts with his servants. [24]As he began the settlement,
a man who owed him ten thousand talents[a] was brought to him.
[25]Since he was not able to pay, the master ordered that he and
his wife and his children and all that he had be sold to repay the
debt.
[26]"The servant fell on his knees before him. 'Be patient with
me,' he begged, 'and I will pay back everything.' [27]The servant's
master took pity on him, canceled the debt and let him go.
[28]"But when that servant went out, he found one of his fellow
servants who owed him a hundred denarii.[b] He grabbed him and
began to choke him. 'Pay back what you owe me!' he demanded.
[29]"His fellow servant fell to his knees and begged him, 'Be patient with me, and I will pay you back.'
[30]"But he refused. Instead, he went off and had the man thrown
into prison until he could pay the debt. [31]When the other servants
saw what had happened, they were greatly distressed and went
and told their master everything that had happened.
[32]"Then the master called the servant in. 'You wicked servant,'
he said, 'I canceled all that debt of yours because you begged me
to. [33]Shouldn't you have had mercy on your fellow servant just as
I had on you?' [34]In anger his master turned him over to the jailers
to be tortured, until he should pay back all he owed.
[35]"This is how my heavenly Father will treat each of you unless
you forgive your brother from your heart."

Jesus' teaching on forgiveness (vv. 23–35)? In refusing to be merciful to others, what do we deny ourselves (vv. 31–34)? **3.** Do we forgive others so God will forgive us, or does God forgive us so that we will have a forgiving attitude? Explain. **4.** Based on this parable, is God's forgiveness of us limited or unlimited? Conditional or unconditional? Likewise, our forgiveness of others?

♡ **1.** How can we forgive, yet not encourage, irresponsibility? **2.** How can you forgive someone from the distant past who hurt you deeply? **3.** What is the connection between forgiveness, health and wholeness?

[a]*24* That is, millions of dollars [b]*28* That is, a few dollars

Matthew 18:21–35 PARABLE OF THE UNMERCIFUL SERVANT

1. What prompted Peter to ask how many times he needed to forgive?
   a. He was the type to keep score.
   b. Since Jewish tradition dictated forgiving three times, he thought he was being generous.
   c. He wanted to forgive like Jesus.
   d. Someone just irritated him for the eighth time, and Peter wanted to smack him.

2. What is this parable really about?
   a. how to deal with someone who owes you money
   b. how to deal with your anger when you've been wronged
   c. how to keep your relationship with God right
   d. how to avoid the trap of grudges
   e. how to show your thanks for God's forgiveness

3. What is the principle for dealing with someone who has wronged you?
   a. "an eye for an eye"
   b. You can't out-forgive God.
   c. God expects you to be a pushover.
   d. People who can't forgive wind up in their own chains.
   e. Only the forgiven can forgive.

4. What is hardest for you?
   a. forgiving again and again
   b. not punishing those who hurt me
   c. forgiving from my heart—I can say the words but I don't feel them.
   d. wondering how I can forgive without encouraging irresponsibility

5. What have you found helpful in dealing with strained relationships?
   a. being up front with the person
   b. ignoring it and hoping for the best
   c. asking someone else to mediate
   d. writing out my feelings
   e. breaking off the relationship

6. What is the most important thing you have needed (or need now) to be able to forgive "from your heart"?
   a. talking through my pain
   b. receiving counseling
   c. appreciating God's forgiving me
   d. seeing the other person as human and hurting himself/herself
   e. foregoing the pleasure of self-pity

7. If the person who has hurt you most were on his/her knees begging for forgiveness, how would you react?
   a. gladly send them to the dungeon
   b. regretfully send them to the dungeon so they couldn't hurt others
   c. let them go, but not forgive them
   d. forgive them completely
   e. pinch myself to see if I was awake

8. How have you been burned in past relationships? To what extent has that resulted in loneliness in your life now? What does this passage say to you about venturing to risk again?

9. What role does—or should—forgiveness play in your marriage relationship?
   a. It keeps me from keeping score.
   b. It keeps me from giving my spouse the silent treatment.
   c. It keeps me from playing the blame game—because we almost always *both* are to blame!
   d. When I recognize my own "debts," I can forgive my mate a lot easier.
   e. I never do anything that I need to be forgiven for!
   f. I know if I want my relationship with God to be right, my relationship with my mate needs to be right.

What was (or would be) Mom's advice to you about marriage? What was Dad's?

1. What would the Pharisees gain if Jesus opposed Moses? **2.** Why doesn't Jesus debate divorce? Why does he focus on marriage instead? How is he reversing the trap? **3.** What was Moses' intention in allowing divorce? **4.** Does "what God has joined together" apply to non-believers? How might his answer be different if a divorce truly seeking God had asked the question? **5.** How do the disciples see marriage? Why?

1. How can you have the marriage God desires? **2.** When divorce occurs, what hope does Jesus offer?

---

1. If your house were on fire, what three items would you try to save? **2.** What is your ideal annual salary?

1. Why would parents bring their children to Jesus? Why did the disciples discourage this? What is Jesus' view of children and the kingdom? **2.** What appears to be this young man's view on how one obtains eternal life? **3.** Is there a difference between the young man's concern ("eternal life") and Jesus' concern ("life")? **4.** Of the Ten Commandments recorded by Moses (see Ex 20), what is the general subject of the first four? Of the last six? Which one did Jesus omit? Why? Which commandment did Jesus add here which was not part of the original ten? **5.** Had the man truly loved his neighbor? How do you know? **6.** Why is it so difficult for the rich to enter the kingdom? On what basis is it possible for anyone, rich or poor, to enter (vv. 26–30)? **7.** In this passage, how are these four concepts connected: *salvation, discipleship, entering the kingdom of heaven* and *inheriting eternal life*?

1. Jesus hit this man where it hurt—in his wallet. If Jesus were to address you where it hurts, what would be his hot topic? **2.**

Divorce

19 When Jesus had finished saying these things, he left Galilee
and went into the region of Judea to the other side of the
Jordan. 2Large crowds followed him, and he healed them there.
3Some Pharisees came to him to test him. They asked, "Is it
lawful for a man to divorce his wife for any and every reason?"
4"Haven't you read," he replied, "that at the beginning the Creator 'made them male and female,'[a] 5and said, 'For this reason a
man will leave his father and mother and be united to his wife, and
the two will become one flesh'[b]? 6So they are no longer two, but
one. Therefore what God has joined together, let man not separate."
7"Why then," they asked, "did Moses command that a man give
his wife a certificate of divorce and send her away?"
8Jesus replied, "Moses permitted you to divorce your wives because your hearts were hard. But it was not this way from the
beginning. 9I tell you that anyone who divorces his wife, except for
marital unfaithfulness, and marries another woman commits adultery."
10The disciples said to him, "If this is the situation between a
husband and wife, it is better not to marry."
11Jesus replied, "Not everyone can accept this word, but only
those to whom it has been given. 12For some are eunuchs because
they were born that way; others were made that way by men; and
others have renounced marriage[c] because of the kingdom of heav-
en. The one who can accept this should accept it."

The Little Children and Jesus

13Then little children were brought to Jesus for him to place his
hands on them and pray for them. But the disciples rebuked those
who brought them.
14Jesus said, "Let the little children come to me, and do not
hinder them, for the kingdom of heaven belongs to such as these."
15When he had placed his hands on them, he went on from there.

The Rich Young Man

16Now a man came up to Jesus and asked, "Teacher, what good
thing must I do to get eternal life?"
17"Why do you ask me about what is good?" Jesus replied.
"There is only One who is good. If you want to enter life, obey the
commandments."
18"Which ones?" the man inquired.
Jesus replied, " 'Do not murder, do not commit adultery, do not
steal, do not give false testimony, 19honor your father and mother,'[d] and 'love your neighbor as yourself.'[e]"
20"All these I have kept," the young man said. "What do I still
lack?"
21Jesus answered, "If you want to be perfect, go, sell your possessions and give to the poor, and you will have treasure in heaven.
Then come, follow me."
22When the young man heard this, he went away sad, because
he had great wealth.
23Then Jesus said to his disciples, "I tell you the truth, it is hard
for a rich man to enter the kingdom of heaven. 24Again I tell you,
it is easier for a camel to go through the eye of a needle than for a
rich man to enter the kingdom of God."

[a] *4* Gen. 1:27 [b] *5* Gen. 2:24 [c] *12* Or *have made themselves eunuchs*
[d] *19* Exodus 20:12-16; Deut. 5:16-20 [e] *19* Lev. 19:18

25When the disciples heard this, they were greatly astonished
and asked, "Who then can be saved?"
26Jesus looked at them and said, "With man this is impossible,
but with God all things are possible."
27Peter answered him, "We have left everything to follow you!
What then will there be for us?"
28Jesus said to them, "I tell you the truth, at the renewal of all
things, when the Son of Man sits on his glorious throne, you who
have followed me will also sit on twelve thrones, judging the
twelve tribes of Israel. 29And everyone who has left houses or
brothers or sisters or father or mother[a] or children or fields for
my sake will receive a hundred times as much and will inherit
eternal life. 30But many who are first will be last, and many who
are last will be first.

Why is Jesus so tough on riches? **3.** What have you given up to follow Jesus? How is your life different as a result?

The Parable of the Workers in the Vineyard

20 "For the kingdom of heaven is like a landowner who went
out early in the morning to hire men to work in his vineyard. 2He agreed to pay them a denarius for the day and sent them
into his vineyard.
3"About the third hour he went out and saw others standing in
the marketplace doing nothing. 4He told them, 'You also go and
work in my vineyard, and I will pay you whatever is right.' 5So they
went.
"He went out again about the sixth hour and the ninth hour and
did the same thing. 6About the eleventh hour he went out and
found still others standing around. He asked them, 'Why have you
been standing here all day long doing nothing?'

[a]29 Some manuscripts *mother or wife*

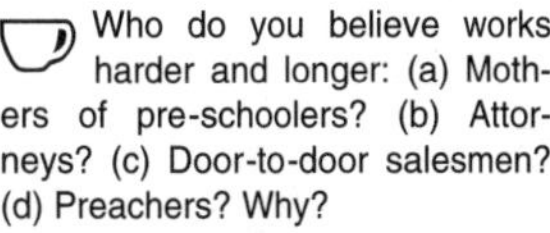

Who do you believe works harder and longer: (a) Mothers of pre-schoolers? (b) Attorneys? (c) Door-to-door salesmen? (d) Preachers? Why?

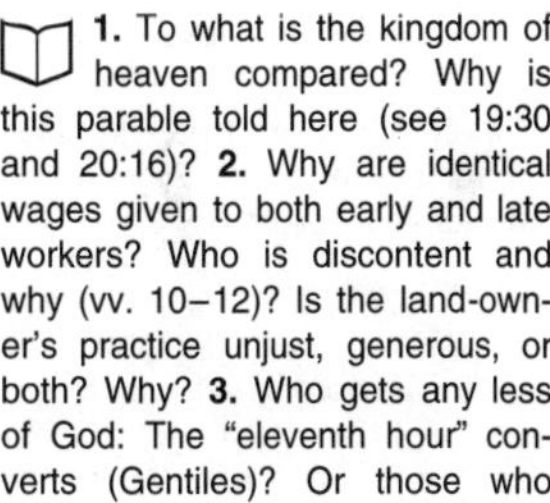

1. To what is the kingdom of heaven compared? Why is this parable told here (see 19:30 and 20:16)? **2.** Why are identical wages given to both early and late workers? Who is discontent and why (vv. 10–12)? Is the land-owner's practice unjust, generous, or both? Why? **3.** Who gets any less of God: The "eleventh hour" converts (Gentiles)? Or those who

Mt 20:1–16 PARABLE OF THE WORKERS IN THE VINEYARD

1. If you were one of the first hired (at 6 a.m), how would you have felt?
   a. I'd have reported the landowner to the Better Business Bureau!
   b. I'd have grumbled behind the landowner's back.
   c. I wouldn't have complained, because I got the pay I agreed to.
   d. I'd have been happy for the workers hired after I was.

2. From an employer's viewpoint, how would you react to the landowner's wage practices?
   a. He was too soft-hearted.
   b. He was unfair to the first workers.
   c. He was right—he could do what he wanted with his money.
   d. He was a compassionate man.
   e. He didn't have a business mind.

3. What does this parable say to you about God and his kingdom?
   a. God is arbitrary and unfair.
   b. God's grace is truly amazing.
   c. God is free to bless who he wants.
   d. God's grace isn't dependent on our merit.
   e. God is gracious no matter how long it takes you to follow him.

4. Would you say you entered God's kingdom early, in the middle or late in the day? Do you ever wish you had waited, or feel jealous of others who waited until the "eleventh hour"?

5. What is the main reason you work?
   a. to survive
   b. to give our children a better life
   c. to obtain material things
   d. because work is fulfilling
   e. because I'd be bored otherwise
   f. because I feel called to

6. What do you consider to be most stressful about your work?
   a. an excessive workload
   b. an unreasonable boss
   c. monotonous work
   d. irritating co-workers
   e. poor pay/benefits/job security
   f. balancing work with the rest of life

7. Comparing your energy level and life perspective to this parable, what time is it in your life right now?
   a. 6 a.m.—I'm raring to go.
   b. 9 a.m.—I'm feeling productive.
   c. Noon—I'm ready for a break.
   d. 3 p.m.—I'm running out of gas.
   e. 5 p.m.—Help, I *am* out of gas!
   f. 6 p.m.—It's so good to be home.

8. Which one of the following—(1) controls what happens in your work; and (2) do you most try to please?
   a. my employer
   b. myself
   c. God

9. How does the tension between work and marriage bother you the most?
   a. stress from work spilling over into our relationship
   b. disagreeing on how much time and energy to give to work
   c. hassles about dividing up household responsibilities
   d. guilt about the toll work takes on our family time
   e. fear about what lasting damage work might bring to our family

should have known God since the "first hour" (the Jews)?

1. How do you feel about recent converts getting the same benefits as you in the kingdom? 2. Would you recommend that people wait until just before they die to come to Christ, so that they won't have to work so hard or give up so much? Why? 3. Do you ever envy God's blessing on others? Why?

---

1. What did your parents want you to be when you grew up? What about you? 2. What are some secret expectations you have for your children?

1. Why does Jesus once again predict his death? Why on this occasion? 2. What in the request of the woman (vv. 20–21) shows that the disciples' view of the kingdom was different from Jesus'? Of what are she (and they) ignorant? 3. In order to share in his kingdom, what "cup" must the disciples share with Jesus (vv. 18–19)? 4. Why were the other 10 disciples so outraged? Were their reactions any more commendable? 5. What contrast does Jesus set up between the Gentile kingdom and God's kingdom? How does Jesus model this new way? 6. How would you compare the attitude of the two blind men with that of the disciples (vv. 20–28)? 7. How do their requests differ? 8. Why are these two singled out for healing? Once healed, what do they do? Why? How does this relate to the disciples' concern (vv. 20–28)?

1. What specific ways can you serve people, using Jesus as your model? Jesus was always saying or doing the unexpected (vv. 26–28). What has he told you that you did not expect? 2. In what ways do you feel spiritually blind? How is your sight better now than six months ago? 3. If Jesus said, "What do you want me to do for you?" how would you answer?

7" 'Because no one has hired us,' they answered.
"He said to them, 'You also go and work in my vineyard.'
8"When evening came, the owner of the vineyard said to his
foreman, 'Call the workers and pay them their wages, beginning
with the last ones hired and going on to the first.'
9"The workers who were hired about the eleventh hour came
and each received a denarius. 10So when those came who were
hired first, they expected to receive more. But each one of them
also received a denarius. 11When they received it, they began to
grumble against the landowner. 12'These men who were hired last
worked only one hour,' they said, 'and you have made them equal
to us who have borne the burden of the work and the heat of the
day.'
13"But he answered one of them, 'Friend, I am not being unfair
to you. Didn't you agree to work for a denarius? 14Take your pay
and go. I want to give the man who was hired last the same as I
gave you. 15Don't I have the right to do what I want with my own
money? Or are you envious because I am generous?'
16"So the last will be first, and the first will be last."

Jesus Again Predicts His Death

17Now as Jesus was going up to Jerusalem, he took the twelve
disciples aside and said to them, 18"We are going up to Jerusalem,
and the Son of Man will be betrayed to the chief priests and the
teachers of the law. They will condemn him to death 19and will
turn him over to the Gentiles to be mocked and flogged and crucified. On the third day he will be raised to life!"

A Mother's Request

20Then the mother of Zebedee's sons came to Jesus with her
sons and, kneeling down, asked a favor of him.
21"What is it you want?" he asked.
She said, "Grant that one of these two sons of mine may sit at
your right and the other at your left in your kingdom."
22"You don't know what you are asking," Jesus said to them.
"Can you drink the cup I am going to drink?"
"We can," they answered.
23Jesus said to them, "You will indeed drink from my cup, but to
sit at my right or left is not for me to grant. These places belong to
those for whom they have been prepared by my Father."
24When the ten heard about this, they were indignant with the
two brothers. 25Jesus called them together and said, "You know
that the rulers of the Gentiles lord it over them, and their high
officials exercise authority over them. 26Not so with you. Instead,
whoever wants to become great among you must be your servant,
27and whoever wants to be first must be your slave— 28just as the
Son of Man did not come to be served, but to serve, and to give his
life as a ransom for many."

Two Blind Men Receive Sight

29As Jesus and his disciples were leaving Jericho, a large crowd
followed him. 30Two blind men were sitting by the roadside, and
when they heard that Jesus was going by, they shouted, "Lord, Son
of David, have mercy on us!"
31The crowd rebuked them and told them to be quiet, but they
shouted all the louder, "Lord, Son of David, have mercy on us!"
32Jesus stopped and called them. "What do you want me to do
for you?" he asked.
33"Lord," they answered, "we want our sight."

34Jesus had compassion on them and touched their eyes. Immediately they received their sight and followed him.

The Triumphal Entry

21 As they approached Jerusalem and came to Bethphage on
the Mount of Olives, Jesus sent two disciples, 2saying to
them, "Go to the village ahead of you, and at once you will find a
donkey tied there, with her colt by her. Untie them and bring them
to me. 3If anyone says anything to you, tell him that the Lord needs
them, and he will send them right away."
4This took place to fulfill what was spoken through the prophet:

> 5"Say to the Daughter of Zion,
> 'See, your king comes to you,
> gentle and riding on a donkey,
> on a colt, the foal of a donkey.' "[a]

6The disciples went and did as Jesus had instructed them. 7They
brought the donkey and the colt, placed their cloaks on them, and
Jesus sat on them. 8A very large crowd spread their cloaks on the
road, while others cut branches from the trees and spread them on
the road. 9The crowds that went ahead of him and those that
followed shouted,

> "Hosanna[b] to the Son of David!"

[a] *5* Zech. 9:9 [b] *9* A Hebrew expression meaning "Save!" which became an exclamation of praise; also in verse 15

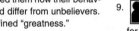

How would you arrange for a visiting President to have maximum exposure in your town: What parades? What TV talk shows or radio call-in programs? Where would he eat? Stay the night?

1. To what town has Jesus come? Why? **2.** Jesus comes on a donkey and not on a stallion. What does that portray? **3.** What kind of kingdom and king were the people expecting? How do their wishes compare with the reality of Jesus? **4.** How might that discrepancy account for the same crowd jeering and shouting later, "Crucify him!"?

1. What difference does it make to you that Jesus is a gentle King, and not like the one described in 20:25? **2.** How would you have reacted if you had been there to greet Jesus riding into town? Do you jump on political or religious bandwagons today? Why or why not? **3.** Does Jesus' humility work for you? Why or why not?

Matthew 20:20–28 A MOTHER'S REQUEST

1. Why do you think James' and John's mother did this?
   a. Her sons put her up to it.
   b. She was just being a mother.
   c. She wanted the best for her sons.
   d. She didn't realize what she was asking.

2. Are you living up to your parents' expectations?
   a. Are you kidding? d. I'm trying.
   b. Yes. e. I quit trying.
   c. They didn't have any.

3. What was Jesus saying by his response in verse 22?
   a. Your request is out of line.
   b. Your sons don't deserve this.
   c. It's not my decision to make.
   d. You don't understand what following me involves.

4. Why were the other 10 disciples angry about the request?
   a. They felt it was dividing them.
   b. They were insecure.
   c. They understood servanthood.
   d. They were angry that they hadn't asked first.

5. How would you describe Jesus' response to this conflict?
   a. He scolded them.
   b. He used it to teach them.
   c. He showed them how their behavior should differ from unbelievers.
   d. He redefined "greatness."

6. In what area of your life do you think God wants you to be more of a servant? How do you feel about that?

7. How would you describe your parents' expectations of you?
   a. My parents expect very little—I wonder if they even care.
   b. My parents expect too much—I could never live up to their expectations.
   c. My parents' expectations are high enough to challenge me, but not too high to discourage me.
   d. My parents have helped me to set my own expectations.

8. When you have a difference with a parent over expectations, what have you found helpful?
   a. Tell them to stay out of my life.
   b. Tell them what they want to hear.
   c. Try to understand their viewpoint.
   d. Talk it through until we agree together on the expectations.

9. What does this story say to you about your expectations for your children?
   a. I need to let my children speak for themselves.
   b. Before I encourage my children to reach for something, I should be sure I know the cost.
   c. I need to help my children focus less on self-glory and more on how they can serve.

10. What would you like to pass on to your kids?
   a. nothing in particular—They need to develop on their own.
   b. a sense of right and wrong
   c. a deep faith
   d. family loyalty
   e. lots of initiative
   f. a significant inheritance
   g. our business or a certain career
   h. other:____________________

"Blessed is he who comes in the name of the
Lord!"[a]

"Hosanna[b] in the highest!"

10When Jesus entered Jerusalem, the whole city was stirred and
asked, "Who is this?"
11The crowds answered, "This is Jesus, the prophet from Nazareth in Galilee."

Jesus at the Temple

12Jesus entered the temple area and drove out all who were
buying and selling there. He overturned the tables of the money
changers and the benches of those selling doves. 13"It is written,"
he said to them, "'My house will be called a house of prayer,'[c]
but you are making it a 'den of robbers.'[d]"
14The blind and the lame came to him at the temple, and he
healed them. 15But when the chief priests and the teachers of the
law saw the wonderful things he did and the children shouting in
the temple area, "Hosanna to the Son of David," they were indignant.
16"Do you hear what these children are saying?" they asked him.
"Yes," replied Jesus, "have you never read,

"'From the lips of children and infants
you have ordained praise'[e]?"

17And he left them and went out of the city to Bethany, where
he spent the night.

The Fig Tree Withers

18Early in the morning, as he was on his way back to the city, he
was hungry. 19Seeing a fig tree by the road, he went up to it but
found nothing on it except leaves. Then he said to it, "May you
never bear fruit again!" Immediately the tree withered.
20When the disciples saw this, they were amazed. "How did the
fig tree wither so quickly?" they asked.
21Jesus replied, "I tell you the truth, if you have faith and do not
doubt, not only can you do what was done to the fig tree, but also
you can say to this mountain, 'Go, throw yourself into the sea,' and
it will be done. 22If you believe, you will receive whatever you ask
for in prayer."

When you see something wrong, are you more likely to act without thinking or think without acting?

1. What upset Jesus so much about what he saw in the temple (see Isa 56:6–7)? **2.** Although the merchants once performed a useful service for out-of-towners, how had it become corrupted? **3.** In this passage, which groups of people did and did not recognize the significance of Jesus? How do you explain that? **4.** How is the fig tree incident a parable about what has happened in the temple and what is to come (see Hos 9:10–17)? **5.** What does this dramatized parable teach about faith? Prayer? Judgment? Jesus?

1. If Jesus were to visit your church, where would he begin "turning over tables"? What about in your life? **2.** Could the promise of verse 22 be abused? How does it encourage you in your prayer?

The Authority of Jesus Questioned

23Jesus entered the temple courts, and, while he was teaching,
the chief priests and the elders of the people came to him. "By
what authority are you doing these things?" they asked. "And who
gave you this authority?"
24Jesus replied, "I will also ask you one question. If you answer
me, I will tell you by what authority I am doing these things.
25John's baptism—where did it come from? Was it from heaven, or
from men?"
They discussed it among themselves and said, "If we say, 'From
heaven,' he will ask, 'Then why didn't you believe him?' 26But if
we say, 'From men'—we are afraid of the people, for they all hold
that John was a prophet."
27So they answered Jesus, "We don't know."

In high school, with what authority figure did you run into trouble? Why?

1. How could Jesus have answered the priests question? Why didn't he? **2.** How did Jesus' counter-question force the issue? **3.** How was Jesus' authority linked to John's?

When it comes right down to it, whose opinion do you care about more—God's or people's? How does that show?

[a] *9* Psalm 118:26 [b] *9* A Hebrew expression meaning "Save!" which became an exclamation of praise; also in verse 15 [c] *13* Isaiah 56:7 [d] *13* Jer. 7:11
[e] *16* Psalm 8:2

Then he said, "Neither will I tell you by what authority I am
doing these things.

The Parable of the Two Sons

28"What do you think? There was a man who had two sons. He
went to the first and said, 'Son, go and work today in the vineyard.'
29" 'I will not,' he answered, but later he changed his mind and
went.
30"Then the father went to the other son and said the same
thing. He answered, 'I will, sir,' but he did not go.
31"Which of the two did what his father wanted?"
"The first," they answered.
Jesus said to them, "I tell you the truth, the tax collectors and
the prostitutes are entering the kingdom of God ahead of you. 32For
John came to you to show you the way of righteousness, and you
did not believe him, but the tax collectors and the prostitutes did.
And even after you saw this, you did not repent and believe him.

As a child, what kind of worker were you? How often did your parents have to yell to get you to work?

1. What links this parable to verses 23–27? **2.** What is the father's request? What does each son say and do? Why? **3.** What group is like which son? How? **4.** How do you suppose the religious leaders felt about this story?

Which son's story is most like your own? Why?

The Parable of the Tenants

33"Listen to another parable: There was a landowner who planted a vineyard. He put a wall around it, dug a winepress in it and
built a watchtower. Then he rented the vineyard to some farmers
and went away on a journey. 34When the harvest time approached,
he sent his servants to the tenants to collect his fruit.
35"The tenants seized his servants; they beat one, killed another,
and stoned a third. 36Then he sent other servants to them, more
than the first time, and the tenants treated them the same way.
37Last of all, he sent his son to them. 'They will respect my son,' he
said.
38"But when the tenants saw the son, they said to each other,
'This is the heir. Come, let's kill him and take his inheritance.'
39So they took him and threw him out of the vineyard and killed
him.
40"Therefore, when the owner of the vineyard comes, what will
he do to those tenants?"
41"He will bring those wretches to a wretched end," they replied, "and he will rent the vineyard to other tenants, who will
give him his share of the crop at harvest time."
42Jesus said to them, "Have you never read in the Scriptures:

> " 'The stone the builders rejected
> has become the capstone[a];
> the Lord has done this,
> and it is marvelous in our eyes'[b]?

43"Therefore I tell you that the kingdom of God will be taken
away from you and given to a people who will produce its fruit.
44He who falls on this stone will be broken to pieces, but he on
whom it falls will be crushed."[c]
45When the chief priests and the Pharisees heard Jesus' parables,
they knew he was talking about them. 46They looked for a way to
arrest him, but they were afraid of the crowd because the people
held that he was a prophet.

1. If you could travel anywhere in the world (money being no problem), where would you go? **2.** If you were an absentee landlord and had to find trustworthy tenants, what would you seek?

1. In this parable, who is represented as the landowner? The vineyard? Tenants? Servants? Son? **2.** What corresponds to the son's death? To the removal of the wretched tenants? **3.** What is ironic about verses 42–44? **4.** At whom does Jesus direct the parable? Why don't they arrest him? Why don't they repent and follow Jesus? **5.** Who will be given the kingdom of God (v. 43)?

1. At different times in your life, how have you received Jesus? **2.** Have you ever felt as though you deserved God's kingdom? **3.** In your life, is Jesus like a *capstone* (the highest point in your building)? Or is he like a *millstone* (a weight that drags you down)? In what ways? **4.** With whom do you identify in this story? Why?

[a] *42* Or *cornerstone* [b] *42* Psalm 118:22,23 [c] *44* Some manuscripts do not have verse 44.

If you could choose one unusual way to do (or redo) your wedding, what would you choose: (a) Recite your vows while parachuting? (b) Hold the service underwater? (c) Dress everyone in costume? (d) Other?

1. Why is this banquet held? **2.** What do you learn about those originally invited? What is so surprising about their response? **3.** Who did the king eventually invite? Why? **4.** What is the problem with one guest (vv. 11–12)? What does it mean to be in the king's presence "without wedding clothes"? Why is this ill-clad guest banished? **5.** What does this parable suggest about the kingdom?

1. When did Jesus first call you to the banquet? How did you respond initially? How many other times did he invite you? **2.** Whom do you identify with in this story? Why? **3.** What can you do this week to encourage attendance and proper dress?

The Parable of the Wedding Banquet

22 Jesus spoke to them again in parables, saying: 2"The kingdom of heaven is like a king who prepared a wedding banquet for his son. 3He sent his servants to those who had been invited to the banquet to tell them to come, but they refused to come.

4"Then he sent some more servants and said, 'Tell those who have been invited that I have prepared my dinner: My oxen and fattened cattle have been butchered, and everything is ready. Come to the wedding banquet.'

5"But they paid no attention and went off—one to his field, another to his business. 6The rest seized his servants, mistreated them and killed them. 7The king was enraged. He sent his army and destroyed those murderers and burned their city.

8"Then he said to his servants, 'The wedding banquet is ready, but those I invited did not deserve to come. 9Go to the street corners and invite to the banquet anyone you find.' 10So the servants went out into the streets and gathered all the people they could find, both good and bad, and the wedding hall was filled with guests.

11"But when the king came in to see the guests, he noticed a man there who was not wearing wedding clothes. 12'Friend,' he asked, 'how did you get in here without wedding clothes?' The man was speechless.

13"Then the king told the attendants, 'Tie him hand and foot, and throw him outside, into the darkness, where there will be weeping and gnashing of teeth.'

14"For many are invited, but few are chosen."

Who can guess how many times the word or numeral "one" is printed on a one dollar bill?

1. What would the social or political consequences have been if Jesus simply said "Pay Caesar"? "Don't pay"? **2.** What does Jesus mean by his answer (v. 21)? What should we give to God? What is he teaching about the relationship of church and state? Which obligation is primary? Why?

1. In your life, what belongs to Caesar ? To God? **2.** How well are you giving to each?

Paying Taxes to Caesar

15Then the Pharisees went out and laid plans to trap him in his words. 16They sent their disciples to him along with the Herodians. "Teacher," they said, "we know you are a man of integrity and that you teach the way of God in accordance with the truth. You aren't swayed by men, because you pay no attention to who they are. 17Tell us then, what is your opinion? Is it right to pay taxes to Caesar or not?"

18But Jesus, knowing their evil intent, said, "You hypocrites, why are you trying to trap me? 19Show me the coin used for paying the tax." They brought him a denarius, 20and he asked them, "Whose portrait is this? And whose inscription?"

21"Caesar's," they replied.

Then he said to them, "Give to Caesar what is Caesar's, and to God what is God's."

22When they heard this, they were amazed. So they left him and went away.

In heaven, who or what on earth would you miss most?

1. Who questions Jesus here (v. 23)? What do they believe? How does their question appear: Mocking? Serious? Scriptural (see Dt 25:5–10)? A trick? **2.** What aspects of their question does Jesus answer? Why is there no marriage in heaven?

Marriage at the Resurrection

23That same day the Sadducees, who say there is no resurrection, came to him with a question. 24"Teacher," they said, "Moses told us that if a man dies without having children, his brother must marry the widow and have children for him. 25Now there were seven brothers among us. The first one married and died, and since he had no children, he left his wife to his brother. 26The same thing happened to the second and third brother, right on down to the seventh. 27Finally, the woman died. 28Now then, at the resurrection, whose wife will she be of the seven, since all of them were married to her?"

29Jesus replied, "You are in error because you do not know the

Scriptures or the power of God. 30At the resurrection people will
neither marry nor be given in marriage; they will be like the angels
in heaven. 31But about the resurrection of the dead—have you not
read what God said to you, 32'I am the God of Abraham, the God of
Isaac, and the God of Jacob'[a]? He is not the God of the dead but
of the living."
33When the crowds heard this, they were astonished at his
teaching.

The Greatest Commandment

34Hearing that Jesus had silenced the Sadducees, the Pharisees
got together. 35One of them, an expert in the law, tested him with
this question: 36"Teacher, which is the greatest commandment in
the Law?"
37Jesus replied: " 'Love the Lord your God with all your heart and
with all your soul and with all your mind.'[b] 38This is the first and
greatest commandment. 39And the second is like it: 'Love your
neighbor as yourself.'[c] 40All the Law and the Prophets hang on
these two commandments."

Whose Son Is the Christ?

41While the Pharisees were gathered together, Jesus asked them,
42"What do you think about the Christ[d]? Whose son is he?"
"The son of David," they replied.
43He said to them, "How is it then that David, speaking by the
Spirit, calls him 'Lord'? For he says,

44" 'The Lord said to my Lord:
"Sit at my right hand
until I put your enemies
under your feet." '[e]

45If then David calls him 'Lord,' how can he be his son?" 46No one
could say a word in reply, and from that day on no one dared to ask
him any more questions.

Seven Woes

23 Then Jesus said to the crowds and to his disciples: 2"The
teachers of the law and the Pharisees sit in Moses' seat. 3So
you must obey them and do everything they tell you. But do not do
what they do, for they do not practice what they preach. 4They tie
up heavy loads and put them on men's shoulders, but they themselves are not willing to lift a finger to move them.
5"Everything they do is done for men to see: They make their
phylacteries[f] wide and the tassels on their garments long; 6they
love the place of honor at banquets and the most important seats in
the synagogues; 7they love to be greeted in the marketplaces and to
have men call them 'Rabbi.'
8"But you are not to be called 'Rabbi,' for you have only one
Master and you are all brothers. 9And do not call anyone on earth
'father,' for you have one Father, and he is in heaven. 10Nor are
you to be called 'teacher,' for you have one Teacher, the Christ.[d]
11The greatest among you will be your servant. 12For whoever
exalts himself will be humbled, and whoever humbles himself will
be exalted.
13"Woe to you, teachers of the law and Pharisees, you hypocrites! You shut the kingdom of heaven in men's faces. You your-

[a]*32* Exodus 3:6 [b]*37* Deut. 6:5 [c]*39* Lev. 19:18 [d]*42,10* Or *Messiah*
[e]*44* Psalm 110:1 [f]*5* That is, boxes containing Scripture verses, worn on forehead and arm

What hope does the resurrection give you? What one question would you like to ask Jesus about life after death?

Who are the three people in this world you love the most?

Why do you think Jesus emphasized loving God with our heart, soul and mind? How is loving God related to loving people?

1. By Jesus' definition, what kind of "lover" are you? **2.** In what way do you want to grow in love right now: Toward God? Toward those in your family? Toward the needy? Toward yourself? **3.** How might you do so?

Would you rather ask questions or answer them? Why?

1. Were the Pharisees expecting the Messiah to be human (David's descendant) or divine (David's Lord)? **2.** Why would it take Jesus' death and resurrection to show that the Messiah is more than just David's descendant?

What does Jesus' humanity mean to you? What does his divinity mean?

---

1. Growing up, what "hot buttons" did you push to get your parents mad? What "hot buttons" do your kids (if any) use on you? **2.** What is your favorite city? Why?

1. What was the seat of Moses? Given Jesus' remarks about the Pharisees in chapters 21–22, what is surprising about his remarks in 23:3? How does he limit his commendation of the Pharisees? **2.** As Jesus sees it, what is the main evil of the Pharisees? How are the disciples to avoid falling into the same evil? Why would it be important that the disciples not allow themselves to be called "Rabbi"? What distinction was Jesus trying to make between his followers and the Pharisees? **3.** Compare the path to greatness followed by the Pharisees with that taught by Jesus (vv. 5–12). What do these two views of greatness teach us about the two views of the kingdom? **4.** Make a list of the seven charges Jesus makes against the Pharisees and the teachers of the Law (vv. 13–32). How do they relate to what Jesus says in verses 2–7? Do you find anything common to all seven charges? How do each of these affect the common people? **5.** How have the religious leaders corrupted the practice of evangelism (vv. 13–15)? Of oath-making (vv. 16–22)? Of tithing (vv. 23–24: see Mic 6:6–8)? Of integrity, where public image matches inner reality (vv. 25–28)? **6.** In what way are these religious leaders condemned to repeat the past because of their failure to learn from their forefathers (vv. 29–36)? How is the punishment in verses 33–36 appropriate to the crimes? **7.** What emotion does Jesus display in verses 37–39? How do you think he likely felt as he was teaching? Why?

♡ **1.** Where does Jesus catch your attention in this passage? What practices touch close to home in your life? How can you avoid "talking the talk" but not "walking the walk"? **2.** How can you avoid making it hard for others to grow spiritually? **3.** What about today's church do you lament over (as Jesus did over Jerusalem)? When have you seen money in a church become more important than what the church stands for? **4.** From reading this passage, what should today's teachers and pastors be especially mindful of? How have you seen the power of the pulpit abused? **5.** What "camels" are easy for you to swallow? What "gnats" are difficult (v. 24)? How will you cheer Jesus when you see him again?

selves do not enter, nor will you let those enter who are trying
to.[a]
15"Woe to you, teachers of the law and Pharisees, you hypocrites! You travel over land and sea to win a single convert, and
when he becomes one, you make him twice as much a son of hell
as you are.
16"Woe to you, blind guides! You say, 'If anyone swears by the
temple, it means nothing; but if anyone swears by the gold of the
temple, he is bound by his oath.' 17You blind fools! Which is
greater: the gold, or the temple that makes the gold sacred? 18You
also say, 'If anyone swears by the altar, it means nothing; but if
anyone swears by the gift on it, he is bound by his oath.' 19You
blind men! Which is greater: the gift, or the altar that makes the
gift sacred? 20Therefore, he who swears by the altar swears by it
and by everything on it. 21And he who swears by the temple
swears by it and by the one who dwells in it. 22And he who swears
by heaven swears by God's throne and by the one who sits on it.
23"Woe to you, teachers of the law and Pharisees, you hypocrites! You give a tenth of your spices—mint, dill and cummin. But
you have neglected the more important matters of the law—justice, mercy and faithfulness. You should have practiced the latter,
without neglecting the former. 24You blind guides! You strain out a
gnat but swallow a camel.
25"Woe to you, teachers of the law and Pharisees, you hypocrites! You clean the outside of the cup and dish, but inside they
are full of greed and self-indulgence. 26Blind Pharisee! First clean
the inside of the cup and dish, and then the outside also will be
clean.
27"Woe to you, teachers of the law and Pharisees, you hypocrites! You are like whitewashed tombs, which look beautiful on
the outside but on the inside are full of dead men's bones and
everything unclean. 28In the same way, on the outside you appear
to people as righteous but on the inside you are full of hypocrisy
and wickedness.
29"Woe to you, teachers of the law and Pharisees, you hypocrites! You build tombs for the prophets and decorate the graves of
the righteous. 30And you say, 'If we had lived in the days of our
forefathers, we would not have taken part with them in shedding
the blood of the prophets.' 31So you testify against yourselves that
you are the descendants of those who murdered the prophets.
32Fill up, then, the measure of the sin of your forefathers!
33"You snakes! You brood of vipers! How will you escape being
condemned to hell? 34Therefore I am sending you prophets and
wise men and teachers. Some of them you will kill and crucify;
others you will flog in your synagogues and pursue from town to
town. 35And so upon you will come all the righteous blood that has
been shed on earth, from the blood of righteous Abel to the blood
of Zechariah son of Berekiah, whom you murdered between the
temple and the altar. 36I tell you the truth, all this will come upon
this generation.
37"O Jerusalem, Jerusalem, you who kill the prophets and stone
those sent to you, how often I have longed to gather your children
together, as a hen gathers her chicks under her wings, but you
were not willing. 38Look, your house is left to you desolate. 39For I
tell you, you will not see me again until you say, 'Blessed is he who
comes in the name of the Lord.'[b]"

[a]*13* Some manuscripts *to. 14Woe to you, teachers of the law and Pharisees, you hypocrites! You devour widows' houses and for a show make lengthy prayers. Therefore you will be punished more severely.* [b]*39* Psalm 118:26

Signs of the End of the Age

24 Jesus left the temple and was walking away when his disciples came up to him to call his attention to its buildings. 2“Do you see all these things?” he asked. “I tell you the truth, not one stone here will be left on another; every one will be thrown down.”

3As Jesus was sitting on the Mount of Olives, the disciples came to him privately. “Tell us,” they said, “when will this happen, and what will be the sign of your coming and of the end of the age?”

4Jesus answered: “Watch out that no one deceives you. 5For many will come in my name, claiming, ‘I am the Christ,[a]’ and will deceive many. 6You will hear of wars and rumors of wars, but see to it that you are not alarmed. Such things must happen, but the end is still to come. 7Nation will rise against nation, and kingdom against kingdom. There will be famines and earthquakes in various places. 8All these are the beginning of birth pains.

9“Then you will be handed over to be persecuted and put to death, and you will be hated by all nations because of me. 10At that time many will turn away from the faith and will betray and hate each other, 11and many false prophets will appear and deceive many people. 12Because of the increase of wickedness, the love of most will grow cold, 13but he who stands firm to the end will be saved. 14And this gospel of the kingdom will be preached in the whole world as a testimony to all nations, and then the end will come.

15“So when you see standing in the holy place ‘the abomination that causes desolation,’[b] spoken of through the prophet Daniel—let the reader understand— 16then let those who are in Judea flee to the mountains. 17Let no one on the roof of his house go down to take anything out of the house. 18Let no one in the field go back to get his cloak. 19How dreadful it will be in those days for pregnant women and nursing mothers! 20Pray that your flight will not take place in winter or on the Sabbath. 21For then there will be great distress, unequaled from the beginning of the world until now—and never to be equaled again. 22If those days had not been cut short, no one would survive, but for the sake of the elect those days will be shortened. 23At that time if anyone says to you, ‘Look, here is the Christ!’ or, ‘There he is!’ do not believe it. 24For false Christs and false prophets will appear and perform great signs and miracles to deceive even the elect—if that were possible. 25See, I have told you ahead of time.

26“So if anyone tells you, ‘There he is, out in the desert,’ do not go out; or, ‘Here he is, in the inner rooms,’ do not believe it. 27For as lightning that comes from the east is visible even in the west, so will be the coming of the Son of Man. 28Wherever there is a carcass, there the vultures will gather.

29“Immediately after the distress of those days

“ ‘the sun will be darkened,
  and the moon will not give its light;
the stars will fall from the sky,
  and the heavenly bodies will be shaken.’[c]

30“At that time the sign of the Son of Man will appear in the sky, and all the nations of the earth will mourn. They will see the Son of Man coming on the clouds of the sky, with power and great glory. 31And he will send his angels with a loud trumpet call, and

When you were growing up, what were you like with building blocks (Lincoln logs, Tinker toys, Legos, etc.): (a) Meticulous in following the instructions step by step? (b) Innovative in designing your own structure? (c) Mischievous in destroying someone else's creation? ?

1. What prompts Jesus' next lesson? **2.** What bombshell does he drop on his disciples (vv. 4–25)? How do the Jewish people (including the disciples) feel about the temple? How must the disciples have felt when they heard Jesus' words in verse 2? **3.** What three questions do the disciples ask (v. 3)? **4.** What events might mislead the disciples into thinking the end had come (vv. 4–7)? **5.** What does Jesus promise for those who endure and don't give in? What must the church continue doing (v. 14)? **6.** What event would signal the start of the great distress? What does “the abomination that causes desolation” mean? (See Da 9:27 and 11:31.) **7.** What should the residents of Jerusalem do when this happens (vv. 16–20)? Why? **8.** What dangerous deceptions would Christians need to guard against (vv. 23–26)? Why would believers be susceptible to such rumors then? **9.** In contrast, what will mark the coming of the true Messiah (vv. 27–29)? What will his second coming be like (vv. 30–31)? **10.** What is the lesson from the fig tree? How does it apply to the disciples' question (v. 3) and Jesus' answer (vv. 33–35)?

1. Some people think this passage anticipated the destruction of Jerusalem in 70 A.D., while others think it refers to the end of the world. What do you think? Could it be both? **2.** How does this passage influence your lifestyle? **3.** If you could ask Jesus one question about either the Second Coming or the end of the world, what would you ask? How do you think he would answer it? **4.** Has your love for others grown cold (v. 12)? What can you do about it?

[a]*5* Or *Messiah*; also in verse 23 [b]*15* Daniel 9:27; 11:31; 12:11 [c]*29* Isaiah 13:10; 34:4

they will gather his elect from the four winds, from one end of the heavens to the other.

32"Now learn this lesson from the fig tree: As soon as its twigs get tender and its leaves come out, you know that summer is near. 33Even so, when you see all these things, you know that it[a] is near, right at the door. 34I tell you the truth, this generation[b] will certainly not pass away until all these things have happened. 35Heaven and earth will pass away, but my words will never pass away.

1. If Jesus returned at 7:00 PM this Tuesday, what would you be doing? **2.** As a child, what was your favorite time of day? Day of the week? Season of the year?

1. In what ways is the Flood like the second coming of Christ? **2.** What does it mean, practically, to be ready for Jesus' return if we do not know when he will come? **3.** In view of Christ's second coming, what does the story of the faithful and wise servant teach you about readiness? About stewardship? Judgment? Responsibility for serving and witnessing to others?

1. Specifically, how are you preparing for the Second Coming? How does the knowledge that Jesus will return some day effect your behavior? **2.** How would you explain the end times and the Second Coming to a seeker? **3.** Over what has God given you stewardship? How would God evaluate the job you're doing?

The Day and Hour Unknown

36"No one knows about that day or hour, not even the angels in heaven, nor the Son,[c] but only the Father. 37As it was in the days of Noah, so it will be at the coming of the Son of Man. 38For in the days before the flood, people were eating and drinking, marrying and giving in marriage, up to the day Noah entered the ark; 39and they knew nothing about what would happen until the flood came and took them all away. That is how it will be at the coming of the Son of Man. 40Two men will be in the field; one will be taken and the other left. 41Two women will be grinding with a hand mill; one will be taken and the other left.

42"Therefore keep watch, because you do not know on what day your Lord will come. 43But understand this: If the owner of the house had known at what time of night the thief was coming, he would have kept watch and would not have let his house be broken into. 44So you also must be ready, because the Son of Man will come at an hour when you do not expect him.

45"Who then is the faithful and wise servant, whom the master has put in charge of the servants in his household to give them their food at the proper time? 46It will be good for that servant whose master finds him doing so when he returns. 47I tell you the truth, he will put him in charge of all his possessions. 48But suppose that servant is wicked and says to himself, 'My master is staying away a long time,' 49and he then begins to beat his fellow servants and to eat and drink with drunkards. 50The master of that servant will come on a day when he does not expect him and at an hour he is not aware of. 51He will cut him to pieces and assign him a place with the hypocrites, where there will be weeping and gnashing of teeth.

If a meeting begins at 7:00 PM, do you get there at 6:45? 7:05? Plan to leave your house at 7:00? Hope everyone else will be late?

1. How does this parable relate to Matthew 24? **2.** In what ways were the 10 girls alike? Different? What unexpected event takes place (vv. 5–6)? With what embarrassing consequence (v. 8)? **3.** What is the point of this parable? **4.** Why is readiness so important in regard to the Second Coming?

1. At the final wedding banquet, where will you be standing? Why? **2.** What is the "oil"

The Parable of the Ten Virgins

25 "At that time the kingdom of heaven will be like ten virgins who took their lamps and went out to meet the bridegroom. 2Five of them were foolish and five were wise. 3The foolish ones took their lamps but did not take any oil with them. 4The wise, however, took oil in jars along with their lamps. 5The bridegroom was a long time in coming, and they all became drowsy and fell asleep.

6"At midnight the cry rang out: 'Here's the bridegroom! Come out to meet him!'

7"Then all the virgins woke up and trimmed their lamps. 8The foolish ones said to the wise, 'Give us some of your oil; our lamps are going out.'

9" 'No,' they replied, 'there may not be enough for both us and you. Instead, go to those who sell oil and buy some for yourselves.'

10"But while they were on their way to buy the oil, the bride-

[a]*33* Or *he* [b]*34* Or *race* [c]*36* Some manuscripts do not have *nor the Son.*

groom arrived. The virgins who were ready went in with him to
the wedding banquet. And the door was shut.
11"Later the others also came. 'Sir! Sir!' they said. 'Open the
door for us!'
12"But he replied, 'I tell you the truth, I don't know you.'
13"Therefore keep watch, because you do not know the day or
the hour.

The Parable of the Talents

14"Again, it will be like a man going on a journey, who called his
servants and entrusted his property to them. 15To one he gave five
talents[a] of money, to another two talents, and to another one
talent, each according to his ability. Then he went on his journey.
16The man who had received the five talents went at once and put
his money to work and gained five more. 17So also, the one with
the two talents gained two more. 18But the man who had received
the one talent went off, dug a hole in the ground and hid his
master's money.
19"After a long time the master of those servants returned and
settled accounts with them. 20The man who had received the five
talents brought the other five. 'Master,' he said, 'you entrusted me
with five talents. See, I have gained five more.'
21"His master replied, 'Well done, good and faithful servant! You
have been faithful with a few things; I will put you in charge of
many things. Come and share your master's happiness!'
22"The man with the two talents also came. 'Master,' he said,
'you entrusted me with two talents; see, I have gained two more.'
23"His master replied, 'Well done, good and faithful servant! You

[a] *15* A talent was worth more than a thousand dollars.

that keeps your "lamp" lit? **3.** Who are you most like in this story? Why?

---

1. Who was one of the most talented people you knew in school? What happened to that person? **2.** What talents were you known for in school?

1. In this parable, who does the master represent? The journey? The talents? The servants? **2.** What happens to the two servants who doubled their investment? To the servant who hides his talent? On what basis were they rewarded? **3.** How does the master's treatment of the one-talent servant seem to you: Fair? Harsh? Lenient? Why? **4.** Why do you think Jesus thought it necessary to repeat his point so many times and in so many different ways (as in ch. 23–25)?

1. If the Master returned today, what would he say about how you've used what he gave you? How have you devel-

Matthew 25:1–13 PARABLE OF THE 10 VIRGINS

This parable was based on wedding customs of the time. Jewish weddings typically took place in the evening, though the exact time was kept secret. Prior to the ceremony the groom would go to the bride's home and lead her, along with the villagers, in a procession to the wedding. The virgins in this story were waiting for the groom, and were probably bridesmaids who had the responsibility to prepare the bride to meet the groom.

1. What made the "wise virgins" different from the "foolish virgins"?
   a. They had been Girl Scouts.
   b. They didn't fall asleep.
   c. They were always prepared.
   d. They made responsible decisions.

2. What would you call the refusal of the five women to share their oil?
   a. wise
   b. shrewd
   c. selfish
   d. just
   e. unjust
   f. mean

3. What did the bridegroom mean when he said, "I don't know you"?
   a. "I don't recognize you."
   b. "You don't have an invitation."
   c. "True friends would take my coming more seriously."
   d. "You're too late."

4. How do you feel about Jesus saying that the door to the kingdom gets closed for some?
   a. It doesn't sound like something a loving God would do.
   b. They had their chance and blew it.
   c. We should just be glad people get invited at all.
   d. I'm glad this is God's business.

5. What is the point of this parable?
   a. Each of us needs our own relationship with the Lord.
   b. You can't obtain faith in Christ just by being around others who do.
   c. There is a limited opportunity to enter God's kingdom.
   d. The second coming of Christ will arrive unexpectedly.
   e. Be prepared for Christ's return.

6. Have you in the past (or in the present) tried to live off the "oil" of someone else's faith? If so, whose faith?
   a. my parents'
   b. my spouse's
   c. my friends'
   d. my church's
   e. my small group's
   f. other:____________

7. What does it mean to *keep watch*?
   a. try to figure out the signs of Christ's return
   b. patiently wait for a future event
   c. actively prepare in the present
   d. be ready when Jesus comes back

8. What does Jesus expect Christians to do with their lives in anticipation of his return?

9. In what ways does Christ's second coming affect the way you live? How are you staying prepared for his return?

10. At the final wedding banquet, will you be escorted inside? How do you know?

oped it? What kind of responsibility do you feel toward God regarding your talents? **2.** When have you observed that the more you used a talent, the more talents God gave you? **3.** What will you do this week with the talents God has given you to prepare for his coming? What can your group do to help you in this regard? **4.** What does sharing your Master's happiness mean to you?

have been faithful with a few things; I will put you in charge of
many things. Come and share your master's happiness!'
24“Then the man who had received the one talent came. ‘Master,’ he said, ‘I knew that you are a hard man, harvesting where
you have not sown and gathering where you have not scattered
seed. 25So I was afraid and went out and hid your talent in the
ground. See, here is what belongs to you.’
26“His master replied, ‘You wicked, lazy servant! So you knew
that I harvest where I have not sown and gather where I have not
scattered seed? 27Well then, you should have put my money on
deposit with the bankers, so that when I returned I would have
received it back with interest.
28“ ‘Take the talent from him and give it to the one who has the
ten talents. 29For everyone who has will be given more, and he will
have an abundance. Whoever does not have, even what he has will
be taken from him. 30And throw that worthless servant outside,
into the darkness, where there will be weeping and gnashing of
teeth.’

1. Where do you keep your prized possessions? **2.** What do you prize the most?

1. Does this story seem more like a parable or a prophecy? Why? **2.** List the six actions Jesus

The Sheep and the Goats

31“When the Son of Man comes in his glory, and all the angels
with him, he will sit on his throne in heavenly glory. 32All the
nations will be gathered before him, and he will separate the people one from another as a shepherd separates the sheep from the
goats. 33He will put the sheep on his right and the goats on his left.

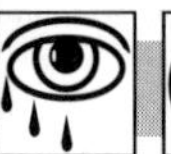

Matthew 25:14–30 PARABLE OF THE TALENTS

The term “talent” was first used for a unit of weight, then for a unit of coins. The present-day use of “talent” as an ability comes from this parable.

1. Why did the servant with one talent hide his money?
   a. He was afraid of his master.
   b. He was afraid to take risks.
   c. He was lazy and irresponsible.
   d. He resented the way the master made his money.

2. What was Jesus saying to the two servants who doubled their money?
   a. I'm proud of you.
   b. Enter into a life of ease.
   c. My investment in you paid off.
   d. You'll get your reward in heaven.
   e. I can trust you with bigger things.

3. What is this parable's message?
   a. God cannot tolerate laziness.
   b. God has given Christians a “job” to do until Jesus returns.
   c. When we use what God has given us for him, God gives us more.
   d. Judgment awaits those who don't invest their lives in God's kingdom.

4. Share two or three “talents” you are using for God. What is your favorite excuse for *not* using them?

5. If the Master returned today, how well would he say you have been using what he gave you? What can you do with your talents this week to prepare for Christ's coming?

6. What help do you need to use your abilities in a way that “measures up”?
   a. help from God to overcome fear
   b. help from God to believe in myself
   c. help from others to see my talents
   d. for others not to be so hard on me
   e. for me not to be so hard on myself

7. What holds you back from taking responsibility for your financial problems?
   a. Like the third servant, I always seem to get the short end.
   b. Compared to others I wasn't given much “ability” to manage money.
   c. I've encountered some circumstances beyond my control.
   d. Something always happens to keep me from “investing” wisely.
   e. Nothing—I take full responsibility.

8. What could you do to have a less stressful life?
   a. have less fear of the “master”—my boss!
   b. be more concerned about the approval of *the* “master”—God
   c. get into a job or vocation that more fully utilizes my talents
   d. use my talents in my current job/vocation in a more fulfilling way
   e. start risking and stop worrying
   f. be more accepting of what God has given me
   g. invest more in my career
   h. invest more in my family

9. To which of the characters in the parable do you relate most in regard to managing your finances?
   a. the first servant—We've been greatly blessed.
   b. the second servant—We've done okay with what we've had to work with.
   c. the third servant—We've blown it.

10. Regarding money, what causes the most conflict in your marriage? What can you do to grow in your communication and agreement about finances?

11. Go around the group and have each person listen silently while others affirm what “talent” God has given to that person to invest in the kingdom of God.

34"Then the King will say to those on his right, 'Come, you who
are blessed by my Father; take your inheritance, the kingdom prepared for you since the creation of the world. 35For I was hungry
and you gave me something to eat, I was thirsty and you gave me
something to drink, I was a stranger and you invited me in, 36I
needed clothes and you clothed me, I was sick and you looked after
me, I was in prison and you came to visit me.'
37"Then the righteous will answer him, 'Lord, when did we see
you hungry and feed you, or thirsty and give you something to
drink? 38When did we see you a stranger and invite you in, or
needing clothes and clothe you? 39When did we see you sick or in
prison and go to visit you?'
40"The King will reply, 'I tell you the truth, whatever you did for
one of the least of these brothers of mine, you did for me.'
41"Then he will say to those on his left, 'Depart from me, you
who are cursed, into the eternal fire prepared for the devil and his
angels. 42For I was hungry and you gave me nothing to eat, I was
thirsty and you gave me nothing to drink, 43I was a stranger and
you did not invite me in, I needed clothes and you did not clothe
me, I was sick and in prison and you did not look after me.'
44"They also will answer, 'Lord, when did we see you hungry or
thirsty or a stranger or needing clothes or sick or in prison, and did
not help you?'
45"He will reply, 'I tell you the truth, whatever you did not do
for one of the least of these, you did not do for me.'
46"Then they will go away to eternal punishment, but the righteous to eternal life."

will use as the basis of judgment. What kinds of acts are these? For whom are they done now and ultimately (v. 40)? How do they benefit the doer? **3.** How are those who don't do the acts and those who do them similar? Different? **4.** What does this section teach about Christian responsibility? Who are "the least of these brothers of mine"? **5.** In summary, what did Jesus teach in chapters 23–25? How were Jesus and his opponents different in actions and attitudes? Is the judgment note in this section consistent with your view of Jesus? Why or why not?

1. When have you been hungry, thirsty, a stranger, in need of clothes, sick or imprisoned, and someone reached out to you? How did it feel? **2.** In these six areas, where do you find yourself serving most naturally? In which areas do you have the most trouble reaching out?

Matthew 25:31–46 THE SHEEP AND THE GOATS

1. If you had been one of the disciples, how do you think you would have felt when you heard this?
   a. confused—I still don't understand.
   b. scared—Am I one of the goats he's talking about?
   c. inspired—I want to be part of this kingdom.
   d. disappointed—I expected Jesus to be a *real* king.

2. On what basis does Jesus say people are divided into sheep and goats?
   a. "eany-meany-miny-moe ..."
   b. their beliefs
   c. their actions
   d. their character
   e. their treatment of others

3. What point is Jesus making when he describes those who will be part of his kingdom?
   a. It is only for the needy.
   b. It is only for those who care for the needy.
   c. It is for those who love the King.
   d. It is a kingdom where people are there for those who are hurting.

4. Who today are the hungry, thirsty, strangers, naked, sick, imprisoned?
   a. the hungry, thirsty, strangers, naked, sick, imprisoned
   b. the down-and-outers
   c. the poorest of the poor
   d. anyone in need
   e. all of us at one time or another

5. When have you been hurting or in need? Who reached out to you?

6. At this point in your life, with whom in this story can you identify?
   a. the sheep
   b. the goats
   c. "one of the least of these"

7. If Jesus were to come today and evaluate your life, how well would he say you have "cared for him"?

8. How would you rate your small group for taking care of each other when someone is hurting or in need?
   a. We do great.
   b. We are learning.
   c. We have a long way to go.
   d. We really don't have any needs.

9. How do you fit together the message of this Scripture with other passages, such as the ones used in the other studies in this course? If you could ask God one question about giving and receiving in general, and one question about your own life—what would you ask?

10. Think of your small group as a community of love in which all of you are hurting in some way. Who would you nominate for the following gifts of caring?
   a. ____________ *I was hungry and you gave me something to eat:* Your sharing of yourself has caused me to grow.
   b. ____________ *I was thirsty and you gave me something to drink:* Your spiritual life and devotion to God helped me find spiritual refreshment.
   c. ____________ *I was a stranger and you invited me in:* Your welcome made me feel at home.
   d. ____________ *I was sick and you looked after me:* Your reaching out when I was down touched me.

If you had a year's wages to blow on one special gift, what would you buy and for whom?

1. Why was Passover an appropriate time for the events of verses 1–5 to unfold? Why might the timing be risky? **2.** What is significant about the setting for this woman's gift to Jesus? **3.** What context in Jesus' life (v. 12) justifies this woman's act? Why are the disciples indignant? **4.** What is Jesus trying to teach his disciples about priorities? **5.** How could this scene relate to what happens in verses 14–16?

1. What "beautiful" thing could you do this week for Jesus (or "the least of these")? **2.** Whereas the woman (v. 7) gave lavishly *for* Jesus, Judas wanted to see what he could get *from* him. In what ways are you like the woman? Like Judas?

As a kid, what were mealtimes like in your family? Where did everyone sit around the table? What behavior was not allowed?

1. What do you know about the Feast of Unleavened Bread (see Ex 12:1–30)? **2.** Why do you think Jesus was so secretive about his arrangements for the Passover meal? **3.** In what stages does Jesus reveal his betrayer (vv. 21,23,25)? Why does he do this? **4.** In what ways do the bread and wine relate to his body and blood?

1. What does Communion mean to you? **2.** How deeply do you know God's forgiveness of your sins? Why do many Christians struggle with guilt if Jesus provides the forgiveness of sins? **3.** What impresses you most about Jesus at the Last Supper?

The Plot Against Jesus

26 When Jesus had finished saying all these things, he said
to his disciples, 2“As you know, the Passover is two days
away—and the Son of Man will be handed over to be crucified.”
3Then the chief priests and the elders of the people assembled in
the palace of the high priest, whose name was Caiaphas, 4and they
plotted to arrest Jesus in some sly way and kill him. 5“But not
during the Feast,” they said, “or there may be a riot among the
people.”

Jesus Anointed at Bethany

6While Jesus was in Bethany in the home of a man known as
Simon the Leper, 7a woman came to him with an alabaster jar of
very expensive perfume, which she poured on his head as he was
reclining at the table.
8When the disciples saw this, they were indignant. “Why this
waste?” they asked. 9“This perfume could have been sold at a high
price and the money given to the poor.”
10Aware of this, Jesus said to them, “Why are you bothering this
woman? She has done a beautiful thing to me. 11The poor you will
always have with you, but you will not always have me. 12When
she poured this perfume on my body, she did it to prepare me for
burial. 13I tell you the truth, wherever this gospel is preached
throughout the world, what she has done will also be told, in
memory of her.”

Judas Agrees to Betray Jesus

14Then one of the Twelve—the one called Judas Iscariot—went
to the chief priests 15and asked, “What are you willing to give me
if I hand him over to you?” So they counted out for him thirty
silver coins. 16From then on Judas watched for an opportunity to
hand him over.

The Lord's Supper

17On the first day of the Feast of Unleavened Bread, the disciples
came to Jesus and asked, “Where do you want us to make preparations for you to eat the Passover?”
18He replied, “Go into the city to a certain man and tell him,
‘The Teacher says: My appointed time is near. I am going to celebrate the Passover with my disciples at your house.’” 19So the
disciples did as Jesus had directed them and prepared the Passover.
20When evening came, Jesus was reclining at the table with the
Twelve. 21And while they were eating, he said, “I tell you the
truth, one of you will betray me.”
22They were very sad and began to say to him one after the
other, “Surely not I, Lord?”
23Jesus replied, “The one who has dipped his hand into the bowl
with me will betray me. 24The Son of Man will go just as it is
written about him. But woe to that man who betrays the Son of
Man! It would be better for him if he had not been born.”
25Then Judas, the one who would betray him, said, “Surely not I,
Rabbi?”

Jesus answered, “Yes, it is you.”[a]
26While they were eating, Jesus took bread, gave thanks and
broke it, and gave it to his disciples, saying, “Take and eat; this is
my body.”
27Then he took the cup, gave thanks and offered it to them,

[a]25 Or *“You yourself have said it”*

saying, "Drink from it, all of you. 28This is my blood of the[a]
covenant, which is poured out for many for the forgiveness of sins.
29I tell you, I will not drink of this fruit of the vine from now on
until that day when I drink it anew with you in my Father's kingdom."

30When they had sung a hymn, they went out to the Mount of
Olives.

Jesus Predicts Peter's Denial

31Then Jesus told them, "This very night you will all fall away on
account of me, for it is written:

> " 'I will strike the shepherd,
> and the sheep of the flock will be scattered.'[b]

32But after I have risen, I will go ahead of you into Galilee."

33Peter replied, "Even if all fall away on account of you, I never
will."

34"I tell you the truth," Jesus answered, "this very night, before
the rooster crows, you will disown me three times."

35But Peter declared, "Even if I have to die with you, I will never
disown you." And all the other disciples said the same.

What very sincere promise did you once make but failed to deliver on?

What emotions and motives accompany Jesus' next prediction? Peter's vow? Jesus' reply? Peter's follow-up vow?

1. When have you felt betrayed? How did you deal with it? **2.** When, if ever, have you had the rooster crow in your relationship with Jesus? How did you and Jesus resolve that issue?

Gethsemane

36Then Jesus went with his disciples to a place called Gethsemane, and he said to them, "Sit here while I go over there and pray."
37He took Peter and the two sons of Zebedee along with him, and
he began to be sorrowful and troubled. 38Then he said to them,
"My soul is overwhelmed with sorrow to the point of death. Stay
here and keep watch with me."

39Going a little farther, he fell with his face to the ground and
prayed, "My Father, if it is possible, may this cup be taken from
me. Yet not as I will, but as you will."

40Then he returned to his disciples and found them sleeping.
"Could you men not keep watch with me for one hour?" he asked
Peter. 41"Watch and pray so that you will not fall into temptation.
The spirit is willing, but the body is weak."

42He went away a second time and prayed, "My Father, if it is
not possible for this cup to be taken away unless I drink it, may
your will be done."

43When he came back, he again found them sleeping, because
their eyes were heavy. 44So he left them and went away once more
and prayed the third time, saying the same thing.

45Then he returned to the disciples and said to them, "Are you
still sleeping and resting? Look, the hour is near, and the Son of
Man is betrayed into the hands of sinners. 46Rise, let us go! Here
comes my betrayer!"

What was the longest night of your life: Delivering your first child? Waiting up for your teenager? Making a major decision?

1. What are the various emotions Jesus must have felt in Gethsemane? What does he ask of his disciples? What does he ask of God? **2.** What is God's will (vv. 39, 42)? What model for our prayers does Jesus provide here?

1. What has been your "Gethsemane"— a place where you really wrestled with God? What was the issue? What do you learn from Jesus' example about praying at those times? **2.** Who would you want to "watch and pray" with you next time you face a "Gethsemane"? **3.** What do you appreciate most about Jesus' emotions in this story?

Jesus Arrested

47While he was still speaking, Judas, one of the Twelve, arrived.
With him was a large crowd armed with swords and clubs, sent
from the chief priests and the elders of the people. 48Now the
betrayer had arranged a signal with them: "The one I kiss is the
man; arrest him." 49Going at once to Jesus, Judas said, "Greetings,
Rabbi!" and kissed him.

50Jesus replied, "Friend, do what you came for."[c]

Then the men stepped forward, seized Jesus and arrested him.
51With that, one of Jesus' companions reached for his sword, drew

How did your favorite adventure hero respond to danger?

1. What kind of Messiah was the large, armed crowd expecting to arrest? Was the sword-wielding disciple's expectation essentially the same as theirs? Why or why not? **2.** What does Jesus' response to Judas, the crowd and the disciple show about the type of Messiah he is?

[a] *28* Some manuscripts *the new* [b] *31* Zech. 13:7 [c] *50* Or *"Friend, why have you come?"*

1. Knowing yourself, how would you have reacted if you had been with Jesus in this scene? 2. Have you ever kissed or showed affection to someone for the wrong reasons? Why?

it out and struck the servant of the high priest, cutting off his ear.
52“Put your sword back in its place,” Jesus said to him, “for all
who draw the sword will die by the sword. 53Do you think I cannot
call on my Father, and he will at once put at my disposal more than
twelve legions of angels? 54But how then would the Scriptures be
fulfilled that say it must happen in this way?”
55At that time Jesus said to the crowd, “Am I leading a rebellion,
that you have come out with swords and clubs to capture me?
Every day I sat in the temple courts teaching, and you did not
arrest me. 56But this has all taken place that the writings of the
prophets might be fulfilled.” Then all the disciples deserted him
and fled.

Have you ever been in a court of law or situation where you felt unfairly treated or felt the judge violated your rights?

1. Who is the Sanhedrin (or Jewish court of elders), and what kind of cases were brought before it (see Ac 4:1–22)? 2. Why take Jesus to the high priest? Why do you think Peter followed? Why would the priests knowingly accept false evidence? Why two witnesses (v. 60; see Dt 19:15)? 3. What is unusual about Jesus' self-defense? Why did he remain silent? How does he view God's kingdom?

Before the Sanhedrin

57Those who had arrested Jesus took him to Caiaphas, the high
priest, where the teachers of the law and the elders had assembled.
58But Peter followed him at a distance, right up to the courtyard of
the high priest. He entered and sat down with the guards to see
the outcome.
59The chief priests and the whole Sanhedrin were looking for
false evidence against Jesus so that they could put him to death.
60But they did not find any, though many false witnesses came
forward.
Finally two came forward 61and declared, “This fellow said, ‘I am
able to destroy the temple of God and rebuild it in three days.’ ”
62Then the high priest stood up and said to Jesus, “Are you not
going to answer? What is this testimony that these men are bringing against you?” 63But Jesus remained silent.

Matthew 26:47–56 JESUS IS ARRESTED

Jesus has just finished an agonizing time of prayer at Gethsemane, during which his disciples kept falling asleep.

1. How do you think Jesus felt when he saw Judas and an armed mob coming toward him?
   a. frightened
   b. surprised
   c. prepared
   d. angry
   e. betrayed
   f. confused
2. How do you think the disciples felt when they saw Judas and an armed mob coming toward them?
   a. frightened
   b. surprised
   c. prepared
   d. angry
   e. betrayed
   f. confused
3. How do you feel about the disciple (identified in John's Gospel as Peter) striking a member of the crowd?
   a. He didn't have very good aim.
   b. He didn't understand Jesus' mission.
   c. He was just trying to help.
   d. He hadn't absorbed Jesus' teachings against violence.
   e. I would probably have done the same thing.
4. Why did the disciples desert Jesus?
   a. They panicked.
   b. Their leader appeared defeated.
   c. They feared for their own lives.
   d. Jesus wasn't the kind of Messiah they thought he was.
   e. They didn't know how else to handle Jesus' acceptance of his arrest.
5. What do you suppose was the hardest thing about this event for Jesus?
   a. being betrayed by a friend
   b. being deserted by all the disciples
   c. knowing what was going to happen to him next
   d. knowing he could have called on multitudes of angels to rescue him
6. In times of crisis or severe stress, how do you respond?
   a. I stay cool—like Jesus.
   b. I get hot—like Peter.
   c. I run off—like the disciples.
7. When have you, like Peter, felt you had a better way to deal with things than Jesus?
8. What is the closest you have come to deserting Christ?
9. On a scale of 1 (lowest) to 10 (highest) how would you rate your level of loyalty to Jesus now?
10. Who has disappointed you the most?
    a. my parent(s)
    b. another family member
    c. my friend(s)
    d. a teacher or coach
    e. other:____________
11. What should you do to deal with the stress of feeling let down or betrayed?
    a. whack somebody's ear
    b. punch a pillow
    c. get some exercise
    d. call on God for help
    e. ask God to sick some angels on the person who hurt me
    f. try to understand where that person is coming from
    g. talk to that person about how I feel

The high priest said to him, “I charge you under oath by the
living God: Tell us if you are the Christ,[a] the Son of God.”
64“Yes, it is as you say,” Jesus replied. “But I say to all of you: In
the future you will see the Son of Man sitting at the right hand of
the Mighty One and coming on the clouds of heaven.”
65Then the high priest tore his clothes and said, “He has spoken
blasphemy! Why do we need any more witnesses? Look, now you
have heard the blasphemy. 66What do you think?”
“He is worthy of death,” they answered.
67Then they spit in his face and struck him with their fists.
Others slapped him 68and said, “Prophesy to us, Christ. Who hit
you?”

Peter Disowns Jesus

69Now Peter was sitting out in the courtyard, and a servant girl
came to him. “You also were with Jesus of Galilee,” she said.
70But he denied it before them all. “I don’t know what you’re
talking about,” he said.
71Then he went out to the gateway, where another girl saw him
and said to the people there, “This fellow was with Jesus of Nazareth.”
72He denied it again, with an oath: “I don’t know the man!”
73After a little while, those standing there went up to Peter and
said, “Surely you are one of them, for your accent gives you away.”
74Then he began to call down curses on himself and he swore to
them, “I don’t know the man!”
Immediately a rooster crowed. 75Then Peter remembered the
word Jesus had spoken: “Before the rooster crows, you will disown
me three times.” And he went outside and wept bitterly.

Judas Hangs Himself

27 Early in the morning, all the chief priests and the elders of
the people came to the decision to put Jesus to death. 2They
bound him, led him away and handed him over to Pilate, the
governor.
3When Judas, who had betrayed him, saw that Jesus was condemned, he was seized with remorse and returned the thirty silver
coins to the chief priests and the elders. 4“I have sinned,” he said,
“for I have betrayed innocent blood.”
“What is that to us?” they replied. “That’s your responsibility.”
5So Judas threw the money into the temple and left. Then he
went away and hanged himself.
6The chief priests picked up the coins and said, “It is against the
law to put this into the treasury, since it is blood money.” 7So they
decided to use the money to buy the potter’s field as a burial place
for foreigners. 8That is why it has been called the Field of Blood to
this day. 9Then what was spoken by Jeremiah the prophet was
fulfilled: “They took the thirty silver coins, the price set on him by
the people of Israel, 10and they used them to buy the potter’s field,
as the Lord commanded me.”[b]

Jesus Before Pilate

11Meanwhile Jesus stood before the governor, and the governor
asked him, “Are you the king of the Jews?”
“Yes, it is as you say,” Jesus replied.
12When he was accused by the chief priests and the elders, he
gave no answer. 13Then Pilate asked him, “Don’t you hear the

[a]*63* Or *Messiah*; also in verse 68 [b]*10* See Zech. 11:12,13; Jer. 19:1-13; 32:6-9.

4. Why would the priests think Jesus was guilty of blasphemy?

1. What impresses you most about Jesus here? **2.** Ever “defend your faith”? How well did you do? How could you give a better answer for the hope you have (1Pe 3:15–16)? **3.** How do you know when to keep silent and when to talk about your faith?

In high school, when did you really disappoint yourself?

1. So far in Matthew, what character traits has Peter exhibited (see 14:22–36; 15:1–20; 16:13–20; 26:31–45)? Here, how do his actions reveal his character? Which character trait dominates this story? **2.** When did Peter realize what was happening? Why then? Why cry?

When have you felt like Peter? When did you cry in regret before God? How did you make a comeback?

Ever wish you could erase words once written, or retrieve words once spoken? Describe.

1. Why is Judas suddenly seized with remorse? Was he expecting a different outcome? **2.** What irony can you see in the story of Jesus’ arrest and trial?

1. Both Peter and Judas caved in under pressure, yet history has treated them differently. Why? **2.** Have you ever felt you were beyond redemption? To whom did you turn?

When have you been in a wild crowd: Rock concert? Football game? Protest march? Public hearing? Serendipity group?

1. At this time in history, it was against Roman law to proclaim yourself king (it was considered treason). The punishment was death. What does this tell us about the Roman view of what a kingdom was? **2.** What is Pilate's overriding concern in this trial: Identifying the Messiah? Hearing out Jesus? Exchanging prisoners? Doing justice? Appeasement? **3.** Is Pilate more concerned about the crowd? His wife? His conscience? Why? How did Pilate know envy was a motive (v. 18)? **4.** What is Pilate's motive in offering the crowd a prisoner exchange? How concerned is Pilate that Jesus is innocent? **5.** Who is ultimately on trial here? For what?

1. Have you ever gone along with the crowd only to regret it later? What happened? How can you more effectively be your own person? **2.** On a scale of 1 (easiest) to 10 (toughest), how difficult is it for you to accept responsibility? **3.** With whom do you identify in this story: Jesus, Pilate, Pilate's wife, the crowd, the chief priests or Barabbas? Why?

---

1. Which of these violent deaths affected you the most: (a) John F. Kennedy, (b) Martin Luther King or (c) John Lennon? **2.** Ultimately, which of these people will be remembered most? Why?

1. Why were the soldiers so cruel in this case? What does that say about their view of Jesus? Of themselves? **2.** Why does Jesus need Simon's help? What shape is he in? **3.** For what "official" reason is Jesus crucified (v. 37)? **4.** What three groups taunt Jesus? Why these particular insults? **5.** How is this scene like a mock coronation? What did Jesus actually deserve?

1. If Jesus came today, who would "crucify" him? What would be the charge against him? Where would you be? **2.** In what way does the agony of these insults deepen your appreciation of what Christ did for you in his death? How have you made Jesus King in your life? **3.** Write a note to Jesus expressing your feelings about his crucifixion.

testimony they are bringing against you?" 14But Jesus made no
reply, not even to a single charge—to the great amazement of the
governor.

15Now it was the governor's custom at the Feast to release a
prisoner chosen by the crowd. 16At that time they had a notorious
prisoner, called Barabbas. 17So when the crowd had gathered, Pilate asked them, "Which one do you want me to release to you:
Barabbas, or Jesus who is called Christ?" 18For he knew it was out
of envy that they had handed Jesus over to him.

19While Pilate was sitting on the judge's seat, his wife sent him
this message: "Don't have anything to do with that innocent man,
for I have suffered a great deal today in a dream because of him."

20But the chief priests and the elders persuaded the crowd to ask
for Barabbas and to have Jesus executed.

21"Which of the two do you want me to release to you?" asked
the governor.

"Barabbas," they answered.

22"What shall I do, then, with Jesus who is called Christ?" Pilate
asked.

They all answered, "Crucify him!"

23"Why? What crime has he committed?" asked Pilate.

But they shouted all the louder, "Crucify him!"

24When Pilate saw that he was getting nowhere, but that instead
an uproar was starting, he took water and washed his hands in
front of the crowd. "I am innocent of this man's blood," he said. "It
is your responsibility!"

25All the people answered, "Let his blood be on us and on our
children!"

26Then he released Barabbas to them. But he had Jesus flogged,
and handed him over to be crucified.

The Soldiers Mock Jesus

27Then the governor's soldiers took Jesus into the Praetorium
and gathered the whole company of soldiers around him. 28They
stripped him and put a scarlet robe on him, 29and then twisted
together a crown of thorns and set it on his head. They put a staff
in his right hand and knelt in front of him and mocked him. "Hail,
king of the Jews!" they said. 30They spit on him, and took the staff
and struck him on the head again and again. 31After they had
mocked him, they took off the robe and put his own clothes on
him. Then they led him away to crucify him.

The Crucifixion

32As they were going out, they met a man from Cyrene, named
Simon, and they forced him to carry the cross. 33They came to a
place called Golgotha (which means The Place of the Skull).
34There they offered Jesus wine to drink, mixed with gall; but after
tasting it, he refused to drink it. 35When they had crucified him,
they divided up his clothes by casting lots.[a] 36And sitting down,
they kept watch over him there. 37Above his head they placed the
written charge against him: THIS IS JESUS, THE KING OF THE JEWS. 38Two
robbers were crucified with him, one on his right and one on his
left. 39Those who passed by hurled insults at him, shaking their
heads 40and saying, "You who are going to destroy the temple and
build it in three days, save yourself! Come down from the cross, if
you are the Son of God!"

[a]*35* A few late manuscripts *lots that the word spoken by the prophet might be fulfilled: "They divided my garments among themselves and cast lots for my clothing"* (Psalm 22:18)

41In the same way the chief priests, the teachers of the law and the elders mocked him. 42"He saved others," they said, "but he can't save himself! He's the King of Israel! Let him come down now from the cross, and we will believe in him. 43He trusts in God. Let God rescue him now if he wants him, for he said, 'I am the Son of God.' " 44In the same way the robbers who were crucified with him also heaped insults on him.

The Death of Jesus

45From the sixth hour until the ninth hour darkness came over all the land. 46About the ninth hour Jesus cried out in a loud voice, *"Eloi, Eloi,*[a] *lama sabachthani?"*—which means, "My God, my God, why have you forsaken me?"[b]

47When some of those standing there heard this, they said, "He's calling Elijah."

48Immediately one of them ran and got a sponge. He filled it with wine vinegar, put it on a stick, and offered it to Jesus to drink. 49The rest said, "Now leave him alone. Let's see if Elijah comes to save him."

50And when Jesus had cried out again in a loud voice, he gave up his spirit.

51At that moment the curtain of the temple was torn in two from top to bottom. The earth shook and the rocks split. 52The tombs broke open and the bodies of many holy people who had died were raised to life. 53They came out of the tombs, and after Jesus' resurrection they went into the holy city and appeared to many people.

54When the centurion and those with him who were guarding Jesus saw the earthquake and all that had happened, they were terrified, and exclaimed, "Surely he was the Son[c] of God!"

55Many women were there, watching from a distance. They had followed Jesus from Galilee to care for his needs. 56Among them were Mary Magdalene, Mary the mother of James and Joses, and the mother of Zebedee's sons.

The Burial of Jesus

57As evening approached, there came a rich man from Arimathea, named Joseph, who had himself become a disciple of Jesus. 58Going to Pilate, he asked for Jesus' body, and Pilate ordered that it be given to him. 59Joseph took the body, wrapped it in a clean linen cloth, 60and placed it in his own new tomb that he had cut out of the rock. He rolled a big stone in front of the entrance to the tomb and went away. 61Mary Magdalene and the other Mary were sitting there opposite the tomb.

The Guard at the Tomb

62The next day, the one after Preparation Day, the chief priests and the Pharisees went to Pilate. 63"Sir," they said, "we remember that while he was still alive that deceiver said, 'After three days I will rise again.' 64So give the order for the tomb to be made secure until the third day. Otherwise, his disciples may come and steal the body and tell the people that he has been raised from the dead. This last deception will be worse than the first."

65"Take a guard," Pilate answered. "Go, make the tomb as secure as you know how." 66So they went and made the tomb secure by putting a seal on the stone and posting the guard.

[a]46 Some manuscripts *Eli, Eli* [b]46 Psalm 22:1 [c]54 Or *a son*

What is the saddest funeral you ever experienced—one where a friend, family member or national figure was taken suddenly and unexpectedly? How did you feel?

1. Why does Jesus cry out in verse 46? What is the significance of this for Jesus? For you? **2.** What do the sympathizers see? Hear? Feel? Do? **3.** What is the significance of each of the supernatural events accompanying Jesus' death? What was significant about the words of the centurion (v. 54)? **4.** What might the disciples believe about Jesus now? **5.** In asking for the body of Jesus, what risks is Joseph taking with Pilate and the Sanhedrin? **6.** By posting the guards at the tomb, do the leaders really believe Jesus will rise again? Or do they think that the disciples will steal the body? Or do they fear something else? Why? What would it cost the Roman guards if Jesus "escaped"?

1. Why does Matthew emphasize the presence of armed guards? Was Jesus separated from the Father in spirit when he was on the cross? For whose sins did he go to the cross? **2.** How do you explain the necessity of Jesus' death to a nonbeliever? **3.** Is Jesus' death for you more a dispassionate fact, or an emotional experience? Why? **4.** How have you tried to guard against God breaking through in your life? Why? What happened?

The Resurrection

28 After the Sabbath, at dawn on the first day of the week,
Mary Magdalene and the other Mary went to look at the
tomb.
2 There was a violent earthquake, for an angel of the Lord came
down from heaven and, going to the tomb, rolled back the stone
and sat on it. 3 His appearance was like lightning, and his clothes
were white as snow. 4 The guards were so afraid of him that they
shook and became like dead men.
5 The angel said to the women, "Do not be afraid, for I know that
you are looking for Jesus, who was crucified. 6 He is not here; he
has risen, just as he said. Come and see the place where he lay.
7 Then go quickly and tell his disciples: 'He has risen from the dead
and is going ahead of you into Galilee. There you will see him.'
Now I have told you."
8 So the women hurried away from the tomb, afraid yet filled
with joy, and ran to tell his disciples. 9 Suddenly Jesus met them.
"Greetings," he said. They came to him, clasped his feet and worshiped him. 10 Then Jesus said to them, "Do not be afraid. Go and
tell my brothers to go to Galilee; there they will see me."

The Guards' Report

11 While the women were on their way, some of the guards went
into the city and reported to the chief priests everything that had
happened. 12 When the chief priests had met with the elders and
devised a plan, they gave the soldiers a large sum of money, 13 telling them, "You are to say, 'His disciples came during the night and

1. What do you like to do first thing Sunday morning? Why? **2.** Of "all the news that's fit to print," what section of the newspaper do you read first? **3.** Which do you believe more: (a) What you hear? (b) What you see? (c) What you want?

1. Who visits the tomb? When? Why now? (See Lk 23:56–24:1.) **2.** How were they feeling on their way to the tomb? What problems do they expect to confront (see 27:60,65–66)? **3.** How do you think they felt as they left the tomb? As they met Jesus? **4.** Why did Jesus appear to these women before he appeared to his own disciples? How do you explain this transformation? In light of 4:10, what is the significance of the fact that they worshiped Jesus? **5.** How might the guards' report have differed from the women's report? **6.** Why would the chief priests and others prefer to believe the falsified story? **7.** Upon seeing the resurrected Jesus, how do the disciples respond (v. 17)? Why is doubt mingled with their worship? What do they doubt? **8.** Of the four actions

Matthew 28:1–20 JESUS' RESURRECTION AND GREAT COMMISSION

After Jesus was crucified, the Jewish religious leaders persuaded the Roman governor to make sure the tomb was sealed securely and guarded.

1. How do you think the women felt on their way to the tomb?
   a. sad
   b. sentimental
   c. worried about facing the soldiers
   d. exhausted
   e. expectant

2. When they found the stone rolled back and an angel sitting on it, how do you think they felt?
   a. scared to death
   b. wondering who took the body
   c. overcome with grief—They could not take any more heartache.
   d. overcome with joy—They knew Jesus would come back!

3. How do you think the women felt when Jesus suddenly met them?
   a. shocked
   b. afraid
   c. overjoyed
   d. full of praise

4. Why did the chief priests and elders want to spread the rumor that Jesus' disciples came and stole his body?
   a. He was a threat to them.
   b. He might file charges against them for falsely accusing him.
   c. The Resurrection would prove he really *was* the Son of God.
   d. They saw him as a troublemaker, and they wanted to keep the peace.

5. How did the reality of Christ's resurrection "dawn" on you?

6. When the disciples saw Jesus in Galilee, why was doubt mingled with their worship? What doubts get mixed in with *your* worship?

7. If you had been one of the disciples, what part of Jesus' "Great Commission" would have been most important to you?
   a. He has authority over everything.
   b. He wants me to spread the word.
   c. He will always be with me.
   d. There will come a time when history would come to a close.

8. What is your favorite way of dodging issues of Christian discipleship, like passing on the good news?
   a. claiming I don't understand
   b. saying I don't have time
   c. thinking others are better at it
   d. just ignoring it

9. What does this Scripture say to you about your own death and life beyond it?
   a. Sure, God would raise his Son, but why would he bother with me?
   b. Hey, this is just a story.
   c. If God can raise Jesus, he can raise me.
   d. It's like the angel and Jesus told the women: "Do not be afraid."

10. What do you do when you don't understand the resurrection of Jesus or your own resurrection?
   a. fall back on what the Bible says
   b. accept the teaching of my church
   c. go with what I was taught as a child
   d. ask God to help me accept it "by faith"
   e. other:________________

11. How has your faith grown or changed as a result of this course?

stole him away while we were asleep.' [14]If this report gets to the
governor, we will satisfy him and keep you out of trouble." [15]So the
soldiers took the money and did as they were instructed. And this
story has been widely circulated among the Jews to this very day.

The Great Commission

[16]Then the eleven disciples went to Galilee, to the mountain
where Jesus had told them to go. [17]When they saw him, they
worshiped him; but some doubted. [18]Then Jesus came to them and
said, "All authority in heaven and on earth has been given to me.
[19]Therefore go and make disciples of all nations, baptizing them
in[a] the name of the Father and of the Son and of the Holy Spirit,
[20]and teaching them to obey everything I have commanded you.
And surely I am with you always, to the very end of the age."

commanded of the disciples (vv. 19–20), which one is central? How are they to make disciples? Of whom? With what resources? Toward what end?

♡ **1.** How did the reality of Jesus' resurrection "dawn" upon you? Were you more of a quick believer or a slow doubter? Why? **2.** How would you argue against the ideas: (a) That the disciples stole the body? (b) That Jesus was only unconscious on the cross, and revived in the cool tomb? (c) That the resurrection was a tale that caught on? **3.** How much authority does Jesus have to give to his disciples to fulfill the Great Commission? In what ways can you fulfill the Great Commission in the context of your family? Work? Community? **4.** How has the Book of Matthew changed your views of: Jesus as the Messiah? The kingdom of God? Jesus' ministry? Your ministry?

[a] *19* Or *into*; see Acts 8:16; 19:5; Romans 6:3; 1 Cor. 1:13; 10:2 and Gal. 3:27.

INTRODUCTION to
MARK

Book Study Outline: If you are using Mark for a study course, here is a 7- or 13-week outline. Use the questions in the margin for your group agenda:

- start meeting / 15 min.
- read & discuss Bible / 30 min.
- close meeting / 15–45 min.

Refer to the Questions and Answers in the front of this Bible for more information.

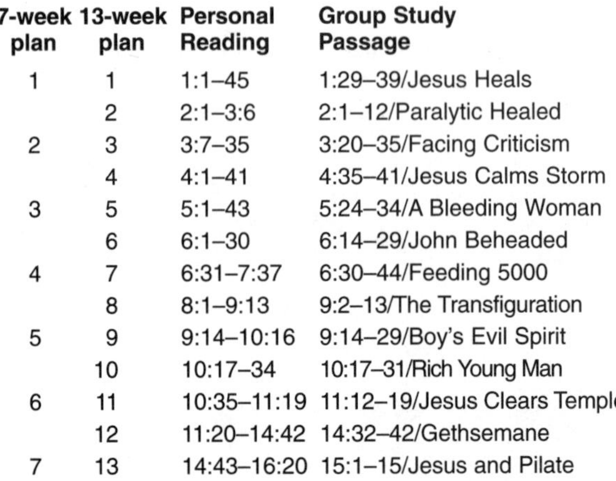

7-week plan	13-week plan	Personal Reading	Group Study Passage
1	1	1:1–45	1:29–39/Jesus Heals
	2	2:1–3:6	2:1–12/Paralytic Healed
2	3	3:7–35	3:20–35/Facing Criticism
	4	4:1–41	4:35–41/Jesus Calms Storm
3	5	5:1–43	5:24–34/A Bleeding Woman
	6	6:1–30	6:14–29/John Beheaded
4	7	6:31–7:37	6:30–44/Feeding 5000
	8	8:1–9:13	9:2–13/The Transfiguration
5	9	9:14–10:16	9:14–29/Boy's Evil Spirit
	10	10:17–34	10:17–31/Rich Young Man
6	11	10:35–11:19	11:12–19/Jesus Clears Temple
	12	11:20–14:42	14:32–42/Gethsemane
7	13	14:43–16:20	15:1–15/Jesus and Pilate

Author: No author is named in the text. However, an early tradition ascribes this Gospel to Mark, the son of Mary (Ac 12:12) and the companion of both Paul (Ac 12:25; Col 4:10; Phm 24) and Peter (1Pe 5:13).

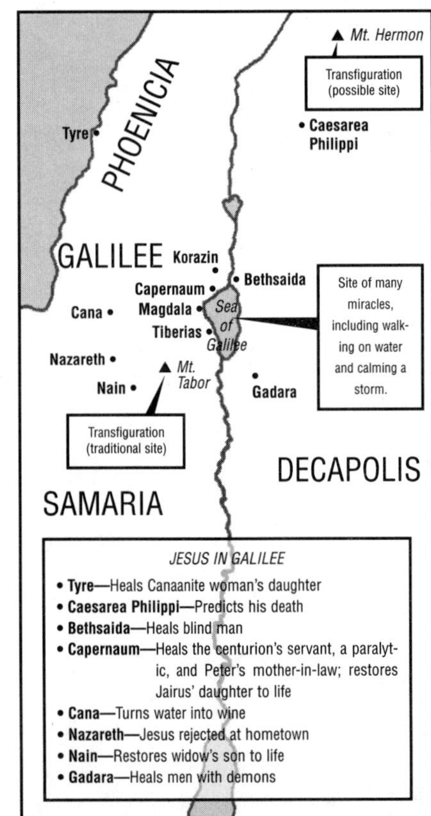
Mt. Hermon
Transfiguration (possible site)
PHOENICIA
Tyre
Caesarea Philippi
GALILEE
Korazin
Bethsaida
Capernaum
Magdala
Cana
Tiberias
Sea of Galilee
Site of many miracles, including walking on water and calming a storm.
Nazareth
Mt. Tabor
Nain
Gadara
Transfiguration (traditional site)
DECAPOLIS
SAMARIA
JESUS IN GALILEE
• Tyre—Heals Canaanite woman's daughter
• Caesarea Philippi—Predicts his death
• Bethsaida—Heals blind man
• Capernaum—Heals the centurion's servant, a paralytic, and Peter's mother-in-law; restores Jairus' daughter to life
• Cana—Turns water into wine
• Nazareth—Jesus rejected at hometown
• Nain—Restores widow's son to life
• Gadara—Heals men with demons

Date: Mark was written somewhere between A.D. 50–70; probably in the mid-60s.

Theme: Jesus the Messiah, the Son of God.

Historical Background: Mark was written for a Gentile audience; traditionally, the church at Rome. It may have been occasioned by the great fire which devastated much of Rome in A.D. 64. Despite his efforts at rebuilding the city, many people believed the Emperor Nero himself had arranged for this fire. To shift the focus off himself, Nero placed the blame for this tragedy on the Christians. This led to an outbreak of severe persecution which tested the faith of many. It was to people in this situation that Mark may have written this Gospel. This book would encourage these suffering believers by showing them Jesus' authority over all types of opposing forces. At the same time, Mark called on them to serve Christ faithfully even as they shared in his sufferings. Mark was probably the first Gospel written, forming the basis for much of Matthew and Luke.

Characteristics: Mark is not so much a biography of Jesus as it is a character sketch. Without any introduction or infancy narrative, Jesus bursts onto the scene as a fully grown man. Three years of ministry are packed into chapters 1–10, while Jesus' final week stretches out through chapters 11–16.

Mark

John the Baptist Prepares the Way

1 The beginning of the gospel about Jesus Christ, the Son of God.[a]

2It is written in Isaiah the prophet:

> "I will send my messenger ahead of you,
> who will prepare your way"[b]—
> 3"a voice of one calling in the desert,
> 'Prepare the way for the Lord,
> make straight paths for him.' "[c]

4And so John came, baptizing in the desert region and preaching a baptism of repentance for the forgiveness of sins. 5The whole Judean countryside and all the people of Jerusalem went out to him. Confessing their sins, they were baptized by him in the Jordan River. 6John wore clothing made of camel's hair, with a leather belt around his waist, and he ate locusts and wild honey. 7And this was his message: "After me will come one more powerful than I, the thongs of whose sandals I am not worthy to stoop down and untie. 8I baptize you with[d] water, but he will baptize you with the Holy Spirit."

The Baptism and Temptation of Jesus

9At that time Jesus came from Nazareth in Galilee and was baptized by John in the Jordan. 10As Jesus was coming up out of the water, he saw heaven being torn open and the Spirit descending on him like a dove. 11And a voice came from heaven: "You are my Son, whom I love; with you I am well pleased."

12At once the Spirit sent him out into the desert, 13and he was in the desert forty days, being tempted by Satan. He was with the wild animals, and angels attended him.

The Calling of the First Disciples

14After John was put in prison, Jesus went into Galilee, proclaiming the good news of God. 15"The time has come," he said. "The kingdom of God is near. Repent and believe the good news!"

16As Jesus walked beside the Sea of Galilee, he saw Simon and his brother Andrew casting a net into the lake, for they were fishermen. 17"Come, follow me," Jesus said, "and I will make you fishers of men." 18At once they left their nets and followed him.

19When he had gone a little farther, he saw James son of Zebedee and his brother John in a boat, preparing their nets. 20Without delay he called them, and they left their father Zebedee in the boat with the hired men and followed him.

Jesus Drives Out an Evil Spirit

21They went to Capernaum, and when the Sabbath came, Jesus went into the synagogue and began to teach. 22The people were amazed at his teaching, because he taught them as one who had authority, not as the teachers of the law. 23Just then a man in

a1 Some manuscripts do not have *the Son of God.* *b2* Mal. 3:1 *c3* Isaiah 40:3
d8 Or *in*

1. When the mail comes, what do you open and read first? **2.** What is the strangest thing you have ever eaten?

1. What do the contexts of the quotes (Mal 3:1; Isa 40:3) teach about the "coming one"? **2.** Why is John's ministry so popular (vv. 4–5)? **3.** Given John's message (vv. 7–8), what type of person is the crowd anticipating (see Isa 32:15–20)? **4.** What do you think the dove and voice (vv. 10–11) meant to Jesus as he came out of the water? As he entered the desert? During his temptations? How would all this prepare him?

1. What from your life illustrates what it means to repent? **2.** John the Baptist prepared "the way for the Lord." Who prepared the way for the Lord in your life? **3.** As Jesus came out of the water as he was being baptized, what did the voice from heaven say? What would you like to hear God say to you? **4.** What do you think would happen if you went away by yourself for 40 days to face your particular temptations?

What is the "good news" according to Jesus? What might this kingdom mean to the disciples?

1. What is it about Jesus that makes you follow him? **2.** Different types of fishermen need different skills: sailing, casting, maintaining nets, reading charts, etc. If Jesus asked you to be a "fisher of men," what skills could you bring?

Who was one of your best teachers? What made that teacher so good?

1. Why do you suppose Jesus started his public ministry in a synagogue? What two things about Jesus amazed the people? Why? **2.** What does it mean to teach "with authority"? What was the nature and source of Jesus' authority?

1. Why do you think Jesus healed people? **2.** On a scale of 1 to 10, how much authority does Jesus have in your life? What would you have to cast out to rate a 10?

---

1. As a child, were you sickly or robust? **2.** What is your solitary place?

1. How does Jesus' healing (vv. 30–31) compare with his exorcism (v. 25)? What new realm of authority is seen here? **2.** How do you picture the scene in verses 32–34? Why does he silence the demons? **3.** After a day like this (vv. 29–34), what pressures could Jesus feel as a new day dawns? What might he pray about? How might this relate to his decision to move on (v. 38)?

1. What do you do when you need to get away and be with

their synagogue who was possessed by an evil[a] spirit cried out,
24"What do you want with us, Jesus of Nazareth? Have you come to
destroy us? I know who you are—the Holy One of God!"
25"Be quiet!" said Jesus sternly. "Come out of him!" 26The evil
spirit shook the man violently and came out of him with a shriek.
27The people were all so amazed that they asked each other,
"What is this? A new teaching—and with authority! He even gives
orders to evil spirits and they obey him." 28News about him spread
quickly over the whole region of Galilee.

Jesus Heals Many

29As soon as they left the synagogue, they went with James and
John to the home of Simon and Andrew. 30Simon's mother-in-law
was in bed with a fever, and they told Jesus about her. 31So he
went to her, took her hand and helped her up. The fever left her
and she began to wait on them.
32That evening after sunset the people brought to Jesus all the
sick and demon-possessed. 33The whole town gathered at the door,
34and Jesus healed many who had various diseases. He also drove
out many demons, but he would not let the demons speak because
they knew who he was.

Jesus Prays in a Solitary Place

35Very early in the morning, while it was still dark, Jesus got up,
left the house and went off to a solitary place, where he prayed.

[a] *23* Greek *unclean*; also in verses 26 and 27

Mark 1:29–39 JESUS HEALS AND PRAYS

After Jesus' baptism and temptation, he immediately launched into his public ministry. As his base of operations during his ministry in Galilee, Jesus uses the Capernaum home of Simon Peter, one of the first disciples.

1. If you were having a private prayer time and the disciples came looking for you, how would you feel?
   a. angry I couldn't have time alone
   b. like telling the disciples to leave so I could keep praying
   c. like inviting the disciples to join me
   d. gratified that I was so needed
   e. guilty that I wasn't around when I was needed
   f. torn between my need to be alone and my desire to help others

2. What do you think the crowds were looking for in Jesus?
   a. a quick fix
   b. a miracle-worker
   c. a teacher of truth
   d. a spiritual leader to follow
   e. a better way to live

3. What do you think Jesus was looking for in the people?
   a. appreciation and applause
   b. faith
   c. followers
   d. He gave with no strings attached.

4. Which of the things Jesus faced cause you the most stress?
   a. being physically crowded (v. 33)
   b. short nights (v. 35)
   c. having routines disrupted (v. 37)
   d. constant demands (v. 37)
   e. always on the go (v. 39)

5. When you need time alone, where do you go and what do you do?

6. What is the greatest obstacle in your personal devotional life?
   a. finding time
   b. finding somewhere quiet
   c. being consistent
   d. staying awake
   e. keeping my concentration
   f. knowing what to do
   g. having the desire

7. What goals would you like to set for your "quiet time"—for example, amount of time, or a Scripture-reading plan?

8. How does this Scripture speak to your life?
   a. Being alone at times is good.
   b. I need more balance between activity and prayer.
   c. I need more balance between being with others and being alone.
   d. I shouldn't stay constantly busy just to keep from being lonely.

9. Which of the following ways do you typically manage stress? Which of these ways could you and your spouse do together to manage stress better?
   a. ignore it
   b. rant and rave
   c. exercise regularly
   d. get out into nature
   e. go out for an evening
   f. take vacations
   g. have quality devotional time
   h. relax with a book or TV
   i. participate in a hobby
   j. draw support from others

10. What difference has getting alone to pray made (or could it make) in handling the stress in your life?

36Simon and his companions went to look for him, 37and when
they found him, they exclaimed: "Everyone is looking for you!"
38Jesus replied, "Let us go somewhere else—to the nearby villages—so I can preach there also. That is why I have come." 39So
he traveled throughout Galilee, preaching in their synagogues and
driving out demons.

A Man With Leprosy

40A man with leprosy[a] came to him and begged him on his
knees, "If you are willing, you can make me clean."
41Filled with compassion, Jesus reached out his hand and
touched the man. "I am willing," he said. "Be clean!" 42Immediate-
ly the leprosy left him and he was cured.
43Jesus sent him away at once with a strong warning: 44"See that
you don't tell this to anyone. But go, show yourself to the priest
and offer the sacrifices that Moses commanded for your cleansing,
as a testimony to them." 45Instead he went out and began to talk
freely, spreading the news. As a result, Jesus could no longer enter
a town openly but stayed outside in lonely places. Yet the people
still came to him from everywhere.

Jesus Heals a Paralytic

2 A few days later, when Jesus again entered Capernaum, the
people heard that he had come home. 2So many gathered that
there was no room left, not even outside the door, and he preached
the word to them. 3Some men came, bringing to him a paralytic,

[a]*40* The Greek word was used for various diseases affecting the skin—not necessarily leprosy.

God? **2.** What insight do you see in these stories about Jesus and the kingdom?

When caught in a crowd (rush hour, Christmas crunch, etc.), what do you do?

Why is the leper unsure of Jesus' desire to help (see Lev 13)? What is significant about Jesus touching the leper prior to healing him? What do the crowds expect?

Where do you need his special touch this week? How can you "touch lepers" in your community?

If in a crisis, even at 3 a.m., which four friends would you call?

1. What would you be seeing and feeling if you were in this crowd (vv. 1–4)? **2.** Why are the teachers so upset? In their minds, how are sin and the authority of

Mark 2:1–12 JESUS HEALS A PARALYTIC

1. If you were one of the paralytic's four friends and saw the crowd where Jesus was, what would you do?
   a. suggest we come back later
   b. politely wait in line
   c. make a hole in the roof
   d. go along with the hole in the roof, but make clear it wasn't my idea

2. How would you feel if you were the paralytic when your friends decided to help you "drop in on Jesus"?
   a. reluctant—You will embarrass me.
   b. scared—You're going to drop me.
   c. grateful—Thanks for your concern.
   d. apprehensive—They are going to throw us out!
   e. mixed—I don't think this is going to work, but I will trust you guys.

3. When the crowd heard the commotion and saw the man lowered into the room, how do you think they felt?
   a. annoyed—Where's their respect?
   b. amused—This is the best show in town!
   c. angry—Throw them out!
   d. admiring—They are really concerned for their friend.

4. Why were the teachers of the Law so upset with Jesus?
   a. They were worried about the roof.
   b. They didn't believe Jesus was the Son of God.
   c. They didn't accept the connection of spiritual and physical healing.
   d. They thought Jesus was being disrespectful to God.

5. What quality do the four men possess that impresses you most?
   a. faith
   b. ingenuity
   c. concern for their friend
   d. determination
   e. boldness

6. How do you need to change to receive more support from friends?
   a. stop trying to be so self-sufficient
   b. learn to take the risk of asking
   c. be more supportive of others
   d. recruit some different friends
   e. I'm doing fine as is.

7. If you had friends who would take you to Jesus for healing today, what kind of healing would you ask for?
   a. physical
   b. spiritual
   c. emotional
   d. relational

8. As your friends help you find healing or comfort, what is the biggest obstacle they may have to help you overcome?
   a. my self-pity
   b. my anger
   c. some family members or friends who don't understand my pain
   d. the distance I feel from God
   e. I'm afraid I don't have friends like that.

9. When it comes to going against the pressure like these guys did, how hard is it for you to stand up against the crowd? Rate yourself from 1 (easy) to 10 (hard) in each of the following categories:
   a. getting wasted on drugs or alcohol
   b. letting others cheat off of you
   c. taking something that isn't yours
   d. lying to your parents to cover for your friends
   e. sex (when your friends are sexually active)
   f. cursing/profanity/dirty jokes
   g. raunchy movies, magazines, etc.
   h. disobeying/disrespecting parents

God linked (see Jn 9:1–3)? **3.** Why didn't Jesus just heal the man like everyone expected? What new insight about the kingdom and himself is he revealing?

♡ **1.** In what ways is sin like paralysis? What freedoms has Jesus' word of forgiveness given to you? Where do you need to hear that word again? **2.** In this story, do you identify more with the paralytic, his friends or the teachers? Why?

carried by four of them. 4Since they could not get him to Jesus
because of the crowd, they made an opening in the roof above
Jesus and, after digging through it, lowered the mat the paralyzed
man was lying on. 5When Jesus saw their faith, he said to the
paralytic, "Son, your sins are forgiven."
6Now some teachers of the law were sitting there, thinking to
themselves, 7"Why does this fellow talk like that? He's blaspheming! Who can forgive sins but God alone?"
8Immediately Jesus knew in his spirit that this was what they
were thinking in their hearts, and he said to them, "Why are you
thinking these things? 9Which is easier: to say to the paralytic,
'Your sins are forgiven,' or to say, 'Get up, take your mat and
walk'? 10But that you may know that the Son of Man has authority
on earth to forgive sins . . . ." He said to the paralytic, 11"I tell you,
get up, take your mat and go home." 12He got up, took his mat and
walked out in full view of them all. This amazed everyone and they
praised God, saying, "We have never seen anything like this!"

If your salary was suddenly tripled, what would you do with the extra money?

The disciples who were fishermen (1:16–19) may have paid inflated taxes to Levi for years. How would they feel when Jesus called him? Why did he do so?

♡ **1.** Describe a time in your life when you felt like you were at odds with the religious establishment. **2.** When have you resented Jesus calling a particular person?

The Calling of Levi

13Once again Jesus went out beside the lake. A large crowd came
to him, and he began to teach them. 14As he walked along, he saw
Levi son of Alphaeus sitting at the tax collector's booth. "Follow
me," Jesus told him, and Levi got up and followed him.
15While Jesus was having dinner at Levi's house, many tax collectors and "sinners" were eating with him and his disciples, for
there were many who followed him. 16When the teachers of the
law who were Pharisees saw him eating with the "sinners" and tax
collectors, they asked his disciples: "Why does he eat with tax
collectors and 'sinners'?"
17On hearing this, Jesus said to them, "It is not the healthy who
need a doctor, but the sick. I have not come to call the righteous,
but sinners."

Do you fix and mend or toss and replace? Why?

1. Why did John's disciples and the Pharisees fast (see Lev 16:29,31; 23:27,29,31)? Why did Jesus' disciples not fast? **2.** How do the three mini-parables (vv. 19–22) answer the question? What is the new wine? The old wineskins?

♡ How has the "wine" of Jesus burst some of your "old wineskins"?

Jesus Questioned About Fasting

18Now John's disciples and the Pharisees were fasting. Some
people came and asked Jesus, "How is it that John's disciples and
the disciples of the Pharisees are fasting, but yours are not?"
19Jesus answered, "How can the guests of the bridegroom fast
while he is with them? They cannot, so long as they have him with
them. 20But the time will come when the bridegroom will be taken
from them, and on that day they will fast.
21"No one sews a patch of unshrunk cloth on an old garment. If
he does, the new piece will pull away from the old, making the tear
worse. 22And no one pours new wine into old wineskins. If he
does, the wine will burst the skins, and both the wine and the
wineskins will be ruined. No, he pours new wine into new wineskins."

Who in your family was (or is) always checking up on you to see if you "do it right"?

1. What is the complaint about Jesus here? **2.** How does David's story apply to Jesus' situation (see 1Sa 21:1–6)? **3.** What causes the tension in the synagogue (3:1–6)? What concerns are shared by the leaders? By Jesus? By the man with the

Lord of the Sabbath

23One Sabbath Jesus was going through the grainfields, and as
his disciples walked along, they began to pick some heads of grain.
24The Pharisees said to him, "Look, why are they doing what is
unlawful on the Sabbath?"
25He answered, "Have you never read what David did when he
and his companions were hungry and in need? 26In the days of
Abiathar the high priest, he entered the house of God and ate the
consecrated bread, which is lawful only for priests to eat. And he
also gave some to his companions."
27Then he said to them, "The Sabbath was made for man, not

man for the Sabbath. 28So the Son of Man is Lord even of the
Sabbath."

3 Another time he went into the synagogue, and a man with a
shriveled hand was there. 2Some of them were looking for a
reason to accuse Jesus, so they watched him closely to see if he
would heal him on the Sabbath. 3Jesus said to the man with the
shriveled hand, "Stand up in front of everyone."

4Then Jesus asked them, "Which is lawful on the Sabbath: to do
good or to do evil, to save life or to kill?" But they remained silent.

5He looked around at them in anger and, deeply distressed at
their stubborn hearts, said to the man, "Stretch out your hand." He
stretched it out, and his hand was completely restored. 6Then the
Pharisees went out and began to plot with the Herodians how they
might kill Jesus.

Crowds Follow Jesus

7Jesus withdrew with his disciples to the lake, and a large crowd
from Galilee followed. 8When they heard all he was doing, many
people came to him from Judea, Jerusalem, Idumea, and the regions across the Jordan and around Tyre and Sidon. 9Because of the
crowd he told his disciples to have a small boat ready for him, to
keep the people from crowding him. 10For he had healed many,
so that those with diseases were pushing forward to touch him.
11Whenever the evil[a] spirits saw him, they fell down before him
and cried out, "You are the Son of God." 12But he gave them strict
orders not to tell who he was.

[a]*11* Greek *unclean*; also in verse 30

shriveled hand? **4.** What prompts Jesus' anger?

1. How have you seen religious rules or institutions hurt people? What causes that? **2.** Have you ever felt angry at a church or religious institution? Why? How has that experience affected you?

1. When have you been attracted to or repelled by large crowds (sporting events, rock concerts, political rallies, opening day at a new mall)? **2.** What do you do to get away from the maddening crowd?

1. From what places were people traveling to see and hear Jesus? What would have motivated you to go? What motives would have pleased Jesus? Why? **2.** What qualities did the 12 disciples possess which might have

Mark 2:23–3:6 LORD OF THE SABBATH

The conflict in these two stories arose from the Pharisees' adherence to traditional interpretations of Old Testament Sabbath laws: "harvesting" of any kind was forbidden, and aid could be given the sick only when the person's life was threatened.

1. How would the *Galilee Gazette* headline these two stories?
   a. New Rules for New Rabbi
   b. Jesus and Pharisees Square Off in Sabbath Spat
   c. Controversial Miracle Occurs in Local Synagogue
   d. Jesus' Popularity Growing ... But Not With Everyone
2. What reasoning did Jesus use to answer the Pharisees' accusation of the disciples breaking the Sabbath?
   a. Lighten up, it's a small infraction.
   b. I'm reinterpreting the Law.
   c. You're concentrating on the letter of the Law, and I'm concerned with the spirit behind it.
   d. The Sabbath should be a help to people, not a burden.
3. What made Jesus so upset with the Pharisees in the synagogue (3:5)?
   a. their refusal to answer his question
   b. their disbelief
   c. their suspicion of him
   d. their lack of compassion
   e. their putting principles over people
4. What made the Pharisees so upset with Jesus?
   a. intolerance
   b. spiritual blindness
   c. righteous indignation
   d. jealousy
   e. legalism
5. Why did Jesus heal the man on the Sabbath?
   a. because there was no reason to wait until the next day
   b. to spite the Pharisees
   c. because he had compassion upon the man
   d. to demonstrate he was Lord of the Sabbath
6. These two confrontations show that Jesus:
   a. liked to stir up trouble.
   b. didn't care what the religious elite thought.
   c. was above Old Testament Law.
   d. came to abolish the Law.
   e. came to restore the Law's intent.
7. How have you seen religious rules or institutions hurt people? How might you be guilty of that yourself?
8. What does "Sabbath" mean for you?
   a. worship
   b. physical rest
   c. inner peace
   d. no work
   e. no anxiety
   f. other:_____
9. What do you regularly give up your Sabbath for? What are the difficult things for you to set aside?
10. Are each of the following true or false for you?
   a. I feel I give my children proper priority.
   b. My children feel I give them proper priority.
   c. Nothing keeps me from fulfilling my commitment to family time.
   d. I feel good about the fun and recreation we enjoy as a family.
   e. I feel good about the spiritual life we share as a family.

caused Jesus to select them? What is their purpose? Why such ordinary guys?

What motivates you to seek Jesus? What does it mean to you to be "with him"? To be "sent out" by him?

What crazy stunt or notorious behavior from your high school days are your classmates likely to remember you by?

1. Why was Jesus' family worried about him? What type of conversation might they have had before deciding to "take charge of him?" **2.** What tensions might these people feel when they hear what the Pharisees say about Jesus? **3.** How do Jesus' parables answer the "teachers of the law?" How do they relate to verse 29? **4.** What did the crowd expect in verses 31–32? What did Jesus say is the basis for a family relationship with him (v. 35)? Is doing God's will

The Appointing of the Twelve Apostles

13 Jesus went up on a mountainside and called to him those he
wanted, and they came to him. 14 He appointed twelve—designating them apostles[a]—that they might be with him and that he
might send them out to preach 15 and to have authority to drive out
demons. 16 These are the twelve he appointed: Simon (to whom he
gave the name Peter); 17 James son of Zebedee and his brother John
(to them he gave the name Boanerges, which means Sons of Thunder); 18 Andrew, Philip, Bartholomew, Matthew, Thomas, James
son of Alphaeus, Thaddaeus, Simon the Zealot 19 and Judas Iscariot,
who betrayed him.

Jesus and Beelzebub

20 Then Jesus entered a house, and again a crowd gathered, so
that he and his disciples were not even able to eat. 21 When his
family heard about this, they went to take charge of him, for they
said, "He is out of his mind."

22 And the teachers of the law who came down from Jerusalem
said, "He is possessed by Beelzebub[b]! By the prince of demons he
is driving out demons."

23 So Jesus called them and spoke to them in parables: "How can
Satan drive out Satan? 24 If a kingdom is divided against itself, that
kingdom cannot stand. 25 If a house is divided against itself, that
house cannot stand. 26 And if Satan opposes himself and is divided,
he cannot stand; his end has come. 27 In fact, no one can enter a
strong man's house and carry off his possessions unless he first ties
up the strong man. Then he can rob his house. 28 I tell you the

[a] *14* Some manuscripts do not have *designating them apostles.* [b] *22* Greek *Beezeboul* or *Beelzeboul*

Mark 3:20–35 JESUS FACES CRITICISM

1. If you were Jesus, what would be the hardest for you to handle?
   a. not getting to eat
   b. my family thinking I was crazy
   c. rejection by religious authorities
   d. accusations of being possessed

2. Why did Jesus' family think he was out of his mind?
   a. No normal person would act the way he did.
   b. They thought he was under excessive stress.
   c. They thought he had "delusions of grandeur."
   d. They really didn't understand who he was.
   e. They were swayed by others.

3. Why did Jesus' family want to "take charge of him"?
   a. They were afraid he would overwork himself.
   b. They were afraid of what his opponents might do to him.
   c. They wanted to teach him proper behavior.
   d. He was embarrassing them.

4. What does it mean to "blaspheme against the Holy Spirit"?
   a. to ridicule the Holy Spirit
   b. to sin repeatedly
   c. to refuse to accept God's forgiveness
   d. to attribute Jesus' works to Satan

5. What would you have thought if you were listening to Jesus when he spoke about his "family"?
   a. Jesus is anti-family.
   b. Jesus sees himself as belonging to the family of all humanity.
   c. I can belong to Jesus' family.
   d. Membership in God's spiritual family is more important than membership in my biological family.
   e. I have to turn my back on my natural family.
   f. I have to obey the will of God.

6. Which of the following statements describe your relationship with the family of God?
   a. I've been in the family a long time.
   b. I'm just a baby in the family.
   c. I'm a "black sheep" in the family.
   d. I generally don't get along with other family members.
   e. I generally get along great with other family members.

7. How can you improve the way you relate to your "brothers and sisters" in the family of God?

8. How can you improve the way you relate to your "Heavenly Father"?

9. Which of the following is *most* true of your family? Which of the following is *least* true?
   a. My parents think I'm weird.
   b. I don't feel very accepted by my parents.
   c. I don't feel like I can do anything right in my parents' eyes.
   d. I feel closer to other people than to my own family.
   e. Our family life is full of tension.

10. How do you think God wants you to deal with the frustrations you feel toward your parents? What *can* you change? What *can't* you change?

truth, all the sins and blasphemies of men will be forgiven them. 29But whoever blasphemes against the Holy Spirit will never be forgiven; he is guilty of an eternal sin."

30He said this because they were saying, "He has an evil spirit."

Jesus' Mother and Brothers

31Then Jesus' mother and brothers arrived. Standing outside, they sent someone in to call him. 32A crowd was sitting around him, and they told him, "Your mother and brothers are outside looking for you."

33"Who are my mother and my brothers?" he asked.

34Then he looked at those seated in a circle around him and said, "Here are my mother and my brothers! 35Whoever does God's will is my brother and sister and mother."

The Parable of the Sower

4 Again Jesus began to teach by the lake. The crowd that gathered around him was so large that he got into a boat and sat in it out on the lake, while all the people were along the shore at the water's edge. 2He taught them many things by parables, and in his teaching said: 3"Listen! A farmer went out to sow his seed. 4As he was scattering the seed, some fell along the path, and the birds came and ate it up. 5Some fell on rocky places, where it did not have much soil. It sprang up quickly, because the soil was shallow. 6But when the sun came up, the plants were scorched, and they withered because they had no root. 7Other seed fell among thorns, which grew up and choked the plants, so that they did not bear grain. 8Still other seed fell on good soil. It came up, grew and produced a crop, multiplying thirty, sixty, or even a hundred times."

9Then Jesus said, "He who has ears to hear, let him hear."

10When he was alone, the Twelve and the others around him asked him about the parables. 11He told them, "The secret of the kingdom of God has been given to you. But to those on the outside everything is said in parables 12so that,

> " 'they may be ever seeing but never perceiving,
> and ever hearing but never understanding;
> otherwise they might turn and be forgiven!'[a]"

13Then Jesus said to them, "Don't you understand this parable? How then will you understand any parable? 14The farmer sows the word. 15Some people are like seed along the path, where the word is sown. As soon as they hear it, Satan comes and takes away the word that was sown in them. 16Others, like seed sown on rocky places, hear the word and at once receive it with joy. 17But since they have no root, they last only a short time. When trouble or persecution comes because of the word, they quickly fall away. 18Still others, like seed sown among thorns, hear the word; 19but the worries of this life, the deceitfulness of wealth and the desires for other things come in and choke the word, making it unfruitful. 20Others, like seed sown on good soil, hear the word, accept it, and produce a crop—thirty, sixty or even a hundred times what was sown."

A Lamp on a Stand

21He said to them, "Do you bring in a lamp to put it under a bowl or a bed? Instead, don't you put it on its stand? 22For what-

[a] *12* Isaiah 6:9,10

an action or a belief (see Lk 6:46; Jn 6:29)?

1. What do you need to do with your life before Jesus can more fully be the Master of your life? **2.** Have you ever experienced a conflict between what God wanted for you and what your family expected of you? **3.** What differences can you identify between the members of your biological family and your spiritual brothers and sisters? **4.** Of the responses to Jesus in this chapter (3:6,8, 21–22,34–35), which best describes your relationship to him now? Why?

---

1. If you were to change careers and become a farmer, what kind of crops would you like to raise? Why? **2.** What is the oldest house plant you own? What is the shortest time you have kept a house plant living?

1. What are the four types of ground on which these seeds fall? What kind of growth occurred in each soil type? **2.** How might this crowd have responded to such a parable? How are the parables like a spiritual hearing test? What blocks understanding? What distinguishes those who are told "the secret of the kingdom" from those "outside"? **3.** Why does the word not take root at all in some people? What causes the second plant to wither? What three things choked off the third plant? **4.** What modern analogy would you use to explain this parable to city kids who have never seen a farm?

1. Which soil would best describe your response to the Gospel when you first heard it? What kind of crop have you been producing lately? **2.** What "worries of life, deceitfulness of wealth and desires for other things" might hinder your ability to produce a bountiful crop? **3.** What do you need to do so your spiritual life is producing an abundant crop?

Of all the different types of lights (such as desk lamps, night lights, torches, candelabras, florescent lights, etc.), which one best describes you?

1. If Jesus is the lamp (v. 21), what is he revealing (see also vv. 11–12)? 2. What is the secret of receiving more from Jesus? 3. In verses 26–29, what part (if any) do people play in the growing kingdom? How does this parable com-plement the one in verses 3–20? 4. What does the contrasting seed and bush teach about the kingdom (vv. 30–32)?

1. In terms of the light of Christ that you shed, are you a 20-, 75-, or 200-watt light bulb? Or a burned out bulb? Why? 2. How comfortable do you feel about everything you've ever concealed being disclosed? 3. How would you live your life differently if you wanted to live it without worrying what was disclosed? 4. Does knowing that the growth of the kingdom is ultimately in God's hands cause you to rest or to work more? Why? 5. At what stage is the kingdom in your life now: Still a seed? Sprouting? Outgrowing the "weeds"? Producing a harvest?

Have you ever been in a natural disaster? What happened?

1. How do you picture the disciples' faces in verses 39–41? Which would frighten you more—the storm or Jesus? 2. What was Jesus showing them about himself in all this?

1. How do you react to Jesus when he seems to be asleep in your life? 2. What is the worst personal "storm" you have faced? How did Jesus help?

---

1. When did a vacation turn into something unpleasant you never expected? 2. What is the most dramatic change you have ever seen in someone's behavior?

1. After a nerve-wracking ride across a lake, how would you react to being accosted by an escapee from a cemetery? 2. What do we learn about demons from the actions of the possessed man? 3. How does his healing take place? What is the man like afterwards? 4. Why do you think the people reacted as they did? Why were they afraid (v. 15) after seeing the man "dressed and in his right mind"? What does this story say

ever is hidden is meant to be disclosed, and whatever is concealed
is meant to be brought out into the open. 23If anyone has ears to
hear, let him hear."
24"Consider carefully what you hear," he continued. "With the
measure you use, it will be measured to you—and even more.
25Whoever has will be given more; whoever does not have, even
what he has will be taken from him."

The Parable of the Growing Seed

26He also said, "This is what the kingdom of God is like. A man
scatters seed on the ground. 27Night and day, whether he sleeps or
gets up, the seed sprouts and grows, though he does not know
how. 28All by itself the soil produces grain—first the stalk, then the
head, then the full kernel in the head. 29As soon as the grain is
ripe, he puts the sickle to it, because the harvest has come."

The Parable of the Mustard Seed

30Again he said, "What shall we say the kingdom of God is like,
or what parable shall we use to describe it? 31It is like a mustard
seed, which is the smallest seed you plant in the ground. 32Yet
when planted, it grows and becomes the largest of all garden
plants, with such big branches that the birds of the air can perch in
its shade."
33With many similar parables Jesus spoke the word to them, as
much as they could understand. 34He did not say anything to them
without using a parable. But when he was alone with his own
disciples, he explained everything.

Jesus Calms the Storm

35That day when evening came, he said to his disciples, "Let us
go over to the other side." 36Leaving the crowd behind, they took
him along, just as he was, in the boat. There were also other boats
with him. 37A furious squall came up, and the waves broke over
the boat, so that it was nearly swamped. 38Jesus was in the stern,
sleeping on a cushion. The disciples woke him and said to him,
"Teacher, don't you care if we drown?"
39He got up, rebuked the wind and said to the waves, "Quiet! Be
still!" Then the wind died down and it was completely calm.
40He said to his disciples, "Why are you so afraid? Do you still
have no faith?"
41They were terrified and asked each other, "Who is this? Even
the wind and the waves obey him!"

The Healing of a Demon-possessed Man

5 They went across the lake to the region of the Gerasenes.[a]
2When Jesus got out of the boat, a man with an evil[b] spirit
came from the tombs to meet him. 3This man lived in the tombs,
and no one could bind him any more, not even with a chain. 4For
he had often been chained hand and foot, but he tore the chains
apart and broke the irons on his feet. No one was strong enough to
subdue him. 5Night and day among the tombs and in the hills he
would cry out and cut himself with stones.
6When he saw Jesus from a distance, he ran and fell on his knees
in front of him. 7He shouted at the top of his voice, "What do you
want with me, Jesus, Son of the Most High God? Swear to God that
you won't torture me!" 8For Jesus had said to him, "Come out of
this man, you evil spirit!"

[a] *1* Some manuscripts *Gadarenes*; other manuscripts *Gergesenes* [b] *2* Greek *unclean*; also in verses 8 and 13

9Then Jesus asked him, "What is your name?"
"My name is Legion," he replied, "for we are many." 10And he
begged Jesus again and again not to send them out of the area.
11A large herd of pigs was feeding on the nearby hillside. 12The
demons begged Jesus, "Send us among the pigs; allow us to go into
them." 13He gave them permission, and the evil spirits came out
and went into the pigs. The herd, about two thousand in number,
rushed down the steep bank into the lake and were drowned.
14Those tending the pigs ran off and reported this in the town
and countryside, and the people went out to see what had happened. 15When they came to Jesus, they saw the man who had
been possessed by the legion of demons, sitting there, dressed and
in his right mind; and they were afraid. 16Those who had seen it
told the people what had happened to the demon-possessed man—
and told about the pigs as well. 17Then the people began to plead
with Jesus to leave their region.
18As Jesus was getting into the boat, the man who had been
demon-possessed begged to go with him. 19Jesus did not let him,
but said, "Go home to your family and tell them how much the
Lord has done for you, and how he has had mercy on you." 20So
the man went away and began to tell in the Decapolis[a] how much
Jesus had done for him. And all the people were amazed.

A Dead Girl and a Sick Woman

21When Jesus had again crossed over by boat to the other side of
the lake, a large crowd gathered around him while he was by the
lake. 22Then one of the synagogue rulers, named Jairus, came

[a]*20* That is, the Ten Cities

about their values? **5.** What do you suppose the demoniac said to his family? **6.** What did the disciples learn about Jesus on this day (4:35–5:20)?

1. When have you felt torn by many conflicting voices and feelings? How did Jesus bring peace to you? How do you need to hear his word of peace right now? **2.** Have you ever told your family how Jesus has shown mercy on you? If so, what happened? If not, why? What would you like to tell them?

---

1. What would you do if the phone rang, the doorbell chimed, your child called for help, and the oven alarm went off all at the same time? **2.** If you could raise

Mark 4:35–41 JESUS CALMS THE STORM

1. If you had been one of the disciples when the boat was about to sink, what would you have done?
   a. started bailing water
   b. jumped overboard
   c. taken command
   d. woken up Jesus

2. Why do you think the disciples awakened Jesus?
   a. They were afraid for his life.
   b. They were afraid for *their* lives.
   c. They wanted help bailing water.
   d. They wanted a miracle.
   e. They were mad that Jesus was sleeping through their crisis.

3. What was the tone in Jesus' voice when he said, "Why are you afraid? Do you still have no faith?"
   a. angry
   b. scolding
   c. disappointed
   d. compassionate

4. Why did Jesus allow a storm to come up in the first place?
   a. He didn't—storms are natural.
   b. He was asleep at the switch.
   c. He wanted to test them.
   d. He wanted to stretch their faith.

5. If you had been there, what would you have told your friends afterward?
   a. "I just about got killed!"
   b. "Jesus sure is a sound sleeper."
   c. "I can't figure Jesus out."
   d. "Only God can do what I just saw."

6. What do you do when "storms" come up in your life?
   a. turn to a person I can trust
   b. turn to God
   c. act like nothing is wrong
   d. get touchy and irritable
   e. take charge of things
   f. panic

7. What brings on most of the storms in your life?
   a. financial difficulties
   b. hassles with relationships
   c. overwhelming demands
   d. insecurity: worry about job/future
   e. disappointment: feelings of failure
   f. tragedy: sickness/death

8. As time goes on, have you seen improvement in the way you handle storms? What difference does your faith in Christ make?

9. How would you compare your life right now to the storm in this story?
   a. smooth sailing—enjoying the ride
   b. choppy water—a storm is brewing
   c. furious squall—sinking fast
   d. storm is over—cleaning up

10. "Quiet! Be still!" If Jesus were to speak these words to you today, what would they mean?

11. What is the most stressful recurring storm you face?
   a. making the grade in school
   b. getting along with my parents
   c. making friends
   d. getting along with friends
   e. other:__________

12.  How does this story relate to the stress in your life?
   a. Like the boat—I feel "nearly swamped"!
   b. Like the disciples—I wonder at times if Jesus really cares.
   c. Like Jesus—it seems like somebody always wants or needs me.
   d. Like the disciples—I know that only Jesus can keep my life calm.

someone from the dead, who would it be? Why?

1. Of all the people pressing for Jesus' attention, two get through to him in this story? Why? **2.** What impressions do you get of the sick woman (vv. 25–26)? This illness made her ritually unclean and thus unable to have contact with other people. What do you think it took for her to touch Jesus? Why do you think Jesus makes the sick woman reveal herself? How was her faith obvious to Jesus? **3.** What impressions do you get of Jairus (vv. 22–23)? How is his situation similar to that of the sick woman? How is it different? **4.** What is Jesus' reaction to the news that the child is dead? Jairus' reaction? Why did Jesus say the child was asleep? As Jairus, what would you say to the crowd outside your house after Jesus left?

1. Jairus, the synagogue ruler, fell at Jesus' feet and begged him to heal his 12-year-old daughter. When was the last time you "fell at Jesus' feet" and begged

there. Seeing Jesus, he fell at his feet 23and pleaded earnestly with
him, "My little daughter is dying. Please come and put your hands
on her so that she will be healed and live." 24So Jesus went with
him.

A large crowd followed and pressed around him. 25And a woman
was there who had been subject to bleeding for twelve years. 26She
had suffered a great deal under the care of many doctors and had
spent all she had, yet instead of getting better she grew worse.
27When she heard about Jesus, she came up behind him in the
crowd and touched his cloak, 28because she thought, "If I just
touch his clothes, I will be healed." 29Immediately her bleeding
stopped and she felt in her body that she was freed from her
suffering.

30At once Jesus realized that power had gone out from him.
He turned around in the crowd and asked, "Who touched my
clothes?"

31"You see the people crowding against you," his disciples answered, "and yet you can ask, 'Who touched me?' "

32But Jesus kept looking around to see who had done it. 33Then
the woman, knowing what had happened to her, came and fell at
his feet and, trembling with fear, told him the whole truth. 34He
said to her, "Daughter, your faith has healed you. Go in peace and
be freed from your suffering."

35While Jesus was still speaking, some men came from the house
of Jairus, the synagogue ruler. "Your daughter is dead," they said.
"Why bother the teacher any more?"

Mark 5:24–34 JESUS HEALS A BLEEDING WOMAN

Jesus had just agreed to go to the home of a man whose young daughter was dying. On the way he encounters a woman who most likely suffered from steady menstrual bleeding. Her affliction was social as well as physical since, according to Old Testament ritual laws, both her and anyone touching her were "unclean."

1. What would you consider to be the worst of this woman's problems?
   a. her physical suffering
   b. spending all her money in vain
   c. being a social outcast
   d. always being religiously impure
   e. guilt and low self-esteem

2. What do you think gave her the courage to touch Jesus' clothes?
   a. She didn't have anything to lose.
   b. She was desperate.
   c. She believed she'd be healed.
   d. She thought she could slip away unnoticed.

3. Why was it so important to Jesus that the person who touched him be identified?
   a. so Jesus could see who it was
   b. so the crowd would know a miracle had taken place
   c. so he could point out that the woman's faith had healed her
   d. so the woman could know she was accepted and given God's peace
   e. so it would be clear her physical healing included social healing

4. What would have caused the woman's fearful reaction in verse 33?
   a. fear of what the crowd would do
   b. fear of Jesus shaming her
   c. fear her healing would be revoked
   d. years of failure and rejection

5. In what way does this woman most remind you of yourself?
   a. having pain that no one can heal
   b. struggling with finances
   c. feeling emotionally alone
   d. feeling spiritually impure
   e. being shy about asking for help
   f. being shy about sharing what Christ has done for me

6. When do you remember being the most desperate for God's help? How did Jesus "touch" you?

7. What causes the most shame associated with the pain in your life?
   a. the guilt I feel just for being sick
   b. that my prayers aren't working
   c. all the money my illness has cost
   d. being such a burden to others
   e. relying on medicine/pain relievers

8. What is the biggest obstacle you need to "push through" in submitting to God as your "Higher Power"? What is your greatest need for that Higher Power?
   a. someone to love me and help me love myself
   b. someone to empower me to overcome my problems
   c. someone who forgives me and helps me forgive myself
   d. someone with such awesome power he commands my respect

9. How would you like the power and love of Jesus to "touch" you?
   a. to heal me physically
   b. to stop the emotional "bleeding" in my life
   c. to help me deal with the disappointment of waiting in life
   d. to give me faith to face the future
   e. to give me peace
   f. to change my circumstances
   g. to change how I view things

36Ignoring what they said, Jesus told the synagogue ruler, "Don't
be afraid; just believe."
37He did not let anyone follow him except Peter, James and John
the brother of James. 38When they came to the home of the synagogue ruler, Jesus saw a commotion, with people crying and wailing loudly. 39He went in and said to them, "Why all this commotion and wailing? The child is not dead but asleep." 40But they
laughed at him.
After he put them all out, he took the child's father and mother
and the disciples who were with him, and went in where the child
was. 41He took her by the hand and said to her, *"Talitha koum!"*
(which means, "Little girl, I say to you, get up!"). 42Immediately
the girl stood up and walked around (she was twelve years old). At
this they were completely astonished. 43He gave strict orders not to
let anyone know about this, and told them to give her something to
eat.

A Prophet Without Honor

6 Jesus left there and went to his hometown, accompanied by his
disciples. 2When the Sabbath came, he began to teach in the
synagogue, and many who heard him were amazed.
"Where did this man get these things?" they asked. "What's this
wisdom that has been given him, that he even does miracles! 3Isn't
this the carpenter? Isn't this Mary's son and the brother of James,
Joseph,[a] Judas and Simon? Aren't his sisters here with us?" And
they took offense at him.
4Jesus said to them, "Only in his hometown, among his relatives
and in his own house is a prophet without honor." 5He could not
do any miracles there, except lay his hands on a few sick people
and heal them. 6And he was amazed at their lack of faith.

Jesus Sends Out the Twelve

Then Jesus went around teaching from village to village. 7Calling
the Twelve to him, he sent them out two by two and gave them
authority over evil[b] spirits.
8These were his instructions: "Take nothing for the journey except a staff—no bread, no bag, no money in your belts. 9Wear
sandals but not an extra tunic. 10Whenever you enter a house, stay
there until you leave that town. 11And if any place will not welcome you or listen to you, shake the dust off your feet when you
leave, as a testimony against them."
12They went out and preached that people should repent. 13They
drove out many demons and anointed many sick people with oil
and healed them.

John the Baptist Beheaded

14King Herod heard about this, for Jesus' name had become well
known. Some were saying,[c] "John the Baptist has been raised
from the dead, and that is why miraculous powers are at work in
him."
15Others said, "He is Elijah."
And still others claimed, "He is a prophet, like one of the prophets of long ago."
16But when Herod heard this, he said, "John, the man I beheaded, has been raised from the dead!"
17For Herod himself had given orders to have John arrested, and
he had him bound and put in prison. He did this because of Herodi-

[a]*3* Greek *Joses,* a variant of *Joseph* [b]*7* Greek *unclean* [c]*14* Some early manuscripts *He was saying*

for help? **2.** The woman with the bleeding problem spent all her money and a great deal of effort to find a solution for her suffering. How likely are you to try every other option before you take your problem to God?

What childhood escapade of yours do you hear about most often when you visit family?

After these two power draining miracles, what happens when Jesus goes home? Why?

1. How has familiarity with Jesus blocked you from really seeing who he is? What helps you get a fresh look? **2.** How does your family react to your faith in Christ? How does that affect you?

Who in your family overpacks for a trip?

1. What does the disciples' assignment tell you about the kingdom of God? What impact would this have on the villages? **2.** How is the disciples' message like that of John (1:4) and Jesus (1:14–15)?

Where has God sent you to tell about the kingdom? How is it going?

---

1. If you were granted one wish for your next birthday, what would it be? **2.** What quality do you have that your family does not fully appreciate?

1. Why include this flashback to Herod between sending out the disciples (vv. 6–13) and their return (vv. 30–31)? **2.** What drew Herod's attention to Jesus? What was the significance of Elijah and John the Baptist to the people of Jesus' day (see Mt 17:9–13)? Why might people mistake Jesus for one of them? **3.** Why does Herod jail John? What does that reveal about Herod? About John? About Herodias? **4.** How do the two "kings"—Jesus and Herod—differ in terms of their kingdoms, character, popularity and use of power?

♡ **1.** What do you do when God's message leaves you puzzled? **2.** Would you consider John's ministry as a success or a tragedy? **3.** What would the story say to someone facing persecution, then and now? **4.** Do you feel like you deserve a first place ribbon for your spiritual life or a consolation prize?

as, his brother Philip's wife, whom he had married. 18For John had
been saying to Herod, "It is not lawful for you to have your brother's wife." 19So Herodias nursed a grudge against John and wanted
to kill him. But she was not able to, 20because Herod feared John
and protected him, knowing him to be a righteous and holy man.
When Herod heard John, he was greatly puzzled[a]; yet he liked to
listen to him.

21Finally the opportune time came. On his birthday Herod gave
a banquet for his high officials and military commanders and the
leading men of Galilee. 22When the daughter of Herodias came in
and danced, she pleased Herod and his dinner guests.

The king said to the girl, "Ask me for anything you want, and I'll
give it to you." 23And he promised her with an oath, "Whatever
you ask I will give you, up to half my kingdom."

24She went out and said to her mother, "What shall I ask for?"

"The head of John the Baptist," she answered.

25At once the girl hurried in to the king with the request: "I
want you to give me right now the head of John the Baptist on a
platter."

26The king was greatly distressed, but because of his oaths and
his dinner guests, he did not want to refuse her. 27So he immediately sent an executioner with orders to bring John's head. The
man went, beheaded John in the prison, 28and brought back his
head on a platter. He presented it to the girl, and she gave it to her
mother. 29On hearing of this, John's disciples came and took his
body and laid it in a tomb.

[a] *20* Some early manuscripts *he did many things*

Mark 6:14–29 JOHN THE BAPTIST BEHEADED

Though subject to Rome, Herod ruled over Galilee. In this story, Herod faces a dilemma after his step-daughter (Salome) performs what was surely a highly sensual dance.

1. If tabloids existed back then, what would the headlines be?
   a. "Prophet Loses Head Over Girl"
   b. "First Lady in Charge at Palace"
   c. "Popular Preacher Pays the Price for Exotic Dancer"
   d. "John the Baptist Returns From the Dead to Haunt Herod"

2. Of the people involved in the death of John the Baptist, whom do you hold most responsible?
   a. Herodias—because she set up the king out of her spite for John
   b. Herodias' daughter—because she let her mother use her "dirty dancing" to ask for John's head
   c. Herod—because he took his brother's wife, and gave the order to have John beheaded

3. What bothered Herod the most about killing John the Baptist?
   a. his conscience
   b. his fear of a revolt by the people
   c. his fear of insulting his guests
   d. his awareness that John was a righteous man
   e. his being forced to do it by his wife

4. Whom have you hurt so badly in the past that it still bothers your conscience?

5. How important is it to you to please others? When does your desire to please others lead you, like Herod, to do wrong?

6. Which of the following statements do you *agree* with, and which do you *disagree* with?
   a. Sexuality is feeling good about being a guy/girl.
   b. Sexuality brings a great deal of pressure to life.
   c. Sexuality is overly identified with sexual activity.
   d. Sexuality is not overemphasized in our society.
   e. You cannot express your sexuality without being sexually active.
   f. When you have sex apart from marriage, you get used and hurt.

7. How close are your views to your parents' about sex and dating? How much conflict do you have about these issues in particular, and your friendships in general? What can you do to reduce it?

8. In what way is your "dark side" like Herod's?
   a. I've been tempted to have an affair.
   b. I struggle with being drawn to images like sexy female dancers.
   c. Sometimes I think I'd do anything to please a particular person.
   d. I've acted violently, and regret it.

9. What do you think you need to do about your "dark side"?
   a. ignore it
   b. admit it
   c. enjoy it
   d. exert more effort to suppress it
   e. ask God to forgive my indulging it
   f. invite God's Spirit to empower me
   g. avoid certain tempting situations

Jesus Feeds the Five Thousand

30 The apostles gathered around Jesus and reported to him all
they had done and taught. 31 Then, because so many people were
coming and going that they did not even have a chance to eat, he
said to them, "Come with me by yourselves to a quiet place and get
some rest."
32 So they went away by themselves in a boat to a solitary place.
33 But many who saw them leaving recognized them and ran on
foot from all the towns and got there ahead of them. 34 When Jesus
landed and saw a large crowd, he had compassion on them, because they were like sheep without a shepherd. So he began teaching them many things.
35 By this time it was late in the day, so his disciples came to him.
"This is a remote place," they said, "and it's already very late.
36 Send the people away so they can go to the surrounding countryside and villages and buy themselves something to eat."
37 But he answered, "You give them something to eat."
They said to him, "That would take eight months of a man's
wages[a]! Are we to go and spend that much on bread and give it to
them to eat?"
38 "How many loaves do you have?" he asked. "Go and see."
When they found out, they said, "Five—and two fish."
39 Then Jesus directed them to have all the people sit down in
groups on the green grass. 40 So they sat down in groups of hun-
dreds and fifties. 41 Taking the five loaves and the two fish and
looking up to heaven, he gave thanks and broke the loaves. Then

[a] 37 Greek *take two hundred denarii*

What was the largest dinner party you ever had? What did you serve? Did everyone have enough to eat?

1. Why did Jesus decide to take the disciples away (v. 31)? What happened as soon as they left? How did the disciples and Jesus differ in the way they viewed the problem? How would you have felt about this intrusion? **2.** What emotions might have been expressed by the disciples in verse 37? **3.** What would you feel as a disciple when you gathered the leftovers? What was the lesson to be learned?

1. How has Jesus fed you when you've been spiritually hungry lately? When you sense that hunger, do you come searching for him, or do you usually try to fill up on something else first? If so, what? Why? **2.** If you went to a solitary place with Jesus, what would you talk about?

Mark 6:30–44 JESUS FEEDS THE FIVE THOUSAND

Jesus had sent the disciples on a ministry trip. After hearing their reports, he now leads them to sail to a different point on the small Sea of Galilee.

1. "Come with me by yourselves to a quiet place and get some rest." If you were one of the disciples, what would you expect?
   a. a quiet little vacation
   b. time to be with Jesus
   c. fun and recreation
   d. anything but people

2. Surprise! There are 5,000 men, plus women and children, waiting on the shore. Now how do you feel?
   a. delighted
   b. overwhelmed
   c. compassionate
   d. angry
   e. whipped
   f. frustrated

3. "You give them something to eat." How would you have reacted to Jesus' statement?
   a. Are you serious?!
   b. We don't have that much "bread"!
   c. I don't believe in giving handouts.
   d. What happened to our vacation?!
   e. Whatever you say, Lord.

4. "How many loaves do you have?" What was Jesus asking the disciples to do?
   a. take inventory of their resources
   b. see how impossible it really was
   c. start with what they had
   d. trust that he had a plan
   e. learn how to give
   f. exercise their faith

5. How do you react when you are faced with an overwhelming sense of need? When do you feel most inadequate and short of resources as you look at the needs around you?

6. Jesus had compassion on the crowd because "they were like sheep without a shepherd." What group of people do you feel the most compassion for? What could you do to act on that compassion? How could this group help you do that?

7. How have you noticed compassion among the people in your group?

8.  What is the biggest reason you work hard?
   a. to feel good about myself
   b. to please others
   c. to be successful
   d. to fulfill a calling
   e. I don't know how to slow down.
   f. I was brought up this way.
   g. I don't work all that hard.

9. Do you think you get enough rest? What would your family say? What would God say? What could you do to have a healthier balance between work and rest?

10. What is sure to ruin a restful family vacation for you?
   a. mosquitoes/jellyfish/ants
   b. car trouble
   c. seven straight days of rain
   d. unfinished business at work/home
   e. standing in long lines
   f. tight time schedules
   g. cranky/misbehaved kids

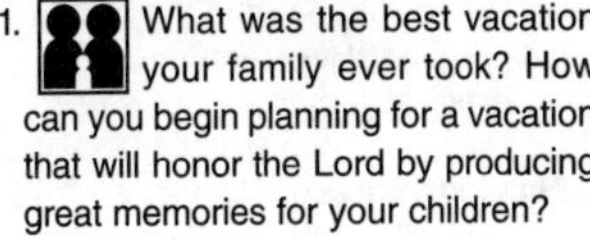

11. What was the best vacation your family ever took? How can you begin planning for a vacation that will honor the Lord by producing great memories for your children?

he gave them to his disciples to set before the people. He also divided the two fish among them all. 42They all ate and were satisfied, 43and the disciples picked up twelve basketfuls of broken pieces of bread and fish. 44The number of the men who had eaten was five thousand.

Do you know how to ice-skate? Windsurf? Water-ski? Float on an inner tube? Have you ever had any memorable experiences while doing any of these things?

1. What is the significance of Jesus' walking on the water and his response to the disciples' terror? How do you think they understood it (see Mt 8:23–27)? **2.** What should they have perceived in the lesson of the loaves that would have prepared them for this? Who is Jesus revealing himself to be?

1. How do Jesus' words (v. 50) speak to that storm? **2.** The disciples did not understand about the loaves and fish because "their hearts were hardened." What in your life needs to be softened?

Jesus Walks on the Water

45Immediately Jesus made his disciples get into the boat and go on ahead of him to Bethsaida, while he dismissed the crowd. 46After leaving them, he went up on a mountainside to pray.

47When evening came, the boat was in the middle of the lake, and he was alone on land. 48He saw the disciples straining at the oars, because the wind was against them. About the fourth watch of the night he went out to them, walking on the lake. He was about to pass by them, 49but when they saw him walking on the lake, they thought he was a ghost. They cried out, 50because they all saw him and were terrified.

Immediately he spoke to them and said, "Take courage! It is I. Don't be afraid." 51Then he climbed into the boat with them, and the wind died down. They were completely amazed, 52for they had not understood about the loaves; their hearts were hardened.

53When they had crossed over, they landed at Gennesaret and anchored there. 54As soon as they got out of the boat, people recognized Jesus. 55They ran throughout that whole region and carried the sick on mats to wherever they heard he was. 56And wherever he went—into villages, towns or countryside—they placed the sick in the marketplaces. They begged him to let them touch even the edge of his cloak, and all who touched him were healed.

1. What is the messiest food that you enjoy the most (fried chicken, cotton candy, sloppy joes, tacos, etc.)? **2.** What is the most fun you ever had getting dirty?

1. What is the issue debated by the Pharisees and Jesus (v. 15)? Given this debate, how would each define what it means to be spiritual? How does the quote from Isaiah address the issue at hand? **2.** Although the traditions were established to help people obey the law, how is it that they ended up overshadowing that law (vv. 8–9)? **3.** Something declared "Corban" meant it was dedicated to God, thus it was no longer able to be given away. What does this illustration show about how traditions twisted the law? **4.** How does Jesus' idea of being unclean differ from that of the Pharisees? Why doesn't Jesus offer any solution to the problem at this time?

1. Jesus told the Pharisees that fulfilling human traditions can interfere with obeying the commands of God. Have you ever felt like a victim of human, religious traditions in your efforts to obey God? **2.** How do you avoid hypocrisy in

Clean and Unclean

7 The Pharisees and some of the teachers of the law who had come from Jerusalem gathered around Jesus and 2saw some of his disciples eating food with hands that were "unclean," that is, unwashed. 3(The Pharisees and all the Jews do not eat unless they give their hands a ceremonial washing, holding to the tradition of the elders. 4When they come from the marketplace they do not eat unless they wash. And they observe many other traditions, such as the washing of cups, pitchers and kettles.[a])

5So the Pharisees and teachers of the law asked Jesus, "Why don't your disciples live according to the tradition of the elders instead of eating their food with 'unclean' hands?"

6He replied, "Isaiah was right when he prophesied about you hypocrites; as it is written:

> " 'These people honor me with their lips,
> but their hearts are far from me.
> 7They worship me in vain;
> their teachings are but rules taught by men.'[b]

8You have let go of the commands of God and are holding on to the traditions of men."

9And he said to them: "You have a fine way of setting aside the commands of God in order to observe[c] your own traditions! 10For Moses said, 'Honor your father and your mother,'[d] and, 'Anyone who curses his father or mother must be put to death.'[e] 11But you say that if a man says to his father or mother: 'Whatever help you

[a] *4* Some early manuscripts *pitchers, kettles and dining couches* [b] *6,7* Isaiah 29:13
[c] *9* Some manuscripts *set up* [d] *10* Exodus 20:12; Deut. 5:16 [e] *10* Exodus 21:17; Lev. 20:9

might otherwise have received from me is Corban' (that is, a gift devoted to God), 12then you no longer let him do anything for his father or mother. 13Thus you nullify the word of God by your tradition that you have handed down. And you do many things like that."

14Again Jesus called the crowd to him and said, "Listen to me, everyone, and understand this. 15Nothing outside a man can make him 'unclean' by going into him. Rather, it is what comes out of a man that makes him 'unclean.'[a]"

17After he had left the crowd and entered the house, his disciples asked him about this parable. 18"Are you so dull?" he asked. "Don't you see that nothing that enters a man from the outside can make him 'unclean'? 19For it doesn't go into his heart but into his stomach, and then out of his body." (In saying this, Jesus declared all foods "clean.")

20He went on: "What comes out of a man is what makes him 'unclean.' 21For from within, out of men's hearts, come evil thoughts, sexual immorality, theft, murder, adultery, 22greed, malice, deceit, lewdness, envy, slander, arrogance and folly. 23All these evils come from inside and make a man 'unclean.'"

your life? **3.** What changes would you make in your own church to more effectively embrace the commands of God? **4.** Have you experienced a conflict between your religious obligations and your obligations to your loved ones? What happened? **5.** What is the nicest thing you have ever done for your parents or guardians?

The Faith of a Syrophoenician Woman

24Jesus left that place and went to the vicinity of Tyre.[b] He entered a house and did not want anyone to know it; yet he could not keep his presence secret. 25In fact, as soon as she heard about him, a woman whose little daughter was possessed by an evil[c] spirit came and fell at his feet. 26The woman was a Greek, born in Syrian Phoenicia. She begged Jesus to drive the demon out of her daughter.

27"First let the children eat all they want," he told her, "for it is not right to take the children's bread and toss it to their dogs."

28"Yes, Lord," she replied, "but even the dogs under the table eat the children's crumbs."

29Then he told her, "For such a reply, you may go; the demon has left your daughter."

30She went home and found her child lying on the bed, and the demon gone.

For what would you walk 100 miles out of your way? Why?

1. What is Jesus' point in going to Tyre (a Gentile area) after the discussion in 7:1–23? **2.** Were Jesus' words overly harsh? How does this woman respond? How does her reply show faith? **3.** What message is Jesus giving by this healing?

How does Jesus care for the "unclean" in your community? How might you be his hands and feet for them?

The Healing of a Deaf and Mute Man

31Then Jesus left the vicinity of Tyre and went through Sidon, down to the Sea of Galilee and into the region of the Decapolis.[d] 32There some people brought to him a man who was deaf and could hardly talk, and they begged him to place his hand on the man.

33After he took him aside, away from the crowd, Jesus put his fingers into the man's ears. Then he spit and touched the man's tongue. 34He looked up to heaven and with a deep sigh said to him, *"Ephphatha!"* (which means, "Be opened!"). 35At this, the man's ears were opened, his tongue was loosened and he began to speak plainly.

36Jesus commanded them not to tell anyone. But the more he did so, the more they kept talking about it. 37People were overwhelmed with amazement. "He has done everything well," they said. "He even makes the deaf hear and the mute speak."

1. If you were to become deaf, what sound would you miss hearing the most? **2.** If you were to become unable to speak, what would you miss saying?

1. Why do you think Jesus used this method to heal the man? **2.** How is the response of these Gentiles (v. 37) like that of the Jews (1:27; 2:12) and the disciples (4:41)? What is Mark's point in emphasizing this?

1. How has your grasp of who Jesus is changed over the past five years? **2.** What can you do this week to show friendship to someone who is alone? **3.** What would you like Jesus to help you hear or say?

[a] *15* Some early manuscripts *'unclean.' 16If anyone has ears to hear, let him hear.*
[b] *24* Many early manuscripts *Tyre and Sidon* [c] *25* Greek *unclean* [d] *31* That is, the Ten Cities

How did your parents complete this sentence when you were a child: "How many times do I have to tell you . . ."?

1. How does this feeding compare and contrast with that of 6:30–44? **2.** In light of all the miracles that Jesus had already done, why would the Pharisees "demand a sign from heaven"? How would they have responded if Jesus had provided one? **3.** From what you have seen of the Pharisees and Herod so far, what does Jesus mean by his warning in verse 15? How does their "yeast" differ from Jesus' "bread"? How do the disciples interpret Jesus' comments here? **4.** With what tone of voice do you hear Jesus saying verses 17–21? Why? **5.** What is Jesus' point in highlighting the numbers "12" and "7"? What should the disciples understand about Jesus from these numbers? How are they like and unlike the Pharisees (vv. 11–12)?

1. Do you sometimes doubt Jesus' ability to meet your needs? How so? How are you discovering that he really can shepherd you? In what areas are you still unsure about that? **2.** How can you recognize where the "yeast of the Pharisees and Herod" is still active today? How does it show in the way people relate to God? To one another? **3.** What does "hardness of heart" mean to you? How has Jesus made your heart softer? What part is still hard?

If you lost your sight, what would you miss seeing the most?

1. Why does Jesus take the man outside the city to heal him? **2.** What is Jesus' point in healing him in stages, not all at once?

As for understanding Jesus, are you: (a) Almost blind? (b) Seeing blurred shapes? (c) Enjoying 20/20 vision? Explain.

Jesus Feeds the Four Thousand

8 During those days another large crowd gathered. Since they
had nothing to eat, Jesus called his disciples to him and said,
2"I have compassion for these people; they have already been with
me three days and have nothing to eat. 3If I send them home
hungry, they will collapse on the way, because some of them have
come a long distance."
4His disciples answered, "But where in this remote place can
anyone get enough bread to feed them?"
5"How many loaves do you have?" Jesus asked.
"Seven," they replied.
6He told the crowd to sit down on the ground. When he had
taken the seven loaves and given thanks, he broke them and gave
them to his disciples to set before the people, and they did so.
7They had a few small fish as well; he gave thanks for them also
and told the disciples to distribute them. 8The people ate and were
satisfied. Afterward the disciples picked up seven basketfuls of
broken pieces that were left over. 9About four thousand men were
present. And having sent them away, 10he got into the boat with
his disciples and went to the region of Dalmanutha.
11The Pharisees came and began to question Jesus. To test him,
they asked him for a sign from heaven. 12He sighed deeply and
said, "Why does this generation ask for a miraculous sign? I tell you
the truth, no sign will be given to it." 13Then he left them, got back
into the boat and crossed to the other side.

The Yeast of the Pharisees and Herod

14The disciples had forgotten to bring bread, except for one loaf
they had with them in the boat. 15"Be careful," Jesus warned them.
"Watch out for the yeast of the Pharisees and that of Herod."
16They discussed this with one another and said, "It is because
we have no bread."
17Aware of their discussion, Jesus asked them: "Why are you
talking about having no bread? Do you still not see or understand?
Are your hearts hardened? 18Do you have eyes but fail to see, and
ears but fail to hear? And don't you remember? 19When I broke the
five loaves for the five thousand, how many basketfuls of pieces did
you pick up?"
"Twelve," they replied.
20"And when I broke the seven loaves for the four thousand,
how many basketfuls of pieces did you pick up?"
They answered, "Seven."
21He said to them, "Do you still not understand?"

The Healing of a Blind Man at Bethsaida

22They came to Bethsaida, and some people brought a blind man
and begged Jesus to touch him. 23He took the blind man by the
hand and led him outside the village. When he had spit on the
man's eyes and put his hands on him, Jesus asked, "Do you see
anything?"
24He looked up and said, "I see people; they look like trees
walking around."
25Once more Jesus put his hands on the man's eyes. Then his
eyes were opened, his sight was restored, and he saw everything
clearly. 26Jesus sent him home, saying, "Don't go into the village.[a]"

[a] 26 Some manuscripts *Don't go and tell anyone in the village*

Peter's Confession of Christ

27Jesus and his disciples went on to the villages around Caesarea
Philippi. On the way he asked them, "Who do people say I am?"
28They replied, "Some say John the Baptist; others say Elijah;
and still others, one of the prophets."
29"But what about you?" he asked. "Who do you say I am?"
Peter answered, "You are the Christ.[a]"
30Jesus warned them not to tell anyone about him.

Jesus Predicts His Death

31He then began to teach them that the Son of Man must suffer
many things and be rejected by the elders, chief priests and teachers of the law, and that he must be killed and after three days rise
again. 32He spoke plainly about this, and Peter took him aside and
began to rebuke him.
33But when Jesus turned and looked at his disciples, he rebuked
Peter. "Get behind me, Satan!" he said. "You do not have in mind
the things of God, but the things of men."
34Then he called the crowd to him along with his disciples and
said: "If anyone would come after me, he must deny himself and
take up his cross and follow me. 35For whoever wants to save his
life[b] will lose it, but whoever loses his life for me and for the
gospel will save it. 36What good is it for a man to gain the whole
world, yet forfeit his soul? 37Or what can a man give in exchange
for his soul? 38If anyone is ashamed of me and my words in this
adulterous and sinful generation, the Son of Man will be ashamed
of him when he comes in his Father's glory with the holy angels."
9 And he said to them, "I tell you the truth, some who are
standing here will not taste death before they see the kingdom
of God come with power."

1. What was your nickname in school? 2. What do you do when someone says something you do not want to hear?

1. Thus far, what answers have been given to Jesus' poll (v. 27; see 3:21–22; 4:41; 6:3, 14–15)? 2. How and why does the tone of the Gospel shift after Peter's declaration? 3. What title does Jesus take on, and why (see Da 7:13–14)? What four things does he prophesy about the Son of Man? Why does Jesus react so strongly to Peter? 4. How would you paraphrase what Jesus says in verse 34? How do Herod and John (6:14–29) display the "life-saving" principle (vv. 35–36)? What does it really mean to believe in Jesus?

1. What do you do when you are angry at God? 2. How has your relationship with Jesus affected your lifestyle? Relationships? Priorities? Politics? 3. Where does Jesus' way conflict with your way? What do you stand to lose by following Christ? What do you stand to gain?

The Transfiguration

2After six days Jesus took Peter, James and John with him and
led them up a high mountain, where they were all alone. There he
was transfigured before them. 3His clothes became dazzling white,
whiter than anyone in the world could bleach them. 4And there
appeared before them Elijah and Moses, who were talking with
Jesus.
5Peter said to Jesus, "Rabbi, it is good for us to be here. Let us
put up three shelters—one for you, one for Moses and one for
Elijah." 6(He did not know what to say, they were so frightened.)
7Then a cloud appeared and enveloped them, and a voice came
from the cloud: "This is my Son, whom I love. Listen to him!"
8Suddenly, when they looked around, they no longer saw anyone
with them except Jesus.
9As they were coming down the mountain, Jesus gave them
orders not to tell anyone what they had seen until the Son of Man
had risen from the dead. 10They kept the matter to themselves,
discussing what "rising from the dead" meant.
11And they asked him, "Why do the teachers of the law say that
Elijah must come first?"
12Jesus replied, "To be sure, Elijah does come first, and restores
all things. Why then is it written that the Son of Man must suffer
much and be rejected? 13But I tell you, Elijah has come, and they
have done to him everything they wished, just as it is written about
him."

1. If you could take three people up a mountain to meet God, whom would you take and why? 2. Where is one outdoor location you feel especially close to God?

1. What is the connection between 9:1 and this event? 2. What do you imagine this scene was like? What is the significance of Moses' and Elijah's presence? Of the voice (see 1:11)? Why would this event be important for the disciples? 3. Who played the role of Elijah (see Mt 17:10–13)? With what result (6:14–29)? How could John the Baptist's experience help the disciples understand the nature of Jesus' Messiahship?

1. Where have you grasped a bit of Jesus' glory in a special way? 2. How does the picture of a suffering Messiah shape your view of what the Christian life is all about?

[a]29 Or *Messiah.* "The Christ" (Greek) and "the Messiah" (Hebrew) both mean "the Anointed One." [b]35 The Greek word means either *life* or *soul*; also in verse 36.

When you were a child, what issues were most likely to trigger an argument within your family?

1. While the three disciples were up on the mountain, what problem were the other nine having? How did they deal with it? What do you think the argument was about in verse 14? 2. As the boy's father, how would you feel during this argument? 3. How do the contrasts between this story and the transfiguration account for Jesus' response (v. 19)? 4. What is the major difference between Jesus' teaching in 8:31 and 9:30–32? What is significant about this difference?

1. Whom do you identify with in the story of the demon-possessed boy: Someone watching from the crowd? The Pharisees? The disciples? The little boy? The boy's father? 2. When have you felt like the father in verse 24? How do prayer and faith relate for you at those times? 3. Where do you learn more—during spiritual highs or lows? 4. How can you live with the full reality of evil and yet with strong awareness of

The Healing of a Boy With an Evil Spirit

14 When they came to the other disciples, they saw a large crowd
around them and the teachers of the law arguing with them. 15 As
soon as all the people saw Jesus, they were overwhelmed with
wonder and ran to greet him.
16 "What are you arguing with them about?" he asked.
17 A man in the crowd answered, "Teacher, I brought you my
son, who is possessed by a spirit that has robbed him of speech.
18 Whenever it seizes him, it throws him to the ground. He foams at
the mouth, gnashes his teeth and becomes rigid. I asked your
disciples to drive out the spirit, but they could not."
19 "O unbelieving generation," Jesus replied, "how long shall I
stay with you? How long shall I put up with you? Bring the boy
to me."
20 So they brought him. When the spirit saw Jesus, it immediately
threw the boy into a convulsion. He fell to the ground and rolled
around, foaming at the mouth.
21 Jesus asked the boy's father, "How long has he been like
this?"
"From childhood," he answered. 22 "It has often thrown him into
fire or water to kill him. But if you can do anything, take pity on us
and help us."
23 " 'If you can'?" said Jesus. "Everything is possible for him who
believes."
24 Immediately the boy's father exclaimed, "I do believe; help me
overcome my unbelief!"
25 When Jesus saw that a crowd was running to the scene, he

Mark 9:2–13 THE TRANSFIGURATION

1. Why do you think Jesus took time for a trip to the mountains not long before his death?
   a. to get away from people
   b. to spend time with God
   c. to prepare for what was ahead
   d. to reveal himself in his glorified state to his three closest disciples
   e. to receive Moses' and Elijah's encouragement
   f. for these two great Old Testament characters to bear witness that Jesus was the Messiah
2. How would you have felt if you had been there when Jesus' form changed and Elijah and Moses appeared?
   a. totally awed
   b. out of place
   c. scared spitless
   d. on a high
   e. like hiding
3. Why did Peter suggest building three shelters?
   a. to honor Elijah, Moses and Jesus
   b. to memorialize the occasion
   c. to keep the mountaintop feeling
   d. He enjoyed camping.
   e. He had "foot in mouth disease."
   f. He hoped this meant Jesus had come into his kingdom without the suffering he had told them about.
4. What is the meaning of the words, "This is my Son, whom I love. Listen to him"?
   a. Shut up a minute.
   b. Forget about building anything.
   c. The splendor you have seen is proof that Jesus is my Son.
   d. My Son has all my authority.
5. As they came down the mountain, what do you think the disciples concluded about Jesus' words regarding his suffering and death?
   a. It makes sense.
   b. It doesn't make sense.
   c. We need more information.
   d. It conflicts with what we know about the Messiah.
6. How did you come to realize that Jesus was the one above all others you should listen to? What keeps you from being a better listener?
7. What spot for you is like the Mount of Transfiguration—where you grasped Jesus' glory in a special way?
8. When was your most recent mountaintop experience with God?
   a. a long time ago
   b. recently
   c. right now
   d. I've never had one.
9. How would you describe your relationship with God now?
   a. in the valley
   b. climbing the mountain
   c. on the mountaintop
   d. on the rocks
10. Jesus was perfect and complete in and of himself. What needs to happen for you to feel like a "whole in one" as a single person? How has this course helped you in that process?
11. Have each person listen in silence as other group members affirm how that person demonstrates one aspect of personal "wholeness."

rebuked the evil[a] spirit. "You deaf and mute spirit," he said, "I
command you, come out of him and never enter him again."
26The spirit shrieked, convulsed him violently and came out. The
boy looked so much like a corpse that many said, "He's dead."
27But Jesus took him by the hand and lifted him to his feet, and he
stood up.
28After Jesus had gone indoors, his disciples asked him privately,
"Why couldn't we drive it out?"
29He replied, "This kind can come out only by prayer.[b]"
30They left that place and passed through Galilee. Jesus did not
want anyone to know where they were, 31because he was teaching
his disciples. He said to them, "The Son of Man is going to be
betrayed into the hands of men. They will kill him, and after three
days he will rise." 32But they did not understand what he meant
and were afraid to ask him about it.

God's transforming power? In what way do you feel that tension now? **5.** What possibilities and what abuses come to mind when you ponder the fact that "everything is possible for him who believes" (v. 23)?

Who Is the Greatest?

33They came to Capernaum. When he was in the house, he
asked them, "What were you arguing about on the road?" 34But
they kept quiet because on the way they had argued about who
was the greatest.
35Sitting down, Jesus called the Twelve and said, "If anyone
wants to be first, he must be the very last, and the servant of all."
36He took a little child and had him stand among them. Taking
him in his arms, he said to them, 37"Whoever welcomes one of
these little children in my name welcomes me; and whoever welcomes me does not welcome me but the one who sent me."

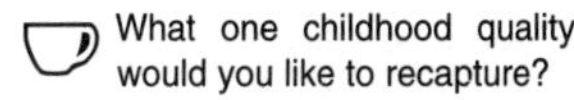

What one childhood quality would you like to recapture?

1. As a disciple, how would you feel when Jesus asked about the argument? Why does Jesus use the child as an object lesson on true greatness in the kingdom? **2.** What does it mean to do something "in Jesus' name"?

1. What can you do in Jesus' name? **2.** How does Jesus' idea of success differ from success portrayed by television or pursued

[a] *25* Greek *unclean* [b] *29* Some manuscripts *prayer and fasting*

Mark 9:14–29 THE HEALING OF A BOY WITH AN EVIL SPIRIT

1. How would you describe the father in this story?
   a. a parent who had been disappointed a few too many times
   b. a skeptic who had little faith
   c. a man who was doing his best to have faith
   d. a person of faith who was honest enough to admit his doubts

2. Whom do you identify with most in this story?
   a. the disciples—because I never seem to give people the help they need
   b. the boy—because I often feel like I'm controlled by evil
   c. the father—because I find it hard to believe sometimes
   d. Jesus—because I get called in to fix things when others mess up

3. What do you learn about evil spirits from this story?
   a. I think there must be some other explanation.
   b. They are very real.
   c. They are very powerful.
   d. Jesus has authority over them.
   e. Some are harder to cast out than others.
   f. Confronting them should be done with prayer.

4. What would you call the father's statement, "I do believe; help me overcome my unbelief"?
   a. contradictory
   b. wishy-washy
   c. an honest statement, because no one is entirely without doubt
   d. a good example, for we all need God's help to overcome unbelief
   e. encouraging, because it shows that healing from God is not dependent on our having perfect faith

5. When Jesus tells you, "Everything is possible for him who believes," which aspect of the father's response is closer to your own: "I believe" or "Help me overcome my unbelief"?

6. What do you have the hardest time believing?
   a. that God exists at all
   b. that Jesus is God's Son
   c. that a good God controls the world
   d. that there is life after death
   e. that God loves me
   f. that miracles can occur today
   g. other:________________

7. What do you believe that you wish you could believe more intensely?

8. What kind of doubts hit you the hardest?
   a. spiritual—questions like "Can my life please God?"
   b. family—questions like "Am I failing as a husband/father?"
   c. vocational—questions like "Will I make it in my work life?"
   d. personal—questions like "Will I always have these weaknesses and struggles?"

9. What would help silence the doubts you feel?
   a. admit that I have them
   b. more Bible study and prayer
   c. gleaning from those who can share how God helped them
   d. some miracle, like in the Bible
   e. people who will pray for me

by most people? Have you ever let your relationship with Christ get polluted by using your relationship with him for status, power or earthly success? What happened? **3.** What Christian groups do you tend to bad-mouth because they are "not one of us"? Why? What is Jesus' point for you here?

Whoever Is Not Against Us Is for Us

38"Teacher," said John, "we saw a man driving out demons in your name and we told him to stop, because he was not one of us."

39"Do not stop him," Jesus said. "No one who does a miracle in my name can in the next moment say anything bad about me, 40for whoever is not against us is for us. 41I tell you the truth, anyone who gives you a cup of water in my name because you belong to Christ will certainly not lose his reward.

If you had to give up a hand, a foot or an eye, which would you give up and why?

1. What four things does Jesus say are "better"? What is his point in using this hyperbole? **2.** How does the admonition to be at peace (v. 50) relate to verses 42–49?

1. Short of amputating body parts, what do you need to cut out of your life in order to avoid sin? **2.** What can you do to "salt" your relationships with peace this week?

Causing to Sin

42"And if anyone causes one of these little ones who believe in me to sin, it would be better for him to be thrown into the sea with a large millstone tied around his neck. 43If your hand causes you to sin, cut it off. It is better for you to enter life maimed than with two hands to go into hell, where the fire never goes out.[a] 45And if your foot causes you to sin, cut it off. It is better for you to enter life crippled than to have two feet and be thrown into hell.[b] 47And if your eye causes you to sin, pluck it out. It is better for you to enter the kingdom of God with one eye than to have two eyes and be thrown into hell, 48where

> " 'their worm does not die,
> and the fire is not quenched.'[c]

49Everyone will be salted with fire.

50"Salt is good, but if it loses its saltiness, how can you make it salty again? Have salt in yourselves, and be at peace with each other."

Who had the best marriage you have ever seen? Why was it so special?

1. How were the Pharisees trying to test Jesus by their question? What was their view on divorce (see Dt 24:1,3)? **2.** Instead of answering their question, how does Jesus test them by emphasizing God's intent for marriage (see Mt 19:1–12)?

1. How can you apply the principles of marriage underlined here? **2.** Do you think Jesus would respond the same to someone in a troubled marriage who was sincerely asking the question in verse 2? Why or why not?

Divorce

10 Jesus then left that place and went into the region of Judea and across the Jordan. Again crowds of people came to him, and as was his custom, he taught them.

2Some Pharisees came and tested him by asking, "Is it lawful for a man to divorce his wife?"

3"What did Moses command you?" he replied.

4They said, "Moses permitted a man to write a certificate of divorce and send her away."

5"It was because your hearts were hard that Moses wrote you this law," Jesus replied. 6"But at the beginning of creation God 'made them male and female.'[d] 7'For this reason a man will leave his father and mother and be united to his wife,[e] 8and the two will become one flesh.'[f] So they are no longer two, but one. 9Therefore what God has joined together, let man not separate."

10When they were in the house again, the disciples asked Jesus about this. 11He answered, "Anyone who divorces his wife and marries another woman commits adultery against her. 12And if she divorces her husband and marries another man, she commits adultery."

---

1. When are you most likely to lose patience with little children? When do you really like them? **2.** Did you choose the job you are in for (a) money, (b) fulfillment, or (c) the chance to make a contribution ?

1. Why would the disciples want to keep the children away from Jesus? What childlike qualities was Jesus encouraging

The Little Children and Jesus

13People were bringing little children to Jesus to have him touch them, but the disciples rebuked them. 14When Jesus saw this, he was indignant. He said to them, "Let the little children come to me, and do not hinder them, for the kingdom of God belongs to such as these. 15I tell you the truth, anyone who will not receive

[a]*43* Some manuscripts *out, 44where / " 'their worm does not die, / and the fire is not quenched.'* [b]*45* Some manuscripts *hell, 46where / " 'their worm does not die, / and the fire is not quenched.'* [c]*48* Isaiah 66:24 [d]*6* Gen. 1:27 [e]*7* Some early manuscripts do not have *and be united to his wife.* [f]*8* Gen. 2:24

the kingdom of God like a little child will never enter it." 16 And he
took the children in his arms, put his hands on them and blessed
them.

The Rich Young Man

17 As Jesus started on his way, a man ran up to him and fell on his
knees before him. "Good teacher," he asked, "what must I do to
inherit eternal life?"
18 "Why do you call me good?" Jesus answered. "No one is
good—except God alone. 19 You know the commandments: 'Do not
murder, do not commit adultery, do not steal, do not give false
testimony, do not defraud, honor your father and mother.'[a]"
20 "Teacher," he declared, "all these I have kept since I was a
boy."
21 Jesus looked at him and loved him. "One thing you lack," he
said. "Go, sell everything you have and give to the poor, and you
will have treasure in heaven. Then come, follow me."
22 At this the man's face fell. He went away sad, because he had
great wealth.
23 Jesus looked around and said to his disciples, "How hard it is
for the rich to enter the kingdom of God!"
24 The disciples were amazed at his words. But Jesus said again,
"Children, how hard it is[b] to enter the kingdom of God! 25 It is
easier for a camel to go through the eye of a needle than for a rich
man to enter the kingdom of God."
26 The disciples were even more amazed, and said to each other,
"Who then can be saved?"

[a] *19* Exodus 20:12-16; Deut. 5:16-20 [b] *24* Some manuscripts *is for those who trust in riches*

(vv. 13–16)? **2.** How does the man's question (v. 17) compare with what Jesus had just taught about the kingdom (v. 15)? What was his assumption about how one gains the kingdom? **3.** What is Jesus trying to drive home by responding to the way the man addressed him? **4.** Jesus quizzes the man on only a partial list of the Ten Commandments (see Ex 20). How well might the man have obeyed the ones relating directly to God? **5.** Why does Jesus command the man as he does (v. 21; see also 8:34)? What does his response reveal which had been hidden by his good works? **6.** What does the disciples' shock reveal about them? On what basis is it possible for anyone to receive the kingdom? **7.** How is the promise (vv. 29–30) to come true for believers?

1. Are you more like the rich young man or the children (vv. 13–16) in terms of the way you approach God? Why? **2.** What has helped you to see the impossibility of earning the kingdom? As a result, how have you experienced the gift of the kingdom as described in verses 29–30? **3.** What in your life could Jesus point to as something

Mark 10:17–31 THE RICH YOUNG MAN

1. What do you think motivated the man to ask Jesus his question?
   a. He was testing Jesus' knowledge as a teacher.
   b. He was sincerely searching to know spiritual truth.
   c. He was feeling self-righteous and wanted affirmation from Jesus.
   d. He had everything, except an "eternal life insurance policy."

2. What did Jesus mean by his reply, "Why do you call me good? No one is good—except God alone"?
   a. Take a close look at who I am.
   b. I'm not "good."
   c. I'm not on God's level.
   d. Your only hope for goodness is to rely on God.

3. Jesus asked the man to sell all his possessions and give the money to the poor because Jesus knew:
   a. the poor needed the money.
   b. the man was greedy.
   c. as long as the man was rich he wouldn't be able to trust God.
   d. the man's money was his god.

4. By choosing his wealth over a relationship with Jesus, what was the rich man gaining? What was he losing?

5. According to verses 29–31, what might you lose by following Christ? What will you gain? Which carries the greater sacrifice?

6. What is Jesus teaching us in this passage?
   a. Commitment to him must be total.
   b. Wealth is evil.
   c. Following Jesus means sacrifice.
   d. Eternal life is more important than earthly life.
   e. Giving is part of discipleship.
   f. We can only be saved by God's doing, not our own.

7. What would you do if Jesus asked you to sell everything you had and give the proceeds to the poor?
   a. have my hearing checked
   b. compute my net worth and think about it
   c. hold a garage sale this Saturday
   d. increase my pledge to the church
   e. sadly walk away

8. Jesus "looked at him and loved him" and invited the man to follow him. Have you ever had to choose between material comforts and Christ's love?

9. Name one thing you can do this week to let go of material things and embrace God's kingdom more fully.

10. If Jesus were to evaluate your life and say, "One thing you lack"—what do you think that one thing would be?

11. What does this story say about "success"? What would you say is your greatest success unrelated to your profession (or making money)?

12. What holds you back from being totally committed to Christ?
   a. wealth
   b. apathy
   c. pride
   d. habits or temptations
   e. doubts about issues of faith
   f. fear of being labeled a fanatic

[27]Jesus looked at them and said, "With man this is impossible,
but not with God; all things are possible with God."
[28]Peter said to him, "We have left everything to follow you!"
[29]"I tell you the truth," Jesus replied, "no one who has left home
or brothers or sisters or mother or father or children or fields for
me and the gospel [30]will fail to receive a hundred times as much in
this present age (homes, brothers, sisters, mothers, children and
fields—and with them, persecutions) and in the age to come, eternal life. [31]But many who are first will be last, and the last first."

that is preventing you from receiving the kingdom?

---

1. If you had one week to live, how would you spend your time? **2.** What did your parents want you to be when you grew up?

1. Why would going to Jerusalem cause the disciples to be astonished and afraid? **2.** When Jesus said, "What do you want me to do for you?" to James and John, what tone of voice do you think he used? **3.** What view of the kingdom are James and John still clinging to? How could they respond like this in light of verses 33–34? **4.** What is the *cup*, the *baptism* and the *glory* as each applies to Jesus? As each applies to the disciples? **5.** What made the other disciples indignant? **6.** How does Jesus use

Jesus Again Predicts His Death

[32]They were on their way up to Jerusalem, with Jesus leading
the way, and the disciples were astonished, while those who followed were afraid. Again he took the Twelve aside and told them
what was going to happen to him. [33]"We are going up to Jerusalem," he said, "and the Son of Man will be betrayed to the chief
priests and teachers of the law. They will condemn him to death
and will hand him over to the Gentiles, [34]who will mock him and
spit on him, flog him and kill him. Three days later he will rise."

The Request of James and John

[35]Then James and John, the sons of Zebedee, came to him.
"Teacher," they said, "we want you to do for us whatever we ask."
[36]"What do you want me to do for you?" he asked.
[37]They replied, "Let one of us sit at your right and the other at
your left in your glory."
[38]"You don't know what you are asking," Jesus said. "Can you

Mark 10:35–45 THE REQUEST OF JAMES AND JOHN

Jesus has just taken the 12 disciples aside to tell them about his approaching death. Now two of the disciples, James and his brother John, come to Jesus with a request.

1. What were James and John really wanting in their request?
   a. a close relationship with God
   b. power and position
   c. special recognition
   d. spiritual security
   e. parental approval

2. "You don't know what you are asking?" What did Jesus' reply mean?
   a. You've got to be kidding!
   b. What you ask is impossible.
   c. You don't deserve it.
   d. It's not my decision to make.
   e. You don't understand what following me is all about.

3. What was Jesus referring to when he asked, "Can you drink the cup I am going to drink?"
   a. royal dinnerware
   b. divine authority
   c. suffering and death
   d. future glory

4. Why were the other 10 disciples upset with James and John? How did Jesus use this uproar to convey new insights about the meaning of true greatness?

5. Which of the following is typical of people in positions of authority?
   a. expecting others to serve them
   b. taking advantage of other people
   c. using their position to serve
   d. using their position to get ahead
   e. not caring about other people

6. What does being a "slave of all" mean?
   a. doing menial tasks for everyone
   b. following the example of Christ
   c. allowing others to treat you poorly
   d. considering others' interests over your own

7. Who has been an example to you of a Christlike servant? What effect has that person had on your life?

8. How does Jesus practice what he preached—as the ultimate servant? When and how have you responded to Christ as your "ransom"?

9. What is the *best* thing about your relationships at work?
   a. Say what?!
   b. humor and camaraderie
   c. accomplishing goals together
   d. spending time together after hours
   e. working with other Christians
   f. other:____________

10. What is the *worst* thing about your relationships at work?
   a. employer/employee tensions
   b. backbiting and gossip
   c. jealousy and competition
   d. authority issues
   e. personality clashes
   f. clashes regarding faith or values
   g. other:____________

11. What advantages does being single have when it comes to serving God and others? Would getting married have a positive or negative effect on your servanthood?

12.  How have you experienced Christlike servanthood in this group?

drink the cup I drink or be baptized with the baptism I am baptized
with?”
39“We can,” they answered.
Jesus said to them, “You will drink the cup I drink and be
baptized with the baptism I am baptized with, 40but to sit at my
right or left is not for me to grant. These places belong to those for
whom they have been prepared.”
41When the ten heard about this, they became indignant with
James and John. 42Jesus called them together and said, “You know
that those who are regarded as rulers of the Gentiles lord it over
them, and their high officials exercise authority over them. 43Not
so with you. Instead, whoever wants to become great among you
must be your servant, 44and whoever wants to be first must be
slave of all. 45For even the Son of Man did not come to be served,
but to serve, and to give his life as a ransom for many.”

this uproar to convey new insights into his greatness? **7.** How does Jesus practice what he preached? In this context, what is a “ransom for many”? How is the death of Christ the ultimate service to all?

1. Do you find yourself desiring to sit next to God? **2.** Do you resist following the servant's path to greatness? Why? **3.** What one way could you serve this week?

Blind Bartimaeus Receives His Sight

46Then they came to Jericho. As Jesus and his disciples, together
with a large crowd, were leaving the city, a blind man, Bartimaeus
(that is, the Son of Timaeus), was sitting by the roadside begging.
47When he heard that it was Jesus of Nazareth, he began to shout,
“Jesus, Son of David, have mercy on me!”
48Many rebuked him and told him to be quiet, but he shouted all
the more, “Son of David, have mercy on me!”
49Jesus stopped and said, “Call him.”
So they called to the blind man, “Cheer up! On your feet! He's
calling you.” 50Throwing his cloak aside, he jumped to his feet and
came to Jesus.
51“What do you want me to do for you?” Jesus asked him.
The blind man said, “Rabbi, I want to see.”
52“Go,” said Jesus, “your faith has healed you.” Immediately he
received his sight and followed Jesus along the road.

How do you respond when a beggar approaches you on the street? Why?

1. What is significant about the way Bartimaeus addresses Jesus? How does Bartimaeus show his faith (while the crowd does not)? **2.** How is Bartimaeus different from the rich young man in 10:17–22? **3.** Why is there no “order of silence” here (as in 7:36)?

If Jesus asked you, “What do you want me to do for you?” what would you say?

The Triumphal Entry

11 As they approached Jerusalem and came to Bethphage and
Bethany at the Mount of Olives, Jesus sent two of his disciples, 2saying to them, “Go to the village ahead of you, and just as
you enter it, you will find a colt tied there, which no one has ever
ridden. Untie it and bring it here. 3If anyone asks you, ‘Why are
you doing this?’ tell him, ‘The Lord needs it and will send it back
here shortly.’ ”
4They went and found a colt outside in the street, tied at a
doorway. As they untied it, 5some people standing there asked,
“What are you doing, untying that colt?” 6They answered as Jesus
had told them to, and the people let them go. 7When they brought
the colt to Jesus and threw their cloaks over it, he sat on it. 8Many
people spread their cloaks on the road, while others spread
branches they had cut in the fields. 9Those who went ahead and
those who followed shouted,

“Hosanna![a]”

“Blessed is he who comes in the name of the
Lord!”[b]

10“Blessed is the coming kingdom of our father
David!”

“Hosanna in the highest!”

What is the closest you have come to meeting a world leader or celebrity?

1. Jesus always does the unexpected. What was unexpected about the way he entered Jerusalem? **2.** In light of the response he received, what were the expectations of the crowd? The disciples (see 10:37)? Jesus? **3.** What do you find most significant about the triumphal entry into Jerusalem?

1. How did Jesus ride into your life: As a Conquering Hero forcing you into submission? As a Gentle King bearing peace? As a White Knight rescuing you? How about now? **2.** Have you ever misunderstood Jesus' purposes, praising him one day and despairing the next?

[a]9 A Hebrew expression meaning “Save!” which became an exclamation of praise; also in verse 10 [b]9 Psalm 118:25,26

[11]Jesus entered Jerusalem and went to the temple. He looked
around at everything, but since it was already late, he went out to
Bethany with the Twelve.

If you could change one thing about modern Christianity, what would it be?

1. How does the story of the fig tree relate to the clearing of the temple (vv. 13–14, 20–21)? In what ways did the Pharisees cover their fruitlessness with flashy foliage? 2. This profiteering on the sale of sacrificial animals took place in the only area where Gentiles could worship. Why would that especially anger Jesus (see Isa 56:6–8)? What was Jesus threatening when he called the temple a "den of robbers" (see Jer 7:9–15)? 3. Why was Peter amazed (vv. 20–21)? Should he have been? What conditions for effective prayer are upheld here?

1. If you were a tree, what would help you produce more fruit: Pruning? Watering? Staking? Transplanting? Fertilizing? Why? 2. Like the temple, no church is perfect. What have you

Jesus Clears the Temple

[12]The next day as they were leaving Bethany, Jesus was hungry.
[13]Seeing in the distance a fig tree in leaf, he went to find out if it
had any fruit. When he reached it, he found nothing but leaves,
because it was not the season for figs. [14]Then he said to the tree,
"May no one ever eat fruit from you again." And his disciples
heard him say it.
[15]On reaching Jerusalem, Jesus entered the temple area and
began driving out those who were buying and selling there. He
overturned the tables of the money changers and the benches of
those selling doves, [16]and would not allow anyone to carry merchandise through the temple courts. [17]And as he taught them, he
said, "Is it not written:

" 'My house will be called
a house of prayer for all nations'[a]?

But you have made it 'a den of robbers.'[b]"
[18]The chief priests and the teachers of the law heard this and
began looking for a way to kill him, for they feared him, because
the whole crowd was amazed at his teaching.
[19]When evening came, they[c] went out of the city.

[a]17 Isaiah 56:7 [b]17 Jer. 7:11 [c]19 Some early manuscripts *he*

Mark 11:12–19 JESUS CLEARS THE TEMPLE

As Passover approaches, Jesus confronts abuses in the temple. Pilgrims needed to buy animals approved for sacrifice and have their money changed into the local currency for the annual temple tax. They were grossly cheated in both transactions. In addition, these chaotic activities took place in the court of the Gentiles, the only part of the temple in which God-fearing non-Jews could worship and pray.

1. What does Jesus resemble here?
   a. bouncer
   b. fiery prophet
   c. Marine sergeant
   d. political activist
   e. bull in a china shop

2. What were the temple merchants doing that made Jesus so upset?
   a. not paying rent to use the temple
   b. mixing worship and business
   c. ripping off the people
   d. robbing the temple of its holiness
   e. ruining the Gentiles' area of prayer

3. Why did the religious authorities of the time want to kill Jesus?

4. What does this story tell you about anger?
   a. Even Jesus expressed anger.
   b. At times it's okay to throw things.
   c. After you get angry, it's best to leave town.
   d. The reason for your anger should always be clearly expressed.

5. When was the last time something happened that aroused "righteous anger" within you?

6. On a scale of 1 ("peace at any price") to 10 ("let's have it out"), how would you rate yourself on taking a stand that could lead to conflict?

7. If Jesus came to clean up your community, where would he start?
   a. crime district
   b. city hall
   c. the schools
   d. the media
   e. the churches
   f. my house

8. How is God calling you now to get involved?
   a. to overturn a few tables
   b. to reach leaders in my community
   c. to win people to Christ
   d. to get involved politically
   e. to get involved in programs helping those in need
   f. to bring change to my church

9. What keeps you from making your life more of a "house of prayer"?

10. What is your biggest problem regarding anger?
   a. being argumentative
   b. running away to avoid letting people know I'm angry
   c. dwelling on revenge
   d. hurting someone else verbally
   e. hurting someone else physically
   f. hurting myself by holding it in

11. In what way do you need to be more of a "tough guy"?
   a. more assertive/open with anger
   b. more courage to share my faith
   c. more tolerance for pain or stress
   d. more disciplined devotional life
   e. more resistant of temptation
   f. more spiritual leadership at home
   g. more involved in disciplining and directing my children

The Withered Fig Tree

20In the morning, as they went along, they saw the fig tree
withered from the roots. 21Peter remembered and said to Jesus,
"Rabbi, look! The fig tree you cursed has withered!"
22"Have[a] faith in God," Jesus answered. 23"I tell you the truth,
if anyone says to this mountain, 'Go, throw yourself into the sea,'
and does not doubt in his heart but believes that what he says will
happen, it will be done for him. 24Therefore I tell you, whatever
you ask for in prayer, believe that you have received it, and it will
be yours. 25And when you stand praying, if you hold anything
against anyone, forgive him, so that your Father in heaven may
forgive you your sins.[b]"

done to make your church a better place? **3.** How do you feel about expressing anger? Have you ever expressed righteous anger? What happened? **4.** What amazing answer to prayer can you remember receiving? How much faith did it take?

The Authority of Jesus Questioned

27They arrived again in Jerusalem, and while Jesus was walking
in the temple courts, the chief priests, the teachers of the law and
the elders came to him. 28"By what authority are you doing these
things?" they asked. "And who gave you authority to do this?"
29Jesus replied, "I will ask you one question. Answer me, and I
will tell you by what authority I am doing these things. 30John's
baptism—was it from heaven, or from men? Tell me!"
31They discussed it among themselves and said, "If we say,
'From heaven,' he will ask, 'Then why didn't you believe him?'
32But if we say, 'From men' . . . ." (They feared the people, for
everyone held that John really was a prophet.)
33So they answered Jesus, "We don't know."
Jesus said, "Neither will I tell you by what authority I am doing
these things."

What authority figures do you still trust completely? Which do you distrust? Why?

1. Why were the leaders concerned about authority? Who had legitimate authority? **2.** What dilemma does this pose for Jesus? Why doesn't he answer them directly? How does he cause the leaders' trickery to backfire?

The religious leaders in Jerusalem considered Jesus a threat. Have you ever felt like Jesus was a threat to you? Why?

The Parable of the Tenants

12 He then began to speak to them in parables: "A man planted a vineyard. He put a wall around it, dug a pit for the
winepress and built a watchtower. Then he rented the vineyard to
some farmers and went away on a journey. 2At harvest time he
sent a servant to the tenants to collect from them some of the fruit
of the vineyard. 3But they seized him, beat him and sent him away
empty-handed. 4Then he sent another servant to them; they struck
this man on the head and treated him shamefully. 5He sent still
another, and that one they killed. He sent many others; some of
them they beat, others they killed.
6"He had one left to send, a son, whom he loved. He sent him
last of all, saying, 'They will respect my son.'
7"But the tenants said to one another, 'This is the heir. Come,
let's kill him, and the inheritance will be ours.' 8So they took him
and killed him, and threw him out of the vineyard.
9"What then will the owner of the vineyard do? He will come
and kill those tenants and give the vineyard to others. 10Haven't
you read this scripture:

> " 'The stone the builders rejected
> has become the capstone[c];
> 11the Lord has done this,
> and it is marvelous in our eyes'[d]?"

12Then they looked for a way to arrest him because they knew
he had spoken the parable against them. But they were afraid of
the crowd; so they left him and went away.

1. If you owned a garden or an orchard, what would you grow? **2.** If you had to entrust your business or belongings to someone outside your family, whom would you choose? Why?

1. What does the vineyard represent? Who is the owner? The son? Who are the tenants? The servants? The "others"? What was Jesus prophesying by telling this story? **2.** How does the Scripture Jesus quotes relate to the parable? Who is the capstone? **3.** How did this parable answer the question about Jesus' authority (11:28)?

1. How do you make Jesus feel welcome in your life each day? What actions of yours might make him feel unwelcome? **2.** In what ways is Jesus the capstone in your life? In what ways is he not?

[a] *22* Some early manuscripts *If you have* [b] *25* Some manuscripts *sins. 26But if you do not forgive, neither will your Father who is in heaven forgive your sins.* [c] *10* Or *cornerstone* [d] *11* Psalm 118:22,23

Which taxes do you hate paying the most? Which ones are you less bothered by paying?

1. What was dangerous about this trap? Why do the Herodians (allied to Rome) and the Pharisees make strange partners? How was Jesus a threat to each? **2.** What if Jesus had just said yes? If he had said no?

What do you give to Caesar, what do you give to God? What prevents you from giving to God what is God's?

Paying Taxes to Caesar

13Later they sent some of the Pharisees and Herodians to Jesus to
catch him in his words. 14They came to him and said, "Teacher,
we know you are a man of integrity. You aren't swayed by men,
because you pay no attention to who they are; but you teach the
way of God in accordance with the truth. Is it right to pay taxes to
Caesar or not? 15Should we pay or shouldn't we?"
But Jesus knew their hypocrisy. "Why are you trying to trap
me?" he asked. "Bring me a denarius and let me look at it." 16They
brought the coin, and he asked them, "Whose portrait is this? And
whose inscription?"
"Caesar's," they replied.
17Then Jesus said to them, "Give to Caesar what is Caesar's and
to God what is God's."
And they were amazed at him.

No one knows exactly what heaven is like, but what would make heaven especially "heavenly" for you?

1. What was odd about the Sadducees' question? Why ask it? **2.** What is the source of the Sadducees' false assumption (v. 24)? **3.** How does Exodus 3:6 (quoted in v. 26) demonstrate the fact of the resurrection?

Marriage at the Resurrection

18Then the Sadducees, who say there is no resurrection, came to
him with a question. 19"Teacher," they said, "Moses wrote for us
that if a man's brother dies and leaves a wife but no children, the
man must marry the widow and have children for his brother.
20Now there were seven brothers. The first one married and died
without leaving any children. 21The second one married the widow, but he also died, leaving no child. It was the same with the
third. 22In fact, none of the seven left any children. Last of all, the
woman died too. 23At the resurrection[a] whose wife will she be,
since the seven were married to her?"

[a]23 Some manuscripts *resurrection, when men rise from the dead,*

$ *Mark 12:13–17* PAYING TAXES TO CAESAR

In their disdain for Jesus, the Pharisees (religious conservatives) and the Herodians (supporters of Rome) had become strange allies. If Jesus answered their explosive question by saying the Jews should *not* pay taxes to Caesar, he could be arrested. If he said they *should* pay, he could lose his popular support.

1. What would you call the Pharisees' and Herodians' approach to Jesus?
   a. sneaky
   b. respectful
   c. flattering
   d. hypocritical
2. How would you describe Jesus' response to their question?
   a. evasive
   b. smart
   c. compromising
   d. balanced
3. What is implied in Jesus saying, "Give to Caesar what is Caesar's and to God what is God's"?
   a. Both God and the government should be given their due.
   b. Government has rightful authority, but final authority must be to God.
   c. Paying taxes is a spiritual as well as a political obligation.
   d. Don't do any more for the government than you have to do.
4. Which of the following do you think Jesus would encourage or condone?
   a. cheating on income taxes
   b. minimizing taxes with "loopholes"
   c. refusing to pay taxes because of an unjust war or program
   d. protesting a government policy
   e. disobeying what you believe is an unchristian law
   f. disrespecting government officials
5. What do you have the most trouble with in giving "Caesar" what is his?
   a. submitting to authority—I don't like to be told what to do.
   b. paying so much money in taxes
   c. supporting a government I don't agree with
6. How did you demonstrate rebellion in your younger days? What is your attitude toward authority now?
   a. highly obedient/compliant
   b. moderately obedient/compliant
   c. moderately rebellious
   d. highly rebellious
7. What can you give to God that you cannot give to the government? What often prevents you from doing so?
8. $ Which of the following do you think would violate Jesus' teaching in this story?
   a. avoiding government safety or environmental regulations
   b. inaccurately completing required reports to the government
   c. overcharging on government contracts
   d. disobeying a government policy which is bad for business
9. $ In your business dealings, when have you been in trouble due to rebelliousness? Were there times you felt it was *good* to be a little rebellious?
10. $ Rank the following in order of the loyalty you believe you should give them (1 being highest and 6 being lowest).
    a. country
    b. family
    c. self
    d. God
    e. my business
    f. people in general

24 Jesus replied, "Are you not in error because you do not know
the Scriptures or the power of God? 25 When the dead rise, they
will neither marry nor be given in marriage; they will be like the
angels in heaven. 26 Now about the dead rising—have you not read
in the book of Moses, in the account of the bush, how God said to
him, 'I am the God of Abraham, the God of Isaac, and the God of
Jacob'[a]? 27 He is not the God of the dead, but of the living. You are
badly mistaken!"

Which do you know more about—the Scriptures or the power of God? What are your hopes for growing in the other area?

The Greatest Commandment

28 One of the teachers of the law came and heard them debating.
Noticing that Jesus had given them a good answer, he asked him,
"Of all the commandments, which is the most important?"
29 "The most important one," answered Jesus, "is this: 'Hear,
O Israel, the Lord our God, the Lord is one.[b] 30 Love the Lord your
God with all your heart and with all your soul and with all your
mind and with all your strength.'[c] 31 The second is this: 'Love
your neighbor as yourself.'[d] There is no commandment greater
than these."
32 "Well said, teacher," the man replied. "You are right in saying
that God is one and there is no other but him. 33 To love him
with all your heart, with all your understanding and with all your
strength, and to love your neighbor as yourself is more important
than all burnt offerings and sacrifices."
34 When Jesus saw that he had answered wisely, he said to him,
"You are not far from the kingdom of God." And from then on no
one dared ask him any more questions.

What subject is guaranteed to spark a debate in your house? Sports? Politics? Religion? Other?

1. Why are these two commandments the greatest? How do the Ten Commandments relate to these two? **2.** How was this teacher's attitude different from that of many others who questioned Jesus (11:28; 12:13–14; 12:18–19)? What does Jesus' response to this man teach you about Jesus? About the kingdom of God?

1. In the three possibilities of love relationships (with God, neighbors and self), where are you the strongest? The weakest? **2.** How do you show your love for God?

Whose Son Is the Christ?

35 While Jesus was teaching in the temple courts, he asked, "How
is it that the teachers of the law say that the Christ[e] is the son of
David? 36 David himself, speaking by the Holy Spirit, declared:

> " 'The Lord said to my Lord:
> "Sit at my right hand
> until I put your enemies
> under your feet." '[f]

37 David himself calls him 'Lord.' How then can he be his son?"
The large crowd listened to him with delight.
38 As he taught, Jesus said, "Watch out for the teachers of the
law. They like to walk around in flowing robes and be greeted in
the marketplaces, 39 and have the most important seats in the synagogues and the places of honor at banquets. 40 They devour widows' houses and for a show make lengthy prayers. Such men will
be punished most severely."

The Widow's Offering

41 Jesus sat down opposite the place where the offerings were put
and watched the crowd putting their money into the temple treasury. Many rich people threw in large amounts. 42 But a poor widow came and put in two very small copper coins,[g] worth only a
fraction of a penny.[h]
43 Calling his disciples to him, Jesus said, "I tell you the truth,
this poor widow has put more into the treasury than all the others.
44 They all gave out of their wealth; but she, out of her poverty, put
in everything—all she had to live on."

1. Whom did your parents tell you to avoid? **2.** Do you know more rich uncles or more poor widows? Do you treat them any differently? If so, how?

1. What issue lies behind Jesus' question (vv. 35–37)? How will the answer to this question answer all the others directed at Jesus in 11:27–12:34? **2.** How would you describe the lifestyle of these teachers of the Law (vv. 38–40)? By contrast, what should the attitude of a Christian leader look like (see 10:42–45)? **3.** What is Jesus' point in contrasting their situation with that of the poor widow? **4.** When is "more" actually "less"? When is a "little" a "lot"?

1. How do people use religion to make themselves look good? How have you been tempted to do so? **2.** Why do you give to God's work? What do you give besides money?

[a] 26 Exodus 3:6 [b] 29 Or *the Lord our God is one Lord* [c] 30 Deut. 6:4,5
[d] 31 Lev. 19:18 [e] 35 Or *Messiah* [f] 36 Psalm 110:1 [g] 42 Greek *two lepta*
[h] 42 Greek *kodrantes*

1. If you could take two things with you to heaven, what would they be? **2.** In school or at work, did you ever get burned because you stood by the truth or refused to go along with the crowd? Was it worth it? Why or why not?

1. Why do you think that Jesus used the discussion about the temple to begin his discourse about the end of the age? What made the temple so significant for the disciples? What would its destruction symbolize for them? **2.** Upon hearing this bombshell, what two questions do the disciples ask (v. 4)? What events might deceive them into thinking the end times had come (vv. 5–8)? Of what will these events be a sign? **3.** After that, what things will happen to the disciples and the early church (vv. 9–13)? What comfort and advocate will aid them to endure their trials? **4.** What dreadful event (v. 14; see Da 9:26; 11:31; 12:11) will bring "days of distress" unequalled in human history? What deceptive signs will accompany that distress (vv. 21–22)? **5.** How

Signs of the End of the Age

13 As he was leaving the temple, one of his disciples said to
him, "Look, Teacher! What massive stones! What magnifi-
cent buildings!"
2"Do you see all these great buildings?" replied Jesus. "Not one
stone here will be left on another; every one will be thrown
down."
3As Jesus was sitting on the Mount of Olives opposite the temple, Peter, James, John and Andrew asked him privately, 4"Tell us,
when will these things happen? And what will be the sign that
they are all about to be fulfilled?"
5Jesus said to them: "Watch out that no one deceives you. 6Many
will come in my name, claiming, 'I am he,' and will deceive many.
7When you hear of wars and rumors of wars, do not be alarmed.
Such things must happen, but the end is still to come. 8Nation will
rise against nation, and kingdom against kingdom. There will be
earthquakes in various places, and famines. These are the beginning of birth pains.
9"You must be on your guard. You will be handed over to the
local councils and flogged in the synagogues. On account of me you
will stand before governors and kings as witnesses to them. 10And
the gospel must first be preached to all nations. 11Whenever you
are arrested and brought to trial, do not worry beforehand about
what to say. Just say whatever is given you at the time, for it is not
you speaking, but the Holy Spirit.
12"Brother will betray brother to death, and a father his child.
Children will rebel against their parents and have them put to

Mark 12:41–44 THE WIDOW'S OFFERING

This story takes place in the temple in the court of women, where the treasury was located. It contained 13 trumpet-shaped receptacles used to collect donations for the temple.

1. Why do you think Jesus was watching people give to the temple?
   a. He was just killing time.
   b. He was curious.
   c. He was rating the givers.
   d. He was setting up a teaching situation for his disciples.

2. What do you think motivated the widow to give all she had?
   a. She was senile.
   b. She loved God very deeply.
   c. She was grateful for what she did have.
   d. She thought it would earn her some "brownie points" with God.

3. What was Jesus trying to teach the disciples?
   a. Poor people are better than rich people.
   b. Everyone should give to God.
   c. You should give your all to God.
   d. Your giving should be sacrificial.

4. What is your opinion of the widow's actions?
   a. Her actions were admirable, but I wouldn't do it.
   b. She was foolhardy and not using common sense.
   c. She was doing exactly what God wanted her to do.
   d. She should have talked to a financial planner.

5. What is the message of this story?
   a. We should be completely "sold-out" to God.
   b. A willing attitude, not a large amount, is all that matters.
   c. You don't need a big bank balance to be a big giver.
   d. It's not how much you give, but how much is left over, that counts with God.

6. In your opinion, why do most people give money to churches?

7. What kind of faith did the widow possess in order to give the way she did? How does the way you give financial offerings reflect your faith?

8. Why do you give to God's work? What do you give besides money?

9. Imagine yourself in this woman's place—surrounded by people who were vastly out-giving her. How do you think she felt about herself? How would it affect her view of herself to hear Jesus' affirmation of her offering?

10. How does this story make you feel about the financial stress in your life?
    a. I hate when people scrutinize my financial management.
    b. I long for the day I can "throw in large amounts" like these rich people.
    c. Like this widow, I feel all alone in trying to make ends meet.
    d. I wish I had this woman's faith.

11. What have you appreciated about this course? Go around your group and tell each person one thing you have appreciated about their giving of themselves to God or to the group.

death. 13All men will hate you because of me, but he who stands
firm to the end will be saved.
14"When you see 'the abomination that causes desolation'[a]
standing where it[b] does not belong—let the reader understand—
then let those who are in Judea flee to the mountains. 15Let no one
on the roof of his house go down or enter the house to take
anything out. 16Let no one in the field go back to get his cloak.
17How dreadful it will be in those days for pregnant women and
nursing mothers! 18Pray that this will not take place in winter,
19because those will be days of distress unequaled from the beginning, when God created the world, until now—and never to be
equaled again. 20If the Lord had not cut short those days, no one
would survive. But for the sake of the elect, whom he has chosen,
he has shortened them. 21At that time if anyone says to you, 'Look,
here is the Christ[c]!' or, 'Look, there he is!' do not believe it. 22For
false Christs and false prophets will appear and perform signs and
miracles to deceive the elect—if that were possible. 23So be on
your guard; I have told you everything ahead of time.
24"But in those days, following that distress,

" 'the sun will be darkened,
and the moon will not give its light;
25the stars will fall from the sky,
and the heavenly bodies will be shaken.'[d]

26"At that time men will see the Son of Man coming in clouds
with great power and glory. 27And he will send his angels and
gather his elect from the four winds, from the ends of the earth to
the ends of the heavens.
28"Now learn this lesson from the fig tree: As soon as its twigs
get tender and its leaves come out, you know that summer is near.
29Even so, when you see these things happening, you know that it
is near, right at the door. 30I tell you the truth, this generation[e]
will certainly not pass away until all these things have happened.
31Heaven and earth will pass away, but my words will never pass
away.

The Day and Hour Unknown

32"No one knows about that day or hour, not even the angels
in heaven, nor the Son, but only the Father. 33Be on guard! Be
alert[f]! You do not know when that time will come. 34It's like a
man going away: He leaves his house and puts his servants in
charge, each with his assigned task, and tells the one at the door to
keep watch.
35"Therefore keep watch because you do not know when the
owner of the house will come back—whether in the evening, or at
midnight, or when the rooster crows, or at dawn. 36If he comes
suddenly, do not let him find you sleeping. 37What I say to you, I
say to everyone: 'Watch!' "

Jesus Anointed at Bethany

14 Now the Passover and the Feast of Unleavened Bread were
only two days away, and the chief priests and the teachers
of the law were looking for some sly way to arrest Jesus and kill
him. 2"But not during the Feast," they said, "or the people may
riot."
3While he was in Bethany, reclining at the table in the home of
a man known as Simon the Leper, a woman came with an alabaster

[a] 14 Daniel 9:27; 11:31; 12:11 [b] 14 Or *he*; also in verse 29 [c] 21 Or *Messiah*
[d] 25 Isaiah 13:10; 34:4 [e] 30 Or *race* [f] 33 Some manuscripts *alert and pray*

will the Son of Man come (vv. 24–27)? **6.** How does the "fig tree" lesson (vv. 28–29) answer the disciples' questions from verse 4 (also 11:12–14,20–21)? **7.** What promises does Jesus give in verses 30–31? How would this comfort (or discomfort) the disciples? What impact do these promises have on you, 21 centuries later? **8.** How do you reconcile Jesus' predictions of the destruction of Jerusalem with his predictions of his return? **9.** Why do you think the Father has kept the time secret (v. 32)? What is the responsibility of believers in the meantime?

1. Have you ever faced persecution for your faith? What happened? **2.** When you see the forces of evil apparently winning, do you feel like withdrawing from the battle and perching on the rooftop? Or rolling up your sleeves and getting into the fray? **3.** What is the most exciting thing to you about the Second Coming? The most distressing? What questions would you like to ask Jesus about it? **4.** Specifically, how can you fulfill verses 33 and 37: "Be on guard! Be alert ... Watch!"?

If you had a year's wages to blow on friends, which would you choose: (a) Big party for all? (b) Glorious trip for a few? or (c) Extravagant gift for one?

1. How does this woman's action (v. 3) strike you: Thoughtful, but misguided? Tasteful, but extravagant? Wasteful, no buts about it? Honoring to the Nth degree? **2.** Do you think the perfume could have been better used? Why? How was her action justified by Jesus (vv. 6–9) and used by Judas (vv. 10–11)?

1. What "beautiful thing" (v. 6) would you like to do for Jesus that some might see as wasteful? 2. What is the most beautiful, touching thing you have ever seen one person do for another? What is the most beautiful, touching thing another person has ever done for you?

jar of very expensive perfume, made of pure nard. She broke the jar
and poured the perfume on his head.
4 Some of those present were saying indignantly to one another,
"Why this waste of perfume? 5 It could have been sold for more
than a year's wages[a] and the money given to the poor." And they
rebuked her harshly.
6 "Leave her alone," said Jesus. "Why are you bothering her? She
has done a beautiful thing to me. 7 The poor you will always have
with you, and you can help them any time you want. But you will
not always have me. 8 She did what she could. She poured perfume
on my body beforehand to prepare for my burial. 9 I tell you the
truth, wherever the gospel is preached throughout the world, what
she has done will also be told, in memory of her."
10 Then Judas Iscariot, one of the Twelve, went to the chief
priests to betray Jesus to them. 11 They were delighted to hear this
and promised to give him money. So he watched for an opportunity
to hand him over.

1. What is one of your favorite places to eat? What makes it special? 2. What favorite meal does Mom prepare on your special days?

1. How does this meal relate to the Passover (see Ex 12)? 2. Why would secrecy be needed as this meal was planned? What risk was involved? 3. What does Jesus say about his betrayer? How do the disciples react to that bombshell? 4. What new meaning did Jesus give to the Passover bread? The wine? What vow did he make? 5. How much do you think the disciples understood when Jesus spoke about his body and blood?

1. How would you have felt if you had been at that meal? 2. What is your focus when you partake of Communion? Why is Communion important to a body of believers? 3. What do you think the disciples were thinking when Jesus said, "this is my body" and "this is my blood"?

The Lord's Supper

12 On the first day of the Feast of Unleavened Bread, when it was
customary to sacrifice the Passover lamb, Jesus' disciples asked
him, "Where do you want us to go and make preparations for you
to eat the Passover?"
13 So he sent two of his disciples, telling them, "Go into the city,
and a man carrying a jar of water will meet you. Follow him. 14 Say
to the owner of the house he enters, 'The Teacher asks: Where is
my guest room, where I may eat the Passover with my disciples?'
15 He will show you a large upper room, furnished and ready. Make
preparations for us there."
16 The disciples left, went into the city and found things just as
Jesus had told them. So they prepared the Passover.
17 When evening came, Jesus arrived with the Twelve. 18 While
they were reclining at the table eating, he said, "I tell you the
truth, one of you will betray me—one who is eating with me."
19 They were saddened, and one by one they said to him, "Surely
not I?"
20 "It is one of the Twelve," he replied, "one who dips bread into
the bowl with me. 21 The Son of Man will go just as it is written
about him. But woe to that man who betrays the Son of Man! It
would be better for him if he had not been born."
22 While they were eating, Jesus took bread, gave thanks and
broke it, and gave it to his disciples, saying, "Take it; this is my
body."
23 Then he took the cup, gave thanks and offered it to them, and
they all drank from it.
24 "This is my blood of the[b] covenant, which is poured out for
many," he said to them. 25 "I tell you the truth, I will not drink
again of the fruit of the vine until that day when I drink it anew in
the kingdom of God."
26 When they had sung a hymn, they went out to the Mount of
Olives.

Where do you go (or what do you do) when you're facing difficult situations? Do you prefer to be alone at these times, or in the company of close friends?

Jesus Predicts Peter's Denial

27 "You will all fall away," Jesus told them, "for it is written:

> " 'I will strike the shepherd,
> and the sheep will be scattered.'[c]

[a] 5 Greek *than three hundred denarii* [b] 24 Some manuscripts *the new*
[c] 27 Zech. 13:7

28But after I have risen, I will go ahead of you into Galilee."
29Peter declared, "Even if all fall away, I will not."
30"I tell you the truth," Jesus answered, "today—yes, tonight—
before the rooster crows twice[a] you yourself will disown me three
times."
31But Peter insisted emphatically, "Even if I have to die with
you, I will never disown you." And all the others said the same.

Gethsemane

32They went to a place called Gethsemane, and Jesus said to his
disciples, "Sit here while I pray." 33He took Peter, James and John
along with him, and he began to be deeply distressed and troubled.
34"My soul is overwhelmed with sorrow to the point of death," he
said to them. "Stay here and keep watch."
35Going a little farther, he fell to the ground and prayed that if
possible the hour might pass from him. 36*"Abba,*[b] Father," he
said, "everything is possible for you. Take this cup from me. Yet
not what I will, but what you will."
37Then he returned to his disciples and found them sleeping.
"Simon," he said to Peter, "are you asleep? Could you not keep
watch for one hour? 38Watch and pray so that you will not fall into
temptation. The spirit is willing, but the body is weak."
39Once more he went away and prayed the same thing. 40When
he came back, he again found them sleeping, because their eyes
were heavy. They did not know what to say to him.
41Returning the third time, he said to them, "Are you still sleep-

[a]30 Some early manuscripts do not have *twice.* [b]36 Aramaic for *Father*

1. How does Peter see himself in relation to the other disciples? Was Peter sincere in verse 29? **2.** Why do you think Jesus warned the disciples (especially Peter) of their upcoming denial? **3.** Why did Jesus take Peter, James and John with him to pray (v. 33)? **4.** Why don't the disciples share Jesus' sense of urgency? How does this relate to their statements in the previous passage? **5.** Why did this woman know to prepare Jesus for his burial when the disciples did not? **6.** Why did Jesus urge Peter specifically to "watch and pray" (v. 34)?

1. How do you feel, realizing that Jesus knows your weaknesses and failures? **2.** When, if ever, have you faced a Gethsemane? What happened? **3.** What determines for whom and what you pray? How will the Gethsemane story change the way you pray this week?

Mark 14:32–42 JESUS IN GETHSEMANE

Just after the Last Supper and before his arrest, Jesus goes to a garden (or orchard) outside Jerusalem to pray.

1. Why do you think Jesus went to Gethsemane to pray?
   a. It was part of his routine.
   b. He was stressed out and knew he needed strength and guidance.
   c. He wanted to provide a good example for his disciples.
   d. It was his last chance to ask God for a plan other than the cross.

2. Why did Jesus take Peter, James and John along with him?
   a. He wanted them on the lookout.
   b. He needed their support.
   c. He was testing their endurance.
   d. He wanted them to pray for him.
   e. He knew they needed to pray for themselves.

3. If Jesus knew his mission was to go to the cross, why was he flinching at doing God's will?
   a. Being human, he was scared.
   b. He faced the same battle we face—submitting to God's will.
   c. He knew the cross was painful.
   d. He dreaded taking the sins of the world upon himself.
   e. The closer he got to the cross, the worse the pressure became.

4. How do you think Jesus felt when he said to his disciples, "Could you not keep watch for one hour?"
   a. let down
   b. sympathetic
   c. unimportant
   d. angry
   e. lonely
   f. sad

5. What is more of a struggle for you?
   a. finding God's will for my life
   b. doing what I know God wants
   c. standing alone without the support of others
   d. watching someone I love struggle

6. What is the closest you have come to going through a time of stress and soul-searching like Jesus did here?

7. When has there been a time you felt you relied on friends and they "fell asleep on you"? How did you react?

8. If you were to go through a time of agony like Jesus did in this story, what three people (not in this group) would you choose to be with you?

9. Which of the following experiences of loneliness have you had in the last month?
   a. feeling alone in a crowd
   b. feeling abandoned by friends
   c. feeling desperate for close friends
   d. feeling nobody understands me
   e. feeling everyone was out to get me
   f. having no one just to have fun with

10. How does this story relate to your situation in life?
   a. It's not wrong for me to ask God for my situation to change.
   b. Part of prayer is becoming willing to submit to God's plan for my life.
   c. God's will for my life may not be easy, but it is best.
   d. God can give me strength and grace to be alone.
   e. My "spirit" is willing to be single, but my "body" would rather not.

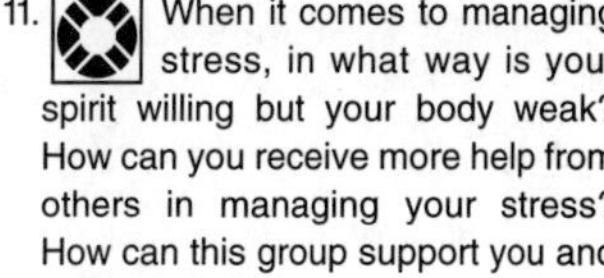

11. When it comes to managing stress, in what way is your spirit willing but your body weak? How can you receive more help from others in managing your stress? How can this group support you and pray for you?

ing and resting? Enough! The hour has come. Look, the Son of Man
is betrayed into the hands of sinners. 42Rise! Let us go! Here comes
my betrayer!"

How would you react if one of your kids (or parents!) was arrested?

1. Why is the crowd armed (v. 48)? What does this tell you about Judas' misunderstanding of Jesus' mission? **2.** How do you account for the disciples' reactions (vv. 47,50,51)?

In times of crisis, how do you respond: Like the impulsive disciple? Like Judas? Like the naked disciple? What would help you respond like Jesus did?

Jesus Arrested

43Just as he was speaking, Judas, one of the Twelve, appeared.
With him was a crowd armed with swords and clubs, sent from the
chief priests, the teachers of the law, and the elders.
44Now the betrayer had arranged a signal with them: "The one I
kiss is the man; arrest him and lead him away under guard."
45Going at once to Jesus, Judas said, "Rabbi!" and kissed him.
46The men seized Jesus and arrested him. 47Then one of those
standing near drew his sword and struck the servant of the high
priest, cutting off his ear.
48"Am I leading a rebellion," said Jesus, "that you have come out
with swords and clubs to capture me? 49Every day I was with you,
teaching in the temple courts, and you did not arrest me. But the
Scriptures must be fulfilled." 50Then everyone deserted him and
fled.
51A young man, wearing nothing but a linen garment, was following Jesus. When they seized him, 52he fled naked, leaving his
garment behind.

Have you ever gotten a bad deal from a judge or a policeman? How did it make you feel?

1. What does the fact that Peter has followed Jesus (at a distance) tell you about Peter's character? **2.** What perversions of justice do you find in Jesus' trial? Why do you think that Jesus, for the most part, remains silent? **3.** What is the significance of Jesus' messianic acknowledgement, the first direct confession recorded in Mark (v. 62; see Ps 110:1 and Da 7:13)? **4.** If the high priest, chief priests, elders and teachers of the law were waiting for the Messiah, why would they consider it blasphemy when the actual Messiah, who is right in front of them, identifies himself?

1. How does Jesus' behavior differ from that of the priests, elders and teachers? What does this say about the character of each? **2.** What would your reaction be to seeing Jesus spit on, blindfolded, struck and mocked?

Before the Sanhedrin

53They took Jesus to the high priest, and all the chief priests,
elders and teachers of the law came together. 54Peter followed him
at a distance, right into the courtyard of the high priest. There he
sat with the guards and warmed himself at the fire.
55The chief priests and the whole Sanhedrin were looking for
evidence against Jesus so that they could put him to death, but they
did not find any. 56Many testified falsely against him, but their
statements did not agree.
57Then some stood up and gave this false testimony against him:
58"We heard him say, 'I will destroy this man-made temple and in
three days will build another, not made by man.' " 59Yet even then
their testimony did not agree.
60Then the high priest stood up before them and asked Jesus,
"Are you not going to answer? What is this testimony that these
men are bringing against you?" 61But Jesus remained silent and
gave no answer.

Again the high priest asked him, "Are you the Christ,[a] the Son
of the Blessed One?"
62"I am," said Jesus. "And you will see the Son of Man sitting at
the right hand of the Mighty One and coming on the clouds of
heaven."
63The high priest tore his clothes. "Why do we need any more
witnesses?" he asked. 64"You have heard the blasphemy. What do
you think?"

They all condemned him as worthy of death. 65Then some began
to spit at him; they blindfolded him, struck him with their fists,
and said, "Prophesy!" And the guards took him and beat him.

When in your life were you most disappointed with yourself?

1. Peter is brave enough to follow Jesus to the high priest's house. Why do you think he now denies Christ (v. 68)? Do

Peter Disowns Jesus

66While Peter was below in the courtyard, one of the servant
girls of the high priest came by. 67When she saw Peter warming
himself, she looked closely at him.

"You also were with that Nazarene, Jesus," she said.

[a]*61* Or *Messiah*

68 But he denied it. "I don't know or understand what you're
talking about," he said, and went out into the entryway.[a]
69 When the servant girl saw him there, she said again to those
standing around, "This fellow is one of them." 70 Again he denied it.
After a little while, those standing near said to Peter, "Surely you
are one of them, for you are a Galilean."
71 He began to call down curses on himself, and he swore to
them, "I don't know this man you're talking about."
72 Immediately the rooster crowed the second time.[b] Then Peter remembered the word Jesus had spoken to him: "Before the
rooster crows twice[c] you will disown me three times." And he
broke down and wept.

Jesus Before Pilate

15 Very early in the morning, the chief priests, with the elders, the teachers of the law and the whole Sanhedrin,
reached a decision. They bound Jesus, led him away and handed
him over to Pilate.
2 "Are you the king of the Jews?" asked Pilate.
"Yes, it is as you say," Jesus replied.
3 The chief priests accused him of many things. 4 So again Pilate
asked him, "Aren't you going to answer? See how many things
they are accusing you of."
5 But Jesus still made no reply, and Pilate was amazed.

[a] 68 Some early manuscripts *entryway and the rooster crowed* [b] 72 Some early manuscripts do not have *the second time.* [c] 72 Some early manuscripts do not have *twice.*

you think he realized what he was doing? Why? **2.** How were the three denials similar? Different?

1. When, if ever, have you felt that your failures had made it impossible for Christ to use you again? **2.** What "rooster" reminds you of failure and guilt? What helps then?

---

1. As a child, would you rather have been punished by Mom or by Dad? Why? **2.** Were you ever bullied as a child? What happened? How did it feel?

1. What insights into Pilate's and Jesus' character does this story offer? Why is Pilate indecisive (v. 12)? Why is Jesus silent? **2.** Why do the people, after witnessing Jesus' miracles, hearing his teachings, and praising him with hosannas, now demand that Jesus be crucified? **3.** Why does Pilate grant their request? **4.** What insights into the Gospel do you see

Mark 15:1–15 JESUS BEFORE PILATE

The night before this, Jesus had been arrested and brought before the Sanhedrin (Jewish high court consisting of 71 religious leaders). He was found guilty of blasphemy—a crime punishable by death. However, the Sanhedrin's power was limited by Roman rule; so now they bring Jesus to Pilate, the Roman governor, with a request for his execution.

1. If you were a film director, how would you portray Pilate?
   a. a smooth politician
   b. a wimp
   c. a victim of circumstances
   d. a pragmatist—going with the flow

2. Why was Jesus so silent throughout his trials?
   a. His words had been so twisted against him, there was no point in speaking.
   b. He trusted God's plan.
   c. The ears of his accusers were sealed against him.
   d. The Old Testament prophesied the Messiah's silence before his accusers.

3. Do you think the Roman governor knew Jesus was innocent?
   a. absolutely
   b. probably
   c. It's hard to say.
   d. If he didn't, he was blind.

4. Why did Pilate offer to release a prisoner chosen by the crowd?
   a. to check out their motives
   b. to expose their hypocrisy
   c. to get Jesus off the hook
   d. to keep everybody happy
   e. to avoid making a decision

5. Who ended up the biggest winner and who ended up the biggest loser in Jesus' sentence of crucifixion?
   a. Pilate d. Jesus
   b. Sanhedrin e. the crowd
   c. Barabbas f. me

6. How can you relate to each of the following?
   a. Pilate—selling short my convictions in exchange for "peace"
   b. Jesus—acting on my convictions and suffering the consequences
   c. Barabbas—guilty, yet released

7. What do you find most amazing about this story?
   a. that Jesus was so silent
   b. that the people turned on Jesus
   c. that Jesus was so misunderstood
   d. that Jesus was so mistreated
   e. that a murderer was released instead of the Messiah
   f. that Jesus took my place so my sins could be forgiven
   g. that Jesus allowed all this to happen when he could have used his great powers to escape

8. At what point in your life did you ask Jesus to forgive your sins, realizing he died as your substitute?
   a. as a child
   b. years ago
   c. just recently
   d. I don't know that I have.

9. Close with a time of silent prayer—thanking Christ for his sacrifice, confessing your need for forgiveness, and committing/recommitting your life to him.

6 Now it was the custom at the Feast to release a prisoner whom
the people requested. 7 A man called Barabbas was in prison with
the insurrectionists who had committed murder in the uprising.
8 The crowd came up and asked Pilate to do for them what he
usually did.
9 "Do you want me to release to you the king of the Jews?" asked
Pilate, 10 knowing it was out of envy that the chief priests had
handed Jesus over to him. 11 But the chief priests stirred up the
crowd to have Pilate release Barabbas instead.
12 "What shall I do, then, with the one you call the king of the
Jews?" Pilate asked them.
13 "Crucify him!" they shouted.
14 "Why? What crime has he committed?" asked Pilate.
But they shouted all the louder, "Crucify him!"
15 Wanting to satisfy the crowd, Pilate released Barabbas to them.
He had Jesus flogged, and handed him over to be crucified.

The Soldiers Mock Jesus

16 The soldiers led Jesus away into the palace (that is, the Praetorium) and called together the whole company of soldiers. 17 They
put a purple robe on him, then twisted together a crown of thorns
and set it on him. 18 And they began to call out to him, "Hail, king
of the Jews!" 19 Again and again they struck him on the head with
a staff and spit on him. Falling on their knees, they paid homage to
him. 20 And when they had mocked him, they took off the purple
robe and put his own clothes on him. Then they led him out to
crucify him.

The Crucifixion

21 A certain man from Cyrene, Simon, the father of Alexander
and Rufus, was passing by on his way in from the country, and they
forced him to carry the cross. 22 They brought Jesus to the place
called Golgotha (which means The Place of the Skull). 23 Then they
offered him wine mixed with myrrh, but he did not take it. 24 And
they crucified him. Dividing up his clothes, they cast lots to see
what each would get.
25 It was the third hour when they crucified him. 26 The written
notice of the charge against him read: THE KING OF THE JEWS. 27 They
crucified two robbers with him, one on his right and one on his
left.[a] 29 Those who passed by hurled insults at him, shaking their
heads and saying, "So! You who are going to destroy the temple
and build it in three days, 30 come down from the cross and save
yourself!"
31 In the same way the chief priests and the teachers of the law
mocked him among themselves. "He saved others," they said, "but
he can't save himself! 32 Let this Christ,[b] this King of Israel, come
down now from the cross, that we may see and believe." Those
crucified with him also heaped insults on him.

The Death of Jesus

33 At the sixth hour darkness came over the whole land until the
ninth hour. 34 And at the ninth hour Jesus cried out in a loud voice,
"Eloi, Eloi, lama sabachthani?"—which means, "My God, my
God, why have you forsaken me?"[c]
35 When some of those standing near heard this, they said, "Listen, he's calling Elijah."
36 One man ran, filled a sponge with wine vinegar, put it on a

[a] *27* Some manuscripts *left, 28and the scripture was fulfilled which says, "He was counted with the lawless ones"* (Isaiah 53:12) [b] *32* Or *Messiah* [c] *34* Psalm 22:1

in the release of Barabbas in exchange for Jesus (see 8:37; 10:45)? **5.** What mental, physical and emotional brutality do the soldiers inflict on Jesus? Why? Does their mockery stem from fear, anger, unbelief or what?

1. Why did Jesus go through this trial and torture when he could easily have used his great powers and escaped? How does this make you feel? What does it make you want to do? **2.** If you were the only person in the world, would Jesus have done the same thing? **3.** Have your actions ever mocked the name of Jesus? What can you do to resist this kind of behavior?

---

1. Have you ever sat with someone who was dying? What was it like? **2.** How do you feel deep down when you attend funerals and burials?

1. Why is Simon needed to carry Jesus' cross (see 14:65; 15:15,19)? How might that affect him? **2.** What kinds of people were usually crucified (v. 27)? How is Jesus like them? **3.** What further insults are added to injury (vv. 29–32)? **4.** What ironies do you see here: In the places occupied by the robbers (see 10:37)? In the call for Jesus to save himself by coming down from the cross? In the officially posted reason for Jesus' death? **5.** What aspect of the crucifixion was the worst for Jesus: The physical pain? Feeling forsaken by God? What does this say about our part in his crucifixion? **6.** How are the cry of Jesus (v. 34; also Ps 22:1), the tearing of the temple curtain (v. 38; see Mt 27:51–53; Heb 10:19–22), and the faith of the centurion (v. 39) all related? **7.** What do you learn about Joseph (vv. 43–46)? What risks does a man of his status take by this action? **8.** What is significant about the centurion's confirmation of Jesus' death? About the eyewitnesses of his burial (Mt 28:11–15)?

stick, and offered it to Jesus to drink. "Now leave him alone. Let's see if Elijah comes to take him down," he said.

37With a loud cry, Jesus breathed his last.

38The curtain of the temple was torn in two from top to bottom. 39And when the centurion, who stood there in front of Jesus, heard his cry and[a] saw how he died, he said, "Surely this man was the Son[b] of God!"

40Some women were watching from a distance. Among them were Mary Magdalene, Mary the mother of James the younger and of Joses, and Salome. 41In Galilee these women had followed him and cared for his needs. Many other women who had come up with him to Jerusalem were also there.

The Burial of Jesus

42It was Preparation Day (that is, the day before the Sabbath). So as evening approached, 43Joseph of Arimathea, a prominent member of the Council, who was himself waiting for the kingdom of God, went boldly to Pilate and asked for Jesus' body. 44Pilate was surprised to hear that he was already dead. Summoning the centurion, he asked him if Jesus had already died. 45When he learned from the centurion that it was so, he gave the body to Joseph. 46So Joseph bought some linen cloth, took down the body, wrapped it in the linen, and placed it in a tomb cut out of rock. Then he rolled a stone against the entrance of the tomb. 47Mary Magdalene and Mary the mother of Joses saw where he was laid.

The Resurrection

16 When the Sabbath was over, Mary Magdalene, Mary the mother of James, and Salome bought spices so that they might go to anoint Jesus' body. 2Very early on the first day of the week, just after sunrise, they were on their way to the tomb 3and they asked each other, "Who will roll the stone away from the entrance of the tomb?"

4But when they looked up, they saw that the stone, which was very large, had been rolled away. 5As they entered the tomb, they saw a young man dressed in a white robe sitting on the right side, and they were alarmed.

6"Don't be alarmed," he said. "You are looking for Jesus the Nazarene, who was crucified. He has risen! He is not here. See the place where they laid him. 7But go, tell his disciples and Peter, 'He is going ahead of you into Galilee. There you will see him, just as he told you.' "

8Trembling and bewildered, the women went out and fled from the tomb. They said nothing to anyone, because they were afraid.

[The earliest manuscripts and some other ancient witnesses do not have Mark 16:9–20.]

9When Jesus rose early on the first day of the week, he appeared first to Mary Magdalene, out of whom he had driven seven demons. 10She went and told those who had been with him and who were mourning and weeping. 11When they heard that Jesus was alive and that she had seen him, they did not believe it.

12Afterward Jesus appeared in a different form to two of them

[a]39 Some manuscripts do not have *heard his cry and* [b]39 Or *a son*

1. Read Isaiah 53:12. How would you paraphrase it to explain what Jesus' death was all about? **2.** What curtain do you feel still separates you from God? How does Jesus' death relate to that? **3.** What is the riskiest thing you have ever done because of your faith in Jesus? Why did you do it? **4.** When did the crucifixion begin to make a difference in your own life?

---

1. What do you like to do on Sunday mornings? **2.** What was the most incredible event you have ever seen? Convince your small group it really happened. What difficulties do you experience in the retelling of your eyewitness account?

1. Mary Magdalene and Mary, the mother of James and Salome, were never very far away during the crucifixion and entombment of Christ (see 15:40–41). What does this tell you about the faith of these women? What does this tell you about the role of women in Jesus' life? **2.** What potential problem looms ahead (v. 3)? What do they find instead? What do they fear? Seeing the empty tomb and the man sitting beside it, what thoughts are racing through their heads? **3.** Do you think they believed the man (v. 8)? How do their actions support your answer? **4.** Why do you think the angel asked them specifically to speak to Peter? What does this tell you about Jesus' plans for Peter?

1. Would you have had trouble believing the angel's words? Why or why not? **2.** Who did Jesus send to you to tell you he had risen? Did you have trouble believing that person? How were you finally convinced of Jesus' resurrection? **3.** To whom is Jesus sending you with this message? How will you accomplish this mission? **4.** Where is your spiritual life focused these days: On Good Friday? Easter Sunday? Or in between? **5.** How would your life be different if Jesus was not risen from the dead? **6.** What will you remember most from the Gospel of Mark to sharpen your focus of who Jesus really is?

while they were walking in the country. 13 These returned and
reported it to the rest; but they did not believe them either.

14 Later Jesus appeared to the Eleven as they were eating; he
rebuked them for their lack of faith and their stubborn refusal to
believe those who had seen him after he had risen.

15 He said to them, “Go into all the world and preach the good
news to all creation. 16 Whoever believes and is baptized will be
saved, but whoever does not believe will be condemned. 17 And
these signs will accompany those who believe: In my name they
will drive out demons; they will speak in new tongues; 18 they will
pick up snakes with their hands; and when they drink deadly
poison, it will not hurt them at all; they will place their hands on
sick people, and they will get well.”

19 After the Lord Jesus had spoken to them, he was taken up into
heaven and he sat at the right hand of God. 20 Then the disciples
went out and preached everywhere, and the Lord worked with
them and confirmed his word by the signs that accompanied it.

INTRODUCTION to
LUKE

Book Study Outline: If you are using Luke for a study course, here is a 7- or 13-week outline. Use the margin questions for your group agenda:

- start meeting / 15 min.
- read & discuss Bible / 30 min.
- close meeting / 15–45 min.

Refer to the Questions and Answers in front of Bible for more information.

7-week plan	13-week plan	Personal Reading	Group Study Passage
	1	1:1–38	1:26–38/Jesus Foretold
1	2	1:39–2:20	2:1–20/Birth of Jesus
	3	2:21–4:30	4:14–30/Jesus Rejected
2	4	4:31–7:50	5:27–39/Levi; Wineskins
	5	8:1–10:37	10:25–37/Good Samaritan
3	6	10:38–12:12	10:38–42/Martha and Mary
	7	12:13–15:10	12:13–21/The Rich Fool
4	8	15:11–16:18	15:11–32/The Prodigal Son
	9	16:19–18:8	16:19–31/Heaven and Hell
5	10	18:9–22:6	18:9–14/Two Prayers
	11	22:7–23:43	22:7–34/Last Supper
6	12	23:44–24:12	23:44–49/Jesus' Death
7	13	24:13–53	24:13–35/Road to Emmaus

Author: While the book itself is anonymous, traditionally it is thought to be the work of Luke the physician, Paul's coworker and companion (Col 4:14; 2Ti 4:11). Luke is the only non-Jewish author in the New Testament. The Gospel of Luke is Volume I ("The Story of Jesus") in Luke's two-part account. The Acts of the Apostles is Volume II ("The Story of the Church").

Date: Uncertain, probably sometime after the fall of Jerusalem in A.D. 70.

Theme: Jesus is the Savior of the whole world.

Historical Background: Luke wrote this record of Jesus' life for a Gentile audience. In 1:3 he addresses the book to Theophilus, an unknown but probably wealthy Roman aristocrat.

Characteristics: Luke is the longest book in the NT. While using much of the same material as Mark and Matthew, Luke adds his own distinctive flavor to the story. This Gospel is marked by joy (1:46–47; 15:8–32; 24:52–53), songs of praise (1:46–55,68–79; 2:14,29–32), and an interest in the relationship of Jesus with people considered outcasts by his fellow countrymen (e.g., women, children, the poor, tax collectors and Samaritans). Luke's Gentile orientation is seen in the fact that Jesus' genealogy is traced back to Adam, the founder of the human race, rather than back to Abraham, the founder of the Jewish race (as Matthew does). Luke seldom quotes the OT, and he translates Hebrew words into their Greek equivalents. This is a book that tells how the promised Jewish Messiah is indeed the Savior of the whole world.

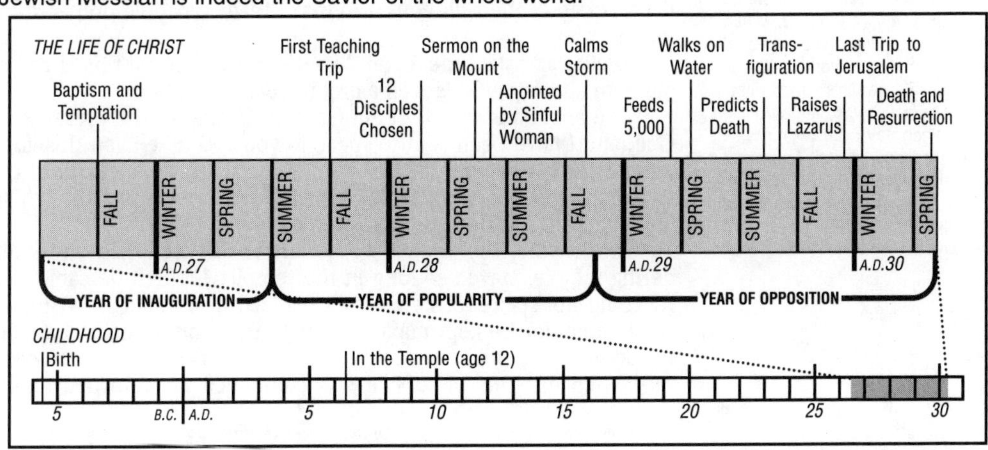

Luke

1. Have you drawn up your last will and testament? What important facts did you include? Who would you choose as the biographer of your life story, and why? **2.** What is a recent surprise that your family has experienced: A job promotion? A new addition to the family? Your child earned all "A's"? You joined this Bible study?

1. What do you learn from verses 1–4 about Luke? About the reason he wrote this Gospel? About his sources? **2.** What stands out to you about Zechariah and Elizabeth (vv. 5–7)? What feelings might the couple have had in light of their barrenness? **3.** What was the significance of the task for which Zechariah was chosen (see 1Ch 23:13)? Since many priests never had the chance to go into the temple and burn incense, what might he be feeling as he prepares for it? How about when the angel appears? **4.** What is the connection between alcohol and the Holy Spirit (see Eph 5:18)? **5.** How would the birth of this son affect Zechariah and Elizabeth? Describe the child's mission in your own words. Why would Zechariah doubt? **6.** In the meantime, how were the people feeling (v. 21)? What did they think when Zechariah emerged from the temple, mute?

1. Of the major characters in this story—Zechariah, Elizabeth, John—with whom do you identify most? Why? With whom do you identify least? Why? **2.** When was the last time you doubted God? What caused your doubt? **3.** Consider Zechariah's and Elizabeth's character (v. 6) and struggle (v. 7). When have you been obedient to God and still felt forgotten? What does this story tell you? **4.** How is John's mission a model for your mission today? How might you "prepare" people for the Lord?

Introduction

1 Many have undertaken to draw up an account of the things that have been fulfilled[a] among us, 2just as they were handed down to us by those who from the first were eyewitnesses and servants of the word. 3Therefore, since I myself have carefully investigated everything from the beginning, it seemed good also to me to write an orderly account for you, most excellent Theophilus, 4so that you may know the certainty of the things you have been taught.

The Birth of John the Baptist Foretold

5In the time of Herod king of Judea there was a priest named Zechariah, who belonged to the priestly division of Abijah; his wife Elizabeth was also a descendant of Aaron. 6Both of them were upright in the sight of God, observing all the Lord's commandments and regulations blamelessly. 7But they had no children, because Elizabeth was barren; and they were both well along in years.

8Once when Zechariah's division was on duty and he was serving as priest before God, 9he was chosen by lot, according to the custom of the priesthood, to go into the temple of the Lord and burn incense. 10And when the time for the burning of incense came, all the assembled worshipers were praying outside.

11Then an angel of the Lord appeared to him, standing at the right side of the altar of incense. 12When Zechariah saw him, he was startled and was gripped with fear. 13But the angel said to him: "Do not be afraid, Zechariah; your prayer has been heard. Your wife Elizabeth will bear you a son, and you are to give him the name John. 14He will be a joy and delight to you, and many will rejoice because of his birth, 15for he will be great in the sight of the Lord. He is never to take wine or other fermented drink, and he will be filled with the Holy Spirit even from birth.[b] 16Many of the people of Israel will he bring back to the Lord their God. 17And he will go on before the Lord, in the spirit and power of Elijah, to turn the hearts of the fathers to their children and the disobedient to the wisdom of the righteous—to make ready a people prepared for the Lord."

18Zechariah asked the angel, "How can I be sure of this? I am an old man and my wife is well along in years."

19The angel answered, "I am Gabriel. I stand in the presence of God, and I have been sent to speak to you and to tell you this good news. 20And now you will be silent and not able to speak until the day this happens, because you did not believe my words, which will come true at their proper time."

21Meanwhile, the people were waiting for Zechariah and wondering why he stayed so long in the temple. 22When he came out, he could not speak to them. They realized he had seen a vision in the temple, for he kept making signs to them but remained unable to speak.

23When his time of service was completed, he returned home.

[a] *1* Or *been surely believed* [b] *15* Or *from his mother's womb*

24After this his wife Elizabeth became pregnant and for five months
remained in seclusion. 25"The Lord has done this for me," she said.
"In these days he has shown his favor and taken away my disgrace
among the people."

The Birth of Jesus Foretold

26In the sixth month, God sent the angel Gabriel to Nazareth, a
town in Galilee, 27to a virgin pledged to be married to a man
named Joseph, a descendant of David. The virgin's name was
Mary. 28The angel went to her and said, "Greetings, you who are
highly favored! The Lord is with you."

29Mary was greatly troubled at his words and wondered what
kind of greeting this might be. 30But the angel said to her, "Do not
be afraid, Mary, you have found favor with God. 31You will be with
child and give birth to a son, and you are to give him the name
Jesus. 32He will be great and will be called the Son of the Most
High. The Lord God will give him the throne of his father David,
33and he will reign over the house of Jacob forever; his kingdom
will never end."

34"How will this be," Mary asked the angel, "since I am a virgin?"

35The angel answered, "The Holy Spirit will come upon you, and
the power of the Most High will overshadow you. So the holy one
to be born will be called[a] the Son of God. 36Even Elizabeth your
relative is going to have a child in her old age, and she who was
said to be barren is in her sixth month. 37For nothing is impossible
with God."

If told that you (or your parents) were to have a child this year, how would you react?

1. How does Gabriel's word to Mary compare with his word to Zechariah (1:13–17)? **2.** How does Mary (vv. 34,38) respond differently than Zechariah (vv. 12,18)? **3.** What truths about Jesus are emphasized here? What expectations must have been raised in Mary?

1. What would it mean to doubt and fear God? When were you recently fearful but believing? How did God meet you? **2.** In what area of your life do you need to believe that nothing is impossible with God? What keeps you from believing this?

[a]35 Or *So the child to be born will be called holy,*

Luke 1:26–38 THE BIRTH OF JESUS FORETOLD

1. What was Mary's initial reaction to the appearance of the angel?
   a. fear
   b. curiosity
   c. confusion
   d. doubt
   e. faith
   f. concern

2. If you had been Mary, what would have been hardest to comprehend?
   a. being favored by God
   b. getting pregnant as a virgin
   c. who her child was going to be
   d. how to explain this to others, especially Joseph and her family

3. How do you think Mary felt about giving birth to the Messiah?
   a. scared
   b. honored
   c. burdened
   d. overjoyed
   e. lonely
   f. clueless

4. If an angel were to reveal God's plan for my life today, I would:
   a. ask a lot of questions.
   b. wonder if I had any say about it.
   c. rejoice that God could use me.
   d. worry about my ability to do it.
   e. run away scared.
   f. tell the angel I would rather not know my future.

5. What point about Jesus sticks out to you the most?
   a. his conception—by the Holy Spirit and a virgin
   b. his nature—God's holy Son
   c. his authority—as an eternal King
   d. his mission—as Savior (*Jesus* means "the Lord saves")

6. My understanding of who Jesus is:
   a. came as an instantaneous insight.
   b. came over time.
   c. has begun and is still coming.
   d. hasn't come very clearly yet.
   e. other:____________________

7. Who was the "angel" God sent to help explain the truth about Jesus Christ to you?

8. In what area of your life do you need to believe that "nothing is impossible with God"? What keeps you from believing him?

9. What did you think of Jesus and his birth when you were younger?
   a. Santa Claus was more exciting.
   b. It made for a nice children's play.
   c. Jesus seemed more "spiritual" than real.
   d. I can't remember not wanting Jesus to be first in my life.

10. What do you think of Jesus and his birth *now?*

11. How do you feel about being in a group studying about "becoming a Christian"?
   a. eager
   b. nervous
   c. out of place
   d. embarrassed
   e. cautious
   f. comfortable

12. How would you describe your commitment to Jesus Christ?
   a. I have lots of questions.
   b. I'm still recovering from bad experiences in the past.
   c. I'm drawn to Christ but unsure what that involves.
   d. I'm committed to Christ and want to find out all I need to know.
   e. other:____________________

38“I am the Lord’s servant,” Mary answered. “May it be to me as
you have said.” Then the angel left her.

Whom do you call first when you have good news to share?

How might Mary have felt when Elizabeth greeted her? How is she “blessed” and encouraged?

How is Mary’s faith an example to you?

Mary Visits Elizabeth

39At that time Mary got ready and hurried to a town in the hill
country of Judea, 40where she entered Zechariah’s home and greeted Elizabeth. 41When Elizabeth heard Mary’s greeting, the baby
leaped in her womb, and Elizabeth was filled with the Holy Spirit.
42In a loud voice she exclaimed: “Blessed are you among women,
and blessed is the child you will bear! 43But why am I so favored,
that the mother of my Lord should come to me? 44As soon as the
sound of your greeting reached my ears, the baby in my womb
leaped for joy. 45Blessed is she who has believed that what the Lord
has said to her will be accomplished!”

What song has been playing in your head lately? When has the song in your head annoyed you? Inspired you?

1. For what does Mary praise God in this song? What contrasts does she make in verses 51–53? How do these reflect her feelings about God? About herself? **2.** Who are the “proud,” the “rulers” and the “rich,” whose overthrow she celebrates? How will Jesus fulfill the themes of this song?

Mary’s Song

46And Mary said:

“My soul glorifies the Lord
47 and my spirit rejoices in God my Savior,
48for he has been mindful
of the humble state of his servant.
From now on all generations will call me blessed,
49 for the Mighty One has done great things for me—
holy is his name.
50His mercy extends to those who fear him,
from generation to generation.
51He has performed mighty deeds with his arm;

Luke 1:39–56 MARY VISITS ELIZABETH

The angel Gabriel appeared to Mary, telling her that, though she was a virgin, she would become the mother of the Messiah. The angel also reported that Mary’s relative Elizabeth was pregnant as well. Elizabeth was six months pregnant with the child who would be known as John the Baptist.

1. Why did Mary go to Elizabeth’s house?
   a. for a little “female bonding”
   b. to share her exciting news
   c. to share in the joy of another pregnant woman
   d. to get some advice from an older and wiser relative
   e. to get away from the talk about her “illegitimate” pregnancy

2. Why did Elizabeth’s baby leap in her womb when Mary arrived?
   a. He was a hyper child.
   b. He was filled with joy.
   c. The Lord was demonstrating how special these babies—especially Mary’s—were.
   d. Elizabeth just imagined it.

3. Why did God choose Mary to give birth to his Son?
   a. She was at the right place at the right time.
   b. She earned the honor by her holy life.
   c. God had her in mind from the beginning.
   d. Only God knows why he did.

4. How did Mary envision herself?
   a. a lowly servant
   b. a surrogate mother
   c. an ordinary person
   d. greatly blessed
   e. deserving of her recognition
   f. as someone who would never be forgotten

5. What do you need to share with an “Elizabeth” right now?
   a. a joy I’ve been wanting to share
   b. a burden I need to talk about
   c. some questions about my faith
   d. just a good time

6. Which of the words found in Mary’s song best describes how you are feeling about your spiritual life?
   a. rejoicing
   b. humble
   c. blessed
   d. proud
   e. lifted up
   f. filled
   g. hungry
   h. empty

7. What do you appreciate most about Mary?
   a. She had a humble background.
   b. She had a humble spirit.
   c. She gave God all the glory for her blessings.
   d. She had faith to believe that the amazing things she heard would be accomplished.
   e. She didn’t let what others would think about her (like getting pregnant out of wedlock) control her.

8. In what way would you like to be more like Mary?

9. What have you really appreciated about this course? Conclude your time together by affirming each other like Elizabeth affirmed Mary: One at a time, have each group member simply listen as others share with them an affirmation or blessing.

he has scattered those who are proud in their
inmost thoughts.
52He has brought down rulers from their thrones
but has lifted up the humble.
53He has filled the hungry with good things
but has sent the rich away empty.
54He has helped his servant Israel,
remembering to be merciful
55to Abraham and his descendants forever,
even as he said to our fathers."

56Mary stayed with Elizabeth for about three months and then
returned home.

The Birth of John the Baptist

57When it was time for Elizabeth to have her baby, she gave
birth to a son. 58Her neighbors and relatives heard that the Lord
had shown her great mercy, and they shared her joy.
59On the eighth day they came to circumcise the child, and they
were going to name him after his father Zechariah, 60but his mother spoke up and said, "No! He is to be called John."
61They said to her, "There is no one among your relatives who
has that name."
62Then they made signs to his father, to find out what he would
like to name the child. 63He asked for a writing tablet, and to
everyone's astonishment he wrote, "His name is John." 64Immedi-
ately his mouth was opened and his tongue was loosed, and he
began to speak, praising God. 65The neighbors were all filled with
awe, and throughout the hill country of Judea people were talking
about all these things. 66Everyone who heard this wondered about
it, asking, "What then is this child going to be?" For the Lord's
hand was with him.

Zechariah's Song

67His father Zechariah was filled with the Holy Spirit and prophesied:

68"Praise be to the Lord, the God of Israel,
because he has come and has redeemed his
people.
69He has raised up a horn[a] of salvation for us
in the house of his servant David
70(as he said through his holy prophets of long ago),
71salvation from our enemies
and from the hand of all who hate us—
72to show mercy to our fathers
and to remember his holy covenant,
73 the oath he swore to our father Abraham:
74to rescue us from the hand of our enemies,
and to enable us to serve him without fear
75 in holiness and righteousness before him all our
days.

76And you, my child, will be called a prophet of the
Most High;
for you will go on before the Lord to prepare
the way for him,
77to give his people the knowledge of salvation

[a]69 *Horn* here symbolizes strength.

1. Of the attributes of God celebrated in Mary's song, which do you appreciate the most? Which challenges you the most? Why? **2.** Considering Mary, what level of social status do you need to fulfill God's purposes? Does that encourage you? Why? **3.** Would Mary consider you God's humble servant or a proud, rich ruler?

What is your nickname and how did you get it?

1. How did John's birth fulfill the words of the angel in verses 13–17? **2.** How did the neighbors and relatives respond to these events? How does all this begin to promote the Gospel? **3.** As Zechariah's neighbor, what would you think about his son?

1. Describe a time when you, like Zechariah, took a step of faith and began speaking, praising God. **2.** How was "the Lord's hand" seen in John's life? In your life?

How did you (or would you) celebrate the birth of your first child?

1. Make a list of the things for which Zechariah praises God. How does his song compare and contrast with Mary's (vv. 46–55)? **2.** What does it mean that Zechariah was "filled with the Holy Spirit"? Is that the same experience with the Spirit that believers experience today? Why or why not? **3.** What, according to this song, is the purpose of salvation? How does Zechariah's song show God's unfolding plan from OT days to the coming of the Messiah?

1. Of the promises listed in this song, which one means the most to you? Why? **2.** How has God unfolded his plan of salvation in your life? Who helped prepare the way? What were some key events that led you to your commitment to Jesus? **3.** Write a verse of praise to God using the special events from your own spiritual journey.

through the forgiveness of their sins,
78because of the tender mercy of our God,
by which the rising sun will come to us from
heaven
79to shine on those living in darkness
and in the shadow of death,
to guide our feet into the path of peace."

80And the child grew and became strong in spirit; and he lived in
the desert until he appeared publicly to Israel.

What is one way your hometown is different now than when you grew up? Is it still home to you? Why or why not?

In light of the promises of 1:30–35, how might Mary feel as she awaits delivery in a stable? How does this tie into God's plan (Mic 5:2)?

How did God take your "hopeless situation" and use it for good? What does that teach you?

When does your Christmas tree go up? Who trims it? How? What other traditions do you observe from your childhood?

The Birth of Jesus

2 In those days Caesar Augustus issued a decree that a census
should be taken of the entire Roman world. 2(This was the first
census that took place while Quirinius was governor of Syria.)
3And everyone went to his own town to register.
4So Joseph also went up from the town of Nazareth in Galilee to
Judea, to Bethlehem the town of David, because he belonged to the
house and line of David. 5He went there to register with Mary,
who was pledged to be married to him and was expecting a child.
6While they were there, the time came for the baby to be born,
7and she gave birth to her firstborn, a son. She wrapped him in
cloths and placed him in a manger, because there was no room for
them in the inn.

The Shepherds and the Angels

8And there were shepherds living out in the fields nearby, keeping watch over their flocks at night. 9An angel of the Lord appeared
to them, and the glory of the Lord shone around them, and they

Luke 2:1–20 THE BIRTH OF JESUS

1. Pregnant before marriage. Broke. Homeless. If you were Mary and Joseph's friend, what chance would you have given them?
   a. none
   b. 50/50
   c. uphill all the way
   d. a great way to begin

2. Why do you suppose the Savior of the world was born in an obscure village and laid in a manger?
   a. to fulfill Old Testament prophecy
   b. to show he was an ordinary person
   c. It just happened that way.
   d. He demanded no special favors.
   e. God didn't want to draw attention to his son's birth.
   f. No place would have been as grand as he deserved.

3. What effect did the angelic visit have on the shepherds?
   a. They wondered if they had been dreaming.
   b. They saw God in a new way.
   c. Their lives were changed forever.
   d. It was soon business as usual.

4. What do you think the shepherds were most excited to tell others?
   a. about hearing the angels sing
   b. about seeing the newborn baby
   c. God's plan for their salvation
   d. that the angel's words were true
   e. that the wait for Messiah was over

5. Do you think Mary and Joseph understood the full significance of the child they brought into the world?
   a. probably not
   b. up to a point
   c. Mary could have.
   d. They must have.
   e. They couldn't have.

6. What effect has the news of Christ's birth had on you?
   a. business as usual
   b. spiritual commitment
   c. an awakened sense of joy
   d. hope for the future
   e. thankfulness for God's forgiveness
   f. confusion about God's plan

7. How would you describe your relationship with Jesus Christ now?

8. If you were to spread the word about what Jesus has done for you, with whom would you speak first?

9. How would Mary and Joseph's humble beginnings prepare them for parenting?
   a. It gave them a dose of real life.
   b. It caused them to grow up fast.
   c. It caused them to depend on God.
   d. It showed them that struggle is the best teacher.

10. How would you compare your start to Jesus' parents'?
    a. We were also very young.
    b. We didn't have much either.
    c. We were also under much stress.
    d. Our start was much easier.

11. What was your reaction when you found out you were going to have your first baby? Reflecting back, how prepared were you to be a parent?
    a. I was totally prepared.
    b. I was basically prepared.
    c. I was basically unprepared.
    d. I was totally unprepared.

were terrified. 10But the angel said to them, "Do not be afraid. I
bring you good news of great joy that will be for all the people.
11Today in the town of David a Savior has been born to you; he is
Christ[a] the Lord. 12This will be a sign to you: You will find a baby
wrapped in cloths and lying in a manger."
13Suddenly a great company of the heavenly host appeared with
the angel, praising God and saying,

14"Glory to God in the highest,
and on earth peace to men on whom his favor
rests."

15When the angels had left them and gone into heaven, the
shepherds said to one another, "Let's go to Bethlehem and see this
thing that has happened, which the Lord has told us about."
16So they hurried off and found Mary and Joseph, and the baby,
who was lying in the manger. 17When they had seen him, they
spread the word concerning what had been told them about this
child, 18and all who heard it were amazed at what the shepherds
said to them. 19But Mary treasured up all these things and pon-
dered them in her heart. 20The shepherds returned, glorifying and
praising God for all the things they had heard and seen, which
were just as they had been told.

Jesus Presented in the Temple

21On the eighth day, when it was time to circumcise him, he
was named Jesus, the name the angel had given him before he had
been conceived.
22When the time of their purification according to the Law of
Moses had been completed, Joseph and Mary took him to Jerusalem to present him to the Lord 23(as it is written in the Law of the
Lord, "Every firstborn male is to be consecrated to the Lord"[b]),
24and to offer a sacrifice in keeping with what is said in the Law of
the Lord: "a pair of doves or two young pigeons."[c]
25Now there was a man in Jerusalem called Simeon, who was
righteous and devout. He was waiting for the consolation of Israel,
and the Holy Spirit was upon him. 26It had been revealed to him by
the Holy Spirit that he would not die before he had seen the Lord's
Christ. 27Moved by the Spirit, he went into the temple courts.
When the parents brought in the child Jesus to do for him what the
custom of the Law required, 28Simeon took him in his arms and
praised God, saying:

29"Sovereign Lord, as you have promised,
you now dismiss[d] your servant in peace.
30For my eyes have seen your salvation,
31 which you have prepared in the sight of all
people,
32a light for revelation to the Gentiles
and for glory to your people Israel."

33The child's father and mother marveled at what was said about
him. 34Then Simeon blessed them and said to Mary, his mother:
"This child is destined to cause the falling and rising of many in
Israel, and to be a sign that will be spoken against, 35so that the
thoughts of many hearts will be revealed. And a sword will pierce
your own soul too."
36There was also a prophetess, Anna, the daughter of Phanuel, of

[a] 11 Or *Messiah.* "The Christ" (Greek) and "the Messiah" (Hebrew) both mean "the Anointed One"; also in verse 26. [b] 23 Exodus 13:2,12 [c] 24 Lev. 12:8
[d] 29 Or *promised, / now dismiss*

1. How does the shepherds' experience with the angels compare to that of Zechariah (1:8–9) and Mary (1:26–27)? **2.** Of all the people the angels could have visited, why did God send them to the shepherds? How does that relate to Mary's song (1:46–55)?

1. God appeared to Zechariah, Mary and the shepherds when they were just being themselves. What does that imply about what it means to be "spiritual"? How has God spoken to you in the ordinary flow of life? **2.** What precious event has God done that you "treasure in your heart"?

---

1. When you were growing up, what teacher, coach or relative made you feel special? How did that person make you feel good? **2.** Who is the oldest person you know?

1. What Mosaic laws are being fulfilled by this presentation (see Lev 12:1–8, Ex 13:2, 12,13)? How do these events foreshadow Jesus' mission? **2.** What does this temple ceremony reveal about the parents of Jesus: They were very poor? Religious? Proud? Dedicated? Fearful of their salvation? **3.** In Simeon's two prophecies (vv. 29–32,34–35), what was he predicting about the work of Jesus? His effect on people? The pain of his parents? **4.** Do you know anyone like dear old, saintly Anna? How does she complement Simeon's prophecy? **5.** What impact would these startling predictions by Simeon and Anna have on all who were listening that day? On the parents of Jesus as they returned home (vv. 33,39)? **6.** What do you learn about Mary and Joseph in this passage? About Jesus? About God?

1. How has Christ brought "light" to your life? How is he still the cause of "the falling and rising" of people that you know? **2.** Did your parents dedicate you to the Lord? How did they help you mature spiritually? **3.** When has God brought along a "Simeon" and "Anna" to confirm something in your life? How did this affect you?

the tribe of Asher. She was very old; she had lived with her husband seven years after her marriage, 37and then was a widow until
she was eighty-four.[a] She never left the temple but worshiped
night and day, fasting and praying. 38Coming up to them at that
very moment, she gave thanks to God and spoke about the child to
all who were looking forward to the redemption of Jerusalem.

39When Joseph and Mary had done everything required by the
Law of the Lord, they returned to Galilee to their own town of
Nazareth. 40And the child grew and became strong; he was filled
with wisdom, and the grace of God was upon him.

The Boy Jesus at the Temple

41Every year his parents went to Jerusalem for the Feast of the
Passover. 42When he was twelve years old, they went up to the
Feast, according to the custom. 43After the Feast was over, while
his parents were returning home, the boy Jesus stayed behind in
Jerusalem, but they were unaware of it. 44Thinking he was in their
company, they traveled on for a day. Then they began looking for
him among their relatives and friends. 45When they did not find
him, they went back to Jerusalem to look for him. 46After three
days they found him in the temple courts, sitting among the teachers, listening to them and asking them questions. 47Everyone who
heard him was amazed at his understanding and his answers.
48When his parents saw him, they were astonished. His mother
said to him, "Son, why have you treated us like this? Your father
and I have been anxiously searching for you."

49"Why were you searching for me?" he asked. "Didn't you

[a]37 Or *widow for eighty-four years*

---

1. What was your best family trip? **2.** Ever get lost as a child? What happened?

1. What was the significance of this feast, which was an annual tradition with Jesus' parents (see Dt 16:1–6)? **2.** What do Jesus' character traits revealed in this passage (vv. 43–51) tell us about him? **3.** How much does he seem to know about his mission? How much do his parents know? **4.** Why do you think Luke included this episode of Jesus' life?

Has your hunger for God ever been misunderstood by your family? How? How do you maintain a balance between daily responsibilities and serving God?

Luke 2:21–40 — JESUS PRESENTED IN THE TEMPLE

Joseph and Mary now fulfill three Old Testament requirements for parents: circumcision, the ritual purification of the mother and the dedication of the firstborn.

1. If you were Joseph or Mary and experienced the events in this story, what would have been the first thing you wrote in your diary for that day?
   a. "Everybody loved him—I was so proud!"
   b. "Old people say such strange things sometimes!"
   c. "I never had so much to thank the Lord for as I do now!"
   d. "I wonder what that man meant about a sword piercing my soul."

2. Why do you suppose this was such a meaningful occasion for Simeon?
   a. He had been expecting to see the Christ.
   b. He had waited so long for this moment.
   c. God had not forgotten about his promise of the Messiah.
   d. He marveled at how God could use a baby to bring his salvation.

3. Why do you suppose this was such a meaningful occasion for Anna?
   a. Years of prayer were answered.
   b. Her heart was filled with praise.
   c. God showed her this baby was the Messiah.
   d. She was privileged to introduce the Messiah to others.

4. In Simeon's prophetic words about the child, what was he predicting?
   a. Jesus would bring the light of salvation to both Jews and Gentiles.
   b. Israel would reject their Messiah.
   c. People will respond to Jesus strongly—one way or the other.
   d. Both Jesus and Mary would suffer greatly.

5. How did your parents dedicate you to the Lord (if at all)? How did they help you mature spiritually?

6. How has Christ brought "light" to your life in the past? What is he illuminating about your spiritual life now?

7. What family or young person might God want you to "bless"? How will you go about doing that—A letter? A phone call? A personal visit? Your prayers?

8. Which of the following were or are on your list for doing "everything required" by the Lord?
   a. circumcision
   b. baptism or dedication
   c. taking my child to church
   d. praying *for* my child
   e. praying *with* my child
   f. teaching my child about God
   g. disciplining my child
   h. spending lots of time with my child

9. Which of those actions are your top two priorities right now? Which of them do you have the hardest time doing?

10. What would be the crowning joy for you in your old age?
    a. to see my children's children
    b. to see my family serving God
    c. to strike it rich
    d. to leave the world a better place
    e. to feel I have done God's will
    f. to know I've spent my days walking with the Lord

know I had to be in my Father's house?" [50]But they did not understand what he was saying to them.
[51]Then he went down to Nazareth with them and was obedient
to them. But his mother treasured all these things in her heart.
[52]And Jesus grew in wisdom and stature, and in favor with God and
men.

John the Baptist Prepares the Way

3 In the fifteenth year of the reign of Tiberius Caesar—when
Pontius Pilate was governor of Judea, Herod tetrarch of Galilee,
his brother Philip tetrarch of Iturea and Traconitis, and Lysanias
tetrarch of Abilene— [2]during the high priesthood of Annas and
Caiaphas, the word of God came to John son of Zechariah in the
desert. [3]He went into all the country around the Jordan, preaching
a baptism of repentance for the forgiveness of sins. [4]As is written
in the book of the words of Isaiah the prophet:

"A voice of one calling in the desert,
'Prepare the way for the Lord,
make straight paths for him.
[5]Every valley shall be filled in,
every mountain and hill made low.
The crooked roads shall become straight,
the rough ways smooth.
[6]And all mankind will see God's salvation.' "[a]

[a]6 Isaiah 40:3-5

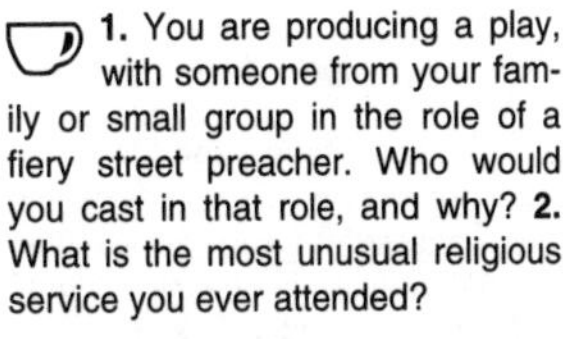

1. You are producing a play, with someone from your family or small group in the role of a fiery street preacher. Who would you cast in that role, and why? **2.** What is the most unusual religious service you ever attended?

1. How much time passes between appearances of John the Baptist here and in 1:80? What was John doing in those intervening years (Mt 3:1–6; Mk 1:4–6)? Why? **2.** Why does Luke list all the political and religious figures in verses 1–2? **3.** How would you describe John's message and style? **4.** What's radical about John's message? What does the "root" and "fruit" signify (v. 9)? Is he advocating social upheaval? Or inner transformation? Is he preaching or meddling? Why? Why would

Luke 2:41–52 YOUNG JESUS AT THE TEMPLE

1. What do you think of Jesus' behavior in this story?
   a. He disobeyed his parents.
   b. He was oblivious to his parents.
   c. He behaved like any 12-year-old.
   d. He put his heavenly Father's concerns over his parents' concerns.

2. What do you think of Mary and Joseph's behavior in this story?
   a. They were negligent parents.
   b. They behaved like any parents would.
   c. They gave Jesus more freedom than parents can today.
   d. They were confused about who Jesus really was.

3. If you had been Mary or Joseph, what would you have said to Jesus?
   a. "Why did you run off like that?!"
   b. "You had us worried sick!"
   c. "I'm so sorry we forgot you!"
   d. "You're grounded for a month!"
   e. "I understand why you are here."

4. This event was important in Jesus' development because it showed he:
   a. had become independent.
   b. was choosing to honor his Father.
   c. could now teach his elders.
   d. knew he was God's Son.

5. In what ways are you growing "in wisdom and stature, and in favor with God and men"?

6. What similar tension have you experienced with your parents? (How can you reduce it?)
   a. My parents don't understand me.
   b. I probably confuse my parents too.
   c. My parents don't like some of the places I hang out.
   d. I go through hassles about what time I have to come home.

7. As a parent, how can you relate to this story?
   a. This sounds like my kid!
   b. My child is a lot like Jesus, except for the "obedient" part!
   c. Like Mary, I often ask or think "Why have you treated us like this?"
   d. It illustrates that strong-willed children are full of potential.
   e. It illustrates how perplexing "gifted" children can be.
   f. Like Joseph and Mary must have felt, I feel like nobody else can understand what I go through.

8. What are your biggest anxieties about parenting teens or adolescent-aged children?

9. How does this story give you comfort or insight?
   a. Even Jesus' parents had to go through stress and challenges.
   b. Even Jesus did things that disturbed his parents.
   c. Developing independence is necessary in growing up.
   d. Sometimes we misjudge children.
   e. Sometimes children mature without us really noticing.

10. How much stress have you experienced due to the changes in your family? How do you deal with that stress?

11. What does this story say to you about your relationships?
    a. I need to do what God wants regardless of what others think.
    b. Like Mary, if I'm upset with someone I should voice my concerns.
    c. Like Jesus, if I know I'm doing what's right I shouldn't apologize.
    d. In all my relationships, I have to be at peace with myself.

12. How have you noticed your group growing in wisdom and in relationship with God and each other?

anyone go out of their way to hear such a preacher? **5.** Why is John confused with Christ (v. 15; Jn 1:19–28)? By contrast, how does John differentiate himself and his ministry? What does the "wheat" and "chaff" signify (v. 17)? **6.** What is the beginning of the end for John's ministry (vv. 19–20)? What does this illustrate about John?

1. Who have been "John the Baptists" in your life—people who have shown you the way, led you to Christ and encouraged you? **2.** If you asked John, "What should we do?" how would he answer? **3.** What *one* action will you take this week to produce fruit in keeping with your repentance? **4.** How can you emulate John's attitude toward Jesus as seen in verse 16?

---

1. Who is the historian in your family? What has he/she done to help you know more about your ancestors? **2.** If you were to explore in more detail the life of one of your ancestors, whose life would you investigate? Why? **3.** Whose life would you prefer not to know about?

1. What is significant about Jesus being baptized at the same time as "all the people"? What three things happen at Jesus' baptism that make it unlike the others' (vv. 21–22)? Was Jesus any different after his baptism? Why or why not? **2.** How does this account of Jesus' baptism compare and contrast with the other accounts (Mt 3:13–17; Mk 1:9–11; Jn 1:32–34)? **3.** If Matthew's genealogy starts with Abraham to demonstrate God's working through the chosen people (Mt 1:1–17), what is Luke's point in going all the way back to Adam (v. 38)? What do Adam and Jesus have in common? Why else might Luke include this genealogy (see 1:27,32,69)? **4.** In this genealogy, which names stand out to you? What do you know about them? What can you conclude about Jesus' earthly ancestry

7John said to the crowds coming out to be baptized by him, "You
brood of vipers! Who warned you to flee from the coming wrath?
8Produce fruit in keeping with repentance. And do not begin to say
to yourselves, 'We have Abraham as our father.' For I tell you that
out of these stones God can raise up children for Abraham. 9The ax
is already at the root of the trees, and every tree that does not
produce good fruit will be cut down and thrown into the fire."
10"What should we do then?" the crowd asked.
11John answered, "The man with two tunics should share with
him who has none, and the one who has food should do the same."
12Tax collectors also came to be baptized. "Teacher," they asked,
"what should we do?"
13"Don't collect any more than you are required to," he told
them.
14Then some soldiers asked him, "And what should we do?"
He replied, "Don't extort money and don't accuse people falsely—be content with your pay."
15The people were waiting expectantly and were all wondering
in their hearts if John might possibly be the Christ.[a] 16John answered them all, "I baptize you with[b] water. But one more powerful than I will come, the thongs of whose sandals I am not worthy
to untie. He will baptize you with the Holy Spirit and with fire.
17His winnowing fork is in his hand to clear his threshing floor and
to gather the wheat into his barn, but he will burn up the chaff
with unquenchable fire." 18And with many other words John exhorted the people and preached the good news to them.
19But when John rebuked Herod the tetrarch because of Herodias, his brother's wife, and all the other evil things he had done,
20Herod added this to them all: He locked John up in prison.

The Baptism and Genealogy of Jesus

21When all the people were being baptized, Jesus was baptized
too. And as he was praying, heaven was opened 22and the Holy
Spirit descended on him in bodily form like a dove. And a voice
came from heaven: "You are my Son, whom I love; with you I am
well pleased."
23Now Jesus himself was about thirty years old when he began
his ministry. He was the son, so it was thought, of Joseph,

the son of Heli, 24the son of Matthat,
the son of Levi, the son of Melki,
the son of Jannai, the son of Joseph,
25the son of Mattathias, the son of Amos,
the son of Nahum, the son of Esli,
the son of Naggai, 26the son of Maath,
the son of Mattathias, the son of Semein,
the son of Josech, the son of Joda,
27the son of Joanan, the son of Rhesa,
the son of Zerubbabel, the son of Shealtiel,
the son of Neri, 28the son of Melki,
the son of Addi, the son of Cosam,
the son of Elmadam, the son of Er,
29the son of Joshua, the son of Eliezer,
the son of Jorim, the son of Matthat,
the son of Levi, 30the son of Simeon,
the son of Judah, the son of Joseph,
the son of Jonam, the son of Eliakim,
31the son of Melea, the son of Menna,

[a] *15* Or *Messiah* [b] *16* Or *in*

the son of Mattatha, the son of Nathan,
the son of David, 32the son of Jesse,
the son of Obed, the son of Boaz,
the son of Salmon,[a] the son of Nahshon,
33the son of Amminadab, the son of Ram,[b]
the son of Hezron, the son of Perez,
the son of Judah, 34the son of Jacob,
the son of Isaac, the son of Abraham,
the son of Terah, the son of Nahor,
35the son of Serug, the son of Reu,
the son of Peleg, the son of Eber,
the son of Shelah, 36the son of Cainan,
the son of Arphaxad, the son of Shem,
the son of Noah, the son of Lamech,
37the son of Methuselah, the son of Enoch,
the son of Jared, the son of Mahalalel,
the son of Kenan, 38the son of Enosh,
the son of Seth, the son of Adam,
the son of God.

from what you know of this genealogy?

1. How has Jesus been like a "new Adam" for you—giving you a fresh start at life? How does Jesus' sonship (v. 22) form the basis for the way the Father sees you? What kinship do you sense with Jesus? 2. What means the most to you about your own baptism? 3. When in your life have you felt God's special touch, as if something new were beginning for you? What happened?

The Temptation of Jesus

4 Jesus, full of the Holy Spirit, returned from the Jordan and was
led by the Spirit in the desert, 2where for forty days he was
tempted by the devil. He ate nothing during those days, and at the
end of them he was hungry.
3The devil said to him, "If you are the Son of God, tell this stone
to become bread."
4Jesus answered, "It is written: 'Man does not live on bread
alone.'[c]"
5The devil led him up to a high place and showed him in an
instant all the kingdoms of the world. 6And he said to him, "I will
give you all their authority and splendor, for it has been given to
me, and I can give it to anyone I want to. 7So if you worship me, it
will all be yours."
8Jesus answered, "It is written: 'Worship the Lord your God and
serve him only.'[d]"
9The devil led him to Jerusalem and had him stand on the highest point of the temple. "If you are the Son of God," he said,
"throw yourself down from here. 10For it is written:

"'He will command his angels concerning you
to guard you carefully;
11they will lift you up in their hands,
so that you will not strike your foot against a
stone.'[e]"

12Jesus answered, "It says: 'Do not put the Lord your God to the
test.'[f]"
13When the devil had finished all this tempting, he left him until
an opportune time.

1. What's one of your all-time favorite foods? How often do you eat it? 2. If you were the emperor of the world, what would be your first decree?

1. Under what circumstances (vv. 1–2) was Jesus tempted: After a spiritual high? At a weak moment? At a new stage in life? 2. In each temptation, what was its appeal? Its price? How does Jesus resist them? How does Satan's use of Scripture differ from the way Jesus uses it? 3. How are the three temptations similar? Different? 4. Why were the temptations directed at Jesus immediately after he was affirmed by God at his baptism (3:22)?

1. What does it mean to you that all the authority and splendor of the kingdoms of the world has been given to Satan (vv. 5–6)? 2. If the devil had three shots at you, what three temptations would he use? 3. What can help you resist? What encouragement does this story provide?

Jesus Rejected at Nazareth

14Jesus returned to Galilee in the power of the Spirit, and news
about him spread through the whole countryside. 15He taught in
their synagogues, and everyone praised him.
16He went to Nazareth, where he had been brought up, and on
the Sabbath day he went into the synagogue, as was his custom.

1. What do you like best about the hometown where you grew up? 2. What was the symbol or sign of having "made it" in your hometown?

1. Compare 3:21; 4:1,14,18. What is the common element in each of these verses? What does this tell us about the source of Jesus' power? 2. What is signifi-

[a]32 Some early manuscripts *Sala* [b]33 Some manuscripts *Amminadab, the son of Admin, the son of Arni*; other manuscripts vary widely. [c]4 Deut. 8:3 [d]8 Deut. 6:13 [e]11 Psalm 91:11,12 [f]12 Deut. 6:16

cant about the time, place and posture (vv. 16,21–22) for Jesus' reading from Isaiah? **3.** What is Jesus' five-fold mission (vv. 18–19)? How did Jesus fulfill it then? Now? **4.** What expectations stirred in the people as a result of Jesus' claim (vv. 21–22)? **5.** What is Jesus saying through the proverb (v. 23)? Through the Elijah and Elisha stories (vv. 24–27)? Why does this turn their amazement (v. 22) into anger (vv. 28–29)? How does all this relate to the prophetic statements in 2:14, 2:32 and 3:6?

1. If all five areas of Jesus' mission are to be carried on by the church as a whole, which area of concern do you give priority and which do you tend to neglect: (a) Preaching the Gospel? (b) Helping people to be free to live for God? (c) Performing acts of mercy? (d) Working for fair and just social structures? (e) Explaining God's grace to disheartened people? **2.** Who are the "Gentiles" (2:32) God desires you to care for? How might you do so?

And he stood up to read. 17 The scroll of the prophet Isaiah was
handed to him. Unrolling it, he found the place where it is written:

> 18 "The Spirit of the Lord is on me,
> because he has anointed me
> to preach good news to the poor.
> He has sent me to proclaim freedom for the prisoners
> and recovery of sight for the blind,
> to release the oppressed,
> 19 to proclaim the year of the Lord's favor."[a]

20 Then he rolled up the scroll, gave it back to the attendant and
sat down. The eyes of everyone in the synagogue were fastened on
him, 21 and he began by saying to them, "Today this scripture is
fulfilled in your hearing."
22 All spoke well of him and were amazed at the gracious words
that came from his lips. "Isn't this Joseph's son?" they asked.
23 Jesus said to them, "Surely you will quote this proverb to me:
'Physician, heal yourself! Do here in your hometown what we
have heard that you did in Capernaum.' "
24 "I tell you the truth," he continued, "no prophet is accepted in
his hometown. 25 I assure you that there were many widows in
Israel in Elijah's time, when the sky was shut for three and a half
years and there was a severe famine throughout the land. 26 Yet
Elijah was not sent to any of them, but to a widow in Zarephath in
the region of Sidon. 27 And there were many in Israel with lepro-

[a] *19* Isaiah 61:1,2

Luke 4:14–30 JESUS REJECTED AT NAZARETH

Though Jesus was born in the town of Bethlehem, he grew up in the town of Nazareth in Galilee. Now, early in his ministry, he returns to Nazareth.

1. How would you describe the reception Jesus got in his hometown?
   a. thunderous applause
   b. faint praise
   c. mixed reviews
   d. a drastic change in public opinion

2. Why did people in Nazareth have a problem accepting Jesus?
   a. They were spiritually blind.
   b. He was just a carpenter's son.
   c. There were rumors about his "illegitimate birth."
   d. He sounded like a traitor—affirming Gentiles and condemning Israel.

3. In the end, why were Jesus' hometown neighbors so furious?
   a. They felt put down.
   b. They felt he was blasphemous.
   c. He felt he was better than them.
   d. He would rather go to non-Jews who would accept his claims.

4. How was Jesus affected when he was rejected by his hometown?
   a. He anticipated rejection and was not bothered much by it.
   b. He was upset, but didn't show it.
   c. Being human, he was hurt by it.
   d. Being divine, he wasn't affected by it at all.

5. In verses 18–21 Jesus applied five points from an Old Testament passage to his mission. Of these five ministries, which do you have a need for in your life—either literally/physically or symbolically/spiritually?
   a. good news to the poor
   b. freedom for the prisoners
   c. recovery of sight for the blind
   d. release for the oppressed
   e. proclaiming the year of the Lord's favor (celebrating God's grace to "debtors")

6. In which of the five ministries do you feel God is calling you to invest yourself toward serving others?

7. How do you deal with feelings of rejection?

8. Where do you find it hardest to be accepted as a person of value? How do feelings of rejection affect your participation in a group like this?

9. How does this story speak to your financial stress?
   a. I need some "good news."
   b. I have felt a lot of rejection because of my financial problems.
   c. I feel imprisoned and oppressed by financial pressures.
   d. I feel like others are saying, "You made this mess—'heal yourself!' "
   e. I wish I could be like Jesus and "walk right through" my creditors!

10. Do you think Jesus was a real man, with hair on his chest?
   a. I've never really thought about it.
   b. Yes—though he was divine, he was no less a man than I am.
   c. No—I like the stained glass Jesus.

11. What did your father think being a man meant? When you were an adolescent, how did you fare with the "tests of manhood"?

sy[a] in the time of Elisha the prophet, yet not one of them was
cleansed—only Naaman the Syrian."
28All the people in the synagogue were furious when they heard
this. 29They got up, drove him out of the town, and took him to the
brow of the hill on which the town was built, in order to throw
him down the cliff. 30But he walked right through the crowd and
went on his way.

Jesus Drives Out an Evil Spirit

31Then he went down to Capernaum, a town in Galilee, and on
the Sabbath began to teach the people. 32They were amazed at his
teaching, because his message had authority.
33In the synagogue there was a man possessed by a demon, an
evil[b] spirit. He cried out at the top of his voice, 34"Ha! What do
you want with us, Jesus of Nazareth? Have you come to destroy us?
I know who you are—the Holy One of God!"
35"Be quiet!" Jesus said sternly. "Come out of him!" Then the
demon threw the man down before them all and came out without
injuring him.
36All the people were amazed and said to each other, "What is
this teaching? With authority and power he gives orders to evil
spirits and they come out!" 37And the news about him spread
throughout the surrounding area.

Who was your favorite teacher in secondary school?

1. How is this story related to the one before, especially verses 18–19? What similarities and differences do you see? **2.** What strikes you most about the behavior of the evil spirit?

1. How has Jesus' authority grabbed your attention recently? **2.** How is his authority bringing freedom to you?

Jesus Heals Many

38Jesus left the synagogue and went to the home of Simon. Now
Simon's mother-in-law was suffering from a high fever, and they
asked Jesus to help her. 39So he bent over her and rebuked the
fever, and it left her. She got up at once and began to wait on them.
40When the sun was setting, the people brought to Jesus all who
had various kinds of sickness, and laying his hands on each one, he
healed them. 41Moreover, demons came out of many people, shouting, "You are the Son of God!" But he rebuked them and would not
allow them to speak, because they knew he was the Christ.[c]
42At daybreak Jesus went out to a solitary place. The people were
looking for him and when they came to where he was, they tried to
keep him from leaving them. 43But he said, "I must preach the
good news of the kingdom of God to the other towns also, because
that is why I was sent." 44And he kept on preaching in the synagogues of Judea.[d]

When you need a break from pressure, where do you go? What do you do?

1. How has Jesus' life changed since his temptation? What in this section (vv. 38–42) shows that Jesus is beginning to feel the effects of this change? **2.** Why does Jesus find it necessary to retreat at this time (vv. 42–44)? What pressure is he facing? What are his priorities?

Jesus is obviously busy, yet he takes time to be alone. How do you discern God's long-range call to you amidst all the shouting of the urgent needs?

The Calling of the First Disciples

5 One day as Jesus was standing by the Lake of Gennesaret,[e]
with the people crowding around him and listening to the
word of God, 2he saw at the water's edge two boats, left there by
the fishermen, who were washing their nets. 3He got into one of
the boats, the one belonging to Simon, and asked him to put out a
little from shore. Then he sat down and taught the people from the
boat.
4When he had finished speaking, he said to Simon, "Put out into
deep water, and let down[f] the nets for a catch."
5Simon answered, "Master, we've worked hard all night and
haven't caught anything. But because you say so, I will let down
the nets."
6When they had done so, they caught such a large number of

What was your first paying job you had?

1. What do you think Simon was thinking and feeling in verse 5? 7? 8? **2.** How did this miracle affect Peter? Why does this have a more profound effect on him than the healing of his mother-in-law? What is he beginning to grasp about Jesus? About sin? About belief in himself?

[a] 27 The Greek word was used for various diseases affecting the skin—not necessarily leprosy. [b] 33 Greek *unclean*; also in verse 36 [c] 41 Or *Messiah* [d] 44 Or *the land of the Jews*; some manuscripts *Galilee* [e] 1 That is, Sea of Galilee [f] 4 The Greek verb is plural.

1. When was the first time, if ever, that you responded to Jesus like Peter did in verse 8? **2.** In *your* "fishing business," how do you see Jesus: (a) Interesting, but a slightly irrelevant teacher? (b) Potentially a great business partner—if you could hire him to work for you? (c) The one who calls all the shots?

fish that their nets began to break. 7So they signaled their partners
in the other boat to come and help them, and they came and filled
both boats so full that they began to sink.
8When Simon Peter saw this, he fell at Jesus' knees and said,
"Go away from me, Lord; I am a sinful man!" 9For he and all his
companions were astonished at the catch of fish they had taken,
10and so were James and John, the sons of Zebedee, Simon's partners.
Then Jesus said to Simon, "Don't be afraid; from now on you will
catch men." 11So they pulled their boats up on shore, left everything and followed him.

The Man With Leprosy

What illness are you most afraid of catching? Why?

1. By touching the leper before he heals him, what is Jesus demonstrating? **2.** Why does Jesus try to silence him?

1. When have you felt shunned, like a leper? How did Jesus "touch" you then? **2.** Who are the "lepers" in your life? What would it mean for you to touch them for Christ?

12While Jesus was in one of the towns, a man came along who
was covered with leprosy.[a] When he saw Jesus, he fell with his
face to the ground and begged him, "Lord, if you are willing, you
can make me clean."
13Jesus reached out his hand and touched the man. "I am willing," he said. "Be clean!" And immediately the leprosy left him.
14Then Jesus ordered him, "Don't tell anyone, but go, show
yourself to the priest and offer the sacrifices that Moses commanded for your cleansing, as a testimony to them."
15Yet the news about him spread all the more, so that crowds of

[a] 12 The Greek word was used for various diseases affecting the skin—not necessarily leprosy.

Luke 5:1–11 CALLING OF THE FIRST DISCIPLES

1. If you had been Simon Peter when Jesus said, "Put out into deep water, and let down the nets for a catch," what would you have done?
   a. wondered who he thought he was
   b. told Jesus I was too tired
   c. suggested another time when the fish were biting
   d. politely told Jesus to stick to his preaching
   e. grudgingly complied with the idea

2. When they caught so many fish that their nets began to break, how do you think Peter felt?
   a. overjoyed
   b. dumfounded
   c. terrible about what he had said
   d. aware of who Jesus was

3. "Go away from me, Lord; I am a sinful man!" What did Peter mean?
   a. "Your power frightens me."
   b. "I feel unworthy to be around you because of my sinful life."
   c. "I know you are all you say you are, but I'm not ready to give up my life and follow you."
   d. "I'm afraid of what you might ask me to do."

4. Compared to Peter, how would you describe your spiritual beginning?
   a. pretty tame
   b. more intellectual
   c. just as confusing
   d. even crazier
   e. different, but just as real

5. What would Jesus have in mind if he asked you right now to launch out into the deep and let down your nets?

6. What will it take to get you going the right direction in your spiritual life?
   a. time to consider the cost
   b. time to get myself together
   c. a little support from others
   d. a good kick in the pants
   e. help to clean up my life
   f. an end to feeling that Christ can't accept me because of my past
   g. I am already feeling pretty good about following Jesus.

7. How do these fishermen's decisions to leave everything strike you?
   a. How silly to give up a respectable career for who knows what.
   b. How exciting to try something new.
   c. It would take a lot more than this to get me to change careers.
   d. Following Jesus is more important than any career.

8. What connection can you see between your career or job and the call to follow Jesus? Can you let God use you more where you're at, or would you be more useful for God's purposes elsewhere?

9. What issues about working or about a career are most unsettling to you?
   a. knowing *if* or *how much* I should work
   b. adjusting to a new job or career
   c. deciding whether I should change jobs or careers
   d. balancing work and family
   e. discerning how work and career issues relate to following Christ

10. In order to "catch" people for Jesus, what do you have going for you to help draw them?
    a. my ability to make friends
    b. my knowledge of the Bible
    c. my willingness to help people
    d. my willingness to take risks
    e. my willingness to "walk my talk"

11. Where have you grown in your understanding of yourself in this course? Where have you seen growth in other members of your group?

people came to hear him and to be healed of their sicknesses. 16But
Jesus often withdrew to lonely places and prayed.

Jesus Heals a Paralytic

17One day as he was teaching, Pharisees and teachers of the law,
who had come from every village of Galilee and from Judea and
Jerusalem, were sitting there. And the power of the Lord was
present for him to heal the sick. 18Some men came carrying a
paralytic on a mat and tried to take him into the house to lay him
before Jesus. 19When they could not find a way to do this because
of the crowd, they went up on the roof and lowered him on his mat
through the tiles into the middle of the crowd, right in front of
Jesus.
20When Jesus saw their faith, he said, "Friend, your sins are
forgiven."
21The Pharisees and the teachers of the law began thinking to
themselves, "Who is this fellow who speaks blasphemy? Who can
forgive sins but God alone?"
22Jesus knew what they were thinking and asked, "Why are you
thinking these things in your hearts? 23Which is easier: to say,
'Your sins are forgiven,' or to say, 'Get up and walk'? 24But that you
may know that the Son of Man has authority on earth to forgive
sins. . . ." He said to the paralyzed man, "I tell you, get up, take
your mat and go home." 25Immediately he stood up in front of
them, took what he had been lying on and went home praising
God. 26Everyone was amazed and gave praise to God. They were
filled with awe and said, "We have seen remarkable things today."

Who were your four closest friends in high school? What was one memorable prank you pulled off together?

1. How might the Pharisees and teachers have felt in verses 17–19? Verse 20? Verses 21–23? Verses 24–26? **2.** The man came for *healing*, so why did Jesus raise the issue of *forgiveness*? How would the friends react to Jesus' words (v. 20)? To his actions (v. 24)? **3.** What new realm of Jesus' authority is demonstrated here? **4.** What motivates the Pharisees to respond as they do to the situation?

1. Who are you most like in this story? Why? **2.** Are you a little paralyzed now—emotionally, spiritually, relationally? What needs to happen for you to "take your mat and go home"?

The Calling of Levi

27After this, Jesus went out and saw a tax collector by the name
of Levi sitting at his tax booth. "Follow me," Jesus said to him,
28and Levi got up, left everything and followed him.
29Then Levi held a great banquet for Jesus at his house, and a
large crowd of tax collectors and others were eating with them.
30But the Pharisees and the teachers of the law who belonged to
their sect complained to his disciples, "Why do you eat and drink
with tax collectors and 'sinners'?"
31Jesus answered them, "It is not the healthy who need a doctor,
but the sick. 32I have not come to call the righteous, but sinners to
repentance."

Jesus Questioned About Fasting

33They said to him, "John's disciples often fast and pray, and so
do the disciples of the Pharisees, but yours go on eating and drinking."
34Jesus answered, "Can you make the guests of the bridegroom
fast while he is with them? 35But the time will come when the
bridegroom will be taken from them; in those days they will fast."
36He told them this parable: "No one tears a patch from a new
garment and sews it on an old one. If he does, he will have torn the
new garment, and the patch from the new will not match the old.
37And no one pours new wine into old wineskins. If he does, the
new wine will burst the skins, the wine will run out and the
wineskins will be ruined. 38No, new wine must be poured into
new wineskins. 39And no one after drinking old wine wants the
new, for he says, 'The old is better.' "

A famous person you admire is coming to dine with you tomorrow. What would you do to get ready?

1. Tax collectors lined their pockets with money they collected. How might the disciples (5:1–11) feel about Jesus' choice? **2.** Why choose Levi? What is the irony here (vv. 31–32)? **3.** Why is Jesus questioned about fasting? **4.** What is Jesus implying by the parable in verses 34–35? In verses 36–39? How does this relate to Levi's call and to the disciples' not fasting? **5.** What is the new cloth? Old garment? New wine? Old wineskins?

1. In this story, what do you have to do to qualify as a disciple? **2.** In the way you relate to "undesirable types," are you more like Levi (inviting them to your party), the Pharisees (looking down on them), or the disciples (unsure what to do)? Why?

As a child, what family rules did you consider stupid? How do you view those rules now?

1. How are things developing in the Pharisees' ongoing investigation of Jesus (5:17,30, 33)? What is the main issue here for the Pharisees? For Jesus? **2.** How does the story of David (1Sa 21:1–6) apply to Jesus and his disciples? **3.** How does Jesus clarify the Sabbath issue (vv. 5,9)? **4.** Why does Jesus provoke the Pharisees' wrath by healing on the Sabbath? Why not wait a day? **5.** What is Jesus' attitude about formalized religion in 5:27–6:10?

1. When have you felt tension between obeying religious *principles* and helping *people*? What causes that tension? What relieves it? **2.** As you try to follow Jesus, are you becoming more free to love others, or becoming more constrained by religious rules? Why?

What was one of the best teams you ever belonged to?

Lord of the Sabbath

6 One Sabbath Jesus was going through the grainfields, and his
disciples began to pick some heads of grain, rub them in their
hands and eat the kernels. 2Some of the Pharisees asked, "Why are
you doing what is unlawful on the Sabbath?"
3Jesus answered them, "Have you never read what David did
when he and his companions were hungry? 4He entered the house
of God, and taking the consecrated bread, he ate what is lawful
only for priests to eat. And he also gave some to his companions."
5Then Jesus said to them, "The Son of Man is Lord of the Sabbath."
6On another Sabbath he went into the synagogue and was teaching, and a man was there whose right hand was shriveled. 7The
Pharisees and the teachers of the law were looking for a reason to
accuse Jesus, so they watched him closely to see if he would heal
on the Sabbath. 8But Jesus knew what they were thinking and said
to the man with the shriveled hand, "Get up and stand in front of
everyone." So he got up and stood there.
9Then Jesus said to them, "I ask you, which is lawful on the
Sabbath: to do good or to do evil, to save life or to destroy it?"
10He looked around at them all, and then said to the man,
"Stretch out your hand." He did so, and his hand was completely
restored. 11But they were furious and began to discuss with one
another what they might do to Jesus.

The Twelve Apostles

12One of those days Jesus went out to a mountainside to pray,
and spent the night praying to God. 13When morning came, he
called his disciples to him and chose twelve of them, whom he also

Luke 5:27–39 THE CALLING OF LEVI; NEW WINESKINS

This story illustrates the disdain of two groups of people: (1) "sinners"—those who were notoriously evil, as well as those who refused to follow the Pharisees' interpretations of the Law of Moses; (2) tax collectors like Levi (also known as Matthew)—Jewish agents for the Roman government who were detested both by the religious authorities and common people for their disloyalty and cheating.

1. Why did Jesus call a despised tax collector like Levi to follow him?
   a. He saw his potential.
   b. He overlooked his faults.
   c. Levi must have been honest.
   d. He was calling him to repentance.
   e. He was looking for followers from a variety of backgrounds.

2. How do you think the other disciples felt when Jesus asked Levi to join their group?
   a. angry that Jesus did such a thing
   b. embarrassed for Levi to join them
   c. hopeful about their future tax bills
   d. delighted to accept a new recruit

3. Why do you think Jesus attended a dinner party with a bunch of tax collectors and "sinners"?
   a. to show he accepted them
   b. to convert them
   c. to enjoy himself
   d. to offend the self-righteousness of the Pharisees
   e. I'm not sure—I don't think I would have gone.

4. What did Jesus mean when he said, "I have not come to call the righteous, but sinners to repentance"?
   a. The Pharisees didn't need Jesus.
   b. Jesus came for sinners—not for Pharisees.
   c. Jesus came for sinners—anyone recognizing themselves as such.
   d. Only admitted sinners can see their need for salvation.
   e. You can lead a horse to water, but you can't make it drink.

5. Why weren't Jesus' disciples fasting? When would they?

6. Generally, how receptive are you to "new wine"?
   a. I like to keep things as they are.
   b. I accept change slowly, but with God's help I can handle it.
   c. I'm all for change if I'm sure it's God's doing.
   d. I'm a revolutionary—let's turn the world upside down!

7. Why do you suppose Levi and the other disciples responded to Jesus' call so readily? If you were in their position, how readily do you think you would have responded?

8. When was the first time you recall feeling Jesus' tug on your heart? What was it about Jesus that first drew you to him?

9. How has (or should) Jesus' "new wine" burst some of your "old wineskins"—your religious rituals or ruts?

10. How do you relate to "undesirable types"? Do you look down on them? Do you invite them to your parties? How can your group reach out to "sinners" and persons considered unacceptable?

designated apostles: 14Simon (whom he named Peter), his brother
Andrew, James, John, Philip, Bartholomew, 15Matthew, Thomas,
James son of Alphaeus, Simon who was called the Zealot, 16Judas
son of James, and Judas Iscariot, who became a traitor.

Blessings and Woes

17He went down with them and stood on a level place. A large
crowd of his disciples was there and a great number of people from
all over Judea, from Jerusalem, and from the coast of Tyre and
Sidon, 18who had come to hear him and to be healed of their
diseases. Those troubled by evil[a] spirits were cured, 19and the
people all tried to touch him, because power was coming from him
and healing them all.
20Looking at his disciples, he said:

"Blessed are you who are poor,
for yours is the kingdom of God.
21Blessed are you who hunger now,
for you will be satisfied.
Blessed are you who weep now,
for you will laugh.
22Blessed are you when men hate you,
when they exclude you and insult you
and reject your name as evil,
because of the Son of Man.

23"Rejoice in that day and leap for joy, because great is your
reward in heaven. For that is how their fathers treated the prophets.

24"But woe to you who are rich,
for you have already received your comfort.
25Woe to you who are well fed now,
for you will go hungry.
Woe to you who laugh now,
for you will mourn and weep.
26Woe to you when all men speak well of you,
for that is how their fathers treated the false
prophets.

Love for Enemies

27"But I tell you who hear me: Love your enemies, do good to
those who hate you, 28bless those who curse you, pray for those
who mistreat you. 29If someone strikes you on one cheek, turn to
him the other also. If someone takes your cloak, do not stop him
from taking your tunic. 30Give to everyone who asks you, and if
anyone takes what belongs to you, do not demand it back. 31Do to
others as you would have them do to you.
32"If you love those who love you, what credit is that to you?
Even 'sinners' love those who love them. 33And if you do good to
those who are good to you, what credit is that to you? Even 'sinners' do that. 34And if you lend to those from whom you expect
repayment, what credit is that to you? Even 'sinners' lend to 'sinners,' expecting to be repaid in full. 35But love your enemies, do
good to them, and lend to them without expecting to get anything
back. Then your reward will be great, and you will be sons of the
Most High, because he is kind to the ungrateful and wicked. 36Be
merciful, just as your Father is merciful.

[a]18 Greek *unclean*

In the context of chapter 6, what is significant about Jesus calling these men? What do you know about them? Who are brothers? Buddies? Antagonists?

Describe a time recently when something you dreaded or something you wished for was disappointing.

1. Who is in the crowd? Why have they come? How does Jesus meet their needs? How do his actions (vv. 18–19) relate to his teaching (vv. 20–22)? **2.** What four qualities ought to characterize "kingdom people" (vv. 20–22)? How would you define each of these? What blessing is promised for each? Are these present blessings or future blessings? **3.** Who is Jesus addressing (vv. 24–26)? How would you define each warning he gives here?

1. How do the values Jesus talks about here compare with the values you are sold every day on TV? What values do you and your family accept? Reject? **2.** If you could add another "blessed" and another "woe" to counteract modern values, what would you want to add?

As a child, who were the bad guys on your favorite Saturday morning cartoons or TV show?

1. Why has Jesus made a shift in the object of love (see Lev 19:18)? What specifically are we to do to enemies? **2.** Since applying verses 29–30 literally could reinforce someone's bad behavior, what is Jesus' point (see vv. 31, 36)?

1. How does this description of love challenge you? **2.** How can that be a model for relating to someone you find difficult? **3.** Have you ever shown love to an enemy? How?

1. Would you rather be a movie director or a movie critic? Why? 2. Where would you like to locate your "dream house"? Why?

1. What activities does Jesus condemn and commend (vv. 37–38)? What does the promise (v. 38) mean in this context? 2. Does verse 37 say that we must love others before God will love us? Why or why not? 3. What's the point of this parable (vv. 39–40) in this context? 4. What is the point of the speck and the plank? 5. How does the tree and its fruit (vv. 43–45) help you recognize a "kingdom person"? How does this relate to verses 37–42? 6. Compare the two houses and their owner-builders (vv. 46–49). How does this lesson relate to verses 41–45?

1. In light of this three-fold passage (vv. 41–45), how would you recommend approaching people who need help or correction? 2. What quality of fruit would your acquaintances say you are producing: Grade A-1? So-so? Wormy? Why? What would Jesus need to do to make it good? 3. During the last storm to hit your life, what did you learn about your life's foundation?

Judging Others

37“Do not judge, and you will not be judged. Do not condemn, and you will not be condemned. Forgive, and you will be forgiven. 38Give, and it will be given to you. A good measure, pressed down, shaken together and running over, will be poured into your lap. For with the measure you use, it will be measured to you.”

39He also told them this parable: “Can a blind man lead a blind man? Will they not both fall into a pit? 40A student is not above his teacher, but everyone who is fully trained will be like his teacher.

41“Why do you look at the speck of sawdust in your brother's eye and pay no attention to the plank in your own eye? 42How can you say to your brother, ‘Brother, let me take the speck out of your eye,’ when you yourself fail to see the plank in your own eye? You hypocrite, first take the plank out of your eye, and then you will see clearly to remove the speck from your brother's eye.

A Tree and Its Fruit

43“No good tree bears bad fruit, nor does a bad tree bear good fruit. 44Each tree is recognized by its own fruit. People do not pick figs from thornbushes, or grapes from briers. 45The good man brings good things out of the good stored up in his heart, and the evil man brings evil things out of the evil stored up in his heart. For out of the overflow of his heart his mouth speaks.

The Wise and Foolish Builders

46“Why do you call me, ‘Lord, Lord,’ and do not do what I say? 47I will show you what he is like who comes to me and hears my words and puts them into practice. 48He is like a man building a house, who dug down deep and laid the foundation on rock. When a flood came, the torrent struck that house but could not shake it, because it was well built. 49But the one who hears my words and does not put them into practice is like a man who built a house on the ground without a foundation. The moment the torrent struck that house, it collapsed and its destruction was complete.”

What is the most dramatic “near death” experience you've ever had: An accident? Illness? Showing your father a bad report card? Stock market crash?

1. Describe the faith of the centurion in this story. How are Roman centurions portrayed elsewhere (see Mt 27:26,54; 28:4, 11–15; Ac 10:2; 23:17–18; 27:43)? In what way is this related to 6:43–45? 2. On what basis did the elders request Jesus' help? How does their approach differ from the centurion's (vv. 6–8)? How does this relate to Jesus' commandment (v. 9)? 3. What quality of faith is exhibited here?

Describe a time when you let go and let God accomplish his purposes.

The Faith of the Centurion

7 When Jesus had finished saying all this in the hearing of the people, he entered Capernaum. 2There a centurion's servant, whom his master valued highly, was sick and about to die. 3The centurion heard of Jesus and sent some elders of the Jews to him, asking him to come and heal his servant. 4When they came to Jesus, they pleaded earnestly with him, “This man deserves to have you do this, 5because he loves our nation and has built our synagogue.” 6So Jesus went with them.

He was not far from the house when the centurion sent friends to say to him: “Lord, don't trouble yourself, for I do not deserve to have you come under my roof. 7That is why I did not even consider myself worthy to come to you. But say the word, and my servant will be healed. 8For I myself am a man under authority, with soldiers under me. I tell this one, ‘Go,’ and he goes; and that one, ‘Come,’ and he comes. I say to my servant, ‘Do this,’ and he does it.”

9When Jesus heard this, he was amazed at him, and turning to the crowd following him, he said, “I tell you, I have not found such great faith even in Israel.” 10Then the men who had been sent returned to the house and found the servant well.

Jesus Raises a Widow's Son

11 Soon afterward, Jesus went to a town called Nain, and his
disciples and a large crowd went along with him. 12 As he approached the town gate, a dead person was being carried out—the
only son of his mother, and she was a widow. And a large crowd
from the town was with her. 13 When the Lord saw her, his heart
went out to her and he said, "Don't cry."

14 Then he went up and touched the coffin, and those carrying it
stood still. He said, "Young man, I say to you, get up!" 15 The dead
man sat up and began to talk, and Jesus gave him back to his
mother.

16 They were all filled with awe and praised God. "A great prophet has appeared among us," they said. "God has come to help his
people." 17 This news about Jesus spread throughout Judea[a] and
the surrounding country.

Jesus and John the Baptist

18 John's disciples told him about all these things. Calling two of
them, 19 he sent them to the Lord to ask, "Are you the one who was
to come, or should we expect someone else?"

20 When the men came to Jesus, they said, "John the Baptist sent
us to you to ask, 'Are you the one who was to come, or should we
expect someone else?' "

21 At that very time Jesus cured many who had diseases, sicknesses and evil spirits, and gave sight to many who were blind.
22 So he replied to the messengers, "Go back and report to John
what you have seen and heard: The blind receive sight, the lame
walk, those who have leprosy[b] are cured, the deaf hear, the dead
are raised, and the good news is preached to the poor. 23 Blessed is
the man who does not fall away on account of me."

24 After John's messengers left, Jesus began to speak to the crowd
about John: "What did you go out into the desert to see? A reed
swayed by the wind? 25 If not, what did you go out to see? A man
dressed in fine clothes? No, those who wear expensive clothes and
indulge in luxury are in palaces. 26 But what did you go out to see?
A prophet? Yes, I tell you, and more than a prophet. 27 This is the
one about whom it is written:

" 'I will send my messenger ahead of you,
who will prepare your way before you.'[c]

28 I tell you, among those born of women there is no one greater
than John; yet the one who is least in the kingdom of God is
greater than he."

29 (All the people, even the tax collectors, when they heard Jesus'
words, acknowledged that God's way was right, because they had
been baptized by John. 30 But the Pharisees and experts in the law
rejected God's purpose for themselves, because they had not been
baptized by John.)

31 "To what, then, can I compare the people of this generation?
What are they like? 32 They are like children sitting in the marketplace and calling out to each other:

" 'We played the flute for you,
and you did not dance;
we sang a dirge,
and you did not cry.'

[a] 17 Or *the land of the Jews* [b] 22 The Greek word was used for various diseases affecting the skin—not necessarily leprosy. [c] 27 Mal. 3:1

What national hero do you associate with the "good ol' days"?

This story resembles the one in 2 Kings 4:8–37. Why did Jesus perform this miracle in Nain (near Shunem)? What did he reveal about himself? What impact did he have on others?

How does Jesus' power over death affect the way you live your life?

---

1. (For the married:) When did you know that the person you married was "the one"? (For the unmarried:) What is the "sign" you look for as that decisive signal you have found the "right one"? **2.** What situation recently has frustrated you because you weren't sure what to do?

1. How does John receive information about Jesus? Why can't he get it firsthand (see 3:20)? What question does John tell his men to ask Jesus (v. 20)? Why? **2.** How does Jesus answer the question (vv. 21–23)? Why doesn't he answer directly? What six things characterize Jesus' ministry? **3.** From Isaiah 29:18–19; 35:5–6; 61:1, how might John interpret Jesus' reply? How might he take Jesus' added blessing (v. 23)? **4.** What questions does Jesus put to the people (vv. 24–28)? How does Jesus affirm John? **5.** How does the people's response to John contrast to that of the Pharisees (v. 29)? How are the followers of the Pharisees like children?

1. When did you come to the place in your spiritual pilgrimage when you knew Jesus was "the one" you were looking for? How did you come to this understanding? What difference has it made? **2.** Looking at verses 33–34, are you more like John or Jesus in your lifestyle? Would you be more effective if you lived differently? Why or why not? **3.** If you could ask Jesus one question today about a decision you are facing, what would it be?

33For John the Baptist came neither eating bread nor drinking
wine, and you say, 'He has a demon.' 34The Son of Man came
eating and drinking, and you say, 'Here is a glutton and a drunkard,
a friend of tax collectors and "sinners."' 35But wisdom is proved
right by all her children."

Jesus Anointed by a Sinful Woman

36Now one of the Pharisees invited Jesus to have dinner with
him, so he went to the Pharisee's house and reclined at the table.
37When a woman who had lived a sinful life in that town learned
that Jesus was eating at the Pharisee's house, she brought an alabaster jar of perfume, 38and as she stood behind him at his feet
weeping, she began to wet his feet with her tears. Then she wiped
them with her hair, kissed them and poured perfume on them.
39When the Pharisee who had invited him saw this, he said to
himself, "If this man were a prophet, he would know who is
touching him and what kind of woman she is—that she is a sinner."
40Jesus answered him, "Simon, I have something to tell you."
"Tell me, teacher," he said.
41"Two men owed money to a certain moneylender. One owed
him five hundred denarii,[a] and the other fifty. 42Neither of them
had the money to pay him back, so he canceled the debts of both.
Now which of them will love him more?"

[a]41 A denarius was a coin worth about a day's wages.

1. What is one special gift you've received from your children or parents? **2.** What parties do you enjoy? Dislike?

1. What risk was this "sinful woman" taking in coming to the house of Simon, the Pharisee? What does this tell you about her state of mind? **2.** What is your impression of Simon? What do you think Jesus' purpose was in telling the parable in verses 41–43? Why didn't he just accuse Simon of not loving enough? **3.** What does Jesus see in this woman that Simon does not? How does this affect Jesus' actions toward her? In this passage, what seems to be Jesus' main concern? Simon's concern? **4.** Who do you think was a greater sinner, the woman or Simon? Why? How important is it to

Luke 7:36–50 JESUS ANOINTED BY A SINFUL WOMAN

1. Why do you think this woman, an apparent prostitute, came to the Pharisee's house?
   a. to ruin the party
   b. to upset Simon the Pharisee
   c. to seek forgiveness
   d. to minister to Jesus

2. How do you think Jesus felt when she began crying, wetting his feet with her tears, wiping them with her hair, then kissing his feet and pouring perfume on them?
   a. surprised
   b. flattered
   c. upset
   d. embarrassed
   e. moved
   f. uncomfortable

3. Why do you suppose the woman expressed her repentance and devotion like she did, instead of verbally?

4. What are the implications of Jesus' words and parable?
   a. The more you have sinned the more you will love God.
   b. You can't experience grace until you recognize you are a sinner.
   c. Our love for Christ is the basis of our forgiveness.
   d. Our love for Christ is the evidence of our forgiveness.

5. Whom do you identify with most in this story?
   a. the woman—because I feel bad about my past
   b. the Pharisee—because I have a tendency to be judgmental
   c. Jesus—because hypocritical attitudes make me angry

6. Who in your life has played the role of Simon, questioning your value? Who has played the role of Jesus, believing in and sticking up for you?

7. How has the kindness and caring of others in this group "touched" you?

8. When in your life have you most felt like an outsider (like this woman) who didn't belong? How closely can you relate to her ability to be herself regardless of how she appeared to others?

9. Which of the following expresses your attitude toward touching and being touched?
   a. I want and need to be touched and hugged more.
   b. I'm suspicious of people who want to touch me.
   c. I want to be touched and hugged, but worry if it's okay.
   d. People should avoid touching—it brings too much temptation.
   e. To be close emotionally, you have to be able to touch physically.

10. What needs to happen for you to feel the kind of forgiveness this woman felt?
    a. I need to get my life straightened out first.
    b. I need to find someone to talk to who is as sympathetic as Jesus.
    c. I need to stop listening to the "Pharisees" who condemn me.
    d. I need to accept the forgiveness which Jesus has already offered.

11. What have you appreciated about this course? In your journey to come home to God, do you feel you have a clean slate? How can the group pray for you?

12. Conclude with a time of silent prayer and reflection: Do you need to ask God's forgiveness for failures sexually or for other sins in your life? Do you need to seek out someone to share with concerning these issues or failures?

[43]Simon replied, "I suppose the one who had the bigger debt canceled."

"You have judged correctly," Jesus said.

[44]Then he turned toward the woman and said to Simon, "Do you
see this woman? I came into your house. You did not give me any
water for my feet, but she wet my feet with her tears and wiped
them with her hair. [45]You did not give me a kiss, but this woman,
from the time I entered, has not stopped kissing my feet. [46]You did
not put oil on my head, but she has poured perfume on my feet.
[47]Therefore, I tell you, her many sins have been forgiven—for she
loved much. But he who has been forgiven little loves little."

[48]Then Jesus said to her, "Your sins are forgiven."

[49]The other guests began to say among themselves, "Who is this who even forgives sins?"

[50]Jesus said to the woman, "Your faith has saved you; go in peace."

this woman that Jesus loves and forgives her?

1. How difficult is it for you to express your love in a relationship with Jesus? 2. What is the most loving thing you have ever done for Jesus? For someone else? How was Jesus part of it? 3. What have you learned from this story that you could apply this week?

The Parable of the Sower

8 After this, Jesus traveled about from one town and village to
another, proclaiming the good news of the kingdom of God.
The Twelve were with him, [2]and also some women who had been
cured of evil spirits and diseases: Mary (called Magdalene) from
whom seven demons had come out; [3]Joanna the wife of Cuza, the
manager of Herod's household; Susanna; and many others. These
women were helping to support them out of their own means.

[4]While a large crowd was gathering and people were coming to
Jesus from town after town, he told this parable: [5]"A farmer went
out to sow his seed. As he was scattering the seed, some fell along
the path; it was trampled on, and the birds of the air ate it up.
[6]Some fell on rock, and when it came up, the plants withered
because they had no moisture. [7]Other seed fell among thorns,
which grew up with it and choked the plants. [8]Still other seed fell
on good soil. It came up and yielded a crop, a hundred times more
than was sown."

When he said this, he called out, "He who has ears to hear, let him hear."

[9]His disciples asked him what this parable meant. [10]He said,
"The knowledge of the secrets of the kingdom of God has been
given to you, but to others I speak in parables, so that,

> " 'though seeing, they may not see;
> though hearing, they may not understand.'[a]

[11]"This is the meaning of the parable: The seed is the word of
God. [12]Those along the path are the ones who hear, and then the
devil comes and takes away the word from their hearts, so that
they may not believe and be saved. [13]Those on the rock are the
ones who receive the word with joy when they hear it, but they
have no root. They believe for a while, but in the time of testing
they fall away. [14]The seed that fell among thorns stands for those
who hear, but as they go on their way they are choked by life's
worries, riches and pleasures, and they do not mature. [15]But the
seed on good soil stands for those with a noble and good heart,
who hear the word, retain it, and by persevering produce a crop.

What kind of luck have you had with growing things? Are you a "green thumb" or a "brown thumb"? What is your secret of success (or reason for failure)?

1. What is Jesus' ministry style here (v. 1)? Who travels with him? What strikes you about them? **2.** What is a parable? Why does Jesus use parables? **3.** What is the reason why the disciples receive an explanation, while the others do not? How would the parable help the disciples to better understand what is happening in their ministry? **4.** In Jesus' explanation of this parable, what is the seed? The birds? The soils? The fruit? The farmer? **5.** What does it really mean to "hear"? How would you explain this parable to children who have never been on a farm? What modern analogy would you use? **6.** What does Jesus mean to be "a noble and good heart"?

1. What kind of "soil" best represents you now? Five years ago? **2.** When it comes to hearing God right now, are you: (a) Locked in on the station? (b) Getting a lot of static? (c) Barely picking up the signal? Why? The disciples were always asking Jesus questions (even dumb ones). How comfortable are you taking your questions to Jesus? **3.** What help do you get from this parable about sharing your faith with others?

A Lamp on a Stand

[16]"No one lights a lamp and hides it in a jar or puts it under a
bed. Instead, he puts it on a stand, so that those who come in can

If I looked under your bed right now, what would I find? (A suitcase, old socks, dust balls!)

[a]*10* Isaiah 6:9

1. If Jesus and his message are the lamp of truth, what is this parable saying about the kingdom of God? What is the promise for those who do and don't listen? **2.** How does Jesus expand on this in verses 19–21?

1. How do you feel about verse 17? **2.** Are you closer to your church family or your family of origin? Why?

see the light. 17For there is nothing hidden that will not be disclosed, and nothing concealed that will not be known or brought out into the open. 18Therefore consider carefully how you listen. Whoever has will be given more; whoever does not have, even what he thinks he has will be taken from him."

Jesus' Mother and Brothers

19Now Jesus' mother and brothers came to see him, but they were not able to get near him because of the crowd. 20Someone told him, "Your mother and brothers are standing outside, wanting to see you."

21He replied, "My mother and brothers are those who hear God's word and put it into practice."

What is the worst storm you remember?

1. What is Jesus teaching his disciples by ignoring and then rebuking the storm? **2.** What tone did Jesus use in verse 25?

Comparing your life to a storm, what would it be like right now: Partly cloudy? Lightning? Raging? Clearing up? What do you wish Jesus would do for you?

Jesus Calms the Storm

22One day Jesus said to his disciples, "Let's go over to the other side of the lake." So they got into a boat and set out. 23As they sailed, he fell asleep. A squall came down on the lake, so that the boat was being swamped, and they were in great danger.

24The disciples went and woke him, saying, "Master, Master, we're going to drown!"

He got up and rebuked the wind and the raging waters; the storm subsided, and all was calm. 25"Where is your faith?" he asked his disciples.

In fear and amazement they asked one another, "Who is this? He commands even the winds and the water, and they obey him."

When did a vacation turn into something you never expected? What happened?

1. After verses 22–25, how might the disciples be feeling: As they arrive on the other side of the lake? Once they realize they are near a graveyard? As the demoniac runs toward them? **2.** How does Jesus treat the man differently than the way others have? What is the net result? **3.** How do the pig farmers respond? The townspeople? Why are they afraid? **4.** Usually doing the opposite, why does Jesus tell this man to tell others what happened?

1. In your life right now, what is the thing that makes you feel like a "legion" (6,000 soldiers) is marching through your head, keeping you awake at night or filled with anxiety? **2.** When, if ever, have you wanted Jesus to leave you alone? To get out of your life? To let you hurt yourself? **3.** What is the most dramatic transformation you have seen Jesus work in someone's life? **4.** When you first met Jesus, how did he treat you? How was this different from the way others treated you?

The Healing of a Demon-possessed Man

26They sailed to the region of the Gerasenes,[a] which is across the lake from Galilee. 27When Jesus stepped ashore, he was met by a demon-possessed man from the town. For a long time this man had not worn clothes or lived in a house, but had lived in the tombs. 28When he saw Jesus, he cried out and fell at his feet, shouting at the top of his voice, "What do you want with me, Jesus, Son of the Most High God? I beg you, don't torture me!" 29For Jesus had commanded the evil[b] spirit to come out of the man. Many times it had seized him, and though he was chained hand and foot and kept under guard, he had broken his chains and had been driven by the demon into solitary places.

30Jesus asked him, "What is your name?"

"Legion," he replied, because many demons had gone into him. 31And they begged him repeatedly not to order them to go into the Abyss.

32A large herd of pigs was feeding there on the hillside. The demons begged Jesus to let them go into them, and he gave them permission. 33When the demons came out of the man, they went into the pigs, and the herd rushed down the steep bank into the lake and was drowned.

34When those tending the pigs saw what had happened, they ran off and reported this in the town and countryside, 35and the people went out to see what had happened. When they came to Jesus, they found the man from whom the demons had gone out, sitting at Jesus' feet, dressed and in his right mind; and they were afraid. 36Those who had seen it told the people how the demon-possessed man had been cured. 37Then all the people of the region of the Gerasenes asked Jesus to leave them, because they were overcome with fear. So he got into the boat and left.

[a]*26* Some manuscripts *Gadarenes*; other manuscripts *Gergesenes*; also in verse 37
[b]*29* Greek *unclean*

[38]The man from whom the demons had gone out begged to go
with him, but Jesus sent him away, saying, [39]"Return home and tell
how much God has done for you." So the man went away and told
all over town how much Jesus had done for him.

A Dead Girl and a Sick Woman

[40]Now when Jesus returned, a crowd welcomed him, for they
were all expecting him. [41]Then a man named Jairus, a ruler of the
synagogue, came and fell at Jesus' feet, pleading with him to come
to his house [42]because his only daughter, a girl of about twelve,
was dying.

As Jesus was on his way, the crowds almost crushed him. [43]And
a woman was there who had been subject to bleeding for twelve
years,[a] but no one could heal her. [44]She came up behind him
and touched the edge of his cloak, and immediately her bleeding
stopped.

[45]"Who touched me?" Jesus asked.

When they all denied it, Peter said, "Master, the people are
crowding and pressing against you."

[46]But Jesus said, "Someone touched me; I know that power has
gone out from me."

[47]Then the woman, seeing that she could not go unnoticed,
came trembling and fell at his feet. In the presence of all the
people, she told why she had touched him and how she had been
instantly healed. [48]Then he said to her, "Daughter, your faith has
healed you. Go in peace."

[49]While Jesus was still speaking, someone came from the house

What is the most astonishing event you have ever witnessed?

1. Of all the people pressing for Jesus' attention, two get through to him—how so? **2.** Why do you think Jesus makes the sick woman reveal herself? For his sake? Or for her sake (vv. 46–48)? **3.** What else do you learn about her character before and after she touches Jesus' garment? How was her faith obvious to Jesus? **4.** What do you know about Jairus' daughter from verses 41,42,49 and 53? **5.** Why does Jesus say she will be healed, or that she is "only asleep," when the facts speak otherwise? **6.** What part does Jairus' intense desire have in the raising of the dead girl? **7.** Why does Jesus sometimes tell those he healed to be silent (v. 56; also 5:14), but other times orders the healed person to first go home and tell all (see 5:24; 8:39)?

[a]*43* Many manuscripts *years, and she had spent all she had on doctors*

Luke 8:26–39 THE HEALING OF A DEMON-POSSESSED MAN

1. Stepping off the boat, how do you think Jesus reacted to the demon-possessed man?
   a. with kindness
   b. with fear
   c. with authority
   d. with uncertainty about the situation
   e. instantly recognizing the Enemy

2. What impresses you most about "Legion"?
   a. their number
   b. their power
   c. their fear of Jesus
   d. their path to destruction

3. Why do you think Jesus granted the demons' request to be allowed to go into the pigs?
   a. Sometimes you have to compromise with a powerful opponent.
   b. It was a dramatic way to get rid of the demons.
   c. Being a Jew, he didn't like pigs.
   d. The pigs (and demons) rushing into the lake were symbolic of the demons' defeat.
   e. He didn't—it just looked that way.

4. After the demons left him, how did the man feel?
   a. empty
   b. healthy
   c. hopeful
   d. in control of his choices
   e. desiring to belong again
   f. committed to Jesus

5. Why did the people of the region want Jesus to leave town?
   a. They were afraid of his power.
   b. They were afraid he might send more pigs into the lake.
   c. They were afraid he might cast out *their* demons.
   d. They were afraid he might be God.

6. Why did Jesus want the healed man to go home instead of with him?

7. What image from this story best describes you at this time?
   a. in solitary places
   b. crying out to Jesus
   c. experiencing God's healing
   d. sitting at Jesus' feet
   e. telling everyone what Jesus has done for me

8. If you could be freed from one specific thing, what would you choose?

9. In what way do you most identify with this demon-possessed man?
   a. My addiction has ruined my life.
   b. The things that afflict me are many.
   c. Sometimes I feel I am driven by an evil force inside of me.
   d. Sometimes I resist God.
   e. Sometimes I resist the people who are trying to help me.
   f. I can't beat this on my own.
   g. God has had great mercy on me.

10. Which of the following would you name as possible sources of your affliction? And what would you like Jesus to do for you in that area (or areas)?
    a. a poor self-image
    b. inherited tendencies to addiction
    c. trying to rely on myself alone
    d. relational or spiritual loneliness
    e. real demons
    f. a painful childhood or loss
    g. spiritual weakness

1. When have you been as desperate as Jairus and the bleeding woman? How did Jesus respond to you? **2.** Have you ever been too frightened to come to God with a problem? Why? **3.** From the stories in 8:2–56, what stands out to you about Jesus' power? His purposes? How might this make a difference as you face desperate situations?

What is one memorable camping trip you have had?

1. What decision does Jesus make about his ministry? Why? **2.** What are the disciples told to do? Why? **3.** How does King Herod react (vv. 7–9)? Why?

1. Who is someone you admire because they dared to give their life to a mission? **2.** What is your mission in life, other than to keep food on the table? How does God's kingdom fit in?

How do you unwind when you return from work or a trip: Eat? Read? Sleep? Play? TV?

1. Why does Jesus take his disciples away with him upon their return? **2.** How do you account for the differences in the way Jesus and the disciples view the crowd? **3.** What thoughts must the disciples have as they collect the leftovers?

From what do you need a rest: Work hassles? Family? Church activities? Community activities? School deadlines? How would you cope if God gave you a new challenge instead?

When you were a teenager, how did peer pressure affect your choice of clothes? Music? Friends?

of Jairus, the synagogue ruler. "Your daughter is dead," he said. "Don't bother the teacher any more."

50Hearing this, Jesus said to Jairus, "Don't be afraid; just believe, and she will be healed."

51When he arrived at the house of Jairus, he did not let anyone go in with him except Peter, John and James, and the child's father and mother. 52Meanwhile, all the people were wailing and mourning for her. "Stop wailing," Jesus said. "She is not dead but asleep."

53They laughed at him, knowing that she was dead. 54But he took her by the hand and said, "My child, get up!" 55Her spirit returned, and at once she stood up. Then Jesus told them to give her something to eat. 56Her parents were astonished, but he ordered them not to tell anyone what had happened.

Jesus Sends Out the Twelve

9 When Jesus had called the Twelve together, he gave them power and authority to drive out all demons and to cure diseases, 2and he sent them out to preach the kingdom of God and to heal the sick. 3He told them: "Take nothing for the journey—no staff, no bag, no bread, no money, no extra tunic. 4Whatever house you enter, stay there until you leave that town. 5If people do not welcome you, shake the dust off your feet when you leave their town, as a testimony against them." 6So they set out and went from village to village, preaching the gospel and healing people everywhere.

7Now Herod the tetrarch heard about all that was going on. And he was perplexed, because some were saying that John had been raised from the dead, 8others that Elijah had appeared, and still others that one of the prophets of long ago had come back to life. 9But Herod said, "I beheaded John. Who, then, is this I hear such things about?" And he tried to see him.

Jesus Feeds the Five Thousand

10When the apostles returned, they reported to Jesus what they had done. Then he took them with him and they withdrew by themselves to a town called Bethsaida, 11but the crowds learned about it and followed him. He welcomed them and spoke to them about the kingdom of God, and healed those who needed healing.

12Late in the afternoon the Twelve came to him and said, "Send the crowd away so they can go to the surrounding villages and countryside and find food and lodging, because we are in a remote place here."

13He replied, "You give them something to eat."

They answered, "We have only five loaves of bread and two fish—unless we go and buy food for all this crowd." 14(About five thousand men were there.)

But he said to his disciples, "Have them sit down in groups of about fifty each." 15The disciples did so, and everybody sat down. 16Taking the five loaves and the two fish and looking up to heaven, he gave thanks and broke them. Then he gave them to the disciples to set before the people. 17They all ate and were satisfied, and the disciples picked up twelve basketfuls of broken pieces that were left over.

Peter's Confession of Christ

18Once when Jesus was praying in private and his disciples were with him, he asked them, "Who do the crowds say I am?"

19They replied, "Some say John the Baptist; others say Elijah;

and still others, that one of the prophets of long ago has come back to life."

20"But what about you?" he asked. "Who do you say I am?"

Peter answered, "The Christ[a] of God."

21Jesus strictly warned them not to tell this to anyone. 22And he said, "The Son of Man must suffer many things and be rejected by the elders, chief priests and teachers of the law, and he must be killed and on the third day be raised to life."

23Then he said to them all: "If anyone would come after me, he must deny himself and take up his cross daily and follow me. 24For whoever wants to save his life will lose it, but whoever loses his life for me will save it. 25What good is it for a man to gain the whole world, and yet lose or forfeit his very self? 26If anyone is ashamed of me and my words, the Son of Man will be ashamed of him when he comes in his glory and in the glory of the Father and of the holy angels. 27I tell you the truth, some who are standing here will not taste death before they see the kingdom of God."

The Transfiguration

28About eight days after Jesus said this, he took Peter, John and James with him and went up onto a mountain to pray. 29As he was praying, the appearance of his face changed, and his clothes became as bright as a flash of lightning. 30Two men, Moses and Elijah, 31appeared in glorious splendor, talking with Jesus. They spoke about his departure, which he was about to bring to fulfillment at Jerusalem. 32Peter and his companions were very sleepy, but when they became fully awake, they saw his glory and the two men standing with him. 33As the men were leaving Jesus, Peter said to him, "Master, it is good for us to be here. Let us put up three shelters—one for you, one for Moses and one for Elijah." (He did not know what he was saying.)

34While he was speaking, a cloud appeared and enveloped them, and they were afraid as they entered the cloud. 35A voice came from the cloud, saying, "This is my Son, whom I have chosen; listen to him." 36When the voice had spoken, they found that Jesus was alone. The disciples kept this to themselves, and told no one at that time what they had seen.

The Healing of a Boy With an Evil Spirit

37The next day, when they came down from the mountain, a large crowd met him. 38A man in the crowd called out, "Teacher, I beg you to look at my son, for he is my only child. 39A spirit seizes him and he suddenly screams; it throws him into convulsions so that he foams at the mouth. It scarcely ever leaves him and is destroying him. 40I begged your disciples to drive it out, but they could not."

41"O unbelieving and perverse generation," Jesus replied, "how long shall I stay with you and put up with you? Bring your son here."

42Even while the boy was coming, the demon threw him to the ground in a convulsion. But Jesus rebuked the evil[b] spirit, healed the boy and gave him back to his father. 43And they were all amazed at the greatness of God.

While everyone was marveling at all that Jesus did, he said to his disciples, 44"Listen carefully to what I am about to tell you: The Son of Man is going to be betrayed into the hands of men." 45But they did not understand what this meant. It was hidden from them,

[a]*20* Or *Messiah* [b]*42* Greek *unclean*

1. Why would Jesus be interested in this opinion poll? **2.** Why does Jesus ask the follow-up question (v. 20)? **3.** Why doesn't Jesus want them to tell anyone he is the Christ? **4.** How might the disciples have felt about verse 22? **5.** What activities or attitudes are key to following Christ (v. 23)?

1. What does it mean specifically to you to: (a) deny yourself, (b) take up your cross daily, (c) follow Christ, and (d) lose your life? **2.** Have you ever been ashamed of Jesus? When? **3.** Knowing what you do now, would you reconsider your commitment to Christ? Why or why not?

When did you last say something you regretted?

1. Why would Jesus take these three disciples to witness this event? How is this related to: (a) Peter's confession (vv. 18–20)? (b) Jesus' prophecy (v. 22)? (c) The preceding saying (v. 27)? (d) The radiant face of Moses (Ex 34:29–30)? **2.** Why is this event misunderstood by Peter? Underscored by God (vv. 34–35)?

1. When have you experienced God in an unusual way? What happened? **2.** When it comes to listening to Jesus, how hard of hearing are you?

Can you remember a tantrum you threw as a child? What happened?

1. What has evidently been going on while Jesus was gone? **2.** What feelings are behind Jesus' words in verse 41? **3.** After the healing, what does Jesus teach his disciples? What's the significance of this teaching?

1. If you had been one of the disciples who couldn't solve the boy's problem only days after you had been on a *mission* trip, how would you feel? **2.** What spiritual low has recently followed a spiritual high for you?

What is the one thing you are best at doing?

1. In verses 46–50, how are the disciples gauging "greatness"? How does Jesus do so? 2. In John's concern (v. 49), what's the root desire? The irony (see v. 40)? 3. How does Jesus' "timetable" meet further resistance (vv. 51–56)? Why from the Samaritans? Why from his own disciples? How must Jesus be feeling by now?

1. What have you done for someone recently "in Jesus' name"? 2. How can you enact "he who is least among you all ... he is the greatest"? How did you picture "greatness" as a child? As an adult?

What's your favorite excuse for not doing something (e.g., "dog ate my homework")?

How does Jesus respond to the excuses offered by the three men (vv. 57,59,61)? In your own words, what do each of Jesus' sayings mean? What's his point?

Of the issues listed here (comfort, social obligations, family concerns), which one would tempt you to not follow Jesus?

If you had to sell something door to door, what would you choose: Fuller brushes? Encyclopedias? Jewelry? Cosmetics? Subscriptions? Serendipity Bibles? Why?

1. Why does he send the disciples out two-by-two? What are they looking for (v. 2)? 2. How is the Christian disciple like a "worker in the harvest"? A "lamb among wolves"? 3. What was the purpose of traveling light (v. 4)? Of praying first, going later? 4. What kind of household guests are they to be (v. 5)? Why? 5. How are they related to the town of which they are a part (vv. 8–12)? What is their basic message? 6. How do verses 1–12 show the urgency Jesus himself senses for evangelism? What is the reason for this urgency? 7.

so that they did not grasp it, and they were afraid to ask him
about it.

Who Will Be the Greatest?

46An argument started among the disciples as to which of them
would be the greatest. 47Jesus, knowing their thoughts, took a little
child and had him stand beside him. 48Then he said to them,
"Whoever welcomes this little child in my name welcomes me;
and whoever welcomes me welcomes the one who sent me. For he
who is least among you all—he is the greatest."
49"Master," said John, "we saw a man driving out demons in
your name and we tried to stop him, because he is not one of us."
50"Do not stop him," Jesus said, "for whoever is not against you
is for you."

Samaritan Opposition

51As the time approached for him to be taken up to heaven,
Jesus resolutely set out for Jerusalem. 52And he sent messengers on
ahead, who went into a Samaritan village to get things ready for
him; 53but the people there did not welcome him, because he was
heading for Jerusalem. 54When the disciples James and John saw
this, they asked, "Lord, do you want us to call fire down from
heaven to destroy them[a]?" 55But Jesus turned and rebuked them,
56and[b] they went to another village.

The Cost of Following Jesus

57As they were walking along the road, a man said to him, "I will
follow you wherever you go."
58Jesus replied, "Foxes have holes and birds of the air have
nests, but the Son of Man has no place to lay his head."
59He said to another man, "Follow me."
But the man replied, "Lord, first let me go and bury my father."
60Jesus said to him, "Let the dead bury their own dead, but you
go and proclaim the kingdom of God."
61Still another said, "I will follow you, Lord; but first let me go
back and say good-by to my family."
62Jesus replied, "No one who puts his hand to the plow and
looks back is fit for service in the kingdom of God."

Jesus Sends Out the Seventy-two

10 After this the Lord appointed seventy-two[c] others and sent
them two by two ahead of him to every town and place
where he was about to go. 2He told them, "The harvest is plentiful,
but the workers are few. Ask the Lord of the harvest, therefore, to
send out workers into his harvest field. 3Go! I am sending you out
like lambs among wolves. 4Do not take a purse or bag or sandals;
and do not greet anyone on the road.
5"When you enter a house, first say, 'Peace to this house.' 6If a
man of peace is there, your peace will rest on him; if not, it will
return to you. 7Stay in that house, eating and drinking whatever
they give you, for the worker deserves his wages. Do not move
around from house to house.
8"When you enter a town and are welcomed, eat what is set
before you. 9Heal the sick who are there and tell them, 'The kingdom of God is near you.' 10But when you enter a town and are not

[a] 54 Some manuscripts *them, even as Elijah did* [b] 55,56 Some manuscripts *them. And he said, "You do not know what kind of spirit you are of, for the Son of Man did not come to destroy men's lives, but to save them." 56And* [c] 1 Some manuscripts *seventy*; also in verse 17

welcomed, go into its streets and say, 11‘Even the dust of your town
that sticks to our feet we wipe off against you. Yet be sure of this:
The kingdom of God is near.’ 12I tell you, it will be more bearable
on that day for Sodom than for that town.

13“Woe to you, Korazin! Woe to you, Bethsaida! For if the miracles that were performed in you had been performed in Tyre and
Sidon, they would have repented long ago, sitting in sackcloth and
ashes. 14But it will be more bearable for Tyre and Sidon at the
judgment than for you. 15And you, Capernaum, will you be lifted
up to the skies? No, you will go down to the depths.[a]

16“He who listens to you listens to me; he who rejects you
rejects me; but he who rejects me rejects him who sent me.”

17The seventy-two returned with joy and said, “Lord, even the
demons submit to us in your name.”

18He replied, “I saw Satan fall like lightning from heaven. 19I
have given you authority to trample on snakes and scorpions and to
overcome all the power of the enemy; nothing will harm you.
20However, do not rejoice that the spirits submit to you, but rejoice
that your names are written in heaven.”

21At that time Jesus, full of joy through the Holy Spirit, said, “I
praise you, Father, Lord of heaven and earth, because you have
hidden these things from the wise and learned, and revealed them
to little children. Yes, Father, for this was your good pleasure.

22“All things have been committed to me by my Father. No one
knows who the Son is except the Father, and no one knows who
the Father is except the Son and those to whom the Son chooses to
reveal him.”

23Then he turned to his disciples and said privately, “Blessed are
the eyes that see what you see. 24For I tell you that many prophets
and kings wanted to see what you see but did not see it, and to
hear what you hear but did not hear it.”

What do you know about Sodom (see Ge 19:24–28)? Korazin and Bethsaida? About Capernaum (see Mt 4:13)? Tyre and Sidon (see Ez 28)? **8.** What is the comfort and the danger of aligning oneself with Jesus (v. 16)? **9.** Upon their return, what does Jesus say to them (vv. 18–20)? What in their report gives Jesus reason for joy (v. 21)? **10.** Consider verse 23. Do you think the disciples appreciate the privilege of being with Jesus? Why or why not?

1. How do you feel about the harvest where you live? Are people ripe for the Gospel? What would it take for you to be more involved in the harvest? **2.** When have you felt like a lamb among wolves? What did you learn from that experience? **3.** What do these verses show you about the privileges you have in Jesus Christ? Of these privileges, which are you experiencing now? **4.** What does verse 22 tell you about those who claim to know God without Christ?

The Parable of the Good Samaritan

25On one occasion an expert in the law stood up to test Jesus.
“Teacher,” he asked, “what must I do to inherit eternal life?”

26“What is written in the Law?” he replied. “How do you
read it?”

27He answered: “ ‘Love the Lord your God with all your heart
and with all your soul and with all your strength and with all your
mind’[b]; and, ‘Love your neighbor as yourself.’[c]”

28“You have answered correctly,” Jesus replied. “Do this and you
will live.”

29But he wanted to justify himself, so he asked Jesus, “And who
is my neighbor?”

30In reply Jesus said: “A man was going down from Jerusalem to
Jericho, when he fell into the hands of robbers. They stripped him
of his clothes, beat him and went away, leaving him half dead. 31A
priest happened to be going down the same road, and when he saw
the man, he passed by on the other side. 32So too, a Levite, when
he came to the place and saw him, passed by on the other side.
33But a Samaritan, as he traveled, came where the man was; and
when he saw him, he took pity on him. 34He went to him and
bandaged his wounds, pouring on oil and wine. Then he put the
man on his own donkey, took him to an inn and took care of him.
35The next day he took out two silver coins[d] and gave them to the
innkeeper. ‘Look after him,’ he said, ‘and when I return, I will
reimburse you for any extra expense you may have.’

Have you ever helped a stranger in distress? What happened?

1. Who’s testing whom in this story? **2.** Does the lawyer seem to think he has passed the test in verse 28? How so? **3.** Why does Jesus answer with a story instead of a straight answer? **4.** How might one justify the actions of the priest and the Levite (see Lev 21:1–3; Nu 19:11–22)? **5.** Given the divisions between Jews and Samaritans (see Jn 4), what’s unusual about the plot twist in this story? What is Jesus’ point here?

1. What attitude or behavior does God want you to have that is the most difficult to accept? **2.** Who have been Good Samaritans in your life? What makes a Good Samaritan really *good*? **3.** To whom will you be a Good Samaritan this week?

[a] *15* Greek *Hades* [b] *27* Deut. 6:5 [c] *27* Lev. 19:18 [d] *35* Greek *two denarii*

36"Which of these three do you think was a neighbor to the man
who fell into the hands of robbers?"
37The expert in the law replied, "The one who had mercy on
him."
Jesus told him, "Go and do likewise."

At the Home of Martha and Mary

38As Jesus and his disciples were on their way, he came to a
village where a woman named Martha opened her home to him.
39She had a sister called Mary, who sat at the Lord's feet listening
to what he said. 40But Martha was distracted by all the preparations
that had to be made. She came to him and asked, "Lord, don't you
care that my sister has left me to do the work by myself? Tell her
to help me!"
41"Martha, Martha," the Lord answered, "you are worried and
upset about many things, 42but only one thing is needed.[a] Mary
has chosen what is better, and it will not be taken away from her."

Jesus' Teaching on Prayer

11 One day Jesus was praying in a certain place. When he
finished, one of his disciples said to him, "Lord, teach us to
pray, just as John taught his disciples."
2He said to them, "When you pray, say:

> " 'Father,[b]
> hallowed be your name,
> your kingdom come.[c]

[a]42 Some manuscripts *but few things are needed—or only one* [b]2 Some manuscripts *Our Father in heaven* [c]2 Some manuscripts *come. May your will be done on earth as it is in heaven.*

How do these two sisters differ? Is Mary's choice better? What about Jesus' call to servanthood? What is Jesus' point?

Describe a time when you used your work responsibilities or social obligations to avoid Jesus. How do you seek to serve while also keeping God-given priorities?

---

1. Recite a prayer you said as a child. **2.** What's the funniest prayer you've heard a child say?

1. What motivates the disciples to ask about prayer at this point (v. 1)? **2.** In Jesus' model prayer (vv. 2–4), what two concerns related to God come first? Why? What personal concerns then follow? How do prayer and forgiveness relate? **3.** What does the parable in verses 5–8 teach

Luke 10:25–37 PARABLE OF THE GOOD SAMARITAN

1. In the parable Jesus told, why do you think the priest and the Levite (an assistant to the priests) refused to stop and help the mugging victim?
   a. They were in a big hurry.
   b. They didn't want to be bothered.
   c. Traveling on a notoriously dangerous road, they were afraid this was a trap to rob them.
   d. They thought the man was already dead.
   e. They were afraid to get too close, because the Law didn't allow them to touch a dead body.
2. Why did the Samaritan—whose people the Jews despised as half-breeds both physically and spiritually—stop and help the man?
   a. He evidently knew the man.
   b. The man was hurt, so it didn't matter to the Samaritan who he was.
   c. He put the wounded man's safety above his own.
   d. He didn't care about the religious problem of touching a corpse.
   e. He knew what it was like to be hurt and have others pass by.
3. Why do you think Jesus told this parable in response to the lawyer's question, "Who is my neighbor?"
   a. to let him answer his own question
   b. to catch him in a moral dilemma
   c. to use the "case study" approach that lawyers use
   d. to show how the expert in the Law failed to practice what he preached
   e. because the real question was, "To whom must I *be* a neighbor?"
4. After reading this parable, whom would you say is your "neighbor"?
   a. any person in need
   b. those I have a reasonable hope of being able to help
   c. those I'm most afraid of helping
   d. everyone—even my enemies
5. With whom do you identify most in this parable right now?
   a. the legal expert—always asking tough questions
   b. Jesus—under great pressure to say or do the right thing
   c. the mugging victim—bruised and bleeding
   d. the priest and Levite—too busy or too afraid
   e. the Good Samaritan—fulfilled by passing on God's love
   f. the innkeeper—constantly being asked to take care of someone
6. How do you feel when your efforts help others? How do you feel when your efforts don't seem to help?
7. Who has been a Good Samaritan in your life? How can you be a Good Samaritan to someone this week?
8. What does this story say about each of the following?
   a. how I should spend my life
   b. in whom I should invest my energy
   c. what kind of risks I should take
9. What would be the costs of investing in others the way God may be calling you to do?
   a. loss of time
   b. loss of energy
   c. financial sacrifice
   d. strain on relationships
   e. strain on my emotions

3Give us each day our daily bread.
4Forgive us our sins,
for we also forgive everyone who sins against
us.[a]
And lead us not into temptation.[b]' "

5Then he said to them, "Suppose one of you has a friend, and he
goes to him at midnight and says, 'Friend, lend me three loaves of
bread, 6because a friend of mine on a journey has come to me, and
I have nothing to set before him.'
7"Then the one inside answers, 'Don't bother me. The door is
already locked, and my children are with me in bed. I can't get up
and give you anything.' 8I tell you, though he will not get up and
give him the bread because he is his friend, yet because of the
man's boldness[c] he will get up and give him as much as he needs.
9"So I say to you: Ask and it will be given to you; seek and you
will find; knock and the door will be opened to you. 10For everyone
who asks receives; he who seeks finds; and to him who knocks, the
door will be opened.
11"Which of you fathers, if your son asks for[d] a fish, will give
him a snake instead? 12Or if he asks for an egg, will give him a
scorpion? 13If you then, though you are evil, know how to give

[a]4 Greek *everyone who is indebted to us* [b]4 Some manuscripts *temptation but deliver us from the evil one* [c]8 Or *persistence* [d]11 Some manuscripts *for bread, will give him a stone; or if he asks for*

about prayer? How do verses 9–10 relate to the parable? What attitude is implied in verses 9–10? How do verses 11–13 clarify the intent of verses 9–10?

1. What should be the relationship between this prayer and our own? How do you usually pray? Do you have a set time? A set place? Or are you more spontaneous when you pray? **2.** What do you use to prepare for prayer: Read a psalm? A devotional guide? A hymn? **3.** What concerns occupy most of your time in prayer: Praise? Confession? Petition? Why? In which area do you want to grow? **4.** What is the most valuable gift God can give (v. 13)? How much do you want that gift? Why? **5.** What one thing would you like to obtain from the Father?

Lk 10:38–42 AT THE HOME OF MARTHA & MARY

1. How would you describe the difference between Martha and Mary as you meet them in this story?
   a. a normal person vs. a lazy bum who lets others do all the work
   b. a normal person vs. an over-bearing workaholic who needs to relax
   c. a person who values responsibility vs. one who values relationships
   d. a person who needs to be needed vs. one who needs to be served

2. If you were Martha, how would you have responded to Jesus' words?
   a. flown off the handle
   b. thought to myself: "He doesn't have to live with my sister."
   c. left the room and pouted
   d. accepted the correction, sat down with Mary and forgot about supper

3. If Jesus could take Mary aside, what advice would he likely give her?
   a. Be a little more understanding of Martha.
   b. You are pushing your sister's buttons by being so laid back.
   c. You need to work on some of your own weaknesses—like sharing responsibilities in the kitchen.
   d. God made you and your sister different and you need each other.

4. What was Jesus saying to Martha?
   a. She should be more like Mary.
   b. She had her priorities messed up.
   c. People are more important than housework.
   d. "Sitting at Jesus' feet" is more important than anything else.

5. From this story, how would you describe the different personalities of Mary and Martha? What are their strengths and weaknesses? Which one are you more like?

6. If Jesus dropped in on you, what might he point out that distracts *you* from the really important things in life like spending time with him?

7. Are you more responsible or carefree? More focused on other people or yourself? Should you try to change your personality?

8. Regarding giving to others, how often do you experience each of the following motivations—seldom, sometimes or frequently?
   a. to feel in control
   b. to feel needed
   c. to receive in return
   d. to get people to like me
   e. out of obligation

9. In light of your answers to the last question, what course of action do you need to take?
   a. admit my need to change
   b. open my life more to God's love
   c. keep in touch with my motivations
   d. set limits on what I do for others
   e. keep doing what I'm doing

10. On a scale of 1 (very relaxed) to 10 (very tense), rate yourself on the following. What can you do to reduce your total score?
    a. driven/competitive/forceful
    b. find it hard to relax or play
    c. overloaded with activities
    d. impatient with delays
    e. easily angered by people/events
    f. very conscious of deadlines
    g. anxious about what others think

11. In each of the following, which quality is more true of you? Which is more true of your spouse? How can your different personalities bring you together rather than apart?
    a. *task* or *relational* oriented
    b. *work* or *quality-of-life* oriented
    c. *practical* or *idea* oriented
    d. *uptight* or *laid-back*
    e. *physically* or *spiritually* oriented

good gifts to your children, how much more will your Father in
heaven give the Holy Spirit to those who ask him!"

How well did you keep your bedroom when you were growing up? How have your habits changed with age?

1. How does the crowd react to Jesus' miracle (vv. 14–16)? **2.** How does Jesus show the foolishness of the claim that he drives out demons by Beelzebub? What does Jesus' ability to drive out demons say about the kingdom of God (v. 20)? **3.** What is Jesus' point in verses 24–26? To whom is the point addressed? Why is the final condition worse than the first? **4.** Why does Jesus turn around the blessing shouted to him in verse 27? What is he emphasizing here?

If you compared your life right now to a fortress, what is it like: (a) The Rock of Gibraltar? (b) Slowly eroding? (c) Quickly crumbling? Are you spiritually on the attack or feeling besieged? How's the battle going?

Jesus and Beelzebub

14Jesus was driving out a demon that was mute. When the demon left, the man who had been mute spoke, and the crowd was
amazed. 15But some of them said, "By Beelzebub,[a] the prince of
demons, he is driving out demons." 16Others tested him by asking
for a sign from heaven.

17Jesus knew their thoughts and said to them: "Any kingdom
divided against itself will be ruined, and a house divided against
itself will fall. 18If Satan is divided against himself, how can his
kingdom stand? I say this because you claim that I drive out demons by Beelzebub. 19Now if I drive out demons by Beelzebub, by
whom do your followers drive them out? So then, they will be your
judges. 20But if I drive out demons by the finger of God, then the
kingdom of God has come to you.

21"When a strong man, fully armed, guards his own house, his
possessions are safe. 22But when someone stronger attacks and
overpowers him, he takes away the armor in which the man trusted and divides up the spoils.

23"He who is not with me is against me, and he who does not
gather with me, scatters.

24"When an evil[b] spirit comes out of a man, it goes through
arid places seeking rest and does not find it. Then it says, 'I will
return to the house I left.' 25When it arrives, it finds the house
swept clean and put in order. 26Then it goes and takes seven other
spirits more wicked than itself, and they go in and live there. And
the final condition of that man is worse than the first."

27As Jesus was saying these things, a woman in the crowd called
out, "Blessed is the mother who gave you birth and nursed you."

28He replied, "Blessed rather are those who hear the word of
God and obey it."

Who is the wisest person you have ever known?

1. Why is Jesus upset about "this generation"? **2.** What is the sign of Jonah (see Jnh 1:17)? How is Jesus like that? **3.** Who is this Queen (1Ki 10:1–15)? Who condemns whom? **4.** What is Jesus' point?

What sign would it take for your generation to turn to God? What's the problem with relying on "signs" to do the trick?

The Sign of Jonah

29As the crowds increased, Jesus said, "This is a wicked generation. It asks for a miraculous sign, but none will be given it except
the sign of Jonah. 30For as Jonah was a sign to the Ninevites, so also
will the Son of Man be to this generation. 31The Queen of the
South will rise at the judgment with the men of this generation and
condemn them; for she came from the ends of the earth to listen to
Solomon's wisdom, and now one[c] greater than Solomon is here.
32The men of Nineveh will stand up at the judgment with this
generation and condemn it; for they repented at the preaching of
Jonah, and now one greater than Jonah is here.

How many flashlights do you own? How many work?

What does the light represent? The eye? The body? The darkness?

How would you score on a spiritual sight exam: 20/20? 20/80? Colorblind? Why?

The Lamp of the Body

33"No one lights a lamp and puts it in a place where it will be
hidden, or under a bowl. Instead he puts it on its stand, so that
those who come in may see the light. 34Your eye is the lamp of
your body. When your eyes are good, your whole body also is full
of light. But when they are bad, your body also is full of darkness.
35See to it, then, that the light within you is not darkness. 36There-
fore, if your whole body is full of light, and no part of it dark, it will
be completely lighted, as when the light of a lamp shines on you."

[a] *15* Greek *Beezeboul* or *Beelzeboul*; also in verses 18 and 19 [b] *24* Greek *unclean*
[c] *31* Or *something*; also in verse 32

Six Woes

37When Jesus had finished speaking, a Pharisee invited him to
eat with him; so he went in and reclined at the table. 38But the
Pharisee, noticing that Jesus did not first wash before the meal,
was surprised.
39Then the Lord said to him, "Now then, you Pharisees clean the
outside of the cup and dish, but inside you are full of greed and
wickedness. 40You foolish people! Did not the one who made the
outside make the inside also? 41But give what is inside ⌞the dish⌟[a]
to the poor, and everything will be clean for you.
42"Woe to you Pharisees, because you give God a tenth of your
mint, rue and all other kinds of garden herbs, but you neglect
justice and the love of God. You should have practiced the latter
without leaving the former undone.
43"Woe to you Pharisees, because you love the most important
seats in the synagogues and greetings in the marketplaces.
44"Woe to you, because you are like unmarked graves, which
men walk over without knowing it."
45One of the experts in the law answered him, "Teacher, when
you say these things, you insult us also."
46Jesus replied, "And you experts in the law, woe to you, because you load people down with burdens they can hardly carry,
and you yourselves will not lift one finger to help them.
47"Woe to you, because you build tombs for the prophets, and it
was your forefathers who killed them. 48So you testify that you
approve of what your forefathers did; they killed the prophets, and
you build their tombs. 49Because of this, God in his wisdom said, 'I
will send them prophets and apostles, some of whom they will kill
and others they will persecute.' 50Therefore this generation will be
held responsible for the blood of all the prophets that has been
shed since the beginning of the world, 51from the blood of Abel to
the blood of Zechariah, who was killed between the altar and the
sanctuary. Yes, I tell you, this generation will be held responsible
for it all.
52"Woe to you experts in the law, because you have taken away
the key to knowledge. You yourselves have not entered, and you
have hindered those who were entering."
53When Jesus left there, the Pharisees and the teachers of the
law began to oppose him fiercely and to besiege him with questions, 54waiting to catch him in something he might say.

When you were a child, who insisted that you wash up before meals? Who insisted that you wear clean clothes? How did you react to this fussing?

1. What is the natural and the surprising thing Jesus does to open this scene (v. 38)? **2.** How does the Lord turn the tables on his host? What is his basic point about the Pharisees (vv. 39–41)? **3.** In your own words, what is the meaning of these three woes directed at the Pharisees (vv. 42–44)? Given the Pharisees' view of tombs and the dead (see Nu 19:16), what is the significance of the unmarked graves (v. 44)? **4.** What is the point of these criticisms? **5.** In your own words, what is the meaning of the next three woes (vv. 46–52)? In the sixth woe (v. 52), what does Jesus mean by the key of knowledge? **6.** How does this Pharisee dinner compare with the one in 7:36–50? Why the difference?

1. Typically, Jesus is thought of as "meek and mild." What is the significance of this passage's presentation of Jesus for you? **2.** Of the three woes directed to the Pharisees, which one is Jesus directing most to you? Why? **3.** Of the three woes directed to the lawyers, which one has your name on it? Why? **4.** How would you like your life to change this week in light of what you've read here?

Warnings and Encouragements

12 Meanwhile, when a crowd of many thousands had gathered, so that they were trampling on one another, Jesus
began to speak first to his disciples, saying: "Be on your guard
against the yeast of the Pharisees, which is hypocrisy. 2There is
nothing concealed that will not be disclosed, or hidden that will
not be made known. 3What you have said in the dark will be heard
in the daylight, and what you have whispered in the ear in the
inner rooms will be proclaimed from the roofs.
4"I tell you, my friends, do not be afraid of those who kill the
body and after that can do no more. 5But I will show you whom
you should fear: Fear him who, after the killing of the body, has
power to throw you into hell. Yes, I tell you, fear him. 6Are not five
sparrows sold for two pennies[b]? Yet not one of them is forgotten
by God. 7Indeed, the very hairs of your head are all numbered.
Don't be afraid; you are worth more than many sparrows.

As a kid, who was the disciplinarian at home? What was the unpardonable sin in terms of breaking the rules?

1. Why does this crowd grow? **2.** What warnings (vv. 1–3) does Jesus issue the disciples? **3.** How does hypocrisy work like yeast (see 11:37–54)? **4.** Why does Jesus encourage his disciples to fear, yet be fearless (vv. 4–7)? **5.** What does it mean to "blaspheme against the Holy Spirit" (v. 10; see Lev 24:16)? How is the contrite person assured of not having done this? **6.** What does Jesus teach about the believer's security when facing human opposition (vv. 11–12)?

[a] 41 Or *what you have*   [b] 6 Greek *two assaria*

1. How do you feel knowing that everything done in secret will someday be revealed? **2.** When have you taken a risk and stood for Jesus in a public way? What happened? What did you learn?

8"I tell you, whoever acknowledges me before men, the Son of Man will also acknowledge him before the angels of God. 9But he who disowns me before men will be disowned before the angels of God. 10And everyone who speaks a word against the Son of Man will be forgiven, but anyone who blasphemes against the Holy Spirit will not be forgiven.

11"When you are brought before synagogues, rulers and authorities, do not worry about how you will defend yourselves or what you will say, 12for the Holy Spirit will teach you at that time what you should say."

What did you like to collect as a child? Now?

In response to the man's plea, Jesus tells a parable. What is the man's problem? His solution? Why is he a fool? What is the punch line?

1. When have you been like the man in this story? **2.** Advertising is dedicated to making us believe the opposite of verse 15. What differences in lifestyle result from believing Jesus versus advertisements? **3.** In planning an investment portfolio to become "rich toward God," what will you do this week? This year?

The Parable of the Rich Fool

13Someone in the crowd said to him, "Teacher, tell my brother to divide the inheritance with me."

14Jesus replied, "Man, who appointed me a judge or an arbiter between you?" 15Then he said to them, "Watch out! Be on your guard against all kinds of greed; a man's life does not consist in the abundance of his possessions."

16And he told them this parable: "The ground of a certain rich man produced a good crop. 17He thought to himself, 'What shall I do? I have no place to store my crops.'

18"Then he said, 'This is what I'll do. I will tear down my barns and build bigger ones, and there I will store all my grain and my goods. 19And I'll say to myself, "You have plenty of good things laid up for many years. Take life easy; eat, drink and be merry." '

20"But God said to him, 'You fool! This very night your life will be demanded from you. Then who will get what you have prepared for yourself?'

Luke 12:13–21 PARABLE OF THE RICH FOOL

1. After Jesus' response, how do you think the man who asked Jesus to settle his dispute with his brother felt?
   a. like slinking back into the crowd
   b. upset his dispute wasn't settled
   c. ashamed of his greed
   d. mad he was used to make a point

2. How would you describe the rich man in the parable?
   a. a show-off
   b. brilliant
   c. dumb
   d. content
   e. unhappy
   f. selfish

3. After dying, how would the local paper describe him in the obituaries?
   a. a tireless worker
   b. a success story
   c. foolish
   d. enterprising

4. God's response to the rich man was so harsh because God is:
   a. intolerant of self-indulgent people.
   b. compassionate for poor people.
   c. down on rich people.
   d. jealous of all other "gods."

5. How do you react to the idea that a person's "life does not consist in the abundance of his possessions"?
   a. It sounds like the teaching of someone poor and jealous.
   b. It's what a preacher should say.
   c. Yeah, but people with nice houses and cars sure *seem* happy!
   d. Yes, the best things in life are free.

6. What is Jesus saying in this story?
   a. People who try to be a financial success are motivated by greed.
   b. It's okay to be successful, but remember your highest priority.
   c. To really prepare for the future, you have to look beyond finances.
   d. When you think you have it made, think again.
   e. You can't take it with you.
   f. Life is short, so get all the gusto you can.
   g. Material things provide the greatest test of our spiritual devotion.

7. In harvest terms, how is your life going? Are your barns closer to bursting with grain, or empty from drought?

8. What changes would be required for you to be "rich toward God"?

9. How can this group help you make spiritual preparations for your future?

10. What do you value most in life?
    a. my loved ones
    b. my assets
    c. my good health
    d. my work
    e. my faith
    f. my integrity
    g. my memories
    h. my time

11. I would like to be remembered as a person who:
    a. had a lot.
    b. gave a lot.
    c. built it all single-handedly.
    d. enjoyed what he/she had.
    e. sacrificed to be rich toward God.

12. What does an investment portfolio guided by a desire to be rich toward God contain in areas like savings, retirement and estate planning? How are you handling these issues?

13. If your life ended "this very night," what would be your biggest regret? What can you do now and in the future to change that?

21"This is how it will be with anyone who stores up things for
himself but is not rich toward God."

Do Not Worry

22Then Jesus said to his disciples: "Therefore I tell you, do not
worry about your life, what you will eat; or about your body, what
you will wear. 23Life is more than food, and the body more than
clothes. 24Consider the ravens: They do not sow or reap, they have
no storeroom or barn; yet God feeds them. And how much more
valuable you are than birds! 25Who of you by worrying can add a
single hour to his life[a]? 26Since you cannot do this very little
thing, why do you worry about the rest?

27"Consider how the lilies grow. They do not labor or spin. Yet
I tell you, not even Solomon in all his splendor was dressed like
one of these. 28If that is how God clothes the grass of the field,
which is here today, and tomorrow is thrown into the fire, how
much more will he clothe you, O you of little faith! 29And do not
set your heart on what you will eat or drink; do not worry about it.
30For the pagan world runs after all such things, and your Father
knows that you need them. 31But seek his kingdom, and these
things will be given to you as well.

32"Do not be afraid, little flock, for your Father has been pleased
to give you the kingdom. 33Sell your possessions and give to the
poor. Provide purses for yourselves that will not wear out, a treasure in heaven that will not be exhausted, where no thief comes
near and no moth destroys. 34For where your treasure is, there
your heart will be also.

Which situation is most worrisome to you: Overdrawn at the bank? Gained 10 pounds? Child expelled? Nobody called all weekend? Mother-in-law stays two weeks? Business folds?

1. How does this section relate to the preceding parable about riches? **2.** What does Jesus tell the disciples *not* to do (v. 22)? Why? What does Jesus urge them to do instead (v. 33)? Why? What will result? **3.** What does Jesus teach here about seeking the kingdom of God?

1. On a scale from 1 ("no sweat") to 10 ("panic"), what is the worry quotient in your life right now? Why? **2.** How can you transfer your treasure from Wall Street to Heaven's Gate? **3.** How would your life be different if you lived the way Jesus sets forth in this passage?

Watchfulness

35"Be dressed ready for service and keep your lamps burning,
36like men waiting for their master to return from a wedding banquet, so that when he comes and knocks they can immediately
open the door for him. 37It will be good for those servants whose
master finds them watching when he comes. I tell you the truth,
he will dress himself to serve, will have them recline at the table
and will come and wait on them. 38It will be good for those servants whose master finds them ready, even if he comes in the
second or third watch of the night. 39But understand this: If the
owner of the house had known at what hour the thief was coming,
he would not have let his house be broken into. 40You also must be
ready, because the Son of Man will come at an hour when you do
not expect him."

41Peter asked, "Lord, are you telling this parable to us, or to
everyone?"

42The Lord answered, "Who then is the faithful and wise manager, whom the master puts in charge of his servants to give them
their food allowance at the proper time? 43It will be good for that
servant whom the master finds doing so when he returns. 44I tell
you the truth, he will put him in charge of all his possessions. 45But
suppose the servant says to himself, 'My master is taking a long
time in coming,' and he then begins to beat the menservants and
maidservants and to eat and drink and get drunk. 46The master of
that servant will come on a day when he does not expect him and
at an hour he is not aware of. He will cut him to pieces and assign
him a place with the unbelievers.

47"That servant who knows his master's will and does not get
ready or does not do what his master wants will be beaten with

Are you a night owl or an early bird? Ever fall asleep at the wheel? On a date? On duty?

1. What is the relationship between watchfulness and worry (verses 22–34)? **2.** Explain the role reversal described in verse 37. Why does Peter ask the question in verse 41? Why does Jesus answer as he does? **3.** Why does Jesus say they should be ready (vv. 39–40)? Who is the thief? **4.** What should be the attitude and actions of the faithful and wise manager (vv. 42-–43)? What could tempt the servants to do wrong (v. 45)? **5.** What is the meaning of verse 48? How would the disciples have interpreted it?

1. Consider verse 37. How do you feel about Jesus serving you? **2.** What dangers is Jesus warning you about in this section? Which danger is most likely to be a problem for you? **3.** What has God entrusted to you as his manager? If you knew that in 30 days Jesus was returning, what would you do to get things ready for inspection?

[a]25 Or *single cubit to his height*

many blows. 48But the one who does not know and does things
deserving punishment will be beaten with few blows. From everyone who has been given much, much will be demanded; and from
the one who has been entrusted with much, much more will be
asked.

What discussion topics are taboo at your family table or at family reunions? Why?

1. Of what "fire" is Jesus speaking? What "baptism"? What division? How and why does Jesus bring division? Why do you think Jesus wishes the fire was already kindled? How does this relate to "Peace on Earth, goodwill toward men"? **2.** How has the crowd misread Jesus? In verses 54–59, would Jesus speak the same way to a Gentile audience?

1. What has Christ brought to your family and friends: division or peace? Why? **2.** How can you tell if it is your faith that strains a relationship, or the way you live your faith? **3.** What signs in your own life indicate how you are doing? Using a weather map to describe your spiritual life, what does it forecast?

Not Peace but Division

49"I have come to bring fire on the earth, and how I wish it were
already kindled! 50But I have a baptism to undergo, and how distressed I am until it is completed! 51Do you think I came to bring
peace on earth? No, I tell you, but division. 52From now on there
will be five in one family divided against each other, three against
two and two against three. 53They will be divided, father against
son and son against father, mother against daughter and daughter
against mother, mother-in-law against daughter-in-law and daughter-in-law against mother-in-law."

Interpreting the Times

54He said to the crowd: "When you see a cloud rising in the
west, immediately you say, 'It's going to rain,' and it does. 55And
when the south wind blows, you say, 'It's going to be hot,' and it
is. 56Hypocrites! You know how to interpret the appearance of the
earth and the sky. How is it that you don't know how to interpret
this present time?

57"Why don't you judge for yourselves what is right? 58As you
are going with your adversary to the magistrate, try hard to be
reconciled to him on the way, or he may drag you off to the judge,
and the judge turn you over to the officer, and the officer throw
you into prison. 59I tell you, you will not get out until you have paid
the last penny.[a]"

What was the worst tragedy in your community last year?

1. What is the danger of associating someone's misfortune with sin? **2.** In verses 6–9, who does the tree represent: The owner? Farmer? Why the urgency?

1. If you had "one more year" like the fig tree to turn your life around, what would you do? **2.** What fruit do you want to be producing by this time next year?

Repent or Perish

13 Now there were some present at that time who told Jesus
about the Galileans whose blood Pilate had mixed with
their sacrifices. 2Jesus answered, "Do you think that these Galileans were worse sinners than all the other Galileans because they
suffered this way? 3I tell you, no! But unless you repent, you too
will all perish. 4Or those eighteen who died when the tower in
Siloam fell on them—do you think they were more guilty than all
the others living in Jerusalem? 5I tell you, no! But unless you
repent, you too will all perish."

6Then he told this parable: "A man had a fig tree, planted in his
vineyard, and he went to look for fruit on it, but did not find any.
7So he said to the man who took care of the vineyard, 'For three
years now I've been coming to look for fruit on this fig tree and
haven't found any. Cut it down! Why should it use up the soil?'

8" 'Sir,' the man replied, 'leave it alone for one more year, and
I'll dig around it and fertilize it. 9If it bears fruit next year, fine! If
not, then cut it down.' "

Are you more of a "the-rules-are-meant-to-be-broken" or a "play-it-by-the-book" type of person? Why? Give an example.

1. What does verse 11 tell you about Dr. Luke's knowledge of medicine? Of spiritual phe-

A Crippled Woman Healed on the Sabbath

10On a Sabbath Jesus was teaching in one of the synagogues,
11and a woman was there who had been crippled by a spirit for
eighteen years. She was bent over and could not straighten up at
all. 12When Jesus saw her, he called her forward and said to her,
"Woman, you are set free from your infirmity." 13Then he put his

[a]59 Greek *lepton*

hands on her, and immediately she straightened up and praised
God.
14 Indignant because Jesus had healed on the Sabbath, the synagogue ruler said to the people, "There are six days for work. So
come and be healed on those days, not on the Sabbath."
15 The Lord answered him, "You hypocrites! Doesn't each of you
on the Sabbath untie his ox or donkey from the stall and lead it out
to give it water? 16 Then should not this woman, a daughter of
Abraham, whom Satan has kept bound for eighteen long years, be
set free on the Sabbath day from what bound her?"
17 When he said this, all his opponents were humiliated, but the
people were delighted with all the wonderful things he was doing.

nomenon? **2.** How does Jesus expose the ruler's hypocrisy?

1. What tensions between caring for *people* and keeping religious *rules* do you experience? **2.** How do you reconcile this connection between physical and spiritual healing?

The Parables of the Mustard Seed and the Yeast

18 Then Jesus asked, "What is the kingdom of God like? What
shall I compare it to? 19 It is like a mustard seed, which a man took
and planted in his garden. It grew and became a tree, and the birds
of the air perched in its branches."
20 Again he asked, "What shall I compare the kingdom of God
to? 21 It is like yeast that a woman took and mixed into a large
amount[a] of flour until it worked all through the dough."

What is your favorite story about someone with humble beginnings who greatly succeeds?

What does the contrast between the seed and bush teach about the power of God's kingdom? What does yeast teach about it?

How can a little faith influence *your* everyday life?

The Narrow Door

22 Then Jesus went through the towns and villages, teaching as
he made his way to Jerusalem. 23 Someone asked him, "Lord, are
only a few people going to be saved?"
He said to them, 24 "Make every effort to enter through the
narrow door, because many, I tell you, will try to enter and will not
be able to. 25 Once the owner of the house gets up and closes the
door, you will stand outside knocking and pleading, 'Sir, open the
door for us.'
"But he will answer, 'I don't know you or where you come
from.'
26 "Then you will say, 'We ate and drank with you, and you
taught in our streets.'
27 "But he will reply, 'I don't know you or where you come from.
Away from me, all you evildoers!'
28 "There will be weeping there, and gnashing of teeth, when
you see Abraham, Isaac and Jacob and all the prophets in the
kingdom of God, but you yourselves thrown out. 29 People will
come from east and west and north and south, and will take their
places at the feast in the kingdom of God. 30 Indeed there are those
who are last who will be first, and first who will be last."

What happened the last time you were locked out of your house or car? How did you get in?

1. According to Jesus, who will make it through the narrow door and who won't (v. 30)? **2.** If God loves people, why isn't the door wider? Who are the ones outside? Why isn't eating and drinking with Jesus enough? **3.** What do you think Jesus means by "evildoers"? In the end, do you think only a few or many or all people will be saved? Why?

How do you know whether you are inside or outside the kingdom? How can you be sure?

Jesus' Sorrow for Jerusalem

31 At that time some Pharisees came to Jesus and said to him,
"Leave this place and go somewhere else. Herod wants to kill you."
32 He replied, "Go tell that fox, 'I will drive out demons and heal
people today and tomorrow, and on the third day I will reach my
goal.' 33 In any case, I must keep going today and tomorrow and the
next day—for surely no prophet can die outside Jerusalem!
34 "O Jerusalem, Jerusalem, you who kill the prophets and stone
those sent to you, how often I have longed to gather your children
together, as a hen gathers her chicks under her wings, but you
were not willing! 35 Look, your house is left to you desolate. I tell
you, you will not see me again until you say, 'Blessed is he who
comes in the name of the Lord.'[b]"

What place do you identify with your spiritual roots?

1. What does Jesus reveal here (vv. 32–33) about his intentions? What does his response reveal about him? **2.** What strikes you about Jesus' prophecy?

What would it mean for each of us to gather under Jesus' wings?

[a] 21 Greek *three satas* (probably about 1/2 bushel or 22 liters) [b] 35 Psalm 118:26

Jesus at a Pharisee's House

14 One Sabbath, when Jesus went to eat in the house of a prominent Pharisee, he was being carefully watched.
2There in front of him was a man suffering from dropsy. 3Jesus
asked the Pharisees and experts in the law, "Is it lawful to heal on
the Sabbath or not?" 4But they remained silent. So taking hold of
the man, he healed him and sent him away.
5Then he asked them, "If one of you has a son[a] or an ox that
falls into a well on the Sabbath day, will you not immediately pull
him out?" 6And they had nothing to say.
7When he noticed how the guests picked the places of honor at
the table, he told them this parable: 8"When someone invites you
to a wedding feast, do not take the place of honor, for a person
more distinguished than you may have been invited. 9If so, the
host who invited both of you will come and say to you, 'Give this
man your seat.' Then, humiliated, you will have to take the least
important place. 10But when you are invited, take the lowest place,
so that when your host comes, he will say to you, 'Friend, move up
to a better place.' Then you will be honored in the presence of all
your fellow guests. 11For everyone who exalts himself will be humbled, and he who humbles himself will be exalted."
12Then Jesus said to his host, "When you give a luncheon or
dinner, do not invite your friends, your brothers or relatives, or
your rich neighbors; if you do, they may invite you back and so you
will be repaid. 13But when you give a banquet, invite the poor, the
crippled, the lame, the blind, 14and you will be blessed. Although
they cannot repay you, you will be repaid at the resurrection of the
righteous."

If you could have the best seats in the house, what would you choose: Super Bowl? A rock concert? Philharmonic orchestra? Indy 500? Royal wedding?

1. What's the situation here: The day? Host? Atmosphere? **2.** What does Jesus do to heal the man and to trap the Pharisees (vv. 2–6)? What does their silence mean? **3.** How does Jesus' view of honor (vv. 7–11) vary from that held by others at the meal? **4.** What does this passage teach you about the differences between kingdom values vs. social values? In verse 7 Jesus observes subtle social behavior. What does that tell you about his ability to observe your behavior?

1. How do things like customs and status get in the way of loving others in your family? Church? Work place? Community? **2.** If you threw a party for the "poor," "crippled," "lame" and "blind," who would you invite? How might you do this?

The Parable of the Great Banquet

15When one of those at the table with him heard this, he said to
Jesus, "Blessed is the man who will eat at the feast in the kingdom
of God."
16Jesus replied: "A certain man was preparing a great banquet
and invited many guests. 17At the time of the banquet he sent his
servant to tell those who had been invited, 'Come, for everything
is now ready.'
18"But they all alike began to make excuses. The first said, 'I
have just bought a field, and I must go and see it. Please excuse me.'
19"Another said, 'I have just bought five yoke of oxen, and I'm
on my way to try them out. Please excuse me.'
20"Still another said, 'I just got married, so I can't come.'
21"The servant came back and reported this to his master. Then
the owner of the house became angry and ordered his servant, 'Go
out quickly into the streets and alleys of the town and bring in the
poor, the crippled, the blind and the lame.'
22"'Sir,' the servant said, 'what you ordered has been done, but
there is still room.'
23"Then the master told his servant, 'Go out to the roads and
country lanes and make them come in, so that my house will be
full. 24I tell you, not one of those men who were invited will get a
taste of my banquet.'"

What was one of your best parties? How so?

1. Do you think that the man in verse 15 understood Jesus' teaching and blessing in the previous passage? Why or why not? **2.** In this parable, who are the invited guests? Why don't they come? What happens to them? Who eventually comes? **3.** On what basis is one invited? How might Jesus' servant fulfill the command of verse 23? What does this parable teach about the kingdom?

From your experience, what excuses do people make to avoid God's "banquet"? What can you say or do to help people overcome their hesitation?

The Cost of Being a Disciple

25Large crowds were traveling with Jesus, and turning to them
he said: 26"If anyone comes to me and does not hate his father and

If you were on a TV game show, would you try for the $50,000 grand prize, even though you might lose the $25,000 you had won so far? Why?

[a]5 Some manuscripts *donkey*

mother, his wife and children, his brothers and sisters—yes, even
his own life—he cannot be my disciple. 27And anyone who does
not carry his cross and follow me cannot be my disciple.
28"Suppose one of you wants to build a tower. Will he not first
sit down and estimate the cost to see if he has enough money to
complete it? 29For if he lays the foundation and is not able to finish
it, everyone who sees it will ridicule him, 30saying, 'This fellow
began to build and was not able to finish.'
31"Or suppose a king is about to go to war against another king.
Will he not first sit down and consider whether he is able with ten
thousand men to oppose the one coming against him with twenty
thousand? 32If he is not able, he will send a delegation while the
other is still a long way off and will ask for terms of peace. 33In the
same way, any of you who does not give up everything he has
cannot be my disciple.
34"Salt is good, but if it loses its saltiness, how can it be made
salty again? 35It is fit neither for the soil nor for the manure pile; it
is thrown out.
"He who has ears to hear, let him hear."

1. What is Jesus saying about family? What does he mean by "hate"? By carrying a cross? **2.** What do each of the three parables tell us about how to give our lives to Jesus? **3.** What does the salt analogy emphasize about discipleship? **4.** In summary, what kingdom values are taught? Why such tough talk from Jesus?

1. When did you realize that following Jesus was costly? How so? **2.** Is it worth it? What keeps you going?

The Parable of the Lost Sheep

15 Now the tax collectors and "sinners" were all gathering
around to hear him. 2But the Pharisees and the teachers
of the law muttered, "This man welcomes sinners and eats with
them."
3Then Jesus told them this parable: 4"Suppose one of you has a
hundred sheep and loses one of them. Does he not leave the
ninety-nine in the open country and go after the lost sheep until he
finds it? 5And when he finds it, he joyfully puts it on his shoulders

Which of your possessions were recently lost? Recently found?

1. Who is in Jesus' audience? How do they respond to him? **2.** How does Jesus' parable of the sheep relate to the muttering of the Pharisees? What is Jesus' point (v. 7)? **3.** How do you

Luke 14:15–24 PARABLE OF THE GREAT BANQUET

1. The three people in the parable accepted the initial banquet invitation, then backed out with flimsy excuses the day of the party. How would you have felt if you had been the host?
   a. furious
   b. hurt
   c. curious about the real reason
   d. indifferent
   e. understanding
2. Why did the three invited guests refuse to come?
   a. They weren't interested.
   b. They were interested, but had more important things to do.
   c. Their relationship with the host was not important to them.
   d. They didn't know how good the party was going to be.
3. Who are the poor, crippled, blind and lame who are invited to take the others' place?
   a. losers and outcasts
   b. the party crowd
   c. people hungry for spiritual things
   d. Gentiles outside of the covenant
   e. everybody who knows they don't deserve God's grace
4. What exactly is this great banquet?
   a. the kingdom of God here and now
   b. deeper spiritual things
   c. Jesus himself
   d. the banquet at the return of Christ
5. What does it take to get into God's banquet? Do you have a personal reservation?
6. Why do so many people say "No" to God's banquet? Who in particular comes to your mind? What can you say or do to help them come in?
7. What is the lesson of this passage for you?
   a. God is throwing a party, and it is for everyone.
   b. God is calling me to go and invite others to feast with him.
   c. God desires my fellowship.
   d. I've got to have an appetite for spiritual things.
   e. I need to get my priorities in line with my commitments.
8. Which of the following "kingdom priorities" do you struggle with the most? Which do you struggle with the least?
   a. personal devotional time
   b. family devotional time
   c. regular church participation
   d. regular small group participation
   e. sharing my gifts and talents
   f. sharing my material resources
   g. sharing my faith
9. What excuses do you use for staying away from God's banquet of fellowship with him and your fellow invited guests?
   a. It's my parents' fault—they gave me a bunch of hang-ups instead of a foundation.
   b. It's my spouse's fault—he/she doesn't give me encouragement.
   c. It's a great idea, but unfortunately I don't have the time.
   d. I am what I am, and I can't help it.
   e. No excuses, I just don't want to go!
   f. No excuses, I'm on the way to the banquet!
10. How would Jesus confront you about your excuses?

6and goes home. Then he calls his friends and neighbors together and says, 'Rejoice with me; I have found my lost sheep.' 7I tell you that in the same way there will be more rejoicing in heaven over one sinner who repents than over ninety-nine righteous persons who do not need to repent.

The Parable of the Lost Coin

8"Or suppose a woman has ten silver coins[a] and loses one. Does she not light a lamp, sweep the house and search carefully until she finds it? 9And when she finds it, she calls her friends and neighbors together and says, 'Rejoice with me; I have found my lost coin.' 10In the same way, I tell you, there is rejoicing in the presence of the angels of God over one sinner who repents."

The Parable of the Lost Son

11Jesus continued: "There was a man who had two sons. 12The younger one said to his father, 'Father, give me my share of the estate.' So he divided his property between them.

13"Not long after that, the younger son got together all he had, set off for a distant country and there squandered his wealth in wild living. 14After he had spent everything, there was a severe famine in that whole country, and he began to be in need. 15So he went and hired himself out to a citizen of that country, who sent him to his fields to feed pigs. 16He longed to fill his stomach with the pods that the pigs were eating, but no one gave him anything.

17"When he came to his senses, he said, 'How many of my father's hired men have food to spare, and here I am starving to death! 18I will set out and go back to my father and say to him: Father, I have sinned against heaven and against you. 19I am no longer worthy to be called your son; make me like one of your hired men.' 20So he got up and went to his father.

"But while he was still a long way off, his father saw him and was filled with compassion for him; he ran to his son, threw his arms around him and kissed him.

21"The son said to him, 'Father, I have sinned against heaven and against you. I am no longer worthy to be called your son.[b]'

22"But the father said to his servants, 'Quick! Bring the best robe and put it on him. Put a ring on his finger and sandals on his feet. 23Bring the fattened calf and kill it. Let's have a feast and celebrate. 24For this son of mine was dead and is alive again; he was lost and is found.' So they began to celebrate.

25"Meanwhile, the older son was in the field. When he came near the house, he heard music and dancing. 26So he called one of the servants and asked him what was going on. 27'Your brother has come,' he replied, 'and your father has killed the fattened calf because he has him back safe and sound.'

28"The older brother became angry and refused to go in. So his father went out and pleaded with him. 29But he answered his father, 'Look! All these years I've been slaving for you and never disobeyed your orders. Yet you never gave me even a young goat so I could celebrate with my friends. 30But when this son of yours who has squandered your property with prostitutes comes home, you kill the fattened calf for him!'

31" 'My son,' the father said, 'you are always with me, and everything I have is yours. 32But we had to celebrate and be glad, because this brother of yours was dead and is alive again; he was lost and is found.' "

[a]*8* Greek *ten drachmas,* each worth about a day's wages [b]*21* Some early manuscripts *son. Make me like one of your hired men.*

picture the woman searching for her money (vv. 8–9)? What is Jesus' point here?

1. Have you ever strayed from the Christian faith? How did God bring you back? **2.** How do these stories make you feel about your value to God? **3.** How could these stories affect your relationships with those you know who wander from the faith?

---

1. Did you ever run away from home? Where did you go? What happened? **2.** Who was (or is) the "obedient type" in your family? The "wild one"? Which were (or are) you? How did (or do) these types get along?

1. What stages does the younger son go through on his pilgrimage? What brings him to his senses? What does he realize then? With what sort of attitude does he approach his father? **2.** How does the father receive his son? Why? **3.** How does the older brother feel about his younger brother's return? Why? How does the father answer the older brother's objection? **4.** What's Jesus' point with this parable? What does this story teach about sin, repentance and God's love? **5.** In summary, how do these three parables answer the Pharisee's objection in verse 2? What does Jesus want to teach the Pharisees in verses 25–31? In light of the context (v. 2), why does Jesus leave the story open-ended as to how the older brother responded to his father's plea?

1. Comparing yourself to the two brothers in this story, who are you most like? Why? Are you quietly "at home"? Living only for today? Paying the consequences for yesterday? On the way home? Whom would you have identified with 10 years ago, or in your youth? **2.** How have you experienced God as similar to this father? **3.** When have you been like the older brother, quietly resentful of God's lavishness to less deserving people? Why? **4.** Consider verse 31. What does God have to give you that you have not taken?

The Parable of the Shrewd Manager

16 Jesus told his disciples: "There was a rich man whose manager was accused of wasting his possessions. 2So he called
him in and asked him, 'What is this I hear about you? Give an
account of your management, because you cannot be manager any
longer.'
3"The manager said to himself, 'What shall I do now? My master
is taking away my job. I'm not strong enough to dig, and I'm
ashamed to beg— 4I know what I'll do so that, when I lose my job
here, people will welcome me into their houses.'
5"So he called in each one of his master's debtors. He asked the
first, 'How much do you owe my master?'
6" 'Eight hundred gallons[a] of olive oil,' he replied.
"The manager told him, 'Take your bill, sit down quickly, and
make it four hundred.'

[a]6 Greek *one hundred batous* (probably about 3 kiloliters)

Which job would best fit your personality: Ringmaster at a circus? Movie producer? Sculptor? Librarian? Skydiving instructor? Gourmet chef? Church pastor?

1. Why would it be important for Jesus' disciples to hear this parable? **2.** In what crisis does the manager find himself? What plan does he devise? In light of this scheme, why does the owner commend the manager (v. 8)? **3.** How does Jesus summarize this parable (v. 9)? What do you think he's commending here? How do verses 10–12 help you understand his point? **4.** What's the problem with trying to serve two masters (v. 13)? What characterizes the attitude of

Lk 15:11–32 **PRODIGAL SON**

1. Why do you think the younger son decided to leave home?
   a. to try to make it on his own
   b. to experience the "fast lane"
   c. to be free of his father's values
   d. to get away from his older brother

2. What made the son come home?
   a. He got homesick.
   b. He got hungry.
   c. He felt sorry for his father.
   d. He felt sorry for himself.
   e. He felt guilty for what he had done.

3. If you were the father, what would have been your attitude when your son returned?
   a. Good to see you—but you're grounded!
   b. You have disgraced the family.
   c. Where's the money?
   d. I don't approve of what you've done, but you're still my son.
   e. Welcome home, son—I love you!

4. If you were the older brother, how would you have felt when you found out your father was throwing a party for your younger brother?
   a. angry
   b. confused
   c. happy
   d. resentful

5. In your life do you identify most with the father, with the younger son or with the older son?

6. Which relationship in your family generates the most conflict? What would need to happen for your family to want to celebrate the way the father did with his son?

7. If you likened your spiritual journey to the younger son's, where are you right now?
   a. never left home
   b. still at home, but itching to leave
   c. in a distant country, having a blast
   d. starting to realize I'm in a pigpen
   e. nervously on my way home
   f. back home and enjoying the party

8. How does this parable remind you of your own story? What are the roadblocks you have faced (or still face) on your way "home"?

9. What is the closest you have come to hitting bottom financially? What have you learned through financial hard times?
   a. that I can fail
   b. that forgiveness awaits when I admit my failure
   c. that I can't control everything that happens in life
   d. that it's never too late to make things right

10. Which of the patterns for resolving family conflict are typical of you and/or your family? (And how would you like things to be different?) I/We usually:
   a. enforce towing the line (because "father knows best").
   b. lovingly let people suffer the consequences of their own decisions.
   c. avoid conflict, and let time heal all wounds.
   d. allow the expression of disappointment and anger.

11. How does this story relate to the following four of the "12 Steps" which pertain to confession?
   a. Made a searching and fearless moral inventory of ourselves.
   b. Admitted to God, to ourselves, and to another human being the exact nature of our wrongs.
   c. Were entirely ready to have God remove these defects of character.
   d. Humbly asked him to remove our shortcomings.

12. On your road to recovery, how are you dong in practicing these four steps? Is there anything you want to confess to the group right now?

13. If you were to have a party to celebrate the most positive thing about you and your parents' relationship, what would you celebrate? What can you do to make your relationship better?

14. Which of the father's qualities do you most need?
   a. his willingness to let his son make mistakes
   b. his patience in waiting for change
   c. his capacity to forgive
   d. his understanding in dealing with both his children
   e. his ability to celebrate life

15. What has brought you the most joy as a parent? What have you appreciated the most about this course? How would you like the group to remember you in prayer?

the Pharisees (v. 14)? How does the parable speak to them?

1. How do you view your money: (a) It's mine, keep your hands off? (b) It's my creditors'? (c) It's God's—I just manage it? Why? How could you use it for the sake of the kingdom? **2.** Who (or what) are some of the masters you've served in the past? What masters *pull* at you for allegiance now? How do you deal with these pressures in light of your commitment to Christ?

---

1. How has the coming of the kingdom supplanted the law? Reinforced it? **2.** How is verse 18 to be applied today?

7"Then he asked the second, 'And how much do you owe?'
" 'A thousand bushels[a] of wheat,' he replied.
"He told him, 'Take your bill and make it eight hundred.'
8"The master commended the dishonest manager because he
had acted shrewdly. For the people of this world are more shrewd
in dealing with their own kind than are the people of the light. 9I
tell you, use worldly wealth to gain friends for yourselves, so that
when it is gone, you will be welcomed into eternal dwellings.
10"Whoever can be trusted with very little can also be trusted
with much, and whoever is dishonest with very little will also be
dishonest with much. 11So if you have not been trustworthy in
handling worldly wealth, who will trust you with true riches?
12And if you have not been trustworthy with someone else's property, who will give you property of your own?
13"No servant can serve two masters. Either he will hate the one
and love the other, or he will be devoted to the one and despise
the other. You cannot serve both God and Money."
14The Pharisees, who loved money, heard all this and were
sneering at Jesus. 15He said to them, "You are the ones who justify
yourselves in the eyes of men, but God knows your hearts. What is
highly valued among men is detestable in God's sight.

Additional Teachings

16"The Law and the Prophets were proclaimed until John. Since
that time, the good news of the kingdom of God is being preached,
and everyone is forcing his way into it. 17It is easier for heaven and

[a]7 Greek *one hundred korous* (probably about 35 kiloliters)

Luke 16:1–15 PARABLE OF THE SHREWD MANAGER

1. What did the manager do when he saw he was about to get fired?
   a. He moved quickly to cut his boss's losses.
   b. He hurried to cover his tracks.
   c. He tried to get even with his boss.
   d. He tried to wheel and deal his way out of trouble.
   e. He created obligations he could "call in" later.

2. Why did the master commend the manager?
   a. because he had given up on collecting the debts
   b. because he admired shrewdness
   c. because some payment was better than none
   d. because the manager had acted quickly and decisively

3. What was Jesus teaching here?
   a. Dishonesty is the best policy.
   b. We should use money shrewdly.
   c. We should use money to buy friends.
   d. We should extend God's kingdom by sharing with those in need.
   e. We should be as diligent as unbelievers are in managing money.
   f. Our spiritual growth is directly related to our faithfulness with money.

4. What does it mean to you to be "trustworthy in handling worldly wealth"?
   a. to put profits first
   b. to make smart financial decisions
   c. to implement the decisions of my superiors
   d. to handle wealth with the conviction that God owns it all
   e. to always be honest and ethical
   f. to use money in a way that will reap eternal dividends

5. How do you view your money?
   a. It's mine—keep your hands off!
   b. It's my creditors'.
   c. It's God's—I just manage it.

6. How do you feel about Jesus' black and white words: "You cannot serve both God and Money"? What practical changes can you make in your life to make you less of a servant or slave to money?

7. Have you faced a crisis where, like the manager in this story, you thought you might lose your business or job because of a particular decision or a money management failure? What did you do?

8. What is God calling you to do as a result of this study?
   a. view money management in the business world as an obligation to God to be trustworthy
   b. make wise, but honest, business decisions
   c. stop serving money and start serving God more
   d. give more money to help people

9. In what way are you currently experiencing the most internal conflict regarding money? How does that conflict affect your relationships with God and others?

10. What is the toughest decision you need to make concerning your finances? How does this passage speak to that decision? How can this group pray for you?

earth to disappear than for the least stroke of a pen to drop out of
the Law.
[18]"Anyone who divorces his wife and marries another woman
commits adultery, and the man who marries a divorced woman
commits adultery.

The Rich Man and Lazarus

[19]"There was a rich man who was dressed in purple and fine
linen and lived in luxury every day. [20]At his gate was laid a beggar
named Lazarus, covered with sores [21]and longing to eat what fell
from the rich man's table. Even the dogs came and licked his sores.
[22]"The time came when the beggar died and the angels carried
him to Abraham's side. The rich man also died and was buried.
[23]In hell,[a] where he was in torment, he looked up and saw Abraham far away, with Lazarus by his side. [24]So he called to him,
'Father Abraham, have pity on me and send Lazarus to dip the tip
of his finger in water and cool my tongue, because I am in agony in
this fire.'
[25]"But Abraham replied, 'Son, remember that in your lifetime
you received your good things, while Lazarus received bad things,
but now he is comforted here and you are in agony. [26]And besides
all this, between us and you a great chasm has been fixed, so that
those who want to go from here to you cannot, nor can anyone
cross over from there to us.'
[27]"He answered, 'Then I beg you, father, send Lazarus to my

[a]23 Greek *Hades*

1. To clarify this passage, what would you ask Jesus? **2.** How have you tried to force your way into the kingdom of heaven?

For what occasions do you feel like dressing to the hilt? When are you permitted and content to dress just in rags?

1. How do the lives of the rich man and Lazarus compare on earth (vv. 19–21)? After death (vv. 22–24)? **2.** What determines who enters heaven? Why does this poor man qualify while the rich man is kept out? **3.** What does this story teach you about comfort? Suffering? Why is it so difficult for people to be convinced of God's ways? How is verse 31 prophetic? **4.** What does this passage teach about the afterlife? **5.** What should we do with our lives on earth?

1. On a scale of 1 (the rich man and his brothers) to 10 (Lazarus), where do you stand? Why there? **2.** Since lack of knowledge is not the brothers' problem, what is? How do you see that ten-

Luke 16:19–31 THE RICH MAN AND LAZARUS

1. Whom do you feel most sorry for?
   a. Lazarus in the beginning of the story
   b. the rich man in the middle of the story
   c. the rich man's brothers in the end of the story
2. What caused the rich man to be condemned?
   a. his great wealth
   b. his luxurious self-indulgence
   c. his oppression of the poor
   d. his hardness of heart toward God
   e. his apathy toward people's needs
   f. his lack of faith
   g. his refusal to listen and submit to Scripture
3. Why do you think Lazarus was qualified for heaven while the rich man was kept out?
4. How do you feel about discussing the subject of hell?
5. If Jesus commented on our view of wealth today, what might he say?
   a. The "Lifestyles of the Rich and Famous" is not the way to go.
   b. You are grabbing for it all, but missing the true meaning of life.
   c. It's difficult to see any difference between Christian values and secular values.
   d. You have so much, but you are spiritually bankrupt.
6. What does this story teach about the dark side of human nature?
   a. People can be very selfish.
   b. People can block out the needs of those around them.
   c. People can shut out God's Word.
   d. People can resist the testimony of miracles.
   e. People can ignore Jesus Christ in general and his resurrection in particular.
7. To which of the preceding offenses are you most vulnerable?
8. If you suddenly came into a great deal of money, what would you do with it?
9. Being totally honest, what are your top three priorities in life right now?
   a. a good time
   b. a good marriage/family
   c. good friendships
   d. making lots of money
   e. having nice things
   f. financial independence/security
   g. greater intimacy with God
   h. developing my spiritual gifts
   i. making a contribution to humanity
   j. being true to myself
   k. other:____________________
10. How have your values changed since you gave your life to Christ? How do you think God might want them to change some more?
11. If you died tonight, what could be said about you? Finish the following sentences with the first thing that comes to mind.
    a. Last night (fill in your name) died suddenly.
    b. He/she will always be remembered for his/her ...
    c. He/she always had time for ...
    d. He/she felt possessions were ...
    e. He/she treated people like ...

dency in yourself? **3.** How do you feel about discussing Judgment Day with friends?

father's house, 28for I have five brothers. Let him warn them, so
that they will not also come to this place of torment.'
29"Abraham replied, 'They have Moses and the Prophets; let
them listen to them.'
30" 'No, father Abraham,' he said, 'but if someone from the dead
goes to them, they will repent.'
31"He said to him, 'If they do not listen to Moses and the Prophets, they will not be convinced even if someone rises from the
dead.' "

As a child, what was a surefire way that your siblings or parents could get your goat?

1. What might be an example of Jesus' meaning in verse 1? **2.** How could you practice verses 3–4 without reinforcing someone's bad behavior? **3.** How might the disciples' plea (v. 5) relate to Jesus' statement (vv. 3–4)? What does Jesus' response (v. 6) really mean? **4.** What attitudes should Jesus' followers have in serving him (vv. 7–10)?

Which quality of discipleship do you have the most difficulty with? How might dealing with this affect the other qualities?

Sin, Faith, Duty

17 Jesus said to his disciples: "Things that cause people to sin
are bound to come, but woe to that person through whom
they come. 2It would be better for him to be thrown into the sea
with a millstone tied around his neck than for him to cause one of
these little ones to sin. 3So watch yourselves.
"If your brother sins, rebuke him, and if he repents, forgive him.
4If he sins against you seven times in a day, and seven times comes
back to you and says, 'I repent,' forgive him."
5The apostles said to the Lord, "Increase our faith!"
6He replied, "If you have faith as small as a mustard seed, you
can say to this mulberry tree, 'Be uprooted and planted in the sea,'
and it will obey you.
7"Suppose one of you had a servant plowing or looking after the
sheep. Would he say to the servant when he comes in from the
field, 'Come along now and sit down to eat'? 8Would he not rather
say, 'Prepare my supper, get yourself ready and wait on me while
I eat and drink; after that you may eat and drink'? 9Would he thank
the servant because he did what he was told to do? 10So you also,
when you have done everything you were told to do, should say,
'We are unworthy servants; we have only done our duty.' "

When it comes to thank you notes are you: (a) Miss Manners? (b) Sir Sometimes? (c) Father Forgetful? Why?

1. What is it like to be a leper? What would healing mean for them? **2.** As one of the nine, how would you rationalize not going back to Jesus to say thanks? **3.** What is significant about the one being a Samaritan?

How do you express your gratitude to Jesus?

Ten Healed of Leprosy

11Now on his way to Jerusalem, Jesus traveled along the border
between Samaria and Galilee. 12As he was going into a village, ten
men who had leprosy[a] met him. They stood at a distance 13and
called out in a loud voice, "Jesus, Master, have pity on us!"
14When he saw them, he said, "Go, show yourselves to the
priests." And as they went, they were cleansed.
15One of them, when he saw he was healed, came back, praising
God in a loud voice. 16He threw himself at Jesus' feet and thanked
him—and he was a Samaritan.
17Jesus asked, "Were not all ten cleansed? Where are the other
nine? 18Was no one found to return and give praise to God except
this foreigner?" 19Then he said to him, "Rise and go; your faith has
made you well."

What are you looking forward to or waiting for right now?

1. In answering the Pharisees' question, what does Jesus say about the kingdom—as to when, how or where it is? Does he view the kingdom as an inward, spiritual reality *within* people? Or an outward, social manifestation *among* them? Or is he speaking of their failure to recognize who he is?

The Coming of the Kingdom of God

20Once, having been asked by the Pharisees when the kingdom
of God would come, Jesus replied, "The kingdom of God does not
come with your careful observation, 21nor will people say, 'Here
it is,' or 'There it is,' because the kingdom of God is within[b]
you."
22Then he said to his disciples, "The time is coming when you
will long to see one of the days of the Son of Man, but you will not

[a] *12* The Greek word was used for various diseases affecting the skin—not necessarily leprosy. [b] *21* Or *among*

see it. 23 Men will tell you, 'There he is!' or 'Here he is!' Do not go
running off after them. 24 For the Son of Man in his day[a] will be
like the lightning, which flashes and lights up the sky from one end
to the other. 25 But first he must suffer many things and be rejected
by this generation.
26 "Just as it was in the days of Noah, so also will it be in the days
of the Son of Man. 27 People were eating, drinking, marrying and
being given in marriage up to the day Noah entered the ark. Then
the flood came and destroyed them all.
28 "It was the same in the days of Lot. People were eating and
drinking, buying and selling, planting and building. 29 But the day
Lot left Sodom, fire and sulfur rained down from heaven and destroyed them all.
30 "It will be just like this on the day the Son of Man is revealed.
31 On that day no one who is on the roof of his house, with his
goods inside, should go down to get them. Likewise, no one in
the field should go back for anything. 32 Remember Lot's wife!
33 Whoever tries to keep his life will lose it, and whoever loses his
life will preserve it. 34 I tell you, on that night two people will be
in one bed; one will be taken and the other left. 35 Two women
will be grinding grain together; one will be taken and the other
left.[b]"
37 "Where, Lord?" they asked.
He replied, "Where there is a dead body, there the vultures will
gather."

[a] 24 Some manuscripts do not have *in his day.* [b] 35 Some manuscripts *left.* 36 *Two men will be in the field; one will be taken and the other left.*

2. What did Jesus mean by "one of the days of the Son of Man"? **3.** How will those days be like the days of Noah and Lot? What is so bad about the lives people were living in verses 27–28? What is meant by the warning about Lot's wife (see Ge 19:17–26)? **4.** Verse 37 was a common proverb, implying that something will happen in its proper time. Why does Jesus say this?

♡ **1.** While you live "in the kingdom" waiting for "the Son of Man" to come, what do you see in this section about the way you ought to apply verses 32–33? **2.** Do you ever look back to your pre-Christ lifestyle? In what way?

Luke 17:11–19 TEN HEALED OF LEPROSY

In this story Jesus meets a group of 10 men with leprosy. Because of their disease, lepers were considered "unclean" and were required to keep a distance from others. Only after being declared healed and "clean" by a priest could a leper re-enter society. At least one of the 10 was a Samaritan—whom Jews generally despised as ethnic and religious half-breeds.

1. Why did Jesus send the lepers to the priests rather than healing them on the spot?
   a. He was tired of healing people.
   b. He didn't want to get close enough to them to heal them.
   c. He was testing their obedience.
   d. He wanted them to exercise faith themselves.
   e. He wanted to show that healing doesn't always happen instantly.
2. Why did all but one of the lepers fail to come back and thank Jesus?
   a. They couldn't find him.
   b. They weren't grateful enough to make the effort.
   c. They had what they wanted.
   d. They thought it was time something good happened to them.
   e. They were too busy telling others their good news.
   f. They were too busy getting reunited with their families and friends.
   g. They were only interested in the miracle, not the one providing it.
3. What was significant about the man who did return to thank Jesus?
   a. As a Samaritan, being looked down on made him more grateful.
   b. The others received physical healing, but only he received salvation.
   c. His being a foreigner shows that Jesus came for *all* people.
   d. He provides an example for our attitude toward Jesus.
4. Which of the following can you relate to personally? In what way?
   a. the pain of a physical condition
   b. the pain of social barriers
   c. being more interested in what God can do for me than in God himself
   d. neglecting to thank God or others
5. Whom do you need to thank for what they have done for you? How will you go about conveying your thanks to them?
   a. Jesus
   b. my parents
   c. my spouse
   d. my children
   e. a friend
   f. a pastor
   g. a doctor
   h. a teacher
   i. a coach/mentor
   j. other:________
6. The man who was healed praised God in a loud voice and threw himself at Jesus' feet. What keeps you from being that expressive of your thanks to Jesus?
   a. Jesus hasn't done anything that exciting for me.
   b. I'm not the emotional type.
   c. I don't want to look like a fanatic.
   d. Our culture is more restrained.
   e. We aren't like that at my church.
   f. If Jesus were here, I would.
   g. I'd like to, but it's not easy.
   h. Nothing—that's how I am.
7. How has Jesus healed you before?
8. How do you need healing now? How can this group pray for you?

What did you use to do to get your way with your parents: Sulk? Cry? Bribe? Persist? Force? Wit? What worked best?

1. What method did this woman use as she approached the judge? **2.** How is God like and unlike the judge?

1. As for prayer, are you more likely to give up or hang tough? Why? **2.** Does this story mean you should *keep* praying to get rich or to see the coming of God's kingdom? Why?

---

1. What group of people would be the Pharisees today? The tax collectors? What would be the "Pharisee's Prayer"? **2.** How does this parable complement the one on persistence (vv. 1–8)? How do both demonstrate faith?

1. When have you been like the Pharisee? Like the tax collector? What accounts for the difference? **2.** Right now, considering your attitude toward others, who are you most like? **3.** How are you humble before God (Mic 6:8)?

The Parable of the Persistent Widow

18 Then Jesus told his disciples a parable to show them that
they should always pray and not give up. 2He said: "In a
certain town there was a judge who neither feared God nor cared
about men. 3And there was a widow in that town who kept coming
to him with the plea, 'Grant me justice against my adversary.'
4"For some time he refused. But finally he said to himself, 'Even
though I don't fear God or care about men, 5yet because this
widow keeps bothering me, I will see that she gets justice, so that
she won't eventually wear me out with her coming!' "
6And the Lord said, "Listen to what the unjust judge says. 7And
will not God bring about justice for his chosen ones, who cry out to
him day and night? Will he keep putting them off? 8I tell you, he
will see that they get justice, and quickly. However, when the Son
of Man comes, will he find faith on the earth?"

The Parable of the Pharisee and the Tax Collector

9To some who were confident of their own righteousness and
looked down on everybody else, Jesus told this parable: 10"Two
men went up to the temple to pray, one a Pharisee and the other
a tax collector. 11The Pharisee stood up and prayed about[a] himself: 'God, I thank you that I am not like other men—robbers,
evildoers, adulterers—or even like this tax collector. 12I fast twice
a week and give a tenth of all I get.'
13"But the tax collector stood at a distance. He would not even
look up to heaven, but beat his breast and said, 'God, have mercy
on me, a sinner.'

[a] *11* Or *to*

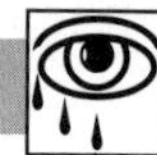

Luke 18:1–8 PARABLE OF THE PERSISTENT WIDOW

Secular judges in Jesus' time were notoriously corrupt. Without influence or bribe money, plaintiffs might find it impossible to get their case settled.

1. What was this woman's problem?
   a. a corrupt judge
   b. no husband
   c. no lawyer
   d. nagging

2. What did she have going for her?
   a. not much
   b. stubbornness
   c. faith
   d. power and influence
   e. persistence
   f. God
   g. justice

3. How is God like this judge?
   a. God *is* the Judge.
   b. God *does* grant justice.
   c. Sometimes God *does* take a long time to act.

4. How is God unlike this judge?
   a. God *does* care about people.
   b. God *doesn't* have to be hounded to bring about justice.
   c. God *doesn't* get worn out by our unceasing prayers.

5. What is the point of this parable?
   a. If at first you don't succeed—try, try again.
   b. If an unjust judge is compelled by persistence to render justice, how much more will God answer justly?
   c. If you really love God, you will never get tired of praying.
   d. If you really have faith, God will answer all your prayers.

6. For whose sake do you think Jesus spoke this parable?
   a. for crooked judges—to clean up their act
   b. for Christians in need—to persist in prayer
   c. for Christians suffering persecution—to persist in their faith
   d. for all Christians—to endure faithfully until "the Son of Man" returns

7. When it comes to prayer, what are you most likely to do?
   a. cry out to God day and night
   b. worry constantly, rather than pray
   c. hang tough
   d. give up

8. If you were in desperate need in the middle of the night, whom outside your family would you call?

9. What is your most urgent plea for the Lord right now? How can this group support you and join you in that prayer?

10. As you struggle with pain, what from this story do you need the most?
    a. justice
    b. faith
    c. a persistent prayer life
    d. the persistent prayers of others
    e. strength not to give up on life
    f. strength not to give up hope of getting better
    g. strength to cope with my situation

11. What difference has this course made in your ability to cope with pain? Have one person at a time listen silently as others share with them a word of encouragement or affirmation.

14“I tell you that this man, rather than the other, went home
justified before God. For everyone who exalts himself will be humbled, and he who humbles himself will be exalted.”

The Little Children and Jesus

15People were also bringing babies to Jesus to have him touch
them. When the disciples saw this, they rebuked them. 16But Jesus
called the children to him and said, “Let the little children come to
me, and do not hinder them, for the kingdom of God belongs to
such as these. 17I tell you the truth, anyone who will not receive
the kingdom of God like a little child will never enter it.”

The Rich Ruler

18A certain ruler asked him, “Good teacher, what must I do to
inherit eternal life?”
19“Why do you call me good?” Jesus answered. “No one is
good—except God alone. 20You know the commandments: ‘Do not
commit adultery, do not murder, do not steal, do not give false
testimony, honor your father and mother.’[a]”
21“All these I have kept since I was a boy,” he said.
22When Jesus heard this, he said to him, “You still lack one
thing. Sell everything you have and give to the poor, and you will
have treasure in heaven. Then come, follow me.”
23When he heard this, he became very sad, because he was a
man of great wealth. 24Jesus looked at him and said, “How hard it
is for the rich to enter the kingdom of God! 25Indeed, it is easier for

[a]*20* Exodus 20:12-16; Deut. 5:16-20

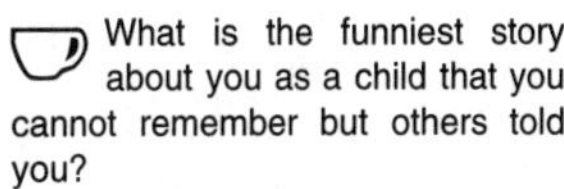

What is the funniest story about you as a child that you cannot remember but others told you?

1. How did the disciples feel about all these parents bringing their babies to Jesus? Why would they try to stop them? **2.** What does the ruler's question (v. 18) imply about his viewpoint on eternal life? What is Jesus' point in his response (v. 19)? Considering the man's religious obedience, what is ironic about verses 23–25? **3.** Since wealth was commonly considered a sign of God's blessing, what was the problem for the disciples (v. 26)? **4.** What is the way into the kingdom (vv. 27–30)? How do the children (vv. 15–17) reflect this attitude better than the rich man?

1. Are you more like the ruler or the children in how you approach God? Why? **2.** What has helped you see the impossibility of

Lk 18:9–14 THE PHARISEE AND THE TAX COLLECTOR

This parable is about two very different men. The Pharisees were a religious sect whose prime concern was keeping the Law of Moses. Tax collectors were considered traitors and thieves, because they collected taxes for the Romans from their fellow Jews—usually with great personal profit.

1. Why do you think the Pharisee acted the way he did?
   a. He was grateful to God.
   b. He was arrogantly self-righteous.
   c. He sincerely wanted to honor God.
   d. He wouldn't be real with others.
   e. He wouldn't be real with himself.

2. Why do you think the tax collector acted the way he did?
   a. He knew he had done wrong.
   b. He wanted sympathy.
   c. He had a poor self-image.
   d. He was plea bargaining with God.
   e. He had hit rock bottom.

3. What is Jesus teaching here?
   a. God hates self-righteous religion.
   b. God loves humble repentance.
   c. Good works can't earn salvation.
   d. God knows what's in our hearts.

4. Which character would you feel more comfortable being around—the Pharisee or the tax collector?

5. Why did you choose that person?
   a. He is more spiritual.
   b. He is more honest.
   c. He is more like me.
   d. He is more like who I want to be.
   e. He could better understand me.

6. How would the Pharisee be accepted in this small group? How about the tax collector?

7. Being really honest, when have you been like the Pharisee—patting yourself on the back for your accomplishments or righteousness?

8. When have you been like the tax collector? When was the first time you cried out, “God, have mercy on me, a sinner”? When was the last time?

9. How did the tax collector demonstrate healthy humility? In each of the following, which is closer to how you view yourself?
   a. I make excuses for my faults *or* I take responsibility for my faults.
   b. I put myself down *or* I see myself like God does.
   c. I have a self-defeating attitude *or* I have a God-confident attitude.
   d. I'm a reject *or* I'm wanted.

10. Why do you think so many people confess their sins in bars rather than in churches? With whom do you share your problems?

11. How do you feel about opening up with this group?
   a. What did I get myself into?!
   b. I'm nervous, but I know I need it.
   c. I hope things stay confidential.
   d. I'm looking forward to it.
   e. I'll let you know later.

12. In what areas do you most often put yourself down?
   a. grades
   b. looks
   c. athletics
   d. spiritual commitment
   e. physical strength
   f. willpower
   g. coordination

13. What addiction do you battle? How have you tried to deny it? How can you be more like the tax collector on your road to recovery?

earning the kingdom? As a result, how have you experienced the gift of the kingdom (vv. 29–30)?

a camel to go through the eye of a needle than for a rich man to enter the kingdom of God."

26Those who heard this asked, "Who then can be saved?"

27Jesus replied, "What is impossible with men is possible with God."

28Peter said to him, "We have left all we had to follow you!"

29"I tell you the truth," Jesus said to them, "no one who has left home or wife or brothers or parents or children for the sake of the kingdom of God 30will fail to receive many times as much in this age and, in the age to come, eternal life."

In light of all the talk about the kingdom of God coming, why is this new teaching misunderstood?

What is the greatest dilemma you have faced in your spiritual life? How did you respond?

Jesus Again Predicts His Death

31Jesus took the Twelve aside and told them, "We are going up to Jerusalem, and everything that is written by the prophets about the Son of Man will be fulfilled. 32He will be handed over to the Gentiles. They will mock him, insult him, spit on him, flog him and kill him. 33On the third day he will rise again."

34The disciples did not understand any of this. Its meaning was hidden from them, and they did not know what he was talking about.

Who is the most famous person you have seen up close? What were the circumstances?

1. What do the disciples still fail to see about Jesus (v. 39; compare to 18:15)? About his kingdom? **2.** From this story, what do you know of the beggar's handicap? His faith? His intensity?

1. Have you ever felt Jesus was too busy for you? Why? How do we inadvertently communicate that idea to children or people with chronic needs? **2.** If Jesus asked, "What do you *want* me to do for you?" what would you say?

A Blind Beggar Receives His Sight

35As Jesus approached Jericho, a blind man was sitting by the roadside begging. 36When he heard the crowd going by, he asked what was happening. 37They told him, "Jesus of Nazareth is passing by."

38He called out, "Jesus, Son of David, have mercy on me!"

39Those who led the way rebuked him and told him to be quiet, but he shouted all the more, "Son of David, have mercy on me!"

40Jesus stopped and ordered the man to be brought to him. When he came near, Jesus asked him, 41"What do you want me to do for you?"

"Lord, I want to see," he replied.

42Jesus said to him, "Receive your sight; your faith has healed you." 43Immediately he received his sight and followed Jesus, praising God. When all the people saw it, they also praised God.

If you could pick an ideal height, how tall would you be?

1. How does Zacchaeus compare with the rich, young ruler (18:18–30) in his approach and response to Jesus? **2.** Why does Jesus dine with him? Why does this bother others? Do you think Jesus' words (vv. 9–10) stopped the crowd's muttering?

1. Where did Jesus first find you? (Up a tree? Out on a limb?) **2.** How did he get you to join him? **3.** What wrongs do you need to make right?

Zacchaeus the Tax Collector

19 Jesus entered Jericho and was passing through. 2A man was there by the name of Zacchaeus; he was a chief tax collector and was wealthy. 3He wanted to see who Jesus was, but being a short man he could not, because of the crowd. 4So he ran ahead and climbed a sycamore-fig tree to see him, since Jesus was coming that way.

5When Jesus reached the spot, he looked up and said to him, "Zacchaeus, come down immediately. I must stay at your house today." 6So he came down at once and welcomed him gladly.

7All the people saw this and began to mutter, "He has gone to be the guest of a 'sinner.' "

8But Zacchaeus stood up and said to the Lord, "Look, Lord! Here and now I give half of my possessions to the poor, and if I have cheated anybody out of anything, I will pay back four times the amount."

9Jesus said to him, "Today salvation has come to this house, because this man, too, is a son of Abraham. 10For the Son of Man came to seek and to save what was lost."

The Parable of the Ten Minas

11While they were listening to this, he went on to tell them a
parable, because he was near Jerusalem and the people thought
that the kingdom of God was going to appear at once. 12He said: "A
man of noble birth went to a distant country to have himself appointed king and then to return. 13So he called ten of his servants
and gave them ten minas.[a] 'Put this money to work,' he said,
'until I come back.'
14"But his subjects hated him and sent a delegation after him to
say, 'We don't want this man to be our king.'
15"He was made king, however, and returned home. Then he
sent for the servants to whom he had given the money, in order to
find out what they had gained with it.
16"The first one came and said, 'Sir, your mina has earned ten
more.'
17" 'Well done, my good servant!' his master replied. 'Because
you have been trustworthy in a very small matter, take charge of
ten cities.'
18"The second came and said, 'Sir, your mina has earned five
more.'
19"His master answered, 'You take charge of five cities.'
20"Then another servant came and said, 'Sir, here is your mina;
I have kept it laid away in a piece of cloth. 21I was afraid of you,

[a]13 A mina was about three months' wages.

1. What is the best financial investment you have ever made? **2.** Describe a time when you lost money.

1. Where does the man of noble birth go? Why? What are his servants to do in his absence? **2.** What is the meaning of verses 14 and 27? Who are the enemies? **3.** What has happened to the 10 minas given to the first servant? The second servant? How does the master reply to them? How is the third servant's report influenced by a faulty perception of his master? Hence, what is his "reward"? **4.** Does verse 26 contradict Jesus' words to the ruler in 18:18–30? Why or why not? **5.** How does this parable speak to the misconception in verse 11?

1. What talents and resources do you think Jesus has left with you? How do you feel about the way you have invested them? How could you be more pru-

Lk 19:1–10 ZACCHAEUS THE TAX COLLECTOR

1. If you had been Zacchaeus when Jesus stopped and told him to come down, how would you have felt?
   - a. flabbergasted
   - b. embarrassed
   - c. overwhelmed with joy
   - d. both excited *and* afraid

2. Why did Jesus single him out?
   - a. He was wealthy.
   - b. He was short.
   - c. He was trying to hide.
   - d. He was the worst sinner in town.
   - e. Jesus could see his potential.

3. Why do you think Jesus invited himself to Zacchaeus' house?
   - a. He needed a place to stay.
   - b. He wanted to talk to him about his shady business practices.
   - c. He wanted to show everyone that Zacchaeus wasn't really a sinner.
   - d. He wanted to help this "little guy."
   - e. He knew that Zacchaeus was a seeker looking for more in life.

4. "Today salvation has come to this house, because this man, too, is a son of Abraham." What was Jesus saying about Zacchaeus?
   - a. He has followed the example of Abraham's faith.
   - b. He was "lost" but now is "found."
   - c. Others see him as an outcast, but God loves and accepts him.
   - d. His generous decision shows that his heart has changed.

5. How do you think Zacchaeus felt when he and Jesus parted?
   - a. clean
   - b. loved
   - c. included in God's family
   - d. broke
   - e. brand new

6. Who was the person early in your life who affirmed you like Jesus did with Zacchaeus? Who is the person who builds you up now?

7. What most helps you to feel good about yourself?
   - a. to be treated as a person and not a category
   - b. for people to spend time with me
   - c. for people to ignore the negative talk about me from the crowd
   - d. for people to show that they need me and what I can contribute
   - e. to assert myself beyond my comfort zone like Zacchaeus did
   - f. to be assured and reminded that I am accepted by God

8. Complete each sentence with how that person sees you as special or unique:
   - a. My parents see me as ...
   - b. My teachers see me as ...
   - c. My close friends see me as ...
   - d. People who don't know me very well see me as ...
   - e. I see myself as ...

9. What is God calling you to do right now?
   - a. stop "watching" Jesus from a safe distance
   - b. accept Jesus' invitation to get to know him better
   - c. lay claim to God's gift of salvation
   - d. celebrate God's acceptance
   - e. make restitution for my wrongs

10. Why did Zacchaeus volunteer to make such generous restitution to those he had cheated?
    - a. He was already in a 12 Step program.
    - b. He felt guilty.
    - c. His heart was full of love and gratitude toward Jesus.
    - d. He wanted to be accepted by the community.
    - e. A miracle had happened in his life.

11. To whom do you need to make amends? How are you planning to do so?

dent in the way you invest? **2.** Is fear ever a motive in your relationship with Christ? Why?

How do you make your grand entry when you come home: With a silent grunt? A big splash? A hug and kiss? Yelling, "What's for dinner?"

1. How close is Jesus to Jerusalem now (v. 29)? **2.** What task does he give two of his disciples? Why? What problems might they have encountered in such a job? **3.** How do you picture the scene in verses 35–38? What do you see? Hear? Feel? **4.** What were the people expecting Jesus to do when he reached Jerusalem (v. 11; see Zec 9:9)? How are their expectations different from his? How does this help to explain Jesus' words and emotions in verses 41–44? **5.** What does Jesus' reply to the Pharisees (vv. 39–40) imply about him? **6.** How do verses 45–48 relate to Jesus' concern about Jerusalem? Why does he take such extreme action?

1. What kind of reception would Jesus get: (a) If he rode into your town today? (b) After the people heard the message? **2.** How would he be treated by the local media? By elected officials? The guys in the tavern? The ladies in the bridge club? **3.** What person or group of people do you weep for? **4.** How has Jesus "turned over tables" in your life? What has he been cleaning out recently?

because you are a hard man. You take out what you did not put in
and reap what you did not sow.'
22"His master replied, 'I will judge you by your own words, you
wicked servant! You knew, did you, that I am a hard man, taking
out what I did not put in, and reaping what I did not sow? 23Why
then didn't you put my money on deposit, so that when I came
back, I could have collected it with interest?'
24"Then he said to those standing by, 'Take his mina away from
him and give it to the one who has ten minas.'
25" 'Sir,' they said, 'he already has ten!'
26"He replied, 'I tell you that to everyone who has, more will be
given, but as for the one who has nothing, even what he has will
be taken away. 27But those enemies of mine who did not want me
to be king over them—bring them here and kill them in front
of me.' "

The Triumphal Entry

28After Jesus had said this, he went on ahead, going up to Jerusalem. 29As he approached Bethphage and Bethany at the hill called
the Mount of Olives, he sent two of his disciples, saying to them,
30"Go to the village ahead of you, and as you enter it, you will find
a colt tied there, which no one has ever ridden. Untie it and bring
it here. 31If anyone asks you, 'Why are you untying it?' tell him,
'The Lord needs it.' "
32Those who were sent ahead went and found it just as he had
told them. 33As they were untying the colt, its owners asked them,
"Why are you untying the colt?"
34They replied, "The Lord needs it."
35They brought it to Jesus, threw their cloaks on the colt and put
Jesus on it. 36As he went along, people spread their cloaks on the
road.
37When he came near the place where the road goes down the
Mount of Olives, the whole crowd of disciples began joyfully to
praise God in loud voices for all the miracles they had seen:

38"Blessed is the king who comes in the name of
the Lord!"[a]

"Peace in heaven and glory in the highest!"

39Some of the Pharisees in the crowd said to Jesus, "Teacher,
rebuke your disciples!"
40"I tell you," he replied, "if they keep quiet, the stones will cry
out."
41As he approached Jerusalem and saw the city, he wept over it
42and said, "If you, even you, had only known on this day what
would bring you peace—but now it is hidden from your eyes.
43The days will come upon you when your enemies will build an
embankment against you and encircle you and hem you in on
every side. 44They will dash you to the ground, you and the children within your walls. They will not leave one stone on another,
because you did not recognize the time of God's coming to you."

Jesus at the Temple

45Then he entered the temple area and began driving out those
who were selling. 46"It is written," he said to them, " 'My house
will be a house of prayer'[b]; but you have made it 'a den of
robbers.'[c]"
47Every day he was teaching at the temple. But the chief priests,

[a]*38* Psalm 118:26 [b]*46* Isaiah 56:7 [c]*46* Jer. 7:11

the teachers of the law and the leaders among the people were trying to kill him. [48]Yet they could not find any way to do it, because all the people hung on his words.

The Authority of Jesus Questioned

20 One day as he was teaching the people in the temple courts and preaching the gospel, the chief priests and the teachers of the law, together with the elders, came up to him. [2]"Tell us by what authority you are doing these things," they said. "Who gave you this authority?"

[3]He replied, "I will also ask you a question. Tell me, [4]John's baptism—was it from heaven, or from men?"

[5]They discussed it among themselves and said, "If we say, 'From heaven,' he will ask, 'Why didn't you believe him?' [6]But if we say, 'From men,' all the people will stone us, because they are persuaded that John was a prophet."

[7]So they answered, "We don't know where it was from."

[8]Jesus said, "Neither will I tell you by what authority I am doing these things."

The Parable of the Tenants

[9]He went on to tell the people this parable: "A man planted a vineyard, rented it to some farmers and went away for a long time. [10]At harvest time he sent a servant to the tenants so they would give him some of the fruit of the vineyard. But the tenants beat him and sent him away empty-handed. [11]He sent another servant, but that one also they beat and treated shamefully and sent away empty-handed. [12]He sent still a third, and they wounded him and threw him out.

As a teenager, what authority figure (parent, teacher, minister) upset you most? Why?

1. What "things" (v. 2) has Jesus been doing? What about these things would worry the chief priests? **2.** What interests are they trying to protect from Jesus' probing question? Why does Jesus evade their question?

What people, things or events led you to recognize Jesus' authority? What authority does he have (or demand) now?

When have you recently experienced "three-strikes-and-you're-out": Employment? Dating? School? Family? How do you handle rejection?

1. How does this parable relate to the question of authority raised in verses 1–8? **2.** What does the landowner do? How do

Luke 19:28–44 THE TRIUMPHAL ENTRY

With Passover just a few days away, Jerusalem would have been filled with travelers. Jesus makes an entrance into the "holy city" on the first day of this, the last week of his life.

1. What would you have said if you were one of the two disciples Jesus sent to go and get a colt?
   a. "I could get arrested for this!"
   b. "This sounds important."
   c. "This sounds impossible—How will we find this colt?"
   d. "No problem."

2. What would you have said if you owned the colt and saw two men taking it?
   a. "What are you doing?!"
   b. "Who is 'the Lord' who needs my donkey?"
   c. "Quick! Somebody call the police!"
   d. "No problem."

3. Why did Jesus arrange this "triumphal entry"?
   a. to confuse people about his mission and identity
   b. to receive people's praise
   c. to fulfill Old Testament prophecy
   d. to declare openly that he was the Messiah
   e. to start the countdown to the cross

4. Why did the crowd respond the way they did?
   a. because it was Palm Sunday
   b. because of the miracles Jesus did
   c. because they realized Jesus was the Messiah
   d. because they thought Jesus was acting like a deliverer and king
   e. because Jesus deserved their praise and honor

5. What caused Jesus to weep over Jerusalem?
   a. He was angry at the people's hardness of heart.
   b. He was grieved by their rejection.
   c. He foresaw the city's destruction.
   d. He knew that destruction could have been prevented.
   e. He knew how the tide of public opinion would turn against him.
   f. He realized how misunderstood he and his mission were.
   g. He was sad that God's people failed to recognize "God's coming."

6. What kind of king did the crowd think Jesus was? What kind of King do you think Jesus was, and is? When have you had wrong assumptions about how God works?

7. How did Jesus enter your life?
   a. as a knight on a white horse
   b. as a warrior on a chariot
   c. as a rabbi with an armful of scrolls
   d. as an authoritative king with a penetrating gaze
   e. as a humble servant on a colt

8. Has there ever been a "Jerusalem" in your life, when you knew that once you arrived you would be doing God's will at great personal sacrifice?

9. What person or group of people do you yearn to see come to God?

10. If the Pharisees were here now, how much joyful praise would they find to criticize in your church? In your small group? In your own life?

the tenants respond? Why? **3.** What do the landowner, the tenants, the servants and the son represent? **4.** How does the quoted Scripture (vv. 17–18) relate to the parable (vv. 9–16)? **5.** How does the parable and the quote affect the religious leaders? Why don't they act? Why choose this time to tell such a parable?

1. At different times in your life, how have you received Jesus? How do you receive him now? **2.** Is Jesus more like a *millstone* (weight) or a *capstone* (one that holds everything together) in your life? Why?

13“Then the owner of the vineyard said, ‘What shall I do? I will send my son, whom I love; perhaps they will respect him.’

14“But when the tenants saw him, they talked the matter over. ‘This is the heir,’ they said. ‘Let's kill him, and the inheritance will be ours.’ 15So they threw him out of the vineyard and killed him.

“What then will the owner of the vineyard do to them? 16He will come and kill those tenants and give the vineyard to others.”

When the people heard this, they said, “May this never be!”

17Jesus looked directly at them and asked, “Then what is the meaning of that which is written:

“ ‘The stone the builders rejected
has become the capstone[a]’[b]?

18Everyone who falls on that stone will be broken to pieces, but he on whom it falls will be crushed.”

19The teachers of the law and the chief priests looked for a way to arrest him immediately, because they knew he had spoken this parable against them. But they were afraid of the people.

When do you pay your taxes: Early, late, or never? Why?

1. Why ask this question (v. 22)? **2.** What's the trap here: If Jesus said, “Pay Caesar,” what would have happened to his crowd support? If Jesus had said, “Don't pay,” how would the rulers have responded? **3.** What's so insightful about Jesus' response?

In giving yourself to God, are you in the 15, 28, 45, or 100 percent “tax bracket”? Why?

Paying Taxes to Caesar

20Keeping a close watch on him, they sent spies, who pretended to be honest. They hoped to catch Jesus in something he said so that they might hand him over to the power and authority of the governor. 21So the spies questioned him: “Teacher, we know that you speak and teach what is right, and that you do not show partiality but teach the way of God in accordance with the truth. 22Is it right for us to pay taxes to Caesar or not?”

23He saw through their duplicity and said to them, 24“Show me a denarius. Whose portrait and inscription are on it?”

25“Caesar's,” they replied.

He said to them, “Then give to Caesar what is Caesar's, and to God what is God's.”

26They were unable to trap him in what he had said there in public. And astonished by his answer, they became silent.

What was the last big exam you had to really prepare for? How did you do?

1. Why would the Sadducees, an elite religious and political group, pose a question like this to Jesus? **2.** How seriously does Jesus treat this absurd question? What if he had ridiculed it? **3.** What does Jesus teach about life after death (vv. 34–36)? **4.** How does he then “prove” the resurrection? (Note the verb tense in this Ex 3:6 quote and recall *when* this burning bush incident took place.) **5.** How do the teachers of the law differ in their response? Why?

How do you deal with someone who wants to argue a point in the Bible? What if the person has honest questions and you don't have the answer?

The Resurrection and Marriage

27Some of the Sadducees, who say there is no resurrection, came to Jesus with a question. 28“Teacher,” they said, “Moses wrote for us that if a man's brother dies and leaves a wife but no children, the man must marry the widow and have children for his brother. 29Now there were seven brothers. The first one married a woman and died childless. 30The second 31and then the third married her, and in the same way the seven died, leaving no children. 32Finally, the woman died too. 33Now then, at the resurrection whose wife will she be, since the seven were married to her?”

34Jesus replied, “The people of this age marry and are given in marriage. 35But those who are considered worthy of taking part in that age and in the resurrection from the dead will neither marry nor be given in marriage, 36and they can no longer die; for they are like the angels. They are God's children, since they are children of the resurrection. 37But in the account of the bush, even Moses showed that the dead rise, for he calls the Lord ‘the God of Abraham, and the God of Isaac, and the God of Jacob.’[c] 38He is not the God of the dead, but of the living, for to him all are alive.”

39Some of the teachers of the law responded, “Well said, teacher!” 40And no one dared to ask him any more questions.

[a] *17* Or *cornerstone* [b] *17* Psalm 118:22 [c] *37* Exodus 3:6

Whose Son Is the Christ?

41Then Jesus said to them, "How is it that they say the Christ[a] is the Son of David? 42David himself declares in the Book of Psalms:

> "'The Lord said to my Lord:
> "Sit at my right hand
> 43until I make your enemies
> a footstool for your feet." '[b]

44David calls him 'Lord.' How then can he be his son?"

45While all the people were listening, Jesus said to his disciples, 46"Beware of the teachers of the law. They like to walk around in flowing robes and love to be greeted in the marketplaces and have the most important seats in the synagogues and the places of honor at banquets. 47They devour widows' houses and for a show make lengthy prayers. Such men will be punished most severely."

The Widow's Offering

21 As he looked up, Jesus saw the rich putting their gifts into the temple treasury. 2He also saw a poor widow put in two very small copper coins.[c] 3"I tell you the truth," he said, "this poor widow has put in more than all the others. 4All these people gave their gifts out of their wealth; but she out of her poverty put in all she had to live on."

Signs of the End of the Age

5Some of his disciples were remarking about how the temple was adorned with beautiful stones and with gifts dedicated to God. But Jesus said, 6"As for what you see here, the time will come when not one stone will be left on another; every one of them will be thrown down."

7"Teacher," they asked, "when will these things happen? And what will be the sign that they are about to take place?"

8He replied: "Watch out that you are not deceived. For many will come in my name, claiming, 'I am he,' and, 'The time is near.' Do not follow them. 9When you hear of wars and revolutions, do not be frightened. These things must happen first, but the end will not come right away."

10Then he said to them: "Nation will rise against nation, and kingdom against kingdom. 11There will be great earthquakes, famines and pestilences in various places, and fearful events and great signs from heaven.

12"But before all this, they will lay hands on you and persecute you. They will deliver you to synagogues and prisons, and you will be brought before kings and governors, and all on account of my name. 13This will result in your being witnesses to them. 14But make up your mind not to worry beforehand how you will defend yourselves. 15For I will give you words and wisdom that none of your adversaries will be able to resist or contradict. 16You will be betrayed even by parents, brothers, relatives and friends, and they will put some of you to death. 17All men will hate you because of me. 18But not a hair of your head will perish. 19By standing firm you will gain life.

20"When you see Jerusalem being surrounded by armies, you will know that its desolation is near. 21Then let those who are in Judea flee to the mountains, let those in the city get out, and let those in the country not enter the city. 22For this is the time of punishment in fulfillment of all that has been written. 23How

[a] 41 Or *Messiah* [b] 43 Psalm 110:1 [c] 2 Greek *two lepta*

As a child, what "hot buttons" did you push to make your parents mad?

1. Given the issue of authority in this chapter, why does Jesus continue to challenge traditional values? **2.** What undermines the authority of the religious leaders (vv. 45–47)? **3.** How does the poor widow differ from these leaders? What is Jesus' point in making this contrast?

1. When have you "used" religion to get something for yourself (attention, respect, good feelings) rather than for love of God? What helps get you back on track? **2.** Do you give to God off the top (at the outset of the month), or from what is left over (at month's end)? Explain.

What is the tallest building you have been in? What could you see from the top?

1. What prompts Jesus' next lesson? **2.** What bombshell does he drop on his disciples (v. 6)? Considering how the Jews felt about the temple, how must they have felt when they heard Jesus' words? **3.** The disciples identified the destruction of the temple with the end times, but Jesus separates them. In verses 8–19, which is he teaching about? **4.** What will happen to the disciples and the church during tribulation (v. 10)? What comfort will come in the midst of these trials? **5.** In A.D. 70, Jerusalem was destroyed by the Romans. Why would Jesus warn of this event in verses 20–24? Why will Jerusalem be devastated (see 11:49–51; 13:34–35 and 19:41–44)? How does Jesus describe this time (vv. 21–24)? What does he tell the people to do? Why? **6.** In verses 25–28, which event (the coming of the end or Jerusalem's destruction) is in view? What do the two events have in common? What is significant about the way the Son of Man will come (v. 27; see Da 7:13–14)? What should be the attitude of believers when they see the Son of Man coming (v. 28)? **7.** What is the lesson of the fig tree (vv. 29–31)? How does this lesson answer the disciples' question from verse 7? **8.** How would the promises (vv.

32–33) have been a comfort to the disciples? A discomfort? What impact do they have on you? **9.** In the midst of this heavy news, how does Jesus caution his followers (vv. 34–35)?

1. When were you a bold witness for Christ? What happened? How did God give you insight and wisdom? **2.** When reading the parable of the fig tree today, how near is the fig tree to sprouting? What makes you think this? How does this affect the way you live your life? **3.** How well does your life reflect verse 36? What will you do this week to become better at watching and praying?

When you were growing up, what were mealtimes like? Where did everyone sit around the table? What one vivid memory do you have about each family member at that time?

1. What was the significance of Passover? The Passover lamb (see Ex 12:1–13,21–28)? **2.** In light of 19:39–48, why are the priests and teachers so determined to kill Jesus? How does that relate to the roundabout way Jesus has the disciples arrange for the Passover feast? **3.** Besides the desire to be with friends, why might Jesus "eagerly desire" to share this particular Passover feast with the disciples? How will Passover really be "fulfilled" in the kingdom of God (v. 16)? How does Jesus' use of the bread and wine change the emphasis of Passover? What is the meaning of verse 18? Verse 19? From Jeremiah 31:31–33, how would you describe the "new covenant" Jesus brought about? **4.** If you were there, how would you have reacted to the news about Jesus' unnamed betrayer (vv. 21–22)? How might that lead to the argument in verse 24? How does

dreadful it will be in those days for pregnant women and nursing mothers! There will be great distress in the land and wrath against this people. 24They will fall by the sword and will be taken as prisoners to all the nations. Jerusalem will be trampled on by the Gentiles until the times of the Gentiles are fulfilled.

25"There will be signs in the sun, moon and stars. On the earth, nations will be in anguish and perplexity at the roaring and tossing of the sea. 26Men will faint from terror, apprehensive of what is coming on the world, for the heavenly bodies will be shaken. 27At that time they will see the Son of Man coming in a cloud with power and great glory. 28When these things begin to take place, stand up and lift up your heads, because your redemption is drawing near."

29He told them this parable: "Look at the fig tree and all the trees. 30When they sprout leaves, you can see for yourselves and know that summer is near. 31Even so, when you see these things happening, you know that the kingdom of God is near.

32"I tell you the truth, this generation[a] will certainly not pass away until all these things have happened. 33Heaven and earth will pass away, but my words will never pass away.

34"Be careful, or your hearts will be weighed down with dissipation, drunkenness and the anxieties of life, and that day will close on you unexpectedly like a trap. 35For it will come upon all those who live on the face of the whole earth. 36Be always on the watch, and pray that you may be able to escape all that is about to happen, and that you may be able to stand before the Son of Man."

37Each day Jesus was teaching at the temple, and each evening he went out to spend the night on the hill called the Mount of Olives, 38and all the people came early in the morning to hear him at the temple.

Judas Agrees to Betray Jesus

22 Now the Feast of Unleavened Bread, called the Passover, was approaching, 2and the chief priests and the teachers of the law were looking for some way to get rid of Jesus, for they were afraid of the people. 3Then Satan entered Judas, called Iscariot, one of the Twelve. 4And Judas went to the chief priests and the officers of the temple guard and discussed with them how he might betray Jesus. 5They were delighted and agreed to give him money. 6He consented, and watched for an opportunity to hand Jesus over to them when no crowd was present.

The Last Supper

7Then came the day of Unleavened Bread on which the Passover lamb had to be sacrificed. 8Jesus sent Peter and John, saying, "Go and make preparations for us to eat the Passover."

9"Where do you want us to prepare for it?" they asked.

10He replied, "As you enter the city, a man carrying a jar of water will meet you. Follow him to the house that he enters, 11and say to the owner of the house, 'The Teacher asks: Where is the guest room, where I may eat the Passover with my disciples?' 12He will show you a large upper room, all furnished. Make preparations there."

13They left and found things just as Jesus had told them. So they prepared the Passover.

14When the hour came, Jesus and his apostles reclined at the table. 15And he said to them, "I have eagerly desired to eat this

[a]*32* Or *race*

Passover with you before I suffer. 16For I tell you, I will not eat it again until it finds fulfillment in the kingdom of God."

17After taking the cup, he gave thanks and said, "Take this and divide it among you. 18For I tell you I will not drink again of the fruit of the vine until the kingdom of God comes."

19And he took bread, gave thanks and broke it, and gave it to them, saying, "This is my body given for you; do this in remembrance of me."

20In the same way, after the supper he took the cup, saying, "This cup is the new covenant in my blood, which is poured out for you. 21But the hand of him who is going to betray me is with mine on the table. 22The Son of Man will go as it has been decreed, but woe to that man who betrays him." 23They began to question among themselves which of them it might be who would do this.

24Also a dispute arose among them as to which of them was considered to be greatest. 25Jesus said to them, "The kings of the Gentiles lord it over them; and those who exercise authority over them call themselves Benefactors. 26But you are not to be like that. Instead, the greatest among you should be like the youngest, and the one who rules like the one who serves. 27For who is greater, the one who is at the table or the one who serves? Is it not the one who is at the table? But I am among you as one who serves. 28You are those who have stood by me in my trials. 29And I confer on you a kingdom, just as my Father conferred one on me, 30so that you may eat and drink at my table in my kingdom and sit on thrones, judging the twelve tribes of Israel.

Jesus resolve that argument (vv. 25–27)? What does he mean by the promise in verses 28–30? **5.** How must Peter feel in verses 31–34? What are the differences between Judas (vv. 1–6) and Peter, since both failed Jesus? **6.** What is Jesus trying to impress upon Peter (v. 33) and the others in verses 35–38: (a) They should fight? (b) They really will be left on their own once he's gone? (c) He is indeed going to die, and will not be able to care for them? or (d) Other? Why?

1. What does sharing in Communion or the Lord's Supper mean to you? **2.** What would it mean to apply Jesus' words about service (v. 27) in your family life? Work or school relationships? Use of money? Why apply this principle in those areas? Why not? **3.** With which disciple do you identify most and why: (a) Judas—I've sold out on Jesus? (b) Those arguing—I want to follow Jesus, but I still want to be successful in the eyes of others? or (c) Peter—I am passionately committed to

Luke 22:7–34 THE LAST SUPPER

1. How do you think Jesus felt at this "last supper"?
   a. nostalgic
   b. sad
   c. relaxed
   d. uptight
   e. anxious to get things over with

2. Rank the following reasons why it was important to Jesus to have this supper with his disciples, from 1 to 5 (most to least significant):
   a. to celebrate the traditional Jewish Passover
   b. to tie his impending death to the Passover and redemption
   c. to share one last time of fellowship
   d. to share some final teaching
   e. to institute the Lord's Supper as an ongoing sacrament/ordinance

3. Probably the hardest thing for the disciples to understand in this passage was what Jesus meant:
   a. by the mysterious preparations.
   b. about eating the Passover again when the kingdom of God comes.
   c. about the bread and the cup.
   d. about one of them betraying him.
   e. about servants being the greatest.
   f. about one day "judging," or ruling, the 12 tribes of Israel.
   g. about Satan and his sifting.

4. Which of the previous points are hardest for *you* to understand?

5. What do you think is the most striking parallel between Passover and the meaning of the Last Supper?
   a. Both involved a sacrificial "lamb."
   b. God was rescuing his people through both.
   c. Contrary to Passover, Jesus' sacrifice never needs to be repeated.
   d. Passover is a remembrance of deliverance from slavery; the Last Supper is a remembrance of deliverance from sin.

6. What was Jesus' response to the disciples' dispute about which of them was considered to be greatest?
   a. His followers shouldn't argue.
   b. His followers shouldn't compete, unless it's competing to serve.
   c. His followers shouldn't flaunt their authority or position.
   d. His followers should think of themselves as equals.

7. Do you think Peter was sincere when he said, "Lord, I am ready to go with you to prison and to death"? Why can it be so hard for *you* to take a stand for Christ?

8. Why is the Last Supper important to believers? What can you do in preparing for Communion to make it more significant for you?

9. Through both Passover and Christ's death, God brought people freedom. What do you need to be free from?

10. In what relationship(s) or area of life do you find it hardest to be a servant? What is God calling you to do to make your life more service-oriented?

11. What are your family's most meaningful traditions? How could you involve your children more in planning and celebrating them?
   a. birthdays and anniversaries
   b. holidays, especially___________
   c. family nights
   d. special meals
   e. family communion services

Jesus, but sometimes I fall flat on my face? **4.** Does verse 37 apply to you? Why?

31“Simon, Simon, Satan has asked to sift you[a] as wheat. 32But I have prayed for you, Simon, that your faith may not fail. And when you have turned back, strengthen your brothers.”

33But he replied, “Lord, I am ready to go with you to prison and to death.”

34Jesus answered, “I tell you, Peter, before the rooster crows today, you will deny three times that you know me.”

35Then Jesus asked them, “When I sent you without purse, bag or sandals, did you lack anything?”

“Nothing,” they answered.

36He said to them, “But now if you have a purse, take it, and also a bag; and if you don’t have a sword, sell your cloak and buy one. 37It is written: ‘And he was numbered with the transgressors’[b]; and I tell you that this must be fulfilled in me. Yes, what is written about me is reaching its fulfillment.”

38The disciples said, “See, Lord, here are two swords.”

“That is enough,” he replied.

In times of crisis, do you stay cool, get hot, panic or dig in? Where do you go to be alone?

1. What strikes you about Jesus’ prayer? In saying, “your will be done,” is Jesus: (a) Helplessly submitting to fate? (b) Admitting defeat before a power that beat him? (c) Bitterly resigning himself to the inevitable? or (d) Quietly trusting in God’s love? **2.** Why is the crowd so large and armed (v. 52)? What do they fear? Why are their fears unfounded? **3.** What is the irony in Judas’ betrayal? How do you reconcile 22:38 and Jesus’ behavior in verses 50–51? **4.** What does Jesus mean by “your hour” (v. 53; in contrast to his own, v. 42)?

1. What do *you* mean when you pray, “your will be done”? **2.** How would you compare Jesus’ attitudes and actions with those of his disciples? His enemies? What impresses you most about him?

Jesus Prays on the Mount of Olives

39Jesus went out as usual to the Mount of Olives, and his disciples followed him. 40On reaching the place, he said to them, “Pray that you will not fall into temptation.” 41He withdrew about a stone’s throw beyond them, knelt down and prayed, 42“Father, if you are willing, take this cup from me; yet not my will, but yours be done.” 43An angel from heaven appeared to him and strengthened him. 44And being in anguish, he prayed more earnestly, and his sweat was like drops of blood falling to the ground.[c]

45When he rose from prayer and went back to the disciples, he found them asleep, exhausted from sorrow. 46“Why are you sleeping?” he asked them. “Get up and pray so that you will not fall into temptation.”

Jesus Arrested

47While he was still speaking a crowd came up, and the man who was called Judas, one of the Twelve, was leading them. He approached Jesus to kiss him, 48but Jesus asked him, “Judas, are you betraying the Son of Man with a kiss?”

49When Jesus’ followers saw what was going to happen, they said, “Lord, should we strike with our swords?” 50And one of them struck the servant of the high priest, cutting off his right ear.

51But Jesus answered, “No more of this!” And he touched the man’s ear and healed him.

52Then Jesus said to the chief priests, the officers of the temple guard, and the elders, who had come for him, “Am I leading a rebellion, that you have come with swords and clubs? 53Every day I was with you in the temple courts, and you did not lay a hand on me. But this is your hour—when darkness reigns.”

When have you felt like crawling into a hole, never to return: When you gave up the winning run in a baseball game? Hit the wrong note in your orchestra solo? Other?

1. How would you describe Peter’s personality? **2.** Given verse 33, what accounts for Peter’s actions now? What questions must he have had about himself?

Peter Disowns Jesus

54Then seizing him, they led him away and took him into the house of the high priest. Peter followed at a distance. 55But when they had kindled a fire in the middle of the courtyard and had sat down together, Peter sat down with them. 56A servant girl saw him seated there in the firelight. She looked closely at him and said, “This man was with him.”

57But he denied it. “Woman, I don’t know him,” he said.

[a] *31* The Greek is plural. [b] *37* Isaiah 53:12 [c] *44* Some early manuscripts do not have verses 43 and 44.

58A little later someone else saw him and said, “You also are one
of them.”
“Man, I am not!” Peter replied.
59About an hour later another asserted, “Certainly this fellow
was with him, for he is a Galilean.”
60Peter replied, “Man, I don’t know what you’re talking about!”
Just as he was speaking, the rooster crowed. 61The Lord turned and
looked straight at Peter. Then Peter remembered the word the
Lord had spoken to him: “Before the rooster crows today, you will
disown me three times.” 62And he went outside and wept bitterly.

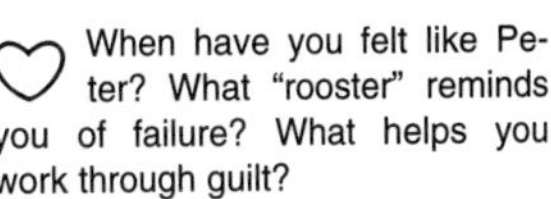
When have you felt like Peter? What “rooster” reminds you of failure? What helps you work through guilt?

The Guards Mock Jesus

63The men who were guarding Jesus began mocking and beating
him. 64They blindfolded him and demanded, “Prophesy! Who hit
you?” 65And they said many other insulting things to him.

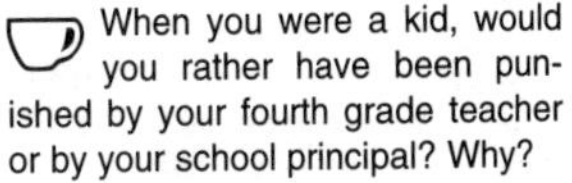
When you were a kid, would you rather have been punished by your fourth grade teacher or by your school principal? Why?

Jesus Before Pilate and Herod

66At daybreak the council of the elders of the people, both the
chief priests and teachers of the law, met together, and Jesus was
led before them. 67“If you are the Christ,[a]” they said, “tell us.”
Jesus answered, “If I tell you, you will not believe me, 68and if I
asked you, you would not answer. 69But from now on, the Son of
Man will be seated at the right hand of the mighty God.”
70They all asked, “Are you then the Son of God?”
He replied, “You are right in saying I am.”

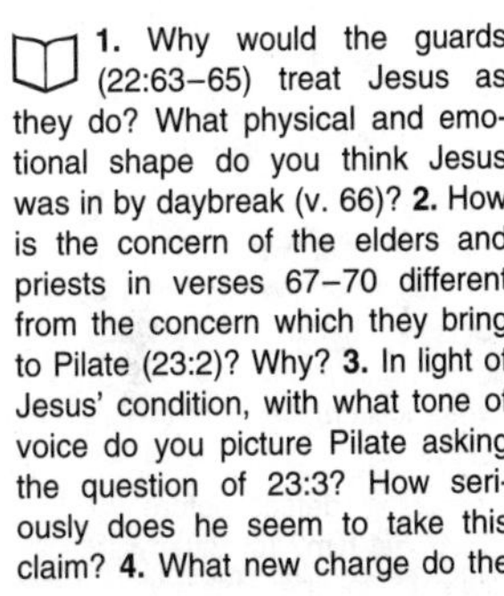
1. Why would the guards (22:63–65) treat Jesus as they do? What physical and emotional shape do you think Jesus was in by daybreak (v. 66)? **2.** How is the concern of the elders and priests in verses 67–70 different from the concern which they bring to Pilate (23:2)? Why? **3.** In light of Jesus’ condition, with what tone of voice do you picture Pilate asking the question of 23:3? How seriously does he seem to take this claim? **4.** What new charge do the

[a]67 Or *Messiah*

Luke 22:54–62 PETER DISOWNS JESUS

1. After Jesus was arrested, what made Peter deny knowing him?
   a. momentary insanity
   b. spiritual weakness
   c. personality weakness
   d. fear for his own life

2. If you could put in a good word for Peter, what would it be?
   a. He meant well.
   b. He was the only disciple to follow Jesus to his trial.
   c. He was only human.
   d. He came back to Christ in the end.
   e. I wouldn’t have done any better.

3. How do you think Peter felt when Jesus looked at him?
   a. He realized how stupid he’d been.
   b. He felt ashamed of his behavior.
   c. He was humiliated by his failure.
   d. He was afraid Jesus would never forgive him.

4. The impact this failure had on Peter’s future was that it probably:
   a. made him less cocky.
   b. took away all his self-confidence.
   c. made him more sensitive.
   d. helped make him into the man of God he became.

5. How do you usually react to failure, and how would you like to react differently?
   a. kick myself for days
   b. try to be extra good for awhile
   c. shrug it off
   d. admit it and get on with life
   e. become afraid to try again
   f. talk to God about it

6. How has failure changed you?
   a. I’m more caring and empathetic.
   b. I’m more determined.
   c. I’m more humble.
   d. I’m more realistic.
   e. I look out for myself more.
   f. I’m emotionally fragile.
   g. I don’t feel I can serve God again.

7. What failure in your life comes closest to hitting you like Peter’s failure hit him?
   a. when I went through a divorce
   b. when I lost my job
   c. when I went through bankruptcy or financial failure
   d. when I “fell off the wagon”
   e. when I failed my wife or children
   f. when I had a chance to talk about Christ, but didn’t

8. How does this story relate to you and your child?
   a. I have blown it as a parent.
   b. My child has really let me down.
   c. One of us has been in denial about some things in our relationship.
   d. Fortunately, like Jesus and Peter, our relationship has been restored.
   e. Fortunately, we haven’t gone through anything like this.

9. What has brought you the most pain as a parent? How can identifying with Christ’s pain (and/or your child’s pain) help you cope with your own pain?

10. Would you give yourself a “plus” or a “minus” for each of the following characteristics:
    a. bouncing back after you blow it
    b. forgiving those who fail you
    c. standing up for Christ
    d. spiritual desire
    e. spiritual consistency

11. How has this course, and especially those in your group, helped you learn to deal better with stress?

71 Then they said, "Why do we need any more testimony? We
have heard it from his own lips."
23 Then the whole assembly rose and led him off to Pilate.
2 And they began to accuse him, saying, "We have found
this man subverting our nation. He opposes payment of taxes to
Caesar and claims to be Christ,[a] a king."
3 So Pilate asked Jesus, "Are you the king of the Jews?"
"Yes, it is as you say," Jesus replied.
4 Then Pilate announced to the chief priests and the crowd, "I
find no basis for a charge against this man."
5 But they insisted, "He stirs up the people all over Judea[b] by his
teaching. He started in Galilee and has come all the way here."
6 On hearing this, Pilate asked if the man was a Galilean. 7 When
he learned that Jesus was under Herod's jurisdiction, he sent him
to Herod, who was also in Jerusalem at that time.
8 When Herod saw Jesus, he was greatly pleased, because for a
long time he had been wanting to see him. From what he had
heard about him, he hoped to see him perform some miracle. 9 He
plied him with many questions, but Jesus gave him no answer.
10 The chief priests and the teachers of the law were standing there,
vehemently accusing him. 11 Then Herod and his soldiers ridiculed
and mocked him. Dressing him in an elegant robe, they sent him
back to Pilate. 12 That day Herod and Pilate became friends—before
this they had been enemies.
13 Pilate called together the chief priests, the rulers and the people, 14 and said to them, "You brought me this man as one who was
inciting the people to rebellion. I have examined him in your
presence and have found no basis for your charges against him.
15 Neither has Herod, for he sent him back to us; as you can see, he
has done nothing to deserve death. 16 Therefore, I will punish him
and then release him.[c]"
18 With one voice they cried out, "Away with this man! Release
Barabbas to us!" 19 (Barabbas had been thrown into prison for an
insurrection in the city, and for murder.)
20 Wanting to release Jesus, Pilate appealed to them again. 21 But
they kept shouting, "Crucify him! Crucify him!"
22 For the third time he spoke to them: "Why? What crime has
this man committed? I have found in him no grounds for the death
penalty. Therefore I will have him punished and then release him."
23 But with loud shouts they insistently demanded that he be
crucified, and their shouts prevailed. 24 So Pilate decided to grant
their demand. 25 He released the man who had been thrown into
prison for insurrection and murder, the one they asked for, and
surrendered Jesus to their will.

The Crucifixion

26 As they led him away, they seized Simon from Cyrene, who
was on his way in from the country, and put the cross on him and
made him carry it behind Jesus. 27 A large number of people followed him, including women who mourned and wailed for him.
28 Jesus turned and said to them, "Daughters of Jerusalem, do not
weep for me; weep for yourselves and for your children. 29 For the
time will come when you will say, 'Blessed are the barren women,
the wombs that never bore and the breasts that never nursed!'
30 Then

[a] 2 Or *Messiah*; also in verses 35 and 39 [b] 5 Or *over the land of the Jews*
[c] 16 Some manuscripts *him." 17 Now he was obliged to release one man to them at the Feast.*

elders bring against Jesus in verse 5? What does Pilate's referral of the case to Herod show about the seriousness with which he viewed "the Jesus threat"? **5.** What do you learn about Herod's character from verses 8–11? What do you think he asked Jesus? Why wouldn't Jesus answer him at all? How do you account for the new friendship (v. 12)? **6.** Although Pilate and Herod both found Jesus innocent, why does Pilate finally give in to the leaders? What would you have done in his place? **7.** What ironies do you see in the fact that Barabbas (his name means "son of the father") was released, while Jesus was condemned? What does that show about the leaders? About Pilate?

1. In 19:45, Jesus confronted injustice with action, but here he was silent. Why? What particular form of injustice makes your blood boil? How do you decide when to fight for what is right, and when not to? Has that decision faced you recently? **2.** What contrasts do you see between Jesus' kingship and the authority of Pilate and Herod? What difference does it make to you that Jesus is not the type of king they were? **3.** How do you feel as you consider what Jesus experienced during his trial?

Which childhood chore (cleaning your room, mowing the lawn, caring for pets, doing the dishes), was your least favorite? Most favorite?

1. By now, how is Jesus faring (see Mk 14:65; 15:15–19)? Why would someone have to help Jesus carry the cross? **2.** Why would Jesus rather have no one weep for him (vv. 28–31; see 21:20–24)? Does Jesus address these women as his followers or as citizens of Jerusalem? How would you paraphrase what he meant by

" 'they will say to the mountains, "Fall on us!"
and to the hills, "Cover us!" '[a]

31For if men do these things when the tree is green, what will
happen when it is dry?"
32Two other men, both criminals, were also led out with him to
be executed. 33When they came to the place called the Skull, there
they crucified him, along with the criminals—one on his right, the
other on his left. 34Jesus said, "Father, forgive them, for they do not
know what they are doing."[b] And they divided up his clothes by
casting lots.
35The people stood watching, and the rulers even sneered at
him. They said, "He saved others; let him save himself if he is the
Christ of God, the Chosen One."
36The soldiers also came up and mocked him. They offered him
wine vinegar 37and said, "If you are the king of the Jews, save
yourself."
38There was a written notice above him, which read: THIS IS THE
KING OF THE JEWS.
39One of the criminals who hung there hurled insults at him:
"Aren't you the Christ? Save yourself and us!"
40But the other criminal rebuked him. "Don't you fear God," he
said, "since you are under the same sentence? 41We are punished
justly, for we are getting what our deeds deserve. But this man has
done nothing wrong."
42Then he said, "Jesus, remember me when you come into your
kingdom.[c]"
43Jesus answered him, "I tell you the truth, today you will be
with me in paradise."

Jesus' Death

44It was now about the sixth hour, and darkness came over the
whole land until the ninth hour, 45for the sun stopped shining. And
the curtain of the temple was torn in two. 46Jesus called out with a
loud voice, "Father, into your hands I commit my spirit." When he
had said this, he breathed his last.
47The centurion, seeing what had happened, praised God and
said, "Surely this was a righteous man." 48When all the people who
had gathered to witness this sight saw what took place, they beat
their breasts and went away. 49But all those who knew him, including the women who had followed him from Galilee, stood at a
distance, watching these things.

Jesus' Burial

50Now there was a man named Joseph, a member of the Council,
a good and upright man, 51who had not consented to their decision
and action. He came from the Judean town of Arimathea and he
was waiting for the kingdom of God. 52Going to Pilate, he asked for
Jesus' body. 53Then he took it down, wrapped it in linen cloth and
placed it in a tomb cut in the rock, one in which no one had yet
been laid. 54It was Preparation Day, and the Sabbath was about to
begin.
55The women who had come with Jesus from Galilee followed
Joseph and saw the tomb and how his body was laid in it. 56Then
they went home and prepared spices and perfumes. But they rested
on the Sabbath in obedience to the commandment.

[a] *30* Hosea 10:8 [b] *34* Some early manuscripts do not have this sentence.
[c] *42* Some manuscripts *come with your kingly power*

the proverb in verse 31? **3.** What attitudes and motives do you see in the crowd following this death-march? In the rulers? The criminals? The soldiers? The sign maker (v. 38)? In Jesus? **4.** What aspects of the Gospel message do you see in verses 40–43?

1. How do you view the crucifixion: Necessary evil? Cruel and unusual punishment? Sacrifice for sin? Triumph over injustice? Why? **2.** When did the meaning of the death of Christ begin to make sense to you? How would you explain the crucifixion to a non-Christian friend? **3.** Who in this story do you identify with most? With least? Why? **4.** How do people today similarly reflect the profound misunderstanding expressed in verse 35?

Whose death (family, friend or national figure) has affected you most? Why?

1. What is the meaning of the darkness (see 22:53)? The torn curtain (Heb 9)? Jesus' prayer (Ps 31:5)? The centurion's confession (v. 47)? **2.** What do you learn about Joseph of Arimathea? Why would he risk his reputation and status at this point?

1. From the elements here, how would you describe to someone what Jesus' death was all about? How does it make a difference in your view of sin and failure? Your confidence in God's love? **2.** Jesus had apparently failed, but Joseph and the women did not abandon him. What do you learn from this for your life? **3.** What does Jesus' crucifixion teach you about success, power, wealth and status?

Describe a time recently when you woke up very early to do something outside your normal routine.

1. Given what these women experienced in the last few days (19:37ff; 23:26–49, 55), how would they feel as they went to the tomb? When they find it empty? When the two men spoke to them? **2.** Why wouldn't the Eleven believe them? What must be going through Peter's mind?

1. How did the meaning of the resurrection first "dawn" upon you? What difference does the resurrection make to you? **2.** Where is your spiritual life focused: On Good Friday? Easter Sunday? Or in between?

The Resurrection

24 On the first day of the week, very early in the morning, the
women took the spices they had prepared and went to the
tomb. 2They found the stone rolled away from the tomb, 3but when
they entered, they did not find the body of the Lord Jesus. 4While
they were wondering about this, suddenly two men in clothes that
gleamed like lightning stood beside them. 5In their fright the wom-
en bowed down with their faces to the ground, but the men said to
them, "Why do you look for the living among the dead? 6He is not
here; he has risen! Remember how he told you, while he was still
with you in Galilee: 7'The Son of Man must be delivered into the
hands of sinful men, be crucified and on the third day be raised
again.' " 8Then they remembered his words.

9When they came back from the tomb, they told all these things
to the Eleven and to all the others. 10It was Mary Magdalene,
Joanna, Mary the mother of James, and the others with them who
told this to the apostles. 11But they did not believe the women,
because their words seemed to them like nonsense. 12Peter, however, got up and ran to the tomb. Bending over, he saw the strips
of linen lying by themselves, and he went away, wondering to
himself what had happened.

If you were laid off from work today or your job was terminated, where would you go to get yourself together?

On the Road to Emmaus

13Now that same day two of them were going to a village called
Emmaus, about seven miles[a] from Jerusalem. 14They were talking
with each other about everything that had happened. 15As they

[a] *13* Greek *sixty stadia* (about 11 kilometers)

Luke 23:44–49 JESUS' DEATH

1. How would you illustrate this story?
   a. a black cloud blocking the sun, representing such an ominous day
   b. a sunset, representing the end of an era
   c. a sunrise, representing the hope of the new day to come
   d. the torn curtain of the temple, representing the way to God opened

2. Why did darkness cover the land from about noon until 3 p.m.?
   a. There was probably an eclipse.
   b. The forces of evil were at the height of their power.
   c. God was dealing with the darkness of sin.
   d. God was so upset he didn't want anyone to see these events.
   e. God was mad at the world.

3. What is so significant about the temple curtain (which shielded the Most Holy Place) being torn in two?
   a. The barrier between God and us was removed.
   b. Everyone can approach God directly now.
   c. There's no more need for mystery.
   d. There's no more need for blood sacrifices.
   e. Fellowship between God and people has been restored.

4. What do you think the Roman centurion in charge of the crucifixion, who gave God praise, did the next day?
   a. tried to forget all about this
   b. figured he had let his fears and emotions get the best of him
   c. searched out Jesus' followers to find out more about Jesus
   d. asked God to forgive him for his role in Jesus' death

5. What caused those witnessing the crucifixion (other than Jesus' followers) to leave the cross beating their breasts?
   a. awe at the day's events
   b. guilt for their earlier mocking
   c. grief for Jesus' death
   d. fear for their own future

6. Do you see Jesus' crucifixion as a tragedy or a victory? How does the story of his death make you feel?

7. When did you come to realize that Jesus died for you?

8. How would you describe the way Jesus' death has impacted your lifestyle and value system?
   a. a little bit
   b. a whole lot
   c. not as much as it should
   d. a lot more than it used to
   e. I'm not sure.

9. What kind of man does the story of Jesus' death show him to be?
   a. a *real* man
   b. a righteous man
   c. no ordinary man
   d. a defeated man
   e. a triumphant man

10. How has this course affected your views of masculinity? How can you be more like Jesus?

11. One at a time, listen silently as other group members share what Christlike qualities that person demonstrates.

talked and discussed these things with each other, Jesus himself
came up and walked along with them; 16but they were kept from
recognizing him.
17He asked them, "What are you discussing together as you walk
along?"
They stood still, their faces downcast. 18One of them, named
Cleopas, asked him, "Are you only a visitor to Jerusalem and do not
know the things that have happened there in these days?"
19"What things?" he asked.
"About Jesus of Nazareth," they replied. "He was a prophet,
powerful in word and deed before God and all the people. 20The
chief priests and our rulers handed him over to be sentenced to
death, and they crucified him; 21but we had hoped that he was the
one who was going to redeem Israel. And what is more, it is the
third day since all this took place. 22In addition, some of our wom-
en amazed us. They went to the tomb early this morning 23but
didn't find his body. They came and told us that they had seen a
vision of angels, who said he was alive. 24Then some of our companions went to the tomb and found it just as the women had said,
but him they did not see."
25He said to them, "How foolish you are, and how slow of heart
to believe all that the prophets have spoken! 26Did not the Christ[a]
have to suffer these things and then enter his glory?" 27And beginning with Moses and all the Prophets, he explained to them what
was said in all the Scriptures concerning himself.
28As they approached the village to which they were going, Jesus
acted as if he were going farther. 29But they urged him strongly,

1. What are the two disciples talking about as they walk (see vv. 19–24)? What tones of voice do you hear? What hopes are dashed? What plans might they be making? How do they react to the "stranger"? **2.** From your knowledge of OT prophecy, what passages might "the stranger" have discussed with them in verses 25–27 (see list in Introduction to Hosea)? Why did Jesus do a roundabout Bible study rather than just reveal his identity immediately and directly? **3.** Why did Jesus act as if he was going further? **4.** What has happened to the other disciples that has caused them to change their minds from verse 11? Why a special appearance to Peter?

1. Where is your "Road to Emmaus"—the place where Jesus surprised you recently? What happened? Did you urge him to stay (v. 29)? Why or why not? **2.** How well do you think you can explain the life, death and resurrection of Jesus Christ, and the way a person can have a relationship with him? Try rehearsing or role playing

a26 Or *Messiah*; also in verse 46

Luke 24:13–35 ON THE ROAD TO EMMAUS

This story happened late in the day in which Jesus rose from the dead.

1. What do you think caused these two disciples to leave town?
   a. fear—They feared for their lives.
   b. disillusionment—They thought they lost their political liberator.
   c. overload—Jesus' suffering and crucifixion had wiped them out.
   d. loneliness—They wanted to get back home.
   e. despair—They lost their hope along with their spiritual leader.

2. Why didn't they recognize Jesus when he joined them?
   a. They were preoccupied.
   b. They refused to believe their eyes.
   c. Jesus wasn't recognizable in his resurrected body.
   d. God supernaturally prevented them from recognizing him.

3. What opened their eyes?
   a. a sudden burst of insight
   b. Jesus taking bread and breaking it
   c. the Holy Spirit
   d. putting two and two together

4. Why did the two disciples want to return to Jerusalem?
   a. to confirm the women's report
   b. to be with their friends
   c. to tell everybody the good news
   d. to rejoin the team they had quit

5. What is the thing that triggers a spiritual crisis for you?
   a. financial panic
   b. anger with God over personal tragedy
   c. disappointment in a relationship
   d. family problems
   e. questions/doubts about my faith
   f. disillusionment with my church
   g. lack of direction from God

6. What is the closest you have come to "throwing in the towel" spiritually?

7. What helps you recognize Jesus alongside you when you are down?
   a. spending time alone with God
   b. talking with someone who cares
   c. getting away from the situation
   d. taking Communion
   e. reading Scripture
   f. fellowshipping with others

8. How would you describe your relationship with Christ right now?
   a. headed the wrong direction
   b. headed the right direction
   c. up and down
   d. a special case of "heartburn" (like the disciples in this story)

9. Imagine Jesus suddenly coming and walking beside you. What would he talk about?
   a. the troubles I'm experiencing
   b. my anger with God over a tragedy
   c. my lack of direction from God
   d. questions/doubts about my faith
   e. disillusionment with the church
   f. He probably wouldn't say too much—he would just be there.

10. What would it take for you to recognize the presence of Christ in your life?
   a. a "burning" in my heart
   b. an obvious miracle
   c. the elimination of my problems
   d. a change in *me*—a willingness to commit to the "unseen"
   e. I already recognize his presence.

this in your group. Who could you communicate these truths with today?

What favorite slogan or pep talk do you recall from your mentors (parents, a coach, music teacher, etc.)? How were you treated when you blew it?

1. How is "Peace be with you" a good summary of the Gospel? **2.** Why are the disciples having such difficulty believing: (a) Not using their eyes? (b) Not enough evidence? (c) Not enough faith? (d) Too much excitement? Why was it necessary for them to see that Jesus was not a ghost? **3.** What interpretation from Jesus helps them to believe? **4.** What task does he give them? With what promise? How must they have felt? **5.** Why do the disciples react so differently when Jesus is taken away now (vv. 50–53; compare when he was taken away by the crucifixion, v. 46)?

1. Why is it important to you that Jesus' mission was anticipated far beforehand in the Old Testament? **2.** How would you live differently if Jesus was not currently reigning in heaven, but was only another noble martyr? **3.** In light of your circumstances, where is the mission field Jesus has sent you? Who are some of the people you can witness to by your life? By your words? Who are the disciples in your life who encourage your service to Christ? **4.** How do you respond to his mission for you: (a) Let's get going!? (b) I couldn't possibly do that!? (c) He didn't mean me? (d) I'm scared, but I'll trust him? Why? **5.** What has been the high point for you in this study of Luke?

"Stay with us, for it is nearly evening; the day is almost over." So
he went in to stay with them.
30When he was at the table with them, he took bread, gave
thanks, broke it and began to give it to them. 31Then their eyes
were opened and they recognized him, and he disappeared from
their sight. 32They asked each other, "Were not our hearts burning
within us while he talked with us on the road and opened the
Scriptures to us?"
33They got up and returned at once to Jerusalem. There they
found the Eleven and those with them, assembled together 34and
saying, "It is true! The Lord has risen and has appeared to Simon."
35Then the two told what had happened on the way, and how Jesus
was recognized by them when he broke the bread.

Jesus Appears to the Disciples

36While they were still talking about this, Jesus himself stood
among them and said to them, "Peace be with you."
37They were startled and frightened, thinking they saw a ghost.
38He said to them, "Why are you troubled, and why do doubts rise
in your minds? 39Look at my hands and my feet. It is I myself!
Touch me and see; a ghost does not have flesh and bones, as you
see I have."
40When he had said this, he showed them his hands and feet.
41And while they still did not believe it because of joy and amazement, he asked them, "Do you have anything here to eat?" 42They
gave him a piece of broiled fish, 43and he took it and ate it in their
presence.
44He said to them, "This is what I told you while I was still with
you: Everything must be fulfilled that is written about me in the
Law of Moses, the Prophets and the Psalms."
45Then he opened their minds so they could understand the
Scriptures. 46He told them, "This is what is written: The Christ
will suffer and rise from the dead on the third day, 47and repentance and forgiveness of sins will be preached in his name to all
nations, beginning at Jerusalem. 48You are witnesses of these
things. 49I am going to send you what my Father has promised; but
stay in the city until you have been clothed with power from on
high."

The Ascension

50When he had led them out to the vicinity of Bethany, he lifted
up his hands and blessed them. 51While he was blessing them, he
left them and was taken up into heaven. 52Then they worshiped
him and returned to Jerusalem with great joy. 53And they stayed
continually at the temple, praising God.

INTRODUCTION to
JOHN

Book Study Outline: If you are using John for a study course, here is a 7- or 13-week outline. Use the margin questions for your group agenda:

start meeting / 15 min.

read & discuss Bible / 30 min.

close meeting / 15–45 min.

Refer to the Questions and Answers in the front of this Bible for more information.

7-week plan	13-week plan	Personal Reading	Group Study Passage
	1	1:1–2:11	2:1–11/Water to Wine
1	2	2:12–3:21	3:1–21/Nicodemus
2	3	3:22–4:30	4:7–30/A Samaritan Woman
	4	4:31–5:15	5:1–15/Healing at the Pool
3	5	5:16–8:11	7:53–8:11/Adulterous Woman
	6	8:12–9:34	9:1–34/Blind Man Healed
4	7	9:35–11:44	11:1–44/Lazarus Raised
5	8	11:45–13:17	13:1–17/Washing of Feet
	9	13:18–16:33	15:1–17/Vine and Branches
6	10	17:1–19:27	19:16–27/The Crucifixion
	11	19:28–20:18	20:1–18/Appearance to Mary
7	12	20:19–31	20:24–31/Thomas Doubts
	13	21:1–25	21:1–25/Peter Reinstated

Author: According to tradition, John, "the beloved disciple" (21:20–24), wrote this Gospel. John was prominent in the early church but is not mentioned by name in this book—which would be natural if he wrote it. For more information about John's long life, see the timeline in the Introduction to 1 John.

Date: Uncertain; estimates range anywhere from the A.D. 50s to 90s.

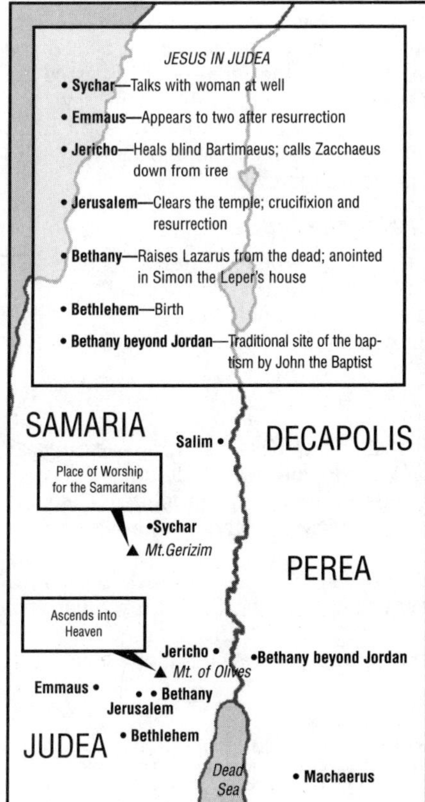
JESUS IN JUDEA
• Sychar—Talks with woman at well
• Emmaus—Appears to two after resurrection
• Jericho—Heals blind Bartimaeus; calls Zacchaeus down from tree
• Jerusalem—Clears the temple; crucifixion and resurrection
• Bethany—Raises Lazarus from the dead; anointed in Simon the Leper's house
• Bethlehem—Birth
• Bethany beyond Jordan—Traditional site of the baptism by John the Baptist
SAMARIA
Salim
DECAPOLIS
Place of Worship for the Samaritans
Sychar
Mt.Gerizim
PEREA
Ascends into Heaven
Jericho
Mt. of Olives
Bethany beyond Jordan
Emmaus
Bethany
Jerusalem
JUDEA
Bethlehem
Dead Sea
Machaerus

Theme: Jesus is the giver of life (20:31).

Historical Background: Of all the Gospels, John's is most clearly not meant to be a chronological account of Jesus' life. Instead it is a meditation on the significance of his death—a reality which is present right from the beginning of the Gospel (e.g., 1:29).

Characteristics: One commentator writes that years of studying John "do not leave one with a feeling of having mastered it, but rather with the conviction that it is still strange, restless and unfamiliar" (Morris). In many ways this Gospel is very different from the others. The action centers in Jerusalem rather than in Galilee. Jesus' teaching is given in long discourses instead of pithy parables. The call to faith and the promise of eternal life are repeatedly emphasized. Stories not in the other Gospels about people like Nicodemus, the woman at the well and Lazarus, are highlighted. The "I am" statements of Jesus, as well as the beautiful prologue (1:1–18), are unique. Irony, words with double meanings, and metaphors invite the reader to reflect upon the richness and depth of Jesus. Chapters 1–12 focus on a few public miracles which are expressly meant as "signs" pointing to Jesus' identity, while in chapters 13–21, Jesus is basically alone with his disciples teaching them about his mission, the Holy Spirit and his command to love.

John

1. What is your full name? 2. What is your nickname? Where did the names come from?

1. Why does this Gospel begin "In the beginning" rather than at Jesus' birth? 2. What facts about "the Word" can you find in verses 1–5? Verses 10–18? 3. What is John the Baptist's role as a witness? 4. Who or what fails to comprehend the light (vv. 5, 10–11)? Why? 5. From the image of "receiving" someone (v. 12), how would you explain what faith is about? What is the result of this type of faith? 6. How would someone "full of grace and truth" treat others? 7. From this passage, how can a person come to know God?

1. Are you keeping Jesus at the door? In certain rooms? Why? Or have you given him the keys? 2. What does John's emphasis on the pre-existent, creative Christ mean to you?

The Word Became Flesh

1 In the beginning was the Word, and the Word was with God,
and the Word was God. 2 He was with God in the beginning.
3 Through him all things were made; without him nothing was
made that has been made. 4 In him was life, and that life was the
light of men. 5 The light shines in the darkness, but the darkness
has not understood[a] it.
6 There came a man who was sent from God; his name was John.
7 He came as a witness to testify concerning that light, so that
through him all men might believe. 8 He himself was not the light;
he came only as a witness to the light. 9 The true light that gives
light to every man was coming into the world.[b]
10 He was in the world, and though the world was made through
him, the world did not recognize him. 11 He came to that which
was his own, but his own did not receive him. 12 Yet to all who
received him, to those who believed in his name, he gave the right
to become children of God— 13 children born not of natural descent,[c] nor of human decision or a husband's will, but born of
God.
14 The Word became flesh and made his dwelling among us. We
have seen his glory, the glory of the One and Only,[d] who came
from the Father, full of grace and truth.
15 John testifies concerning him. He cries out, saying, "This was
he of whom I said, 'He who comes after me has surpassed me
because he was before me.' " 16 From the fullness of his grace we
have all received one blessing after another. 17 For the law was
given through Moses; grace and truth came through Jesus Christ.
18 No one has ever seen God, but God the One and Only,[d,e] who
is at the Father's side, has made him known.

Have you ever been embarrassed by mistaking a stranger for an acquaintance? What happened?

1. What questions do the priests and Levites ask John? What do these questions reveal about the reason why they were sent? 2. Why does John respond so abruptly? What would you have said in his situation? 3. What is John's purpose in life (vv. 22–23,26–27; also Isa 40:3–5)? 4. How does John finally answer their question about his baptism (vv. 30–31)? What does he mean by calling Jesus the "Lamb of God" (v. 29; see Ex 12:1–13; Isa 53:7) and the "Son of God" (v. 34)? What proof supports these claims (Ps 2:7)?

1. Who "made straight the way for the Lord" in your life? 2. How could you incorporate the

John the Baptist Denies Being the Christ

19 Now this was John's testimony when the Jews of Jerusalem
sent priests and Levites to ask him who he was. 20 He did not fail to
confess, but confessed freely, "I am not the Christ.[f]"
21 They asked him, "Then who are you? Are you Elijah?"
He said, "I am not."
"Are you the Prophet?"
He answered, "No."
22 Finally they said, "Who are you? Give us an answer to take
back to those who sent us. What do you say about yourself?"
23 John replied in the words of Isaiah the prophet, "I am the
voice of one calling in the desert, 'Make straight the way for the
Lord.' "[g]
24 Now some Pharisees who had been sent 25 questioned him,
"Why then do you baptize if you are not the Christ, nor Elijah, nor
the Prophet?"
26 "I baptize with[h] water," John replied, "but among you stands

[a]5 Or *darkness, and the darkness has not overcome* [b]9 Or *This was the true light that gives light to every man who comes into the world* [c]13 Greek *of bloods* [d]14,18 Or *the Only Begotten* [e]18 Some manuscripts *but the only* (or *only begotten*) *Son* [f]20 Or *Messiah.* "The Christ" (Greek) and "the Messiah" (Hebrew) both mean "the Anointed One"; also in verse 25. [g]23 Isaiah 40:3 [h]26 Or *in*; also in verses 31 and 33

one you do not know. 27He is the one who comes after me, the
thongs of whose sandals I am not worthy to untie."
28This all happened at Bethany on the other side of the Jordan,
where John was baptizing.

Jesus the Lamb of God

29The next day John saw Jesus coming toward him and said,
"Look, the Lamb of God, who takes away the sin of the world!
30This is the one I meant when I said, 'A man who comes after me
has surpassed me because he was before me.' 31I myself did not
know him, but the reason I came baptizing with water was that he
might be revealed to Israel."
32Then John gave this testimony: "I saw the Spirit come down
from heaven as a dove and remain on him. 33I would not have
known him, except that the one who sent me to baptize with
water told me, 'The man on whom you see the Spirit come down
and remain is he who will baptize with the Holy Spirit.' 34I have
seen and I testify that this is the Son of God."

Jesus' First Disciples

35The next day John was there again with two of his disciples.
36When he saw Jesus passing by, he said, "Look, the Lamb of God!"
37When the two disciples heard him say this, they followed
Jesus. 38Turning around, Jesus saw them following and asked,
"What do you want?"
They said, "Rabbi" (which means Teacher), "where are you staying?"
39"Come," he replied, "and you will see."
So they went and saw where he was staying, and spent that day
with him. It was about the tenth hour.
40Andrew, Simon Peter's brother, was one of the two who heard
what John had said and who had followed Jesus. 41The first thing
Andrew did was to find his brother Simon and tell him, "We have
found the Messiah" (that is, the Christ). 42And he brought him to
Jesus.
Jesus looked at him and said, "You are Simon son of John. You
will be called Cephas" (which, when translated, is Peter[a]).

Jesus Calls Philip and Nathanael

43The next day Jesus decided to leave for Galilee. Finding Philip,
he said to him, "Follow me."
44Philip, like Andrew and Peter, was from the town of Bethsaida.
45Philip found Nathanael and told him, "We have found the one
Moses wrote about in the Law, and about whom the prophets also
wrote—Jesus of Nazareth, the son of Joseph."
46"Nazareth! Can anything good come from there?" Nathanael
asked.
"Come and see," said Philip.
47When Jesus saw Nathanael approaching, he said of him, "Here
is a true Israelite, in whom there is nothing false."
48"How do you know me?" Nathanael asked.
Jesus answered, "I saw you while you were still under the fig
tree before Philip called you."
49Then Nathanael declared, "Rabbi, you are the Son of God; you
are the King of Israel."
50Jesus said, "You believe[b] because I told you I saw you under
the fig tree. You shall see greater things than that." 51He then

[a]*42* Both *Cephas* (Aramaic) and *Peter* (Greek) mean *rock*. [b]*50* Or *Do you believe. . . ?*

submissive, sacrificial lifestyle of the Lamb of God into your own life? Of the titles for Jesus given so far (the Word, the Light, the Christ, the Lamb of God, the Son of God), which means the most to you? Why? **3.** What does baptism mean to you? What about baptism with the Holy Spirit?

---

1. When you get some good news, who is the first person you want to share it with? Why? **2.** As a child, what would it take for you to believe something your brother or sister told you?

1. In light of verses 30–31, how do you think John felt when his disciples left him to follow Jesus? What does this say about John? **2.** What motivated the disciples of John to follow Jesus? What motivated Andrew to tell Simon about him? **3.** How do you think Simon felt when Jesus changed his name to Cephas (meaning "rock")? **4.** What type of person is Nathanael? Why might he find it hard to believe Philip's statement? Why would Jesus call Philip and Nathanael in such different ways? How do you think Nathanael felt when Jesus spoke to him? **5.** Of the five people in verses 35–48 to follow Jesus: (a) How was the contact made for each one? (b) How much did each one know about Jesus when he decided to follow him? (c) How does each decision for Christ illustrate the point of the prologue (vv. 1–17) about the light of John and the true light of Christ?

1. What was your motive for initially following Jesus? What were the circumstances that led you to do so? How much did you know about him? **2.** Consider verse 48. In your life, how has Jesus shown his ability to know all about you?

added, “I tell you[a] the truth, you[a] shall see heaven open, and the
angels of God ascending and descending on the Son of Man.”

What is the funniest thing you've witnessed at a wedding?

1. Jesus is not known as a miracle-worker, so why does Mary approach him (v. 3)? What do you learn about Jesus and his mother from this story? **2.** How does this passage affect your belief in the consumption of alcohol? **3.** What part does the function and size of the jars play in this story? How does the quantity and quality of the wine demonstrate Jesus' glory?

Where is the wine level (zest for life) in your life right now: Full? Half full? Empty? What is draining you? What area seems like stale water in an old jug? How could Jesus bring celebration back into your life?

Jesus Changes Water to Wine

2 On the third day a wedding took place at Cana in Galilee.
Jesus' mother was there, 2and Jesus and his disciples had also
been invited to the wedding. 3When the wine was gone, Jesus'
mother said to him, “They have no more wine.”
4“Dear woman, why do you involve me?” Jesus replied. “My
time has not yet come.”
5His mother said to the servants, “Do whatever he tells you.”
6Nearby stood six stone water jars, the kind used by the Jews for
ceremonial washing, each holding from twenty to thirty gallons.[b]
7Jesus said to the servants, “Fill the jars with water”; so they
filled them to the brim.
8Then he told them, “Now draw some out and take it to the
master of the banquet.”
They did so, 9and the master of the banquet tasted the water that
had been turned into wine. He did not realize where it had come
from, though the servants who had drawn the water knew. Then
he called the bridegroom aside 10and said, “Everyone brings out
the choice wine first and then the cheaper wine after the guests
have had too much to drink; but you have saved the best till now.”
11This, the first of his miraculous signs, Jesus performed at Cana
in Galilee. He thus revealed his glory, and his disciples put their
faith in him.

[a]*51* The Greek is plural. [b]*6* Greek *two to three metretes* (probably about 75 to 115 liters)

John 2:1–11 JESUS CHANGES WATER TO WINE

Weddings in Jesus' time were important events. Relatives and townspeople would gather to celebrate, often for up to a week! To run out of wine would be a great social embarrassment.

1. Why do you think Jesus went to this wedding?
   a. to please his mother
   b. to perform a miracle
   c. because everyone was invited
   d. because weddings are always fun

2. Why did Jesus' mother ask Jesus to do something about the wine?
   a. Mothers are that way.
   b. She was catering the party.
   c. She was concerned for the guests.
   d. She wanted to save the bridegroom from embarrassment.
   e. She had faith that Jesus could take care of things.
   f. She wanted to show what her son could do.

3. How do you think Jesus felt?
   a. annoyed
   b. embarrassed
   c. manipulated
   d. honored
   e. reluctant
   f. willing

4. How do you think the bridegroom felt when he heard about the new wine?
   a. perplexed
   b. amazed
   c. delighted
   d. relieved

5. Why do you think Jesus performed his first miracle at a wedding feast?
   a. It just happened that way.
   b. His mother twisted his arm.
   c. He saw a need and met it.
   d. Wine had a special significance.
   e. Weddings had (and still have) a special significance.

6. In verse 11 what does John, the author of this Gospel, mean by calling Jesus' miracles “signs”?

7. What “sign” led you to put your faith in Jesus?
   a. the miracles Jesus did in the Bible
   b. a specific miracle Jesus did for me
   c. the wrong direction my life was going
   d. the resurrection of Jesus and the fact that he is still alive
   e. the change in heart I experienced
   f. the changes I saw in others
   g. Nothing else made sense.

8. What is the “wine” level (zest for living) in your life at the moment?
   a. overflowing
   b. half-full
   c. running out fast
   d. empty

9. What is draining you? What in your life feels like stale water in an old jug? How could Jesus change things?

10. How often do you feel pressure from an extended family member to do something you really don't want to do? How much conflict do your extended families cause your marriage? What could reduce that conflict?

11. In what area(s) do your parents ask something of you that really irritates you? (And what can you do about these hassles?)
    a. chores
    b. grades
    c. curfew
    d. clothes
    e. hair
    f. friends
    g. keeping my room clean
    h. going to church/youth group
    i. dating
    j. manners
    k. language
    l. music/TV
    m. using the phone
    n. driving the car

Jesus Clears the Temple

12After this he went down to Capernaum with his mother and
brothers and his disciples. There they stayed for a few days.
13When it was almost time for the Jewish Passover, Jesus went
up to Jerusalem. 14In the temple courts he found men selling cattle,
sheep and doves, and others sitting at tables exchanging money.
15So he made a whip out of cords, and drove all from the temple
area, both sheep and cattle; he scattered the coins of the money
changers and overturned their tables. 16To those who sold doves he
said, "Get these out of here! How dare you turn my Father's house
into a market!"
17His disciples remembered that it is written: "Zeal for your
house will consume me."[a]
18Then the Jews demanded of him, "What miraculous sign can
you show us to prove your authority to do all this?"
19Jesus answered them, "Destroy this temple, and I will raise it
again in three days."
20The Jews replied, "It has taken forty-six years to build this
temple, and you are going to raise it in three days?" 21But the
temple he had spoken of was his body. 22After he was raised from
the dead, his disciples recalled what he had said. Then they believed the Scripture and the words that Jesus had spoken.
23Now while he was in Jerusalem at the Passover Feast, many
people saw the miraculous signs he was doing and believed in his
name.[b] 24But Jesus would not entrust himself to them, for he
knew all men. 25He did not need man's testimony about man, for
he knew what was in a man.

Jesus Teaches Nicodemus

3 Now there was a man of the Pharisees named Nicodemus, a
member of the Jewish ruling council. 2He came to Jesus at
night and said, "Rabbi, we know you are a teacher who has come
from God. For no one could perform the miraculous signs you are
doing if God were not with him."
3In reply Jesus declared, "I tell you the truth, no one can see the
kingdom of God unless he is born again.[c]"
4"How can a man be born when he is old?" Nicodemus asked.
"Surely he cannot enter a second time into his mother's womb to
be born!"
5Jesus answered, "I tell you the truth, no one can enter the
kingdom of God unless he is born of water and the Spirit. 6Flesh
gives birth to flesh, but the Spirit[d] gives birth to spirit. 7You
should not be surprised at my saying, 'You[e] must be born again.'
8The wind blows wherever it pleases. You hear its sound, but you
cannot tell where it comes from or where it is going. So it is with
everyone born of the Spirit."
9"How can this be?" Nicodemus asked.
10"You are Israel's teacher," said Jesus, "and do you not understand these things? 11I tell you the truth, we speak of what we
know, and we testify to what we have seen, but still you people do
not accept our testimony. 12I have spoken to you of earthly things
and you do not believe; how then will you believe if I speak of
heavenly things? 13No one has ever gone into heaven except the
one who came from heaven—the Son of Man.[f] 14Just as Moses
lifted up the snake in the desert, so the Son of Man must be lifted
up, 15that everyone who believes in him may have eternal life.[g]

[a] *17* Psalm 69:9 [b] *23* Or *and believed in him* [c] *3* Or *born from above*; also in verse 7 [d] *6* Or *but spirit* [e] *7* The Greek is plural. [f] *13* Some manuscripts *Man, who is in heaven* [g] *15* Or *believes may have eternal life in him*

What room or area of yours is cleanest? Dirtiest?

1. The sellers and money-changers were set up to provide sacrificial animals for sale at the temple as a help to Jews from far away. How might this once useful practice have deteriorated into a racket? Why else was Jesus angry (Ps 69:9)? **2.** As one of the sellers, how would you feel about Jesus' actions? As one of the disciples, how would you feel? **3.** How is Jesus challenged (v. 19)? Why? What effect does his response have on them? **4.** Why doesn't Jesus entrust himself to the crowd in verses 23–25?

If you compare your spiritual life to the rooms of a house, which room do you think Jesus might want to clean up: (a) Library—the reading room? (b) Dining room—appetites, desires? (c) Workshop—where you keep your skills? (d) Recreation room—where you hang out after work? (e) Family room—where most of your relationships are lived out? or (f) Closet—where your hang-ups are?

What were you first told about where babies came from? How old were you when you learned the real story?

1. What can you find out about Nicodemus in verses 1–2? What is significant about his coming to Jesus? Why at night (see vv. 19–20)? Why was Jesus so direct with him? **2.** What two ideas about birth are Jesus and Nicodemus thinking of? What point is Jesus making by comparing spiritual birth to the wind? How does Jesus account for Nicodemus' lack of understanding? **3.** What does Jesus claim about himself in verses 13–15? **4.** From verses 16–18, what stands out to you about God? About what he wants to do? About how a person is condemned? How will belief show itself (vv. 15–21)? **5.** How is Jesus' use of the words "born again" similar to and different from the way it is used today? How would you define "born again" in your own words?

1. What first aroused your interest in Jesus? Why? **2.** Where are you right now in the birthing process of spiritual life: Not yet conceived? Developing, but not so anyone could tell? Heavy with child and waiting? Kicking and screaming like an infant? Growing daily? Explain. **3.** When did you begin to see God as saving you, rather than condemning you?

16"For God so loved the world that he gave his one and only
Son,[a] that whoever believes in him shall not perish but have
eternal life. 17For God did not send his Son into the world to
condemn the world, but to save the world through him. 18Whoever
believes in him is not condemned, but whoever does not believe
stands condemned already because he has not believed in the
name of God's one and only Son.[b] 19This is the verdict: Light has
come into the world, but men loved darkness instead of light because their deeds were evil. 20Everyone who does evil hates the
light, and will not come into the light for fear that his deeds will be
exposed. 21But whoever lives by the truth comes into the light, so
that it may be seen plainly that what he has done has been done
through God."[c]

---

1. What did you and your brother or sister fight about? How would you try to get your way? **2.** At family reunions, what subject (e.g., politics or religion) is bound to start an argument?

1. Given the different ideas about baptism, what do you think had happened at the river? What do you think the "certain Jew" had said (v. 25)? How would you have felt if you had been one of John's disciples at this point? **2.** How does John the Baptist respond (vv. 27–36)? What is the point of the allegory or story about the bride and bridegroom? What

John the Baptist's Testimony About Jesus

22After this, Jesus and his disciples went out into the Judean
countryside, where he spent some time with them, and baptized.
23Now John also was baptizing at Aenon near Salim, because there
was plenty of water, and people were constantly coming to be
baptized. 24(This was before John was put in prison.) 25An argument developed between some of John's disciples and a certain
Jew[d] over the matter of ceremonial washing. 26They came to John
and said to him, "Rabbi, that man who was with you on the other
side of the Jordan—the one you testified about—well, he is baptizing, and everyone is going to him."
27To this John replied, "A man can receive only what is given

[a]16 Or *his only begotten Son* [b]18 Or *God's only begotten Son* [c]21 Some interpreters end the quotation after verse 15. [d]25 Some manuscripts *and certain Jews*

John 3:1–21 JESUS TEACHES NICODEMUS

1. Why did Nicodemus come to Jesus by night?
   a. He worked during the day.
   b. He couldn't wait until morning.
   c. He was afraid of being seen.
   d. He wanted time alone with Jesus.

2. When Jesus brought up the need for a person to be "born again," how did Nicodemus react?
   a. He got curious.
   b. He got defensive.
   c. He got interested.
   d. He got confused.

3. What did Jesus mean when he said you have to be born again to see the kingdom of God?
   a. We have to be able to point to a specific conversion experience.
   b. We can only be accepted into God's kingdom by turning our lives over to him.
   c. Our spirits are destroyed by sin and need God's intervention to be reborn.
   d. Our spiritual lives have a beginning just like our physical lives.

4. How do you think Nicodemus came away from this meeting with Jesus?
   a. turned off
   b. enlightened
   c. totally confused
   d. with a lot to think about
   e. a secret follower of Jesus
   f. convinced in his mind but not in his heart

5. Which of the following describes your openness to the light God might shed on your life?
   a. It's so dark I can't find a light.
   b. There's still a lot of me that I want to hide in the darkness.
   c. I want to leave the darkness, but the light hurts my eyes.
   d. The more I follow the light, the brighter it becomes.
   e. I am completely open to God's light and grateful for it.

6. What is the most important point in this passage for you right now?
   a. Spiritual rebirth is indeed possible (vv. 3–7).
   b. Heaven is waiting for those who believe in Jesus Christ (vv. 14–16).
   c. God loved us enough to give us his only Son (v. 16).
   d. God doesn't desire to condemn us, but to save us (vv. 17–18).
   e. If we are open to being enlightened, light will come (vv. 19–21).

7. To receive Christ's promise of new life, I need to:
   a. stop being so literal and rational.
   b. ask God to forgive me for some things.
   c. forgive myself for some things.
   d. realize I'm not too old to change—to be reborn.
   e. open my heart to Christ.
   f. do nothing—I have already claimed this promise.

8. If you came to Jesus with one question that you were a little embarrassed to ask, what would it be? What other person could you go to with questions about your spiritual journey?

him from heaven. 28You yourselves can testify that I said, 'I am not
the Christ[a] but am sent ahead of him.' 29The bride belongs to the
bridegroom. The friend who attends the bridegroom waits and
listens for him, and is full of joy when he hears the bridegroom's
voice. That joy is mine, and it is now complete. 30He must become
greater; I must become less.

31"The one who comes from above is above all; the one who is
from the earth belongs to the earth, and speaks as one from the
earth. The one who comes from heaven is above all. 32He testifies
to what he has seen and heard, but no one accepts his testimony.
33The man who has accepted it has certified that God is truthful.
34For the one whom God has sent speaks the words of God, for
God[b] gives the Spirit without limit. 35The Father loves the Son
and has placed everything in his hands. 36Whoever believes in the
Son has eternal life, but whoever rejects the Son will not see life,
for God's wrath remains on him."[c]

Jesus Talks With a Samaritan Woman

4 The Pharisees heard that Jesus was gaining and baptizing more
disciples than John, 2although in fact it was not Jesus who
baptized, but his disciples. 3When the Lord learned of this, he left
Judea and went back once more to Galilee.

4Now he had to go through Samaria. 5So he came to a town in
Samaria called Sychar, near the plot of ground Jacob had given to
his son Joseph. 6Jacob's well was there, and Jesus, tired as he was
from the journey, sat down by the well. It was about the sixth
hour.

7When a Samaritan woman came to draw water, Jesus said to
her, "Will you give me a drink?" 8(His disciples had gone into the
town to buy food.)

9The Samaritan woman said to him, "You are a Jew and I am a
Samaritan woman. How can you ask me for a drink?" (For Jews do
not associate with Samaritans.[d])

10Jesus answered her, "If you knew the gift of God and who it is
that asks you for a drink, you would have asked him and he would
have given you living water."

11"Sir," the woman said, "you have nothing to draw with and
the well is deep. Where can you get this living water? 12Are you
greater than our father Jacob, who gave us the well and drank from
it himself, as did also his sons and his flocks and herds?"

13Jesus answered, "Everyone who drinks this water will be
thirsty again, 14but whoever drinks the water I give him will never
thirst. Indeed, the water I give him will become in him a spring of
water welling up to eternal life."

15The woman said to him, "Sir, give me this water so that I
won't get thirsty and have to keep coming here to draw water."

16He told her, "Go, call your husband and come back."

17"I have no husband," she replied.

Jesus said to her, "You are right when you say you have no
husband. 18The fact is, you have had five husbands, and the man
you now have is not your husband. What you have just said is quite
true."

19"Sir," the woman said, "I can see that you are a prophet. 20Our
fathers worshiped on this mountain, but you Jews claim that the
place where we must worship is in Jerusalem."

21Jesus declared, "Believe me, woman, a time is coming when
you will worship the Father neither on this mountain nor in Jerusa-

[a]28 Or *Messiah* [b]34 Greek *he* [c]36 Some interpreters end the quotation after verse 30. [d]9 Or *do not use dishes Samaritans have used*

does John's response tell you about him? **3.** What facts about Jesus does John bring out in verses 31–36? **4.** How does the phrase "rejecting the Son" stand in contrast to what belief really means?

1. Consider verse 27. What have you received from heaven? How do you use what you have received? **2.** How can you apply verse 30 in your own life?

When you were growing up, who were the people you were told to avoid? What part of the city or country would you be warned about? What would have happened if you had gone there?

1. What is significant about this story taking place in Samaria? **2.** Since "nice" girls did not come to draw water at noontime ("the sixth hour"), why do you think Jesus risked his reputation to ask a favor of this woman? **3.** How would you describe the woman's response? **4.** How did Jesus turn the tables on her in verse 10? **5.** In the woman's reply, what is she really saying? How is she like Nicodemus (3:1–21)? **6.** Why does Jesus change the topic of conversation so abruptly to her personal life (v. 16–18)? What strikes you about the way he responds to her claim not to have a husband? **7.** Why do you think this woman changed the conversation to focus on a religious controversy? In this story, what does Jesus mean by telling her that God is interested in worshippers who will do so in "spirit and truth"? **8.** What is significant about Jesus choosing this woman as the first person to whom he revealed himself (see vv. 39–42)?

1. What social, ethnic or religious barriers have you overcome in Jesus' name? **2.** What aspects of Jesus' conversation could you use as a model for your own discussions with searching friends? **3.** What are you constantly "thirsting" for? How has Jesus satisfied you?

lem. 22You Samaritans worship what you do not know; we worship
what we do know, for salvation is from the Jews. 23Yet a time is
coming and has now come when the true worshipers will worship
the Father in spirit and truth, for they are the kind of worshipers
the Father seeks. 24God is spirit, and his worshipers must worship
in spirit and in truth."
25The woman said, "I know that Messiah" (called Christ) "is
coming. When he comes, he will explain everything to us."
26Then Jesus declared, "I who speak to you am he."

What causes you to skip a meal? To eat too much unintentionally?

1. Why were the disciples surprised to find Jesus with this woman? 2. What does "leaving her water jar" reveal about Jesus' impact on the woman? How did she affect others? 3. How is Jesus' figurative speech once again misunderstood (see 2:19; 3:3; 4:10)? Why does he continue to speak like this? In what ways is God's will like food for him? 4. How does the parable of harvesting apply to the disciples? 5. Given the social barriers between Jews and Samaritans, what do verses 40–42 teach you about Jesus?

The Disciples Rejoin Jesus

27Just then his disciples returned and were surprised to find him
talking with a woman. But no one asked, "What do you want?" or
"Why are you talking with her?"
28Then, leaving her water jar, the woman went back to the town
and said to the people, 29"Come, see a man who told me everything I ever did. Could this be the Christ[a]?" 30They came out of
the town and made their way toward him.
31Meanwhile his disciples urged him, "Rabbi, eat something."
32But he said to them, "I have food to eat that you know nothing
about."
33Then his disciples said to each other, "Could someone have
brought him food?"
34"My food," said Jesus, "is to do the will of him who sent me
and to finish his work. 35Do you not say, 'Four months more and
then the harvest'? I tell you, open your eyes and look at the fields!

[a]29 Or *Messiah*

John 4:7–30 JESUS TALKS WITH A SAMARITAN WOMAN

Instead of avoiding Samaria as Jews often did, Jesus passed through this area that Jews considered inhabited by spiritual and ethnic half-breeds.

1. How would you describe this woman's response for most of her conversation with Jesus?
   a. Searching—"Is it possible this is what I've been looking for?"
   b. Avoidance—"I think I'd better try to change the subject."
   c. Skeptical—"Who does this guy think he is?!"

2. What most influenced the woman to consider that the man she was talking to was the Messiah?
   a. what he said about "living water"
   b. the way he knew so much about her without being told
   c. his accepting her though she was a loose-living Samaritan woman
   d. when he claimed, "I who speak to you am he"

3. What was Jesus saying about worshiping God?
   a. The Jews' worship is better than the Samaritans' worship.
   b. The object of true worship—the Messiah—comes from the Jews.
   c. Focusing on where to worship misses the point.
   d. True worship is from the heart.

4. What was this woman thirsting for?
   a. intimacy in her relationships
   b. intimacy with God
   c. acceptance of who she was
   d. forgiveness for the life she had led
   e. meaning and purpose in life
   f. basic survival in life

5. What are *you* really thirsting for?

6. What did it take for Jesus and this woman to get past their cultural differences to communicate like this? What can you do to help overcome barriers that exist in your "world"?

7. What have been the most significant changes you have gone through in your spiritual life?
   a. a conversion experience
   b. a spiritual crisis
   c. changes in my beliefs
   d. different choices than my family
   e. switching churches/denominations

8. In what ways have the changes in your spiritual life been stressful or unsettling? How have you worked through that?

9. What differences exist between you as a couple?
   a. religious differences
   b. racial or ethnic differences
   c. political differences
   d. differences about handling money
   e. different ideas about leisure time
   f. differences in how we see our roles as husband and wife
   g. other:____________

10. What helps you get past your differences?
   a. willingness to listen and learn
   b. willingness to see past certain controversies between us
   c. determination to make our marriage work
   d. the fact we don't just tolerate our differences—we enjoy them!

11. What do you appreciate about this group? How have the members of your group helped you become refreshed by God's living water?

They are ripe for harvest. [36]Even now the reaper draws his wages,
even now he harvests the crop for eternal life, so that the sower
and the reaper may be glad together. [37]Thus the saying 'One sows
and another reaps' is true. [38]I sent you to reap what you have not
worked for. Others have done the hard work, and you have reaped
the benefits of their labor."

Many Samaritans Believe

[39]Many of the Samaritans from that town believed in him because of the woman's testimony, "He told me everything I ever
did." [40]So when the Samaritans came to him, they urged him to
stay with them, and he stayed two days. [41]And because of his
words many more became believers.

[42]They said to the woman, "We no longer believe just because of what you said; now we have heard for ourselves, and we know that this man really is the Savior of the world."

Jesus Heals the Official's Son

[43]After the two days he left for Galilee. [44](Now Jesus himself had
pointed out that a prophet has no honor in his own country.)
[45]When he arrived in Galilee, the Galileans welcomed him. They had seen all that he had done in Jerusalem at the Passover Feast, for they also had been there.

[46]Once more he visited Cana in Galilee, where he had turned the water into wine. And there was a certain royal official whose
son lay sick at Capernaum. [47]When this man heard that Jesus had
arrived in Galilee from Judea, he went to him and begged him to come and heal his son, who was close to death.

[48]"Unless you people see miraculous signs and wonders," Jesus told him, "you will never believe."

[49]The royal official said, "Sir, come down before my child dies."

[50]Jesus replied, "You may go. Your son will live."

The man took Jesus at his word and departed. [51]While he was
still on the way, his servants met him with the news that his boy
was living. [52]When he inquired as to the time when his son got
better, they said to him, "The fever left him yesterday at the seventh hour."

[53]Then the father realized that this was the exact time at which Jesus had said to him, "Your son will live." So he and all his household believed.

[54]This was the second miraculous sign that Jesus performed, having come from Judea to Galilee.

The Healing at the Pool

5 Some time later, Jesus went up to Jerusalem for a feast of the
Jews. [2]Now there is in Jerusalem near the Sheep Gate a pool,
which in Aramaic is called Bethesda[a] and which is surrounded by
five covered colonnades. [3]Here a great number of disabled people
used to lie—the blind, the lame, the paralyzed.[b] [5]One who was
there had been an invalid for thirty-eight years. [6]When Jesus saw
him lying there and learned that he had been in this condition for a long time, he asked him, "Do you want to get well?"

[7]"Sir," the invalid replied, "I have no one to help me into the pool when the water is stirred. While I am trying to get in, someone else goes down ahead of me."

[a]2 Some manuscripts *Bethzatha*; other manuscripts *Bethsaida* [b]3 Some less important manuscripts *paralyzed—and they waited for the moving of the waters. [4]From time to time an angel of the Lord would come down and stir up the waters. The first one into the pool after each such disturbance would be cured of whatever disease he had.*

1. Considering your interest in "spiritual things," are you more like the disciples or the woman? Why? **2.** Is doing God's will as essential to you as eating food? Why? **3.** What do you learn from the woman about telling others about Jesus? From the parable (vv. 35–38)?

When you were a child, what was the most serious illness or injury you ever had?

1. Now that Jesus is home again, what motivates the people to welcome him? **2.** How do you account for the contrast between the crowd's welcome (v. 45) and Jesus' comments in verses 44 and 48? How are the Galileans alike and unlike the Samaritans in verses 39–42? **3.** What motivates the royal official to travel so far? How would you have responded to what Jesus told him to do? What does this miracle tell you about Jesus?

1. When you bring your problem to God (such as a sickness in the family), do you tend to accept his word or keep fretting and fussing? **2.** When have you taken God at his word (even though the circumstances were seemingly impossible), and discovered that he did exactly what was promised?

When you get sick, what are you like: Oscar the Grouch? Superman? Rip Van Winkle?

1. How do you picture the setting of this story (vv. 2–4)? What is the smell? The noises? The atmosphere? **2.** How would you picture the invalid (vv. 5–7)? What does Jesus mean by his question in verse 6? What did the invalid hope Jesus might do? **3.** As the invalid, what would you feel in verses 8–9? In verses 10–13? In verse 14? **4.** Why were the leaders so upset? How do you suppose they responded to the healed man's testimony (v. 15)?

1. In what ways do people today try to be healed without Christ? 2. How would you respond to someone who said all sickness is a result of sin? 3. Why would Jesus ask, "Do you want to get well"? Describe a time when you would have said "No." How about "Yes"?

As you get older, do you find yourself becoming more, or less, like your parents? Why?

1. What was the result for Jesus of healing the invalid (vv. 1–15)? 2. How did his response to the Jewish leaders only heighten their opposition? Why would Jesus do this? 3. In what ways is Jesus equal with the Father (vv. 26–27)? What terms are used to show the kind of relation-

8 Then Jesus said to him, "Get up! Pick up your mat and walk."
9 At once the man was cured; he picked up his mat and walked.
The day on which this took place was a Sabbath, 10 and so the
Jews said to the man who had been healed, "It is the Sabbath; the
law forbids you to carry your mat."
11 But he replied, "The man who made me well said to me, 'Pick
up your mat and walk.' "
12 So they asked him, "Who is this fellow who told you to pick it
up and walk?"
13 The man who was healed had no idea who it was, for Jesus had
slipped away into the crowd that was there.
14 Later Jesus found him at the temple and said to him, "See, you
are well again. Stop sinning or something worse may happen to
you." 15 The man went away and told the Jews that it was Jesus
who had made him well.

Life Through the Son

16 So, because Jesus was doing these things on the Sabbath, the
Jews persecuted him. 17 Jesus said to them, "My Father is always at
his work to this very day, and I, too, am working." 18 For this
reason the Jews tried all the harder to kill him; not only was he
breaking the Sabbath, but he was even calling God his own Father,
making himself equal with God.
19 Jesus gave them this answer: "I tell you the truth, the Son can
do nothing by himself; he can do only what he sees his Father
doing, because whatever the Father does the Son also does. 20 For
the Father loves the Son and shows him all he does. Yes, to your

John 5:1–15 THE HEALING AT THE POOL

This story happened at a pool that evidently had a reputation for bringing healing to the first person to get in when its waters were stirred.

1. How do you think this man felt after being an invalid for 38 years?
   a. bitter and angry
   b. helpless and dependent
   c. discouraged and depressed
   d. comfortable with his condition

2. Jesus asked the man, "Do you want to get well?" because the man:
   a. hadn't asked Jesus for help.
   b. didn't know who Jesus was.
   c. was likely a beggar and could lose his income if he were healed.
   d. may have lost the will to get well.
   e. may have had a psychosomatic illness.

3. What was the man really saying by his response to Jesus' question?
   a. "Are you crazy—Would I be lying here if I didn't want to get well?!"
   b. "I don't know—I'm so helpless."
   c. "If you help me into the pool when the water stirs, I might get well."
   d. "I've been sick for so long I can't take responsibility for my life."

4. What did Jesus mean later when he said to the man: "See, you are well again. Stop sinning or something worse may happen to you"?
   a. "You were sick because of sin."
   b. "You lost 38 years; don't lose any more."
   c. "The eternal consequences of sin are worse than your illness."
   d. "You've got a fresh start in life—don't blow it."

5. What is the closest Jesus has come to saying to you, "Get up! Pick up your mat and walk"?
   a. when I turned my life over to him
   b. when I experienced his healing
   c. when I had a self-pity problem
   d. when I was overly dependent on others
   e. when I lost my will to get better

6. What connection between your physical and spiritual health have you noticed? When have you found yourself getting physically sick over problems in other areas of your life?

7. If Jesus were to stop by the "watering hole" where you hang out, what would he probably ask you?
   a. Do you want to get well?
   b. What are you doing with your life?
   c. Are you satisfied with what you are doing?
   d. Are you looking for the real thing?

8. Briefly share the story of the pain in your life. How often have you asked, "Where is God when I hurt?" What are your hopes and expectations for this group?

9. What about your health causes you the most stress?
   a. battling a chronic condition
   b. dealing with the financial burden
   c. coping with added time pressures, such as missing work
   d. facing health problems alone
   e. other:________________

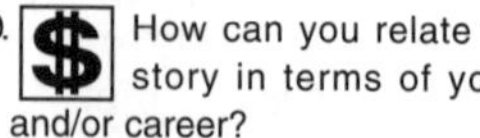

10. How can you relate to this story in terms of your job and/or career?
   a. I feel like I've been stuck where I'm at for 38 years!
   b. Someone else always seems to get in ahead of me.
   c. I feel powerless to change things.
   d. I'm really not sure why I'm doing what I'm doing.

amazement he will show him even greater things than these. 21For
just as the Father raises the dead and gives them life, even so the
Son gives life to whom he is pleased to give it. 22Moreover, the
Father judges no one, but has entrusted all judgment to the Son,
23that all may honor the Son just as they honor the Father. He who
does not honor the Son does not honor the Father, who sent him.
24"I tell you the truth, whoever hears my word and believes him
who sent me has eternal life and will not be condemned; he has
crossed over from death to life. 25I tell you the truth, a time is
coming and has now come when the dead will hear the voice of
the Son of God and those who hear will live. 26For as the Father
has life in himself, so he has granted the Son to have life in himself.
27And he has given him authority to judge because he is the Son of
Man.
28"Do not be amazed at this, for a time is coming when all who
are in their graves will hear his voice 29and come out—those who
have done good will rise to live, and those who have done evil will
rise to be condemned. 30By myself I can do nothing; I judge only as
I hear, and my judgment is just, for I seek not to please myself but
him who sent me.

Testimonies About Jesus

31"If I testify about myself, my testimony is not valid. 32There is
another who testifies in my favor, and I know that his testimony
about me is valid.
33"You have sent to John and he has testified to the truth. 34Not
that I accept human testimony; but I mention it that you may be
saved. 35John was a lamp that burned and gave light, and you chose
for a time to enjoy his light.
36"I have testimony weightier than that of John. For the very
work that the Father has given me to finish, and which I am doing,
testifies that the Father has sent me. 37And the Father who sent me
has himself testified concerning me. You have never heard his
voice nor seen his form, 38nor does his word dwell in you, for you
do not believe the one he sent. 39You diligently study[a] the Scriptures because you think that by them you possess eternal life.
These are the Scriptures that testify about me, 40yet you refuse to
come to me to have life.
41"I do not accept praise from men, 42but I know you. I know
that you do not have the love of God in your hearts. 43I have come
in my Father's name, and you do not accept me; but if someone
else comes in his own name, you will accept him. 44How can you
believe if you accept praise from one another, yet make no effort to
obtain the praise that comes from the only God[b]?
45"But do not think I will accuse you before the Father. Your
accuser is Moses, on whom your hopes are set. 46If you believed
Moses, you would believe me, for he wrote about me. 47But since
you do not believe what he wrote, how are you going to believe
what I say?"

Jesus Feeds the Five Thousand

6 Some time after this, Jesus crossed to the far shore of the Sea
of Galilee (that is, the Sea of Tiberias), 2and a great crowd of
people followed him because they saw the miraculous signs he had
performed on the sick. 3Then Jesus went up on a mountainside and
sat down with his disciples. 4The Jewish Passover Feast was near.
5When Jesus looked up and saw a great crowd coming toward

[a]39 Or *Study diligently* (the imperative) [b]44 Some early manuscripts *the Only One*

ship between the two? **4.** What claims does Jesus make about himself in verse 24? What is the promise? **5.** What happens to those who hear and believe (vv. 24–30)? To those who do not? **6.** How would you describe the business that God the Father and God the Son are in?

1. If you had to explain to someone what verse 24 means in your own words, how would you put it? **2.** In your own spiritual journey, when did you come to understand this truth? How did it affect your self-image? Your lifestyle? Your life goals?

Whom do you still admire today who was a hero to you as a child? Who was a hero who turned out to be a disappointment?

1. Who or what testifies in favor of Jesus (v. 33)? How do you think the religious leaders felt when Jesus referred to these witnesses (already discounted by the authorities)? **2.** How does Jesus refute the religious leaders with their own Scripture?

1. What witnesses have convinced you that Jesus is indeed the one who gives life? **2.** Have you ever seen anyone put the study of the Scriptures before their love for Christ? Have you ever done this? **3.** Is the love of God in your heart? How can you use Scripture to cultivate the love of God in you?

Do you prefer to socialize at large parties, have a dinner for four, or spend a quiet evening with a friend? Why?

1. Why did the crowd follow Jesus (v. 2)? What did they think about him? **2.** What was the test that Jesus was using on Philip (v. 5)? From their responses, what grades would you give Philip and Andrew? **3.** Why was there more food after the feeding than before? **4.** How could the nearness of the Passover feast (when Jews from all over came to Jerusalem) fuel the desires of the people (vv. 14–15)? What does Jesus' response indicate about his idea of his kingship?

1. When has God stretched your limited resources (physically or emotionally) far beyond what you could have imagined? In what way do you need to trust him to do so now? **2.** How are you like Philip and Andrew—failing to remember something about Jesus when you face a difficult situation?

What was one of your greatest childhood fears: Bugs? High places? Darkness? Water?

1. How would you have reacted if you saw Jesus on the water? When he climbed aboard? **2.** What did the disciples fail to see in the feeding of the 5,000 that could have helped them here?

1. Has Jesus ever frightened you? How? **2.** Where in your life do you need Jesus to say "It is I, don't be afraid"?

What type of bread are you today: All natural? Rye? Moldy? Crusty? Fresh? Easy to butter up?

1. Why are the crowds still searching for Jesus (vv. 24–26)? **2.** How does Jesus' response to their question show the difference between his interests and theirs? **3.** How are they to work for the food that leads to eternal life (v. 29)? **4.** What does the crowd ask Jesus to do in order that they can believe him? What is their real interest? **5.** How does Jesus use their interest in food to illustrate what he wants them to understand? What are the similarities and differences between manna (Ex 16) and the "bread of life" (v. 35)? **6.** What claims does Jesus

him, he said to Philip, "Where shall we buy bread for these people
to eat?" 6He asked this only to test him, for he already had in mind
what he was going to do.
7Philip answered him, "Eight months' wages[a] would not buy
enough bread for each one to have a bite!"
8Another of his disciples, Andrew, Simon Peter's brother, spoke
up, 9"Here is a boy with five small barley loaves and two small fish,
but how far will they go among so many?"
10Jesus said, "Have the people sit down." There was plenty of
grass in that place, and the men sat down, about five thousand of
them. 11Jesus then took the loaves, gave thanks, and distributed to
those who were seated as much as they wanted. He did the same
with the fish.
12When they had all had enough to eat, he said to his disciples,
"Gather the pieces that are left over. Let nothing be wasted." 13So
they gathered them and filled twelve baskets with the pieces of the
five barley loaves left over by those who had eaten.
14After the people saw the miraculous sign that Jesus did, they
began to say, "Surely this is the Prophet who is to come into the
world." 15Jesus, knowing that they intended to come and make
him king by force, withdrew again to a mountain by himself.

Jesus Walks on the Water

16When evening came, his disciples went down to the lake,
17where they got into a boat and set off across the lake for Capernaum. By now it was dark, and Jesus had not yet joined them. 18A
strong wind was blowing and the waters grew rough. 19When they
had rowed three or three and a half miles,[b] they saw Jesus approaching the boat, walking on the water; and they were terrified.
20But he said to them, "It is I; don't be afraid." 21Then they were
willing to take him into the boat, and immediately the boat reached
the shore where they were heading.
22The next day the crowd that had stayed on the opposite shore
of the lake realized that only one boat had been there, and that
Jesus had not entered it with his disciples, but that they had gone
away alone. 23Then some boats from Tiberias landed near the place
where the people had eaten the bread after the Lord had given
thanks. 24Once the crowd realized that neither Jesus nor his disciples were there, they got into the boats and went to Capernaum in
search of Jesus.

Jesus the Bread of Life

25When they found him on the other side of the lake, they asked
him, "Rabbi, when did you get here?"
26Jesus answered, "I tell you the truth, you are looking for me,
not because you saw miraculous signs but because you ate the
loaves and had your fill. 27Do not work for food that spoils, but for
food that endures to eternal life, which the Son of Man will give
you. On him God the Father has placed his seal of approval."
28Then they asked him, "What must we do to do the works God
requires?"
29Jesus answered, "The work of God is this: to believe in the one
he has sent."
30So they asked him, "What miraculous sign then will you give
that we may see it and believe you? What will you do? 31Our
forefathers ate the manna in the desert; as it is written: 'He gave
them bread from heaven to eat.'[c]"

[a] *7* Greek *two hundred denarii* [b] *19* Greek *rowed twenty-five or thirty stadia* (about 5 or 6 kilometers) [c] *31* Exodus 16:4; Neh. 9:15; Psalm 78:24,25

32Jesus said to them, "I tell you the truth, it is not Moses who
has given you the bread from heaven, but it is my Father who gives
you the true bread from heaven. 33For the bread of God is he who
comes down from heaven and gives life to the world."
34"Sir," they said, "from now on give us this bread."
35Then Jesus declared, "I am the bread of life. He who comes to
me will never go hungry, and he who believes in me will never be
thirsty. 36But as I told you, you have seen me and still you do not
believe. 37All that the Father gives me will come to me, and whoever comes to me I will never drive away. 38For I have come down
from heaven not to do my will but to do the will of him who sent
me. 39And this is the will of him who sent me, that I shall lose
none of all that he has given me, but raise them up at the last day.
40For my Father's will is that everyone who looks to the Son and
believes in him shall have eternal life, and I will raise him up at the
last day."
41At this the Jews began to grumble about him because he said,
"I am the bread that came down from heaven." 42They said, "Is
this not Jesus, the son of Joseph, whose father and mother we
know? How can he now say, 'I came down from heaven'?"
43"Stop grumbling among yourselves," Jesus answered. 44"No
one can come to me unless the Father who sent me draws him,
and I will raise him up at the last day. 45It is written in the
Prophets: 'They will all be taught by God.'[a] Everyone who listens
to the Father and learns from him comes to me. 46No one has seen
the Father except the one who is from God; only he has seen the
Father. 47I tell you the truth, he who believes has everlasting life.
48I am the bread of life. 49Your forefathers ate the manna in the
desert, yet they died. 50But here is the bread that comes down from
heaven, which a man may eat and not die. 51I am the living bread
that came down from heaven. If anyone eats of this bread, he will
live forever. This bread is my flesh, which I will give for the life of
the world."
52Then the Jews began to argue sharply among themselves,
"How can this man give us his flesh to eat?"
53Jesus said to them, "I tell you the truth, unless you eat the
flesh of the Son of Man and drink his blood, you have no life in
you. 54Whoever eats my flesh and drinks my blood has eternal life,
and I will raise him up at the last day. 55For my flesh is real food
and my blood is real drink. 56Whoever eats my flesh and drinks my
blood remains in me, and I in him. 57Just as the living Father sent
me and I live because of the Father, so the one who feeds on me
will live because of me. 58This is the bread that came down from
heaven. Your forefathers ate manna and died, but he who feeds on
this bread will live forever." 59He said this while teaching in the
synagogue in Capernaum.

Many Disciples Desert Jesus

60On hearing it, many of his disciples said, "This is a hard teaching. Who can accept it?"
61Aware that his disciples were grumbling about this, Jesus said
to them, "Does this offend you? 62What if you see the Son of Man
ascend to where he was before! 63The Spirit gives life; the flesh
counts for nothing. The words I have spoken to you are spirit[b]
and they are life. 64Yet there are some of you who do not believe."
For Jesus had known from the beginning which of them did not
believe and who would betray him. 65He went on to say, "This is

[a]*45* Isaiah 54:13 [b]*63* Or *Spirit*

make in verses 35–40? What do these claims emphasize about his being the bread of life? About the will of the Father? **7.** In verses 41–42, how do the crowds respond to his claims? How is the principle of the hometown prophet (see 4:44) played out here? **8.** What part is played by God and by the people in the process of coming to know Jesus (vv. 44–45)? What promise is repeated three times for those who do come to him? Why the emphasis on this? **9.** How is the "bread" he gives greater than that of Moses (vv. 32,49)? **10.** Why does Jesus develop the food analogy even more graphically (vv. 53–58)? **11.** What does Jesus mean by "eating his flesh" and "drinking his blood" (vv. 51–58)?

1. What is the main reason you follow Jesus? **2.** How would you describe your daily spiritual diet: Junk food? Frozen food? Baby food? TV microwave food? Leftovers? Meat and potatoes? Pure bread and wine? **3.** Has your familiarity with Jesus (from Sunday School stories, parochial school, etc.) ever kept you from seeing who he really is? What can remove the blinders? **4.** If someone asked, "How do you hunger and thirst after God," what counsel could you offer?

How did you feel when you were first rejected by a friend or sweetheart?

1. What teaching do Jesus' followers find so unacceptable (6:54–56)? **2.** Why do you think Peter and the others decided to stay? How does this relate to verse 65?

1. What words of Jesus are hard for you to accept? **2.** Have you known anyone who stopped following Jesus? How did their action affect you? **3.** How do people today make Jesus into an errand boy for their own personal agendas? How have you been tempted to do so?

why I told you that no one can come to me unless the Father has
enabled him."
66From this time many of his disciples turned back and no longer
followed him.
67"You do not want to leave too, do you?" Jesus asked the
Twelve.
68Simon Peter answered him, "Lord, to whom shall we go? You
have the words of eternal life. 69We believe and know that you are
the Holy One of God."
70Then Jesus replied, "Have I not chosen you, the Twelve? Yet
one of you is a devil!" 71(He meant Judas, the son of Simon Iscariot,
who, though one of the Twelve, was later to betray him.)

Were you ever dared by your brothers or sisters to do something dangerous? What happened?

1. Why did the religious leaders want to kill Jesus (see 5:18)? **2.** In urging Jesus to attend this feast, are the brothers being wise or worldly (vv. 2–5; see 6:42,66)? **3.** What rumors are circulating about Jesus in Jerusalem (vv. 12–13)? Hence, why do you think he chose to go secretly?

1. Do you face any family opposition to, or ridicule of your faith? How do you deal with it? How does Jesus' situation help? **2.** Are you loved or hated by the world (v. 7)? Why? **3.** Are you more likely to be cautious in sharing your faith with your family? Why?

Jesus Goes to the Feast of Tabernacles

7 After this, Jesus went around in Galilee, purposely staying
away from Judea because the Jews there were waiting to take
his life. 2But when the Jewish Feast of Tabernacles was near,
3Jesus' brothers said to him, "You ought to leave here and go to
Judea, so that your disciples may see the miracles you do. 4No one
who wants to become a public figure acts in secret. Since you are
doing these things, show yourself to the world." 5For even his own
brothers did not believe in him.
6Therefore Jesus told them, "The right time for me has not yet
come; for you any time is right. 7The world cannot hate you, but it
hates me because I testify that what it does is evil. 8You go to the
Feast. I am not yet[a] going up to this Feast, because for me the
right time has not yet come." 9Having said this, he stayed in Galilee.
10However, after his brothers had left for the Feast, he went also,
not publicly, but in secret. 11Now at the Feast the Jews were
watching for him and asking, "Where is that man?"
12Among the crowds there was widespread whispering about
him. Some said, "He is a good man."
Others replied, "No, he deceives the people." 13But no one
would say anything publicly about him for fear of the Jews.

From your school days, what rule seemed pointless or silly? Did you break it?

1. Given the risk, why did Jesus go to the Passover (v. 16)? How did the people react to Jesus' teaching? Why? **2.** What do Jesus' responses reveal about his authority? **3.** How would you respond if you were in the crowd? **4.** What point are the leaders missing?

1. How does Jesus reveal himself to you today? Are you ever upset by what he says? Why? **2.** When have you seen religious principles put ahead of love?

Jesus Teaches at the Feast

14Not until halfway through the Feast did Jesus go up to the
temple courts and begin to teach. 15The Jews were amazed and
asked, "How did this man get such learning without having stud-
ied?"
16Jesus answered, "My teaching is not my own. It comes from
him who sent me. 17If anyone chooses to do God's will, he will find
out whether my teaching comes from God or whether I speak on
my own. 18He who speaks on his own does so to gain honor for
himself, but he who works for the honor of the one who sent him
is a man of truth; there is nothing false about him. 19Has not Moses
given you the law? Yet not one of you keeps the law. Why are you
trying to kill me?"
20"You are demon-possessed," the crowd answered. "Who is
trying to kill you?"
21Jesus said to them, "I did one miracle, and you are all astonished. 22Yet, because Moses gave you circumcision (though actually
it did not come from Moses, but from the patriarchs), you circumcise a child on the Sabbath. 23Now if a child can be circumcised on
the Sabbath so that the law of Moses may not be broken, why are

[a]8 Some early manuscripts do not have *yet*.

you angry with me for healing the whole man on the Sabbath?
[24]Stop judging by mere appearances, and make a right judgment."

Is Jesus the Christ?

[25]At that point some of the people of Jerusalem began to ask,
"Isn't this the man they are trying to kill? [26]Here he is, speaking
publicly, and they are not saying a word to him. Have the authorities really concluded that he is the Christ[a]? [27]But we know where
this man is from; when the Christ comes, no one will know where
he is from."
[28]Then Jesus, still teaching in the temple courts, cried out, "Yes,
you know me, and you know where I am from. I am not here on
my own, but he who sent me is true. You do not know him, [29]but
I know him because I am from him and he sent me."
[30]At this they tried to seize him, but no one laid a hand on him,
because his time had not yet come. [31]Still, many in the crowd put
their faith in him. They said, "When the Christ comes, will he do
more miraculous signs than this man?"
[32]The Pharisees heard the crowd whispering such things about
him. Then the chief priests and the Pharisees sent temple guards to
arrest him.
[33]Jesus said, "I am with you for only a short time, and then I go
to the one who sent me. [34]You will look for me, but you will not
find me; and where I am, you cannot come."
[35]The Jews said to one another, "Where does this man intend to
go that we cannot find him? Will he go where our people live
scattered among the Greeks, and teach the Greeks? [36]What did he
mean when he said, 'You will look for me, but you will not find
me,' and 'Where I am, you cannot come'?"
[37]On the last and greatest day of the Feast, Jesus stood and said
in a loud voice, "If anyone is thirsty, let him come to me and drink.
[38]Whoever believes in me, as[b] the Scripture has said, streams of
living water will flow from within him." [39]By this he meant the
Spirit, whom those who believed in him were later to receive. Up
to that time the Spirit had not been given, since Jesus had not yet
been glorified.
[40]On hearing his words, some of the people said, "Surely this
man is the Prophet."
[41]Others said, "He is the Christ."
Still others asked, "How can the Christ come from Galilee?
[42]Does not the Scripture say that the Christ will come from David's
family[c] and from Bethlehem, the town where David lived?"
[43]Thus the people were divided because of Jesus. [44]Some wanted to
seize him, but no one laid a hand on him.

Unbelief of the Jewish Leaders

[45]Finally the temple guards went back to the chief priests and
Pharisees, who asked them, "Why didn't you bring him in?"
[46]"No one ever spoke the way this man does," the guards declared.
[47]"You mean he has deceived you also?" the Pharisees retorted.
[48]"Has any of the rulers or of the Pharisees believed in him? [49]No!
But this mob that knows nothing of the law—there is a curse on
them."
[50]Nicodemus, who had gone to Jesus earlier and who was one of

[a]*26* Or *Messiah*; also in verses 27, 31, 41 and 42 [b]*37,38* Or / *If anyone is thirsty, let him come to me. / And let him drink, [38]who believes in me. / As* [c]*42* Greek *seed*

When you played "hide and seek" as a kid (or with your kids), did you prefer hiding or seeking? Where was one of your best hiding spots? Did you stay hidden long, or did you jump out to scare the one seeking you?

1. Who is saying what about Jesus in this passage? What is causing the confusion? **2.** Why does Jesus' teaching in verses 14–29 provoke the responses of verses 30–31? How do you account for the wide range of opinions about him? For the timing involved? **3.** Every day at this feast, water would be poured out as a symbol of thanks for God's provision. In this context, what does Jesus' statement in verses 37–38 mean? What are some ways that the Spirit's work is like water (compare 4:13–14)? How is the Spirit received? **4.** How does the confusion over Jesus' birthplace (vv. 41–42) cloud the issue of his identity?

1. What evidence can you offer of the presence of the Holy Spirit in your life? How is his presence like flowing water? **2.** What is the relationship for you between believing the promises of Christ and experiencing the power of the Holy Spirit? **3.** What different opinions about Christ do you hear today? Why does that confusion exist?

When has someone jumped to a wrong conclusion about you? How did you feel?

1. Why do the guards keep hands off? What tensions do they feel? **2.** What justification do the Pharisees offer in refuting the guards? Nicodemus (vv. 48,50)? Why would Nicodemus risk defending Jesus?

When have you been ridiculed because of your faith? What did you do?

their own number, asked, 51"Does our law condemn anyone without first hearing him to find out what he is doing?"
52They replied, "Are you from Galilee, too? Look into it, and you
will find that a prophet[a] does not come out of Galilee."

[The earliest manuscripts and many
other ancient witnesses do not
have John 7:53–8:11.]

53Then each went to his own home.
8 But Jesus went to the Mount of Olives. 2At dawn he appeared
again in the temple courts, where all the people gathered
around him, and he sat down to teach them. 3The teachers of the
law and the Pharisees brought in a woman caught in adultery. They
made her stand before the group 4and said to Jesus, "Teacher, this
woman was caught in the act of adultery. 5In the Law Moses
commanded us to stone such women. Now what do you say?"
6They were using this question as a trap, in order to have a basis
for accusing him.
But Jesus bent down and started to write on the ground with his
finger. 7When they kept on questioning him, he straightened up
and said to them, "If any one of you is without sin, let him be the
first to throw a stone at her." 8Again he stooped down and wrote
on the ground.
9At this, those who heard began to go away one at a time, the

[a]52 Two early manuscripts *the Prophet*

Describe a time in your childhood when someone tattled on you.

1. How is this situation a trap for Jesus? What would the Pharisees accuse Jesus of if he told them to let her go? If he told them to stone her? How does he spring the trap (v. 7)? **2.** How would the woman just caught in adultery have felt? What was the significance of Jesus' question in verse 10? **3.** How does Jesus' response to the woman exemplify "grace and truth" (1:17)?

1. How does the way Jesus treated this woman help you face your sins? **2.** Jesus accepts you "as is." Does that free you to

John 7:53–8:11 THE WOMAN CAUGHT IN ADULTERY

1. Whom do you feel most sorry for?
   a. the woman—for being publicly humiliated
   b. Jesus—for being put on the spot
   c. the religious leaders—for stooping this low
2. Since adultery was a violation by both parties, why didn't the accusers also bring the man caught in the act?
   a. He got away.
   b. Men and women were treated differently.
   c. He was part of a plot that was staged to trap Jesus.
3. In Jesus' situation, what would you feel most pressured to do?
   a. go along with the crowd
   b. do what Moses' Law required
   c. compromise my moral convictions
   d. be compassionate and forgiving
4. Why do you think Jesus bent down and wrote on the ground?
   a. to cool off
   b. to divert attention from the woman
   c. to give himself time to think
   d. to force the accusers to think
   e. to write something for the accusers to see—maybe *their* sins
5. Why did the accusers slip away?
   a. They had all committed adultery.
   b. None of them could claim they were without sin.
   c. Jesus made them think by asking for one person to step forward.
   d. Jesus had their number.
6. What was the tone of Jesus' voice and what did he mean when he said, "Neither do I condemn you. Go now and leave your life of sin"?
   a. guilt trip: "You've been bad and I'm ashamed of you."
   b. acquittal: "You did nothing wrong."
   c. warning: "I'll let you off this time, but don't do it again."
   d. encouragement: "You're a beautiful person and you don't have to live like you used to."
   e. challenge: "The evidence of forgiveness is a changed life."
7. When did you come to truly believe that Jesus values you as a person?
   a. when I committed my life to him
   b. when I fully understood what he did for me
   c. when I felt his healing or forgiveness during a difficult time
   d. when I discovered acceptance in my church
   e. when a few close friends really got to know me and still accepted me
   f. I'm not sure how to answer that.
8. What do you do when you blow it?
   a. crawl into a hole
   b. try to be extra good
   c. confess it to God and move on
   d. confess it to another person
   e. shrug it off
9. How could the way Jesus related to this woman help you face the sins you struggle with?
10. Who has affirmed you and helped you recognize your full potential as a woman?
11. How do you struggle the most to measure up in a glitzy world? What woman do you see as a role model for real beauty?

older ones first, until only Jesus was left, with the woman still standing there. 10Jesus straightened up and asked her, "Woman, where are they? Has no one condemned you?"

11"No one, sir," she said.

"Then neither do I condemn you," Jesus declared. "Go now and leave your life of sin."

change, or does it support your bad behavior? How so? **3.** What can you learn from Jesus about helping a friend who has fallen?

The Validity of Jesus' Testimony

12When Jesus spoke again to the people, he said, "I am the light of the world. Whoever follows me will never walk in darkness, but will have the light of life."

13The Pharisees challenged him, "Here you are, appearing as your own witness; your testimony is not valid."

14Jesus answered, "Even if I testify on my own behalf, my testimony is valid, for I know where I came from and where I am going. But you have no idea where I come from or where I am going. 15You judge by human standards; I pass judgment on no one. 16But if I do judge, my decisions are right, because I am not alone. I stand with the Father, who sent me. 17In your own Law it is written that the testimony of two men is valid. 18I am one who testifies for myself; my other witness is the Father, who sent me."

19Then they asked him, "Where is your father?"

"You do not know me or my Father," Jesus replied. "If you knew me, you would know my Father also." 20He spoke these words while teaching in the temple area near the place where the offerings were put. Yet no one seized him, because his time had not yet come.

21Once more Jesus said to them, "I am going away, and you will look for me, and you will die in your sin. Where I go, you cannot come."

22This made the Jews ask, "Will he kill himself? Is that why he says, 'Where I go, you cannot come'?"

23But he continued, "You are from below; I am from above. You are of this world; I am not of this world. 24I told you that you would die in your sins; if you do not believe that I am ⌊the one I claim to be⌋,[a] you will indeed die in your sins."

25"Who are you?" they asked.

"Just what I have been claiming all along," Jesus replied. 26"I have much to say in judgment of you. But he who sent me is reliable, and what I have heard from him I tell the world."

27They did not understand that he was telling them about his Father. 28So Jesus said, "When you have lifted up the Son of Man, then you will know that I am ⌊the one I claim to be⌋ and that I do nothing on my own but speak just what the Father has taught me. 29The one who sent me is with me; he has not left me alone, for I always do what pleases him." 30Even as he spoke, many put their faith in him.

What is your most vivid memory as a child in a dark place (cave, tunnel, power blackout)? What feelings do you associate with darkness?

1. What is Jesus really claiming in verse 12? What is the promise? What does Jesus mean by "light" and "darkness"? **2.** With what does Jesus bolster his claim (see 5:31–40)? What does it matter that Jesus knows where he comes from (vv. 14,21–23; see 7:41–42)? **3.** What does the Pharisees' question in verse 19 reveal about their relationship with the Father? **4.** What is at stake in this whole discussion (v. 24)? Why does everything hinge on who Jesus really is (v. 25) and who sent him (vv. 16,18,26,29)? **5.** What does Jesus mean by each phrase in verse 28? How will this show people he is the Christ? **6.** What is the significance of verse 30 in light of the total misunderstanding of the Pharisees? How do the Pharisees exemplify darkness in this scene?

1. How is following Jesus like following someone with a light through a dark place for you? **2.** How do people you know misunderstand Jesus? How do their lives exemplify darkness? How can you be a light-bearer to them?

The Children of Abraham

31To the Jews who had believed him, Jesus said, "If you hold to my teaching, you are really my disciples. 32Then you will know the truth, and the truth will set you free."

33They answered him, "We are Abraham's descendants[b] and have never been slaves of anyone. How can you say that we shall be set free?"

1. Where did your ancestors come from? How did they get to this country? **2.** Who is one of the more colorful characters in your family tree? **3.** Who, in your family tree, do you look to as a spiritual patriarch or matriarch?

[a] *24* Or *I am he*; also in verse 28 [b] *33* Greek *seed*; also in verse 37

1. What does Jesus want to emphasize to the people who believed him? What does he mean by *disciples*? *Truth*? *Freedom*? **2.** What false assumptions confuse the issue of spiritual freedom for Abraham's descendants? How does Jesus undermine their base of confidence? What issues does he force them to confront (vv. 34–41)? **3.** How does Jesus undermine their claim in verse 41? What does he say is the ultimate test to show who "belongs to God" (vv. 42–47)? How does he account for their misunderstanding of him (vv. 37,43,45,47)? **4.** Why does Jesus continue to address his relationship with the Father? **5.** What is the critical question raised by his claim in verse 51 (also v. 24)? How is this issue central to the whole argument in 7:4–8:58? How does Jesus use their loyalty to Abraham against them? Why does Jesus' final claim cause such an outrage (see Ex 3:14)?

1. What are you proud of in your religious heritage? In what ways has it been a handicap? **2.** What has knowing the truth set you free to do? How can you be sure that there is room in your life for his Word? What needs to be cleaned out so there is room? **3.** Of the four claims Jesus makes in this chapter (vv. 12,32,51,58), which means the most to you? Why? **4.** What does Jesus' association between the devil and telling lies mean to you? From this passage, what can you do for someone who is honestly seeking God? What in your spiritual journey might help?

34Jesus replied, "I tell you the truth, everyone who sins is a slave to sin. 35Now a slave has no permanent place in the family, but a son belongs to it forever. 36So if the Son sets you free, you will be free indeed. 37I know you are Abraham's descendants. Yet you are ready to kill me, because you have no room for my word. 38I am telling you what I have seen in the Father's presence, and you do what you have heard from your father.[a]"

39"Abraham is our father," they answered.

"If you were Abraham's children," said Jesus, "then you would[b] do the things Abraham did. 40As it is, you are determined to kill me, a man who has told you the truth that I heard from God. Abraham did not do such things. 41You are doing the things your own father does."

"We are not illegitimate children," they protested. "The only Father we have is God himself."

The Children of the Devil

42Jesus said to them, "If God were your Father, you would love me, for I came from God and now am here. I have not come on my own; but he sent me. 43Why is my language not clear to you? Because you are unable to hear what I say. 44You belong to your father, the devil, and you want to carry out your father's desire. He was a murderer from the beginning, not holding to the truth, for there is no truth in him. When he lies, he speaks his native language, for he is a liar and the father of lies. 45Yet because I tell the truth, you do not believe me! 46Can any of you prove me guilty of sin? If I am telling the truth, why don't you believe me? 47He who belongs to God hears what God says. The reason you do not hear is that you do not belong to God."

The Claims of Jesus About Himself

48The Jews answered him, "Aren't we right in saying that you are a Samaritan and demon-possessed?"

49"I am not possessed by a demon," said Jesus, "but I honor my Father and you dishonor me. 50I am not seeking glory for myself; but there is one who seeks it, and he is the judge. 51I tell you the truth, if anyone keeps my word, he will never see death."

52At this the Jews exclaimed, "Now we know that you are demon-possessed! Abraham died and so did the prophets, yet you say that if anyone keeps your word, he will never taste death. 53Are you greater than our father Abraham? He died, and so did the prophets. Who do you think you are?"

54Jesus replied, "If I glorify myself, my glory means nothing. My Father, whom you claim as your God, is the one who glorifies me. 55Though you do not know him, I know him. If I said I did not, I would be a liar like you, but I do know him and keep his word. 56Your father Abraham rejoiced at the thought of seeing my day; he saw it and was glad."

57"You are not yet fifty years old," the Jews said to him, "and you have seen Abraham!"

58"I tell you the truth," Jesus answered, "before Abraham was born, I am!" 59At this, they picked up stones to stone him, but Jesus hid himself, slipping away from the temple grounds.

[a] *38* Or *presence. Therefore do what you have heard from the Father.* [b] *39* Some early manuscripts *"If you are Abraham's children," said Jesus, "then*

Jesus Heals a Man Born Blind

9 As he went along, he saw a man blind from birth. 2His disciples asked him, "Rabbi, who sinned, this man or his parents,
that he was born blind?"
3"Neither this man nor his parents sinned," said Jesus, "but this
happened so that the work of God might be displayed in his life.
4As long as it is day, we must do the work of him who sent me.
Night is coming, when no one can work. 5While I am in the world,
I am the light of the world."
6Having said this, he spit on the ground, made some mud with
the saliva, and put it on the man's eyes. 7"Go," he told him, "wash
in the Pool of Siloam" (this word means Sent). So the man went
and washed, and came home seeing.
8His neighbors and those who had formerly seen him begging
asked, "Isn't this the same man who used to sit and beg?" 9Some
claimed that he was.
Others said, "No, he only looks like him."
But he himself insisted, "I am the man."
10"How then were your eyes opened?" they demanded.
11He replied, "The man they call Jesus made some mud and put
it on my eyes. He told me to go to Siloam and wash. So I went and
washed, and then I could see."
12"Where is this man?" they asked him.
"I don't know," he said.

Describe an adventure you had with mud when you were a child.

1. What idea lies behind the disciples' question (v. 1): Curiosity? Guilt-tripping? A trap? Compassion? **2.** What does Jesus' answer (vv. 3–5) reveal about how he views the man's suffering? **3.** In this story, what is the "work of God" (v. 3)? The "night" that is coming (v. 4)? The "light of the world" (v. 5)? How are sin and suffering related?

1. What physical or emotional misfortune in your life has turned into an opportunity for God to demonstrate his power? **2.** When you hear about another person's misfortune, do you react like the disciples or Jesus? Why?

John 9:1–34 JESUS HEALS A MAN BORN BLIND

1. What was behind the disciples' question, "Who sinned, this man or his parents, that he was born blind?"
   a. judgmentalism c. curiosity
   b. compassion d. a trap

2. What did Jesus' reply show about how he viewed the man's affliction?
   a. He and his parents were sinless.
   b. He was an exception to the rule.
   c. The standard theology of the day was full of baloney.
   d. The man was born blind so that Jesus could miraculously heal him.
   e. Suffering like this just happens.
   f. The purpose of the blindness was more important than its cure.

3. Why did Jesus spit and make mud in healing the man?
   a. to add variety to his practices of healing people
   b. to provoke the Pharisees by breaking their Sabbath rules, since treating illness and making mud were considered "work"
   c. to gain the man's confidence since saliva was believed to have healing properties
   d. to give the man a part in the healing process

4. Why did some of the Pharisees take a stand against Jesus?
   a. because he violated their Sabbath restrictions
   b. because he violated their concept of the Messiah
   c. because it never occurred to them their regulations might be wrong
   d. because they started from their own bias instead of the miracle
   e. because *they* were "blind"

5. How does this story illustrate Jesus' statement in verse 5: "I am the light of the world"?

6. The man progressed in his understanding of Jesus: from a man (v. 11), to a prophet (v. 17), to one worthy of following (v. 27), to one "from God" (v. 33), to one who should be worshiped (v. 38). How has your view of Jesus and your commitment to him progressed over time?

7. How would you measure your spiritual vision now (and how could it be corrected)?
   a. 20/20 d. near-sighted
   b. 20/200 e. far-sighted
   c. legally blind f. a few blind spots

8. What hard questions do you have about life, particularly regarding suffering? In spite of them are you able to affirm the basic spiritual reality—"One thing I do know. I was blind but now I see"?

9. How can you relate to the blame this man lived with from a society that said he was blind because of sin? From whom have you felt blame for your pain?
   a. my family e. myself
   b. my friends f. God
   c. the church g. other:________
   d. the medical community

10. How are you, as opposed to the blind man's fearful parents, helping your children progress in their understanding of Jesus? How much of your spiritual journey have you shared with them? How can you formally (e.g. family devotions) and informally (throughout your daily routine) communicate lasting values to your children?

11. What can you affirm about this group? How will your family time have more lasting value?

Describe a time when an authority figure (your boss, a policeman, your pastor) pulled you over for a talk.

1. What convinces some of the Pharisees to stand against Jesus (v. 16; see also 5:9–10,23)? What question bothers others? Why does Jesus keep healing on the Sabbath when it upsets the Pharisees so much? **2.** In light of their divided opinion, why do the Pharisees question the man's parents (vv. 18–23)? How would you feel if you were his father or mother? **3.** Note the conflicting claims to knowledge and certainty on the part of the Pharisees, the parents and the man born blind. What is each party sure of? Not sure of? **4.** In the course of this investigation, what is the man able to see about Jesus (vv. 12, 17,25,27,30–33,36, 38)? About the Pharisees? How is his attitude changing? **5.** In contrast to the man's growing spiritual insight, how are the Pharisees progressing? **6.** What is the Pharisees' real motive in questioning the man (vv. 28,34)? What in the man's response finally puts them "over the top"?

1. Who has been the toughest person for you to explain your faith to? Why? What have you found to be helpful in dealing with people who ridicule your faith? **2.** Has your faith in Jesus led to your exclusion from any group? How has this hurt or helped you? **3.** Have you ever been afraid of religious leaders? Why?

The Pharisees Investigate the Healing

13They brought to the Pharisees the man who had been blind.
14Now the day on which Jesus had made the mud and opened the
man's eyes was a Sabbath. 15Therefore the Pharisees also asked
him how he had received his sight. "He put mud on my eyes," the
man replied, "and I washed, and now I see."

16Some of the Pharisees said, "This man is not from God, for he
does not keep the Sabbath."

But others asked, "How can a sinner do such miraculous signs?"
So they were divided.

17Finally they turned again to the blind man, "What have you to
say about him? It was your eyes he opened."

The man replied, "He is a prophet."

18The Jews still did not believe that he had been blind and had
received his sight until they sent for the man's parents. 19"Is this
your son?" they asked. "Is this the one you say was born blind?
How is it that now he can see?"

20"We know he is our son," the parents answered, "and we
know he was born blind. 21But how he can see now, or who
opened his eyes, we don't know. Ask him. He is of age; he will
speak for himself." 22His parents said this because they were afraid
of the Jews, for already the Jews had decided that anyone who
acknowledged that Jesus was the Christ[a] would be put out of the
synagogue. 23That was why his parents said, "He is of age; ask
him."

24A second time they summoned the man who had been blind.
"Give glory to God,[b]" they said. "We know this man is a sinner."

25He replied, "Whether he is a sinner or not, I don't know. One
thing I do know. I was blind but now I see!"

26Then they asked him, "What did he do to you? How did he
open your eyes?"

27He answered, "I have told you already and you did not listen.
Why do you want to hear it again? Do you want to become his
disciples, too?"

28Then they hurled insults at him and said, "You are this fellow's
disciple! We are disciples of Moses! 29We know that God spoke to
Moses, but as for this fellow, we don't even know where he comes
from."

30The man answered, "Now that is remarkable! You don't know
where he comes from, yet he opened my eyes. 31We know that
God does not listen to sinners. He listens to the godly man who
does his will. 32Nobody has ever heard of opening the eyes of a
man born blind. 33If this man were not from God, he could do
nothing."

34To this they replied, "You were steeped in sin at birth; how
dare you lecture us!" And they threw him out.

What 24-hour period in your life had the most ups and downs?

1. Why does Jesus wait until now to fully present himself? How is the man, only now, able to affirm Jesus as Lord? **2.** What blindness is the result of sin (vv. 39–41)? How do such guilty people see again?

Spiritual Blindness

35Jesus heard that they had thrown him out, and when he found
him, he said, "Do you believe in the Son of Man?"

36"Who is he, sir?" the man asked. "Tell me so that I may
believe in him."

37Jesus said, "You have now seen him; in fact, he is the one
speaking with you."

38Then the man said, "Lord, I believe," and he worshiped him.

39Jesus said, "For judgment I have come into this world, so that
the blind will see and those who see will become blind."

[a]22 Or *Messiah* [b]24 A solemn charge to tell the truth (see Joshua 7:19)

40 Some Pharisees who were with him heard him say this and asked, “What? Are we blind too?”

41 Jesus said, “If you were blind, you would not be guilty of sin; but now that you claim you can see, your guilt remains.

The Shepherd and His Flock

10 “I tell you the truth, the man who does not enter the sheep pen by the gate, but climbs in by some other way, is a thief and a robber. 2 The man who enters by the gate is the shepherd of his sheep. 3 The watchman opens the gate for him, and the sheep listen to his voice. He calls his own sheep by name and leads them out. 4 When he has brought out all his own, he goes on ahead of them, and his sheep follow him because they know his voice. 5 But they will never follow a stranger; in fact, they will run away from him because they do not recognize a stranger’s voice.” 6 Jesus used this figure of speech, but they did not understand what he was telling them.

7 Therefore Jesus said again, “I tell you the truth, I am the gate for the sheep. 8 All who ever came before me were thieves and robbers, but the sheep did not listen to them. 9 I am the gate; whoever enters through me will be saved.[a] He will come in and go out, and find pasture. 10 The thief comes only to steal and kill and destroy; I have come that they may have life, and have it to the full.

11 “I am the good shepherd. The good shepherd lays down his life for the sheep. 12 The hired hand is not the shepherd who owns the sheep. So when he sees the wolf coming, he abandons the sheep and runs away. Then the wolf attacks the flock and scatters it. 13 The man runs away because he is a hired hand and cares nothing for the sheep.

14 “I am the good shepherd; I know my sheep and my sheep know me— 15 just as the Father knows me and I know the Father—and I lay down my life for the sheep. 16 I have other sheep that are not of this sheep pen. I must bring them also. They too will listen to my voice, and there shall be one flock and one shepherd. 17 The reason my Father loves me is that I lay down my life—only to take it up again. 18 No one takes it from me, but I lay it down of my own accord. I have authority to lay it down and authority to take it up again. This command I received from my Father.”

19 At these words the Jews were again divided. 20 Many of them said, “He is demon-possessed and raving mad. Why listen to him?”

21 But others said, “These are not the sayings of a man possessed by a demon. Can a demon open the eyes of the blind?”

The Unbelief of the Jews

22 Then came the Feast of Dedication[b] at Jerusalem. It was winter, 23 and Jesus was in the temple area walking in Solomon’s Colonnade. 24 The Jews gathered around him, saying, “How long will you keep us in suspense? If you are the Christ,[c] tell us plainly.”

25 Jesus answered, “I did tell you, but you do not believe. The miracles I do in my Father’s name speak for me, 26 but you do not believe because you are not my sheep. 27 My sheep listen to my voice; I know them, and they follow me. 28 I give them eternal life, and they shall never perish; no one can snatch them out of my hand. 29 My Father, who has given them to me, is greater than all[d]; no one can snatch them out of my Father’s hand. 30 I and the Father are one.”

[a] 9 Or *kept safe* [b] 22 That is, Hanukkah [c] 24 Or *Messiah* [d] 29 Many early manuscripts *What my Father has given me is greater than all*

Describe your own spiritual sight: 20–20? Near-sighted? Far-sighted? A few “blind spots”? Why? What could correct this?

As a child, what was your favorite pet? How did this pet respond when it heard your voice?

1. What do the sheep, shepherd, the sheep pen and stranger represent? How does the story in chapter 9 provide one example of what this parable is about? **2.** How do the sheep respond to the shepherd? How does this relate to the Pharisees’ difficulty in understanding Jesus? **3.** What does Jesus mean by likening himself to a gate for the sheepfold? Who are these “thieves and robbers”? How is Jesus unlike them? **4.** How does Jesus identify himself with the “good shepherd” (vv. 11–15)? How does Jesus’ death relate to his promise in verse 10? **5.** Who are the “other sheep” he must bring also? What characterizes his flock? **6.** What final claim does Jesus make (vv. 17–18)? Why do his listeners respond as they do? How would you have responded?

1. What was the turning point for you in terms of hearing “God’s voice” and responding? **2.** How do you discern his voice from all the voices that vie for your attention? **3.** How does it make you feel to think of God caring for you as the Good Shepherd?

---

1. What is the big annual “feast day” for your family? Who usually comes? What is served? What is the big pastime? **2.** What family traditions are you going to preserve for your children?

1. Given the meaning of the Feast of Hanukkah (when Jews remember their deliverance during the Maccabean revolt, 168–165 B.C.), what feelings about Rome’s authority might surface among the crowds? How would Roman authorities prepare for this feast? What might be the real intent of the Pharisees’ question in verse 24? **2.** How do the leaders interpret Jesus' claim to be one with God? How does Jesus sidetrack them (v. 34; Ps 82:6)? **3.** What could account for the difference in reception Jesus received across the Jordan (vv. 40–42)?

1. What has convinced you that Jesus is the Messiah? What "old ways" of looking at Jesus must you overcome by faith? **2.** What difference does it make that Jesus is God and not just a man? Would the promise of verse 28 mean much otherwise?

31Again the Jews picked up stones to stone him, 32but Jesus said
to them, "I have shown you many great miracles from the Father.
For which of these do you stone me?"
33"We are not stoning you for any of these," replied the Jews,
"but for blasphemy, because you, a mere man, claim to be God."
34Jesus answered them, "Is it not written in your Law, 'I have
said you are gods'[a]? 35If he called them 'gods,' to whom the word
of God came—and the Scripture cannot be broken— 36what about
the one whom the Father set apart as his very own and sent into
the world? Why then do you accuse me of blasphemy because I
said, 'I am God's Son'? 37Do not believe me unless I do what my
Father does. 38But if I do it, even though you do not believe me,
believe the miracles, that you may know and understand that the
Father is in me, and I in the Father." 39Again they tried to seize
him, but he escaped their grasp.
40Then Jesus went back across the Jordan to the place where
John had been baptizing in the early days. Here he stayed 41and
many people came to him. They said, "Though John never performed a miraculous sign, all that John said about this man was
true." 42And in that place many believed in Jesus.

Describe the sickest you have ever been.

1. How would you describe Jesus' relationship with this family (vv. 1–5)? Why does Jesus deliberately delay (v. 6)? **2.** Given his disciples' objection (v. 8), what do you think Jesus means by his parable (vv. 9–10)? **3.** Why is Jesus returning to Lazarus at this time (vv. 11–15)? What do the disciples fear instead (vv. 8,16)?

1. Have you ever felt like God was not listening when you prayed? How did you deal with this? How does the way in which Jesus postponed his response to the sisters' request help you in understanding your own prayer life? **2.** Have you, like Thomas (v. 16), ever felt Jesus was calling you to do something very risky? What happened?

The Death of Lazarus

11 Now a man named Lazarus was sick. He was from Bethany,
the village of Mary and her sister Martha. 2This Mary,
whose brother Lazarus now lay sick, was the same one who poured
perfume on the Lord and wiped his feet with her hair. 3So the
sisters sent word to Jesus, "Lord, the one you love is sick."
4When he heard this, Jesus said, "This sickness will not end in
death. No, it is for God's glory so that God's Son may be glorified
through it." 5Jesus loved Martha and her sister and Lazarus. 6Yet
when he heard that Lazarus was sick, he stayed where he was two
more days.
7Then he said to his disciples, "Let us go back to Judea."
8"But Rabbi," they said, "a short while ago the Jews tried to
stone you, and yet you are going back there?"
9Jesus answered, "Are there not twelve hours of daylight? A man
who walks by day will not stumble, for he sees by this world's
light. 10It is when he walks by night that he stumbles, for he has no
light."
11After he had said this, he went on to tell them, "Our friend
Lazarus has fallen asleep; but I am going there to wake him up."
12His disciples replied, "Lord, if he sleeps, he will get better."
13Jesus had been speaking of his death, but his disciples thought he
meant natural sleep.
14So then he told them plainly, "Lazarus is dead, 15and for your
sake I am glad I was not there, so that you may believe. But let us
go to him."
16Then Thomas (called Didymus) said to the rest of the disciples,
"Let us also go, that we may die with him."

If you could raise one person from the dead, who would it be? Why?

1. How long had Lazarus been dead by the time Jesus arrived? How would you feel if you were Martha or Mary and you heard that Jesus had finally come? **2.** What do you learn about Martha

Jesus Comforts the Sisters

17On his arrival, Jesus found that Lazarus had already been in the
tomb for four days. 18Bethany was less than two miles[b] from
Jerusalem, 19and many Jews had come to Martha and Mary to
comfort them in the loss of their brother. 20When Martha heard
that Jesus was coming, she went out to meet him, but Mary stayed
at home.

[a] *34* Psalm 82:6 [b] *18* Greek *fifteen stadia* (about 3 kilometers)

21“Lord,” Martha said to Jesus, “if you had been here, my brother would not have died. 22But I know that even now God will give
you whatever you ask.”
23Jesus said to her, “Your brother will rise again.”
24Martha answered, “I know he will rise again in the resurrection at the last day.”
25Jesus said to her, “I am the resurrection and the life. He who
believes in me will live, even though he dies; 26and whoever lives
and believes in me will never die. Do you believe this?”
27“Yes, Lord,” she told him, “I believe that you are the Christ,[a]
the Son of God, who was to come into the world.”
28And after she had said this, she went back and called her sister
Mary aside. “The Teacher is here,” she said, “and is asking for
you.” 29When Mary heard this, she got up quickly and went to
him. 30Now Jesus had not yet entered the village, but was still at
the place where Martha had met him. 31When the Jews who had
been with Mary in the house, comforting her, noticed how quickly
she got up and went out, they followed her, supposing she was
going to the tomb to mourn there.
32When Mary reached the place where Jesus was and saw him,

[a]*27* Or *Messiah*

from the way she talks with Jesus in verses 21–27? How does Jesus stretch her faith by his claim in verse 25? How does this relate to his claim in 10:9? **3.** What does Martha's statement (v. 27) sound like to you: (a) Stab in the dark? (b) Hope against hope? (c) Intellectual assent? (d) Active commitment? Why do you think so? **4.** How is Mary's greeting (v. 32) like and unlike Martha's? Since Jesus knew he was going to raise Lazarus (11:11), how do you account for his weeping (vv. 33–35)? **5.** What lies behind the comments of the mourners in verses 36–37? **6.** How does Martha's objection in verse 39 contrast with her confidence in verse 22?

♡ **1.** When have you been faced with a tough situation that ended up stretching your faith? What would have been different for

John 11:1–44 JESUS RAISES LAZARUS

1. Why do you think Jesus didn't go immediately to help Lazarus?
   a. He was afraid he would get killed if he went back to Judea.
   b. He didn't always do what people wanted.
   c. He was waiting for the "go ahead" from his Father.
   d. God would receive more glory if Jesus waited until Lazarus died.

2. How would you have felt if you were Mary or Martha and you heard that Jesus was about to arrive?
   a. despondent—It's too late.
   b. angry—It's about time!
   c. consoled—Better late than never.
   d. hopeful—With Jesus, it's never too late.

3. What do you learn about Jesus from his coming to the tomb?
   a. He was a very emotional person.
   b. He was profoundly affected by the reality and power of death.
   c. He empathized with suffering.
   d. He loved people deeply.

4. Why did Jesus raise Lazarus from the dead?
   a. to see his friend again
   b. to relieve Mary and Martha's grief
   c. to demonstrate he was God's Son
   d. to illustrate that he is "the resurrection and the life"
   e. to glorify his Father

5. If you compared your spiritual life to Lazarus, where would you be?
   a. still in the grave
   b. alive but still wrapped with grave clothes
   c. alive and free of the grave clothes

6. What are some old "grave clothes" that still need to be shed for you to feel completely free in Christ?

7. What means the most to you?
   a. Jesus' promise that believers will "never die"
   b. Jesus' words, "I am the resurrection and the life"
   c. the anticipation of seeing Jesus after I die
   d. the anticipation of seeing my loved ones in heaven

8. If you had been there and saw Jesus crying, how would you have felt?
   a. embarrassed for him—Grown men don't cry.
   b. relieved—It's okay to cry.
   c. mad—He could have prevented this and now all he can do is bawl.
   d. inspired—He really cared.

9. When you were a child, how tender would you say your mother was? How about your father? How tender are you? What keeps you from being more tender than you are?

10. What is the greatest challenge for you related to being assertive? Specifically, how hard is it for you to follow Jesus' example in the following areas:
    a. not dropping everything to answer the requests of others
    b. not feeling like I should be everywhere, meeting every need
    c. not always giving in when there is a difference of opinion

11. How does this story speak to you as a person living with pain?
    a. I know what it's like to wonder why Jesus hasn't intervened sooner.
    b. I'm glad to know Jesus can handle our getting upset and frustrated.
    c. It's comforting to know that, no matter what, Jesus is the resurrection and the life.
    d. It touches me to realize how deeply Jesus was touched.
    e. There's nothing wrong with expressing my sorrow and tears.
    f. I'm confident that someday I will be liberated from my pain.

12. What word of hope or encouragement would you like to share with your group or with a particular member? Close in prayer by thanking God for the promises of this Scripture and for Christ's continual comfort and presence with you.

you if that struggle had simply been avoided? **2.** Have you ever attended a funeral where there was no sense of eternal life, as in verses 25–26? How did you go away from that experience? What difference does this hope make for you? **3.** How does Jesus' response to Lazarus' death and Mary's weeping (v. 35) help you to trust him more? **4.** On a scale of 1 (none) to 10 (completely) how confident are you that you will live eternally? What evidence is there supporting your level of confidence? How would you live your life differently if you were more confident? **5.** What are some "old grave clothes" that still must be shed for you to feel truly free in Christ?

she fell at his feet and said, "Lord, if you had been here, my brother would not have died."

33When Jesus saw her weeping, and the Jews who had come along with her also weeping, he was deeply moved in spirit and troubled. 34"Where have you laid him?" he asked.

"Come and see, Lord," they replied.

35Jesus wept.

36Then the Jews said, "See how he loved him!"

37But some of them said, "Could not he who opened the eyes of the blind man have kept this man from dying?"

Jesus Raises Lazarus From the Dead

38Jesus, once more deeply moved, came to the tomb. It was a cave with a stone laid across the entrance. 39"Take away the stone," he said.

"But, Lord," said Martha, the sister of the dead man, "by this time there is a bad odor, for he has been there four days."

40Then Jesus said, "Did I not tell you that if you believed, you would see the glory of God?"

41So they took away the stone. Then Jesus looked up and said, "Father, I thank you that you have heard me. 42I knew that you always hear me, but I said this for the benefit of the people standing here, that they may believe that you sent me."

43When he had said this, Jesus called in a loud voice, "Lazarus, come out!" 44The dead man came out, his hands and feet wrapped with strips of linen, and a cloth around his face.

Jesus said to them, "Take off the grave clothes and let him go."

When have you challenged company policy? What happened?

1. What responses does the Lazarus miracle produce? Why? **2.** What are the chief concerns of the leaders? How do they misunderstand the role of the Messiah? How does Caiaphas propose to solve "the Jesus problem"? How does Caiaphas' murderous threat unwittingly convey prophetic truth about Jesus' death (see 3:16)? **3.** How does Jesus respond to this new situation?

1. What would you have done if you had been on the Sanhedrin? Would politics or truth win out with you? **2.** In what ways are you most likely to misunderstand who Jesus is? **3.** How have you tried to keep Jesus in line with your religious traditions?

The Plot to Kill Jesus

45Therefore many of the Jews who had come to visit Mary, and had seen what Jesus did, put their faith in him. 46But some of them went to the Pharisees and told them what Jesus had done. 47Then the chief priests and the Pharisees called a meeting of the Sanhedrin.

"What are we accomplishing?" they asked. "Here is this man performing many miraculous signs. 48If we let him go on like this, everyone will believe in him, and then the Romans will come and take away both our place[a] and our nation."

49Then one of them, named Caiaphas, who was high priest that year, spoke up, "You know nothing at all! 50You do not realize that it is better for you that one man die for the people than that the whole nation perish."

51He did not say this on his own, but as high priest that year he prophesied that Jesus would die for the Jewish nation, 52and not only for that nation but also for the scattered children of God, to bring them together and make them one. 53So from that day on they plotted to take his life.

54Therefore Jesus no longer moved about publicly among the Jews. Instead he withdrew to a region near the desert, to a village called Ephraim, where he stayed with his disciples.

55When it was almost time for the Jewish Passover, many went up from the country to Jerusalem for their ceremonial cleansing before the Passover. 56They kept looking for Jesus, and as they stood in the temple area they asked one another, "What do you think? Isn't he coming to the Feast at all?" 57But the chief priests and Pharisees had given orders that if anyone found out where Jesus was, he should report it so that they might arrest him.

a48 Or *temple*

Jesus Anointed at Bethany

12 Six days before the Passover, Jesus arrived at Bethany, where Lazarus lived, whom Jesus had raised from the dead. 2Here a dinner was given in Jesus' honor. Martha served, while Lazarus was among those reclining at the table with him. 3Then Mary took about a pint[a] of pure nard, an expensive perfume; she poured it on Jesus' feet and wiped his feet with her hair. And the house was filled with the fragrance of the perfume.

4But one of his disciples, Judas Iscariot, who was later to betray him, objected, 5"Why wasn't this perfume sold and the money given to the poor? It was worth a year's wages.[b]" 6He did not say this because he cared about the poor but because he was a thief; as keeper of the money bag, he used to help himself to what was put into it.

7"Leave her alone," Jesus replied. "⌊It was intended⌋ that she should save this perfume for the day of my burial. 8You will always have the poor among you, but you will not always have me."

9Meanwhile a large crowd of Jews found out that Jesus was there and came, not only because of him but also to see Lazarus, whom he had raised from the dead. 10So the chief priests made plans to kill Lazarus as well, 11for on account of him many of the Jews were going over to Jesus and putting their faith in him.

If you had a year's wages to spend on friends, which would you choose: (a) Big party? (b) Glorious trip for a few? (c) Extravagant gift for one?

1. Given the value of the perfume (v. 5), how would you have reacted as you watched Mary? Why? **2.** How does Jesus interpret Mary's action? How is his comment in verse 8 especially applicable to Judas? **3.** How is the blindness of the priests shown by their reaction to Lazarus?

1. If you had a year's salary or time to use for Christ, how would you use it? How is that reflected in your budget and priorities now? **2.** If you gave a dinner in Jesus' honor, whom would you invite?

The Triumphal Entry

12The next day the great crowd that had come for the Feast heard that Jesus was on his way to Jerusalem. 13They took palm branches and went out to meet him, shouting,

> "Hosanna![c]"
>
> "Blessed is he who comes in the name of the
> Lord!"[d]
>
> "Blessed is the King of Israel!"

14Jesus found a young donkey and sat upon it, as it is written,

> 15"Do not be afraid, O Daughter of Zion;
> see, your king is coming,
> seated on a donkey's colt."[e]

16At first his disciples did not understand all this. Only after Jesus was glorified did they realize that these things had been written about him and that they had done these things to him.

17Now the crowd that was with him when he called Lazarus from the tomb and raised him from the dead continued to spread the word. 18Many people, because they had heard that he had given this miraculous sign, went out to meet him. 19So the Pharisees said to one another, "See, this is getting us nowhere. Look how the whole world has gone after him!"

1. What do you like *best* about parades: Bands? Food Venders? Clowns? **2.** What do you like *least:* Traffic? Pickpockets? Tall people?

1. What previous stories stand in contrast to the unity and enthusiasm the people are expressing here? **2.** How could you tie in their hope that Jesus will do at *this* Passover what God did at the *first* Passover? **3.** Why a lowly donkey for Jesus (see Zec 9:9)? **4.** What do you think the crowds, the disciples and the Jewish leaders must be feeling now? One week later? Had you been there, what would you be feeling: Fanaticism, fickleness, faith or fear? Why?

1. What convinced you that Jesus is your King? What is the best thing you've seen about the type of King he is? **2.** Is your worship life like a hero's victory or a funeral dirge? Why?

Jesus Predicts His Death

20Now there were some Greeks among those who went up to worship at the Feast. 21They came to Philip, who was from Bethsaida in Galilee, with a request. "Sir," they said, "we would like to see Jesus." 22Philip went to tell Andrew; Andrew and Philip in turn told Jesus.

23Jesus replied, "The hour has come for the Son of Man to be glorified. 24I tell you the truth, unless a kernel of wheat falls to the

Are you more likely to panic in the *big* crises or the *little* ones? Explain.

1. What brings Gentiles to Jerusalem during a time of a Jewish feast? **2.** What was so unique about their request that Philip would first filter it through Andrew? **3.** Jesus said several times that "his time had not come" (2:4; 7:6,30). What regarding this request caused him to say that now it

a3 Greek *a litra* (probably about 0.5 liter) *b5* Greek *three hundred denarii*
c13 A Hebrew expression meaning "Save!" which became an exclamation of praise
d13 Psalm 118:25, 26 *e15* Zech. 9:9

has come? **4.** In Jesus' parable (v. 24), who is the kernel of wheat? How is this related to the Gentiles' request? **5.** What is he calling his disciples to do in verses 25–26? What promise do they receive? **6.** In verses 27–32, what is about to occur "now"? How does this affect Jesus? Why did the crowd deny the reality of Jesus' future death (vv. 32–34)?

1. In what area of your life are you in denial? **2.** Where is Jesus calling you to *die* so that you might *live*? What do you tend to hold on to rather than follow Jesus? **3.** Do you feel like you are walking in the dark, the light, or in some shadowland right now? Why?

Are you more like the salesman who could sell an icebox to an Eskimo, or more like the Eskimo who buys one?

1. What are some of the miraculous signs Jesus has done in this Gospel? How do the prophecies from Isaiah 53:1 and 6:10 account for the people's disbelief in spite of these signs? **2.** What is the author implying about Jesus in verse 41 (see 8:58)? **3.** What inhibits the leaders from speaking? How does this illustrate 12:25–26? **4.** What is Jesus claiming in verses 44–45? How do verses 44–46 relate to 1:1–5? How is Jesus like a light? **5.** What does Jesus emphasize in verses 47–50? As a last public statement, why is this one especially appropriate? How is it that Jesus' words can either judge a person or lead one to life?

1. Where do you find it most difficult to live your faith: At home or work? Why? **2.** If you had to sacrifice social status or certain relationships to follow Jesus, what would you get in return? **3.** How do you let people know where you stand with God?

ground and dies, it remains only a single seed. But if it dies, it produces many seeds. **25**The man who loves his life will lose it, while the man who hates his life in this world will keep it for eternal life. **26**Whoever serves me must follow me; and where I am, my servant also will be. My Father will honor the one who serves me.

27"Now my heart is troubled, and what shall I say? 'Father, save me from this hour'? No, it was for this very reason I came to this hour. **28**Father, glorify your name!"

Then a voice came from heaven, "I have glorified it, and will glorify it again." **29**The crowd that was there and heard it said it had thundered; others said an angel had spoken to him.

30Jesus said, "This voice was for your benefit, not mine. **31**Now is the time for judgment on this world; now the prince of this world will be driven out. **32**But I, when I am lifted up from the earth, will draw all men to myself." **33**He said this to show the kind of death he was going to die.

34The crowd spoke up, "We have heard from the Law that the Christ[a] will remain forever, so how can you say, 'The Son of Man must be lifted up'? Who is this 'Son of Man'?"

35Then Jesus told them, "You are going to have the light just a little while longer. Walk while you have the light, before darkness overtakes you. The man who walks in the dark does not know where he is going. **36**Put your trust in the light while you have it, so that you may become sons of light." When he had finished speaking, Jesus left and hid himself from them.

The Jews Continue in Their Unbelief

37Even after Jesus had done all these miraculous signs in their presence, they still would not believe in him. **38**This was to fulfill the word of Isaiah the prophet:

"Lord, who has believed our message
and to whom has the arm of the Lord been
revealed?"[b]

39For this reason they could not believe, because, as Isaiah says elsewhere:

40"He has blinded their eyes
and deadened their hearts,
so they can neither see with their eyes,
nor understand with their hearts,
nor turn—and I would heal them."[c]

41Isaiah said this because he saw Jesus' glory and spoke about him.

42Yet at the same time many even among the leaders believed in him. But because of the Pharisees they would not confess their faith for fear they would be put out of the synagogue; **43**for they loved praise from men more than praise from God.

44Then Jesus cried out, "When a man believes in me, he does not believe in me only, but in the one who sent me. **45**When he looks at me, he sees the one who sent me. **46**I have come into the world as a light, so that no one who believes in me should stay in darkness.

47"As for the person who hears my words but does not keep them, I do not judge him. For I did not come to judge the world, but to save it. **48**There is a judge for the one who rejects me and does not accept my words; that very word which I spoke will

[a]*34* Or *Messiah* [b]*38* Isaiah 53:1 [c]*40* Isaiah 6:10

condemn him at the last day. 49For I did not speak of my own
accord, but the Father who sent me commanded me what to say
and how to say it. 50I know that his command leads to eternal life.
So whatever I say is just what the Father has told me to say."

Jesus Washes His Disciples' Feet

13 It was just before the Passover Feast. Jesus knew that the
time had come for him to leave this world and go to the
Father. Having loved his own who were in the world, he now
showed them the full extent of his love.[a]
2The evening meal was being served, and the devil had already
prompted Judas Iscariot, son of Simon, to betray Jesus. 3Jesus knew
that the Father had put all things under his power, and that he had
come from God and was returning to God; 4so he got up from the
meal, took off his outer clothing, and wrapped a towel around his
waist. 5After that, he poured water into a basin and began to wash
his disciples' feet, drying them with the towel that was wrapped
around him.
6He came to Simon Peter, who said to him, "Lord, are you going
to wash my feet?"
7Jesus replied, "You do not realize now what I am doing, but
later you will understand."
8"No," said Peter, "you shall never wash my feet."

[a] *1* Or *he loved them to the last*

1. What were the special meals in your family: Thanksgiving? Sunday lunch? Birthday dinners? Christmas? What was usually served? **2.** Who would you nominate for the "Mother Teresa Award" in your family or church for selfless, tireless servanthood?

1. What does Jesus *know* that escapes the disciples' attention (vv. 1,3,11)? Hence, what impresses you about Jesus washing their feet? **2.** If you were Peter, would you have reacted as he did? Why or why not? While Peter is taking the washing of his feet literally, what do you think Jesus meant by his statement in verse 8? In verse 10? **3.** How does Jesus challenge their idea of what it means to be the chief followers of

John 13:1–17 JESUS WASHES THE DISCIPLES' FEET

It was customary in Jesus' day for people's dusty, sandaled feet to be washed, usually by the lowest ranking servant, before a meal was served.

1. Why didn't the disciples wash their feet before supper?
   a. They forgot.
   b. They were slobs.
   c. It wasn't their job.
   d. There weren't any servants there.

2. What would you have done if Jesus wanted to wash your feet?
   a. left the room
   b. objected like Peter did
   c. insisted that I wash *his* feet
   d. kept quiet but felt uncomfortable
   e. felt honored by his caring act

3. What did Jesus mean when he said, "Unless I wash you, you have no part with me"?
   a. "I don't want to share a room with anyone with dirty feet."
   b. "To be part of me you have to learn to receive."
   c. "You have to let my coming sacrifice cleanse you from your sin."
   d. "As long as you live you will need cleansing and forgiveness."
   e. "Unless you're a servant like I am, you can't be my disciple."

4. Why did Jesus wash his disciples' feet?
   a. to shame them
   b. to be an example of servanthood
   c. to illustrate his whole mission
   d. to show them real leadership
   e. to show his deep love for them before he died

5. How did Jesus expect the disciples to follow his example?
   a. to wash each other's feet literally
   b. to be willing to do the "dirty work"
   c. to take care of each other
   d. to observe footwashing regularly in the church, like Communion

6. Why do you think Christians don't serve each other more than they do?

7. What one thing will you do at home, work or church this week to follow Jesus' example of serving?

8. What would it mean to practice footwashing in your marriage relationship?
   a. to serve my spouse more
   b. to let my spouse serve me
   c. to listen to my spouse more
   d. to show more affection
   e. to show more appreciation
   f. to be more patient and forgiving
   g. to serve with no strings attached
   h. to do things that aren't "my job"
   i. to work at sharing unpleasant tasks

9. Growing up, how often did your family sit down and eat together? How much did you visit around the table? How does that compare to your current lifestyle?

10. How can you better serve your children?
   a. spend more time with them
   b. give them my undivided attention
   c. give them more affection
   d. bless them more with special meals and other fun occasions

11. Which of the following is true about your job?
   a. My job has nothing to do with serving—it's about making money.
   b. Jesus' example of servanthood is what keeps me going in my job.
   c. I have to do many servant tasks, most of which are pleasant.
   d. I have to do many servant tasks, most of which are unpleasant.
   e. Feeling underqualified for my job, I'd welcome more servant tasks.
   f. Feeling overqualified, I do more servant tasks than I would like.

the Messiah (vv. 12–17)? What role reversals do you see here?

1. In your spiritual life, who is one person who has demonstrated what it means to "wash feet"? What did he or she do? 2. Specifically, how will you put Jesus' teaching into practice in at least one relationship this week at home, work or church?

Jesus answered, "Unless I wash you, you have no part with me."

9"Then, Lord," Simon Peter replied, "not just my feet but my hands and my head as well!"

10Jesus answered, "A person who has had a bath needs only to wash his feet; his whole body is clean. And you are clean, though not every one of you." 11For he knew who was going to betray him, and that was why he said not every one was clean.

12When he had finished washing their feet, he put on his clothes and returned to his place. "Do you understand what I have done for you?" he asked them. 13"You call me 'Teacher' and 'Lord,' and rightly so, for that is what I am. 14Now that I, your Lord and Teacher, have washed your feet, you also should wash one another's feet. 15I have set you an example that you should do as I have done for you. 16I tell you the truth, no servant is greater than his master, nor is a messenger greater than the one who sent him. 17Now that you know these things, you will be blessed if you do them.

When you are troubled, what symptoms show on your face? In your spirit?

1. If you were a movie director, how would you capture the drama of verses 18–22? If you had been sitting at this table, what would you be feeling? Saying? 2. In foretelling his betrayal, what do you sense in Jesus: Resolution? Resignation? Restlessness? What do you sense in his disciples? In Judas? 3. Is Judas to be excused or held responsible when "Satan entered into him" (v. 27; also 6:70; 12:4–6; 13:2)?

1. If you knew ahead of time that someone would stab you in the back, how would you treat that person? How does Jesus show you what love is all about? 2. Given three years of very intimate fellowship with Jesus, how could Judas turn around and betray him? Have you ever betrayed Jesus? If so, how?

Jesus Predicts His Betrayal

18"I am not referring to all of you; I know those I have chosen. But this is to fulfill the scripture: 'He who shares my bread has lifted up his heel against me.'[a]

19"I am telling you now before it happens, so that when it does happen you will believe that I am He. 20I tell you the truth, whoever accepts anyone I send accepts me; and whoever accepts me accepts the one who sent me."

21After he had said this, Jesus was troubled in spirit and testified, "I tell you the truth, one of you is going to betray me."

22His disciples stared at one another, at a loss to know which of them he meant. 23One of them, the disciple whom Jesus loved, was reclining next to him. 24Simon Peter motioned to this disciple and said, "Ask him which one he means."

25Leaning back against Jesus, he asked him, "Lord, who is it?"

26Jesus answered, "It is the one to whom I will give this piece of bread when I have dipped it in the dish." Then, dipping the piece of bread, he gave it to Judas Iscariot, son of Simon. 27As soon as Judas took the bread, Satan entered into him.

"What you are about to do, do quickly," Jesus told him, 28but no one at the meal understood why Jesus said this to him. 29Since Judas had charge of the money, some thought Jesus was telling him to buy what was needed for the Feast, or to give something to the poor. 30As soon as Judas had taken the bread, he went out. And it was night.

What trait do you share with other family members?

1. Why did Jesus wait until Judas had gone to share the message in verses 31–35? 2. What does he call the disciples to do (v. 34)? 3. What type of person is Peter (vv. 6–9,36–37)? How do you think he felt after verse 38?

1. How do your good intentions compare to Peter's? 2. On a scale from 1 to 10, how does your church rank against the standard of love? How could you increase its score?

Jesus Predicts Peter's Denial

31When he was gone, Jesus said, "Now is the Son of Man glorified and God is glorified in him. 32If God is glorified in him,[b] God will glorify the Son in himself, and will glorify him at once.

33"My children, I will be with you only a little longer. You will look for me, and just as I told the Jews, so I tell you now: Where I am going, you cannot come.

34"A new command I give you: Love one another. As I have loved you, so you must love one another. 35By this all men will know that you are my disciples, if you love one another."

36Simon Peter asked him, "Lord, where are you going?"

Jesus replied, "Where I am going, you cannot follow now, but you will follow later."

[a] *18* Psalm 41:9 [b] *32* Many early manuscripts do not have *If God is glorified in him.*

37Peter asked, "Lord, why can't I follow you now? I will lay down my life for you."

38Then Jesus answered, "Will you really lay down your life for me? I tell you the truth, before the rooster crows, you will disown me three times!

Jesus Comforts His Disciples

14 "Do not let your hearts be troubled. Trust in God[a]; trust also in me. 2In my Father's house are many rooms; if it were not so, I would have told you. I am going there to prepare a place for you. 3And if I go and prepare a place for you, I will come back and take you to be with me that you also may be where I am. 4You know the way to the place where I am going."

Jesus the Way to the Father

5Thomas said to him, "Lord, we don't know where you are going, so how can we know the way?"

6Jesus answered, "I am the way and the truth and the life. No one comes to the Father except through me. 7If you really knew me, you would know[b] my Father as well. From now on, you do know him and have seen him."

8Philip said, "Lord, show us the Father and that will be enough for us."

9Jesus answered: "Don't you know me, Philip, even after I have been among you such a long time? Anyone who has seen me has seen the Father. How can you say, 'Show us the Father'? 10Don't you believe that I am in the Father, and that the Father is in me? The words I say to you are not just my own. Rather, it is the Father, living in me, who is doing his work. 11Believe me when I say that I am in the Father and the Father is in me; or at least believe on the evidence of the miracles themselves. 12I tell you the truth, anyone who has faith in me will do what I have been doing. He will do even greater things than these, because I am going to the Father. 13And I will do whatever you ask in my name, so that the Son may bring glory to the Father. 14You may ask me for anything in my name, and I will do it.

1. What is your favorite room in the house? Why? **2.** Can you remember a time when you got lost? What happened?

1. What comfort does Jesus offer his disciples? **2.** Look at 13:36, 14:6,8, and 22. What problems are the disciples struggling with? **3.** Put Jesus' statement in 14:6–7 in your own words. **4.** How does 1:18 relate to what Jesus says in 14:9? With what tone of voice do you imagine Jesus speaking in verses 9–14? What evidence does Jesus give for his claims? **5.** Do you think the promises Jesus makes in verses 12–14 are "blank check" promises about prayer? In verse 12, does he mean the church will do works greater in *power*? Greater in *scope*? How could this be?

1. If Jesus is the Way, do you feel you are on a bumpy dead-end street, or on a four-lane highway? Why? **2.** In light of 14:6, how would you respond to someone who says, "there are many ways to God"?

Jesus Promises the Holy Spirit

15"If you love me, you will obey what I command. 16And I will ask the Father, and he will give you another Counselor to be with you forever— 17the Spirit of truth. The world cannot accept him, because it neither sees him nor knows him. But you know him, for he lives with you and will be[c] in you. 18I will not leave you as orphans; I will come to you. 19Before long, the world will not see me anymore, but you will see me. Because I live, you also will live. 20On that day you will realize that I am in my Father, and you are in me, and I am in you. 21Whoever has my commands and obeys them, he is the one who loves me. He who loves me will be loved by my Father, and I too will love him and show myself to him."

22Then Judas (not Judas Iscariot) said, "But, Lord, why do you intend to show yourself to us and not to the world?"

23Jesus replied, "If anyone loves me, he will obey my teaching. My Father will love him, and we will come to him and make our home with him. 24He who does not love me will not obey my teaching. These words you hear are not my own; they belong to the Father who sent me.

25"All this I have spoken while still with you. 26But the Counsel-

Who was the best counselor you ever had? Why was this person so special?

1. How are the disciples to show love to each other (13:34)? To Jesus (14:15)? Why is this idea repeated four times (vv. 15,21,23–24)? **2.** What do you learn about the Holy Spirit in verses 16–17 and 25–27? What is the relationship of the Father, Jesus and the Holy Spirit to the believer? To each other? **3.** What is the difference between how *Jesus* gives peace and how the *world* does?

1. How at home are the Father, Son and Holy Spirit in your life? Are they more like owners, or temporary guests? **2.** On a scale from 1 (smooth sailing) to 10 (furious storm), what is your peace quotient? Why? Where do you need Jesus' peace? Where can you find

[a] *1* Or *You trust in God* [b] *7* Some early manuscripts *If you really have known me, you will know* [c] *17* Some early manuscripts *and is*

hope in this passage? **3.** How has the Holy Spirit revealed Jesus in your life? **4.** Of all the promises made here (vv. 16–18,21,23,26–27), which one means the most to you? Why?

or, the Holy Spirit, whom the Father will send in my name, will
teach you all things and will remind you of everything I have said
to you. 27Peace I leave with you; my peace I give you. I do not give
to you as the world gives. Do not let your hearts be troubled and do
not be afraid.
28"You heard me say, 'I am going away and I am coming back to
you.' If you loved me, you would be glad that I am going to the
Father, for the Father is greater than I. 29I have told you now
before it happens, so that when it does happen you will believe. 30I
will not speak with you much longer, for the prince of this world is
coming. He has no hold on me, 31but the world must learn that I
love the Father and that I do exactly what my Father has commanded me.
"Come now; let us leave.

What plant best describes you now: Towering oak? Weeping willow? Tumbleweed? Crab apple tree? Explain.

1. If vine branches were human lives, what pain would be associated with pruning? What tools? What fruit? **2.** Jesus repeats *remain in me*, *love* and *bear fruit*. How are these words related? What is the "fruit that will last" (v. 16)? **3.** How do verses 9 and 12 tie together? How is love the essential dynamic of the Christian life? How does your relationship with Jesus change once you start practicing his example of love? **4.** What is the link between obedience and prayer (vv. 7,16; see 14:13–14)?

1. As a branch on Christ's vine, how would you describe the fruit in your life: Grade A–1? Juicy? Green? Wormy? Why? **2.** Do you feel more like Jesus' servant or his friend? What helps develop the friendship?

The Vine and the Branches

15 "I am the true vine, and my Father is the gardener. 2He
cuts off every branch in me that bears no fruit, while every
branch that does bear fruit he prunes[a] so that it will be even more
fruitful. 3You are already clean because of the word I have spoken
to you. 4Remain in me, and I will remain in you. No branch can
bear fruit by itself; it must remain in the vine. Neither can you bear
fruit unless you remain in me.
5"I am the vine; you are the branches. If a man remains in me
and I in him, he will bear much fruit; apart from me you can do
nothing. 6If anyone does not remain in me, he is like a branch that
is thrown away and withers; such branches are picked up, thrown
into the fire and burned. 7If you remain in me and my words
remain in you, ask whatever you wish, and it will be given you.
8This is to my Father's glory, that you bear much fruit, showing
yourselves to be my disciples.
9"As the Father has loved me, so have I loved you. Now remain
in my love. 10If you obey my commands, you will remain in my
love, just as I have obeyed my Father's commands and remain in
his love. 11I have told you this so that my joy may be in you and
that your joy may be complete. 12My command is this: Love each
other as I have loved you. 13Greater love has no one than this, that
he lay down his life for his friends. 14You are my friends if you do
what I command. 15I no longer call you servants, because a servant
does not know his master's business. Instead, I have called you
friends, for everything that I learned from my Father I have made
known to you. 16You did not choose me, but I chose you and
appointed you to go and bear fruit—fruit that will last. Then the
Father will give you whatever you ask in my name. 17This is my
command: Love each other.

Have you ever been to a large group or reunion of someone else's family? How did you feel?

1. Since the emphasis in 15:9–17 was on love, why does Jesus now talk about hate? What does Jesus mean here by "the world"? How is the relationship of the disciples to the world like that of Jesus' relationship to it? **2.** What do you see in the relationship between the Father, Jesus and the disciples? **3.** How has Jesus' com-

The World Hates the Disciples

18"If the world hates you, keep in mind that it hated me first. 19If
you belonged to the world, it would love you as its own. As it is,
you do not belong to the world, but I have chosen you out of the
world. That is why the world hates you. 20Remember the words I
spoke to you: 'No servant is greater than his master.'[b] If they
persecuted me, they will persecute you also. If they obeyed my
teaching, they will obey yours also. 21They will treat you this way
because of my name, for they do not know the One who sent me.
22If I had not come and spoken to them, they would not be guilty
of sin. Now, however, they have no excuse for their sin. 23He who

[a]2 The Greek for *prunes* also means *cleans*. [b]20 John 13:16

hates me hates my Father as well. 24If I had not done among them
what no one else did, they would not be guilty of sin. But now they
have seen these miracles, and yet they have hated both me and my
Father. 25But this is to fulfill what is written in their Law: 'They
hated me without reason.'[a]
26"When the Counselor comes, whom I will send to you from
the Father, the Spirit of truth who goes out from the Father, he will
testify about me. 27And you also must testify, for you have been
with me from the beginning.

16 "All this I have told you so that you will not go astray.
2They will put you out of the synagogue; in fact, a time is
coming when anyone who kills you will think he is offering a
service to God. 3They will do such things because they have not
known the Father or me. 4I have told you this, so that when the
time comes you will remember that I warned you. I did not tell you
this at first because I was with you.

The Work of the Holy Spirit

5"Now I am going to him who sent me, yet none of you asks me,
'Where are you going?' 6Because I have said these things, you are
filled with grief. 7But I tell you the truth: It is for your good that I
am going away. Unless I go away, the Counselor will not come to
you; but if I go, I will send him to you. 8When he comes, he will
convict the world of guilt[b] in regard to sin and righteousness and
judgment: 9in regard to sin, because men do not believe in me; 10in
regard to righteousness, because I am going to the Father, where
you can see me no longer; 11and in regard to judgment, because
the prince of this world now stands condemned.
12"I have much more to say to you, more than you can now bear.
13But when he, the Spirit of truth, comes, he will guide you into all
truth. He will not speak on his own; he will speak only what he
hears, and he will tell you what is yet to come. 14He will bring
glory to me by taking from what is mine and making it known to
you. 15All that belongs to the Father is mine. That is why I said the
Spirit will take from what is mine and make it known to you.
16"In a little while you will see me no more, and then after a
little while you will see me."

The Disciples' Grief Will Turn to Joy

17Some of his disciples said to one another, "What does he mean
by saying, 'In a little while you will see me no more, and then after
a little while you will see me,' and 'Because I am going to the
Father'?" 18They kept asking, "What does he mean by 'a little
while'? We don't understand what he is saying."
19Jesus saw that they wanted to ask him about this, so he said to
them, "Are you asking one another what I meant when I said, 'In
a little while you will see me no more, and then after a little while
you will see me'? 20I tell you the truth, you will weep and mourn
while the world rejoices. You will grieve, but your grief will turn to
joy. 21A woman giving birth to a child has pain because her time
has come; but when her baby is born she forgets the anguish
because of her joy that a child is born into the world. 22So with
you: Now is your time of grief, but I will see you again and you will
rejoice, and no one will take away your joy. 23In that day you will
no longer ask me anything. I tell you the truth, my Father will give
you whatever you ask in my name. 24Until now you have not asked

[a] 25 Psalms 35:19; 69:4 [b] 8 Or *will expose the guilt of the world*

ing highlighted the reality and evil of sin (vv. 22,24)?

1. When have you found that speaking truth and showing love can lead to hostility from others? How do you explain that? **2.** How do you handle people who are religious but not godly?

How are you at saying "goodbye"? Is it harder for you to be the one leaving home, or the one left behind? Explain.

1. What are the disciples feeling now? What is their grief keeping them from understanding (v. 17)? **2.** How would you paraphrase the three goals of the Spirit's work (vv. 8–11)? Therefore, why is it good that Jesus goes away? **3.** If you were a disciple, how would you feel after hearing verse 16?

1. Of the various roles of the Holy Spirit described here, which one have you come to appreciate recently? **2.** Has Jesus ever said things to you that you could hardly bear (v. 12)? What happened?

Did your parents ever tell you about your birth experience? What was it like for them?

1. What tones of voice do you hear in verses 17–18? If you were there, would Jesus' answer encourage you, or confuse you more? **2.** What event is Jesus referring to in verses 20–22? In what ways does the world's "joy" (v. 20) contrast with the joy the disciples will experience (v. 22)? How is this similar to what Jesus said about dying (12:24)? About peace (14:27)? **3.** What characterizes the relationship we can have with the Father because of Jesus (vv. 23–27)? **4.** Do you think the disciples truly grasp what Jesus says in verse 28? Why?

1. Both Jesus and the world offer a form of peace (14:27; 16:33), joy (15:11; 16:22–24) and love (13:34–35; 15:9–19). How have you experienced each of these? What is different between them? **2.** How do you deal with change? Moves? Job transfers? Transitions from one stage of your life to another? How has pain helped you to grow? **3.** From your experience, how could you comfort someone going through change? **4.** How do you desire joy? How do you experience it?

for anything in my name. Ask and you will receive, and your joy
will be complete.
25“Though I have been speaking figuratively, a time is coming
when I will no longer use this kind of language but will tell you
plainly about my Father. 26In that day you will ask in my name. I
am not saying that I will ask the Father on your behalf. 27No, the
Father himself loves you because you have loved me and have
believed that I came from God. 28I came from the Father and
entered the world; now I am leaving the world and going back to
the Father.”
29Then Jesus' disciples said, “Now you are speaking clearly and
without figures of speech. 30Now we can see that you know all
things and that you do not even need to have anyone ask you
questions. This makes us believe that you came from God.”
31“You believe at last!”[a] Jesus answered. 32“But a time is coming, and has come, when you will be scattered, each to his own
home. You will leave me all alone. Yet I am not alone, for my
Father is with me.
33“I have told you these things, so that in me you may have
peace. In this world you will have trouble. But take heart! I have
overcome the world.”

---

1. What going-away gift have you received or given that still warms your heart or brings a smile? **2.** What is the *best* reason you have heard for *not* believing in Jesus as Savior?

1. What event is it now “time” for (v. 1; 12:23–24)? **2.** What does it mean to “glorify” someone (vv. 4–5,10,22,24)? How is Jesus' deity emphasized here? **3.** Who is the focal point of Jesus' prayer in verses 6–19? Why? If you had to file a report to the Father on Jesus' activities, how would you verify verses 6–8? **4.** What is Jesus' concern in verses 11 and 15? What does he mean by “the name you gave me” (see 8:58; Ex 3:14)? What do the events surrounding the original revelation of this name show about its power to save (Ex 3:7–10)? **5.** What does he mean by his request in verse 17? What is its purpose? **6.** Who is the focus of Jesus' prayer in verses 20–26? Toward what end? What kind of unity exists between God and Jesus that we should copy? **7.** What does Jesus' ultimate desire (v. 24) reveal about his love for us? **8.** How do verses 25–26 sum up the major concerns of Jesus in chapters 13–16?

1. This week, whom have you glorified by the way you lived? How so? **2.** What two phrases sum up your goal for the past year? How does this relate to God's purpose? **3.** How are your prayers for others like and unlike Jesus' prayer? Do your prayers re-

Jesus Prays for Himself

17 After Jesus said this, he looked toward heaven and prayed:
“Father, the time has come. Glorify your Son, that your Son
may glorify you. 2For you granted him authority over all people that he might give eternal life to all those you have given
him. 3Now this is eternal life: that they may know you, the
only true God, and Jesus Christ, whom you have sent. 4I have
brought you glory on earth by completing the work you gave
me to do. 5And now, Father, glorify me in your presence with
the glory I had with you before the world began.

Jesus Prays for His Disciples

6“I have revealed you[b] to those whom you gave me out of
the world. They were yours; you gave them to me and they
have obeyed your word. 7Now they know that everything you
have given me comes from you. 8For I gave them the words
you gave me and they accepted them. They knew with certainty that I came from you, and they believed that you sent
me. 9I pray for them. I am not praying for the world, but for
those you have given me, for they are yours. 10All I have is
yours, and all you have is mine. And glory has come to me
through them. 11I will remain in the world no longer, but they
are still in the world, and I am coming to you. Holy Father,
protect them by the power of your name—the name you gave
me—so that they may be one as we are one. 12While I was
with them, I protected them and kept them safe by that name
you gave me. None has been lost except the one doomed to
destruction so that Scripture would be fulfilled.
13“I am coming to you now, but I say these things while I
am still in the world, so that they may have the full measure
of my joy within them. 14I have given them your word and the
world has hated them, for they are not of the world any more
than I am of the world. 15My prayer is not that you take them
out of the world but that you protect them from the evil one.

[a] *31* Or *“Do you now believe?”* [b] *6* Greek *your name*; also in verse 26

16They are not of the world, even as I am not of it. 17Sancti-
fy[a] them by the truth; your word is truth. 18As you sent me
into the world, I have sent them into the world. 19For them I
sanctify myself, that they too may be truly sanctified.

Jesus Prays for All Believers

20"My prayer is not for them alone. I pray also for those
who will believe in me through their message, 21that all of
them may be one, Father, just as you are in me and I am in
you. May they also be in us so that the world may believe that
you have sent me. 22I have given them the glory that you gave
me, that they may be one as we are one: 23I in them and you
in me. May they be brought to complete unity to let the world
know that you sent me and have loved them even as you have
loved me.

24"Father, I want those you have given me to be with me
where I am, and to see my glory, the glory you have given me
because you loved me before the creation of the world.

25"Righteous Father, though the world does not know you,
I know you, and they know that you have sent me. 26I have
made you known to them, and will continue to make you
known in order that the love you have for me may be in them
and that I myself may be in them."

Jesus Arrested

18 When he had finished praying, Jesus left with his disciples
and crossed the Kidron Valley. On the other side there was
an olive grove, and he and his disciples went into it.

2Now Judas, who betrayed him, knew the place, because Jesus
had often met there with his disciples. 3So Judas came to the grove,
guiding a detachment of soldiers and some officials from the chief
priests and Pharisees. They were carrying torches, lanterns and
weapons.

4Jesus, knowing all that was going to happen to him, went out
and asked them, "Who is it you want?"

5"Jesus of Nazareth," they replied.

"I am he," Jesus said. (And Judas the traitor was standing there
with them.) 6When Jesus said, "I am he," they drew back and fell
to the ground.

7Again he asked them, "Who is it you want?"

And they said, "Jesus of Nazareth."

8"I told you that I am he," Jesus answered. "If you are looking
for me, then let these men go." 9This happened so that the words
he had spoken would be fulfilled: "I have not lost one of those you
gave me."[b]

10Then Simon Peter, who had a sword, drew it and struck the
high priest's servant, cutting off his right ear. (The servant's name
was Malchus.)

11Jesus commanded Peter, "Put your sword away! Shall I not
drink the cup the Father has given me?"

Jesus Taken to Annas

12Then the detachment of soldiers with its commander and the
Jewish officials arrested Jesus. They bound him 13and brought him
first to Annas, who was the father-in-law of Caiaphas, the high
priest that year. 14Caiaphas was the one who had advised the Jews
that it would be good if one man died for the people.

[a] *17* Greek *hagiazo (set apart for sacred use* or *make holy)*; also in verse 19
[b] *9* John 6:39

flect the short-term urgent, or the long-term important needs that people have? What can you apply to your prayer skills from this chapter? **4.** How does the fact that Jesus existed before the world began affect the way you live? **5.** How important to you is unity with other believers? With whom do you share this unity? How can you experience more unity?

Where do you go when you need to prepare yourself for a very stressful time?

1. Why do the Pharisees want to take advantage of the night to arrest Jesus (see 3:19–20; 12:35; 13:30)? **2.** How do you think the disciples felt when they saw these menacing-looking people coming? Jesus used many "I am . . ." sayings (vine, light, bread). How do you explain verse 6? **3.** Seeing how he deals with the soldiers (vv. 4,8) and Peter (v. 11), what do you learn about Jesus? **4.** How does Peter show he still doesn't grasp what is going on? **5.** What is "the cup" which Jesus must drink (v. 11)? **6.** Given his pacifism, why is Jesus bound (v. 12)? Who's afraid of whom here? Why?

1. Have you ever tried to obey Jesus, only to be overzealous and ending up hurting someone? What happened? **2.** How does Jesus' decision to "drink the cup" (v. 11) help you in your obedience to God? What issue of obedience is challenging you?

1. As a child, what was one "big" thing you really messed up on: Missing the catch for the final out? Forgetting the crucial line in the school play? Leaving something behind, never to be recovered? **2.** After forgetting a name or messing up, what did you do?

1. What do you think Peter and the other disciple hoped to do? How do you account for the difference between Peter here (v. 17) and in the garden (18:10)? **2.** What is ironic about the high priest's questioning of Jesus? **3.** How do Jesus' answers expose this trial as a mockery (v. 23)? If you were there, what would you have done on Jesus' behalf? **4.** What feelings must Peter have had after the rooster crowed (v. 27; see 13:37–38)? What do you suppose Peter did at that point?

1. How does the story of Peter both humble and encourage you? When have you felt like Peter? **2.** How do you explain the ups and downs in your own spiritual life? **3.** When have you dealt with someone whose mind was so made up that the facts didn't matter? How do you deal with this when it relates to your faith?

As a child, were you ever blamed for something you didn't do? How did you react?

1. Where was Jesus taken next? When? Why are the Jewish leaders rushing this trial? **2.** What is the irony in verse 28? **3.** What reason do they finally give Pilate for bringing Jesus to him (vv. 33–34)? Why would Pilate take this seriously? How are Pilate's fears like those of the Jewish leaders in 11:48? **4.** What does Jesus tell Pilate about his kingdom (vv. 36–37)? Who is included in it? What do you think Pilate meant by his concerns in verse 38? **5.** In his pursuit of "truth," is Pilate trying to absolve himself, or Jesus? Why do you think so?

1. Since both Peter and Pilate caved in under pressure, why do we tend to scorn Pilate but honor Peter? **2.** Do you see any of

Peter's First Denial

15Simon Peter and another disciple were following Jesus. Because this disciple was known to the high priest, he went with Jesus into the high priest's courtyard, 16but Peter had to wait outside at the door. The other disciple, who was known to the high priest, came back, spoke to the girl on duty there and brought Peter in.

17"You are not one of his disciples, are you?" the girl at the door asked Peter.

He replied, "I am not."

18It was cold, and the servants and officials stood around a fire they had made to keep warm. Peter also was standing with them, warming himself.

The High Priest Questions Jesus

19Meanwhile, the high priest questioned Jesus about his disciples and his teaching.

20"I have spoken openly to the world," Jesus replied. "I always taught in synagogues or at the temple, where all the Jews come together. I said nothing in secret. 21Why question me? Ask those who heard me. Surely they know what I said."

22When Jesus said this, one of the officials nearby struck him in the face. "Is this the way you answer the high priest?" he demanded.

23"If I said something wrong," Jesus replied, "testify as to what is wrong. But if I spoke the truth, why did you strike me?" 24Then Annas sent him, still bound, to Caiaphas the high priest.[a]

Peter's Second and Third Denials

25As Simon Peter stood warming himself, he was asked, "You are not one of his disciples, are you?"

He denied it, saying, "I am not."

26One of the high priest's servants, a relative of the man whose ear Peter had cut off, challenged him, "Didn't I see you with him in the olive grove?" 27Again Peter denied it, and at that moment a rooster began to crow.

Jesus Before Pilate

28Then the Jews led Jesus from Caiaphas to the palace of the Roman governor. By now it was early morning, and to avoid ceremonial uncleanness the Jews did not enter the palace; they wanted to be able to eat the Passover. 29So Pilate came out to them and asked, "What charges are you bringing against this man?"

30"If he were not a criminal," they replied, "we would not have handed him over to you."

31Pilate said, "Take him yourselves and judge him by your own law."

"But we have no right to execute anyone," the Jews objected. 32This happened so that the words Jesus had spoken indicating the kind of death he was going to die would be fulfilled.

33Pilate then went back inside the palace, summoned Jesus and asked him, "Are you the king of the Jews?"

34"Is that your own idea," Jesus asked, "or did others talk to you about me?"

35"Am I a Jew?" Pilate replied. "It was your people and your chief priests who handed you over to me. What is it you have done?"

[a]*24* Or *(Now Annas had sent him, still bound, to Caiaphas the high priest.)*

36Jesus said, "My kingdom is not of this world. If it were, my
servants would fight to prevent my arrest by the Jews. But now my
kingdom is from another place."
37"You are a king, then!" said Pilate.
Jesus answered, "You are right in saying I am a king. In fact, for
this reason I was born, and for this I came into the world, to testify
to the truth. Everyone on the side of truth listens to me."
38"What is truth?" Pilate asked. With this he went out again to
the Jews and said, "I find no basis for a charge against him. 39But
it is your custom for me to release to you one prisoner at the time
of the Passover. Do you want me to release 'the king of the Jews'?"
40They shouted back, "No, not him! Give us Barabbas!" Now
Barabbas had taken part in a rebellion.

Pilate's qualities in yourself? **3.** How does Barabbas' freedom at Christ's expense illustrate the Gospel?

Jesus Sentenced to be Crucified

19 Then Pilate took Jesus and had him flogged. 2The soldiers
twisted together a crown of thorns and put it on his head.
They clothed him in a purple robe 3and went up to him again and
again, saying, "Hail, king of the Jews!" And they struck him in the
face.
4Once more Pilate came out and said to the Jews, "Look, I am
bringing him out to you to let you know that I find no basis for a
charge against him." 5When Jesus came out wearing the crown of
thorns and the purple robe, Pilate said to them, "Here is the man!"
6As soon as the chief priests and their officials saw him, they
shouted, "Crucify! Crucify!"
But Pilate answered, "You take him and crucify him. As for me,
I find no basis for a charge against him."
7The Jews insisted, "We have a law, and according to that law he
must die, because he claimed to be the Son of God."
8When Pilate heard this, he was even more afraid, 9and he went
back inside the palace. "Where do you come from?" he asked
Jesus, but Jesus gave him no answer. 10"Do you refuse to speak to
me?" Pilate said. "Don't you realize I have power either to free you
or to crucify you?"
11Jesus answered, "You would have no power over me if it were
not given to you from above. Therefore the one who handed me
over to you is guilty of a greater sin."
12From then on, Pilate tried to set Jesus free, but the Jews kept
shouting, "If you let this man go, you are no friend of Caesar.
Anyone who claims to be a king opposes Caesar."
13When Pilate heard this, he brought Jesus out and sat down on
the judge's seat at a place known as the Stone Pavement (which in
Aramaic is Gabbatha). 14It was the day of Preparation of Passover
Week, about the sixth hour.
"Here is your king," Pilate said to the Jews.
15But they shouted, "Take him away! Take him away! Crucify
him!"
"Shall I crucify your king?" Pilate asked.
"We have no king but Caesar," the chief priests answered.
16Finally Pilate handed him over to them to be crucified.

Were you ever bullied as a kid? What happened?

1. In view of Pilate's convictions (see 18:38; 19:4,6), why would he allow Jesus to be struck? Are the soldiers cruel, or are there deeper hates and fears involved? Despite the mock coronation (vv. 2–3), what did Jesus actually deserve? **2.** Why do the Jewish leaders clamor for Jesus to be crucified? What does Pilate's fearful response to that charge show about him? How might his conversation with Jesus in 18:33–37 have influenced him? **3.** What is the implied threat to Pilate in verse 12? **4.** What does the priests' reply (v. 15) indicate about their spiritual condition? Why is this especially ironic (see 8:33,41)? **5.** Pretend you are Pilate. How would you explain to your wife later that night why you finally let Jesus be killed?

When have you made a decision based on fear and ambition, rather than on what is right? How do you feel about that now? How can you guard against it in the future?

The Crucifixion

So the soldiers took charge of Jesus. 17Carrying his own cross, he
went out to the place of the Skull (which in Aramaic is called
Golgotha). 18Here they crucified him, and with him two others—
one on each side and Jesus in the middle.
19Pilate had a notice prepared and fastened to the cross. It read:
JESUS OF NAZARETH, THE KING OF THE JEWS. 20Many of the Jews read this

What movie or book (such as "Jesus Christ Superstar," "Godspell," or "Jesus of Nazareth") brought home to you most vividly the events of the crucifixion?

1. According to the sign on Jesus' cross, for what "official" reason was he crucified? What meaning does this title have for Pilate (18:33–37)? For the soldiers (19:14–15)? The chief priests (19:14–15)? Is this title being used here sincerely or mockingly? Why is it in all three common languages? **2.** As Jesus may have recited Psalm 22 from the cross (Mt 27:46), how might he have felt as he watched the soldiers take his clothes (vv. 23–24; Ps 22:18)? **3.** Given Jesus' mother's faith in him at the outset of his public ministry (2:3–5), what must she be feeling now at the end? Why is Old Testament prophecy about Jesus' death (Ex 12:46; Zech 12:10) so important in this chapter? **4.** From here and throughout John's Gospel, we see that Jesus' death has special paradoxical meaning: In what sense was Jesus' death necessary, yet voluntary? Triumphant, yet tragic? Pre-ordained, yet avoidable? Lifted up, yet laid down? Unjust, yet just? Finished, yet ongoing?

♡ **1.** If Jesus preached the same Gospel today that he preached in the first century, who might be the "chief priests," the "Peters" and "Pilates"? Who would

sign, for the place where Jesus was crucified was near the city, and
the sign was written in Aramaic, Latin and Greek. 21The chief
priests of the Jews protested to Pilate, "Do not write 'The King of
the Jews,' but that this man claimed to be king of the Jews."
22Pilate answered, "What I have written, I have written."
23When the soldiers crucified Jesus, they took his clothes, dividing them into four shares, one for each of them, with the undergar-
ment remaining. This garment was seamless, woven in one piece
from top to bottom.
24"Let's not tear it," they said to one another. "Let's decide by
lot who will get it."
This happened that the scripture might be fulfilled which said,

"They divided my garments among them
and cast lots for my clothing."[a]

So this is what the soldiers did.
25Near the cross of Jesus stood his mother, his mother's sister,
Mary the wife of Clopas, and Mary Magdalene. 26When Jesus saw
his mother there, and the disciple whom he loved standing nearby,
he said to his mother, "Dear woman, here is your son," 27and to
the disciple, "Here is your mother." From that time on, this disciple took her into his home.

The Death of Jesus

28Later, knowing that all was now completed, and so that the
Scripture would be fulfilled, Jesus said, "I am thirsty." 29A jar of
wine vinegar was there, so they soaked a sponge in it, put the

[a]*24* Psalm 22:18

John 19:16–27 THE CRUCIFIXION

1. Why did the chief priests, who plotted Jesus' crucifixion, protest to Pilate about the sign he fastened to the cross: "Jesus of Nazareth, the King of the Jews"?
   a. The sign was too confusing.
   b. They thought Pilate was mocking them.
   c. The truth hurts.
   d. No matter how they tried, they couldn't escape Jesus' claims.
2. How do you think Jesus felt about the soldiers entertaining themselves by gambling for his clothes?
   a. humiliated
   b. angry
   c. forgiving
   d. too distraught to notice
   e. aware that an Old Testament Scripture was being fulfilled
   f. aware that everything happening was somehow part of God's plan
3. What motivated Jesus to go through with this humiliating death when he could have used his tremendous power to avoid it?
4. What feelings do you think Mary had as she watched her son die?
   a. She was confused.
   b. She really wasn't surprised.
   c. She felt incredible anguish.
   d. She realized Jesus' death was necessary, so she was at peace.
   e. She was angry at the injustice.
5. What feelings do you think Jesus had when he saw his mother?
   a. He was in too much agony to be concerned.
   b. He felt helpless.
   c. He felt compassion for her.
   d. He loved her and wanted to look out for her welfare.
6. Why do you think Jesus charged John ("the disciple whom he loved") with taking care of his mother?
   a. Mary's husband Joseph must have been dead.
   b. Jesus' brothers must not have believed in him yet.
   c. John was Jesus' favorite disciple.
   d. Jesus recognized the importance of a "spiritual family."
7. Can you picture the scene of Jesus' crucifixion? What makes Good Friday "good"? For whom?
8. When, and how, did the crucifixion begin to make a difference in your life? How could you explain the need for Jesus' death to someone who really wanted to understand?
9. What does Jesus entrusting his mother and John to each other say to you about relationships?
   a. Biological family is important to Jesus.
   b. Spiritual family is important to Jesus.
   c. Our relationships with other Christians are indeed *family* relationships.
   d. My spiritual family can help fill the void of my biological family's lack of spiritual commitment.
10. How have the people in this group become a spiritual family for you? How can they continue to support you in prayer?

sponge on a stalk of the hyssop plant, and lifted it to Jesus' lips. 30When he had received the drink, Jesus said, "It is finished." With that, he bowed his head and gave up his spirit.

31Now it was the day of Preparation, and the next day was to be a special Sabbath. Because the Jews did not want the bodies left on the crosses during the Sabbath, they asked Pilate to have the legs broken and the bodies taken down. 32The soldiers therefore came and broke the legs of the first man who had been crucified with Jesus, and then those of the other. 33But when they came to Jesus and found that he was already dead, they did not break his legs. 34Instead, one of the soldiers pierced Jesus' side with a spear, bringing a sudden flow of blood and water. 35The man who saw it has given testimony, and his testimony is true. He knows that he tells the truth, and he testifies so that you also may believe. 36These things happened so that the scripture would be fulfilled: "Not one of his bones will be broken,"[a] 37and, as another scripture says, "They will look on the one they have pierced."[b]

The Burial of Jesus

38Later, Joseph of Arimathea asked Pilate for the body of Jesus. Now Joseph was a disciple of Jesus, but secretly because he feared the Jews. With Pilate's permission, he came and took the body away. 39He was accompanied by Nicodemus, the man who earlier had visited Jesus at night. Nicodemus brought a mixture of myrrh and aloes, about seventy-five pounds.[c] 40Taking Jesus' body, the two of them wrapped it, with the spices, in strips of linen. This was in accordance with Jewish burial customs. 41At the place where Jesus was crucified, there was a garden, and in the garden a new tomb, in which no one had ever been laid. 42Because it was the Jewish day of Preparation and since the tomb was nearby, they laid Jesus there.

The Empty Tomb

20 Early on the first day of the week, while it was still dark, Mary Magdalene went to the tomb and saw that the stone had been removed from the entrance. 2So she came running to Simon Peter and the other disciple, the one Jesus loved, and said, "They have taken the Lord out of the tomb, and we don't know where they have put him!"

3So Peter and the other disciple started for the tomb. 4Both were running, but the other disciple outran Peter and reached the tomb first. 5He bent over and looked in at the strips of linen lying there but did not go in. 6Then Simon Peter, who was behind him, arrived and went into the tomb. He saw the strips of linen lying there, 7as well as the burial cloth that had been around Jesus' head. The cloth was folded up by itself, separate from the linen. 8Finally the other disciple, who had reached the tomb first, also went inside. He saw and believed. 9(They still did not understand from Scripture that Jesus had to rise from the dead.)

Jesus Appears to Mary Magdalene

10Then the disciples went back to their homes, 11but Mary stood outside the tomb crying. As she wept, she bent over to look into the tomb 12and saw two angels in white, seated where Jesus' body had been, one at the head and the other at the foot.

13They asked her, "Woman, why are you crying?"

"They have taken my Lord away," she said, "and I don't know

[a]*36* Exodus 12:46; Num. 9:12; Psalm 34:20 [b]*37* Zech. 12:10 [c]*39* Greek *a hundred litrai* (about 34 kilograms)

you be? **2.** How would you explain the need for the crucifixion to someone else? **3.** How is Jesus' death real to you? How have Jesus' "blood" and "water" touched your life? What would your life be like without them?

What kind of burial would you like: Large? Small? Somber? Boisterous? Where would you prefer to be buried? Why?

1. Why did secret believers, Joseph and Nicodemus, risk public exposure now? **2.** Some say Jesus did not really die, but revived in the tomb. How do 19:1,18,32–34 and 40 disprove this notion?

1. How does your fear of others and your love for Jesus sometimes conflict? **2.** In spite of past failures and fears, what will you do this week to show love for Jesus?

When something upsets you, who is the first one you tell?

1. Put yourself in the place of Mary. What is your emotional state two days after the crucifixion? Why do you visit the tomb so early? Realizing the body is gone, how do you react? **2.** If John was "the other disciple," why did he refer to himself as "the one Jesus loved"?

1. When a loved one dies, how does the resurrection of Jesus help you to deal with your pain? **2.** What is your proof that Jesus rose from the dead?

Describe a time when you mistook someone for the wrong person.

1. Would you have responded more like Mary or like the disciples? Why? **2.** Does Mary appear to be quietly grieving, or more hysterical? What finally breaks through her grief and confusion

(v. 16)? **3.** What term (v. 17) does Jesus use for his disciples here? What is new in their relationship from now on (see 15:15)?

1. How has Jesus spoken your name in a time of grief? How did it affect you? **2.** What does it mean to you that Jesus is your brother?

where they have put him." 14At this, she turned around and saw
Jesus standing there, but she did not realize that it was Jesus.
15"Woman," he said, "why are you crying? Who is it you are
looking for?"
Thinking he was the gardener, she said, "Sir, if you have carried
him away, tell me where you have put him, and I will get him."
16Jesus said to her, "Mary."
She turned toward him and cried out in Aramaic, "Rabboni!"
(which means Teacher).
17Jesus said, "Do not hold on to me, for I have not yet returned
to the Father. Go instead to my brothers and tell them, 'I am
returning to my Father and your Father, to my God and your
God.' "
18Mary Magdalene went to the disciples with the news: "I have
seen the Lord!" And she told them that he had said these things to
her.

Have you ever gone to your room and locked the door? Why?

1. Why are the disciples fearful now? **2.** Of all the things Jesus must have said, why does John record "peace be with you" three times (vv. 19,21,26)? How does this relate to their fears? To their being sent? **3.** How does Thomas' personality compare to Mary's (v. 13)? To the other disci-

Jesus Appears to His Disciples

19On the evening of that first day of the week, when the disciples were together, with the doors locked for fear of the Jews, Jesus
came and stood among them and said, "Peace be with you!" 20After
he said this, he showed them his hands and side. The disciples
were overjoyed when they saw the Lord.
21Again Jesus said, "Peace be with you! As the Father has sent
me, I am sending you." 22And with that he breathed on them and
said, "Receive the Holy Spirit. 23If you forgive anyone his sins, they
are forgiven; if you do not forgive them, they are not forgiven."

John 20:1–18 JESUS APPEARS TO MARY MAGDALENE

Though the other Gospels record that a few women went to the tomb early Easter morning, John's focus is only on Mary Magdalene. One of several women who traveled with Jesus and the disciples, Mary at some point had seven demons cast out of her.

1. What do you think motivated Mary Magdalene to come to the tomb?
   a. grief and loss
   b. curiosity
   c. loneliness
   d. loyalty
   e. love

2. What would you have thought if you were Mary or one of the disciples and saw that the tomb was empty?
   a. Someone had taken Jesus' body.
   b. Jesus had returned to heaven.
   c. Jesus had risen, but was still on earth.

3. What word would you use to describe Mary's behavior until Jesus appeared to her?
   a. confused
   b. hysterical
   c. impulsive
   d. understandable

4. How did Jesus respond to Mary?
   a. He let her cool off.
   b. He calmed her by using her name.
   c. He opened her eyes.
   d. He spoke to her heart.
   e. He restored her hope.

5. Why did Jesus say to Mary, "Do not hold on to me"?
   a. It was not appropriate for her to touch him after his resurrection.
   b. She would have opportunities to see Jesus again.
   c. She had a message to give.
   d. She would "hold on" to him in an even more personal way when he sent the Holy Spirit.

6. What do you think the disciples said when she told them the news: "I have seen the Lord!"?
   a. "Yeah. Sure!"
   b. "It's that woman again."
   c. "Wait a minute—she could be telling the truth."
   d. "Let's submit this report to a committee for further study."
   e. "Let's get moving."

7. How has Jesus spoken your name in a time of grief or trouble? What effect did that have on you?

8. What do you rely on for evidence that Jesus rose from the dead?

9. What is the evidence that Jesus is alive in your life today?

10. Has your life lately been more like the darkness of Good Friday or the joy of Easter? Or somewhere in between? How can this group support you in your spiritual journey?

11. What have been the hardest "goodbyes" in your life? How can the resurrection of Jesus and the comfort of God's Spirit help you deal with that kind of pain and disappointment?

12. How have the people in this group been a Christ-like model for you in dealing with life's challenges? Go around and have each person listen silently while others share their appreciation.

Jesus Appears to Thomas

[24]Now Thomas (called Didymus), one of the Twelve, was not
with the disciples when Jesus came. [25]So the other disciples told
him, "We have seen the Lord!"

But he said to them, "Unless I see the nail marks in his hands and put my finger where the nails were, and put my hand into his side, I will not believe it."

[26]A week later his disciples were in the house again, and Thomas was with them. Though the doors were locked, Jesus came and
stood among them and said, "Peace be with you!" [27]Then he said
to Thomas, "Put your finger here; see my hands. Reach out your hand and put it into my side. Stop doubting and believe."

[28]Thomas said to him, "My Lord and my God!"

[29]Then Jesus told him, "Because you have seen me, you have believed; blessed are those who have not seen and yet have believed."

[30]Jesus did many other miraculous signs in the presence of his
disciples, which are not recorded in this book. [31]But these are
written that you may[a] believe that Jesus is the Christ, the Son of God, and that by believing you may have life in his name.

ples' (vv. 9,19)? **4.** How does Jesus deal with Thomas' doubt (v. 29)? What is significant about the way Thomas responds? How did your first confession of Christ's lordship sound? **5.** What is the author's purpose for writing this Gospel (vv. 30–31; 21:24–25)?

♡ **1.** Where could you use Jesus' "peace" right now: In some relationship? In some inner fear? In your work? **2.** What doubts or questions about God are you struggling with? What have you found helpful in dealing with doubts? **3.** Have you received the gift of the Holy Spirit? How has it changed you?

Jesus and the Miraculous Catch of Fish

21 Afterward Jesus appeared again to his disciples, by the Sea
of Tiberias.[b] It happened this way: [2]Simon Peter, Thomas
(called Didymus), Nathanael from Cana in Galilee, the sons of
Zebedee, and two other disciples were together. [3]"I'm going out to

1. What has been your best fishing, hunting or camping? **2.** What is your favorite food on a cookout?

1. The seven disciples have returned to the Galilee district, about 90 miles from the place

[a]31 Some manuscripts *may continue to*
[b]1 That is, Sea of Galilee

John 20:24–31 — JESUS APPEARS TO THOMAS

1. Why do you think Thomas was not with the rest of the disciples Easter night when Jesus appeared to them?
   a. He was a loner.
   b. He was sorting things out.
   c. He thought it was all over.
   d. He just happened to be in the wrong place at the wrong time.
2. "Unless I see the nail marks in his hands and put my finger where the nails were, and put my hand into his side, I will not believe it." What was Thomas saying?
   a. "You guys are crazy."
   b. "I need proof."
   c. "I want to believe, but ..."
   d. "Don't break my heart again."
3. How did Jesus deal with Thomas?
   a. harshly
   b. tenderly
   c. by waiting until Thomas was ready
   d. with the evidence he asked for
4. What do you suppose happened to Thomas' faith after this?
   a. He learned his lesson, and believed from this point on.
   b. He never did get past his doubts.
   c. Voicing his doubts helped him have a stronger faith than those who never admit such things.
   d. He always felt guilty for doubting, which crippled his faith.
5. What did Jesus mean when he said, "Blessed are those who have not seen and yet have believed"?
   a. "You will be happier if you do not doubt."
   b. "You don't have to see me to believe in me."
   c. "God calls you to be faithful even when you can't see clearly."
   d. "You blew it, Thomas."
6. What do you rely upon for spiritual "proof"?
   a. a feeling of peace
   b. simple faith
   c. what my church teaches
   d. what is logical and makes sense
   e. what the Bible says
   f. what my Christian friends say
7. When you have struggles in your faith, what have you found helpful?
8. When you have spiritual doubts, what does that indicate?
   a. My faith is weak.
   b. I need some more information.
   c. I need a spiritual "checkup."
   d. Growth may be taking place.
9. If you could ask God one question about your struggles, what would it be?
   a. How do I deal with doubt?
   b. What if I don't always feel like a Christian?
   c. Why can't I feel closer to Jesus?
   d. Where is God when I'm hurting?
10. Do you have doubts about being sure you are a Christian? How does it make you feel to know that ...
    a. Jesus invited Thomas to inspect his wounds?
    b. Jesus said those who believe without seeing are "blessed"?
    c. John wrote this so "you may believe that Jesus is the Christ, the Son of God, and that by believing you may have life in his name"?

Jesus was killed and rose again. What might they have discussed on the way? **2.** In fishing all night, using nets, do you think Peter just wanted something to do, or did he return to his old business? **3.** Why did Jesus' followers have difficulty recognizing him after the resurrection? **4.** How would you feel if you had been fishing with the disciples all night? How does Jesus' preparation of breakfast relate to what he did for them in 13:1–17?

1. Where do you go to get away from it all? How does God meet you there? **2.** When was the last time you received a bountiful blessing? Did Jesus get your attention through this blessing?

fish," Simon Peter told them, and they said, "We'll go with you."
So they went out and got into the boat, but that night they caught
nothing.
4Early in the morning, Jesus stood on the shore, but the disciples
did not realize that it was Jesus.
5He called out to them, "Friends, haven't you any fish?"
"No," they answered.
6He said, "Throw your net on the right side of the boat and you
will find some." When they did, they were unable to haul the net
in because of the large number of fish.
7Then the disciple whom Jesus loved said to Peter, "It is the
Lord!" As soon as Simon Peter heard him say, "It is the Lord," he
wrapped his outer garment around him (for he had taken it off) and
jumped into the water. 8The other disciples followed in the boat,
towing the net full of fish, for they were not far from shore, about
a hundred yards.[a] 9When they landed, they saw a fire of burning
coals there with fish on it, and some bread.
10Jesus said to them, "Bring some of the fish you have just
caught."
11Simon Peter climbed aboard and dragged the net ashore. It was
full of large fish, 153, but even with so many the net was not torn.
12Jesus said to them, "Come and have breakfast." None of the
disciples dared ask him, "Who are you?" They knew it was the
Lord. 13Jesus came, took the bread and gave it to them, and did
the same with the fish. 14This was now the third time Jesus appeared to his disciples after he was raised from the dead.

[a]8 Greek *about two hundred cubits* (about 90 meters)

John 21:1–25 JESUS REINSTATES PETER

1. Why do you think Peter and the other disciples went back to Peter's home territory of Galilee?
   a. to relax and do some fishing
   b. to go back to their old occupation
   c. to put their lives back together
   d. to forget about Jesus
   e. to obey Jesus' instructions to go to Galilee and wait for him there

2. Why did Jesus provide a miraculous catch of fish and then make breakfast for the disciples?
   a. to remind them of the miraculous catch of fish that first got them "hooked" as disciples
   b. to assure them they were still called to be "fishers of men"
   c. to show, by eating with them, that he forgave them for failing him
   d. to remind them of the significance of the Last Supper

3. Why do you think Jesus pressed Peter three times with the question, "Do you love me?"
   a. to get Peter's attention
   b. to shame Peter for denying Jesus three times
   c. to make Peter face his failure
   d. to show Peter he had forgiven him
   e. to be sure Peter accepted his love

4. If you had been Peter, how would you have felt by the end of the third question?
   a. angry
   b. hurt
   c. guilty
   d. humiliated
   e. healed
   f. frustrated

5. "Feed my lambs ... Take care of my sheep ... Feed my sheep." What was Jesus saying to Peter?
   a. You would make a better shepherd than fisherman.
   b. Your job is caring for my followers.
   c. Prove that you love me.
   d. I'm still counting on you.
   e. Don't blow it again.
   f. Lay down your life for people—like I did.

6. What is the closest you have come to going back on your promise to follow Jesus? What did you discover about God through that experience? What did you discover about yourself?

7. If Jesus said to you, "Take care of my sheep"—what would he mean?
   a. Pick yourself up and get going.
   b. I need you to carry on my work.
   c. Get your eyes off of yourself.
   d. Do something about others' needs.
   e. Use your gifts.

8. What evidence is there in your life that you truly love Jesus?
   a. I want to spend time with him.
   b. Scripture has come alive to me.
   c. I want to go to church/small group.
   d. It's easier to show love to others.
   e. His joy has been my strength.
   f. My concern for others has grown.
   g. I want to share my faith.

9. What has caused you to want to return to God?
   a. healing from a hurt
   b. the influence of my Christian friends/family
   c. taking time to pray
   d. getting back into Scripture
   e. a desire for my family to be active in the church
   f. a mysterious yearning in my heart
   g. other:__________________

Jesus Reinstates Peter

15 When they had finished eating, Jesus said to Simon Peter,
"Simon son of John, do you truly love me more than these?"
"Yes, Lord," he said, "you know that I love you."
Jesus said, "Feed my lambs."
16 Again Jesus said, "Simon son of John, do you truly love me?"
He answered, "Yes, Lord, you know that I love you."
Jesus said, "Take care of my sheep."
17 The third time he said to him, "Simon son of John, do you
love me?"
Peter was hurt because Jesus asked him the third time, "Do you
love me?" He said, "Lord, you know all things; you know that I
love you."
Jesus said, "Feed my sheep. 18 I tell you the truth, when you
were younger you dressed yourself and went where you wanted;
but when you are old you will stretch out your hands, and someone
else will dress you and lead you where you do not want to go."
19 Jesus said this to indicate the kind of death by which Peter would
glorify God. Then he said to him, "Follow me!"
20 Peter turned and saw that the disciple whom Jesus loved was
following them. (This was the one who had leaned back against
Jesus at the supper and had said, "Lord, who is going to betray
you?") 21 When Peter saw him, he asked, "Lord, what about him?"
22 Jesus answered, "If I want him to remain alive until I return,
what is that to you? You must follow me." 23 Because of this, the
rumor spread among the brothers that this disciple would not die.
But Jesus did not say that he would not die; he only said, "If I want
him to remain alive until I return, what is that to you?"
24 This is the disciple who testifies to these things and who wrote
them down. We know that his testimony is true.
25 Jesus did many other things as well. If every one of them were
written down, I suppose that even the whole world would not have
room for the books that would be written.

1. Have you ever been kicked off the team, out of the club, out of the house or out of school? Why? **2.** Who was expected to do the most chores around your house when you were a kid? Who got off the easiest?

1. Why do you think Jesus repeated the same question and charge to Peter three times? How is Peter supposed to demonstrate his love and loyalty to Jesus now? In light of 10:15, what would Jesus' shepherd image mean to Peter? **2.** What does Jesus mean by his prediction in verse 18? Why did Peter ask about John? **3.** What is the crucial issue revealed in Jesus' response to Peter (v. 22)? How is this linked with verses 15–17?

1. What is the closest you have come to blowing it so badly that you thought God was never going to speak to you again? What did you discover about God in that experience? **2.** When have you compared yourself with someone else and wondered why his or her life was the way it was? How did that affect your desire to do what you were supposed to do? **3.** Whom do you know who needs to feel forgiven by God? What will you do to tell them they are forgiven? **4.** If you were writing a book about Jesus' work in your life, what would be some of the chapter titles? **5.** What has been brought to light for you through studying John's Gospel?

INTRODUCTION to

ACTS

Book Study Outline: If you are using Acts for a study course, here is a 7- or 13-week outline. Use the margin questions for your group agenda:

start meeting / 15 min.

read & discuss Bible / 30 min.

close meeting / 15–45 min.

Refer to the Questions and Answers in front of Bible for more information.

7-week plan	13-week plan	Personal Reading	Group Study Passage
	1	1:1–26	1:1–11/Jesus Taken
1	2	2:1–41	2:1–24,36–41/Pentecost
2	3	2:42–3:26	2:42–47/Fellowship
	4	4:1–37	4:1–31/Before Sanhedrin
3	5	5:1–8:25	5:1–11/Ananias and Sapphira
	6	8:26–40	8:26–40/The Ethiopian
4	7	9:1–43	9:1–19/Saul's Conversion
5	8	10:1–11:30	10:1–23/Peter's Vision
	9	12:1–16:15	12:1–19/Peter's Escape
6	10	16:16–17:34	16:16–40/In Prison
	11	18:1–21:36	18:5–17/Paul's Vision
	12	21:37–25:27	21:37–22:29/Paul Speaks
7	13	26:1–28:30	26:1–32/Before Agrippa

Author: The writer is unknown; however, because of the "we" passages (e.g., 16:10–17) it seems likely that the author is Luke, the physician who joined Paul on some of his journeys.

Date: The final events recorded here took place in early A.D. 60, so Acts must have been compiled some time after that.

Theme: The spread of the Gospel to all the known world (1:8).

Historical Background: In 30 short years, the church grew from what was considered an insignificant Jewish sect to a major force in the Roman Empire. Luke wrote Acts as a companion piece to his Gospel to show how Christianity was *not* a political threat to Rome, but rather the work of God's Spirit in building up a spiritual "kingdom," one comprised of all who live by faith in Jesus. Luke does this by focusing on the two leading figures in the church: Peter, the apostle to the Jews (ch. 1–12), and Paul, the apostle to the Gentiles (ch. 13–28).

Characteristics: The theme of Acts is defined in 1:8. Luke records the growth of the church in Jerusalem and Judea (1:1–6:7), Galilee and Samaria (6:8–9:31), Antioch, which became a missionary launching pad to the Gentile world (9:32–12:24), Asia (12:25–16:5), Europe (16:6–19:20), and Rome (19:21–28:31). Luke centers in on Paul. By doing so, he affirms Paul's authority as an apostle, as well as his innocence of the charges brought against him. Acts provides essential background information about the churches Paul founded and to whom he wrote his epistles.

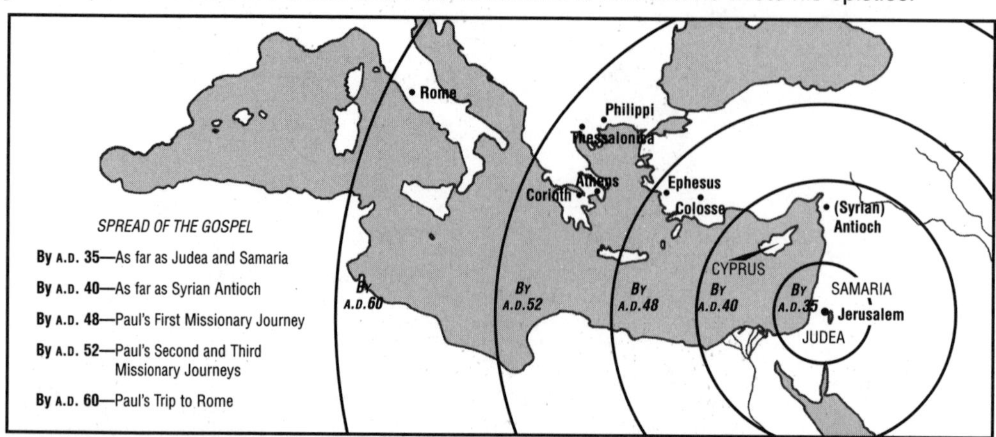

Acts

Jesus Taken Up Into Heaven

1 In my former book, Theophilus, I wrote about all that Jesus
began to do and to teach 2until the day he was taken up to
heaven, after giving instructions through the Holy Spirit to the
apostles he had chosen. 3After his suffering, he showed himself to
these men and gave many convincing proofs that he was alive. He
appeared to them over a period of forty days and spoke about the
kingdom of God. 4On one occasion, while he was eating with
them, he gave them this command: "Do not leave Jerusalem, but
wait for the gift my Father promised, which you have heard me
speak about. 5For John baptized with[a] water, but in a few days
you will be baptized with the Holy Spirit."

6So when they met together, they asked him, "Lord, are you at
this time going to restore the kingdom to Israel?"

7He said to them: "It is not for you to know the times or dates
the Father has set by his own authority. 8But you will receive
power when the Holy Spirit comes on you; and you will be my
witnesses in Jerusalem, and in all Judea and Samaria, and to the
ends of the earth."

9After he said this, he was taken up before their very eyes, and
a cloud hid him from their sight.

Who would you want to write the biography of your life? Why that person? What does this person know about you that you would like your group to know?

1. How does this book pick up where Luke 24:45–53 leaves off? **2.** What do the disciples think will happen when they receive the Holy Spirit (v. 6)? How does their idea of the kingdom differ from Jesus' (vv. 7–8)? **3.** As a disciple, what is the impact on you of Jesus' words (v. 8)? Of Jesus' departure (v. 9)? Of the angels' promise (v. 11)?

1. How would you explain the effects of the Resurrection to your non-believing friends? **2.** To which "Jerusalem" are you called to bear witness? How do you need the Spirit to help you?

[a]5 Or *in*

Acts 1:1–11 JESUS TAKEN UP INTO HEAVEN

1. How do you think the disciples felt about Jesus leaving them?
   a. terrified
   b. confused
   c. excited about what was ahead
   d. abandoned
   e. angry

2. What would you call Jesus' ascension to heaven?
   a. sad—the end of his ministry
   b. hopeful—the start of a new phase of his ministry
   c. glorious—He will return!

3. What chance would you have given the followers of Jesus at this point to change the world?
   a. a lot
   b. some
   c. a little
   d. none

4. Why do you think Jesus insisted his followers wait in Jerusalem?
   a. They needed mutual support.
   b. They couldn't make it without the Holy Spirit.
   c. They needed to help each other understand what was going on.
   d. They needed to develop a strategy for spreading the message.

5. What do you think the disciples did during the 10 days of waiting for the Holy Spirit to come?
   a. grieved over the loss of Jesus
   b. praised God with much joy
   c. talked about their mixed-up feelings and encouraged each other
   d. recalled Jesus' teachings and tried to understand what was going on
   e. sat in silence—waiting for something to happen

6. What do you see as the key point of this passage?
   a. God's kingdom isn't a matter of one people's destiny (including Israel's), but a spiritual realm involving the whole world.
   b. Jesus will return, but don't stand around waiting for him.
   c. Jesus continues his mission and ministry through his followers.
   d. The power of the Holy Spirit is crucial to every Christian's life.
   e. Following Jesus and relying on the Spirit leads to both Christian community and evangelism.

7. How was the disciples' idea of the kingdom of God different than Jesus'? When have you been confused about God's plans or ways?

8. What proof do you have of Jesus' resurrection that would make sense to unbelievers? What holds you back from spreading the word about Jesus to them?
   a. lack of knowledge
   b. lack of concern
   c. lack of unbelieving family/friends
   d. lack of courage
   e. nothing—I'm doing it!

9. Where are you called to be Christ's witness? How do you sense a need for the Holy Spirit to help you?

10. How has this course and this group been a witness and testimony to you of God's love, Christ's presence and the Holy Spirit's power? Have one person at a time listen silently while others share how they appreciate him or her.

10They were looking intently up into the sky as he was going, when suddenly two men dressed in white stood beside them. 11"Men of Galilee," they said, "why do you stand here looking into the sky? This same Jesus, who has been taken from you into heaven, will come back in the same way you have seen him go into heaven."

Matthias Chosen to Replace Judas

12Then they returned to Jerusalem from the hill called the Mount of Olives, a Sabbath day's walk[a] from the city. 13When they arrived, they went upstairs to the room where they were staying. Those present were Peter, John, James and Andrew; Philip and Thomas, Bartholomew and Matthew; James son of Alphaeus and Simon the Zealot, and Judas son of James. 14They all joined together constantly in prayer, along with the women and Mary the mother of Jesus, and with his brothers.

15In those days Peter stood up among the believers[b] (a group numbering about a hundred and twenty) 16and said, "Brothers, the Scripture had to be fulfilled which the Holy Spirit spoke long ago through the mouth of David concerning Judas, who served as guide for those who arrested Jesus— 17he was one of our number and shared in this ministry."

18(With the reward he got for his wickedness, Judas bought a field; there he fell headlong, his body burst open and all his intestines spilled out. 19Everyone in Jerusalem heard about this, so they called that field in their language Akeldama, that is, Field of Blood.)

20"For," said Peter, "it is written in the book of Psalms,

> " 'May his place be deserted;
> let there be no one to dwell in it,'[c]

and,

> " 'May another take his place of leadership.'[d]

21Therefore it is necessary to choose one of the men who have been with us the whole time the Lord Jesus went in and out among us, 22beginning from John's baptism to the time when Jesus was taken up from us. For one of these must become a witness with us of his resurrection."

23So they proposed two men: Joseph called Barsabbas (also known as Justus) and Matthias. 24Then they prayed, "Lord, you know everyone's heart. Show us which of these two you have chosen 25to take over this apostolic ministry, which Judas left to go where he belongs." 26Then they cast lots, and the lot fell to Matthias; so he was added to the eleven apostles.

The Holy Spirit Comes at Pentecost

2 When the day of Pentecost came, they were all together in one place. 2Suddenly a sound like the blowing of a violent wind came from heaven and filled the whole house where they were sitting. 3They saw what seemed to be tongues of fire that separated and came to rest on each of them. 4All of them were filled with the Holy Spirit and began to speak in other tongues[e] as the Spirit enabled them.

5Now there were staying in Jerusalem God-fearing Jews from every nation under heaven. 6When they heard this sound, a crowd came together in bewilderment, because each one heard them speaking in his own language. 7Utterly amazed, they asked: "Are

[a] *12* That is, about 3/4 mile (about 1,100 meters) [b] *15* Greek *brothers*
[c] *20* Psalm 69:25 [d] *20* Psalm 109:8 [e] *4* Or *languages*; also in verse 11

What was your favorite board game as a child? Did it involve luck of the draw, taking risks or strategy? Which is your favorite game now, and why?

1. Who was present at this meeting? From Mark 3:20–21,31–35 and John 7:1–5, how do you account for this change in Jesus' "family"? Why weren't "the women" mentioned by name? **2.** In light of Peter's denial of Jesus, how might the others feel about his leadership? How would the events of John 21:15–19 calm any fears they have? **3.** Given verses 6–8, how would you be praying if you were in this group? What emotions would you express? **4.** What was the role of Scripture, prayer, discussion, qualifications, and trust in God when the disciples selected a replacement for Judas?

1. What have been your best experiences in group prayer? How is praying with others for a common mission (one that is beyond your natural ability) different from private prayer about your individual concerns? **2.** How does the pattern of decision-making here compare with the way you, your family or your church make important decisions? Which of the ingredients listed here do you need to utilize more?

Have you ever traveled where you did not speak the language? What happened?

1. Why did God wait until Pentecost, a Jewish harvest festival (Dt 16:9–10) to give the Holy Spirit? **2.** How far have these pilgrims come (vv. 9–11)? What attracts them to the disciples? How does being filled with the Spirit relate to bearing witness to Jesus?

1. Would you respond more like those in verse 12, or those in verse 13? Why? **2.** Have you ever seen the gift of tongues

not all these men who are speaking Galileans? [8]Then how is it that
each of us hears them in his own native language? [9]Parthians,
Medes and Elamites; residents of Mesopotamia, Judea and Cappadocia, Pontus and Asia, [10]Phrygia and Pamphylia, Egypt and the
parts of Libya near Cyrene; visitors from Rome [11](both Jews and
converts to Judaism); Cretans and Arabs—we hear them declaring
the wonders of God in our own tongues!" [12]Amazed and perplexed, they asked one another, "What does this mean?"
[13]Some, however, made fun of them and said, "They have had
too much wine.[a]"

Peter Addresses the Crowd

[14]Then Peter stood up with the Eleven, raised his voice and
addressed the crowd: "Fellow Jews and all of you who live in
Jerusalem, let me explain this to you; listen carefully to what I say.
[15]These men are not drunk, as you suppose. It's only nine in the
morning! [16]No, this is what was spoken by the prophet Joel:

[17]" 'In the last days, God says,
I will pour out my Spirit on all people.
Your sons and daughters will prophesy,
your young men will see visions,
your old men will dream dreams.
[18]Even on my servants, both men and women,
I will pour out my Spirit in those days,
and they will prophesy.
[19]I will show wonders in the heaven above
and signs on the earth below,
blood and fire and billows of smoke.
[20]The sun will be turned to darkness
and the moon to blood
before the coming of the great and glorious day
of the Lord.
[21]And everyone who calls
on the name of the Lord will be saved.'[b]

[22]"Men of Israel, listen to this: Jesus of Nazareth was a man
accredited by God to you by miracles, wonders and signs, which
God did among you through him, as you yourselves know. [23]This
man was handed over to you by God's set purpose and foreknowledge; and you, with the help of wicked men,[c] put him to death by
nailing him to the cross. [24]But God raised him from the dead,
freeing him from the agony of death, because it was impossible for
death to keep its hold on him. [25]David said about him:

" 'I saw the Lord always before me.
Because he is at my right hand,
I will not be shaken.
[26]Therefore my heart is glad and my tongue
rejoices;
my body also will live in hope,
[27]because you will not abandon me to the grave,
nor will you let your Holy One see decay.
[28]You have made known to me the paths of life;
you will fill me with joy in your presence.'[d]

[29]"Brothers, I can tell you confidently that the patriarch David
died and was buried, and his tomb is here to this day. [30]But he was
a prophet and knew that God had promised him on oath that he

[a]*13* Or *sweet wine* [b]*21* Joel 2:28-32 [c]*23* Or *of those not having the law* (that is, Gentiles) [d]*28* Psalm 16:8-11

used this way? Another way? **3.** When have you experienced an empowering from God to witness about Christ?

What are you usually doing at 9:00 in the morning on a Saturday? On Sunday? On a weekday?

1. Compare Peter and the other disciples in John 18:25–27 and 20:19 with their actions here: What accounts for the great difference? **2.** In what way is Luke 24:44–49 reflected in this sermon? Given the audience, why would Peter quote from the Old Testament? **3.** What is the point Peter wants the people to understand about current events (vv. 15, 17–18)? How do you understand verses 19–21? What tells you Joel's prophecy is coming true now? **4.** How familiar were these people with the events of Jesus' life? How might they be dealing with the rumors of the empty tomb? Given that, why does Peter emphasize the resurrection (vv. 24, 31–32)? **5.** What are the implications of the resurrection and ascension for Jesus (vv. 24,30–31,33–36)? For the people? What would it mean to the people that Jesus is a spiritual King far greater than their greatest earthly king (vv. 35–36)? **6.** How would you put Peter's answer (vv. 38–40) in your own words to explain what it means to become a Christian? What is required? What is promised? **7.** How does the resurrection prove that Jesus is the Messiah? Remembering where these 3,000 came from (vv. 8–11), in what way is 1:8 partially fulfilled here? What news will the people bring home with them?

1. To repent and be baptized in Jesus' name means to turn away from all your sin and affirm allegiance to Jesus. Does that present a challenge to you? How have you experienced the reality of God's promises for answering his call? **2.** From Peter's sermon, what facts about Jesus would be key for non-believers to understand (vv. 29–33)? **3.** When did you make your initial commitment to Christ?

Who was influential in that process? What convinced you of your need for Christ? **4.** What difference does it make that Jesus truly is the reigning King over all? How does that truth affect your daily life? **5.** When was the last time you seized an opportunity to witness for Jesus? What happened? Who stood with you at that time? How are you like Peter? Unlike him? What encourages you as you watch Peter? Why?

would place one of his descendants on his throne. 31Seeing what
was ahead, he spoke of the resurrection of the Christ,[a] that he
was not abandoned to the grave, nor did his body see decay. 32God
has raised this Jesus to life, and we are all witnesses of the fact.
33Exalted to the right hand of God, he has received from the Father
the promised Holy Spirit and has poured out what you now see and
hear. 34For David did not ascend to heaven, and yet he said,

> " 'The Lord said to my Lord:
> "Sit at my right hand
> 35until I make your enemies
> a footstool for your feet." '[b]

36"Therefore let all Israel be assured of this: God has made this
Jesus, whom you crucified, both Lord and Christ."
37When the people heard this, they were cut to the heart and
said to Peter and the other apostles, "Brothers, what shall we do?"
38Peter replied, "Repent and be baptized, every one of you, in
the name of Jesus Christ for the forgiveness of your sins. And you
will receive the gift of the Holy Spirit. 39The promise is for you and
your children and for all who are far off—for all whom the Lord
our God will call."
40With many other words he warned them; and he pleaded with
them, "Save yourselves from this corrupt generation." 41Those who
accepted his message were baptized, and about three thousand
were added to their number that day.

[a]*31* Or *Messiah.* "The Christ" (Greek) and "the Messiah" (Hebrew) both mean "the Anointed One"; also in verse 36. [b]*35* Psalm 110:1

Acts 2:1–24,36–41 THE HOLY SPIRIT COMES AT PENTECOST

1. What would you say was the most impressive evidence of the Holy Spirit on the day of Pentecost?
   a. the sudden, mysterious wind
   b. the tongues of fire that came to rest on each of them
   c. the believers all speaking in unknown tongues or languages
   d. the crowd hearing the disciples declaring the wonders of God in their own languages
   e. the giving of prophecies, visions and dreams to all God's people
   f. the response—3,000 converts

2. If you had been there that day, what would have been your strongest feeling afterward?
   a. That was a once-in-a-lifetime experience.
   b. I hope that wasn't a once-in-a-lifetime experience.
   c. If the Spirit is that powerful, there isn't any problem I can't face.
   d. Give us five days and we'll take the world!
   e. I'm keeping quiet about this—people will think I'm crazy.

3. Why did God pour out the gift of the Holy Spirit upon Jesus' followers?
   a. to bless them with a spiritual high
   b. to empower them to be witnesses
   c. to serve as a miraculous sign to draw others
   d. to get the Christian church off to an explosive start

4. What do the wind and fire, symbolic of the Holy Spirit, suggest to you most strongly?
   a. unpredictability—Like wind and fire, you cannot always predict what God will do.
   b. power—The forces of wind and fire remind us of the Spirit's power.
   c. invisibility—Like the wind and the heat of a fire, you cannot always see the Spirit at work.
   d. change—As wind brings change, the Spirit changes the world.
   e. warmth—As fire brings warmth, the Spirit brings loving warmth.

5. From Peter's message to the crowd, especially his conclusion (vv. 36–39), how would you explain to someone what it means to become a Christian?

6. What preacher or teacher has God used to draw you to Jesus?

7. Compared to the experience of the disciples on the day of Pentecost, how would you describe your initial experience with the Holy Spirit?
   a. rather tame
   b. similar to theirs
   c. quite different, but just as real
   d. something I can't explain

8. How would you describe your experience with the Holy Spirit now?
   a. on fire
   b. up in the air
   c. gone with the wind

9. When have you experienced an empowering from the Holy Spirit to witness about Christ? What are you going to do to be better prepared for God's use?

10. To help add to *your* number, whom can you invite to this group?

The Fellowship of the Believers

42They devoted themselves to the apostles' teaching and to the
fellowship, to the breaking of bread and to prayer. 43Everyone was
filled with awe, and many wonders and miraculous signs were
done by the apostles. 44All the believers were together and had
everything in common. 45Selling their possessions and goods, they
gave to anyone as he had need. 46Every day they continued to meet
together in the temple courts. They broke bread in their homes
and ate together with glad and sincere hearts, 47praising God and
enjoying the favor of all the people. And the Lord added to their
number daily those who were being saved.

What do you devote yourself to *daily*? Anything that would pass for a daily devotion?

What did these 3,000 converts end up doing (vv. 42–47)? How is God with them?

How is your church fellowship like and unlike the fellowship here? How could you help your church be more like this? How will this example affect how you get involved in your church?

Peter Heals the Crippled Beggar

3 One day Peter and John were going up to the temple at the
time of prayer—at three in the afternoon. 2Now a man crippled from birth was being carried to the temple gate called Beautiful, where he was put every day to beg from those going into the
temple courts. 3When he saw Peter and John about to enter, he
asked them for money. 4Peter looked straight at him, as did John.
Then Peter said, "Look at us!" 5So the man gave them his attention, expecting to get something from them.
6Then Peter said, "Silver or gold I do not have, but what I have
I give you. In the name of Jesus Christ of Nazareth, walk." 7Taking
him by the right hand, he helped him up, and instantly the man's
feet and ankles became strong. 8He jumped to his feet and began to
walk. Then he went with them into the temple courts, walking and
jumping, and praising God. 9When all the people saw him walking
and praising God, 10they recognized him as the same man who

Describe a time when you found yourself without money.

1. As the cripple, what would you write as a diary entry for a typical day? When Peter grabs your hand? After the healing? **2.** How does this miracle relate to 2:19 and 2:22?

1. How is Jesus healing some crippled area of your life? **2.** Would you do the same thing as Peter did, or would you ask John for a dime? Why? Could God heal through you? Why or why not?

Acts 2:42–47 THE FELLOWSHIP OF THE BELIEVERS

As a result of the coming of the Holy Spirit on the day of Pentecost, the fellowship of believers described in this passage had grown by about 3,000.

1. Why do you think all these people got together every day?
   a. They loved to eat.
   b. They were excited about their new life and wanted to talk about it.
   c. They had a lot of needs.
   d. They had a lot to learn.
   e. They had nothing else to do.

2. What do you think the atmosphere was like when they got together?
   a. chaotic
   b. fun
   c. boring
   d. caring
   e. life-changing
   f. exciting
   g. claustrophobic
   h. unpredictable

3. What made the early church so appealing to others?
   a. their spiritual vitality
   b. their amazing love for each other
   c. their openness to others
   d. miracles
   e. great preaching from the pulpit
   f. advertising

4. Why do you think the Christian community today does not have the early church's depth of relationships?
   a. We don't have time.
   b. We don't know each other.
   c. We don't want to know each other's needs.
   d. It's not okay to have needs.
   e. Our culture is so different.
   f. Caring for one another is not on the church's agenda.

5. On a scale of 1 to 10, how would you rate your small group (and your church) on the following qualities?
   a. spiritual commitment and growth
   b. spiritual healing
   c. caring for one another materially
   d. intimate fellowship
   e. faithfulness in prayer and worship
   f. reaching out/growing in numbers

6. What aspect of the spiritual life and energy found in the early church do you most desire for yourself? For your small group? For your church? How will this example in Acts affect the way you pray?

7. As a single person, what are your two biggest needs?
   a. loneliness
   b. not feeling like a person of worth
   c. sexual frustrations/anxieties
   d. financial problems
   e. single parenting stresses
   f. healing from past relationships
   g. not fitting into the church
   h. lack of someone supportive to communicate with about my needs
   i. other:________________

8. How could a fellowship of believers like that found in this passage make a difference for singles like yourself? What can you do to help your Christian community be more like the early church?

9. How regularly do you go to church as a family? What is the *most* and *least* positive aspect of your family's church involvement?

10. What can you as a parent do to make your family's church experience—and your children's feelings about it—better?

used to sit begging at the temple gate called Beautiful, and they were filled with wonder and amazement at what had happened to him.

Peter Speaks to the Onlookers

11While the beggar held on to Peter and John, all the people were astonished and came running to them in the place called Solomon's Colonnade. 12When Peter saw this, he said to them: "Men of Israel, why does this surprise you? Why do you stare at us as if by our own power or godliness we had made this man walk? 13The God of Abraham, Isaac and Jacob, the God of our fathers, has glorified his servant Jesus. You handed him over to be killed, and you disowned him before Pilate, though he had decided to let him go. 14You disowned the Holy and Righteous One and asked that a murderer be released to you. 15You killed the author of life, but God raised him from the dead. We are witnesses of this. 16By faith in the name of Jesus, this man whom you see and know was made strong. It is Jesus' name and the faith that comes through him that has given this complete healing to him, as you can all see.

17"Now, brothers, I know that you acted in ignorance, as did your leaders. 18But this is how God fulfilled what he had foretold through all the prophets, saying that his Christ[a] would suffer. 19Repent, then, and turn to God, so that your sins may be wiped out, that times of refreshing may come from the Lord, 20and that he may send the Christ, who has been appointed for you—even Jesus. 21He must remain in heaven until the time comes for God to restore everything, as he promised long ago through his holy prophets. 22For Moses said, 'The Lord your God will raise up for you a prophet like me from among your own people; you must listen to everything he tells you. 23Anyone who does not listen to him will be completely cut off from among his people.'[b]

24"Indeed, all the prophets from Samuel on, as many as have spoken, have foretold these days. 25And you are heirs of the prophets and of the covenant God made with your fathers. He said to Abraham, 'Through your offspring all peoples on earth will be blessed.'[c] 26When God raised up his servant, he sent him first to you to bless you by turning each of you from your wicked ways."

Peter and John Before the Sanhedrin

4 The priests and the captain of the temple guard and the Sadducees came up to Peter and John while they were speaking to the people. 2They were greatly disturbed because the apostles were teaching the people and proclaiming in Jesus the resurrection of the dead. 3They seized Peter and John, and because it was evening, they put them in jail until the next day. 4But many who heard the message believed, and the number of men grew to about five thousand.

5The next day the rulers, elders and teachers of the law met in Jerusalem. 6Annas the high priest was there, and so were Caiaphas, John, Alexander and the other men of the high priest's family. 7They had Peter and John brought before them and began to question them: "By what power or what name did you do this?"

8Then Peter, filled with the Holy Spirit, said to them: "Rulers and elders of the people! 9If we are being called to account today for an act of kindness shown to a cripple and are asked how he was healed, 10then know this, you and all the people of Israel: It is by the name of Jesus Christ of Nazareth, whom you crucified but

---

What refreshes you the most? A cool shower? A swim? A glass of lemonade? A massage? Air conditioning?

1. How is this situation like the one in 2:1–12? **2.** List all the facts about Jesus which Peter mentions here (vv. 13–16). How does this profile of Jesus compare with the one in 2:22–24? **3.** Restate verse 16 in your own words. **4.** What does Peter say about the people? How would you feel being accused: "You killed . . ." (v. 15)? **5.** From Peter's second recorded sermon, how would you sum up what it means to become a Christian? **6.** Despite what Peter says about them (vv. 13–15), how does he give the people hope in verses 24–26? How are "blessing" and "turning" related?

1. When is it proper to come on strong against a person's sin, like Peter did in verses 13–15? In coming to Christ, did you need to be hit over the head with your sin first? **2.** What does Peter's use of the OT indicate about its benefits to your faith in Christ? How can you start to increase your knowledge of it? **3.** How has repentance and turning to God brought "times of refreshing" (v. 19) to you? How can that be used as a means of encouraging others to come to Christ? **4.** What does Jesus as "the author of life" (v. 15) mean to you?

Describe a time when you felt right about breaking the rules.

1. What roles did the priest, captain of the guard and the Sadducees play in the ministry of Jesus (see Lk 20:27–40; 22:6,52)? Why would the Sadducees oppose the disciples' preaching (v. 2)? What would you feel if you were one of the believers who saw Peter and John taken away? If you were Peter or John? **2.** What is the high priest's family trying to do (v. 7)—seek information or intimidate the disciples? Why (see v. 2; 3:16)? **3.** If you were one of the authorities, what would be your reaction to Peter's bold answer? How does Peter "filled with the Holy Spirit" (vv. 8–12) compare with the purpose of the filling in 2:4 (see also Lk

---

[a] *18* Or *Messiah*; also in verse 20 [b] *23* Deut. 18:15,18,19 [c] *25* Gen. 22:18; 26:4

whom God raised from the dead, that this man stands before you
healed. 11He is

> " 'the stone you builders rejected,
> which has become the capstone.'[a][b]

12Salvation is found in no one else, for there is no other name
under heaven given to men by which we must be saved."
13When they saw the courage of Peter and John and realized
that they were unschooled, ordinary men, they were astonished
and they took note that these men had been with Jesus. 14But
since they could see the man who had been healed standing there
with them, there was nothing they could say. 15So they ordered
them to withdraw from the Sanhedrin and then conferred together. 16"What are we going to do with these men?" they asked.
"Everybody living in Jerusalem knows they have done an outstanding miracle, and we cannot deny it. 17But to stop this thing
from spreading any further among the people, we must warn these
men to speak no longer to anyone in this name."
18Then they called them in again and commanded them not to
speak or teach at all in the name of Jesus. 19But Peter and John
replied, "Judge for yourselves whether it is right in God's sight to
obey you rather than God. 20For we cannot help speaking about
what we have seen and heard."
21After further threats they let them go. They could not decide
how to punish them, because all the people were praising God for
what had happened. 22For the man who was miraculously healed
was over forty years old.

21:12–13)? **4.** How is the leader's response similar to their response to the Lazarus episode (see Jn 11:45–53; 12:10–11)? Why are they reacting like this?

♡ **1.** When, if ever, do you feel that Peter's response to his political and religious leaders would be appropriate for a Christian today? How do you reconcile this passage (vv. 18–21) with Romans 13:1–4? **2.** What is the most persecution you have experienced due to your faith? How did you take it? **3.** On a scale of 1 (low) to 10 (high), how sure are you of Peter's statement in verse 12? What has built your assurance the most? What doubts still linger? **4.** How has knowing Jesus shaped your character"?

[a]11 Or *cornerstone* [b]11 Psalm 118:22

Acts 4:1–31 PETER AND JOHN BEFORE THE SANHEDRIN

When the Holy Spirit came upon the disciples on the day of Pentecost they were empowered to be witnesses for Jesus, their risen Lord. On their way to the temple, Peter and John brought healing in the name of Jesus to a man who had been crippled from birth. As a result, Peter was able to proclaim the Gospel to the crowd that gathered.

1. Why did the religious leaders object to Peter and John's preaching?
   a. They were mad that these uneducated laymen taught in the temple.
   b. This Jesus business was getting out of hand.
   c. They were jealous.
   d. They didn't accept Jesus' followers any more than they did Jesus.
2. If you were Peter or John, how would you have felt when you got thrown into jail?
   a. This reminds me too much of what happened to Jesus.
   b. Help! Somebody please help me!
   c. I'm not surprised—Jesus said we would be persecuted.
   d. What an honor to suffer for Jesus.
3. What impresses you about the believers' prayer (and how can you apply it to your prayer life)?
   a. their faith that God was in control
   b. their desire for boldness in spite of persecution
   c. their confidence in God's power to do miracles
   d. the results—the place shaken and the believers filled with the Spirit
4. Under what circumstances should a Christian disobey civil or religious authorities? Have you ever done so?
5. How strongly do you believe "salvation is found in no one" but Jesus? How do you see the claim to his exclusive role challenged today? If Jesus is the only means of salvation, what does that mean for our mission?
6. When are you most aware of the Holy Spirit?
   a. reading Scripture
   b. worshiping or praying with others
   c. sharing in a group like this
   d. when I am alone with God
   e. when I am spiritually desperate
7. In what way do you most need the power of the Holy Spirit?
   a. for my shyness about witnessing
   b. for the heat I take as a Christian
   c. to pray more effectively
   d. to believe that I can change
   e. to empower me to make a difference in the world
   f. to face my fear of __________
   g. other:________________
8. From this story, what aspect about the Holy Spirit is most striking to you?
   a. how personal the Spirit is—"They were all filled with the Holy Spirit."
   b. how inspiring the Spirit is—They became so bold and courageous.
   c. how powerful the Spirit is—The place got shook up, literally!
9. Comparing your spiritual life to a car's gas tank, how would you describe your relationship with the Holy Spirit?
   a. full to the brim
   b. running low
   c. on empty
   d. at the pump, refueling

What bold move are you contemplating: Dating someone new? Singing a solo? Leading a group? Starting a new career?

1. How do the Sanhedrin (4:15–17) and the disciples each view themselves and God? **2.** Why would the disciples begin the prayer by recalling God's sovereignty (vv. 24–28)? **3.** Did God allow, direct or anticipate Jesus' crucifixion (see 2:23; 3:17–18)? **4.** How might 1:8 be shaping the disciples' prayer in verses 29–30? **5.** What is one purpose of the Holy Spirit (see 2:4; 4:8,31)?

1. How are your prayers in crises like and unlike this prayer (vv. 24–30)? Why would it be beneficial to recall God's character and actions in history? **2.** How is your Christian life characterized by boldness?

The Believers' Prayer

23 On their release, Peter and John went back to their own people and reported all that the chief priests and elders had said to
them. 24 When they heard this, they raised their voices together in
prayer to God. "Sovereign Lord," they said, "you made the heaven
and the earth and the sea, and everything in them. 25 You spoke by
the Holy Spirit through the mouth of your servant, our father David:

" 'Why do the nations rage
and the peoples plot in vain?
26 The kings of the earth take their stand
and the rulers gather together
against the Lord
and against his Anointed One.'[a][b]

27 Indeed Herod and Pontius Pilate met together with the Gentiles
and the people[c] of Israel in this city to conspire against your holy
servant Jesus, whom you anointed. 28 They did what your power
and will had decided beforehand should happen. 29 Now, Lord,
consider their threats and enable your servants to speak your word
with great boldness. 30 Stretch out your hand to heal and perform
miraculous signs and wonders through the name of your holy servant Jesus."
31 After they prayed, the place where they were meeting was
shaken. And they were all filled with the Holy Spirit and spoke the
word of God boldly.

With what group have you sensed the most unity: A team? Bible study? Family?

Compare verses 32–35 with 2:42–47. What qualities mark this church?

How well does verse 32 describe your relationship with others in your church? What would have to change for such sharing to be possible?

The Believers Share Their Possessions

32 All the believers were one in heart and mind. No one claimed
that any of his possessions was his own, but they shared everything
they had. 33 With great power the apostles continued to testify to
the resurrection of the Lord Jesus, and much grace was upon them
all. 34 There were no needy persons among them. For from time to
time those who owned lands or houses sold them, brought the
money from the sales 35 and put it at the apostles' feet, and it was
distributed to anyone as he had need.
36 Joseph, a Levite from Cyprus, whom the apostles called Barnabas (which means Son of Encouragement), 37 sold a field he owned
and brought the money and put it at the apostles' feet.

What religious practice did you once do just because everyone else did it that way, but you have since outgrown?

1. Were Ananias and Sapphira required to sell the land and lay all the money at the apostles' feet (see 4:32–37)? Why or why not? What was their sin? **2.** What would Ananias and Sapphira gain by lying about the money they received? **3.** How come many people who deceive God and their church today do not come to a dramatic end like Ananias and Sapphira? **4.** How might great fear or uncompromising honesty be useful to God? **5.** How would the incident with Ananias and Sapphira lead to the response of people in verses

Ananias and Sapphira

5 Now a man named Ananias, together with his wife Sapphira,
also sold a piece of property. 2 With his wife's full knowledge
he kept back part of the money for himself, but brought the rest
and put it at the apostles' feet.
3 Then Peter said, "Ananias, how is it that Satan has so filled your
heart that you have lied to the Holy Spirit and have kept for yourself some of the money you received for the land? 4 Didn't it belong
to you before it was sold? And after it was sold, wasn't the money
at your disposal? What made you think of doing such a thing? You
have not lied to men but to God."
5 When Ananias heard this, he fell down and died. And great fear
seized all who heard what had happened. 6 Then the young men
came forward, wrapped up his body, and carried him out and
buried him.
7 About three hours later his wife came in, not knowing what had

[a] *26* That is, Christ or Messiah [b] *26* Psalm 2:1,2 [c] *27* The Greek is plural.

happened. 8Peter asked her, "Tell me, is this the price you and
Ananias got for the land?"
"Yes," she said, "that is the price."
9Peter said to her, "How could you agree to test the Spirit of the
Lord? Look! The feet of the men who buried your husband are at
the door, and they will carry you out also."
10At that moment she fell down at his feet and died. Then the
young men came in and, finding her dead, carried her out and
buried her beside her husband. 11Great fear seized the whole
church and all who heard about these events.

The Apostles Heal Many

12The apostles performed many miraculous signs and wonders
among the people. And all the believers used to meet together in
Solomon's Colonnade. 13No one else dared join them, even though
they were highly regarded by the people. 14Nevertheless, more and
more men and women believed in the Lord and were added to
their number. 15As a result, people brought the sick into the streets
and laid them on beds and mats so that at least Peter's shadow
might fall on some of them as he passed by. 16Crowds gathered also
from the towns around Jerusalem, bringing their sick and those
tormented by evil[a] spirits, and all of them were healed.

The Apostles Persecuted

17Then the high priest and all his associates, who were members
of the party of the Sadducees, were filled with jealousy. 18They
arrested the apostles and put them in the public jail. 19But during

13–14? What words might outsiders use to describe this church? **6.** Is coming to Jesus or his disciples for healing the same as giving him your life? Why or why not?

1. When have you tried to fool God? What happened? **2.** How have you experienced the "fear of the Lord"? How has that changed your life?

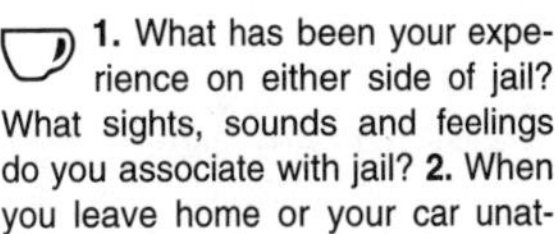

1. What has been your experience on either side of jail? What sights, sounds and feelings do you associate with jail? **2.** When you leave home or your car unat-

[a]*16* Greek *unclean*

Acts 4:32–37 THE BELIEVERS SHARE THEIR POSSESSIONS

1. What would you call the way these first Christians shared their possessions with each other?
   a. radical
   b. ridiculous
   c. exciting
   d. cultish
   e. beautiful
   f. foolish
2. How do you think they felt about their church?
   a. It was really important to them.
   b. It was all they had.
   c. They could take it or leave it.
   d. It felt like family—or even closer.
3. Why did the early church do such a good job of looking after each other?
   a. They were totally committed to it.
   b. They knew each other's needs.
   c. They didn't have government welfare programs, so they had to.
   d. They had the Old Testament model of caring for the poor.
   e. They had small house churches where needs could be shared.
4. How is your church like, and unlike, the fellowship of believers described here? Where does most of the caregiving take place in your church?
5. If you had been invited to join this community, what would your initial reaction have been?
   a. This sounds too much like socialism to me.
   b. This sounds like heaven—where do I sign up?!
   c. I have some things that I wouldn't sell for anyone!
   d. I might try it for awhile.
   e. It's fine for others, but not for me.
6. What is the closest you have come to experiencing the kind of fellowship the early church enjoyed?
7. Whom do you (or your group) know with an urgent need? How can you (or your group) help meet that need?
8. What has the church meant to you?
   a. the Sunday thing to do
   b. a social club
   c. brothers and sisters in the family of God
   d. one more activity to fit in
   e. where my closest friends are
   f. just a building
9. What is necessary for you to feel "one in heart and mind" with a church fellowship?
   a. They can't act super-religious.
   b. It needs to be a place where I can honestly question things.
   c. They have to show they care by their actions.
   d. They need to stand firm for the things I believe.
   e. They have to let me be myself.
   f. They have to be Christ-centered.
10. What questions does this passage raise about your financial stress?
   a. Where is a guy like Barnabas when you need him?!
   b. Why don't Christians do more of this today?
   c. Who determines who is "needy" and how much they should get?
   d. When will I be on the giving end instead of needing to receive?
11. If you had to go to someone with a financial need in your life, to whom would you go?

tended do you always lock it? Why or why not?

1. How do you account for the jealousy of the Sadducees? **2.** As an apostle, how would you feel during the events of verses 18–21? What would you expect to happen next? **3.** Of what do they accuse the apostles in 5:28? How is this different from what bothered them in 4:2? **4.** What assertions in Peter's response (vv. 29–32) would arouse their fury? Why is Peter being so direct (see 4:1–12; 5:19–20)? **5.** Prior to Jesus, there were many Jewish zealots who led rebellions against Rome. What is Gamaliel's point in recalling two such leaders (vv. 36–37)? Do you think he might be one of the secret believers mentioned in John 12:42? Or a political opportunist not wanting to arouse the public? Why? How do you think Peter's statement in verse 29 (and 4:19) may have influenced Gamaliel? **6.** Flogging sometimes resulted in death. Why do you think the disciples considered it worth rejoicing that they suffered in Jesus' name? **7.** How might proclaiming Jesus as risen Prince and Savior in Jerusalem immediately after his crucifix-

the night an angel of the Lord opened the doors of the jail and
brought them out. 20“Go, stand in the temple courts,” he said,
“and tell the people the full message of this new life.”
21At daybreak they entered the temple courts, as they had been
told, and began to teach the people.
When the high priest and his associates arrived, they called
together the Sanhedrin—the full assembly of the elders of Israel—
and sent to the jail for the apostles. 22But on arriving at the jail, the
officers did not find them there. So they went back and reported,
23“We found the jail securely locked, with the guards standing at
the doors; but when we opened them, we found no one inside.”
24On hearing this report, the captain of the temple guard and the
chief priests were puzzled, wondering what would come of this.
25Then someone came and said, “Look! The men you put in jail
are standing in the temple courts teaching the people.” 26At that,
the captain went with his officers and brought the apostles. They
did not use force, because they feared that the people would stone
them.
27Having brought the apostles, they made them appear before
the Sanhedrin to be questioned by the high priest. 28“We gave you
strict orders not to teach in this name,” he said. “Yet you have
filled Jerusalem with your teaching and are determined to make us
guilty of this man's blood.”
29Peter and the other apostles replied: “We must obey God rather than men! 30The God of our fathers raised Jesus from the dead—
whom you had killed by hanging him on a tree. 31God exalted him
to his own right hand as Prince and Savior that he might give
repentance and forgiveness of sins to Israel. 32We are witnesses of

Acts 5:1–11 ANANIAS AND SAPPHIRA

As the previous passage demonstrates, members of the early church cared for each other so much they even sold their possessions and brought the proceeds to the apostles for distribution to those in need.

1. Where did Ananias and Sapphira go wrong?
   a. They shouldn't have sold the land.
   b. They shouldn't have kept part of the proceeds for themselves.
   c. They shouldn't have dishonestly claimed to donate all the proceeds.
   d. They shouldn't have been dishonest about the selling price.

2. What did Ananias and Sapphira have to gain by lying about the amount of money they gave?
   a. enjoyment of the portion they kept
   b. people's praise for their generosity
   c. status in the community
   d. a boost for their egos
   e. nothing, in the long run

3. How would you have felt if you were one of those who carried out and buried Ananias and Sapphira?
   a. shocked
   b. sobered
   c. afraid
   d. full of respect for God
   e. I would have gotten God's point.
   f. saddened
   g. sickened

4. Why do you think God punished Ananias and Sapphira so severely?
   a. to keep them from continuing in their greed and deceit
   b. to deter others from their sin
   c. to show that, with God, honesty is the *only* policy
   d. to demonstrate that God cannot be deceived
   e. to make it clear at the church's outset that a holy God will not tolerate such hypocrisy and deceit
   f. because the trust and integrity of the fellowship was threatened

5. How have you seen people try to use God and the church to further their own ends?

6. In your personal or professional life, in what situations are you most tempted to be dishonest, unethical or lack integrity in some way?

7. When have you tried to "fool" God? On the other hand, when have you experienced the "fear of the Lord"?

8. What do you think is God's attitude toward us "getting ahead"?
   a. He's all for it!
   b. It's okay as long as no one else gets hurt.
   c. It's wrong if it is for selfish reasons.
   d. "Get ahead" for God and not for yourself.
   e. Greater wealth brings greater responsibility.

9. Rank the following questions according to how you make business decisions, from 1 (most important) to 6 (least important):
   a. Will it help me realize my dream?
   b. Will I make more money?
   c. Is God calling me to do it?
   d. Will it bring me more respect or prestige?
   e. Does it lack integrity in any way?
   f. How will it affect those with whom I work?

these things, and so is the Holy Spirit, whom God has given to
those who obey him."
33When they heard this, they were furious and wanted to put
them to death. 34But a Pharisee named Gamaliel, a teacher of the
law, who was honored by all the people, stood up in the Sanhedrin
and ordered that the men be put outside for a little while. 35Then
he addressed them: "Men of Israel, consider carefully what you
intend to do to these men. 36Some time ago Theudas appeared,
claiming to be somebody, and about four hundred men rallied to
him. He was killed, all his followers were dispersed, and it all came
to nothing. 37After him, Judas the Galilean appeared in the days of
the census and led a band of people in revolt. He too was killed,
and all his followers were scattered. 38Therefore, in the present
case I advise you: Leave these men alone! Let them go! For if their
purpose or activity is of human origin, it will fail. 39But if it is from
God, you will not be able to stop these men; you will only find
yourselves fighting against God."
40His speech persuaded them. They called the apostles in and
had them flogged. Then they ordered them not to speak in the
name of Jesus, and let them go.
41The apostles left the Sanhedrin, rejoicing because they had
been counted worthy of suffering disgrace for the Name. 42Day
after day, in the temple courts and from house to house, they never
stopped teaching and proclaiming the good news that Jesus is the
Christ.[a]

The Choosing of the Seven

6 In those days when the number of disciples was increasing,
the Grecian Jews among them complained against the Hebraic
Jews because their widows were being overlooked in the daily
distribution of food. 2So the Twelve gathered all the disciples together and said, "It would not be right for us to neglect the ministry of the word of God in order to wait on tables. 3Brothers, choose
seven men from among you who are known to be full of the Spirit
and wisdom. We will turn this responsibility over to them 4and will
give our attention to prayer and the ministry of the word."
5This proposal pleased the whole group. They chose Stephen, a
man full of faith and of the Holy Spirit; also Philip, Procorus, Nica-
nor, Timon, Parmenas, and Nicolas from Antioch, a convert to
Judaism. 6They presented these men to the apostles, who prayed
and laid their hands on them.
7So the word of God spread. The number of disciples in Jerusalem increased rapidly, and a large number of priests became obedient to the faith.

Stephen Seized

8Now Stephen, a man full of God's grace and power, did great
wonders and miraculous signs among the people. 9Opposition
arose, however, from members of the Synagogue of the Freedmen
(as it was called)—Jews of Cyrene and Alexandria as well as the
provinces of Cilicia and Asia. These men began to argue with
Stephen, 10but they could not stand up against his wisdom or the
Spirit by whom he spoke.
11Then they secretly persuaded some men to say, "We have
heard Stephen speak words of blasphemy against Moses and
against God."
12So they stirred up the people and the elders and the teachers of

[a]42 Or *Messiah*

ion be different than proclaiming Jesus as risen Prince and Savior over 6000 miles away 2000 years later?

1. How do you think you would feel if you were sent to jail for what you believe? How would your family feel? What would this do for your faith? **2.** In what way has God set you free to honor him more fully? **3.** How do you explain why God sometimes delivers you out of hardships, but at other times he allows you to go through them? **4.** Describe a recent event when you had to choose between God and man (v. 29).

Which responsibility at home or work would you gladly give up? Never give up?

1. Given 2:44–45 and 4:32, how could the widows be neglected? **2.** How do the apostles resolve this problem? **3.** Why did they choose men "full of the Spirit and wisdom"? **4.** Consider verse 6. Why such attention to a seemingly minor task?

1. What secondary issues hinder your church from fulfilling Acts 1:8? **2.** Does your church require high credentials and offer great blessing for the minor tasks? What if it did?

Are you more likely to "rock-the-boat" or keep "peace-at-any-price"?

1. What do you think Stephen was like? **2.** Immigrant Jews often formed their own synagogues in Jerusalem. How is their opposition to Stephen like and unlike the opposition the apostles faced from the Sanhedrin (5:27–28)?

What two adjectives best describe your spiritual life? What would be different if you were "full of grace and power"?

---

1. As a child, who was the best storyteller you ever heard? What made that person so effective? **2.** Where did your ancestors come from? Do you have any heroes in your family? Any black sheep? **3.** What's the longest speech you've ever listened to? Was it exciting or boring? Why? What makes a speech or sermon interesting to you? **4.** In which ways are you "just like your mother" or "just like your father"?

1. From 6:13–14, how would you write up the formal charges against Stephen? **2.** What does Stephen's storytelling (in effect a history lesson) reveal about his respect for the Mosaic Law? **3.** Why does Stephen spend the bulk of his history lesson talking about Moses? What parallels does he draw between Moses and Jesus? How does this relate to the charges against him in 6:13–14? How does the quote in verse 37 begin to turn the tables on his accusers (regarding who is really rejecting Moses)? **4.** From verses 44–50, what is his point about the temple and God's presence? How is he turning the tables against his accusers once again? **5.** What does Stephen mean by the phrase "uncircumcised hearts and ears" (v. 51)? In this context, what is Stephen really saying about the Sanhedrin's regard for Moses and the Law? **6.** Of what does he accuse them in verses 51–53? How does his charge reveal the reason why he gave them this history lesson? **7.** Considering this oppressive situation, what type of person is Stephen?

1. Since the Sanhedrin knew religious history every bit as well as Stephen, how do you account for their radically different response to Jesus? To fully understand Jesus, what is needed in your life besides well-rehearsed knowledge? **2.** How do people hold on to religious rituals and heroes today, while missing the whole point of what those ceremonies and people represent? **3.** In what

the law. They seized Stephen and brought him before the Sanhedrin. 13 They produced false witnesses, who testified, "This fellow
never stops speaking against this holy place and against the law.
14 For we have heard him say that this Jesus of Nazareth will destroy this place and change the customs Moses handed down
to us."
15 All who were sitting in the Sanhedrin looked intently at Stephen, and they saw that his face was like the face of an angel.

Stephen's Speech to the Sanhedrin

7 Then the high priest asked him, "Are these charges true?"
2 To this he replied: "Brothers and fathers, listen to me! The
God of glory appeared to our father Abraham while he was still in
Mesopotamia, before he lived in Haran. 3 'Leave your country and
your people,' God said, 'and go to the land I will show you.'[a]
4 "So he left the land of the Chaldeans and settled in Haran. After
the death of his father, God sent him to this land where you are
now living. 5 He gave him no inheritance here, not even a foot of
ground. But God promised him that he and his descendants after
him would possess the land, even though at that time Abraham had
no child. 6 God spoke to him in this way: 'Your descendants will be
strangers in a country not their own, and they will be enslaved and
mistreated four hundred years. 7 But I will punish the nation they
serve as slaves,' God said, 'and afterward they will come out of that
country and worship me in this place.'[b] 8 Then he gave Abraham
the covenant of circumcision. And Abraham became the father of
Isaac and circumcised him eight days after his birth. Later Isaac
became the father of Jacob, and Jacob became the father of the
twelve patriarchs.
9 "Because the patriarchs were jealous of Joseph, they sold him as
a slave into Egypt. But God was with him 10 and rescued him from
all his troubles. He gave Joseph wisdom and enabled him to gain
the goodwill of Pharaoh king of Egypt; so he made him ruler over
Egypt and all his palace.
11 "Then a famine struck all Egypt and Canaan, bringing great
suffering, and our fathers could not find food. 12 When Jacob heard
that there was grain in Egypt, he sent our fathers on their first visit.
13 On their second visit, Joseph told his brothers who he was, and
Pharaoh learned about Joseph's family. 14 After this, Joseph sent for
his father Jacob and his whole family, seventy-five in all. 15 Then
Jacob went down to Egypt, where he and our fathers died. 16 Their
bodies were brought back to Shechem and placed in the tomb that
Abraham had bought from the sons of Hamor at Shechem for a
certain sum of money.
17 "As the time drew near for God to fulfill his promise to Abraham, the number of our people in Egypt greatly increased. 18 Then
another king, who knew nothing about Joseph, became ruler of
Egypt. 19 He dealt treacherously with our people and oppressed our
forefathers by forcing them to throw out their newborn babies so
that they would die.
20 "At that time Moses was born, and he was no ordinary child.[c]
For three months he was cared for in his father's house. 21 When he
was placed outside, Pharaoh's daughter took him and brought him
up as her own son. 22 Moses was educated in all the wisdom of the
Egyptians and was powerful in speech and action.
23 "When Moses was forty years old, he decided to visit his fellow Israelites. 24 He saw one of them being mistreated by an Egyp-

[a] *3* Gen. 12:1 [b] *7* Gen. 15:13,14 [c] *20* Or *was fair in the sight of God*

tian, so he went to his defense and avenged him by killing the
Egyptian. 25Moses thought that his own people would realize that
God was using him to rescue them, but they did not. 26The next
day Moses came upon two Israelites who were fighting. He tried to
reconcile them by saying, 'Men, you are brothers; why do you
want to hurt each other?'

27"But the man who was mistreating the other pushed Moses
aside and said, 'Who made you ruler and judge over us? 28Do you
want to kill me as you killed the Egyptian yesterday?'[a] 29When
Moses heard this, he fled to Midian, where he settled as a foreigner
and had two sons.

30"After forty years had passed, an angel appeared to Moses in
the flames of a burning bush in the desert near Mount Sinai.
31When he saw this, he was amazed at the sight. As he went over
to look more closely, he heard the Lord's voice: 32'I am the God of
your fathers, the God of Abraham, Isaac and Jacob.'[b] Moses trem-
bled with fear and did not dare to look.

33"Then the Lord said to him, 'Take off your sandals; the place
where you are standing is holy ground. 34I have indeed seen the
oppression of my people in Egypt. I have heard their groaning and
have come down to set them free. Now come, I will send you back
to Egypt.'[c]

35"This is the same Moses whom they had rejected with the
words, 'Who made you ruler and judge?' He was sent to be their
ruler and deliverer by God himself, through the angel who appeared to him in the bush. 36He led them out of Egypt and did
wonders and miraculous signs in Egypt, at the Red Sea[d] and for
forty years in the desert.

37"This is that Moses who told the Israelites, 'God will send you
a prophet like me from your own people.'[e] 38He was in the assembly in the desert, with the angel who spoke to him on Mount Sinai,
and with our fathers; and he received living words to pass on to us.

39"But our fathers refused to obey him. Instead, they rejected
him and in their hearts turned back to Egypt. 40They told Aaron,
'Make us gods who will go before us. As for this fellow Moses who
led us out of Egypt—we don't know what has happened to him!'[f]
41That was the time they made an idol in the form of a calf. They
brought sacrifices to it and held a celebration in honor of what
their hands had made. 42But God turned away and gave them over
to the worship of the heavenly bodies. This agrees with what is
written in the book of the prophets:

"'Did you bring me sacrifices and offerings
forty years in the desert, O house of Israel?
43You have lifted up the shrine of Molech
and the star of your god Rephan,
the idols you made to worship.
Therefore I will send you into exile'[g] beyond
Babylon.

44"Our forefathers had the tabernacle of the Testimony with
them in the desert. It had been made as God directed Moses,
according to the pattern he had seen. 45Having received the tabernacle, our fathers under Joshua brought it with them when they
took the land from the nations God drove out before them. It
remained in the land until the time of David, 46who enjoyed God's

[a]*28* Exodus 2:14 [b]*32* Exodus 3:6 [c]*34* Exodus 3:5,7,8,10 [d]*36* That is, Sea of Reeds [e]*37* Deut. 18:15 [f]*40* Exodus 32:1 [g]*43* Amos 5:25-27

ways could the charges that Stephen makes against the leaders be made against you? How might you be "stiff-necked" this week? How will you begin to bow to God in that area now? **4.** Has Stephen's review of OT history encouraged you? Challenged you? Confused you? Would you say that the OT is more like a stranger or a close friend to you? How does this speech show the importance of the OT to the early Christians? What will you do to let its importance grow for you? **5.** When Jesus was brought to trial, he was basically quiet before the Sanhedrin; yet Stephen spoke very boldly. How do you decide when to speak and when to be quiet before opposition? **6.** What has been your experience with people who seem overly concerned with religious arguments?

favor and asked that he might provide a dwelling place for the God of Jacob.[a] 47But it was Solomon who built the house for him.

48"However, the Most High does not live in houses made by men. As the prophet says:

49" 'Heaven is my throne,
 and the earth is my footstool.
What kind of house will you build for me?
 says the Lord.
 Or where will my resting place be?
50Has not my hand made all these things?'[b]

51"You stiff-necked people, with uncircumcised hearts and ears! You are just like your fathers: You always resist the Holy Spirit! 52Was there ever a prophet your fathers did not persecute? They even killed those who predicted the coming of the Righteous One. And now you have betrayed and murdered him— 53you who have received the law that was put into effect through angels but have not obeyed it."

What do you do when you feel angry enough to resort to sticks and stones?

1. Why are Stephen's listeners so enraged (see Da 7:13–14)? **2.** Stephen's death was illegal (see Jn 18:31). What does that reveal about the desperation of the Sanhedrin? **3.** This begins phase two ("Judea and Samaria") of God's plan (see 1:8). How would you sum up the "Jerusalem phase" (ch. 2–7)?

1. What is one very traumatic event that happened to you in your formative years? Can you see now how God has used it for good? **2.** Peter's speech led to mass conversion (ch. 2), while Stephen's led to his death. What does that teach about success in one's service to God?

The Stoning of Stephen

54When they heard this, they were furious and gnashed their teeth at him. 55But Stephen, full of the Holy Spirit, looked up to heaven and saw the glory of God, and Jesus standing at the right hand of God. 56"Look," he said, "I see heaven open and the Son of Man standing at the right hand of God."

57At this they covered their ears and, yelling at the top of their voices, they all rushed at him, 58dragged him out of the city and began to stone him. Meanwhile, the witnesses laid their clothes at the feet of a young man named Saul.

59While they were stoning him, Stephen prayed, "Lord Jesus, receive my spirit." 60Then he fell on his knees and cried out, "Lord, do not hold this sin against them." When he had said this, he fell asleep.

8 And Saul was there, giving approval to his death.

The Church Persecuted and Scattered

On that day a great persecution broke out against the church at Jerusalem, and all except the apostles were scattered throughout Judea and Samaria. 2Godly men buried Stephen and mourned deeply for him. 3But Saul began to destroy the church. Going from house to house, he dragged off men and women and put them in prison.

Who was your hero when you were 10? A movie star? An athlete? A comic book character? What ability did they have that you wanted for yourself?

1. What did Simon and Phillip have in common (vv. 5–11)? How were they different? How did the crowd respond to both men? **2.** Given that the Samaritans were considered outcasts by the Jews (see Jn 4:9), why would Peter and John come to them? **3.** Why would the Father delay pouring out his Spirit until Peter and John were on the scene? Do you think this was a lesson for the Samaritans or for the

Philip in Samaria

4Those who had been scattered preached the word wherever they went. 5Philip went down to a city in Samaria and proclaimed the Christ[c] there. 6When the crowds heard Philip and saw the miraculous signs he did, they all paid close attention to what he said. 7With shrieks, evil[d] spirits came out of many, and many paralytics and cripples were healed. 8So there was great joy in that city.

Simon the Sorcerer

9Now for some time a man named Simon had practiced sorcery in the city and amazed all the people of Samaria. He boasted that he was someone great, 10and all the people, both high and low,

[a] *46* Some early manuscripts *the house of Jacob* [b] *50* Isaiah 66:1,2 [c] *5* Or *Messiah* [d] *7* Greek *unclean*

gave him their attention and exclaimed, "This man is the divine
power known as the Great Power." 11They followed him because
he had amazed them for a long time with his magic. 12But when
they believed Philip as he preached the good news of the kingdom
of God and the name of Jesus Christ, they were baptized, both men
and women. 13Simon himself believed and was baptized. And he
followed Philip everywhere, astonished by the great signs and miracles he saw.

14When the apostles in Jerusalem heard that Samaria had accepted the word of God, they sent Peter and John to them. 15When
they arrived, they prayed for them that they might receive the Holy
Spirit, 16because the Holy Spirit had not yet come upon any of
them; they had simply been baptized into[a] the name of the Lord
Jesus. 17Then Peter and John placed their hands on them, and they
received the Holy Spirit.

18When Simon saw that the Spirit was given at the laying on of
the apostles' hands, he offered them money 19and said, "Give me
also this ability so that everyone on whom I lay my hands may
receive the Holy Spirit."

20Peter answered: "May your money perish with you, because
you thought you could buy the gift of God with money! 21You have
no part or share in this ministry, because your heart is not right
before God. 22Repent of this wickedness and pray to the Lord.
Perhaps he will forgive you for having such a thought in your heart.
23For I see that you are full of bitterness and captive to sin."

24Then Simon answered, "Pray to the Lord for me so that nothing you have said may happen to me."

25When they had testified and proclaimed the word of the Lord,
Peter and John returned to Jerusalem, preaching the gospel in
many Samaritan villages.

apostles? **4.** In what ways does Simon's reaction to the apostles (vv. 18–19) show his deep misunderstanding about the Gospel? **5.** Do you think that Simon's words in verse 24 reveal a change in his heart?

1. What prejudices were you brought up with? How is the Gospel breaking through those prejudices in your life? **2.** What was your primary motivation in first receiving Jesus Christ as Savior? What is your primary motivation for continuing in the faith? **3.** How has jealousy of other Christians affected your faith?

Philip and the Ethiopian

26Now an angel of the Lord said to Philip, "Go south to the
road—the desert road—that goes down from Jerusalem to Gaza."
27So he started out, and on his way he met an Ethiopian[b] eunuch,
an important official in charge of all the treasury of Candace, queen
of the Ethiopians. This man had gone to Jerusalem to worship,
28and on his way home was sitting in his chariot reading the book
of Isaiah the prophet. 29The Spirit told Philip, "Go to that chariot
and stay near it."

30Then Philip ran up to the chariot and heard the man reading
Isaiah the prophet. "Do you understand what you are reading?"
Philip asked.

31"How can I," he said, "unless someone explains it to me?" So
he invited Philip to come up and sit with him.

32The eunuch was reading this passage of Scripture:

"He was led like a sheep to the slaughter,
and as a lamb before the shearer is silent,
so he did not open his mouth.
33In his humiliation he was deprived of justice.
Who can speak of his descendants?
For his life was taken from the earth."[c]

34The eunuch asked Philip, "Tell me, please, who is the prophet
talking about, himself or someone else?" 35Then Philip began with
that very passage of Scripture and told him the good news about
Jesus.

What experience have you had with being tutored, or with tutoring others?

1. Why does the eunuch visit Jerusalem (see 2:1–11)? **2.** The eunuch was reading Isaiah 53. In what ways does Jesus fit the picture of the one described there? **3.** How did God pave the way for his message? What is the relationship between divine preparation and human initiative in this story? **4.** So far, what has been the effect of Stephen's death upon Phillip? Upon the church as a whole?

1. From the way God sets up opportunities to witness (vv. 26–40; 2:5–14; 3:6–16), how does that free you from fears in evangelism? **2.** Deep down, do you think successful VIPs really need the Gospel as much as poor beggars do (3:2)? Why or why not? **3.** Would you know the Bible well enough to address the eunuch's questions? How can you grow in faith so you will be prepared for similar opportunities?

[a]*16* Or *in* [b]*27* That is, from the upper Nile region [c]*33* Isaiah 53:7,8

36As they traveled along the road, they came to some water and
the eunuch said, "Look, here is water. Why shouldn't I be baptized?"[a] 38And he gave orders to stop the chariot. Then both
Philip and the eunuch went down into the water and Philip baptized him. 39When they came up out of the water, the Spirit of the
Lord suddenly took Philip away, and the eunuch did not see him
again, but went on his way rejoicing. 40Philip, however, appeared
at Azotus and traveled about, preaching the gospel in all the towns
until he reached Caesarea.

What is the longest you have been without food or drink: Three days? Three meals? Three hours? Why? How did you feel?

1. What do you know about Saul to this point? **2.** Saul's former teacher was Gamaliel (see 22:3). What had Gamaliel advised the Sanhedrin regarding Christians in 5:34–39? How is Saul responding to this advice? What does this show about him? **3.** Describe what happened in verses 3–9 from the viewpoint of one of Saul's companions? **4.** Was Saul's heart open to Jesus' arrival? Why or why not? **5.** How do you think Saul felt when confronted by Jesus (vv. 4–6)? Given his previous activities, what would he be thinking about during

Saul's Conversion

9 Meanwhile, Saul was still breathing out murderous threats
against the Lord's disciples. He went to the high priest 2and
asked him for letters to the synagogues in Damascus, so that if he
found any there who belonged to the Way, whether men or wom-
en, he might take them as prisoners to Jerusalem. 3As he neared
Damascus on his journey, suddenly a light from heaven flashed
around him. 4He fell to the ground and heard a voice say to him,
"Saul, Saul, why do you persecute me?"
5"Who are you, Lord?" Saul asked.
"I am Jesus, whom you are persecuting," he replied. 6"Now get
up and go into the city, and you will be told what you must do."
7The men traveling with Saul stood there speechless; they heard
the sound but did not see anyone. 8Saul got up from the ground,
but when he opened his eyes he could see nothing. So they led him

[a]36 Some late manuscripts *baptized?" 37Philip said, "If you believe with all your heart, you may." The eunuch answered, "I believe that Jesus Christ is the Son of God."*

Acts 8:26–40 PHILIP AND THE ETHIOPIAN

1. What is your impression of Philip, one of the church's first evangelists, in this story?
   a. He really got around!
   b. He instantly obeyed the Lord.
   c. He seemed kind of pushy.
   d. I wish I were as bold as he was.
   e. I'm surprised how quick he was to baptize the Ethiopian eunuch.

2. What is your impression of the Ethiopian official in this story?
   a. As a Gentile interested in the Jewish religion, he was a spiritually hungry seeker.
   b. He was fortunate—he found quick answers to his spiritual questions.
   c. He was "ripe" for the Gospel.
   d. He was decisive—when he found what he wanted, he went for it.

3. How would you have reacted if you were the Ethiopian when Philip ran up and asked, "Do you understand what you are reading?"
   a. "Sorry, I don't pick up hitchhikers!"
   b. "Do I know you?"
   c. "I can figure it out myself."
   d. "I'm always open to someone else's opinion."
   e. "This stuff is over my head—I'd be glad for your help."
   f. "Who made you an authority?!"

4. Compared to this story, how would you rate yourself with Scripture?
   a. I've never been as interested in Scripture as they were.
   b. I share their strong interest.
   c. I share the Ethiopian's confusion!
   d. I may know a little more than the Ethiopian did, but there is still much I don't understand.
   e. I have questions but, like Philip, I have a good grasp of Scripture and what it says about my faith.
   f. Like Philip, I am fulfilled by helping others understand Scripture.

5. The Ethiopian was traveling along a desert road. How would you describe the "road" you've been traveling?
   a. also a desert road—lonely, with little life around
   b. a scenic mountain road—off the main highway, but beautiful
   c. a highway under construction—smoother some places than others
   d. a freeway—a nice, relaxeo trip

6. Who along the road has been like Philip and shown you the way to a more meaningful life? What was the most important spiritual truth that person taught you?

7. On a scale of 1 to 10, what degree of meaning have you received from your work (or other main activity) at the following times?
   a. right now
   b. five years ago
   c. 10 years ago
   d. when I was most fulfilled—at the time I was doing ____________

8. What is it that makes work meaningful or not meaningful for you?
   a. whether I see results
   b. whether I am working mainly with people or not
   c. whether it has lasting value
   d. whether I am using strengths and skills I enjoy using
   e. whether I believe what I do truly helps people
   f. whether the business I am in is operated ethically
   g. other:____________

by the hand into Damascus. [9]For three days he was blind, and did
not eat or drink anything.
[10]In Damascus there was a disciple named Ananias. The Lord
called to him in a vision, "Ananias!"
"Yes, Lord," he answered.
[11]The Lord told him, "Go to the house of Judas on Straight Street
and ask for a man from Tarsus named Saul, for he is praying. [12]In
a vision he has seen a man named Ananias come and place his
hands on him to restore his sight."
[13]"Lord," Ananias answered, "I have heard many reports about
this man and all the harm he has done to your saints in Jerusalem.
[14]And he has come here with authority from the chief priests to
arrest all who call on your name."
[15]But the Lord said to Ananias, "Go! This man is my chosen
instrument to carry my name before the Gentiles and their kings
and before the people of Israel. [16]I will show him how much he
must suffer for my name."
[17]Then Ananias went to the house and entered it. Placing his
hands on Saul, he said, "Brother Saul, the Lord—Jesus, who appeared to you on the road as you were coming here—has sent me
so that you may see again and be filled with the Holy Spirit."
[18]Immediately, something like scales fell from Saul's eyes, and he
could see again. He got up and was baptized, [19]and after taking
some food, he regained his strength.

Saul in Damascus and Jerusalem

Saul spent several days with the disciples in Damascus. [20]At
once he began to preach in the synagogues that Jesus is the Son of

those three days of blindness and fasting (v. 9)? **6.** How would you feel in Ananias' place? Since Jesus had already appeared to Saul directly, why this time would he want a person to go to him? What is significant about the way Ananias addresses Saul (v. 17)?

1. How did the Lord first get your attention? Was it in some dramatic event or something more subtle? Have you had a post-encounter experience like Saul did? **2.** Do you assume some people are beyond God's reach? How does this story challenge those assumptions? **3.** When have you, like Ananias, obeyed the Lord even when you had doubts? What happened? **4.** Who has played the role of Ananias in your life? To whom does the Lord want you to play that part?

Who do people say you look like? Why?

Acts 9:1–19 SAUL'S CONVERSION

While the early church was growing rapidly, Saul the Pharisee—who would become known as the apostle Paul—was trying to destroy it.

1. How might the medical profession today explain what happened to Saul on the road to Damascus?
   a. He was struck by lightning.
   b. He had a physical breakdown.
   c. He had a mental breakdown.
   d. He had a partial stroke that rendered him temporarily blind.
   e. He had a psychological crisis due to an overly-religious personality.
   f. He suffered from repressed guilt for his role in persecuting people.

2. How do you think Saul felt during his three days of blindness?
   a. wiped out
   b. terrified
   c. confused
   d. humbled
   e. angry
   f. repentant

3. If you were Ananias, how would you have reacted when God told you to go and lay hands on Saul?
   a. "I'll lay hands on him all right!"
   b. "This is just a dream, right God?"
   c. "Don't you know who this guy is?"
   d. "I love a challenge!"
   e. "If you really want me to, I'll do it."

4. What was the most significant thing that happened to Saul after Ananias prayed for him?
   a. His physical vision was restored.
   b. His spiritual vision was corrected.
   c. He believed and was baptized.
   d. He was filled with the Holy Spirit.
   e. He was accepted as a "brother" in God's family.
   f. He was commissioned to represent Christ around the world.

5. How would you compare your conversion to Saul's conversion?
   a. Mine was almost as dramatic.
   b. Mine was a lot more gradual.
   c. I'm still sorting out what has happened to me.
   d. I'm on my way back to God and I still have a lot of questions.

6. Who has played the role of Ananias in your life? To whom might the Lord want you to play the part?

7. In what area of your life have you seen the most change since you committed your life to Christ? And in what area do you sense God calling you to allow him to bring additional change?
   a. priorities
   b. relationships
   c. attitudes
   d. beliefs
   e. goals
   f. values

8. Why do you think that, as other Scriptures show, Saul (Paul) saw his singleness as a gift?
   a. He probably saw it as a fulfillment of verse 16: "I will show him how much he must *suffer*"!
   b. He realized he could serve God and others more wholeheartedly as a single.
   c. He was such an intense person that he knew it would be better for him to remain single.
   d. He saw it as part of his calling.

9. How do you feel about the possibility that God has given *you* the gift of singleness?
   a. That doesn't sound like a gift!
   b. It makes sense to me.
   c. I'll have to think about it.
   d. If that's what God wants, that's what I want.

1. What would others have expected Saul to say when he came to the synagogue? When he proceeds to preach about Christ, how do they react (v. 23)? Why? **2.** Why would the Jerusalem disciples still fear Saul? What risk is Barnabas taking? **3.** People in Damascus and Jerusalem wanted to kill Saul. What does that say about him? **4.** How is the story of Saul related to 1:8?

1. What changes did people notice when you began following Jesus? How did they react? **2.** Who has been a Barnabas to you? How? Whom have you served as a Barnabas? **3.** What does "living in the fear of the Lord" (v. 31) mean to you?

God. 21All those who heard him were astonished and asked, "Isn't
he the man who raised havoc in Jerusalem among those who call
on this name? And hasn't he come here to take them as prisoners
to the chief priests?" 22Yet Saul grew more and more powerful and
baffled the Jews living in Damascus by proving that Jesus is the
Christ.[a]

23After many days had gone by, the Jews conspired to kill him,
24but Saul learned of their plan. Day and night they kept close
watch on the city gates in order to kill him. 25But his followers took
him by night and lowered him in a basket through an opening in
the wall.

26When he came to Jerusalem, he tried to join the disciples, but
they were all afraid of him, not believing that he really was a
disciple. 27But Barnabas took him and brought him to the apostles.
He told them how Saul on his journey had seen the Lord and
that the Lord had spoken to him, and how in Damascus he had
preached fearlessly in the name of Jesus. 28So Saul stayed with
them and moved about freely in Jerusalem, speaking boldly in the
name of the Lord. 29He talked and debated with the Grecian Jews,
but they tried to kill him. 30When the brothers learned of this, they
took him down to Caesarea and sent him off to Tarsus.

31Then the church throughout Judea, Galilee and Samaria enjoyed a time of peace. It was strengthened; and encouraged by the Holy Spirit, it grew in numbers, living in the fear of the Lord.

Aeneas and Dorcas

32As Peter traveled about the country, he went to visit the saints
in Lydda. 33There he found a man named Aeneas, a paralytic who

[a]22 Or *Messiah*

Acts 9:20–31 SAUL IN DAMASCUS AND JERUSALEM

As a zealous Pharisee, Saul became a vehement opponent of Christianity. But on his way to Damascus to arrest believers, Saul had a life-changing encounter with the risen Christ. The result was that he not only became a Christian himself, but eventually the renowned "apostle Paul."

1. What would be the most intriguing scene of a movie about this story?
   a. Jesus suddenly appearing to Saul on the road to Damascus (v. 27)
   b. people's reaction when the persecutor of Christians turned out to be a preacher of Christ (vv. 20–21)
   c. Saul being lowered in a basket to escape the threat on his life (v. 25)
   d. the Jerusalem disciples' fear and distrust of Saul (v. 26)
   e. Barnabas' courage to step forward and speak up for Saul (v. 27)
   f. Saul threatened again, but spared by his new "brothers" (vv. 29–30)
2. How would you have felt if you were part of the church in Jerusalem when Saul wanted to join it?
   a. I would be afraid he was faking a conversion to infiltrate our group.
   b. I would rejoice in his claim to faith and welcome him with open arms.
   c. I would let him in but keep a close eye on him.
   d. I would have required him to make up for his past wrongs.
3. How would you have felt if you met the kind of suspicion Saul did?
   a. I would be hurt.
   b. I would be angry.
   c. I would think I didn't deserve to be accepted.
   d. I would withdraw and give up.
   e. I would take it as a challenge to prove myself.
4. What led Barnabas to help Saul?
   a. He felt sorry for him.
   b. He let Saul tell his story.
   c. He could discern Saul's heart.
   d. He had the gift of encouragement.
   e. He was motivated by love rather than fear.
   f. His belief in Saul outweighed the risks of being rejected himself.
5. Who has been a Barnabas to you—encouraging you or helping you feel accepted? Whom have you, or could you, serve like Barnabas did?
6. How do other people respond to you as a Christian? Have you ever experienced rejection for your faith?
7. Where is it hardest for you to feel accepted?
   a. in my family
   b. at school
   c. at church/youth group
   d. at parties/social gatherings
   e. by the opposite sex
   f. into groups or cliques
8. What do you do when you feel like you don't fit in?
   a. I don't let it bother me.
   b. I *act* like it doesn't bother me.
   c. I try even harder to fit in.
   d. I back off or quit trying.
   e. I find somewhere else to fit in.
9. How accepted do you feel by God? How can God's acceptance help when you don't fit in?

had been bedridden for eight years. 34“Aeneas,” Peter said to him, “Jesus Christ heals you. Get up and take care of your mat.” Immediately Aeneas got up. 35All those who lived in Lydda and Sharon saw him and turned to the Lord.

36In Joppa there was a disciple named Tabitha (which, when translated, is Dorcas[a]), who was always doing good and helping the poor. 37About that time she became sick and died, and her body was washed and placed in an upstairs room. 38Lydda was near Joppa; so when the disciples heard that Peter was in Lydda, they sent two men to him and urged him, “Please come at once!”

39Peter went with them, and when he arrived he was taken upstairs to the room. All the widows stood around him, crying and showing him the robes and other clothing that Dorcas had made while she was still with them.

40Peter sent them all out of the room; then he got down on his knees and prayed. Turning toward the dead woman, he said, “Tabitha, get up.” She opened her eyes, and seeing Peter she sat up. 41He took her by the hand and helped her to her feet. Then he called the believers and the widows and presented her to them alive. 42This became known all over Joppa, and many people believed in the Lord. 43Peter stayed in Joppa for some time with a tanner named Simon.

Cornelius Calls for Peter

10 At Caesarea there was a man named Cornelius, a centurion in what was known as the Italian Regiment. 2He and all his family were devout and God-fearing; he gave generously to those in need and prayed to God regularly. 3One day at about three in the afternoon he had a vision. He distinctly saw an angel of God, who came to him and said, “Cornelius!”

4Cornelius stared at him in fear. “What is it, Lord?” he asked.

The angel answered, “Your prayers and gifts to the poor have come up as a memorial offering before God. 5Now send men to Joppa to bring back a man named Simon who is called Peter. 6He is staying with Simon the tanner, whose house is by the sea.”

7When the angel who spoke to him had gone, Cornelius called two of his servants and a devout soldier who was one of his attendants. 8He told them everything that had happened and sent them to Joppa.

Peter’s Vision

9About noon the following day as they were on their journey and approaching the city, Peter went up on the roof to pray. 10He became hungry and wanted something to eat, and while the meal was being prepared, he fell into a trance. 11He saw heaven opened and something like a large sheet being let down to earth by its four corners. 12It contained all kinds of four-footed animals, as well as reptiles of the earth and birds of the air. 13Then a voice told him, “Get up, Peter. Kill and eat.”

14“Surely not, Lord!” Peter replied. “I have never eaten anything impure or unclean.”

15The voice spoke to him a second time, “Do not call anything impure that God has made clean.”

16This happened three times, and immediately the sheet was taken back to heaven.

17While Peter was wondering about the meaning of the vision, the men sent by Cornelius found out where Simon’s house was and

[a]36 Both *Tabitha* (Aramaic) and *Dorcas* (Greek) mean *gazelle.*

What does it take to get you out of bed in the morning?

1. What is the purpose of these signs and wonders (vv. 35, 41–42; also 2:22,43; 4:30; 5:12–14)? **2.** Although Peter had healed many people, he had never raised anyone from death. What might he be feeling as he goes to Tabitha’s home? **3.** Which of Jesus’ miracles do these two incidents remind you of?

1. Why is it that Tabitha was raised, but Stephen died, even though Peter was there too (8:2)? How would you explain God’s ways to Stephen’s widow or mother? How does the results of Stephen’s death and Tabitha’s resurrection help you to understand God’s plans? **2.** Do miracles like these happen in the same way today? Why or why not?

What dream (or nightmare) has inspired (or haunted) you?

What is Cornelius like (vv. 1–2)? Since he is part of an occupying army, what is unusual about him? About his encounter with God?

1. Are you very “God-fearing”? If evaluated by how you treated others this week, what would they say? **2.** How does Cornelius’ life challenge you?

As a child, what foods did you refuse to eat? What foods do you still dislike today?

1. Look at Leviticus 11:4–7, 13–19 and 29–30. With these restrictions, how do you think Peter felt when he heard the voice ordering him to eat these animals? Why was it repeated three times? What would the new principle given in verse 15 mean to him? How does it fit with the story of Cornelius (vv. 1–10, 23–34)? **2.** How might Peter feel when the men sent by Cornelius showed up?

1. What principles or beliefs do you hold that limit your ability to reach out to people “different” from you? How would others around you feel if you moved beyond these limits? **2.** What new relationships has God given you recently? How has he brought these people into your life? How have you influenced each other?

stopped at the gate. 18They called out, asking if Simon who was
known as Peter was staying there.
19While Peter was still thinking about the vision, the Spirit said
to him, "Simon, three[a] men are looking for you. 20So get up and
go downstairs. Do not hesitate to go with them, for I have sent
them."
21Peter went down and said to the men, "I'm the one you're
looking for. Why have you come?"
22The men replied, "We have come from Cornelius the centurion. He is a righteous and God-fearing man, who is respected by all
the Jewish people. A holy angel told him to have you come to his
house so that he could hear what you have to say." 23Then Peter
invited the men into the house to be his guests.

Did you grow up isolated from or associating with other ethnic groups? How much contact do you have with people from other ethnic groups today?

1. Given Peter's experience in verses 9–23 and what you know of Cornelius, how do you think each man was feeling as they greeted one another? **2.** Jews regarded even people like Cornelius as pagans, unless they fully submitted to Jewish practices (see 11:3). Hence, what would verse 28 have meant to Cornelius? Why is

Peter at Cornelius' House

The next day Peter started out with them, and some of the
brothers from Joppa went along. 24The following day he arrived in
Caesarea. Cornelius was expecting them and had called together
his relatives and close friends. 25As Peter entered the house, Cornelius met him and fell at his feet in reverence. 26But Peter made
him get up. "Stand up," he said, "I am only a man myself."
27Talking with him, Peter went inside and found a large gathering of people. 28He said to them: "You are well aware that it is
against our law for a Jew to associate with a Gentile or visit him.
But God has shown me that I should not call any man impure or
unclean. 29So when I was sent for, I came without raising any
objection. May I ask why you sent for me?"

[a]19 One early manuscript *two*; other manuscripts do not have the number.

Acts 10:1–23 PETER'S VISION

1. Why do you think this story got into the Bible?
   a. It shows that God doesn't care what Christians eat.
   b. It shows that Gentiles are on equal terms as Jews before God.
   c. It teaches Christians not to put limits on God.
   d. Cornelius and his close friends and relatives would be the first Gentiles to become Christians.
   e. It was a turning point in the expansion of the church.
2. Why do you think God gave Peter a vision of "unclean" animals instead of directly telling him what he wanted?
   a. God doesn't like to do things the easy way.
   b. Peter was hungry, so God started where he was at.
   c. God likes to use symbolism.
   d. If God was more direct, Peter might have been more resistant.
3. What do you think Peter's first reaction was to eating animals that "Law-abiding Jews" religiously avoided?
   a. I must be having a crazy dream.
   b. God can't be serious about this.
   c. Why is God changing the rules in midstream?
   d. Is God trying to test my obedience to him?
4. What was God saying through the vision and Cornelius' messengers?
   a. It's okay to eat anything you want.
   b. You can overlook ceremonial laws.
   c. Anybody can become a Christian.
   d. You need to accept non-Jews into the church.
5. Who would it be harder for you to accept into your group or church?
   a. someone like Peter with a very religious mindset
   b. someone like Cornelius with a pagan, unchurched background
   c. We could accept either.
   d. We would have trouble with both.
6. What kind of walls have you permitted between yourself and others?
   a. racial d. political
   b. religious e. moral
   c. economic f. denominational
7. What are some types of people you have written off? What principles or beliefs have limited your ability to reach out to these persons?
8. Considering the makeup of your community and church or small group, would some people assume your church or group is not for them? If so, how can you change that?
9. What does this story say to you about following Christ?
   a. God is pleased by prayer and giving to the poor.
   b. If I were more diligent in prayer, God might speak to me more clearly.
   c. I need to have a teachable spirit.
   d. I need to say no to prejudice.
   e. I need to break down social barriers within my sphere of influence.
   f. other:__________________
10. If God gave you a vision or sent an angel to you with a message, what do you think the Spirit would tell you to do? Would you have any hesitation to obey?

30 Cornelius answered: "Four days ago I was in my house praying
at this hour, at three in the afternoon. Suddenly a man in shining
clothes stood before me 31 and said, 'Cornelius, God has heard your
prayer and remembered your gifts to the poor. 32 Send to Joppa for
Simon who is called Peter. He is a guest in the home of Simon the
tanner, who lives by the sea.' 33 So I sent for you immediately, and
it was good of you to come. Now we are all here in the presence
of God to listen to everything the Lord has commanded you to
tell us."
34 Then Peter began to speak: "I now realize how true it is that
God does not show favoritism 35 but accepts men from every nation
who fear him and do what is right. 36 You know the message God
sent to the people of Israel, telling the good news of peace through
Jesus Christ, who is Lord of all. 37 You know what has happened
throughout Judea, beginning in Galilee after the baptism that John
preached— 38 how God anointed Jesus of Nazareth with the Holy
Spirit and power, and how he went around doing good and healing
all who were under the power of the devil, because God was with
him.
39 "We are witnesses of everything he did in the country of the
Jews and in Jerusalem. They killed him by hanging him on a tree,
40 but God raised him from the dead on the third day and caused
him to be seen. 41 He was not seen by all the people, but by
witnesses whom God had already chosen—by us who ate and
drank with him after he rose from the dead. 42 He commanded us to
preach to the people and to testify that he is the one whom God
appointed as judge of the living and the dead. 43 All the prophets
testify about him that everyone who believes in him receives forgiveness of sins through his name."
44 While Peter was still speaking these words, the Holy Spirit
came on all who heard the message. 45 The circumcised believers
who had come with Peter were astonished that the gift of the Holy
Spirit had been poured out even on the Gentiles. 46 For they heard
them speaking in tongues[a] and praising God.
Then Peter said, 47 "Can anyone keep these people from being
baptized with water? They have received the Holy Spirit just as we
have." 48 So he ordered that they be baptized in the name of Jesus
Christ. Then they asked Peter to stay with them for a few days.

Peter Explains His Actions

11 The apostles and the brothers throughout Judea heard that
the Gentiles also had received the word of God. 2 So when
Peter went up to Jerusalem, the circumcised believers criticized
him 3 and said, "You went into the house of uncircumcised men
and ate with them."
4 Peter began and explained everything to them precisely as it
had happened: 5 "I was in the city of Joppa praying, and in a trance
I saw a vision. I saw something like a large sheet being let down
from heaven by its four corners, and it came down to where I was.
6 I looked into it and saw four-footed animals of the earth, wild
beasts, reptiles, and birds of the air. 7 Then I heard a voice telling
me, 'Get up, Peter. Kill and eat.'
8 "I replied, 'Surely not, Lord! Nothing impure or unclean has
ever entered my mouth.'
9 "The voice spoke from heaven a second time, 'Do not call
anything impure that God has made clean.' 10 This happened three
times, and then it was all pulled up to heaven again.

[a]46 Or *other languages*

the story of Cornelius so important in Acts (vv. 28,34–35,43)? **3.** What is the main point in Peter's sermon? How does that compare with his sermons in 2:36–39 and 3:17–23? From these sermons, what do you see as central to the Gospel message? **4.** In light of the astonished reaction of the Jews (v. 45), what did it mean that the Gentiles could speak in tongues? How does this reinforce Peter's private vision in 10:9–23?

1. Using this story, how would you respond to the question: "Can people who have never heard the Gospel be saved"? If your answer is "yes," why then did God send Peter to preach (see also 11:14)? If it is "no," how do you explain verses 34–35? **2.** Consider the makeup of your church (ethnically, socially, politically, agewise, etc.). Are there some people who would just assume that your church is not for them? Are there some forms or practices you could change to remove those barriers? How would you feel about making those changes?

What was the wrong crowd to hang out with when you were in school? Did you anyway?

1. Why did Luke take the time and space to record the events of 10:9–46 all over again? **2.** Of what importance is the gift of the Holy Spirit in Peter's argument? Why would this have such a strong effect on the Jerusalem believers? Why is this gift misunderstood (see vv. 5–8)? **3.** Why do you think God chose Peter to be the first to go to the Gentiles? Would any other disciple have been as successful in both Caesarea and Jerusalem? Why or why not? **4.** How do you explain the change in attitudes from verse 2 to verse 18? How does this story relate to 1:8?

1. How can the principle of God bestowing his Spirit on non-Jews affect the way you treat unacceptable people you meet? **2.** How have you been criticized for breaking religious traditions? What did you feel was at stake? **3.** The lesson of 10:34–35 and 11:18 was not easily learned, even by Peter (see Gal 2:11–14). What might have happened if the early church ignored this principle?

11 “Right then three men who had been sent to me from Caesarea stopped at the house where I was staying. 12 The Spirit told me
to have no hesitation about going with them. These six brothers
also went with me, and we entered the man’s house. 13 He told us
how he had seen an angel appear in his house and say, ‘Send to
Joppa for Simon who is called Peter. 14 He will bring you a message
through which you and all your household will be saved.’

15 “As I began to speak, the Holy Spirit came on them as he had
come on us at the beginning. 16 Then I remembered what the Lord
had said: ‘John baptized with[a] water, but you will be baptized
with the Holy Spirit.’ 17 So if God gave them the same gift as he
gave us, who believed in the Lord Jesus Christ, who was I to think
that I could oppose God?”

18 When they heard this, they had no further objections and
praised God, saying, “So then, God has granted even the Gentiles
repentance unto life.”

What is the farthest from home you have ever been? Why were you there?

1. Antioch was the third largest city in the Roman empire. What might the apostles feel as they hear the Gospel is taking root there (v. 23)? **2.** Write a character reference for Barnabas based on verses 22–26 (also 4:36–37). From this profile, why did Barnabus recruit Saul (9:27–28)?

1. With whom do you associate that no minister would normally contact? How do you share the Gospel with those people? **2.** Would these people be comfortable in your church? **3.** What is the most unusual thing the Holy Spirit has done in your life?

The Church in Antioch

19 Now those who had been scattered by the persecution in connection with Stephen traveled as far as Phoenicia, Cyprus and
Antioch, telling the message only to Jews. 20 Some of them, however, men from Cyprus and Cyrene, went to Antioch and began to
speak to Greeks also, telling them the good news about the Lord
Jesus. 21 The Lord’s hand was with them, and a great number of
people believed and turned to the Lord.

22 News of this reached the ears of the church at Jerusalem, and
they sent Barnabas to Antioch. 23 When he arrived and saw the
evidence of the grace of God, he was glad and encouraged them all
to remain true to the Lord with all their hearts. 24 He was a good
man, full of the Holy Spirit and faith, and a great number of people
were brought to the Lord.

25 Then Barnabas went to Tarsus to look for Saul, 26 and when he
found him, he brought him to Antioch. So for a whole year Barnabas and Saul met with the church and taught great numbers of
people. The disciples were called Christians first at Antioch.

27 During this time some prophets came down from Jerusalem to
Antioch. 28 One of them, named Agabus, stood up and through the
Spirit predicted that a severe famine would spread over the entire
Roman world. (This happened during the reign of Claudius.) 29 The
disciples, each according to his ability, decided to provide help for
the brothers living in Judea. 30 This they did, sending their gift to
the elders by Barnabas and Saul.

---

1. Who was the most surprising person to ever show up at your door? **2.** If you were arrested by a dictatorial government for being a Christian, what evidence might they point to as proof of your guilt? What could some “well-meaning” character witnesses point to as proof of your innocence?

1. This Herod is the nephew of the Herod who ruled in Jesus’ day. What do you learn about his character in verses 20–23? Why would his choice to arrest (vv. 2–4) Peter please the Jewish leaders? Why do you think

Peter’s Miraculous Escape From Prison

12 It was about this time that King Herod arrested some who
belonged to the church, intending to persecute them. 2 He
had James, the brother of John, put to death with the sword.
3 When he saw that this pleased the Jews, he proceeded to seize
Peter also. This happened during the Feast of Unleavened Bread.
4 After arresting him, he put him in prison, handing him over to be
guarded by four squads of four soldiers each. Herod intended to
bring him out for public trial after the Passover.

5 So Peter was kept in prison, but the church was earnestly praying to God for him.

6 The night before Herod was to bring him to trial, Peter was
sleeping between two soldiers, bound with two chains, and sen-
tries stood guard at the entrance. 7 Suddenly an angel of the Lord

a16 Or *in*

appeared and a light shone in the cell. He struck Peter on the side
and woke him up. "Quick, get up!" he said, and the chains fell off
Peter's wrists.
8Then the angel said to him, "Put on your clothes and sandals."
And Peter did so. "Wrap your cloak around you and follow me,"
the angel told him. 9Peter followed him out of the prison, but he
had no idea that what the angel was doing was really happening;
he thought he was seeing a vision. 10They passed the first and
second guards and came to the iron gate leading to the city. It
opened for them by itself, and they went through it. When they
had walked the length of one street, suddenly the angel left him.
11Then Peter came to himself and said, "Now I know without a
doubt that the Lord sent his angel and rescued me from Herod's
clutches and from everything the Jewish people were anticipating."
12When this had dawned on him, he went to the house of Mary
the mother of John, also called Mark, where many people had
gathered and were praying. 13Peter knocked at the outer entrance,
and a servant girl named Rhoda came to answer the door. 14When
she recognized Peter's voice, she was so overjoyed she ran back
without opening it and exclaimed, "Peter is at the door!"
15"You're out of your mind," they told her. When she kept
insisting that it was so, they said, "It must be his angel."
16But Peter kept on knocking, and when they opened the door
and saw him, they were astonished. 17Peter motioned with his
hand for them to be quiet and described how the Lord had brought
him out of prison. "Tell James and the brothers about this," he
said, and then he left for another place.
18In the morning, there was no small commotion among the
soldiers as to what had become of Peter. 19After Herod had a

Herod, as a Roman official, would now join in the Jewish opposition to the church? **2.** When Rhoda announced who was at the door, what would you have said if you had been there? **3.** How do you feel about the fact that God saved Peter but not James? In light of John 21:18–19, how might Peter respond to this question? **4.** Who is the James of verse 17 (see Gal 1:18–19)? Why do you think he is mentioned? What does this tell you about his importance in the Jerusalem church? **5.** Putting yourself in the place of the soldiers (v. 18), what would you say to each other in the morning? **6.** In verses 20–22, what contrasts do you see between Herod's power and God's? **7.** What do you make of Herod's death (vv. 21–23)? **8.** In this "Judea and Samaria" phase (ch. 8–12) of God's plan (1:8), how has the church fared? What opposition has it faced so far? How far has it expanded?

1. Who truly has power here: Herod or the Lord? What does this tell you about how Christians ought to deal with opposition and persecution? What worldly forces seem all-powerful to you?

Acts 12:1–19 PETER'S MIRACULOUS ESCAPE FROM PRISON

Persecution of the first Christians now resumes—at the hands of the Roman representative King, Herod Agrippa I (nephew of Herod Antipas, who questioned Jesus before his death).

1. If one of the people in your group were put to death and another were thrown into jail, what would that do to your group?
   a. It would bring us closer together.
   b. It would cause us to really pray.
   c. We would stand up for our faith.
   d. We would likely go into hiding.
   e. We would likely give up our faith.
   f. I don't know what we would do.

2. Why do you suppose Herod wanted to kill Peter?
   a. Peter was a threat to his authority.
   b. Peter wouldn't stop preaching.
   c. Herod hated Christians.
   d. Herod wanted to stay on the good side of the Jewish leaders.

3. If the Christians were asking God to deliver Peter from jail, why were they so surprised when he showed up at the door?
   a. They knew how tight the security would be.
   b. They didn't really expect God to answer their prayer.
   c. They were afraid it was a trick.
   d. They were caught off guard.
   e. They reacted the same way I probably would have.

4. If you had been present at this prayer meeting, what would this miracle have done for you?
   a. given me courage
   b. boosted my prayer life
   c. made me ashamed for doubting
   d. drawn our group closer together

5. When has God surprised you by intervening in a situation that you thought was hopeless?

6. Where do you find yourself in prison, so to speak, right now?
   a. in my family relationships
   b. to a craving that holds me captive
   c. to a physical limitation that holds me back
   d. to feelings of low self-worth
   e. to a stagnant spiritual life

7. What would most help you to find freedom from this?
   a. an angel rescuing me
   b. some friends praying for me, and really believing it can happen
   c. my own confidence in God's ability to help me
   d. my own desire to change

8. How can this group assist you in your situation?
   a. leave me alone
   b. pray for me
   c. help me deal with the relationship that binds me
   d. call me every now and then
   e. hold me accountable
   f. other:______________________

9. How are you doing in your quest for an addiction-free lifestyle? What about this course and this group has been the greatest help in your road to recovery?

10. Who is supporting you and praying for you and your recovery? How can this group continue to support and pray for you?

How does this chapter put them in perspective? **2.** How are you like the people at the prayer meeting in this story (v. 12)? **3.** If you were arrested by a dictatorial government for being a Christian, what evidence might they use as proof of your guilt?

What were you called as a child? Did you ever want a new name besides the one you were given?

1. What was the scene when the Holy Spirit spoke to the leaders at Antioch? How do you think he may have spoken? How does he speak today? **2.** Cyprus is a 150-mile sail from Seleucia, and was Barnabas' home (4:36). What might these two men be talking about as they travel? **3.** Since Gentiles were already welcome in the church (11:18), why would Barnabas and Saul go to the synagogue? **4.** The change of Saul's name to Paul (v. 9) may be related to the beginning of his ministry to the Gentiles. Why do you think names are so important to God?

1. With what types of people do you feel most comfortable talking about the Lord? Why? **2.** When have people tried to turn you from your faith? What happened? How do you deal with such pressures? **3.** When should you strongly confront people who oppose Jesus?

---

1. Some great speeches in history are worth committing to memory, at least in part. What famous lines or stanzas from a famous speech can you recall? **2.** Are you the kind of person who can commit things (names, birthdates, phone numbers, clothing sizes) to memory easily? Who in your group

thorough search made for him and did not find him, he cross-examined the guards and ordered that they be executed.

Herod's Death

Then Herod went from Judea to Caesarea and stayed there a
while. 20He had been quarreling with the people of Tyre and Sidon;
they now joined together and sought an audience with him. Having
secured the support of Blastus, a trusted personal servant of the
king, they asked for peace, because they depended on the king's
country for their food supply.
21On the appointed day Herod, wearing his royal robes, sat on
his throne and delivered a public address to the people. 22They
shouted, "This is the voice of a god, not of a man." 23Immediately,
because Herod did not give praise to God, an angel of the Lord
struck him down, and he was eaten by worms and died.
24But the word of God continued to increase and spread.
25When Barnabas and Saul had finished their mission, they returned from[a] Jerusalem, taking with them John, also called Mark.

Barnabas and Saul Sent Off

13 In the church at Antioch there were prophets and teachers:
Barnabas, Simeon called Niger, Lucius of Cyrene, Manaen
(who had been brought up with Herod the tetrarch) and Saul.
2While they were worshiping the Lord and fasting, the Holy Spirit
said, "Set apart for me Barnabas and Saul for the work to which I
have called them." 3So after they had fasted and prayed, they
placed their hands on them and sent them off.

On Cyprus

4The two of them, sent on their way by the Holy Spirit, went
down to Seleucia and sailed from there to Cyprus. 5When they
arrived at Salamis, they proclaimed the word of God in the Jewish
synagogues. John was with them as their helper.
6They traveled through the whole island until they came to Paphos. There they met a Jewish sorcerer and false prophet named
Bar-Jesus, 7who was an attendant of the proconsul, Sergius Paulus.
The proconsul, an intelligent man, sent for Barnabas and Saul because he wanted to hear the word of God. 8But Elymas the sorcerer
(for that is what his name means) opposed them and tried to turn
the proconsul from the faith. 9Then Saul, who was also called Paul,
filled with the Holy Spirit, looked straight at Elymas and said,
10"You are a child of the devil and an enemy of everything that is
right! You are full of all kinds of deceit and trickery. Will you never
stop perverting the right ways of the Lord? 11Now the hand of the
Lord is against you. You are going to be blind, and for a time you
will be unable to see the light of the sun."
Immediately mist and darkness came over him, and he groped
about, seeking someone to lead him by the hand. 12When the
proconsul saw what had happened, he believed, for he was amazed
at the teaching about the Lord.

In Pisidian Antioch

13From Paphos, Paul and his companions sailed to Perga in Pamphylia, where John left them to return to Jerusalem. 14From Perga
they went on to Pisidian Antioch. On the Sabbath they entered the
synagogue and sat down. 15After the reading from the Law and the
Prophets, the synagogue rulers sent word to them, saying, "Broth-

[a]25 Some manuscripts *to*

ers, if you have a message of encouragement for the people, please speak."

16Standing up, Paul motioned with his hand and said: "Men of Israel and you Gentiles who worship God, listen to me! 17The God of the people of Israel chose our fathers; he made the people prosper during their stay in Egypt, with mighty power he led them out of that country, 18he endured their conduct[a] for about forty years in the desert, 19he overthrew seven nations in Canaan and gave their land to his people as their inheritance. 20All this took about 450 years.

"After this, God gave them judges until the time of Samuel the prophet. 21Then the people asked for a king, and he gave them Saul son of Kish, of the tribe of Benjamin, who ruled forty years. 22After removing Saul, he made David their king. He testified concerning him: 'I have found David son of Jesse a man after my own heart; he will do everything I want him to do.'

23"From this man's descendants God has brought to Israel the Savior Jesus, as he promised. 24Before the coming of Jesus, John preached repentance and baptism to all the people of Israel. 25As John was completing his work, he said: 'Who do you think I am? I am not that one. No, but he is coming after me, whose sandals I am not worthy to untie.'

26"Brothers, children of Abraham, and you God-fearing Gentiles, it is to us that this message of salvation has been sent. 27The people of Jerusalem and their rulers did not recognize Jesus, yet in condemning him they fulfilled the words of the prophets that are read every Sabbath. 28Though they found no proper ground for a death sentence, they asked Pilate to have him executed. 29When they had carried out all that was written about him, they took him down from the tree and laid him in a tomb. 30But God raised him from the dead, 31and for many days he was seen by those who had traveled with him from Galilee to Jerusalem. They are now his witnesses to our people.

32"We tell you the good news: What God promised our fathers 33he has fulfilled for us, their children, by raising up Jesus. As it is written in the second Psalm:

> " 'You are my Son;
> today I have become your Father.[b]'[c]

34The fact that God raised him from the dead, never to decay, is stated in these words:

> " 'I will give you the holy and sure blessings
> promised to David.'[d]

35So it is stated elsewhere:

> " 'You will not let your Holy One see decay.'[e]

36"For when David had served God's purpose in his own generation, he fell asleep; he was buried with his fathers and his body decayed. 37But the one whom God raised from the dead did not see decay.

38"Therefore, my brothers, I want you to know that through Jesus the forgiveness of sins is proclaimed to you. 39Through him everyone who believes is justified from everything you could not be justified from by the law of Moses. 40Take care that what the prophets have said does not happen to you:

[a] *18* Some manuscripts *and cared for them* [b] *33* Or *have begotten you*
[c] *33* Psalm 2:7 [d] *34* Isaiah 55:3 [e] *35* Psalm 16:10

can recall the phone number of a previous residence where you once lived? **3.** What failure of memory is most embarrassing to you?

1. From Cyprus to Pisidian Antioch is about 350 miles by sea and land. What does their willingness to travel so far show about Paul and Barnabas? Why do you think John Mark (12:12; 13:5) may have left them to go back to his home? What consequence will this have for Paul and Barnabus later (see 15:36–41)? **2.** What is significant about Paul's audience (v. 15)? **3.** From verses 17–23, list all the things Paul says God has done. How do God's actions prepare the way for Paul to speak about Jesus in verse 23? **4.** Compare verses 22–23 and 36–37 with Romans 1:3 and Acts 2:29–31: What is the connection between David and Jesus? Why is this so important to Paul and Peter? **5.** What things about Jesus is Paul emphasizing by recalling three famous quotes in verses 33–35? The Resurrection is mentioned four times in verses 30–37. How does the Resurrection confirm the meaning of these quotes? **6.** In verses 38–39, what does Paul say is the central meaning of the Resurrection for his listeners? Compare verse 39 with Romans 3:20–24 and 8:3–4. From these verses, how would you explain what Paul means by being "justified"? **7.** Why does Paul end his sermon with this OT quote, "a warning of judgment" (v. 41)? **8.** What feelings and emotions are created by this sermon in the various groups of people mentioned in verses 42–51? How do you explain such a variety of reactions and responses?

1. If you were to emphasize one central truth about the Gospel, what would it be? Why? **2.** What difference would it make to your faith if there were no Easter to celebrate, but only Good Friday to remember? **3.** How do you think Paul would respond to a modern-day skeptic who felt Jesus was a noble, but misguided, martyr? What role would the OT play in Paul's answer? How would knowing the OT, even memorizing it, help you to understand and share your faith better? **4.** What kind of opposition have you faced because of your faith? How do you usually respond to opposition? Does it make you stronger? Why? Would it be tougher for you to face opposition from community leaders or from family members? Why? **5.** Do you "honor the word of the Lord" (v. 48)? Why or why not? **6.** What has God given you that causes you to consider yourself worthy to have eternal life (v. 46)? The Spirit? Spiritual gifts? Forgiveness? A place in God's purpose? Other?

41" 'Look, you scoffers,
wonder and perish,
for I am going to do something in your days
that you would never believe,
even if someone told you.'[a]"

42As Paul and Barnabas were leaving the synagogue, the people
invited them to speak further about these things on the next Sabbath. 43When the congregation was dismissed, many of the Jews
and devout converts to Judaism followed Paul and Barnabas, who
talked with them and urged them to continue in the grace of God.
44On the next Sabbath almost the whole city gathered to hear
the word of the Lord. 45When the Jews saw the crowds, they were
filled with jealousy and talked abusively against what Paul was
saying.
46Then Paul and Barnabas answered them boldly: "We had to
speak the word of God to you first. Since you reject it and do not
consider yourselves worthy of eternal life, we now turn to the
Gentiles. 47For this is what the Lord has commanded us:

" 'I have made you[b] a light for the Gentiles,
that you[b] may bring salvation to the ends of
the earth.'[c]"

48When the Gentiles heard this, they were glad and honored the
word of the Lord; and all who were appointed for eternal life
believed.
49The word of the Lord spread through the whole region. 50But
the Jews incited the God-fearing women of high standing and the
leading men of the city. They stirred up persecution against Paul
and Barnabas, and expelled them from their region. 51So they
shook the dust from their feet in protest against them and went to
Iconium. 52And the disciples were filled with joy and with the Holy
Spirit.

In your youthful idealism, for what social, political or religious causes were you willing to "go to the mat," if need be? Did you ever have to?

1. How does Paul and Barnabas' experience in Iconium differ from their experience in Antioch? How is it similar? **2.** What is the purpose of signs and wonders here (see also 6:8)? Why are the people divided (v. 4)? **3.** What was religious life like in Lystra? **4.** Compare 14:8–13 with 3:1–11. How are the two stories alike and different? What results from each healing? **5.** What does Paul emphasize about God in his speech? How is his speech to this crowd (vv. 15–17) different from his previous sermon in the synagogue (see 13:17–41)? Why the difference? **6.** Since Antioch was 100 miles away, what does that tell you about the nature of Paul's opposition? **7.** How would you feel if you were one of these new believers (vv. 21–25) and you heard about the treatment Paul and Barnabas had received?

In Iconium

14 At Iconium Paul and Barnabas went as usual into the Jewish
synagogue. There they spoke so effectively that a great
number of Jews and Gentiles believed. 2But the Jews who refused
to believe stirred up the Gentiles and poisoned their minds against
the brothers. 3So Paul and Barnabas spent considerable time there,
speaking boldly for the Lord, who confirmed the message of his
grace by enabling them to do miraculous signs and wonders. 4The
people of the city were divided; some sided with the Jews, others
with the apostles. 5There was a plot afoot among the Gentiles and
Jews, together with their leaders, to mistreat them and stone them.
6But they found out about it and fled to the Lycaonian cities of
Lystra and Derbe and to the surrounding country, 7where they
continued to preach the good news.

In Lystra and Derbe

8In Lystra there sat a man crippled in his feet, who was lame
from birth and had never walked. 9He listened to Paul as he was
speaking. Paul looked directly at him, saw that he had faith to be
healed 10and called out, "Stand up on your feet!" At that, the man
jumped up and began to walk.
11When the crowd saw what Paul had done, they shouted in the
Lycaonian language, "The gods have come down to us in human
form!" 12Barnabas they called Zeus, and Paul they called Hermes

[a]*41* Hab. 1:5 [b]*47* The Greek is singular. [c]*47* Isaiah 49:6

because he was the chief speaker. 13The priest of Zeus, whose
temple was just outside the city, brought bulls and wreaths to the city
gates because he and the crowd wanted to offer sacrifices to them.
14But when the apostles Barnabas and Paul heard of this, they
tore their clothes and rushed out into the crowd, shouting:
15"Men, why are you doing this? We too are only men, human like
you. We are bringing you good news, telling you to turn from these
worthless things to the living God, who made heaven and earth
and sea and everything in them. 16In the past, he let all nations go
their own way. 17Yet he has not left himself without testimony: He
has shown kindness by giving you rain from heaven and crops in
their seasons; he provides you with plenty of food and fills your
hearts with joy." 18Even with these words, they had difficulty keeping the crowd from sacrificing to them.
19Then some Jews came from Antioch and Iconium and won the
crowd over. They stoned Paul and dragged him outside the city,
thinking he was dead. 20But after the disciples had gathered around
him, he got up and went back into the city. The next day he and
Barnabas left for Derbe.

The Return to Antioch in Syria

21They preached the good news in that city and won a large
number of disciples. Then they returned to Lystra, Iconium and
Antioch, 22strengthening the disciples and encouraging them to
remain true to the faith. "We must go through many hardships to
enter the kingdom of God," they said. 23Paul and Barnabas appointed elders[a] for them in each church and, with prayer and fasting,
committed them to the Lord, in whom they had put their trust.
24After going through Pisidia, they came into Pamphylia, 25and
when they had preached the word in Perga, they went down to
Attalia.
26From Attalia they sailed back to Antioch, where they had been
committed to the grace of God for the work they had now completed. 27On arriving there, they gathered the church together and
reported all that God had done through them and how he had
opened the door of faith to the Gentiles. 28And they stayed there a
long time with the disciples.

The Council at Jerusalem

15 Some men came down from Judea to Antioch and were
teaching the brothers: "Unless you are circumcised, according to the custom taught by Moses, you cannot be saved." 2This
brought Paul and Barnabas into sharp dispute and debate with
them. So Paul and Barnabas were appointed, along with some
other believers, to go up to Jerusalem to see the apostles and elders
about this question. 3The church sent them on their way, and as
they traveled through Phoenicia and Samaria, they told how the
Gentiles had been converted. This news made all the brothers very
glad. 4When they came to Jerusalem, they were welcomed by the
church and the apostles and elders, to whom they reported everything God had done through them.
5Then some of the believers who belonged to the party of the
Pharisees stood up and said, "The Gentiles must be circumcised
and required to obey the law of Moses."
6The apostles and elders met to consider this question. 7After
much discussion, Peter got up and addressed them: "Brothers, you
know that some time ago God made a choice among you that the

[a]23 Or *Barnabas ordained elders*; or *Barnabas had elders elected*

8. Reviewing this journey of about 1100 miles (13:1–14:26), what do you learn about Paul? About the Gospel?

1. Seeing Paul and Barnabas' courage, faith and endurance, how are you challenged to serve the Lord more completely? **2.** What does the difference between Paul's sermon (13:17–41) and his speech in verses 15–17 teach you about sharing your faith with various groups of people? **3.** The people Paul and Barnabas encountered along the way interpreted the Gospel through their own lenses, even calling them Hermes and Zeus. How do people you know interpret the Gospel by their own prejudices and beliefs? **4.** What was one of the biggest misunderstandings about Christianity you had to overcome before you could believe? **5.** How would you share the Gospel differently with a Jewish person than you would a non-Jewish person?

What were some of the expected, extra-biblical rules you were supposed to follow in the church where you grew up? When you became a Christian?

1. What other things would these teachers say the Gentiles must do (vv. 1,5 see Mk 2:16, 18,24; 7:1–5)? **2.** If you were a Gentile hearing that these regulations were required, how would you feel about your new faith? As a strict Jew, why would these rules be important to you? **3.** What is the main issue as Paul sees it (vv. 1–2; see Gal 2:21; 3:5,10–14)? **4.** How would you describe Peter's struggle with this issue (vv. 7–11; see 10:28,34–35; Gal 2:11–13)? How does Paul's teaching in Galatians 2:15–16 show its influence on Peter here? **5.** Knowing Paul's

Pharisaic background (26:5) and Peter's desire to keep the law (10:14), how would their testimony carry the day? **6.** What has led James to change his mind? **7.** What is the significance of the council's decision in light of 1:8? Why were the conditions of verse 20 added (see 1Co 8)?

1. What roles do experience, theology and practical considerations play in the decision-making process of this council? What issues, now troubling your church, could be resolved by looking at them with these three perspectives? **2.** Is there some area of your faith where you feel like Peter—going back and forth because you are not sure of what is right? How could verse 11 relate to this concern? **3.** What additions to the Gospel might a new believer encounter in your church? What should you do about that?

What experience have you had in a church with a worship style different than what you were used to?

1. Why would a letter *and* representatives from the Jerusalem church be a good way to communicate the apostles' decision? **2.** What is the tone of the letter? Its main points (vv. 22–29)? **3.** How do Judas and Silas personally add to this letter? What else brings unity to the primarily Jewish church in Jerusalem and the primarily Gentile church in Antioch? **4.** How would things be different if those in 15:5 had been successful?

1. From the debate, the resulting letter, and the way in which it was delivered, what do you learn about the way to solve disagreements among Christians? What conflicts are active in your church? Is your church's style of handling disagreements similar to the way the issue was handled in chapter 15? **2.** In your community's churches, what are the ethnic, social and racial lines of division?

Gentiles might hear from my lips the message of the gospel and
believe. 8God, who knows the heart, showed that he accepted
them by giving the Holy Spirit to them, just as he did to us. 9He
made no distinction between us and them, for he purified their
hearts by faith. 10Now then, why do you try to test God by putting
on the necks of the disciples a yoke that neither we nor our fathers
have been able to bear? 11No! We believe it is through the grace of
our Lord Jesus that we are saved, just as they are."

12The whole assembly became silent as they listened to Barnabas
and Paul telling about the miraculous signs and wonders God had
done among the Gentiles through them. 13When they finished,
James spoke up: "Brothers, listen to me. 14Simon[a] has described
to us how God at first showed his concern by taking from the
Gentiles a people for himself. 15The words of the prophets are in
agreement with this, as it is written:

16" 'After this I will return
and rebuild David's fallen tent.
Its ruins I will rebuild,
and I will restore it,
17that the remnant of men may seek the Lord,
and all the Gentiles who bear my name,
says the Lord, who does these things'[b]
18 that have been known for ages.[c]

19"It is my judgment, therefore, that we should not make it
difficult for the Gentiles who are turning to God. 20Instead we
should write to them, telling them to abstain from food polluted by
idols, from sexual immorality, from the meat of strangled animals
and from blood. 21For Moses has been preached in every city from
the earliest times and is read in the synagogues on every Sabbath."

The Council's Letter to Gentile Believers

22Then the apostles and elders, with the whole church, decided
to choose some of their own men and send them to Antioch with
Paul and Barnabas. They chose Judas (called Barsabbas) and Silas,
two men who were leaders among the brothers. 23With them they
sent the following letter:

The apostles and elders, your brothers,

To the Gentile believers in Antioch, Syria and Cilicia:

Greetings.

24We have heard that some went out from us without our
authorization and disturbed you, troubling your minds by
what they said. 25So we all agreed to choose some men and
send them to you with our dear friends Barnabas and Paul—
26men who have risked their lives for the name of our Lord
Jesus Christ. 27Therefore we are sending Judas and Silas to
confirm by word of mouth what we are writing. 28It seemed
good to the Holy Spirit and to us not to burden you with
anything beyond the following requirements: 29You are to abstain from food sacrificed to idols, from blood, from the meat
of strangled animals and from sexual immorality. You will do
well to avoid these things.

Farewell.

[a] *14* Greek *Simeon*, a variant of *Simon*; that is, Peter [b] *17* Amos 9:11,12
[c] *17,18* Some manuscripts *things'— / 18known to the Lord for ages is his work*

30The men were sent off and went down to Antioch, where they gathered the church together and delivered the letter. 31The people read it and were glad for its encouraging message. 32Judas and Silas, who themselves were prophets, said much to encourage and strengthen the brothers. 33After spending some time there, they were sent off by the brothers with the blessing of peace to return to those who had sent them.[a] 35But Paul and Barnabas remained in Antioch, where they and many others taught and preached the word of the Lord.

What is your relationship like with believers in these different churches?

Disagreement Between Paul and Barnabas

36Some time later Paul said to Barnabas, "Let us go back and visit the brothers in all the towns where we preached the word of the Lord and see how they are doing." 37Barnabas wanted to take John, also called Mark, with them, 38but Paul did not think it wise to take him, because he had deserted them in Pamphylia and had not continued with them in the work. 39They had such a sharp disagreement that they parted company. Barnabas took Mark and sailed for Cyprus, 40but Paul chose Silas and left, commended by the brothers to the grace of the Lord. 41He went through Syria and Cilicia, strengthening the churches.

Timothy Joins Paul and Silas

16 He came to Derbe and then to Lystra, where a disciple named Timothy lived, whose mother was a Jewess and a believer, but whose father was a Greek. 2The brothers at Lystra and Iconium spoke well of him. 3Paul wanted to take him along on the journey, so he circumcised him because of the Jews who lived in that area, for they all knew that his father was a Greek. 4As they traveled from town to town, they delivered the decisions reached by the apostles and elders in Jerusalem for the people to obey. 5So the churches were strengthened in the faith and grew daily in numbers.

What "break-up" was hardest for you and why: Moving? Losing your first girl/boyfriend? Empty nest? Closing shop?

1. Role play how you think Paul and Barnabas split up. With which one would you have sided? Why? **2.** Given the decision in Chapter 15, why did Paul circumcise Timothy? How could this be justified (see 1Co 9:19–23)?

1. When have you given up your "rights" in order to better represent Christ to others? How can you do so now? **2.** Have you ever lost a friendship because of a religious dispute? What happened?

Paul's Vision of the Man of Macedonia

6Paul and his companions traveled throughout the region of Phrygia and Galatia, having been kept by the Holy Spirit from preaching the word in the province of Asia. 7When they came to the border of Mysia, they tried to enter Bithynia, but the Spirit of Jesus would not allow them to. 8So they passed by Mysia and went down to Troas. 9During the night Paul had a vision of a man of Macedonia standing and begging him, "Come over to Macedonia and help us." 10After Paul had seen the vision, we got ready at once to leave for Macedonia, concluding that God had called us to preach the gospel to them.

Lydia's Conversion in Philippi

11From Troas we put out to sea and sailed straight for Samothrace, and the next day on to Neapolis. 12From there we traveled to Philippi, a Roman colony and the leading city of that district of Macedonia. And we stayed there several days.

13On the Sabbath we went outside the city gate to the river, where we expected to find a place of prayer. We sat down and began to speak to the women who had gathered there. 14One of those listening was a woman named Lydia, a dealer in purple cloth from the city of Thyatira, who was a worshiper of God. The Lord

What was the best idea or invention you ever came up with? How did it turn out?

1. Note the change from "they" (v. 8) to "we" (v. 10): How does this relate to Luke 1:3–4? **2.** How does this closed door point to another opportunity? **3.** Compare verse 13 with 14:1 and 17:2. What does the lack of a synagogue in Philippi indicate about Jewish community there? How did that affect Paul's strategy for mission? **4.** What do you make of Lydia's career and conversion?

1. How did the Lord open your heart to respond to the Gospel? Who did he use as part of the process? **2.** Where do you have an "open door" for ministry now: In your home? School? Work? Community? How will you take advantage of it?

[a]33 Some manuscripts *them,* 34*but Silas decided to remain there*

opened her heart to respond to Paul's message. 15When she and
the members of her household were baptized, she invited us to her
home. "If you consider me a believer in the Lord," she said, "come
and stay at my house." And she persuaded us.

Paul and Silas in Prison

16Once when we were going to the place of prayer, we were met
by a slave girl who had a spirit by which she predicted the future.
She earned a great deal of money for her owners by fortune-telling.
17This girl followed Paul and the rest of us, shouting, "These men
are servants of the Most High God, who are telling you the way to
be saved." 18She kept this up for many days. Finally Paul became so
troubled that he turned around and said to the spirit, "In the name
of Jesus Christ I command you to come out of her!" At that moment the spirit left her.
19When the owners of the slave girl realized that their hope of
making money was gone, they seized Paul and Silas and dragged
them into the marketplace to face the authorities. 20They brought
them before the magistrates and said, "These men are Jews, and
are throwing our city into an uproar 21by advocating customs unlawful for us Romans to accept or practice."
22The crowd joined in the attack against Paul and Silas, and the
magistrates ordered them to be stripped and beaten. 23After they
had been severely flogged, they were thrown into prison, and the
jailer was commanded to guard them carefully. 24Upon receiving
such orders, he put them in the inner cell and fastened their feet in
the stocks.
25About midnight Paul and Silas were praying and singing hymns
to God, and the other prisoners were listening to them. 26Suddenly

---

What type of music lifts your spirits? What music reminds you of the "good ol' days"?

1. How do you think a shouting slave girl affected the apostles' mood? Their goals? **2.** Retell verses 17–21 from the perspective of the owners of the girl: What do you feel about her? About your money? About these missionaries? **3.** Since there was no synagogue in Philippi (v. 13), and since the Gentile missionaries (Luke and Timothy) were not seized, how could racism be a factor in the actions described in verses 19–24? What might be meant by the charge against them? **4.** In light of what happened, how do you think Paul and Silas felt in verse 25? If you were falsely accused, severely beaten and thrown into a dark jail, would you still trust in God' plan (vv. 23–30)? Why or why not? **5.** What does the response of Paul and Silas show about them? If you were the jailer, what would you

Acts 16:11–15 LYDIA'S CONVERSION

The apostle Paul's missionary travels brought him to Philippi. Paul's practice was first to preach at each city's synagogue. But there were so few Jews in Philippi that there was no synagogue there. In such cities it was common for the Jews and those Gentiles interested in Judaism ("worshippers of God," like Lydia in this story) to gather outdoors near running water.

1. Which of the following words best describes your impression of Lydia?
   a. persuasive
   b. spiritual
   c. trusting
   d. industrious
   e. hospitable
   f. impulsive
   g. naive
   h. friendly
2. Which of the following do you find most impressive about Lydia?
   a. She was a businesswoman at a time when few women were.
   b. Her heart was immediately receptive to the Gospel.
   c. She convinced her household to be baptized.
   d. She was willing to open her home to strangers.
3. Lydia managed to care for her business, her spiritual life and her household. On a scale from 1 to 10, how would you rate yourself in each area:
   a. business/professional life
   b. spiritual life
   c. home life
4. What step do you need to take to put your work life, spiritual life and family life in better balance?
5. Lydia's "place of prayer" was by a river. What is your favorite place to meet God?
   a. in church
   b. with others in a small group
   c. alone in my home
   d. outside in natural surroundings
   e. at special meetings or retreats
   f. other:____________________
6. How did the Lord open your heart to respond to the Gospel? What people did God use as part of the process?
7. In comparison, how open to the Lord is your heart right now? What would make it, and keep it, more open?
8. When you were little, what did you want to be when you grew up?
9. Regarding career and family, what are your hopes and dreams now? What would you change about your life if you could?
10. Lydia's status appears to have been "single head of household." What example from her life would you like to apply to your life?
    a. She didn't seem to resent her situation in life.
    b. She made the most of her life both vocationally and spiritually.
    c. She used her situation in life to hospitably serve others.
    d. She avoided loneliness by taking initiative to reach out to people.
11. What have you appreciated about this course, and how has this group served you? Have one person at a time listen silently while others share their thanks or affirmation of that person.

there was such a violent earthquake that the foundations of the
prison were shaken. At once all the prison doors flew open, and
everybody's chains came loose. [27]The jailer woke up, and when he
saw the prison doors open, he drew his sword and was about to kill
himself because he thought the prisoners had escaped. [28]But Paul
shouted, "Don't harm yourself! We are all here!"
[29]The jailer called for lights, rushed in and fell trembling before
Paul and Silas. [30]He then brought them out and asked, "Sirs, what
must I do to be saved?"
[31]They replied, "Believe in the Lord Jesus, and you will be
saved—you and your household." [32]Then they spoke the word of
the Lord to him and to all the others in his house. [33]At that hour of
the night the jailer took them and washed their wounds; then
immediately he and all his family were baptized. [34]The jailer
brought them into his house and set a meal before them; he was
filled with joy because he had come to believe in God—he and his
whole family.
[35]When it was daylight, the magistrates sent their officers to the
jailer with the order: "Release those men." [36]The jailer told Paul,
"The magistrates have ordered that you and Silas be released. Now
you can leave. Go in peace."
[37]But Paul said to the officers: "They beat us publicly without a
trial, even though we are Roman citizens, and threw us into prison.
And now do they want to get rid of us quietly? No! Let them come
themselves and escort us out."
[38]The officers reported this to the magistrates, and when they
heard that Paul and Silas were Roman citizens, they were alarmed.
[39]They came to appease them and escorted them from the prison,
requesting them to leave the city. [40]After Paul and Silas came out of

think of Paul and Silas singing? Remaining? **6.** What kind of man was the jailer before his salvation? In what ways does the jailer express his new faith in Jesus? **7.** Given the charge against them (vv. 20–21), why would Paul insist on his rights as a Roman citizen?

1. The girl's owners rejected the Gospel because it cost them financially. What financial concerns keep some people from faith today? Are any of these a factor for you? **2.** About 12 years later, Paul wrote the letter to the Philippians from another prison. How could the events here be the basis for what Paul said in Philippians 4:4–7,12–13? What can you learn from his example about knowing peace and joy, even in hard times? **3.** If asked, "What must I do to be saved?" how would you answer?

Acts 16:16–40 PAUL AND SILAS IN PRISON

These events take place in the city of Philippi, a Roman colony, during the apostle Paul's second missionary trip.

1. How would you have felt if someone kept shouting, "These men are servants of the Most High God, who are telling you the way to be saved"?
   a. This is good advertising!
   b. This is spooky!
   c. This is driving me crazy!
   d. The words are true, but I'm afraid this is doing more harm than good.

2. What motivated the slave girl's owners to seize Paul and Silas and bring charges against them?
   a. anger
   b. legal issues
   c. anti-Semitism
   d. greed
   e. fear
   f. spite

3. How would you have felt if you were falsely accused, flogged and put in stocks in a dark prison cell?
   a. like getting out of missionary work
   b. like praying and singing hymns
   c. like suing for police brutality
   d. like thanking God for the honor of suffering for him

4. What caused the jailer to want to be saved?
   a. Paul and Silas' example of faith
   b. hearing about their preaching and the slave girl's deliverance
   c. hearing them pray and sing
   d. the earthquake
   e. Paul and Silas' concern that he not take his own life
   f. all of the above

5. In what ways did the jailer demonstrate his new-found faith in the Lord Jesus?

6. How much joy did you have when you first committed your life to Christ? How much joy do you have now?

7. If someone asked you, "What must I do to be saved?"—how would you answer?

8. What does this story say to you about dealing with hard times? How hard is it for you to pray and be thankful in the midst of chaotic or difficult experiences?

9. How does this story relate to the stress in your life?
   a. I feel like I'm constantly hounded by people or demands (v. 18).
   b. I worry about my "hope of making money" disappearing (v. 19).
   c. I'm facing criticism, false accusation or discrimination (vv. 20–21).
   d. I feel trapped ("fastened in the stocks") in a bad situation (v. 24).
   e. I have to take the blame for things out of my control (v. 27).
   f. I need someone to support me and "wash my wounds" (v. 33).

10. What is the closest your marriage has come to a powerful shared spiritual experience like that of the jailer and his family? How can your faith, and in particular your prayer lives, strengthen and support your marriage in the area of communication and conflict?

11. Who are the Paul and Silas type people who challenge and support your marriage? How could greater support from others help strengthen your marriage?

the prison, they went to Lydia's house, where they met with the brothers and encouraged them. Then they left.

In Thessalonica

17 When they had passed through Amphipolis and Apollonia, they came to Thessalonica, where there was a Jewish synagogue. 2As his custom was, Paul went into the synagogue, and on three Sabbath days he reasoned with them from the Scriptures, 3explaining and proving that the Christ[a] had to suffer and rise from the dead. "This Jesus I am proclaiming to you is the Christ,[a]" he said. 4Some of the Jews were persuaded and joined Paul and Silas, as did a large number of God-fearing Greeks and not a few prominent women.

5But the Jews were jealous; so they rounded up some bad characters from the marketplace, formed a mob and started a riot in the city. They rushed to Jason's house in search of Paul and Silas in order to bring them out to the crowd.[b] 6But when they did not find them, they dragged Jason and some other brothers before the city officials, shouting: "These men who have caused trouble all over the world have now come here, 7and Jason has welcomed them into his house. They are all defying Caesar's decrees, saying that there is another king, one called Jesus." 8When they heard this, the crowd and the city officials were thrown into turmoil. 9Then they made Jason and the others post bond and let them go.

In Berea

10As soon as it was night, the brothers sent Paul and Silas away to Berea. On arriving there, they went to the Jewish synagogue. 11Now the Bereans were of more noble character than the Thessalonians, for they received the message with great eagerness and examined the Scriptures every day to see if what Paul said was true. 12Many of the Jews believed, as did also a number of prominent Greek women and many Greek men.

13When the Jews in Thessalonica learned that Paul was preaching the word of God at Berea, they went there too, agitating the crowds and stirring them up. 14The brothers immediately sent Paul to the coast, but Silas and Timothy stayed at Berea. 15The men who escorted Paul brought him to Athens and then left with instructions for Silas and Timothy to join him as soon as possible.

What has been your most exciting experience in a crowd? Your scariest experience?

1. Thessalonica was a wealthy trading city on a major road from the Adriatic Sea to the Black Sea (see map in Introduction to Acts). How is Paul received (see 1Th 1:4–10; 3:1–4)? **2.** What accusations has Paul encountered so far (vv. 5–7; also 16:20–21)? What lies behind these accusations? **3.** Since his conversion, this is the sixth time Paul has been forced by persecution to leave an area. How would you view your mission if that happened to you? How does your response compare with Paul's (see 1Th 2:1–6)? **4.** Compared with the Thessalonians (vv. 2–4), how do the Bereans receive the Gospel (vv. 11–12)? **5.** How is Paul's teaching on the diversity of gifts (1Co 12) illustrated here in the functions of Paul, Silas and Timothy?

1. Whether Jesus or Caesar was Lord became a real issue for Christians. When has your faith in Christ led to conflict with other authorities claiming your loyalty? **2.** In terms of time, consistency and intensity, how would you rate your Bible study? Is it at all like the Bereans?

In Athens

16While Paul was waiting for them in Athens, he was greatly distressed to see that the city was full of idols. 17So he reasoned in the synagogue with the Jews and the God-fearing Greeks, as well as in the marketplace day by day with those who happened to be there. 18A group of Epicurean and Stoic philosophers began to dispute with him. Some of them asked, "What is this babbler trying to say?" Others remarked, "He seems to be advocating foreign gods." They said this because Paul was preaching the good news about Jesus and the resurrection. 19Then they took him and brought him to a meeting of the Areopagus, where they said to him, "May we know what this new teaching is that you are presenting? 20You are bringing some strange ideas to our ears, and we want to know what they mean." 21(All the Athenians and the foreigners who lived there spent their time doing nothing but talking about and listening to the latest ideas.)

22Paul then stood up in the meeting of the Areopagus and said:

If someone made a statue of you, what pose would be most appropriate? What inscription?

1. To be noticed by the Greek philosophers of Athens, how extensive was Paul's activity? **2.** What previous understanding of Christianity did these philosophers have? **3.** The Stoics believed in pantheism while the Epicureans had little or no belief in God. What does Paul emphasize about God (vv. 23–30)? How does Paul use their own culture and ideas to help them see the weaknesses in the way they relate to deity? **4.** How is this sermon unlike the one to Jews in 13:16–41? Is not using Scripture here a strength or a weakness? Why? How are the

[a]3 Or *Messiah* [b]5 Or *the assembly of the people*

"Men of Athens! I see that in every way you are very religious. 23For as I walked around and looked carefully at your objects of worship, I even found an altar with this inscription: TO AN UNKNOWN GOD. Now what you worship as something unknown I am going to proclaim to you.

24"The God who made the world and everything in it is the Lord of heaven and earth and does not live in temples built by hands. 25And he is not served by human hands, as if he needed anything, because he himself gives all men life and breath and everything else. 26From one man he made every nation of men, that they should inhabit the whole earth; and he determined the times set for them and the exact places where they should live. 27God did this so that men would seek him and perhaps reach out for him and find him, though he is not far from each one of us. 28'For in him we live and move and have our being.' As some of your own poets have said, 'We are his offspring.'

29"Therefore since we are God's offspring, we should not think that the divine being is like gold or silver or stone—an image made by man's design and skill. 30In the past God overlooked such ignorance, but now he commands all people everywhere to repent. 31For he has set a day when he will judge the world with justice by the man he has appointed. He has given proof of this to all men by raising him from the dead."

32When they heard about the resurrection of the dead, some of them sneered, but others said, "We want to hear you again on this subject." 33At that, Paul left the Council. 34A few men became followers of Paul and believed. Among them was Dionysius, a member of the Areopagus, also a woman named Damaris, and a number of others.

In Corinth

18 After this, Paul left Athens and went to Corinth. 2There he met a Jew named Aquila, a native of Pontus, who had recently come from Italy with his wife Priscilla, because Claudius had ordered all the Jews to leave Rome. Paul went to see them, 3and because he was a tentmaker as they were, he stayed and worked with them. 4Every Sabbath he reasoned in the synagogue, trying to persuade Jews and Greeks.

5When Silas and Timothy came from Macedonia, Paul devoted himself exclusively to preaching, testifying to the Jews that Jesus was the Christ.[a] 6But when the Jews opposed Paul and became abusive, he shook out his clothes in protest and said to them, "Your blood be on your own heads! I am clear of my responsibility. From now on I will go to the Gentiles."

7Then Paul left the synagogue and went next door to the house of Titius Justus, a worshiper of God. 8Crispus, the synagogue ruler, and his entire household believed in the Lord; and many of the Corinthians who heard him believed and were baptized.

9One night the Lord spoke to Paul in a vision: "Do not be afraid; keep on speaking, do not be silent. 10For I am with you, and no one is going to attack and harm you, because I have many people in this city." 11So Paul stayed for a year and a half, teaching them the word of God.

12While Gallio was proconsul of Achaia, the Jews made a united attack on Paul and brought him into court. 13"This man," they charged, "is persuading the people to worship God in ways contrary to the law."

[a]5 Or *Messiah;* also in verse 28

sermons alike in terms of what they teach about Jesus? **5.** How does the response in Athens (17:21,32–34) compare with Berea (17:12) and Thessalonica (17:4)?

1. What distresses you spiritually about the area in which you live? What specific needs do you see? What do you feel God is calling you to do about it? **2.** Whom do you know who has very little, or no background, in the Gospel? Could you share the Gospel with someone without quoting Bible verses? Why or why not? **3.** Paul uses idols and Greek poetry as points of contact with these people. What could you use as a point of contact with people today in your efforts to relate the Gospel?

What skill do you have from a hobby or interest that you could use to make money in a full-time job?

1. Claudius' order (v. 2) was given in A.D. 50 after a Jewish riot in Rome over the preaching of Christ. What else reveals a Roman attitude toward Christianity (vv. 12–17)? Would this help or hinder Christian witness? **2.** How did Paul's ministry change after Timothy and Silas came to him (see 2Co 11:9)? **3.** How might Paul feel about the beginning of his ministry at Corinth (see 1Co 2:3)? How might the vision from God (vv. 9–10) and the gift from the Philippians encourage him?

1. With what missions or missionaries have you entered into financial partnership? If you were called to the foreign mission field, would you seek such partners, or would you become a "tentmaker"? Why? **2.** How could your present job be "tentmaking" to support your family while you engage in God's kingdom work?

14Just as Paul was about to speak, Gallio said to the Jews, "If you
Jews were making a complaint about some misdemeanor or serious
crime, it would be reasonable for me to listen to you. 15But since it
involves questions about words and names and your own law—settle the matter yourselves. I will not be a judge of such things." 16So
he had them ejected from the court. 17Then they all turned on
Sosthenes the synagogue ruler and beat him in front of the court.
But Gallio showed no concern whatever.

Priscilla, Aquila and Apollos

18Paul stayed on in Corinth for some time. Then he left the
brothers and sailed for Syria, accompanied by Priscilla and Aquila.
Before he sailed, he had his hair cut off at Cenchrea because of a
vow he had taken. 19They arrived at Ephesus, where Paul left
Priscilla and Aquila. He himself went into the synagogue and reasoned with the Jews. 20When they asked him to spend more time
with them, he declined. 21But as he left, he promised, "I will come
back if it is God's will." Then he set sail from Ephesus. 22When he
landed at Caesarea, he went up and greeted the church and then
went down to Antioch.

23After spending some time in Antioch, Paul set out from there
and traveled from place to place throughout the region of Galatia
and Phrygia, strengthening all the disciples.

24Meanwhile a Jew named Apollos, a native of Alexandria, came
to Ephesus. He was a learned man, with a thorough knowledge of
the Scriptures. 25He had been instructed in the way of the Lord,
and he spoke with great fervor[a] and taught about Jesus accurately,

[a]25 Or *with fervor in the Spirit*

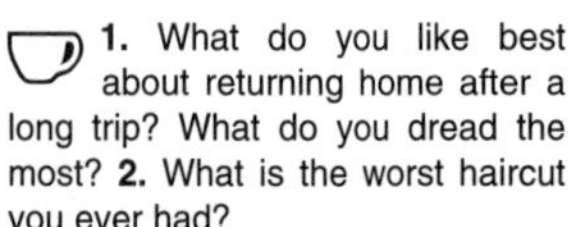

1. What do you like best about returning home after a long trip? What do you dread the most? **2.** What is the worst haircut you ever had?

1. What do you make of his companions Priscilla and Aquila? What type of person was Apollos (vv. 24–26)? **2.** What influence did Apollos have in Achaia, specifically Corinth (vv. 27–28; see 1Co 3:4–6)? How did Priscilla and Aquila assist him? What does this tell you about the role of women in the New Testament?

1. Who was very helpful to you when you were young and enthusiastic about the faith? How did this person help? Who could you help now? How? **2.** Where do you sense God has equipped you to serve? **3.** What

Acts 18:5–17 PAUL'S VISION IN CORINTH

In Acts 18 the apostle Paul comes to Corinth. As usual, his missionary work begins in the Jewish synagogue.

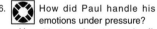

1. What was Paul's attitude toward the Jews when they rejected his message and became abusive?
   a. "I've had it with you people."
   b. "If you go to hell, don't blame me."
   c. "You can lead a horse to water, but you can't make it drink."
   d. "You've had your chance—I'm going where the fish are biting."
2. What *really* caused the Jews to charge Paul in the Roman court?
   a. Unlike Judaism, they felt Paul was advocating a religion not recognized by Roman law.
   b. They were mad that Paul started a church next to the synagogue.
   c. They were jealous and scared because of losing members.
   d. They were spiritually blind.
3. How would you describe Gallio's attitude about the case?
   a. apathetic—"I couldn't care less."
   b. confused—"This is over my head."
   c. angry—"You're wasting my time."
   d. convinced—"Paul is innocent."
4. What effect do you suppose Paul's vision of Christ had on him?
   a. It renewed his courage.
   b. It took away all his problems.
   c. It kept him going for a long time.
   d. It gave him confidence that he was doing what God wanted him to do.
   e. It reminded him that both the Lord and other people were with him.
5. Which of these might the Lord be saying to you right now?
   a. "Do not be afraid."
   b. "Keep on speaking (or doing what you are called to do)."
   c. "Do not be silent (about Christ)."
   d. "I am with you."
   e. "No one is going to attack and harm you."
   f. "I have many people in this city (to help you)."
6.  How did Paul handle his emotions under pressure?
   a. He got testy and wrote people off.
   b. He dealt with conflict directly.
   c. He showed a lot of flexibility by shifting his focus to the Gentiles.
   d. He let the Lord calm his fears.
   e. He found peace in Christ.
7. What happens to your emotions when you are under pressure? How would you like to respond differently?
8. Who are your competitors in your work? What does this story say to you about how to relate to them?
   a. If they want to play hardball, so can I.
   b. Because of God's help, I have nothing to fear.
   c. The main thing is that I am faithful to do what God wants me to do.
   d. I can be content with whatever success comes my way.
9. What have you appreciated about this course? Go around the circle and answer this question: How has the person to your left been a gift to you and to your group?

though he knew only the baptism of John. 26He began to speak
boldly in the synagogue. When Priscilla and Aquila heard him, they
invited him to their home and explained to him the way of God
more adequately.
27When Apollos wanted to go to Achaia, the brothers encouraged him and wrote to the disciples there to welcome him. On
arriving, he was a great help to those who by grace had believed.
28For he vigorously refuted the Jews in public debate, proving from
the Scriptures that Jesus was the Christ.

role do women have in your church? How do you feel about that? **4.** How does your church balance evangelism with the strengthening and equipping of believers?

Paul in Ephesus

19 While Apollos was at Corinth, Paul took the road through
the interior and arrived at Ephesus. There he found some
disciples 2and asked them, "Did you receive the Holy Spirit
when[a] you believed?"
They answered, "No, we have not even heard that there is a
Holy Spirit."
3So Paul asked, "Then what baptism did you receive?"
"John's baptism," they replied.
4Paul said, "John's baptism was a baptism of repentance. He told
the people to believe in the one coming after him, that is, in
Jesus." 5On hearing this, they were baptized into[b] the name of
the Lord Jesus. 6When Paul placed his hands on them, the Holy

[a] 2 Or *after* [b] 5 Or *in*

What experiences have you had with religious counterfeits (relics, forgeries, hoaxes, cults and the like)? Any that have really scared you?

1. Why do you think Paul went to Ephesus on his next trip (see 18:19–21)? **2.** Apollos was from Egypt (18:24–25), and these disciples were about 800 miles from Jerusalem. What does the fact that they were followers of John the Baptist tell you about the extent of his influence? How would their awareness of John be good preparation for them to hear the Gospel (see Jn 1:19–34)? **3.** Since

  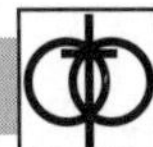

Acts 18:1–4,18–28 PRISCILLA, AQUILA AND APOLLOS

1. What surprises you most?
   a. that the apostle Paul supported himself by making tents (v. 3)
   b. that Paul had his hair cut off because of a vow (v. 18)
   c. that Priscilla, a woman, was so active in ministry, and her name was even mentioned before her husband's (vv. 18–19, 26)
   d. that Apollos with all his fervor and knowledge did not understand Christian baptism (vv. 24–25)
2. What best illustrates Priscilla and Aquila's virtues as servant-leaders?
   a. their tentmaking business partnership with Paul
   b. their invitation and willingness to travel with Paul
   c. Paul's leaving them in Ephesus to start forming a new church there
   d. their ability to teach Apollos
   e. their hospitality toward Paul in Corinth and Apollos in Ephesus
3. How do you envision Apollos?
   a. a silver-tongued orator
   b. an absent-minded professor
   c. a fiery preacher
   d. a sophisticated philosopher
   e. an argumentative bulldog
4. In their lives, Priscilla and Aquila encountered Paul and Apollos—one was a teacher to them and one they taught. Who was one of your early mentors? Whom have you in turn mentored—or could you mentor?
5. What are the primary gifts God has given you for Christian service?
6. On a scale of 1 (totally disagree) to 10 (totally agree), how do you feel about each of the following statements:
   a. Women in leadership was acceptable in the New Testament church.
   b. Women in leadership is acceptable in the church today.
   c. God encourages women to be all that they can be.
   d. Women can realize their full potential in the church.
   e. Gender doesn't matter; what matters is using our gifts for Christ.
7. What type of role do you have in the church? What role would you like to have? What keeps you from that?
8. Priscilla and Aquila were a model of partnership in marriage. Regarding the possibility of discovering a mate, it's important to me to find someone ...
   a. who knows how to make tents.
   b. who shares my faith and values.
   c. whom I find attractive.
   d. who complements my personality and gifts.
   e. with whom I can serve the Lord.
   f. who likes to do everything I like.
9. How can you as a couple use your gifts to serve God and others? How would finding a ministry or service project in which to share affect your marriage?
   a. disastrous—We don't have much free time the way it is.
   b. mostly bad—It would keep our focus off of our marriage.
   c. mostly good—It would force us to spend more time together.
   d. wonderful—A common fulfillment would bind us together.
   e. We are already doing this.
10. How has this course helped strengthen your marriage? Share with the group one word of affirmation for your spouse, then one word for the group.

Spirit came on them, and they spoke in tongues[a] and prophesied. 7There were about twelve men in all.

8Paul entered the synagogue and spoke boldly there for three months, arguing persuasively about the kingdom of God. 9But some of them became obstinate; they refused to believe and publicly maligned the Way. So Paul left them. He took the disciples with him and had discussions daily in the lecture hall of Tyrannus. 10This went on for two years, so that all the Jews and Greeks who lived in the province of Asia heard the word of the Lord.

11God did extraordinary miracles through Paul, 12so that even handkerchiefs and aprons that had touched him were taken to the sick, and their illnesses were cured and the evil spirits left them.

13Some Jews who went around driving out evil spirits tried to invoke the name of the Lord Jesus over those who were demon-possessed. They would say, "In the name of Jesus, whom Paul preaches, I command you to come out." 14Seven sons of Sceva, a Jewish chief priest, were doing this. 15⌊One day⌋ the evil spirit answered them, "Jesus I know, and I know about Paul, but who are you?" 16Then the man who had the evil spirit jumped on them and overpowered them all. He gave them such a beating that they ran out of the house naked and bleeding.

17When this became known to the Jews and Greeks living in Ephesus, they were all seized with fear, and the name of the Lord Jesus was held in high honor. 18Many of those who believed now came and openly confessed their evil deeds. 19A number who had practiced sorcery brought their scrolls together and burned them publicly. When they calculated the value of the scrolls, the total came to fifty thousand drachmas.[b] 20In this way the word of the Lord spread widely and grew in power.

21After all this had happened, Paul decided to go to Jerusalem, passing through Macedonia and Achaia. "After I have been there," he said, "I must visit Rome also." 22He sent two of his helpers, Timothy and Erastus, to Macedonia, while he stayed in the province of Asia a little longer.

The Riot in Ephesus

23About that time there arose a great disturbance about the Way. 24A silversmith named Demetrius, who made silver shrines of Artemis, brought in no little business for the craftsmen. 25He called them together, along with the workmen in related trades, and said: "Men, you know we receive a good income from this business. 26And you see and hear how this fellow Paul has convinced and led astray large numbers of people here in Ephesus and in practically the whole province of Asia. He says that man-made gods are no gods at all. 27There is danger not only that our trade will lose its good name, but also that the temple of the great goddess Artemis will be discredited, and the goddess herself, who is worshiped throughout the province of Asia and the world, will be robbed of her divine majesty."

28When they heard this, they were furious and began shouting: "Great is Artemis of the Ephesians!" 29Soon the whole city was in an uproar. The people seized Gaius and Aristarchus, Paul's traveling companions from Macedonia, and rushed as one man into the theater. 30Paul wanted to appear before the crowd, but the disciples would not let him. 31Even some of the officials of the province, friends of Paul, sent him a message begging him not to venture into the theater.

[a] *6* Or *other languages* [b] *19* A drachma was a silver coin worth about a day's wages.

Paul had to teach these people about Jesus (v. 4), they apparently had not heard about him or the Holy Spirit (v. 2). From 2:38; 10:43–44 and this passage, what do you learn about the relationship between faith in Jesus and receiving the Holy Spirit? **4.** What seems to be the signal throughout Acts for Paul to stop teaching in the synagogues? Why do you think this is so? What do these "stop and go" signals teach you about ministry in general? **5.** Compare verses 8–9 with 13–15: How do these two groups of Jews view Jesus differently? If you were one of Sceva's sons, what would you say about Jesus after being jumped by this evil spirit (v. 16)? **6.** From the reaction of the crowd in verses 17–19, how would you describe the general response to Jesus prior to verses 13–16? Why would those events change people's ideas so much?

1. How do people try to use Jesus for their own purposes today? What is the difference between that and real faith in Christ? **2.** What do you need to "burn" in order to live for God? What will it cost you?

What can you make by using your own hands?

1. Why would Demetrius rally people against Paul (vv. 25–27; see 17:24–29)? Since this temple was one of the seven wonders of the ancient world, what businesses would Paul be affecting? **2.** Consider the crowd (vv. 32–34). What do they see and hear? Why are they there? Why are the Jews trying to get a speaker to represent them? Why would Alexander be shouted down? **3.** How do the concerns of the city clerk and Demetrius compare?

1. Success, money and independence are some cultural idols. What others come to mind? How has your faith affected your relationship to idols? **2.** Could Demetrius have become a Christian *and* kept his business? Can you think of situations today where someone in a respectable trade would be forced to choose between

32The assembly was in confusion: Some were shouting one
thing, some another. Most of the people did not even know why
they were there. 33The Jews pushed Alexander to the front, and
some of the crowd shouted instructions to him. He motioned for
silence in order to make a defense before the people. 34But when
they realized he was a Jew, they all shouted in unison for about
two hours: "Great is Artemis of the Ephesians!"

35The city clerk quieted the crowd and said: "Men of Ephesus,
doesn't all the world know that the city of Ephesus is the guardian
of the temple of the great Artemis and of her image, which fell
from heaven? 36Therefore, since these facts are undeniable, you
ought to be quiet and not do anything rash. 37You have brought
these men here, though they have neither robbed temples nor
blasphemed our goddess. 38If, then, Demetrius and his fellow
craftsmen have a grievance against anybody, the courts are open
and there are proconsuls. They can press charges. 39If there is
anything further you want to bring up, it must be settled in a legal
assembly. 40As it is, we are in danger of being charged with rioting
because of today's events. In that case we would not be able to
account for this commotion, since there is no reason for it." 41After
he had said this, he dismissed the assembly.

that trade and Christ? How have your business dealings been affected by your faith? **3.** Many people, even believers, would find it difficult to do what Paul did. Do you think Paul was happy? Why or why not? **4.** What began as Artemis-*worship* became Artemis-*business.* How can Christians fall into the same trap and make Jesus-worship into Jesus-business?

Through Macedonia and Greece

20 When the uproar had ended, Paul sent for the disciples and,
after encouraging them, said good-by and set out for Macedonia. 2He traveled through that area, speaking many words of
encouragement to the people, and finally arrived in Greece, 3where
he stayed three months. Because the Jews made a plot against him
just as he was about to sail for Syria, he decided to go back through
Macedonia. 4He was accompanied by Sopater son of Pyrrhus from
Berea, Aristarchus and Secundus from Thessalonica, Gaius from
Derbe, Timothy also, and Tychicus and Trophimus from the province of Asia. 5These men went on ahead and waited for us at Troas.
6But we sailed from Philippi after the Feast of Unleavened Bread,
and five days later joined the others at Troas, where we stayed
seven days.

Eutychus Raised From the Dead at Troas

7On the first day of the week we came together to break bread.
Paul spoke to the people and, because he intended to leave the
next day, kept on talking until midnight. 8There were many lamps
in the upstairs room where we were meeting. 9Seated in a window
was a young man named Eutychus, who was sinking into a deep
sleep as Paul talked on and on. When he was sound asleep, he fell
to the ground from the third story and was picked up dead. 10Paul
went down, threw himself on the young man and put his arms
around him. "Don't be alarmed," he said. "He's alive!" 11Then he
went upstairs again and broke bread and ate. After talking until
daylight, he left. 12The people took the young man home alive and
were greatly comforted.

Describe a time when, much to your embarrassment, you took a spill or fell "off your rocker."

1. One reason for this trip was to collect money for Christians in Judea (see Ro 15:25–29). Why then would Paul want companions for this task (see 2Co 8:16–23; 1Co 16:1–4)? Why else might Paul want to present these Gentiles to the church in Jerusalem (see ch. 15)? **2.** What can you learn about Paul and the church in Troas from this lengthy meeting?

1. Paul's companions protect him from anyone accusing him of misusing funds. How could churches and other ministries today be helped by such accountability? How would this enhance outsiders' opinions of Christian integrity? **2.** Are you at all related to Eutychus: Do sermons put you to sleep? Or are you wide awake spiritually? How can you keep from falling flat? **3.** What is the role of miracles in God's purposes today?

Paul's Farewell to the Ephesian Elders

13We went on ahead to the ship and sailed for Assos, where we
were going to take Paul aboard. He had made this arrangement
because he was going there on foot. 14When he met us at Assos,
we took him aboard and went on to Mitylene. 15The next day we
set sail from there and arrived off Kios. The day after that we
crossed over to Samos, and on the following day arrived at Miletus.
16Paul had decided to sail past Ephesus to avoid spending time in

How do you say goodbye to people you love? Quick and painless? Long or drawn out? Weeping and wailing? Like it's no big deal? Other?

1. Why "sail past" Ephesus to reach Jerusalem for Pentecost (see 2:1)? **2.** What has characterized Paul's ministry so far? Why does he emphasize how he lived among them? **3.** What kinds of hardships has Paul already encountered? How would you explain what motivates Paul to keep on (compare 20:24 with Php 3:7–8)? **4.** What does it mean to "keep watch" (v. 28; see 1Ti 4:11–16)? How and why is their appointment as elders divine, humbling and dangerous (vv. 28–31)? **5.** How does the message of grace (v. 32) and the example of Paul (vv. 33–35) protect them from these dangers? Some people viewed the office of elder as a way of gaining power and wealth (see 1Ti 6:6–10; 1Pe 5:3). How does Paul oppose that idea here? **6.** What do you suppose the Ephesians will miss about Paul?

1. Suddenly, Paul is more the loving friend than hard-driving missionary. Has your preoccupation with the task of ministry ever caused you to miss out on loving people? **2.** Who makes up the "flock" for whom you are responsible? In what specific way can you shepherd them? **3.** How would you complete this sentence: "The one thing I must accomplish at any cost is _____?" How does it relate to Paul's goal in verse 24? **4.** In the race of doing God's will, are you in the front of the pack, one of the stragglers, or an onlooker?

the province of Asia, for he was in a hurry to reach Jerusalem, if
possible, by the day of Pentecost.
17From Miletus, Paul sent to Ephesus for the elders of the
church. 18When they arrived, he said to them: "You know how I
lived the whole time I was with you, from the first day I came into
the province of Asia. 19I served the Lord with great humility and
with tears, although I was severely tested by the plots of the Jews.
20You know that I have not hesitated to preach anything that would
be helpful to you but have taught you publicly and from house to
house. 21I have declared to both Jews and Greeks that they must
turn to God in repentance and have faith in our Lord Jesus.
22"And now, compelled by the Spirit, I am going to Jerusalem,
not knowing what will happen to me there. 23I only know that in
every city the Holy Spirit warns me that prison and hardships are
facing me. 24However, I consider my life worth nothing to me, if
only I may finish the race and complete the task the Lord Jesus has
given me—the task of testifying to the gospel of God's grace.
25"Now I know that none of you among whom I have gone about
preaching the kingdom will ever see me again. 26Therefore, I declare to you today that I am innocent of the blood of all men. 27For
I have not hesitated to proclaim to you the whole will of God.
28Keep watch over yourselves and all the flock of which the Holy
Spirit has made you overseers.[a] Be shepherds of the church of
God,[b] which he bought with his own blood. 29I know that after I
leave, savage wolves will come in among you and will not spare the
flock. 30Even from your own number men will arise and distort the
truth in order to draw away disciples after them. 31So be on your
guard! Remember that for three years I never stopped warning
each of you night and day with tears.
32"Now I commit you to God and to the word of his grace, which
can build you up and give you an inheritance among all those who
are sanctified. 33I have not coveted anyone's silver or gold or clothing. 34You yourselves know that these hands of mine have supplied
my own needs and the needs of my companions. 35In everything I
did, I showed you that by this kind of hard work we must help the
weak, remembering the words the Lord Jesus himself said: 'It is
more blessed to give than to receive.'"
36When he had said this, he knelt down with all of them and
prayed. 37They all wept as they embraced him and kissed him.
38What grieved them most was his statement that they would never see his face again. Then they accompanied him to the ship.

What place did your parents have to drag you to, because you were scared to go there: Circus? Dentist's? Elsewhere?

1. How is Paul interpreting these warnings differently than his friends do (vv. 4,10–13; see 20:22–23)? Why doesn't he listen to their advice? **2.** What else do you know about Agabus (see 11:27–29) that gives more credence to his prophecy? Does Paul strike you as courageous or foolish, given this belt-tightening message? Why? **3.** Why does he want to go to Jerusalem?

On to Jerusalem

21 After we had torn ourselves away from them, we put out to
sea and sailed straight to Cos. The next day we went to
Rhodes and from there to Patara. 2We found a ship crossing over
to Phoenicia, went on board and set sail. 3After sighting Cyprus
and passing to the south of it, we sailed on to Syria. We landed at
Tyre, where our ship was to unload its cargo. 4Finding the disciples
there, we stayed with them seven days. Through the Spirit they
urged Paul not to go on to Jerusalem. 5But when our time was up,
we left and continued on our way. All the disciples and their wives
and children accompanied us out of the city, and there on the
beach we knelt to pray. 6After saying good-by to each other, we
went aboard the ship, and they returned home.
7We continued our voyage from Tyre and landed at Ptolemais,
where we greeted the brothers and stayed with them for a day.

[a]28 Traditionally *bishops* [b]28 Many manuscripts *of the Lord*

8Leaving the next day, we reached Caesarea and stayed at the
house of Philip the evangelist, one of the Seven. 9He had four
unmarried daughters who prophesied.
10After we had been there a number of days, a prophet named
Agabus came down from Judea. 11Coming over to us, he took Paul's
belt, tied his own hands and feet with it and said, "The Holy Spirit
says, 'In this way the Jews of Jerusalem will bind the owner of this
belt and will hand him over to the Gentiles.' "
12When we heard this, we and the people there pleaded with
Paul not to go up to Jerusalem. 13Then Paul answered, "Why are
you weeping and breaking my heart? I am ready not only to be
bound, but also to die in Jerusalem for the name of the Lord Jesus."
14When he would not be dissuaded, we gave up and said, "The
Lord's will be done."
15After this, we got ready and went up to Jerusalem. 16Some of
the disciples from Caesarea accompanied us and brought us to the
home of Mnason, where we were to stay. He was a man from
Cyprus and one of the early disciples.

1. In your eyes, did Paul make the right decision to go to Jerusalem, even though godly people through the Spirit urged him not to go? 2. When have you made decisions against the wishes of people you admired and trusted? What happened? In retrospect, were your decisions wise ones? Explain.

Paul's Arrival at Jerusalem

17When we arrived at Jerusalem, the brothers received us warmly. 18The next day Paul and the rest of us went to see James, and all
the elders were present. 19Paul greeted them and reported in detail
what God had done among the Gentiles through his ministry.
20When they heard this, they praised God. Then they said to
Paul: "You see, brother, how many thousands of Jews have believed, and all of them are zealous for the law. 21They have been
informed that you teach all the Jews who live among the Gentiles
to turn away from Moses, telling them not to circumcise their
children or live according to our customs. 22What shall we do?
They will certainly hear that you have come, 23so do what we tell
you. There are four men with us who have made a vow. 24Take
these men, join in their purification rites and pay their expenses,
so that they can have their heads shaved. Then everybody will
know there is no truth in these reports about you, but that you
yourself are living in obedience to the law. 25As for the Gentile
believers, we have written to them our decision that they should
abstain from food sacrificed to idols, from blood, from the meat of
strangled animals and from sexual immorality."
26The next day Paul took the men and purified himself along
with them. Then he went to the temple to give notice of the date
when the days of purification would end and the offering would be
made for each of them.

What "rites of passage" have been significant for you in maturing in your faith, and why: Baptism/Confirmation? Summer mission project? Ordination? Marriage? Raising your children as believers?

1. What pressure do James and the elders face as Paul comes to Jerusalem? How would Paul's teaching cause strict Jews to be upset (vv. 21–26)? 2. This issue was supposedly settled at least six years earlier (see ch. 15). Why do these tensions still plague Jerusalem believers? 3. How would James' suggestion to Paul solve the problem for both of them (15:19–21)? Why remind the Gentile believers what to do (v. 25; 15:20)?

How do you decide when you should bend for the sake of others, and when you should stand for your principles?

Paul Arrested

27When the seven days were nearly over, some Jews from the
province of Asia saw Paul at the temple. They stirred up the whole
crowd and seized him, 28shouting, "Men of Israel, help us! This is
the man who teaches all men everywhere against our people and
our law and this place. And besides, he has brought Greeks into
the temple area and defiled this holy place." 29(They had previously
seen Trophimus the Ephesian in the city with Paul and assumed
that Paul had brought him into the temple area.)
30The whole city was aroused, and the people came running
from all directions. Seizing Paul, they dragged him from the temple, and immediately the gates were shut. 31While they were trying
to kill him, news reached the commander of the Roman troops that
the whole city of Jerusalem was in an uproar. 32He at once took
some officers and soldiers and ran down to the crowd. When the

What is the strangest thing you have ever seen done in the name of religion?

1. Why would Asian Jews be especially upset when they saw Paul (19:8–10)? 2. Gentiles were forbidden from entering the temple. How would the accusation of verse 28 fuel the suspicions of James (v. 21)? 3. Compare the reaction against Paul (vv. 30–31) with that against Stephen (6:11–13) 20 years earlier. What does this reveal about Christian-Jewish relationships in Jerusalem during this period?

What group is critical of the church today? How might the church provoke this group? What could be done to lessen this animosity? What can you do to help?

---

1. When have you wished you could understand another language better? How did you do in languages in school? **2.** What is one thing you have seen that no one else in your group has seen?

1. From 21:30–36, why would the commander mistake Paul for the Egyptian revolutionary (v. 38)? **2.** Under the circumstances, why did Paul think it so important to address this hostile crowd? How would Jewish-Christian relationships erode even further if the charges of 21:28 were left unanswered? **3.** Many foreign-born Jews did not speak Aramaic well. How does Paul's use of this language (along with the content of his speech) force these Jews to listen? **4.** This speech (22:1–10) recounts the events of 9:1–18. What points of identification does Paul make with his hostile audience? What is he hoping to achieve by this? **5.** Why does Paul's reference to the Gentiles (v. 21) upset the crowd (v. 22), whereas they did not react to his speaking about Jesus? What was the real sticking point about the Gospel for the Jews? What does this tell you about them? **6.** How was Paul's status as a Roman citizen an asset in his ministry to Gentiles (vv. 25–29; see also 16:37–38)?

1. Paul told his own story instead of preaching a sermon to this crowd. When do you find your story most effective and helpful to others? If you have not already done so, share the story of your relationship with Christ with the small group—in three minutes or less. **2.** How has your faith in Jesus redirected your life in a surprising way? How do you struggle with that redirection? In what ways have you embraced some of these changes for yourself? **3.** What is one of the hardest things you have had to experience because of your faith? **4.** Paul's citizenship became an asset in his efforts to share the

rioters saw the commander and his soldiers, they stopped beating
Paul.
33The commander came up and arrested him and ordered him to
be bound with two chains. Then he asked who he was and what he
had done. 34Some in the crowd shouted one thing and some another, and since the commander could not get at the truth because
of the uproar, he ordered that Paul be taken into the barracks.
35When Paul reached the steps, the violence of the mob was so
great he had to be carried by the soldiers. 36The crowd that followed kept shouting, "Away with him!"

Paul Speaks to the Crowd

37As the soldiers were about to take Paul into the barracks, he
asked the commander, "May I say something to you?"
"Do you speak Greek?" he replied. 38"Aren't you the Egyptian
who started a revolt and led four thousand terrorists out into the
desert some time ago?"
39Paul answered, "I am a Jew, from Tarsus in Cilicia, a citizen of
no ordinary city. Please let me speak to the people."
40Having received the commander's permission, Paul stood on
the steps and motioned to the crowd. When they were all silent, he
22 said to them in Aramaic[a]: 1"Brothers and fathers, listen
now to my defense."
2When they heard him speak to them in Aramaic, they became
very quiet.
Then Paul said: 3"I am a Jew, born in Tarsus of Cilicia, but
brought up in this city. Under Gamaliel I was thoroughly trained in
the law of our fathers and was just as zealous for God as any of you
are today. 4I persecuted the followers of this Way to their death,
arresting both men and women and throwing them into prison, 5as
also the high priest and all the Council can testify. I even obtained
letters from them to their brothers in Damascus, and went there to
bring these people as prisoners to Jerusalem to be punished.
6"About noon as I came near Damascus, suddenly a bright light
from heaven flashed around me. 7I fell to the ground and heard a
voice say to me, 'Saul! Saul! Why do you persecute me?'
8" 'Who are you, Lord?' I asked.
" 'I am Jesus of Nazareth, whom you are persecuting,' he replied. 9My companions saw the light, but they did not understand
the voice of him who was speaking to me.
10" 'What shall I do, Lord?' I asked.
" 'Get up,' the Lord said, 'and go into Damascus. There you will
be told all that you have been assigned to do.' 11My companions led
me by the hand into Damascus, because the brilliance of the light
had blinded me.
12"A man named Ananias came to see me. He was a devout
observer of the law and highly respected by all the Jews living
there. 13He stood beside me and said, 'Brother Saul, receive your
sight!' And at that very moment I was able to see him.
14"Then he said: 'The God of our fathers has chosen you to know
his will and to see the Righteous One and to hear words from his
mouth. 15You will be his witness to all men of what you have seen
and heard. 16And now what are you waiting for? Get up, be baptized and wash your sins away, calling on his name.'
17"When I returned to Jerusalem and was praying at the temple,
I fell into a trance 18and saw the Lord speaking. 'Quick!' he said to

[a] *40* Or possibly *Hebrew*; also in 22:2

me. 'Leave Jerusalem immediately, because they will not accept
your testimony about me.'
19"'Lord,' I replied, 'these men know that I went from one
synagogue to another to imprison and beat those who believe in
you. 20And when the blood of your martyr[a] Stephen was shed, I
stood there giving my approval and guarding the clothes of those
who were killing him.'
21"Then the Lord said to me, 'Go; I will send you far away to the
Gentiles.' "

Paul the Roman Citizen

22The crowd listened to Paul until he said this. Then they raised
their voices and shouted, "Rid the earth of him! He's not fit to
live!"
23As they were shouting and throwing off their cloaks and fling-
ing dust into the air, 24the commander ordered Paul to be taken
into the barracks. He directed that he be flogged and questioned in
order to find out why the people were shouting at him like this.
25As they stretched him out to flog him, Paul said to the centurion
standing there, "Is it legal for you to flog a Roman citizen who
hasn't even been found guilty?"
26When the centurion heard this, he went to the commander
and reported it. "What are you going to do?" he asked. "This man
is a Roman citizen."
27The commander went to Paul and asked, "Tell me, are you a
Roman citizen?"
"Yes, I am," he answered.
28Then the commander said, "I had to pay a big price for my
citizenship."
"But I was born a citizen," Paul replied.
29Those who were about to question him withdrew immediately.
The commander himself was alarmed when he realized that he had
put Paul, a Roman citizen, in chains.

Before the Sanhedrin

30The next day, since the commander wanted to find out exactly
why Paul was being accused by the Jews, he released him and
ordered the chief priests and all the Sanhedrin to assemble. Then
he brought Paul and had him stand before them.
23 Paul looked straight at the Sanhedrin and said, "My brothers, I have fulfilled my duty to God in all good conscience to
this day." 2At this the high priest Ananias ordered those standing
near Paul to strike him on the mouth. 3Then Paul said to him,
"God will strike you, you whitewashed wall! You sit there to judge
me according to the law, yet you yourself violate the law by commanding that I be struck!"
4Those who were standing near Paul said, "You dare to insult
God's high priest?"
5Paul replied, "Brothers, I did not realize that he was the high
priest; for it is written: 'Do not speak evil about the ruler of your
people.'[b]"
6Then Paul, knowing that some of them were Sadducees and the
others Pharisees, called out in the Sanhedrin, "My brothers, I am a
Pharisee, the son of a Pharisee. I stand on trial because of my hope
in the resurrection of the dead." 7When he said this, a dispute
broke out between the Pharisees and the Sadducees, and the assembly was divided. 8(The Sadducees say that there is no resurrec-

[a]20 Or *witness* [b]5 Exodus 22:28

Gospel with Gentiles. What traits, skills or experiences do you have which can help you share the Gospel with others?

What was the most frightening thing that happened to you last week?

1. What sparks this exchange of accusations (see 21:21,28)? **2.** Why (and how) does Paul show his respect for the Jewish Law (vv. 1–5)? **3.** Why does Paul change the focus of attention from keeping the Law to his hope in the Resurrection? Given the tensions between the Pharisees and Sadducees on this issue, describe what you think the next few minutes of the assembly must have been like. **4.** What effect does the split have on Paul's case (vv. 7–10)? **5.** We last heard God speak to Paul in 18:9–10, after he had experienced a series of setbacks. How would the Lord's message here (v. 11) help Paul again? How would this help Paul remember what the Lord said about him to Ananias in 9:15–16?

tion, and that there are neither angels nor spirits, but the Pharisees acknowledge them all.)

9There was a great uproar, and some of the teachers of the law who were Pharisees stood up and argued vigorously. "We find nothing wrong with this man," they said. "What if a spirit or an angel has spoken to him?" 10The dispute became so violent that the commander was afraid Paul would be torn to pieces by them. He ordered the troops to go down and take him away from them by force and bring him into the barracks.

11The following night the Lord stood near Paul and said, "Take courage! As you have testified about me in Jerusalem, so you must also testify in Rome."

1. When facing death, what duty do you want to have fulfilled before God? How can you pursue that course this week? **2.** How has the Lord encouraged you during hard times? **3.** What could be your "Rome"—the next crucial step in your spiritual journey?

The Plot to Kill Paul

Who is your favorite relative? What incident brought the two of you closer?

1. How do you explain the fierce determination of these Jews to kill Paul (see Ro 10:2)? Why do they think he is so dangerous? **2.** Given verse 11, how would you feel if you were Paul and you heard this news from your nephew (vv. 12–16)? **3.** By sending his nephew to the commander, is Paul showing a lack of faith in God's promise? Why or why not?

1. The Gentile soldier and the Jews take different sides in Paul's situation. When have you seen a non-Christian behave more righteously than a believer? **2.** What risks did Paul's nephew take in this story? How might you be called upon this week to take a risk and stand up for someone whom others dislike?

12The next morning the Jews formed a conspiracy and bound themselves with an oath not to eat or drink until they had killed Paul. 13More than forty men were involved in this plot. 14They went to the chief priests and elders and said, "We have taken a solemn oath not to eat anything until we have killed Paul. 15Now then, you and the Sanhedrin petition the commander to bring him before you on the pretext of wanting more accurate information about his case. We are ready to kill him before he gets here."

16But when the son of Paul's sister heard of this plot, he went into the barracks and told Paul.

17Then Paul called one of the centurions and said, "Take this young man to the commander; he has something to tell him." 18So he took him to the commander.

The centurion said, "Paul, the prisoner, sent for me and asked me to bring this young man to you because he has something to tell you."

19The commander took the young man by the hand, drew him aside and asked, "What is it you want to tell me?"

20He said: "The Jews have agreed to ask you to bring Paul before the Sanhedrin tomorrow on the pretext of wanting more accurate information about him. 21Don't give in to them, because more than forty of them are waiting in ambush for him. They have taken an oath not to eat or drink until they have killed him. They are ready now, waiting for your consent to their request."

22The commander dismissed the young man and cautioned him, "Don't tell anyone that you have reported this to me."

Paul Transferred to Caesarea

What was the most life-changing letter you ever received?

1. How does the commander's provision for Paul contrast with the way Pilate dealt with Jesus (see Lk 23:1–25)? Why do you think this is the case? **2.** What has the commander decided to do with the "Paul problem"? Why the elaborate security precautions and the constant passing the buck? How does all this relate to 9:15? **3.** How would you feel if you were one of the men in 23:12–13, and you found out the next day that Paul was gone?

23Then he called two of his centurions and ordered them, "Get ready a detachment of two hundred soldiers, seventy horsemen and two hundred spearmen[a] to go to Caesarea at nine tonight. 24Provide mounts for Paul so that he may be taken safely to Governor Felix."

25He wrote a letter as follows:

26Claudius Lysias,

To His Excellency, Governor Felix:

Greetings.

27This man was seized by the Jews and they were about to kill him, but I came with my troops and rescued him, for I had learned that he is a Roman citizen. 28I wanted to know why

a*23* The meaning of the Greek for this word is uncertain.

they were accusing him, so I brought him to their Sanhedrin.
29I found that the accusation had to do with questions about
their law, but there was no charge against him that deserved
death or imprisonment. 30When I was informed of a plot to be
carried out against the man, I sent him to you at once. I also
ordered his accusers to present to you their case against him.

31So the soldiers, carrying out their orders, took Paul with them
during the night and brought him as far as Antipatris. 32The next
day they let the cavalry go on with him, while they returned to the
barracks. 33When the cavalry arrived in Caesarea, they delivered
the letter to the governor and handed Paul over to him. 34The
governor read the letter and asked what province he was from.
Learning that he was from Cilicia, 35he said, "I will hear your case
when your accusers get here." Then he ordered that Paul be kept
under guard in Herod's palace.

The Trial Before Felix

24 Five days later the high priest Ananias went down to Caesarea with some of the elders and a lawyer named Tertullus,
and they brought their charges against Paul before the governor.
2When Paul was called in, Tertullus presented his case before Felix: "We have enjoyed a long period of peace under you, and your
foresight has brought about reforms in this nation. 3Everywhere
and in every way, most excellent Felix, we acknowledge this with
profound gratitude. 4But in order not to weary you further, I would
request that you be kind enough to hear us briefly.

5"We have found this man to be a troublemaker, stirring up riots
among the Jews all over the world. He is a ringleader of the Nazarene sect 6and even tried to desecrate the temple; so we seized
him. 8By[a] examining him yourself you will be able to learn the
truth about all these charges we are bringing against him."

9The Jews joined in the accusation, asserting that these things
were true.

10When the governor motioned for him to speak, Paul replied: "I
know that for a number of years you have been a judge over this
nation; so I gladly make my defense. 11You can easily verify that no
more than twelve days ago I went up to Jerusalem to worship.
12My accusers did not find me arguing with anyone at the temple,
or stirring up a crowd in the synagogues or anywhere else in the
city. 13And they cannot prove to you the charges they are now
making against me. 14However, I admit that I worship the God of
our fathers as a follower of the Way, which they call a sect. I
believe everything that agrees with the Law and that is written in
the Prophets, 15and I have the same hope in God as these men,
that there will be a resurrection of both the righteous and the
wicked. 16So I strive always to keep my conscience clear before
God and man.

17"After an absence of several years, I came to Jerusalem to bring
my people gifts for the poor and to present offerings. 18I was ceremonially clean when they found me in the temple courts doing
this. There was no crowd with me, nor was I involved in any
disturbance. 19But there are some Jews from the province of Asia,
who ought to be here before you and bring charges if they have
anything against me. 20Or these who are here should state what
crime they found in me when I stood before the Sanhedrin—

[a]6-8 Some manuscripts *him and wanted to judge him according to our law. 7But the commander, Lysias, came and with the use of much force snatched him from our hands 8and ordered his accusers to come before you. By*

1. How do Paul's experiences with Roman authority here shed light on his comments in Romans 13:1–7? How does this contrast with Peter's experience with the Jewish authorities in Acts 4:8–20? **2.** What do these two incidents show you about the Christian's relationship with civil authority? Where should you show your support of government authority? Where should you challenge it?

If someone were to bribe you to do a favor for them, what's the most effective incentive they could use: A return favor? Your favorite meal? Free babysitting? Money? Flattery? Other?

1. Felix had a reputation of violently suppressing rebellions against Rome. How might Tertullus hope that would compensate for the lack of evidence he can offer? **2.** What difference can you see in the style Tertullus uses (vv. 2–4) to present his case to Felix compared to Paul's style? **3.** How would all the charges in verses 5–6 seem true to Ananias and Tertullus? What does their reference to Christians as the "Nazarene sect" show about their view of Christianity? **4.** How then does Paul defend himself (vv. 11–19)? **5.** Put yourself in the place of Felix. In light of the riot in Jerusalem over Paul (if you only had Lysias' letter [23:26–30], the accusations of the Jews, and Paul's word to go on), what would you do? **6.** What do you learn about Felix from verses 22–26? Why does he merely put Paul under house arrest? **7.** In light of Acts 23:11, what must Paul be feeling as time wears on and no progress at all is made?

1. How has your desire to serve Christ been misunderstood by others? How did you feel then? **2.** What's the difference between being "well acquainted with the Way" (v. 22) and being a true believer? How long were you "well acquainted" before you became a believer? **3.** Have you ever felt there was a period in your life that was "dead time"—when nothing seemed to be happening at all (as seems to be the case with Paul)? Why do you think God allows such times in our lives? **4.** Consider verse 25. When have discussions on righteousness, self-control and judgment troubled you? Why?

Name three laws or rules you have never broken.

1. Two years have passed since the trial before Felix (24:27). Why hasn't the opposition to Paul by the Jewish leaders dissipated during this time? **2.** Paul has come a long way since the events of 9:1–2. What irony do you see in that? How could 9:1–2 also account in part for their animosity? **3.** How is Paul like a pawn to these Roman officials (v. 9; see 24:27)? How might this account for his decision to appeal to Caesar?

1. What laws conflict with your efforts to emulate Jesus Christ? **2.** What was one circumstance that threatened to ambush you in your spiritual life? How did you deal with it? **3.** If someone wanted to prove you were a Christian, what evidence from this past week could they use?

If you could be king or queen for a day, what new law would you enact?

1. How fair is Festus in describing the case? How much does he seem to know about Judaism? About Christianity? How would this have affected any decision he would have made in the case? Do you think he is honestly

21 unless it was this one thing I shouted as I stood in their presence: 'It is concerning the resurrection of the dead that I am on trial before you today.' "

22 Then Felix, who was well acquainted with the Way, adjourned the proceedings. "When Lysias the commander comes," he said, "I will decide your case." 23 He ordered the centurion to keep Paul under guard but to give him some freedom and permit his friends to take care of his needs.

24 Several days later Felix came with his wife Drusilla, who was a Jewess. He sent for Paul and listened to him as he spoke about faith in Christ Jesus. 25 As Paul discoursed on righteousness, self-control and the judgment to come, Felix was afraid and said, "That's enough for now! You may leave. When I find it convenient, I will send for you." 26 At the same time he was hoping that Paul would offer him a bribe, so he sent for him frequently and talked with him.

27 When two years had passed, Felix was succeeded by Porcius Festus, but because Felix wanted to grant a favor to the Jews, he left Paul in prison.

The Trial Before Festus

25 Three days after arriving in the province, Festus went up from Caesarea to Jerusalem, 2 where the chief priests and Jewish leaders appeared before him and presented the charges against Paul. 3 They urgently requested Festus, as a favor to them, to have Paul transferred to Jerusalem, for they were preparing an ambush to kill him along the way. 4 Festus answered, "Paul is being held at Caesarea, and I myself am going there soon. 5 Let some of your leaders come with me and press charges against the man there, if he has done anything wrong."

6 After spending eight or ten days with them, he went down to Caesarea, and the next day he convened the court and ordered that Paul be brought before him. 7 When Paul appeared, the Jews who had come down from Jerusalem stood around him, bringing many serious charges against him, which they could not prove.

8 Then Paul made his defense: "I have done nothing wrong against the law of the Jews or against the temple or against Caesar."

9 Festus, wishing to do the Jews a favor, said to Paul, "Are you willing to go up to Jerusalem and stand trial before me there on these charges?"

10 Paul answered: "I am now standing before Caesar's court, where I ought to be tried. I have not done any wrong to the Jews, as you yourself know very well. 11 If, however, I am guilty of doing anything deserving death, I do not refuse to die. But if the charges brought against me by these Jews are not true, no one has the right to hand me over to them. I appeal to Caesar!"

12 After Festus had conferred with his council, he declared: "You have appealed to Caesar. To Caesar you will go!"

Festus Consults King Agrippa

13 A few days later King Agrippa and Bernice arrived at Caesarea to pay their respects to Festus. 14 Since they were spending many days there, Festus discussed Paul's case with the king. He said: "There is a man here whom Felix left as a prisoner. 15 When I went to Jerusalem, the chief priests and elders of the Jews brought charges against him and asked that he be condemned.

16 "I told them that it is not the Roman custom to hand over any man before he has faced his accusers and has had an opportunity to

defend himself against their charges. [17]When they came here with
me, I did not delay the case, but convened the court the next day
and ordered the man to be brought in. [18]When his accusers got up
to speak, they did not charge him with any of the crimes I had
expected. [19]Instead, they had some points of dispute with him
about their own religion and about a dead man named Jesus who
Paul claimed was alive. [20]I was at a loss how to investigate such
matters; so I asked if he would be willing to go to Jerusalem and
stand trial there on these charges. [21]When Paul made his appeal to
be held over for the Emperor's decision, I ordered him held until I
could send him to Caesar."

[22]Then Agrippa said to Festus, "I would like to hear this man
myself."

He replied, "Tomorrow you will hear him."

Paul Before Agrippa

[23]The next day Agrippa and Bernice came with great pomp and
entered the audience room with the high ranking officers and the
leading men of the city. At the command of Festus, Paul was
brought in. [24]Festus said: "King Agrippa, and all who are present
with us, you see this man! The whole Jewish community has peti-
tioned me about him in Jerusalem and here in Caesarea, shouting
that he ought not to live any longer. [25]I found he had done nothing
deserving of death, but because he made his appeal to the Emperor
I decided to send him to Rome. [26]But I have nothing definite to
write to His Majesty about him. Therefore I have brought him
before all of you, and especially before you, King Agrippa, so that as
a result of this investigation I may have something to write. [27]For
I think it is unreasonable to send on a prisoner without specifying
the charges against him."

26 Then Agrippa said to Paul, "You have permission to speak
for yourself."

So Paul motioned with his hand and began his defense: [2]"King
Agrippa, I consider myself fortunate to stand before you today as I
make my defense against all the accusations of the Jews, [3]and
especially so because you are well acquainted with all the Jewish
customs and controversies. Therefore, I beg you to listen to me
patiently.

[4]"The Jews all know the way I have lived ever since I was a
child, from the beginning of my life in my own country, and also in
Jerusalem. [5]They have known me for a long time and can testify, if
they are willing, that according to the strictest sect of our religion,
I lived as a Pharisee. [6]And now it is because of my hope in what
God has promised our fathers that I am on trial today. [7]This is the
promise our twelve tribes are hoping to see fulfilled as they earnestly serve God day and night. O king, it is because of this hope
that the Jews are accusing me. [8]Why should any of you consider it
incredible that God raises the dead?

[9]"I too was convinced that I ought to do all that was possible to
oppose the name of Jesus of Nazareth. [10]And that is just what I did
in Jerusalem. On the authority of the chief priests I put many of the
saints in prison, and when they were put to death, I cast my vote
against them. [11]Many a time I went from one synagogue to another
to have them punished, and I tried to force them to blaspheme. In
my obsession against them, I even went to foreign cities to persecute them.

[12]"On one of these journeys I was going to Damascus with the
authority and commission of the chief priests. [13]About noon,

trying to find the truth in this matter? Why? **2.** This Agrippa was the son of the Herod in 12:1–23. Why would he be especially interested in hearing from Paul?

When you have questions about your faith, to whom do you turn? Why? How else do you seek input?

---

1. When have you had to publicly appear before an important or powerful person and put your fate in his/her hands: (a) Defending yourself in a tax audit? (b) Asking for a pay raise or an allowance hike? (c) Asking parents for approval and blessing to marry? (d) Asking for liability damages? (e) Submitting to the dentist or surgeon? **2.** How did you feel as you thought about what to say?

1. What is the problem Festus faces? Why doesn't he simply let Paul go? How could Agrippa be in a position to help (26:3)? **2.** According to Paul, what issue is the real source of his conflict with the Jewish leaders (see 23:6; 24:21; 26:6–8)? Why do you think his adversaries never directly bring this out (see 18:15)? How does his conviction about the Resurrection differ from that of the Pharisees, who in theory believed in a general resurrection as well? **3.** Compare 26:20 with 20:21. How could you tell someone what it means to be a Christian from these two verses? **4.** How does faith in Jesus relate to a repentant change in lifestyle? Would you describe Paul's speech as a legal defense or a personal testimony? How are the two related? Do you think Paul's primary goal in this speech is to convince Agrippa of his innocence, or of the truth of Christianity's claims? Why? **5.** From 25:19 and 26:24, how convinced is Festus regarding the resurrection of Jesus? How might Paul's response in verses 25–27 surprise Festus? **6.** If you were in this hall, what impressions would you have of Paul as he concluded his speech? **7.** Up to this point, the Romans considered Christians and Jews as basically one and the same. From this speech, can the Romans begin to see some differences?

♡ **1.** What difference does it make to you that Jesus truly rose from the dead? What would be different about your faith if that were not the case? **2.** How does verse 18 fit as a description of your spiritual journey? Which other images describe what coming to faith was like for you? **3.** In verse 14, Paul adds a comment not found in his conversion story in chapters 9 or 22. When has God pointed out to you that your struggle has been against him all along? How has he redirected you since then? **4.** Paul considered himself a servant and a witness. In what way is God's call to you similar to or different from his call to Paul? **5.** Paul's obedience to Jesus resulted in a trial very similar to Jesus' trial. How has your obedience to Jesus resulted in similarities to Jesus' experience? **6.** How has Christ brought light into your life? How can you pass on that light to someone else this week?

O king, as I was on the road, I saw a light from heaven, brighter
than the sun, blazing around me and my companions. 14We all fell
to the ground, and I heard a voice saying to me in Aramaic,[a] 'Saul,
Saul, why do you persecute me? It is hard for you to kick against
the goads.'
15"Then I asked, 'Who are you, Lord?'
" 'I am Jesus, whom you are persecuting,' the Lord replied.
16'Now get up and stand on your feet. I have appeared to you to
appoint you as a servant and as a witness of what you have seen of
me and what I will show you. 17I will rescue you from your own
people and from the Gentiles. I am sending you to them 18to open
their eyes and turn them from darkness to light, and from the
power of Satan to God, so that they may receive forgiveness of sins
and a place among those who are sanctified by faith in me.'
19"So then, King Agrippa, I was not disobedient to the vision
from heaven. 20First to those in Damascus, then to those in Jerusalem and in all Judea, and to the Gentiles also, I preached that they
should repent and turn to God and prove their repentance by their
deeds. 21That is why the Jews seized me in the temple courts and
tried to kill me. 22But I have had God's help to this very day, and
so I stand here and testify to small and great alike. I am saying
nothing beyond what the prophets and Moses said would happen— 23that the Christ[b] would suffer and, as the first to rise from
the dead, would proclaim light to his own people and to the Gentiles."
24At this point Festus interrupted Paul's defense. "You are out of

[a]*14* Or *Hebrew* [b]*23* Or *Messiah*

Acts 26:1–32 PAUL BEFORE AGRIPPA

The apostle Paul's trial before Festus, the Roman governor of Judea, ended with Paul appealing to Caesar. Now Festus has King Herod Agrippa II, himself a Jew, hear Paul to help Festus better understand the case for his report to be sent with Paul to Rome.

1. Why did Paul begin by saying to King Agrippa, "I consider myself fortunate to stand before you today"?
   a. It was just a formality.
   b. Paul was buttering him up.
   c. Since Agrippa should understand the issues, Paul thought he could convince him of his innocence.
   d. Paul wanted to challenge Agrippa to become a Christian.

2. What was the main point Paul wanted to make?
   a. that he was still a faithful Jew
   b. that the real reason he was on trial was his belief that Jesus was the Messiah God raised from the dead
   c. that he was a personal witness to the resurrection of Jesus
   d. that his preaching was doing what God had called him to do

3. If you had been at Paul's defense, how would you describe him?
   a. insane
   b. logical
   c. fearful
   d. full of passion
   e. full of the Spirit
   f. convincing

4. How do you handle situations where your faith is criticized or questioned?
   a. I don't allow myself to get in those situations.
   b. I ask God to give me strength.
   c. I thrive on those situations.
   d. I wilt.

5. Which image from Paul's summary of the Gospel in verse 18 best describes your spiritual journey?
   a. having my eyes opened
   b. turning from darkness to light
   c. turning from Satan's power to God

6. What is the closest you have come to Paul's experience of having your entire focus in life change?

7. Where do you need God's transforming power in your life now?

8. $ What is the most important variable in whether or not you have a passion for what you are doing in life?
   a. believing in God's direction
   b. knowing yourself and your talents
   c. having an ability to focus on something other than yourself
   d. having a purpose greater than the material aspects of life
   e. not being too philosophical, since the purpose of life is survival
   f. other:________________

9. $ If you compared where you are right now in your career and sense of calling to Paul's conversion, where would you be?
   a. on the road to Damascus—pursuing my own passion
   b. hearing God call my name and wondering what he's trying to say
   c. starting to sort out God's call on my vocational life
   d. letting God give me *his* passion

10. $ How has this course and this group affected your sense of purpose in life? Close by thanking God for the gift of Jesus and for the gift of each other.

your mind, Paul!” he shouted. “Your great learning is driving you
insane.”
25“I am not insane, most excellent Festus,” Paul replied. “What
I am saying is true and reasonable. 26The king is familiar with these
things, and I can speak freely to him. I am convinced that none of
this has escaped his notice, because it was not done in a corner.
27King Agrippa, do you believe the prophets? I know you do.”
28Then Agrippa said to Paul, “Do you think that in such a short
time you can persuade me to be a Christian?”
29Paul replied, “Short time or long—I pray God that not only you
but all who are listening to me today may become what I am,
except for these chains.”
30The king rose, and with him the governor and Bernice and
those sitting with them. 31They left the room, and while talking
with one another, they said, “This man is not doing anything that
deserves death or imprisonment.”
32Agrippa said to Festus, “This man could have been set free if
he had not appealed to Caesar.”

Paul Sails for Rome

27 When it was decided that we would sail for Italy, Paul and
some other prisoners were handed over to a centurion
named Julius, who belonged to the Imperial Regiment. 2We board-
ed a ship from Adramyttium about to sail for ports along the coast
of the province of Asia, and we put out to sea. Aristarchus, a
Macedonian from Thessalonica, was with us.
3The next day we landed at Sidon; and Julius, in kindness to
Paul, allowed him to go to his friends so they might provide for his
needs. 4From there we put out to sea again and passed to the lee of
Cyprus because the winds were against us. 5When we had sailed
across the open sea off the coast of Cilicia and Pamphylia, we
landed at Myra in Lycia. 6There the centurion found an Alexandrian ship sailing for Italy and put us on board. 7We made slow
headway for many days and had difficulty arriving off Cnidus.
When the wind did not allow us to hold our course, we sailed to
the lee of Crete, opposite Salmone. 8We moved along the coast
with difficulty and came to a place called Fair Havens, near the
town of Lasea.
9Much time had been lost, and sailing had already become dangerous because by now it was after the Fast.[a] So Paul warned
them, 10“Men, I can see that our voyage is going to be disastrous
and bring great loss to ship and cargo, and to our own lives also.”
11But the centurion, instead of listening to what Paul said, followed
the advice of the pilot and of the owner of the ship. 12Since the
harbor was unsuitable to winter in, the majority decided that we
should sail on, hoping to reach Phoenix and winter there. This was
a harbor in Crete, facing both southwest and northwest.

The Storm

13When a gentle south wind began to blow, they thought they
had obtained what they wanted; so they weighed anchor and sailed
along the shore of Crete. 14Before very long, a wind of hurricane
force, called the “northeaster,” swept down from the island. 15The
ship was caught by the storm and could not head into the wind; so
we gave way to it and were driven along. 16As we passed to the lee
of a small island called Cauda, we were hardly able to make the
lifeboat secure. 17When the men had hoisted it aboard, they passed

a9 That is, the Day of Atonement (Yom Kippur)

1. If you could take a honeymoon cruise anywhere, where would you go? Why? **2.** Have you ever been seasick? What happened? How did you recover?

1. As Paul sets sail for Rome (consult the map in the Introduction to Romans), what points of interest can you locate along the way from Paul's diary? **2.** From verses 1–3 and 43, what do you know about the centurion in charge? How does his concern for Paul indicate the way Paul used his time while imprisoned in Caesarea? **3.** If you were the ship's owner or pilot, how would you react to Paul's warning about the 50-mile trip they wanted to make (v. 10)? Would you have responded any differently than Julius did to Paul's concern? **4.** What in verses 13–20 reveals how severe this storm was? Verse 27 indicates this situation lasted two weeks. How would you be feeling by the end of the first week? What would a page from your ship's diary sound like? **5.** As a sailor on board, how would you feel about Paul's message in verses 21–26? **6.** After being in Caesarea for at least two years, why would Paul need to hear the promise of 23:11 repeated (v. 24)? **7.** Compare verse 31 with verse 11. How does the centurion feel about Paul now? About the God Paul serves? **8.** How do Paul's words and his example serve to encourage the others? How would your estimation of Paul change during the two weeks of the storm? **9.** What do you imagine the scene in verses 39–44 was like? What was said? How did people look? Feel? **10.** How do Paul's attitudes and actions compare with those of the sailors? To what would you attribute Paul's ability to remain calm under pressure?

1. When have you felt caught in a "northeaster," driven along by the wind? What happened? What did you learn from the situation? **2.** In terms of a weather report, how would you describe your life at present? Your life five years ago? **3.** In a crisis, Paul reacted with urgent forewarnings, maintaining hope, counseling, common sense, giving thanks, remaining calm, persevering to the end. In comparison, how do you react to crisis? **4.** What is the greatest pressure situation you're facing now? How can Paul's example and the principles you've learned from his experience help you? What is your part and what is God's part in the resolution of your storm? **5.** When have you been tempted to bail out of a stormy situation and slip away in a lifeboat? What happened? What did you learn?

ropes under the ship itself to hold it together. Fearing that they would run aground on the sandbars of Syrtis, they lowered the sea anchor and let the ship be driven along. 18We took such a violent battering from the storm that the next day they began to throw the cargo overboard. 19On the third day, they threw the ship's tackle overboard with their own hands. 20When neither sun nor stars appeared for many days and the storm continued raging, we finally gave up all hope of being saved.

21After the men had gone a long time without food, Paul stood up before them and said: "Men, you should have taken my advice not to sail from Crete; then you would have spared yourselves this damage and loss. 22But now I urge you to keep up your courage, because not one of you will be lost; only the ship will be destroyed. 23Last night an angel of the God whose I am and whom I serve stood beside me 24and said, 'Do not be afraid, Paul. You must stand trial before Caesar; and God has graciously given you the lives of all who sail with you.' 25So keep up your courage, men, for I have faith in God that it will happen just as he told me. 26Nevertheless, we must run aground on some island."

The Shipwreck

27On the fourteenth night we were still being driven across the Adriatic[a] Sea, when about midnight the sailors sensed they were approaching land. 28They took soundings and found that the water was a hundred and twenty feet[b] deep. A short time later they took soundings again and found it was ninety feet[c] deep. 29Fearing that we would be dashed against the rocks, they dropped four anchors from the stern and prayed for daylight. 30In an attempt to escape from the ship, the sailors let the lifeboat down into the sea, pretending they were going to lower some anchors from the bow. 31Then Paul said to the centurion and the soldiers, "Unless these men stay with the ship, you cannot be saved." 32So the soldiers cut the ropes that held the lifeboat and let it fall away.

33Just before dawn Paul urged them all to eat. "For the last fourteen days," he said, "you have been in constant suspense and have gone without food—you haven't eaten anything. 34Now I urge you to take some food. You need it to survive. Not one of you will lose a single hair from his head." 35After he said this, he took some bread and gave thanks to God in front of them all. Then he broke it and began to eat. 36They were all encouraged and ate some food themselves. 37Altogether there were 276 of us on board. 38When they had eaten as much as they wanted, they lightened the ship by throwing the grain into the sea.

39When daylight came, they did not recognize the land, but they saw a bay with a sandy beach, where they decided to run the ship aground if they could. 40Cutting loose the anchors, they left them in the sea and at the same time untied the ropes that held the rudders. Then they hoisted the foresail to the wind and made for the beach. 41But the ship struck a sandbar and ran aground. The bow stuck fast and would not move, and the stern was broken to pieces by the pounding of the surf.

42The soldiers planned to kill the prisoners to prevent any of them from swimming away and escaping. 43But the centurion wanted to spare Paul's life and kept them from carrying out their plan. He ordered those who could swim to jump overboard first

[a]*27* In ancient times the name referred to an area extending well south of Italy.
[b]*28* Greek *twenty orguias* (about 37 meters) [c]*28* Greek *fifteen orguias* (about 27 meters)

and get to land. [44]The rest were to get there on planks or on pieces of the ship. In this way everyone reached land in safety.

Ashore on Malta

28 Once safely on shore, we found out that the island was called Malta. [2]The islanders showed us unusual kindness. They built a fire and welcomed us all because it was raining and cold. [3]Paul gathered a pile of brushwood and, as he put it on the fire, a viper, driven out by the heat, fastened itself on his hand. [4]When the islanders saw the snake hanging from his hand, they said to each other, "This man must be a murderer; for though he escaped from the sea, Justice has not allowed him to live." [5]But Paul shook the snake off into the fire and suffered no ill effects. [6]The people expected him to swell up or suddenly fall dead, but after waiting a long time and seeing nothing unusual happen to him, they changed their minds and said he was a god.

[7]There was an estate nearby that belonged to Publius, the chief official of the island. He welcomed us to his home and for three days entertained us hospitably. [8]His father was sick in bed, suffering from fever and dysentery. Paul went in to see him and, after prayer, placed his hands on him and healed him. [9]When this had happened, the rest of the sick on the island came and were cured. [10]They honored us in many ways and when we were ready to sail, they furnished us with the supplies we needed.

Arrival at Rome

[11]After three months we put out to sea in a ship that had wintered in the island. It was an Alexandrian ship with the figurehead of the twin gods Castor and Pollux. [12]We put in at Syracuse and stayed there three days. [13]From there we set sail and arrived at Rhegium. The next day the south wind came up, and on the following day we reached Puteoli. [14]There we found some brothers who invited us to spend a week with them. And so we came to Rome. [15]The brothers there had heard that we were coming, and they traveled as far as the Forum of Appius and the Three Taverns to meet us. At the sight of these men Paul thanked God and was encouraged. [16]When we got to Rome, Paul was allowed to live by himself, with a soldier to guard him.

Paul Preaches at Rome Under Guard

[17]Three days later he called together the leaders of the Jews. When they had assembled, Paul said to them: "My brothers, although I have done nothing against our people or against the customs of our ancestors, I was arrested in Jerusalem and handed over to the Romans. [18]They examined me and wanted to release me, because I was not guilty of any crime deserving death. [19]But when the Jews objected, I was compelled to appeal to Caesar—not that I had any charge to bring against my own people. [20]For this reason I have asked to see you and talk with you. It is because of the hope of Israel that I am bound with this chain."

[21]They replied, "We have not received any letters from Judea concerning you, and none of the brothers who have come from there has reported or said anything bad about you. [22]But we want to hear what your views are, for we know that people everywhere are talking against this sect."

[23]They arranged to meet Paul on a certain day, and came in even larger numbers to the place where he was staying. From morning till evening he explained and declared to them the kingdom of God and tried to convince them about Jesus from the Law of Moses and

---

Whom would you elect as "Mr. or Mrs. Hospitality" at work? In your neighborhood? In your church? In your family?

1. In light of the fact God wanted Paul to get to Rome, why do you think he allowed all the events of 27:1–28:9 to happen? What stories would the centurion tell his fellow officers once they arrive? **2.** How could this set the stage for Paul to write about the way his imprisonment at Rome served to advance the Gospel (see Php 1:12–13)? **3.** How do you see Acts 1:8 still being carried out?

How has God used a disaster in your life for ministry? What have you learned from this?

---

1. As a child, whose visit would you be so excited about that you would wait outside (or by the window) until they arrived? Why? **2.** If in jail, what three items would you want most (a file, saw or key is not permitted!)?

1. Given the long delay, his shipwreck at sea, and his continuing status as a prisoner, how would Paul feel upon finally arriving in Rome? What must the believers' reunion with Paul have been like (vv. 14–15)? **2.** Why might Paul take the initiative to call this meeting with the Jewish leaders in Rome (vv. 17–20)? **3.** How do Paul's statements in 23:6, 24:21; 26:8 and 28:20 illustrate what he means by being a "prisoner for the Lord" (see Eph 4:1; Php 1:13–14; Col 4:3; Phm 1)? How does the existence of these "prison epistles" demonstrate the way Paul made the best of his situation? **4.** In light of all that Paul has been through, how do you think he felt when he heard the Jews' response in verse 21? How is their attitude different from that of the Jews in Jerusalem? How do you account for this difference? **5.** How does Isaiah's "hardening ministry" (vv. 25–28) bridge the gap in perception between those who view Christianity as a narrow Jewish sect (v. 21) and those who view Christianity as a faith for all peoples (v. 28)? How does this thematic bridge relate to 1:8? To 9:15–16? To 26:22–23? **6.** Verse 31 is similar to other summary verses in Acts (see 6:7; 9:31; 12:24; 16:5; 19:20). What does this ending reveal about Luke's central concern in writing this book?

♡ **1.** What bothers your non-Christian friends about the faith? How can you help them overcome those barriers? **2.** When limitations are placed upon you by circumstances beyond your control, how do you react? How can you serve the Lord within these limits? **3.** How does verse 31 set the stage for the way your life could become a continuation of Acts 28? In what way would you like to contribute an "Acts, chapter 29" to this movement of God during the next two years? **4.** Probably within a few years, Paul was killed by the emperor Nero. How would verse 31 serve as a fitting epitaph on Paul's grave? What do you need to build into your life now, so that your faith in Christ will be what people remember about you at death?

from the Prophets. [24]Some were convinced by what he said, but
others would not believe. [25]They disagreed among themselves and
began to leave after Paul had made this final statement: "The Holy
Spirit spoke the truth to your forefathers when he said through
Isaiah the prophet:

[26]" 'Go to this people and say,
"You will be ever hearing but never
understanding;
you will be ever seeing but never perceiving."
[27]For this people's heart has become calloused;
they hardly hear with their ears,
and they have closed their eyes.
Otherwise they might see with their eyes,
hear with their ears,
understand with their hearts
and turn, and I would heal them.'[a]

[28]"Therefore I want you to know that God's salvation has been
sent to the Gentiles, and they will listen!"[b]

[30]For two whole years Paul stayed there in his own rented house
and welcomed all who came to see him. [31]Boldly and without
hindrance he preached the kingdom of God and taught about the
Lord Jesus Christ.

[a]*27* Isaiah 6:9,10 [b]*28* Some manuscripts *listen!"* [29]*After he said this, the Jews left, arguing vigorously among themselves.*

INTRODUCTION to
ROMANS

Book Study Outline: If you are using Romans for a study course, here is a 7- or 13-week outline. Use the margin questions for your group agenda:

- start meeting / 15 min.
- read & discuss Bible / 30 min.
- close meeting / 15–45 min.

Refer to the Questions and Answers in front of Bible for more information.

7-week plan	13-week plan	Personal Reading	Group Study Passage
1	1	1:1–17	1:1–17/The Gospel of Christ
	2	1:18–2:32	1:18–32/The Bad News
2	3	3:1–31	3:21–31/The Good News
	4	4:1–25	4:1–25/An Example of Faith
3	5	5:1–21	5:12–21/Grace Reigns!
	6	6:1–7:6	6:1–14/Alive in Christ
4	7	7:7–25	7:7–25/The Law of Sin
	8	8:1–39	8:28–39/More Than Conquerors
5	9	9:1–11:36	9:1–29/God's Word Is True
	10	12:1–21	12:1–8/Responding to God
6	11	13:1–14	13:8–14/Love One Another
	12	14:1–15:13	14:1–15:13/Life Together
7	13	15:14–16:27	16:1–27/The Living Church

Author: The apostle Paul.

Date: Probably A.D. 56–57, but no later than A.D. 59.

Theme: Being right with God through faith in Christ.

Historical Background: Paul wrote this letter to introduce himself to the church at Rome. He intended to stop there *en route* to Spain. He was eager to assure the Roman Christians that, in spite of any rumors they might have heard, his message was indeed the Gospel of the grace of God in Christ Jesus. The church at Rome had not been planted by Paul. It may have been started by Roman Jews who were converted on the Day of Pentecost (Ac 2:10–11). The church was a mixture of Jewish and Gentile believers. At that point in time they were experiencing some tensions between these two groups.

Characteristics: The big issue in this letter is how anyone can be right with God on the final Day of Judgment. In his most precise theological statement in the New Testament, Paul asserts that right standing comes only through faith in Jesus Christ who died for us as a sacrifice for sin. In light of the Jewish-Gentile tensions in the church, Paul makes it clear that no one has an "edge" on God; rather, all stand condemned before him because no one has kept his Law. Having driven that truth home, he then declares the good news that forgiveness, acceptance and the new life of the Spirit come to all as God's gift to be received by faith. Chapters 1–11 speak of what God has done for all who believe, while chapters 12–16 show how believers ought to live in response to the lavish grace of God.

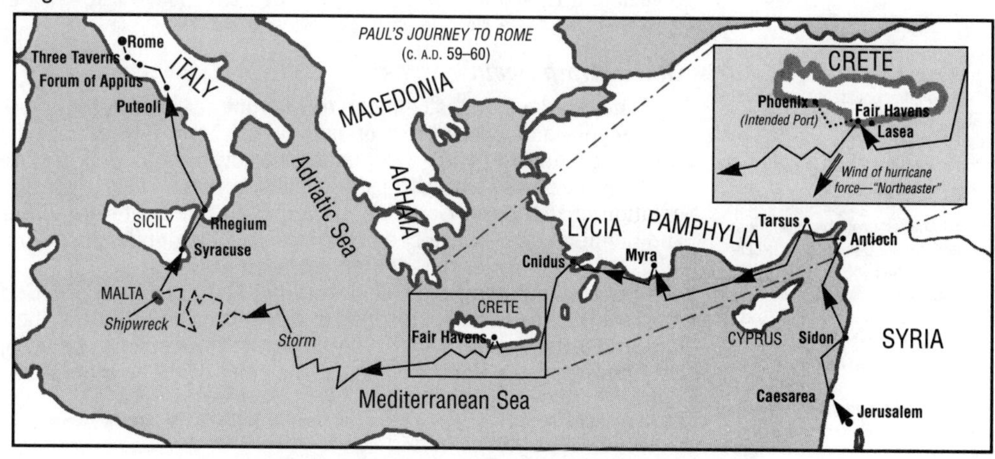

Romans

1 Paul, a servant of Christ Jesus, called to be an apostle and set apart for the gospel of God— 2the gospel he promised beforehand through his prophets in the Holy Scriptures 3regarding his Son, who as to his human nature was a descendant of David, 4and who through the Spirit[a] of holiness was declared with power to be the Son of God[b] by his resurrection from the dead: Jesus Christ our Lord. 5Through him and for his name's sake, we received grace and apostleship to call people from among all the Gentiles to the obedience that comes from faith. 6And you also are among those who are called to belong to Jesus Christ.

7To all in Rome who are loved by God and called to be saints:

Grace and peace to you from God our Father and from the Lord Jesus Christ.

Paul's Longing to Visit Rome

8First, I thank my God through Jesus Christ for all of you, because your faith is being reported all over the world. 9God, whom I serve with my whole heart in preaching the gospel of his Son, is my witness how constantly I remember you 10in my prayers at all times; and I pray that now at last by God's will the way may be opened for me to come to you.

11I long to see you so that I may impart to you some spiritual gift to make you strong— 12that is, that you and I may be mutually encouraged by each other's faith. 13I do not want you to be unaware, brothers, that I planned many times to come to you (but have been prevented from doing so until now) in order that I might have a harvest among you, just as I have had among the other Gentiles.

14I am obligated both to Greeks and non-Greeks, both to the wise and the foolish. 15That is why I am so eager to preach the gospel also to you who are at Rome.

16I am not ashamed of the gospel, because it is the power of God for the salvation of everyone who believes: first for the Jew, then for the Gentile. 17For in the gospel a righteousness from God is revealed, a righteousness that is by faith from first to last,[c] just as it is written: "The righteous will live by faith."[d]

God's Wrath Against Mankind

18The wrath of God is being revealed from heaven against all the godlessness and wickedness of men who suppress the truth by their wickedness, 19since what may be known about God is plain to them, because God has made it plain to them. 20For since the creation of the world God's invisible qualities—his eternal power and divine nature—have been clearly seen, being understood from what has been made, so that men are without excuse.

21For although they knew God, they neither glorified him as God nor gave thanks to him, but their thinking became futile and their foolish hearts were darkened. 22Although they claimed to be wise, they became fools 23and exchanged the glory of the immortal God

[a]4 Or *who as to his spirit* [b]4 Or *was appointed to be the Son of God with power*
[c]17 Or *is from faith to faith* [d]17 Hab. 2:4

1. When you write a letter, are you more likely to write until you run out of paper, or keep it short and to the point? **2.** What is one place you have never seen that you would like to visit?

1. If you received a letter from Paul (a missionary) saying he wanted to visit your family or small group, how would you react? **2.** What do you know about Rome in the first century? What are the circumstances that caused Paul to write this letter? (Read Introduction to Romans.) **3.** Note all the "I" statements. What do you learn about Paul in this passage? **4.** What do you learn about Jesus Christ in this passage? **5.** Reading between the lines, what is the problem in the church in Rome that Paul addresses in this letter?

1. When did you first feel Jesus' call in your life? How has that call changed your goals? Your sense of obligation to others? How is that reflected in your prayers? Your actions? **2.** How would you compare your commitment to the Gospel to Paul's in verse 16? **3.** Who was the Paul in your life who encouraged you in the rookie year of your spiritual life?

---

1. Who in your family is a lover of the great outdoors? **2.** What causes you to stand in awe of God? Being in the mountains? Walking along the seashore? Working in the garden?

1. This is probably the most descriptive passage in the Bible on the "fall of mankind." In verse 18, what did mankind do when given "the truth" about God? **2.** How did God expect mankind to know "the truth" before Jesus Christ came into the world (vv. 19–20)? **3.** Why then do people tend to worship the creation rather

for images made to look like mortal man and birds and animals and reptiles.

24Therefore God gave them over in the sinful desires of their hearts to sexual impurity for the degrading of their bodies with one another. 25They exchanged the truth of God for a lie, and worshiped and served created things rather than the Creator—who is forever praised. Amen.

26Because of this, God gave them over to shameful lusts. Even their women exchanged natural relations for unnatural ones. 27In the same way the men also abandoned natural relations with women and were inflamed with lust for one another. Men committed indecent acts with other men, and received in themselves the due penalty for their perversion.

28Furthermore, since they did not think it worthwhile to retain the knowledge of God, he gave them over to a depraved mind, to do what ought not to be done. 29They have become filled with every kind of wickedness, evil, greed and depravity. They are full of envy, murder, strife, deceit and malice. They are gossips, 30slanderers, God-haters, insolent, arrogant and boastful; they invent ways of doing evil; they disobey their parents; 31they are senseless, faithless, heartless, ruthless. 32Although they know God's righteous decree that those who do such things deserve death, they not only continue to do these very things but also approve of those who practice them.

than the Creator (vv. 21–23,25)? **4.** How does God respond to these evil attitudes? When mankind did not follow the truth, what did God let them do (vv. 24,26,28)?

1. Do you think our society has changed for the better or the worse since Paul wrote this description? **2.** Paul explains in this passage that the root cause for the ills in our society is a "depraved mind" or the sin nature in all of us. How does this view differ from what modern psychology teaches? **3.** If you could take a social psychologist on a tour of your community for a good look at the depraved mind in action, where would you take this person? What would you show this psychologist within your own life?

God's Righteous Judgment

2 You, therefore, have no excuse, you who pass judgment on someone else, for at whatever point you judge the other, you are condemning yourself, because you who pass judgment do the same things. 2Now we know that God's judgment against those who do such things is based on truth. 3So when you, a mere man, pass judgment on them and yet do the same things, do you think you will escape God's judgment? 4Or do you show contempt for the riches of his kindness, tolerance and patience, not realizing that God's kindness leads you toward repentance?

5But because of your stubbornness and your unrepentant heart, you are storing up wrath against yourself for the day of God's wrath, when his righteous judgment will be revealed. 6God "will give to each person according to what he has done."[a] 7To those who by persistence in doing good seek glory, honor and immortality, he will give eternal life. 8But for those who are self-seeking and who reject the truth and follow evil, there will be wrath and anger. 9There will be trouble and distress for every human being who does evil: first for the Jew, then for the Gentile; 10but glory, honor and peace for everyone who does good: first for the Jew, then for the Gentile. 11For God does not show favoritism.

12All who sin apart from the law will also perish apart from the law, and all who sin under the law will be judged by the law. 13For it is not those who hear the law who are righteous in God's sight, but it is those who obey the law who will be declared righteous. 14(Indeed, when Gentiles, who do not have the law, do by nature things required by the law, they are a law for themselves, even though they do not have the law, 15since they show that the requirements of the law are written on their hearts, their consciences also bearing witness, and their thoughts now accusing, now even defending them.) 16This will take place on the day when

When you were young, which of your parents was more strict? Merciful? Consistent?

1. Who is Paul talking about in this passage (see v. 17)? **2.** Reading between the lines, what is going on in the church between the Jews and the Gentile converts? Who are the outsiders? Why? **3.** When Paul accuses the readers of doing the "same things" (v. 3), is he referring to the same specific sins, or to the same root causes of sin? **4.** If "the righteous will live by faith" (1:17), why does Paul emphasize doing good (v. 7) and obeying the law (v. 13)?

1. From your experience, is it easier for those who grew up in a Christian home to appreciate God's grace, or someone who had no religious training as a child? **2.** As you grow older in your spiritual life, does your appreciation of God's grace grow stronger ... or is it likely to be taken for granted? **3.** Are you more likely to get upset by the immaturity of new Christians in the gray areas ... or be upset at those who get upset over issues in the gray areas, such as social drinking?

[a]6 Psalm 62:12; Prov. 24:12

God will judge men's secrets through Jesus Christ, as my gospel declares.

The Jews and the Law

17Now you, if you call yourself a Jew; if you rely on the law and brag about your relationship to God; 18if you know his will and approve of what is superior because you are instructed by the law; 19if you are convinced that you are a guide for the blind, a light for those who are in the dark, 20an instructor of the foolish, a teacher of infants, because you have in the law the embodiment of knowledge and truth— 21you, then, who teach others, do you not teach yourself? You who preach against stealing, do you steal? 22You who say that people should not commit adultery, do you commit adultery? You who abhor idols, do you rob temples? 23You who brag about the law, do you dishonor God by breaking the law? 24As it is written: "God's name is blasphemed among the Gentiles because of you."[a]

25Circumcision has value if you observe the law, but if you break the law, you have become as though you had not been circumcised. 26If those who are not circumcised keep the law's requirements, will they not be regarded as though they were circumcised? 27The one who is not circumcised physically and yet obeys the law will condemn you who, even though you have the[b] written code and circumcision, are a lawbreaker.

28A man is not a Jew if he is only one outwardly, nor is circumcision merely outward and physical. 29No, a man is a Jew if he is one inwardly; and circumcision is circumcision of the heart, by the Spirit, not by the written code. Such a man's praise is not from men, but from God.

God's Faithfulness

3 What advantage, then, is there in being a Jew, or what value is there in circumcision? 2Much in every way! First of all, they have been entrusted with the very words of God.

3What if some did not have faith? Will their lack of faith nullify God's faithfulness? 4Not at all! Let God be true, and every man a liar. As it is written:

> "So that you may be proved right when you speak
> and prevail when you judge."[c]

5But if our unrighteousness brings out God's righteousness more clearly, what shall we say? That God is unjust in bringing his wrath on us? (I am using a human argument.) 6Certainly not! If that were so, how could God judge the world? 7Someone might argue, "If my falsehood enhances God's truthfulness and so increases his glory, why am I still condemned as a sinner?" 8Why not say—as we are being slanderously reported as saying and as some claim that we say—"Let us do evil that good may result"? Their condemnation is deserved.

No One Is Righteous

9What shall we conclude then? Are we any better[d]? Not at all! We have already made the charge that Jews and Gentiles alike are all under sin. 10As it is written:

> "There is no one righteous, not even one;
> 11 there is no one who understands,

[a]*24* Isaiah 52:5; Ezek. 36:22 [b]*27* Or *who, by means of a* [c]*4* Psalm 51:4
[d]*9* Or *worse*

Does your conscience trouble you when you violate the speed limit?

1. If you were a Christian in the church in Rome and you came from a Jewish background that practiced circumcision, how would you feel about Gentiles if they wanted to come into the church without being circumcised? **2.** What was the original intent of the Law and of circumcision (see Ge 17:1–14)? How is that being twisted here? **3.** Why is Paul (a Jew) so vocal about Gentiles not having to be circumcised to come into the church? **4.** What does Paul mean by "circumcision of the heart" (v. 29; see Dt 10:16; 30:6; Jer 4:4; 9:25–26)? What is the real mark of God's family?

1. How open are you to receiving someone into your own small group or circle of friends who is seeking God but struggling with alcohol? **2.** Where might you be hypocritical regarding your spirituality? Bible knowledge? Wisdom? Maturity? Morality? Lack of hypocrisy? Political convictions?

Among your relatives, who comes closest to being the family's spiritual "patriarch"?

1. If you are in a group, have two people read verses 1–8 aloud. Reader #1—verses 1,3,5 and 7. Reader #2—verses 2,4,6 and 8. What are the issues in each question and how does Paul address them? **2.** Do you think it is easier for a prodigal who has "hit bottom" to come to God in repentance and faith than it is for someone who has had good religious training? **3.** From verses 10–18, list what is said regarding human thought, direction, speech and action. How does this list make you feel? **4.** From verse 20, would you say that the law is *descriptive* (more like a doctor's thermometer)? Or *prescriptive* (more like medicine to a sick patient)? What is its purpose?

1. When did you first truly sense your sin and need for God? **2.** In raising your own children, what are you going to insist on in their religious training ... and what are you going to let them de-

no one who seeks God.
12All have turned away,
they have together become worthless;
there is no one who does good,
not even one."[a]
13"Their throats are open graves;
their tongues practice deceit."[b]
"The poison of vipers is on their lips."[c]
14 "Their mouths are full of cursing and
bitterness."[d]
15"Their feet are swift to shed blood;
16 ruin and misery mark their ways,
17and the way of peace they do not know."[e]
18 "There is no fear of God before their eyes."[f]

19Now we know that whatever the law says, it says to those who
are under the law, so that every mouth may be silenced and the
whole world held accountable to God. 20Therefore no one will be
declared righteous in his sight by observing the law; rather,
through the law we become conscious of sin.

Righteousness Through Faith

21But now a righteousness from God, apart from law, has been
made known, to which the Law and the Prophets testify. 22This
righteousness from God comes through faith in Jesus Christ to all
who believe. There is no difference, 23for all have sinned and fall
short of the glory of God, 24and are justified freely by his grace
through the redemption that came by Christ Jesus. 25God presented him as a sacrifice of atonement,[g] through faith in his blood. He
did this to demonstrate his justice, because in his forbearance he
had left the sins committed beforehand unpunished— 26he did it
to demonstrate his justice at the present time, so as to be just and
the one who justifies those who have faith in Jesus.
27Where, then, is boasting? It is excluded. On what principle?
On that of observing the law? No, but on that of faith. 28For we
maintain that a man is justified by faith apart from observing the
law. 29Is God the God of Jews only? Is he not the God of Gentiles
too? Yes, of Gentiles too, 30since there is only one God, who will
justify the circumcised by faith and the uncircumcised through that
same faith. 31Do we, then, nullify the law by this faith? Not at all!
Rather, we uphold the law.

Abraham Justified by Faith

4 What then shall we say that Abraham, our forefather, discovered in this matter? 2If, in fact, Abraham was justified by
works, he had something to boast about—but not before God.
3What does the Scripture say? "Abraham believed God, and it was
credited to him as righteousness."[h]
4Now when a man works, his wages are not credited to him as
a gift, but as an obligation. 5However, to the man who does not
work but trusts God who justifies the wicked, his faith is credited
as righteousness. 6David says the same thing when he speaks of the
blessedness of the man to whom God credits righteousness apart
from works:

7"Blessed are they
whose transgressions are forgiven,

[a] *12* Psalms 14:1-3; 53:1-3; Eccles. 7:20 [b] *13* Psalm 5:9 [c] *13* Psalm 140:3 [d] *14* Psalm 10:7 [e] *17* Isaiah 59:7,8 [f] *18* Psalm 36:1 [g] *25* Or *as the one who would turn aside his wrath, taking away sin* [h] *3* Gen. 15:6; also in verse 22

cide? **3.** Up to this point in Romans, what has Paul been trying to prove? How important is this to a full understanding of the Gospel? **4.** What can you learn about witnessing from Paul's example in chapters 2–3? What kinds of people may need to be approached like this?

How close have you come to getting in trouble with the law?

1. If you were the person who was deserving of the death penalty, what would the word "justify" mean? **2.** If you were a slave, what would the word "redemption" mean to you? **3.** If you were a Jew who brought a yearly sacrifice to "postpone" God's judgment on you, what would the word "atonement" mean to you? **4.** How does this section break down barriers between Jews and Gentiles?

Martin Luther, John Wesley, Karl Barth—This passage, changed their lives ... and world history. How is the message of grace impacting your life?

---

1. When you were growing up, what chores were you expected to do around the house? Did your parents pay you? **2.** What is the biggest scam or junk mail offer you have fallen for—that promised something for nothing?

1. What is Paul doing when he calls Abraham to the witness stand to testify in his case for "justification by faith," not "by works?" **2.** Why would the example of Abraham be so important to the Jewish people? **3.** Why is circumcision so significant to the church in Rome in Paul's day? **4.** What do you learn about faith from the example in verses 18–21? How would you feel in Abraham's place? **5.** How does Abraham's faith relate to what God calls us to believe in verses 23–25? **6.** In some religions, forgiveness or grace as a free gift is a foreign concept. You "earn" your way to heaven by doing good deeds. What would have happened to Christianity if Paul had given in on the issue of circumcision?

1. What does it matter to you—practically or emotionally—whether a right relationship with God is a *gift* to be received or a *prize* to be earned? **2.** In what area of your life do you need to take a lesson from Abraham and focus not on "working" but on "believing"?

In your family, who tried to keep the peace? Mom or Dad?

1. How does "justification" change things in our relationship with God? What happened to the wrath of God Paul talked about in verses 9 and 1:18? **2.** How does Paul describe mankind's condition before Christ in verses 6, 8 and 10? How has this changed? **3.** How should a Christian look upon suffering and stress? Upon disappointment?

1. How much of God's peace and hope need to begin with a *feeling* and how much must begin with *head knowledge* and *con-*

whose sins are covered.
8Blessed is the man
whose sin the Lord will never count against
him."[a]

9Is this blessedness only for the circumcised, or also for the uncircumcised? We have been saying that Abraham's faith was credited to him as righteousness. 10Under what circumstances was it credited? Was it after he was circumcised, or before? It was not after, but before! 11And he received the sign of circumcision, a seal of the righteousness that he had by faith while he was still uncircumcised. So then, he is the father of all who believe but have not been circumcised, in order that righteousness might be credited to them. 12And he is also the father of the circumcised who not only are circumcised but who also walk in the footsteps of the faith that our father Abraham had before he was circumcised.

13It was not through law that Abraham and his offspring received the promise that he would be heir of the world, but through the righteousness that comes by faith. 14For if those who live by law are heirs, faith has no value and the promise is worthless, 15because law brings wrath. And where there is no law there is no transgression.

16Therefore, the promise comes by faith, so that it may be by grace and may be guaranteed to all Abraham's offspring—not only to those who are of the law but also to those who are of the faith of Abraham. He is the father of us all. 17As it is written: "I have made you a father of many nations."[b] He is our father in the sight of God, in whom he believed—the God who gives life to the dead and calls things that are not as though they were.

18Against all hope, Abraham in hope believed and so became the father of many nations, just as it had been said to him, "So shall your offspring be."[c] 19Without weakening in his faith, he faced the fact that his body was as good as dead—since he was about a hundred years old—and that Sarah's womb was also dead. 20Yet he did not waver through unbelief regarding the promise of God, but was strengthened in his faith and gave glory to God, 21being fully persuaded that God had power to do what he had promised. 22This is why "it was credited to him as righteousness." 23The words "it was credited to him" were written not for him alone, 24but also for us, to whom God will credit righteousness—for us who believe in him who raised Jesus our Lord from the dead. 25He was delivered over to death for our sins and was raised to life for our justification.

Peace and Joy

5 Therefore, since we have been justified through faith, we[d] have peace with God through our Lord Jesus Christ, 2through whom we have gained access by faith into this grace in which we now stand. And we[d] rejoice in the hope of the glory of God. 3Not only so, but we[d] also rejoice in our sufferings, because we know that suffering produces perseverance; 4perseverance, character; and character, hope. 5And hope does not disappoint us, because God has poured out his love into our hearts by the Holy Spirit, whom he has given us.

6You see, at just the right time, when we were still powerless, Christ died for the ungodly. 7Very rarely will anyone die for a righteous man, though for a good man someone might possibly dare to die. 8But God demonstrates his own love for us in this: While we were still sinners, Christ died for us.

[a] *8* Psalm 32:1,2 [b] *17* Gen. 17:5 [c] *18* Gen. 15:5 [d] *1,2,3* Or *let us*

9Since we have now been justified by his blood, how much more
shall we be saved from God's wrath through him! 10For if, when
we were God's enemies, we were reconciled to him through the
death of his Son, how much more, having been reconciled, shall
we be saved through his life! 11Not only is this so, but we also
rejoice in God through our Lord Jesus Christ, through whom we
have now received reconciliation.

Death Through Adam, Life Through Christ

12Therefore, just as sin entered the world through one man, and
death through sin, and in this way death came to all men, because
all sinned— 13for before the law was given, sin was in the world.
But sin is not taken into account when there is no law. 14Neverthe-
less, death reigned from the time of Adam to the time of Moses,
even over those who did not sin by breaking a command, as did
Adam, who was a pattern of the one to come.
15But the gift is not like the trespass. For if the many died by the
trespass of the one man, how much more did God's grace and the
gift that came by the grace of the one man, Jesus Christ, overflow
to the many! 16Again, the gift of God is not like the result of the
one man's sin: The judgment followed one sin and brought condemnation, but the gift followed many trespasses and brought justification. 17For if, by the trespass of the one man, death reigned
through that one man, how much more will those who receive
God's abundant provision of grace and of the gift of righteousness
reign in life through the one man, Jesus Christ.
18Consequently, just as the result of one trespass was condemnation for all men, so also the result of one act of righteousness was
justification that brings life for all men. 19For just as through the
disobedience of the one man the many were made sinners, so also
through the obedience of the one man the many will be made
righteous.
20The law was added so that the trespass might increase. But
where sin increased, grace increased all the more, 21so that, just as
sin reigned in death, so also grace might reign through righteousness to bring eternal life through Jesus Christ our Lord.

Dead to Sin, Alive in Christ

6 What shall we say, then? Shall we go on sinning so that grace
may increase? 2By no means! We died to sin; how can we live
in it any longer? 3Or don't you know that all of us who were
baptized into Christ Jesus were baptized into his death? 4We were
therefore buried with him through baptism into death in order
that, just as Christ was raised from the dead through the glory of
the Father, we too may live a new life.
5If we have been united with him like this in his death, we will
certainly also be united with him in his resurrection. 6For we know
that our old self was crucified with him so that the body of sin
might be done away with,[a] that we should no longer be slaves to
sin— 7because anyone who has died has been freed from sin.
8Now if we died with Christ, we believe that we will also live
with him. 9For we know that since Christ was raised from the
dead, he cannot die again; death no longer has mastery over him.
10The death he died, he died to sin once for all; but the life he
lives, he lives to God.
11In the same way, count yourselves dead to sin but alive to God
in Christ Jesus. 12Therefore do not let sin reign in your mortal body

a6 Or *be rendered powerless*

scious claiming of peace and hope? **2.** What incident in your life can you look back on and see the truth of verses 3–5?

Who do you take after in your temperament, your mother or your father? How about your body build? Your musical ability?

1. Before DNA testing proved the likelihood of a single source for all of mankind, Paul was saying that the disease of sin came from a single source: Adam. What do you remember about the story in the Old Testament of Adam and his "fall" (Ge 3:1–24)? **2.** How has the sin of Adam affected his descendants to the present day? How would you describe this in medical terms? A disease? An epidemic? An infection that attacks the immune system? **3.** From chapter 5, what do you see that God has done through Jesus for us? How does this add to your understanding of God's grace (vv. 1,15, 17, 20–21)? How does this chapter illustrate why "Grace and peace to you" (1:7) is such an appropriate greeting for Christians?

Does the Gospel message excite you as it does Paul? Why or why not? What could help you to experience its life and vitality again?

What is the closest you have come to losing your life?

1. What is Paul's short answer to the addict who says he is a slave to his habit? **2.** The idea of death and resurrection is mentioned 15 times in this passage. What is Paul trying to say? **3.** What do you do with the flashbacks and voices in the night that keep reminding you of your past mistakes? **4.** If we are dead to sin, how is it that Christians still sin? What does it mean to practice the teaching in verses 11–13?

How does the knowledge of your death to sin affect your struggle with sin, or how can it? How can it affect your prayer life?

so that you obey its evil desires. 13Do not offer the parts of your body to sin, as instruments of wickedness, but rather offer yourselves to God, as those who have been brought from death to life; and offer the parts of your body to him as instruments of righteousness. 14For sin shall not be your master, because you are not under law, but under grace.

Slaves to Righteousness

15What then? Shall we sin because we are not under law but under grace? By no means! 16Don't you know that when you offer yourselves to someone to obey him as slaves, you are slaves to the one whom you obey—whether you are slaves to sin, which leads to death, or to obedience, which leads to righteousness? 17But thanks be to God that, though you used to be slaves to sin, you wholeheartedly obeyed the form of teaching to which you were entrusted. 18You have been set free from sin and have become slaves to righteousness.

19I put this in human terms because you are weak in your natural selves. Just as you used to offer the parts of your body in slavery to impurity and to ever-increasing wickedness, so now offer them in slavery to righteousness leading to holiness. 20When you were slaves to sin, you were free from the control of righteousness. 21What benefit did you reap at that time from the things you are now ashamed of? Those things result in death! 22But now that you have been set free from sin and have become slaves to God, the benefit you reap leads to holiness, and the result is eternal life. 23For the wages of sin is death, but the gift of God is eternal life in[a] Christ Jesus our Lord.

An Illustration From Marriage

7 Do you not know, brothers—for I am speaking to men who know the law—that the law has authority over a man only as long as he lives? 2For example, by law a married woman is bound to her husband as long as he is alive, but if her husband dies, she is released from the law of marriage. 3So then, if she marries another man while her husband is still alive, she is called an adulteress. But if her husband dies, she is released from that law and is not an adulteress, even though she marries another man.

4So, my brothers, you also died to the law through the body of Christ, that you might belong to another, to him who was raised from the dead, in order that we might bear fruit to God. 5For when we were controlled by the sinful nature,[b] the sinful passions aroused by the law were at work in our bodies, so that we bore fruit for death. 6But now, by dying to what once bound us, we have been released from the law so that we serve in the new way of the Spirit, and not in the old way of the written code.

Struggling With Sin

7What shall we say, then? Is the law sin? Certainly not! Indeed I would not have known what sin was except through the law. For I would not have known what coveting really was if the law had not said, "Do not covet."[c] 8But sin, seizing the opportunity afforded by the commandment, produced in me every kind of covetous desire. For apart from law, sin is dead. 9Once I was alive apart from law; but when the commandment came, sin sprang to life and I died. 10I found that the very commandment that was intended to bring life actually brought death. 11For sin, seizing the opportunity

[a]23 Or *through* [b]5 Or *the flesh*; also in verse 25 [c]7 Exodus 20:17; Deut. 5:21

Who was your first "boss"? Was this person easy to work for or a slave driver?

1. If you find yourself once again being a slave to sin, what does this passage ask you to do? **2.** From this passage (and also in 1:18–32) what were the members of this church doing before they turned over their lives to Christ? **3.** What would Paul say to the modern psychologist who says that you can't change inherited behavior? **4.** What is the difference between the pension plan that the old slave owner of your life offered ... and the new owner's plan?

1. If Paul were around today, what would he say enslaves our society? What about the Christian community? **2.** If you had acted as God's willing servant this week, what would have changed in your attitudes and actions?

When you were dating, did you ever get caught two-timing? Did anyone two-time you?

1. When Paul talks about the "authority" of the law, what does he mean? **2.** Using the allegory of marriage, who were you married to originally? How did that marriage work out? **3.** When Paul says you are "released" from the obligations of a religious life, is he discouraging spiritual discipline?

1. What were some of the "rules" that were taught in your religious upbringing? **2.** Do you feel more "married" to the living Christ, or to some religious code? Explain.

---

1. When you were a teenager, what was one of your biggest struggles? **2.** What New Year's resolution have you started with good intentions only to have it fizzle out?

1. Is the struggle that Paul describes here in verse 18 the struggle *before* he became a Christian ... or the struggle *after* he

afforded by the commandment, deceived me, and through the commandment put me to death. [12]So then, the law is holy, and the
commandment is holy, righteous and good.

[13]Did that which is good, then, become death to me? By no
means! But in order that sin might be recognized as sin, it produced death in me through what was good, so that through the
commandment sin might become utterly sinful.

[14]We know that the law is spiritual; but I am unspiritual, sold as
a slave to sin. [15]I do not understand what I do. For what I want to
do I do not do, but what I hate I do. [16]And if I do what I do not
want to do, I agree that the law is good. [17]As it is, it is no longer I
myself who do it, but it is sin living in me. [18]I know that nothing
good lives in me, that is, in my sinful nature.[a] For I have the
desire to do what is good, but I cannot carry it out. [19]For what I do
is not the good I want to do; no, the evil I do not want to do—this
I keep on doing. [20]Now if I do what I do not want to do, it is no
longer I who do it, but it is sin living in me that does it.

[21]So I find this law at work: When I want to do good, evil is right
there with me. [22]For in my inner being I delight in God's law;
[23]but I see another law at work in the members of my body,
waging war against the law of my mind and making me a prisoner
of the law of sin at work within my members. [24]What a wretched
man I am! Who will rescue me from this body of death? [25]Thanks
be to God—through Jesus Christ our Lord!

So then, I myself in my mind am a slave to God's law, but in the
sinful nature a slave to the law of sin.

Life Through the Spirit

8 Therefore, there is now no condemnation for those who are in
Christ Jesus,[b] [2]because through Christ Jesus the law of the
Spirit of life set me free from the law of sin and death. [3]For what
the law was powerless to do in that it was weakened by the sinful
nature,[c] God did by sending his own Son in the likeness of sinful
man to be a sin offering.[d] And so he condemned sin in
sinful man,[e] [4]in order that the righteous requirements of the law
might be fully met in us, who do not live according to the sinful
nature but according to the Spirit.

[5]Those who live according to the sinful nature have their minds
set on what that nature desires; but those who live in accordance
with the Spirit have their minds set on what the Spirit desires.
[6]The mind of sinful man[f] is death, but the mind controlled by the
Spirit is life and peace; [7]the sinful mind[g] is hostile to God. It does
not submit to God's law, nor can it do so. [8]Those controlled by the
sinful nature cannot please God.

[9]You, however, are controlled not by the sinful nature but by the
Spirit, if the Spirit of God lives in you. And if anyone does not have
the Spirit of Christ, he does not belong to Christ. [10]But if Christ is
in you, your body is dead because of sin, yet your spirit is alive
because of righteousness. [11]And if the Spirit of him who raised
Jesus from the dead is living in you, he who raised Christ from the
dead will also give life to your mortal bodies through his Spirit,
who lives in you.

[12]Therefore, brothers, we have an obligation—but it is not to
the sinful nature, to live according to it. [13]For if you live according
to the sinful nature, you will die; but if by the Spirit you put to

[a]*18* Or *my flesh* [b]*1* Some later manuscripts *Jesus, who do not live according to the sinful nature but according to the Spirit,* [c]*3* Or *the flesh*; also in verses 4, 5, 8, 9, 12 and 13 [d]*3* Or *man, for sin* [e]*3* Or *in the flesh* [f]*6* Or *mind set on the flesh* [g]*7* Or *the mind set on the flesh*

became a Christian? **2.** If you feel that Paul is talking about his pre-Christian life, where did he get his "desire" to do good? **3.** If you think he is talking about his Christian life, why is he struggling when God is the new owner of his life? **4.** When have you come to the place where you cried out like Paul in verse 24? **5.** Why do you think God's law was given: (a) Means to follow *in order* to be saved? (b) Guide to follow *once we are* saved by grace? (c) Stumbling block, impossible to follow, which only points the sinner to God's grace? How do verses 10, 12 and 22 support your answer?

1. In light of your own struggles with sin, how do you feel about Paul's conflict? How is this a model for a healthy, realistic self-image? How is it a model for taking appropriate responsibility? **2.** What is the struggle in your spiritual life right now?

When you were young, who caused you to change your behavior by their powerful influence?

1. The next time the travel agent for your old nature tries to send you on a guilt trip, what does Paul want you to keep in mind? **2.** What do you remember about the Ascension of Jesus Christ and his promise to send the Holy Spirit to indwell his followers at Pentecost (Acts 1)? **3.** In verses 5–11, what does Paul say about the option Christians have in living their life? **4.** Where is the battle for the control of your life going to be fought ... and won or lost? **5.** Since we are not set right with God by doing good works, what is the motive for changing our lives? How are we to deal with our sinful nature (vv. 13–14; see 6:13,19)? **6.** What does it mean to be "led by the Spirit" (v. 14)? How does the Spirit help us fight our battles? Give an example.

1. If there were a pollution control device on your thoughts right now, what would it register? GREEN (no problem); ORANGE (Warning signs) or RED (Fire alert zone). **2.** What does it mean to you that you are not God's slave, but his child?

death the misdeeds of the body, you will live, 14because those who are led by the Spirit of God are sons of God. 15For you did not receive a spirit that makes you a slave again to fear, but you received the Spirit of sonship.[a] And by him we cry, *"Abba,*[b] Father." 16The Spirit himself testifies with our spirit that we are God's children. 17Now if we are children, then we are heirs—heirs of God and co-heirs with Christ, if indeed we share in his sufferings in order that we may also share in his glory.

Future Glory

18I consider that our present sufferings are not worth comparing with the glory that will be revealed in us. 19The creation waits in eager expectation for the sons of God to be revealed. 20For the creation was subjected to frustration, not by its own choice, but by the will of the one who subjected it, in hope 21that[c] the creation itself will be liberated from its bondage to decay and brought into the glorious freedom of the children of God.

22We know that the whole creation has been groaning as in the pains of childbirth right up to the present time. 23Not only so, but we ourselves, who have the firstfruits of the Spirit, groan inwardly as we wait eagerly for our adoption as sons, the redemption of our bodies. 24For in this hope we were saved. But hope that is seen is no hope at all. Who hopes for what he already has? 25But if we hope for what we do not yet have, we wait for it patiently.

26In the same way, the Spirit helps us in our weakness. We do not know what we ought to pray for, but the Spirit himself intercedes for us with groans that words cannot express. 27And he who searches our hearts knows the mind of the Spirit, because the Spirit intercedes for the saints in accordance with God's will.

What signs of aging or weathering are you starting to feel in your bones?

1. What do you remember about the persecution of Christians in Rome during this time that would help explain Paul's words of comfort in this passage? **2.** What is the closest you have come to feeling a "groaning" in your spirit to see the final triumph over sin and death? What would a world like ours be like if there were no decay or death? No expectation or delay? **3.** What does the Holy Spirit do for us when we do not know how to pray? When is the last time you did not know how to pray and the Holy Spirit helped and comforted you?

What is the difference between the hope of a Christian and wishful thinking?

More Than Conquerors

28And we know that in all things God works for the good of those who love him,[d] who[e] have been called according to his purpose. 29For those God foreknew he also predestined to be conformed to the likeness of his Son, that he might be the firstborn among many brothers. 30And those he predestined, he also called; those he called, he also justified; those he justified, he also glorified.

31What, then, shall we say in response to this? If God is for us, who can be against us? 32He who did not spare his own Son, but gave him up for us all—how will he not also, along with him, graciously give us all things? 33Who will bring any charge against those whom God has chosen? It is God who justifies. 34Who is he that condemns? Christ Jesus, who died—more than that, who was raised to life—is at the right hand of God and is also interceding for us. 35Who shall separate us from the love of Christ? Shall trouble or hardship or persecution or famine or nakedness or danger or sword? 36As it is written:

> "For your sake we face death all day long;
> we are considered as sheep to be
> slaughtered."[f]

37No, in all these things we are more than conquerors through him who loved us. 38For I am convinced that neither death nor life, neither angels nor demons,[g] neither the present nor the future,

Do you tend to see the glass half full or half empty?

1. What confidence does verse 28 give you about events that occur in your life? Do you say the same thing when suffering (v. 18) comes your way? **2.** In verses 29–30, what five verbs describe what God has already done for you? **3.** If you received this letter and you were facing possible arrest, torture and physical death for your faith in Christ, how would verses 31–39 comfort you? **4.** How could the forces in verses 38–39 disrupt your trust in God's love? **5.** When has it been hardest for you to believe Romans 8:28?

1. How are you doing in the school of hard knocks right now? **2.** What is the closest you have come to feeling the despair and loneliness of being separated from God like Paul describes in verses 31–39?

[a] *15* Or *adoption* [b] *15* Aramaic for *Father* [c] *20,21* Or *subjected it in hope. 21For* [d] *28* Some manuscripts *And we know that all things work together for good to those who love God* [e] *28* Or *works together with those who love him to bring about what is good—with those who* [f] *36* Psalm 44:22 [g] *38* Or *nor heavenly rulers*

nor any powers, 39neither height nor depth, nor anything else in all creation, will be able to separate us from the love of God that is in Christ Jesus our Lord.

God's Sovereign Choice

9 I speak the truth in Christ—I am not lying, my conscience confirms it in the Holy Spirit— 2I have great sorrow and unceasing anguish in my heart. 3For I could wish that I myself were cursed and cut off from Christ for the sake of my brothers, those of my own race, 4the people of Israel. Theirs is the adoption as sons; theirs the divine glory, the covenants, the receiving of the law, the temple worship and the promises. 5Theirs are the patriarchs, and from them is traced the human ancestry of Christ, who is God over all, forever praised![a] Amen.

6It is not as though God's word had failed. For not all who are descended from Israel are Israel. 7Nor because they are his descendants are they all Abraham's children. On the contrary, "It is through Isaac that your offspring will be reckoned."[b] 8In other words, it is not the natural children who are God's children, but it is the children of the promise who are regarded as Abraham's offspring. 9For this was how the promise was stated: "At the appointed time I will return, and Sarah will have a son."[c]

10Not only that, but Rebekah's children had one and the same father, our father Isaac. 11Yet, before the twins were born or had done anything good or bad—in order that God's purpose in election might stand: 12not by works but by him who calls—she was told, "The older will serve the younger."[d] 13Just as it is written: "Jacob I loved, but Esau I hated."[e]

14What then shall we say? Is God unjust? Not at all! 15For he says to Moses,

> "I will have mercy on whom I have mercy,
> and I will have compassion on whom I have compassion."[f]

16It does not, therefore, depend on man's desire or effort, but on God's mercy. 17For the Scripture says to Pharaoh: "I raised you up for this very purpose, that I might display my power in you and that my name might be proclaimed in all the earth."[g] 18Therefore God has mercy on whom he wants to have mercy, and he hardens whom he wants to harden.

19One of you will say to me: "Then why does God still blame us? For who resists his will?" 20But who are you, O man, to talk back to God? "Shall what is formed say to him who formed it, 'Why did you make me like this?' "[h] 21Does not the potter have the right to make out of the same lump of clay some pottery for noble purposes and some for common use?

22What if God, choosing to show his wrath and make his power known, bore with great patience the objects of his wrath—prepared for destruction? 23What if he did this to make the riches of his glory known to the objects of his mercy, whom he prepared in advance for glory— 24even us, whom he also called, not only from the Jews but also from the Gentiles? 25As he says in Hosea:

> "I will call them 'my people' who are not my people;

[a]5 Or *Christ, who is over all. God be forever praised!* Or *Christ. God who is over all be forever praised!* [b]7 Gen. 21:12 [c]9 Gen. 18:10,14 [d]12 Gen. 25:23 [e]13 Mal. 1:2,3 [f]15 Exodus 33:19 [g]17 Exodus 9:16 [h]20 Isaiah 29:16; 45:9

---

1. What was one thing about which your folks used to say, "Wait 'till you're older, you'll understand then"? **2.** When have you won something unexpected? A trip? Award of achievement? Class officer elections? The big game?

1. How should each of the benefits Paul mentions in verses 4–5 have drawn the Jewish people to Christ? How does he account for their unbelief in spite of such advantages (vv. 6–9; see 4:11–12)? **2.** How would this link to Abraham help resolve conflicts between Jews and Gentiles? **3.** What would be just and fair for each of us to receive from God (see 3:9–20)? **4.** Is God fair? What does Paul says in verses 14–15? How does he respond to further questions about God's fairness in choosing some but not others (v. 19)? What is God's overriding purpose?

1. How deeply do you hurt for unbelievers? As much as Paul? **2.** If you were God, would you choose "you" to be part of your plan for the universe? How do you feel about God's authority to choose who will be "objects of his mercy" (v. 23)? **3.** Who are some non-Christians God has used to help you on your way to spiritual maturity? How so? In light of this passage, how should Christians approach witnessing? Is there any point? **4.** Where are you growing in your understanding of God's will for your life? What questions would you like to ask God about this? **5.** Suppose salvation did depend on human desire and effort. What grade would God give you: "E" for effort? "C" for creativity? "A" for accomplishment? "F" for failure to follow directions? If God graded on a curve, would you have a better chance of passing? Would "cribsheets" help? How about polishing a few apples and becoming the teacher's pet? How does this passage make you feel about your own salvation?

and I will call her 'my loved one' who is not
my loved one,"[a]

26 and,

"It will happen that in the very place where it
was said to them,
'You are not my people,'
they will be called 'sons of the living God.' "[b]

27 Isaiah cries out concerning Israel:

"Though the number of the Israelites be like the
sand by the sea,
only the remnant will be saved.
28 For the Lord will carry out
his sentence on earth with speed and
finality."[c]

29 It is just as Isaiah said previously:

"Unless the Lord Almighty
had left us descendants,
we would have become like Sodom,
we would have been like Gomorrah."[d]

Israel's Unbelief

30 What then shall we say? That the Gentiles, who did not pursue
righteousness, have obtained it, a righteousness that is by faith;
31 but Israel, who pursued a law of righteousness, has not attained
it. 32 Why not? Because they pursued it not by faith but as if it were
by works. They stumbled over the "stumbling stone." 33 As it is
written:

"See, I lay in Zion a stone that causes men to
stumble
and a rock that makes them fall,
and the one who trusts in him will never be put
to shame."[e]

10 Brothers, my heart's desire and prayer to God for the Israelites is that they may be saved. 2 For I can testify about them
that they are zealous for God, but their zeal is not based on knowledge. 3 Since they did not know the righteousness that comes from
God and sought to establish their own, they did not submit to
God's righteousness. 4 Christ is the end of the law so that there may
be righteousness for everyone who believes.
5 Moses describes in this way the righteousness that is by the
law: "The man who does these things will live by them."[f] 6 But
the righteousness that is by faith says: "Do not say in your heart,
'Who will ascend into heaven?'[g]" (that is, to bring Christ down)
7 "or 'Who will descend into the deep?'[h]" (that is, to bring Christ
up from the dead). 8 But what does it say? "The word is near you;
it is in your mouth and in your heart,"[i] that is, the word of faith
we are proclaiming: 9 That if you confess with your mouth, "Jesus is
Lord," and believe in your heart that God raised him from the
dead, you will be saved. 10 For it is with your heart that you believe
and are justified, and it is with your mouth that you confess and are
saved. 11 As the Scripture says, "Anyone who trusts in him will
never be put to shame."[j] 12 For there is no difference between

a25 Hosea 2:23 b26 Hosea 1:10 c28 Isaiah 10:22,23 d29 Isaiah 1:9
e33 Isaiah 8:14; 28:16 f5 Lev. 18:5 g6 Deut. 30:12 h7 Deut. 30:13
i8 Deut. 30:14 j11 Isaiah 28:16

---

1. When you were a child, what did you do to earn your allowance? **2.** In elementary school, what was your hardest subject? What did you do to try to improve your grades? **3.** What were some of the hard and fast rules observed in your house when your were growing up?

1. Is Paul anti-Semitic? What hope does he have for the Israelites in the first verse of Chapter 10? **2.** In what characteristic way did Jews seek to be right with God (9:32)? What was the basic problem in this approach (see 3:20; 7:7–11)? **3.** On the basis of 10:1–2, how would you respond to someone who said, *"What* you believe doesn't matter as long as you are *sincere"?* How can zeal for God sometimes get in the way of knowing him? **4.** What is the only way to be saved according to Paul in 10:9–10? **5.** How would the attitude of a person coming to God on the basis of his or her performance (v. 5) be different from that of someone coming to him by faith in Christ (vv. 8–9)? **6.** What does it mean to confess "Jesus is Lord"? How does this tie in with belief? **7.** What is the purpose of Paul's series of questions in verses 14–17? How does this underscore the importance of evangelism? **8.** In general, what is the world's view today of going to heaven?

1. When did you first come to realize that it isn't so much what you do for God, but what he's

Jew and Gentile—the same Lord is Lord of all and richly blesses all who call on him, 13for, "Everyone who calls on the name of the Lord will be saved."[a]

14How, then, can they call on the one they have not believed in? And how can they believe in the one of whom they have not heard? And how can they hear without someone preaching to them? 15And how can they preach unless they are sent? As it is written, "How beautiful are the feet of those who bring good news!"[b]

16But not all the Israelites accepted the good news. For Isaiah says, "Lord, who has believed our message?"[c] 17Consequently, faith comes from hearing the message, and the message is heard through the word of Christ. 18But I ask: Did they not hear? Of course they did:

> "Their voice has gone out into all the earth,
> their words to the ends of the world."[d]

19Again I ask: Did Israel not understand? First, Moses says,

> "I will make you envious by those who are not a nation;
> I will make you angry by a nation that has no understanding."[e]

20And Isaiah boldly says,

> "I was found by those who did not seek me;
> I revealed myself to those who did not ask for me."[f]

21But concerning Israel he says,

> "All day long I have held out my hands
> to a disobedient and obstinate people."[g]

The Remnant of Israel

11 I ask then: Did God reject his people? By no means! I am an Israelite myself, a descendant of Abraham, from the tribe of Benjamin. 2God did not reject his people, whom he foreknew. Don't you know what the Scripture says in the passage about Elijah—how he appealed to God against Israel: 3"Lord, they have killed your prophets and torn down your altars; I am the only one left, and they are trying to kill me"[h]? 4And what was God's answer to him? "I have reserved for myself seven thousand who have not bowed the knee to Baal."[i] 5So too, at the present time there is a remnant chosen by grace. 6And if by grace, then it is no longer by works; if it were, grace would no longer be grace.[j]

7What then? What Israel sought so earnestly it did not obtain, but the elect did. The others were hardened, 8as it is written:

> "God gave them a spirit of stupor,
> eyes so that they could not see
> and ears so that they could not hear,
> to this very day."[k]

9And David says:

> "May their table become a snare and a trap,
> a stumbling block and a retribution for them.

[a] 13 Joel 2:32 [b] 15 Isaiah 52:7 [c] 16 Isaiah 53:1 [d] 18 Psalm 19:4
[e] 19 Deut. 32:21 [f] 20 Isaiah 65:1 [g] 21 Isaiah 65:2 [h] 3 1 Kings 19:10,14
[i] 4 1 Kings 19:18 [j] 6 Some manuscripts *by grace. But if by works, then it is no longer grace; if it were, work would no longer be work.* [k] 8 Deut. 29:4; Isaiah 29:10

done for you? **2.** The central affirmation of the early church was "Jesus is Lord"; everyone else was saying "Caesar is Lord." Who (or what) are some gods that compete with your allegiance to Christ? **3.** How hard is it for you to accept the fact that "the same Lord is Lord of all" (v. 12)? What about rapists and child abusers? What about people of other nations? What about your neighbors?

---

1. As a child, what item did a friend or sibling possess that made you jealous? **2.** What moments of rejection in your teen years do you remember vividly? Getting cut from the team? Not being invited to a big party? Turned down for a date? **3.** What have been the benefits of healthy competition in your life?

1. Has God rejected the Jews (vv. 1,5)? How might Paul's comments in 9:25 and 10:21 lead someone to ask the question in verse 1? **2.** On what basis are Paul and others of the remnant chosen? Why would this be so difficult for his fellow Israelites to grasp (see 10:3)? **3.** What relationships does Paul see between the Gentiles and the Jews in verse 11? **4.** Why does Paul want his Gentile readers to be aware of God's plan (v. 25)? Why would pride become a danger for them? **5.** Does Paul mean in verses 25–32 that every Jewish person will ultimately be saved or that the nation as a whole will experience the salvation of those who believe in faith? **6.** What is Paul's ultimate hope for Israel (vv. 26–27)? For Gentiles (v. 32)? How does this tie in with Paul's teaching in 3:21–24? **7.** How does the song in verses 33–36 relate to: (a) Paul's argument in verses 25–32? (b) Any questions that may have been raised by chapters 9–11? **8.** Which traits of God does Paul celebrate here? Why these?

♡ **1.** How is it possible for someone to try so hard to please God that they actually resist his love for them? When have you experienced this? **2.** Like the Jews in Paul's day, are churchgoers today relying more on performance of rituals than on God's grace? How? **3.** How does the church itself struggle with works versus grace? In what ways are works still important? **4.** How has arrogance between groups of Christians hurt your church experience? When have you found yourself exhibiting this attitude too? **5.** When someone else receives God's blessing and grace in their life, does that spur you on to seek God all the more, or does it leave you feeling on the short end of the stick? Why? **6.** Why is the end of this chapter a good place for a doxology—Paul's, yours and your group's?

10 May their eyes be darkened so they cannot see,
and their backs be bent forever."[a]

Ingrafted Branches

11 Again I ask: Did they stumble so as to fall beyond recovery?
Not at all! Rather, because of their transgression, salvation has
come to the Gentiles to make Israel envious. 12 But if their transgression means riches for the world, and their loss means riches for
the Gentiles, how much greater riches will their fullness bring!
13 I am talking to you Gentiles. Inasmuch as I am the apostle to
the Gentiles, I make much of my ministry 14 in the hope that I may
somehow arouse my own people to envy and save some of them.
15 For if their rejection is the reconciliation of the world, what will
their acceptance be but life from the dead? 16 If the part of the
dough offered as firstfruits is holy, then the whole batch is holy; if
the root is holy, so are the branches.
17 If some of the branches have been broken off, and you, though
a wild olive shoot, have been grafted in among the others and now
share in the nourishing sap from the olive root, 18 do not boast over
those branches. If you do, consider this: You do not support the
root, but the root supports you. 19 You will say then, "Branches
were broken off so that I could be grafted in." 20 Granted. But they
were broken off because of unbelief, and you stand by faith. Do not
be arrogant, but be afraid. 21 For if God did not spare the natural
branches, he will not spare you either.
22 Consider therefore the kindness and sternness of God: sternness to those who fell, but kindness to you, provided that you
continue in his kindness. Otherwise, you also will be cut off. 23 And
if they do not persist in unbelief, they will be grafted in, for God is
able to graft them in again. 24 After all, if you were cut out of an
olive tree that is wild by nature, and contrary to nature were
grafted into a cultivated olive tree, how much more readily will
these, the natural branches, be grafted into their own olive tree!

All Israel Will Be Saved

25 I do not want you to be ignorant of this mystery, brothers, so
that you may not be conceited: Israel has experienced a hardening
in part until the full number of the Gentiles has come in. 26 And so
all Israel will be saved, as it is written:

"The deliverer will come from Zion;
he will turn godlessness away from Jacob.
27 And this is[b] my covenant with them
when I take away their sins."[c]

28 As far as the gospel is concerned, they are enemies on your
account; but as far as election is concerned, they are loved on
account of the patriarchs, 29 for God's gifts and his call are irrevoca-
ble. 30 Just as you who were at one time disobedient to God have
now received mercy as a result of their disobedience, 31 so they too
have now become disobedient in order that they too may now[d]
receive mercy as a result of God's mercy to you. 32 For God has
bound all men over to disobedience so that he may have mercy on
them all.

Doxology

33 Oh, the depth of the riches of the wisdom and[e]
knowledge of God!

[a]*10* Psalm 69:22,23 [b]*27* Or *will be* [c]*27* Isaiah 59:20,21; 27:9; Jer. 31:33,34
[d]*31* Some manuscripts do not have *now.* [e]*33* Or *riches and the wisdom and the*

How unsearchable his judgments,
and his paths beyond tracing out!
34“Who has known the mind of the Lord?
Or who has been his counselor?”[a]
35“Who has ever given to God,
that God should repay him?”[b]
36For from him and through him and to him are all
things.
To him be the glory forever! Amen.

Living Sacrifices

12 Therefore, I urge you, brothers, in view of God’s mercy, to
offer your bodies as living sacrifices, holy and pleasing to
God—this is your spiritual[c] act of worship. 2Do not conform any
longer to the pattern of this world, but be transformed by the
renewing of your mind. Then you will be able to test and approve
what God’s will is—his good, pleasing and perfect will.
3For by the grace given me I say to every one of you: Do not
think of yourself more highly than you ought, but rather think of
yourself with sober judgment, in accordance with the measure of
faith God has given you. 4Just as each of us has one body with
many members, and these members do not all have the same
function, 5so in Christ we who are many form one body, and each
member belongs to all the others. 6We have different gifts, according to the grace given us. If a man’s gift is prophesying, let him use
it in proportion to his[d] faith. 7If it is serving, let him serve; if it is
teaching, let him teach; 8if it is encouraging, let him encourage; if
it is contributing to the needs of others, let him give generously; if
it is leadership, let him govern diligently; if it is showing mercy, let
him do it cheerfully.

As a teen, how did peer pressure affect the way you dressed? How you acted?

1. How can you offer your "body" as a living sacrifice? **2.** What does verse 1 add to your understanding of true worship (see also 6:13; 8:13)? **3.** In what ways do you tend to conform to the world? How does the "renewing of your mind" happen (v. 2)?

1. How clear is your sense of the gifts God has given you? Are you inclined to "think of yourself more highly than you ought" (v. 3) or put yourself down? **2.** What holds you back from using your gifts more fully?

Love

9Love must be sincere. Hate what is evil; cling to what is good.
10Be devoted to one another in brotherly love. Honor one another
above yourselves. 11Never be lacking in zeal, but keep your spiritual fervor, serving the Lord. 12Be joyful in hope, patient in affliction,
faithful in prayer. 13Share with God’s people who are in need.
Practice hospitality.
14Bless those who persecute you; bless and do not curse. 15Re-
joice with those who rejoice; mourn with those who mourn. 16Live
in harmony with one another. Do not be proud, but be willing to
associate with people of low position.[e] Do not be conceited.
17Do not repay anyone evil for evil. Be careful to do what is right
in the eyes of everybody. 18If it is possible, as far as it depends
on you, live at peace with everyone. 19Do not take revenge, my
friends, but leave room for God’s wrath, for it is written: “It is
mine to avenge; I will repay,”[f] says the Lord. 20On the contrary:

“If your enemy is hungry, feed him;
if he is thirsty, give him something to drink.
In doing this, you will heap burning coals on his
head.”[g]

21Do not be overcome by evil, but overcome evil with good.

As a child, who was the troublemaker in your family? Who was the peacemaker?

1. How does this section explain what Paul means in verses 1–2? **2.** When is it harder to practice love—when you are hurt by someone close to you? Or by an acquaintance? Why? **3.** How are love (v. 9) and peace (v. 18) the basis for all the other guidelines here?

1. Of the commands listed in these verses, which two are easiest for you to keep? Which two are the most difficult? **2.** Is loving your enemies: (a) nice, but unrealistic; (b) for Jesus and apostle Paul types only; or (c) a result of following Christ? How is Christ helping you to love? **3.** What relationship in your life most needs this lesson? Take a moment in silence to ask for God's forgiveness, understanding, patience and power for this relationship.

[a]*34* Isaiah 40:13 [b]*35* Job 41:11 [c]*1* Or *reasonable* [d]*6* Or *in agreement with the* [e]*16* Or *willing to do menial work* [f]*19* Deut. 32:35 [g]*20* Prov. 25:21,22

When was the last time you got a traffic ticket? How did you feel about the police officer?

1. Why does Paul say we should submit to governing authorities? Compare this passage with Acts 5:27–32. What principles do you find for helping you deal with authority? **2.** Who are the authorities in your life? How well have you related to them? How could you do better?

What would Paul advise people in a modern democracy who face injustice? Those in countries banning Christianity?

Submission to the Authorities

13 Everyone must submit himself to the governing authorities,
for there is no authority except that which God has established. The authorities that exist have been established by God.
2Consequently, he who rebels against the authority is rebelling
against what God has instituted, and those who do so will bring
judgment on themselves. 3For rulers hold no terror for those who
do right, but for those who do wrong. Do you want to be free from
fear of the one in authority? Then do what is right and he will
commend you. 4For he is God's servant to do you good. But if you
do wrong, be afraid, for he does not bear the sword for nothing. He
is God's servant, an agent of wrath to bring punishment on the
wrongdoer. 5Therefore, it is necessary to submit to the authorities,
not only because of possible punishment but also because of conscience.
6This is also why you pay taxes, for the authorities are God's
servants, who give their full time to governing. 7Give everyone
what you owe him: If you owe taxes, pay taxes; if revenue, then
revenue; if respect, then respect; if honor, then honor.

What was the occasion of your first debt or loan?

1. What is the greatest example of love you have ever experienced or observed? How did it make you feel? **2.** How does the law help us know what it means to love? How does this differ from popular notions of love? **3.** How do you obtain the "clothing" in verse 14? How would you use this section to explain holiness?

How would your life be different if you consciously tried to "wear" Jesus Christ? What must change to ensure a better fit?

Love, for the Day Is Near

8Let no debt remain outstanding, except the continuing debt to
love one another, for he who loves his fellowman has fulfilled the
law. 9The commandments, "Do not commit adultery," "Do not
murder," "Do not steal," "Do not covet,"[a] and whatever other
commandment there may be, are summed up in this one rule:
"Love your neighbor as yourself."[b] 10Love does no harm to its
neighbor. Therefore love is the fulfillment of the law.
11And do this, understanding the present time. The hour has
come for you to wake up from your slumber, because our salvation
is nearer now than when we first believed. 12The night is nearly
over; the day is almost here. So let us put aside the deeds of
darkness and put on the armor of light. 13Let us behave decently, as
in the daytime, not in orgies and drunkenness, not in sexual immorality and debauchery, not in dissension and jealousy. 14Rather,
clothe yourselves with the Lord Jesus Christ, and do not think
about how to gratify the desires of the sinful nature.[c]

---

1. What, if any, rules did your family have for what you could or could not do on Sunday? **2.** What did you, or do you, refuse to eat or drink?

1. Paul is writing about "gray areas"—issues over which equally committed Christians disagree. What are some controversial, gray areas in your life, family, small group or church? **2.** Regarding these gray areas, do you need to hear: (a) Paul's challenge not to look down on those who have strict convictions; or (b) his challenge not to condemn those with more lenient convictions? **3.** How can both sides stop judging one another and start accepting each other? **4.** When you are tempted to judge someone's behavior, is it more out of your own codependency—a need to help the

The Weak and the Strong

14 Accept him whose faith is weak, without passing judgment
on disputable matters. 2One man's faith allows him to eat
everything, but another man, whose faith is weak, eats only vegeta-
bles. 3The man who eats everything must not look down on him
who does not, and the man who does not eat everything must not
condemn the man who does, for God has accepted him. 4Who are
you to judge someone else's servant? To his own master he stands
or falls. And he will stand, for the Lord is able to make him stand.
5One man considers one day more sacred than another; another
man considers every day alike. Each one should be fully convinced
in his own mind. 6He who regards one day as special, does so to
the Lord. He who eats meat, eats to the Lord, for he gives thanks to
God; and he who abstains, does so to the Lord and gives thanks
to God. 7For none of us lives to himself alone and none of us dies
to himself alone. 8If we live, we live to the Lord; and if we die, we
die to the Lord. So, whether we live or die, we belong to the Lord.
9For this very reason, Christ died and returned to life so that he
might be the Lord of both the dead and the living. 10You, then,

[a] 9 Exodus 20:13-15,17; Deut. 5:17-19,21 [b] 9 Lev. 19:18 [c] 14 Or *the flesh*

why do you judge your brother? Or why do you look down on your brother? For we will all stand before God's judgment seat. 11It is written:

> " 'As surely as I live,' says the Lord,
> 'every knee will bow before me;
> every tongue will confess to God.' "[a]

12So then, each of us will give an account of himself to God.

13Therefore let us stop passing judgment on one another. Instead, make up your mind not to put any stumbling block or obstacle in your brother's way. 14As one who is in the Lord Jesus, I am fully convinced that no food[b] is unclean in itself. But if anyone regards something as unclean, then for him it is unclean. 15If your brother is distressed because of what you eat, you are no longer acting in love. Do not by your eating destroy your brother for whom Christ died. 16Do not allow what you consider good to be spoken of as evil. 17For the kingdom of God is not a matter of eating and drinking, but of righteousness, peace and joy in the Holy Spirit, 18because anyone who serves Christ in this way is pleasing to God and approved by men.

19Let us therefore make every effort to do what leads to peace and to mutual edification. 20Do not destroy the work of God for the sake of food. All food is clean, but it is wrong for a man to eat anything that causes someone else to stumble. 21It is better not to eat meat or drink wine or to do anything else that will cause your brother to fall.

22So whatever you believe about these things keep between yourself and God. Blessed is the man who does not condemn himself by what he approves. 23But the man who has doubts is condemned if he eats, because his eating is not from faith; and everything that does not come from faith is sin.

15 We who are strong ought to bear with the failings of the weak and not to please ourselves. 2Each of us should please his neighbor for his good, to build him up. 3For even Christ did not please himself but, as it is written: "The insults of those who insult you have fallen on me."[c] 4For everything that was written in the past was written to teach us, so that through endurance and the encouragement of the Scriptures we might have hope.

5May the God who gives endurance and encouragement give you a spirit of unity among yourselves as you follow Christ Jesus, 6so that with one heart and mouth you may glorify the God and Father of our Lord Jesus Christ.

7Accept one another, then, just as Christ accepted you, in order to bring praise to God. 8For I tell you that Christ has become a servant of the Jews[d] on behalf of God's truth, to confirm the promises made to the patriarchs 9so that the Gentiles may glorify God for his mercy, as it is written:

> "Therefore I will praise you among the Gentiles;
> I will sing hymns to your name."[e]

10Again, it says,

> "Rejoice, O Gentiles, with his people."[f]

[a] *11* Isaiah 45:23 [b] *14* Or *that nothing* [c] *3* Psalm 69:9 [d] *8* Greek *circumcision* [e] *9* 2 Samuel 22:50; Psalm 18:49 [f] *10* Deut. 32:43

other person do it "right"—or out of your own defensiveness—a need to declare your own behavior as "right"? **5.** Instead of judging, what should occupy our energy (14:13,17–18; 15:2)? **6.** What does Paul mean by the words "stumble" and "fall" in 14: 20–21? **7.** What is the essential motivation for this lifestyle of putting others first (15:3,7)? **8.** What should characterize the church (14:17; 15:13)? How would obeying Paul's instructions in this passage free us for this goal? **9.** By instructing the Romans not to judge each other, does Paul mean we are never to judge between right and wrong where others are concerned? Why or why not? Give an example.

♡ **1.** When has your freedom been a stumbling block to someone else? What happened? **2.** As time has passed, how has your sensitivity to the consciences of other Christians changed? Where do you draw the line on trying to please everyone? **3.** Romans 15:7 states, "Accept one another, then, just as Christ accepted you, in order to bring praise to God." What individual or types of people are you stretching to accept? Can you commit that to the Lord?

11And again,

"Praise the Lord, all you Gentiles,
and sing praises to him, all you peoples."[a]

12And again, Isaiah says,

"The Root of Jesse will spring up,
one who will arise to rule over the nations;
the Gentiles will hope in him."[b]

13May the God of hope fill you with all joy and peace as you trust
in him, so that you may overflow with hope by the power of the
Holy Spirit.

1. As a child, what did you want to be when you grew up? 2. What do you remember about the first time you were away from home without a parent?

1. Why would Paul feel the need to write an encouraging word at this point (vv. 14–15)? What are some of the major points Paul has stressed in Romans? 2. Why do you think Paul now switches to writing so much about himself? 3. What motivates and inspires Paul (see vv. 16–22)? 4. Illyricum (v. 19) is in present-day Yugoslavia. How far is that from Jerusalem? Likewise, how far away is Spain (v. 29)? What does this tell you about Paul? 5. Why do you think the collection for the needy believers in Jerusalem was so important to Paul (see also 2Co 8:1–15)? What does he mean when he says that the Gentiles owe this to the Jews (v. 27)?

1. To whom are you indebted for your spiritual blessings? 2. Looking over your schedule and priorities this past month, what would you say is your ambition in life? Is that what you want it to be? How do your ambitions compare with Paul's in terms of clarity? Value? Concern for God's kingdom? 3. What could you begin to work on regarding your ambitions? 4. Where do you sense God calling you in furthering his kingdom? Prayer for the world? Commitment to the poor? Sharing your life of faith with unbelievers you know? Teaching God's values to children?

Paul the Minister to the Gentiles

14I myself am convinced, my brothers, that you yourselves are
full of goodness, complete in knowledge and competent to instruct
one another. 15I have written you quite boldly on some points, as if
to remind you of them again, because of the grace God gave me
16to be a minister of Christ Jesus to the Gentiles with the priestly
duty of proclaiming the gospel of God, so that the Gentiles might
become an offering acceptable to God, sanctified by the Holy Spirit.
17Therefore I glory in Christ Jesus in my service to God. 18I will
not venture to speak of anything except what Christ has accomplished through me in leading the Gentiles to obey God by what
I have said and done— 19by the power of signs and miracles,
through the power of the Spirit. So from Jerusalem all the way
around to Illyricum, I have fully proclaimed the gospel of Christ.
20It has always been my ambition to preach the gospel where
Christ was not known, so that I would not be building on someone
else's foundation. 21Rather, as it is written:

"Those who were not told about him will see,
and those who have not heard will
understand."[c]

22This is why I have often been hindered from coming to you.

Paul's Plan to Visit Rome

23But now that there is no more place for me to work in these
regions, and since I have been longing for many years to see you,
24I plan to do so when I go to Spain. I hope to visit you while
passing through and to have you assist me on my journey there,
after I have enjoyed your company for a while. 25Now, however, I
am on my way to Jerusalem in the service of the saints there. 26For
Macedonia and Achaia were pleased to make a contribution for the
poor among the saints in Jerusalem. 27They were pleased to do it,
and indeed they owe it to them. For if the Gentiles have shared in
the Jews' spiritual blessings, they owe it to the Jews to share with
them their material blessings. 28So after I have completed this task
and have made sure that they have received this fruit, I will go to
Spain and visit you on the way. 29I know that when I come to you,
I will come in the full measure of the blessing of Christ.
30I urge you, brothers, by our Lord Jesus Christ and by the love
of the Spirit, to join me in my struggle by praying to God for me.
31Pray that I may be rescued from the unbelievers in Judea and that

[a] *11* Psalm 117:1 [b] *12* Isaiah 11:10 [c] *21* Isaiah 52:15

my service in Jerusalem may be acceptable to the saints there, 32so
that by God's will I may come to you with joy and together with
you be refreshed. 33The God of peace be with you all. Amen.

Personal Greetings

16 I commend to you our sister Phoebe, a servant[a] of the
church in Cenchrea. 2I ask you to receive her in the Lord in
a way worthy of the saints and to give her any help she may need
from you, for she has been a great help to many people, including me.

3Greet Priscilla[b] and Aquila, my fellow workers in Christ Jesus.
4They risked their lives for me. Not only I but all the churches of the Gentiles are grateful to them.
5Greet also the church that meets at their house.
Greet my dear friend Epenetus, who was the first convert to Christ in the province of Asia.
6Greet Mary, who worked very hard for you.
7Greet Andronicus and Junias, my relatives who have been in prison with me. They are outstanding among the apostles, and they were in Christ before I was.
8Greet Ampliatus, whom I love in the Lord.
9Greet Urbanus, our fellow worker in Christ, and my dear friend Stachys.
10Greet Apelles, tested and approved in Christ.
Greet those who belong to the household of Aristobulus.
11Greet Herodion, my relative.
Greet those in the household of Narcissus who are in the Lord.
12Greet Tryphena and Tryphosa, those women who work hard in the Lord.
Greet my dear friend Persis, another woman who has worked very hard in the Lord.
13Greet Rufus, chosen in the Lord, and his mother, who has been a mother to me, too.
14Greet Asyncritus, Phlegon, Hermes, Patrobas, Hermas and the brothers with them.
15Greet Philologus, Julia, Nereus and his sister, and Olympas and all the saints with them.
16Greet one another with a holy kiss.
All the churches of Christ send greetings.

17I urge you, brothers, to watch out for those who cause divisions and put obstacles in your way that are contrary to the teaching you have learned. Keep away from them. 18For such people are
not serving our Lord Christ, but their own appetites. By smooth
talk and flattery they deceive the minds of naive people. 19Every-
one has heard about your obedience, so I am full of joy over you;
but I want you to be wise about what is good, and innocent about
what is evil.
20The God of peace will soon crush Satan under your feet.
The grace of our Lord Jesus be with you.
21Timothy, my fellow worker, sends his greetings to you, as do
Lucius, Jason and Sosipater, my relatives.
22I, Tertius, who wrote down this letter, greet you in the Lord.
23Gaius, whose hospitality I and the whole church here enjoy,
sends you his greetings.

[a]*1* Or *deaconess* [b]*3* Greek *Prisca*, a variant of *Priscilla*

---

1. Describe briefly your first best friend. **2.** What "old friends" do you keep in touch with? Why? How often?

1. What kinds of things does Paul commend in the persons mentioned in verses 1–16? What does this say about how we ought to judge "success"? Whom we ought to choose for friends? **2.** In your opinion, how close did Paul let people get to him? How close do you let people get to you? **3.** Looking at this list, how balanced would you say Paul was in his friendships with both genders? How many women are named here? (In v. 7, "Junias" is most likely "Junia," a woman's name.) What roles do these women have in the church? **4.** Although Paul had never been to Rome, what does this greeting show about his perception of the church? **5.** What divisions and obstacles are the people to avoid (vv. 17–20; see 3:8; 6:1,15; 7:7; 9:14; also Gal 5:2–6)? Is there a contradiction here when compared with Paul's prior instructions on not passing judgment on *disputable* matters (14:1–4)?

1. What does it mean to you that in these final chapters, God is described as the "God of hope" (15:13) and the "God of peace" (15:33; 16:20)? How can we know God in this way, especially since Paul began this letter by revealing the God of wrath? **2.** What are some of the teachings that divide the church today? How do you work for a balance between the desire for unity and the desire to maintain truth? How do you handle individuals who cause strife and division (vv. 17–18): Avoid them? Talk about them? Confront them? Worry about them? **3.** Who are some people you know whom you consider real servants of Christ? What impresses you about them? **4.** What can you, or your group, do to increase your participation in God's plan to lead all nations to believe and obey him? Do you view this task more as a grim duty, or as a tremendous privilege? What does this show about your heart attitude toward the Gospel?

Erastus, who is the city's director of public works, and our brother Quartus send you their greetings.[a]
25Now to him who is able to establish you by my gospel and the
proclamation of Jesus Christ, according to the revelation of the
mystery hidden for long ages past, 26but now revealed and made
known through the prophetic writings by the command of the
eternal God, so that all nations might believe and obey him— 27to
the only wise God be glory forever through Jesus Christ! Amen.

[a]23 Some manuscripts *their greetings. 24May the grace of our Lord Jesus Christ be with all of you. Amen.*

INTRODUCTION to

1 CORINTHIANS

Book Study Outline: If you are using 1 Corinthians for a study course, here is a 7- or 13-week outline. Use the margin questions for your group agenda:

- start meeting / 15 min.
- read & discuss Bible / 30 min.
- close meeting / 15–45 min.

Refer to the Questions and Answers in front of Bible for more information.

7-week plan	13-week plan	Personal Reading	Group Study Passage
1	1	1:1–2:5	1:18–2:5/True Wisdom
	2	2:6–3:23	3:1–23/God's Temple
2	3	4:1–21	4:1–21/Foolish or Wise?
	4	5:1–13	5:1–13/Proud Immorality
3	5	6:1–20	6:12–20/Sexual Immorality
	6	7:1–40	7:1–40/To Marry or Not?
4	7	8:1–13	8:1–13/Exercising Freedom
	8	9:1–27	9:1–27/Run the Race
5	9	10:1–11:1	10:14–11:1/Glorifying God
	10	11:2–34	11:17–34/Lord's Supper
6	11	12:1–31	12:1–31/Spiritual Gifts
	12	13:1–14:40	13:1–13/Love Is Supreme
7	13	15:1–16:24	15:12–34/The Resurrection

Author: The apostle Paul.

Date: A.D. 53–55.

Theme: Christian lifestyle in a pagan society.

Historical Background: Corinth was a large, bustling, wealthy city. Because of its location, goods and people from around the world flowed in and out of its ports. It was a center for art, philosophy and religion. It contained a number of pagan temples including large ones to Apollo and Aphrodite. The city had a reputation for vice, immorality and debauchery. Paul spent 18 months establishing a church in Corinth during his second missionary journey (Ac 18:1–18). This letter, composed three or four years later, was written in response to reports Paul received concerning problems in the church.

Characteristics: The Corinthian church destroys the myth of the early church as the model for us to imitate! Seduction by the surrounding pagan culture and a hyper-spirituality had led this church into a host of problems. As a result, 1 Corinthians is full of information about how a Christian lifestyle differs from that of the culture as a whole. At points, there is difficulty in understanding 1 Corinthians because all we possess are Paul's responses. Thus commentators differ on whether some passages in the letter are meant as Paul's advice, or if he is quoting from their letter before refuting that position (e.g. 7:1; 10:23). Structurally, the letter falls into two parts. Part one (ch. 1–6) deals with four problems reported to Paul (1:11), while part two (ch. 7–16) looks at a variety of issues about which the Corinthians had written to Paul (7:1).

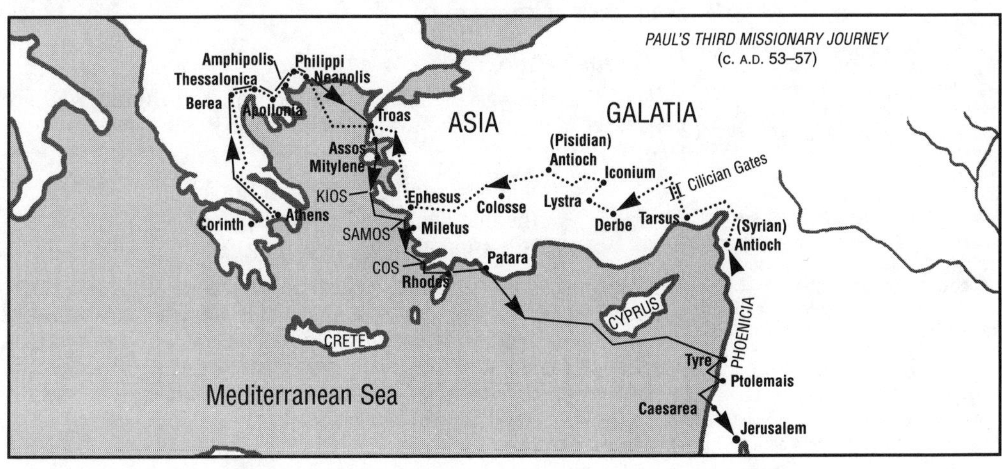

1 Corinthians

1 Paul, called to be an apostle of Christ Jesus by the will of God, and our brother Sosthenes,

[2]To the church of God in Corinth, to those sanctified in Christ Jesus and called to be holy, together with all those everywhere who call on the name of our Lord Jesus Christ—their Lord and ours:

[3]Grace and peace to you from God our Father and the Lord Jesus Christ.

Thanksgiving

[4]I always thank God for you because of his grace given you in Christ Jesus. [5]For in him you have been enriched in every way—in all your speaking and in all your knowledge— [6]because our testimony about Christ was confirmed in you. [7]Therefore you do not lack any spiritual gift as you eagerly wait for our Lord Jesus Christ to be revealed. [8]He will keep you strong to the end, so that you will be blameless on the day of our Lord Jesus Christ. [9]God, who has called you into fellowship with his Son Jesus Christ our Lord, is faithful.

Divisions in the Church

[10]I appeal to you, brothers, in the name of our Lord Jesus Christ, that all of you agree with one another so that there may be no divisions among you and that you may be perfectly united in mind and thought. [11]My brothers, some from Chloe's household have informed me that there are quarrels among you. [12]What I mean is this: One of you says, "I follow Paul"; another, "I follow Apollos"; another, "I follow Cephas[a]"; still another, "I follow Christ."

[13]Is Christ divided? Was Paul crucified for you? Were you baptized into[b] the name of Paul? [14]I am thankful that I did not baptize any of you except Crispus and Gaius, [15]so no one can say that you were baptized into my name. [16](Yes, I also baptized the household of Stephanas; beyond that, I don't remember if I baptized anyone else.) [17]For Christ did not send me to baptize, but to preach the gospel—not with words of human wisdom, lest the cross of Christ be emptied of its power.

Christ the Wisdom and Power of God

[18]For the message of the cross is foolishness to those who are perishing, but to us who are being saved it is the power of God. [19]For it is written:

> "I will destroy the wisdom of the wise;
> the intelligence of the intelligent I will
> frustrate."[c]

[20]Where is the wise man? Where is the scholar? Where is the philosopher of this age? Has not God made foolish the wisdom of the world? [21]For since in the wisdom of God the world through its wisdom did not know him, God was pleased through the foolishness of what was preached to save those who believe. [22]Jews de-

[a] *12* That is, Peter [b] *13* Or *in*; also in verse 15 [c] *19* Isaiah 29:14

---

1. When you were 8, who was your hero? **2.** Have you ever felt like you were a part of a close-knit team? When?

1. What kind of place was Corinth? How would life in Corinth affect a young church? (See Introduction to 1 Corinthians.) **2.** Paul spent 18 months in Corinth, his second longest stay with any of the new churches he started. What kind of feelings or emotional connection do you think he had with the people in those churches? **3.** Why would Paul emphasize in verse 1 that he is an apostle? **4.** What divides the church in Corinth (vv. 11–12,15)? Who was Apollos (see Ac 18:24–19:1)?

1. Do you feel like the thanksgiving in verses 4–9 describes you? Why or why not? **2.** Have you ever been a part of a church that was divided? What was it like? Have you ever been a part of a church that was single-minded and unified? What was it like? **3.** Have you been baptized? Did your personal relationship with Christ begin before or after your baptism? Share about that beginning. **4.** Who has been or is your spiritual hero? Why? **5.** Have you ever put your spiritual hero above Christ? Why or why not?

---

1. What was the least useful class you had to take in school? Why? **2.** How do you feel about speaking before a group?

1. What do the Jews seek? What do the Greeks want? What is "Christ crucified" to the Jews? To the Gentile Greeks? How does Christ fulfill what both groups are looking for (vv. 22–25)? **2.** What was the "wisdom and strength" which was so attractive to the Corinthians (1:20–21,26; 2:1, 4–5)? What does this reveal about the division in 1:12? **3.** In contrast, what was the "wisdom and power" of God? **4.** Is Paul rejecting educa-

mand miraculous signs and Greeks look for wisdom, 23but we
preach Christ crucified: a stumbling block to Jews and foolishness
to Gentiles, 24but to those whom God has called, both Jews and
Greeks, Christ the power of God and the wisdom of God. 25For the
foolishness of God is wiser than man's wisdom, and the weakness
of God is stronger than man's strength.
26Brothers, think of what you were when you were called. Not
many of you were wise by human standards; not many were influential; not many were of noble birth. 27But God chose the foolish
things of the world to shame the wise; God chose the weak things
of the world to shame the strong. 28He chose the lowly things of
this world and the despised things—and the things that are not—
to nullify the things that are, 29so that no one may boast before
him. 30It is because of him that you are in Christ Jesus, who has
become for us wisdom from God—that is, our righteousness, holiness and redemption. 31Therefore, as it is written: "Let him who
boasts boast in the Lord."[a]

2 When I came to you, brothers, I did not come with eloquence
or superior wisdom as I proclaimed to you the testimony about
God.[b] 2For I resolved to know nothing while I was with you
except Jesus Christ and him crucified. 3I came to you in weakness
and fear, and with much trembling. 4My message and my preaching were not with wise and persuasive words, but with a demonstration of the Spirit's power, 5so that your faith might not rest on
men's wisdom, but on God's power.

tion itself, or some related and prideful assumptions?

1. What pictures come to mind when you think of powerful, successful people? How do these images sometimes conflict with knowing Christ? **2.** How do people today confuse the world's power with God's power? How does that affect you? **3.** What do you think Paul means when he says that the foolish and lowly things will shame the wise and strong? How does your own life reflect this principle?

Wisdom From the Spirit

6We do, however, speak a message of wisdom among the mature, but not the wisdom of this age or of the rulers of this age,
who are coming to nothing. 7No, we speak of God's secret wisdom,
a wisdom that has been hidden and that God destined for our glory
before time began. 8None of the rulers of this age understood it, for
if they had, they would not have crucified the Lord of glory. 9How-
ever, as it is written:

> "No eye has seen,
> no ear has heard,
> no mind has conceived
> what God has prepared for those who love
> him"[c]—

10but God has revealed it to us by his Spirit.
The Spirit searches all things, even the deep things of God. 11For
who among men knows the thoughts of a man except the man's
spirit within him? In the same way no one knows the thoughts of
God except the Spirit of God. 12We have not received the spirit of
the world but the Spirit who is from God, that we may understand
what God has freely given us. 13This is what we speak, not in
words taught us by human wisdom but in words taught by the
Spirit, expressing spiritual truths in spiritual words.[d] 14The man
without the Spirit does not accept the things that come from the
Spirit of God, for they are foolishness to him, and he cannot understand them, because they are spiritually discerned. 15The spiritual
man makes judgments about all things, but he himself is not subject to any man's judgment:

1. How well did you keep secrets when you were a child? How about since then? **2.** What person in your circle of family and friends has the most wisdom?

1. From the references to "wisdom" in this passage, what differences do you see between human wisdom and God's? **2.** What is secret about God's wisdom (vv. 7,9)? **3.** How do you feel about verse 9? How is your outlook on life affected by the promises in this verse? **4.** Philosophers were respected as people who could search out deep truths; in contrast, how does Paul say the truth of the Gospel is discovered (vv. 10–13)? Why is that significant for the Corinthians' unity?

1. The Corinthians were measuring "truth and success" by how powerful, influential and articulate someone was. How is that idea communicated today? How does it square with the Gospel? **2.** What can you do to exercise "the mind of Christ" (v. 16) more fully in your life?

[a] *31* Jer. 9:24 [b] *1* Some manuscripts *as I proclaimed to you God's mystery*
[c] *9* Isaiah 64:4 [d] *13* Or *Spirit, interpreting spiritual truths to spiritual men*

16"For who has known the mind of the Lord
that he may instruct him?"[a]

But we have the mind of Christ.

When you were a child, what did you make that you were proud of?

1. What does Paul mean by infants? Milk? Solid food (v. 2)? 2. What were Paul's and Apollos' contributions to the church in Corinth? 3. Who did the planting in your spiritual life? Who did the watering? 4. How do Paul's illustrations help to make his point (vv. 5–15)? 5. What is the wise way to build a foundation for your life? What do the building materials in verse 12 refer to? 6. Paul tells the Corinthians as a church they are "God's temple" (v. 16). What evidence do you have that your church or your body is a dwelling place for God's Spirit?

1. What is the difference between respecting a Christian leader and the problem Paul deals with here? 2. What does it mean to be a "fool" for Christ? What would being a fool for Christ mean in your life? 3. If you could describe your spiritual condition as a building, what kind of building would it be? A cathedral? A health club? A junkyard? A library? A skyscraper? 4. Name one thing you can do this week to build the foundation of your life with "gold, silver and costly stones."

On Divisions in the Church

3 Brothers, I could not address you as spiritual but as worldly—mere infants in Christ. 2I gave you milk, not solid food, for you were not yet ready for it. Indeed, you are still not ready. 3You are still worldly. For since there is jealousy and quarreling among you, are you not worldly? Are you not acting like mere men? 4For when one says, "I follow Paul," and another, "I follow Apollos," are you not mere men?

5What, after all, is Apollos? And what is Paul? Only servants, through whom you came to believe—as the Lord has assigned to each his task. 6I planted the seed, Apollos watered it, but God made it grow. 7So neither he who plants nor he who waters is anything, but only God, who makes things grow. 8The man who plants and the man who waters have one purpose, and each will be rewarded according to his own labor. 9For we are God's fellow workers; you are God's field, God's building.

10By the grace God has given me, I laid a foundation as an expert builder, and someone else is building on it. But each one should be careful how he builds. 11For no one can lay any foundation other than the one already laid, which is Jesus Christ. 12If any man builds on this foundation using gold, silver, costly stones, wood, hay or straw, 13his work will be shown for what it is, because the Day will bring it to light. It will be revealed with fire, and the fire will test the quality of each man's work. 14If what he has built survives, he will receive his reward. 15If it is burned up, he will suffer loss; he himself will be saved, but only as one escaping through the flames.

16Don't you know that you yourselves are God's temple and that God's Spirit lives in you? 17If anyone destroys God's temple, God will destroy him; for God's temple is sacred, and you are that temple.

18Do not deceive yourselves. If any one of you thinks he is wise by the standards of this age, he should become a "fool" so that he may become wise. 19For the wisdom of this world is foolishness in God's sight. As it is written: "He catches the wise in their craftiness"[b]; 20and again, "The Lord knows that the thoughts of the wise are futile."[c] 21So then, no more boasting about men! All things are yours, 22whether Paul or Apollos or Cephas[d] or the world or life or death or the present or the future—all are yours, 23and you are of Christ, and Christ is of God.

1. What is the most menial job you ever had? What did you like or dislike about it? 2. Who has been a parent figure in your life, outside of your parents?

1. Paul, when talking about judging himself, claims that even his conscience is not dependable (vv. 3–4). Has your conscience ever differed with God's will for you? What happened? 2. How do you feel about the Lord "bringing to light" what is hidden and exposing the motives of our

Apostles of Christ

4 So then, men ought to regard us as servants of Christ and as those entrusted with the secret things of God. 2Now it is required that those who have been given a trust must prove faithful. 3I care very little if I am judged by you or by any human court; indeed, I do not even judge myself. 4My conscience is clear, but that does not make me innocent. It is the Lord who judges me. 5Therefore judge nothing before the appointed time; wait till the Lord comes. He will bring to light what is hidden in darkness and will expose the motives of men's hearts. At that time each will receive his praise from God.

[a] *16* Isaiah 40:13 [b] *19* Job 5:13 [c] *20* Psalm 94:11 [d] *22* That is, Peter

6 Now, brothers, I have applied these things to myself and Apollos for your benefit, so that you may learn from us the meaning of the saying, "Do not go beyond what is written." Then you will not take pride in one man over against another. 7 For who makes you different from anyone else? What do you have that you did not receive? And if you did receive it, why do you boast as though you did not?

8 Already you have all you want! Already you have become rich! You have become kings—and that without us! How I wish that you really had become kings so that we might be kings with you! 9 For it seems to me that God has put us apostles on display at the end of the procession, like men condemned to die in the arena. We have been made a spectacle to the whole universe, to angels as well as to men. 10 We are fools for Christ, but you are so wise in Christ! We are weak, but you are strong! You are honored, we are dishonored! 11 To this very hour we go hungry and thirsty, we are in rags, we are brutally treated, we are homeless. 12 We work hard with our own hands. When we are cursed, we bless; when we are persecuted, we endure it; 13 when we are slandered, we answer kindly. Up to this moment we have become the scum of the earth, the refuse of the world.

14 I am not writing this to shame you, but to warn you, as my dear children. 15 Even though you have ten thousand guardians in Christ, you do not have many fathers, for in Christ Jesus I became your father through the gospel. 16 Therefore I urge you to imitate me. 17 For this reason I am sending to you Timothy, my son whom I love, who is faithful in the Lord. He will remind you of my way of life in Christ Jesus, which agrees with what I teach everywhere in every church.

18 Some of you have become arrogant, as if I were not coming to you. 19 But I will come to you very soon, if the Lord is willing, and then I will find out not only how these arrogant people are talking, but what power they have. 20 For the kingdom of God is not a matter of talk but of power. 21 What do you prefer? Shall I come to you with a whip, or in love and with a gentle spirit?

hearts (v. 5)? How can we live so that what is revealed will be less surprising and embarrassing? **3.** Corinthian factions judged one another by the reputation of the leader they followed. What then does Paul mean by the proverb in verse 6? How should they apply it? **4.** Read verse 7. What do you have that you did not receive from God? Of everything God has given you, what do you tend to take credit for yourself? **5.** Paul tells the Corinthians to imitate his way of life. How does this square with not following one leader or another?

1. How would Paul respond to the phrase: "God wants you to be happy, healthy and successful"? **2.** In verses 8–13 Paul rather sarcastically compares his situation with the Corinthians', who have a mistaken idea of wisdom and power. Would you characterize your Christian life as more like the Corinthians' or Paul's? Why? **3.** A role model or mentor is someone you want to emulate. Who has fulfilled these roles in your life? In what ways do you still feel the need? **4.** Reflecting honestly on verse 20, is your Christian life more a matter of talk or of power?

Expel the Immoral Brother!

5 It is actually reported that there is sexual immorality among you, and of a kind that does not occur even among pagans: A man has his father's wife. 2 And you are proud! Shouldn't you rather have been filled with grief and have put out of your fellowship the man who did this? 3 Even though I am not physically present, I am with you in spirit. And I have already passed judgment on the one who did this, just as if I were present. 4 When you are assembled in the name of our Lord Jesus and I am with you in spirit, and the power of our Lord Jesus is present, 5 hand this man over to Satan, so that the sinful nature[a] may be destroyed and his spirit saved on the day of the Lord.

6 Your boasting is not good. Don't you know that a little yeast works through the whole batch of dough? 7 Get rid of the old yeast that you may be a new batch without yeast—as you really are. For Christ, our Passover lamb, has been sacrificed. 8 Therefore let us keep the Festival, not with the old yeast, the yeast of malice and wickedness, but with bread without yeast, the bread of sincerity and truth.

9 I have written you in my letter not to associate with sexually

How did your parents, teachers or church leaders talk to you about sex? Openly? Only negatively? Not at all?

1. Why would the Corinthians be proud of such an immoral situation (vv. 1–2)? Have you ever seen a church proud of something typically considered immoral? **2.** How can handing someone over to Satan result in their salvation on the Day of the Lord (v. 5)? **3.** From the yeast imagery (vv. 6–8), what is Paul's concern if this situation is allowed to go on without discipline? **4.** Why does Paul set forth one standard for relating to people in the church who are living in sin, and another for "people of this world" (vv. 9–13)? **5.** How do you reconcile Paul's teaching here with that in 4:3–5? What is the point of each?

[a]5 Or *that his body*; or *that the flesh*

What happens when a church is more concerned with judging those outside the church than evaluating their own behavior and motives?

immoral people— [10]not at all meaning the people of this world who are immoral, or the greedy and swindlers, or idolaters. In that case you would have to leave this world. [11]But now I am writing you that you must not associate with anyone who calls himself a brother but is sexually immoral or greedy, an idolater or a slanderer, a drunkard or a swindler. With such a man do not even eat.

[12]What business is it of mine to judge those outside the church? Are you not to judge those inside? [13]God will judge those outside. "Expel the wicked man from among you."[a]

Have you ever been on jury duty? What was it like?

1. Why is Paul so upset that members of the young church in Corinth are taking their disputes to a civil, secular court? What does Paul mean when he tells the Corinthians that they have been "defeated already" (v. 7)? **2.** Why do lawsuits, and other kinds of conflict or indiscretion, cast a shadow over the church? **3.** Do you agree with Paul that it is better to be cheated than to go to court against a fellow believer? Why? **4.** Does Paul mean that believers who do the things in verses 9–10 will not enter heaven?

What attitudes in conflict situations do you see in yourself: An insistence on "my rights"? A desire for revenge? Peace at any cost? Apathy about my example to non-believers?

Lawsuits Among Believers

6 If any of you has a dispute with another, dare he take it before the ungodly for judgment instead of before the saints? [2]Do you not know that the saints will judge the world? And if you are to judge the world, are you not competent to judge trivial cases? [3]Do you not know that we will judge angels? How much more the things of this life! [4]Therefore, if you have disputes about such matters, appoint as judges even men of little account in the church![b] [5]I say this to shame you. Is it possible that there is nobody among you wise enough to judge a dispute between believers? [6]But instead, one brother goes to law against another—and this in front of unbelievers!

[7]The very fact that you have lawsuits among you means you have been completely defeated already. Why not rather be wronged? Why not rather be cheated? [8]Instead, you yourselves cheat and do wrong, and you do this to your brothers.

[9]Do you not know that the wicked will not inherit the kingdom of God? Do not be deceived: Neither the sexually immoral nor idolaters nor adulterers nor male prostitutes nor homosexual offenders [10]nor thieves nor the greedy nor drunkards nor slanderers nor swindlers will inherit the kingdom of God. [11]And that is what some of you were. But you were washed, you were sanctified, you were justified in the name of the Lord Jesus Christ and by the Spirit of our God.

What is the best thing you've done for your health?

1. Some of the Corinthians felt that what they did in the "flesh" had no bearing on their spiritual lives (vv. 19–20). What do you think? **2.** How does God care for your physical self—your appetites, sexuality, diet, habits? **3.** Why would uniting yourself with a prostitute and being "one with her in body" be harmful to a Christian? What other activities would be harmful for similar reasons?

In what ways do you struggle with what is permissible and what is beneficial? How can you keep your "temple" pure?

Sexual Immorality

[12]"Everything is permissible for me"—but not everything is beneficial. "Everything is permissible for me"—but I will not be mastered by anything. [13]"Food for the stomach and the stomach for food"—but God will destroy them both. The body is not meant for sexual immorality, but for the Lord, and the Lord for the body. [14]By his power God raised the Lord from the dead, and he will raise us also. [15]Do you not know that your bodies are members of Christ himself? Shall I then take the members of Christ and unite them with a prostitute? Never! [16]Do you not know that he who unites himself with a prostitute is one with her in body? For it is said, "The two will become one flesh."[c] [17]But he who unites himself with the Lord is one with him in spirit.

[18]Flee from sexual immorality. All other sins a man commits are outside his body, but he who sins sexually sins against his own body. [19]Do you not know that your body is a temple of the Holy Spirit, who is in you, whom you have received from God? You are not your own; [20]you were bought at a price. Therefore honor God with your body.

[a] *13* Deut. 17:7; 19:19; 21:21; 22:21,24; 24:7 [b] *4* Or *matters, do you appoint as judges men of little account in the church?* [c] *16* Gen. 2:24

Marriage

7 Now for the matters you wrote about: It is good for a man not
to marry.[a] 2But since there is so much immorality, each man
should have his own wife, and each woman her own husband.
3The husband should fulfill his marital duty to his wife, and likewise the wife to her husband. 4The wife's body does not belong to
her alone but also to her husband. In the same way, the husband's
body does not belong to him alone but also to his wife. 5Do not
deprive each other except by mutual consent and for a time, so that
you may devote yourselves to prayer. Then come together again so
that Satan will not tempt you because of your lack of self-control. 6I
say this as a concession, not as a command. 7I wish that all men
were as I am. But each man has his own gift from God; one has this
gift, another has that.

8Now to the unmarried and the widows I say: It is good for them
to stay unmarried, as I am. 9But if they cannot control themselves,
they should marry, for it is better to marry than to burn with
passion.

10To the married I give this command (not I, but the Lord): A
wife must not separate from her husband. 11But if she does, she
must remain unmarried or else be reconciled to her husband. And
a husband must not divorce his wife.

12To the rest I say this (I, not the Lord): If any brother has a wife
who is not a believer and she is willing to live with him, he must
not divorce her. 13And if a woman has a husband who is not a
believer and he is willing to live with her, she must not divorce
him. 14For the unbelieving husband has been sanctified through
his wife, and the unbelieving wife has been sanctified through her
believing husband. Otherwise your children would be unclean, but
as it is, they are holy.

15But if the unbeliever leaves, let him do so. A believing man or
woman is not bound in such circumstances; God has called us to
live in peace. 16How do you know, wife, whether you will save
your husband? Or, how do you know, husband, whether you will
save your wife?

17Nevertheless, each one should retain the place in life that the
Lord assigned to him and to which God has called him. This is the
rule I lay down in all the churches. 18Was a man already circumcised when he was called? He should not become uncircumcised.
Was a man uncircumcised when he was called? He should not be
circumcised. 19Circumcision is nothing and uncircumcision is
nothing. Keeping God's commands is what counts. 20Each one
should remain in the situation which he was in when God called
him. 21Were you a slave when you were called? Don't let it trouble
you—although if you can gain your freedom, do so. 22For he who
was a slave when he was called by the Lord is the Lord's freedman;
similarly, he who was a free man when he was called is Christ's
slave. 23You were bought at a price; do not become slaves of men.
24Brothers, each man, as responsible to God, should remain in the
situation God called him to.

25Now about virgins: I have no command from the Lord, but I
give a judgment as one who by the Lord's mercy is trustworthy.
26Because of the present crisis, I think that it is good for you to
remain as you are. 27Are you married? Do not seek a divorce. Are
you unmarried? Do not look for a wife. 28But if you do marry, you
have not sinned; and if a virgin marries, she has not sinned. But

[a] *1* Or "*It is good for a man not to have sexual relations with a woman.*"

Are you more like Garfield ("I hate getting up") or Odie ("Life is fun, fun, fun!")?

1. What do verses 3–5 tell you about the role of sex in marriage? Did God create sex to be merely a physical act or a time of mutual edification? **2.** What do verses 5 and 9 say about the human body and sexuality?

Some Corinthian Christians considered sex with their marital partners impure or unspiritual. How have your ideas of sex been skewed? How do you need God's help?

If married, tell your "love story." How did you meet? What attracted you? If single, share what you know about your parents' love story.

1. What obligation does a believing spouse have to an unbelieving mate? What are the limits to this obligation? **2.** What does it mean for an unbeliever to be "sanctified" by their believing spouse (vv. 12–14; see Ro 15:15–16)? **3.** How do verses 12–14 encourage someone who is married to an unbeliever regarding his or her spouse's salvation and that of their children? **4.** In verses 17–24, Paul is saying that Christians should not use their new life in Christ to climb the social ladder or be someone they are not. Have you ever been tempted to do this? What does someone stand to lose by doing this? **5.** Is Paul saying in these verses that a person should not set goals for him or herself?

What questions do you have about these verses? Where do you feel a special need for God's wisdom and power as you seek to "live in peace" (v. 15)?

Whom do you know who has chosen to remain single?

1. Why will those who marry "face many troubles" in life (v. 28)? **2.** What concerns do those who are married have that singles do not? **3.** How does Paul's advice

those who marry will face many troubles in this life, and I want to
spare you this.
29What I mean, brothers, is that the time is short. From now on
those who have wives should live as if they had none; 30those who
mourn, as if they did not; those who are happy, as if they were not;
those who buy something, as if it were not theirs to keep; 31those
who use the things of the world, as if not engrossed in them. For
this world in its present form is passing away.
32I would like you to be free from concern. An unmarried man is
concerned about the Lord's affairs—how he can please the Lord.
33But a married man is concerned about the affairs of this world—
how he can please his wife— 34and his interests are divided. An
unmarried woman or virgin is concerned about the Lord's affairs:
Her aim is to be devoted to the Lord in both body and spirit. But a
married woman is concerned about the affairs of this world—how
she can please her husband. 35I am saying this for your own good,
not to restrict you, but that you may live in a right way in undivided devotion to the Lord.
36If anyone thinks he is acting improperly toward the virgin he is
engaged to, and if she is getting along in years and he feels he
ought to marry, he should do as he wants. He is not sinning. They
should get married. 37But the man who has settled the matter in
his own mind, who is under no compulsion but has control over
his own will, and who has made up his mind not to marry the
virgin—this man also does the right thing. 38So then, he who
marries the virgin does right, but he who does not marry her does
even better.[a]
39A woman is bound to her husband as long as he lives. But if
her husband dies, she is free to marry anyone she wishes, but he
must belong to the Lord. 40In my judgment, she is happier if she
stays as she is—and I think that I too have the Spirit of God.

Food Sacrificed to Idols

8 Now about food sacrificed to idols: We know that we all possess knowledge.[b] Knowledge puffs up, but love builds up.
2The man who thinks he knows something does not yet know as
he ought to know. 3But the man who loves God is known by God.
4So then, about eating food sacrificed to idols: We know that an
idol is nothing at all in the world and that there is no God but one.
5For even if there are so-called gods, whether in heaven or on
earth (as indeed there are many "gods" and many "lords"), 6yet for
us there is but one God, the Father, from whom all things came
and for whom we live; and there is but one Lord, Jesus Christ,
through whom all things came and through whom we live.
7But not everyone knows this. Some people are still so accus-
tomed to idols that when they eat such food they think of it as
having been sacrificed to an idol, and since their conscience is
weak, it is defiled. 8But food does not bring us near to God; we are
no worse if we do not eat, and no better if we do.
9Be careful, however, that the exercise of your freedom does not
become a stumbling block to the weak. 10For if anyone with a weak
conscience sees you who have this knowledge eating in an idol's
temple, won't he be emboldened to eat what has been sacrificed to

[a] *36-38* Or *36If anyone thinks he is not treating his daughter properly, and if she is getting along in years, and he feels she ought to marry, he should do as he wants. He is not sinning. He should let her get married. 37But the man who has settled the matter in his own mind, who is under no compulsion but has control over his own will, and who has made up his mind to keep the virgin unmarried—this man also does the right thing. 38So then, he who gives his virgin in marriage does right, but he who does not give her in marriage does even better.* [b] *1* Or *"We all possess knowledge," as you say*

to the married (v. 29) relate to his teaching in Ephesians 5:21–32.

1. How can an unmarried person find emotional fulfillment and intimacy if they have chosen to remain single in order to be more fully devoted to the Lord? **2.** A close look at the Epistles reveals meaningful and touching relationships among believers. Do we expect marriage to bring the kind of intimacy and fulfillment that God intended the church to bring?

---

1. Paul presents singleness as an option some should consider. What reasons does he give? **2.** Whether people marry or not, what is the overriding issue here?

Is singleness more of a calling or a choice? What role does God play? How do you feel about your role?

Have you ever been superstitious? In what ways?

1. Why would eating food sacrificed to idols be difficult for some people? **2.** How is it that what is not sin for one group is sin for another? What general principle is Paul applying here (v. 9)? **3.** Some of the Corinthian Christians knew that food sacrificed to idols was just that, food. What could those people have done to help those who were not comfortable with eating food sacrificed to idols? **4.** In verse 2, Paul points out that if you are focused on what you know, you are likely to exclude empathy and concern for others. Do you ever get focused on knowing something *about God* at the expense of being known *by God* (v. 3)? Explain. **5.** What might hinder you from loving new Christians or those believers who do not know something you know?

1. Where in your experience is one person's "freedom" another person's "stumbling block"? Alcohol? Certain styles of clothes? Dance? Music? Lifestyle? Political idols? 11So this weak brother, for whom Christ died, is destroyed by your knowledge. 12When you sin against your brothers in this way and wound their weak conscience, you sin against Christ. 13Therefore, if what I eat causes my brother to fall into sin, I will never eat meat again, so that I will not cause him to fall.

The Rights of an Apostle

9 Am I not free? Am I not an apostle? Have I not seen Jesus our Lord? Are you not the result of my work in the Lord? 2Even though I may not be an apostle to others, surely I am to you! For you are the seal of my apostleship in the Lord.

3This is my defense to those who sit in judgment on me. 4Don't we have the right to food and drink? 5Don't we have the right to take a believing wife along with us, as do the other apostles and the Lord's brothers and Cephas[a]? 6Or is it only I and Barnabas who must work for a living?

7Who serves as a soldier at his own expense? Who plants a vineyard and does not eat of its grapes? Who tends a flock and does not drink of the milk? 8Do I say this merely from a human point of view? Doesn't the Law say the same thing? 9For it is written in the Law of Moses: "Do not muzzle an ox while it is treading out the grain."[b] Is it about oxen that God is concerned? 10Surely he says this for us, doesn't he? Yes, this was written for us, because when the plowman plows and the thresher threshes, they ought to do so in the hope of sharing in the harvest. 11If we have sown spiritual seed among you, is it too much if we reap a material harvest from you? 12If others have this right of support from you, shouldn't we have it all the more?

But we did not use this right. On the contrary, we put up with anything rather than hinder the gospel of Christ. 13Don't you know that those who work in the temple get their food from the temple, and those who serve at the altar share in what is offered on the altar? 14In the same way, the Lord has commanded that those who preach the gospel should receive their living from the gospel.

15But I have not used any of these rights. And I am not writing this in the hope that you will do such things for me. I would rather die than have anyone deprive me of this boast. 16Yet when I preach the gospel, I cannot boast, for I am compelled to preach. Woe to me if I do not preach the gospel! 17If I preach voluntarily, I have a reward; if not voluntarily, I am simply discharging the trust committed to me. 18What then is my reward? Just this: that in preaching the gospel I may offer it free of charge, and so not make use of my rights in preaching it.

19Though I am free and belong to no man, I make myself a slave to everyone, to win as many as possible. 20To the Jews I became like a Jew, to win the Jews. To those under the law I became like one under the law (though I myself am not under the law), so as to win those under the law. 21To those not having the law I became like one not having the law (though I am not free from God's law but am under Christ's law), so as to win those not having the law. 22To the weak I became weak, to win the weak. I have become all things to all men so that by all possible means I might save some. 23I do all this for the sake of the gospel, that I may share in its blessings.

24Do you not know that in a race all the runners run, but only one gets the prize? Run in such a way as to get the prize. 25Everyone who competes in the games goes into strict training. They do

[a]5 That is, Peter [b]9 Deut. 25:4

issues? **2.** Have you done anything lately to wound the conscience of a fellow believer (v. 12)? How is this sinning against Christ?

---

1. Describe a time when you were overqualified for a particular job. Describe a time when you felt underqualified. **2.** Describe a volunteer position you held which was especially fulfilling.

1. Why would some of the Corinthians try and shed doubt on Paul's authority as an apostle? **2.** What is your response when you hear a message from God (i.e. a Bible teacher, a sermon, a wise word from a Christian friend) that you don't want to hear? **3.** Some of the rights apostles could claim included monetary payment, bringing a wife along, and eating and drinking with freedom. What was gained by Paul denying himself of these rights? **4.** How do you reconcile 8:24 and the principle of integrity with Paul's practice in verses 19–23? **5.** Have you ever denied yourself of any basic rights for the sake of the Gospel? Explain your answer. **6.** In verses 16–18 Paul refers to his deep passion for preaching the Gospel. What is your passion when it comes to living for God?

1. Consider verses 19–23, what group of people are you especially aware of who need God's love? The poor? The homeless? Homosexuals? Those in nursing homes? Troubled youngsters? What barriers are there between you and these groups? What "rights" would you be willing to discard to love them? **2.** Paul summarizes this passage in verses 24–27 by emphasizing the importance of discipline in the Christian life (discipline which includes sacrificing personal rights and comforts for the sake of others). How would you describe your "Gospel readiness" training program? (a) I haven't found the gym; (b) I'm not sure I'm ready to make the necessary sacrifices; (c) I'm ready anytime, if only I had a team of people to train with me; (d) I've run the race and I'm exhausted; (e) I'm rarin' to go!

it to get a crown that will not last; but we do it to get a crown that
will last forever. 26Therefore I do not run like a man running
aimlessly; I do not fight like a man beating the air. 27No, I beat my
body and make it my slave so that after I have preached to others,
I myself will not be disqualified for the prize.

What is the most expensive vacation you've taken?

1. In verses 1–5 Paul asserts that the baptism and spiritual food and drink of the Israelites did not guarantee their protection from God's judgment. What do you tend to look to as your guarantee from God's judgment? **2.** In verses 6–10, what four things did the Israelites do that resulted in God's judgment? **3.** Which of these four "examples" are you most susceptible to doing? **4.** If you think you've "got it together," why do you become vulnerable (v. 12)?

1. What helps satisfy your urges before they grow into temptations and sin? **2.** How can the promises in verse 13 help you in your spiritual battles? **3.** How can being in this group help you stand up under temptations?

Warnings From Israel's History

10 For I do not want you to be ignorant of the fact, brothers,
that our forefathers were all under the cloud and that they
all passed through the sea. 2They were all baptized into Moses in
the cloud and in the sea. 3They all ate the same spiritual food 4and
drank the same spiritual drink; for they drank from the spiritual
rock that accompanied them, and that rock was Christ. 5Neverthe-
less, God was not pleased with most of them; their bodies were
scattered over the desert.

6Now these things occurred as examples[a] to keep us from setting our hearts on evil things as they did. 7Do not be idolaters, as
some of them were; as it is written: "The people sat down to eat
and drink and got up to indulge in pagan revelry."[b] 8We should
not commit sexual immorality, as some of them did—and in one
day twenty-three thousand of them died. 9We should not test the
Lord, as some of them did—and were killed by snakes. 10And do
not grumble, as some of them did—and were killed by the destroying angel.

11These things happened to them as examples and were written
down as warnings for us, on whom the fulfillment of the ages has
come. 12So, if you think you are standing firm, be careful that you
don't fall! 13No temptation has seized you except what is common
to man. And God is faithful; he will not let you be tempted beyond
what you can bear. But when you are tempted, he will also provide
a way out so that you can stand up under it.

1. What is the strangest food you have ever eaten? **2.** Were you raised in a permissive environment or in a strict, but forgiving, one? Give an example.

1. How is drinking the cup of thanksgiving a participation in the blood of Christ? How is breaking the bread a participation in the body of Christ? **2.** Why does Paul mention eating the OT sacrifices (v. 18) in this context? **3.** When you partake in the body and blood of Christ during Communion, what does it mean to you? **4.** How have you been involved in something that God would consider idolatry? **5.** In what ways is a Christian free (vv. 23–24)? How do you exercise your freedom in Christ? **6.** In verse 24, Paul says, "Nobody should seek his own good, but the good of others." How can you receive the love and care you need if you live by that verse?

1. Is there anything you do that does not bother your conscience but might bother the conscience of someone else? Explain. **2.** Verses 27–33 describe

Idol Feasts and the Lord's Supper

14Therefore, my dear friends, flee from idolatry. 15I speak to
sensible people; judge for yourselves what I say. 16Is not the cup of
thanksgiving for which we give thanks a participation in the blood
of Christ? And is not the bread that we break a participation in the
body of Christ? 17Because there is one loaf, we, who are many, are
one body, for we all partake of the one loaf.

18Consider the people of Israel: Do not those who eat the sacrifices participate in the altar? 19Do I mean then that a sacrifice
offered to an idol is anything, or that an idol is anything? 20No, but
the sacrifices of pagans are offered to demons, not to God, and I do
not want you to be participants with demons. 21You cannot drink
the cup of the Lord and the cup of demons too; you cannot have a
part in both the Lord's table and the table of demons. 22Are we
trying to arouse the Lord's jealousy? Are we stronger than he?

The Believer's Freedom

23"Everything is permissible"—but not everything is beneficial.
"Everything is permissible"—but not everything is constructive.
24Nobody should seek his own good, but the good of others.

25Eat anything sold in the meat market without raising questions
of conscience, 26for, "The earth is the Lord's, and everything
in it."[c]

27If some unbeliever invites you to a meal and you want to go,
eat whatever is put before you without raising questions of con-

[a]6 Or *types*; also in verse 11 [b]7 Exodus 32:6 [c]26 Psalm 24:1

science. 28But if anyone says to you, "This has been offered in
sacrifice," then do not eat it, both for the sake of the man who told
you and for conscience' sake[a]— 29the other man's conscience, I
mean, not yours. For why should my freedom be judged by another's conscience? 30If I take part in the meal with thankfulness, why
am I denounced because of something I thank God for?

31So whether you eat or drink or whatever you do, do it all for
the glory of God. 32Do not cause anyone to stumble, whether Jews,
Greeks or the church of God— 33even as I try to please everybody
in every way. For I am not seeking my own good but the good of
11 many, so that they may be saved. 1Follow my example, as I
follow the example of Christ.

Propriety in Worship

2I praise you for remembering me in everything and for holding
to the teachings,[b] just as I passed them on to you.

3Now I want you to realize that the head of every man is Christ,
and the head of the woman is man, and the head of Christ is God.
4Every man who prays or prophesies with his head covered dishonors his head. 5And every woman who prays or prophesies with her
head uncovered dishonors her head—it is just as though her head
were shaved. 6If a woman does not cover her head, she should
have her hair cut off; and if it is a disgrace for a woman to have her
hair cut or shaved off, she should cover her head. 7A man ought
not to cover his head,[c] since he is the image and glory of God; but
the woman is the glory of man. 8For man did not come from
woman, but woman from man; 9neither was man created for woman, but woman for man. 10For this reason, and because of the
angels, the woman ought to have a sign of authority on her head.

11In the Lord, however, woman is not independent of man, nor
is man independent of woman. 12For as woman came from man,
so also man is born of woman. But everything comes from God.
13Judge for yourselves: Is it proper for a woman to pray to God with
her head uncovered? 14Does not the very nature of things teach
you that if a man has long hair, it is a disgrace to him, 15but that if
a woman has long hair, it is her glory? For long hair is given to her
as a covering. 16If anyone wants to be contentious about this, we
have no other practice—nor do the churches of God.

The Lord's Supper

17In the following directives I have no praise for you, for your
meetings do more harm than good. 18In the first place, I hear that
when you come together as a church, there are divisions among
you, and to some extent I believe it. 19No doubt there have to be
differences among you to show which of you have God's approval.
20When you come together, it is not the Lord's Supper you eat,
21for as you eat, each of you goes ahead without waiting for anybody else. One remains hungry, another gets drunk. 22Don't you
have homes to eat and drink in? Or do you despise the church of
God and humiliate those who have nothing? What shall I say to
you? Shall I praise you for this? Certainly not!

23For I received from the Lord what I also passed on to you: The
Lord Jesus, on the night he was betrayed, took bread, 24and when

[a] *28* Some manuscripts *conscience' sake, for "the earth is the Lord's and everything in it"*
[b] *2* Or *traditions* [c] *4-7* Or *4Every man who prays or prophesies with long hair dishonors his head. 5And every woman who prays or prophesies with no covering ⌞of hair⌟ on her head dishonors her head—she is just like one of the "shorn women." 6If a woman has no covering, let her be for now with short hair, but since it is a disgrace for a woman to have her hair shorn or shaved, she should grow it again. 7A man ought not to have long hair*

what a believer should do in a relationship with an unbeliever. Do Paul's instructions sound hypocritical? Do you act differently around Christians and non-Christians? How come?

How did you wear your hair 10 years ago? 20?

1. In Greek, the word "head" (v. 3) means "origin." Why was it important for Paul to state the relationship of women to God, Christ and man? How do verses 11 and 12 fit into your answer? **2.** Paul assumes that women in the Corinthian church will pray and prophesy just as the men do. How do you feel about women leading worship? Have you ever been inspired to worship God because of a woman's efforts? **3.** Pagan cults in Corinth practiced ecstatic worship which frequently involved loose hair and nudity. How does this information shed light on the situation in Corinth?

Concern for the glory of God, the interdependence of men and women, and sensitivity to the culture are three principles here. How do these principles apply in your church? In your marriage?

What is the biggest party you've ever given? What food and drink did you serve?

1. How would you describe the scene if you were observing the Lord's Supper at the Corinthian church? **2.** What changes would the Corinthians need to make to ensure that it really was the "Lord's supper"? **3.** Have you ever been in a church that was affected by divisions among the members? What happened? **4.** How do you respond when you hear the words of verses 23–26 during Communion? **5.** What does Paul mean by eating in "an unworthy manner" (v. 27)? By "not recognizing the body of the Lord" (v. 29)? By self-examination (v. 28)? By judging oneself (v. 31)?

1. When do you tend to approach worship or a part of the worship experience too lightly? **2.** The poor in Corinth weren't able to participate fully in the Lord's Supper. How do churches today discriminate? How could your church be more inclusive of the types of people where you live?

he had given thanks, he broke it and said, "This is my body, which
is for you; do this in remembrance of me." 25In the same way, after
supper he took the cup, saying, "This cup is the new covenant in
my blood; do this, whenever you drink it, in remembrance of me."
26For whenever you eat this bread and drink this cup, you proclaim
the Lord's death until he comes.

27Therefore, whoever eats the bread or drinks the cup of the
Lord in an unworthy manner will be guilty of sinning against the
body and blood of the Lord. 28A man ought to examine himself
before he eats of the bread and drinks of the cup. 29For anyone
who eats and drinks without recognizing the body of the Lord eats
and drinks judgment on himself. 30That is why many among you
are weak and sick, and a number of you have fallen asleep. 31But if
we judged ourselves, we would not come under judgment. 32When
we are judged by the Lord, we are being disciplined so that we will
not be condemned with the world.

33So then, my brothers, when you come together to eat, wait for
each other. 34If anyone is hungry, he should eat at home, so that
when you meet together it may not result in judgment.

And when I come I will give further directions.

What was the most fulfilling job you ever had?

1. What was life like when you first began to believe that "Jesus is Lord"? **2.** Verses 4–6 indicate that some Corinthians felt certain spiritual gifts were better than others. Have you ever encountered a similar attitude? In yourself? **3.** How is the diversity of the gifts related to the unity of the Father, Son and Holy Spirit?

1. Of the spiritual gifts listed, which have you received? Is this list all-inclusive? **2.** How have you used your gift for the common good? Have you ever seen a spiritual gift not used for the common good?

Spiritual Gifts

12 Now about spiritual gifts, brothers, I do not want you to be
ignorant. 2You know that when you were pagans, somehow
or other you were influenced and led astray to mute idols. 3There-
fore I tell you that no one who is speaking by the Spirit of God says,
"Jesus be cursed," and no one can say, "Jesus is Lord," except by
the Holy Spirit.

4There are different kinds of gifts, but the same Spirit. 5There
are different kinds of service, but the same Lord. 6There are different kinds of working, but the same God works all of them in all
men.

7Now to each one the manifestation of the Spirit is given for the
common good. 8To one there is given through the Spirit the message of wisdom, to another the message of knowledge by means of
the same Spirit, 9to another faith by the same Spirit, to another
gifts of healing by that one Spirit, 10to another miraculous powers,
to another prophecy, to another distinguishing between spirits, to
another speaking in different kinds of tongues,[a] and to still another the interpretation of tongues.[a] 11All these are the work of one
and the same Spirit, and he gives them to each one, just as he
determines.

What is one skill you secretly possess?

1. Why is verse 12 such a good illustration of verse 13? **2.** What could be an example of a "weaker" part of the body of Christ (v. 22)? Of a "less honorable" part (v. 23)? Of a "presentable" part (v. 24)? Does each receive the treatment it should in your church? **3.** From Paul's rhetorical questions in verses 29–30, what is another problem in this church?

1. Regardless of your church's doctrinal position, what attitudes toward spiritual gifts dominate: (a) For pastors only? (b)

One Body, Many Parts

12The body is a unit, though it is made up of many parts; and
though all its parts are many, they form one body. So it is with
Christ. 13For we were all baptized by[b] one Spirit into one body—
whether Jews or Greeks, slave or free—and we were all given the
one Spirit to drink.

14Now the body is not made up of one part but of many. 15If the
foot should say, "Because I am not a hand, I do not belong to the
body," it would not for that reason cease to be part of the body.
16And if the ear should say, "Because I am not an eye, I do not
belong to the body," it would not for that reason cease to be part of
the body. 17If the whole body were an eye, where would the sense
of hearing be? If the whole body were an ear, where would the
sense of smell be? 18But in fact God has arranged the parts in the

[a] *10* Or *languages*; also in verse 28 [b] *13* Or *with*; or *in*

body, every one of them, just as he wanted them to be. 19If they
were all one part, where would the body be? 20As it is, there are
many parts, but one body.

21The eye cannot say to the hand, "I don't need you!" And the
head cannot say to the feet, "I don't need you!" 22On the contrary,
those parts of the body that seem to be weaker are indispensable,
23and the parts that we think are less honorable we treat with
special honor. And the parts that are unpresentable are treated
with special modesty, 24while our presentable parts need no special
treatment. But God has combined the members of the body and
has given greater honor to the parts that lacked it, 25so that there
should be no division in the body, but that its parts should have
equal concern for each other. 26If one part suffers, every part suffers with it; if one part is honored, every part rejoices with it.

27Now you are the body of Christ, and each one of you is a part
of it. 28And in the church God has appointed first of all apostles,
second prophets, third teachers, then workers of miracles, also
those having gifts of healing, those able to help others, those with
gifts of administration, and those speaking in different kinds of
tongues. 29Are all apostles? Are all prophets? Are all teachers? Do
all work miracles? 30Do all have gifts of healing? Do all speak in
tongues[a]? Do all interpret? 31But eagerly desire[b] the greater gifts.

Love

And now I will show you the most excellent way.

13 If I speak in the tongues[c] of men and of angels, but have
not love, I am only a resounding gong or a clanging cymbal.
2If I have the gift of prophecy and can fathom all mysteries and all
knowledge, and if I have a faith that can move mountains, but have
not love, I am nothing. 3If I give all I possess to the poor and
surrender my body to the flames,[d] but have not love, I gain nothing.

4Love is patient, love is kind. It does not envy, it does not boast,
it is not proud. 5It is not rude, it is not self-seeking, it is not easily
angered, it keeps no record of wrongs. 6Love does not delight in
evil but rejoices with the truth. 7It always protects, always trusts,
always hopes, always perseveres.

8Love never fails. But where there are prophecies, they will
cease; where there are tongues, they will be stilled; where there is
knowledge, it will pass away. 9For we know in part and we prophesy in part, 10but when perfection comes, the imperfect disappears.
11When I was a child, I talked like a child, I thought like a child, I
reasoned like a child. When I became a man, I put childish ways
behind me. 12Now we see but a poor reflection as in a mirror; then
we shall see face to face. Now I know in part; then I shall know
fully, even as I am fully known.

13And now these three remain: faith, hope and love. But the
greatest of these is love.

Gifts of Prophecy and Tongues

14 Follow the way of love and eagerly desire spiritual gifts,
especially the gift of prophecy. 2For anyone who speaks in a
tongue[e] does not speak to men but to God. Indeed, no one understands him; he utters mysteries with his spirit.[f] 3But everyone
who prophesies speaks to men for their strengthening, encouragement and comfort. 4He who speaks in a tongue edifies himself, but

[a]30 Or *other languages* [b]31 Or *But you are eagerly desiring* [c]1 Or *languages*
[d]3 Some early manuscripts *body that I may boast* [e]2 Or *another language*; also in verses 4, 13, 14, 19, 26 and 27 [f]2 Or *by the Spirit*

For all believers? (c) For the good of others? (d) For the first-century church only? (e) For believers who have a post-conversion experience? (f) More spiritual gifts for the more spiritually mature? **2.** How do these verses make you feel about your place in the body of Christ? About your need for others? **3.** Take turns affirming each person in the group with which spiritual gifts and Christ-like qualities you have noticed in them.

---

1. What was one of your favorite love songs when you were a teenager? **2.** When in your life have you felt the most loved?

1. Given the Corinthians' quest for spiritual gifts and power, what is Paul's point in verses 1–3? What have you *done* that has become a substitute for really loving others? **2.** In what ways has God loved you according to the qualities of love you found in verses 4–8? What have you done lately that is an example of what love is *not*? **3.** Have you ever done a religious act without love? What was it like?

1. In your opinion, what is the best way to develop the ability to love others? **2.** How do verses 8–10 help to put your church in perspective? Your personal life? **3.** What does it mean to you that you will see Jesus face to face?

---

1. Describe a time when you were in a country or area where you couldn't speak the language. Was it funny? Frustrating? Humbling? **2.** If you could play any musical instrument, what would it be? What songs would you like to play?

1. What is the difference between speaking in tongues and prophesying (vv. 2–4)? **2.** During Corinthian worship services far too much time was spent speaking in tongues. The result was chaos. How is this another mark of their immaturity (v. 20; see also 3:1–4)? **3.** What are Paul's corrective instructions to the spiritually proud Corinthians (v. 12)? **4.** What are the values and limits of tongues (vv. 4,9,13–19,21–25)? **5.** What is Paul saying about the need for balance between the mind and the emotions in worship?

1. Have you ever been in a worship service that was chaotic and disorderly? What was it like? **2.** Have you ever seen someone exercise a spiritual gift without regard for "building up the church"? **3.** How does the gift of tongues edify an individual? What do you do that edifies you alone? What do you do to edify others in your church? **4.** The Corinthians presumably were partial to ecstatic or flamboyant spirituality. What exciting experiences do you wish your Christian life could have? Which experiences do you wish your church would tone down? **5.** Whether or not your church practices the gifts of tongues and prophecy, what principles for church life need to be exercised more fully in your church?

What was your favorite song as a child?

1. In verse 26, Paul describes a worship service where everyone seems to have something to offer. How could your church better include the contributions of more people in worship? **2.** Verses 29–33 contain instructions about prophecy. What is prophe-

he who prophesies edifies the church. 5I would like every one of
you to speak in tongues,[a] but I would rather have you prophesy.
He who prophesies is greater than one who speaks in tongues,[a]
unless he interprets, so that the church may be edified.

6Now, brothers, if I come to you and speak in tongues, what
good will I be to you, unless I bring you some revelation or knowledge or prophecy or word of instruction? 7Even in the case of
lifeless things that make sounds, such as the flute or harp, how will
anyone know what tune is being played unless there is a distinction in the notes? 8Again, if the trumpet does not sound a clear call,
who will get ready for battle? 9So it is with you. Unless you speak
intelligible words with your tongue, how will anyone know what
you are saying? You will just be speaking into the air. 10Undoubted-
ly there are all sorts of languages in the world, yet none of them is
without meaning. 11If then I do not grasp the meaning of what
someone is saying, I am a foreigner to the speaker, and he is a
foreigner to me. 12So it is with you. Since you are eager to have
spiritual gifts, try to excel in gifts that build up the church.

13For this reason anyone who speaks in a tongue should pray
that he may interpret what he says. 14For if I pray in a tongue, my
spirit prays, but my mind is unfruitful. 15So what shall I do? I will
pray with my spirit, but I will also pray with my mind; I will sing
with my spirit, but I will also sing with my mind. 16If you are
praising God with your spirit, how can one who finds himself
among those who do not understand[b] say "Amen" to your thanksgiving, since he does not know what you are saying? 17You may be
giving thanks well enough, but the other man is not edified.

18I thank God that I speak in tongues more than all of you. 19But
in the church I would rather speak five intelligible words to instruct others than ten thousand words in a tongue.

20Brothers, stop thinking like children. In regard to evil be infants, but in your thinking be adults. 21In the Law it is written:

"Through men of strange tongues
and through the lips of foreigners
I will speak to this people,
but even then they will not listen to me,"[c]

says the Lord.

22Tongues, then, are a sign, not for believers but for unbelievers;
prophecy, however, is for believers, not for unbelievers. 23So if the
whole church comes together and everyone speaks in tongues, and
some who do not understand[d] or some unbelievers come in, will
they not say that you are out of your mind? 24But if an unbeliever
or someone who does not understand[e] comes in while everybody
is prophesying, he will be convinced by all that he is a sinner and
will be judged by all, 25and the secrets of his heart will be laid bare.
So he will fall down and worship God, exclaiming, "God is really
among you!"

Orderly Worship

26What then shall we say, brothers? When you come together,
everyone has a hymn, or a word of instruction, a revelation, a
tongue or an interpretation. All of these must be done for the
strengthening of the church. 27If anyone speaks in a tongue, two—
or at the most three—should speak, one at a time, and someone

[a] *5* Or *other languages;* also in verses 6, 18, 22, 23 and 39 [b] *16* Or *among the inquirers* [c] *21* Isaiah 28:11,12 [d] *23* Or *some inquirers* [e] *24* Or *or some inquirer*

must interpret. 28If there is no interpreter, the speaker should keep
quiet in the church and speak to himself and God.
29Two or three prophets should speak, and the others should
weigh carefully what is said. 30And if a revelation comes to someone who is sitting down, the first speaker should stop. 31For you
can all prophesy in turn so that everyone may be instructed and
encouraged. 32The spirits of prophets are subject to the control of
prophets. 33For God is not a God of disorder but of peace.
As in all the congregations of the saints, 34women should remain
silent in the churches. They are not allowed to speak, but must be
in submission, as the Law says. 35If they want to inquire about
something, they should ask their own husbands at home; for it is
disgraceful for a woman to speak in the church.
36Did the word of God originate with you? Or are you the only
people it has reached? 37If anybody thinks he is a prophet or spiritually gifted, let him acknowledge that what I am writing to you is
the Lord's command. 38If he ignores this, he himself will be ignored.[a]
39Therefore, my brothers, be eager to prophesy, and do not forbid speaking in tongues. 40But everything should be done in a
fitting and orderly way.

The Resurrection of Christ

15 Now, brothers, I want to remind you of the gospel I
preached to you, which you received and on which you
have taken your stand. 2By this gospel you are saved, if you hold
firmly to the word I preached to you. Otherwise, you have believed
in vain.
3For what I received I passed on to you as of first importance[b]:
that Christ died for our sins according to the Scriptures, 4that he
was buried, that he was raised on the third day according to the
Scriptures, 5and that he appeared to Peter,[c] and then to the
Twelve. 6After that, he appeared to more than five hundred
the the brothers at the same time, most of whom are still living,
though some have fallen asleep. 7Then he appeared to James, then
to all the apostles, 8and last of all he appeared to me also, as to one
abnormally born.
9For I am the least of the apostles and do not even deserve to be
called an apostle, because I persecuted the church of God. 10But by
the grace of God I am what I am, and his grace to me was not
without effect. No, I worked harder than all of them—yet not I,
but the grace of God that was with me. 11Whether, then, it was I
or they, this is what we preach, and this is what you believed.

The Resurrection of the Dead

12But if it is preached that Christ has been raised from the dead,
how can some of you say that there is no resurrection of the dead?
13If there is no resurrection of the dead, then not even Christ has
been raised. 14And if Christ has not been raised, our preaching is
useless and so is your faith. 15More than that, we are then found to
be false witnesses about God, for we have testified about God that
he raised Christ from the dead. But he did not raise him if in fact
the dead are not raised. 16For if the dead are not raised, then Christ
has not been raised either. 17And if Christ has not been raised,
your faith is futile; you are still in your sins. 18Then those also who
have fallen asleep in Christ are lost. 19If only for this life we have
hope in Christ, we are to be pitied more than all men.

[a]*38* Some manuscripts *If he is ignorant of this, let him be ignorant* [b]*3* Or *you at the first* [c]*5* Greek *Cephas*

cy? What do you think about two or three prophets speaking during a worship service? Has anything ever popped into your head that you wanted to share with the entire congregation? What would become of your church if that were allowed to happen? **3.** In light of 11:5, verses 34–35 are difficult to understand. What type of talk, contributing to general disorder, might be in view here?

1. What *positive* qualities about public worship could you and your church learn from the Corinthian church's enthusiasm? **2.** What was the most inspiring part of the worship service you attended most recently? The sermon? A prayer? The music? A greeting from someone?

What is one piece of advice you were told as a child that you have never forgotten?

1. How had the Corinthians taken their stand on the Gospel? **2.** In verse 2, what does it mean to "hold firmly to the word I preached to you"? **3.** What do you think it means to "believe in vain"? **4.** Why did Paul go to such detail listing who saw Jesus after he was resurrected?

1. What does "Christ died for our sins" mean to you? How does the Gospel affect your life on a daily basis? **2.** What evidence can you offer that Christ is alive in your life?

When you were a child, what friend or other person was a negative influence on you?

1. What false teaching is being spread among the Corinthians (v. 12)? **2.** How do you connect Christ's resurrection with your own hope of resurrection from death? **3.** Paul puts the Resurrection in perspective with the Second Coming and the end of time. How does it make you feel that in the end Christ will be victorious? **4.** How would your life be different without your hope that you will be resurrected? **5.** It seems that some Corinthians had begun the practice of vicarious baptism—the baptism of a living person on behalf of someone who was dead (v. 29). Why does Paul speak of this absurd practice when making his arguments (vv. 30–32)? **6.** Paul says, "I die every day," referring to his willingness to sacrifice his present rights for the salvation of others (knowing he will be raised from the dead). In what ways do you "die every day"?

1. Though reaching out to unbelievers is important (v. 33), how can too close an association with unbelievers affect your faith? Have you ever gotten too wrapped up in the lives of unbelievers, to the detriment of your relationship with Christ? How? **2.** What difference has Christ's resurrection and your resulting victory over death made to you in terms of hope and courage? In terms of purpose for life? **3.** What arguments have you found helpful in showing unbelieving friends that Christ did rise from the dead?

During what stage of your life did you change the most? In what ways did you change?

1. What practical problem is causing some to question their belief in the Resurrection (v. 35)? **2.** What would Resurrection Day be like if everyone's bodies came back to life without some kind of transformation? How would Hollywood film this scene? **3.** How do the analogies of the seed and the different types of bodies deal with doubts about the Resurrection of the dead (vv. 36–44)? **4.** What is the point of the comparison between Adam and Christ (vv. 45–49; also vv. 21–22)? **5.** Have you ever been face-to-face with death? How did that experience affect you? **6.** How does it make you feel to think of being part of what happens in verses 50–55? **7.** How does the hope of the Resurrection comfort you?

1. What is most comforting when you consider the reality of your own death? What is hardest for you to understand? **2.** What can you do now to reveal the likeness of Christ? How can your small group help you do that? **3.** What motivates you to obey God? Fear of judgment? God's anger? Worry about not being resurrected? Love

20But Christ has indeed been raised from the dead, the firstfruits
of those who have fallen asleep. 21For since death came through a
man, the resurrection of the dead comes also through a man. 22For
as in Adam all die, so in Christ all will be made alive. 23But each in
his own turn: Christ, the firstfruits; then, when he comes, those
who belong to him. 24Then the end will come, when he hands over
the kingdom to God the Father after he has destroyed all dominion,
authority and power. 25For he must reign until he has put all his
enemies under his feet. 26The last enemy to be destroyed is death.
27For he "has put everything under his feet."[a] Now when it says
that "everything" has been put under him, it is clear that this does
not include God himself, who put everything under Christ. 28When
he has done this, then the Son himself will be made subject to him
who put everything under him, so that God may be all in all.

29Now if there is no resurrection, what will those do who are
baptized for the dead? If the dead are not raised at all, why are
people baptized for them? 30And as for us, why do we endanger
ourselves every hour? 31I die every day—I mean that, brothers—
just as surely as I glory over you in Christ Jesus our Lord. 32If I
fought wild beasts in Ephesus for merely human reasons, what
have I gained? If the dead are not raised,

> "Let us eat and drink,
> for tomorrow we die."[b]

33Do not be misled: "Bad company corrupts good character."
34Come back to your senses as you ought, and stop sinning; for
there are some who are ignorant of God—I say this to your shame.

The Resurrection Body

35But someone may ask, "How are the dead raised? With what
kind of body will they come?" 36How foolish! What you sow does
not come to life unless it dies. 37When you sow, you do not plant
the body that will be, but just a seed, perhaps of wheat or of
something else. 38But God gives it a body as he has determined,
and to each kind of seed he gives its own body. 39All flesh is not
the same: Men have one kind of flesh, animals have another, birds
another and fish another. 40There are also heavenly bodies and
there are earthly bodies; but the splendor of the heavenly bodies is
one kind, and the splendor of the earthly bodies is another. 41The
sun has one kind of splendor, the moon another and the stars
another; and star differs from star in splendor.

42So will it be with the resurrection of the dead. The body that
is sown is perishable, it is raised imperishable; 43it is sown in
dishonor, it is raised in glory; it is sown in weakness, it is raised in
power; 44it is sown a natural body, it is raised a spiritual body.

If there is a natural body, there is also a spiritual body. 45So it is
written: "The first man Adam became a living being"[c]; the last
Adam, a life-giving spirit. 46The spiritual did not come first, but the
natural, and after that the spiritual. 47The first man was of the dust
of the earth, the second man from heaven. 48As was the earthly
man, so are those who are of the earth; and as is the man from
heaven, so also are those who are of heaven. 49And just as we have
borne the likeness of the earthly man, so shall we[d] bear the
likeness of the man from heaven.

50I declare to you, brothers, that flesh and blood cannot inherit
the kingdom of God, nor does the perishable inherit the imperishable. 51Listen, I tell you a mystery: We will not all sleep, but we

[a] *27* Psalm 8:6 [b] *32* Isaiah 22:13 [c] *45* Gen. 2:7 [d] *49* Some early manuscripts *so let us*

will all be changed— 52in a flash, in the twinkling of an eye, at the last trumpet. For the trumpet will sound, the dead will be raised imperishable, and we will be changed. 53For the perishable must clothe itself with the imperishable, and the mortal with immortality. 54When the perishable has been clothed with the imperishable, and the mortal with immortality, then the saying that is written will come true: "Death has been swallowed up in victory."[a]

> 55"Where, O death, is your victory?
> Where, O death, is your sting?"[b]

56The sting of death is sin, and the power of sin is the law. 57But thanks be to God! He gives us the victory through our Lord Jesus Christ.

58Therefore, my dear brothers, stand firm. Let nothing move you. Always give yourselves fully to the work of the Lord, because you know that your labor in the Lord is not in vain.

The Collection for God's People

16 Now about the collection for God's people: Do what I told the Galatian churches to do. 2On the first day of every week, each one of you should set aside a sum of money in keeping with his income, saving it up, so that when I come no collections will have to be made. 3Then, when I arrive, I will give letters of introduction to the men you approve and send them with your gift to Jerusalem. 4If it seems advisable for me to go also, they will accompany me.

Personal Requests

5After I go through Macedonia, I will come to you—for I will be going through Macedonia. 6Perhaps I will stay with you awhile, or even spend the winter, so that you can help me on my journey, wherever I go. 7I do not want to see you now and make only a passing visit; I hope to spend some time with you, if the Lord permits. 8But I will stay on at Ephesus until Pentecost, 9because a great door for effective work has opened to me, and there are many who oppose me.

10If Timothy comes, see to it that he has nothing to fear while he is with you, for he is carrying on the work of the Lord, just as I am. 11No one, then, should refuse to accept him. Send him on his way in peace so that he may return to me. I am expecting him along with the brothers.

12Now about our brother Apollos: I strongly urged him to go to you with the brothers. He was quite unwilling to go now, but he will go when he has the opportunity.

13Be on your guard; stand firm in the faith; be men of courage; be strong. 14Do everything in love.

15You know that the household of Stephanas were the first converts in Achaia, and they have devoted themselves to the service of the saints. I urge you, brothers, 16to submit to such as these and to everyone who joins in the work, and labors at it. 17I was glad when Stephanas, Fortunatus and Achaicus arrived, because they have supplied what was lacking from you. 18For they refreshed my spirit and yours also. Such men deserve recognition.

Final Greetings

19The churches in the province of Asia send you greetings. Aquila and Priscilla[c] greet you warmly in the Lord, and so does the

[a] *54* Isaiah 25:8 [b] *55* Hosea 13:14 [c] *19* Greek *Prisca*, a variant of *Priscilla*

from God? Love for God? Hope of being with God? How does verse 58 encourage and motivate you?

---

1. Who is one person you would like to visit? **2.** When you travel, do you like to plan things thoroughly, or just go and see what happens?

1. Why did Paul ask for a collection of money (vv. 1–4; see Ac 11:30; 24:17; Ro 15:25–28; 2Co 8:13–14)? **2.** How do you feel about giving money to your church? What motivates you to give? **3.** What do you think Paul's reunion with the Corinthian church was like (vv. 6–8)? Beneath all his corrective instruction, how do you think Paul felt about the Corinthians? **4.** What was the greatest door of effective work that ever opened for you? What happened? **5.** What should the Corinthians imitate regarding Stephanas and the others (vv. 15–18)? **6.** Who in your life, or in this group, has helped to refresh your spirit?

1. Which of Paul's concluding exhortations in verses 13–14 do you want to apply at this time: (a) "Be on your guard"? (b) "Stand firm in your faith"? (c) "Have courage"? (d) "Be strong"? (e) "Do everything in love"? How will you apply it to your life? **2.** As a member of your church and small group, how has this letter helped you? Challenged you? In what way would you like to grow from here?

church that meets at their house. 20All the brothers here send you
greetings. Greet one another with a holy kiss.
21I, Paul, write this greeting in my own hand.
22If anyone does not love the Lord—a curse be on him. Come,
O Lord[a]!
23The grace of the Lord Jesus be with you.
24My love to all of you in Christ Jesus. Amen.[b]

[a] *22* In Aramaic the expression *Come, O Lord* is *Marana tha.*
[b] *24* Some manuscripts do not have *Amen*.

INTRODUCTION to

2 CORINTHIANS

Book Study Outline: If you are using 2 Corinthians for a study course, here is a 7- or 13-week outline. Use the margin questions for your group agenda:

start meeting / 15 min.

read & discuss Bible / 30 min.

close meeting / 15–45 min.

Refer to the Questions and Answers in front of Bible for more information.

7-week plan	13-week plan	Personal Reading	Group Study Passage
1	1	1:1–2:4	1:1–11/God's Comfort
	2	2:5–3:6	2:12–3:6/An Aroma of Life
2	3	3:7–18	3:7–18/The New Covenant
	4	4:1–18	4:1–18/Our Treasure
3	5	5:1–6:2	5:11–6:2/Reconciliation
	6	6:3–7:1	6:14–7:1/Be Separate!
4	7	7:2–16	7:2–16/Peace Restored
	8	8:1–24	8:1–15/Our Giving
5	9	9:1–15	9:6–15/God's Giving
	10	10:1–18	10:1–18/Paul's Defense
6	11	11:1–33	11:16–33/Paul's Credentials
	12	12:1–21	12:1–10/Paul's Strength
7	13	13:1–14	13:1–14/True Power

Author: The apostle Paul.

Date: A.D. 55–56.

Theme: The strength of weakness.

Historical Background: Since much of this letter is devoted to explaining Paul's actions since the time he wrote 1 Corinthians, it is important to have a clear idea of what happened in this time period. The problem is that no one really knows! What follows is a "best guess." That Paul promised to visit the Corinthians a second time is clear (1Co 16:5–6). This visit apparently resulted in severe conflict with the "false apostles." Although they attacked Paul vigorously, what really hurt was the fact that the Corinthians did not rally to his support. This letter was written to prepare them for a third visit. The background is further complicated by two factors. First, Paul refers to a "painful letter" he wrote which has not been preserved. Second, because the fierce tone of chapters 10–13 stands in sharp contrast to the reconciling tone of chapters 1–9, 2 Corinthians may actually be a combination of two letters! According to this view, chapters 1–9 were written on the basis of Titus' report that the situation had been rectified (7:6–13). However, when Titus returned to Corinth he found that the "super-apostles" were back in charge. On hearing this, Paul wrote another letter which is chapters 10–13.

Characteristics: This letter, as much as any other, allows us to see inside Paul: his passion for the Gospel, his deep love for his churches, the pain he felt over misunderstanding, rejection and attack, and the cost of his sufferings.

STRUCTURE OF THE NEW TESTAMENT

39 Books in the Old Testament + **27** Books in the New Testament = **66** Books in the Bible

Historical Books	Paul's Epistles	General Letters	Prophetic Books
Matthew Mark Luke John Acts	Romans 1 Corinthians 2 Corinthians Galatians Ephesians Philippians Colossians 1 Thessalonians 2 Thessalonians 1 Timothy 2 Timothy Titus Philemon	Hebrews James 1 Peter 2 Peter 1 John 2 John 3 John Jude	Revelation

2 Corinthians

When sick or hurt as a child, what expression of care did you find most comforting?

1. What's the relationship between God's ability to comfort us and our ability to comfort others (v. 5)? **2.** When have you been the recipient of this comfort? How are Christ's and Paul's sufferings related to the Corinthians? What pressures is Paul facing that would cause him to despair even of life (see 7:5–7 and Ac 19:23–41)? **3.** What pressures are causing you to despair?

1. Paul found that intense pressures led him to depend on God all the more (v. 9). How do you respond to intense pressures? Do they deepen your walk with God or drive you away from him? **2.** Whom do you know who is under intense pressure? How would Paul have you pray for them? **3.** A friend asks, "Why do you have to bother praying, since God knows what's going to happen anyway?" What is your answer?

---

1. What was one accomplishment as a teenager of which you felt proud? If you were permitted to brag a little about your kids or grandkids (if any) what would you boast about? **2.** From which parent could you bank on a "no" reply? A "yes" reply? Which one waffled? Why was that?

1. In what does Paul boast (v. 12)? What is the basis for his integrity? **2.** How does a leader who uses his authority according to "worldly wisdom" differ from one who does so by "God's grace" (1:12)? **3.** From 1:15–17, of what may Paul have been accused? How does he account for his change of plans (1:23–2:2)? **4.** What does it mean that Jesus is the "Yes" of God's promise to us? How does this relate to Paul's argument? **5.** Corinth was the commercial center of the region: What do the three trading metaphors in 1:22 indicate that Jesus has done

1 Paul, an apostle of Christ Jesus by the will of God, and Timothy our brother,

To the church of God in Corinth, together with all the saints throughout Achaia:

2 Grace and peace to you from God our Father and the Lord Jesus Christ.

The God of All Comfort

3 Praise be to the God and Father of our Lord Jesus Christ, the Father of compassion and the God of all comfort, 4 who comforts us in all our troubles, so that we can comfort those in any trouble with the comfort we ourselves have received from God. 5 For just as the sufferings of Christ flow over into our lives, so also through Christ our comfort overflows. 6 If we are distressed, it is for your comfort and salvation; if we are comforted, it is for your comfort, which produces in you patient endurance of the same sufferings we suffer. 7 And our hope for you is firm, because we know that just as you share in our sufferings, so also you share in our comfort.

8 We do not want you to be uninformed, brothers, about the hardships we suffered in the province of Asia. We were under great pressure, far beyond our ability to endure, so that we despaired even of life. 9 Indeed, in our hearts we felt the sentence of death. But this happened that we might not rely on ourselves but on God, who raises the dead. 10 He has delivered us from such a deadly peril, and he will deliver us. On him we have set our hope that he will continue to deliver us, 11 as you help us by your prayers. Then many will give thanks on our[a] behalf for the gracious favor granted us in answer to the prayers of many.

Paul's Change of Plans

12 Now this is our boast: Our conscience testifies that we have conducted ourselves in the world, and especially in our relations with you, in the holiness and sincerity that are from God. We have done so not according to worldly wisdom but according to God's grace. 13 For we do not write you anything you cannot read or understand. And I hope that, 14 as you have understood us in part, you will come to understand fully that you can boast of us just as we will boast of you in the day of the Lord Jesus.

15 Because I was confident of this, I planned to visit you first so that you might benefit twice. 16 I planned to visit you on my way to Macedonia and to come back to you from Macedonia, and then to have you send me on my way to Judea. 17 When I planned this, did I do it lightly? Or do I make my plans in a worldly manner so that in the same breath I say, "Yes, yes" and "No, no"?

18 But as surely as God is faithful, our message to you is not "Yes" and "No." 19 For the Son of God, Jesus Christ, who was preached among you by me and Silas[b] and Timothy, was not "Yes" and "No," but in him it has always been "Yes." 20 For no matter how many promises God has made, they are "Yes" in Christ. And so through him the "Amen" is spoken by us to the glory of God.

[a] *11* Many manuscripts *your* [b] *19* Greek *Silvanus,* a variant of *Silas*

[21]Now it is God who makes both us and you stand firm in Christ. He anointed us, [22]set his seal of ownership on us, and put his Spirit in our hearts as a deposit, guaranteeing what is to come.

[23]I call God as my witness that it was in order to spare you that I did not return to Corinth. [24]Not that we lord it over your faith, but we work with you for your joy, because it is by faith you stand firm. **2** [1]So I made up my mind that I would not make another painful visit to you. [2]For if I grieve you, who is left to make me glad but you whom I have grieved? [3]I wrote as I did so that when I came I should not be distressed by those who ought to make me rejoice. I had confidence in all of you, that you would all share my joy. [4]For I wrote you out of great distress and anguish of heart and with many tears, not to grieve you but to let you know the depth of my love for you.

for us? **6.** What are the causes of joy and grief for Paul and the Corinthians (1:23–2:5)? **7.** What must Paul's grievous letter have been about (see 2:3–9; 7:8–12)? **8.** What has happened since the letter was received (2:6–8)? How might their continuation of punishment be a scheme of Satan (vv. 9–11)?

1. What does Paul's example mean for you in terms of how you relate to others? **2.** Paraphrase the "business deal" of 1:22 in modern terms. How have you experienced this spiritual "new deal"? **3.** How does this passage apply to church discipline and restoration of fallen leaders today? Is there someone you need to forgive and comfort (no names)? Why not now?

Forgiveness for the Sinner

[5]If anyone has caused grief, he has not so much grieved me as he has grieved all of you, to some extent—not to put it too severely. [6]The punishment inflicted on him by the majority is sufficient for him. [7]Now instead, you ought to forgive and comfort him, so that he will not be overwhelmed by excessive sorrow. [8]I urge you, therefore, to reaffirm your love for him. [9]The reason I wrote you was to see if you would stand the test and be obedient in everything. [10]If you forgive anyone, I also forgive him. And what I have forgiven—if there was anything to forgive—I have forgiven in the sight of Christ for your sake, [11]in order that Satan might not outwit us. For we are not unaware of his schemes.

Ministers of the New Covenant

[12]Now when I went to Troas to preach the gospel of Christ and found that the Lord had opened a door for me, [13]I still had no peace of mind, because I did not find my brother Titus there. So I said good-by to them and went on to Macedonia.

[14]But thanks be to God, who always leads us in triumphal procession in Christ and through us spreads everywhere the fragrance of the knowledge of him. [15]For we are to God the aroma of Christ among those who are being saved and those who are perishing. [16]To the one we are the smell of death; to the other, the fragrance of life. And who is equal to such a task? [17]Unlike so many, we do not peddle the word of God for profit. On the contrary, in Christ we speak before God with sincerity, like men sent from God.

3 Are we beginning to commend ourselves again? Or do we need, like some people, letters of recommendation to you or from you? [2]You yourselves are our letter, written on our hearts, known and read by everybody. [3]You show that you are a letter from Christ, the result of our ministry, written not with ink but with the Spirit of the living God, not on tablets of stone but on tablets of human hearts.

[4]Such confidence as this is ours through Christ before God. [5]Not that we are competent in ourselves to claim anything for ourselves, but our competence comes from God. [6]He has made us competent as ministers of a new covenant—not of the letter but of the Spirit; for the letter kills, but the Spirit gives life.

What is the most memorable parade you've seen or taken part in?

1. Until Titus returns with "good news" (see 7:6–13), Paul has "no peace of mind" (2:13): What does that say about Paul's concern for this church? **2.** How can the same Gospel be either the smell of death or the fragrance of life? **3.** What might be happening in Corinth (2:17–3:1)? Although preachers often had letters of recommendation when they traveled to new areas (3Jn 5–8), why does Paul need no such letter? **4.** Why should the Corinthians listen to Paul (1:1–3:6)?

1. How can you spread the aroma of Christ in the environment of your home? In your workplace? **2.** If you were the only "Bible" someone else had to read, how much of the Gospel would they grasp?

The Glory of the New Covenant

[7]Now if the ministry that brought death, which was engraved in letters on stone, came with glory, so that the Israelites could not look steadily at the face of Moses because of its glory, fading though

When did you last experience suddenly understanding something that once confused and puzzled you?

1. How does Paul here (also vv. 3,6) contrast the old and new covenants? **2.** Compare Exodus 34:27–35 and Jeremiah 32:31–34 with Romans 3:19–24. Why did that once-glorious covenant of Moses have to be replaced by the everlasting covenant of Christ? **3.** What then is the basis for Paul's (and our) hope and boldness? **4.** What are the practical results of this new covenant (vv. 16–18)?

1. Who or what helped to remove the cobwebs which once veiled your "dull mind"? **2.** What changes have you noticed since you "turned to the Lord"?

---

1. Do you feel more like a disposable cup or a crystal goblet this week? Why? **2.** What thought, song or verse encourages you?

1. How does the way Paul *received* his ministry (vv. 1,6) make a difference in the way he *conducts* that ministry (vv. 2–5)? **2.** What do you learn from Paul about sharing your faith (vv. 1–6)? About its content? About the lack of response? **3.** What about the ministry is most like a struggle (vv. 7–11)? How does Paul's struggle show God's power and reflect Jesus' life? How is this true in your own life? **4.** What does "death at work" and "life at work" (v. 12) mean to you? Which is at work in your life? Why? **5.** What truths keep Paul going in spite of his hardships? Why does God allow Paul to go through them?

1. How did the light of Christ first break through to you? **2.** Why is being a servant to others essential for sharing the Gospel? What is one way you could be more of a servant to someone you are concerned about? **3.** How do verses 7–12 and 16–18 help you cope with your present anxieties? **4.** How does this section challenge common ideas of "success"?

it was, 8will not the ministry of the Spirit be even more glorious? 9If the ministry that condemns men is glorious, how much more glorious is the ministry that brings righteousness! 10For what was glorious has no glory now in comparison with the surpassing glory. 11And if what was fading away came with glory, how much greater is the glory of that which lasts!

12Therefore, since we have such a hope, we are very bold. 13We are not like Moses, who would put a veil over his face to keep the Israelites from gazing at it while the radiance was fading away. 14But their minds were made dull, for to this day the same veil remains when the old covenant is read. It has not been removed, because only in Christ is it taken away. 15Even to this day when Moses is read, a veil covers their hearts. 16But whenever anyone turns to the Lord, the veil is taken away. 17Now the Lord is the Spirit, and where the Spirit of the Lord is, there is freedom. 18And we, who with unveiled faces all reflect[a] the Lord's glory, are being transformed into his likeness with ever-increasing glory, which comes from the Lord, who is the Spirit.

Treasures in Jars of Clay

4 Therefore, since through God's mercy we have this ministry, we do not lose heart. 2Rather, we have renounced secret and shameful ways; we do not use deception, nor do we distort the word of God. On the contrary, by setting forth the truth plainly we commend ourselves to every man's conscience in the sight of God. 3And even if our gospel is veiled, it is veiled to those who are perishing. 4The god of this age has blinded the minds of unbelievers, so that they cannot see the light of the gospel of the glory of Christ, who is the image of God. 5For we do not preach ourselves, but Jesus Christ as Lord, and ourselves as your servants for Jesus' sake. 6For God, who said, "Let light shine out of darkness,"[b] made his light shine in our hearts to give us the light of the knowledge of the glory of God in the face of Christ.

7But we have this treasure in jars of clay to show that this all-surpassing power is from God and not from us. 8We are hard pressed on every side, but not crushed; perplexed, but not in despair; 9persecuted, but not abandoned; struck down, but not destroyed. 10We always carry around in our body the death of Jesus, so that the life of Jesus may also be revealed in our body. 11For we who are alive are always being given over to death for Jesus' sake, so that his life may be revealed in our mortal body. 12So then, death is at work in us, but life is at work in you.

13It is written: "I believed; therefore I have spoken."[c] With that same spirit of faith we also believe and therefore speak, 14because we know that the one who raised the Lord Jesus from the dead will also raise us with Jesus and present us with you in his presence. 15All this is for your benefit, so that the grace that is reaching more and more people may cause thanksgiving to overflow to the glory of God.

16Therefore we do not lose heart. Though outwardly we are wasting away, yet inwardly we are being renewed day by day. 17For our light and momentary troubles are achieving for us an eternal glory that far outweighs them all. 18So we fix our eyes not on what is seen, but on what is unseen. For what is seen is temporary, but what is unseen is eternal.

[a]*18* Or *contemplate* [b]*6* Gen. 1:3 [c]*13* Psalm 116:10

Our Heavenly Dwelling

5 Now we know that if the earthly tent we live in is destroyed, we have a building from God, an eternal house in heaven, not built by human hands. 2Meanwhile we groan, longing to be clothed with our heavenly dwelling, 3because when we are clothed, we will not be found naked. 4For while we are in this tent, we groan and are burdened, because we do not wish to be unclothed but to be clothed with our heavenly dwelling, so that what is mortal may be swallowed up by life. 5Now it is God who has made us for this very purpose and has given us the Spirit as a deposit, guaranteeing what is to come.

6Therefore we are always confident and know that as long as we are at home in the body we are away from the Lord. 7We live by faith, not by sight. 8We are confident, I say, and would prefer to be away from the body and at home with the Lord. 9So we make it our goal to please him, whether we are at home in the body or away from it. 10For we must all appear before the judgment seat of Christ, that each one may receive what is due him for the things done while in the body, whether good or bad.

Complete this sentence: "Home is where . . ."

1. How does Paul's confidence in his future relate to 4:16–18? To John 14:1–3? What role does faith play in this? How does Paul's "home" affect his daily living (vv. 6–10)? **2.** What is this "heavenly dwelling" like? **3.** Is Paul motivated more by the desire to be with Christ, or by fear of judgment? Which motivates you?

1. How does God's purpose (v. 5) apply to a current crisis of yours? **2.** How can knowing the location of your ultimate "home" affect your attitude toward aging? How can it encourage you to be more hospitable to others now?

The Ministry of Reconciliation

11Since, then, we know what it is to fear the Lord, we try to persuade men. What we are is plain to God, and I hope it is also plain to your conscience. 12We are not trying to commend ourselves to you again, but are giving you an opportunity to take pride in us, so that you can answer those who take pride in what is seen rather than in what is in the heart. 13If we are out of our mind, it is for the sake of God; if we are in our right mind, it is for you. 14For Christ's love compels us, because we are convinced that one died for all, and therefore all died. 15And he died for all, that those who live should no longer live for themselves but for him who died for them and was raised again.

16So from now on we regard no one from a worldly point of view. Though we once regarded Christ in this way, we do so no longer. 17Therefore, if anyone is in Christ, he is a new creation; the old has gone, the new has come! 18All this is from God, who reconciled us to himself through Christ and gave us the ministry of reconciliation: 19that God was reconciling the world to himself in Christ, not counting men's sins against them. And he has committed to us the message of reconciliation. 20We are therefore Christ's ambassadors, as though God were making his appeal through us. We implore you on Christ's behalf: Be reconciled to God. 21God made him who had no sin to be sin[a] for us, so that in him we might become the righteousness of God.

6 As God's fellow workers we urge you not to receive God's grace in vain. 2For he says,

> "In the time of my favor I heard you,
> and in the day of salvation I helped you."[b]

I tell you, now is the time of God's favor, now is the day of salvation.

If you were appointed as an ambassador, where would you like to be sent?

1. What is Paul's motive for evangelism in verses 10–11? In verse 14? How do they fit together? How would someone motivated by these values stand in contrast to someone motivated by those mentioned in 2:17 and 5:12? **2.** What does Paul mean by what he says about Christ and our response to him (vv. 15–17; see also Ro 6:5–13)? How does this make you feel about your past life? Your life now? **3.** What does "reconciliation" mean? What story from your life illustrates this? **4.** What does God do through Christ (v. 18)? Through us (v. 20)? For us (vv. 17–18)?

1. What motivation does Paul give to share your faith (see 6:1–2)? What motivates you? What inhibits you? **2.** In light of your experiences of alienation and reconciliation in other relationships, at what stage is your relationship with God: A family feud, a truce or have you made up?

Paul's Hardships

3We put no stumbling block in anyone's path, so that our ministry will not be discredited. 4Rather, as servants of God we commend ourselves in every way: in great endurance; in troubles, hardships and distresses; 5in beatings, imprisonments and riots; in

1. How does Paul defend the authenticity of his ministry here? How does this differ from the ways those who are challenging him assert their authority (see 3:1; 4:2; 5:12; 11:23–29)? By appealing to these things instead of his supernatural conversion or mira-

[a]21 Or *be a sin offering* [b]2 Isaiah 49:8

cles (Ac 9:3 – 5; 19:11–12), what is he saying the real test of faith is? **2.** What is Paul asking the Corinthians (and us) to do in verses 11–13 (see 3:2–3; 4:15)?

1. By what standards do you gauge success? Why? How do they compare with verses 4–10? Would Paul be a success by your standards? Would you? **2.** What, from Paul's example, do you want to incorporate into your life? Into your vocational pursuits?

What food are you most likely to spill on yourself? Tell about a "bad spill."

1. What is a yoke? How is *unequal* yoking an apt metaphor in this context? **2.** From verses 16–18, what is necessary if we want to have God as our Father? What does this imply about choosing a spouse? About where we should look for dates and close friends?

1. What does it mean that you are the dwelling place of God? What contaminants can affect your body? Your spirit? Is there something contaminating you now? **2.** How can a believer be a friend and witness to an unbeliever without becoming "yoked"?

---

1. What does "homecoming" mean to you? **2.** What finally gets your attention: Tough talk? Slammed door? Tears? Letter? Walkout? Give a recent example.

1. Why does Paul want this church to open up to him (vv. 2–4; see 6:11–13)? Hence, do you think Titus' report (v. 7) was entirely positive? Why or why not? **2.** In verse 5, Paul picks up the account of his travels (of which he left off in 2:12–13). How does his account in verses 5–7 illustrate why he began this letter with thanks to God for his comfort (1:3–7)? **3.** What was the result of Paul's previous letter to them (vv. 8–13; see also 2:3–4)? What intentions does Paul clarify here? Practically, how does godly sorrow differ from worldly sorrow? **4.** What tone of voice do you hear in verse 16? In light of his previous hurtful letter, why would he underscore his present joy and confidence? If you were the first to read this, how would you feel?

hard work, sleepless nights and hunger; 6in purity, understanding,
patience and kindness; in the Holy Spirit and in sincere love; 7in
truthful speech and in the power of God; with weapons of righteousness in the right hand and in the left; 8through glory and
dishonor, bad report and good report; genuine, yet regarded as
impostors; 9known, yet regarded as unknown; dying, and yet we
live on; beaten, and yet not killed; 10sorrowful, yet always rejoicing; poor, yet making many rich; having nothing, and yet possessing everything.
11We have spoken freely to you, Corinthians, and opened wide
our hearts to you. 12We are not withholding our affection from you,
but you are withholding yours from us. 13As a fair exchange—I
speak as to my children—open wide your hearts also.

Do Not Be Yoked With Unbelievers

14Do not be yoked together with unbelievers. For what do righteousness and wickedness have in common? Or what fellowship
can light have with darkness? 15What harmony is there between
Christ and Belial[a]? What does a believer have in common with an
unbeliever? 16What agreement is there between the temple of God
and idols? For we are the temple of the living God. As God has
said: "I will live with them and walk among them, and I will be
their God, and they will be my people."[b]

17"Therefore come out from them
and be separate,
says the Lord.
Touch no unclean thing,
and I will receive you."[c]
18"I will be a Father to you,
and you will be my sons and daughters,
says the Lord Almighty."[d]

7 Since we have these promises, dear friends, let us purify ourselves from everything that contaminates body and spirit, perfecting holiness out of reverence for God.

Paul's Joy

2Make room for us in your hearts. We have wronged no one, we
have corrupted no one, we have exploited no one. 3I do not say
this to condemn you; I have said before that you have such a place
in our hearts that we would live or die with you. 4I have great
confidence in you; I take great pride in you. I am greatly encouraged; in all our troubles my joy knows no bounds.
5For when we came into Macedonia, this body of ours had no
rest, but we were harassed at every turn—conflicts on the outside,
fears within. 6But God, who comforts the downcast, comforted us
by the coming of Titus, 7and not only by his coming but also by the
comfort you had given him. He told us about your longing for me,
your deep sorrow, your ardent concern for me, so that my joy was
greater than ever.
8Even if I caused you sorrow by my letter, I do not regret it.
Though I did regret it—I see that my letter hurt you, but only for
a little while— 9yet now I am happy, not because you were made
sorry, but because your sorrow led you to repentance. For you
became sorrowful as God intended and so were not harmed in any
way by us. 10Godly sorrow brings repentance that leads to salvation
and leaves no regret, but worldly sorrow brings death. 11See what

[a] *15* Greek *Beliar,* a variant of *Belial* [b] *16* Lev. 26:12; Jer. 32:38; Ezek. 37:27
[c] *17* Isaiah 52:11; Ezek. 20:34,41 [d] *18* 2 Samuel 7:14; 7:8

this godly sorrow has produced in you: what earnestness, what eagerness to clear yourselves, what indignation, what alarm, what longing, what concern, what readiness to see justice done. At every point you have proved yourselves to be innocent in this matter. 12So even though I wrote to you, it was not on account of the one who did the wrong or of the injured party, but rather that before God you could see for yourselves how devoted to us you are. 13By all this we are encouraged.

In addition to our own encouragement, we were especially delighted to see how happy Titus was, because his spirit has been refreshed by all of you. 14I had boasted to him about you, and you have not embarrassed me. But just as everything we said to you was true, so our boasting about you to Titus has proved to be true as well. 15And his affection for you is all the greater when he remembers that you were all obedient, receiving him with fear and trembling. 16I am glad I can have complete confidence in you.

1. Have you ever been confronted with a wrong you have done by someone who loves you? How did you feel about that person at the time? **2.** When is it more loving to confront someone with their sin than to ignore it? What attitudes are needed to keep loving confrontation from becoming judgmental? How do you see those attitudes in Paul? **3.** When did godly sorrow motivate you to make a real change? How do you feel about that change now?

Generosity Encouraged

8 And now, brothers, we want you to know about the grace that God has given the Macedonian churches. 2Out of the most severe trial, their overflowing joy and their extreme poverty welled up in rich generosity. 3For I testify that they gave as much as they were able, and even beyond their ability. Entirely on their own, 4they urgently pleaded with us for the privilege of sharing in this service to the saints. 5And they did not do as we expected, but they gave themselves first to the Lord and then to us in keeping with God's will. 6So we urged Titus, since he had earlier made a beginning, to bring also to completion this act of grace on your part. 7But just as you excel in everything—in faith, in speech, in knowledge, in complete earnestness and in your love for us[a]—see that you also excel in this grace of giving.

8I am not commanding you, but I want to test the sincerity of your love by comparing it with the earnestness of others. 9For you know the grace of our Lord Jesus Christ, that though he was rich, yet for your sakes he became poor, so that you through his poverty might become rich.

10And here is my advice about what is best for you in this matter: Last year you were the first not only to give but also to have the desire to do so. 11Now finish the work, so that your eager willingness to do it may be matched by your completion of it, according to your means. 12For if the willingness is there, the gift is acceptable according to what one has, not according to what he does not have.

13Our desire is not that others might be relieved while you are hard pressed, but that there might be equality. 14At the present time your plenty will supply what they need, so that in turn their plenty will supply what you need. Then there will be equality, 15as it is written: "He who gathered much did not have too much, and he who gathered little did not have too little."[b]

1. With what are you generous: Your money? Time? Talents? Toys? With what are you stingy? **2.** What were you doing last year at this time which still needs to be completed?

1. From 1 Corinthians 16:1–4 (written about a year earlier) and Romans 15:25–27 (written either during or shortly after Paul had revisited Corinth), what is this collection all about? **2.** What do you learn about the Macedonians from their giving? In light of the struggles in Corinth, why would Paul draw their attention to the Macedonian example? What would this test of generosity reveal? **3.** What principles about giving do you observe?

1. If you were to evaluate your zeal for God in light of your checkbook, what grade would you give yourself? **2.** What from Jesus' example (v. 9) prompts you to be generous with your money, time and energy? What inhibits you? **3.** How can the equality principle (vv. 13–15) help you decide what cause needs your immediate attention? **4.** What does this principle say about getting your own needs met?

Titus Sent to Corinth

16I thank God, who put into the heart of Titus the same concern I have for you. 17For Titus not only welcomed our appeal, but he is coming to you with much enthusiasm and on his own initiative. 18And we are sending along with him the brother who is praised by all the churches for his service to the gospel. 19What is more, he was chosen by the churches to accompany us as we carry the

Whom do you trust with money: (a) Your kids? (b) Bank? (c) Broker? (d) Government? (e) No one but God? (f) What money, I'm broke? Why is that?

[a]7 Some manuscripts *in our love for you* [b]15 Exodus 16:18

1. Why is this gift for the Jerusalem church so important? What dangers or suspicions accompany Paul? How does Paul attempt to diminish these criticisms? 2. What commends Titus for his role of ensuring fiscal accountability in this mission relief work? 3. Does Paul expect Titus and the others to be well-received (see 8:16–24)? Why or why not? 4. Why does Paul expect the Corinthians to be generous (9:1–5)? In what ways?

1. How do the groups you contribute to practice Paul's principle in 20–21? Why is this especially critical for Christian organizations? 2. If Macedonians came to visit you, would they find your generosity lacking or overflowing? With what else besides money are you generous? 3. To become more generous, what would have to change: Your job, time priorities, spending habits, mission vision?

offering, which we administer in order to honor the Lord himself and to show our eagerness to help. [20]We want to avoid any criticism of the way we administer this liberal gift. [21]For we are taking pains to do what is right, not only in the eyes of the Lord but also in the eyes of men.

[22]In addition, we are sending with them our brother who has often proved to us in many ways that he is zealous, and now even more so because of his great confidence in you. [23]As for Titus, he is my partner and fellow worker among you; as for our brothers, they are representatives of the churches and an honor to Christ. [24]Therefore show these men the proof of your love and the reason for our pride in you, so that the churches can see it.

9 There is no need for me to write to you about this service to the saints. [2]For I know your eagerness to help, and I have been boasting about it to the Macedonians, telling them that since last year you in Achaia were ready to give; and your enthusiasm has stirred most of them to action. [3]But I am sending the brothers in order that our boasting about you in this matter should not prove hollow, but that you may be ready, as I said you would be. [4]For if any Macedonians come with me and find you unprepared, we—not to say anything about you—would be ashamed of having been so confident. [5]So I thought it necessary to urge the brothers to visit you in advance and finish the arrangements for the generous gift you had promised. Then it will be ready as a generous gift, not as one grudgingly given.

What is one lesson about money you can recall learning from your parents?

1. By "sowing and reaping" imagery, is Paul saying that if you give $100 you will get $1,000? Why or why not? 2. What do you make of the three "alls" in verse 8? 3. For what purpose will God materially bless these people? How does generosity effect righteousness, and the ever-widening circles of people giving thanks to God? 4. How is giving contagious? How does it reflect God's grace? 5. Why is being able to receive also important (v. 12)?

1. What have you reaped by being generous to others? 2. How can God's promise (v. 8) enable you to be more generous? To persevere in your work? 3. How do generosity and financial planning and responsibility fit together?

Sowing Generously

[6]Remember this: Whoever sows sparingly will also reap sparingly, and whoever sows generously will also reap generously. [7]Each man should give what he has decided in his heart to give, not reluctantly or under compulsion, for God loves a cheerful giver. [8]And God is able to make all grace abound to you, so that in all things at all times, having all that you need, you will abound in every good work. [9]As it is written:

> "He has scattered abroad his gifts to the poor;
> his righteousness endures forever."[a]

[10]Now he who supplies seed to the sower and bread for food will also supply and increase your store of seed and will enlarge the harvest of your righteousness. [11]You will be made rich in every way so that you can be generous on every occasion, and through us your generosity will result in thanksgiving to God.

[12]This service that you perform is not only supplying the needs of God's people but is also overflowing in many expressions of thanks to God. [13]Because of the service by which you have proved yourselves, men will praise God for the obedience that accompanies your confession of the gospel of Christ, and for your generosity in sharing with them and with everyone else. [14]And in their prayers for you their hearts will go out to you, because of the surpassing grace God has given you. [15]Thanks be to God for his indescribable gift!

Is "authority" more of a positive or a negative word to you? How so? Why is that?

1. Things have improved in Corinth since Paul wrote his last letter (7:8–16; see also Introduction to 2 Corinthians), but not al-

Paul's Defense of His Ministry

10 By the meekness and gentleness of Christ, I appeal to you—I, Paul, who am "timid" when face to face with you, but "bold" when away! [2]I beg you that when I come I may not have to be as bold as I expect to be toward some people who think that we

[a]9 Psalm 112:9

live by the standards of this world. [3]For though we live in the world, we do not wage war as the world does. [4]The weapons we fight with are not the weapons of the world. On the contrary, they have divine power to demolish strongholds. [5]We demolish arguments and every pretension that sets itself up against the knowledge of God, and we take captive every thought to make it obedient to Christ. [6]And we will be ready to punish every act of disobedience, once your obedience is complete.

[7]You are looking only on the surface of things.[a] If anyone is confident that he belongs to Christ, he should consider again that we belong to Christ just as much as he. [8]For even if I boast somewhat freely about the authority the Lord gave us for building you up rather than pulling you down, I will not be ashamed of it. [9]I do not want to seem to be trying to frighten you with my letters. [10]For some say, "His letters are weighty and forceful, but in person he is unimpressive and his speaking amounts to nothing." [11]Such people should realize that what we are in our letters when we are absent, we will be in our actions when we are present.

[12]We do not dare to classify or compare ourselves with some who commend themselves. When they measure themselves by themselves and compare themselves with themselves, they are not wise. [13]We, however, will not boast beyond proper limits, but will confine our boasting to the field God has assigned to us, a field that reaches even to you. [14]We are not going too far in our boasting, as would be the case if we had not come to you, for we did get as far as you with the gospel of Christ. [15]Neither do we go beyond our limits by boasting of work done by others.[b] Our hope is that, as your faith continues to grow, our area of activity among you will greatly expand, [16]so that we can preach the gospel in the regions beyond you. For we do not want to boast about work already done in another man's territory. [17]But, "Let him who boasts boast in the Lord."[c] [18]For it is not the one who commends himself who is approved, but the one whom the Lord commends.

Paul and the False Apostles

11 I hope you will put up with a little of my foolishness; but you are already doing that. [2]I am jealous for you with a godly jealousy. I promised you to one husband, to Christ, so that I might present you as a pure virgin to him. [3]But I am afraid that just as Eve was deceived by the serpent's cunning, your minds may somehow be led astray from your sincere and pure devotion to Christ. [4]For if someone comes to you and preaches a Jesus other than the Jesus we preached, or if you receive a different spirit from the one you received, or a different gospel from the one you accepted, you put up with it easily enough. [5]But I do not think I am in the least inferior to those "super-apostles." [6]I may not be a trained speaker, but I do have knowledge. We have made this perfectly clear to you in every way.

[7]Was it a sin for me to lower myself in order to elevate you by preaching the gospel of God to you free of charge? [8]I robbed other churches by receiving support from them so as to serve you. [9]And when I was with you and needed something, I was not a burden to anyone, for the brothers who came from Macedonia supplied what I needed. I have kept myself from being a burden to you in any

[a]7 Or *Look at the obvious facts* [b]13-15 Or [13]*We, however, will not boast about things that cannot be measured, but we will boast according to the standard of measurement that the God of measure has assigned us—a measurement that relates even to you.* [14]*. . . .* [15]*Neither do we boast about things that cannot be measured in regard to the work done by others.* [c]17 Jer. 9:24

together. How is Paul discredited (vv. 1–2,9–11)? How is Paul's gentleness and meekness being misunderstood? Where have you seen Paul's strength and concern for others? **2.** How is Paul's exercise of authority (vv. 3–8) different than his usurpers, the so-called "super-apostles" (see 11:5,20)? How and why does he play upon their boastful attitude? **3.** How do you feel about Paul's "reprimand" here in defense of himself? Do you see it as strength or weakness when a person admits his or her limitations? Why?

1. From Paul's example here, what is supposed to be the "normal" way Christians exercise leadership over one another? On a scale from 1–10, how well do you demonstrate Christ's gentleness and meekness in leading others? **2.** What will you work on this week that demonstrates your interest in building others up? **3.** When is it right to show "tough love" by demanding that someone change? What risks does this involve? **4.** As an act of "tough love," what worldly, anti-God thoughts prevail in your circle of friends or family which you can "take captive" and "make obedient to Christ" (v. 5)?

What springs to mind when you hear the word "Satan"?

1. What upsets Paul about these "super-apostles"? How does this relate to 6:14? **2.** Why do you think Paul refused to be supported by the Corinthians, yet accepted help from the Macedonian churches? How is Paul's servant-attitude being distorted by the false apostles? How do their motives compare with his? **3.** What is Paul's final conclusion about these teachers (vv. 13–15)? What tensions would you feel as a Corinthian Christian when you read this accusation?

1. Spiritually, you have been promised to one husband who is Christ (v. 2). How are you getting ready for that upcoming wedding? **2.** What "different gospel" has at one point or another pulled you away from Jesus? How did you become aware of its deceitfulness? **3.** Sin rarely approaches us as evil, but as "virtue in disguisc." From verses 2–4, how can you guard yourself against this satanic strategy?

way, and will continue to do so. 10As surely as the truth of Christ
is in me, nobody in the regions of Achaia will stop this boasting of
mine. 11Why? Because I do not love you? God knows I do! 12And I
will keep on doing what I am doing in order to cut the ground from
under those who want an opportunity to be considered equal with
us in the things they boast about.

13For such men are false apostles, deceitful workmen, masquer-
ading as apostles of Christ. 14And no wonder, for Satan himself
masquerades as an angel of light. 15It is not surprising, then, if his
servants masquerade as servants of righteousness. Their end will
be what their actions deserve.

Where was the last place you felt you were really in danger of being hurt? Would you put yourself in that position again?

1. In 10:1, Paul made it clear how he would like to appeal to them, so why does he sarcastically resort to "boasting," as the false apostles were doing? What is the irony that galls Paul (see also 12:11–13)? **2.** What has Paul already boasted about (see 1:12; 9:2; 10:8; 11:10)? How does this differ from the boasting of the false teachers? **3.** The false teachers were apparently Palestinian Jews (11:22), preaching a distorted gospel (11:4). How does Paul validate his claim to serve Christ more than they? How is his suffering a more eloquent witness to his authority than fine speech? **4.** How would you regard a minister who had been through these experiences (vv. 23–33)? Would you feel grateful, guilty or what? **5.** How do you need to embrace Paul's attitude in light of the pressures and demands in your life?

1. Both Jesus' and Paul's gentleness was misunderstood as weakness. How has that resulted in blessing (see Mt 5:5)? **2.** Would Paul have been more popular if he had pushed his weight around? How would that have misrepresented the Gospel? **3.** In your witness, where are you caught "between a rock and a hard place"?

Paul Boasts About His Sufferings

16I repeat: Let no one take me for a fool. But if you do, then
receive me just as you would a fool, so that I may do a little
boasting. 17In this self-confident boasting I am not talking as the
Lord would, but as a fool. 18Since many are boasting in the way the
world does, I too will boast. 19You gladly put up with fools since
you are so wise! 20In fact, you even put up with anyone who
enslaves you or exploits you or takes advantage of you or pushes
himself forward or slaps you in the face. 21To my shame I admit
that we were too weak for that!

What anyone else dares to boast about—I am speaking as a
fool—I also dare to boast about. 22Are they Hebrews? So am I. Are
they Israelites? So am I. Are they Abraham's descendants? So am I.
23Are they servants of Christ? (I am out of my mind to talk like
this.) I am more. I have worked much harder, been in prison more
frequently, been flogged more severely, and been exposed to death
again and again. 24Five times I received from the Jews the forty
lashes minus one. 25Three times I was beaten with rods, once I was
stoned, three times I was shipwrecked, I spent a night and a day in
the open sea, 26I have been constantly on the move. I have been in
danger from rivers, in danger from bandits, in danger from my own
countrymen, in danger from Gentiles; in danger in the city, in
danger in the country, in danger at sea; and in danger from false
brothers. 27I have labored and toiled and have often gone without
sleep; I have known hunger and thirst and have often gone without
food; I have been cold and naked. 28Besides everything else, I face
daily the pressure of my concern for all the churches. 29Who is
weak, and I do not feel weak? Who is led into sin, and I do not
inwardly burn?

30If I must boast, I will boast of the things that show my weakness. 31The God and Father of the Lord Jesus, who is to be praised
forever, knows that I am not lying. 32In Damascus the governor
under King Aretas had the city of the Damascenes guarded in order
to arrest me. 33But I was lowered in a basket from a window in the
wall and slipped through his hands.

How often do you remember your dreams? What was your most recent or bizarre dream?

1. So far, how has Paul authenticated his apostleship (see 11:21–30; 6:3–10)? How would this sound if you read it on a minister's resume? **2.** Why doesn't Paul play the boasting game of the false apostles (see 4:5–7; 10:12–18)? **3.** How has Paul's "thorn" affected his life?

Paul's Vision and His Thorn

12 I must go on boasting. Although there is nothing to be
gained, I will go on to visions and revelations from the
Lord. 2I know a man in Christ who fourteen years ago was caught
up to the third heaven. Whether it was in the body or out of the
body I do not know—God knows. 3And I know that this man—
whether in the body or apart from the body I do not know, but God
knows— 4was caught up to paradise. He heard inexpressible
things, things that man is not permitted to tell. 5I will boast about
a man like that, but I will not boast about myself, except about my
weaknesses. 6Even if I should choose to boast, I would not be a

fool, because I would be speaking the truth. But I refrain, so no one will think more of me than is warranted by what I do or say.

7To keep me from becoming conceited because of these surpassingly great revelations, there was given me a thorn in my flesh, a messenger of Satan, to torment me. 8Three times I pleaded with the Lord to take it away from me. 9But he said to me, "My grace is sufficient for you, for my power is made perfect in weakness." Therefore I will boast all the more gladly about my weaknesses, so that Christ's power may rest on me. 10That is why, for Christ's sake, I delight in weaknesses, in insults, in hardships, in persecutions, in difficulties. For when I am weak, then I am strong.

1. How do you react when God appears to be silent in answer to your urgent request? How do you feel about God's promise in verse 9? Why doesn't God simply take the hurt away? **2.** How has God worked in and through you during a time of weakness? What will you do to develop trust in God during times of weakness?

Paul's Concern for the Corinthians

11I have made a fool of myself, but you drove me to it. I ought to have been commended by you, for I am not in the least inferior to the "super-apostles," even though I am nothing. 12The things that mark an apostle—signs, wonders and miracles—were done among you with great perseverance. 13How were you inferior to the other churches, except that I was never a burden to you? Forgive me this wrong!

14Now I am ready to visit you for the third time, and I will not be a burden to you, because what I want is not your possessions but you. After all, children should not have to save up for their parents, but parents for their children. 15So I will very gladly spend for you everything I have and expend myself as well. If I love you more, will you love me less? 16Be that as it may, I have not been a burden to you. Yet, crafty fellow that I am, I caught you by trickery! 17Did I exploit you through any of the men I sent you? 18I urged Titus to go to you and I sent our brother with him. Titus did not exploit you, did he? Did we not act in the same spirit and follow the same course?

19Have you been thinking all along that we have been defending ourselves to you? We have been speaking in the sight of God as those in Christ; and everything we do, dear friends, is for your strengthening. 20For I am afraid that when I come I may not find you as I want you to be, and you may not find me as you want me to be. I fear that there may be quarreling, jealousy, outbursts of anger, factions, slander, gossip, arrogance and disorder. 21I am afraid that when I come again my God will humble me before you, and I will be grieved over many who have sinned earlier and have not repented of the impurity, sexual sin and debauchery in which they have indulged.

What is one way your parents sacrificed for you? How did you feel about that unselfish sacrifice then? Now?

1. What led Paul to write this letter (vv. 11–13)? How have the false "super-apostles" distorted his ministry (see also 2:17; 11:7)? **2.** How does Paul distance himself from the superior-sounding leaders (vv. 14–15)? What must he be feeling as he thinks about the Corinthians? **3.** What do Paul's rhetorical questions (vv. 17–19) reveal about his intentions versus their perception of him? **4.** How would you feel about visiting a ministry you love which is behaving like verses 20–21? How persistent would you be in loving them?

To whom is God leading you to minister? How can you show the spirit of verses 14–15 to them? What will that cost you? How will you prepare for that? How will you keep from being a burden on those to whom God is sending you to minister?

Final Warnings

13 This will be my third visit to you. "Every matter must be established by the testimony of two or three witnesses."[a] 2I already gave you a warning when I was with you the second time. I now repeat it while absent: On my return I will not spare those who sinned earlier or any of the others, 3since you are demanding proof that Christ is speaking through me. He is not weak in dealing with you, but is powerful among you. 4For to be sure, he was crucified in weakness, yet he lives by God's power. Likewise, we are weak in him, yet by God's power we will live with him to serve you.

5Examine yourselves to see whether you are in the faith; test yourselves. Do you not realize that Christ Jesus is in you—unless, of course, you fail the test? 6And I trust that you will discover that

[a] Deut. 19:15

In high school or college, what did you do to prepare yourself for big exams?

1. Acts 18 records Paul's first visit to Corinth, and Acts 20:2–3 alludes to what must have been his third visit. Given that he stayed there three months, what do you think happened as a result of this letter? **2.** Paul prefers to come to them in "the gentleness and meekness of Christ" (10:1), and as a loving parent (12:14–15). How will he come, instead, if repentance has not occurred? How does this relate to the ministry of Jesus? **3.** While they have been critical of

Paul's "credentials" as an apostle all along, what does he tell them to do in verse 5? Whether or not they approve of him, what does he pray for them in verses 7–9? **4.** What does he hope for as he considers his upcoming visit (vv. 10–11)? **5.** Considering the problems of this church, how would his benediction in verse 14 be appropriate?

♡ **1.** Misunderstanding gentleness and compassion as negative traits was a real problem in Corinth. How is that same problem true in your community? In your church? **2.** If you were searching for a new pastor or new small group leaders, what leadership profile (modeled by Paul) would you look for? How do you fit that profile? **3.** In which area of your spiritual life will you aim for "perfection" (13:9) this week? In which area will you be content with "weakness" (12:9–10)? How can others pray for and encourage you? **4.** As you leave this last study, give a "benediction" to each other, praying specifically for one another's needs.

we have not failed the test. 7Now we pray to God that you will not
do anything wrong. Not that people will see that we have stood the
test but that you will do what is right even though we may seem to
have failed. 8For we cannot do anything against the truth, but only
for the truth. 9We are glad whenever we are weak but you are
strong; and our prayer is for your perfection. 10This is why I write
these things when I am absent, that when I come I may not have
to be harsh in my use of authority—the authority the Lord gave me
for building you up, not for tearing you down.

Final Greetings

11Finally, brothers, good-by. Aim for perfection, listen to my
appeal, be of one mind, live in peace. And the God of love and
peace will be with you.

12Greet one another with a holy kiss. 13All the saints send their
greetings.

14May the grace of the Lord Jesus Christ, and the love of God,
and the fellowship of the Holy Spirit be with you all.

INTRODUCTION to

GALATIANS

Book Study Outline: If you are using Galatians for a study course, here is a 6- or 12-week outline. Use the margin questions for your group agenda:

start meeting / 15 min.

read & discuss Bible / 30 min.

close meeting / 15–45 min.

Refer to the Questions and Answers in front of Bible for more information.

6-week plan	12-week plan	Group Study Passage
1	1	1:1–10/Paul's Passion
	2	1:11–24/Paul's Call
2	3	2:1–10/Paul's Acceptance
	4	2:11–21/Paul's Gospel
3	5	3:1–14/Faith and the Law
	6	3:15–25/Law and Promise
4	7	3:26–4:7/Sonship and Unity
	8	4:8–20/Joy and Zeal
5	9	4:21–31/Hagar and Sarah
	10	5:1–15/Freedom in Christ
6	11	5:16–26/Life by the Spirit
	12	6:1–18/A New Creation

Author: The apostle Paul.

Date: Two possible dates have been proposed depending upon whether Paul is writing to congregations in North or South Galatia. If the first date is correct (between A.D. 48–50) then this is the earliest surviving letter of Paul. The second date, A.D. 51–53, places this work closer to the writing of Romans with which Galatians shares a close thematic connection.

Theme: Justification by faith alone.

Historical Background: Paul founded the churches in Galatia during his first missionary journey (Ac 13–14). After leaving the area, apparently some Jewish Christians arrived. Accusing Paul of omitting crucial parts of the Gospel, they said that the Galatians needed to submit to Jewish law and customs (such as circumcision) in order to be truly Christian (see also Ac 15). Although Paul was willing to accommodate Jewish sensitivities (Ac 16:3), he vehemently opposed this as a requirement. This letter is a ringing declaration that salvation is God's free gift, and a hard-hitting rejection of any hint that it must—or can—somehow be earned.

Characteristics: Paul's passion for Christ and the Gospel are evident in his anger and surprise at the Galatians' acceptance of these false teachers (1:6–9; 3:1; 5:12). Galatians is like a rough-hewn Romans (see the Introduction to Romans). Whereas the argument for justification by faith in that letter is carefully developed and calmly logical, Galatians is an emotionally charged response to a challenge that Paul felt very deeply.

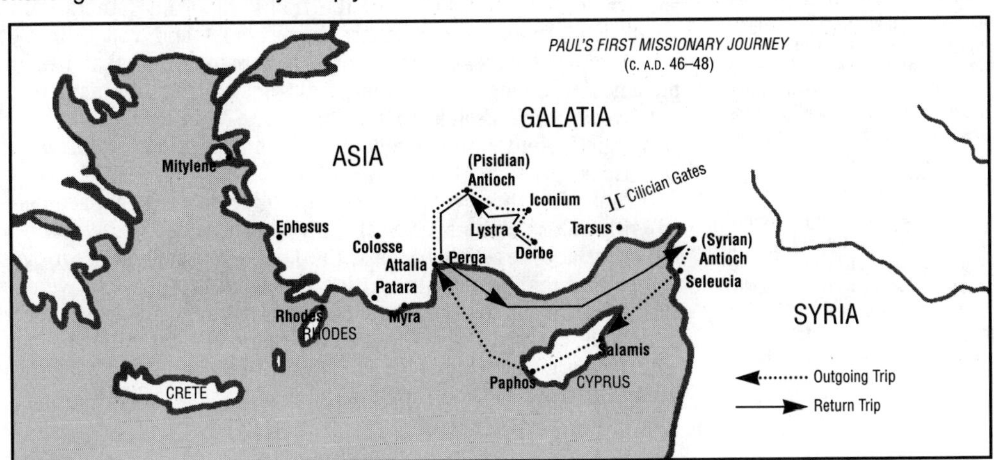

Galatians

In high school, how loyal were your friends? How loyal were you to them?

1. What, according to Paul's claim in verse 1, gives him the right to be heard? **2.** What kind of contrary "gospel" was being preached that led the Galatians astray? (See background in Introduction to Galatians.) How does Paul feel about the Judaizers' message? **3.** What does Paul say will happen to anyone who promotes a "gospel" other than that which he preached—the good news of grace (vv. 8–9)? **4.** What accusation is Paul refuting in verse 10? How does this reflect Jesus' life? How true would this accusation be of you?

Who has been an "apostle Paul" in your life, contributing to your spiritual growth?

---

1. At age 18, what career were you preparing for or starting? How does that relate to your life now? **2.** How important is it to you to consult others on major decisions you make?

1. In a letter of correction like this, how significant is it that Paul still refers to the Galatians as "brothers" (v. 11)? **2.** How was Paul's life changed? **3.** By whom (and what) was Paul called (v. 15)? What was he specifically called to do (v. 16)? **4.** Why did Paul stress the fact that he functioned independently from others? How does that independence relate to Paul's major point here?

1. If you had to argue for the reality of the Gospel by giving one example of how you have changed as a result of your faith, what would you share? **2.** How do you include your personal experience of Christ changing your life in your witness to others?

1 Paul, an apostle—sent not from men nor by man, but by Jesus Christ and God the Father, who raised him from the dead— 2and all the brothers with me,

To the churches in Galatia:

3Grace and peace to you from God our Father and the Lord Jesus Christ, 4who gave himself for our sins to rescue us from the present evil age, according to the will of our God and Father, 5to whom be glory for ever and ever. Amen.

No Other Gospel

6I am astonished that you are so quickly deserting the one who called you by the grace of Christ and are turning to a different gospel— 7which is really no gospel at all. Evidently some people are throwing you into confusion and are trying to pervert the gospel of Christ. 8But even if we or an angel from heaven should preach a gospel other than the one we preached to you, let him be eternally condemned! 9As we have already said, so now I say again: If anybody is preaching to you a gospel other than what you accepted, let him be eternally condemned!

10Am I now trying to win the approval of men, or of God? Or am I trying to please men? If I were still trying to please men, I would not be a servant of Christ.

Paul Called by God

11I want you to know, brothers, that the gospel I preached is not something that man made up. 12I did not receive it from any man, nor was I taught it; rather, I received it by revelation from Jesus Christ.

13For you have heard of my previous way of life in Judaism, how intensely I persecuted the church of God and tried to destroy it. 14I was advancing in Judaism beyond many Jews of my own age and was extremely zealous for the traditions of my fathers. 15But when God, who set me apart from birth[a] and called me by his grace, was pleased 16to reveal his Son in me so that I might preach him among the Gentiles, I did not consult any man, 17nor did I go up to Jerusalem to see those who were apostles before I was, but I went immediately into Arabia and later returned to Damascus.

18Then after three years, I went up to Jerusalem to get acquainted with Peter[b] and stayed with him fifteen days. 19I saw none of the other apostles—only James, the Lord's brother. 20I assure you before God that what I am writing you is no lie. 21Later I went to Syria and Cilicia. 22I was personally unknown to the churches of Judea that are in Christ. 23They only heard the report: "The man who formerly persecuted us is now preaching the faith he once tried to destroy." 24And they praised God because of me.

[a] *15* Or *from my mother's womb* [b] *18* Greek *Cephas*

Paul Accepted by the Apostles

2 Fourteen years later I went up again to Jerusalem, this time with Barnabas. I took Titus along also. [2]I went in response to a revelation and set before them the gospel that I preach among the Gentiles. But I did this privately to those who seemed to be leaders, for fear that I was running or had run my race in vain. [3]Yet not even Titus, who was with me, was compelled to be circumcised, even though he was a Greek. [4]⌞This matter arose⌟ because some false brothers had infiltrated our ranks to spy on the freedom we have in Christ Jesus and to make us slaves. [5]We did not give in to them for a moment, so that the truth of the gospel might remain with you.

[6]As for those who seemed to be important—whatever they were makes no difference to me; God does not judge by external appearance—those men added nothing to my message. [7]On the contrary, they saw that I had been entrusted with the task of preaching the gospel to the Gentiles,[a] just as Peter had been to the Jews.[b] [8]For God, who was at work in the ministry of Peter as an apostle to the Jews, was also at work in my ministry as an apostle to the Gentiles. [9]James, Peter[c] and John, those reputed to be pillars, gave me and Barnabas the right hand of fellowship when they recognized the grace given to me. They agreed that we should go to the Gentiles, and they to the Jews. [10]All they asked was that we should continue to remember the poor, the very thing I was eager to do.

Are you the type of person who usually "goes with the crowd" or "does your own thing"?

1. The "false brothers" had caused some believers to become "slaves" (v. 4). To what? **2.** What was the outcome of this meeting? What did the leaders add to Paul's message (v. 6)? **3.** What did the spiritual "pillars" of the Jerusalem church recognize about Paul (v. 9)? **4.** How is grace the critical issue of Galatians, and this passage in particular? **5.** How does caring for the poor (v. 10) relate to proclaiming the Gospel of grace?

How do you feel when your beliefs are contrary to popular opinion? On what issue do you need to stand alone? How much was at stake—for Paul, and for you now?

Paul Opposes Peter

[11]When Peter came to Antioch, I opposed him to his face, because he was clearly in the wrong. [12]Before certain men came from James, he used to eat with the Gentiles. But when they arrived, he began to draw back and separate himself from the Gentiles because he was afraid of those who belonged to the circumcision group. [13]The other Jews joined him in his hypocrisy, so that by their hypocrisy even Barnabas was led astray.

[14]When I saw that they were not acting in line with the truth of the gospel, I said to Peter in front of them all, "You are a Jew, yet you live like a Gentile and not like a Jew. How is it, then, that you force Gentiles to follow Jewish customs?

[15]"We who are Jews by birth and not 'Gentile sinners' [16]know that a man is not justified by observing the law, but by faith in Jesus Christ. So we, too, have put our faith in Christ Jesus that we may be justified by faith in Christ and not by observing the law, because by observing the law no one will be justified.

[17]"If, while we seek to be justified in Christ, it becomes evident that we ourselves are sinners, does that mean that Christ promotes sin? Absolutely not! [18]If I rebuild what I destroyed, I prove that I am a lawbreaker. [19]For through the law I died to the law so that I might live for God. [20]I have been crucified with Christ and I no longer live, but Christ lives in me. The life I live in the body, I live by faith in the Son of God, who loved me and gave himself for me. [21]I do not set aside the grace of God, for if righteousness could be gained through the law, Christ died for nothing!"[d]

Have you ever "opposed" a boss? What was the outcome?

1. In the past, God had dramatically led Peter to break Jewish custom by fellowshipping and eating with Gentiles (Acts 11:1–18). What causes Peter to reverse course now? **2.** How quickly would you stand up and rebuke the leader of the church (v. 14)? What does this incident say about the need for accountability among believers? **3.** In the Christian life, what dies and what gets resurrected (vv. 19–20)? How is that made possible? **4.** According to verse 21, if you can be in right standing with God through your own efforts—for example, by being a "good person"—what did Christ die for?

1. When are you guilty of double standards? How do you communicate—probably by example—"Do as I say, not as I do"? **2.** How would you explain verse 16 to a non-Christian, particularly one with high moral standards? **3.** Applying the spiritual concept of verse 20, who is "alive" in your life right now—"I," or "Christ in me"? **4.** If you are a self-made person who likes to see everyone pay their own way, how does this Gospel of undeserved grace strike you?

[a]*7* Greek *uncircumcised* [b]*7* Greek *circumcised*; also in verses 8 and 9
[c]*9* Greek *Cephas*; also in verses 11 and 14 [d]*21* Some interpreters end the quotation after verse 14.

When you were dating, were you ever dropped for someone else? What did that do to your emotions?

1. To what extent was the Galatians' conversion experience related to observing the Law? **2.** Why would anyone revert from a liberating spiritual life of faith to a legalistic spiritual life of works and performance? When have you gone in that direction? What caused it to happen? **3.** Was Abraham considered righteous by God through his faith or through his works (vv. 6–9)? **4.** Who are the true children of Abraham? Who is eligible to be one? **5.** How does Jesus solve the problem that no one can earn their right standing with God (vv. 10–14)?

What "additions" to faith might outsiders sense in your Christian circles regarding what they should do to be approved? How can you help break down these barriers?

Faith or Observance of the Law

3 You foolish Galatians! Who has bewitched you? Before your
very eyes Jesus Christ was clearly portrayed as crucified. 2 I
would like to learn just one thing from you: Did you receive the
Spirit by observing the law, or by believing what you heard? 3 Are
you so foolish? After beginning with the Spirit, are you now trying
to attain your goal by human effort? 4 Have you suffered so much for
nothing—if it really was for nothing? 5 Does God give you his Spirit
and work miracles among you because you observe the law, or
because you believe what you heard?

6 Consider Abraham: "He believed God, and it was credited to
him as righteousness."[a] 7 Understand, then, that those who believe are children of Abraham. 8 The Scripture foresaw that God
would justify the Gentiles by faith, and announced the gospel in
advance to Abraham: "All nations will be blessed through you."[b]
9 So those who have faith are blessed along with Abraham, the man
of faith.

10 All who rely on observing the law are under a curse, for it is
written: "Cursed is everyone who does not continue to do everything written in the Book of the Law."[c] 11 Clearly no one is justified before God by the law, because, "The righteous will live by
faith."[d] 12 The law is not based on faith; on the contrary, "The
man who does these things will live by them."[e] 13 Christ redeemed us from the curse of the law by becoming a curse for us,
for it is written: "Cursed is everyone who is hung on a tree."[f]
14 He redeemed us in order that the blessing given to Abraham
might come to the Gentiles through Christ Jesus, so that by faith
we might receive the promise of the Spirit.

When you think of babysitters you had growing up, who comes to mind? How did you feel about that person?

1. In what way is a human covenant—a will—like God's covenant-promise with Abraham and his seed (vv. 15–16)? **2.** Who is the Seed through whom the promise to Abraham will be fulfilled? **3.** Since the Law was not to take the place of the promise, what was its purpose? Was it temporary or permanent? **4.** Can the Law give "life" (v. 21)? How (v. 22)? **5.** How is attempting to be right with God through keeping the Law like being in prison (v. 23)? Like having a babysitter (vv. 24–25)?

1. How would you share this passage with someone who thinks keeping the Ten Commandments or Golden Rule is enough to be right with God? Or to someone who was brought up believing that keeping rules wins approval? **2.** How has, and is, your faith liberating you from spiritual bondage?

The Law and the Promise

15 Brothers, let me take an example from everyday life. Just as no
one can set aside or add to a human covenant that has been duly
established, so it is in this case. 16 The promises were spoken to
Abraham and to his seed. The Scripture does not say "and to
seeds," meaning many people, but "and to your seed,"[g] meaning
one person, who is Christ. 17 What I mean is this: The law, introduced 430 years later, does not set aside the covenant previously
established by God and thus do away with the promise. 18 For if the
inheritance depends on the law, then it no longer depends on a
promise; but God in his grace gave it to Abraham through a promise.

19 What, then, was the purpose of the law? It was added because
of transgressions until the Seed to whom the promise referred had
come. The law was put into effect through angels by a mediator.
20 A mediator, however, does not represent just one party; but God
is one.

21 Is the law, therefore, opposed to the promises of God? Absolutely not! For if a law had been given that could impart life, then
righteousness would certainly have come by the law. 22 But the
Scripture declares that the whole world is a prisoner of sin, so that
what was promised, being given through faith in Jesus Christ,
might be given to those who believe.

23 Before this faith came, we were held prisoners by the law,
locked up until faith should be revealed. 24 So the law was put in
charge to lead us to Christ[h] that we might be justified by faith.

[a] *6* Gen. 15:6 [b] *8* Gen. 12:3; 18:18; 22:18 [c] *10* Deut. 27:26 [d] *11* Hab. 2:4 [e] *12* Lev. 18:5 [f] *13* Deut. 21:23 [g] *16* Gen. 12:7; 13:15; 24:7 [h] *24* Or *charge until Christ came*

[25]Now that faith has come, we are no longer under the supervision
of the law.

Sons of God

[26]You are all sons of God through faith in Christ Jesus, [27]for all of
you who were baptized into Christ have clothed yourselves with
Christ. [28]There is neither Jew nor Greek, slave nor free, male nor
female, for you are all one in Christ Jesus. [29]If you belong to Christ,
then you are Abraham's seed, and heirs according to the promise.
4 What I am saying is that as long as the heir is a child, he is no
different from a slave, although he owns the whole estate. [2]He
is subject to guardians and trustees until the time set by his father.
[3]So also, when we were children, we were in slavery under the
basic principles of the world. [4]But when the time had fully come,
God sent his Son, born of a woman, born under law, [5]to redeem
those under law, that we might receive the full rights of sons.
[6]Because you are sons, God sent the Spirit of his Son into our
hearts, the Spirit who calls out, *"Abba,*[a] Father." [7]So you are no
longer a slave, but a son; and since you are a son, God has made
you also an heir.

Paul's Concern for the Galatians

[8]Formerly, when you did not know God, you were slaves to
those who by nature are not gods. [9]But now that you know God—
or rather are known by God—how is it that you are turning back to
those weak and miserable principles? Do you wish to be enslaved
by them all over again? [10]You are observing special days and
months and seasons and years! [11]I fear for you, that somehow I
have wasted my efforts on you.

[12]I plead with you, brothers, become like me, for I became like
you. You have done me no wrong. [13]As you know, it was because
of an illness that I first preached the gospel to you. [14]Even though
my illness was a trial to you, you did not treat me with contempt or
scorn. Instead, you welcomed me as if I were an angel of God, as if
I were Christ Jesus himself. [15]What has happened to all your joy? I
can testify that, if you could have done so, you would have torn out
your eyes and given them to me. [16]Have I now become your enemy
by telling you the truth?

[17]Those people are zealous to win you over, but for no good.
What they want is to alienate you ⌊from us⌋, so that you may be
zealous for them. [18]It is fine to be zealous, provided the purpose is
good, and to be so always and not just when I am with you. [19]My
dear children, for whom I am again in the pains of childbirth until
Christ is formed in you, [20]how I wish I could be with you now and
change my tone, because I am perplexed about you!

Hagar and Sarah

[21]Tell me, you who want to be under the law, are you not aware
of what the law says? [22]For it is written that Abraham had two
sons, one by the slave woman and the other by the free woman.
[23]His son by the slave woman was born in the ordinary way; but
his son by the free woman was born as the result of a promise.

[24]These things may be taken figuratively, for the women represent two covenants. One covenant is from Mount Sinai and bears
children who are to be slaves: This is Hagar. [25]Now Hagar stands
for Mount Sinai in Arabia and corresponds to the present city of
Jerusalem, because she is in slavery with her children. [26]But the

[a]6 Aramaic for *Father*

How affectionate was, or is, your relationship with your parents?

1. What effect does being "in Christ" have on relationships among believers (3:28)? **2.** How is being under the Law like being an heir who is still a minor (4:1–3)? How has Jesus changed all that?

1. What are some social and cultural barriers in our time? How can you increase the sense of oneness in Christ in your "world"? **2.** How affectionate is your relationship with God?

How much joy did you have in the beginning phase of your Christian life?

1. Prior to their conversion, the Galatians worshiped pagan gods. How are they now doing the same with Jewish observances? **2.** What is the difference between celebrating religious holidays (Christmas, Easter) and what the Galatians were doing? **3.** Overall, was Paul more concerned for himself or the Galatians?

1. How has your relationship with God changed from being one based on zealous love and trust to one based on performance and keeping the rules? **2.** Have you slipped back into any bad habits or old ways, from which Christ once delivered you? What can you do about it?

What story do (or did) your parents tell about your birth?

1. What do you remember about the story in Genesis of Hagar and Sarah and their sons—Ishmael and Isaac (Ge 16,17,21)? What was extraordinary about Isaac's birth? **2.** Normally, the Jews would regard Sarah as their spiritual mother and Hagar as the mother of the Gentiles. Why does Paul turn the tables and indicate that the Jews are actually the ones in slavery with Hagar (v. 25)? **3.** How does verse 30 give a stern warning to the Judaizers?

Are you living like a "child of the free woman"—liberated from the bondage of trying to win God's approval? How can you live out your "freedom" in Christ, and still please him with your sacrificial obedience?

How do you feel and react when others cut in on you while driving, shopping, speaking, waiting in line, etc.?

1. What does Paul mean by a "yoke of slavery" (v. 1)? **2.** Is circumcision wrong in and of itself, or only if it is a symbol of the "yoke of slavery"? **3.** Since our own efforts and achievements aren't the way to God, what is (vv. 5–6)? **4.** How is Paul's call to serve one another in love (vv. 13–15) reconcilable with his own attitude toward the Judaizers (especially in v. 12)? How good is Paul at demonstrating "tough love"?

1. How have you seen Christian freedom abused? How do verses 6 and 13 address those who think their freedom in Christ allows them to do anything they want? How do they challenge you? **2.** In the past, who or what has cut in and side-tracked you from a child-like faith "expressing itself through love"?

On a scale of 0 to 10, how many "wild oats" did you sow in your youth?

1. Paul has warned the Galatians about being enslaved to legalism. What does he warn them about being enslaved to in this passage? **2.** What two things are in conflict (v. 17)? **3.** If we were made alive by the Spirit, why do we still struggle with sin? How are we "led by" the Spirit? **4.** Is Paul condemning everyone who sins, or those whose sin is part of their lifestyle?

Jerusalem that is above is free, and she is our mother. 27For it is
written:

> "Be glad, O barren woman,
> who bears no children;
> break forth and cry aloud,
> you who have no labor pains;
> because more are the children of the desolate
> woman
> than of her who has a husband."[a]

28Now you, brothers, like Isaac, are children of promise. 29At
that time the son born in the ordinary way persecuted the son born
by the power of the Spirit. It is the same now. 30But what does the
Scripture say? "Get rid of the slave woman and her son, for the
slave woman's son will never share in the inheritance with the free
woman's son."[b] 31Therefore, brothers, we are not children of the
slave woman, but of the free woman.

Freedom in Christ

5 It is for freedom that Christ has set us free. Stand firm, then,
and do not let yourselves be burdened again by a yoke of
slavery.

2Mark my words! I, Paul, tell you that if you let yourselves be
circumcised, Christ will be of no value to you at all. 3Again I
declare to every man who lets himself be circumcised that he is
obligated to obey the whole law. 4You who are trying to be justified
by law have been alienated from Christ; you have fallen away from
grace. 5But by faith we eagerly await through the Spirit the righteousness for which we hope. 6For in Christ Jesus neither circumcision nor uncircumcision has any value. The only thing that
counts is faith expressing itself through love.

7You were running a good race. Who cut in on you and kept you
from obeying the truth? 8That kind of persuasion does not come
from the one who calls you. 9"A little yeast works through the
whole batch of dough." 10I am confident in the Lord that you will
take no other view. The one who is throwing you into confusion
will pay the penalty, whoever he may be. 11Brothers, if I am still
preaching circumcision, why am I still being persecuted? In that
case the offense of the cross has been abolished. 12As for those
agitators, I wish they would go the whole way and emasculate
themselves!

13You, my brothers, were called to be free. But do not use your
freedom to indulge the sinful nature[c]; rather, serve one another
in love. 14The entire law is summed up in a single command: "Love
your neighbor as yourself."[d] 15If you keep on biting and devouring
each other, watch out or you will be destroyed by each other.

Life by the Spirit

16So I say, live by the Spirit, and you will not gratify the desires
of the sinful nature. 17For the sinful nature desires what is contrary
to the Spirit, and the Spirit what is contrary to the sinful nature.
They are in conflict with each other, so that you do not do what
you want. 18But if you are led by the Spirit, you are not under law.

19The acts of the sinful nature are obvious: sexual immorality,
impurity and debauchery; 20idolatry and witchcraft; hatred, dis-
cord, jealousy, fits of rage, selfish ambition, dissensions, factions
21and envy; drunkenness, orgies, and the like. I warn you, as I did

[a] *27* Isaiah 54:1 [b] *30* Gen. 21:10 [c] *13* Or *the flesh*; also in verses 16, 17, 19 and 24 [d] *14* Lev. 19:18

before, that those who live like this will not inherit the kingdom of God.

22But the fruit of the Spirit is love, joy, peace, patience, kindness, goodness, faithfulness, 23gentleness and self-control. Against such things there is no law. 24Those who belong to Christ Jesus have crucified the sinful nature with its passions and desires. 25Since we live by the Spirit, let us keep in step with the Spirit. 26Let us not become conceited, provoking and envying each other.

Doing Good to All

6 Brothers, if someone is caught in a sin, you who are spiritual should restore him gently. But watch yourself, or you also may be tempted. 2Carry each other's burdens, and in this way you will fulfill the law of Christ. 3If anyone thinks he is something when he is nothing, he deceives himself. 4Each one should test his own actions. Then he can take pride in himself, without comparing himself to somebody else, 5for each one should carry his own load.

6Anyone who receives instruction in the word must share all good things with his instructor.

7Do not be deceived: God cannot be mocked. A man reaps what he sows. 8The one who sows to please his sinful nature, from that nature[a] will reap destruction; the one who sows to please the Spirit, from the Spirit will reap eternal life. 9Let us not become weary in doing good, for at the proper time we will reap a harvest if we do not give up. 10Therefore, as we have opportunity, let us do good to all people, especially to those who belong to the family of believers.

Not Circumcision but a New Creation

11See what large letters I use as I write to you with my own hand!

12Those who want to make a good impression outwardly are trying to compel you to be circumcised. The only reason they do this is to avoid being persecuted for the cross of Christ. 13Not even those who are circumcised obey the law, yet they want you to be circumcised that they may boast about your flesh. 14May I never boast except in the cross of our Lord Jesus Christ, through which[b] the world has been crucified to me, and I to the world. 15Neither circumcision nor uncircumcision means anything; what counts is a new creation. 16Peace and mercy to all who follow this rule, even to the Israel of God.

17Finally, let no one cause me trouble, for I bear on my body the marks of Jesus.

18The grace of our Lord Jesus Christ be with your spirit, brothers. Amen.

[a]*8* Or *his flesh, from the flesh* [b]*14* Or *whom*

---

1. Is the crucifixion of the sinful nature done *to* or *by* the Christian? **2.** What sinful acts are dead and buried in your life? Alive and well? **3.** Which spiritual fruit is blossoming in your life? Which are still in the bud?

What kind of garden have you tended? What did you enjoy about it? What did you dread?

1. How do verses 1–2 illustrate ways of helping someone to "keep in step with the Spirit" (5:25)? What is the "law of Christ" (see 5:14)? **2.** How can you restore a brother caught in sin, and avoid feeling superior to him or being victimized by it yourself? **3.** How does verse 5 relate to verse 2? Are they contradictory? (The word "load" in verse 5 does not mean a crushing burden, but rather a small, individual pack.) What sort of burdens do your friends or family carry? How do you (or could you) help them with these burdens? **4.** What is the main point of Paul's teaching on the Spirit-filled life (vv. 7–10)? Where in your life do you need to sow to please the Spirit instead of your sinful nature? **5.** How does Paul sum up the motives of the false teachers (vv. 12–13)? His own motives (v. 14)? **6.** Is your concern for creating a good outward impression greater or lesser than it used to be? Why? **7.** Why does Paul call these Gentile Galatians the "Israel of God" (v. 16; see 3:6–9)? How is that a final rebuke to those who would compel these believers to obey Jewish rules? **8.** What does Paul mean by bearing on his body the marks of Jesus (v. 17; see 2Co 11:23–30)? Why would Paul's willingness to suffer be a further rebuke to the false teachers? Do you bear any "marks of Jesus"?

1. As you reflect on what you have sown this year, what harvest are you expecting: Weeds? A bumper crop? Spindly plants? Why? **2.** In what ways do people tamper with the Gospel to make it less offensive to others? Have you been tempted to do so? **3.** In what way has God greatly inspired or convicted you through your study of Galatians? **4.** How has your group contributed to what God has done in your life through this study?

INTRODUCTION to

EPHESIANS

Book Study Outline: If you are using Ephesians for a study course, here is a 6- or 11-week outline. Use the margin questions for your group agenda:

start meeting / 15 min.

read & discuss Bible / 30 min.

close meeting / 15–45 min.

Refer to the Questions and Answers in front of Bible for more information.

6-week plan	11-week plan	Group Study Passage
1	1	1:1–14/To God Be the Glory!
	2	1:15–23/Fullness of Christ
2	3	2:1–10/Raised Up With Christ
	4	2:11–22/End of Hostility
3	5	3:1–13/Mystery of Grace
	6	3:14–21/Power to Know Love
4	7	4:1–16/Working Out Our Unity
	8	4:17–32/Children of Light
5	9	5:1–21/Imitators of God
	10	5:22–6:9/Relationships in Christ
6	11	6:10–24/Armor of God

Author: The apostle Paul.

Date: Probably in the early A.D. 60s.

Theme: God's new society.

Historical Background: Ephesians, Colossians and Philemon were all written from prison at about the same time. Because over half of the verses in this letter are found in Colossians, it seems that Paul first developed these themes in that letter while dealing with a local problem, and then expanded them into a more universal setting for this one. It is unclear which imprisonment produced these letters (see 2Co 11:23), but most likely Paul was at Rome (Ac 28).

Characteristics: In this letter, Paul takes us to the mountaintops of Christian truth and invites us to look at the breathtaking view! When we do so, we see that it is Jesus Christ who dominates that view. We see him breaking down the wall between God and humanity. We see him subduing the hostile cosmic powers. We see him creating the church, a new social order of love and unity that transcends the racial, ethnic and social distinctions between people. In conveying this vision, Paul reaches into eternity past and eternity future to demonstrate how God, out of his love and glory, calls people to be reconciled to himself and to one another through the cross of Christ. The cross provides forgiveness of sins, a new life and a new people. Between Paul's greeting (1:1–2) and salutation (6:21–24), the letter divides easily into two parts. Part one (ch. 1–3) focuses on *doctrine*, specifically, the new life and new society God has created through Jesus. Part two (ch. 4–6) focuses on *ethics*, specifically, the new standards and new relationships expected of believers.

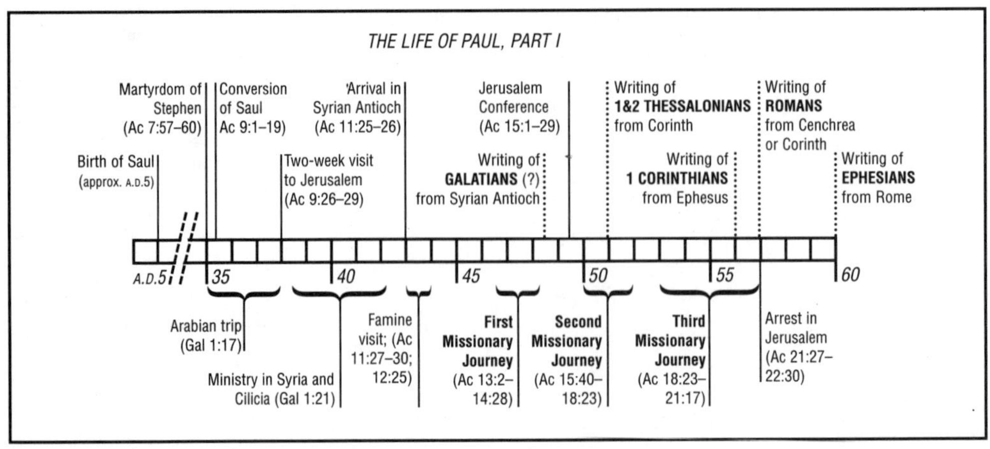

Ephesians

1 Paul, an apostle of Christ Jesus by the will of God,

To the saints in Ephesus,[a] the faithful[b] in Christ Jesus:

2Grace and peace to you from God our Father and the Lord Jesus Christ.

Whom do you know who has been adopted?

1. The large capital city of Ephesus was a center for trade. It featured the renowned Temple of Artemis. In this letter, what does Paul write about that is truly wonderful? **2.** In your words, describe the "blessings in Christ" (vv. 3–9). **3.** What are seven things that God has done for us, starting in verse 4? **4.** How does being chosen by God (v. 4) relate to our believing and salvation (v. 13)?

1. When did you come to appreciate all that God has done for you in Jesus Christ? **2.** How do you know if you are "chosen"? How does knowing you are adopted change your view of yourself and God? **3.** How do you feel about the quality of love of the One who has chosen you? How does this affect your love for others?

Spiritual Blessings in Christ

3Praise be to the God and Father of our Lord Jesus Christ, who has blessed us in the heavenly realms with every spiritual blessing in Christ. 4For he chose us in him before the creation of the world to be holy and blameless in his sight. In love 5he[c] predestined us to be adopted as his sons through Jesus Christ, in accordance with his pleasure and will— 6to the praise of his glorious grace, which he has freely given us in the One he loves. 7In him we have redemption through his blood, the forgiveness of sins, in accordance with the riches of God's grace 8that he lavished on us with all wisdom and understanding. 9And he[d] made known to us the mystery of his will according to his good pleasure, which he purposed in Christ, 10to be put into effect when the times will have reached their fulfillment—to bring all things in heaven and on earth together under one head, even Christ.

11In him we were also chosen,[e] having been predestined according to the plan of him who works out everything in conformity with the purpose of his will, 12in order that we, who were the first to hope in Christ, might be for the praise of his glory. 13And you also were included in Christ when you heard the word of truth, the gospel of your salvation. Having believed, you were marked in him with a seal, the promised Holy Spirit, 14who is a deposit guaranteeing our inheritance until the redemption of those who are God's possession—to the praise of his glory.

What do you remember from your childhood about Thanksgiving Day? Who keeps your family traditions alive now?

1. If the Christians in Ephesus were millionaires in Christ spiritually, what was wrong with them? How were they living? **2.** In your own words, what does Paul pray for the Ephesians? **3.** When a Christian plugs into God's energy source, what kind of power can be expected? **4.** How does Jesus give hope and power?

1. How would you change if your group prayed verses 17–19 every week for each other? Try it and see. **2.** How much of God's energy are you using at the moment? God put into your bank account all of his resources. What is keeping you from transferring them into your checking account?

Thanksgiving and Prayer

15For this reason, ever since I heard about your faith in the Lord Jesus and your love for all the saints, 16I have not stopped giving thanks for you, remembering you in my prayers. 17I keep asking that the God of our Lord Jesus Christ, the glorious Father, may give you the Spirit[f] of wisdom and revelation, so that you may know him better. 18I pray also that the eyes of your heart may be enlightened in order that you may know the hope to which he has called you, the riches of his glorious inheritance in the saints, 19and his incomparably great power for us who believe. That power is like the working of his mighty strength, 20which he exerted in Christ when he raised him from the dead and seated him at his right hand in the heavenly realms, 21far above all rule and authority, power and dominion, and every title that can be given, not only in the present age but also in the one to come. 22And God placed all things under his feet and appointed him to be head over everything for the church, 23which is his body, the fullness of him who fills everything in every way.

[a] *1* Some early manuscripts do not have *in Ephesus.* [b] *1* Or *believers who are*
[c] *4,5* Or *sight in love. 5He* [d] *8,9* Or *us. With all wisdom and understanding, 9he*
[e] *11* Or *were made heirs* [f] *17* Or *a spirit*

What special gift have you received recently?

1. Paul divides your life into two periods. What are they? Who owned you in the first period? What was the result? **2.** For what purpose did God take over your life? **3.** What is the difference between cosmetic surgery (to remove wrinkles) and the surgery God performs? **4.** Is a Christian ever completely rid of the cravings of the past—lust, selfishness, pride, etc.?

What in your life is due only to God's presence and goodness?

Made Alive in Christ

2 As for you, you were dead in your transgressions and sins, 2 in which you used to live when you followed the ways of this world and of the ruler of the kingdom of the air, the spirit who is now at work in those who are disobedient. 3 All of us also lived among them at one time, gratifying the cravings of our sinful nature[a] and following its desires and thoughts. Like the rest, we were by nature objects of wrath. 4 But because of his great love for us, God, who is rich in mercy, 5 made us alive with Christ even when we were dead in transgressions—it is by grace you have been saved. 6 And God raised us up with Christ and seated us with him in the heavenly realms in Christ Jesus, 7 in order that in the coming ages he might show the incomparable riches of his grace, expressed in his kindness to us in Christ Jesus. 8 For it is by grace you have been saved, through faith—and this not from yourselves, it is the gift of God— 9 not by works, so that no one can boast. 10 For we are God's workmanship, created in Christ Jesus to do good works, which God prepared in advance for us to do.

From where did your ancestors emigrate? What did their new citizenship mean to them?

1. What is the problem in this church? Who are the "in" people? Who are the "out" people? **2.** How did God resolve this problem (v. 13)? **3.** What is the difference between Hitler's "superior race" and Paul's idea of "one body"? How has your life changed through this "one body"(v. 16)? **4.** How do you think the practicing Jews felt when these Gentiles started coming to their church, but didn't want to adopt the Jewish custom of circumcision?

1. If Paul wrote a letter to your church today, what stand would he take on issues that threaten to tear the church apart? **2.** What relationship in your life still has walls to be knocked down?

One in Christ

11 Therefore, remember that formerly you who are Gentiles by birth and called "uncircumcised" by those who call themselves "the circumcision" (that done in the body by the hands of men)— 12 remember that at that time you were separate from Christ, excluded from citizenship in Israel and foreigners to the covenants of the promise, without hope and without God in the world. 13 But now in Christ Jesus you who once were far away have been brought near through the blood of Christ.

14 For he himself is our peace, who has made the two one and has destroyed the barrier, the dividing wall of hostility, 15 by abolishing in his flesh the law with its commandments and regulations. His purpose was to create in himself one new man out of the two, thus making peace, 16 and in this one body to reconcile both of them to God through the cross, by which he put to death their hostility. 17 He came and preached peace to you who were far away and peace to those who were near. 18 For through him we both have access to the Father by one Spirit.

19 Consequently, you are no longer foreigners and aliens, but fellow citizens with God's people and members of God's household, 20 built on the foundation of the apostles and prophets, with Christ Jesus himself as the chief cornerstone. 21 In him the whole building is joined together and rises to become a holy temple in the Lord. 22 And in him you too are being built together to become a dwelling in which God lives by his Spirit.

Who is your favorite mystery writer? What is a favorite mystery movie?

1. What exactly is the mystery Paul is talking about? What does Paul have to do with this mystery? Where does the church come in? **2.** When did this mystery take on meaning in your life? **3.** Is Paul being hard on himself in verse 8, or just appropriately humble? Why? **4.** How would you compare Paul's passion to share this mystery to your own passion?

Paul the Preacher to the Gentiles

3 For this reason I, Paul, the prisoner of Christ Jesus for the sake of you Gentiles—

2 Surely you have heard about the administration of God's grace that was given to me for you, 3 that is, the mystery made known to me by revelation, as I have already written briefly. 4 In reading this, then, you will be able to understand my insight into the mystery of Christ, 5 which was not made known to men in other generations as it has now been revealed by the Spirit to God's holy apostles and prophets. 6 This mystery is that through the gospel the Gentiles are heirs together with Israel, members together of one body, and sharers together in the promise in Christ Jesus.

[a] 3 Or *our flesh*

7I became a servant of this gospel by the gift of God's grace given
me through the working of his power. 8Although I am less than the
least of all God's people, this grace was given me: to preach to the
Gentiles the unsearchable riches of Christ, 9and to make plain to
everyone the administration of this mystery, which for ages past
was kept hidden in God, who created all things. 10His intent was
that now, through the church, the manifold wisdom of God should
be made known to the rulers and authorities in the heavenly
realms, 11according to his eternal purpose which he accomplished
in Christ Jesus our Lord. 12In him and through faith in him we may
approach God with freedom and confidence. 13I ask you, therefore,
not to be discouraged because of my sufferings for you, which are
your glory.

A Prayer for the Ephesians

14For this reason I kneel before the Father, 15from whom his
whole family[a] in heaven and on earth derives its name. 16I pray
that out of his glorious riches he may strengthen you with power
through his Spirit in your inner being, 17so that Christ may dwell
in your hearts through faith. And I pray that you, being rooted and
established in love, 18may have power, together with all the saints,
to grasp how wide and long and high and deep is the love of Christ,
19and to know this love that surpasses knowledge—that you may
be filled to the measure of all the fullness of God.

20Now to him who is able to do immeasurably more than all we
ask or imagine, according to his power that is at work within us,
21to him be glory in the church and in Christ Jesus throughout all
generations, for ever and ever! Amen.

Unity in the Body of Christ

4 As a prisoner for the Lord, then, I urge you to live a life worthy
of the calling you have received. 2Be completely humble and
gentle; be patient, bearing with one another in love. 3Make every
effort to keep the unity of the Spirit through the bond of peace.
4There is one body and one Spirit— just as you were called to one
hope when you were called— 5one Lord, one faith, one baptism;
6one God and Father of all, who is over all and through all and in
all.

7But to each one of us grace has been given as Christ appor-
tioned it. 8This is why it[b] says:

> "When he ascended on high,
> he led captives in his train
> and gave gifts to men."[c]

9(What does "he ascended" mean except that he also descended to
the lower, earthly regions[d]? 10He who descended is the very one
who ascended higher than all the heavens, in order to fill the
whole universe.) 11It was he who gave some to be apostles, some
to be prophets, some to be evangelists, and some to be pastors and
teachers, 12to prepare God's people for works of service, so that the
body of Christ may be built up 13until we all reach unity in the
faith and in the knowledge of the Son of God and become mature,
attaining to the whole measure of the fullness of Christ.

14Then we will no longer be infants, tossed back and forth by the
waves, and blown here and there by every wind of teaching and by
the cunning and craftiness of men in their deceitful scheming.

[a] *15* Or *whom all fatherhood* [b] *8* Or *God* [c] *8* Psalm 68:18 [d] *9* Or *the depths of the earth*

5. How would you explain the way one can know God (2:18; 3:12)?

1. If Paul lived in your community, who in particular would he go after for Christ? **2.** Where does the unifying Gospel (v. 6) challenge you: e.g. issues of racism? Sexism? Missions? Concern for the poor and elderly? **3.** Where is God calling you to be an ambassador for him? Why has he chosen you?

---

1. What is Paul asking God to do? **2.** In this passage, who is the lover? Who is being loved? **3.** When have you felt overwhelmed by the love of God?

1. If a person knew only rejection and pain in their relationships, how can this person come to understand the love of God in a personal way? **2.** What does the promise in verse 20 mean? How have you seen it to be true?

What is your favorite team sport?

1. Would you say this church has more "servants" or more "masters"? What's wrong? From some of the things that Paul says, what are they doing? Not doing? **2.** How do the qualities in verses 2 and 3 promote unity? How does viewing God as our Father add to our unity? **3.** What does Paul recommend in verse 11? How would he go about building a successful management team? What would be the goal? **4.** If Paul were a management consultant appraising the productivity in the church today, what would he say? How would he go about changing things?

1. Are you living up to the "calling you have received" (v. 1)? In your work? Your home? Your relationships? Why or why not? **2.** Of the four jobs he describes for a management team, which job would you choose based on your understanding of your gifts: apostle (pioneer and church planter), prophet (motivator and encourager), evangelist (soul winner) or pastor/teacher (trainer and coach)? How can you develop this

[15]Instead, speaking the truth in love, we will in all things grow up into him who is the Head, that is, Christ. [16]From him the whole body, joined and held together by every supporting ligament, grows and builds itself up in love, as each part does its work.

Living as Children of Light

[17]So I tell you this, and insist on it in the Lord, that you must no longer live as the Gentiles do, in the futility of their thinking. [18]They are darkened in their understanding and separated from the life of God because of the ignorance that is in them due to the hardening of their hearts. [19]Having lost all sensitivity, they have given themselves over to sensuality so as to indulge in every kind of impurity, with a continual lust for more.

[20]You, however, did not come to know Christ that way. [21]Surely you heard of him and were taught in him in accordance with the truth that is in Jesus. [22]You were taught, with regard to your former way of life, to put off your old self, which is being corrupted by its deceitful desires; [23]to be made new in the attitude of your minds; [24]and to put on the new self, created to be like God in true righteousness and holiness.

[25]Therefore each of you must put off falsehood and speak truthfully to his neighbor, for we are all members of one body. [26]"In your anger do not sin"[a]: Do not let the sun go down while you are still angry, [27]and do not give the devil a foothold. [28]He who has been stealing must steal no longer, but must work, doing something useful with his own hands, that he may have something to share with those in need.

[29]Do not let any unwholesome talk come out of your mouths, but only what is helpful for building others up according to their needs, that it may benefit those who listen. [30]And do not grieve the Holy Spirit of God, with whom you were sealed for the day of redemption. [31]Get rid of all bitterness, rage and anger, brawling and slander, along with every form of malice. [32]Be kind and compassionate to one another, forgiving each other, just as in Christ God forgave you.

5 Be imitators of God, therefore, as dearly loved children [2]and live a life of love, just as Christ loved us and gave himself up for us as a fragrant offering and sacrifice to God.

[3]But among you there must not be even a hint of sexual immorality, or of any kind of impurity, or of greed, because these are improper for God's holy people. [4]Nor should there be obscenity, foolish talk or coarse joking, which are out of place, but rather thanksgiving. [5]For of this you can be sure: No immoral, impure or greedy person—such a man is an idolater—has any inheritance in the kingdom of Christ and of God.[b] [6]Let no one deceive you with empty words, for because of such things God's wrath comes on those who are disobedient. [7]Therefore do not be partners with them.

[8]For you were once darkness, but now you are light in the Lord. Live as children of light [9](for the fruit of the light consists in all goodness, righteousness and truth) [10]and find out what pleases the Lord. [11]Have nothing to do with the fruitless deeds of darkness, but rather expose them. [12]For it is shameful even to mention what the disobedient do in secret. [13]But everything exposed by the light becomes visible, [14]for it is light that makes everything visible. This is why it is said:

[a]*26* Psalm 4:4 [b]*5* Or *kingdom of the Christ and God*

gift? **3.** Are you more likely to "speak the truth" or "in love" try to keep the peace at any price? To achieve a balance, what do you need to learn?

What is the best piece of clothing you have had for years and can't seem to discard?

1. According to verses 17–19, how do the mind, heart and conscience influence the actions of non-believers? How are Christians to deal with these realities? **2.** How does Paul describe the behavior of the "old" self? The "new" self? **3.** How would you compare moral standards today with the moral standards in Paul's day? **4.** How do you go about "putting off" and "putting on"? Can the Christian ever attain a complete transformation in this life?

1. What are the positive and/or negative motivations which prompt you to live a Christian life? Where do you feel you are making progress in your Christian life? **2.** Of the challenges Paul gives to the Christian in the last two paragraphs, what are the top two you need to work on?

Did you ever get your mouth washed out with soap? What were your parents' rules about language in your home?

1. Ephesus was known for sexual immorality. The Temple of Diana had 300 prostitutes. Sexual pleasure was part of the "religion" of the city. How does the apostle Paul confront this pagan culture? **2.** What is the standard Paul sets for Christians in verses 1 and 8? What does verse 6 say about resisting "peer pressure"? **3.** What is the difference between "foolish talk or coarse joking" (v. 4) and a good belly-laugh? Between the "fruitless deeds of darkness" (v. 11) and good clean fun? **4.** What contrasts does Paul draw between the old and the new life in verses 15–21? What sights, sounds, feelings, attitudes and actions define this new life?

"Wake up, O sleeper,
rise from the dead,
and Christ will shine on you."

15 Be very careful, then, how you live—not as unwise but as wise, 16 making the most of every opportunity, because the days are evil. 17 Therefore do not be foolish, but understand what the Lord's will is. 18 Do not get drunk on wine, which leads to debauchery. Instead, be filled with the Spirit. 19 Speak to one another with psalms, hymns and spiritual songs. Sing and make music in your heart to the Lord, 20 always giving thanks to God the Father for everything, in the name of our Lord Jesus Christ.

21 Submit to one another out of reverence for Christ.

Wives and Husbands

22 Wives, submit to your husbands as to the Lord. 23 For the husband is the head of the wife as Christ is the head of the church, his body, of which he is the Savior. 24 Now as the church submits to Christ, so also wives should submit to their husbands in everything.

25 Husbands, love your wives, just as Christ loved the church and gave himself up for her 26 to make her holy, cleansing[a] her by the washing with water through the word, 27 and to present her to himself as a radiant church, without stain or wrinkle or any other blemish, but holy and blameless. 28 In this same way, husbands ought to love their wives as their own bodies. He who loves his wife loves himself. 29 After all, no one ever hated his own body, but he feeds and cares for it, just as Christ does the church— 30 for we are members of his body. 31 "For this reason a man will leave his father and mother and be united to his wife, and the two will become one flesh."[b] 32 This is a profound mystery—but I am talking about Christ and the church. 33 However, each one of you also must love his wife as he loves himself, and the wife must respect her husband.

Children and Parents

6 Children, obey your parents in the Lord, for this is right. 2 "Honor your father and mother"—which is the first commandment with a promise— 3 "that it may go well with you and that you may enjoy long life on the earth."[c]

4 Fathers, do not exasperate your children; instead, bring them up in the training and instruction of the Lord.

Slaves and Masters

5 Slaves, obey your earthly masters with respect and fear, and with sincerity of heart, just as you would obey Christ. 6 Obey them not only to win their favor when their eye is on you, but like slaves of Christ, doing the will of God from your heart. 7 Serve wholeheartedly, as if you were serving the Lord, not men, 8 because you know that the Lord will reward everyone for whatever good he does, whether he is slave or free.

9 And masters, treat your slaves in the same way. Do not threaten them, since you know that he who is both their Master and yours is in heaven, and there is no favoritism with him.

The Armor of God

10 Finally, be strong in the Lord and in his mighty power. 11 Put on the full armor of God so that you can take your stand against the

[a] 26 Or *having cleansed* [b] 31 Gen. 2:24 [c] 3 Deut. 5:16

---

1. As you look back over your life since becoming a Christian, what positive changes have you seen in your motives and desires? **2.** As you compare the life that you lived *before* Christ to the life you live *today*, where have you seen the greatest change? In your language? Your desires? Your values? The way you treat your spouse? Your children?

Which of these TV families reflects your family: Cleavers? Flintstones? Bradys? Huxtables? Waltons? Simpsons?

1. How do verses 18–21, on the Holy Spirit's infilling, affect your attitude toward these verses on submission? **2.** In the culture of his day—which addressed women through their husbands, and by Jewish law termed a woman a "thing"—would Paul be considered a "chauvinist" or a "radical feminist"? **3.** Christ's love led him to *die* for us. What would it mean for a husband to *live* with his wife with this type of love (vv. 25–33)? How did Christ act out his headship? **4.** How did your parents approach marriage? Two masters? Two servants? One master, one servant? What is the goal of Christian marriage (v. 31)? What role does sex play? **5.** What does it mean to "honor your parents"? To bring up children in the Lord without exasperating them? **6.** If you work for someone, how are you to look upon your job? If you are the boss, how are you to look upon your employees? Can you hold to these principles today in your business and still make it?

1. What does a wife do when the husband does not take spiritual leadership? **2.** Whom do you look up to as a good role model for marriage? **3.** What is God saying to you about your spouse? Family?

What were some of your (or your kids') favorite dress-up costumes? Why those?

1. From his prison cell awaiting trial, Paul looks up and sees a battle raging (vv. 12–13). What is this battle? What is it over? **2.** What are the six armors for the Christian? Which of these are offensive weapons? Defensive weapons? **3.** What attitude should we have as we face these forces? How does prayer fit into this spiritual battle?

1. If you had to compare your spiritual armor to this list, where are you strong? Weak? What do you need to do to prepare for battle? What is at stake if you don't? **2.** What evidence do you see of the battle in your life? Your church? Your community? Your nation? The world? What would it mean for you "to stand" in these particular battlefields?

devil's schemes. [12]For our struggle is not against flesh and blood, but against the rulers, against the authorities, against the powers of this dark world and against the spiritual forces of evil in the heavenly realms. [13]Therefore put on the full armor of God, so that when the day of evil comes, you may be able to stand your ground, and after you have done everything, to stand. [14]Stand firm then, with the belt of truth buckled around your waist, with the breastplate of righteousness in place, [15]and with your feet fitted with the readiness that comes from the gospel of peace. [16]In addition to all this, take up the shield of faith, with which you can extinguish all the flaming arrows of the evil one. [17]Take the helmet of salvation and the sword of the Spirit, which is the word of God. [18]And pray in the Spirit on all occasions with all kinds of prayers and requests. With this in mind, be alert and always keep on praying for all the saints.

[19]Pray also for me, that whenever I open my mouth, words may be given me so that I will fearlessly make known the mystery of the gospel, [20]for which I am an ambassador in chains. Pray that I may declare it fearlessly, as I should.

Final Greetings

[21]Tychicus, the dear brother and faithful servant in the Lord, will tell you everything, so that you also may know how I am and what I am doing. [22]I am sending him to you for this very purpose, that you may know how we are, and that he may encourage you.

[23]Peace to the brothers, and love with faith from God the Father and the Lord Jesus Christ. [24]Grace to all who love our Lord Jesus Christ with an undying love.

INTRODUCTION to

PHILIPPIANS

Book Study Outline: If you are using Philippians for a study course, here is a 4- or 8-week outline. Use the margin questions for your group agenda:

start meeting / 15 min.

read & discuss Bible / 30 min.

close meeting / 15–45 min.

Refer to the Questions and Answers in front of Bible for more information.

4-week plan	8-week plan	Group Study Passage
1	1	1:1–11/Partners in Christ's Gospel
	2	1:12–30/Suffering for Christ's Sake
2	3	2:1–11/Imitating Christ's Humility
	4	2:12–30/Examples of Christ's Service
3	5	3:1–11/Knowing Christ's Suffering
	6	3:12–4:1/Pursuing Christ's Call
4	7	4:2–9/Joy in Christ's Nearness
	8	4:10–23/Receiving Christ's Riches

Author: The apostle Paul.

Date: Probably around A.D. 61–63, a dozen or so years after Paul had founded the church in Philippi (the first one in Europe; see Ac 16).

Theme: The joy of knowing Jesus.

Historical Background: Paul was in prison (most likely at Rome; see Ac 28:11–31) when Epaphroditus arrived with a gift from the church at Philippi, an important Roman colony in northern Greece. Paul had at least four motives as he wrote this letter in return. For one, it served as a "thank you" to them for their love and partnership in the Gospel (1:5; 4:10–19). Secondly, he wanted them to know he was not discouraged even though he was in prison (1:12–26; 4:10–19). Thirdly, reports of how false teachers were bringing their damaging doctrines into the church prompted him to warn them to stand firm against these errors (1:27–28; 3:2–4,18–19). Finally, he was concerned about a serious clash between two women in the church whose disagreement was apparently affecting the unity of the whole body (4:2–3).

Characteristics: Philippians radiates with joy in the Lord and with love for these old friends and warm supporters. Paul's joy while in prison flows from his awareness of Jesus' presence (1:21–24), his confidence that he is in Christ's hands (1:20; 2:9–13; 3:20–21), his pleasure over the advancement of the Gospel (1:12–14) and his single-minded desire to know Jesus (1:21; 3:7–10). His concern is that the Philippians reflect the same attitudes through a life of mutual service (1:27–2:11), steadfastness in the truth (3:2–4:1) and dedication to the things of Christ (4:4–9).

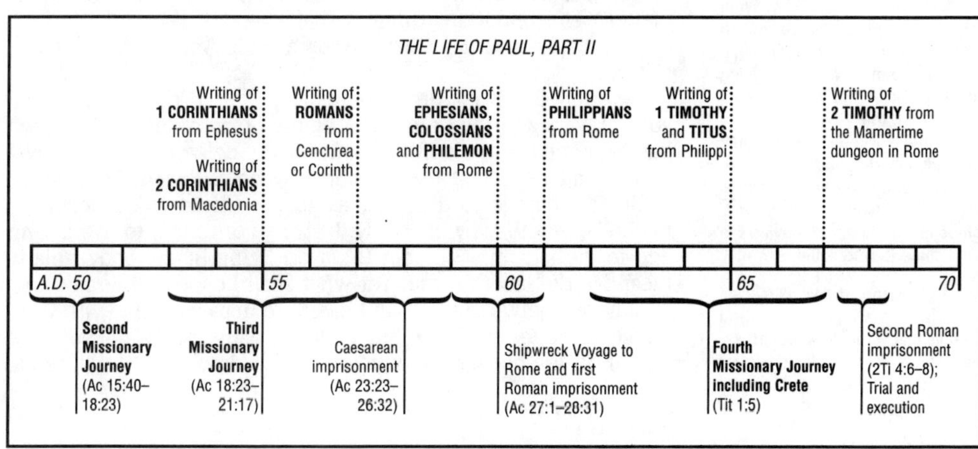

Philippians

1 Paul and Timothy, servants of Christ Jesus,

To all the saints in Christ Jesus at Philippi, together with the
overseers[a] and deacons:

2Grace and peace to you from God our Father and the Lord Jesus
Christ.

Thanksgiving and Prayer

3I thank my God every time I remember you. 4In all my prayers
for all of you, I always pray with joy 5because of your partnership in
the gospel from the first day until now, 6being confident of this,
that he who began a good work in you will carry it on to completion until the day of Christ Jesus.
7It is right for me to feel this way about all of you, since I have
you in my heart; for whether I am in chains or defending and
confirming the gospel, all of you share in God's grace with me.
8God can testify how I long for all of you with the affection of
Christ Jesus.
9And this is my prayer: that your love may abound more and
more in knowledge and depth of insight, 10so that you may be able
to discern what is best and may be pure and blameless until the
day of Christ, 11filled with the fruit of righteousness that comes
through Jesus Christ—to the glory and praise of God.

Paul's Chains Advance the Gospel

12Now I want you to know, brothers, that what has happened to
me has really served to advance the gospel. 13As a result, it has
become clear throughout the whole palace guard[b] and to everyone else that I am in chains for Christ. 14Because of my chains,
most of the brothers in the Lord have been encouraged to speak
the word of God more courageously and fearlessly.
15It is true that some preach Christ out of envy and rivalry, but
others out of goodwill. 16The latter do so in love, knowing that I am
put here for the defense of the gospel. 17The former preach Christ
out of selfish ambition, not sincerely, supposing that they can stir
up trouble for me while I am in chains.[c] 18But what does it
matter? The important thing is that in every way, whether from
false motives or true, Christ is preached. And because of this I
rejoice.
Yes, and I will continue to rejoice, 19for I know that through
your prayers and the help given by the Spirit of Jesus Christ, what
has happened to me will turn out for my deliverance.[d] 20I eagerly
expect and hope that I will in no way be ashamed, but will have
sufficient courage so that now as always Christ will be exalted in
my body, whether by life or by death. 21For to me, to live is Christ
and to die is gain. 22If I am to go on living in the body, this will
mean fruitful labor for me. Yet what shall I choose? I do not know!
23I am torn between the two: I desire to depart and be with Christ,
which is better by far; 24but it is more necessary for you that I
remain in the body. 25Convinced of this, I know that I will remain,

[a] *1* Traditionally *bishops* [b] *13* Or *whole palace* [c] *16,17* Some late manuscripts have verses 16 and 17 in reverse order. [d] *19* Or *salvation*

What mail do you open first: Bills? Official looking stuff? Personal mail? Love letter?

1. Where is Paul writing from? Why? To whom is he writing? (See Introduction to Philippians.) **2.** What are Paul's feelings for this church? What does that show about his leadership style? **3.** How is God at work in a believer's life according to verses 6 and 9–11? How does this make you feel about uncertainties in your life?

1. Who was the "apostle Paul" in your spiritual life, who introduced you to Jesus Christ and cared about your spiritual growth? **2.** Who is your spiritual cheerleader now?

---

1. When you have had a bad day, what do you do? **2.** Are you the kind of person who sees the glass half-empty or half-full?

1. What is the difference between Paul's view of life and the view of the Stoics (grin and bear it) and the Epicureans (eat, drink and be merry)? **2.** How does Paul decide if an event (like his jailing) is good or bad? How would this example encourage others? **3.** What motives for preaching does Paul speak of (vv. 15–17)? **4.** What is Paul's overriding attitude toward his uncertain future (v. 21)? What does he mean? What reasoning helps him decide? **5.** What conduct is worthy of the Gospel (v. 27)? Why is that so important to Paul? How seriously do you take this? **6.** What difference has your personal faith in Jesus Christ made in your attitude toward death and dying? In your attitude toward suffering?

1. "For me, to live is_____." Given your priorities and schedule this week, how would you honestly fill in the blank? What would change if you wrote "Christ"? **2.** Since churches often divide

and I will continue with all of you for your progress and joy in the
faith, 26so that through my being with you again your joy in Christ
Jesus will overflow on account of me.
27Whatever happens, conduct yourselves in a manner worthy of
the gospel of Christ. Then, whether I come and see you or only
hear about you in my absence, I will know that you stand firm in
one spirit, contending as one man for the faith of the gospel 28with-
out being frightened in any way by those who oppose you. This is
a sign to them that they will be destroyed, but that you will be
saved—and that by God. 29For it has been granted to you on behalf
of Christ not only to believe on him, but also to suffer for him,
30since you are going through the same struggle you saw I had, and
now hear that I still have.

along denominational, cultural, theological and social lines, what would it mean to apply verse 27 in your community in concrete ways? What would have to change in you to make such unity possible?

Imitating Christ's Humility

2 If you have any encouragement from being united with Christ,
if any comfort from his love, if any fellowship with the Spirit,
if any tenderness and compassion, 2then make my joy complete by
being like-minded, having the same love, being one in spirit and
purpose. 3Do nothing out of selfish ambition or vain conceit, but
in humility consider others better than yourselves. 4Each of you
should look not only to your own interests, but also to the interests
of others.
5Your attitude should be the same as that of Christ Jesus:

6Who, being in very nature[a] God,
did not consider equality with God something
to be grasped,
7but made himself nothing,
taking the very nature[b] of a servant,
being made in human likeness.
8And being found in appearance as a man,
he humbled himself
and became obedient to death—
even death on a cross!
9Therefore God exalted him to the highest place
and gave him the name that is above every
name,
10that at the name of Jesus every knee should bow,
in heaven and on earth and under the earth,
11and every tongue confess that Jesus Christ is Lord,
to the glory of God the Father.

1. Who takes out the trash in your home? Cleans the toilet? **2.** What is your pet peeve at home?

1. Reading between the lines, what was wrong with the church in Philippi? **2.** What does it mean to consider someone "better than yourself" (v. 3)? How does humility differ from being a doormat? **3.** What do you think it was like for Jesus to leave heaven and become human? To take on himself all of the sin of mankind?

1. How does this passage challenge the Madison Avenue advertising image of success? **2.** Who do you admire because they truly put the interests of others ahead of their own interests? **3.** What is the closest you have come to being in a fellowship that cared for one another like Paul describes here: Your buddies in the war? Your college sorority? Your sports team? An AA recovery group?

Shining as Stars

12Therefore, my dear friends, as you have always obeyed—not
only in my presence, but now much more in my absence—continue to work out your salvation with fear and trembling, 13for it is
God who works in you to will and to act according to his good
purpose.
14Do everything without complaining or arguing, 15so that you
may become blameless and pure, children of God without fault in
a crooked and depraved generation, in which you shine like stars
in the universe 16as you hold out[c] the word of life—in order that
I may boast on the day of Christ that I did not run or labor for
nothing. 17But even if I am being poured out like a drink offering
on the sacrifice and service coming from your faith, I am glad and
rejoice with all of you. 18So you too should be glad and rejoice
with me.

Who are you like in the morning: Big Bird or Oscar the Grouch?

1. Who does Paul sound like in this passage: Your dad? Army sergeant? Coach at halftime? **2.** What does it mean to "work out your salvation" (v. 12; see also 2:1–4)? **3.** What makes God's people "shine like stars"?

How brightly do you "shine" in your universe?

[a]6 Or *in the form of* [b]7 Or *the form* [c]16 Or *hold on to*

1. Who would look after your children if something happened to you and your spouse? **2.** Who would look after your business or personal affairs?

1. How do Timothy and Epaphroditus illustrate 2:1–4? **2.** Consider verses 20–22 and 30. How true is verse 21 today? How rare are people like these two men? Who is one person you know who resembles them?

1. When you were growing up, did your father praise you the way Paul praises Timothy? **2.** Who are the people in your life who have helped shape your own self-image by their praise or lack of praise? **3.** Do you give praise easily … or do you find this hard to do? Where do you need to improve?

Timothy and Epaphroditus

19I hope in the Lord Jesus to send Timothy to you soon, that I
also may be cheered when I receive news about you. 20I have no
one else like him, who takes a genuine interest in your welfare.
21For everyone looks out for his own interests, not those of Jesus
Christ. 22But you know that Timothy has proved himself, because
as a son with his father he has served with me in the work of the
gospel. 23I hope, therefore, to send him as soon as I see how things
go with me. 24And I am confident in the Lord that I myself will
come soon.

25But I think it is necessary to send back to you Epaphroditus,
my brother, fellow worker and fellow soldier, who is also your
messenger, whom you sent to take care of my needs. 26For he longs
for all of you and is distressed because you heard he was ill. 27In-
deed he was ill, and almost died. But God had mercy on him, and
not on him only but also on me, to spare me sorrow upon sorrow.
28Therefore I am all the more eager to send him, so that when you
see him again you may be glad and I may have less anxiety. 29Wel-
come him in the Lord with great joy, and honor men like him,
30because he almost died for the work of Christ, risking his life to
make up for the help you could not give me.

What skill do you have that you could brag about?

1. Why is Paul so concerned about the influence of the "dogs" on this Christian community? **2.** If this problem with those promoting circumcision had gone unchallenged, how would this have hurt the Gospel? **3.** Paul lived a "good" life before he became a Christian. Was he trying to put down his religious background?

1. How would you compare your upbringing to Paul's? Your passion for Christ to Paul's? **2.** Do you need to walk away from something in your past keeping you from becoming new in Christ?

No Confidence in the Flesh

3 Finally, my brothers, rejoice in the Lord! It is no trouble for me
to write the same things to you again, and it is a safeguard for
you.

2Watch out for those dogs, those men who do evil, those mutila-
tors of the flesh. 3For it is we who are the circumcision, we who
worship by the Spirit of God, who glory in Christ Jesus, and who
put no confidence in the flesh— 4though I myself have reasons for
such confidence.

If anyone else thinks he has reasons to put confidence in the
flesh, I have more: 5circumcised on the eighth day, of the people of
Israel, of the tribe of Benjamin, a Hebrew of Hebrews; in regard to
the law, a Pharisee; 6as for zeal, persecuting the church; as for
legalistic righteousness, faultless.

7But whatever was to my profit I now consider loss for the sake
of Christ. 8What is more, I consider everything a loss compared
to the surpassing greatness of knowing Christ Jesus my Lord, for
whose sake I have lost all things. I consider them rubbish, that I
may gain Christ 9and be found in him, not having a righteousness
of my own that comes from the law, but that which is through faith
in Christ—the righteousness that comes from God and is by faith.
10I want to know Christ and the power of his resurrection and the
fellowship of sharing in his sufferings, becoming like him in his
death, 11and so, somehow, to attain to the resurrection from the
dead.

In your dreams of the ideal life, are you more like the pioneer (always pushing on) or the settler (settling down)?

1. Using the imagery of a track race, where does Paul picture himself in his spiritual life? What prize is he after? How is he going to reach it? **2.** From what Paul says in this passage (particu-

Pressing on Toward the Goal

12Not that I have already obtained all this, or have already been
made perfect, but I press on to take hold of that for which Christ
Jesus took hold of me. 13Brothers, I do not consider myself yet to
have taken hold of it. But one thing I do: Forgetting what is behind
and straining toward what is ahead, 14I press on toward the goal to
win the prize for which God has called me heavenward in Christ
Jesus.

15All of us who are mature should take such a view of things.

And if on some point you think differently, that too God will make clear to you. [16]Only let us live up to what we have already attained.

[17]Join with others in following my example, brothers, and take note of those who live according to the pattern we gave you. [18]For, as I have often told you before and now say again even with tears, many live as enemies of the cross of Christ. [19]Their destiny is destruction, their god is their stomach, and their glory is in their shame. Their mind is on earthly things. [20]But our citizenship is in heaven. And we eagerly await a Savior from there, the Lord Jesus Christ, [21]who, by the power that enables him to bring everything under his control, will transform our lowly bodies so that they will be like his glorious body.

4 Therefore, my brothers, you whom I love and long for, my joy and crown, that is how you should stand firm in the Lord, dear friends!

Exhortations

[2]I plead with Euodia and I plead with Syntyche to agree with each other in the Lord. [3]Yes, and I ask you, loyal yokefellow,[a] help these women who have contended at my side in the cause of the gospel, along with Clement and the rest of my fellow workers, whose names are in the book of life.

[4]Rejoice in the Lord always. I will say it again: Rejoice! [5]Let your gentleness be evident to all. The Lord is near. [6]Do not be anxious about anything, but in everything, by prayer and petition, with thanksgiving, present your requests to God. [7]And the peace of God, which transcends all understanding, will guard your hearts and your minds in Christ Jesus.

[8]Finally, brothers, whatever is true, whatever is noble, whatever is right, whatever is pure, whatever is lovely, whatever is admirable—if anything is excellent or praiseworthy—think about such things. [9]Whatever you have learned or received or heard from me, or seen in me—put it into practice. And the God of peace will be with you.

Thanks for Their Gifts

[10]I rejoice greatly in the Lord that at last you have renewed your concern for me. Indeed, you have been concerned, but you had no opportunity to show it. [11]I am not saying this because I am in need, for I have learned to be content whatever the circumstances. [12]I know what it is to be in need, and I know what it is to have plenty. I have learned the secret of being content in any and every situation, whether well fed or hungry, whether living in plenty or in want. [13]I can do everything through him who gives me strength.

[14]Yet it was good of you to share in my troubles. [15]Moreover, as you Philippians know, in the early days of your acquaintance with the gospel, when I set out from Macedonia, not one church shared with me in the matter of giving and receiving, except you only; [16]for even when I was in Thessalonica, you sent me aid again and again when I was in need. [17]Not that I am looking for a gift, but I am looking for what may be credited to your account. [18]I have received full payment and even more; I am amply supplied, now that I have received from Epaphroditus the gifts you sent. They are a fragrant offering, an acceptable sacrifice, pleasing to God. [19]And

[a]3 Or *loyal Syzygus*

larly the second half), what do you think is going on in this Christian community? **3.** In contrast, what should characterize the "citizens of heaven"?

1. If you had to compare your life in Christ right now to a track race, where would you be: Sitting on the sidelines? Warming up? At the starting blocks? Giving it your all? **2.** What are you passionate about? Are you more likely to strive for excellence in your secular life or your spiritual life? **3.** How would you finish the sentence in verse 13: "But one thing I do ..."

What is the best thing that happened to you this week?

1. How are these women harming the church? **2.** What is Paul's prescription for stress? Compare it to that of modern psychology and New Age religions. **3.** What is Paul's solution to thought pollution? What would he say to the church today about leisure time, reading matter, R-rated movies and football all weekend long on TV? What would he suggest?

On a scale from 1 to 10, what is the stress level in your life? What is your body saying to you?

What do you look back on as the happiest days of your life? Were they really that good?

1. What is Paul's secret to contentment? Where do you think he learned this: From devotional books? Going to church? Graduating from the school of hard knocks? **2.** What is the closest you have come to experiencing what Paul talks about here: Rebounding from loss of freedom? Loss of some physical skill? Loss of some vocational opportunity? Loss of a partner in your life? Or loss of financial security? **3.** What do you learn from Paul in this passage about both contentment and giving and receiving help from others? **4.** In light of Paul's imprisonment for the sake of his preaching, could

my God will meet all your needs according to his glorious riches in
Christ Jesus.
20To our God and Father be glory for ever and ever. Amen.

Final Greetings

21Greet all the saints in Christ Jesus. The brothers who are with
me send greetings. 22All the saints send you greetings, especially
those who belong to Caesar's household.
23The grace of the Lord Jesus Christ be with your spirit. Amen.[a]

some "tongue in cheek" irony be intended in verse 22? (Hint: Caesar Augustus was emperor of Rome at the time.)

♡ **1.** What *outside* force is most likely to upset your contentment? Since God does not always change negative outside forces, what can he change *in you* so that contentment is possible? How can you and your group help the process (see 4:4–8)? **2.** Take turns having one person sit silently while the others share something they are thankful to have received from that person during these study sessions. **3.** What one thing from Philippians do you especially want to apply in your life? In your church?

[a]*23* Some manuscripts do not have *Amen*.

INTRODUCTION to

COLOSSIANS

Book Study Outline: If you are using Colossians for a study course, here is a 4- or 6-week outline. Use the margin questions for your group agenda:

- start meeting / 15 min.
- read & discuss Bible / 30 min.
- close meeting / 15–45 min.

4-week plan	6-week plan	Group Study Passage
1	1	1:1–14/Eternal Redemption in Christ
	2	1:15–23/All Reconciled in Christ
2	3	1:24–2:5/Full Riches in Christ
	4	2:6–23/Firmly Rooted in Christ
3	5	3:1–4:1/Newly Robed in Christ
4	6	4:2–18/New Relationships in Christ

Refer to the Questions and Answers in front of Bible for more information.

Author: The apostle Paul.

Date: Probably in the early A.D. 60s.

Theme: Fullness and freedom in Christ.

Historical Background: Although Paul never visited Colosse, a town about 100 miles east of Ephesus, the church there was probably established as a result of his extended ministry in Ephesus (Ac 19:8–10). Although it had once been a prosperous commercial center, by Paul's day its prominence had diminished. While in prison (see the Introduction to Ephesians), Paul was visited by Epaphras, a native of Colosse who may have founded the church there. His report of a developing problem in the Colosse church prompted Paul to write. It seems that the church was coming under the influence of certain false teachers. The problem for the church seems to have been that of syncretism, i.e., combining various teachings from different religions to come up with something new. Apparently, Greek philosophy, cultic practices, Christianity and Jewish speculations were blended together to offer a "fuller" type of of spiritual experience. Jesus was seen as one of several "deities" through which one approaches the Divine. Rigorous ascetic disciplines were used as a means to experience trance-like "visions." In contrast, Paul presents Jesus as the true Lord of the universe (1:15–18; 2:9–10) and highlights love, thankfulness and forgiveness as the marks of true spirituality (3:12–17).

Characteristics: Jesus Christ is central as Paul demonstrates that "in everything he (has) supremacy" (1:18). Chapters 1–2 outline the cosmic nature of Christ who has reconciled all things to himself through his death on the cross, independently of any effort on our part. Chapters 3–4 give the implications of Christ's lordship in terms of how those in union with him are meant to live.

THE LETTERS OF PAUL

Book	Time of Writing (A.D.)	Place of Writing	Theme
Galatians	48–50 or 51–53	Syrian Antioch or Corinth	Justification by faith alone (Gal)
1 Thessalonians	51	Corinth	Christian living in an immoral world (1Th)
2 Thessalonians	51	Corinth	Life in the light of the coming Christ (2Th)
1 Corinthians	53–55	Ephesus	Glorifying God through Christian living (1Co)
2 Corinthians	55–56	Macedonia	Finding strength in God's true power (2Co)
Romans	56–57	Corinth	Being right with God through faith in Christ (Ro)
Philemon	60	Rome	Mercy and unlimited forgiveness (Phm)
Colossians	60	Rome	Fullness and freedom in Christ (Col)
Ephesians	60	Rome	God's new social order (Eph)
Philippians	61–63	Rome	Joy in Christ, despite hardships (Php)
Titus	63–65	Macedonia	Devotion to duty and doing good (Tit)
1 Timothy	63–65	Macedonia	Faithful leadership through Christ (1Ti)
2 Timothy	67–68	Rome	Exhortation to carry on the ministry (2Ti)

Colossians

Who were your favorite TV or comic book heroes as a child?

1. Paul hasn't met these believers (2:1), yet he is attracted to them. Why? What types of people are you attracted to when you enter a new church group? **2.** Why are faith and love the products of hope (v. 5)? Why must hope exist first? **3.** When did you first come to know the hope offered through Christ in the Gospel? **4.** What does it mean to tell the whole truth about God's grace (v. 6)? Conversely, how does one betray grace? What truth about grace do you see in verses 12–14? **5.** How does what Paul prays for (vv. 9–11) compare with what he thanks God for (vv. 12–14)?

1. How does your prayer for others compare with Paul's: (a) In intensity? (b) In thankfulness? (c) In clarity? (d) In faithfulness? **2.** How is the fruit of hope, faith and love growing in your life: Developing well? Suffering from drought? Destroyed by the last storm? Budding? How will you help this "crop" develop?

1 Paul, an apostle of Christ Jesus by the will of God, and Timothy
our brother,

2To the holy and faithful[a] brothers in Christ at Colosse:

Grace and peace to you from God our Father.[b]

Thanksgiving and Prayer

3We always thank God, the Father of our Lord Jesus Christ,
when we pray for you, 4because we have heard of your faith in
Christ Jesus and of the love you have for all the saints— 5the faith
and love that spring from the hope that is stored up for you in
heaven and that you have already heard about in the word of truth,
the gospel 6that has come to you. All over the world this gospel is
bearing fruit and growing, just as it has been doing among you
since the day you heard it and understood God's grace in all its
truth. 7You learned it from Epaphras, our dear fellow servant, who
is a faithful minister of Christ on our[c] behalf, 8and who also told
us of your love in the Spirit.
9For this reason, since the day we heard about you, we have not
stopped praying for you and asking God to fill you with the knowledge of his will through all spiritual wisdom and understanding.
10And we pray this in order that you may live a life worthy of the
Lord and may please him in every way: bearing fruit in every good
work, growing in the knowledge of God, 11being strengthened with
all power according to his glorious might so that you may have
great endurance and patience, and joyfully 12giving thanks to the
Father, who has qualified you[d] to share in the inheritance of the
saints in the kingdom of light. 13For he has rescued us from
the dominion of darkness and brought us into the kingdom of the
Son he loves, 14in whom we have redemption,[e] the forgiveness of
sins.

What was your favorite animal at the zoo as a child? Your favorite now?

1. The "firstborn" has the rights of an heir. What rights does Jesus have (vv. 15–18)? What is his relationship to "all things"? Why emphasize this? **2.** What is his relationship to God and the church? What does "fullness" imply (v. 19)? **3.** Why did all things need to be reconciled to God (v. 20)? How was this achieved by Jesus? **4.** How much do you identify with verse 21, even now? Do you still sense "evil" in your mind? How do verses 22–23 make you feel?

At times, what people (or forces) seem to be more powerful than Jesus? Why? How do you respond to the fact that

The Supremacy of Christ

15He is the image of the invisible God, the firstborn over all
creation. 16For by him all things were created: things in heaven
and on earth, visible and invisible, whether thrones or powers or
rulers or authorities; all things were created by him and for him.
17He is before all things, and in him all things hold together. 18And
he is the head of the body, the church; he is the beginning and the
firstborn from among the dead, so that in everything he might have
the supremacy. 19For God was pleased to have all his fullness dwell
in him, 20and through him to reconcile to himself all things, whether things on earth or things in heaven, by making peace through
his blood, shed on the cross.
21Once you were alienated from God and were enemies in your
minds because of[f] your evil behavior. 22But now he has reconciled you by Christ's physical body through death to present you
holy in his sight, without blemish and free from accusation— 23if
you continue in your faith, established and firm, not moved from

[a] *2* Or *believing* [b] *2* Some manuscripts *Father and the Lord Jesus Christ* [c] *7* Some manuscripts *your* [d] *12* Some manuscripts *us* [e] *14* A few late manuscripts *redemption through his blood* [f] *21* Or *minds, as shown by*

the hope held out in the gospel. This is the gospel that you heard and that has been proclaimed to every creature under heaven, and of which I, Paul, have become a servant.

Paul's Labor for the Church

24Now I rejoice in what was suffered for you, and I fill up in my flesh what is still lacking in regard to Christ's afflictions, for the sake of his body, which is the church. 25I have become its servant by the commission God gave me to present to you the word of God in its fullness— 26the mystery that has been kept hidden for ages and generations, but is now disclosed to the saints. 27To them God has chosen to make known among the Gentiles the glorious riches of this mystery, which is Christ in you, the hope of glory.

28We proclaim him, admonishing and teaching everyone with all wisdom, so that we may present everyone perfect in Christ. 29To this end I labor, struggling with all his energy, which so powerfully works in me.

2 I want you to know how much I am struggling for you and for those at Laodicea, and for all who have not met me personally. 2My purpose is that they may be encouraged in heart and united in love, so that they may have the full riches of complete understanding, in order that they may know the mystery of God, namely, Christ, 3in whom are hidden all the treasures of wisdom and knowledge. 4I tell you this so that no one may deceive you by fine-sounding arguments. 5For though I am absent from you in body, I am present with you in spirit and delight to see how orderly you are and how firm your faith in Christ is.

Freedom From Human Regulations Through Life With Christ

6So then, just as you received Christ Jesus as Lord, continue to live in him, 7rooted and built up in him, strengthened in the faith as you were taught, and overflowing with thankfulness.

8See to it that no one takes you captive through hollow and deceptive philosophy, which depends on human tradition and the basic principles of this world rather than on Christ.

9For in Christ all the fullness of the Deity lives in bodily form, 10and you have been given fullness in Christ, who is the head over every power and authority. 11In him you were also circumcised, in the putting off of the sinful nature,[a] not with a circumcision done by the hands of men but with the circumcision done by Christ, 12having been buried with him in baptism and raised with him through your faith in the power of God, who raised him from the dead.

13When you were dead in your sins and in the uncircumcision of your sinful nature,[b] God made you[c] alive with Christ. He forgave us all our sins, 14having canceled the written code, with its regulations, that was against us and that stood opposed to us; he took it away, nailing it to the cross. 15And having disarmed the powers and authorities, he made a public spectacle of them, triumphing over them by the cross.[d]

16Therefore do not let anyone judge you by what you eat or drink, or with regard to a religious festival, a New Moon celebration or a Sabbath day. 17These are a shadow of the things that were to come; the reality, however, is found in Christ. 18Do not let anyone who delights in false humility and the worship of angels disqualify you for the prize. Such a person goes into great detail

[a] *11* Or *the flesh* [b] *13* Or *your flesh* [c] *13* Some manuscripts *us* [d] *15* Or *them in him*

even these are under Christ's authority?

What memories do you have as a child hunting for "buried treasure" or Easter eggs?

1. In what sense are Paul's sufferings a continuation of Jesus' sufferings? Why would this lead him to rejoice (see 2Co 12:9–10)? **2.** In 2:3–4, Paul contrasts clever speech and true wisdom. What does this indicate about false teaching infecting the church?

1. Is Paul's stated purpose (1:28; 2:2) a reality in your life? Or are you still somewhere along the way? **2.** What "fine sounding arguments" hinder you in following Jesus? How does Paul speak to your concerns? **3.** How has finding Christ been like uncovering long-lost buried treasure?

---

1. As a child, what did you think a "religious" person was like? How did you feel about that person? **2.** Did you consider your parents "permissive" or "strict"? Why? (Did they have a lot of rules for you, or just a few? Which one was the biggie?)

1. What does "living in Christ" (v. 6) involve (see 1:10–12)? What does the phrase "rooted and built up" imply to you? **2.** What are "the basic principles of this world" (vv. 8,20) and the "powers and authorities" (vv. 10,15)? How did Christ give the Colossians victory over these? **3.** What kind of circumcision is done by Christ (v. 11)? How did he do it (vv. 12–15)? **4.** What experiences does the believer share with Christ (vv. 9–13)? What implications are drawn from this (vv. 13,16–17, 20–23)? **5.** What is the result of trying to base one's relationship with God on rule keeping or on private visions, as the false teachers were doing?

1. When have you felt as if the "roots" of your faith in Christ were barely below the surface? What helps you to sink those roots deeper? **2.** What additions to the faith have you encountered from people who try to encourage you to be "more spiritual"? **3.** What convinced you that trying to live up to religious rules couldn't change you on the inside? In what area are you still susceptible to getting caught up in rule keeping?

In buying clothes, are you a name-brand buyer? A bargain hunter? Spouse conscious? Quality conscious? Style conscious? (Or could you care less what others think?—Really?)

1. How are we to grow in our spiritual life (vv. 1–4)? How does that contrast with the things that don't lead to growth (see 2:16–23)? How is setting your mind and heart on Christ related to what he *has already done* for us (v. 1)? To what he *will do* for us (v. 4)? **2.** How much contrast is there between the "clothes" of the earthly nature (vv. 5–11) and those of God's chosen people (vv. 12–17)? How hard would it seem to take off the first and put on the second? How is it possible (see 2:6–7,10)? **3.** What practical difference does this "new clothing" make in the relationship between wives and husbands? Between parents and children? Slaves and masters? **4.** What confirms that all these relationships are to be built around Christ? **5.** Is the person in verses 12–17 calm, cool and in control or self-controlled but also lavish in his or her love for others? Do you seek to resemble the first or the second?

1. We get all too used to "earthly nature" clothing. Which aspect of your old nature feels like a comfortable old T-shirt to you now? Why is it difficult to shed or remove? **2.** With what piece of Christ's wardrobe would you like to replace it? Which aspect of Christ's character do you need to clothe yourself with, in relation to your husband or wife? Your parents or children? Your employer or employees? A changing relationship? **3.** How can your small group help with your clothing selection?

about what he has seen, and his unspiritual mind puffs him up
with idle notions. 19He has lost connection with the Head, from
whom the whole body, supported and held together by its liga-
ments and sinews, grows as God causes it to grow.
20Since you died with Christ to the basic principles of this world,
why, as though you still belonged to it, do you submit to its rules:
21"Do not handle! Do not taste! Do not touch!"? 22These are all
destined to perish with use, because they are based on human
commands and teachings. 23Such regulations indeed have an appearance of wisdom, with their self-imposed worship, their false
humility and their harsh treatment of the body, but they lack any
value in restraining sensual indulgence.

Rules for Holy Living

3 Since, then, you have been raised with Christ, set your hearts
on things above, where Christ is seated at the right hand of
God. 2Set your minds on things above, not on earthly things. 3For
you died, and your life is now hidden with Christ in God. 4When
Christ, who is your[a] life, appears, then you also will appear with
him in glory.
5Put to death, therefore, whatever belongs to your earthly nature: sexual immorality, impurity, lust, evil desires and greed,
which is idolatry. 6Because of these, the wrath of God is coming.[b]
7You used to walk in these ways, in the life you once lived. 8But
now you must rid yourselves of all such things as these: anger,
rage, malice, slander, and filthy language from your lips. 9Do not lie
to each other, since you have taken off your old self with its
practices 10and have put on the new self, which is being renewed
in knowledge in the image of its Creator. 11Here there is no Greek
or Jew, circumcised or uncircumcised, barbarian, Scythian, slave or
free, but Christ is all, and is in all.
12Therefore, as God's chosen people, holy and dearly loved,
clothe yourselves with compassion, kindness, humility, gentleness
and patience. 13Bear with each other and forgive whatever griev-
ances you may have against one another. Forgive as the Lord forgave you. 14And over all these virtues put on love, which binds
them all together in perfect unity.
15Let the peace of Christ rule in your hearts, since as members
of one body you were called to peace. And be thankful. 16Let the
word of Christ dwell in you richly as you teach and admonish one
another with all wisdom, and as you sing psalms, hymns and spiritual songs with gratitude in your hearts to God. 17And whatever
you do, whether in word or deed, do it all in the name of the Lord
Jesus, giving thanks to God the Father through him.

Rules for Christian Households

18Wives, submit to your husbands, as is fitting in the Lord.
19Husbands, love your wives and do not be harsh with them.
20Children, obey your parents in everything, for this pleases the
Lord.
21Fathers, do not embitter your children, or they will become
discouraged.
22Slaves, obey your earthly masters in everything; and do it, not
only when their eye is on you and to win their favor, but with
sincerity of heart and reverence for the Lord. 23Whatever you do,
work at it with all your heart, as working for the Lord, not for men,
24since you know that you will receive an inheritance from the

[a]4 Some manuscripts *our* [b]6 Some early manuscripts *coming on those who are disobedient*

Lord as a reward. It is the Lord Christ you are serving. 25Anyone
who does wrong will be repaid for his wrong, and there is no
favoritism.

4 Masters, provide your slaves with what is right and fair, because you know that you also have a Master in heaven.

Further Instructions

2Devote yourselves to prayer, being watchful and thankful. 3And
pray for us, too, that God may open a door for our message, so that
we may proclaim the mystery of Christ, for which I am in chains.
4Pray that I may proclaim it clearly, as I should. 5Be wise in the
way you act toward outsiders; make the most of every opportunity.
6Let your conversation be always full of grace, seasoned with salt,
so that you may know how to answer everyone.

Final Greetings

7Tychicus will tell you all the news about me. He is a dear
brother, a faithful minister and fellow servant in the Lord. 8I am
sending him to you for the express purpose that you may know
about our[a] circumstances and that he may encourage your hearts.
9He is coming with Onesimus, our faithful and dear brother, who is
one of you. They will tell you everything that is happening here.
10My fellow prisoner Aristarchus sends you his greetings, as does
Mark, the cousin of Barnabas. (You have received instructions
about him; if he comes to you, welcome him.) 11Jesus, who is
called Justus, also sends greetings. These are the only Jews among
my fellow workers for the kingdom of God, and they have proved
a comfort to me. 12Epaphras, who is one of you and a servant of
Christ Jesus, sends greetings. He is always wrestling in prayer for
you, that you may stand firm in all the will of God, mature and fully
assured. 13I vouch for him that he is working hard for you and for
those at Laodicea and Hierapolis. 14Our dear friend Luke, the doctor, and Demas send greetings. 15Give my greetings to the brothers
at Laodicea, and to Nympha and the church in her house.
16After this letter has been read to you, see that it is also read in
the church of the Laodiceans and that you in turn read the letter
from Laodicea.
17Tell Archippus: "See to it that you complete the work you have
received in the Lord."
18I, Paul, write this greeting in my own hand. Remember my
chains. Grace be with you.

In high school, who were two of your best friends? What was one quality about them that stands out to you?

1. In advancing the Gospel (vv. 2–6), what role is played by prayer? Watchfulness? Thankfulness? Open doors? Closed doors or chains? Wise actions? Opportunism? Graceful talk? Salty talk? **2.** Why is thankfulness such a key ingredient in a Christian's life (see 2:7; 3:15,17)? **3.** What type of friend is Tychicus (vv.7–8; see Ac 20:4; Eph 6:21; 2Ti 4:12; Tit 3:12)? **4.** Likewise, what do you know about Onesimus (v. 9; see Phm 10–16)? Which of Paul's rules, instructions and greetings would be appropriate in preparing to receive this runaway slave from Colosse? How might the Colossians feel about him? **5.** Aristarchus (Ac 19:29; 27:2; Phm 24), John Mark (Ac 12:12; 13:5,13; 15:36–40 and the author of Mark), Luke (the author of Luke and Acts), and Demas (Phm 24; 2Ti 4:10) were all with Paul at various times. Why would he include them in his greetings to the church? **6.** In light of the influence of the false teachings, why would Paul's commendation of Epaphras be especially important (1:7; 4:12–13)?

1. What has helped you to grow the most in your prayer life? **2.** From verses 5–6, what principles do you want to build into your life as you relate to non-believers? **3.** Seeing how Paul operated with a team of fellow Christians, what does that imply for you? For your small group? **4.** Of the qualities used to describe these people, which one would you like others to say about you in five years? How do 2:6–7 and 3:1–2 suggest you can get moving in that direction? **5.** How has your respect and love for Christ grown through this study of Colossians? What from this book has helped you to develop a more thankful heart?

[a] 8 Some manuscripts *that he may know about your*

INTRODUCTION to
1 THESSALONIANS

Book Study Outline: If you are using 1 Thessalonians for a study course, here is a 3- or 6-week outline. Use the margin questions for your group agenda:

start meeting / 15 min.

read & discuss Bible / 30 min.

close meeting / 15–45 min.

3-week plan	6-week plan	Group Study Passage
1	1	1:1–10/Legendary Model of Faith
	2	2:1–16/Lasting Model of Ministry
2	3	2:17–3:13/Longing to Visit This Church
	4	4:1–12/Living to Please God
3	5	4:13–5:11/Living in Light of His Coming
	6	5:12–28/Living in Peace With Others

Refer to the Questions and Answers in the front of this Bible for more information.

Author: The apostle Paul.

Date: Around A.D. 51; either 1 and 2 Thessalonians or Galatians are the earliest letters of Paul in the New Testament.

Theme: Living in light of the coming of Christ.

Historical Background: Paul visited Thessalonica, an important city in Northern Greece, during his second missionary journey (Ac 17:1–9). After preaching for three weeks, he was forced to leave due to mob violence. Jewish leaders accused him of sedition against Caesar. Paul's enemies then used his departure as evidence that he was only a "fly-by-night" religious charlatan (2:3). Concerned about the welfare of the new converts, Paul sent Timothy to encourage them. What Timothy found was twofold. On the one hand, the converts were standing fast in their faith despite persecution and Paul's hasty departure from the city. On the other hand, they were (not unexpectedly) experiencing some problems. Some of the converts had not fully understood the ethical implications of the Gospel. They showed laxity in sexual matters (4:3–8). Furthermore, it seems that some felt it unnecessary to work (in light of the imminence of the Second Coming?) and had become a burden to the others (4:11–12; 5:14). The main problem was that there was a fundamental misunderstanding about the Second Coming (see Introduction for 2 Thessalonians). Timothy later rejoined Paul in Corinth where 1 and 2 Thessalonians were written.

Characteristics: Paul expresses joy at the progress the new converts are making despite their lack of teaching. He then instructs them about the life of holiness they ought to lead as they await the return of Jesus. We catch a glimpse of Paul's approach to ministry (2:1–12; 2:17–3:10) and beautiful summaries of what Christian living is all about (see 1Th 3:11–13; 2Th 1:11–12; 2:16–17).

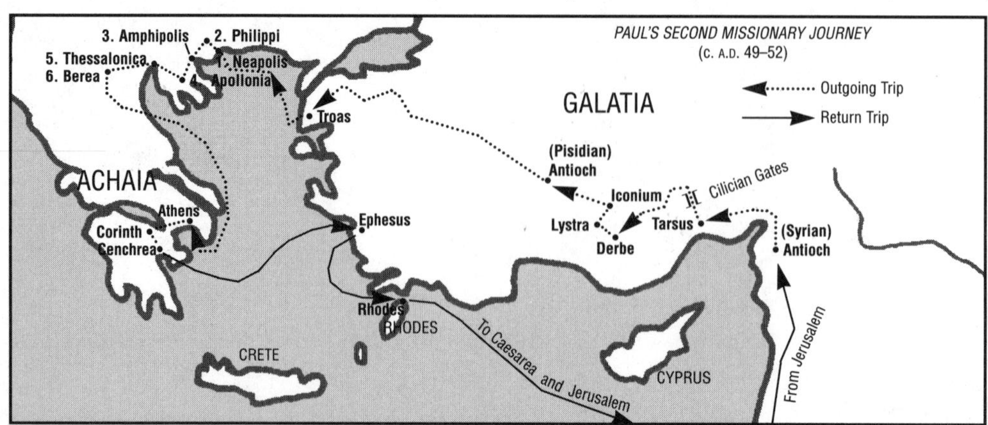

1 Thessalonians

1 Paul, Silas[a] and Timothy,

To the church of the Thessalonians in God the Father and the
Lord Jesus Christ:

Grace and peace to you.[b]

Thanksgiving for the Thessalonians' Faith

2We always thank God for all of you, mentioning you in our
prayers. 3We continually remember before our God and Father
your work produced by faith, your labor prompted by love, and
your endurance inspired by hope in our Lord Jesus Christ.
4For we know, brothers loved by God, that he has chosen you,
5because our gospel came to you not simply with words, but also
with power, with the Holy Spirit and with deep conviction. You
know how we lived among you for your sake. 6You became imitators of us and of the Lord; in spite of severe suffering, you welcomed the message with the joy given by the Holy Spirit. 7And so
you became a model to all the believers in Macedonia and Achaia.
8The Lord's message rang out from you not only in Macedonia and
Achaia—your faith in God has become known everywhere. Therefore we do not need to say anything about it, 9for they themselves
report what kind of reception you gave us. They tell how you
turned to God from idols to serve the living and true God, 10and to
wait for his Son from heaven, whom he raised from the dead—
Jesus, who rescues us from the coming wrath.

What teams did you belong to (or aspire to) as a child? Of which team were you most proud?

1. What do you know about the Thessalonian church from Paul's experiences in Acts 17:1–9? **2.** What convinced Paul that the Thessalonians were indeed chosen by God? **3.** How did they first become imitators of, and then models for, the faith (vv. 6–10)? What does this tell you about their growth in Christ? **4.** In an age without mass media, how do you suppose their faith became so legendary?

1. What kind of "model" are you in matters of faith: Still on the drawing board? A work in progress? Secured in a private collection? On display at the National Museum? **2.** Which of the qualities in verse 3 do you most wish to see developed in your life now? How can the group help?

Paul's Ministry in Thessalonica

2 You know, brothers, that our visit to you was not a failure. 2We
had previously suffered and been insulted in Philippi, as you
know, but with the help of our God we dared to tell you his gospel
in spite of strong opposition. 3For the appeal we make does not
spring from error or impure motives, nor are we trying to trick you.
4On the contrary, we speak as men approved by God to be entrusted with the gospel. We are not trying to please men but God, who
tests our hearts. 5You know we never used flattery, nor did we put
on a mask to cover up greed—God is our witness. 6We were not
looking for praise from men, not from you or anyone else.
As apostles of Christ we could have been a burden to you, 7but
we were gentle among you, like a mother caring for her little
children. 8We loved you so much that we were delighted to share
with you not only the gospel of God but our lives as well, because
you had become so dear to us. 9Surely you remember, brothers,
our toil and hardship; we worked night and day in order not to be
a burden to anyone while we preached the gospel of God to you.
10You are witnesses, and so is God, of how holy, righteous and
blameless we were among you who believed. 11For you know that
we dealt with each of you as a father deals with his own children,
12encouraging, comforting and urging you to live lives worthy of
God, who calls you into his kingdom and glory.
13And we also thank God continually because, when you re-

What was one of your most memorable failures in junior or senior high school?

1. What rumors about Paul have been spread by his opposition (vv. 1–6)? Does Paul sound reassuring to you? What concerns might linger? **2.** From verses 1–12, what does *ethical* evangelism look like? What would its opposite look like? What do the images of being a mother (v. 7) and father (v. 11) add to this picture? What do these images say about caring for your own children or for "young" believers? **3.** What difficulties were the Thessalonians facing (vv. 14–15)? How would Paul's example of perseverance in the face of persecution encourage them?

1. List the characteristics of a faithful Christian worker given in this passage. Which do you possess? Which do you want to develop? **2.** Who has been a positive influence on you for godly living? How so? How can *you* be a positive influence for someone this week? **3.** What turns you off about

[a] *1* Greek *Silvanus,* a variant of *Silas* [b] *1* Some early manuscripts *you from God our Father and the Lord Jesus Christ*

the way some people present the Gospel? How are you attempting to avoid these mistakes, and yet maintain a strong witness? **4.** What opposition to your faith are you facing? What encourages you to persevere?

ceived the word of God, which you heard from us, you accepted it not as the word of men, but as it actually is, the word of God, which is at work in you who believe. 14For you, brothers, became imitators of God's churches in Judea, which are in Christ Jesus: You suffered from your own countrymen the same things those churches suffered from the Jews, 15who killed the Lord Jesus and the prophets and also drove us out. They displease God and are hostile to all men 16in their effort to keep us from speaking to the Gentiles so that they may be saved. In this way they always heap up their sins to the limit. The wrath of God has come upon them at last.[a]

---

1. As a child, when and where did homesickness strike hard? What did you do about it? **2.** What room in your childhood home fills you with warm memories? What happened there?

1. Why do you think Paul called the Thessalonian church his "hope," "joy" and "crown"? **2.** If Paul promised them trials and persecution when he was with them (3:4), why is he writing to them about it now? **3.** What in Timothy's report particularly encourages Paul? What does this tell you about Paul's desires and concerns for the Thessalonians? **4.** What guidelines can you find in Paul's desires, concerns and prayers for those who disciple new Christians today?

1. If someone were to tell you that God promises a trouble-free life to those who are true Christians, how would you respond? What are you struggling with most right now? **2.** In what specific ways have you been encouraged by someone else's faith? Have you told them about it? **3.** Which of Paul's prayer requests would you want someone to pray for you? Do likewise for someone in your small group.

Paul's Longing to See the Thessalonians

17But, brothers, when we were torn away from you for a short time (in person, not in thought), out of our intense longing we made every effort to see you. 18For we wanted to come to you—certainly I, Paul, did, again and again—but Satan stopped us. 19For what is our hope, our joy, or the crown in which we will glory in the presence of our Lord Jesus when he comes? Is it not you? 20Indeed, you are our glory and joy.

3 So when we could stand it no longer, we thought it best to be left by ourselves in Athens. 2We sent Timothy, who is our brother and God's fellow worker[b] in spreading the gospel of Christ, to strengthen and encourage you in your faith, 3so that no one would be unsettled by these trials. You know quite well that we were destined for them. 4In fact, when we were with you, we kept telling you that we would be persecuted. And it turned out that way, as you well know. 5For this reason, when I could stand it no longer, I sent to find out about your faith. I was afraid that in some way the tempter might have tempted you and our efforts might have been useless.

Timothy's Encouraging Report

6But Timothy has just now come to us from you and has brought good news about your faith and love. He has told us that you always have pleasant memories of us and that you long to see us, just as we also long to see you. 7Therefore, brothers, in all our distress and persecution we were encouraged about you because of your faith. 8For now we really live, since you are standing firm in the Lord. 9How can we thank God enough for you in return for all the joy we have in the presence of our God because of you? 10Night and day we pray most earnestly that we may see you again and supply what is lacking in your faith.

11Now may our God and Father himself and our Lord Jesus clear the way for us to come to you. 12May the Lord make your love increase and overflow for each other and for everyone else, just as ours does for you. 13May he strengthen your hearts so that you will be blameless and holy in the presence of our God and Father when our Lord Jesus comes with all his holy ones.

What was the last thing you made from scratch?

1. What three areas of lifestyle, discussed here, most affect a Christian's ministry? How so? **2.** What "behavioral psychology" is Paul using here? What is the guiding principle behind Paul's commands and warnings? What does this passage say to someone

Living to Please God

4 Finally, brothers, we instructed you how to live in order to please God, as in fact you are living. Now we ask you and urge you in the Lord Jesus to do this more and more. 2For you know what instructions we gave you by the authority of the Lord Jesus.

3It is God's will that you should be sanctified: that you should avoid sexual immorality; 4that each of you should learn to control

[a] *16* Or *them fully* [b] *2* Some manuscripts *brother and fellow worker*; other manuscripts *brother and God's servant*

his own body[a] in a way that is holy and honorable, 5not in passionate lust like the heathen, who do not know God; 6and that in
this matter no one should wrong his brother or take advantage of
him. The Lord will punish men for all such sins, as we have already
told you and warned you. 7For God did not call us to be impure,
but to live a holy life. 8Therefore, he who rejects this instruction
does not reject man but God, who gives you his Holy Spirit.

9Now about brotherly love we do not need to write to you, for
you yourselves have been taught by God to love each other. 10And
in fact, you do love all the brothers throughout Macedonia. Yet we
urge you, brothers, to do so more and more.

11Make it your ambition to lead a quiet life, to mind your own
business and to work with your hands, just as we told you, 12so
that your daily life may win the respect of outsiders and so that you
will not be dependent on anybody.

The Coming of the Lord

13Brothers, we do not want you to be ignorant about those who
fall asleep, or to grieve like the rest of men, who have no hope.
14We believe that Jesus died and rose again and so we believe that
God will bring with Jesus those who have fallen asleep in him.
15According to the Lord's own word, we tell you that we who are
still alive, who are left till the coming of the Lord, will certainly not
precede those who have fallen asleep. 16For the Lord himself will
come down from heaven, with a loud command, with the voice of
the archangel and with the trumpet call of God, and the dead in
Christ will rise first. 17After that, we who are still alive and are left
will be caught up together with them in the clouds to meet the
Lord in the air. And so we will be with the Lord forever. 18There-
fore encourage each other with these words.

5 Now, brothers, about times and dates we do not need to write
to you, 2for you know very well that the day of the Lord will
come like a thief in the night. 3While people are saying, "Peace and
safety," destruction will come on them suddenly, as labor pains on
a pregnant woman, and they will not escape.

4But you, brothers, are not in darkness so that this day should
surprise you like a thief. 5You are all sons of the light and sons of
the day. We do not belong to the night or to the darkness. 6So
then, let us not be like others, who are asleep, but let us be alert
and self-controlled. 7For those who sleep, sleep at night, and those
who get drunk, get drunk at night. 8But since we belong to the day,
let us be self-controlled, putting on faith and love as a breastplate,
and the hope of salvation as a helmet. 9For God did not appoint us
to suffer wrath but to receive salvation through our Lord Jesus
Christ. 10He died for us so that, whether we are awake or asleep,
we may live together with him. 11Therefore encourage one another
and build each other up, just as in fact you are doing.

Final Instructions

12Now we ask you, brothers, to respect those who work hard
among you, who are over you in the Lord and who admonish you.
13Hold them in the highest regard in love because of their work.
Live in peace with each other. 14And we urge you, brothers, warn
those who are idle, encourage the timid, help the weak, be patient
with everyone. 15Make sure that nobody pays back wrong for
wrong, but always try to be kind to each other and to everyone
else.

[a]4 Or *learn to live with his own wife*; or *learn to acquire a wife*

who has already made sexual mistakes? **3.** When urged to love "more and more," how do you suppose the Thessalonians felt?

1. How will a lifestyle that bears witness to God affect sexual morality? Work relationships? Time priorities? Small group dynamics? **2.** What do you say to someone who believes you can do anything you want, as long as you mind your own business (v. 11) and no one gets hurt (v. 6)? Would you say anything different to a Christian who believes the same thing about sexual freedom? If so, what?

Who was the first family member you recall dying? Who have you been closest to through their dying days? How did this affect you? What else has shaped your view of death and dying?

1. How would the Thessalonians have felt if they had remained ignorant of the Christian's resurrection and of Christ's return? How would Paul's words have encouraged them? **2.** Do Paul's words about Christ coming as "a thief in the night" (at an unknown time) calm, or stir up fear? How does Paul's analogy of night and day speak to this fear? **3.** How do *faith, love* and *hope* sum up what it means to "belong to the day" (5:8; see 1:3)?

1. Of all the places you live (at home, work, school or church) where do you feel the need for more faith, more hope or more love? How can your group help you? **2.** How can you be better prepared for Christ's return? **3.** How does this passage help you as you consider your own death?

What causes you to "blow a gasket": Traffic jams? Christmas shopping? Bickering children? Burned dinners? Or what?

1. From this passage, people make up the Christian community? **2.** What attitudes underlie Paul's various commands here? What impressions of the Christian life do these commands give you? **3.** How would you summarize the goal and hope of the Christian life

(vv. 23–24) in your own words? **4.** How do the many commands in verses 12–22 relate to the multi-dimensional blessing of verse 23? To the promise of verse 24? To the requests of verses 25–27? To the benediction of verse 28?

1. Of the various commands, which are most relevant to your church? Your small group? Your workplace? You? Which do you feel you already are practicing well? Which one will you work on this week? How? **2.** What encouragement, sanctification and grace do you receive from God to fulfill these commands? How has your small group been a help to you in this regard?

16Be joyful always; 17pray continually; 18give thanks in all circumstances, for this is God's will for you in Christ Jesus.
19Do not put out the Spirit's fire; 20do not treat prophecies with
contempt. 21Test everything. Hold on to the good. 22Avoid every
kind of evil.
23May God himself, the God of peace, sanctify you through and
through. May your whole spirit, soul and body be kept blameless at
the coming of our Lord Jesus Christ. 24The one who calls you is
faithful and he will do it.

25Brothers, pray for us. 26Greet all the brothers with a holy kiss.
27I charge you before the Lord to have this letter read to all the
brothers.
28The grace of our Lord Jesus Christ be with you.

INTRODUCTION to

2 THESSALONIANS

Book Study Outline: If you are using 2 Thessalonians for a study course, here is a 3-week outline. Use the margin questions for your group agenda:

start meeting / 15 min.

read & discuss Bible / 30 min.

close meeting / 15–45 min.

3-week plan	Group Study Passage
1	1:1–12/Perseverance and God's Judgment
2	2:1–17/Lawlessness and Christ's Coming
3	3:1–18/Idleness and Paul's Authority

Refer to the Questions and Answers in the front of this Bible for more information.

Author: The apostle Paul.

Date: Around A.D. 51; 1 and 2 Thessalonians or Galatians are the earliest letters of Paul in the NT.

Theme: Living in light of the coming of Christ.

Historical Background: First and Second Thessalonians are very much alike (see the Introduction to 1 Thessalonians). The second letter was written within months, if not weeks, of the first. Why was this necessary? The answer may well be that Paul's first letter to these young, untaught Christians produced a serious misunderstanding that necessitated a second, clarifying letter. Specifically, his teaching that "the day of the Lord will come like a thief in the night" (1Th 5:2) may have encouraged people to abandon normal pursuits to prepare for the Second Coming. Thus in 2 Thessalonians 2:1–12 he outlines the events, including the great rebellion, that must take place prior to the return of Christ. The Second Coming is not so imminent that they have to stop everything. Then he goes on to reiterate what he said in his earlier letter: Stand firm and do not be idle. Thus Paul encourages the Thessalonians in responsible Christian living as well as trying to correct some of the misunderstandings they had about the nature and implications of the second coming of Christ.

THE PURPOSE OF 1 AND 2 THESSALONIANS

Paul had left Thessalonica rather abruptly (see Ac 17:5–10) after a brief stay. Recent converts from paganism (1Th 1:9) were thus left with little external support in the midst of persecution. Paul's purpose in writing these letters was:

1. To encourage persecuted believers
(1Th 3:2–5; 2Th 1:3–10)

2. To exhort the Thessalonians to be steadfast, godly and to work for a living
(1Th 4:1–8,11–12; 2Th 2:13–3:15)

3. To correct a misunderstanding and give assurance concerning the Lord's return and the future of believers
(1Th 4:13–15; 2Th 2:1–12)

Characteristics: 1 and 2 Thessalonians contain much of the material we have from Paul about the Second Coming. Why did he need to expound on this theme so much at Thessalonica? One suggestion is he may have made use of a popular pagan myth as a point of contact for preaching the Gospel when he was in the city (we have an example of Paul doing something like this when he preached in Athens in Ac 17). Since this myth focused on the hope that one day a hero would return and help the needy, especially those in Thessalonica, Paul would have a ready-made point of entry to tell of the mission of Jesus. His emphasis on the Second Coming in these letters shows that the people may not have fully grasped the differences between Jesus' return and that of their expected hero, especially as it related to their lifestyle.

2 Thessalonians

1 Paul, Silas[a] and Timothy,

To the church of the Thessalonians in God our Father and the
Lord Jesus Christ:

2Grace and peace to you from God the Father and the Lord Jesus
Christ.

Thanksgiving and Prayer

3We ought always to thank God for you, brothers, and rightly so,
because your faith is growing more and more, and the love every
one of you has for each other is increasing. 4Therefore, among
God's churches we boast about your perseverance and faith in all
the persecutions and trials you are enduring.

5All this is evidence that God's judgment is right, and as a result
you will be counted worthy of the kingdom of God, for which you
are suffering. 6God is just: He will pay back trouble to those who
trouble you 7and give relief to you who are troubled, and to us as
well. This will happen when the Lord Jesus is revealed from heav-
en in blazing fire with his powerful angels. 8He will punish those
who do not know God and do not obey the gospel of our Lord
Jesus. 9They will be punished with everlasting destruction and shut
out from the presence of the Lord and from the majesty of his
power 10on the day he comes to be glorified in his holy people and
to be marveled at among all those who have believed. This includes
you, because you believed our testimony to you.

11With this in mind, we constantly pray for you, that our God
may count you worthy of his calling, and that by his power he may
fulfill every good purpose of yours and every act prompted by your
faith. 12We pray this so that the name of our Lord Jesus may be
glorified in you, and you in him, according to the grace of our God
and the Lord Jesus Christ.[b]

The Man of Lawlessness

2 Concerning the coming of our Lord Jesus Christ and our being
gathered to him, we ask you, brothers, 2not to become easily
unsettled or alarmed by some prophecy, report or letter supposed
to have come from us, saying that the day of the Lord has already
come. 3Don't let anyone deceive you in any way, for ⌞that day will
not come⌟ until the rebellion occurs and the man of lawlessness[c]
is revealed, the man doomed to destruction. 4He will oppose and
will exalt himself over everything that is called God or is worshiped, so that he sets himself up in God's temple, proclaiming
himself to be God.

5Don't you remember that when I was with you I used to tell
you these things? 6And now you know what is holding him back,
so that he may be revealed at the proper time. 7For the secret
power of lawlessness is already at work; but the one who now
holds it back will continue to do so till he is taken out of the way.

[a] *1* Greek *Silvanus,* a variant of *Silas* [b] *12* Or *God and Lord, Jesus Christ* [c] *3* Some manuscripts *sin*

What did your parents do right in raising you? What rewards and punishments worked best?

1. What has happened since Paul wrote 1 Thessalonians (v. 4)? How has persecution affected this church? **2.** What is the evidence that they are "worthy" of God's kingdom (v. 5)? **3.** Who is on trial here? Who is on the witness stand? In the judge's chambers? **4.** Why is God waiting until the Second Coming to punish these persecutors? Who benefits from this delayed justice? How so? **5.** What quality do you think Paul admires most in these Christians? **6.** What do you see as the net effect of Paul's thanksgiving and prayer?

1. How will you exercise faith and love this week in a specific way or relationship? **2.** Which of your current struggles are a result of being a Christian? **3.** How do you feel about the punishment mentioned in verses 8–9? How might you feel if you were being severely oppressed? **4.** Pray Paul's prayer (vv. 11–12) in your own words for one another this week.

At what stage in life were you "rebellious"? What memory (painful or humorous) is associated with those times of conflict?

1. What must have been happening in Thessalonica to lead Paul to write this (see also Introduction to 2 Thessalonians)? **2.** How much time was Paul able to spend with the Thessalonians (see Ac 17:2)? How would this affect their willingness to believe rumors about Christ's return (v. 2)? **3.** Whom do you think is the restrainer of this lawless one (vv. 6–7)? How do you think this "restraining order" is enforced? **4.** What is God's ultimate purpose in allowing the "man of lawlessness" to deceive people? What signs mark his appearing? **5.**

8And then the lawless one will be revealed, whom the Lord Jesus will overthrow with the breath of his mouth and destroy by the splendor of his coming. 9The coming of the lawless one will be in accordance with the work of Satan displayed in all kinds of counterfeit miracles, signs and wonders, 10and in every sort of evil that deceives those who are perishing. They perish because they refused to love the truth and so be saved. 11For this reason God sends them a powerful delusion so that they will believe the lie 12and so that all will be condemned who have not believed the truth but have delighted in wickedness.

Stand Firm

13But we ought always to thank God for you, brothers loved by the Lord, because from the beginning God chose you[a] to be saved through the sanctifying work of the Spirit and through belief in the truth. 14He called you to this through our gospel, that you might share in the glory of our Lord Jesus Christ. 15So then, brothers, stand firm and hold to the teachings[b] we passed on to you, whether by word of mouth or by letter.

16May our Lord Jesus Christ himself and God our Father, who loved us and by his grace gave us eternal encouragement and good hope, 17encourage your hearts and strengthen you in every good deed and word.

Request for Prayer

3 Finally, brothers, pray for us that the message of the Lord may spread rapidly and be honored, just as it was with you. 2And pray that we may be delivered from wicked and evil men, for not everyone has faith. 3But the Lord is faithful, and he will strengthen and protect you from the evil one. 4We have confidence in the Lord that you are doing and will continue to do the things we command. 5May the Lord direct your hearts into God's love and Christ's perseverance.

Warning Against Idleness

6In the name of the Lord Jesus Christ, we command you, brothers, to keep away from every brother who is idle and does not live according to the teaching[c] you received from us. 7For you yourselves know how you ought to follow our example. We were not idle when we were with you, 8nor did we eat anyone's food without paying for it. On the contrary, we worked night and day, laboring and toiling so that we would not be a burden to any of you. 9We did this, not because we do not have the right to such help, but in order to make ourselves a model for you to follow. 10For even when we were with you, we gave you this rule: "If a man will not work, he shall not eat."

11We hear that some among you are idle. They are not busy; they are busybodies. 12Such people we command and urge in the Lord Jesus Christ to settle down and earn the bread they eat. 13And as for you, brothers, never tire of doing what is right.

14If anyone does not obey our instruction in this letter, take special note of him. Do not associate with him, in order that he may feel ashamed. 15Yet do not regard him as an enemy, but warn him as a brother.

[a]13 Some manuscripts *because God chose you as his firstfruits* [b]15 Or *traditions*
[c]6 Or *tradition*

How will those who refuse Christ respond to this "man"? How does the "powerful delusion" sent by God differ from the deceptive evil of this "man" (vv. 10–12)? **6.** How and why will God save his people (vv. 13–14)? In response to God's initiative and Paul's ministry, what are the people to do?

1. How does this passage on Christ's Second Coming, and what will precede it, make you feel? Afraid? Relieved? Rather not think about it? Why? How do you think Paul would have wanted you to feel? **2.** What encouragement do verses 13–14 give you as you face hard times? Where do you need encouragement and strength from God now? **3.** Put this prayer (vv. 16–17) in your own words and pray it for one another this week.

---

1. What is one prayer you were taught to memorize? **2.** What was your first paid job? How long or hard did you work at it? What did you do with your money?

1. Paul has twice prayed for these people (1:11–12; 2:16–17). How does he want them to pray for him and his companions? How would the encouragements in verses 3–5 help them in their trials? **2.** How might a misunderstanding of Paul's earlier teaching (1Th 5:1–3) have led to the problem of idleness? Why would Paul see that as a serious problem *then* (see 1Th 4:11–12) and *now* (see v. 6)? What model does Paul leave for the others to follow (vv. 7–13)? What does this have to do with taking responsibility? **3.** Why does Paul call attention to his handwriting (v. 17)? How else is the close of the letter similar to its beginning? Why do you think Paul emphasizes grace and peace? What does it say about God's will?

1. On a scale from 1 (high anxiety) to 10 (blissfully peaceful), where would you rate your sense of God's peace now? Where in particular do you need group prayer and support? **2.** How are God's love and Christ's perseverance needed in your life now? **3.** What have you found helpful in encouraging you to pray for missionaries? For whom do you regularly pray? What types of pressures may he or she face in that part of the world? **4.** Are you idle, a busybody, a worrywart or a workaholic? What is God's message to you in 2 Thessalonians?

Final Greetings

16Now may the Lord of peace himself give you peace at all times
and in every way. The Lord be with all of you.
17I, Paul, write this greeting in my own hand, which is the
distinguishing mark in all my letters. This is how I write.
18The grace of our Lord Jesus Christ be with you all.

INTRODUCTION to
1 TIMOTHY

Book Study Outline: If you are using 1 Timothy for a study course, here is a 6- or 8-week outline. Use the margin questions for your agenda:

start meeting / 15 min.

read & discuss Bible / 30 min.

close meeting / 15–45 min.

Refer to the Questions and Answers in front of Bible for more information.

6-week plan	8-week plan	Group Study Passage
1	1	1:1–11/False Teachers of the Law
	2	1:12–20/True Mercy for Sinners
2	3	2:1–15/Orderly Worship
3	4	3:1–16/Faithful Leadership
4	5	4:1–16/Redemptive Ministry
5	6	5:1–6:2/Widows, Elders and Slaves
6	7	6:3–10/Love of Money
	8	6:11–21/Fighting the Good Fight

Author: The apostle Paul. However, based on considerations of vocabulary and style, the Pauline authorship of the Pastoral Epistles (1 and 2 Timothy, Titus) has been questioned by some scholars.

Date: About A.D. 63–65.

Theme: A faithful ministry.

Historical Background: Timothy, a young man from Lystra, was probably converted during Paul's first missionary journey. When Paul returned to the area a year or two later, Timothy was recommended to him as a faithful disciple of Christ who would make a good traveling companion (Ac 16). From that time on,Timothy is associated with Paul. After Paul was released from his imprisonment in Rome (Ac 28), he,Titus and Timothy went on a preaching tour (see the Introduction to Titus). At Ephesus, Paul discovered that heresy was rotting away the church. It seems that the false teaching involved speculation about obscure matters rather than exposition about Christ and the Christian lifestyle of love. The teachers were characterized as proud, arrogant, contentious and greedy. As a result, Paul excommunicated two of the erring elders (1:19–20) and put Timothy in charge of helping the church recover from its problems (1:3–4). Paul then went on to Macedonia where he wrote this letter to encourage Timothy in his restorative work.

Characteristics: As a result of being called the "Pastoral Epistles," 1 and 2 Timothy and Titus have typically been viewed as manuals for church structure and order. However, 1 Timothy, as well as the other two letters, is a response to a particular crisis in a particular church, not a general commentary on how a church should be run. Its value is not to be found so much in trying to determine church structure (which in the NT appears to be quite fluid), but in determining the character of people who ought to be in leadership. (See the list of qualifications in the Introduction to Titus.)

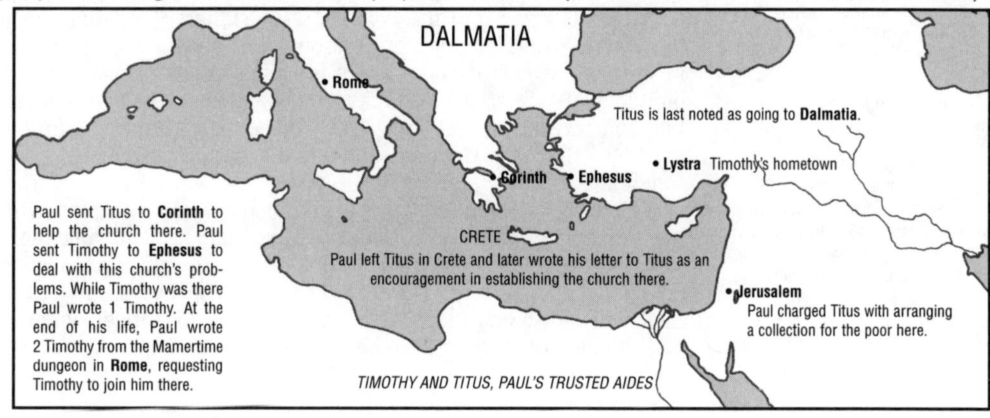

DALMATIA
Rome
Titus is last noted as going to Dalmatia.
Lystra Timothy's hometown
Corinth
Ephesus
Paul sent Titus to Corinth to help the church there. Paul sent Timothy to Ephesus to deal with this church's problems. While Timothy was there Paul wrote 1 Timothy. At the end of his life, Paul wrote 2 Timothy from the Mamertime dungeon in Rome, requesting Timothy to join him there.
CRETE
Paul left Titus in Crete and later wrote his letter to Titus as an encouragement in establishing the church there.
Jerusalem
Paul charged Titus with arranging a collection for the poor here.

TIMOTHY AND TITUS, PAUL'S TRUSTED AIDES

1 Timothy

1. Growing up, what was your father's occupation? Your mother's? **2.** How did they settle sibling fights?

1. What were the problems plaguing the church in Ephesus (vv. 3–4)? How do you think Timothy felt being left in charge of this situation? **2.** What does Paul want Timothy to work toward (v. 5)? How does this differ from the false teachers' work (v. 7)? **3.** For whom is the Law really intended (vv. 9–11)?

1. When did God become your "hope" (v. 1)? In your experience, has God been more of a "lawgiver" or a "lover"? Has your understanding of God changed as you've come to know him? How? **2.** Who in your life would think of you as their "son or daughter in the faith" as Paul addresses Timothy?

1 Paul, an apostle of Christ Jesus by the command of God our Savior and of Christ Jesus our hope,

2To Timothy my true son in the faith:

Grace, mercy and peace from God the Father and Christ Jesus our Lord.

Warning Against False Teachers of the Law

3As I urged you when I went into Macedonia, stay there in Ephesus so that you may command certain men not to teach false doctrines any longer 4nor to devote themselves to myths and endless genealogies. These promote controversies rather than God's work—which is by faith. 5The goal of this command is love, which comes from a pure heart and a good conscience and a sincere faith. 6Some have wandered away from these and turned to meaningless talk. 7They want to be teachers of the law, but they do not know what they are talking about or what they so confidently affirm.

8We know that the law is good if one uses it properly. 9We also know that law[a] is made not for the righteous but for lawbreakers and rebels, the ungodly and sinful, the unholy and irreligious; for those who kill their fathers or mothers, for murderers, 10for adulterers and perverts, for slave traders and liars and perjurers—and for whatever else is contrary to the sound doctrine 11that conforms to the glorious gospel of the blessed God, which he entrusted to me.

Who holds the record in your group for most speeding tickets? Most times "grounded"?

1. What are Paul's credentials—what gives him authority over the false teachers (v. 12)? **2.** Why is someone like Paul such a good witness to unbelievers (v. 16)? How do you feel about talking about your past when you share your faith? **3.** What do you know about Timothy and his relationship with Paul? (See Acts 16:1–5 and Introduction to 1 Timothy.)

1. What was your life like before you knew Christ? **2.** How would you put verse 15 into your own words to share the Gospel with a friend? When have you done this? **3.** Should our response to those who act in "ignorance and unbelief" (v. 13) be different from those who "have shipwrecked their faith" (v. 19)? Why? How so?

The Lord's Grace to Paul

12I thank Christ Jesus our Lord, who has given me strength, that he considered me faithful, appointing me to his service. 13Even though I was once a blasphemer and a persecutor and a violent man, I was shown mercy because I acted in ignorance and unbelief. 14The grace of our Lord was poured out on me abundantly, along with the faith and love that are in Christ Jesus.

15Here is a trustworthy saying that deserves full acceptance: Christ Jesus came into the world to save sinners—of whom I am the worst. 16But for that very reason I was shown mercy so that in me, the worst of sinners, Christ Jesus might display his unlimited patience as an example for those who would believe on him and receive eternal life. 17Now to the King eternal, immortal, invisible, the only God, be honor and glory for ever and ever. Amen.

18Timothy, my son, I give you this instruction in keeping with the prophecies once made about you, so that by following them you may fight the good fight, 19holding on to faith and a good conscience. Some have rejected these and so have shipwrecked their faith. 20Among them are Hymenaeus and Alexander, whom I have handed over to Satan to be taught not to blaspheme.

[a]9 Or *that the law*

Instructions on Worship

2 I urge, then, first of all, that requests, prayers, intercession and
thanksgiving be made for everyone— 2for kings and all those
in authority, that we may live peaceful and quiet lives in all godliness and holiness. 3This is good, and pleases God our Savior, 4who
wants all men to be saved and to come to a knowledge of the truth.
5For there is one God and one mediator between God and men,
the man Christ Jesus, 6who gave himself as a ransom for all men—
the testimony given in its proper time. 7And for this purpose I was
appointed a herald and an apostle—I am telling the truth, I am not
lying—and a teacher of the true faith to the Gentiles.
8I want men everywhere to lift up holy hands in prayer, without
anger or disputing.
9I also want women to dress modestly, with decency and propriety, not with braided hair or gold or pearls or expensive clothes,
10but with good deeds, appropriate for women who profess to
worship God.
11A woman should learn in quietness and full submission. 12I do
not permit a woman to teach or to have authority over a man; she
must be silent. 13For Adam was formed first, then Eve. 14And
Adam was not the one deceived; it was the woman who was
deceived and became a sinner. 15But women[a] will be saved[b]
through childbearing—if they continue in faith, love and holiness
with propriety.

Overseers and Deacons

3 Here is a trustworthy saying: If anyone sets his heart on being
an overseer,[c] he desires a noble task. 2Now the overseer
must be above reproach, the husband of but one wife, temperate,
self-controlled, respectable, hospitable, able to teach, 3not given to
drunkenness, not violent but gentle, not quarrelsome, not a lover
of money. 4He must manage his own family well and see that his
children obey him with proper respect. 5(If anyone does not know
how to manage his own family, how can he take care of God's
church?) 6He must not be a recent convert, or he may become
conceited and fall under the same judgment as the devil. 7He must
also have a good reputation with outsiders, so that he will not fall
into disgrace and into the devil's trap.
8Deacons, likewise, are to be men worthy of respect, sincere,
not indulging in much wine, and not pursuing dishonest gain.
9They must keep hold of the deep truths of the faith with a clear
conscience. 10They must first be tested; and then if there is nothing
against them, let them serve as deacons.
11In the same way, their wives[d] are to be women worthy of
respect, not malicious talkers but temperate and trustworthy in
everything.
12A deacon must be the husband of but one wife and must
manage his children and his household well. 13Those who have
served well gain an excellent standing and great assurance in their
faith in Christ Jesus.
14Although I hope to come to you soon, I am writing you these
instructions so that, 15if I am delayed, you will know how people
ought to conduct themselves in God's household, which is the
church of the living God, the pillar and foundation of the truth.
16Beyond all question, the mystery of godliness is great:

Did you go to church as a child? Was worship inspiring?

1. For whom is Paul asking that prayers for salvation be made (vv. 1,4,6–7)? Have you felt certain people were too far gone for salvation? What would Paul say? **2.** What seemed to be going on in worship in Ephesus (vv. 8–12)? **3.** Are verses 9–15 meant for all times and places, or for a problem at Ephesus (see 1:3–4; 2Ti 3:6–7)? What other principles from Scripture or your experience of God help you decide what women's God-given roles are?

1. What worship attitudes do you want to cultivate? **2.** Often the church has not allowed women to use God-given gifts. How does Christ affirm your worth even when others do not?

---

1. As a child, how did you treat your babysitters? How did they treat you? **2.** Do you enjoy babysitting?

1. Why is this list of leadership qualifications focused on the outward as well as the inward? Why is this important considering the Ephesian church's problem with false teachers (v. 5)? **2.** How do you interpret "the husband of but one wife" (v. 2)? Does that mean the overseer must not be single? Divorced? Widowed? Remarried? A polygamist? Or does it demand sexual fidelity if married (see also 5:9)? **3.** How do you interpret verse 4? What if a godly man who meets the other qualifications has a child who is rebellious and a troublemaker? **4.** What central facts about Jesus are summed up in the hymn (v. 16)?

1. Although applied specifically to leaders here, why are these qualities important for all Christians? **2.** Of these qualities, what are two or three you have made progress with in this past year? In which area do you want to grow now? How can this group help you? **3.** What positions in your church are the equivalent to those of overseers and deacons? Are these basic guidelines followed?

[a] *15* Greek *she* [b] *15* Or *restored* [c] *1* Traditionally *bishop*; also in verse 2
[d] *11* Or *way, deaconesses*

He[a] appeared in a body,[b]
  was vindicated by the Spirit,
was seen by angels,
  was preached among the nations,
was believed on in the world,
  was taken up in glory.

What do you do to keep in shape? How physically fit are you?

1. Why is it hypocritical to preach abstinence from marriage and certain foods (see Mk 7:18–19)? What do the teachings in verse 3 imply about these teachers' views of spirituality? **2.** What are the limits to the "freedom" principle of verses 4–5? **3.** What does Paul mean by "train yourself to be godly" (vv. 7,11–16)?

1. How do you identify hypocrisy versus human imperfection? **2.** Do you spend more time and energy on physical training or godliness training? How intense has your godliness training been this year? In the past? With your children? Have you neglected the use of any God-given gifts (v. 14)? **3.** What disciplines should be part of a person's spiritual growth program? Which do you want to work on? **4.** Some of your coworkers may have been hurt by the church in some way. What in this passage might you practice to influence them toward Christ?

Instructions to Timothy

4 The Spirit clearly says that in later times some will abandon the faith and follow deceiving spirits and things taught by demons. 2Such teachings come through hypocritical liars, whose consciences have been seared as with a hot iron. 3They forbid people to marry and order them to abstain from certain foods, which God created to be received with thanksgiving by those who believe and who know the truth. 4For everything God created is good, and nothing is to be rejected if it is received with thanksgiving, 5because it is consecrated by the word of God and prayer.

6If you point these things out to the brothers, you will be a good minister of Christ Jesus, brought up in the truths of the faith and of the good teaching that you have followed. 7Have nothing to do with godless myths and old wives' tales; rather, train yourself to be godly. 8For physical training is of some value, but godliness has value for all things, holding promise for both the present life and the life to come.

9This is a trustworthy saying that deserves full acceptance 10(and for this we labor and strive), that we have put our hope in the living God, who is the Savior of all men, and especially of those who believe.

11Command and teach these things. 12Don't let anyone look down on you because you are young, but set an example for the believers in speech, in life, in love, in faith and in purity. 13Until I come, devote yourself to the public reading of Scripture, to preaching and to teaching. 14Do not neglect your gift, which was given you through a prophetic message when the body of elders laid their hands on you.

15Be diligent in these matters; give yourself wholly to them, so that everyone may see your progress. 16Watch your life and doctrine closely. Persevere in them, because if you do, you will save both yourself and your hearers.

Growing up, what proverb best described the way your family used money: "Waste not, want not"? "Eat, drink and be merry"? "You can't take it with you"? "A penny saved is a penny earned"? "Penny wise, pound foolish"?

1. Reading between the lines, what was the problem with widows in the church? **2.** What possible abuses of care for the needy does Paul imply in verses 4–8? Verses 9–10? Verses 11–15? Is a different response to each person in need appropriate in today's church as well? **3.** Why are church elders in general to receive "double honor" (v. 17)? Do they receive this honor in your church? Why do some elders deserve pub-

Advice About Widows, Elders and Slaves

5 Do not rebuke an older man harshly, but exhort him as if he were your father. Treat younger men as brothers, 2older women as mothers, and younger women as sisters, with absolute purity.

3Give proper recognition to those widows who are really in need. 4But if a widow has children or grandchildren, these should learn first of all to put their religion into practice by caring for their own family and so repaying their parents and grandparents, for this is pleasing to God. 5The widow who is really in need and left all alone puts her hope in God and continues night and day to pray and to ask God for help. 6But the widow who lives for pleasure is dead even while she lives. 7Give the people these instructions, too, so that no one may be open to blame. 8If anyone does not provide for his relatives, and especially for his immediate family, he has denied the faith and is worse than an unbeliever.

9No widow may be put on the list of widows unless she is over

[a] *16* Some manuscripts *God* [b] *16* Or *in the flesh*

sixty, has been faithful to her husband,[a] 10 and is well known for
her good deeds, such as bringing up children, showing hospitality,
washing the feet of the saints, helping those in trouble and devot-
ing herself to all kinds of good deeds.
11 As for younger widows, do not put them on such a list. For
when their sensual desires overcome their dedication to Christ,
they want to marry. 12 Thus they bring judgment on themselves,
because they have broken their first pledge. 13 Besides, they get
into the habit of being idle and going about from house to house.
And not only do they become idlers, but also gossips and busybodies, saying things they ought not to. 14 So I counsel younger widows
to marry, to have children, to manage their homes and to give the
enemy no opportunity for slander. 15 Some have in fact already
turned away to follow Satan.
16 If any woman who is a believer has widows in her family, she
should help them and not let the church be burdened with them,
so that the church can help those widows who are really in need.
17 The elders who direct the affairs of the church well are worthy
of double honor, especially those whose work is preaching and
teaching. 18 For the Scripture says, "Do not muzzle the ox while
it is treading out the grain,"[b] and "The worker deserves his
wages."[c] 19 Do not entertain an accusation against an elder unless
it is brought by two or three witnesses. 20 Those who sin are to be
rebuked publicly, so that the others may take warning.
21 I charge you, in the sight of God and Christ Jesus and the elect
angels, to keep these instructions without partiality, and to do
nothing out of favoritism.
22 Do not be hasty in the laying on of hands, and do not share in
the sins of others. Keep yourself pure.
23 Stop drinking only water, and use a little wine because of your
stomach and your frequent illnesses.
24 The sins of some men are obvious, reaching the place of judgment ahead of them; the sins of others trail behind them. 25 In the
same way, good deeds are obvious, and even those that are not
cannot be hidden.

6 All who are under the yoke of slavery should consider their
masters worthy of full respect, so that God's name and our
teaching may not be slandered. 2 Those who have believing masters
are not to show less respect for them because they are brothers.
Instead, they are to serve them even better, because those who
benefit from their service are believers, and dear to them. These
are the things you are to teach and urge on them.

Love of Money

3 If anyone teaches false doctrines and does not agree to the
sound instruction of our Lord Jesus Christ and to godly teaching,
4 he is conceited and understands nothing. He has an unhealthy
interest in controversies and quarrels about words that result in
envy, strife, malicious talk, evil suspicions 5 and constant friction
between men of corrupt mind, who have been robbed of the truth
and who think that godliness is a means to financial gain.
6 But godliness with contentment is great gain. 7 For we brought
nothing into the world, and we can take nothing out of it. 8 But if
we have food and clothing, we will be content with that. 9 People
who want to get rich fall into temptation and a trap and into many
foolish and harmful desires that plunge men into ruin and destruc-

[a]9 Or *has had but one husband* [b]18 Deut. 25:4 [c]18 Luke 10:7

lic rebuke? **4.** Why doesn't Paul proclaim slavery to be wrong? **5.** Why might a Christian slave's lack of respect for his master result in the slander of God's name and Christian teaching (6:1–2)? How does this instruction relate to your work situation?

1. Have you or someone you have known ever suddenly become single? What was that time like? Who in your church needs some help that you or your group can provide? **2.** What should be the Christian's/Church's response to the welfare issue?

What was your first job? How much did you get paid?

1. How is the life of one who follows verses 6–8 different from one in verses 9–10? How can you distinguish between them? **2.** What is the "great gain" in "godliness with contentment"?

1. When have you struggled most financially? When have you been tempted to be a "lover of money"? **2.** Is there a difference between enjoying money and being a lover of money? How fine is the line?

tion. 10For the love of money is a root of all kinds of evil. Some
people, eager for money, have wandered from the faith and pierced
themselves with many griefs.

Paul's Charge to Timothy

11But you, man of God, flee from all this, and pursue righteousness, godliness, faith, love, endurance and gentleness. 12Fight the
good fight of the faith. Take hold of the eternal life to which you
were called when you made your good confession in the presence
of many witnesses. 13In the sight of God, who gives life to everything, and of Christ Jesus, who while testifying before Pontius
Pilate made the good confession, I charge you 14to keep this command without spot or blame until the appearing of our Lord Jesus
Christ, 15which God will bring about in his own time—God, the
blessed and only Ruler, the King of kings and Lord of lords, 16who
alone is immortal and who lives in unapproachable light, whom no
one has seen or can see. To him be honor and might forever.
Amen.

17Command those who are rich in this present world not to be
arrogant nor to put their hope in wealth, which is so uncertain, but
to put their hope in God, who richly provides us with everything
for our enjoyment. 18Command them to do good, to be rich in good
deeds, and to be generous and willing to share. 19In this way they
will lay up treasure for themselves as a firm foundation for the
coming age, so that they may take hold of the life that is truly life.
20Timothy, guard what has been entrusted to your care. Turn
away from godless chatter and the opposing ideas of what is falsely
called knowledge, 21which some have professed and in so doing
have wandered from the faith.

Grace be with you.

---

1. Growing up, did your parents tend to overprotect you, or push you beyond your limits? **2.** With your children, what are you going to do (or have you done) differently when it comes to risk-taking versus playing it safe?

1. What is Timothy told to flee? To pursue (v. 11)? How does a person pursue these qualities? Which one do you particularly want to pursue? **2.** How do you think Timothy felt reading the challenge in verses 12–16? How would you respond to this challenge? Why? **3.** Why does Paul use battle imagery in verse 12? What does this tell you about what we must expect in the Christian life? **4.** Why do you think Paul added more instructions to the wealthy (vv. 17–19)? In your opinion, is it easier for a rich person or a poor person to follow the command in verse 18? Why?

1. What grade would God give you for verse 11? Verses 18–19? **2.** What kinds of "godless chatter" and "false knowledge" (v. 20) do Christians need to turn away from today? Which do you need to be especially cautious of? **3.** Who in your life may be a "Timothy" for whom God would have you be a "Paul"? **4.** What false teachings are you aware of and concerned about today? How can you help your church to be on guard, and to present a strong offense?

INTRODUCTION to

2 TIMOTHY

Book Study Outline: If you are using 2 Timothy for a study course, here is a 4-week outline. Use the margin questions for your group agenda:

start meeting / 15 min.

read & discuss Bible / 30 min.

close meeting / 15–45 min.

4-week plan	Group Study Passage
1	1:3–2:13/Be Strong in Christ
2	2:14–26/Be a Good Workman
3	3:10–4:8/Be Faithful
4	4:9–22/To God Be the Glory

Refer to the Questions and Answers in front of Bible for more information.

Author: The apostle Paul. However, based on considerations of vocabulary and style, the Pauline authorship of the Pastoral Epistles (1 and 2 Timothy, Titus) has been questioned by some scholars.

Date: Near the end of Paul's life, c. A.D. 67–68.

Theme: Guard the Gospel.

Historical Background: In the spring following the writing of 1 Timothy, Paul was on his way to Ephesus when he was arrested, taken back to Rome, and thrown into prison. It was the time of Nero's insane persecution of Christians, and so he was put in a dungeon "like a criminal" (2:9). He had had a preliminary trial (4:16). His full trial was ahead but Paul did not expect to be released (4:6). In this letter he writes to Timothy encouraging him to hold on to the faith no matter what, and to come to him as soon as he could. Whether he ever saw Timothy again is not known. According to tradition, Paul was beheaded shortly after this letter was written.

THE LAST WORDS OF PAUL

To Timothy

"...fan into flame the gift of God..."
2Ti 1:6

"...do not be ashamed to testify about our Lord..."
2Ti 1:8

"Endure hardship with us like a good soldier of Christ Jesus."
2Ti 2:3

"Do your best to present yourself to God as one approved, a workman who does not need to be ashamed and who correctly handles the word of truth."
2Ti 2:15

"Preach the word; be prepared in season and out of season..."
2Ti 4:2

About Himself

"...I am not ashamed, because I know whom I have believed, and am convinced that he is able to guard what I have entrusted to him for that day."
2Ti 1:12

"I am already being poured out like a drink offering, and the time has come for my departure."
2Ti 4:6

"I have fought the good fight, I have finished the race, I have kept the faith."
2Ti 4:7

"The Lord will rescue me from every evil attack and will bring me safely to his heavenly kingdom."
2Ti 4:18

Characteristics: Although similar in some ways to 1 Timothy and Titus, 2 Timothy is far more personal in tone. The other two letters were somewhat "business-like" in their discussion of the problems facing the church. This one is the deeply intimate testimony of a man who, having invested his life in the cause of Jesus Christ, wishes to pass on that commitment to a younger man who will carry the torch further. Timothy was the logical choice for this responsibility. He had been a trusted colleague of Paul's for over 15 years and had proved his loyalty to Jesus Christ again and again. This was a critical time for the churches in Europe and Asia. Under Nero's persecution, Rome, which had previously protected the rights of Christians whom they viewed as simply a sect of Jews, had turned against Christianity. Furthermore, there had been widespread apostasy in Asia (1:15). Paul, the missionary who had worked so hard in establishing these churches, was facing death. Now it would be up to Timothy and others to guard the Gospel. Yet, despite the problems, there is a clear note of triumph in this letter. The Gospel cannot be chained (2:9); the church will prevail (4:8); and Paul will be with the Lord (4:18).

2 Timothy

1 Paul, an apostle of Christ Jesus by the will of God, according to
the promise of life that is in Christ Jesus,

[2]To Timothy, my dear son:

Grace, mercy and peace from God the Father and Christ Jesus
our Lord.

Encouragement to Be Faithful

[3]I thank God, whom I serve, as my forefathers did, with a clear
conscience, as night and day I constantly remember you in my
prayers. [4]Recalling your tears, I long to see you, so that I may be
filled with joy. [5]I have been reminded of your sincere faith, which
first lived in your grandmother Lois and in your mother Eunice
and, I am persuaded, now lives in you also. [6]For this reason I
remind you to fan into flame the gift of God, which is in you
through the laying on of my hands. [7]For God did not give us a spirit
of timidity, but a spirit of power, of love and of self-discipline.

[8]So do not be ashamed to testify about our Lord, or ashamed of
me his prisoner. But join with me in suffering for the gospel, by the
power of God, [9]who has saved us and called us to a holy life—not
because of anything we have done but because of his own purpose
and grace. This grace was given us in Christ Jesus before the
beginning of time, [10]but it has now been revealed through the
appearing of our Savior, Christ Jesus, who has destroyed death and
has brought life and immortality to light through the gospel. [11]And
of this gospel I was appointed a herald and an apostle and a teacher. [12]That is why I am suffering as I am. Yet I am not ashamed,
because I know whom I have believed, and am convinced that he
is able to guard what I have entrusted to him for that day.

[13]What you heard from me, keep as the pattern of sound teaching, with faith and love in Christ Jesus. [14]Guard the good deposit
that was entrusted to you—guard it with the help of the Holy Spirit
who lives in us.

[15]You know that everyone in the province of Asia has deserted
me, including Phygelus and Hermogenes.

[16]May the Lord show mercy to the household of Onesiphorus,
because he often refreshed me and was not ashamed of my chains.
[17]On the contrary, when he was in Rome, he searched hard for me
until he found me. [18]May the Lord grant that he will find mercy
from the Lord on that day! You know very well in how many ways
he helped me in Ephesus.

2 You then, my son, be strong in the grace that is in Christ Jesus.
[2]And the things you have heard me say in the presence of
many witnesses entrust to reliable men who will also be qualified
to teach others. [3]Endure hardship with us like a good soldier of
Christ Jesus. [4]No one serving as a soldier gets involved in civilian
affairs—he wants to please his commanding officer. [5]Similarly, if
anyone competes as an athlete, he does not receive the victor's
crown unless he competes according to the rules. [6]The hardwork-
ing farmer should be the first to receive a share of the crops.
[7]Reflect on what I am saying, for the Lord will give you insight into
all this.

1. What physical traits have you inherited from your father's side of the family? Your mother's? **2.** Of all your friends from high school, who are still your friends today?

1. What do you know or remember about Timothy? (See Introductions to 1 and 2 Timothy; Ac 16:1–3.) **2.** What kind of spiritual heritage did Timothy receive from his family? How does that compare with your spiritual heritage? **3.** Along with being reminded of Timothy's sincere faith, what does Paul remind Timothy to do? **4.** What is one weakness that Timothy has and what does Paul remind him of regarding it (v. 7)? **5.** What pressures might pull at Timothy to be ashamed of the Gospel or of Paul? What kept Paul from being ashamed himself (v. 12)? What keeps you from being ashamed of the Gospel? **6.** How is Timothy to ensure that the message of Christ will live on (2:1–2)? Given Paul's outlook that his days are numbered (see Introduction to 2 Timothy), why was this point particularly crucial to him? **7.** What do the examples of the soldier, athlete and farmer (2:3–7) teach about the Christian life? How would these illustrations encourage Timothy to steadfastly endure his own suffering? **8.** In spite of his suffering, what keeps Paul from giving up (2:8–10)? What has kept you going in times of suffering? **9.** How does the hymn in 2:11–13 pull together the key themes of this passage?

1. What were the key factors and events in your life that led to what Paul calls a "sincere faith"? **2.** Have you had a spiritual parent or mentor like Paul? If so, who? **3.** Have you had a spiritual child or trainee like Timothy? If so, who? **4.** When you first decided to follow Jesus, did you assume it would be a bed of roses or a bed of nails? What have you learned about the cost of following Jesus since then? **5.** What role do suffering and endurance play in your life?

8Remember Jesus Christ, raised from the dead, descended from David. This is my gospel, 9for which I am suffering even to the point of being chained like a criminal. But God's word is not chained. 10Therefore I endure everything for the sake of the elect, that they too may obtain the salvation that is in Christ Jesus, with eternal glory.

11Here is a trustworthy saying:

> If we died with him,
> we will also live with him;
> 12if we endure,
> we will also reign with him.
> If we disown him,
> he will also disown us;
> 13if we are faithless,
> he will remain faithful,
> for he cannot disown himself.

A Workman Approved by God

14Keep reminding them of these things. Warn them before God against quarreling about words; it is of no value, and only ruins those who listen. 15Do your best to present yourself to God as one approved, a workman who does not need to be ashamed and who correctly handles the word of truth. 16Avoid godless chatter, because those who indulge in it will become more and more ungodly. 17Their teaching will spread like gangrene. Among them are Hymenaeus and Philetus, 18who have wandered away from the truth. They say that the resurrection has already taken place, and they destroy the faith of some. 19Nevertheless, God's solid foundation stands firm, sealed with this inscription: "The Lord knows those who are his,"[a] and, "Everyone who confesses the name of the Lord must turn away from wickedness."

20In a large house there are articles not only of gold and silver, but also of wood and clay; some are for noble purposes and some for ignoble. 21If a man cleanses himself from the latter, he will be an instrument for noble purposes, made holy, useful to the Master and prepared to do any good work.

22Flee the evil desires of youth, and pursue righteousness, faith, love and peace, along with those who call on the Lord out of a pure heart. 23Don't have anything to do with foolish and stupid arguments, because you know they produce quarrels. 24And the Lord's servant must not quarrel; instead, he must be kind to everyone, able to teach, not resentful. 25Those who oppose him he must gently instruct, in the hope that God will grant them repentance leading them to a knowledge of the truth, 26and that they will come to their senses and escape from the trap of the devil, who has taken them captive to do his will.

What did you and your siblings quarrel about as kids?

1. Looking over this passage, what should you pursue (the "Dos"), and flee (the Don'ts)? **2.** What are the effects of false teaching (vv. 17–18)? **3.** What security and challenge do the inscriptions of verse 19 give the church today? **4.** Since repentance means "changing directions," how does repentance (v. 25) relate to fleeing and pursuing (v. 22)?

1. How do you know if you are "quarreling about words" or standing up against false teaching? Which do most Christians spend more time doing? How about you? **2.** Can you be a "noble vessel" (vv. 20–21)? How? **3.** What do you need to flee: Being vulnerable to false teaching and side issues? Arguing about theology? Being a "know-it-all"? Sharing your views unkindly? **4.** What do you need to pursue: Righteousness? Faith? Love? Peace? Other?

Godlessness in the Last Days

3 But mark this: There will be terrible times in the last days. 2People will be lovers of themselves, lovers of money, boastful, proud, abusive, disobedient to their parents, ungrateful, unholy, 3without love, unforgiving, slanderous, without self-control, brutal, not lovers of the good, 4treacherous, rash, conceited, lovers of pleasure rather than lovers of God— 5having a form of godliness but denying its power. Have nothing to do with them.

1. Contrast the people described here to one who lives by a pure love (see Mt 22:37,39). **2.** According to Jewish tradition, Jannes and Jambres were Egyptian court magicians (see Ex 7:11, 22; 8:7,18). How do "those who oppose the truth" exhibit what Paul means by a "form of godliness"? Why are they dangerous?

[a] *19* Num. 16:5 (see Septuagint)

1. When have you "looked godly" but lacked a true heart for God? **2.** When Paul says, "Have nothing to do with them," (v. 5) is he talking about all evil-doers or only "professing" Christians? Do you reach out to sinners or withdraw into a safe haven?

[6]They are the kind who worm their way into homes and gain control over weak-willed women, who are loaded down with sins and are swayed by all kinds of evil desires, [7]always learning but never able to acknowledge the truth. [8]Just as Jannes and Jambres opposed Moses, so also these men oppose the truth—men of depraved minds, who, as far as the faith is concerned, are rejected. [9]But they will not get very far because, as in the case of those men, their folly will be clear to everyone.

Have your parents written a will? Have you written one? Why or why not?

1. What areas of Paul's life does he ask Timothy to consider (3:10–13)? **2.** What is the crux of what Paul has to say about Timothy's life (3:14–17)? **3.** What does Paul state about the origin and purpose of Scripture (3:16)? **4.** What nine final orders does Paul solemnly charge Timothy to fulfill (4:1–5)? **5.** In the climax of this letter—the last recorded message Paul wrote—how does the apostle sum up his life and ministry.

1. Do you share Paul's hope for the future? How does it motivate you now? **2.** How do Paul's words challenge your life? Are you fighting "the good fight" no matter what persecution and suffering you face? **3.** How does this Scripture challenge your ministry? What are you doing to build it into your life, and how bold are you to share it faithfully rather than to tell people what they want to hear?

Paul's Charge to Timothy

[10]You, however, know all about my teaching, my way of life, my purpose, faith, patience, love, endurance, [11]persecutions, sufferings—what kinds of things happened to me in Antioch, Iconium and Lystra, the persecutions I endured. Yet the Lord rescued me from all of them. [12]In fact, everyone who wants to live a godly life in Christ Jesus will be persecuted, [13]while evil men and impostors will go from bad to worse, deceiving and being deceived. [14]But as for you, continue in what you have learned and have become convinced of, because you know those from whom you learned it, [15]and how from infancy you have known the holy Scriptures, which are able to make you wise for salvation through faith in Christ Jesus. [16]All Scripture is God-breathed and is useful for teaching, rebuking, correcting and training in righteousness, [17]so that the man of God may be thoroughly equipped for every good work.

4 In the presence of God and of Christ Jesus, who will judge the living and the dead, and in view of his appearing and his kingdom, I give you this charge: [2]Preach the Word; be prepared in season and out of season; correct, rebuke and encourage—with great patience and careful instruction. [3]For the time will come when men will not put up with sound doctrine. Instead, to suit their own desires, they will gather around them a great number of teachers to say what their itching ears want to hear. [4]They will turn their ears away from the truth and turn aside to myths. [5]But you, keep your head in all situations, endure hardship, do the work of an evangelist, discharge all the duties of your ministry.

[6]For I am already being poured out like a drink offering, and the time has come for my departure. [7]I have fought the good fight, I have finished the race, I have kept the faith. [8]Now there is in store for me the crown of righteousness, which the Lord, the righteous Judge, will award to me on that day—and not only to me, but also to all who have longed for his appearing.

If you "left home without it," what would be the first thing you'd ask someone to send?

1. What do you learn about Paul, the man, in these personal remarks? How do you think he felt—in a cold prison cell, virtually alone because his friends were either busy or had deserted him? **2.** What do you remember about the young man Mark, who had accompanied Paul on a missionary trip years earlier (see Ac 13:13; 15:36–41)? What is the lesson here for you? **3.** What has the Lord done and what will he do for Paul in the future (vv. 17–18)?

Personal Remarks

[9]Do your best to come to me quickly, [10]for Demas, because he loved this world, has deserted me and has gone to Thessalonica. Crescens has gone to Galatia, and Titus to Dalmatia. [11]Only Luke is with me. Get Mark and bring him with you, because he is helpful to me in my ministry. [12]I sent Tychicus to Ephesus. [13]When you come, bring the cloak that I left with Carpus at Troas, and my scrolls, especially the parchments.

[14]Alexander the metalworker did me a great deal of harm. The Lord will repay him for what he has done. [15]You too should be on your guard against him, because he strongly opposed our message.

[16]At my first defense, no one came to my support, but everyone deserted me. May it not be held against them. [17]But the Lord stood at my side and gave me strength, so that through me the message might be fully proclaimed and all the Gentiles might hear it. And I

was delivered from the lion's mouth. 18The Lord will rescue me
from every evil attack and will bring me safely to his heavenly
kingdom. To him be glory for ever and ever. Amen.

Final Greetings

19Greet Priscilla[a] and Aquila and the household of Onesiphorus. 20Erastus stayed in Corinth, and I left Trophimus sick in Miletus. 21Do your best to get here before winter. Eubulus greets you,
and so do Pudens, Linus, Claudia and all the brothers.
22The Lord be with your spirit. Grace be with you.

♡ **1.** How does Paul's faith and hope, in spite of his suffering, inspire you? **2.** Who are some people who have ministered to you or with you in the past? Why not try to get together again, at least by letter or phone? **3.** What do you most want to apply to your life from 2 Timothy?

a *19* Greek *Prisca,* a variant of *Priscilla*

INTRODUCTION to

TITUS

Book Study Outline: If you are using Titus for a study course, here is a 3-week outline. Use the margin questions for your group agenda:

- start meeting / 15 min.
- read & discuss Bible / 30 min.
- close meeting / 15–45 min.

3-week plan	Group Study Passage
1	1:1–16/Reliable Leaders
2	2:1–15/Sound Doctrine
3	3:1–15/Doing Good

Refer to the Questions and Answers in the front of this Bible for more information.

Author: The apostle Paul. However, based on considerations of vocabulary and style, the Pauline authorship of the Pastoral Epistles (1 and 2 Timothy, Titus) has been questioned by some scholars.

Date: About A.D. 63–65 (at the same time 1 Timothy was written).

Theme: Be devoted to what is good.

Historical Background: Titus was a Gentile who was probably converted through Paul's ministry. He accompanied Paul on his crucial second visit to Jerusalem (Gal 2:1–10). Titus was Paul's trusted friend, sent on difficult assignments. On this trip he was also charged with arranging for a collection for the poor in Jerusalem (2Co 8:16–20). After Paul was released from prison in Rome, Titus and Timothy traveled with him to Crete as part of a preaching tour. Titus was left behind to establish the church they founded there. This letter was written from Macedonia as an encouragement to Titus in that task. Presumably, Titus spent the winter with Paul in Nicopolis after his replacement arrived (see 3:12). In the spring, on their way to Ephesus, Paul was arrested and imprisoned again, probably for the last time. Titus was sent to Dalmatia on yet another mission (2Ti 4:10).

Characteristics: Apart from the greeting and two small sections (2:11–14; 3:3–7, which may be creedal statements), all the material in Titus is parallel to that found in 1 Timothy. Still, differences are notable. Timothy had been left to straighten out an established church that had gone sour because of the false teaching and ungodly lifestyles of its own elders. Titus, on the other hand, had the job of appointing new elders for a new church unstained by such turmoil and controversy. There are no appeals to "keep the faith"; there are few imperatives ("Do this"); there is no mention of the need to endure. Rather, it is primarily a reminder for Christians to live so as to make the teaching about God our Savior attractive to all.

QUALIFICATIONS FOR ELDERS AND DEACONS

Self-controlled	**ELDER**	1Ti 3:2; Tit 1:8
Hospitable	**ELDER**	1Ti 3:2; Tit 1:8
Able to teach	**ELDER**	1Ti 3:2; 5:17; Tit1:9
Not violent but gentle	**ELDER**	1Ti 3:3; Tit 1:7
Not quarrelsome	**ELDER**	1Ti 3:3
Not a lover of money	**ELDER**	1Ti 3:3
Not a recent convert	**ELDER**	1Ti 3:6
Has a good reputation with outsiders	**ELDER**	1Ti 3:7
Not overbearing	**ELDER**	Tit 1:7
Not quick-tempered	**ELDER**	Tit 1:7
Loves what is good	**ELDER**	Tit 1:8
Upright, holy	**ELDER**	Tit 1:8
Disciplined	**ELDER**	Tit 1:8
Above reproach	**ELDER**	1Ti 3:2; Tit 1:6
(blameless)	***DEACON***	1Ti 3:9
Husband of one wife	**ELDER**	1Ti 3:2; Tit 1:6
	DEACON	1Ti 3:12
Temperate	**ELDER**	1Ti 3:2; Tit 1:7
	DEACON	1Ti 3:8
Respectable	**ELDER**	1Ti 3:2
	DEACON	1Ti 3:8
Not given to	**ELDER**	1Ti 3:3; Tit 1:7
drunkenness	***DEACON***	1Ti 3:8
Manages his own	**ELDER**	1Ti 3:4
family well	***DEACON***	1Ti 3:12
Sees that his children	**ELDER**	1Ti 3:4-5; Tit 1:6
obey him	***DEACON***	1Ti 3:12
Does not pursue	**ELDER**	Tit 1:7
dishonest gain	***DEACON***	1Ti 3:8
Holds to the Truth	**ELDER**	Tit 1:9
	DEACON	1TI 3:9
Sincere	***DEACON***	1Ti 3:8
Tested	***DEACON***	1Ti 3:10

Titus

1 Paul, a servant of God and an apostle of Jesus Christ for the faith of God's elect and the knowledge of the truth that leads to godliness— 2a faith and knowledge resting on the hope of eternal life, which God, who does not lie, promised before the beginning of time, 3and at his appointed season he brought his word to light through the preaching entrusted to me by the command of God our Savior,

4To Titus, my true son in our common faith:

Grace and peace from God the Father and Christ Jesus our Savior.

Titus' Task on Crete

5The reason I left you in Crete was that you might straighten out what was left unfinished and appoint[a] elders in every town, as I directed you. 6An elder must be blameless, the husband of but one wife, a man whose children believe and are not open to the charge of being wild and disobedient. 7Since an overseer[b] is entrusted with God's work, he must be blameless—not overbearing, not quick-tempered, not given to drunkenness, not violent, not pursuing dishonest gain. 8Rather he must be hospitable, one who loves what is good, who is self-controlled, upright, holy and disciplined. 9He must hold firmly to the trustworthy message as it has been taught, so that he can encourage others by sound doctrine and refute those who oppose it.

10For there are many rebellious people, mere talkers and deceivers, especially those of the circumcision group. 11They must be silenced, because they are ruining whole households by teaching things they ought not to teach—and that for the sake of dishonest gain. 12Even one of their own prophets has said, "Cretans are always liars, evil brutes, lazy gluttons." 13This testimony is true. Therefore, rebuke them sharply, so that they will be sound in the faith 14and will pay no attention to Jewish myths or to the commands of those who reject the truth. 15To the pure, all things are pure, but to those who are corrupted and do not believe, nothing is pure. In fact, both their minds and consciences are corrupted. 16They claim to know God, but by their actions they deny him. They are detestable, disobedient and unfit for doing anything good.

What Must Be Taught to Various Groups

2 You must teach what is in accord with sound doctrine. 2Teach the older men to be temperate, worthy of respect, self-controlled, and sound in faith, in love and in endurance.

3Likewise, teach the older women to be reverent in the way they live, not to be slanderers or addicted to much wine, but to teach what is good. 4Then they can train the younger women to love their husbands and children, 5to be self-controlled and pure, to be busy at home, to be kind, and to be subject to their husbands, so that no one will malign the word of God.

6Similarly, encourage the young men to be self-controlled. 7In everything set them an example by doing what is good. In your

[a]5 Or *ordain* [b]7 Traditionally *bishop*

1. While growing up, who always sent you a card or a gift for your birthday? **2.** Are you more likely to keep your letters short and to the point, or do you write until you run out of paper?

1. What do you know about the circumstances under which Paul wrote this letter to Titus (see Introduction to Titus). **2.** Why is Paul's list of leadership qualifications focused mostly on "being" and not on "doing" (vv. 6–9)? **3.** How do you interpret "the husband of but one wife" (v. 6)? Does this exclude bachelors or remarried men? **4.** What was going on in Crete that made the appointment of such elders important (vv. 10–16)? Does any of this go on in the church today? In what way?

1. When did you come to a knowledge of the truth of Christ that Paul speaks of in verses 1 and 2? **2.** Who in your Christian community have you especially respected for their godly leadership? Which qualities from this passage did you appreciate in them? **3.** Which of these qualities do you feel you need to develop in your own life? How can your group help you?

---

1. As a teenager or college student, how did you decorate your room or living space so that it was really "you"? **2.** Who is your favorite elderly person?

1. What is Paul implying about the importance of mentors (trusted guides or models)? **2.** What difference does our salvation make in our behavior in this "present age" (v. 12)? What conflicts does this verse imply Christians will face? **3.** Why does Paul emphasize "self control" (1:8–10; 2:2,5–6,12; 3:3) and doing "what is good" (2:3,7,14; 3:1,8)? **4.** How does our new lifestyle relate to Jesus' death (v. 14)? To his glorious appearing (v. 13)?

1. What one quality in each of the groups mentioned do you feel is most important for Christians in our society (look at older men, older women, young women, young men and employees)? **2.** Which group do you fall into? What quality Paul lists for your group catches your attention? Why? **3.** How much have you focused on self-control and doing what is good in your own life? How can you improve?

In what situation do you least exhibit your faith: In a checkout line? In a fender bender? After a tough exam? At the company picnic? In athletics? Other?

1. Why do you think Paul again stresses "doing good" (vv. 1,8,14)? What about human nature makes such reminders necessary (v. 3)? **2.** What do verses 4–7 say about God's character? His work in us? **3.** How does a true understanding of these verses promote humility? Gratitude? A life of service? Have you seen this happen in your life? **4.** What is going on with the people in verses 9–11 (see 2Ti 2:25–26; 3:1–5)? How do Paul's instructions reflect both "tough love" and uncompromising righteousness? What similar situations are occurring in today's church?

1. Does verse 3 paint an accurate picture of you in the past? To what degree? Were these characteristics an obvious part of your life, or more of an underlying reality? **2.** In doing good, what motivates you: (a) Call of duty? (b) Fear of judgment? (c) Hope of Christ's return? (d) Gratitude for what God has done? (e) Desire to make peace in your relationships? (f) Needs of others? **3.** What "good" do you do at home? At church? In your city, state or nation? (Or are you "up to no good"?) **4.** Over the past year, where have you sensed growth in leading a "productive" life for God (see v. 14)?

teaching show integrity, seriousness [8]and soundness of speech that
cannot be condemned, so that those who oppose you may be
ashamed because they have nothing bad to say about us.
[9]Teach slaves to be subject to their masters in everything, to try
to please them, not to talk back to them, [10]and not to steal from
them, but to show that they can be fully trusted, so that in every
way they will make the teaching about God our Savior attractive.
[11]For the grace of God that brings salvation has appeared to all
men. [12]It teaches us to say "No" to ungodliness and worldly passions, and to live self-controlled, upright and godly lives in this
present age, [13]while we wait for the blessed hope—the glorious
appearing of our great God and Savior, Jesus Christ, [14]who gave
himself for us to redeem us from all wickedness and to purify for
himself a people that are his very own, eager to do what is good.
[15]These, then, are the things you should teach. Encourage and
rebuke with all authority. Do not let anyone despise you.

Doing What Is Good

3 Remind the people to be subject to rulers and authorities, to be
obedient, to be ready to do whatever is good, [2]to slander no
one, to be peaceable and considerate, and to show true humility
toward all men.
[3]At one time we too were foolish, disobedient, deceived and
enslaved by all kinds of passions and pleasures. We lived in malice
and envy, being hated and hating one another. [4]But when the
kindness and love of God our Savior appeared, [5]he saved us, not
because of righteous things we had done, but because of his mercy.
He saved us through the washing of rebirth and renewal by the
Holy Spirit, [6]whom he poured out on us generously through Jesus
Christ our Savior, [7]so that, having been justified by his grace, we
might become heirs having the hope of eternal life. [8]This is a
trustworthy saying. And I want you to stress these things, so that
those who have trusted in God may be careful to devote themselves to doing what is good. These things are excellent and profit-
able for everyone.
[9]But avoid foolish controversies and genealogies and arguments
and quarrels about the law, because these are unprofitable and
useless. [10]Warn a divisive person once, and then warn him a second time. After that, have nothing to do with him. [11]You may be
sure that such a man is warped and sinful; he is self-condemned.

Final Remarks

[12]As soon as I send Artemas or Tychicus to you, do your best to
come to me at Nicopolis, because I have decided to winter there.
[13]Do everything you can to help Zenas the lawyer and Apollos on
their way and see that they have everything they need. [14]Our
people must learn to devote themselves to doing what is good, in
order that they may provide for daily necessities and not live unproductive lives.
[15]Everyone with me sends you greetings. Greet those who love
us in the faith.

Grace be with you all.

INTRODUCTION to
PHILEMON

Book Study Outline: If you are using Philemon for a study course, spend one to two meetings on this short book. Use the questions in the margin for your group agenda:

start meeting / 15 min.	read & discuss Bible / 30 min.	close meeting / 15–45 min.

Refer to the Questions and Answers in the front of this Bible for more information.

Author: The apostle Paul.

Date: Probably in the early A.D. 60s.

Theme: Radical forgiveness.

Historical Background: At this point in history, the 60 million slaves in the Roman Empire made up a critical component of Rome's social and economic structure. Runaways were considered criminals who were punishable by severe measures including death. Philemon, a member of the church at Colosse, was the owner of a slave (Onesimus) who had run away from him. Somehow Onesimus got to Rome, met Paul and became a Christian. We may wonder why Paul did not take this opportunity simply to condemn slavery. The reason is partially clear. For one thing, conditions were not yet right for such a massive social upheaval. The Romans would never have voluntarily freed their slaves. Any revolt would have been savagely crushed. For another thing, unlike the American experience, Roman slavery was not a permanent condition based on race. This meant that slaves could purchase their freedom and enter the mainstream of society. Still, Paul did strike the first note for emancipation by his teaching on how Christians, regardless of race or economic condition, are one "family" in Christ (v. 16; Col. 3:11). This letter is Paul's attempt to persuade Philemon to forgive the crime and receive Onesimus as he would receive Paul himself. Onesimus carried this letter (and possibly Colossians and Ephesians) back to his home (Col. 4:9). The outcome of this story is not recorded in Scripture, but about A.D. 110 Bishop Ignatius of Antioch wrote a letter to the bishop of Ephesus, who was a man named Onesimus. In it, he used the same wordplay on his name as Paul does here in verse 11. Since many scholars think that the first collection of Paul's letters was made at Ephesus, Onesimus the bishop may have included this personal note as a vivid demonstration of how Christ can transform and use even a runaway slave.

Characteristics: Philemon is the shortest of Paul's letters, and it is his only private letter preserved in the New Testament. As such, it gives us a valuable glimpse into Paul's personality. He is deeply sympathetic to the plight of Onesimus, so much so that he is willing to deprive himself of Onesimus' help as well as to pay Philemon for any loss Onesimus has caused him (vv. 18–19). This is Christian compassion in action.

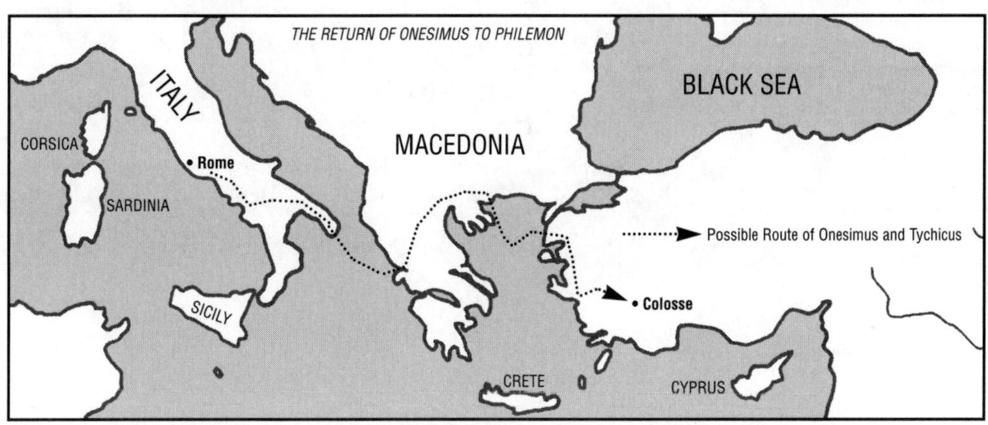

Philemon

1Paul, a prisoner of Christ Jesus, and Timothy our brother,

To Philemon our dear friend and fellow worker, 2to Apphia our
sister, to Archippus our fellow soldier and to the church that meets
in your home:

3Grace to you and peace from God our Father and the Lord Jesus
Christ.

Thanksgiving and Prayer

4I always thank my God as I remember you in my prayers,
5because I hear about your faith in the Lord Jesus and your love for
all the saints. 6I pray that you may be active in sharing your faith,
so that you will have a full understanding of every good thing we
have in Christ. 7Your love has given me great joy and encouragement, because you, brother, have refreshed the hearts of the saints.

Paul's Plea for Onesimus

8Therefore, although in Christ I could be bold and order you to
do what you ought to do, 9yet I appeal to you on the basis of love.
I then, as Paul—an old man and now also a prisoner of Christ
Jesus— 10I appeal to you for my son Onesimus,[a] who became my
son while I was in chains. 11Formerly he was useless to you, but
now he has become useful both to you and to me.
12I am sending him—who is my very heart—back to you. 13I
would have liked to keep him with me so that he could take your
place in helping me while I am in chains for the gospel. 14But I did
not want to do anything without your consent, so that any favor
you do will be spontaneous and not forced. 15Perhaps the reason he
was separated from you for a little while was that you might have
him back for good— 16no longer as a slave, but better than a slave,
as a dear brother. He is very dear to me but even dearer to you,
both as a man and as a brother in the Lord.
17So if you consider me a partner, welcome him as you would
welcome me. 18If he has done you any wrong or owes you anything, charge it to me. 19I, Paul, am writing this with my own
hand. I will pay it back—not to mention that you owe me your
very self. 20I do wish, brother, that I may have some benefit
from you in the Lord; refresh my heart in Christ. 21Confident of
your obedience, I write to you, knowing that you will do even
more than I ask.
22And one thing more: Prepare a guest room for me, because I
hope to be restored to you in answer to your prayers.

23Epaphras, my fellow prisoner in Christ Jesus, sends you greetings. 24And so do Mark, Aristarchus, Demas and Luke, my fellow
workers.
25The grace of the Lord Jesus Christ be with your spirit.

What name were you given at birth? What nicknames have you been given since? What do they mean? How are you living up to their meaning?

1. What qualities in Philemon does Paul commend (vv. 4–7)? How does this prepare the way for Paul's plea in verses 8–10? **2.** Given the seriousness of the crime committed by Onesimus (see Introduction to Philemon), what impact will his return have on Philemon's household? On Paul's relationship with Philemon? On Onesimus himself? **3.** Does the fact that Onesimus has become a Christian lessen the seriousness of his crime? Why or why not? **4.** What is radical about Paul's view of Onesimus (vv. 10–18)? **5.** Given Paul's concern and need for Onesimus, why does Paul return Onesimus to Philemon, anyway? Why doesn't Paul exert his apostolic authority, declare Onesimus free, and keep him as a partner in the Gospel? **6.** What do you think the chances are that Philemon will do what Paul asks? In what way would Philemon be right to refuse Paul?

1. Which of the qualities in Philemon (vv. 4–7) do you wish to develop for yourself? How could doing so cause you to grow in new areas? **2.** Like Onesimus, do you have something you need to return to and make right? Do you have someone like Paul who can help you do that? **3.** When do you feel obligated to forgive someone: When they confess their sin? When they later change their behavior? When someone else intercedes for the offending party? **4.** For whom might you serve as a "Paul" in bringing about reconciliation?

[a] *10 Onesimus* means *useful.*

INTRODUCTION to

HEBREWS

Book Study Outline: If you are using Hebrews for a study course, here is a 7- or 13-week outline. Use the questions in the margin for your group agenda:

start meeting / 15 min.

read & discuss Bible / 30 min.

close meeting / 15–45 min.

Refer to the Questions and Answers in the front of this Bible for more information.

7-week plan	13-week plan	Personal Reading	Group Study Passage
1	1	1:1–14	1:1–14/The Son Reigns
	2	2:1–18	2:5–18/Christ Our Helper
2	3	3:1–19	3:7–19/Don't Turn Back!
	4	4:1–13	4:1–13/The Promised Rest
3	5	4:14–5:10	4:14–5:10/The Great Priest
	6	5:11–6:20	5:11–6:12/Don't Fall Away!
4	7	7:1–28	7:1–28/The New Priest
	8	8:1–13	8:1–13/The New Covenant
5	9	9:1–28	9:11–28/The New Sacrifice
	10	10:1–39	10:19–39/Hold On!
6	11	11:1–40	11:1–40/Examples of Faith
	12	12:1–28	12:1–13/Run the Race!
7	13	13:1–25	13:1–25/A Life of Praise

Author: The author of this letter is nowhere named. Possible authors include Barnabas (Ac 4:36) or Apollos (Ac 18:24).

Date: It is impossible to affix a date to the composition of this letter. However, it seems likely that it was written prior to the destruction of the temple (A.D. 70) since the author consistently refers to it in the present tense.

Theme: The superiority of Jesus.

Historical Background: Hebrews appears to be a written sermon directed to Jewish Christians who were considering whether or not it was worth holding on to Christ any longer. While it is clear that they had suffered great persecution (10:32–34), the nature of their present struggle is less certain. They may have been facing new persecution, rejection by their kin, or the seduction of other teachings that seemed to offer an easier way than the way of Jesus. It appears that they may have been considering a return to Judaism as a way of lessening these tensions. In any case, the temptation to apostasy or reversion was severe enough that the letter to the Hebrews had to be written to encourage these beleaguered Christians to "hold on" (3:6), to "persevere" (10:36), and to "hold unswervingly to the hope we profess" (10:23) lest they compromise Christ and lose the blessings he has won for them.

Characteristics: Hebrews is a marvelous portrait of Jesus Christ seen through the lens of the Old Testament. The author's intent is to show the superiority of Jesus over the prophets, angels, Moses, priests and the whole Old Testament system. Jesus is the new priest with the new sacrifice that establishes a new covenant between people and God.

HEBREWS 11: HEROES OF FAITH

Abel
By faith offered the better sacrifice (v. 4)

Enoch
By faith pleased God and escaped death (v. 5)

Noah
By faith built the ark (v. 7)

Abraham
By faith made his home in a foreign promised land (v. 8)
Abraham and Sarah
By faith became parents when past age (v. 11)
Abraham
By faith offered his son as a sacrifice (vv. 17–19)

Isaac
By faith blessed his sons (v. 20)

Jacob
By faith blessed his grandsons (v. 21)

Joseph
By faith prophesied the Exodus (v. 22)

Moses' Parents
By faith concealed Moses from Pharaoh (v. 23)

Moses
By faith chose mistreatment, left Egypt, and kept the Passover (vv. 24–28)

The Israelites
By faith passed through the Red Sea, and marched around Jericho (vv. 29–30)

Rahab
By faith welcomed the Israelite spies (v. 31)

Hebrews

1. How are you like your mother or father: In artistic talent? Mechanical ability? Athletic ability? Forgetfulness? Distinctive features? **2.** What does your father do? Would you like to take over his business? Why or why not?

1. To what (or whom) is Jesus compared here? **2.** What was the function of the OT prophets (v. 1)? In what ways was Jesus' function similar? How was it different (vv. 2–3)? How is Jesus superior to the prophets? What is the difference between "the past" (v. 1) and "these last days" (v. 2)? **3.** How does Jesus compare with God in terms of activity, authority and relationship (vv. 1–3)? **4.** In verses 5–14, what new facts does the author add to this portrait of Jesus? Which of these OT quotes, first said of the Lord God, is now applied to the Son Jesus? What does that imply? **5.** What do you suppose these readers thought of angels and of prophets that caused the author to write as he does? What counterpoint is the author trying to make about each?

1. When did Jesus become more than just a name to you? **2.** Of all the qualities of Jesus mentioned in verses 2–4, which one are you beginning to appreciate more and more? **3.** Of what help is it for the Christian that God has indeed spoken "at many times and in various ways"? Why not in just one way? Which seems to be God's chosen way of speaking especially to you? **4.** Does this passage imply that Jesus is God's *final* revelation? Most *authoritative* revelation? Most *complete* revelation? Only *self*-revelation? In each instance, tell why you think so.

The Son Superior to Angels

1 In the past God spoke to our forefathers through the prophets at many times and in various ways, [2]but in these last days he has spoken to us by his Son, whom he appointed heir of all things, and through whom he made the universe. [3]The Son is the radiance of God's glory and the exact representation of his being, sustaining all things by his powerful word. After he had provided purification for sins, he sat down at the right hand of the Majesty in heaven. [4]So he became as much superior to the angels as the name he has inherited is superior to theirs.

[5]For to which of the angels did God ever say,

> "You are my Son;
> today I have become your Father[a]"[b]?

Or again,

> "I will be his Father,
> and he will be my Son"[c]?

[6]And again, when God brings his firstborn into the world, he says,

> "Let all God's angels worship him."[d]

[7]In speaking of the angels he says,

> "He makes his angels winds,
> his servants flames of fire."[e]

[8]But about the Son he says,

> "Your throne, O God, will last for ever and ever,
> and righteousness will be the scepter of your kingdom.
> [9]You have loved righteousness and hated wickedness;
> therefore God, your God, has set you above your companions
> by anointing you with the oil of joy."[f]

[10]He also says,

> "In the beginning, O Lord, you laid the foundations of the earth,
> and the heavens are the work of your hands.
> [11]They will perish, but you remain;
> they will all wear out like a garment.
> [12]You will roll them up like a robe;
> like a garment they will be changed.
> But you remain the same,
> and your years will never end."[g]

[13]To which of the angels did God ever say,

> "Sit at my right hand

[a]*5* Or *have begotten you* [b]*5* Psalm 2:7 [c]*5* 2 Samuel 7:14; 1 Chron. 17:13
[d]*6* Deut. 32:43 (see Dead Sea Scrolls and Septuagint) [e]*7* Psalm 104:4
[f]*9* Psalm 45:6,7 [g]*12* Psalm 102:25-27

until I make your enemies
a footstool for your feet"[a]?

14Are not all angels ministering spirits sent to serve those who will
inherit salvation?

Warning to Pay Attention

2 We must pay more careful attention, therefore, to what we
have heard, so that we do not drift away. 2For if the message
spoken by angels was binding, and every violation and disobedience received its just punishment, 3how shall we escape if we
ignore such a great salvation? This salvation, which was first announced by the Lord, was confirmed to us by those who heard
him. 4God also testified to it by signs, wonders and various miracles, and gifts of the Holy Spirit distributed according to his will.

Jesus Made Like His Brothers

5It is not to angels that he has subjected the world to come,
about which we are speaking. 6But there is a place where someone
has testified:

"What is man that you are mindful of him,
the son of man that you care for him?
7You made him a little[b] lower than the angels;
you crowned him with glory and honor
8 and put everything under his feet."[c]

In putting everything under him, God left nothing that is not subject to him. Yet at present we do not see everything subject to him.
9But we see Jesus, who was made a little lower than the angels,
now crowned with glory and honor because he suffered death, so
that by the grace of God he might taste death for everyone.
10In bringing many sons to glory, it was fitting that God, for
whom and through whom everything exists, should make the author of their salvation perfect through suffering. 11Both the one
who makes men holy and those who are made holy are of the same
family. So Jesus is not ashamed to call them brothers. 12He says,

"I will declare your name to my brothers;
in the presence of the congregation I will sing
your praises."[d]

13And again,

"I will put my trust in him."[e]

And again he says,

"Here am I, and the children God has given
me."[f]

14Since the children have flesh and blood, he too shared in their
humanity so that by his death he might destroy him who holds the
power of death—that is, the devil— 15and free those who all their
lives were held in slavery by their fear of death. 16For surely it is
not angels he helps, but Abraham's descendants. 17For this reason
he had to be made like his brothers in every way, in order that he
might become a merciful and faithful high priest in service to God,
and that he might make atonement for[g] the sins of the people.

[a] *13* Psalm 110:1 [b] *7* Or *him for a little while*; also in verse 9 [c] *8* Psalm 8:4-6
[d] *12* Psalm 22:22 [e] *13* Isaiah 8:17 [f] *13* Isaiah 8:18 [g] *17* Or *and that he might turn aside God's wrath, taking away*

1. Back in school, what subject matter were you least attentive to? Why? **2.** When your parents went away, who were you "subject to" as a child? How did you look upon this person or the rules imposed on you?

1. What danger faces these people? What does it mean to "drift away" (v. 1)? **2.** What is the answer to the rhetorical question in verse 3? **3.** In contrast to the popular expectation of that day (v. 5), to whom does God subject the world (vv. 6–8a)? Why is this rule not yet complete or universal? Who rules instead? **4.** In comparing people and angels (vv. 5–8), how are we both lower and higher? What is the ultimate destiny of humanity? **5.** To what does the phrase "the world to come" refer (v. 5)? How can the kingdom of God exist in both the present (in Jesus, in history) and the future (at the end of time)? **6.** In what respects was Jesus "made lower than the angels" (v. 9)? What elevated him above them? What does Jesus share in common with humanity (vv. 7,9)? In which respect is Jesus unique? **7.** Why did we need someone with flesh and blood like us—not an angel—to die in our place (vv. 14–18)? What did Jesus accomplish by his death as one of us? What is the goal of our salvation (vv. 10–11)? What does it mean that Jesus *authors* salvation? **8.** What is the difference between the way Jesus made atonement (v. 17) and the way the priests mediate atonement?

1. When (if ever) did you drift away from the faith? Why? What evidences for faith helped bring you back? **2.** At what points might you be tempted to lose your faith: After a big loss? When you seem to be making it very well on your own? When things are not going your way? When Christianity is mocked on TV talk shows? **3.** How do the achievements and example of Jesus described here encourage you at such times? **4.** Of Jesus' three titles (brother, v. 11; author of salvation, v. 10; high priest, v. 17) which one means most to you now? Why?

18Because he himself suffered when he was tempted, he is able to help those who are being tempted.

1. When lost on a trip, what do you do: Stop and ask directions? Check the map? Wander around until you find the way? **2.** Are you usually early or late getting to places, even to your small group? Why?

1. What is the significance of "therefore" (v. 1)? What are the practical implications of what has been written about Jesus in chapters 1 and 2? How is Jesus like an apostle? **2.** In what ways are Jesus and Moses similar? In what ways is Jesus greater? Why is that important? **3.** What new warning is given (vv. 8,12)? How does this compare with verse 6 and 2:1–4? **4.** To what incident does the quotation from Psalms refer (vv. 7–11; see Nu 14)? How did the people of Israel harden their hearts? With what results (vv. 10–11)? What does it mean to turn away from the living God (v. 12)? **5.** What role does the Christian community play in keeping each other true to God (v. 13)? What will be the outcome of faithfulness (vv. 14–18)? **6.** What does it mean to "enter God's rest" (vv. 11,18–19; see 4:1–11; Mt 11:28–30)?

1. What are some ways your church or small group could put verse 13 into practice? How can that help you? What apprehensions does it cause? **2.** What was one of the most rebellious times in your spiritual life? What resulted from it? Who (or what) helped to bring you back? **3.** How would you describe your heart now: Soft? Hard? Cold? Warm? Why is that?

Jesus Greater Than Moses

3 Therefore, holy brothers, who share in the heavenly calling, fix your thoughts on Jesus, the apostle and high priest whom we confess. 2He was faithful to the one who appointed him, just as Moses was faithful in all God's house. 3Jesus has been found worthy of greater honor than Moses, just as the builder of a house has greater honor than the house itself. 4For every house is built by someone, but God is the builder of everything. 5Moses was faithful as a servant in all God's house, testifying to what would be said in the future. 6But Christ is faithful as a son over God's house. And we are his house, if we hold on to our courage and the hope of which we boast.

Warning Against Unbelief

7So, as the Holy Spirit says:

"Today, if you hear his voice,
8 do not harden your hearts
as you did in the rebellion,
during the time of testing in the desert,
9where your fathers tested and tried me
and for forty years saw what I did.
10That is why I was angry with that generation,
and I said, 'Their hearts are always going astray,
and they have not known my ways.'
11So I declared on oath in my anger,
'They shall never enter my rest.' "[a]

12See to it, brothers, that none of you has a sinful, unbelieving heart that turns away from the living God. 13But encourage one another daily, as long as it is called Today, so that none of you may be hardened by sin's deceitfulness. 14We have come to share in Christ if we hold firmly till the end the confidence we had at first. 15As has just been said:

"Today, if you hear his voice,
do not harden your hearts
as you did in the rebellion."[b]

16Who were they who heard and rebelled? Were they not all those Moses led out of Egypt? 17And with whom was he angry for forty years? Was it not with those who sinned, whose bodies fell in the desert? 18And to whom did God swear that they would never enter his rest if not to those who disobeyed[c]? 19So we see that they were not able to enter, because of their unbelief.

What is your favorite way to spend a Sunday afternoon?

1. What is the author warning his readers about from the story of Israel's rebellion? What "message" (v. 2) was given each community (see Ex 3:7; Nu 14:7–9)? With what reception and results? Why is "hearing" not enough? **2.** What is this "rest"

A Sabbath-Rest for the People of God

4 Therefore, since the promise of entering his rest still stands, let us be careful that none of you be found to have fallen short of it. 2For we also have had the gospel preached to us, just as they did; but the message they heard was of no value to them, because those who heard did not combine it with faith.[d] 3Now we who have believed enter that rest, just as God has said,

[a] *11* Psalm 95:7-11 [b] *15* Psalm 95:7,8 [c] *18* Or *disbelieved* [d] *2* Many manuscripts *because they did not share in the faith of those who obeyed*

"So I declared on oath in my anger,
'They shall never enter my rest.' "[a]

And yet his work has been finished since the creation of the world.
4For somewhere he has spoken about the seventh day in these
words: "And on the seventh day God rested from all his work."[b]
5And again in the passage above he says, "They shall never enter
my rest."
6It still remains that some will enter that rest, and those who
formerly had the gospel preached to them did not go in, because of
their disobedience. 7Therefore God again set a certain day, calling
it Today, when a long time later he spoke through David, as was
said before:

"Today, if you hear his voice,
do not harden your hearts."[c]

8For if Joshua had given them rest, God would not have spoken
later about another day. 9There remains, then, a Sabbath-rest for
the people of God; 10for anyone who enters God's rest also rests
from his own work, just as God did from his. 11Let us, therefore,
make every effort to enter that rest, so that no one will fall by
following their example of disobedience.
12For the word of God is living and active. Sharper than any
double-edged sword, it penetrates even to dividing soul and spirit,
joints and marrow; it judges the thoughts and attitudes of the heart.
13Nothing in all creation is hidden from God's sight. Everything is
uncovered and laid bare before the eyes of him to whom we must
give account.

Jesus the Great High Priest

14Therefore, since we have a great high priest who has gone
through the heavens,[d] Jesus the Son of God, let us hold firmly to
the faith we profess. 15For we do not have a high priest who is
unable to sympathize with our weaknesses, but we have one who
has been tempted in every way, just as we are—yet was without
sin. 16Let us then approach the throne of grace with confidence, so
that we may receive mercy and find grace to help us in our time of
need.
5 Every high priest is selected from among men and is appointed
to represent them in matters related to God, to offer gifts and
sacrifices for sins. 2He is able to deal gently with those who are
ignorant and are going astray, since he himself is subject to weakness. 3This is why he has to offer sacrifices for his own sins, as well
as for the sins of the people.
4No one takes this honor upon himself; he must be called by
God, just as Aaron was. 5So Christ also did not take upon himself
the glory of becoming a high priest. But God said to him,

"You are my Son;
today I have become your Father.[e]"[f]

6And he says in another place,

"You are a priest forever,
in the order of Melchizedek."[g]

7During the days of Jesus' life on earth, he offered up prayers and
petitions with loud cries and tears to the one who could save him
from death, and he was heard because of his reverent submission.

a3 Psalm 95:11; also in verse 5 b4 Gen. 2:2 c7 Psalm 95:7,8 d14 Or *gone into heaven* e5 Or *have begotten you* f5 Psalm 2:7 g6 Psalm 110:4

promised by God: The promised land? Sunday off? Heaven? God's presence? How do verses 3b–10 support your answer? **3.** What is the proper response to the warning in verses 1 and 11? What does it mean that God's Word is "living"? Active? That it penetrates? How has the author used the "Word of God" thus far?

1. How would you explain the "promised rest" to someone who is not a Christian? What situations today would make this type of exhortation necessary? **2.** What efforts (v. 11) can help you enter into God's rest (see Mt 11:28–30; Jn 6:27–29)? **3.** What evidence do you have that the Word of God is living and active in your group study?

---

1. When you "blew it" as a child, how did you feel about the mistake? About yourself? About others involved? **2.** From whom did you then draw comfort: A parent? Sibling? Friend? Your dog?

1. What about Jesus' priesthood is most encouraging (4:14–15; see 2:17; 3:1)? **2.** How does the role of the Jewish high priest compare to Jesus' role in terms of: (a) How each is chosen? (5:1) (b) How each relates to sinners? (5:2) (c) How each relates to God? (5:3) **3.** What two qualities of Jesus allows the comparison to Melchizedek (5:6,10; see ch. 7; Ge 14:18; Ps 110:4)? **4.** What is the significance for our eternal salvation and current situation that Jesus was *fully human*? That Jesus was *without sin*?

1. Why is it hard for many people to trust the love of God? How would you explain the meaning of the priesthood of Jesus to a non-Christian? To someone who doesn't understand the OT sacrificial system? **2.** What has made you consider turning away from Christ? At those times, what advantage was it to you to remember Jesus as your high priest?

8Although he was a son, he learned obedience from what he suffered 9and, once made perfect, he became the source of eternal
salvation for all who obey him 10and was designated by God to be
high priest in the order of Melchizedek.

What do you like hot out of the oven with a glass of cold milk: Chocolate chip cookies? Pound cake? Homemade bread? Apple pie?

1. Why does the author hesitate to give his readers further details? How does solid food help one mature in Christ (5:14)? **2.** What's wrong with this prolonged immaturity (6:4–6)? What does each descriptive phrase mean? **3.** Is their fate (6:6) reversible? Why (see also Mt 10:33)? What does the agricultural analogy suggest (6:7–8)? **4.** Who are these people: (a) True believers gone bad? (b) Those who "hung around" true believers, but ultimately turned away (see 3:16)? (c) Borderline believers who must examine themselves? **5.** How and why does the author encourage his readers to do "better" (6:9–12)? What parental logic (positive and negative incentives, praising and prodding) is used here?

1. How would you describe your spiritual appetite now: (a) "I'll just nibble"? (b) "A good meal now and then is nice"? (c) "I'm famished for all I can get"? Why? **2.** When have you been spiritually lazy? What motivated you again?

Warning Against Falling Away

11We have much to say about this, but it is hard to explain
because you are slow to learn. 12In fact, though by this time you
ought to be teachers, you need someone to teach you the elementary truths of God's word all over again. You need milk, not solid
food! 13Anyone who lives on milk, being still an infant, is not
acquainted with the teaching about righteousness. 14But solid food
is for the mature, who by constant use have trained themselves to
distinguish good from evil.

6 Therefore let us leave the elementary teachings about Christ
and go on to maturity, not laying again the foundation of repentance from acts that lead to death,[a] and of faith in God, 2in-
struction about baptisms, the laying on of hands, the resurrection
of the dead, and eternal judgment. 3And God permitting, we will
do so.

4It is impossible for those who have once been enlightened, who
have tasted the heavenly gift, who have shared in the Holy Spirit,
5who have tasted the goodness of the word of God and the powers
of the coming age, 6if they fall away, to be brought back to repentance, because[b] to their loss they are crucifying the Son of God all
over again and subjecting him to public disgrace.

7Land that drinks in the rain often falling on it and that produces
a crop useful to those for whom it is farmed receives the blessing of
God. 8But land that produces thorns and thistles is worthless and is
in danger of being cursed. In the end it will be burned.

9Even though we speak like this, dear friends, we are confident
of better things in your case—things that accompany salvation.
10God is not unjust; he will not forget your work and the love you
have shown him as you have helped his people and continue to
help them. 11We want each of you to show this same diligence to
the very end, in order to make your hope sure. 12We do not want
you to become lazy, but to imitate those who through faith and
patience inherit what has been promised.

What tries your patience more: Slow elevators? Slow food service? Traffic jams? Christmas sales lines?

1. How does Abraham's example help these people understand God's promise (see 3:12; 6:6)? **2.** What effect did God's promise and oath have on Abraham's descendants? How does this affect Christians now?

1. Where in your life does trusting in God come hardest? Easiest? Why? **2.** What promises of God are your anchor?

The Certainty of God's Promise

13When God made his promise to Abraham, since there was no
one greater for him to swear by, he swore by himself, 14saying, "I
will surely bless you and give you many descendants."[c] 15And so
after waiting patiently, Abraham received what was promised.

16Men swear by someone greater than themselves, and the oath
confirms what is said and puts an end to all argument. 17Because
God wanted to make the unchanging nature of his purpose very
clear to the heirs of what was promised, he confirmed it with an
oath. 18God did this so that, by two unchangeable things in which
it is impossible for God to lie, we who have fled to take hold of the
hope offered to us may be greatly encouraged. 19We have this hope
as an anchor for the soul, firm and secure. It enters the inner
sanctuary behind the curtain, 20where Jesus, who went before us,
has entered on our behalf. He has become a high priest forever, in
the order of Melchizedek.

[a] *1* Or *from useless rituals* [b] *6* Or *repentance while* [c] *14* Gen. 22:17

Melchizedek the Priest

7 This Melchizedek was king of Salem and priest of God Most
High. He met Abraham returning from the defeat of the kings
and blessed him, 2and Abraham gave him a tenth of everything.
First, his name means "king of righteousness"; then also, "king of
Salem" means "king of peace." 3Without father or mother, without
genealogy, without beginning of days or end of life, like the Son of
God he remains a priest forever.

4Just think how great he was: Even the patriarch Abraham gave
him a tenth of the plunder! 5Now the law requires the descendants
of Levi who become priests to collect a tenth from the people—
that is, their brothers—even though their brothers are descended
from Abraham. 6This man, however, did not trace his descent from
Levi, yet he collected a tenth from Abraham and blessed him who
had the promises. 7And without doubt the lesser person is blessed
by the greater. 8In the one case, the tenth is collected by men who
die; but in the other case, by him who is declared to be living.
9One might even say that Levi, who collects the tenth, paid the
tenth through Abraham, 10because when Melchizedek met Abraham, Levi was still in the body of his ancestor.

Jesus Like Melchizedek

11If perfection could have been attained through the Levitical
priesthood (for on the basis of it the law was given to the people),
why was there still need for another priest to come—one in the
order of Melchizedek, not in the order of Aaron? 12For when there
is a change of the priesthood, there must also be a change of the
law. 13He of whom these things are said belonged to a different
tribe, and no one from that tribe has ever served at the altar. 14For
it is clear that our Lord descended from Judah, and in regard to that
tribe Moses said nothing about priests. 15And what we have said is
even more clear if another priest like Melchizedek appears, 16one
who has become a priest not on the basis of a regulation as to his
ancestry but on the basis of the power of an indestructible life.
17For it is declared:

"You are a priest forever,
in the order of Melchizedek."[a]

18The former regulation is set aside because it was weak and
useless 19(for the law made nothing perfect), and a better hope is
introduced, by which we draw near to God.

20And it was not without an oath! Others became priests without
any oath, 21but he became a priest with an oath when God said to
him:

"The Lord has sworn
and will not change his mind:
'You are a priest forever.'"[a]

22Because of this oath, Jesus has become the guarantee of a better
covenant.

23Now there have been many of those priests, since death prevented them from continuing in office; 24but because Jesus lives
forever, he has a permanent priesthood. 25Therefore he is able to
save completely[b] those who come to God through him, because
he always lives to intercede for them.

26Such a high priest meets our need—one who is holy, blameless, pure, set apart from sinners, exalted above the heavens. 27Un-

[a] *17,21* Psalm 110:4 [b] *25* Or *forever*

1. As a child, who was your favorite super-hero? What could he or she do that you wished you could: Fly? Display super-strength? Always win? Talk his way out of anything? **2.** If you could live to be 100, but could retain either the *body* or the *mind* of a 30-year-old, which would you choose? Why?

1. Chapter 7 picks up where 5:10 left off. From verses 1–10, what do we know about Melchizedek (see also Ge 14:17–20)? How did Abraham regard him? **2.** What is the main point in the comparison between Melchizedek and Abraham? How does Abraham's tithe and the blessing of Melchizedek demonstrate the greatness of Melchizedek? How is his priesthood superior to that which descended from Levi and Aaron (v. 11)? Why is another type of priesthood needed? **3.** In what ways is Jesus like the Melchizedek portrayed here (vv. 12–17)? **4.** Why was the law set aside (vv. 18–19)? In what sense had it failed? How does the argument in verse 18 parallel that in verse 11? What are the two features of the Jewish religious system that have been superseded? **5.** In what ways is Jesus a better priest than those under the Jewish system (vv. 20–28)? What is the relationship between the law and the oath? Why is the oath better?

1. The author was showing Jesus' superiority over the priests to Jews who were tempted to go back to their old ways. What are some of the "old ways" that tempt you to turn from Jesus? How is Jesus superior to those old ways in your life? **2.** What difference does Jesus' "once-for-all" sacrifice make to you in terms of your security with God? Your self-image? Your desire to follow Christ?

like the other high priests, he does not need to offer sacrifices day after day, first for his own sins, and then for the sins of the people. He sacrificed for their sins once for all when he offered himself.
[28]For the law appoints as high priests men who are weak; but the oath, which came after the law, appointed the Son, who has been made perfect forever.

The High Priest of a New Covenant

8 The point of what we are saying is this: We do have such a high priest, who sat down at the right hand of the throne of the Majesty in heaven, [2]and who serves in the sanctuary, the true tabernacle set up by the Lord, not by man.

[3]Every high priest is appointed to offer both gifts and sacrifices, and so it was necessary for this one also to have something to offer.
[4]If he were on earth, he would not be a priest, for there are already men who offer the gifts prescribed by the law. [5]They serve at a sanctuary that is a copy and shadow of what is in heaven. This is why Moses was warned when he was about to build the tabernacle: "See to it that you make everything according to the pattern shown you on the mountain."[a] [6]But the ministry Jesus has received is as superior to theirs as the covenant of which he is mediator is superior to the old one, and it is founded on better promises.

[7]For if there had been nothing wrong with that first covenant, no place would have been sought for another. [8]But God found fault with the people and said[b]:

> "The time is coming, declares the Lord,
> when I will make a new covenant
> with the house of Israel
> and with the house of Judah.
> [9]It will not be like the covenant
> I made with their forefathers
> when I took them by the hand
> to lead them out of Egypt,
> because they did not remain faithful to my covenant,
> and I turned away from them,
> declares the Lord.
> [10]This is the covenant I will make with the house of Israel
> after that time, declares the Lord.
> I will put my laws in their minds
> and write them on their hearts.
> I will be their God,
> and they will be my people.
> [11]No longer will a man teach his neighbor,
> or a man his brother, saying, 'Know the Lord,'
> because they will all know me,
> from the least of them to the greatest.
> [12]For I will forgive their wickedness
> and will remember their sins no more."[c]

[13]By calling this covenant "new," he has made the first one obsolete; and what is obsolete and aging will soon disappear.

[a]*5* Exodus 25:40 [b]*8* Some manuscripts may be translated *fault and said to the people.* [c]*12* Jer. 31:31-34

---

1. What are you best at forgetting: Names? Chores? Birthdays? Scripture references? **2.** If your car develops chronic problems, are you the type to keep fixing it up, or to buy a new one? How do you decide it's got to go?

1. What's the point of the previous argument (vv. 1–2)? How would this offer a strong incentive not to turn away from Christianity, as some were considering? **2.** Contrast the location, nature and function of the two priesthoods (vv. 1–5; see 5:14–15; 6:19–20; 7:23–28). How does an OT priest prefigure what Jesus would really do? **3.** What is a covenant? What is the significance of the fact that God initiates and guarantees it? What is a mediator? Why is one needed? **4.** From Exodus 19:5–6, 20:1–17 and 29:35–41, what characterized the old covenant administered by the priests? How does the new covenant mediated by Jesus differ (vv. 10–12)? What four promises does this new covenant involve? **5.** Why was a new covenant needed (vv. 7–9,13)?

1. Which aspect of the new covenant brings great joy to you, and why: (a) Having God's law on your heart? (b) Being one of God's people? (c) Knowing God? (d) Having your sins forgiven? **2.** Which aspect of the covenant do you wish to experience more? Why? **3.** Has your experience of these promises been sudden and dramatic, a gradual awareness, or both? **4.** The old covenant ended up focusing on the people's ability (or inability) to measure up to God's demands. How do you still try to come to God on that basis? What happens? What does it mean to you that the new covenant is based on God's actions in Christ, and not on your efforts?

Worship in the Earthly Tabernacle

9 Now the first covenant had regulations for worship and also an
earthly sanctuary. 2A tabernacle was set up. In its first room
were the lampstand, the table and the consecrated bread; this was
called the Holy Place. 3Behind the second curtain was a room
called the Most Holy Place, 4which had the golden altar of incense
and the gold-covered ark of the covenant. This ark contained the
gold jar of manna, Aaron's staff that had budded, and the stone
tablets of the covenant. 5Above the ark were the cherubim of the
Glory, overshadowing the atonement cover.[a] But we cannot discuss these things in detail now.

6When everything had been arranged like this, the priests entered regularly into the outer room to carry on their ministry. 7But
only the high priest entered the inner room, and that only once a
year, and never without blood, which he offered for himself and for
the sins the people had committed in ignorance. 8The Holy Spirit
was showing by this that the way into the Most Holy Place had not
yet been disclosed as long as the first tabernacle was still standing.
9This is an illustration for the present time, indicating that the gifts
and sacrifices being offered were not able to clear the conscience of
the worshiper. 10They are only a matter of food and drink and
various ceremonial washings—external regulations applying until
the time of the new order.

The Blood of Christ

11When Christ came as high priest of the good things that are
already here,[b] he went through the greater and more perfect
tabernacle that is not man-made, that is to say, not a part of this
creation. 12He did not enter by means of the blood of goats and
calves; but he entered the Most Holy Place once for all by his own
blood, having obtained eternal redemption. 13The blood of goats
and bulls and the ashes of a heifer sprinkled on those who are
ceremonially unclean sanctify them so that they are outwardly
clean. 14How much more, then, will the blood of Christ, who
through the eternal Spirit offered himself unblemished to God,
cleanse our consciences from acts that lead to death,[c] so that we
may serve the living God!

15For this reason Christ is the mediator of a new covenant, that
those who are called may receive the promised eternal inheritance—now that he has died as a ransom to set them free from the
sins committed under the first covenant.

16In the case of a will,[d] it is necessary to prove the death of the
one who made it, 17because a will is in force only when somebody
has died; it never takes effect while the one who made it is living.
18This is why even the first covenant was not put into effect without blood. 19When Moses had proclaimed every commandment of
the law to all the people, he took the blood of calves, together with
water, scarlet wool and branches of hyssop, and sprinkled the scroll
and all the people. 20He said, "This is the blood of the covenant,
which God has commanded you to keep."[e] 21In the same way, he
sprinkled with the blood both the tabernacle and everything used
in its ceremonies. 22In fact, the law requires that nearly everything
be cleansed with blood, and without the shedding of blood there is
no forgiveness.

23It was necessary, then, for the copies of the heavenly things to
be purified with these sacrifices, but the heavenly things them-

[a]5 Traditionally *the mercy seat*
[b]11 Some early manuscripts *are to come*
[c]14 Or *from useless rituals*
[d]16 Same Greek word as *covenant*; also in verse 17
[e]20 Exodus 24:8

In your childhood home, what place was off limits? What thing were you told, "Don't touch"?

1. How do you picture the earthly sanctuary described in verses 1–5? What is the significance of each item in the Holy Place? In the Most Holy Place? If your group wants to "discuss these things in detail now" (v. 5), read Exodus 25–31 and 35–40. **2.** What goes on in the outer room (vv. 6–10)? In the inner room (see Lev 16:14–16)? **3.** What did not happen here at this time (vv. 8–9)? Why were their gifts and sacrifices not sufficient to clear their consciences?

1. Does church ever feel like a labyrinth to you? Why? **2.** When you feel guilty, how do you try to clear your conscience?

---

1. What event have you gone through once, but have since vowed "never again"? **2.** Have you ever seen a blood and gore movie? Which one? How did you feel about it?

1. Jesus' priesthood is exercised here in what setting? By what right (v. 12)? How often? **2.** How is the priesthood of Christ distinguished from the old system (vv. 12–14)? What types of cleansing did the two sacrificial systems bring about? Why does Christ's sacrifice have an everlasting result? **3.** How is Christ's mediation like a "ransom" (v. 15): Who are the hostages? Hostage to what? What is the ransom price? Are those who lived and died before Christ covered by this ransom also (see Ro 3:25)? **4.** How is Christ's death like a "will" made good (vv. 16–18): Who are the beneficiaries? What is their inheritance? What puts the will in force? **5.** Why the emphasis on shed blood (vv. 19–22): Whose blood? What for? How extensive is the application? How effective? **6.** What are the "copies" in this next analogy (vv. 23–24)? What is the real thing? What makes that reality "better" (vv. 24–26)? **7.** In the last analogy here (vv. 27–28), how is the once-and-for-allness of Christ's death illustrated?

1. The author used OT analogies to explain the meaning of Christ's death to religious Jews. What analogies might clarify this with non-religious people today? **2.** In telling others that Christ died to take away their sins, what responses do you get: Lazy indifference? Sincere gratitude? Zealous devotion? What would help your message to have more impact?

What repetitious activity do you dislike most: (a) Cleaning the bathroom? (b) Mowing the lawn? (c) Shaving? (d) Driving to and from work? (e) Doing the dishes? (f) Getting out of bed? Why? What daily rituals do you enjoy most?

1. Why is the Law insufficient? Knowing how a shadow is produced, how then is the Law a "shadow" of reality? Where is true reality? **2.** What is one positive function of animal sacrifice? **3.** In what ways does Christ replace the inadequate sacrifices of the Law? How does Jesus' obedience relate to our holiness (vv. 9–10)? **4.** What is the significance of the contrasts between the old sacrificial system and the new (vv. 11–13)? How did Jesus' once-and-for-all sacrifice make future sacrifices unnecessary? **5.** In the context of verse 14, in what sense are Christians *already* made perfect, while *still in the process* of being made holy?

1. How much of your time is spent with a gnawing and vague sense of guilt: (a) All the time? (b) Most of the time? (c) Some of the time? (d) A fraction of the time? Why is that? **2.** Do you live your life as if you were being made holy (v. 14)? Why or why not? In what way is God calling you to practice greater holiness? **3.** If you were asked to memorize one verse from this section, which would you choose and why?

selves with better sacrifices than these. 24For Christ did not enter a man-made sanctuary that was only a copy of the true one; he entered heaven itself, now to appear for us in God's presence. 25Nor did he enter heaven to offer himself again and again, the way the high priest enters the Most Holy Place every year with blood that is not his own. 26Then Christ would have had to suffer many times since the creation of the world. But now he has appeared once for all at the end of the ages to do away with sin by the sacrifice of himself. 27Just as man is destined to die once, and after that to face judgment, 28so Christ was sacrificed once to take away the sins of many people; and he will appear a second time, not to bear sin, but to bring salvation to those who are waiting for him.

Christ's Sacrifice Once for All

10 The law is only a shadow of the good things that are coming—not the realities themselves. For this reason it can never, by the same sacrifices repeated endlessly year after year, make perfect those who draw near to worship. 2If it could, would they not have stopped being offered? For the worshipers would have been cleansed once for all, and would no longer have felt guilty for their sins. 3But those sacrifices are an annual reminder of sins, 4because it is impossible for the blood of bulls and goats to take away sins.

5Therefore, when Christ came into the world, he said:

"Sacrifice and offering you did not desire,
  but a body you prepared for me;
6with burnt offerings and sin offerings
  you were not pleased.
7Then I said, 'Here I am—it is written about me in
    the scroll—
  I have come to do your will, O God.' "[a]

8First he said, "Sacrifices and offerings, burnt offerings and sin offerings you did not desire, nor were you pleased with them" (although the law required them to be made). 9Then he said, "Here I am, I have come to do your will." He sets aside the first to establish the second. 10And by that will, we have been made holy through the sacrifice of the body of Jesus Christ once for all.

11Day after day every priest stands and performs his religious duties; again and again he offers the same sacrifices, which can never take away sins. 12But when this priest had offered for all time one sacrifice for sins, he sat down at the right hand of God. 13Since that time he waits for his enemies to be made his footstool, 14because by one sacrifice he has made perfect forever those who are being made holy.

15The Holy Spirit also testifies to us about this. First he says:

16"This is the covenant I will make with them
  after that time, says the Lord.
I will put my laws in their hearts,
  and I will write them on their minds."[b]

17Then he adds:

"Their sins and lawless acts
  I will remember no more."[c]

18And where these have been forgiven, there is no longer any sacrifice for sin.

[a] *7* Psalm 40:6-8 (see Septuagint) [b] *16* Jer. 31:33 [c] *17* Jer. 31:34

A Call to Persevere

19Therefore, brothers, since we have confidence to enter the
Most Holy Place by the blood of Jesus, 20by a new and living way
opened for us through the curtain, that is, his body, 21and since we
have a great priest over the house of God, 22let us draw near to
God with a sincere heart in full assurance of faith, having our
hearts sprinkled to cleanse us from a guilty conscience and having
our bodies washed with pure water. 23Let us hold unswervingly to
the hope we profess, for he who promised is faithful. 24And let us
consider how we may spur one another on toward love and good
deeds. 25Let us not give up meeting together, as some are in the
habit of doing, but let us encourage one another—and all the more
as you see the Day approaching.
26If we deliberately keep on sinning after we have received the
knowledge of the truth, no sacrifice for sins is left, 27but only a
fearful expectation of judgment and of raging fire that will consume
the enemies of God. 28Anyone who rejected the law of Moses died
without mercy on the testimony of two or three witnesses. 29How
much more severely do you think a man deserves to be punished
who has trampled the Son of God under foot, who has treated as an
unholy thing the blood of the covenant that sanctified him, and
who has insulted the Spirit of grace? 30For we know him who said,
"It is mine to avenge; I will repay,"[a] and again, "The Lord will
judge his people."[b] 31It is a dreadful thing to fall into the hands of
the living God.
32Remember those earlier days after you had received the light,
when you stood your ground in a great contest in the face of
suffering. 33Sometimes you were publicly exposed to insult and
persecution; at other times you stood side by side with those who
were so treated. 34You sympathized with those in prison and joyfully accepted the confiscation of your property, because you knew
that you yourselves had better and lasting possessions.
35So do not throw away your confidence; it will be richly rewarded. 36You need to persevere so that when you have done the will of
God, you will receive what he has promised. 37For in just a very
little while,

> "He who is coming will come and will not delay.
> 38 But my righteous one[c] will live by faith.
> And if he shrinks back,
> I will not be pleased with him."[d]

39But we are not of those who shrink back and are destroyed, but
of those who believe and are saved.

How did you meet your spouse or "friend"? What was your first date with him or her?

1. Based on Christ's sacrifice (vv. 19–20; 9:1–10:18) and priesthood (v. 21; 7:1–8:13), what attitudes and actions follow? Note the four "let us" statements in verses 22–25. What does each one mean? What incentives are given? **2.** How do verses 19–25 parallel 4:14–16? Why does the author need to stress this to these readers? **3.** If they habitually reject Christ in favor of sin, what do they forfeit (v. 26; also 3:14; 6:4–6)? What can they expect instead (vv. 27,30–31)? Why is this fate not so unexpected (vv. 28–29; also Dt 17:2–7)? **4.** In rejecting Christ, of what three grievous sins would they be guilty (v. 29)? With what consequence (v. 31)? What false security would make such a warning necessary (see 4:12–13; 6:8)? **5.** After such a dire warning, how does the author appeal to previous testing, present action and future events—all to encourage the Hebrews (vv. 32–39)? Which appeal do you find persuasive?

1. In what specific ways can you spur another Christian on toward love and good deeds? How have you been spurred on by others in your group? Whose exhortation, example or encouragement means the most to you? **2.** How have you seen the difference between someone *assured* of their salvation (vv. 19–25) and someone *presumptuous* about it (vv. 26–31)? How can you develop confidence without presumption? **3.** How does the promise of the Second Coming help you to "keep on keeping on"?

By Faith

11 Now faith is being sure of what we hope for and certain of
what we do not see. 2This is what the ancients were commended for.
3By faith we understand that the universe was formed at God's
command, so that what is seen was not made out of what was
visible.
4By faith Abel offered God a better sacrifice than Cain did. By
faith he was commended as a righteous man, when God spoke well
of his offerings. And by faith he still speaks, even though he is
dead.
5By faith Enoch was taken from this life, so that he did not

[a]*30* Deut. 32:35 [b]*30* Deut. 32:36; Psalm 135:14 [c]*38* One early manuscript *But the righteous* [d]*38* Hab. 2:3,4

As you consider the people in your small group, what's one positive adjective you would use to describe each person?

1. What are the connections between 10:35–39 and the themes of chapter 11? **2.** In the definition and focus of faith in verses 1 and 6, what verbs describe faith? What is the object of these verbs? Is our faith directed toward the future, toward the present, or toward both? Toward God alone, or people as well? Why do you conclude this? Write your own expanded definition of faith as you try to capture the meaning of verse 1. **3.** How does verse 3 illustrate this understanding of faith? **4.** Why is Abel's sacrifice regarded as better than Cain's (see Ge 4:1–12)? How did Abel's sacrifice prefigure Christ's ultimate sacrifice in a way Cain's did not (recall ch. 9–10)? **5.** What aspect of faith (v. 1) is demonstrated by Enoch (v. 5; Ge 5: 21–24)? By Noah (v. 7; Ge 6:5–22; 7:11–12)? **6.** How is faith demonstrated or explained in each of the three examples from Abraham's life (vv. 8–12,17–19)? What obstacles had to be overcome? What changed for him? For his family? **7.** What group of people does the author use next to illustrate faith (vv. 17–31)? Recall each Old Testament story which is referred to: What do the stories in verses 17–22 have in common? **8.** What do you learn about faith from the example of Moses (vv. 24–28)? **9.** In verses 29–38, what great achievements were accomplished as a result of faith? What price was paid? What came of such faith (vv. 39–40)? How do verses 29–40 encourage you in light of your own suffering and the questions that suffering brings on?

♡ **1.** What are some verbs that describe your present level of faith? Why these? **2.** Of the people mentioned in this section, with whom do you feel you have the most in common? Why? With whom do you have the least in common? Why? Which situation would have been the most difficult for you to face? Why? What does it mean to you that not all these people of faith met with "success"? **3.** How has your life changed as a result of your faith in God? What has your faith cost you? How has your faith affected your neighbors? **4.** Read aloud verses 13–16. What does it mean to *you* to be an alien and a stranger on earth? In what ways do you feel like a stranger in this world? **5.** Who are some contemporary heroes of faith who inspire you today?

experience death; he could not be found, because God had taken
him away. For before he was taken, he was commended as one
who pleased God. 6And without faith it is impossible to please God,
because anyone who comes to him must believe that he exists and
that he rewards those who earnestly seek him.
7By faith Noah, when warned about things not yet seen, in holy
fear built an ark to save his family. By his faith he condemned the
world and became heir of the righteousness that comes by faith.
8By faith Abraham, when called to go to a place he would later
receive as his inheritance, obeyed and went, even though he did
not know where he was going. 9By faith he made his home in the
promised land like a stranger in a foreign country; he lived in tents,
as did Isaac and Jacob, who were heirs with him of the same
promise. 10For he was looking forward to the city with foundations,
whose architect and builder is God.
11By faith Abraham, even though he was past age—and Sarah
herself was barren—was enabled to become a father because he[a]
considered him faithful who had made the promise. 12And so from
this one man, and he as good as dead, came descendants as numerous as the stars in the sky and as countless as the sand on the
seashore.
13All these people were still living by faith when they died. They
did not receive the things promised; they only saw them and welcomed them from a distance. And they admitted that they were
aliens and strangers on earth. 14People who say such things show
that they are looking for a country of their own. 15If they had been
thinking of the country they had left, they would have had opportunity to return. 16Instead, they were longing for a better country—a
heavenly one. Therefore God is not ashamed to be called their
God, for he has prepared a city for them.
17By faith Abraham, when God tested him, offered Isaac as a
sacrifice. He who had received the promises was about to sacrifice
his one and only son, 18even though God had said to him, "It is
through Isaac that your offspring[b] will be reckoned."[c] 19Abra-
ham reasoned that God could raise the dead, and figuratively speaking, he did receive Isaac back from death.
20By faith Isaac blessed Jacob and Esau in regard to their future.
21By faith Jacob, when he was dying, blessed each of Joseph's
sons, and worshiped as he leaned on the top of his staff.
22By faith Joseph, when his end was near, spoke about the exodus of the Israelites from Egypt and gave instructions about his
bones.
23By faith Moses' parents hid him for three months after he was
born, because they saw he was no ordinary child, and they were
not afraid of the king's edict.
24By faith Moses, when he had grown up, refused to be known
as the son of Pharaoh's daughter. 25He chose to be mistreated along
with the people of God rather than to enjoy the pleasures of sin for
a short time. 26He regarded disgrace for the sake of Christ as of
greater value than the treasures of Egypt, because he was looking
ahead to his reward. 27By faith he left Egypt, not fearing the king's
anger; he persevered because he saw him who is invisible. 28By
faith he kept the Passover and the sprinkling of blood, so that the
destroyer of the firstborn would not touch the firstborn of Israel.
29By faith the people passed through the Red Sea[d] as on dry
land; but when the Egyptians tried to do so, they were drowned.

[a] *11* Or *By faith even Sarah, who was past age, was enabled to bear children because she*
[b] *18* Greek *seed* [c] *18* Gen. 21:12 [d] *29* That is, Sea of Reeds

[30]By faith the walls of Jericho fell, after the people had marched
around them for seven days.
[31]By faith the prostitute Rahab, because she welcomed the spies,
was not killed with those who were disobedient.[a]
[32]And what more shall I say? I do not have time to tell about
Gideon, Barak, Samson, Jephthah, David, Samuel and the prophets,
[33]who through faith conquered kingdoms, administered justice,
and gained what was promised; who shut the mouths of lions,
[34]quenched the fury of the flames, and escaped the edge of the
sword; whose weakness was turned to strength; and who became
powerful in battle and routed foreign armies. [35]Women received
back their dead, raised to life again. Others were tortured and
refused to be released, so that they might gain a better resurrection. [36]Some faced jeers and flogging, while still others were
chained and put in prison. [37]They were stoned[b]; they were sawed
in two; they were put to death by the sword. They went about in
sheepskins and goatskins, destitute, persecuted and mistreated—
[38]the world was not worthy of them. They wandered in deserts and
mountains, and in caves and holes in the ground.
[39]These were all commended for their faith, yet none of them
received what had been promised. [40]God had planned something
better for us so that only together with us would they be made
perfect.

God Disciplines His Sons

12 Therefore, since we are surrounded by such a great cloud of
witnesses, let us throw off everything that hinders and the
sin that so easily entangles, and let us run with perseverance the
race marked out for us. [2]Let us fix our eyes on Jesus, the author
and perfecter of our faith, who for the joy set before him endured
the cross, scorning its shame, and sat down at the right hand of the
throne of God. [3]Consider him who endured such opposition from
sinful men, so that you will not grow weary and lose heart.
[4]In your struggle against sin, you have not yet resisted to the
point of shedding your blood. [5]And you have forgotten that word of
encouragement that addresses you as sons:

> "My son, do not make light of the Lord's
> discipline,
> and do not lose heart when he rebukes you,
> [6]because the Lord disciplines those he loves,
> and he punishes everyone he accepts as a
> son."[c]

[7]Endure hardship as discipline; God is treating you as sons. For
what son is not disciplined by his father? [8]If you are not disciplined
(and everyone undergoes discipline), then you are illegitimate children and not true sons. [9]Moreover, we have all had human fathers
who disciplined us and we respected them for it. How much more
should we submit to the Father of our spirits and live! [10]Our fathers
disciplined us for a little while as they thought best; but God
disciplines us for our good, that we may share in his holiness. [11]No
discipline seems pleasant at the time, but painful. Later on, however, it produces a harvest of righteousness and peace for those who
have been trained by it.
[12]Therefore, strengthen your feeble arms and weak knees.
[13]"Make level paths for your feet,"[d] so that the lame may not be
disabled, but rather healed.

[a]31 Or *unbelieving* [b]37 Some early manuscripts *stoned; they were put to the test;*
[c]6 Prov. 3:11,12 [d]13 Prov. 4:26

---

1. What discipline did you sometimes resent as a child that you appreciate now: Practicing piano? Having a place for everything and everything in its place? Submitting work on time? Not overspending your allowance? **2.** Do you perform better before a crowd or in private? Why is that?

1. How should Christians "run the race"? What does it mean to throw off sin and hindrances? To "run with perseverance"? To "fix our eyes on Jesus"? **2.** What does hardship demonstrate about a person's relationship to God? How should a person respond to God when disciplined? How does Christ's discipline differ from human discipline? What benefits does discipline bring?

1. What comfort do you get from knowing that a cloud of witnesses is watching you run the Christian race? **2.** What are two obstacles that hinder and entangle you in your race? Why? **3.** What have you discovered that helps you keep your eyes fixed on Jesus? **4.** How has God disciplined you in the past? How did his discipline lead to peace for you? **5.** What's the hardest thing you're going through right now? How is God using this in your life?

If you could choose any city to move to with the right job, by what criteria would you choose: Friends or family? Climate? Housing? Cultural or athletic pursuits?

1. How do the instructions and Esau's example (vv. 14–17; see Ge 25:29–34) relate to disciplining your weaker members (vv. 12–13)? **2.** What is the point of the comparison between Mt. Sinai (vv. 18–21) and Mt. Zion (vv. 22–24)? **3.** What is the "better word" (v. 24) in contrast to "no further word" (v. 19)? What do the words "once more" convey (vv. 26–27)? **4.** How does this play on words sum up the author's argument throughout the book? What happens to any who *refuse* to hear God's voice (vv. 18–21,25–29)? To those who *heed* his call?

1. What efforts have you made to "live in peace with all"? **2.** In relationships that fail, do you believe it is because one or both parties didn't try hard enough? What can be done to see that people who are torn apart, despite their best efforts, do not also miss the grace of God? **3.** What in this passage comforts you? What makes you uneasy? What thrills you most about the city of the living God?

---

1. In one or two words, how would you describe the relationship you had with your brothers and sisters when you were growing up? **2.** Who has been as close to you as a brother?

1. In what areas should "brotherly love" define Christians (vv. 1–7)? What consequences are spelled out here for those who do? For those who don't? What help is offered for those who struggle (vv. 6,8)? **2.** What does verse 5 say about priorities when making financial decisions? What reason do we have to be worry-free when it comes to money? How are we to regard our leaders (vv. 7,17) and why? How does this reflect our regard for the changeless Christ? What do these verses say about the importance of considering our leaders as Christ's messengers? **3.** What "strange teaching" was a particular temptation to Hebrew Christians (vv. 9–10)? What rituals, mores and

Warning Against Refusing God

14Make every effort to live in peace with all men and to be holy; without holiness no one will see the Lord. 15See to it that no one misses the grace of God and that no bitter root grows up to cause trouble and defile many. 16See that no one is sexually immoral, or is godless like Esau, who for a single meal sold his inheritance rights as the oldest son. 17Afterward, as you know, when he wanted to inherit this blessing, he was rejected. He could bring about no change of mind, though he sought the blessing with tears.

18You have not come to a mountain that can be touched and that is burning with fire; to darkness, gloom and storm; 19to a trumpet blast or to such a voice speaking words that those who heard it begged that no further word be spoken to them, 20because they could not bear what was commanded: "If even an animal touches the mountain, it must be stoned."[a] 21The sight was so terrifying that Moses said, "I am trembling with fear."[b]

22But you have come to Mount Zion, to the heavenly Jerusalem, the city of the living God. You have come to thousands upon thousands of angels in joyful assembly, 23to the church of the firstborn, whose names are written in heaven. You have come to God, the judge of all men, to the spirits of righteous men made perfect, 24to Jesus the mediator of a new covenant, and to the sprinkled blood that speaks a better word than the blood of Abel.

25See to it that you do not refuse him who speaks. If they did not escape when they refused him who warned them on earth, how much less will we, if we turn away from him who warns us from heaven? 26At that time his voice shook the earth, but now he has promised, "Once more I will shake not only the earth but also the heavens."[c] 27The words "once more" indicate the removing of what can be shaken—that is, created things—so that what cannot be shaken may remain.

28Therefore, since we are receiving a kingdom that cannot be shaken, let us be thankful, and so worship God acceptably with reverence and awe, 29for our "God is a consuming fire."[d]

Concluding Exhortations

13 Keep on loving each other as brothers. 2Do not forget to entertain strangers, for by so doing some people have entertained angels without knowing it. 3Remember those in prison as if you were their fellow prisoners, and those who are mistreated as if you yourselves were suffering.

4Marriage should be honored by all, and the marriage bed kept pure, for God will judge the adulterer and all the sexually immoral. 5Keep your lives free from the love of money and be content with what you have, because God has said,

> "Never will I leave you;
> never will I forsake you."[e]

6So we say with confidence,

> "The Lord is my helper; I will not be afraid.
> What can man do to me?"[f]

7Remember your leaders, who spoke the word of God to you. Consider the outcome of their way of life and imitate their faith. 8Jesus Christ is the same yesterday and today and forever.

9Do not be carried away by all kinds of strange teachings. It is

[a] 20 Exodus 19:12,13 [b] 21 Deut. 9:19 [c] 26 Haggai 2:6 [d] 29 Deut. 4:24
[e] 5 Deut. 31:6 [f] 6 Psalm 118:6,7

good for our hearts to be strengthened by grace, not by ceremonial
foods, which are of no value to those who eat them. 10We have an
altar from which those who minister at the tabernacle have no
right to eat.

11The high priest carries the blood of animals into the Most Holy
Place as a sin offering, but the bodies are burned outside the camp.
12And so Jesus also suffered outside the city gate to make the
people holy through his own blood. 13Let us, then, go to him
outside the camp, bearing the disgrace he bore. 14For here we do
not have an enduring city, but we are looking for the city that is to
come.

15Through Jesus, therefore, let us continually offer to God a
sacrifice of praise—the fruit of lips that confess his name. 16And do
not forget to do good and to share with others, for with such
sacrifices God is pleased.

17Obey your leaders and submit to their authority. They keep
watch over you as men who must give an account. Obey them so
that their work will be a joy, not a burden, for that would be of no
advantage to you.

18Pray for us. We are sure that we have a clear conscience and
desire to live honorably in every way. 19I particularly urge you to
pray so that I may be restored to you soon.

20May the God of peace, who through the blood of the eternal
covenant brought back from the dead our Lord Jesus, that great
Shepherd of the sheep, 21equip you with everything good for doing
his will, and may he work in us what is pleasing to him, through
Jesus Christ, to whom be glory for ever and ever. Amen.

22Brothers, I urge you to bear with my word of exhortation, for
I have written you only a short letter.

23I want you to know that our brother Timothy has been released. If he arrives soon, I will come with him to see you.

24Greet all your leaders and all God's people. Those from Italy
send you their greetings.

25Grace be with you all.

other forms of legalism tempt believers of any age? Why? **4.** What is the point of the argument in verses 9–14? Based on his argument, what types of "sacrifices" is God concerned with (vv. 15–16)? **5.** Why does the author desire their prayers (vv. 18–19)? How would you paraphrase his prayer for them (vv. 20–21)? **6.** From verses 1–19, how would you sum up the Christian lifestyle?

♡ **1.** In which of these six areas have you made the most progress this year: (a) Loving one another as brothers and sisters? (b) Providing hospitality? (c) Caring for those suffering for their faith? (d) Keeping your marriage strong? (e) Staying free from the love of money? (f) Submitting to leaders in authority? Which area do you need the most work on? **2.** In which of these six areas is your church the strongest? The weakest? Would you say an obedient congregation prays for its leaders? Or would you say "a praying congregation obeys its leaders"? What's the difference? **3.** Considering all you have seen about Jesus in this book, write out a "sacrifice of praise" to him reflecting on all he has done for us. What sacrifice of "doing good and sharing" can you offer this week? **4.** What is the most significant thing you've learned from studying Hebrews? How has this affected your life?

INTRODUCTION to

JAMES

Book Study Outline: If you are using James for a study course, here is a 5- or 9-week outline. Use the questions in the margin for your group agenda:

start meeting / 15 min.

read & discuss Bible / 30 min.

close meeting / 15–45 min.

Refer to the Questions and Answers in the front of this Bible for more information.

5-week plan	9-week plan	Group Study Passage
1	1	1:1–18/Trials and Temptations
	2	1:19–27/Listening and Doing
2	3	2:1–13/Mercy and Judgment
	4	2:14–26/Faith and Works
3	5	3:1–12/Taming the Tongue
	6	3:13–18/True and False Wisdom
4	7	4:1–12/Friendship With God
	8	4:13–5:6/Investing in the Future
5	9	5:7–20/Suffering and Prayer

Author: Traditionally, it has been assumed that the James who wrote this epistle was the brother of Jesus (Mk 6:3), and the leader of the church in Jerusalem (Ac 12:17; Gal 1:19).

Date: Uncertain. Some consider James to be the first New Testament book written (about A.D. 45), while others date it quite late.

Theme: Christianity in action.

THE PROMINENCE OF JAMES IN THE EARLY CHURCH

James was probably the oldest of Christ's several brothers and sisters since he heads the list in Matthew 13:55. At first he did not believe in Jesus and even challenged him and misunderstood his mission (Jn 7:2–5). Later James became a committed disciple. Before his martyrdom c. A.D. 62, James was very prominent in the church:

1. James was one of the select individuals Christ appeared to after his resurrection (1Co 15:7).
2. Paul called him a "pillar" of the church (Gal 2:9).
3. Paul, on his first post-conversion visit to Jerusalem, saw James (Gal 1:19).
4. Paul did the same on his last visit (Ac 21:18).
5. When Peter was rescued from prison, he told his friends to tell James (Ac 12:17).
6. James was a leader in the important council of Jerusalem (Ac 15:13).
7. Jude could identify himself simply as a "brother of James" (Jude 1:1), so well-known was James.

Historical Background: It is not clear to whom James is writing. The inscription in 1:1 ("to the twelve tribes") could refer to Jewish Christians. However, elsewhere in the New Testament this term is used for Gentile believers who, by faith, have become the new Israel. The author's familiarity with the OT and his concern with the Law coupled with his use of Greek literary structure, language and metaphors hint that he may have been writing to God-fearing Gentiles who, having once been attracted to Judaism, were now becoming Christians.

Characteristics: James is closer in style to the book of Proverbs than it is to any New Testament book. James reflects the sermonic style of both Greek philosophers and Jewish rabbis in that it is loosely structured, there is conversation with a hypothetical opponent (2:18ff; 5:13–16), it uses questions to introduce new topics (2:14; 4:1), there are frequent commands (over half of the verses in James are imperatives!), and it proves points by quotes and examples (e.g., 1:11,17). This diversity may be evidence that James is a collection of short sermons on different topics. In terms of content, James has little doctrine; it says surprisingly little about Jesus (it does not mention his atonement or resurrection); nor is the Holy Spirit mentioned. James' focus is not on doctrine, but on how the Christian faith is to be lived on a day-to-day basis. Although Jesus is seldom referred to or quoted, his teaching on the Sermon on the Mount (Mt 5–7) underlies much of this letter.

James

1 James, a servant of God and of the Lord Jesus Christ,

To the twelve tribes scattered among the nations:

Greetings.

Trials and Temptations

2Consider it pure joy, my brothers, whenever you face trials of
many kinds, 3because you know that the testing of your faith develops perseverance. 4Perseverance must finish its work so that you
may be mature and complete, not lacking anything. 5If any of you
lacks wisdom, he should ask God, who gives generously to all
without finding fault, and it will be given to him. 6But when he
asks, he must believe and not doubt, because he who doubts is like
a wave of the sea, blown and tossed by the wind. 7That man should
not think he will receive anything from the Lord; 8he is a double-
minded man, unstable in all he does.

9The brother in humble circumstances ought to take pride in his
high position. 10But the one who is rich should take pride in his
low position, because he will pass away like a wild flower. 11For
the sun rises with scorching heat and withers the plant; its blossom
falls and its beauty is destroyed. In the same way, the rich man will
fade away even while he goes about his business.

12Blessed is the man who perseveres under trial, because when
he has stood the test, he will receive the crown of life that God has
promised to those who love him.

13When tempted, no one should say, "God is tempting me." For
God cannot be tempted by evil, nor does he tempt anyone; 14but
each one is tempted when, by his own evil desire, he is dragged
away and enticed. 15Then, after desire has conceived, it gives birth
to sin; and sin, when it is full-grown, gives birth to death.

16Don't be deceived, my dear brothers. 17Every good and perfect
gift is from above, coming down from the Father of the heavenly
lights, who does not change like shifting shadows. 18He chose to
give us birth through the word of truth, that we might be a kind of
firstfruits of all he created.

Listening and Doing

19My dear brothers, take note of this: Everyone should be quick
to listen, slow to speak and slow to become angry, 20for man's
anger does not bring about the righteous life that God desires.
21Therefore, get rid of all moral filth and the evil that is so preva-
lent and humbly accept the word planted in you, which can save
you.

22Do not merely listen to the word, and so deceive yourselves.
Do what it says. 23Anyone who listens to the word but does not do
what it says is like a man who looks at his face in a mirror 24and,
after looking at himself, goes away and immediately forgets what
he looks like. 25But the man who looks intently into the perfect law
that gives freedom, and continues to do this, not forgetting what he
has heard, but doing it—he will be blessed in what he does.

26If anyone considers himself religious and yet does not keep a
tight rein on his tongue, he deceives himself and his religion is

1. What is the hardest test you remember taking? **2.** What do you do to cheer up when you're down? **3.** In your family, who does everyone lean on in hard times?

1. What do you know about James? (See Introduction to James.) **2.** According to James, what should be a Christian's attitude when facing trials (vv. 2–4)? How realistic is this? **3.** How does a person receive wisdom (v. 5)? When asking God for guidance, what must we guard against (v. 6)? **4.** How does James turn upside down the assumed status of the rich and poor (vv. 9–10)? **5.** What is the promise for one who perseveres under trial (v. 12)? **6.** Is there a difference between God "testing our faith" (v. 3) and "tempting" us (v. 13)? Explain.

1. How often is your attitude like James' during trials? How about with any trials you're facing now? How can this group help you in your attitude? **2.** When have you prayed for and received God's wisdom? What do you do when you pray but still have doubts? **3.** When have you been tempted by something that seemed "good and perfect," but turned out to be disappointing or harmful (vv. 16–17)? What are two good gifts God has given you this year?

Which best describes your temper: Short fuse, big bomb? Long fuse, little fizz? Long fuse, H-bomb?

1. What does James command in verse 19? **2.** What is the "righteous life that God desires" (vv. 20,27)? **3.** How does the term "Sunday Christian" illustrate James' point in verses 22–24? Conversely, what does the life of someone in verse 25 look like?

1. Does James say anger is wrong? How about "righteous anger" (Mk 11:15–18)? How well do you handle anger? How can we process anger in a healthy way without breaking God's command here? **2.** How much are you living out verse 27?

worthless. 27Religion that God our Father accepts as pure and faultless is this: to look after orphans and widows in their distress and to keep oneself from being polluted by the world.

---

1. For what event would you buy the "best seats": The World Series? Carnegie Hall? Your child's school play? **2.** What Third World country, or low-income area, have you spent time in?

1. In general, how do people show favoritism (vv. 1–3)? **2.** What two gifts does God give the poor (v. 5)? Why would the poor be rich in faith? **3.** What did James say the rich were doing to the poor? Does this happen today?

1. Who are the "rich" in our churches and communities? Who are the "poor"? **2.** What does this passage say to you about your own conscious or unconscious treatment of others? **3.** How does the love and mercy commanded here relate to God's love and mercy toward you?

Favoritism Forbidden

2 My brothers, as believers in our glorious Lord Jesus Christ, don't show favoritism. 2Suppose a man comes into your meeting wearing a gold ring and fine clothes, and a poor man in shabby clothes also comes in. 3If you show special attention to the man wearing fine clothes and say, "Here's a good seat for you," but say to the poor man, "You stand there" or "Sit on the floor by my feet," 4have you not discriminated among yourselves and become judges with evil thoughts?

5Listen, my dear brothers: Has not God chosen those who are poor in the eyes of the world to be rich in faith and to inherit the kingdom he promised those who love him? 6But you have insulted the poor. Is it not the rich who are exploiting you? Are they not the ones who are dragging you into court? 7Are they not the ones who are slandering the noble name of him to whom you belong?

8If you really keep the royal law found in Scripture, "Love your neighbor as yourself,"[a] you are doing right. 9But if you show favoritism, you sin and are convicted by the law as lawbreakers. 10For whoever keeps the whole law and yet stumbles at just one point is guilty of breaking all of it. 11For he who said, "Do not commit adultery,"[b] also said, "Do not murder."[c] If you do not commit adultery but do commit murder, you have become a lawbreaker.

12Speak and act as those who are going to be judged by the law that gives freedom, 13because judgment without mercy will be shown to anyone who has not been merciful. Mercy triumphs over judgment!

Are you more likely to act without thinking or think without acting?

1. In a word or phrase what is the focus of this passage? **2.** What kind of faith is James criticizing? **3.** How do you make sense of this passage in light of Galatians 2:20–21? What is the difference between the Law and deeds?

1. Why is Abraham such a good example of faith in action (see Ge 22)? In Abraham's sandals, would your "faith" have prompted you to do what he did, or to "trust" God to find another way, without climbing the mountain? How do you suppose the audiences of these two passages were different? **2.** When have you been challenged to put your faith to the test in a major way? What happened? **3.** If you were arrested for being a Christian, what evidence would be used to prove the point?

Faith and Deeds

14What good is it, my brothers, if a man claims to have faith but has no deeds? Can such faith save him? 15Suppose a brother or sister is without clothes and daily food. 16If one of you says to him, "Go, I wish you well; keep warm and well fed," but does nothing about his physical needs, what good is it? 17In the same way, faith by itself, if it is not accompanied by action, is dead.

18But someone will say, "You have faith; I have deeds."

Show me your faith without deeds, and I will show you my faith by what I do. 19You believe that there is one God. Good! Even the demons believe that—and shudder.

20You foolish man, do you want evidence that faith without deeds is useless[d]? 21Was not our ancestor Abraham considered righteous for what he did when he offered his son Isaac on the altar? 22You see that his faith and his actions were working together, and his faith was made complete by what he did. 23And the scripture was fulfilled that says, "Abraham believed God, and it was credited to him as righteousness,"[e] and he was called God's friend. 24You see that a person is justified by what he does and not by faith alone.

25In the same way, was not even Rahab the prostitute considered righteous for what she did when she gave lodging to the spies and sent them off in a different direction? 26As the body without the spirit is dead, so faith without deeds is dead.

[a] *8* Lev. 19:18 [b] *11* Exodus 20:14; Deut. 5:18 [c] *11* Exodus 20:13; Deut. 5:17
[d] *20* Some early manuscripts *dead* [e] *23* Gen. 15:6

Taming the Tongue

3 Not many of you should presume to be teachers, my brothers, because you know that we who teach will be judged more strictly. 2We all stumble in many ways. If anyone is never at fault in what he says, he is a perfect man, able to keep his whole body in check.

3When we put bits into the mouths of horses to make them obey us, we can turn the whole animal. 4Or take ships as an example. Although they are so large and are driven by strong winds, they are steered by a very small rudder wherever the pilot wants to go. 5Likewise the tongue is a small part of the body, but it makes great boasts. Consider what a great forest is set on fire by a small spark. 6The tongue also is a fire, a world of evil among the parts of the body. It corrupts the whole person, sets the whole course of his life on fire, and is itself set on fire by hell.

7All kinds of animals, birds, reptiles and creatures of the sea are being tamed and have been tamed by man, 8but no man can tame the tongue. It is a restless evil, full of deadly poison.

9With the tongue we praise our Lord and Father, and with it we curse men, who have been made in God's likeness. 10Out of the same mouth come praise and cursing. My brothers, this should not be. 11Can both fresh water and salt[a] water flow from the same spring? 12My brothers, can a fig tree bear olives, or a grapevine bear figs? Neither can a salt spring produce fresh water.

What radio personality do you appreciate for his or her uplifting words? What radio personality *don't* you appreciate? Why?

1. Why is it such a big responsibility to be a teacher, especially of the Scripture? **2.** Why are the illustrations of a bit, a rudder and a fire spark so fitting when talking of the tongue? **3.** If verse 8 is true, why should we even try to control our tongues?

1. In your everyday conversation, how seriously do you take verse 9? What does this verse say about the caution and reverence with which we must choose our words? **2.** Jesus and the apostles Peter and Paul, were not always very "tame" when it came to the tongue. When is harsh language acceptable? **3.** How do verses 2 and 10 make you feel about your tongue? How will they prompt you to pray?

Two Kinds of Wisdom

13Who is wise and understanding among you? Let him show it by his good life, by deeds done in the humility that comes from wisdom. 14But if you harbor bitter envy and selfish ambition in your hearts, do not boast about it or deny the truth. 15Such "wisdom" does not come down from heaven but is earthly, unspiritual, of the devil. 16For where you have envy and selfish ambition, there you find disorder and every evil practice.

17But the wisdom that comes from heaven is first of all pure; then peace-loving, considerate, submissive, full of mercy and good fruit, impartial and sincere. 18Peacemakers who sow in peace raise a harvest of righteousness.

Who deserves the "Wisdom of Solomon Award" in your family?

1. How can you recognize a wise person (v. 13)? **2.** What two behaviors indicate a lack of wisdom (v. 16)? **3.** What does heavenly wisdom produce?

What is the model here for effective managers, teachers, pastors, parents and coworkers? For friends?

Submit Yourselves to God

4 What causes fights and quarrels among you? Don't they come from your desires that battle within you? 2You want something but don't get it. You kill and covet, but you cannot have what you want. You quarrel and fight. You do not have, because you do not ask God. 3When you ask, you do not receive, because you ask with wrong motives, that you may spend what you get on your pleasures.

4You adulterous people, don't you know that friendship with the world is hatred toward God? Anyone who chooses to be a friend of the world becomes an enemy of God. 5Or do you think Scripture says without reason that the spirit he caused to live in us envies intensely?[b] 6But he gives us more grace. That is why Scripture says:

> "God opposes the proud
> but gives grace to the humble."[c]

7Submit yourselves, then, to God. Resist the devil, and he will

1. Whom did you quarrel with most while growing up? **2.** What purchase is highest on your "wish list"?

1. What is at the root of fights and quarrels (vv. 1–2a)? **2.** What are the two reasons we don't have what we want (vv. 2b–3)? What if we ask with a good motive and still don't receive? **3.** When disagreements arise between people, what needs to happen (vv. 2c,7,11)? **4.** What is "the law" in verse 11 (see 1:25; 2:8,12)? What is the difference between slander or judgmentalism and identifying sin in order to stand against it?

1. When you quarrel, do you seek to understand what desire is really motivating you? Do you pray about this desire? Where do you need to improve? **2.** How

[a] *11* Greek *bitter* (see also verse 14) [b] *5* Or *that God jealously longs for the spirit that he made to live in us*; or *that the Spirit he caused to live in us longs jealously*
[c] *6* Prov. 3:34

are you most likely to become a "friend" of the world? Lifestyle? Image? Pleasures of money? How does coming near to God (vv. 7–8) strengthen you? **3.** Can self-assertiveness and humility co-exist? Where does pride come in? **4.** Are Christians supposed to reflect verse 9? When?

---

1. Are you a long-range planner, or do you take one day at a time? **2.** When you were 15, what did you expect to be doing at 25? Were you right?

1. What four areas of life are discussed in 4:13? **2.** What is wrong with this type of planning? Is James putting down long-range planning altogether? Is he against making a profit? **3.** What are the abuses the rich committed (5:4–6)?

1. Do you approach your career planning in these terms? Your "life planning"? **2.** Take 30 seconds to reflect on how 4:17 is true of you. What situation comes to mind? **3.** How do the abuses of the rich occur today? How should Christians be involved?

---

1. What kind of garden or crop have you planted? How long did it take for the flowers or food crop to appear? **2.** What is the sickest you have been?

1. What does James call Christians to wait for patiently (v. 7)? **2.** As we live out our lives, waiting to be united with Christ, what should we guard against (v. 9)? **3.** What do you recall about the suffering Job experienced? Why does James use the illustration of Job (v. 11)? **4.** What is the point of verse 12? How sincere are you in your commitments?

1. How does the farmer image relate to our waiting? What situation in your life could take a lesson from the farmer? **2.** Have you ever prayed over someone who was sick or had someone pray over you? What was the experience like? **3.** Have you ever confessed your sins to other trusted believers and received prayer? In

flee from you. [8]Come near to God and he will come near to you. Wash your hands, you sinners, and purify your hearts, you double-minded. [9]Grieve, mourn and wail. Change your laughter to mourning and your joy to gloom. [10]Humble yourselves before the Lord, and he will lift you up.

[11]Brothers, do not slander one another. Anyone who speaks against his brother or judges him speaks against the law and judges it. When you judge the law, you are not keeping it, but sitting in judgment on it. [12]There is only one Lawgiver and Judge, the one who is able to save and destroy. But you—who are you to judge your neighbor?

Boasting About Tomorrow

[13]Now listen, you who say, "Today or tomorrow we will go to this or that city, spend a year there, carry on business and make money." [14]Why, you do not even know what will happen tomorrow. What is your life? You are a mist that appears for a little while and then vanishes. [15]Instead, you ought to say, "If it is the Lord's will, we will live and do this or that." [16]As it is, you boast and brag. All such boasting is evil. [17]Anyone, then, who knows the good he ought to do and doesn't do it, sins.

Warning to Rich Oppressors

5 Now listen, you rich people, weep and wail because of the misery that is coming upon you. [2]Your wealth has rotted, and moths have eaten your clothes. [3]Your gold and silver are corroded. Their corrosion will testify against you and eat your flesh like fire. You have hoarded wealth in the last days. [4]Look! The wages you failed to pay the workmen who mowed your fields are crying out against you. The cries of the harvesters have reached the ears of the Lord Almighty. [5]You have lived on earth in luxury and self-indulgence. You have fattened yourselves in the day of slaughter.[a] [6]You have condemned and murdered innocent men, who were not opposing you.

Patience in Suffering

[7]Be patient, then, brothers, until the Lord's coming. See how the farmer waits for the land to yield its valuable crop and how patient he is for the autumn and spring rains. [8]You too, be patient and stand firm, because the Lord's coming is near. [9]Don't grumble against each other, brothers, or you will be judged. The Judge is standing at the door!

[10]Brothers, as an example of patience in the face of suffering, take the prophets who spoke in the name of the Lord. [11]As you know, we consider blessed those who have persevered. You have heard of Job's perseverance and have seen what the Lord finally brought about. The Lord is full of compassion and mercy.

[12]Above all, my brothers, do not swear—not by heaven or by earth or by anything else. Let your "Yes" be yes, and your "No," no, or you will be condemned.

The Prayer of Faith

[13]Is any one of you in trouble? He should pray. Is anyone happy? Let him sing songs of praise. [14]Is any one of you sick? He should call the elders of the church to pray over him and anoint him with oil in the name of the Lord. [15]And the prayer offered in faith will make the sick person well; the Lord will raise him up. If he has

[a]5 Or *yourselves as in a day of feasting*

sinned, he will be forgiven. 16Therefore confess your sins to each
other and pray for each other so that you may be healed. The
prayer of a righteous man is powerful and effective.
17Elijah was a man just like us. He prayed earnestly that it would
not rain, and it did not rain on the land for three and a half years.
18Again he prayed, and the heavens gave rain, and the earth produced its crops.
19My brothers, if one of you should wander from the truth and
someone should bring him back, 20remember this: Whoever turns
a sinner from the error of his way will save him from death and
cover over a multitude of sins.

what way can that experience bring forgiveness, healing and new life? **4.** When you see a fellow Christian stray from God, are you prone to watch in disappointment, keep your distance so that you aren't negatively influenced, or seek ways in which God would have you bring this person back? Why? **5.** When have you come the closest to wandering from the faith? What (or who) helped bring you back? How does that demonstrate the healing body of Christ?

INTRODUCTION to
1 PETER

Book Study Outline: If you are using 1 Peter for a study course, here is a 5- or 9-week outline. Use the margin questions for your group agenda:

- start meeting / 15 min.
- read & discuss Bible / 30 min.
- close meeting / 15–45 min.

Refer to the Questions and Answers in front of Bible for more information.

5-week plan	9-week plan	Group Study Passage
1	1	1:1–12/Christ Our Hope
	2	1:13–2:3/Christ Our Sacrifice
2	3	2:4–12/Christ Our Foundation
	4	2:13–25/Christ Our Example ...
3	5	3:1–7/ ... In Our Relationships
	6	3:8–22/Christ Our Lord
4	7	4:1–11/Christ Our Strength
	8	4:12–19/Christ Our Joy
5	9	5:1–14/Christ Our Shepherd

Author: Traditionally, the apostle Peter, but some have questioned whether a Galilean fisherman like Peter could have as sophisticated a command of Greek as found in this letter. However in 5:12 he indicates that Silas helped him draft the letter which may explain the excellent style.

Date: Between the great fire in Rome (A.D. 64) and Peter's death (A.D. 68).

Theme: Hope in the midst of suffering.

Historical Background: In the summer of A.D. 64, a great fire destroyed much of Rome. It was widely believed that the Emperor Nero was responsible. Despite his attempts to help the homeless, Nero was unable to allay suspicion. Thus, needing a scapegoat to blame, he selected the Christians for this dubious honor. Up to this point, Christianity had been viewed as simply a sect of Judaism (a legal religion under the Roman system). However, Christianity was now judged to be distinct from Judaism and it was declared a forbidden religion. Waves of oppression and persecution washed over the Empire. During this period Paul was killed by beheading and Peter was crucified upside down. Peter wrote this as a circular letter to the Christians in the Roman provinces of modern-day Turkey (1:1). They were beginning to experience persecution.

Characteristics: The presence of hope in the midst of suffering is the theme throughout this letter. Peter addresses the question of how to live as a Christian in the face of ultimate issues like death, ridicule, persecution and Satanic attack. Throughout the letter, Jesus is held out as their hope (1:3), their Savior (1:18–19), their example (2:21–24), and their Lord (3:15,21b–22). There are numerous Old Testament quotes and allusions, and passages that echo Peter's own sermons as recorded in Acts.

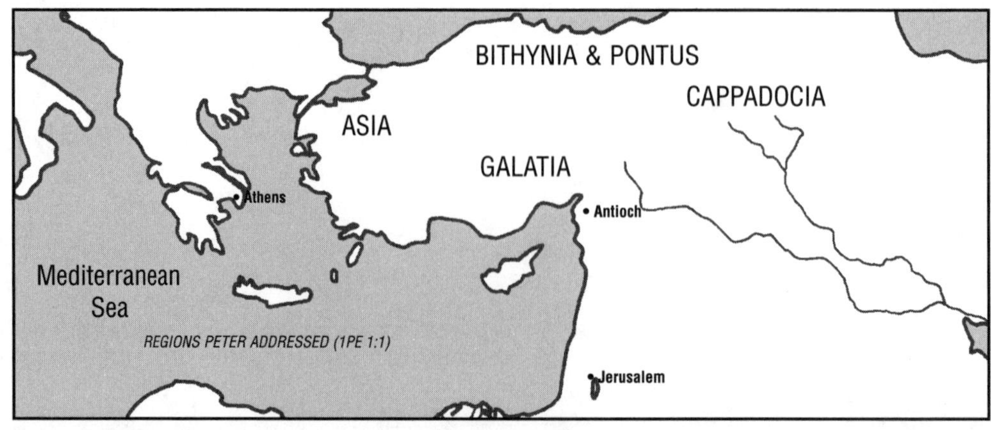

REGIONS PETER ADDRESSED (1PE 1:1)

1 Peter

1 Peter, an apostle of Jesus Christ,

To God's elect, strangers in the world, scattered throughout Pontus, Galatia, Cappadocia, Asia and Bithynia, [2]who have been chosen according to the foreknowledge of God the Father, through the sanctifying work of the Spirit, for obedience to Jesus Christ and sprinkling by his blood:

Grace and peace be yours in abundance.

Praise to God for a Living Hope

[3]Praise be to the God and Father of our Lord Jesus Christ! In his great mercy he has given us new birth into a living hope through the resurrection of Jesus Christ from the dead, [4]and into an inheritance that can never perish, spoil or fade—kept in heaven for you, [5]who through faith are shielded by God's power until the coming of the salvation that is ready to be revealed in the last time. [6]In this you greatly rejoice, though now for a little while you may have had to suffer grief in all kinds of trials. [7]These have come so that your faith—of greater worth than gold, which perishes even though refined by fire—may be proved genuine and may result in praise, glory and honor when Jesus Christ is revealed. [8]Though you have not seen him, you love him; and even though you do not see him now, you believe in him and are filled with an inexpressible and glorious joy, [9]for you are receiving the goal of your faith, the salvation of your souls.

[10]Concerning this salvation, the prophets, who spoke of the grace that was to come to you, searched intently and with the greatest care, [11]trying to find out the time and circumstances to which the Spirit of Christ in them was pointing when he predicted the sufferings of Christ and the glories that would follow. [12]It was revealed to them that they were not serving themselves but you, when they spoke of the things that have now been told you by those who have preached the gospel to you by the Holy Spirit sent from heaven. Even angels long to look into these things.

1. How many times did your family move when you were growing up? Which time was the hardest? **2.** How geographically scattered is your family now? How often do you get together?

1. What was the situation in Rome at the writing of this letter (see Introduction to 1 Peter)? **2.** What, according to verse 2, is God the Father's role in initiating a Christian's salvation? What part does the Holy Spirit play? **3.** What does Peter mean by the "new birth" God, in his mercy, provides (v. 3)? What are God's plans for a Christian's future (vv. 4–5)? **4.** What perspective does Peter give suffering in verses 6–7? **5.** Despite their suffering, how does Peter describe his audience's spiritual relationship and outlook (vv. 8–9)?

1. When have you felt like a "stranger in the world" (v. 1) because of your faith? What helps you through those times? **2.** How has the Spirit stirred a longing for God's forgiveness and holiness within you? **3.** How aware are you of God's shielding power that Peter describes? What part do you play (v. 5)? **4.** In times of personal crisis, do you tend to lean more on God or blame God? Has suffering made you bitter or "better"?

Be Holy

[13]Therefore, prepare your minds for action; be self-controlled; set your hope fully on the grace to be given you when Jesus Christ is revealed. [14]As obedient children, do not conform to the evil desires you had when you lived in ignorance. [15]But just as he who called you is holy, so be holy in all you do; [16]for it is written: "Be holy, because I am holy."[a]

[17]Since you call on a Father who judges each man's work impartially, live your lives as strangers here in reverent fear. [18]For you know that it was not with perishable things such as silver or gold that you were redeemed from the empty way of life handed down to you from your forefathers, [19]but with the precious blood of Christ, a lamb without blemish or defect. [20]He was chosen before the creation of the world, but was revealed in these last times for your sake. [21]Through him you believe in God, who raised him from

1. How did you get ready for exams in school? Keep up? Cram? Get a good night's sleep? **2.** Who was your best coach? How did this person prepare you and help you excel?

1. According to Peter, what does it mean to be holy (1:13–16)? **2.** Why would Peter remind Christians who were facing persecution that God is the Judge, and that they should live in fear? Why might they be prone to self-righteousness? **3.** What is a good test to see if a Christian has really had a change of heart (1:22)? **4.** How is loving deeply and actively possible (1:23–25)?

[a]*16* Lev. 11:44,45; 19:2; 20:7

the dead and glorified him, and so your faith and hope are in God. [22]Now that you have purified yourselves by obeying the truth so that you have sincere love for your brothers, love one another deeply, from the heart.[a] [23]For you have been born again, not of perishable seed, but of imperishable, through the living and enduring word of God. [24]For,

"All men are like grass,
 and all their glory is like the flowers of the
  field;
the grass withers and the flowers fall,
25 but the word of the Lord stands forever."[b]

And this is the word that was preached to you.

2 Therefore, rid yourselves of all malice and all deceit, hypocrisy, envy, and slander of every kind. [2]Like newborn babies, crave pure spiritual milk, so that by it you may grow up in your salvation, [3]now that you have tasted that the Lord is good.

The Living Stone and a Chosen People

[4]As you come to him, the living Stone—rejected by men but chosen by God and precious to him— [5]you also, like living stones, are being built into a spiritual house to be a holy priesthood, offering spiritual sacrifices acceptable to God through Jesus Christ. [6]For in Scripture it says:

"See, I lay a stone in Zion,
 a chosen and precious cornerstone,
and the one who trusts in him
 will never be put to shame."[c]

[7]Now to you who believe, this stone is precious. But to those who do not believe,

"The stone the builders rejected
 has become the capstone,[d]"[e]

[8]and,

"A stone that causes men to stumble
 and a rock that makes them fall."[f]

They stumble because they disobey the message—which is also what they were destined for.

[9]But you are a chosen people, a royal priesthood, a holy nation, a people belonging to God, that you may declare the praises of him who called you out of darkness into his wonderful light. [10]Once you were not a people, but now you are the people of God; once you had not received mercy, but now you have received mercy.

[11]Dear friends, I urge you, as aliens and strangers in the world, to abstain from sinful desires, which war against your soul. [12]Live such good lives among the pagans that, though they accuse you of doing wrong, they may see your good deeds and glorify God on the day he visits us.

Submission to Rulers and Masters

[13]Submit yourselves for the Lord's sake to every authority instituted among men: whether to the king, as the supreme authority, [14]or to governors, who are sent by him to punish those who do wrong and to commend those who do right. [15]For it is God's will that by doing good you should silence the ignorant talk of foolish

[a]*22* Some early manuscripts *from a pure heart* [b]*25* Isaiah 40:6-8
[c]*6* Isaiah 28:16 [d]*7* Or *cornerstone* [e]*7* Psalm 118:22 [f]*8* Isaiah 8:14

---

1. Are you more like a pilgrim, an explorer or a landowner on this earth? Why? **2.** Which of the characteristics in 1:13–16 and 2:1–2 is the greatest challenge for you? **3.** Why are Christians today tempted to be self-righteous and without reverence (see 1:17)? **4.** What has been the "pure spiritual milk" in your life (2:2)? In what way do you still need this milk? **5.** Under stress, what helps you to "set your hope fully on the grace of God," rather than to rely on your own wits to solve the problem?

On which house or apartment have you spent the most time doing improvements, decorating, etc.?

1. What was it about life for first-century Christians that made the words about Jesus in verse 4 especially important (see Introduction to 1 Peter)? **2.** What process is God undertaking right now (v. 5)? Do you usually feel this unity in the church or with other Christians? Why or why not? **3.** How is Christ a cornerstone? Why would people stumble over the stone rather than build their lives on it? **4.** How does verse 10 put the rest of the passage in perspective? **5.** How is our new status with God to influence the way we live?

1. How do you respond to Peter's description of you, and other Christians, in verse 9? **2.** In what dark rooms of your life has God turned on a light? **3.** Does verse 11 encourage you and relieve your anxiety about temptation, or make you feel defeated? What struggle or war within yourself are you facing that only Christ can help you overcome?

Growing up, who was the authority figure in your family? How was disobedience handled?

1. What does Peter say in verses 11–12 that helps to set the stage for this passage? **2.** How are Christians to act toward governmental authority? **3.** When *submit* is used in the NT, it is volun-

men. 16Live as free men, but do not use your freedom as a cover-up
for evil; live as servants of God. 17Show proper respect to everyone:
Love the brotherhood of believers, fear God, honor the king.
18Slaves, submit yourselves to your masters with all respect, not
only to those who are good and considerate, but also to those who
are harsh. 19For it is commendable if a man bears up under the
pain of unjust suffering because he is conscious of God. 20But how
is it to your credit if you receive a beating for doing wrong and
endure it? But if you suffer for doing good and you endure it, this
is commendable before God. 21To this you were called, because
Christ suffered for you, leaving you an example, that you should
follow in his steps.

22"He committed no sin,
and no deceit was found in his mouth."[a]

23When they hurled their insults at him, he did not retaliate; when
he suffered, he made no threats. Instead, he entrusted himself to
him who judges justly. 24He himself bore our sins in his body on
the tree, so that we might die to sins and live for righteousness; by
his wounds you have been healed. 25For you were like sheep going
astray, but now you have returned to the Shepherd and Overseer of
your souls.

Wives and Husbands

3 Wives, in the same way be submissive to your husbands so
that, if any of them do not believe the word, they may be won
over without words by the behavior of their wives, 2when they see
the purity and reverence of your lives. 3Your beauty should not
come from outward adornment, such as braided hair and the wearing of gold jewelry and fine clothes. 4Instead, it should be that of
your inner self, the unfading beauty of a gentle and quiet spirit,
which is of great worth in God's sight. 5For this is the way the
holy women of the past who put their hope in God used to make
themselves beautiful. They were submissive to their own husbands, 6like Sarah, who obeyed Abraham and called him her master. You are her daughters if you do what is right and do not give
way to fear.
7Husbands, in the same way be considerate as you live with your
wives, and treat them with respect as the weaker partner and as
heirs with you of the gracious gift of life, so that nothing will
hinder your prayers.

Suffering for Doing Good

8Finally, all of you, live in harmony with one another; be sympathetic, love as brothers, be compassionate and humble. 9Do not
repay evil with evil or insult with insult, but with blessing, because
to this you were called so that you may inherit a blessing. 10For,

"Whoever would love life
and see good days
must keep his tongue from evil
and his lips from deceitful speech.
11He must turn from evil and do good;
he must seek peace and pursue it.
12For the eyes of the Lord are on the righteous
and his ears are attentive to their prayer,
but the face of the Lord is against those who do
evil."[b]

[a] 22 Isaiah 53:9 [b] 12 Psalm 34:12-16

tary in nature. How is this different from other interpretations of the word today? **4.** What is Peter's response to one whose master is not a Christian or is just a difficult person (v. 18)? **5.** How does Christ's death result in both an ending and a beginning in our lives (v. 24)?

1. In Peter's day, persecution and slavery made submission to authority difficult. What conditions today make it difficult? **2.** How can Jesus' example help you face hardships you can't change? **3.** What should people do whose legal rights are being violated by authority gone bad? Accept suffering? Insist on justice? Confront the authority? (See also Mk 11:15–16; 15:1–15; Ac 16:35–37).

What have you admired about your grandparents' or other older couples' marriage?

1. See question 3 in the previous "BOOK" questions. In this light, how would you define submission for wives? How are husbands to live "in the same way"? **2.** How can God use the spouse of an unbeliever?

1. When appreciating or striving for beauty, on which do you most often focus (vv. 3–4)? **2.** What does a marriage built on voluntary submission and consideration look like? **3.** Is Peter advocating that spouses stay in cruel situations or that wives never say *no*?

As a child, what can you remember fighting about on family trips?

1. How should we live if we want to "love life and see good days" (v. 10)? How would our society answer this? **2.** How does the quote from Psalm 34 sum up all Peter has said in 2:11–3:9? **3.** How can suffering for what is right be a blessing (v. 14)? **4.** Why is verse 15a the key to following all that Peter says? **5.** What hope does Christ's life and death provide? How does the example of Christ encourage those who suffer?

1. How is it really possible to live like verses 8–12? Prayer? Effort? Obedience no matter what? A deepening relationship with Christ? 2. What is the model for evangelism Peter gives in verses 15–16? How closely do you follow this? 3. What fears motivate people today? What fears affect our relationships? How does following Jesus as Lord free you from those fears? 4. How does hope change your behavior and cause people to ask about it? What situation seemed hopeless to you until God brought hope?

13Who is going to harm you if you are eager to do good? 14But
even if you should suffer for what is right, you are blessed. "Do not
fear what they fear[a]; do not be frightened."[b] 15But in your hearts
set apart Christ as Lord. Always be prepared to give an answer to
everyone who asks you to give the reason for the hope that you
have. But do this with gentleness and respect, 16keeping a clear
conscience, so that those who speak maliciously against your good
behavior in Christ may be ashamed of their slander. 17It is better,
if it is God's will, to suffer for doing good than for doing evil. 18For
Christ died for sins once for all, the righteous for the unrighteous,
to bring you to God. He was put to death in the body but made
alive by the Spirit, 19through whom[c] also he went and preached
to the spirits in prison 20who disobeyed long ago when God waited
patiently in the days of Noah while the ark was being built. In it
only a few people, eight in all, were saved through water, 21and
this water symbolizes baptism that now saves you also—not the
removal of dirt from the body but the pledge[d] of a good conscience toward God. It saves you by the resurrection of Jesus
Christ, 22who has gone into heaven and is at God's right hand—
with angels, authorities and powers in submission to him.

How close have you come to dying or being seriously ill?

1. How can suffering change a person's life for the better (vv. 1–2)? 2. Why would a radical change in the lifestyle of Christians be so upsetting to pagan friends or family (v. 4)? 3. How does being clear-minded and self-controlled affect prayer (v. 7)?

1. How have you seen suffering change your own life for the better? 2. How does the reality of judgment (vv. 5–7) and Christ's glory (v. 11) influence your daily behavior? 3. Twice, Peter gives the command to "love each other deeply" (v. 8; 1:22). What comes to mind when you compare your lifestyle of love to this command? 4. Why is using your talents for God important both for yourself and for others?

Living for God

4 Therefore, since Christ suffered in his body, arm yourselves
also with the same attitude, because he who has suffered in his
body is done with sin. 2As a result, he does not live the rest of his
earthly life for evil human desires, but rather for the will of God.
3For you have spent enough time in the past doing what pagans
choose to do—living in debauchery, lust, drunkenness, orgies, carousing and detestable idolatry. 4They think it strange that you do
not plunge with them into the same flood of dissipation, and they
heap abuse on you. 5But they will have to give account to him who
is ready to judge the living and the dead. 6For this is the reason the
gospel was preached even to those who are now dead, so that they
might be judged according to men in regard to the body, but live
according to God in regard to the spirit.

7The end of all things is near. Therefore be clear minded and
self-controlled so that you can pray. 8Above all, love each other
deeply, because love covers over a multitude of sins. 9Offer hospitality to one another without grumbling. 10Each one should use
whatever gift he has received to serve others, faithfully administering God's grace in its various forms. 11If anyone speaks, he should
do it as one speaking the very words of God. If anyone serves, he
should do it with the strength God provides, so that in all things
God may be praised through Jesus Christ. To him be the glory and
the power for ever and ever. Amen.

What kind of pain affects your life the most: physical or emotional?

1. What false assumption does Peter set straight in verse 12? 2. How is rejoicing in suffering different from just enduring suffering? What is meant by "rejoice"? 3. What should be your attitude toward scorn and ridicule of your faith (vv. 16–17)? 4. What is the first and most important course of action amidst suffering (v. 19)?

Suffering for Being a Christian

12Dear friends, do not be surprised at the painful trial you are
suffering, as though something strange were happening to you.
13But rejoice that you participate in the sufferings of Christ, so that
you may be overjoyed when his glory is revealed. 14If you are
insulted because of the name of Christ, you are blessed, for the
Spirit of glory and of God rests on you. 15If you suffer, it should not
be as a murderer or thief or any other kind of criminal, or even
as a meddler. 16However, if you suffer as a Christian, do not be
ashamed, but praise God that you bear that name. 17For it is time
for judgment to begin with the family of God; and if it begins with

[a] 14 Or *not fear their threats* [b] 14 Isaiah 8:12 [c] 18,19 Or *alive in the spirit, 19through which* [d] 21 Or *response*

us, what will the outcome be for those who do not obey the gospel
of God? 18And,

> "If it is hard for the righteous to be saved,
> what will become of the ungodly and the
> sinner?"[a]

19So then, those who suffer according to God's will should commit themselves to their faithful Creator and continue to do good.

To Elders and Young Men

5 To the elders among you, I appeal as a fellow elder, a witness
of Christ's sufferings and one who also will share in the glory
to be revealed: 2Be shepherds of God's flock that is under your
care, serving as overseers—not because you must, but because you
are willing, as God wants you to be; not greedy for money, but
eager to serve; 3not lording it over those entrusted to you, but
being examples to the flock. 4And when the Chief Shepherd appears, you will receive the crown of glory that will never fade
away.
5Young men, in the same way be submissive to those who are
older. All of you, clothe yourselves with humility toward one another, because,

> "God opposes the proud
> but gives grace to the humble."[b]

6Humble yourselves, therefore, under God's mighty hand, that he
may lift you up in due time. 7Cast all your anxiety on him because
he cares for you.
8Be self-controlled and alert. Your enemy the devil prowls
around like a roaring lion looking for someone to devour. 9Resist
him, standing firm in the faith, because you know that your brothers throughout the world are undergoing the same kind of sufferings.
10And the God of all grace, who called you to his eternal glory in
Christ, after you have suffered a little while, will himself restore
you and make you strong, firm and steadfast. 11To him be the
power for ever and ever. Amen.

Final Greetings

12With the help of Silas,[c] whom I regard as a faithful brother, I
have written to you briefly, encouraging you and testifying that this
is the true grace of God. Stand fast in it.
13She who is in Babylon, chosen together with you, sends you
her greetings, and so does my son Mark. 14Greet one another with
a kiss of love.
Peace to all of you who are in Christ.

1. When have you participated in something which was difficult, but eventually became a success (v. 13)? **2.** What form does your suffering for Christ take? How does verse 19 comfort and assure you?

---

1. Were you the youngest, middle or oldest child in your family? How did the family "pecking order" affect your personality? **2.** What is one of the most unruly groups you have had to shepherd: Jr. High kids on a field trip? The church nursery? A small group that wouldn't cooperate? A meeting of competitive professionals?

1. What is Peter warning church leaders about (vv. 2–3)? What are modern-day temptations for leaders? **2.** Who is Peter talking to in verses 5–7? What may be happening in the church? Why might this happen especially during a time of persecution? **3.** How are Christians to deal with stress, tension and hassles (vv. 6–7)? **4.** What theme on suffering in verse 10 summarizes a main theme of 1 Peter? In what way does this promise bring you comfort?

1. Who are the "elders" of our day? **2.** What leadership responsibilities do you have? (We all have some!) How do you score on Peter's leadership test? How can you improve your score? **3.** What specific anxiety or concern do you need to cast humbly on the Lord? What gets in your way? **4.** What should Christians be "alert" to? How does this relate to suffering and tensions between people? How does it relate to your own frame of mind? To your belief in the promise in verse 10? **5.** What picture of Christ has Peter drawn in his letter? How does that picture bring peace (5:14) to you?

[a] *18* Prov. 11:31 [b] *5* Prov. 3:34 [c] *12* Greek *Silvanus,* a variant of *Silas*

INTRODUCTION to

2 PETER

Book Study Outline: If you are using 2 Peter for a study course, here is a 4-week outline. Use the margin questions for your group agenda:

start meeting / 15 min.

read & discuss Bible / 30 min.

close meeting / 15–45 min.

4-week plan	Group Study Passage
1	1:1–11/Keep On Growing in Christ
2	1:12–21/Authority of True Prophets
3	2:1–22/Destruction of False Prophets
4	3:1–18/Second Coming of Christ

Refer to the Questions and Answers in the front of this Bible for more information.

Author: Traditionally, the apostle Peter, although questions about his authorship have existed since the earliest times because the language and style of this letter differs markedly from 1 Peter. The fact that Peter had different secretaries (Silas, Mark, Glaucias) may explain this difference.

Date: Probably near the time of Peter's death in A.D. 68 (see 1:12–15).

Theme: Be eager and on your guard.

Historical Background: See the Introduction to 1 Peter. Although no specific group is addressed, it appears to have been sent to the same group of Christians who received his first letter (3:1). Persecution from Roman authorities (the major issue in Peter's first letter) was not the only problem facing these people. False teachers had arisen. The fact that Jesus had not yet returned was being interpreted as evidence that the apostles (like Peter and Paul) were not to be trusted. These teachers were apparently insinuating that the Second Coming was sort of a "moral club" invented by the apostles to inhibit the Christian's "freedom." For the false teachers, "freedom" meant the right to indulge in sexual immorality, drunkenness and hedonistic pleasure (2:2,10,13–14,18). Peter fights back in this letter by roaring a "Not so!" He asserts that apostolic teaching was not a matter of spinning their own ideas (1:16,20), but that in reality the false teachers' "authority" stemmed from their own minds (1:21), and their "spiritual freedom" really led to depravity (2:19).

Characteristics: Chapter 1 is an exhortation to grow in the Christian virtues. Chapter 2 is very similar to the epistle of Jude (see the Introduction to Jude). A marked contrast is drawn there between the character and teaching of true apostles (like Peter and Paul) and that of the false teachers whose lives are marked by their denial of Jesus, immorality, rejection of authority, enslavement to sin and misuse of Scripture. Chapter 3 addresses the Second Coming of Christ.

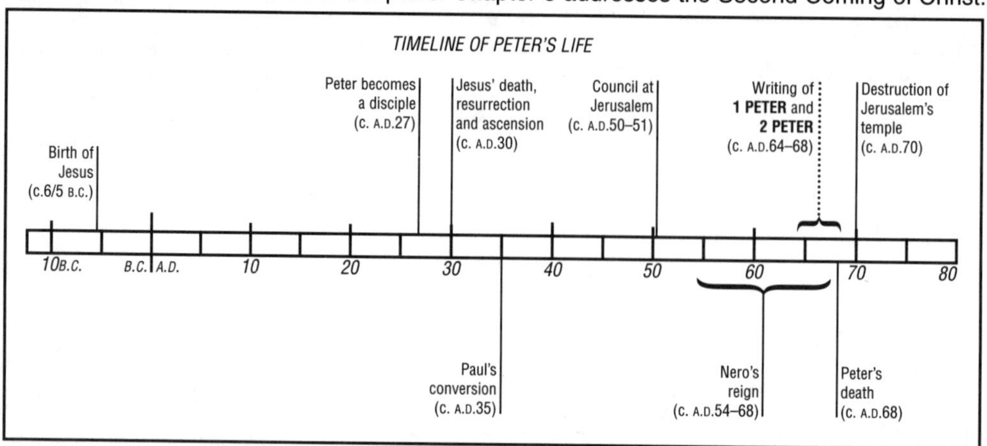

2 Peter

1 Simon Peter, a servant and apostle of Jesus Christ,

To those who through the righteousness of our God and Savior Jesus Christ have received a faith as precious as ours:

2Grace and peace be yours in abundance through the knowledge of God and of Jesus our Lord.

1. As a teenager, what did you desire to do most: Career-wise? Sports-wise? Relationship-wise? 2. How have your desires changed since then?

Making One's Calling and Election Sure

3His divine power has given us everything we need for life and godliness through our knowledge of him who called us by his own glory and goodness. 4Through these he has given us his very great and precious promises, so that through them you may participate in the divine nature and escape the corruption in the world caused by evil desires.

5For this very reason, make every effort to add to your faith goodness; and to goodness, knowledge; 6and to knowledge, self-control; and to self-control, perseverance; and to perseverance, godliness; 7and to godliness, brotherly kindness; and to brotherly kindness, love. 8For if you possess these qualities in increasing measure, they will keep you from being ineffective and unproductive in your knowledge of our Lord Jesus Christ. 9But if anyone does not have them, he is nearsighted and blind, and has forgotten that he has been cleansed from his past sins.

10Therefore, my brothers, be all the more eager to make your calling and election sure. For if you do these things, you will never fall, 11and you will receive a rich welcome into the eternal kingdom of our Lord and Savior Jesus Christ.

1. From verses 3–4, what is "everything we need for life"? **2.** With *everything* given to us, why must we "*add* to our faith"? And with what effort (vv. 5,10)? **3.** What seven qualities are we to zealously desire? How does each fit with the one mentioned before it? **4.** Why is this moral progress and productive knowledge (v. 8) so desirable for believers (vv. 4,10–11)?

1. In what way are verses 5–10 a prescription for one who is feeling disappointed or unfulfilled? **2.** Of the seven qualities in verses 5–7, which two do you possess in the greatest measure? How can you grow in one of the other qualities? How can your group help?

Prophecy of Scripture

12So I will always remind you of these things, even though you know them and are firmly established in the truth you now have. 13I think it is right to refresh your memory as long as I live in the tent of this body, 14because I know that I will soon put it aside, as our Lord Jesus Christ has made clear to me. 15And I will make every effort to see that after my departure you will always be able to remember these things.

16We did not follow cleverly invented stories when we told you about the power and coming of our Lord Jesus Christ, but we were eyewitnesses of his majesty. 17For he received honor and glory from God the Father when the voice came to him from the Majestic Glory, saying, "This is my Son, whom I love; with him I am well pleased."[a] 18We ourselves heard this voice that came from heaven when we were with him on the sacred mountain.

19And we have the word of the prophets made more certain, and you will do well to pay attention to it, as to a light shining in a dark place, until the day dawns and the morning star rises in your hearts. 20Above all, you must understand that no prophecy of Scripture came about by the prophet's own interpretation. 21For prophecy never had its origin in the will of man, but men spoke from God as they were carried along by the Holy Spirit.

How are you like a tent: Always pulling up stakes, moving on? Resistant to winds of change? Cozy with some, cold to others?

1. What event of Jesus' life does Peter recall (vv. 16–18)? **2.** Why (and how) does Peter establish his own authority (v. 16)? Likewise, why does Peter defend the authority and inspiration of the prophets? What problem does this imply his readers may have (vv. 20–21)? **3.** If so much prophecy has already been fulfilled in Christ's first coming, how then are we to regard prophecy yet to be fulfilled?

1. If you could have been with Jesus at one event in his life, which would you choose? Why? **2.** If a non-Christian asked you to prove the Scriptures are God's Word, on what would you base your answer? **3.** How does that answer affect your Bible study habits? Your witness? Your lifestyle?

a *17* Matt. 17:5; Mark 9:7; Luke 9:35

1. If people have pets that are like them in some way, what does your choice of pet say about you? **2.** What "beasts" and other "things which go bump in the night" are you afraid of? Why?

1. Having just commended true prophets (1:12–21), who does Peter now condemn? Why? **2.** If it is so plain that judgment awaits these false teachers, why does anyone follow them (vv. 2–3,14,18–19)? If they are so evil, why do you think God allows them to teach in his church? Isn't God's goodness or greatness brought into question by delaying their judgment? **3.** In response to that implied question, Peter recites God's track record in dealing with evil: What examples are cited in verses 4–9? **4.** If neither angels, the ancient world, nor Sodom and Gomorrah were spared from God's wrath against sin, who does God protect from judgment (v. 9)? Why? How is that a particular comfort to Peter's audience? **5.** Who are the gross sinners in verses 13–16? What are they like? On what basis is Peter assured they will be paid back in kind? **6.** What other imagery does Peter use to further denounce the false prophets (vv. 17–19)? **7.** What "freedom" do they promise: Freedom from sin? From laws? From judgment? From ethical obligations to others and to Christ? All of the above? How is their idea of freedom different from true Christian freedom? **8.** What do verses 20–22 imply about a person's salvation? Can one lose it? Or were these people never converted? Why do you think so?

1. How do you know when a preacher is exploiting you with stories they have made up, or feeding you empty promises as "springs without water"? How could the dangers mentioned by Peter affect you now? **2.** Do such false teachers upset you as much as Peter? Why or why not? Which preacher do you trust more than others? Why? **3.** Amidst all this bad news, what good news is there? Would it be truly good news if there were no judgment? **4.** In your experience, does grace ever come through perverse channels (such as the heretics and wicked men depicted here), or only through pure vessels: Always? Sometimes? Never? Why is that?

False Teachers and Their Destruction

2 But there were also false prophets among the people, just as there will be false teachers among you. They will secretly introduce destructive heresies, even denying the sovereign Lord who bought them—bringing swift destruction on themselves. 2Many will follow their shameful ways and will bring the way of truth into disrepute. 3In their greed these teachers will exploit you with stories they have made up. Their condemnation has long been hanging over them, and their destruction has not been sleeping.

4For if God did not spare angels when they sinned, but sent them to hell,[a] putting them into gloomy dungeons[b] to be held for judgment; 5if he did not spare the ancient world when he brought the flood on its ungodly people, but protected Noah, a preacher of righteousness, and seven others; 6if he condemned the cities of Sodom and Gomorrah by burning them to ashes, and made them an example of what is going to happen to the ungodly; 7and if he rescued Lot, a righteous man, who was distressed by the filthy lives of lawless men 8(for that righteous man, living among them day after day, was tormented in his righteous soul by the lawless deeds he saw and heard)— 9if this is so, then the Lord knows how to rescue godly men from trials and to hold the unrighteous for the day of judgment, while continuing their punishment.[c] 10This is especially true of those who follow the corrupt desire of the sinful nature[d] and despise authority.

Bold and arrogant, these men are not afraid to slander celestial beings; 11yet even angels, although they are stronger and more powerful, do not bring slanderous accusations against such beings in the presence of the Lord. 12But these men blaspheme in matters they do not understand. They are like brute beasts, creatures of instinct, born only to be caught and destroyed, and like beasts they too will perish.

13They will be paid back with harm for the harm they have done. Their idea of pleasure is to carouse in broad daylight. They are blots and blemishes, reveling in their pleasures while they feast with you.[e] 14With eyes full of adultery, they never stop sinning; they seduce the unstable; they are experts in greed—an accursed brood! 15They have left the straight way and wandered off to follow the way of Balaam son of Beor, who loved the wages of wickedness. 16But he was rebuked for his wrongdoing by a donkey—a beast without speech—who spoke with a man's voice and restrained the prophet's madness.

17These men are springs without water and mists driven by a storm. Blackest darkness is reserved for them. 18For they mouth empty, boastful words and, by appealing to the lustful desires of sinful human nature, they entice people who are just escaping from those who live in error. 19They promise them freedom, while they themselves are slaves of depravity—for a man is a slave to whatever has mastered him. 20If they have escaped the corruption of the world by knowing our Lord and Savior Jesus Christ and are again entangled in it and overcome, they are worse off at the end than they were at the beginning. 21It would have been better for them not to have known the way of righteousness, than to have known it and then to turn their backs on the sacred command that was passed on to them. 22Of them the proverbs are true: "A dog returns to its vomit,"[f] and, "A sow that is washed goes back to her wallowing in the mud."

[a]*4* Greek *Tartarus* [b]*4* Some manuscripts *into chains of darkness* [c]*9* Or *unrighteous for punishment until the day of judgment* [d]*10* Or *the flesh* [e]*13* Some manuscripts *in their love feasts* [f]*22* Prov. 26:11

The Day of the Lord

3 Dear friends, this is now my second letter to you. I have
written both of them as reminders to stimulate you to whole-
some thinking. 2I want you to recall the words spoken in the past
by the holy prophets and the command given by our Lord and
Savior through your apostles.
3First of all, you must understand that in the last days scoffers
will come, scoffing and following their own evil desires. 4They will
say, "Where is this 'coming' he promised? Ever since our fathers
died, everything goes on as it has since the beginning of creation."
5But they deliberately forget that long ago by God's word the heavens existed and the earth was formed out of water and by water.
6By these waters also the world of that time was deluged and
destroyed. 7By the same word the present heavens and earth are
reserved for fire, being kept for the day of judgment and destruction of ungodly men.
8But do not forget this one thing, dear friends: With the Lord a
day is like a thousand years, and a thousand years are like a day.
9The Lord is not slow in keeping his promise, as some understand
slowness. He is patient with you, not wanting anyone to perish,
but everyone to come to repentance.
10But the day of the Lord will come like a thief. The heavens will
disappear with a roar; the elements will be destroyed by fire, and
the earth and everything in it will be laid bare.[a]
11Since everything will be destroyed in this way, what kind of
people ought you to be? You ought to live holy and godly lives 12as
you look forward to the day of God and speed its coming.[b] That
day will bring about the destruction of the heavens by fire, and the
elements will melt in the heat. 13But in keeping with his promise
we are looking forward to a new heaven and a new earth, the
home of righteousness.
14So then, dear friends, since you are looking forward to this,
make every effort to be found spotless, blameless and at peace with
him. 15Bear in mind that our Lord's patience means salvation, just
as our dear brother Paul also wrote you with the wisdom that God
gave him. 16He writes the same way in all his letters, speaking in
them of these matters. His letters contain some things that are hard
to understand, which ignorant and unstable people distort, as they
do the other Scriptures, to their own destruction.
17Therefore, dear friends, since you already know this, be on
your guard so that you may not be carried away by the error of
lawless men and fall from your secure position. 18But grow in the
grace and knowledge of our Lord and Savior Jesus Christ. To him
be glory both now and forever! Amen.

1. When did your dad promise a fishing trip, a ballgame or a graduation present and then fail to deliver? How did that make you feel? **2.** When told, "Wait until your birthday," or "Christmas isn't here yet," and "You'd better be good until then," how did that affect your behavior while waiting?

1. Following the digression of chapter 2, to what themes does Peter now return? **2.** What "must" the readers first understand (see also 1:20–21)? **3.** Why does God's creation of the earth support Peter's contention that he will also destroy the earth (v. 10)? Why is that so difficult for people to believe? What does this tell you about their perception of God? **4.** What frustrations does God's patience produce? How is God's patience a benefit (vv. 9,15)? **5.** How does God's view of time differ from the readers' view? In this context (vv. 10–16), is Peter addressing the certainty, the timing or the manner of Christ's coming? How is that an effective inducement to godly living now? **6.** How does Peter's reference to Paul also encourage his readers in right behavior (v. 15)? **7.** What is Peter's final antidote to the false teachers of his day (vv. 17–18)?

1. If you were in charge of the world's clock, would you slow it down or speed it up? Why? **2.** If you were in charge of creating, destroying and redeeming the world, which of these would you take more "time" doing? Why? **3.** In football strategy "the best defense is a good offense," meaning if the other team never gets the ball they can't score against you. How is Peter's strategy like that in his defense against those who would lead us away from the truth? What can you do to "grow in the grace and knowledge of our Lord"?

[a]*10* Some manuscripts *be burned up*

[b]*12* Or *as you wait eagerly for the day of God to come*

INTRODUCTION to
1 JOHN

Book Study Outline: If you are using 1 John for a study course, here is a 4- or 7-week outline. Use the margin questions for your group agenda:

- start meeting / 15 min.
- read & discuss Bible / 30 min.
- close meeting / 15–45 min.

4-week plan	7-week plan	Group Study Passage
1	1	1:1–2:14/Walking in the Light
	2	2:15–27/Warning Against Antichrists
2	3	2:28–3:10/Doing What Is Right
	4	3:11–24/Loving One Another
3	5	4:1–6/Testing the Spirits
	6	4:7–21/Loving God
4	7	5:1–21/Believing in Christ

Refer to the Questions and Answers in the front of this Bible for more information.

Author: Traditionally, the apostle John.

Date: Uncertain, but probably in the late A.D. 80s or early 90s when the heresy which is rebuked here (an early form of Gnosticism) began to flourish.

Theme: Walking in the light.

Historical Background: Since in his later years John resided in Ephesus, this letter was probably addressed to the church there. A group had split off from the church (2:19) and began trying to persuade others to espouse their new and "advanced" views (2:26). To help the church discern truth from error, both in doctrine and lifestyle, John wrote this letter. The secessionists did not believe Jesus was the Messiah (2:22), nor that he had come in the flesh (4:2–3). Furthermore, they didn't need Jesus as Savior or mediator, since they claimed to have direct knowledge of and fellowship with God (1:6; 2:4). This spiritual elitism bypassed morality and love as marks of one's spiritual maturity. What was important to them were visions and spiritual revelations.

Characteristics: First John does not have the neat, logical outline found in many New Testament books. Rather, John seems to have written one paragraph and then he would be reminded of a related idea which became the topic of the next paragraph. The structure is more spiral than linear. This epistle is a distillation of all John, now an old man, wants people to remember about the faith. Its essence is that God is light (1:5); God is love (4:16); Jesus is the Messiah (2:22), the Son of God (4:15) who has come in the flesh (4:2) to make us his children (3:1). As such, we have eternal life (2:25) and are called not to sin (2:1), but to love one another (3:11; 4:7–12).

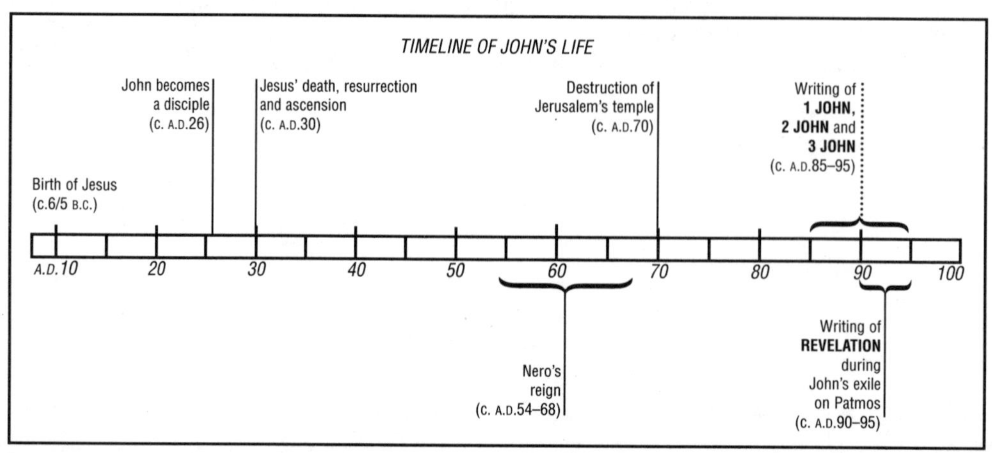

1 John

The Word of Life

1 That which was from the beginning, which we have heard,
which we have seen with our eyes, which we have looked at
and our hands have touched—this we proclaim concerning the
Word of life. 2The life appeared; we have seen it and testify to
it, and we proclaim to you the eternal life, which was with the
Father and has appeared to us. 3We proclaim to you what we have
seen and heard, so that you also may have fellowship with us.
And our fellowship is with the Father and with his Son, Jesus
Christ. 4We write this to make our[a] joy complete.

Walking in the Light

5This is the message we have heard from him and declare to you:
God is light; in him there is no darkness at all. 6If we claim to have
fellowship with him yet walk in the darkness, we lie and do not
live by the truth. 7But if we walk in the light, as he is in the light,
we have fellowship with one another, and the blood of Jesus, his
Son, purifies us from all[b] sin.

8If we claim to be without sin, we deceive ourselves and the
truth is not in us. 9If we confess our sins, he is faithful and just and
will forgive us our sins and purify us from all unrighteousness. 10If
we claim we have not sinned, we make him out to be a liar and his
word has no place in our lives.

2 My dear children, I write this to you so that you will not sin.
But if anybody does sin, we have one who speaks to the Father
in our defense—Jesus Christ, the Righteous One. 2He is the atoning sacrifice for our sins, and not only for ours but also for[c] the
sins of the whole world.

3We know that we have come to know him if we obey his
commands. 4The man who says, "I know him," but does not do
what he commands is a liar, and the truth is not in him. 5But if
anyone obeys his word, God's love[d] is truly made complete in
him. This is how we know we are in him: 6Whoever claims to live
in him must walk as Jesus did.

7Dear friends, I am not writing you a new command but an old
one, which you have had since the beginning. This old command is
the message you have heard. 8Yet I am writing you a new command; its truth is seen in him and you, because the darkness is
passing and the true light is already shining.

9Anyone who claims to be in the light but hates his brother is
still in the darkness. 10Whoever loves his brother lives in the light,
and there is nothing in him[e] to make him stumble. 11But whoever
hates his brother is in the darkness and walks around in the darkness; he does not know where he is going, because the darkness
has blinded him.

12I write to you, dear children,
because your sins have been forgiven on
account of his name.

a4 Some manuscripts *your* b7 Or *every* c2 Or *He is the one who turns aside God's wrath, taking away our sins, and not only ours but also* d5 Or *word, love for God* e10 Or *it*

1. What was your house like at age 7? **2.** What do you remember about your room? **3.** As a child, were you afraid of the dark? What "monsters" were in the dark that scared you?

1. A group in John's church had split off and were teaching that Jesus did not really die. They also believed they were without sin (see Introduction to 1 John). What could not be proclaimed if Jesus hadn't died? **2.** What false claims do John's opponents make (1:6,8)? **3.** What hope does John give when people fail to live in light of God's love (1:9; 2:1–2)? Explain in your own words what it means that Jesus is the advocate, the righteous one and the atoning sacrifice. **4.** How can the command to love God and others (2:7) be new and old at the same time? How is its truth seen in Jesus (think of examples from the Gospels)? **5.** What are the two tests given in this passage for determining whether one really knows God (2:3,10)? How are you doing in each of these areas? **6.** What three things does John stress again in verses 2:12–14?

1. In what ways have you, like John, "seen," "heard" and "touched" Jesus? **2.** Who has been like the apostle John in your life—a person who has cared about your spiritual growth? **3.** What characteristics of light reflect who God is? Has God brought light to your life? Or do you more often feel like you're in the dark? **4.** How do you feel about the consistency of your own life (1:6,8)? Are you living the truth or a lie? In what area do you especially need improvement? **5.** When you know you've sinned, how long do you wait before you confess? What is God's part and your part in the confession process?

13 I write to you, fathers,
because you have known him who is from the beginning.
I write to you, young men,
because you have overcome the evil one.
I write to you, dear children,
because you have known the Father.
14 I write to you, fathers,
because you have known him who is from the beginning.
I write to you, young men,
because you are strong,
and the word of God lives in you,
and you have overcome the evil one.

Are you more likely to err on the side of doing what you shouldn't or not doing what you should?

1. What does John mean by "the world" (vv. 15–17)? Is it wrong to love the outdoors or your pet? Are all human desires contrary to God's will? Why? **2.** What is the anointing in verse 20? How does this anointing help a person to know and remain in the truth (vv. 20,24)? **3.** In what way are the antichrists in this passage foreshadowing the Antichrist to come? What danger do they pose to the church? **4.** Why are there only two options in verse 23?

1. In what areas of your life does love for the world compete with love for God: In your use of money? Time? Priorities? Relationships? Ambitions? **2.** What criteria can you use to distinguish between: (a) new insights into Christian truths that the Holy Spirit brings to light, and (b) new teachings that undermine the Christian faith?

Do Not Love the World

15 Do not love the world or anything in the world. If anyone loves
the world, the love of the Father is not in him. 16 For everything in
the world—the cravings of sinful man, the lust of his eyes and the
boasting of what he has and does—comes not from the Father but
from the world. 17 The world and its desires pass away, but the man
who does the will of God lives forever.

Warning Against Antichrists

18 Dear children, this is the last hour; and as you have heard that
the antichrist is coming, even now many antichrists have come.
This is how we know it is the last hour. 19 They went out from us,
but they did not really belong to us. For if they had belonged to us,
they would have remained with us; but their going showed that
none of them belonged to us.
20 But you have an anointing from the Holy One, and all of you
know the truth.[a] 21 I do not write to you because you do not know
the truth, but because you do know it and because no lie comes
from the truth. 22 Who is the liar? It is the man who denies that
Jesus is the Christ. Such a man is the antichrist—he denies the
Father and the Son. 23 No one who denies the Son has the Father;
whoever acknowledges the Son has the Father also.
24 See that what you have heard from the beginning remains in
you. If it does, you also will remain in the Son and in the Father.
25 And this is what he promised us—even eternal life.
26 I am writing these things to you about those who are trying to
lead you astray. 27 As for you, the anointing you received from him
remains in you, and you do not need anyone to teach you. But as
his anointing teaches you about all things and as that anointing is
real, not counterfeit—just as it has taught you, remain in him.

Who is the "neat freak" in your family? Are you neat or messy?

1. What tell-tale attitudes and actions characterize a person "born of God" (2:29; 3:1b,3,6–7, 10)? **2.** Are Christians sinless (3:6–10)? Does John mean that Christians do not sin: At all? Inadvertently? Deliberately? Habitually? Or is he providing a gauge to evaluate teachers? **3.** John says the main source of tension between the world and Christians is sin. De-

Children of God

28 And now, dear children, continue in him, so that when he
appears we may be confident and unashamed before him at his
coming.
29 If you know that he is righteous, you know that everyone who
does what is right has been born of him.
3 How great is the love the Father has lavished on us, that we
should be called children of God! And that is what we are! The
reason the world does not know us is that it did not know him.
2 Dear friends, now we are children of God, and what we will be
has not yet been made known. But we know that when he ap-

[a]20 Some manuscripts *and you know all things*

pears,[a] we shall be like him, for we shall see him as he is. 3Everyone who has this hope in him purifies himself, just as he is pure.

4Everyone who sins breaks the law; in fact, sin is lawlessness. 5But you know that he appeared so that he might take away our sins. And in him is no sin. 6No one who lives in him keeps on sinning. No one who continues to sin has either seen him or known him.

7Dear children, do not let anyone lead you astray. He who does what is right is righteous, just as he is righteous. 8He who does what is sinful is of the devil, because the devil has been sinning from the beginning. The reason the Son of God appeared was to destroy the devil's work. 9No one who is born of God will continue to sin, because God's seed remains in him; he cannot go on sinning, because he has been born of God. 10This is how we know who the children of God are and who the children of the devil are: Anyone who does not do what is right is not a child of God; nor is anyone who does not love his brother.

Love One Another

11This is the message you heard from the beginning: We should love one another. 12Do not be like Cain, who belonged to the evil one and murdered his brother. And why did he murder him? Because his own actions were evil and his brother's were righteous. 13Do not be surprised, my brothers, if the world hates you. 14We know that we have passed from death to life, because we love our brothers. Anyone who does not love remains in death. 15Anyone who hates his brother is a murderer, and you know that no murderer has eternal life in him.

16This is how we know what love is: Jesus Christ laid down his life for us. And we ought to lay down our lives for our brothers. 17If anyone has material possessions and sees his brother in need but has no pity on him, how can the love of God be in him? 18Dear children, let us not love with words or tongue but with actions and in truth. 19This then is how we know that we belong to the truth, and how we set our hearts at rest in his presence 20whenever our hearts condemn us. For God is greater than our hearts, and he knows everything.

21Dear friends, if our hearts do not condemn us, we have confidence before God 22and receive from him anything we ask, because we obey his commands and do what pleases him. 23And this is his command: to believe in the name of his Son, Jesus Christ, and to love one another as he commanded us. 24Those who obey his commands live in him, and he in them. And this is how we know that he lives in us: We know it by the Spirit he gave us.

Test the Spirits

4 Dear friends, do not believe every spirit, but test the spirits to see whether they are from God, because many false prophets have gone out into the world. 2This is how you can recognize the Spirit of God: Every spirit that acknowledges that Jesus Christ has come in the flesh is from God, 3but every spirit that does not acknowledge Jesus is not from God. This is the spirit of the antichrist, which you have heard is coming and even now is already in the world.

4You, dear children, are from God and have overcome them, because the one who is in you is greater than the one who is in the

[a]2 Or *when it is made known*

spite this tension, what must go hand-in-hand with obedience for a Christian (3:10)? When is it difficult for you to love?

1. How would you feel if Jesus returned right now? Excited? Relieved? Ashamed? **2.** What do verses 1–3 imply about God? What does this mean for our self-image? How have you experienced God's lavish love this week? **3.** How can a Christian recognize and deal with our society's "whatever is right for you" attitude (moral relativism)?

Who was your first "true love" growing up?

1. What do you think Christians in the first century were encountering from the non-Christian world? From each other? **2.** What is the heart of John's message? **3.** Why does John use the story of Cain and Abel here (see Ge 4:1–8)? Where do you see "Cain-like" attitudes in yourself? **4.** What is John's definition of love (vv. 16–18)? How does this differ from contemporary definitions? **5.** What are we assured of through loving others (vv. 14,19–20,24)?

1. How would you like to consciously practice Jesus-like love this week? With your family? A friend? At church? In politics? In social issues? A difficult person? A person in need? How will doing this affect your own need for love? **2.** How are answered prayers and obedience connected (vv. 18–22)? Will obedience affect what we pray for? How has this been true for you?

How do you stay informed on current events?

1. What does John command in verse 1? What else has he said about false prophets (2:18–29)? **2.** How can a Christian distinguish a true prophet from a false (see also 2:20–23)?

1. What do you believe about Jesus' nature? What difference does it make whether he was truly divine? Truly human? **2.** What "power" equips you to overcome false prophets?

What personality trait or strength did you get from your father? Your mother?

1. What is the source of human love? How can God's love be expressed through humans? In our motives? Our actions? Why is it a lie to say you love God but do not show love to your brother (v. 19)? **2.** From verses 8–15, what do you learn about the relationship between the Father, Son and Holy Spirit? About their relationship to us? **3.** How does the message that God's love drives out fear (v. 18) relate to the teaching that God is light (1:5)?

1. Is the love discussed here an action or a feeling? What does this tell you about love? **2.** In your life, when has "love" held too much fear? When has God's love cast out fear? **3.** If you want to do a better job of loving others, how should you go about it? What is the only way to improve (see vv. 15–16)? **4.** How do you want to love sacrificially this week? At home? At work? A difficult relationship? In how you plan your time? Your budget?

---

1. In the Aesop's Fable, "The Tortoise and the Hare," are you more like the steady, persistent tortoise, or the fast-starting, easily distracted hare? How so? **2.** Did you say a bedtime prayer as a child? What kind of prayer? Did Mom or Dad join you?

1. What kind of love comes along with our new birth (vv. 1–3)? Why are God's commands not a burden? **2.** What is the power source for overcoming the world? How have you seen faith (belief), love and obedience to be interconnected in your life? What lie is John combatting (remember the group who had split off from the church, see Introduction to 1 John)? **3.** What are the three witnesses to Jesus Christ (v. 7)? What do water and blood refer to (see 5:6)? What happened at Jesus' baptism (Mk 1:9–11)? Why is it important to emphasize Jesus' death and resurrection? How does the Spirit testify to

world. 5They are from the world and therefore speak from the viewpoint of the world, and the world listens to them. 6We are from God, and whoever knows God listens to us; but whoever is not from God does not listen to us. This is how we recognize the Spirit[a] of truth and the spirit of falsehood.

God's Love and Ours

7Dear friends, let us love one another, for love comes from God. Everyone who loves has been born of God and knows God. 8Whoever does not love does not know God, because God is love. 9This is how God showed his love among us: He sent his one and only Son[b] into the world that we might live through him. 10This is love: not that we loved God, but that he loved us and sent his Son as an atoning sacrifice for[c] our sins. 11Dear friends, since God so loved us, we also ought to love one another. 12No one has ever seen God; but if we love one another, God lives in us and his love is made complete in us.

13We know that we live in him and he in us, because he has given us of his Spirit. 14And we have seen and testify that the Father has sent his Son to be the Savior of the world. 15If anyone acknowledges that Jesus is the Son of God, God lives in him and he in God. 16And so we know and rely on the love God has for us.

God is love. Whoever lives in love lives in God, and God in him. 17In this way, love is made complete among us so that we will have confidence on the day of judgment, because in this world we are like him. 18There is no fear in love. But perfect love drives out fear, because fear has to do with punishment. The one who fears is not made perfect in love.

19We love because he first loved us. 20If anyone says, "I love God," yet hates his brother, he is a liar. For anyone who does not love his brother, whom he has seen, cannot love God, whom he has not seen. 21And he has given us this command: Whoever loves God must also love his brother.

Faith in the Son of God

5 Everyone who believes that Jesus is the Christ is born of God, and everyone who loves the father loves his child as well. 2This is how we know that we love the children of God: by loving God and carrying out his commands. 3This is love for God: to obey his commands. And his commands are not burdensome, 4for everyone born of God overcomes the world. This is the victory that has overcome the world, even our faith. 5Who is it that overcomes the world? Only he who believes that Jesus is the Son of God.

6This is the one who came by water and blood—Jesus Christ. He did not come by water only, but by water and blood. And it is the Spirit who testifies, because the Spirit is the truth. 7For there are three that testify: 8the[d] Spirit, the water and the blood; and the three are in agreement. 9We accept man's testimony, but God's testimony is greater because it is the testimony of God, which he has given about his Son. 10Anyone who believes in the Son of God has this testimony in his heart. Anyone who does not believe God has made him out to be a liar, because he has not believed the testimony God has given about his Son. 11And this is the testimony: God has given us eternal life, and this life is in his Son. 12He

[a]*6* Or *spirit* [b]*9* Or *his only begotten Son* [c]*10* Or *as the one who would turn aside his wrath, taking away* [d]*7,8* Late manuscripts of the Vulgate *testify in heaven: the Father, the Word and the Holy Spirit, and these three are one. 8And there are three that testify on earth: the* (not found in any Greek manuscript before the sixteenth century)

who has the Son has life; he who does not have the Son of God
does not have life.

Concluding Remarks

13I write these things to you who believe in the name of the Son
of God so that you may know that you have eternal life. 14This is
the confidence we have in approaching God: that if we ask anything according to his will, he hears us. 15And if we know that he
hears us—whatever we ask—we know that we have what we
asked of him.
16If anyone sees his brother commit a sin that does not lead to
death, he should pray and God will give him life. I refer to those
whose sin does not lead to death. There is a sin that leads to death.
I am not saying that he should pray about that. 17All wrongdoing is
sin, and there is sin that does not lead to death.
18We know that anyone born of God does not continue to sin;
the one who was born of God keeps him safe, and the evil one
cannot harm him. 19We know that we are children of God, and that
the whole world is under the control of the evil one. 20We know
also that the Son of God has come and has given us understanding,
so that we may know him who is true. And we are in him who is
true—even in his Son Jesus Christ. He is the true God and eternal
life.
21Dear children, keep yourselves from idols.

Jesus? **4.** What is the condition for prayer to be answered (vv. 14–15)? What does it mean to pray in Jesus' name? **5.** How is the assurance of eternal life (v. 13) the key to: (a) Answered prayer (vv. 14–15)? (b) Forgiveness of sin (vv. 16–17)? (c) Deliverance from sin and evil (vv. 18–19)? (d) Avoidance of idols (v. 21)? **6.** What might be the sin that leads to death (see Mk 3:22–30)? Why do the very fears of those who worry about having committed this sin prove that they have not done so?

♡ **1.** How are you doing at loving God? Using the "love test" from verses 1–3, how are you doing at loving others? How does your obedience to God affect your love for others? **2.** What has convinced you that true life is found in Jesus? What further "proof" do you need? **3.** How often are you prompted to pray for someone you see struggling with sin in their life? Who has prayed for you in the past? What was the result? **4.** If 1 John were dropped from the Bible, what would be missing from the story of God's redemptive work in history?

INTRODUCTION to

2 and 3 JOHN

Book Study Outline: If you are using 2 and 3 John for a study course, spend one meeting on each of these short books. Use the questions in the margin for your group agenda:

start meeting / 15 min. | read & discuss Bible / 30 min. | close meeting / 15–45 min.

Refer to the Questions and Answers in the front of this Bible for more information.

Author: Since the style and content of these two letters is similar to 1 John, it is assumed that the author ("the elder") is John the apostle.

Date: Uncertain, but probably in the late A.D. 80s or early 90s, when the heresy which is rebuked here (an early form of Gnosticism) began to flourish.

Theme: Hospitality for itinerant teachers.

Historical Background: Itinerant missionaries were the means by which Christianity spread throughout the Empire. They looked to local churches to aid in their mission by providing hospitality (Roman inns were notorious for being dirty and flea-infested). The problem was that some of the people seeking room and board were false teachers, expounding erroneous doctrines; others were phonies, pretending to be true prophets in order to get free hospitality. Even the pagan Greek author Lucian noticed this sort of abuse. In his satirical work *Peregrinus,* he wrote about a religious charlatan who lived off the generosity of the church simply as a way to avoid working. The *Didache,* an early church manual, set out guidelines to help the churches discern what types of itinerant teachers should and shouldn't be received. For example, it stated that true prophets were indeed to be entertained—for a day or two. But if a prophet stayed three days, this was a sign that he was false. In the same way, 2 and 3 John were written to help certain local churches sort out the problem. In 2 John, the author warns the church to beware of those who teach false doctrine. "Do not welcome such," he says. In 3 John he addresses the opposite problem: the failure of Christians to provide hospitality for genuine teachers. Here he commends a friend by the name of Gaius who opened his house even to strangers. By so doing, he was entering into their work of spreading the truth.

THE ERRORS OF GNOSTICISM

One of the most dangerous heresies of the first two centuries of the church was Gnosticism. Its central teaching was that salvation is a product of knowledge; that spirit is entirely good and matter is entirely evil. From this unbiblical dualism flowed five important errors:

1. Man's body , which is matter, is therefore evil. It is to be contrasted with God, who is wholly spirit and therefore good.

2. Salvation is escape from the body, achieved not by faith in Christ but by special knowledge (the Greek word for "knowledge" is *gnosis*, hence Gnosticism).

3. Christ's humanity was denied in two ways: (1) Some said that Christ only *seemed* to have a body, a view called Docetism, from the Greek *dokeo* ("to seem"), and (2) others said that the divine Christ joined the man Jesus at baptism and left him before he died, a view called Cerinthianism, after its most prominent spokesman, Cerinthus. This view is the background of much of 1 John (see 1:1; 2:22; 4:2–3).

4. Since the body was considered evil, it was to be treated harshly. This ascetic form of Gnosticism is the background of part of the letter to the Colossians (2:21–23).

5. Paradoxically, this dualism also led to licentiousness. The reason was that, since matter—and not the breaking of God's law (1Jn 3:4)—was considered evil, breaking this law was of no moral consequence.

The Gnosticism addressed in the New Testament was an early form of heresy, not the intricately developed system of the second and third centuries. In addition to that seen in Colossians and in John's letters, acquaintance with early Gnosticism is reflected in 1 and 2 Timothy, Titus, 2 Peter and perhaps 1 Corinthians.

Characteristics: These are the shortest letters in the New Testament. They are quite similar in style and content and were undoubtedly written by the same person. There is also a close connection between 1 John and these two shorter letters. They reflect John's concern in his first epistle for *truth* (which is mentioned four times in 2 John and seven times in 3 John) and for *love* (which occurs five times in 2 John and two times in 3 John). These two letters provide a glimpse into the life of the early church, and insight into how we should respond to Christian workers.

2 John

1The elder,

To the chosen lady and her children, whom I love in the truth—and not I only, but also all who know the truth— 2because of the truth, which lives in us and will be with us forever:

3Grace, mercy and peace from God the Father and from Jesus Christ, the Father's Son, will be with us in truth and love.

4It has given me great joy to find some of your children walking in the truth, just as the Father commanded us. 5And now, dear lady, I am not writing you a new command but one we have had from the beginning. I ask that we love one another. 6And this is love: that we walk in obedience to his commands. As you have heard from the beginning, his command is that you walk in love.

7Many deceivers, who do not acknowledge Jesus Christ as coming in the flesh, have gone out into the world. Any such person is the deceiver and the antichrist. 8Watch out that you do not lose what you have worked for, but that you may be rewarded fully. 9Anyone who runs ahead and does not continue in the teaching of Christ does not have God; whoever continues in the teaching has both the Father and the Son. 10If anyone comes to you and does not bring this teaching, do not take him into your house or welcome him. 11Anyone who welcomes him shares in his wicked work.

12I have much to write to you, but I do not want to use paper and ink. Instead, I hope to visit you and talk with you face to face, so that our joy may be complete.

13The children of your chosen sister send their greetings.

1. When you were growing up, where did you gather for family reunions? What was special about those times? Where did the guests stay? **2.** Whose home could you drop in on unexpectedly and know that you would be welcome?

1. How are John's twin themes of truth and love interconnected here? **2.** If the lady addressed in this letter were to show hospitality to these false teachers who traveled around, would her error be on the side of truth, or on the side of love? What's wrong with welcoming such wandering missionaries? **3.** How do John's exhortations to true believers (vv. 4–6) help them resist the deception and wickedness of the religious frauds (vv. 7–11)?

1. Which is easier for you to do—"walk in truth" or "walk in love"? **2.** Have you ever been involved in a deep relationship that had to be terminated because of an overriding issue involving your faith? What happened? **3.** How do you distinguish between those missionaries you ought not to support and those you should? How can you exercise truth and love in that decision? **4.** When was the last time you had someone over who was really hurting, lonely or needing help (no names)? Should you do this more often? What's stopping you?

3 John

1. Did you ever run out of money when you were away from home? What did you do? **2.** Who extended loving hospitality to you when you needed it most?

1. What conflicts were going on in the church that prompted John to write this letter (see Introduction to 2 and 3 John)? What personality issues are involved? What type of character sketch would you draw for Gaius? Diotrephes? Demetrius? **2.** In what ways does this letter tackle the hospitality issue differently than 2 John? Why is John urging that these teachers be cared for in their travels? Why would this be so important at this time?

1. How can you reflect Gaius' desire to be of help to itinerant Christian workers? **2.** Has suspicion about the false motives or messages of some pastors/ teachers soured you against them all? What needs to change so you will not hinder the work of God by failing to encourage his true servants? **3.** Do you find opening up your home (or your small group) to new people easy or difficult? Why is that? **4.** In picking close friends (like Gaius was to John), what do you look for? How can you be that kind of friend to others?

1The elder,

To my dear friend Gaius, whom I love in the truth.

2Dear friend, I pray that you may enjoy good health and that all
may go well with you, even as your soul is getting along well. 3It
gave me great joy to have some brothers come and tell about your
faithfulness to the truth and how you continue to walk in the truth.
4I have no greater joy than to hear that my children are walking in
the truth.
5Dear friend, you are faithful in what you are doing for the
brothers, even though they are strangers to you. 6They have told
the church about your love. You will do well to send them on their
way in a manner worthy of God. 7It was for the sake of the Name
that they went out, receiving no help from the pagans. 8We ought
therefore to show hospitality to such men so that we may work
together for the truth.
9I wrote to the church, but Diotrephes, who loves to be first, will
have nothing to do with us. 10So if I come, I will call attention to
what he is doing, gossiping maliciously about us. Not satisfied with
that, he refuses to welcome the brothers. He also stops those who
want to do so and puts them out of the church.
11Dear friend, do not imitate what is evil but what is good.
Anyone who does what is good is from God. Anyone who does
what is evil has not seen God. 12Demetrius is well spoken of by
everyone—and even by the truth itself. We also speak well of him,
and you know that our testimony is true.
13I have much to write you, but I do not want to do so with pen
and ink. 14I hope to see you soon, and we will talk face to face.

Peace to you. The friends here send their greetings. Greet the friends there by name.

INTRODUCTION to

JUDE

Book Study Outline: If you are using Jude for a study course, spend one to two meetings on this short book. Use the questions in the margin for your group agenda:

start meeting / 15 min. read & discuss Bible / 30 min. close meeting / 15–45 min.

Refer to the Questions and Answers in the front of this Bible for more information.

Author: Traditionally, Jude, the brother of Jesus (Mt 13:55, Jude is a form of the name "Judas"). After the resurrection, Jesus' brothers came to believe in him and they became missionaries (1Co 9:5).

Date: The date of Jude is hard to ascertain. If 2 Peter made use of it, then it would be dated around A.D. 65; otherwise it could be dated as late as A.D. 80.

Theme: Contend for the faith.

Historical Background: This is a sermon/letter meant to be read to a congregation, warning them against false teachers. Jude's opponents are a band of smooth-talking teachers who go from church to church, receiving hospitality in return for their instruction. In this case, the teachers were *antinomians.* They rejected all moral standards and indulged in immoral behavior; particularly of a sexual kind. The root problem was their misunderstanding of the doctrine of grace. They twisted the truth that people are saved by grace to mean that people could therefore do whatever they pleased. Paul, who was apparently accused of this type of teaching, rejected it in no uncertain terms as a perversion of the Gospel (see Ro 6). These teachers rooted their authority largely in their own ecstatic experiences ("God told me"), and therefore they considered their actions beyond criticism. The book of Jude is a fiery call to defend the faith against these heretics who had wormed their way into the church.

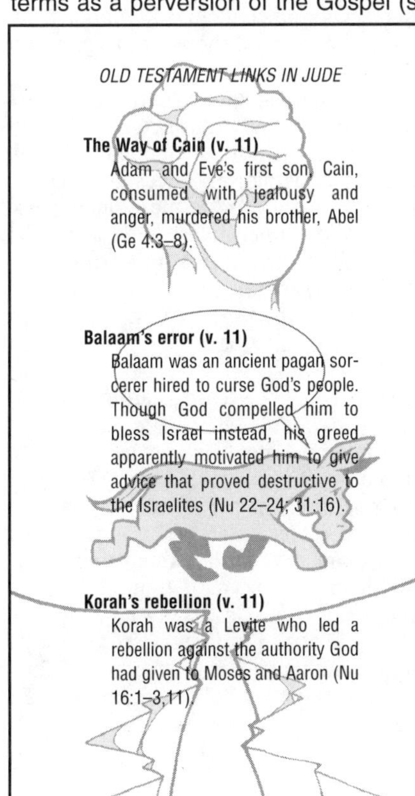

OLD TESTAMENT LINKS IN JUDE
The Way of Cain (v. 11)
Adam and Eve's first son, Cain, consumed with jealousy and anger, murdered his brother, Abel (Ge 4:3–8).
Balaam's error (v. 11)
Balaam was an ancient pagan sorcerer hired to curse God's people. Though God compelled him to bless Israel instead, his greed apparently motivated him to give advice that proved destructive to the Israelites (Nu 22–24; 31:16).
Korah's rebellion (v. 11)
Korah was a Levite who led a rebellion against the authority God had given to Moses and Aaron (Nu 16:1–3,11).

Characteristics: Best known for its doxology (vv. 24–25), Jude is packed with quotes from the Old Testament and the Apocrypha (religious books written by Jews between the time of the Old Testament and New Testament). It uses vivid images and frequent allusions. Jude's themes are summed up in verses 3–4: (a) Christians are to "contend for the faith," and (b) they are to do so against the false teachers who have slipped into their midst. Jude is clearly related to 2 Peter, since 15 of its 25 verses are also found there in whole or in part. However, it is not known which epistle came first, or if they both quoted from a third source. Jude's use of apocryphal literature was of some concern to the early church fathers who concluded (wrongly) that any book that used such literature could not be genuine. However, they failed to recognize that other New Testament writers did the same thing. Paul referred to nonbiblical Jewish writing (2Ti 3:8). He also quoted heathen poets (Ac 17:28; 1Co 15:32–33; Tit 1:12). The author of Hebrews echoes the works of Philo, and James makes reference to nonbiblical sources. The issue is not where the specific words came from but how the New Testament writer used the words to reveal God's truth.

Jude

1Jude, a servant of Jesus Christ and a brother of James,

To those who have been called, who are loved by God the Father
and kept by[a] Jesus Christ:

2Mercy, peace and love be yours in abundance.

The Sin and Doom of Godless Men

3Dear friends, although I was very eager to write to you about
the salvation we share, I felt I had to write and urge you to contend
for the faith that was once for all entrusted to the saints. 4For
certain men whose condemnation was written about[b] long ago
have secretly slipped in among you. They are godless men, who
change the grace of our God into a license for immorality and deny
Jesus Christ our only Sovereign and Lord.

5Though you already know all this, I want to remind you that the
Lord[c] delivered his people out of Egypt, but later destroyed those
who did not believe. 6And the angels who did not keep their
positions of authority but abandoned their own home—these he
has kept in darkness, bound with everlasting chains for judgment
on the great Day. 7In a similar way, Sodom and Gomorrah and the
surrounding towns gave themselves up to sexual immorality and
perversion. They serve as an example of those who suffer the
punishment of eternal fire.

8In the very same way, these dreamers pollute their own bodies,
reject authority and slander celestial beings. 9But even the archangel Michael, when he was disputing with the devil about the body
of Moses, did not dare to bring a slanderous accusation against
him, but said, "The Lord rebuke you!" 10Yet these men speak
abusively against whatever they do not understand; and what
things they do understand by instinct, like unreasoning animals—
these are the very things that destroy them.

11Woe to them! They have taken the way of Cain; they have
rushed for profit into Balaam's error; they have been destroyed in
Korah's rebellion.

12These men are blemishes at your love feasts, eating with you
without the slightest qualm—shepherds who feed only themselves. They are clouds without rain, blown along by the wind;
autumn trees, without fruit and uprooted—twice dead. 13They are
wild waves of the sea, foaming up their shame; wandering stars, for
whom blackest darkness has been reserved forever.

14Enoch, the seventh from Adam, prophesied about these men:
"See, the Lord is coming with thousands upon thousands of his
holy ones 15to judge everyone, and to convict all the ungodly of all
the ungodly acts they have done in the ungodly way, and of all the
harsh words ungodly sinners have spoken against him." 16These
men are grumblers and faultfinders; they follow their own evil
desires; they boast about themselves and flatter others for their
own advantage.

[a] *1* Or *for*; or *in* [b] *4* Or *men who were marked out for condemnation* [c] *5* Some early manuscripts *Jesus*

1. Who was your first boyfriend or girlfriend? Where is that person now? **2.** When was the last time someone "read you the riot act"? What had you done wrong? How did it feel to be soundly rebuked? **3.** What scary experience with fire have you had?

1. What are your first impressions of Jude, the man and his letter? **2.** How does he describe himself and his fellow Christians (vv. 3–5)? From this description, what does it mean to be a Christian? **3.** What concerning these "godless men" (v. 4) is so godless? **4.** How do each of the examples from history (vv. 5–7,11) relate to problems of unbelief, immorality, violence and rebellion? **5.** To someone who questions the certainty, severity or justice of God's judgment, what do these examples teach? How do the vivid images in verses 12–16 further condemn the skeptics? **6.** Should Jude's readers have been surprised by this coming judgment (vv. 17–19)? Why or why not? **7.** How is the good distinguished from the bad in this divided church (vv. 17–21)? **8.** What is our duty to the doubter who is merely flirting with falsehood (v. 22)? To one already singed with evil (v. 23)? How does the rescuer avoid falling into the same danger as those who play with fire? **9.** What role does God play in the believer's safety, sacrificial commitment and sense of joy (v. 24)? How do you explain this picture of God with the contrasting one in verses 5–7?

1. What can make a church vulnerable to false teachers today: (a) Boredom? (b) Lust? (c) Attraction to personalities? (d) Apathy? **2.** What "spiritual body-building" plan could help to keep you strong in God's love (vv. 20–21)? **3.** What goes on daily at your workplace, in your community or even in your church, which would fall within the range of Jude's indicting sermon? **4.** Someone has said, "All it takes for evil to prevail is for a few good men to do nothing." What is one thing you could do this week to help keep this truism from becoming a reality where you live and

A Call to Persevere

17But, dear friends, remember what the apostles of our Lord
Jesus Christ foretold. 18They said to you, "In the last times there
will be scoffers who will follow their own ungodly desires."
19These are the men who divide you, who follow mere natural
instincts and do not have the Spirit.

20But you, dear friends, build yourselves up in your most holy
faith and pray in the Holy Spirit. 21Keep yourselves in God's love as
you wait for the mercy of our Lord Jesus Christ to bring you to
eternal life.

22Be merciful to those who doubt; 23snatch others from the fire
and save them; to others show mercy, mixed with fear—hating
even the clothing stained by corrupted flesh.

Doxology

24To him who is able to keep you from falling and to present you
before his glorious presence without fault and with great joy— 25to
the only God our Savior be glory, majesty, power and authority,
through Jesus Christ our Lord, before all ages, now and forever-
more! Amen.

work? **5.** What has caused you to doubt your faith at times? Who helped you then? How? **6.** In light of the warnings in Jude, what hope do you find in verses 24–25? How does that help as you struggle?

INTRODUCTION to
REVELATION

Book Study Outline: If you are using Revelation for a study course, here is a 7- or 14-week outline. Use the margin questions for your group agenda:

start meeting / 15 min.

read & discuss Bible / 30 min.

close meeting / 15–45 min.

Refer to the Questions and Answers in front of Bible for more information.

7-week plan	14-week plan	Personal Reading	Group Study Passage
1	1	1:1–3:22	1:9–20/Star of the Drama
	2	1:1–3:22	3:14–22/Scene 1: The Church
2	3	4:1–8:1	5:1–14/Scene 2: Heaven
	4	4:1–8:1	6:1–17/The Seven Seals
3	5	8:2–11:18	8:2–9:21/Scene 3: The World
	6	8:2–11:18	11:15–18/The Seventh Trumpet
4	7	11:19–14:20	11:19–13:1a/Scene 4: The Enemy
	8	11:19–14:20	13:1b–10/Worshipping the Enemy
5	9	15:1–16:21	15:1–8/Scene 5: God's Wrath
	10	15:1–16:21	16:1–21/The Seven Bowls
6	11	17:1–19:10	18:1–24/Scene 6: Babylon
	12	17:1–19:10	19:1–10/Song of Praise
7	13	19:11–22:21	20:1–15/Scene 7: God With Us
	14	19:11–22:21	21:1–22:6/The New Jerusalem

Author: Traditionally credited to the apostle John (1:4).

Date: Revelation was written during a time of Roman oppression, probably during Domitian's reign (A.D. 90–95).

Theme: Christ shall overcome!

Historical Background: Near the end of the first century Caesar-worship became a major component of Roman civil religion. Christians, refusing to adulterate their conviction that Jesus is Lord, were persecuted. John the apostle was a victim of this oppression. He was exiled to the island of Patmos in the Aegean Sea where he wrote this book.

Characteristics: Apocalyptic writing (which involves the unveiling of future events) was commonly used by Jewish authors at this time in history. Through bizarre images, vivid pictures of death, supernatural creatures and cryptic language, the writers expressed their hope for a day when judgment would be rendered against all evil powers and peace would be ushered in. Revelation uses this style of writing but anchors its hope in Jesus' authority as King of kings. Revelation has been interpreted in a variety of ways over the centuries; however, the book's central purpose is not to arouse speculation about the future. Rather, it is meant to encourage Christians in every age to maintain their faith despite opposition, and to do so in the confidence that they will share in Jesus' ultimate victory over all forces that oppose him and his people. Revelation consists of a series of scenes, culminating in the triumph of God.

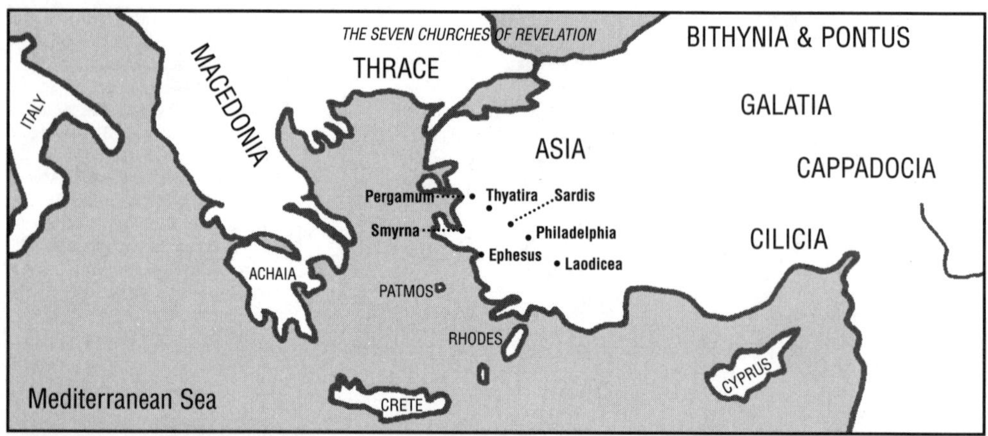

Revelation

Prologue

1 The revelation of Jesus Christ, which God gave him to show
his servants what must soon take place. He made it known by
sending his angel to his servant John, [2]who testifies to everything
he saw—that is, the word of God and the testimony of Jesus
Christ. [3]Blessed is the one who reads the words of this prophecy,
and blessed are those who hear it and take to heart what is written
in it, because the time is near.

Greetings and Doxology

[4]John,

To the seven churches in the province of Asia:

Grace and peace to you from him who is, and who was, and who
is to come, and from the seven spirits[a] before his throne, [5]and
from Jesus Christ, who is the faithful witness, the firstborn from
the dead, and the ruler of the kings of the earth.

To him who loves us and has freed us from our sins by his blood,
[6]and has made us to be a kingdom and priests to serve his God and
Father—to him be glory and power for ever and ever! Amen.

[7]Look, he is coming with the clouds,
    and every eye will see him,
  even those who pierced him;
    and all the peoples of the earth will mourn
        because of him.
                So shall it be! Amen.

[8]"I am the Alpha and the Omega," says the Lord God, "who is,
and who was, and who is to come, the Almighty."

One Like a Son of Man

[9]I, John, your brother and companion in the suffering and kingdom and patient endurance that are ours in Jesus, was on the
island of Patmos because of the word of God and the testimony of
Jesus. [10]On the Lord's Day I was in the Spirit, and I heard behind
me a loud voice like a trumpet, [11]which said: "Write on a scroll
what you see and send it to the seven churches: to Ephesus, Smyrna, Pergamum, Thyatira, Sardis, Philadelphia and Laodicea."
[12]I turned around to see the voice that was speaking to me. And
when I turned I saw seven golden lampstands, [13]and among the
lampstands was someone "like a son of man,"[b] dressed in a robe
reaching down to his feet and with a golden sash around his chest.
[14]His head and hair were white like wool, as white as snow, and
his eyes were like blazing fire. [15]His feet were like bronze glowing
in a furnace, and his voice was like the sound of rushing waters.
[16]In his right hand he held seven stars, and out of his mouth came
a sharp double-edged sword. His face was like the sun shining in all
its brilliance.
[17]When I saw him, I fell at his feet as though dead. Then he

[a]*4* Or *the sevenfold Spirit* [b]*13* Daniel 7:13

1. What kind of book are you: Mystery? Sports? Technical? Adventure? Poetry? Unreadable? Sealed? Open? Explain. **2.** Around the house, are you king, priest or servant? What would your spouse, parent or friend say is your typical role?

1. What is a revelation? In this case, who is revealed? By whom? To whom? For what purpose? **2.** Who is John? Who are the recipient churches (vv. 4,11; see Introduction to Revelation)? **3.** What is significant about the references to God in verses 4 and 8? **4.** What are the meanings of the titles given to Jesus (vv. 5–6)? What three things does Christ do for us? **5.** What theme of the book of Revelation is foreshadowed in verse 7? Why is the phrase "every eye will see him" significant?

1. If asked to share three facts about Jesus that are especially significant to you, what would you say? Why are these facts so important to you? **2.** How will you personalize and pass along the blessing of verse 3?

---

1. What bizarre dream can you still recall, and why? **2.** What religious pictures or statues adorn the walls of your house (or mind)?

1. Why was John on Patmos? What do you know about his assignment there? **2.** What is significant about his spiritual condition and the day when he received this vision? **3.** Close your eyes and have someone read verses 12–18 slowly, several times if necessary. Meditate on it. What do you see? Feel? What do the images in these verses suggest about Christ (Da 7:9)? **4.** What is the meaning of the seven stars? The seven lampstands? What does it mean for a church to be a light?

1. Using the analogy of a lighting fixture to describe the spiritual condition of your church,

placed his right hand on me and said: "Do not be afraid. I am the
First and the Last. 18I am the Living One; I was dead, and behold I
am alive for ever and ever! And I hold the keys of death and Hades.
19"Write, therefore, what you have seen, what is now and what
will take place later. 20The mystery of the seven stars that you saw
in my right hand and of the seven golden lampstands is this: The
seven stars are the angels[a] of the seven churches, and the seven
lampstands are the seven churches.

what kind fits your situation (a chandelier, a nightlight)? What would help create more illumination? **2.** Are you right now "on Patmos" (suffering) or "in the Spirit" (reigning)? Why? Can both happen at once?

What was your "first love" in elementary school like?

1. What do you know about the church at Ephesus (see Ac 19)? **2.** What good things characterize this church? How might its strengths have been the cause of its failure? What do you think their weekly worship was like? **3.** What is repentance? Why is that necessary for the Ephesian church?

1. Of the positive qualities mentioned about this group, which best describes you? Your church? Why? **2.** In what ways have you lost your first love for Christ? What has helped you to keep that love alive?

To the Church in Ephesus

2 "To the angel[b] of the church in Ephesus write:

These are the words of him who holds the seven stars in his
right hand and walks among the seven golden lampstands: 2I
know your deeds, your hard work and your perseverance. I
know that you cannot tolerate wicked men, that you have
tested those who claim to be apostles but are not, and have
found them false. 3You have persevered and have endured
hardships for my name, and have not grown weary.
4Yet I hold this against you: You have forsaken your first
love. 5Remember the height from which you have fallen! Repent and do the things you did at first. If you do not repent, I
will come to you and remove your lampstand from its place.
6But you have this in your favor: You hate the practices of the
Nicolaitans, which I also hate.
7He who has an ear, let him hear what the Spirit says to the
churches. To him who overcomes, I will give the right to eat
from the tree of life, which is in the paradise of God.

If you were rich, what would you like to do?

1. What problems is this church facing? How can they be both poor and rich? **2.** Why is Jesus known as the First and the Last? **3.** What does this passage teach about suffering?

1. Has it been harder to live out your faith when you've been poor, or when you've had enough money? Why? **2.** In what ways do you feel spiritually rich?

To the Church in Smyrna

8"To the angel of the church in Smyrna write:

These are the words of him who is the First and the Last,
who died and came to life again. 9I know your afflictions and
your poverty—yet you are rich! I know the slander of those
who say they are Jews and are not, but are a synagogue of
Satan. 10Do not be afraid of what you are about to suffer. I tell
you, the devil will put some of you in prison to test you, and
you will suffer persecution for ten days. Be faithful, even to
the point of death, and I will give you the crown of life.
11He who has an ear, let him hear what the Spirit says to
the churches. He who overcomes will not be hurt at all by the
second death.

As a child, where was the local "haunted house" in your town? Did you ever dare to go in?

1. What pressures are the Christians in Pergamum facing (v. 13)? At what point are they strong? Where are they tempted? Which do you think is easier to endure: Persecution by enemies or seduction by the culture? Why? **2.** Why is the title by which Christ reveals himself so appropriate to these Christians? **3.** What is the significance of the sword (v. 16)? Of the manna and stone (v. 17)?

To the Church in Pergamum

12"To the angel of the church in Pergamum write:

These are the words of him who has the sharp, double-
edged sword. 13I know where you live—where Satan has his
throne. Yet you remain true to my name. You did not re-
nounce your faith in me, even in the days of Antipas, my
faithful witness, who was put to death in your city—where
Satan lives.
14Nevertheless, I have a few things against you: You have
people there who hold to the teaching of Balaam, who taught
Balak to entice the Israelites to sin by eating food sacrificed to
idols and by committing sexual immorality. 15Likewise you
also have those who hold to the teaching of the Nicolaitans.

[a]20 Or *messengers* [b]1 Or *messenger*; also in verses 8, 12 and 18

16Repent therefore! Otherwise, I will soon come to you and
will fight against them with the sword of my mouth.
17He who has an ear, let him hear what the Spirit says to
the churches. To him who overcomes, I will give some of the
hidden manna. I will also give him a white stone with a new
name written on it, known only to him who receives it.

1. What cultural influences distract you from your relationship with Christ? How subtle are these influences in your life? How direct? **2.** What weapons has God given you to do battle with? Which has proved very helpful?

To the Church in Thyatira

18"To the angel of the church in Thyatira write:

These are the words of the Son of God, whose eyes are like
blazing fire and whose feet are like burnished bronze. 19I
know your deeds, your love and faith, your service and perseverance, and that you are now doing more than you did at
first.
20Nevertheless, I have this against you: You tolerate that
woman Jezebel, who calls herself a prophetess. By her teaching she misleads my servants into sexual immorality and the
eating of food sacrificed to idols. 21I have given her time to
repent of her immorality, but she is unwilling. 22So I will cast
her on a bed of suffering, and I will make those who commit
adultery with her suffer intensely, unless they repent of her
ways. 23I will strike her children dead. Then all the churches
will know that I am he who searches hearts and minds, and I
will repay each of you according to your deeds. 24Now I say to
the rest of you in Thyatira, to you who do not hold to her
teaching and have not learned Satan's so-called deep secrets (I
will not impose any other burden on you): 25Only hold on to
what you have until I come.
26To him who overcomes and does my will to the end, I will
give authority over the nations—

27'He will rule them with an iron scepter;
he will dash them to pieces like
pottery'[a]—

just as I have received authority from my Father. 28I will also
give him the morning star. 29He who has an ear, let him hear
what the Spirit says to the churches.

As a teenager, what person or group influenced you the most? How?

1. What are the strengths of this church? Its weaknesses? **2.** What does the symbolic name "Jezebel" reveal about the woman in this church (1Ki 2:5–25; 2Ki 9:7–37)? **3.** How does Jesus describe himself? How do you interpret this description? What is he saying about himself? Why is this appropriate for the church at Thyatira? **4.** How is the nature and source of the temptation in Thyatira like (and unlike) that in Pergamum? **5.** What do you think Jesus' promise in verses 26–27 means?

1. Which of the qualities in verse 19 apply to you this week? Why? **2.** Who or what has played a role similar to Jezebel in your life (names aren't necessary)? How? How did the Lord free you from that influence? **3.** What do you appreciate most about the promise to overcomers in this section?

To the Church in Sardis

3 "To the angel[b] of the church in Sardis write:

These are the words of him who holds the seven spirits[c] of
God and the seven stars. I know your deeds; you have a
reputation of being alive, but you are dead. 2Wake up!
Strengthen what remains and is about to die, for I have not
found your deeds complete in the sight of my God. 3Remem-
ber, therefore, what you have received and heard; obey it, and
repent. But if you do not wake up, I will come like a thief, and
you will not know at what time I will come to you.
4Yet you have a few people in Sardis who have not soiled
their clothes. They will walk with me, dressed in white, for
they are worthy. 5He who overcomes will, like them, be
dressed in white. I will never blot out his name from the book
of life, but will acknowledge his name before my Father and
his angels. 6He who has an ear, let him hear what the Spirit
says to the churches.

What team or group of yours had a reputation far better than its performance?

1. What is the contrast between reputation and reality in Sardis? What dangers exist for Christians who rely on an image instead of nurturing a genuine spiritual life (v. 2)? **2.** What is the only hope for the survival of the church in Sardis?

1. If Jesus addressed this "wake-up call" to you, what would he want you to strengthen? **2.** Right now, would Jesus need a fire alarm to wake you up, or would a quiet call do it? Why?

[a] *27* Psalm 2:9 [b] *1* Or *messenger*; also in verses 7 and 14 [c] *1* Or *the sevenfold Spirit*

When have you been "locked out"?

1. What does the "key of David" open (vv. 7–8; 4:1; see Isa 22:22–24; Mt 16:19)? 2. How is this church able to persevere? Describe their enemies. How does their reward (v. 12) fit their faithfulness?

1. What open doors has Christ placed before you? How have you taken advantage of the pathways he's made available to you? 2. What are some closed doors he's placed in your career? In your social life? In your schooling? How have you responded to each of these closed doors? 3. In what ways are you like the Christians in Philadelphia? Unlike them? Why? 4. What is the Spirit saying to you now?

To the Church in Philadelphia

7"To the angel of the church in Philadelphia write:

These are the words of him who is holy and true, who holds the key of David. What he opens no one can shut, and what he shuts no one can open. 8I know your deeds. See, I have placed before you an open door that no one can shut. I know that you have little strength, yet you have kept my word and have not denied my name. 9I will make those who are of the synagogue of Satan, who claim to be Jews though they are not, but are liars—I will make them come and fall down at your feet and acknowledge that I have loved you. 10Since you have kept my command to endure patiently, I will also keep you from the hour of trial that is going to come upon the whole world to test those who live on the earth.

11I am coming soon. Hold on to what you have, so that no one will take your crown. 12Him who overcomes I will make a pillar in the temple of my God. Never again will he leave it. I will write on him the name of my God and the name of the city of my God, the new Jerusalem, which is coming down out of heaven from my God; and I will also write on him my new name. 13He who has an ear, let him hear what the Spirit says to the churches.

---

1. What is your favorite cold cereal? Hot cereal? Your favorite drink? 2. If you could invite any famous person for dinner, whom would you ask? Why?

1. What does the "faithful and true witness" see when he looks at the Laodicean church (vv. 15–16)? How does the church view itself? Why the contrast? 2. What does Jesus tell them to do in verse 18? Why? What does this say about true wealth? 3. How would you describe Christ, based on what you have read so far in this book? How does this expand the picture of Jesus in the Gospels?

1. If Jesus took your spiritual temperature today, what would he find? Why? 2. What is Jesus waiting for at the door of your life? Why not let him in?

To the Church in Laodicea

14"To the angel of the church in Laodicea write:

These are the words of the Amen, the faithful and true witness, the ruler of God's creation. 15I know your deeds, that you are neither cold nor hot. I wish you were either one or the other! 16So, because you are lukewarm—neither hot nor cold—I am about to spit you out of my mouth. 17You say, 'I am rich; I have acquired wealth and do not need a thing.' But you do not realize that you are wretched, pitiful, poor, blind and naked. 18I counsel you to buy from me gold refined in the fire, so you can become rich; and white clothes to wear, so you can cover your shameful nakedness; and salve to put on your eyes, so you can see.

19Those whom I love I rebuke and discipline. So be earnest, and repent. 20Here I am! I stand at the door and knock. If anyone hears my voice and opens the door, I will come in and eat with him, and he with me.

21To him who overcomes, I will give the right to sit with me on my throne, just as I overcame and sat down with my Father on his throne. 22He who has an ear, let him hear what the Spirit says to the churches."

What is the most memorable storm you have ever been in? What happened?

1. Where does this scene actually take place: In the afterlife? In some perfect order of things after this world has passed away? Or on the level of spiritual reality here and now (as in Eph 2:6), where good and evil are unmasked to be seen for what they really are? 2. Who is the figure on the throne? What is he like? What are the 24

The Throne in Heaven

4 After this I looked, and there before me was a door standing open in heaven. And the voice I had first heard speaking to me like a trumpet said, "Come up here, and I will show you what must take place after this." 2At once I was in the Spirit, and there before me was a throne in heaven with someone sitting on it. 3And the one who sat there had the appearance of jasper and carnelian. A rainbow, resembling an emerald, encircled the throne. 4Surrounding the throne were twenty-four other thrones, and seated on them were twenty-four elders. They were dressed in white and had crowns of gold on their heads. 5From the throne came flashes of lightning, rumblings and peals of thunder. Before the throne, seven

lamps were blazing. These are the seven spirits[a] of God. 6Also
before the throne there was what looked like a sea of glass, clear as
crystal.
In the center, around the throne, were four living creatures, and
they were covered with eyes, in front and in back. 7The first living
creature was like a lion, the second was like an ox, the third had a
face like a man, the fourth was like a flying eagle. 8Each of the
four living creatures had six wings and was covered with eyes all
around, even under his wings. Day and night they never stop
saying:

"Holy, holy, holy
is the Lord God Almighty,
who was, and is, and is to come."

9Whenever the living creatures give glory, honor and thanks to him
who sits on the throne and who lives for ever and ever, 10the
twenty-four elders fall down before him who sits on the throne,
and worship him who lives for ever and ever. They lay their
crowns before the throne and say:

11"You are worthy, our Lord and God,
to receive glory and honor and power,
for you created all things,
and by your will they were created
and have their being."

The Scroll and the Lamb

5 Then I saw in the right hand of him who sat on the throne a
scroll with writing on both sides and sealed with seven seals.
2And I saw a mighty angel proclaiming in a loud voice, "Who is
worthy to break the seals and open the scroll?" 3But no one in
heaven or on earth or under the earth could open the scroll or even
look inside it. 4I wept and wept because no one was found who
was worthy to open the scroll or look inside. 5Then one of the
elders said to me, "Do not weep! See, the Lion of the tribe of
Judah, the Root of David, has triumphed. He is able to open the
scroll and its seven seals."
6Then I saw a Lamb, looking as if it had been slain, standing in
the center of the throne, encircled by the four living creatures and
the elders. He had seven horns and seven eyes, which are the
seven spirits[a] of God sent out into all the earth. 7He came and
took the scroll from the right hand of him who sat on the throne.
8And when he had taken it, the four living creatures and the
twenty-four elders fell down before the Lamb. Each one had a harp
and they were holding golden bowls full of incense, which are the
prayers of the saints. 9And they sang a new song:

"You are worthy to take the scroll
and to open its seals,
because you were slain,
and with your blood you purchased men for God
from every tribe and language and people and nation.
10You have made them to be a kingdom and priests
to serve our God,
and they will reign on the earth."

[a]5,6 Or *the sevenfold Spirit*

elders like? (Note: 24 seems to represent all of God's people, coming from the 12 tribes before Christ and the 12 apostles after Christ; see 21:12–14.) **3.** What does the scene around the throne include? Note its many OT images (Ge 9:12–17; Ex 19:16–19; 25:31–40; 2Ch 4:2–6; Eze 1). **4.** What about the four living creatures suggests the eternal power of God? What response does the central figure elicit (vv. 7–9)? Why? **5.** What does this say about who God is and how he relates to his creation?

1. Imagine yourself in this scene. What do you see? Hear? Feel? What impresses you about God? **2.** What aspect of creation best demonstrates God's glory and power to you? Why? **3.** How might this vision of God enhance your worship life? Your everyday life?

---

1. What was the best choir or musical group you have ever heard (or participated in)? What was memorable about the group? **2.** Around the house, are you more like a lion or a lamb? Why?

1. What do you think makes the scroll so significant (Jer 36:2–32)? What dilemma does the sealed scroll pose (Isa 29:11)? **2.** Why is Christ the only one worthy enough to open it (vv. 4,9; see Jn 1:29)? What titles are used to describe him? What does it mean that he is both a Lion and a Lamb? Where does he appear? What does this mean for your life? **3.** What is the response when he takes the scroll? Analyze the three songs (vv. 9–10,12–13): How is the Lamb described? Who comprises the first musical group? The second? The third? Who are the true kings and priests on earth? What elements of praise do you sense here?

1. Have different members of your small group try to capture this scene of praise and adoration via a poem, a sketch, a piece of music or a prayer. To do this, put yourself into the scene, seeing and feeling what John saw and felt. Develop a concert of prayer and praise. **2.** What would the visions in chapters 4 and 5 have meant to the persecuted Christians of Asia? What does this vision say to us as we view our out-of-control world? Based on this, what actions will you take this week?

---

1. What kind of horse are you most like: A Clydesdale? A thoroughbred? An Arabian stallion? Why? **2.** How is your group like a team of four horsemen: Are you each pulling in a different direction, or the same? How so?

1. Who (or what) do each of the horsemen represent? Why? **2.** The luxury items (wine and oil) are still available, but the basic foodstuffs are scarce and costly. What does that tell you about their economic situation? **3.** In what sense do the first three horsemen lead to the fourth? How have these forces: conquest (v. 2), strife (v. 3), scarcity (v. 6), and death (v. 8)) operated throughout history? How do they prevail today? What does this mean for the interpretation of the vision? **4.** What is revealed by the opening of the fifth seal (v. 9)? How is this related to the suffering of the Christians in John's day? In our day? **5.** What occurs when the sixth seal is broken (vv. 12–13; see Mk 13)? What elements of the Day of Judgment are described? **6.** Who can stand the wrath of God?

1. Which seal opening makes the greatest impression on you? Why? **2.** What's the *worst* thing that has happened to you because of your faithfulness to the Word of God? **3.** In what area of your life are you trying to hide from God? What do you need to do to come out of hiding? **4.** How does this passage make you feel about the end times? Why? How will this affect your actions this week?

11Then I looked and heard the voice of many angels, numbering
thousands upon thousands, and ten thousand times ten thousand.
They encircled the throne and the living creatures and the elders.
12In a loud voice they sang:

"Worthy is the Lamb, who was slain,
to receive power and wealth and wisdom and
strength
and honor and glory and praise!"

13Then I heard every creature in heaven and on earth and under
the earth and on the sea, and all that is in them, singing:

"To him who sits on the throne and to the Lamb
be praise and honor and glory and power,
for ever and ever!"

14The four living creatures said, "Amen," and the elders fell down
and worshiped.

The Seals

6 I watched as the Lamb opened the first of the seven seals.
Then I heard one of the four living creatures say in a voice like
thunder, "Come!" 2I looked, and there before me was a white
horse! Its rider held a bow, and he was given a crown, and he rode
out as a conqueror bent on conquest.
3When the Lamb opened the second seal, I heard the second
living creature say, "Come!" 4Then another horse came out, a fiery
red one. Its rider was given power to take peace from the earth and
to make men slay each other. To him was given a large sword.
5When the Lamb opened the third seal, I heard the third living
creature say, "Come!" I looked, and there before me was a black
horse! Its rider was holding a pair of scales in his hand. 6Then I
heard what sounded like a voice among the four living creatures,
saying, "A quart[a] of wheat for a day's wages,[b] and three quarts
of barley for a day's wages,[b] and do not damage the oil and the
wine!"
7When the Lamb opened the fourth seal, I heard the voice of the
fourth living creature say, "Come!" 8I looked, and there before me
was a pale horse! Its rider was named Death, and Hades was
following close behind him. They were given power over a fourth
of the earth to kill by sword, famine and plague, and by the wild
beasts of the earth.
9When he opened the fifth seal, I saw under the altar the souls
of those who had been slain because of the word of God and the
testimony they had maintained. 10They called out in a loud voice,
"How long, Sovereign Lord, holy and true, until you judge the
inhabitants of the earth and avenge our blood?" 11Then each of
them was given a white robe, and they were told to wait a little
longer, until the number of their fellow servants and brothers who
were to be killed as they had been was completed.
12I watched as he opened the sixth seal. There was a great
earthquake. The sun turned black like sackcloth made of goat hair,
the whole moon turned blood red, 13and the stars in the sky fell to
earth, as late figs drop from a fig tree when shaken by a strong
wind. 14The sky receded like a scroll, rolling up, and every mountain and island was removed from its place.
15Then the kings of the earth, the princes, the generals, the rich,
the mighty, and every slave and every free man hid in caves and

[a]6 Greek *a choinix* (probably about a liter) [b]6 Greek *a denarius*

among the rocks of the mountains. 16They called to the mountains
and the rocks, "Fall on us and hide us from the face of him who sits
on the throne and from the wrath of the Lamb! 17For the great day
of their wrath has come, and who can stand?"

144,000 Sealed

7 After this I saw four angels standing at the four corners of the
earth, holding back the four winds of the earth to prevent any
wind from blowing on the land or on the sea or on any tree. 2Then
I saw another angel coming up from the east, having the seal of the
living God. He called out in a loud voice to the four angels who had
been given power to harm the land and the sea: 3"Do not harm the
land or the sea or the trees until we put a seal on the foreheads of
the servants of our God." 4Then I heard the number of those who
were sealed: 144,000 from all the tribes of Israel.

5From the tribe of Judah 12,000 were sealed,
from the tribe of Reuben 12,000,
from the tribe of Gad 12,000,
6from the tribe of Asher 12,000,
from the tribe of Naphtali 12,000,
from the tribe of Manasseh 12,000,
7from the tribe of Simeon 12,000,
from the tribe of Levi 12,000,
from the tribe of Issachar 12,000,
8from the tribe of Zebulun 12,000,
from the tribe of Joseph 12,000,
from the tribe of Benjamin 12,000.

What kind of wind (a warm gentle breeze, a cold north wind, a hurricane, etc.) best symbolizes your life? Why?

1. Do you think the work of the four angels is a new woe or a restatement of the events in chapter 6? Why? Likewise, in what sense do the events of chapter 7 come "after" the events in chapter 6: In actual history? Or in John's vision? **2.** What is the message of the fifth angel? Who is sealed? When does this occur? What does it mean (see Ge 4:15; Eze 9:4–6; Eph 1:13–14)? **3.** Is this "144,000" a symbol or a statistic? Why (see 7:9; 14:1–5)?

1. How have you sensed God's protection in the last six months? Before that? **2.** What sort of seal has God placed on your life? How is this seal evident to others?

The Great Multitude in White Robes

9After this I looked and there before me was a great multitude
that no one could count, from every nation, tribe, people and
language, standing before the throne and in front of the Lamb.
They were wearing white robes and were holding palm branches
in their hands. 10And they cried out in a loud voice:

"Salvation belongs to our God,
who sits on the throne,
and to the Lamb."

11All the angels were standing around the throne and around the
elders and the four living creatures. They fell down on their faces
before the throne and worshiped God, 12saying:

"Amen!
Praise and glory
and wisdom and thanks and honor
and power and strength
be to our God for ever and ever.
Amen!"

13Then one of the elders asked me, "These in white robes—who
are they, and where did they come from?"
14I answered, "Sir, you know."
And he said, "These are they who have come out of the great
tribulation; they have washed their robes and made them white in
the blood of the Lamb. 15Therefore,

"they are before the throne of God
and serve him day and night in his temple;
and he who sits on the throne will spread his tent
over them.

What piece of clothing (bathrobe, tennis togs, 3-piece suit, jeans, etc.) do you feel expresses your personality best? How do you feel when wearing it?

1. What does John see next? How does he describe the size of the crowd? Is this multitude the same as the 144,000 (v. 4)? Why or why not? What are they doing? Wearing? Carrying? **2.** What is the significance of the white robes, the palm branches and the washing? What is the new function of those in white robes? What is their future? How would this encourage the Christians of John's day? Of our day? **3.** When the multitude cries out, how do the angels, elders and the four living creatures respond (v. 12)? What does all this say about God's kingdom and Christ's sacrifice? **4.** What qualifies this white-robed crowd to stand before God? What is their new role? What is "the great tribulation"—is it a particular event or a general experience? **5.** Is the safety, security and service of these Christians a *present* life experience for them, or only a promise to be realized in some vague and distant *future*? Or both?

1. Have each person meditate on a word ascribed to God (vv. 9–17) and praise him for part of your group prayer time. **2.** What is your greatest tribulation or persecution? How difficult does that seem next to the majesty of God pictured here? How will you incorporate this glimpse of heavenly worship into your earthly walk?

When home alone, do you like silence, or do you have to have some noise going on? Why?

1. Amid seals and trumpets, why this silence? Why the golden censer? **2.** What do altars and incense teach about prayer (vv. 3–5; see 5:8; 6:9–10; 9:13)?

Does this imagery seem far removed to you? When was the last time you tried silent meditation or cried for justice? What happened?

---

1. What is one of the most excruciating pains you've ever experienced? What happened? **2.** What color would you use to describe your past week? Why? To describe your past year? Why?

1. What events follow the sounding of each of the first four trumpets (vv. 7–12)? What do the trumpets signify: Triumph or doom? Life or death? Or what? **2.** How do these trumpeted events compare with the events inaugurated by the first six seals? **3.** Likewise, how do these events compare with the plagues in Exodus 7–10 and Joel 2:1–11? **4.** What parallels or repeated patterns do you see between the opening of the seals and sounding of the trumpets, which suggest that these two scenes are in reality two sides of the same coin? (Note how the trumpets focus on what will happen to the unbelieving world, whereas the seals focus on what will happen to the church.) **5.** Do these seals and trumpets refer to datable, sequential events or to aspects of the world's condition, which may be true at any point in history? Why? **6.** What happens when the fifth trumpet sounds (9:1–11)? Who can the fallen star be (see Lk 10:18; Isa 14:12)? What power do the locusts have? Describe them.

16Never again will they hunger;
never again will they thirst.
The sun will not beat upon them,
nor any scorching heat.
17For the Lamb at the center of the throne will be their shepherd;
he will lead them to springs of living water.
And God will wipe away every tear from their eyes."

The Seventh Seal and the Golden Censer

8 When he opened the seventh seal, there was silence in heaven
for about half an hour.
2And I saw the seven angels who stand before God, and to them
were given seven trumpets.
3Another angel, who had a golden censer, came and stood at the
altar. He was given much incense to offer, with the prayers of all
the saints, on the golden altar before the throne. 4The smoke of the
incense, together with the prayers of the saints, went up before
God from the angel's hand. 5Then the angel took the censer, filled
it with fire from the altar, and hurled it on the earth; and there
came peals of thunder, rumblings, flashes of lightning and an earthquake.

The Trumpets

6Then the seven angels who had the seven trumpets prepared to
sound them.
7The first angel sounded his trumpet, and there came hail and
fire mixed with blood, and it was hurled down upon the earth. A
third of the earth was burned up, a third of the trees were burned
up, and all the green grass was burned up.
8The second angel sounded his trumpet, and something like a
huge mountain, all ablaze, was thrown into the sea. A third of the
sea turned into blood, 9a third of the living creatures in the sea
died, and a third of the ships were destroyed.
10The third angel sounded his trumpet, and a great star, blazing
like a torch, fell from the sky on a third of the rivers and on the
springs of water— 11the name of the star is Wormwood.[a] A third
of the waters turned bitter, and many people died from the waters
that had become bitter.
12The fourth angel sounded his trumpet, and a third of the sun
was struck, a third of the moon, and a third of the stars, so that a
third of them turned dark. A third of the day was without light, and
also a third of the night.
13As I watched, I heard an eagle that was flying in midair call out
in a loud voice: "Woe! Woe! Woe to the inhabitants of the earth,
because of the trumpet blasts about to be sounded by the other
three angels!"
9 The fifth angel sounded his trumpet, and I saw a star that had
fallen from the sky to the earth. The star was given the key to
the shaft of the Abyss. 2When he opened the Abyss, smoke rose
from it like the smoke from a gigantic furnace. The sun and sky
were darkened by the smoke from the Abyss. 3And out of the
smoke locusts came down upon the earth and were given power
like that of scorpions of the earth. 4They were told not to harm the
grass of the earth or any plant or tree, but only those people who
did not have the seal of God on their foreheads. 5They were not

[a] *11* That is, Bitterness

given power to kill them, but only to torture them for five months.
And the agony they suffered was like that of the sting of a scorpion
when it strikes a man. 6During those days men will seek death, but
will not find it; they will long to die, but death will elude them.
7The locusts looked like horses prepared for battle. On their
heads they wore something like crowns of gold, and their faces
resembled human faces. 8Their hair was like women's hair, and
their teeth were like lions' teeth. 9They had breastplates like
breastplates of iron, and the sound of their wings was like the
thundering of many horses and chariots rushing into battle. 10They
had tails and stings like scorpions, and in their tails they had power
to torment people for five months. 11They had as king over them
the angel of the Abyss, whose name in Hebrew is Abaddon, and in
Greek, Apollyon.[a]
12The first woe is past; two other woes are yet to come.
13The sixth angel sounded his trumpet, and I heard a voice
coming from the horns[b] of the golden altar that is before God. 14It
said to the sixth angel who had the trumpet, "Release the four
angels who are bound at the great river Euphrates." 15And the four
angels who had been kept ready for this very hour and day and
month and year were released to kill a third of mankind. 16The
number of the mounted troops was two hundred million. I heard
their number.
17The horses and riders I saw in my vision looked like this: Their
breastplates were fiery red, dark blue, and yellow as sulfur. The
heads of the horses resembled the heads of lions, and out of their
mouths came fire, smoke and sulfur. 18A third of mankind was
killed by the three plagues of fire, smoke and sulfur that came out
of their mouths. 19The power of the horses was in their mouths
and in their tails; for their tails were like snakes, having heads with
which they inflict injury.
20The rest of mankind that were not killed by these plagues still
did not repent of the work of their hands; they did not stop worshiping demons, and idols of gold, silver, bronze, stone and
wood—idols that cannot see or hear or walk. 21Nor did they repent
of their murders, their magic arts, their sexual immorality or their
thefts.

The Angel and the Little Scroll

10 Then I saw another mighty angel coming down from heav-
en. He was robed in a cloud, with a rainbow above his
head; his face was like the sun, and his legs were like fiery pillars.
2He was holding a little scroll, which lay open in his hand. He
planted his right foot on the sea and his left foot on the land, 3and
he gave a loud shout like the roar of a lion. When he shouted, the
voices of the seven thunders spoke. 4And when the seven thunders
spoke, I was about to write; but I heard a voice from heaven say,
"Seal up what the seven thunders have said and do not write it
down."
5Then the angel I had seen standing on the sea and on the land
raised his right hand to heaven. 6And he swore by him who lives
for ever and ever, who created the heavens and all that is in them,
the earth and all that is in it, and the sea and all that is in it, and
said, "There will be no more delay! 7But in the days when the
seventh angel is about to sound his trumpet, the mystery of God
will be accomplished, just as he announced to his servants the
prophets."

[a] 11 *Abaddon* and *Apollyon* mean *Destroyer.* [b] 13 That is, projections

7. What events are inaugurated by the sixth trumpet (9:13–16)? What response should this woe elicit from the unbelieving world? Why? Why do you suppose this woe failed to bring the majority to repentance, as intended?

1. What do you think of Christians who pray for trouble to strike the unbelieving world? And what do you think of God's answer to such prayers? What modern-day realities does the imagery of these plagues bring to mind for you? How might they have applied equally well in John's day? **2.** How do you feel when you read this account of stranger-than-fiction events? What is the "who" and "why" behind all these events? **3.** How has the star named "Wormwood" or "Bitterness" affected your life? How has your bitterness affected others? What have you discovered as an antidote to bitterness? **4.** What do you have in common with the people mentioned in 9:20–21? What will you do about this today?

Who was one of your fictional heroes when you were a child: Buck Rogers? The Lone Ranger? Superman? Why?

1. Describe the angel who announces the coming of the seventh trumpet? In what ways does this picture contrast with the traditional view of angels? Why would John be forbidden to record the words of the seven thunders (see 2Co 12:3–4)? **2.** What purposes have the disasters of the first six trumpets served? What do you anticipate the seventh trumpet will bring forth? What is the "mystery of God" (v. 7; see Ro 11:25–36; 16:25–27; Eph 1:9–14)? **3.** What happens to the small scroll (v. 9; see also Eze 3:1–3)? How can a revelation from God be both sweet and bitter?

1. When has God led you into a project that you wouldn't have selected for yourself? What happened? 2. What is an experience you once savored for a moment, but that later turned sour? How has God's Word been both sweet and sour to you?

What have been the three greatest years of your life: (a) College? (b) The years without children (or parents) around? (c) The years when the children were _____? (d) The years when you _____? Why do those years stand out?

1. What is John commanded to do? Who will be "measured" (or protected), and why (v. 1)? With the church and the world set in contrast, what do the two indestructible witnesses represent? And their enemies? 2. What happens to these two witnesses (v. 7)? What results from their death and resurrection? 3. If God's witness is faithfully maintained for "1260 days" to offset the "42 months" (which are the times of the Gentiles), then what do the "3 and 1/2 days" mean (vv. 11–12)?

1. What do you learn in this passage about what it means to be a witness? 2. What has been toughest about living out your faith at work? At school? At home? Why is there such difficulty? 3. How have you felt especially empowered by God in the last six months?

What was the most rewarding job you ever had? What was the best part about it?

1. What does this trumpet herald? How is the Second Coming a "good news/bad news" event? 2. For what is God worshiped? What does this tell you about God's power?

1. How do you react to God's power over unbelieving people: to *hurt* them (trumpet 5 or 1st woe), to *kill* them (trumpet 6 or 2nd woe), or to *damn* them (trumpet 7

8Then the voice that I had heard from heaven spoke to me once more: "Go, take the scroll that lies open in the hand of the angel who is standing on the sea and on the land."

9So I went to the angel and asked him to give me the little scroll. He said to me, "Take it and eat it. It will turn your stomach sour, but in your mouth it will be as sweet as honey." 10I took the little scroll from the angel's hand and ate it. It tasted as sweet as honey in my mouth, but when I had eaten it, my stomach turned sour. 11Then I was told, "You must prophesy again about many peoples, nations, languages and kings."

The Two Witnesses

11 I was given a reed like a measuring rod and was told, "Go and measure the temple of God and the altar, and count the worshipers there. 2But exclude the outer court; do not measure it, because it has been given to the Gentiles. They will trample on the holy city for 42 months. 3And I will give power to my two witnesses, and they will prophesy for 1,260 days, clothed in sackcloth." 4These are the two olive trees and the two lampstands that stand before the Lord of the earth. 5If anyone tries to harm them, fire comes from their mouths and devours their enemies. This is how anyone who wants to harm them must die. 6These men have power to shut up the sky so that it will not rain during the time they are prophesying; and they have power to turn the waters into blood and to strike the earth with every kind of plague as often as they want.

7Now when they have finished their testimony, the beast that comes up from the Abyss will attack them, and overpower and kill them. 8Their bodies will lie in the street of the great city, which is figuratively called Sodom and Egypt, where also their Lord was crucified. 9For three and a half days men from every people, tribe, language and nation will gaze on their bodies and refuse them burial. 10The inhabitants of the earth will gloat over them and will celebrate by sending each other gifts, because these two prophets had tormented those who live on the earth.

11But after the three and a half days a breath of life from God entered them, and they stood on their feet, and terror struck those who saw them. 12Then they heard a loud voice from heaven saying to them, "Come up here." And they went up to heaven in a cloud, while their enemies looked on.

13At that very hour there was a severe earthquake and a tenth of the city collapsed. Seven thousand people were killed in the earthquake, and the survivors were terrified and gave glory to the God of heaven.

14The second woe has passed; the third woe is coming soon.

The Seventh Trumpet

15The seventh angel sounded his trumpet, and there were loud voices in heaven, which said:

> "The kingdom of the world has become the
> kingdom of our Lord and of his Christ,
> and he will reign for ever and ever."

16And the twenty-four elders, who were seated on their thrones before God, fell on their faces and worshiped God, 17saying:

> "We give thanks to you, Lord God Almighty,
> the One who is and who was,
> because you have taken your great power
> and have begun to reign.

18The nations were angry;
and your wrath has come.
The time has come for judging the dead,
and for rewarding your servants the prophets
and your saints and those who reverence your
name,
both small and great—
and for destroying those who destroy the earth."

19Then God's temple in heaven was opened, and within his
temple was seen the ark of his covenant. And there came flashes of
lightning, rumblings, peals of thunder, an earthquake and a great
hailstorm.

The Woman and the Dragon

12 A great and wondrous sign appeared in heaven: a woman
clothed with the sun, with the moon under her feet and a
crown of twelve stars on her head. 2She was pregnant and cried
out in pain as she was about to give birth. 3Then another sign
appeared in heaven: an enormous red dragon with seven heads and
ten horns and seven crowns on his heads. 4His tail swept a third of
the stars out of the sky and flung them to the earth. The dragon
stood in front of the woman who was about to give birth, so that he
might devour her child the moment it was born. 5She gave birth to
a son, a male child, who will rule all the nations with an iron
scepter. And her child was snatched up to God and to his throne.
6The woman fled into the desert to a place prepared for her by
God, where she might be taken care of for 1,260 days.
7And there was war in heaven. Michael and his angels fought
against the dragon, and the dragon and his angels fought back. 8But
he was not strong enough, and they lost their place in heaven.
9The great dragon was hurled down—that ancient serpent called
the devil, or Satan, who leads the whole world astray. He was
hurled to the earth, and his angels with him.
10Then I heard a loud voice in heaven say:

"Now have come the salvation and the power and
the kingdom of our God,
and the authority of his Christ.
For the accuser of our brothers,
who accuses them before our God day and
night,
has been hurled down.
11They overcame him
by the blood of the Lamb
and by the word of their testimony;
they did not love their lives so much
as to shrink from death.
12Therefore rejoice, you heavens
and you who dwell in them!
But woe to the earth and the sea,
because the devil has gone down to you!
He is filled with fury,
because he knows that his time is short."

13When the dragon saw that he had been hurled to the earth, he
pursued the woman who had given birth to the male child. 14The
woman was given the two wings of a great eagle, so that she might
fly to the place prepared for her in the desert, where she would be
taken care of for a time, times and half a time, out of the serpent's
reach. 15Then from his mouth the serpent spewed water like a

---

or 3rd woe)? **2.** As God displays this power in response to prayers (8:4), how do you respond to what he has called you to do? What will you pray about? Why?

When you were a child, who was the most important woman in your life besides your mother? Why?

1. Where, in the thematic development of Revelation, does the unveiling of God's heavenly temple and ark of the covenant fit best? (Note: Some or all of the phenomena occurring in 11:19 also occur in 4:5 and 8:5). **2.** Describe the woman, the dragon and the child. Who does the woman represent? The dragon? The child? **3.** Where does the next conflict occur? Who are the protagonists? What is the outcome of this conflict? What is the significance of this outcome for the earth? For Christians? **4.** When do you see this heavenly battle occurring: (a) At some particular time and place in history? (b) Pre-history? (c) Post-history? (d) Any time and any place during the ongoing heavenly battle between the kingdom of God and the kingdom of Satan (that is, in the spiritual realm which is behind *all* of this world's history)? Why do you think so?

1. What do you learn here about conflict between the Christian church and demonic evil? **2.** When has Satan seemed very real to you? Why? How do you overcome Satan (see 12:11)? How could you apply these tactics in your own life? What do you need to do to become stronger for spiritual battle? **3.** How can your Christian friends pray for you in battles you are facing? Likewise, how can you pray for them?

river, to overtake the woman and sweep her away with the torrent.
16But the earth helped the woman by opening its mouth and swal-
lowing the river that the dragon had spewed out of his mouth.
17Then the dragon was enraged at the woman and went off to make
war against the rest of her offspring—those who obey God's com-
13 mandments and hold to the testimony of Jesus. 1And the
dragon[a] stood on the shore of the sea.

The Beast out of the Sea

And I saw a beast coming out of the sea. He had ten horns and
seven heads, with ten crowns on his horns, and on each head a
blasphemous name. 2The beast I saw resembled a leopard, but had
feet like those of a bear and a mouth like that of a lion. The dragon
gave the beast his power and his throne and great authority. 3One
of the heads of the beast seemed to have had a fatal wound, but the
fatal wound had been healed. The whole world was astonished and
followed the beast. 4Men worshiped the dragon because he had
given authority to the beast, and they also worshiped the beast and
asked, "Who is like the beast? Who can make war against him?"
5The beast was given a mouth to utter proud words and blasphemies and to exercise his authority for forty-two months. 6He
opened his mouth to blaspheme God, and to slander his name and
his dwelling place and those who live in heaven. 7He was given
power to make war against the saints and to conquer them. And he
was given authority over every tribe, people, language and nation.
8All inhabitants of the earth will worship the beast—all whose
names have not been written in the book of life belonging to the
Lamb that was slain from the creation of the world.[b]
9He who has an ear, let him hear.

> 10If anyone is to go into captivity,
> into captivity he will go.
> If anyone is to be killed[c] with the sword,
> with the sword he will be killed.

This calls for patient endurance and faithfulness on the part of the saints.

The Beast out of the Earth

11Then I saw another beast, coming out of the earth. He had two
horns like a lamb, but he spoke like a dragon. 12He exercised all
the authority of the first beast on his behalf, and made the earth
and its inhabitants worship the first beast, whose fatal wound had
been healed. 13And he performed great and miraculous signs, even
causing fire to come down from heaven to earth in full view of
men. 14Because of the signs he was given power to do on behalf of
the first beast, he deceived the inhabitants of the earth. He ordered
them to set up an image in honor of the beast who was wounded
by the sword and yet lived. 15He was given power to give breath to
the image of the first beast, so that it could speak and cause all who
refused to worship the image to be killed. 16He also forced everyone, small and great, rich and poor, free and slave, to receive a
mark on his right hand or on his forehead, 17so that no one could
buy or sell unless he had the mark, which is the name of the beast
or the number of his name.
18This calls for wisdom. If anyone has insight, let him calculate
the number of the beast, for it is man's number. His number is
666.

[a]*1* Some late manuscripts *And I* [b]*8* Or *written from the creation of the world in the book of life belonging to the Lamb that was slain* [c]*10* Some manuscripts *anyone kills*

---

1. Who do you think is one of the most charismatic leaders living today? How has charisma helped him or her to lead? **2.** When you were growing up, who was the most patient person in your family?

1. What is this beast from the sea like (v. 2; Isa 27:1)? What is the source of its power? How does it use its power? What is the extent of its power? What is the relationship between the beast and the dragon? **2.** Who worships the beast? **3.** Who do you think the first-century Christians would have identified as this beast (see Da 7 and Ro 13:1)? **4.** What impact will this beast have on the Christians? How ought they to respond? Why?

1. Who are some of the beasts or idols in your life (people, forces, institutions, etc.) that test your allegiance to Christ? How has talk of patriotism and tradition affected your allegiance to Christ? How is God helping you deal with that? **2.** Is your name written in the Book of Life? How do you know? **3.** What kind of grade would you give yourself on patience and faithfulness? Why?

What costume best hid your identity as a child?

1. What is this beast from the earth like? **2.** If the first beast exercises political power, what authority does this second beast exercise? How are true government and religion connected (and mimicked) by these two beasts? **3.** Since "7" is the number of completeness in Revelation, what might "666" mean? **4.** Compare the view of the Roman Empire here with that in Romans 13:1–7. How had Rome changed since Paul's day?

How can we discern false religion and governments?

The Lamb and the 144,000

14 Then I looked, and there before me was the Lamb, standing
on Mount Zion, and with him 144,000 who had his name
and his Father's name written on their foreheads. 2And I heard a
sound from heaven like the roar of rushing waters and like a loud
peal of thunder. The sound I heard was like that of harpists playing
their harps. 3And they sang a new song before the throne and
before the four living creatures and the elders. No one could learn
the song except the 144,000 who had been redeemed from the
earth. 4These are those who did not defile themselves with wom-
en, for they kept themselves pure. They follow the Lamb wherever
he goes. They were purchased from among men and offered as
firstfruits to God and the Lamb. 5No lie was found in their mouths;
they are blameless.

The Three Angels

6Then I saw another angel flying in midair, and he had the
eternal gospel to proclaim to those who live on the earth—to every
nation, tribe, language and people. 7He said in a loud voice, "Fear
God and give him glory, because the hour of his judgment has
come. Worship him who made the heavens, the earth, the sea and
the springs of water."
8A second angel followed and said, "Fallen! Fallen is Babylon the
Great, which made all the nations drink the maddening wine of
her adulteries."
9A third angel followed them and said in a loud voice: "If anyone
worships the beast and his image and receives his mark on the
forehead or on the hand, 10he, too, will drink of the wine of God's
fury, which has been poured full strength into the cup of his wrath.
He will be tormented with burning sulfur in the presence of the
holy angels and of the Lamb. 11And the smoke of their torment
rises for ever and ever. There is no rest day or night for those who
worship the beast and his image, or for anyone who receives the
mark of his name." 12This calls for patient endurance on the part of
the saints who obey God's commandments and remain faithful to
Jesus.
13Then I heard a voice from heaven say, "Write: Blessed are the
dead who die in the Lord from now on."
"Yes," says the Spirit, "they will rest from their labor, for their
deeds will follow them."

The Harvest of the Earth

14I looked, and there before me was a white cloud, and seated on
the cloud was one "like a son of man"[a] with a crown of gold on
his head and a sharp sickle in his hand. 15Then another angel came
out of the temple and called in a loud voice to him who was sitting
on the cloud, "Take your sickle and reap, because the time to reap
has come, for the harvest of the earth is ripe." 16So he who was
seated on the cloud swung his sickle over the earth, and the earth
was harvested.
17Another angel came out of the temple in heaven, and he too
had a sharp sickle. 18Still another angel, who had charge of the fire,
came from the altar and called in a loud voice to him who had the
sharp sickle, "Take your sharp sickle and gather the clusters of
grapes from the earth's vine, because its grapes are ripe." 19The
angel swung his sickle on the earth, gathered its grapes and threw
them into the great winepress of God's wrath. 20They were tram-

[a] *14* Daniel 7:13

What kind of singer are you: Off-Broadway? Off-key?

1. Given the chaos described in chapters 12–13, what comfort do you find in this passage? What sights? Sounds? Feelings? **2.** Who is the Lamb? What has he done? Why are the people following him?

How are you like (and unlike) the 144,000? Why do you follow the Lamb?

Heard any good news lately? Any good news/bad news jokes? Tell one.

1. What is the essence of the "eternal gospel" proclaimed by the angel of grace? Who will hear it? Has this vision yet been fulfilled? What response to the Gospel is called for? **2.** By contrast, what message does the angel of doom spread? Who is the fallen Babylon? Who has been infected by the spirit of Babylon? **3.** How does Satan's system (13:2–10) differ from God's church (14:1–5)? How does Satan's ideology (13:11–18) differ from God's truth (14:6–13)?

1. What have you done to help proclaim the Gospel to every nation, tribe, language and people? **2.** How do you look upon death: As a rest? A reward? A new phase in the journey? **3.** What would you like to be doing when God calls you home?

Ever harvest anything? How hard did you work? Did you enjoy it? Why or why not?

1. Identify the four supernatural beings in this fifth vision. What is the role of each? **2.** What are the differences between the two parts of the vision (vv. 14–16 and 17–20)? What is the nature of the judgment that will occur (see Mt 13:30,39)? **3.** Who might the first figure be (see Da 7:13)?

How ripe do you think the world is now? Do you feel that the end of the world is close at hand? Why or why not? How does this affect your life?

pled in the winepress outside the city, and blood flowed out of the press, rising as high as the horses' bridles for a distance of 1,600 stadia.[a]

Seven Angels With Seven Plagues

15 I saw in heaven another great and marvelous sign: seven angels with the seven last plagues—last, because with them God's wrath is completed. 2And I saw what looked like a sea of glass mixed with fire and, standing beside the sea, those who had been victorious over the beast and his image and over the number of his name. They held harps given them by God 3and sang the song of Moses the servant of God and the song of the Lamb:

"Great and marvelous are your deeds,
Lord God Almighty.
Just and true are your ways,
King of the ages.
4Who will not fear you, O Lord,
and bring glory to your name?
For you alone are holy.
All nations will come
and worship before you,
for your righteous acts have been revealed."

5After this I looked and in heaven the temple, that is, the tabernacle of the Testimony, was opened. 6Out of the temple came the seven angels with the seven plagues. They were dressed in clean, shining linen and wore golden sashes around their chests. 7Then one of the four living creatures gave to the seven angels seven golden bowls filled with the wrath of God, who lives for ever and ever. 8And the temple was filled with smoke from the glory of God and from his power, and no one could enter the temple until the seven plagues of the seven angels were completed.

The Seven Bowls of God's Wrath

16 Then I heard a loud voice from the temple saying to the seven angels, "Go, pour out the seven bowls of God's wrath on the earth."

2The first angel went and poured out his bowl on the land, and ugly and painful sores broke out on the people who had the mark of the beast and worshiped his image.

3The second angel poured out his bowl on the sea, and it turned into blood like that of a dead man, and every living thing in the sea died.

4The third angel poured out his bowl on the rivers and springs of water, and they became blood. 5Then I heard the angel in charge of the waters say:

"You are just in these judgments,
you who are and who were, the Holy One,
because you have so judged;
6for they have shed the blood of your saints and
prophets,
and you have given them blood to drink as they
deserve."

7And I heard the altar respond:

"Yes, Lord God Almighty,
true and just are your judgments."

[a]*20* That is, about 180 miles (about 300 kilometers)

If you could have a bowl full of anything right now, what would you want? Why?

1. How does John describe this new sign? Why does he say these are the last plagues? **2.** What picture does he paint in verse 2? Compare Moses' song of deliverance from Egypt (Ex 15:1–18) with the song sung by those delivered from the beast. What praise is given to God? By whom? **3.** What does John see next? How does the angels' attire contrast with what they are given to do? **4.** What does the temple in heaven mean: A haven of rest and a place to play harps for those who die? Or time to reckon with God's holiness and wrath unveiled in that very temple? Why?

1. How does this passage make you feel? Why? What does it make you want to do? **2.** What great and mighty deeds has God done in your life for which you will praise him today? How appropriate is the song in this passage to your experience with God? Why?

---

1. What firsthand experience have you had with a natural disaster? What happened? What are your most vivid memories about it? **2.** What would be the worst plague for you to experience: Sores all over your body? Intense heat without air conditioning? Total darkness? Or great thirst with very little water? Why?

1. What contents are in each bowl of wrath? Why are these plagues worse than those ushered in by the trumpets (contrast, for example, v. 3 with 8:8)? What was the function of the trumpet plagues? What is the function of the plagues in this passage? **2.** Why does the angel (speaking on behalf of nature) react to the outpouring of God's wrath, not with pain or sorrow, but with recognition of divine justice? **3.** What is described in the interlude (vv. 13–16) between the sixth and seventh bowls? What function did the frogs perform (see Ex 8:2–13)? **4.** How will the just purposes of God and the evil purposes of Satan finally and awfully converge at Armaged-

8The fourth angel poured out his bowl on the sun, and the sun
was given power to scorch people with fire. 9They were seared by
the intense heat and they cursed the name of God, who had control over these plagues, but they refused to repent and glorify him.
10The fifth angel poured out his bowl on the throne of the beast,
and his kingdom was plunged into darkness. Men gnawed their
tongues in agony 11and cursed the God of heaven because of their
pains and their sores, but they refused to repent of what they had
done.
12The sixth angel poured out his bowl on the great river Euphrates, and its water was dried up to prepare the way for the kings
from the East. 13Then I saw three evil[a] spirits that looked like
frogs; they came out of the mouth of the dragon, out of the mouth
of the beast and out of the mouth of the false prophet. 14They are
spirits of demons performing miraculous signs, and they go out to
the kings of the whole world, to gather them for the battle on the
great day of God Almighty.
15"Behold, I come like a thief! Blessed is he who stays awake
and keeps his clothes with him, so that he may not go naked and
be shamefully exposed."
16Then they gathered the kings together to the place that in
Hebrew is called Armageddon.
17The seventh angel poured out his bowl into the air, and out of
the temple came a loud voice from the throne, saying, "It is done!"
18Then there came flashes of lightning, rumblings, peals of thunder
and a severe earthquake. No earthquake like it has ever occurred
since man has been on earth, so tremendous was the quake. 19The
great city split into three parts, and the cities of the nations collapsed. God remembered Babylon the Great and gave her the cup
filled with the wine of the fury of his wrath. 20Every island fled
away and the mountains could not be found. 21From the sky huge
hailstones of about a hundred pounds each fell upon men. And
they cursed God on account of the plague of hail, because the
plague was so terrible.

The Woman on the Beast

17 One of the seven angels who had the seven bowls came and
said to me, "Come, I will show you the punishment of the
great prostitute, who sits on many waters. 2With her the kings of
the earth committed adultery and the inhabitants of the earth were
intoxicated with the wine of her adulteries."
3Then the angel carried me away in the Spirit into a desert.
There I saw a woman sitting on a scarlet beast that was covered
with blasphemous names and had seven heads and ten horns. 4The
woman was dressed in purple and scarlet, and was glittering with
gold, precious stones and pearls. She held a golden cup in her
hand, filled with abominable things and the filth of her adulteries.
5This title was written on her forehead:

MYSTERY
BABYLON THE GREAT
THE MOTHER OF PROSTITUTES
AND OF THE ABOMINATIONS OF THE EARTH.

6I saw that the woman was drunk with the blood of the saints, the
blood of those who bore testimony to Jesus.
When I saw her, I was greatly astonished. 7Then the angel said
to me: "Why are you astonished? I will explain to you the mystery

[a] 13 Greek *unclean*

don (or "hill of Megiddo," an historic crossroads of the Middle East)? With what result (vv. 17–21)? **5.** Compare the seven seals, seven trumpets and seven bowls to each other and to the 10 plagues of Egypt (Ex 7–10). What examples of contrast (e.g., "not only ... but ...") can you find in each section? **6.** What is the connection between the three scenes (of seals, trumpets and bowls)? How would these seals, trumpets and bowls comfort John's original readers?

1. What has God done in your life to help you repent? How receptive are you to admitting your guilt and repenting when you sin? **2.** If "war is hell," could John be envisioning that "hell is war"? What does this passage tell you about God's judgment? **3.** What are the "frogs" that are battling with you? How is the battle going? **4.** How is the book of Revelation making you feel? Why? What has surprised you about God or about this book? How would you explain the necessity of these plagues to someone who is not a Christian?

---

1. If you could be famous for one hour, for what would you like to be known? Why? **2.** What bumper sticker or sign sums up your life now? Why?

1. Who is the central figure in this passage? In what sense is the woman on the Beast influential? Evil? Attractive? Repulsive? Who is she (see also 14:8 and 16:19)? Who appears to be "offstage"? How is the woman and this beast like the first and second beasts of chapter 13? **2.** What here is the ultimate sin (vv. 5–6)? Why? **3.** What does the angel say about the origin of the beast? Its history? Its future (vv. 8–14)? What response does the beast elicit? Why? **4.** Geographically, historically and spiritually, what do you think the beast's seven heads and 10 horns represent (see also Da 7:15–28)? Why do the kings and the beast join forces? With what result? How can evil turn on itself, Satan (in effect) casting out Satan? How does

God's greater purpose triumph in all this? **5.** How are the readers of Revelation comforted by the various "definitions" of the symbols? How do these many symbols draw attention to a single object from different angles?

1. In this passage how does Babylon symbolize what is wrong in society today? For example, what institutions have been overthrown by revolution, only to be replaced by new regimes which surrender to the same godless ideology? **2.** Of society's wrongs, which ones have entrapped you from time to time? How has God enabled you to avoid the snares of "the great prostitute"? **3.** Surely by now you are "calling for a mind with wisdom" (v. 9). What wisdom do you want in the next few weeks? What wisdom do you need in understanding the message of Revelation? **4.** If you have not grasped the full meaning of the various beasts, have you at least been frightened by the power of evil? How will you translate that fear into action or hope?

---

1. If you were a piece of merchandise, would you be made of precious stones, fine linens or costly woods? Why? **2.** Remember as a child when you built a tower of dominoes or blocks, only to have it all fall down—what did you like best about it? Least? Why? **3.** If you could be captain of any kind of ship, what kind would you want? Why?

1. As compelling as the power of evil is, a more compelling authority shouts an overriding double-edged message: one edge cutting Babylon and her followers, the other exhorting God's people. What are the two voices, the two messages and the two responses from the two audiences? How does God's perspective on Babylon (vv. 2–6) differ from Babylon's self-understanding (v. 7)? **2.** How do the voices from the world greet the fall of Babylon (vv. 9–20)? Contemporize each of their laments—make them your own. Why do they mourn? Why would you mourn if you were in their situation? **3.** Compare this passage with the following OT prophecies about the fall of the cities of Sodom and Gomorrah (Ge 19), Babylon (Isa 13,47), and Tyre (Eze 27–28). How is each an

of the woman and of the beast she rides, which has the seven
heads and ten horns. 8The beast, which you saw, once was, now is
not, and will come up out of the Abyss and go to his destruction.
The inhabitants of the earth whose names have not been written in
the book of life from the creation of the world will be astonished
when they see the beast, because he once was, now is not, and yet
will come.

9"This calls for a mind with wisdom. The seven heads are seven
hills on which the woman sits. 10They are also seven kings. Five
have fallen, one is, the other has not yet come; but when he does
come, he must remain for a little while. 11The beast who once was,
and now is not, is an eighth king. He belongs to the seven and is
going to his destruction.

12"The ten horns you saw are ten kings who have not yet received a kingdom, but who for one hour will receive authority as
kings along with the beast. 13They have one purpose and will give
their power and authority to the beast. 14They will make war
against the Lamb, but the Lamb will overcome them because he is
Lord of lords and King of kings—and with him will be his called,
chosen and faithful followers."

15Then the angel said to me, "The waters you saw, where the
prostitute sits, are peoples, multitudes, nations and languages.
16The beast and the ten horns you saw will hate the prostitute.
They will bring her to ruin and leave her naked; they will eat her
flesh and burn her with fire. 17For God has put it into their hearts
to accomplish his purpose by agreeing to give the beast their power
to rule, until God's words are fulfilled. 18The woman you saw is the
great city that rules over the kings of the earth."

The Fall of Babylon

18 After this I saw another angel coming down from heaven.
He had great authority, and the earth was illuminated by
his splendor. 2With a mighty voice he shouted:

"Fallen! Fallen is Babylon the Great!
She has become a home for demons
and a haunt for every evil[a] spirit,
a haunt for every unclean and detestable bird.
3For all the nations have drunk
the maddening wine of her adulteries.
The kings of the earth committed adultery with her,
and the merchants of the earth grew rich from her excessive luxuries."

4Then I heard another voice from heaven say:

"Come out of her, my people,
so that you will not share in her sins,
so that you will not receive any of her plagues;
5for her sins are piled up to heaven,
and God has remembered her crimes.
6Give back to her as she has given;
pay her back double for what she has done.
Mix her a double portion from her own cup.
7Give her as much torture and grief
as the glory and luxury she gave herself.
In her heart she boasts,
'I sit as queen; I am not a widow,

[a]2 Greek *unclean*

and I will never mourn.’
8Therefore in one day her plagues will overtake
her:
death, mourning and famine.
She will be consumed by fire,
for mighty is the Lord God who judges her.

9“When the kings of the earth who committed adultery with her
and shared her luxury see the smoke of her burning, they will
weep and mourn over her. 10Terrified at her torment, they will
stand far off and cry:

“ ‘Woe! Woe, O great city,
O Babylon, city of power!
In one hour your doom has come!’

11“The merchants of the earth will weep and mourn over her
because no one buys their cargoes any more— 12cargoes of gold,
silver, precious stones and pearls; fine linen, purple, silk and scarlet cloth; every sort of citron wood, and articles of every kind made
of ivory, costly wood, bronze, iron and marble; 13cargoes of cinna-
mon and spice, of incense, myrrh and frankincense, of wine and
olive oil, of fine flour and wheat; cattle and sheep; horses and
carriages; and bodies and souls of men.
14“They will say, ‘The fruit you longed for is gone from you. All
your riches and splendor have vanished, never to be recovered.’
15The merchants who sold these things and gained their wealth
from her will stand far off, terrified at her torment. They will weep
and mourn 16and cry out:

“ ‘Woe! Woe, O great city,
dressed in fine linen, purple and scarlet,
and glittering with gold, precious stones and
pearls!
17In one hour such great wealth has been brought
to ruin!’

“Every sea captain, and all who travel by ship, the sailors, and all
who earn their living from the sea, will stand far off. 18When they
see the smoke of her burning, they will exclaim, ‘Was there ever a
city like this great city?’ 19They will throw dust on their heads, and
with weeping and mourning cry out:

“ ‘Woe! Woe, O great city,
where all who had ships on the sea
became rich through her wealth!
In one hour she has been brought to ruin!
20Rejoice over her, O heaven!
Rejoice, saints and apostles and prophets!
God has judged her for the way she treated you.’ ”

21Then a mighty angel picked up a boulder the size of a large
millstone and threw it into the sea, and said:

“With such violence
the great city of Babylon will be thrown down,
never to be found again.
22The music of harpists and musicians, flute players
and trumpeters,
will never be heard in you again.
No workman of any trade
will ever be found in you again.
The sound of a millstone

historical example of the fall of this spiritual Babylon? **4.** What conclusions do you draw concerning the destruction of Babylon from this comparison? What do you learn about God?

1. If you were going to describe your life in terms of a city, what would you say? What kinds of cargoes are coming into it? What activities occur within its walls? How does it compare with Babylon? What would be a fitting name for your city? Why? What do you do to keep the evils listed in this passage out of your city or life? **2.** What “items of merchandise” have you bought at great price and valued highly? Which of these have been too costly because of the resulting loss in your spiritual life? **3.** When has an important part of your life collapsed? What did other individuals say about this demise? What perspective did God bring to your fallen situation? **4.** What is the most important lesson you have learned from this passage? What actions will you take today based on this insight?

will never be heard in you again.
23The light of a lamp
will never shine in you again.
The voice of bridegroom and bride
will never be heard in you again.
Your merchants were the world's great men.
By your magic spell all the nations were led astray.
24In her was found the blood of prophets and of the saints,
and of all who have been killed on the earth."

1. When was the last time your favorite ball team finally won it all? Tell the group about any ticker tape parades and other local celebrations you may have witnessed. **2.** What was the most festive wedding and reception you ever attended? **3.** What funeral have you attended where the eulogy was memorable for its praise of God's salvation?

1. In contrast to the silence that comes with the fall of Babylon (18:22), what characterizes the new scene in heaven? Who participates in this praise? **2.** Compare and contrast the five songs of praise. What is the most frequent refrain? What do you learn about God's character? **3.** Contrast the prostitute of chapters 17 and 18 with the bride of verses 7–8 (see also Eph 5:25–27). What do you find interesting about this contrast? Why? **4.** How is John (and how might we be) tempted to worship the angel or messenger of the good news? **5.** How is the witness of Jesus related to prophecy?

1. What are four things for which you are extremely grateful to God? How do you usually express your gratitude to him about these things? **2.** How has your interest in worshiping God increased or decreased in the last year? Since beginning your study of Revelation? Why? **3.** What sounds of worship do you really appreciate? Why? How will you use them this week to worship God? **4.** How does the defeat and condemnation of Babylon and the triumph and glory of the Lord God affect your overall view of your problems here and now? What is one problem you hope to manage more confidently and joyfully as a result of your study of Revelation?

Hallelujah!

19 After this I heard what sounded like the roar of a great multitude in heaven shouting:

"Hallelujah!
Salvation and glory and power belong to our God,
2 for true and just are his judgments.
He has condemned the great prostitute
who corrupted the earth by her adulteries.
He has avenged on her the blood of his servants."

3And again they shouted:

"Hallelujah!
The smoke from her goes up for ever and ever."

4The twenty-four elders and the four living creatures fell down and worshiped God, who was seated on the throne. And they cried:

"Amen, Hallelujah!"

5Then a voice came from the throne, saying:

"Praise our God,
all you his servants,
you who fear him,
both small and great!"

6Then I heard what sounded like a great multitude, like the roar of rushing waters and like loud peals of thunder, shouting:

"Hallelujah!
For our Lord God Almighty reigns.
7Let us rejoice and be glad
and give him glory!
For the wedding of the Lamb has come,
and his bride has made herself ready.
8Fine linen, bright and clean,
was given her to wear."
(Fine linen stands for the righteous acts of the saints.)

9Then the angel said to me, "Write: 'Blessed are those who are invited to the wedding supper of the Lamb!' " And he added, "These are the true words of God."
10At this I fell at his feet to worship him. But he said to me, "Do not do it! I am a fellow servant with you and with your brothers who hold to the testimony of Jesus. Worship God! For the testimony of Jesus is the spirit of prophecy."

The Rider on the White Horse

11I saw heaven standing open and there before me was a white horse, whose rider is called Faithful and True. With justice he judges and makes war. 12His eyes are like blazing fire, and on his head are many crowns. He has a name written on him that no one knows but he himself. 13He is dressed in a robe dipped in blood, and his name is the Word of God. 14The armies of heaven were following him, riding on white horses and dressed in fine linen, white and clean. 15Out of his mouth comes a sharp sword with which to strike down the nations. "He will rule them with an iron scepter."[a] He treads the winepress of the fury of the wrath of God Almighty. 16On his robe and on his thigh he has this name written:

KING OF KINGS AND LORD OF LORDS.

17And I saw an angel standing in the sun, who cried in a loud voice to all the birds flying in midair, "Come, gather together for the great supper of God, 18so that you may eat the flesh of kings, generals, and mighty men, of horses and their riders, and the flesh of all people, free and slave, small and great."

19Then I saw the beast and the kings of the earth and their armies gathered together to make war against the rider on the horse and his army. 20But the beast was captured, and with him the false prophet who had performed the miraculous signs on his behalf. With these signs he had deluded those who had received the mark of the beast and worshiped his image. The two of them were thrown alive into the fiery lake of burning sulfur. 21The rest of them were killed with the sword that came out of the mouth of the rider on the horse, and all the birds gorged themselves on their flesh.

When you were young, how much did you want a horse? Why? Who was your favorite fictional or real horse? Why?

1. What regarding the horse, the rider and the setting commands your attention? **2.** Who is following Christ: The church *militant* (still on earth)? Or the church *triumphant* (now in heaven)? Why? **3.** What weapon does the rider wield (v. 15)? **4.** How does this supper (vv. 17–18) compare with the wedding supper (19:9)? **5.** Who are the combatants in this war (vv. 19–21)? Who wins? What happens to the enemy leaders? To the army? **6.** How does this "last battle" compare to "previous" ones (16:12–16; 17:14–16) and a "later" one (20:7–10)? Do you think these are different accounts of the same battle? Why?

What hopes and fears does this triumphant picture bring out in you? Why? How has Jesus been your deliverer this year?

The Thousand Years

20 And I saw an angel coming down out of heaven, having the key to the Abyss and holding in his hand a great chain. 2He seized the dragon, that ancient serpent, who is the devil, or Satan, and bound him for a thousand years. 3He threw him into the Abyss, and locked and sealed it over him, to keep him from deceiving the nations anymore until the thousand years were ended. After that, he must be set free for a short time.

4I saw thrones on which were seated those who had been given authority to judge. And I saw the souls of those who had been beheaded because of their testimony for Jesus and because of the word of God. They had not worshiped the beast or his image and had not received his mark on their foreheads or their hands. They came to life and reigned with Christ a thousand years. 5(The rest of the dead did not come to life until the thousand years were ended.) This is the first resurrection. 6Blessed and holy are those who have part in the first resurrection. The second death has no power over them, but they will be priests of God and of Christ and will reign with him for a thousand years.

Satan's Doom

7When the thousand years are over, Satan will be released from his prison 8and will go out to deceive the nations in the four corners of the earth—Gog and Magog—to gather them for battle. In number they are like the sand on the seashore. 9They marched across the breadth of the earth and surrounded the camp of God's people, the city he loves. But fire came down from heaven and

1. When did you last "lose your head"? What happened? **2.** Have you read any good books lately? How do you judge a book?

1. Why is Satan bound? By whom? How? **2.** Where and when will this 1000-year reign begin: On earth or in heaven? Beginning when Christ first came? Or when he comes again? Why? **3.** What will life be like without Satan deceiving the nations, but with the church reigning instead? In what sense is that *already* true? And *not yet* true? **4.** What is the first resurrection? The second death (v. 14; see also 20:11–15)? What do these mean to Christians? To the rest of the dead? **5.** Why do you think Satan will again try to deceive the nations? Why do you suppose God released him and let him out of the Abyss? **6.** Describe this version of the last battle, comparing it to the other versions in Revelation and to Ezekiel 38–39. What is the final fate of the beast and the false prophet? **7.** Who is exempted and who is exhumed at the great white throne of judgment? On what basis?

[a]*15* Psalm 2:9

1. What do you find comforting in this chapter? What disturbs you? Why? **2.** What is your biggest spiritual battle today? What is the outcome so far? What is the hope in this passage for you? **3.** Imagine a book made of your life, with every thought and deed recorded, then read by all. How would you feel? If Jesus edited that book by substituting his works for yours, how would you feel then? How will you then live today?

---

1. Where is one of the most beautiful places you have ever been? What impressed you about that place? **2.** What was one of the most beautiful spots in your hometown when you were growing up? **3.** How do you think your city would be different if God were the mayor?

1. Where will the new world be lived out—on earth or in heaven? Why do you think so? **2.** Who will be the residents of the New Jerusalem and the "wife" of the Lamb (v. 9)? Whose presence is the vision caught up with? What's missing from this picture? Why? **3.** What do you think it will be like living without fear, pain or death and with the continual and direct presence of God? Will this new world to come be recognizable? How so? **4.** What is the significance of the names ascribed to God, especially for those who "overcome" and those who do not (vv. 6–8)? **5.** What is it about the city that John and his readers are meant to notice in particular? Why? What impresses you the most about the city and its central figure? Why? **6.** Compare John's vision of reality here with the related visions in Ezekiel 40–48 and Isaiah 60–66. Accordingly, what was the function of the temple in the old Jerusalem? Why is there no need for a temple in the New Jerusalem? What is more "real": The spiritual things visualized here in the New Jerusalem? Or the physical objects of the old Jerusalem? **7.** What features will be found in the New Jerusalem (22:1–6)? Where else do we see these same features (see Ge 1–3; Eze 47:1–2; Joel 3:18; Zec 14:8)? **8.** Trace the origin of the riv-

devoured them. 10And the devil, who deceived them, was thrown
into the lake of burning sulfur, where the beast and the false
prophet had been thrown. They will be tormented day and night
for ever and ever.

The Dead Are Judged

11Then I saw a great white throne and him who was seated on it.
Earth and sky fled from his presence, and there was no place for
them. 12And I saw the dead, great and small, standing before the
throne, and books were opened. Another book was opened, which
is the book of life. The dead were judged according to what they
had done as recorded in the books. 13The sea gave up the dead that
were in it, and death and Hades gave up the dead that were in
them, and each person was judged according to what he had done.
14Then death and Hades were thrown into the lake of fire. The lake
of fire is the second death. 15If anyone's name was not found
written in the book of life, he was thrown into the lake of fire.

The New Jerusalem

21 Then I saw a new heaven and a new earth, for the first
heaven and the first earth had passed away, and there was
no longer any sea. 2I saw the Holy City, the new Jerusalem, coming
down out of heaven from God, prepared as a bride beautifully
dressed for her husband. 3And I heard a loud voice from the throne
saying, "Now the dwelling of God is with men, and he will live
with them. They will be his people, and God himself will be with
them and be their God. 4He will wipe every tear from their eyes.
There will be no more death or mourning or crying or pain, for the
old order of things has passed away."

5He who was seated on the throne said, "I am making everything new!" Then he said, "Write this down, for these words are
trustworthy and true."

6He said to me: "It is done. I am the Alpha and the Omega, the
Beginning and the End. To him who is thirsty I will give to drink
without cost from the spring of the water of life. 7He who overcomes will inherit all this, and I will be his God and he will be my
son. 8But the cowardly, the unbelieving, the vile, the murderers,
the sexually immoral, those who practice magic arts, the idolaters
and all liars—their place will be in the fiery lake of burning sulfur.
This is the second death."

9One of the seven angels who had the seven bowls full of the
seven last plagues came and said to me, "Come, I will show you
the bride, the wife of the Lamb." 10And he carried me away in the
Spirit to a mountain great and high, and showed me the Holy City,
Jerusalem, coming down out of heaven from God. 11It shone with
the glory of God, and its brilliance was like that of a very precious
jewel, like a jasper, clear as crystal. 12It had a great, high wall with
twelve gates, and with twelve angels at the gates. On the gates
were written the names of the twelve tribes of Israel. 13There were
three gates on the east, three on the north, three on the south and
three on the west. 14The wall of the city had twelve foundations,
and on them were the names of the twelve apostles of the Lamb.

15The angel who talked with me had a measuring rod of gold to
measure the city, its gates and its walls. 16The city was laid out like
a square, as long as it was wide. He measured the city with the rod
and found it to be 12,000 stadia[a] in length, and as wide and high
as it is long. 17He measured its wall and it was 144 cubits[b]

[a]*16* That is, about 1,400 miles (about 2,200 kilometers) [b]*17* That is, about 200 feet (about 65 meters)

thick,[a] by man's measurement, which the angel was using. 18The
wall was made of jasper, and the city of pure gold, as pure as glass.
19The foundations of the city walls were decorated with every kind
of precious stone. The first foundation was jasper, the second sap-
phire, the third chalcedony, the fourth emerald, 20the fifth sardo-
nyx, the sixth carnelian, the seventh chrysolite, the eighth beryl,
the ninth topaz, the tenth chrysoprase, the eleventh jacinth, and
the twelfth amethyst.[b] 21The twelve gates were twelve pearls,
each gate made of a single pearl. The great street of the city was of
pure gold, like transparent glass.
22I did not see a temple in the city, because the Lord God
Almighty and the Lamb are its temple. 23The city does not need the
sun or the moon to shine on it, for the glory of God gives it light,
and the Lamb is its lamp. 24The nations will walk by its light, and
the kings of the earth will bring their splendor into it. 25On no day
will its gates ever be shut, for there will be no night there. 26The
glory and honor of the nations will be brought into it. 27Nothing
impure will ever enter it, nor will anyone who does what is shameful or deceitful, but only those whose names are written in the
Lamb's book of life.

The River of Life

22 Then the angel showed me the river of the water of life, as
clear as crystal, flowing from the throne of God and of the
Lamb 2down the middle of the great street of the city. On each side
of the river stood the tree of life, bearing twelve crops of fruit,
yielding its fruit every month. And the leaves of the tree are for the
healing of the nations. 3No longer will there be any curse. The
throne of God and of the Lamb will be in the city, and his servants
will serve him. 4They will see his face, and his name will be on
their foreheads. 5There will be no more night. They will not need
the light of a lamp or the light of the sun, for the Lord God will give
them light. And they will reign for ever and ever.
6The angel said to me, "These words are trustworthy and true.
The Lord, the God of the spirits of the prophets, sent his angel to
show his servants the things that must soon take place."

Jesus Is Coming

7"Behold, I am coming soon! Blessed is he who keeps the words
of the prophecy in this book."

8I, John, am the one who heard and saw these things. And when
I had heard and seen them, I fell down to worship at the feet of the
angel who had been showing them to me. 9But he said to me, "Do
not do it! I am a fellow servant with you and with your brothers the
prophets and of all who keep the words of this book. Worship
God!"
10Then he told me, "Do not seal up the words of the prophecy of
this book, because the time is near. 11Let him who does wrong
continue to do wrong; let him who is vile continue to be vile; let
him who does right continue to do right; and let him who is holy
continue to be holy."

12"Behold, I am coming soon! My reward is with me, and I will
give to everyone according to what he has done. 13I am the Alpha
and the Omega, the First and the Last, the Beginning and the End.
14"Blessed are those who wash their robes, that they may have

[a]*17* Or *high* [b]*20* The precise identification of some of these precious stones is uncertain.

er and tree of life from its source to its fruit. What does this comparison suggest about the unity of Scripture? The completeness of God's salvation?

1. How must the early Christians have greeted this vision of what was in store for them? How do you feel about knowing that the Holy City will be your hometown? That it will last forever? How do you feel about the fact that this is what Jesus has prepared you for? Does it change your lifestyle? **2.** What has caused you mourning, crying and pain in the past year? What does it mean to you to know that this will pass away? **3.** How has your study of Revelation, and the many parallels to other parts of Scripture enhanced your view of the Bible? Of the completeness of salvation? How has it affected your trust in God? **4.** Now that your study of Revelation is almost over, how do you feel about this book of the Bible? Is this different from how you felt when you began the study? How has God blessed your life through this story? **5.** What do you hope to carry with you from your time spent in the study of Revelation?

If you could give yourself a new name, symbolizing the legacy your family gave you, the God-given potential you have, or some hidden aspiration you have yet to realize, what name would you choose? Why?

1. What words of Christ are repeated three times in this closing (vv. 7,12,20)? How do these words sum up the theme of Revelation? **2.** What significance do you attribute to Jesus' claims and names in verses 12–17? Regarding these claims, how is the final state of humanity determined: By some arbitrary reward system, fixed from eternity? By what we have done in this present life? Or by our response to his *universal* ("whoever thirsts") and *undeserved* ("free gift") invitation to simply "come"? **3.** What then do you make of God's summary of human destiny (vv. 1–6)? Is it ever too late for

the right to the tree of life and may go through the gates into the
city. 15Outside are the dogs, those who practice magic arts, the
sexually immoral, the murderers, the idolaters and everyone who
loves and practices falsehood.
16"I, Jesus, have sent my angel to give you[a] this testimony for
the churches. I am the Root and the Offspring of David, and the
bright Morning Star."

17The Spirit and the bride say, "Come!" And let him who hears
say, "Come!" Whoever is thirsty, let him come; and whoever
wishes, let him take the free gift of the water of life.

18I warn everyone who hears the words of the prophecy of this
book: If anyone adds anything to them, God will add to him the
plagues described in this book. 19And if anyone takes words away
from this book of prophecy, God will take away from him his share
in the tree of life and in the holy city, which are described in this
book.
20He who testifies to these things says, "Yes, I am coming soon."
Amen. Come, Lord Jesus.
21The grace of the Lord Jesus be with God's people. Amen.

people to change their ways and come to Christ? Why or why not? **4.** In the contrast between those "inside" the city and those "outside" (vv. 14–15), what is implied about the basis for our salvation and judgment? What does it mean to "wash" one's "robe"? **5.** What is the meaning of God's final curse in verses 18–19? Knowing what you now do about the seven plagues, the tree of life and the Holy City, how seriously do you take this warning?

♡ **1.** How have you prepared yourself for Christ's second coming? In what way has this study of Revelation helped to prepare you? How is your lifestyle in keeping with verse 7? **2.** How have your perceptions of Jesus, Satan, heaven and hell changed? Why? **3.** How will these new perceptions affect your worship? Your lifestyle? **4.** How would you sum up the central truth of this book?

[a]*16* The Greek is plural.

TABLE OF WEIGHTS AND MEASURES

BIBLICAL UNIT		APPROXIMATE AMERICAN EQUIVALENT	APPROXIMATE METRIC EQUIVALENT
		WEIGHTS	
talent	(60 minas)	75 pounds	34 kilograms
mina	(50 shekels)	1 1/4 pounds	0.6 kilogram
shekel	(2 bekas)	2/5 ounce	11.5 grams
pim	(2/3 shekel)	1/3 ounce	7.6 grams
beka	(10 gerahs)	1/5 ounce	5.5 grams
gerah		1/50 ounce	0.6 gram
		LENGTH	
cubit		18 inches	0.5 meter
span		9 inches	23 centimeters
handbreadth		3 inches	8 centimeters
		CAPACITY	
		Dry Measure	
cor (homer)	(10 ephahs)	6 bushels	220 liters
lethek	(5 ephahs)	3 bushels	110 liters
ephah	(10 omers)	3/5 bushel	22 liters
seah	(1/3 ephah)	7 quarts	7.3 liters
omer	(1/10 ephah)	2 quarts	2 liters
cab	(1/18 ephah)	1 quart	1 liter
		Liquid Measure	
bath	(1 ephah)	6 gallons	22 liters
hin	(1/6 bath)	4 quarts	4 liters
log	(1/72 bath)	1/3 quart	0.3 liter

The figures of the table are calculated on the basis of a shekel equaling 11.5 grams, a cubit equaling 18 inches and an ephah equaling 22 liters. The quart referred to is either a dry quart (slightly larger than a liter) or a liquid quart (slightly smaller than a liter), whichever is applicable. The ton referred to in the footnotes is the American ton of 2,000 pounds.

This table is based upon the best available information, but it is not intended to be mathematically precise; like the measurement equivalents in the footnotes, it merely gives approximate amounts and distances. Weights and measures differed somewhat at various times and places in the ancient world. There is uncertainty particularly about the ephah and the bath; further discoveries may give more light on these units of capacity.

SUBJECT INDEX

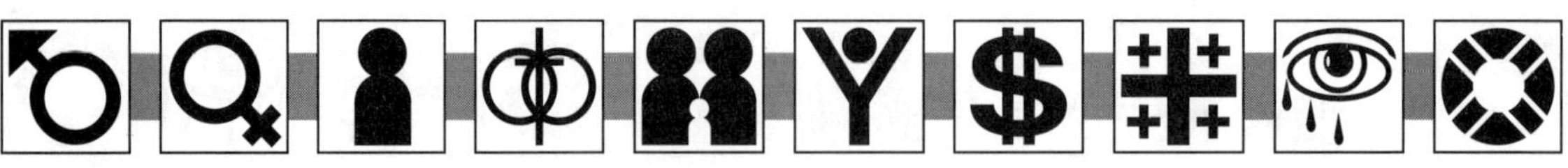

SUBJECT INDEX

Entries and subentries appear in **boldface** type.
Scripture references follow in lightface type.

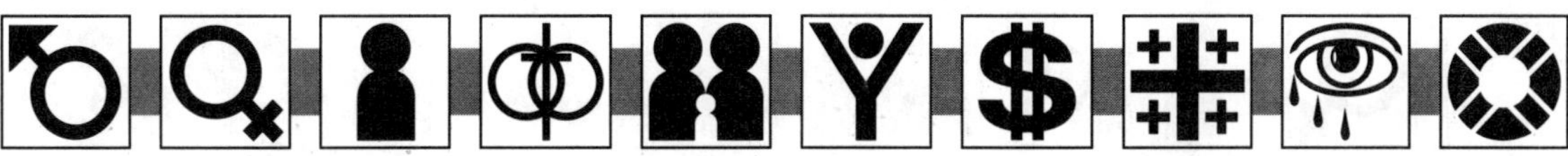

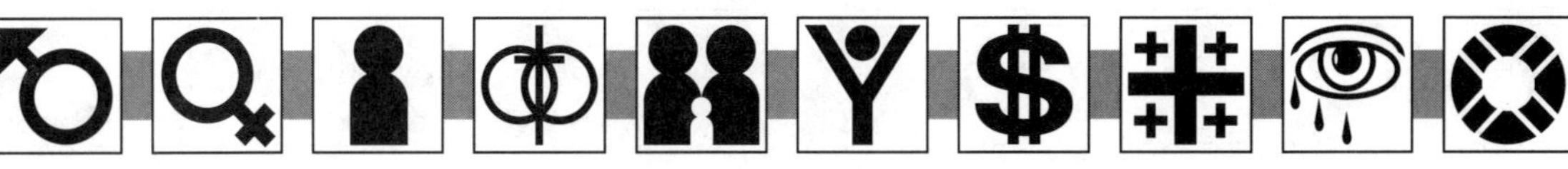

K

L

M

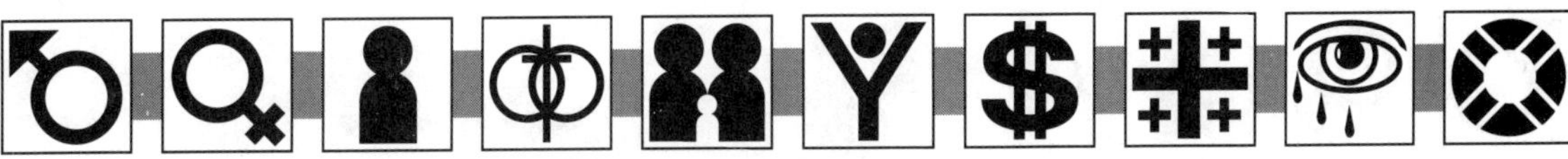

N

O

P

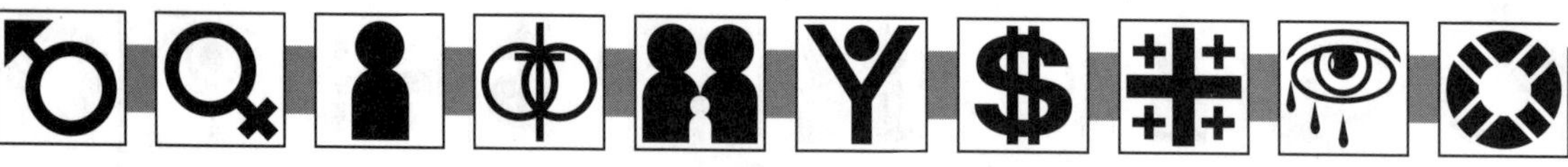

R

S

T

V

W

Z

INDEX OF MAPS AND VISUAL AIDS

NEW TESTAMENT